WORDSPELL

ph=f

Phonetic Dictionary

American English Edition

- Cross-references your word with other words which may sound similar or are spelled similarly (is it petal or pedal or peddle?)

- Provides suffix endings associated with your word and spells them out for you (funny, funnies, funnier, funniest, and so on)

- Provides prefixes with definitions that can be associated with your word (unable, enable, disable, and so on)

- Includes selected commonly used proper nouns (no people or place names)

Diane M. Frank

Summary: Over 70,000 entries of commonly used American English words with multiple misspellings per word based upon their phonetic sound. Brief definitions allow for quickly ascertaining the proper word you wish to use. Extensive cross-referencing allows for words that are either similar in meaning and/or spelling.

All available prefixes are defined. Each correctly spelled word lists all potential suffix endings leaving no guesswork as to how to spell the future and past tense of a word. Use this reference tool as a bridge to go from the sound of your word to a standard dictionary if further comprehension is needed.

Proper nouns are not listed unless they are common in everyday communication. Proper nouns which are included in this resource tool; days of the week, months of the year, common medical and legal terms, common plants, animals and others which can be cross-referenced with a word which may not be a proper noun.

Notice of Rights

Notice of Liability

Authored by Diane M. Frank
Co-authored by Gabrielle M. Purcell
Consultant Editor by Jeremy Sarka
Cover Design by Martian Source Productions
Publisher i.m.Press

Copyright © May, 2015 by i.m.Press
PO Box 412, Rainier, Washington 98576, USA

Library of Congress Cataloging-in-Publication Data
Library of Congress Control Number: 2015939316

Wordspeller Phonetic Dictionary; American English Edition

Summary: Over 70,000 entries of commonly used American English words can be located by how their phonetic sounds. Very brief definitions intended to help you quickly locate your word to bridge you to a standard dictionary. Most proper nouns are not listed unless employed in everyday use (ie. months, days, animals, legal, medical). Extensive cross-referencing allows for words that are either similar in meaning and/or spelling. Defined Prefixes as well as all available Suffix endings for root words are easily located. Use this reference tool as a bridge to go from the sound of your word to a standard dictionary.

www.phoneticdictionary.com
www.wordspeller.net
www.americanwordspeller.com

ISBN 978-0-9830381-0-8

Manufactured in the United States of America

1st Edition

AUTHOR'S WORD

The reasons for creating a dictionary which locates your word by the "way it sounds" are multitudinous. Earning a degree in Communications was not without careful thought and examination. Having witnessed unnecessary embarrassment, the marginalization of many peoples of all types, unfounded pompous arrogance and flaming egos exposes the English language for what it is, a throne. A throne that can seat only a small number of butts. It has been over 200 years, longer than any other country in the world can boast, since a mandate to simplify the language in some form or fashion was brought forth and executed. As every American well knows, mastery of the written language ensures the survival of economic hierarchy. And why this particular language should prevail, despite all the thousands of practical and phonetically matching alphabets of the world, is quite a conundrum and a bit sad since it is the least worthy of such power and rule. Logic would suggest modifying this language to be more user-friendly since communication is primary for everyone.

People of all ages, of all walks of life, from every corner of the globe have been or will be marginalized by this English language at some point in time. Ranging from 'forgetting' the spelling of a word as we dawn into our senior years or suffer head injuries ensuring us of re-learning our own native language all over again. Whether coming into American English via another country or being in your first 6 years of elementary schooling warrants a useful communication tool. Last but not least and more importantly, our friends, neighbors and loved ones who may be experiencing some varying degree of dyslexia, dyspraxia or any of the innumerable afflictions we fondly refer to as 'learning disabilities' that affect over 1/5th of the people in the United States deserve a tool designed with all of them in mind.

Over 50% of populations in all countries are abstract and/or picture thinkers. Words take on lesser meaning when written than when spoken inviting a chasm in communication. The author of this book of reference sees absolutely no reason why communication should be challenged on any level, at any time and for any reason. If American leaders have no intention of leveling the playing field by overhauling the English language so that all people have fair access to a language that is logical and phonetic, then the release of this dictionary should help fill that void where compassion displaces humility.

And while we're at it, let's have a little discussion about...

Dialects, Annunciation and Pronunciation

Perhaps, in my opinion, there is more emphasis placed upon the problems with spelling as it relates to the 'speller' and their perceived disabilities, when, in actuality, more emphasis could be placed upon annunciation or pronunciation by those who speak the English language.

As a child learning EFL (English as a First Language) or a traveler new to this country learning ESL (English as a Second Language) there lies one common trait...hearing the language for the first time on American soil. When it comes to spelling English there are a number of issues facing the speller such as; hearing difficulties (tones, accents, dialects), sight difficulties (irregular neuronet firing, eye muscle control). These challenges are compounded by someone who speaks the language without articulating, pronouncing or annunciating correctly.

Dialects within the United States alone ranges from hundreds to thousands (depending upon whom is citing the study). It's very challenging to take a spelling test with a new teacher who has a strong southern drawl or to grow up in one region of the country where entire letters are dropped from words, letters such as 'r', 't', 'g' and 'd'. In some regions letters are even added that do not belong to a proper English word such as the letters 'r' or 't' or 'd'. Words such as 'something' turn into 'sumthen' and 'children' into 'chilren'. Some people in parts of the country 'warsh' their clothes. Some English speakers may not use the proper tense of a word and interrelate 'forget' with 'forgot' and 'drank' with 'drunk'.

Confusion goes even further with a new speller when, upon hearing a word taken out of context, may experience the inability to grasp and differentiate how to spell the word. Words spoken and not articulated give rise to synonymous sounding words such as 'petal, pedal and peddle' or 'procession', 'precession' and 'precision'.

It behooves us all to ease off on the pressure we place upon those who are challenged with spelling the written word and take responsibility for how we articulate our speech and stop 'warshing our clothes'!

Diane M. Frank

FOREWORD

"Its a damn poor mind that can think of only one way to spell a word."

Andrew Jackson

The literal meaning of the word *dyslexia* – from its Greek roots – is "difficulty with words". And with over 50% of the world experiencing this in varying degrees, we will discuss dyslexia generally and specifically since it is the primary motivation for the creation of this work.

Dr. Maryanne Wolfe, author of *Proust and the Squid: The Story and Science of the Reading Brain*, explains, "the more you know about a word, the faster you can read it." Dr. Virginia Berninger, of the University of Washington, has demonstrated that reading fluency is enhanced for dyslexic students through instruction that focuses on the interrelation between the three "forms" shared by each word: the meaning of the word, its visual appearance, and its sound.

Ronald Davis, author of *The Gift of Dyslexia* (and a man who mastered his autism), builds his program for dyslexia correction upon the insight that word mastery is essential to reading development, using only two essential materials: clay and a dictionary. Students use clay to create three-dimensional models of the meaning of each word, as well as the letters that spell the word. The modeling is needed because dyslexic individuals think mostly in pictures, unable to think with words unless they have mental pictures to go along with them.

But here is where dyslexics encounter their biggest barrier: spelling. The most persistent and pervasive symptom of dyslexia is an orthographic barrier; they have difficulty remembering the conventional spelling of phonetically irregular words. Many educators focus on intensive teaching of phonics, as this provides one avenue for decoding many of the simpler words encountered by beginning readers. English is not a phonetic language, but rather a polyglot and amalgam of words drawn from different languages, often retaining spellings that reflect histories and pronunciations long forgotten.

Through brain scans, Dr. Sally Shaywitz of Yale University has shown that dyslexic readers typically underutilize the "visual word form area" of the brain – the part of the visual cortex believed to be involved in instantaneous recognition of whole words. This is the part of the brain that probably stores a picture of the right letters arranged in the right order, the part that is engaged when you choose the correct spelling because it just *looks* right to you.

It isn't that dyslexic writers are unable to spell a word; with their creative problem-solving strengths, they can easily spell the same word half a dozen different ways. As Andrew Jackson once said, "its a damn poor mind that can think of only one way to spell a word." The problem is in figuring out which spelling is the one that everyone else will use and understand...

If you can't spell a word, you cannot find it in a dictionary.

This is where the most powerful tool – the dictionary – is also the most inaccessible. Because if we err in guessing the first 2 or 3 letters of the word, we will never find it.

And here is where *Wordspeller & Phonetic Dictionary* becomes indispensible – it provides the key to the door that opens the dictionary. This dictionary is the key to independence: it provides the correct spelling and all possible definitions and use of each word. It is where all those phonetic decoding skills emphasized by well-meaning primary school teachers can finally be brought to fruition: *krecher* may not be a word, but it *is* a spelling, albeit an incorrect one. In a regular dictionary, it leads us to the Kremlin, which is not where we wanted to go. But *Wordspeller & Phonetic Dictionary* gives us the answer in exactly the place we have gone to find it: "creature."

Suname leads to tsunami. *Fanomanen* takes us to phenomenon. *Ekselerate* turns into accelerate. And pretty soon, the world of words is ours for the taking. If we already know the meaning of the word, that is all that is needed. The correct spelling is there, in a form that we can copy and use.

If our trip to the dictionary is also a search for meaning, or etymology, or information as to usage, or a set of synonyms, then this *Wordspeller & Phonetic Dictionary* has opened the door for us. By providing the spelling we need, we can access the larger dictionary or thesaurus which can provide us with whatever information we seek.

This reference book should be in every school library, in every classroom, and at home on every student's desk. It is the key to independence for every learner.

-Abigail Marshall, Author of *The Everything Parent's Guide to Children with Dyslexia* and *When Your Child Has ... Dyslexia*. She also manages the *Dyslexia the Gift* site www.dyslexia.com

INTRODUCTION

This American English edition of the *Wordspeller & Phonetic Dictionary* is primarily designed to allow the user to locate their word by the way it sounds (phonetically). As a resource tool, it empowers the user to not only locate their word within seconds...but as a *phonetic* dictionary qualifies it as suitable for ESL, dyslexics and EFL. This reference book (unlike any dictionary ever created) also performs the following functions:

Cross-referencing...

- *emigrant* or *immigrant?*
- *gym* or *gem?*
- *marry* or *merry?*
- *scene* or *seen* or *seine?*
- *pedal* or *petal* or *peddle?*
- *carrot* or *karat* or *caret* or *carat?*

Learn how to spell the word correctly the first time you hear it...

korts, spelled phonetically could lend to words such as:	***bol***, spelled phonetically could be...
quartz	*ball*
courts	*bowl*
quarts	*bawl*
chords	*bull*
cords	

All these words, as well as thousands of others are cross-referenced extensively throughout this phonetic dictionary.

Wordspeller *provides short, concise definitions* to enable the user to quickly identify which word they wish to spell correctly. This lends the user the ability to then consult a standard dictionary for further comprehension of the word if desired.

Misspellings often involve transposing letters which are most commonly misinterpreted in hearing such as:

t	with	*d*		*au*	with	*ow*
b	with	*p*		*ch*	with	*sh*
ph	with	*f*		*ou*	with	*ow*
kn	with	*n*		*th*	with	*f*
qu	with	*kw*		*c*	with	*s*

Another advantage of the Wordspeller is *providing suffix endings for over 70,000 commonly used words to include legal, medical and slang.* Over 12 notable standard dictionaries were required to retrieve every conceivable suffix ending for each word. No single dictionary performs this added feature. As well, the Wordspeller & Phonetic Dictionary has provided *all known 'proper' prefix's as well as their definitions.*

HOW TO USE THIS DICTIONARY
METHODOLOGY: for misspelled words + root words

RULE #1:   If you have a difficult time using this dictionary, refer back to these rules!

RULE #2:   Simply look up the word by the way it SOUNDS...not the way it should/would/could be spelled.

RULE #3:   Look up the **root** word. The root word is the word without suffixes added:

Example of a misspelled word in this dictionary:

baged, bag(gged) / back(ed)

baged, is the misspelled word

= <u>bag</u>(gged) is "bagged" spelled properly ~ <u>bag</u> is the <u>root word</u> to look up in the dictionary to make certain this is the word you want

= <u>back</u>(ed) is "backed" spelled properly ~ <u>back</u> is the <u>root word</u> to look up in the dictionary to make certain this is the word you want

Example:

beder, better / bid(dder) / bitter / bet(ttor)

beder, is the misspelled word

= <u>better</u> is spelled properly

= <u>bid</u>(dder) "bidder" spelled properly~ <u>bid</u> is the <u>root word</u> to look up in the dictionary to make certain this is the word you want

= <u>bitter</u> is spelled properly

= <u>bet</u>(ttor) "bettor" spelled properly~ <u>bet</u> is the <u>root word</u> to look up in the dictionary to make certain this is the word you want

Example:

eksploratory, explore(ratory)

eksploratory is the misspelled word

= <u>explore</u>(ratory) "exploratory" spelled properly ~ <u>explore</u> is the <u>root word</u> to locate in the dictionary to make certain this is the word you want.

METHODOLOGY: for properly spelled words

RULE #1:   If you have a difficult time using this dictionary, refer back to these rules!

RULE #2:   Simply look up the word the way it SOUNDS...not the way it should/would/could be spelled.

RULE #3:   Suffixes (endings for words which describe past, present, future tense) how to:

A.)   The asterisk (*) means to add an "s" to the end of the word.

Example:
receptionist, * = receptionist + 's' = receptionists

B.)   Go back into the latter part of the root word for a letter that matches the beginning letter of the suffix ending.

Example:
paralysis,ytic,yze,yzed,zying,yzation,yzer = **paralytic, paralyze, paralyzed, paralyzing, paralyzation, paralyzer**

C.)   The suffix ending for the word is either added onto the end of the last letter or from a letter towards the end of the word.

Examples:

~ **call,** *,lled,lling,ller
= **called, calling, caller**
(Double 'll' is listed to assure you that there are two 'll's)

~ **reckless,**ssly,ssness
= **recklessly, recklessness**
(Double 'ss' is listed to assure you that there are two 'ss')

~ **balance,** *,ed,cing
= **balances, balanced, balancing**
(Asterisk (*) means "just add an 's)

~ **nag,**gged,gging,ggingly
= **nagged, nagging, nagginly**
(Double 'gg' is listed to assure you that there are two 'gg's)

~ **immaculate,**ely,eness,acy
= **immaculately, immaculateness, immaculacy**

~ **adapt,** *,ted,ting,tive,tively,tation,table,tability
= **adapts, adapted, adapting, adaptive, adaptively, adaptation, adaptable, adaptability**

RULE #4:   DE...If your word begins with a prefix such as 'de', simply remove the first 2 letters - 'de' then look up the remainder of the word (the root word).
Example: deice, '*de*' means "AWAY FROM/DOWN FROM" then look up the root word 'ice'.

RULE #5:   UN... If your word begins with a prefix such as 'un', simply remove the first 2 letters - 'in' then look up the remainder of the word (the root word).
Example: unfavorable, '*un*' means "NOT/REVERSAL" then look up the root word 'favorable'.

a, PREFIX INDICATING 'TO/TOWARDS/ AT' MOST OFTEN MODIFIES THE WORD

ab, PREFIX INDICATING 'FROM/AWAY FROM' MOST OFTEN MODIFIES THE WORD

aback, SURPRISED

abak, aback

abal, able

abalishen, abolition

abalone, A MOLLUSK

abanden, abandon

abandon,*,ned,ning,nment, LEFT ALL ALONE

abaration, aberration

abart, apart

abate,*,ed,ting,table,ement,ements, SUBSIDE/REDUCE/DECREASE

abatizing, appetizing

abaut, about

abawt, about

abazet, opposite

abbey,*, A MONASTERY

abbreveashen, abbreviate(tion)

abbreviate,*,ed,ting,tion,tor,tory, SHORTEN/CONDENSE

abcent, absent

abcerd, absurd

abcint, absent

abcurd, absurd

abdicate,*,ed,ting,tion,tor,able, RELINQUISH

abdikate, abdicate

abdikeit, abdicate

abdiman, abdomen

abdomen,minal,minally, STOMACH AREA

abducate, abdicate

abduct,*,ted,ting,tee,tion,tor, KIDNAP

abdukate, abdicate

abdukt, abduct

abdumen, abdomen

abe, abbey

abed, abet

abedeinse, obedience

abedeint, obedient

abedience, obedience

abel, able / apple / appeal

abelete, ability

abelishen, abolition

abelone, abalone

abeluty, ability

aberant, aberrant

aberegene, aborigine

aberigine, aborigine

aberition, aberration

aberrant,tly,nce,ncy, DEVIATE/STRAY AWAY FROM

aberration,*,nal, DEVIATE FROM THE STANDARD/NORM

abes, abyss

abet,*,tted,tting,tment, BACK UP/ ENCOURAGE/APPROVE

abetchuery, obituary

abeting, abet(tting)

abezit, opposite

abide,*,ed,er,ding,dingly,dance, STAY, WITHSTAND

abidid, abide(d)

abil, able / apple

ability,ties, CAPACITY "prefixes: dis/in"

abilone, abalone

abirant, aberrant

abirition, aberration

abis, abyss

abitchuery, obituary

abituary, obituary

abius, abuse

abl, able / apple

able,ly,bility, CAPABLE "prefixes: dis/en/ un"

ableb, ad-lib

ablederate, obliterate

ableveus, oblivious

ablib, ad-lib

abliveon, oblivion

abliveus, oblivious

abnormal,lly,lity, NOT TYPICAL/ NATURAL

abnormil, abnormal

abnormul, abnormal

aboard, GET ONTO SOMETHING SUCH AS VESSEL/TRAIN/ORGANIZATION (or see about)

abof, above

abol, able / apple

abolesh, abolish

abolish,hes,hed,hing,her,hment,hable, ition, END, TERMINATE

abolishon, abolition

abolition,nist, DESIRES TO END/ TERMINATE SOMETHING

abomanable, abominable

abominable,ly,eness, HORRID

abominuble, abominable

aborant, aberrant

aborchen, abortion

aborchun, abortion

abord, aboard / abort

aboregini, aborigine

aboreginul, aborigine(nal)

aborigine,*,nal, INDIGINEOUS, NATIVE

aborijinul, aborigine(nal)

aborshun, abortion

abort,*,ted,ting,tion, STOP/QUIT ACTION (or see aboard)

abortion,*, CANCEL PROJECT/ PREGNANCY

about, APPROXIMATELY

above, OVER

abowt, about

abpropreate, appropriate

abproximat, approximate

abpruval, approve(val)

abral, apriljanuary

abrasive,ely,eness, ROUGH, SCOURING

abredg, abridge

abreg, abridge

abrehenshun, apprehension

abrel, april

abreveashen, abbreviate(tion)

abreveat, abbreviate

abreveation, abbreviate(tion)

abreviate, abbreviate

abridge,*,ed,ging,er, SHORTEN LENGTH BY CONDENSING/REWRITING

abridged, SHORTEN LENGTH BY CONDENSING/REWRITING

abrig, abridge

abrihenshun, apprehension

abrikot, apricot

abril, april

abroad, LEFT HOME TO GO OVERSEAS

abrod, abroad

abrol, april

abropt, abrupt

abrowtch, approach

abruhensev, apprehensive

abruhenshun, apprehension

abrul, april

abrupt,tly,tness, SUDDEN

abscess,sses,ssed,ssing,ssion, INFECTION IN THE BONE

absence,*, NOT PRESENT, UNAVAILABLE (or see absent(s))

absens, absence / absent(s)

absent,tly,tee,teeism, INTENTIONALLY UNAVAILABLE (or see absence)

abserd, absurd

abserdity, absurd(ity)

abserdly, absurd(ly)

abses, abscess

absilute, absolute
absilutly, absolute(ly)
absins, absence / absent(s)
absint, absent
absintee, absent(ee)
absird, absurd
absirdety, absurd(ity)
absirdly, absurd(ly)
absolute,tely,tion,tism, DEFINITELY
absolve,*,ed,ving,vable,er,lution, FORGIVEN, RELEASED
absorb,*,bed,bing,bingly,bable,ber, bance,bent,rption,rptive,rptivity, COLLECT/ GATHER "prefixes: non"
absorbshen, absorption
absorbtef, absorptive
absorbtion, absorption
absorption, ACCUMULATE/HOLD/ GATHER
absorptive,vity,ion, ACCUMULATES/ HOLDS/GATHERS
absorshen, absorption
absortef, absorptive
absortion, absorption
absortive, absorptive
abstain,*,ned,ning,nment,ner,tinence, DENY, REFRAIN
abstane, abstain
abstinent,nce,tly, VOLUNTARILY DENY/ REFRAIN
abstract,*,ted,ting,tedly,tedness,tion, tionist, APART FROM, THEORETICAL
abstrakt, abstract
abstunent, abstinent
absulootly, absolute(ly)
absulution, absolve(lution)
absunt, absent
absurd,dly,dity,dities,dness, CRAZY
absurdety, absurd(ity)
abtetude, aptitude
abtitude, aptitude
abtumin, abdomen
abuf, above
abul, able
abulishen, abolition
abulone, abalone
abundance,*,nt,ntly, PLENTY
abundince, abundance
abundint, abundance(nt)
aburant, aberrant
aburation, aberration
aburegene, aborigine
aburijene, aborigine
aburition, aberration

abuse,*,sed,sing,sive,siveness, TREAT WRONGLY "prefixes: dis"
abusef, abuse(sive)
abusif, abuse(sive)
abutizing, appetizing
abuve, above
abuze, abuse
abuzet, opposite
aby, abbey
abyss,smal,smally,ssal, CHASM, GREAT DEPTH EITHER PHYSICAL/ EMOTIONAL
abzaulv, absolve
abzdanent, abstinent
abzent, absent
abzilute, absolute
abzint, absent
abzolv, absolve
abzorb, absorb
abzuloot, absolute
abzulute, absolute
abzulution, absolve(lution)
ac, PREFIX INDICATING 'TO/TOWARDS/ AT' MOST OFTEN MODIFIES THE WORD
academic,*,mism,micism,mia,mician, mical,mically, SCHOOLING
academy,mies, SPECIAL SCHOOL
acadume, academy
acamadasions, accomodations
acampany, accompany
accadintul, accident(al)
accedental, accident(al)
accel,*,lled,lerate, ABBREVIATION OF 'ACCELERATE' (or see excel)
accelarate, accelerate
accelerate,*,ed,ting,tion,tor, QUICKEN, FORCE TO GO/MOVE, GAS PEDAL
accelirate, accelerate
accent,*, TONES IN SPEECH, HIGHLIGHTS
accentuate,*,ted,ting,tion, TO EMPHASIZE
accepshen, except(ion)
accept,*,ted,ting,tingly,tance,table, tably,tability,tation, APPROVE (or see except) "prefixes: un"
acceptinse, accept(ance)
acceshen, accession
accesorize, accessory(rize)
access,sses,ssed,ssing,ssible,ssibility, ssion, ENTER "prefixes: in"
accession,*,ned,ning, ENTER "prefixes: de"

accessory,ries,rize,rizing, ADDITIONAL
accident,*,tal,tally, INVOLUNTARILY
acclaim,amatory,amation, LOUD APPROVAL/APPLAUSE (or see acclimate)
acclimate,*,ed,ting,tion,tize,tized,tizing, tization, BECOME ACCUSTOMED TO (or see acclaim(ation))
accomadate, accommodate
accomadation, accommodate(tion)
accomedate, accommodate
accomedashen, accommodate(tion)
accomidation, accommodate(tion)
accommodate,*,ting,tion,tive, ASSIST "prefixes: un"
accomodate, accommodate
accomodation, accommodate(tion)
accompany,nies,nied,nying,niment,nist, GOES ALONG WITH "prefixes: un"
accompeny, accompany
accomplice,*, PARTICIPATED IN A CRIME
accomplish,hes,hed,hing,hment,hable, her, GOAL/IDEA ACHIEVED
accomudation, accommodate(tion)
accord,*,ded,ding,dingly,dance,dant, dantly, GIVE, GRANT TO, IN HARMONY WITH "prefixes: dis"
account,*,ted,ting,tant,tancy,table, tability, RESPONSIBLE/LIABLE FOR "prefixes: un"
accredit,*,ted,ting,table,tation,tive, RESPONSIBLE/LIABLE FOR "prefixes: un"
accrue,*,ual,ed,uing, TO STORE/SAVE UP "prefixes: non/un"
accuate, acuate
accudental, accident(al)
accuiesent, acquiesce(nt)
accumulate,*,ted,ting,tion,tive,tively, tor, GATHER/GROW "prefixes: bio"
accupuncture, acupuncture
accurate,ely,eness,acy, CORRECT "prefixes: in"
accuse,*,ed,sing,singly,satory,satorial, satorially,sative,sation,er, CHARGE OR IMPLY
accustom,med, FAMILIAR, HABITUAL "prefixes: un"
ace,*,ed, A SCORE IN GAME, ON DIE(DICE), TO WIN
acebt, except / accept
acedik, acetic / acidic / ascetic
acempany, accompany

acer, acre
acerens, occur(rrence)
aceshun, accession
acetic,tous, PROPERTIES OF VINEGAR,
SOUR (or see ascetic/acidic)
acetify,fies,fied,fying,fier,fication, OF
ACETIC, CONVERT TO ACID/
VINEGAR (or see acidify)
acewmulate, accumulate
ache,*,ed,hing,hy,hiness, HURT
acheeve, achieve
acheve, achieve
achieve,*,ed,ving,vment,vable,vably,
vability, GAIN "prefixes: over/un/
under"
achin, action
achual, actual
acid,*,dic,dity,dly,dulate,dulated,
dulating,dulation,dulent,dulous,
dulously, CHEMICAL COMPOUND
acidemic, academic
acidental, accident(al)
acidic, CHEMICAL BALANCE, OF ACID
(or see acetic/ascetic)
acidify,fies,fied,fying,fiable,fication,fier,
CONVERT TO ACID (or see acetify)
"prefixes: de"
aciuponcsher, acupuncture
ack, ache
ackawnt, account
acklimation, acclimate(tion) /
acclaim(amation)
acknowledge,*,ed,ging,ement,gable,er,
RECOGNIZE
ackomplish, accomplish
ackord, accord
ackownt, account
ackraget, aggregate
ackred, acrid
ackret, acrid
acks, ax / ache(s) / ask
acksderminate, exterminate
ackseal, axis(ial)
ackses, access / ax(es) / axis
ackseshen, accession
acksesory, accessory
acksglood, exclude
acksul, axil / axle
ackuiesent, acquiesce(nt)
ackumulate, accumulate
ackustumed, accustom(ed)
aclemate, acclimate
aclimate, acclimate

aclimation, acclimate(tion) /
acclaim(amation)
acne, AFFLICTION OF THE SKIN
acnolege, acknowledge
acomadashen, accommodate(tion)
acomblesh, accomplish
acomedate, accommodate
acomidate, accommodate
acomidation, accommodate(tion)
acompany, accompany
acompined, accompany(nied)
acomplise, accomplice
acomplish, accomplish
acompuny, accompany
acomudashen, accommodate(tion)
acomudate, accommodate
acord, accord
acordant, accord(ant)
acount, account
acoustic,*,cal,cally, OF SOUND
acquaint,*,ted,ting,tance, ASSOCIATE
WITH "prefixes: un"
acquaintance,*,eship, FAMILIAR
acquiesce,*,ed,cing,ence,ent,ently,
AGREE/ALLOW IN A HUMBLE/
PASSIVE WAY
acquire,*,red,ring,rement,rable,er,
OBTAIN
acquisition,*,ned,ning,nist, ACQUIRED
acquisitive,ely,eness, READILY
ACQUIRES
acquit,*,tted,tting,ttal,ttance,ttances,
tter, ABSOLVES, FREED
acquittal,*, ABSOLVES, FREE OF
JUDGEMENT
acqwaentense, acquaintance
acqwantinse, acquaintance
acrabats, acrobat(s)
acrad, acrid
acraget, aggregate
acravat, aggravate
acre,*,eage, AMOUNT OF LAND
acred, acrid
acreget, aggregate
acrevat, aggravate
acrid,dity,dly, BITTER/CAUSTIC SMELL
"prefixes: sub"
acriget, aggregate
acrit, acrid
acrivat, aggravate
acro, PREFIX INDICATING 'END/
BEGINNING/HEIGHT' MOST OFTEN
MODIFIES THE WORD

acrobat,*,tic,tics, INVOLVES VARIOUS
CONFIGURATIONS
acroget, aggregate
acronym,*, INITIALS, FIRST LETTER OF
WORDS
across, OVER
acrovat, aggravate
acruget, aggregate
acruvat, aggravate
acseal, axis(ial)
acsebt, except / accept
acsecute, execute
acsel, excel / accel / axle
acselurashen, accelerate(tion)
acsent, accent
acsentric, eccentric
acsepshen, except(ion)
acsept, accept / except
acses, access / excess
acsesurize, accessory(rize)
acshan, action
acshen, action
acshin, action
acshooul, actual
acshual, actual
acshuated, acuate(d)
acshun, action
acsis, access / ax(es) / axis
acsisory, accessory
acsite, excite
acsiul, axis(ial)
acskershin, excursion
acspereanse, experience
act,*,ted,ting,tor, ACTION "prefixes:
over/re/retro/under"
actaf, active
actef, active
actevate, activate
acteve, active
actin, action
action,*,nable,nably, DOING,
MOVEMENT "prefixes: in/re"
activate,*,ed,ting,tion, START "prefixes:
de/in"
active,ely,vity,veness,vate,vation,tor,
vist,vism, MOVING, CAUSE TO ACT
"prefixes: bio/in/over/pro/re/retro"
actovate, activate
actseed, exceed
actual,lly,lity,lization,lize, REAL
actuate,*,ted,ting,tion, INITIATE/BEGIN
ACTIVITY "prefixes: de/un"
actule, actual
actuvate, activate

actuve, active
acudemic, academic
acuemulate, accumulate
acuesativ, acquisitive
acuiesant, acquiesce(nt)
acuisativ, acquisitive
acuital, acquittal
acult, occult
acumpany, accompany
acumpened, accompany(nied)
acumulate, accumulate
acupansy, occupancy
acupuncture,*,rist, TREATMENT FOR
    HEALING BODY
acurate, accurate
acurens, occur(rrence)
acurit, accurate
acuse, accuse
acustic, acoustic
acustumed, accustom(ed)
acute,ely,eness, SHARP
acwatic, aquatic
acwaynt, acquaint
acwayntense, acquaintance
acwazition, acquisition
acweesent, acquiesce(nt)
acwifalent, equivalent
acwire, acquire
acwit, acquit
acwuzeshun, acquisition
acwyre, acquire
ad, PREFIX INDICATING 'TO/TOWARDS'
    MOST OFTEN MODIFIES THE WORD,
    SHORT FOR ADVERTISEMENT (or
    see at/add/aid)
adacity, audacity
adakit, etiquette
adalesint, adolescent
adam, atom
adamant,tly,tine, RELENTLESS, NOT
    PENETRABLE, A METAL
adamently, adamant(ly)
adamize, atom(ize)
adapt,*,ted,ting,tive,tively,tation,table,
    tableness,tability,ter,tor, ADJUST
    (or see adept) "prefixes: pre/retro"
adasity, audacity
adatif, additive
add,*,dded,dding,ddable,dditive,
    ddition,dditional,dditionally,
    ddendum, INCREASE, PLUS, MORE
    THAN BEFORE
addendum,*, SOMETHING ADDED

addict,*,ted,ting,tion,tive, HABITUAL/
    OBSESSIVE USE
additive,*, MORE, AN INCREASE,
    ADDITIONALLY
address,sses,ssed,ssing,ssee, ROUTE/
    LOCATION OF "prefixes: re"
adebt, adapt / adept
adec, attic / addict
adecuasi, adequacy
adecuat, adequate
adek, attic / addict
adekt, addict
adekuasi, adequacy
adekuat, adequate
adelesinse, adolescence
ademant, adamant
adement, adamant
ademize, atom(ize)
ademunt, adamant
adenaficashun, identification
adendum, addendum
adept,tly,tness, SKILLFUL (or see adapt)
adequace, adequacy
adequacy,cies, ABILITY
adequate,ely,eness, SUFFICIENT
    "prefixes: in"
adequise, adequacy
adequot, adequate
ader, adhere
adeshen, edition / add(ition)
adetif, additive
adetion, edition / add(ition)
adetude, attitude
adewlation, adulate(tion)
adgetate, agitate
adgitate, agitate
adgrenalin, adrenaline
adgudekashen, adjudicate(tion)
adgunct, adjunct
adgust, adjust
adhear, adhere
adhere,*,ed,ring,ent,ently,ence,esion,
    esive, STICKS TO
adhesion, STICKS TO
adhesive,*,eness, STICKS TO
adible, audible
adic, attic / addict
adict, addict
adicuasi, adequacy
adieu,*, GOOD-BYE
adik, attic / addict
adikit, etiquette
adikshen, addict(ion)
adikt, addict

adimant, adamant
adimdum, addendum
adimunt, adamant
adindum, addendum
adinefecashin, identification
adiquacy, adequacy
adiquase, adequacy
adiquit, adequate
adiquot, adequate
adishen, edition / add(ition)
aditev, additive
adition, edition / add(ition)
aditiv, additive
aditude, attitude
adiu, adieu
adjacent,tly, NEAR "prefixes: non"
adjasent, adjacent
adjasint, adjacent
adje, etch / edge
adjective,*,val,vally, WORD THAT
    MODIFIES A NOUN
adjewdikashen, adjudicate(tion)
adjewlation, adulate(tion)
adjitate, agitate
adjoin,*,ned,ning,nt,nts, TO JOIN/
    UNITE
adjourn,*,ned,ning,nment, DELAY
adjudicate,*,ed,ting,tion,tor,tive,
    JUDGE
adjudikashen, adjudicate(tion)
adjulation, adulate(tion)
adjunct,*,tive,tly,tion, JOINS/
    ACCOMPANIES
adjust,*,ted,ting,table,tment, CHANGE
    TO NEW CIRCUMSTANCE
adleb, ad-lib
adlesense, adolescence
adlesinse, adolescence
ad-lib,*,bbed,bbing, SPONTANEOUS
    PREPARATION
admenaster, administer
admenastrashen, administrate(tion)
admenester, administer
admenister, administer
admenistration, administrate(tion)
admenustrashen, administrate(tion)
admeshun, admission
admet, admit
admichin, admission
admichun, admission
admided, admit(tted)
adminaster, administer
administer,*,red,ring, SUPERVISE,
    DISPENSE

administrate,*,ed,ting,tion,tive,tively, tor, ONE WHO SUPERVISES
admire,*,er,ring,rable,rably,ration, CHERISH
admisable, admissible
admisef, admission(ive)
admishun, admission
admisible, admissible
admissible,ly,bility, ALLOWABLE "prefixes: in"
admission,*,ive, ENTRANCE, ADMIT TO
admisuf, admission(ive)
admit,*,tted,tting,ttance,ttedly, ALLOW "prefixes: non"
admited, admit(tted)
admizable, admissible
admizible, admissible
admonish,hes,hed,hing,her,hment,ition, itions,itory, WARN/ADVISE/DIRECT AGAINST
admyre, admire
ado, adieu
adobiografe, autobiography
adobt, adopt
adobyografy, autobiography
adograf, autograph
adolecense, adolescence
adolescence,nt, OF YOUTH
adolescent,*, YOUTH
adolesense, adolescence
adolesinse, adolescence
adolesint, adolescent
adolt, adult
adom, atom
adomadik, automatic
adoment, adamant
adometer, odometer
adomider, odometer
adomint, adamant
adomize, atom(ize)
adomobil, automobile
adoo, adieu
adoor, adore
adopt,*,ted,ting,tion,tive,table, ACQUIRE "prefixes: un"
adore,*,ed,ring,ringly,rable,rably, rability,rableness,ration, WORSHIP
adorn,*,ned,ning,nment, ENHANCE
adranalin, adrenaline
adrenaline, HORMONE
adrenulen, adrenaline
adress, address
adrift, MOVE/FLOAT WITHOUT DIRECTION

adroit,tly,tness, NIMBLE, SKILLFUL
adsedura, etcetera
adsetera, etcetera
adshe, etch / edge
adt, eight / ate
adu, adieu
adukit, etiquette
adulate,*,ed,ting,tor,tory,tion, EXCESSIVE PRAISE/COMPLIMENT
adulesinse, adolescence
adulesint, adolescent
adult,*, FULLY MATURE PHYSICALLY
adulterate,*,ed,ting,tion,ant,tor, DEBASE OR ALTER "prefixes: un"
adultery,rous,rously,rer, SEX WITH OTHERS WHEN MARRIED
adum, atom
adumant, adamant
adumint, adamant
adumize, atom(ize)
aduquacy, adequacy
adutif, additive
adutude, attitude
advance,*,ed,cing,ement, PROGRESS "prefixes: under"
advans, advance
advanse, advance
advantage,*,ed,ging,eous,eously, BENEFIT, BETTER CHANCE "prefixes: dis"
advantech, advantage
advantig, advantage
advantuge, advantage
advecate, advocate
advekate, advocate
advencher, adventure
advent,*, EXPECTED/IMPORTANT ARRIVAL
adventure,*,er,rous,rously,esome,ess, EXPLORATION "prefixes: mis"
adverb,*,bial, OF VERBS
advercity, adverse(sity)
advers, adverse
adversarie, adversary
adversary,ries,rial, OPPONENT
adverse,ely,eness,sity,sities,sary,saries, sarial,sative,satively, OPPOSE (or see averse)
adversly, adverse(ly)
advert,*,ted,ting,tence, CHANGE DIRECTION/ATTENTION TOWARDS (or see avert) "prefixes: in"
advertise,*,ed,sing,ement, DECLARE
advertize, advertise

advicate, advocate
advice, RECOMMEND (or see advise)
advikete, advocate
advincher, adventure
advinshure, adventure
advinture, adventure
advirb, adverb
advirsare, adversary
advirse, adverse
advirsere, adversary
advise,*,ed,sing,edly,edness,ement,sor, ser,sory,sable,sably,sability, INFORM (or see advice) "prefixes: in/un"
advize, advise / advice
advizuble, advise(sable)
advocate,*,ed,ting,tory,acy,tion,tor, SUPPORTER
advukate, advocate
advurb, adverb
advurcity, adverse(sity)
advurs, adverse
advursary, adversary
advursle, adverse(ly)
advursudy, adverse(sity)
advurtise, advertise
adyewlation, adulate(tion)
ael, ail
aem, aim
aemeable, amiable
aenckshes, anxious
aengwish, anguish
aenjul, angel
aenkre, angry
aenkshes, anxious
aent, aunt / ant
aenus, anus
aenxiatee, anxiety
aepaloge, apology
aerial, BY AIRCRAFT
aero, PREFIX INDICATING 'AIR' MOST OFTEN MODIFIES THE WORD
aerobic,*, OXYGEN EXERCISE
aerodynamic,*,cal,cally, AIR MOTION
aerosol,*, COMPRESSED CONTENTS IN A CAN
aesthetic,*,cal,cally, PLEASING TO THE EYES
aet, eight / ate
af, PREFIX INDICATING 'TO/TOWARDS' MOST OFTEN MODIFIES THE WORD
afadavit, affidavit
afair, affair
afale, avail

afare, affair
afder, after
afeador, aviator
afeator, aviator
afect, effect / affect
afectation, affect(ation)
afection, affection
afed, aphid
afedavit, affidavit
afekshin, affection
afekt, effect / affect
afektashin, affect(ation)
afektation, affect(ation)
afektion, affection
afeleat, affiliate
afemanit, effeminate
afend, offend
afenity, affinity
afens, offense
afensef, offense(sive)
afensif, offense(sive)
afer, affair / ever
afermative, affirm(ative)
afes, office
afeser, office(r)
afeshent, efficient
afeshul, official
afet, aphid
afeus, effuse
afews, effuse
affadavit, affidavit
affair,*, INTERACTION/BUSINESS
affare, affair
affecient, efficient
affect,*,ted,ting,ter,tation,tive, CAUSE
    SOMETHING TO HAPPEN, TRYING
    TO IMPRESS, PRETENTIOUS (or see
    effect) "prefixes: dis/un"
affection,*,nate,nately,nateness, TO
    EXPRESS FONDNESS
affenity, affinity
affidavit,*, LEGALLY BINDING
    STATEMENT
affiliate,*,ed,ting,tion, ASSOCIATED
    WITH "prefixes: dis/un"
affinity,tive, ATTRACTION
affirm,*,med,ming,mative,mation,
    SUPPORT WITH APPROVAL
    "prefixes: dis/un"
afflict,*,ted,tion,ter,tively, DISTRESS
affluence,*,nt,ntly, ABUNDANCE
affluent,tly, ABUNDANCE
afford,*,ded,dable,dability,dance,
    SPARE "prefixes: un"

affront,*,ted,ting, CONFRONT
affus, effuse
afid, aphid
afileat, affiliate
afimanit, effeminate
afinity, affinity
afinse, offense
afinsef, offense(sive)
afirm, affirm
afis, office
afiser, office(r)
afishensy, efficiency
afishent, efficient
afishinsy, efficiency
afishul, official
afishuly, official(lly)
afit, aphid
aflict, afflict
aflikt, afflict
afloat, FLOATING
aflot, afloat
afluense, affluence
afluent, affluent
afluinse, affluence
afoot, ABOUT TO HAPPEN, IN
    PROGRESS
aford, afford
aforduble, afford(able)
afore, PREFIX INDICATING 'BEFORE'
    MOST OFTEN MODIFIES THE WORD
afortuble, afford(able)
afot, afoot / aphid
afraid, FEARFUL
afrayed, afraid
afrebaudy, every(body)
afrewar, every(where)
afront, affront
afrunt, affront
aften, often
after, PREFIX INDICATING ''AFTER''
    MOST OFTEN MODIFIES THE WORD
    FOLLOWING
aftur, after
afud, aphid
afudavit, affidavit
afurmative, affirm(ative)
afus, office / effuse
afuser, office(r)
afut, afoot
ag, PREFIX INDICATING 'SOIL/FIELD'
    MOST OFTEN MODIFIES THE WORD
again, REPEAT
against, TOWARD, FACING, OPPOSITE
    OF FLOW

agany, agony
agasent, adjacent
agasint, adjacent
agd, age(d)
age,*,ed,ging,eless, MEASURE OF TIME
    "prefixes: over/under"
agen, again / age(ging)
agency,cies, OF BUSINESS, OPERATION
    OF POWER
agenda,*, SCHEDULE/FORMAT/PLAN
agene, agony
agenst, against
agent,*,ncy,ncies, CATALYST,
    INTRODUCED TO PERFORM A TASK
    "prefixes: re"
agenta, agenda
ageny, agony
agern, adjourn
agetat, agitate
agetiv, adjective
agewdicate, adjudicate
aggravate,*,ed,ting,tingly,tion, AGITATE
aggravation, AGITATE
aggregate,*,ed,ting,ely,tion,tive,tor,
    FORM TOGETHER, UNITE "prefixes:
    dis"
aggresef, aggressive
aggresefly, aggressive(ly)
aggreshen, aggression
aggresive, aggressive
aggression,*, OFFENSIVE/ROUGH/
    FORCEFUL
aggressive,ely,eness,ssor, AGGRAVATE/
    AGITATE "prefixes: un"
aggressor,*, ONE WHO AGGRAVATES/
    AGITATES
aggretion, aggression
agile,lity,eness, LIMBER, FLEXIBLE
aginda, agenda
aginst, against
aginsy, agency
agint, agent
aginy, agony
agirn, adjourn
agitate,*,ed,ting,tor,tion,tive,edly,
    AROUSE, AGGRAVATE, AGGRESSIVE
    STIMULATION
ago, PAST
agony,nies,nize,nized,nizing, SUFFER
agorn, adjourn
agrabat, acrobat
agravashen, aggravation
agravate, aggravate
agravation, aggravation

agrecultsher, agriculture
agree,*,eed,eeing,eement,eeable, eeably, CONSENT TO "prefixes: dis"
agregate, aggregate
agrekulcher, agriculture
agrenalin, adrenaline
agresef, aggressive
agreshen, aggression
agresif, aggressive
agresifle, aggressive(ly)
agresion, aggression
agresiv, aggressive
agresor, aggressor
agression, aggression
agressive, aggressive
agretion, aggression
agrevat, aggravate
agri, agree
agribat, acrobat
agricultcher, agriculture
agriculture,*,ral,rist,ralist,ralism, ralization, FARMING
agriget, aggregate
agrikultcher, agriculture
agrivate, aggravate
agrobat, acrobat
agrovat, aggravate
agrubat, acrobat
agruget, aggregate
agruvashen, aggravation
agruvat, aggravate
agruvation, aggravation
agsberament, experiment
agsblane, explain
agsebt, except / accept
agsecutive, executive
agseed, exceed
agsept, except / accept
agsersize, exercise / exorcise
agsert, exert
agspel, expel
agsplan, explain
agsplisit, explicit
agsrem, extreme
agstend, extend
agstenshen, extension
agstenuate, extenuate
agstereor, exterior
agsternal, external
agstinkt, extinct
agstradite, extradite
agstrakt, extract
agstreem, extreme
agstrordenair, extraordinaire

agstrordinery, extraordinary
agsturnal, external
agucolture, agriculture
agudecate, adjudicate
agudikate, adjudicate
agul, agile
agunct, adjunct
agune, agony
agunt, agent
aguny, agony
agust, august
agustible, adjust(able)
agutate, agitate
agutev, adjective
agzemt, exempt
ahead, COMING UP
ahed, ahead
ahod, ahold
ahold, TAKE NOTICE, MAKE CONTACT, GAIN CONTROL
ahpotment, appointment
aid,*,ded,ding, HELP
ail,*,led,ling,lment, SICK/NOT WELL (or see ale/aisle)
aile, aisle
aim,*,med,ming,mless,mlessly, mlessness, FOCUS ON A POINT, DIRECT ATTENTION
ainches, anxious
ainckshes, anxious
ainkshus, anxious
air,*,red,ring,rless, SPACE, A GAS/AURA (or see are/heir/err) "prefixes: un"
airborne, OFF THE GROUND
airea, area
airloom, heirloom
airobic, aerobic
airodynamic, aerodynamic
airoganse, arrogance
airport,*, AIRCRAFT BASE
aisle,*,ed, PASSAGEWAY
ait, eight / ate
aiz, eye(s) / ice
aj, age / edge
ajar, WHEN A DOOR IS NOT CLOSED ALL THE WAY
ajasent, adjacent
ajasint, adjacent
ajative, adjective
ajaur, ajar
aje, age
ajenda, agenda
ajensy, agency
ajent, agent

ajern, adjourn
ajetate, agitate
ajewdicat, adjudicate
ajewdikashen, adjudicate(tion)
ajil, agile
ajilety, agile(lity)
ajinda, agenda
ajinsy, agency
ajint, agent
ajitate, agitate
ajodikate, adjudicate
ajor, ajar
ajorn, adjourn
ajourn, adjourn
ajrenalin, adrenaline
ajudikate, adjudicate
ajul, agile
ajunct, adjunct
ajunt, agent
ajurn, adjourn
ajust, adjust
ajustible, adjust(able)
ajutev, adjective
ak, ache
akademe, academy
akademic, academic
akadume, academy
akamidate, accommodate
akashenul, occasion(al)
akaumplish, accomplish
akawnt, account
akcelaration, accelerate(tion)
akchen, action
akchuel, actual
akchun, action
akedemik, academic
aker, acre
akerens, occur(rrence)
akewmulate, accumulate
akewpunksher, acupuncture
akews, accuse
akewsashen, accuse(sation)
akidemic, academic
akiuponcsher, acupuncture
akiut, acquit
aklemate, acclimate
aklimation, acclimate(tion) / acclaim(amation)
aklumate, acclimate
aknaulig, acknowledge
akne, acne
aknolege, acknowledge
akod, echo(ed)
akomedashen, accommodate(tion)

akomidate, accommodate
akomidation, accommodate(tion)
akomodate, accommodate
akompaned, accompany(nied)
akompeny, accompany
akomplis, accomplice
akomplish, accomplish
akomudate, accommodate
akonume, economy
akord, accord
akordant, accord(ant)
akorinse, occur(rrence)
akount, account
akr, acre
akrabat, acrobat
akrabatek, acrobat(ic)
akrad, acrid
akragate, aggregate
akranem, acronym
akrat, acrid
akrebat, acrobat
akred, acrid
akree, agree
akregate, aggregate
akrenem, acronym
akret, acrid
akrevat, aggravate
akribat, acrobat
akrid, acrid
akrigate, aggregate
akrinem, acronym
akrit, acrid
akrivat, aggravate
akrobat, acrobat
akrogate, aggregate
akronem, acronym
akross, across
akrovat, aggravate
akrugat, aggregate
akruget, aggregate
akrunem, acronym
akruvat, aggravate
aks, ax / ache(s) / ask / ask(ed) / ax(ed)
aksald, excel(lled) / accel(lled)
akschange, exchange
aksd, ax(ed) / ask(ed)
aksderminate, exterminate
aksdurminate, exterminate
akseal, axis(ial)
aksedent, accident
akseed, exceed
aksel, excel / accel / axle
akselarashen, accelerate(tion)
akselarate, accelerate

akselaratur, accelerate(tor)
akseld, excel(lled) / accel(lled)
akselerate, accelerate
akselirashen, accelerate(tion)
akseluratur, accelerate(tor)
aksent, accent
aksentric, eccentric
aksentuate, accentuate
aksepshen, except(ion)
aksept, accept / except
akseptense, accept(ance)
akseptid, accept(ed)
akseptinse, accept(ance)
akses, access / ax(es) / axis / ask(s)
aksesares, accessory(ries)
aksesarize, accessory(rize)
aksesd, access(ed)
aksesible, access(ible)
aksesirize, accessory(rize)
aksesory, accessory
aksesuble, access(ible)
aksesurize, accessory(rize)
aksglude, exclude
aksglute, exclude
akshen, action
akshin, action
akshual, actual
akshuat, actuate
akshuated, acuate(d)
akshuel, actual
akshun, action
aksident, accident
aksidentul, accident(al)
aksil, axle
aksint, accent
aksintuate, accentuate
aksis, ax(es) / axis / access
aksisory, accessory
aksite, excite
aksitment, excite(ment)
akskeus, excuse
akskusis, excuse(s)
aksle, axil / axle
aksol, axil / axle
aksorsize, exercise / exorcise
akspensif, expense(sive)
akspinsif, expense(sive)
aksplan, explain
aksplisit, explicit
akspres, express
akspreshen, express(ion)
aksquse, excuse
akst, ax(ed) / ask(ed)
akstereor, exterior

akstinkt, extinct
aksturnal, external
aksudentul, accident(al)
aksul, axil / axle
aksulens, excel(lled) / accel(lled)
aksus, axis / ax(es)
akt, act / ache(d)
akter, act(or)
aktevate, activate
akteve, active
aktir, act(or)
aktivate, activate
aktive, active
aktober, october
aktovate, activate
aktuate, acuate
aktur, act(or)
aktuvate, activate
aktuve, active
akuazition, acquisition
akudemic, academic
akuiesent, acquiesce(nt)
akult, occult
akumpany, accompany
akumulate, accumulate
akupansy, occupancy
akupunksher, acupuncture
akur, occur / acre
akurense, occur(rrence)
akuret, accurate
akurints, occur(rrence)
akusashen, accuse(sation)
akuse, accuse
akustik, acoustic
akustumed, accustom(ed)
akute, acute
akwa, aqua
akwaent, acquaint
akwantense, acquaintance
akwashin, equation
akwasition, acquisition
akwate, equate
akwater, equator
akwatic, aquatic
akwaynt, acquaint
akwayntinse, acquaintance
akwazeshin, acquisition
akwefer, aquifer
akwesishun, acquisition
akwet, acquit
akwezishun, acquisition
akwinox, equinox
akwipment, equipment
akwire, acquire

akwit, acquit
akwitment, equipment
akwivulense, equivalent(ncy)
akwivulint, equivalent
akwoduct, aqueduct
akwufir, aquifer
akwuzishen, acquisition
akyerit, accurate
akzamen, examine
akzenshuate, accentuate
akzent, accent
akzinshuate, accentuate
akzint, accent
al, PREFIX INDICATING 'TO/TOWARDS'
    MOST OFTEN MODIFIES THE WORD
    (or see ail/ale/all/awl)
alabi, alibi
alactrishun, electrician
alagator, alligator
alagible, eligible
alakwens, eloquence
alakwent, eloquent
alaquens, eloquence
alarm,*,med,ming,mingly,mist, ALERT
alasteck, elastic
alastick, elastic
alastreus, illustrious
alau, allow
alaven, eleven
albem, album
albow, elbow
album,*, MEDIA COLLECTION
alcohol,lic,lism, CHEMICAL
alcove,*, NOOK
alder,*, A TREE (or see altar/alter)
aldir, alder / altar / alter
aldur, alder / altar / alter
ale,*, A BREWED DRINK (or see ail/all/
    alley/awl)
alean, alien
aleas, alias
alebi, alibi
aleby, alibi
alecate, allocate
alech, allege
alechens, allegiance
aleckt, elect
alecktrek, electric
alederite, illiterate
aledge, allege
alee, alley
alef, olive
aleg, allege
alegal, illegal

alegatur, alligator
alege, allege
alegens, allegiance / elegance
alegins, allegiance
alein, alien
aleinashen, alien(ation)
aleinate, alien(ate)
alej, allege
alejanse, allegiance
alejens, allegiance
alejins, allegiance
alekate, allocate
alekshen, elect(ion)
alekt, elect
alektrician, electrician
alektrik, electric
alektrishen, electrician
alekwens, eloquence
alekwent, eloquent
alemenade, eliminate
alemony, alimony
aleon, alien
alequence, eloquence
alequent, eloquent
alerche, allergy
alerchic, allergic
alerge, allergy
alerges, allergy(gies)
alergic, allergic
alert,*,ted,ting,tness, NOTIFY, SHARPLY
    AWARE
alesit, elicit / illicit
alet, elite
aletist, elite(tist)
aleun, alien
aleunashen, alien(ation)
aleunate, alien(ate)
aleus, alias
alev, olive
aleveate, alleviate
aleven, eleven
aleviate, alleviate
alevin, eleven
alevinth, eleven(th)
alevon, eleven
aley, alley
alf, elf
alfabedikul, alphabet(ical)
alfabet, alphabet
alfibetize, alphabet(ize)
alfubedikul, alphabet(ical)
alfubutize, alphabet(ize)
algae, WATER ORGANISM
algebra,aic,aically, TYPE OF MATH

algubra, algebra
ali, ally / alley
alians, alliance
alias,ses, ANOTHER NAME
alibi,*, EXCUSE
alicate, allocate
alid, ally(lied)
aliderate, illiterate
alien,*,nate,nation,nable, FOREIGNER
    (or see alliance) "prefixes: in/un"
alienashen, alien(ation)
alif, olive
aligater, alligator
align,*,ned,ning,nment, STRAIGHTEN
    "prefixes: re"
alikate, allocate
alike, SIMILAR
alikwens, eloquence
alikwent, eloquent
alimenate, eliminate
alimony, MONETARY ALLOWANCE
    AFTER DIVORCE
aline, align
alinment, align(ment)
aliquence, eloquence
aliquent, eloquent
alirt, alert
alis, ally(lies)
alisit, elicit / illicit
aliterate, illiterate
alitest, elite(tist)
aliunate, alien(ate)
alive, NOT DEAD, HAS SPIRIT
alja, algae
aljebra, algebra
aljibra, algebra
alk, elk
alkali,ine,inity,loid, CHEMICAL BALANCE
alkohol, alcohol
alkove, alcove
alkuhol, alcohol
all, EVERYTHING (or see ail/ale/awl)
    "prefixes: over"
allege,*,ed,ging,edly, ASSERT
allegiance,*,nt, LOYALTY
allelo, PREFIX INDICATING 'OTHER/
    ALTERNATE' MOST OFTEN
    MODIFIES THE WORD
allergic, SENSITIVE/REACTION TO
allergy,gies,genic,gic, SENSITIVE/
    REACTION TO
alleviate,*,ed,ting,tion,tive,tory,
    RELIEVE
alley,*,yway, PASSAGEWAY (or see ally)

alli, ally / alley

alliance,*,cing, JOIN "prefixes: mis/pro"

alligator,*, LARGE REPTILE

allocate,*,ed,ting,tion,table,tor, ASSIGN

allow,*,wed,wing,wable,wance,
PERMIT "prefixes: dis/un"

allowance,*, PERMITTED, ALLOTTED

alloy,*, METALS TOGETHER

alltogether, altogether

allude,*,ed,ding,usion,usive, CASUALLY
MAKE REFERENCE TO (or see elude)

allure,*,ed,ring,ement,ringly, TEMPT

allusion,*,ive, TO MENTION
INDIRECTLY/CASUALLY (or see
illusion)

allusive, TO MENTION INDIRECTLY/
CASUALLY (or see elusive/illusive)

ally,llies,llied,llying,lliance, UNITED (or
see alley)

almanac,*, BOOK WITH INFORMATION
AS IT RELATES TO SPACE/STARS

alminak, almanac

almonak, almanac

almost, CLOSE

almozt, almost

almunak, almanac

alof, aloof

alokate, allocate

alone, NO ONE, NOTHING ELSE

aloof,fly,fness, RESERVED/
DISINTERESTED COMPOSURE

aloore, allure

aloosuf, allusive / elusive / illusive

alop, elope

aloquence, eloquence

aloquent, eloquent

alosiv, allusive / elusive / illusive

alow, allow

alowins, allowance

alowy, alloy

aloy, alloy

alphabet,*,tic,tical,tize,tizes,tized,tizing,
tization,tizer, SET OF SYMBOLS/
LETTERS TO FORM WORDS

alphebetical, alphabet(ical)

alphubedikul, alphabet(ical)

already, BY THIS TIME

also, INCLUDED, ALONG WITH

alt, PREFIX INDICATING 'HIGH' MOST
OFTEN MODIFIES THE WORD

altamatum, ultimatum

altar,*, PLATFORM FOR WORSHIP (or
see alter/alder)

altematum, ultimatum

alter,*,red,ring,ration, TO SLIGHTLY
CHANGE/MODIFY (or see alder/
altar) "prefixes: in"

alterashen, alter(ation)

alternate,*,ed,ting,ely,tely,tion,tive,
tively, TO GO BACK AND FORTH
BETWEEN, ROTATE "prefixes: sub"

alternative,*,ely, CHOICES/OPTIONS

alternutiv, alternative

altetude, altitude

although, EVEN THOUGH

alti, PREFIX INDICATING 'HIGH' MOST
OFTEN MODIFIES THE WORD

altimatum, ultimatum

altir, alder / altar / alter

altirashen, alter(ation)

altiration, alter(ation)

altird, alter(ed)

altirnetly, alternate(ly)

altirnitef, alternative

altirnutiv, alternative

altitude,*, HEIGHT

alto, PREFIX INDICATING 'HIGH' MOST
OFTEN MODIFIES THE WORD

altogether, IN ONE PLACE

altumatum, ultimatum

altur, alder / altar / alter

alturashen, alter(ation)

alturation, alter(ation)

alturd, alter(ed)

alturnetly, alternate(ly)

alturnutiv, alternative

altwogether, altogether

aluby, alibi

alucate, allocate

alude, elude

aluf, aloof

alufent, elephant

alugable, eligible

alujen, illusion / allusion

alukate, allocate

alukwens, eloquence

alukwent, eloquent

alumenum, aluminum

aluminate, illuminate

aluminum, A METAL

alumony, alimony

alumunum, aluminum

aluquence, eloquence

aluquent, eloquent

alure, allure

alurgik, allergic

alurjik, allergic

alurt, alert

alusif, allusive / elusive / illusive

alusion, allusion / illusion

alusov, allusive / elusive / illusive

alustrious, illustrious

aluv, olive

always, FOREVER (or see aim)

alwaz, always

aly, ally

alyan, alien

alyke, alike

am, PRESENT TENSE OF "BE/BEING" (or
see aim)

amachur, amateur

amaculet, immaculate

amagen, imagine

amagenation, imagine(nation)

amakewlit, immaculate

amakulit, immaculate

amasher, amateur

amateur,*,rish,rishly,
NONPROFESSIONAL

amatur, amateur

amaunt, amount

amawntuble, amount(able)

amaze,*,ed,edly,zing,zingly,ement,
IMPRESS

ambaquety, ambiguity

ambechis, ambitious

ambegedy, ambiguity

ambegues, ambiguous

ambekyues, ambiguous

ambeshun, ambition

ambeshusnes, ambitious(ness)

ambetious, ambitious

ambi, PREFIX INDICATING 'BOTH/
AROUND' MOST OFTEN MODIFIES
THE WORD

ambichen, ambition

ambiches, ambitious

ambiguity,ties, TWO OR MORE WAYS
AN EXPRESSION COULD BE
INTERPRETED

ambiguous,sly,sness, TWO OR MORE
WAYS AN EXPRESSION COULD BE
INTERPRETED "prefixes: un"

ambiquety, ambiguity

ambishisnes, ambitious(ness)

ambishun, ambition

ambishus, ambitious

ambishusnes, ambitious(ness)

ambition,*, DESIRE TO ACHIEVE A GOAL

ambitious,sly,sness, STRIVING
DILIGENTLY TOWARDS A GOAL

amblanse, ambulance

amblins, ambulance
ambolanse, ambulance
amboosh, ambush
amboshd, ambush(ed)
ambuguedy, ambiguity
ambulance,*,atory,atories, RESCUE
    VEHICLE
ambulence, ambulance
ambush,hes,hed,her, ENTRAP
ambushd, ambush(ed)
ambutashen, amputate(tion)
ame, aim
ameable, amiable
ameba, amoeba
amechur, amateur
amedeat, immediate
ameds, emit / omit
ameible, amiable(ly)
amekibul, amicable
amekuble, amicable
amend,*,ded,ding,dment,dable,datory,
    REPAIR
amense, immense
amensurabl, immensurablee
amenus, ominous
amepa, amoeba
amerchen, immerse(sion)
amergensee, emergency
amerse, immerse / emersed
amershen, immerse(sion)
amertize, amortize
ameshen, omission / emission
ameteut, immediate
amethist, amethyst
amethyst,*, PURPLE QUARTZ
ameuble, amiable / amiable(ly)
amewsd, amuse(d)
amewsmint, amuse(ment)
amiable,eness,ly,bility, GOOD-
    NATURED
amicable,ly,bility, FRIENDLY
amichur, amateur
amikable, amicable
amikuble, amicable
amind, amend
amindment, amend(ment)
aminse, immense
aminsurable, immensurable
aminus, ominous
amirchen, immerse(sion)
amirse, immerse / emersed
amirshen, immerse(sion)
amishen, omission / emission
amit, emit / omit

amithist, amethyst
amitz, emit / omit
amiuble, amiable(ly)
ammonea, ammonia
ammonia,aic, A GAS
ammurshen, immerse(sion)
amne, omni
amnevore, omnivore
amnivore, omnivore
amochure, amateur
amoeba,*,bic, ANIMAL
among,gst, IN THE MIDST OF, WITH
    OTHERS
amonia, ammonia
amonkst, among(st)
amonya, ammonia
amortize,*,zable,tization, IN LOAN
    CALCULATION
amount,*,ted,ting, SUM
amownt, amount
ampakuety, ambiguity
ampegues, ambiguous
ampekuedy, ambiguity
ampel, ample
ampetate, amputate
ampeutashen, amputate(tion)
ampewtation, amputate(tion)
amphi, PREFIX INDICATING 'BOTH/
    AROUND' MOST OFTEN MODIFIES
    THE WORD
ampigewus, ambiguous
ampil, ample
ampition, ambition
amplafikashen, amplify(fication)
ample,er,est,eness, ENOUGH, PLENTY
amplefy, amplify
amplifucation, amplify(fication)
amplify,fies,fied,fier,ying,fiable,fication,
    MAGNIFY SOUND "prefixes: pre"
amplufikashen, amplify(fication)
amplufy, amplify
ampol, ample
amportant, important
ampukuety, ambiguity
ampul, ample
amputashen, amputate(tion)
amputate,*,ed,ting,tion,tee, REMOVE
    LIMB FROM MAIN TORSO
amrold, emerald
amruld, emerald
amune, immune
amunety, immune(nity)
amung, among
amunity, immune(nity)

amunkst, among(st)
amunxt, among(st)
amurchen, immerse(sion)
amurgensee, emergency
amurse, immerse / emersed
amurshen, immerse(sion)
amuse,*,ed,sing,ement, ENTERTAIN
amuthist, amethyst
amuze, amuse
amuzment, amuse(ment)
amythest, amethyst
an, PREFIX INDICATING 'TO/TOWARDS'
    MOST OFTEN MODIFIES THE WORD
ana, PREFIX INDICATING 'UP/BACK/
    AGAIN' MOST OFTEN MODIFIES THE
    WORD
anadot, anecdote
anagma, enigma / enema
anal,lly, NEAR/INVOLVING THE ANUS
    (or see annul)
analesis, analysis
analidek, analytic
analigy, analogy
analitek, analytic
analize, analyze
analog,gous,gously, TYPE OF WAVE/
    SOUND
analogy,gies,gous,gously, LIKENESS
analysis,ses, BREAKDOWN TO STUDY
analyst,*, PERSON WHO STUDIES
    DETAILS
analytic,*,cal,cally, PERSON WHO
    STUDIES DETAILS
analyze,*,ed,zing,er,zable,zation,
    STRICT EXAMINATION/STUDY
    "prefixes: un"
anamashen, animate(tion)
anamation, animate(tion)
anamulistik, animal(istic)
anarchy,hies,hism,hist,histic,hic,hical,
    hically, NO GOVERNMENT/
    CAPITALISM
anarkey, anarchy
anasthesia, anesthesia
anatomy,mic,mical,mically, COMPLETE
    STRUCTURE OF A BODY
anaumely, anomaly
anauns, announce
anbroder, embroider
ancestor,*,ry,tral,trally, LINEAGE
anchor,*,red,ring,rage,rages, STABILITY,
    BOAT HOLD
ancient,*,tness,tly, OLD, GREAT IN AGE
anckshes, anxious

ancorij, encourage / anchor(age)
ancshes, anxious
ancsiuty, anxiety
and, WORD USED AS A CONJUNCTION,
    THIS PLUS THAT, ALSO, INCLUDING
    (or see ant/aunt/end)
andanger, endanger
andefir, endeavor
andevur, endeavor
andlis, endless
andure, endure
ane, any
anebody, anybody
anebreated, inebriate(d)
anecdote,*,tal, STORY (or see antidote)
anedot, anecdote / antidote
anedotul, anecdote(tal)
anegma, enigma / enema
anekdote, anecdote
anekwitable, inequitable
anel, anal / annul
anelidek, analytic
anelog, analog
anelyze, analyze
anemal, animal
anemashen, animate(tion)
anemate, animate
anemation, animate(tion)
aneme, enemy
anemea, anemia
anemek, anemic
anemia, BLOOD HAS A DEFICIENCY/
    NEED (or see enema/enigma)
anemic,cally, BLOOD HAS A
    DEFICIENCY/NEED
anemul, animal
anemulestik, animal(istic)
anequitable, inequitable
aneresm, aneurysm
anerism, aneurysm
anerjetek, energetic
anes, anus
aneshil, initial
anesthesia,iologist,iology, AN
    ANESTHETIC
anesthetic,*,cally,ist,ize, PAIN KILLER
anesthetist,*, ONE WHO ADMINISTERS
    ANESTHESIA
anesthetize,*,ed,zing,zation, TO DULL
    PAIN WITH DRUG
anesthezia, anesthesia
anesthutize, anesthetize
aneurysm,*, WEAK BLOOD VESSEL
    WALL AT BASE OF BRAIN

anew, FRESH/NEW START
anewity, annuity
anewol, annual
anezthetic, anesthetic
anforse, enforce
angaje, engage
angchus, anxious
angel,*,lic,lical,lically, SPIRITUAL BEING
    (or see angle)
angelek, angel(ic)
anger,*,red,ring,gry,grily, MAD
angil, angel / angle
angir, anger
angle,*,ed,ling,er, SLANT/TILT/
    PERSPECTIVE IN DEGREES (or see
    angel)
angrafe, engrave
angrave, engrave
angre, angry
angrele, angrily
angreust, angry(riest)
angri, angry
angrily, OF ANGER
angry,rier,riest, EMOTION OF
    IRRITATED DISAPPOINTMENT
angryest, angry(riest)
angshes, anxious
angshus, anxious
angsiute, anxiety
anguish,hed,hing, SORROW
angul, angle / angel
angwish, anguish
angziute, anxiety
anialate, annihilate
anibreated, inebriate(d)
anidot, anecdote / antidote
anidotul, anecdote(tal)
anikdote, anecdote / antidote
anil, anal / annul
anilate, annihilate
anilidek, analytic
anilize, analyze
anilog, analog
anilyze, analyze
animal,*,listic,lise,lism,list,lity, NOT
    HUMAN
animashen, animate(tion)
animate,*,ed,ting,tion,tic,to,tor, LIVELY,
    AS IF REAL "prefixes: in"
animea, anemia / enema
animec, anemic
animic, anemic
animul, animal
animulistek, animal(istic)

aniresm, aneurysm
anis, anus
anishal, initial
anisthedek, anesthetic
anisthetic, anesthetic
anisthezia, anesthesia
anitiate, initiate
aniulate, annihilate
anjekshen, inject(ion)
anjel, angel
anjelik, angel(ic)
anjil, angel
anjoiment, enjoy(ment)
anjul, angel
ankches, anxious
ankchus, anxious
anker, anchor
ankor, anchor
ankoreg, encourage / anchor(age)
ankreust, angry(riest)
ankry, angry
ankshis, anxious
ankshus, anxious
anksiuty, anxiety
ankulent, inoculate(ant)
ankureg, anchor(age)
ankurig, encourage / anchor(age)
anlarje, enlarge
anliten, enlighten
anmal, animal
annihilate,*,ed,ting,tion,tor, DESTROY
announce,*,ed,cing,ement,er, DECLARE
annoy,*,yed,ying,yance, IRRITATE
annoyents, annoy(ance)
annual,*,lly,lize, YEARLY "prefixes: bi/
    semi"
annuely, annual(lly)
annuity,ties, ANNUAL STIPEND/
    PAYMENT
annul,lment, VOID, REVOKE (or see
    anal)
anoed, annoy(ed)
anoent, anoint
anof, enough
anogreashen, inaugurate(tion)
anogreation, inaugurate(tion)
anoint,*,ted,ting,tment, TO SELECT/
    CONSECRATE
anolidek, analytic
anomale, anomaly
anomaly,lies,lous,lously,listic, NOT
    NORMAL, IRREGULAR
anomile, anomaly
anomulus, anomaly(lous)

anonemous, anonymous
anonemusly, anonymous(ly)
anonimous, anonymous
anonimusly, anonymous(ly)
anonseate, enunciate
anonymity, REMAINS UNKNOWN
anonymous,sly,sness,mity, NOT
    KNOWN
anoqulent, inoculate(ant)
anoresm, aneurysm
anorgee, energy
anorgetek, energetic
anorkey, anarchy
anormus, enormous
another, ADDITIONAL
anothir, another
anough, enough
anounse, announce
anowe, annoy
anownse, announce
anoy, annoy
anoyance, annoy(ance)
anoyd, annoy(ed)
anportant, important
anrich, enrich
anrol, enroll
anrold, enroll(ed)
anser, answer
anseruble, answer(able)
ansestor, ancestor
anshent, ancient
anshunt, ancient
ansiklopedea, encyclopedia
ansir, answer
ansistor, ancestor
ansur, answer
ansuruble, answer(able)
answer,*,red,ring,rable,rably,
    SOLUTION "prefixes: un"
ant,*, SMALL SIX-LEGGED INSECT (or
    see and/ante/anti/aunt)
antagonize,*,ed,ist,istic,istically,
    ENEMY/OPPOSITION
ante, PREFIX INDICATING 'BEFORE/
    PRECEDING' MOST OFTEN
    MODIFIES THE WORD, POKER
    EXPRESSION, TO PRECEDE/COME
    BEFORE (or see anti/aunt(ie))
antebiotik, antibiotic
antecepate, anticipate
antefreeze, antifreeze
antehistamene, antihistamine
anteke, antique
antekwity, antique(uity)

antelope,*, MAMMAL
antena, antenna
antenna, DEVICE TO ATTRACT SIGNALS/
    FREQUENCY
anterior,*,rity,rly, BEFORE, IN FRONT
    OF, TOWARDS THE FRONT (or see
    interior)
antesapashen, anticipate(tion)
antesepate, anticipate
antesupation, anticipate(tion)
anthem,*, SONG
anthim, anthem
anthrapology, anthropology
anthripology, anthropology
anthropology,*gical, STUDY OF
    HUMANITY
anti, OPPOSE/DISAGREE, PREFIX
    INDICATING 'AGAINST' MOST
    OFTEN MODIFIES THE WORD (or
    see aunt(ie)/ante)
antibiotic,*,cally, MANMADE
    CHEMICAL
anticepate, anticipate
anticipate,*,ed,ting,tion,tive,tory,
    EXPECT
antidote,*,tal, USED TO REVERSE
    EFFECTS OF POISON (or see
    anecdote)
antifreeze, SUBSTANCE TO PREVENT
    FREEZING
antihistamine, INACTIVATES
    HISTAMINE
antikwedy, antique(uity)
antilope, antelope
antina, antenna
antique,*,ed,ely,uity,uate,uated,
    ANCIENT
antiquedy, antique(uity)
antireor, anterior / interior
antisapashen, anticipate(tion)
antisupation, anticipate(tion)
antonym,*,mic,mous, WORDS WITH
    OPPOSITE MEANINGS
antorse, endorse / indoor(s)
antser, answer
antulope, antelope
anu, anew
anual, annual
anuale, annual(lly)
anudot, anecdote
anuel, annual
anuety, annuity
anuile, annual(lly)
anuity, annuity

anul, annul
anulidek, analytic
anulise, analyze
anulyze, analyze
anumashen, animate(tion)
anumate, animate
anumation, animate(tion)
anumel, animal
anumilestik, animal(istic)
anunseate, enunciate
anuresm, aneurysm
anurgee, energy
anurjetek, energetic
anus, LOWER ORIFICE
anustheshu, anesthesia
anusthetik, anesthetic
anuther, another
anuzthetek, anesthetic
anvilope, envelope
anvirunmint, environment
anvy, envy
anwritch, enrich
anxiety,ties,ious,iously,iousness,
    UNEASINESS
anxious,iously,iousness, UNEASINESS
any,ybody,yhow,ymore,yone,ything,
    yway,ywhere,ytime, SOME AT
    RANDOM, A PORTION OF
anybody,y's, ANY PERSON
anyerism, aneurysm
anyual, annual
anyurism, aneurysm
aoch, ouch
ap, PREFIX INDICATING 'TO/TOWARDS'
    MOST OFTEN MODIFIES THE WORD
apademic, epidemic
apal, apple / appall
apaloge, apology
aparatus, apparatus
apareshun, apparition
aparint, apparent
aparition, apparition
apart, MAKE INTO SEPARATE PIECES
apartment,*, ROOMS IN DWELLING
apartmint, apartment
apasenter, epicenter
apasom, opossum
apathetic,cal,cally, INDIFFERENT, NO
    EMOTION
apathy,hetic, INDIFFERENT, NO
    EMOTION
apatight, appetite
apatit, appetite
apatizer, appetizer

apatizing, appetizing
apauled, appall(lled)
apaustrufe, apostrophe
apdoman, abdomen
apdukt, abduct
apduman, abdomen
apeal, appeal
apearance, appearance
apecal, apical
apecl, apical
apeel, appeal
apekal, apical
apel, apple / appeal / appall
apendektumy, appendectomy
apenyun, opinion
apera, opera
aperal, apparel
aperant, apparent
aperatus, apparatus
apereshen, apparition
aperil, apparel
aperint, apparent
aperishen, apparition
aperition, apparition
aperul, apparel
aperunt, apparent
apesode, episode
apethetik, apathetic
apetight, appetite
apetit, appetite
apetizer, appetizer
aphed, aphid
aphid,*, INSECT
apical,lly, APEX, TIP/TOP OF "prefixes: sub"
apidemic, epidemic
apikal, apical
apil, apple / able / appeal
apindectemy, appendectomy
apineun, opinion
apinyun, opinion
apiol, appeal
apirans, appearance
apirens, appearance
apiretion, apparition
apithetik, apathetic
apitite, appetite
apitizer, appetizer
aplakashen, application
aplaud, applaud
aplauz, applause
aple, apple
aplecable, applicable
aplecant, applicant

aplecation, application
aplecator, applicator
aplefeus, oblivious
aplekant, applicant
aplekashen, application
aplekator, applicator
aplekuble, applicable
apli, apply
aplianse, appliance
aplicable, applicable
aplicant, applicant
aplicator, applicator
aplid, apply(lied)
apliderate, obliterate
aplifeus, oblivious
aplikashen, application
aplikation, application
aplikator, applicator
aplikuble, applicable
apliveon, oblivion
aplod, applaud
aplos, applause
aplukant, applicant
aplukashen, application
aplukation, application
aplukator, applicator
aply, apply
apodimic, epidemic
apoent, appoint
apoentment, appointment
apoint, appoint
apointment, appointment
apol, apple / able / appall
apold, appall(lled)
apolegize, apology(gize)
apoligize, apology(gize)
apology,gies,gize,gizes,gized,gizing, getic,getically, ASK FORGIVENESS
apolstery, upholstery
apoluge, apology
apolugize, apology(gize)
aponent, opponent
aponit, opponent
apose, oppose
apostrophe,*, SYMBOL IN ENGLISH LANGUAGE
aposum, opossum
apotizing, appetizing
apotment, appointment
apoynt, appoint
apoze, oppose
appal, apple / appall
appall,*,lled,lling,llingly, DISMAYED, SHOCKED, HORRIFIED

apparatus,ses, EQUIPMENT
apparel, CLOTHING
apparent,tly,tness, CLEAR
apparition,*, SPIRIT
appatite, appetite
appatizer, appetizer
appeal,*,led,ling,lingly,lable, CALL FOR MERCY, VIEW FAVORABLY "prefixes: un"
appear,*,red,ring,rance, BECOME VISIBLE "prefixes: dis"
appearance,*, BECOME VISIBLE
appel, appeal / apple
appendectomy,mies, REMOVE APPENDIX FROM BODY
apper, appear
apperal, apparel
apperent, apparent
appetite,*,tive,izing,izer, DESIRE, A HUNGER, A FOOD
appetizer,*, FOOD BEFORE A MEAL
appetizing,gly,zer, DESIRE, A HUNGER, A FOOD
applaud,*,ded,ding,use, USE HANDS TO CLAP
applause, ACCLAIM, USE HANDS TO CLAP
apple,*, FRUIT
appliance,*, SPECIALIZED TOOL/ MACHINE TO PERFORM SPECIFIC TASKS
applicable,eness,ly, RELEVANT, USEFUL "prefixes: in"
applicant,*, CANDIDATE FOR EMPLOYMENT
applicate,*,ed,ting,tion,tor,ant, PUT TO USE, APPLY
application,*, FORM TO APPLY FOR WORK "prefixes: dis"
applicator,*,ting, USED TO APPLY SOMETHING
apply,lies,lied,lying,lier,liable,liableness, licate,lication,licator,licatory, licative,licatively,licable,licably, licability, PUT ON, RELEVANT TO "prefixes: mis/pre/un"
appoint,*,ted,ting,tee,tment, ASSIGN, DESIGNATE "prefixes: dis"
appointment,*, AN ASSIGNED TIME "prefixes: dis"
apprahenshun, apprehension
appraisal,*,ser,sement, EVALUATION
appraise,*,ed,sing,sable,ement,er,sal, EVALUATION

apprapo, apropos
appreciate,*,ed,ting,tion,tory,tive,able, GRATEFUL "prefixes: in/un"
apprehend,*,ded,ding,nsive,nsively, nsiveness,nsion,nsible, TO SEIZE, BE CAUTIOUS "prefixes: mis"
apprehension,*, CAUTIOUS, HESITANT "prefixes: mis"
apprehensive,ely,eness,ion,ible, CAUTIOUS "prefixes: mis"
apprentice,*,ed,cing,eship, LEARNER/IN TRAINING
appresif, oppress(ive)
appripo, apropos
approach,hes,hed,hing,hable,hability, hableness,hably, ADVANCE TOWARDS, NEARING "prefixes: in/un"
appropo, apropos
appropriate,*,ted,ting,ely,eness, PROPER TO, BELONGS ALONG WITH, IN CHARACTER WITH "prefixes: in/mis/non"
approve,*,ed,ving,val,vable,vingly, ACCEPTANCE/COMMENDATION "prefixes: dis"
approximate,ed,ely,ting,tion, AROUND/SOMEWHAT
apprupo, apropos
apracot, apricot
aprahenshun, apprehension
apraisal, appraisal
apraise, appraise
apral, april
aprapo, apropos
aprase, appraise
aprased, appraise(d)
aprasing, appraise(sing)
aprazul, appraisal
apreciate, appreciate
aprehend, apprehend
aprehenshun, apprehension
aprehensive, apprehensive
aprehind, apprehend
aprekot, apricot
aprel, april
apren, apron
aprentis, apprentice
apres, oppress
apresheate, appreciate
apreshen, oppress(ion)
apresif, oppress(ive)
aprhenshun, apprehension
apricot,*, FRUIT

aprikot, apricot
april, A MONTH OF THE YEAR (ENGLISH)
aprin, apron
aprintise, apprentice
apripo, apropos
aproach, approach
aproch, approach
aprol, april
apron,*, CLOTHING PROTECTOR
apropos, SUITABLE IN A PARTICULAR SITUATION/TIME
apropreate, appropriate
apropriate, appropriate
aprotch, approach
aproval, approve(val)
aproxemat, approximate
aproxemation, approximate(tion)
aproximate, approximate
aproxumation, approximate(tion)
apruful, approve(val)
apruhensev, apprehensive
aprul, april
aprupo, apropos
apruvel, approve(val)
apsalutly, absolute(ly)
apsens, absence / absent(s)
apsent, absent
apsentee, absent(ee)
apserd, absurd
apserdle, absurd(ly)
apshen, option
apsiloot, absolute
apsins, absence / absent(s)
apsintee, absent(ee)
apsird, absurd
apsoloot, absolute
apsolute, absolute
apsolution, absolve(lution)
apsolv, absolve
apsorb, absorb
apstane, abstain
apstinent, abstinent
apstract, abstract
apstrukshen, abstract(ion) / obstruct(ion)
apstunent, abstinent
apsulootly, absolute(ly)
apsulute, absolute
apsulutly, absolute(ly)
apsurd, absurd
apsurdly, absurd(ly)
aptetood, aptitude
aptetude, aptitude

aptikate, abdicate
aptimen, abdomen
aptitewd, aptitude
aptitude,*, TENDENCY TOWARDS, AFFINITY FOR
aptomen, abdomen
aptumen, abdomen
apul, apple
aputhetik, apathetic
aputit, appetite
aputizer, appetizer
apuzit, opposite
apzaulv, absolve
apzolv, absolve
apzorb, absorb
aqaint, acquaint
aqefir, aquifer
aqire, acquire
aqiuponcsher, acupuncture
aqiut, acquit
aqua,atic,atics,ueous, WATER, TO DO WITH WATER, A COLOR "prefixes: non/sub"
aquaduct, aqueduct
aquaent, acquaint
aquafer, aquifer
aquaint, acquaint
aquareum, aquarium
aquarium,*, FISH CONTAINER
aquatic,*, IN WATER "prefixes: non/semi/sub"
aqueduct,*, WATER CHANNEL
aquefer, aquifer
aquiesent, acquiesce(nt)
aquifer,*,rous, PROVIDES WATER
aquipd, equip(pped)
aquivalint, equivalent
aqute, acute
aqwazitun, acquisition
aqwiesent, acquiesce(nt)
aqwire, acquire
aqwit, acquit
aqwuzishen, acquisition
ar, are / heir / air / our / hour
ara, array / aura
arachnid,*,noid, WINGLESS ANTHROPODS
aradekate, eradicate
aradic, erratic / erotic
aradikashen, eradicate(tion)
aradikate, eradicate
araign, arraign
araignment, arraign(ment)
arainment, arraign(ment)

arakned, arachnid
arangment, arrange(ment)
aranj, arrange
aranment, arraign(ment)
arase, erase
araser, eraser
arashinal, irrational
aratic, erratic
araudik, erotic
aray, array
arayn, arraign
araze, erase
arazer, eraser
arbeder, arbiter
arbeter, arbiter
arbetrate, arbitrate
arbiter,*,tral, ONE WHO MAKES
    DETERMINATION
arbitrary,rily,riness, RANDOM
    DETERMINATION
arbitrate,*,ed,ting,tion,tor, TO
    DETERMINE
arborne, airborne
arbutrashen, arbitrate(tion)
arbutrate, arbitrate
arc,*, PART OF A CURVE (or see ark/
    arch)
arcade,*,dia, OF GAMES OR ARCHED
    PASSAGEWAY
arcaek, archaic
arch,hes,hed,hing, A CURVED BEND,
    PREFIX INDICATING 'CHIEF/
    BEGINNING' MOST OFTEN
    MODIFIES THE WORD (or see ark/
    arc) "prefixes: over"
archaek, archaic
archaic, OLD-FASHIONED, ANCIENT
archeology,gist,gical, STUDY OF PEOPLE
archer,*,ry, ONE WHO USES BOWS AND
    ARROWS
archetekt, architect
archir, archer
architect,*,ture,tural, BUILDER
archive,*,ed,ving,val,vist, PLACE OF
    PUBLIC RECORDS "prefixes: un"
archur, archer
archure, archer(y)
arckiology, archeology
arctic, NORTH POLE "prefixes: sub"
ardefishal, artificial
ardekle, article
ardent,tly, PASSIONATE
ardery, artery
ardest, artist

ardewous, arduous
ardgewus, arduous
ardifishel, artificial
ardikle, article
ardint, ardent
ardiry, artery
ardist, artist
ardjewous, arduous
ardufishul, artificial
ardukle, article
arduous,sly,sness, DIFFICULT
ardury, artery
are, TO BE, IS (or see air/heir/hour/our)
area,*,al, RANGE OF CONCEPT/EVENT/
    OPERATION
arear, arrear
ared, arid
aregate, irrigate
aregenashen, originate(tion)
aregeno, oregano
aregenul, origin(al)
arejenul, origin(al)
arekshin, erect(ion)
arekt, erect
aren't, CONTRACTION OF THE WORDS
    'ARE NOT'
arena,*, ENCLOSED SPACE
arend, errand
areplasible, irreplaceable
areprochible, irreproachable
arer, error / arrear
arest, arrest
arestokrat, aristocrat
arethmatic, arithmetic
areu, area
areul, aerial
arezt, arrest
argeumint, argument
argew, argue
argkeumint, argument
argue,*,ed,uing,uable,uably, DEBATE,
    DISCUSS "prefixes: in/un"
argument,*,tation,tative,tum, DEBATE,
    DISCUSS
arguous, arduous
arguwus, arduous
aria, area
arid,dity, PARCHED "prefixes: semi"
arie, awry
arife, arrive
ariful, arrival
arigate, irrigate
arigenashen, originate(tion)
ariginul, origin(al)

arijinul, origin(al)
arind, errand
arint, aren't
ariplasible, irreplaceable
arir, error
arisol, aerosol
aristocrat,*,tic,acy, WEALTHY UPPER
    CLASS
arithmetic,cal,cally,cian, MATH
arivd, arrive(d)
arive, arrive
arivul, arrival
arjuwus, arduous
ark,*, BOX/CHEST/CUPBOARD/BOAT(or
    see arc/arch)
arkade, arcade
arkaek, archaic
arkaik, archaic
arkeoligy, archeology
arketekt, architect
arkeu, argue
arkiology, archeology
arkitect, architect
arkiteksher, architect(ure)
arkive, archive
arktic, arctic
arku, argue
arkumint, argument
arkutekshur, architect(ure)
arkyve, archive
arloom, heirloom
arm,*,med,ming,mament, APPENDAGE
    ON UPPER TORSO, TO TAKE UP
    WEAPONS "prefixes: dis/un/under"
armature,*, DEVICE OR STRUCTURE/
    SUPPORT
arme, army
armes, army(mies)
armicher, armature
armonica, harmonica
armor,red,ry,ries,rer, BODY
    PROTECTION, COVERING,
    MILITARY/WEAPONS "prefixes: un"
armucher, armature
armur, armor
army,mies, MANY BODIES
arn, iron
arnamint, ornament
arnge, orange
arnje, orange
arnt, aren't
arnument, ornament
aro, arrow
aroara, aurora

arobek, aerobic
arobik, aerobic
arochun, erosion
arode, erode
arodik, erotic
arodynamic, aerodynamic
aroganse, arrogance
arogate, irrigate
arogent, arrogance(nt)
arogint, arrogance(nt)
aroma,*,atic,atize, ODOR, SMELL
aromadek, aroma(tic)
arond, errand
aronic, ironic
aror, error
arora, aurora
arosef, erosive
aroshin, erosion
arosive, erosive
around, HERE AND THERE
arouse,*,ed,sing,sal, AWAKEN/
    STIMULATE/ACTIVATE
arouzel, arouse(sal)
arow, arrow
arownd, around
arowsul, arouse(sal)
arowze, arouse
arport, airport
arraign,*,ned,ning,nment, ANSWER
    INDICTMENT
arrange,*,ed,ging,ement,er, ADJUST,
    SITUATE "prefixes: dis/un"
arranment, arraign(ment)
array,*,yed, ORDER "prefixes: dis"
arrear,*,rage, PAST DUE
arrest,*,ted,ting,tingly, SUSPEND,
    CAPTURE
arrival,*, BE AT DESTINATION
arrive,*,ed,ving,val, PRESENT AT
    DESTINATION
arrogance,nt,ntly, OVERLY SELF-
    IMPORTANT
arrow,*, SHAFT WITH POINT
arrowgance, arrogance
arsen, arson
arson,*,nist, MALICIOUS/INTENTIONAL
    BURNING
arsunest, arson(ist)
art,*,tist,tistry,tsy,ty,tistic,tistical,
    tistically,tisan,tful,tfully,tfulness,
    tless, tlessly,tlessness,tiness,
    METHOD OF EXPRESSION "prefixes:
    in/non"
arteculate, articulate

artefishel, artificial
artekewlate, articulate
artekulashen, articulate(tion)
artekulate, articulate
artelury, artillery
artereal, arterial
arterial,*, PATH FOR FLOW
artery,ries,ric, CHANNEL FOR
    TRANSPORTATION
artesdik, artist(ic)
artest, artist
artestek, artist(ic)
arthridek, arthritis(ic)
arthridis, arthritis
arthritis,ic, INFLAMMATION
arthudox, orthodox
article,*, PART, ONE OF SEVERAL
articulate,*,ed,ting,tion,tely,eness,
    INTEGRATE, SPECIFIC "prefixes: dis/
    in"
artificial,lly, SIMULATED, NOT REAL
artifishul, artificial
artik, arctic
artikel, article
artikewlate, articulate
artikulashen, articulate(tion)
artikulate, articulate
artillery, FOR WEAPONS
artireal, arterial
artiry, artery
artisdik, artist(ic)
artist,*,tistic,tistically, SKILLED
    "prefixes: in/un"
artistek, artist(ic)
artsh, arch
artsher, archer
artucle, article
artufishul, artificial
artury, artery
arubshen, erupt(ion) / irrupt(ion)
arubt, erupt / irrupt
arubtif, erupt(ive) / irrupt(ive)
arugate, irrigate
arupshen, erupt(ion) / irrupt(ion)
arupt, erupt / irrupt
aruptif, erupt(ive) / irrupt(ive)
aruption, erupt(ion) / irrupt(ion)
arye, awry
aryve, arrive
as, WORD USED TO COMPARE, PREFIX
    INDICATING 'TO/TOWARDS' MOST
    OFTEN MODIFIES THE WORD (or
    see ace)
asaeal, assail

asaee, essay
asail, assail
asalt, assault
asasen, assassin
asault, assault
asay, essay
asbekt, aspect
asberashun, aspirate(tion)
asberegus, asparagus
asbeshulee, especially
asbestos, TYPE OF FIBER
asbir, aspire
asburin, aspirin
ascape, escape
ascend,*,ded,ding,dable,dance,dancy,
    dence,dency,dant,der,nsion,nsional,
    DOMINANT, RISING ABOVE, GO UP
    (or see assent/ascent)
ascendant,*,nce, DOMINANT, RISE
    ABOVE OTHERS
ascension,*,nal, TO GO UP
ascent,*,nsion, MOTION UPWARDS (or
    see assent/ascend)
ascertain,*,ned,ning,nable,nably,ner,
    nment, MAKE SURE "prefixes: un"
ascetic,cal,cally,cism, STRICT, SEVERE,
    EXCESSIVE (or see acetic/acidic)
ascind, ascend / ascent / assent
ascrow, escrow
asd, ask(ed) / ax(ed) / ace(d) / acid
asdeem, esteem
asdonesh, astonish
ased, ask(ed) / ax(ed) / acid / ace(d)
asedek, acetic / acidic / ascetic
asemble, assemble / assemble(ly)
asemetric, asymmetric
asemewlate, assimilate
asemulate, assimilate
asend, ascend / ascent / assent
asendent, ascendant
asense, essence
asenshil, essential
asent, ascend / ascent / assent
asential, essential
asershen, assert(ion)
asert, assert
asertane, ascertain
asertif, assert(ive)
asertion, assert(ion)
ases, assess / access / ace(s)
aseshun, accession
asesible, access(ible)
asesment, assessment
asest, assist

asesuble, access(ible)
aset, acid / asset
asetic, acetic / acidic / ascetic
asexual, NOT SEXUAL
asfalt, asphalt
asfault, asphalt
asfikseate, asphyxiate
asfixiate, asphyxiate
asfolt, asphalt
ashamed,dly, TOUCHED BY SHAME,
  NOT PROUD "prefixes: un"
ashamt, ashamed
asheeve, achieve
asher, assure
ashirense, assure(rance)
ashtarik, asterisk
ashuranse, assure(rance)
asid, acid / aside
aside, SEPARATE FROM
asidic, acetic / acidic / ascetic
asiduous, assiduous
asign, assign
asignment, assignment
asijuous, assiduous
asilum, asylum
asim, awesome
asimble, assemble
asimetric, asymmetric
asimetry, asymmetry
asimilate, assimilate
asimulate, assimilate
asind, ascend
asindent, ascendant
asine, assign
asinment, assignment
asinse, essence
asinshul, essential
asint, ascend / ascent / assent
asirshen, assert(ion)
asirt, assert
asirtane, ascertain
asirtev, assert(ive)
asist, assist
asitic, acetic / acidic / ascetic
ask,*,ked,king, DORMANT STATE
  "prefixes: un"
askalador, escalator
askalater, escalator
askap, escape
askort, escort
askrow, escrow
askt, ask(ed) / ax(ed)
askulader, escalator
asleep, DORMANT STATE

asmu, asthma
asocheate, associate
asociate, associate
asolt, assault
asorded, assorted
asordment, assortment
asorted, assorted
asortment, assortment
asosheate, associate
asoshiate, associate
asparagus, VEGETABLE
aspect,*, OUTLOOK
aspekt, aspect
asperagus, asparagus
asperashun, aspirate(tion)
asperation, aspirate(tion)
asperen, aspirin
asperugus, asparagus
aspeshilee, especially
aspeshulee, especially
aspestus, asbestos
asphalt, MINERAL PITCH
asphixiate, asphyxiate
asphyxiate,*,ed,ting,tion, OF
  BREATHING
aspirashun, aspirate(tion)
aspirate,*,ed,ting,tor,tion,tional,
  AMBITION, OF BREATHING
  "prefixes: un"
aspire,*,ed,ring,er,rate,rant,ration,
  GOAL, DESIRE "prefixes: un"
aspirin,*, PAIN RELIEVER
asprashun, aspirate(tion)
aspren, aspirin
aspurashun, aspirate(tion)
aspuration, aspirate(tion)
aspuren, aspirin
assail,lable,lant, IMPACT UPON
  "prefixes: un"
assasin, assassin
assassin,*,nate,nation, TO MURDER, A
  MURDERER
assault,*,ted,ting, ATTACK WITH
  INTENT TO HARM
assemble,*,ed,ling,lage,ly, PUT
  TOGETHER "prefixes: dis/un"
assent,ted,ting,ter,tor,tingly,tive,tively,
  tiveness, AGREEMENT (or see
  ascent)
assert,*,ted,ting,tion,table,ter,tive,
  tively,tiveness, INSIST
assess,sses,ssed,ssing,ssment,ssable,
  EXAMINE, EVALUATE "prefixes: non"
assessment,*, APPRAISAL, EVALUATION

asset,*, POSSESS SOMETHING
  VALUABLE
assiduous,sly, DILIGENT
assign,*,ned,ning,nment, APPORTION
assignment,*, ASSIGNED WORK
assimetric, asymmetric
assimilate,*,ed,ting,tion, MAKE INTO,
  BECOME LIKE
assint, assent
assist,*,ted,ting,tant,tance, HELP
associate,*,ed,ting,tion,tive,
  CONNECTION TO "prefixes: dis/
  non"
assorted,ting,tment, VARIOUS TYPES
assortment, VARIOUS TYPES
assume,*,ed,ming,mingly,mer,mable,
  mption,mptive, SUPPOSE A FACT
  "prefixes: un"
assumption,*,ive, TAKE FOR GRANTED
assure,*,ed,rance,rances, CERTAINTY
  "prefixes: re"
assymetric, asymmetric
ast, ask / ask(ed) / ax(ed)
asteem, esteem
astemate, estimate
asterik, asterisk
asterisk, LITTLE TEXT STAR
asteroed, asteroid
asteroid,*, PERTAINING TO STAR
asthetik, aesthetic
asthma,atic,atical,atically, DIFFICULTY
  BREATHING
asthmu, asthma
astimate, estimate
astonesh, astonish
astonish,hes,hed,hing,hment,
  SURPRISE/IMPRESS
astragen, estrogen
astral,ly, STELLAR "prefixes: sub"
astrawneme, astronomy
astrek, asterisk
astrengent, astringent
astrenjint, astringent
astrenot, astronaut
astres, estrus
astrik, asterisk
astringent,*,ncy,tly, ACRID "prefixes:
  sub"
astrinot, astronaut
astris, estrus
astroed, asteroid
astrol, astral
astrolegy, astrology

astrology,ger,gic,gical,gically,gist, PREDICT THE FUTURE WITH THE STARS

astronaut,*, PERSON OF SPACE FLIGHT

astroneme, astronomy

astronomic,mical,mically, NUMEROUS/ GREAT PROPORTION

astronomy,mer,mers, OBSERVE CELESTIAL BODIES "prefixes: bio"

astronot, astronaut

astronume, astronomy

astroyd, asteroid

astrugen, estrogen

astrul, astral

astrunot, astronaut

astumate, estimate

astural, astral

asturik, asterisk

asturisk, asterisk

asum, awesome / assume

asumetric, asymmetric

asumpshen, assumption

asumption, assumption

asunse, essence

asurans, assure(rance)

asurants, assure(rance)

asurshen, assert(ion)

asurtif, assert(ive)

asylom, asylum

asylum, REFUGE FOR DESTITUTE

asymetric, asymmetric

asymmetric,cal,ry,ries, OFF-BALANCE

asymmetry,ries, OFF-BALANCE

at, A PREPOSITION EXPRESSING LOCATION OR SOMETHING IN PARTICULAR, PREFIX INDICATING 'TO/TOWARDS' MOST OFTEN MODIFIES THE WORD (or see ate/ eight/add)

atach, attach

atack, attack

ataen, attain

atain, attain

atak, attack

atament, adamant

atamint, adamant

atane, attain

atatch, attach

atcheeve, achieve

ate, PAST TENSE FOR THE WORD 'EAT' (or see eight/add) "prefixes: over"

atec, attic / addict

ated, add(ed)

atek, attic / addict

atekwase, adequacy

atembt, attempt

atemobel, automobile

atempt, attempt

atemt, attempt

atenchin, attention

atend, attend

atendens, attend(ance)

atendent, attend(ant)

atenshin, attention

atentef, attentive

atention, attention

atentive, attentive

atequasy, adequacy

ateqwit, adequate

aternal, eternal

aterney, attorney

atest, attest

atesy, odyssey

atetif, additive

atetude, attitude

atgasent, adjacent

atgasint, adjacent

atgern, adjourn

atgewdikate, adjudicate

atgust, adjust

athear, adhere

atheist,ism,tic,tical,tically, DISBELIEF IN A GOD

athek, ethic

athere, adhere

athesif, adhesive

athic, ethic

athiest, atheist

athik, ethic

athleat, athlete

athlete,*,tic,tics,tically, SPORTS TRAINED, ATHLETE "prefixes: deca"

athletic,*,tically, SPORTS TRAINED, ATHLETE

athnek, ethnic

athnuk, ethnic

athorety, authority

athrek, ether(ic)

athuk, ethic

atic, attic / addict

atid, add(ed)

atikit, etiquette

atikwit, adequate

atikwuse, adequacy

atimant, adamant

atimint, adamant

atimt, attempt

atinchon, attention

atind, attend

atinshun, attention

atipecle, atypical

atipikul, atypical

atiquit, adequate

atiquot, adequate

atire, attire

atisum, autism

atitif, additive

atitude, attitude

atmechen, admission

atmedid, admit(tted)

atmenester, administer

atmenustrashen, administrate(tion)

atmeshen, admission

atmesphere, atmosphere

atmichen, admission

atmided, admit(tted)

atminaster, administer

atminastrashin, administrate(tion)

atminuster, administer

atminustrashen, administrate(tion)

atmird, admire(d)

atmire, admire

atmisef, admission(ive)

atmisfeer, atmosphere

atmishun, admission

atmisphere, atmosphere

atmisuble, admissible

atmit, admit

atmonish, admonish

atmosfear, atmosphere

atmosphere,ric,rical,rically, AROUND A PLANET "prefixes: sub"

atmusfeer, atmosphere

atmusphere, atmosphere

atmyre, admire

atobiografy, autobiography

atograf, autograph

atolesense, adolescence

atolesint, adolescent

atom,*,mic,mically,mize,mizer, PARTICLES OF ELEMENT "prefixes: non/sub"

atomadik, automatic

atomatik, automatic

atomobel, automobile

atonal,*,lity,listic,lly, CANNOT HEAR TRUE TONES

atone,*,eable,nable,ement, MAKE UP FOR, AMEND

atonime, autonomy

atonome, autonomy

atorney, attorney

atracshun, attraction
atract, attract
atraction, attraction
atrakshun, attraction
atrakt, attract
atraktif, attract(ive)
atrebute, attribute
atrefee, atrophy
atrenulen, adrenaline
atress, address
atreum, atrium
atribute, attribute
atriem, atrium
atrifee, atrophy
atriss, address
atrium,*, GLASS ROOM
atrocious,sly,sness, OUTRAGEOUS
atrocity,ties, OUTRAGEOUS
atrocius, atrocious
atrofee, atrophy
atrophy,hies,hied,hic, DEGENERATE
atrosety, atrocity
atroshus, atrocious
atrufee, atrophy
atsetera, etcetera
atsheve, achieve
attach,hes,hed,hing,hment, FASTEN
    "prefixes: un"
attack,*,ked,king,ker, ASSAIL
attain,*,ned,ning,nability,nable,
    nableness,nment, GAIN "prefixes:
    un"
attempt,*,ted,ting, TRY TO
    ACCOMPLISH
attemt, attempt
attenchon, attention
attend,*,ded,ding,dingly,dance,dant,
    der, ACCOMPANY, GO TO "prefixes:
    un"
attention,ive, FOCUS ON "prefixes: in"
attentive,ively,eness, FOCUS ON
    "prefixes: in"
attest,*,ted,ting,tation,tations, BEAR
    WITNESS TO THE TRUTH, CAN BE
    CERTIFIED TO BE CORRECT
attic,*, IN THE ROOF (or see addict)
attichon, attention
attinchon, attention
attire,*,ed,ring, APPAREL
attitude,*,dinal, MENTAL POSTURE
attorney,*, REPRESENTATIVE OF LAW
attotode, attitude
attract,*,ted,ting,tive,tively, TO DRAW
    TOWARDS "prefixes: un"

attraction,*, DRAWN TOWARDS
attribute,*,ed,ting,tion, TO CREDIT
    "prefixes: de"
atukit, etiquette
atulesense, adolescence
atum, atom / autumn
atument, adamant
aturnal, eternal
aturney, attorney
atutif, additive
atutode, attitude
atvacate, advocate
atvanse, advance
atvantech, advantage
atvanteg, advantage
atvantuge, advantage
atvencher, adventure
atvenshure, adventure
atverb, adverb
atverse, adverse
atversery, adversary
atvertize, advertise
atvincher, adventure
atvinsher, adventure
atvirb, adverb
atvirsary, adversary
atvirse, adverse
atvise, advice / advise
atvisuble, advise(sable)
atvize, advise / advice
atvokate, advocate
atvukate, advocate
atvurb, adverb
atvurcity, adverse(sity)
atvursle, adverse(ly)
atvurtize, advertise
atypical, IRREGULAR
aubazit, opposite
aubligate, obligate
aubozit, opposite
aubrebul, operable
aubtemal, optimal
aubuzit, opposite
aucalate, osculate / oscillate
auch, ouch
aucilate, osculate / oscillate
aucshen, auction
auction,*,ning,neer,neering, SELL BY
    BID
aud, odd / ought / out
audacity, WILLING/DARING TO DEAL
    WITH DIFFICULT ISSUE/ SITUATION
audamate, automate
audamotive, automotive

audasity, audacity
audeance, audience
audeble, audible
audej, outage
audem, autumn
audeo, audio
auder, otter / outer / odd(er)
audeshun, audition
audet, audit
audetorium, auditorium
audety, odd(ity)
audfit, outfit
audgo, outgo
audiance, audience
audible,ly,bility,eness, WELL HEARD
    "prefixes: in/sub"
audience,*, GROUP WHO OBSERVES
audimotive, automotive
auding, outing
audio, HEAR
audir, otter / outer
audishun, audition
audit,*,ted,ting,tor,tory, UNDER
    EXAMINATION
audition,*,ned,ning, SUBMIT TO
    EXAMINATION "prefixes: sub"
auditorium,*, FOR PUBLIC AUDIENCE
audity, odd(ity)
audlau, outlaw
audle, odd(ly)
audlieng, outlying
audline, outline
audlook, outlook
audobiography, autobiography
audomotive, automotive
audpost, outpost
audraje, outrage
audrit, outright
audside, outside
audskirt, outskirt
audsmart, outsmart
audstanding, outstand(ing)
audwerd, outward
audwet, outwit
auel, owl
auer, our / hour / oar
auful, awful
auger,*, TOOL TO BORE SOMETHING
augir, auger
augment,*,ted,ting,tation, INCREASE
    SIZE "prefixes: bio"
augre, auger
august, A MONTH OF THE YEAR
    (ENGLISH)

auil, owl
aukshun, auction
auksidize, oxide(dize)
auktober, october
aukward, awkward
aul, owl / all / awl
auldir, alder / altar / alter
aulfubet, alphabet
aulso, also
aultamatum, ultimatum
aultematum, ultimatum
aulter, alter / altar
aulternate, alternate
aultirnetly, alternate(ly)
aultogethur, altogether
aultumatum, ultimatum
aulturnate, alternate
aulways, always
auneng, awning
auns, ounce / own(s)
aunt,*,tie, SISTER OF MOTHER/FATHER
    (or see ant)
auntefrese, antifreeze
aupaset, opposite
auperuble, operable
aupewlent, opulent
aupiruble, operable
aupizit, opposite
aupoyntmint, appointment
aupshen, option
auptemal, optimal
auptimize, optimize
auptumistic, optimist(ic)
aupulent, opulent
aupuset, opposite
aur, hour / our / oar
aura,*,al,ric, LIGHT FIELD
aurajin, origin
aurekel, auricle / oracle
auri, awry
aurickle, auricle / oracle
auricle,*,cular, OF THE EAR (or see
    oracle)
aurikel, auricle / oracle
aurk, arc / ark
aurle, hour(ly)
aurmer, armor
auroara, aurora
aurora,*,al, RADIANT EMISSION
aurthodox, orthodox
ausalate, osculate / oscillate
auselate, osculate / oscillate
ausem, awesome
ausilate, osculate / oscillate

ausim, awesome
auspicious,sly,sness, FAVORABLE
    "prefixes: in"
auspishus, auspicious
auspitious, auspicious
austere,ely, HARSH
ausulate, osculate / oscillate
ausum, awesome
aut, out / ought
autej, outage
autem, autumn
autemate, automate
autemobel, automobile
auteo, audio
auter, otter / outer
autfit, outfit
autgo, outgo
authentic,cally,city,cate,cation,cator,
    VALID, NOT FICTITIOUS OR FAKE
    "prefixes: in"
auther, author
authintik, authentic
authir, author
author,*,red,ring, CREATOR/
    ORIGINATOR
authoretarian, authoritarian
authoritarian, DICTATORIAL
authority,ties,tative,tatively, EXERCISES
    COMMAND
autim, autumn
autimate, automate
autimotive, automotive
auting, outing
autio, audio
autir, otter / outer
autism,stic, BRAIN FIRING MALADY
autlaw, outlaw
autlet, outlet
autlieng, outlying
autline, outline
autlook, outlook
autluk, outlook
autly, odd((ly)
auto, PREFIX INDICATING 'OF OR BY
    ONESELF' MOST OFTEN MODIFIES
    THE WORD
autobiografy, autobiography
autobiography,hies,her,hical,hically,
    WRITTEN BY ONESELF "prefixes:
    semi"
autobyografy, autobiography
autograf, autograph
autograph,*,hed,hing,her,hic,hics,hical,
    hically, AUTHOR'S SIGNATURE

automadik, automatic
automate,*,ed,ting,ticity,tion,tism,
    SELF-CONTROLLING, PERFORMS
    THRU PROGRAMMING
automatic,*,cally, SELF-CONTROLLING,
    PERFORMS THRU PROGRAMMING
    "prefixes: semi"
automobel, automobile
automobile,*, PERSONAL
    TRANSPORTATION
automotive, ASSOCIATED WITH
    VEHICLES
autoname, autonomy
autonime, autonomy
autonomy,mous,mist, INDEPENDENCE
    "prefixes: semi"
autopsy,*, POST-MORTEM
    EXAMINATION
autpost, outpost
autput, output
autragus, outrage(ous)
autraje, outrage
autrite, outright
autset, outset
autside, outside
autskurt, outskirt
autsmart, outsmart
autstanding, outstand(ing)
autumate, automate
autumn, FALL SEASON
autwerd, outward
autwet, outwit
autwit, outwit
autwurd, outward
auxilery, auxiliary
auxiliary,ries, HELP OR AID
avacado, avocado
avacodo, avocado
avacuate, evacuate
avade, evade
avaeleble, available
avail,*,led,ling,lable, READY TO USE/
    HELP "prefixes: un"
available,bly,bility, READY TO USE/HELP
    "prefixes: bio/un"
avaire, aviary
avakuate, evacuate
avalable, available
avalanche,*,ed, COME DOWN/
    DESCEND WITH GREAT
    ACCUMULATION
avale, avail
avalible, available
avaluade, evaluate

avaluashen, evaluate(tion)
avaluate, evaluate
avanew, avenue
avantig, advantage
avantij, advantage
avaperation, evaporate(tion)
avaporashen, evaporate(tion)
avarage, average
avaredge, average
avasef, evasive
avashen, evasion
avashun, aviation
avasive, evasive
avate, evade
avau, avow
aveador, aviator
aveashin, aviation
aveation, aviation
avecado, avocado
avedent, evident
aveere, aviary
avekado, avocado
avekshin, evict(ion)
avekt, evict
avelanch, avalanche
avenchur, adventure
avendful, eventful
avenew, avenue
avenge,*,ed,ging,er, INFLICT PAIN/
    HARM IN RETALIATION
avenje, avenge
avenshuale, event(ually)
avent, event
aventful, eventful
aventshur, adventure
avenue,*, WAY TO PERFORM, STREET/
    ROAD
aver, ever
average,*,ed,ging, IN BETWEEN
averb, adverb
avere, aviary
averege, average
averije, average
aversarie, adversary
averse,ely,eness,sion,sions,sive,sively,
    siveness, AGAINST/OPPOSE (or see
    adverse)
avert,*,ted,ting,table,tible,rsion,rsive,
    GO OFF COURSE, CHANGE
    DIRECTION/ATTENTION AWAY
    FROM (or see advert/overt)
avertise, advertise
averyen, ovary(rian)
aviador, aviator

aviary,ries, PLACE TO KEEP BIRDS
aviashun, aviation
aviation,tor, FLYING TRANSPORTATION
aviator,*, ONE WHO PILOTS AIR SHIPS
avicado, avocado
avicate, advocate
avidens, evidence
avident, evident
aviere, aviary
avikado, avocado
avikd, evict
avikshen, evict(ion)
avikt, evict
avikted, evict(ed)
avilanch, avalanche
avincher, adventure
avindful, eventful
avinew, avenue
avinge, avenge
avinje, avenge
avint, event
avintful, eventful
avinu, avenue
avirage, average
avirej, average
avirse, averse / adverse
avirsere, adversary
avirtize, advertise
avocado,*, EDIBLE FRUIT
avocate, advocate
avoed, avoid
avoid,*,ded,ding,dance,dable,dably,
    STAY CLEAR OF, PURPOSELY STAY
    AWAY FROM "prefixes: un"
avokodo, avocado
avolve, evolve
avow,*,wed,wing,wable,wably,wedly,
    STATE THAT IT'S TRUTH "prefixes:
    dis"
avoyd, avoid
avrag, average
avrebaudy, every(body)
avrebode, every(body)
avree, every
avrege, average
avridge, average
avrige, average
avucate, advocate
avukodo, avocado
avulanch, avalanche
avundful, eventful
avurb, adverb
avurij, average
avurse, averse / adverse

avurt, avert / advert / overt
avurtize, advertise
awa, away
await,*,ted,ting, TO EXPECT
awake,*,en,ening,king, FROM SLEEP
award,*,ded,ding, A PRIZE
aware,eness, CAUTIOUS, ALERT
    "prefixes: un"
awate, await
away, SOMEWHERE ELSE
awayt, await
awbuzit, opposite
awcshen, auction
awd, odd / ought / out
awdacity, audacity
awdamate, automate
awdamotive, automotive
awdasety, audacity
awdeanse, audience
awdeble, audible
awdege, outage
awdeje, outage
awdeo, audio
awder, outer / otter
awdet, audit
awdete, odd(ity)
awdetoreum, auditorium
awdfet, outfit
awdgo, outgo
awdible, audible
awdij, outage
awdimotive, automotive
awding, outing
awdir, outer / otter
awdishun, audition
awdit, audit
awdition, audition
awditorium, auditorium
awdity, odd(ity)
awdlet, outlet
awdlieng, outlying
awdline, outline
awdlook, outlook
awdrit, outright
awdside, outside
awdskirt, outskirt
awdsmart, outsmart
awdstanding, outstand(ing)
awdur, outer / otter
awdwet, outwit
awdwurd, outward
awe,*,ed,wing, TAKEN ABACK,
    STUNNED
awel, owl

awer, our / hour
awesome,ely,eness, IMPRESSIVE
awfil, awful
awful,lly,lness, DREADFUL
awger, auger
awgest, august
awgir, auger
awgist, august
awgment, augment
awgmint, augment
awgre, auger
awgur, auger
awgus, august
awgust, august
awhile, FOR SOME TIME NOW
awil, awhile
awkewpie, occupy
awksedize, oxide(dize)
awksegin, oxygen
awkshun, auction
awkupy, occupy
awkward,dly,dness, BUNGLING OR
    EMBARRASSING
awl,*, TOOL FOR SEWING LEATHER (or
    see owl/all)
awlso, also
awning,*, ROOF OVERHANG
aword, award
awpazit, opposite
awperuble, operable
awposit, opposite
awpuzit, opposite
awr, our / hour
awreginal, origin(al)
awrekt, erect
awrickle, auricle
awrie, awry
awrikle, auricle
awroara, aurora
awrode, erode
awrora, aurora
awru, aura
awry, OFF COURSE
awselate, osculate / oscillate
awsem, awesome
awsilate, osculate / oscillate
awsome, awesome
awspeshus, auspicious
awspitious, auspicious
awstear, austere
awsteer, austere
awsulate, osculate / oscillate
awsum, awesome
awt, out / ought

awtem, autumn
awter, otter / outer
awtesm, autism
awtfit, outfit
awtgo, outgo
awthentik, authentic
awthintik, authentic
awthir, author
awthority, authority
awtim, autumn
awting, outing
awtir, otter / outer
awtism, autism
awtitorium, auditorium
awtizm, autism
awtlaw, outlaw
awtlet, outlet
awtlieng, outlying
awtline, outline
awtlook, outlook
awtluk, outlook
awtlying, outlying
awtobiografy, autobiography
awtopse, autopsy
awtpost, outpost
awtput, output
awtrage, outrage
awtragus, outrage(ous)
awtraje, outrage
awtrite, outright
awtset, outset
awtside, outside
awtskurt, outskirt
awtsmart, outsmart
awtstanding, outstand(ing)
awtum, autumn
awtur, outer / otter
awtward, outward
awtwerd, outward
awtwit, outwit
awtwurd, outward
awul, owl
awur, our / hour
ax,xes,xed,xing, TOOL WITH A SHARP
    BLADE FOR CHOPPING WOOD (or
    see ache(s)/axis/ask)
axcebt, except / accept
axcedent, accident
axceed, exceed
axcelerate, accelerate
axchange, exchange
axchoole, actual
axcident, accident
axclude, exclude

axcurshin, excursion
axderminate, exterminate
axdurminate, exterminate
axebt, except / accept
axecutive, executive
axent, accent
axepshen, except(ion)
axeptinse, accept(ance)
axesory, accessory
axess, access
axeul, axis(ial)
axglood, exclude
axicute, execute
axil,*, ANGLE BETWEEN STEM/BRANCH
    (or see axle)
axint, accent
axis,xes,ial,ially, A PIVOTAL POINT ON
    WHICH SOMETHING IS CENTERED
    (or see ax(es)) "prefixes: bi"
axkerjen, excursion
axklude, exclude
axkuze, excuse
axle,*, ROD WITH TWO WHEELS
    ATTACHED(or see axil)
axol, axil / axle
axplan, explain
axsedintal, accident(al)
axseed, exceed
axselense, excellent
axseluratur, accelerate(tor)
axsenshuate, accentuate
axsent, accent
axsentuate, accentuate
axsept, accept / except
axseptense, accept(ance)
axseptinse, accept(ance)
axses, access / ax(es) / axis
axsesares, accessory(ries)
axsesori, accessory
axsesurize, accessory(rize)
axshule, actual
axshun, action
axsident, accident
axsidental, accident(al)
axsidint, accident
axsint, accent
axsintuate, accentuate
axst, ax(ed) / ask(ed)
axsudentul, accident(al)
axterminate, exterminate
axturminate, exterminate
axturnal, external
axual, actual
axuated, acuate(d)

axukute, execute
axul, axil / axle
axule, actual
azbekt, aspect
azberigus, asparagus
azbestus, asbestos
azburashun, aspirate(tion)
azdragen, estrogen
azemulate, assimilate
azendent, ascendant
azertane, ascertain
azfalt, asphalt
azfault, asphalt
azfikseate, asphyxiate
azfolt, asphalt
azide, aside
azilum, asylum
azinment, assignment
azinshul, essential
azma, asthma
azmu, asthma
azpekt, aspect
azpir, aspire
azpren, aspirin
azspect, aspect
azteem, esteem
azthma, asthma
aztonesh, astonish
aztral, astral
aztranaut, astronaut
aztrawneme, astronomy
aztrengent, astringent
aztringent, astringent
aztroid, asteroid
aztrol, astral
aztrolegy, astrology
aztronume, astronomy
aztrul, astral
aztrunot, astronaut
azumshin, assumption
azurtane, ascertain
b, be / bee
ba, bay
babby, baby
babe, TERM OF ENDEARMENT
babesit, babysit
baby,bies,bied,bying, CHILD UNDER
    THE AGE OF ONE YEAR
babysit,*,tter,tting,babysat, WATCH
    OTHERS CHILDREN
bacen, bacon / bake(king) / basin
bach, back / batch / badge / bash /
    bake / bog / balk / baulk
bachelor,*, UNMARRIED MAN

bacher, badger
bachful, bashful
bachiler, bachelor
bachin, back(ing) / bake(king) /
    batch(ing) / bacon
bachuler, bachelor
bacin, bacon
back,*,ked,king,ker, GO TO THE
    PREVIOUS/PAST, IN THE REAR OF
    (or see bake) "prefixes: un"
backward,*,dness, IN REVERSE
backwurd, backward
bacon, SALTED HOG MEAT/FAT
bacos, because
bacteri, PREFIX INDICATING 'BACTERIA'
    MOST OFTEN MODIFIES THE WORD
bacteria,al,ium, MICROSCOPIC
    ORGANISM "prefixes: non"
bactirea, bacteria
bactireul, bacteria(l)
bactiria, bacteria
bacuerd, backward
bad,dly,dness, NOT GOOD (or see bat/
    bade)
badare, battery
badchelor, bachelor
badder, batter
bade, PAST TENSE FOR THE WORD 'BID'
    (or see bat/bad)
badel, battle
bader, batter
badery, battery
badge,*, INSIGNIA (or see batch)
badger,*,red,ring, TO HECKLE
    SOMEONE, AN ANIMAL
badiry, battery
badje, badge
badjur, badger
badle, battle
badol, battle
badore, battery
badre, battery
badshelor, bachelor
badul, battle
baduly, body(dily)
badur, batter
badury, battery
bae, bay
baege, beige
baej, beige
bael, bail / bale
baenkwit, banquet
baet, bait / bate
bafal, befall

bafileon, pavilion
bafol, befall
bag,*,gged,gging,gger,ggy,ggier,ggiest,
    A CONTAINER TO HOLD ITEMS (or
    see back/beige/batch/badge)
bagage, baggage
bagd, bag(gged) / back(ed)
bage, badge / beige / baggy
baged, bag(gged) / back(ed)
bagege, baggage
bageje, baggage
bagel,*, ROLL WITH A HOLE
bagener, begin(nner)
bager, bag(gger) / badger
baggage, LUGGAGE
baggy,ggies,gily,giness, LOOSE, SAGGY
bagige, baggage
bagil, bagel
baginer, begin(nner)
bagir, badger / bag(gger)
bagle, bagel
baguj, baggage
bagul, bagel
bagur, bag(gger) / badger
bahaf, behave
bahaver, behavior
bahavior, behavior
bahind, behind
baige, beige
baije, beige
bail,*,led,ler, LIBERATE, REMOVE FROM
    (or see bale/bowel)
bailef, bailiff
bailif, bailiff
bailiff,*, CIVIL OFFICER OR
    FUNCTIONARY
bainquet, banquet
bair, bear / bare
bait,*,ted,ting, LURING TO CATCH (or
    see bate/bite)
baj, badge / beige / batch
bajer, badger
bak, back / bake / balk / baulk
bakd, bake(d) / back(ed)
bake,*,ed,king,er, COOK FOOD IN AN
    OVEN (or see back) "prefixes: un"
bakeeny, bikini
baken, bacon
bakene, bikini
bakery,ries, WHERE PASTRIES ARE
    BAKED
bakin, bacon
bakini, bikini
bakiry, bakery

bakose, because
bakry, bakery
bakt, bake(d) / back(ed)
bakterea, bacteria
baktereul, bacteria(l)
baktirea, bacteria
bakuj, baggage
bakwerd, backward
bakwurd, backward
bal, ball / bale / bail / bawl
bala, ballet
balad, ballad / ballade
balance,*,ed,cing, EQUILIBRIUM, CENTERED "prefixes: un"
balarena, ballerina
balat, ballot / ballad / ballade
balay, ballet
balcene, balcony
balcony,nies, PORCH ABOVE THE FIRST STORY ON A BUILDING
balcuny, balcony
bald,ding,dness, LOOSING HAIR (or see bold/ball(ed)/bale(d)/bail(ed))
bale,*,ed,ling,er, TO BUNDLE (or see bail)
baled, bale(d) / bail(ed) / ballad / ballade
baleef, belief
baleeve, believe
balef, bailiff
baleger, beleaguer
balens, balance
balerena, ballerina
balestic, ballistic
balet, ballet / ballot / ballad / ballade
baleve, believe
balevuble, believe(vable)
balid, ballad / ballade
balif, bailiff
balins, balance
balirena, ballerina
balit, ballot / ballet
balk,*,ked,king,ker,kingly, ALSO 'BAULK', EXPRESS UNWILLINGNESS TO DO SOMETHING, HINDER/ PREVENT (or see bulk/baulk) "prefixes: un"
balkeny, balcony
balkune, balcony
ball,*,lled,lling, ROUND OBJECT FOR THROWING/SPORTS, A FORMAL DANCE STYLE (or see bawl/bail/ bale)

ballad,*,dic,dist,dry, SIMPLE SONG/ POEM (or see ballade)
ballade,*, SPECIFIC STYLE OF POEM/ MUSICAL PIECE (or see ballad)
balled, ballad / ballade / ball(ed)
ballerena, ballerina
ballerina,*, FEMALE DANCER
ballet,*, CLASSICAL DANCE (or see ballot)
ballid, ballad / ballade
ballistic,*, PROJECTILE IN AIR
balloon,*,ned,ning, FULL OF AIR
ballot,*,ted,ting,ter, OF VOTING
balm,*, OINTMENT FROM PLANTS
balme, balmy
balmy,mier,miest,mily,miness, OF WARM/MILD CLIMATE
balo, below / bellow / billow
balonee, bologna / baloney
baloney, NONSENSE, MEAT (or see bologna)
balong, belong
baloom, bloom
baloon, balloon
balot, ballot / ballet
balow, below / billow / bellow
bals, bowel(s) / ball(s) / bale(s) / bail(s)
baluf, bailiff
balume, bloom
balune, balloon
balunse, balance
balurena, ballerina
banana,*, EDIBLE FRUIT
band,*,ded,ding, COLLECTION OF PERFORMING MUSICIANS, TO BE GROUPED/BOUND TOGETHER "prefixes: contra/multi"
bandage,*,ed,ging, FOR REPAIRING WOUNDS
bandry, boundary
baneeth, beneath
baner, banner
banesh, banish
banevulense, benevolence
banign, benign
banine, benign
banir, banner
banish,hes,hed,hing,hment, CONDEMNED TO EXILE
bank,*,ked,king,ker, BUSINESS THAT STORES GOODS/CASH, SMALL BERM/HILL "prefixes: under"
bankrupsee, bankrupt(cy)

bankrupt,tcy,tcies, BROKE TO THE BANK, CAN'T PAY
bankwit, banquet
banner,*, TYPE OF SIGN
banquet,*, FEAST WITH FRIENDS
banquit, banquet
bantry, boundary / pantry
banur, banner
baptesm, baptism
baptism,*,mal,ize, REBIRTHING RITUAL
baptize,*,ed,zing, REBIRTHING RITUAL
baptizm, baptism
bar,*,rred,rring, LONG/FLAT SECTION/ COUNTER (or see bare/bear)
bara, barrette / beret
barack, barrack
barbarian,*,ic, UNCIVILIZED PERSON
barbecue,*,ed,uing, GRILLED MEAT
barbekew, barbecue
barbeku, barbecue
barber,*, CUTS HAIR
barberean, barbarian
barberian, barbarian
barbetchuet, barbiturate
barbichuit, barbiturate
barbique, barbecue
barbir, barber
barbitchuet, barbiturate
barbiturate,*, SEDATIVE DRUG "prefixes: non"
barbur, barber
barc, bark
barder, barter
bardur, barter
bare,*,ed,ring,rren, WITHOUT COVER (or see bear/berry/bury)
bareave, bereave
bareck, barrack
bareeve, bereave
bareft, bereft
barel, barrel
baren, barren
bareng, bearing / bar(rring) / bare(ring)
barestur, barrister
baret, barrette / beret
baretone, baritone
bareur, barrier
bargain,*,ned,ning, AFFORDABLE DEAL
barge,*,ed,ging, FLAT-BOTTOM BOAT, BEHAVE LIKE A BOAT
bargen, bargain
bargun, bargain
bargund, bargain(ed)
baricade, barricade

barier, barrier
barikade, barricade
baril, barrel
barin, barren
baring, bearing / bare(ring) / bar(rring)
barister, barrister
barit, barrette / beret
baritone,*, DEEP TONE
barje, barge
bark,*,ked,king,ker, SOUND FROM A
    DOG, COVER ON TREES "prefixes:
    de"
barn,*, LARGE STRUCTURE FOR FARM
    ANIMALS (or see born/barren)
baro, PREFIX INDICATING 'PRESSURE/
    WEIGHT' MOST OFTEN MODIFIES
    THE WORD (or see barrow/borrow)
baroge, barrage
baroje, barrage
barol, barrel
barometer,*,tric, INSTRUMENT
    MEASURING PRESSURE
baromiter, barometer
baron, barren
baroque, TYPE OF MUSIC, WILD,
    UNUSUAL
barow, borrow / burrow / borough
barrack,*, LODGE FOR MANY PEOPLE
barrage,*,ed,ging, ALL AT ONCE
barrel,*,led,ling, DRUM OR GREAT
    SPEED
barren,nly,nness, UNFERTILE
barrette,*, CLASP (or see beret)
barricade,*,ded,ding, BLOCK AGAINST
barrier,*, OBSTRUCTION
barring, EXCEPTING, REFUSAL (or see
    bear(ing)/bar(ing))
barrister,*, LAWYER
barrow, CASTRATED HOG (or see
    borrow)
bartender,*, TENDS BAR
barter,*,red,ring, TRADE
bartinder, bartender
bartur, barter
baruton, baritone
bary, berry / bury
bas, base / bass
basball, baseball
basboll, baseball
base,*,ed,sing,eless, A FOUNDATION,
    FORM IN BASEBALL (or see bass)
    "prefixes: de"
baseach, beseech
baseball, SPORT

baseech, beseech
basek, basic
basekly, basic(ally)
basel, basil
basement,*, UNDER HOUSE
basen, basin
bases, basis / base(s)
baset, basset
bash,hes,hed,hing, A PARTY, TO
    SMASH/DESTROY SOMETHING,
    INSULT SOMEONE
bashfel, bashful
bashful, SHY
basi, PREFIX INDICATING 'BOTTOM/
    BASE' MOST OFTEN MODIFIES THE
    WORD
basic,*,cally, FUNDAMENTAL
baside, beside
basik, basic
basikly, basic(ally)
basil, HERB
basin,*, SHAPED LIKE BOWL
basis, ON WHICH IT STANDS (or see
    base(s))
basit, basset
basket,*, WOVEN CONTAINER
baskit, basket
baskut, basket
basmant, basement
basmint, basement
baso, PREFIX INDICATING 'BOTTOM/
    BASE' MOST OFTEN MODIFIES THE
    WORD
basoon, bassoon
bass,sses,ssist, A FISH, STRINGED
    INSTRUMENT, LEVEL OF SOUND
    TONE/FREQUENCY (or see base)
basset, DOG, HOUND
bassoon, HORN
basuk, basic
basul, basil
basun, basin / bassoon
basurk, berserk
basus, basis / base(s)
basut, basset
bat,*,tted,tting,tter, STUFFING, TOOL
    USED IN BASEBALL, TO HIT (or see
    bate/bait)
batch,hes,hed,hing, INCREMENTS/
    CERTAIN AMOUNTS OF
    SOMETHING AT A TIME (or see
    badge/botch)
batcheler, bachelor
batchuler, bachelor

bate,*,ed,ting, DECREASE, HOLD BACK
    (or see bait)
batel, battle
baten, batten
batenshul, potential
bater, batter
batery, battery
bath,*,hroom, A PLACE TO WASH, TO
    IMMERSE IN LIQUID (or see bathe)
bathe,*,ed,hing,ers, TO WASH UP,
    IMMERSE IN LIQUID (or see bath)
batil, bottle / battle
batin, batten
batinshul, potential
batiry, battery
batle, battle
batom, bottom
baton,*, WAND
batore, battery
batre, battery
batrothed, betrothed
batshelor, bachelor
batshiler, bachelor
batten, SECURE/STRENGTHEN, WOOD
    STRIPS (or see bat(tting))
batter,*,red,ring, FRYING MIXTURE,
    BASEBALL PLAYER, TO BE
    ATTACKED
battery,ries, APPLIES TO MILITARY,
    MECHANICAL, ELECTRICAL,
    BASEBALL
battle,*,ed,ling, FIGHT BETWEEN TWO
    FORCES
batul, battle
batur, batter
batury, battery
batween, between
bauch, botch
bauchulism, botulism
baul, ball / bawl / bail / bale / bowel
baulk,*,ked,king,ker,kingly, ALSO 'BALK',
    EXPRESS UNWILLINGNESS TO DO
    SOMETHING, HINDER/PREVENT (or
    see bulk/balk) "prefixes: un"
baulm, balm
baulme, balmy
bauls, bowel(s) / bawl(s) / ball(s)
baund, bound
baundre, boundary
bauns, bounce / bound(s)
baunse, bounce(cy) / buoyant(ncy)
baunti, bounty
bauntiful, bountiful
bauntre, boundary

baurk, bark
baush, botch
baut, bought / bout
bautel, bottle
bavileon, pavilion
bawdil, bottle
bawildre, bewilder
bawl,*,led,ling,ler, WEEP, SHOUT AT (or see ball)
bawls, bawl(s) / bowel(s) / ball(s)
bawnd, bound
bawnse, bounce / bound(s)
bawntee, bounty
bawntiful, bountiful
bay,*, RELATES TO WINDOW, BARN, DOG HOWLING, SHIP HOSPITAL, AIRCRAFT, SHRUB, OCEAN INLET
bayle, bail / bale
bayond, beyond
bayou, OUTLET OF WATER
bayu, bayou
bazaar,*, SALE OF ARTICLES (or see bizarre)
bazel, basil
bazen, basin
bazil, basil
bazin, basin
bazul, basil
bazurk, berserk
bazzar, bizarre / bazaar
be, A VERB EXPRESSING PRESENT TENSE, A PREFIX INDICATING 'COMPLETELY/INTENSELY' MOST OFTEN MODIFIES THE WORD (or see bee)
beach,hes,hed,hing, SHORELINE (or see beech)
beacon,*, SIGNAL (or see beckon)
bead,*,ded,ding, ROUNDED FORM/ OBJECT (or see beat/beet)
beafy, beef(y)
beagle,*, DOG
beagul, beagle
beak,*, BIRD BILL
beaker,*, VESSEL
beam,*,med,ming, TO SHINE, LINEAR SUPPORT
bean,*, VEGETABLE, TO HURT (or see been/bin)
bear,*,ring,rish,rishly, ANIMAL, PUT PRESSURE ON/AGAINST (or see bare/beer/bearing) "prefixes: over"
bearable, TOLERABLE "prefixes: un"
beard,*,ded, MALE FACIAL HAIR

bearing,*, SUPPORTS, PRESSURE, MACHINE PART, HEADING (or see bare(ring))
beast,*,tly,tliness, ANIMA
beat,*,ting,ten,ter, THRASH/STRIKE/HIT (or see beet) "prefixes: un/up"
beau,*, BOYFRIEND (or see bow/bough)
beauru, bureau
beautician,*, HAIRDRESSER
beautiful,lly, EYE PLEASER
beautishun, beautician
beauty,ties,tify,tiful,tifully,tious,teously, teousness,tification, PLEASING TO THE SENSES, GMP
beaver,*, ANIMAL
bebleografy, bibliography
became, PAST TENSE FOR THE WORD 'BECOME'
because, THE REASON FOR
becin, beckon / beacon / bacon
becken, beckon / beacon / bacon
beckon,*,ned,ning, TO SUMMON/CALL FORTH, ENTICE TO COME (or see beacon/bacon)
beckun, beckon/beacon/bacon
become,*,ming,came, GOING TO BE (or see became) "prefixes: un"
becon, beckon / beacon / bacon
becos, because
becum, become
becun, beckon / beacon / bacon
becus, because
becuz, because
bed,*,dded,dding, SOMETHING TO SLEEP/ LIE DOWN UPON (or see bead/bet/bit/beat)
beded, bet(tted) / bed(dded) / bead(ed)
beder, better / bid(dder) / bitter / bet(ttor)
bedid, bet(tted) / bed(dded)
bedil, beetle
bedir, better / bid(dder) / bitter / bet(ttor)
bedol, beetle
bedraggled, MUSSED UP
bedragled, bedraggled
bedraguled, bedraggled
bedridden, CONFINED TO BED
bedriden, bedridden
bedritin, bedridden
bedrothed, betrothed
bedspread,*, BED COVER
bedspred, bedspread
bedud, bet(tted) / bed(dded)

bedul, beetle
bedur, better / bid(dder) / bitter / bet(ttor)
bedwritin, bedridden
bee,*, FURRY INSECT (or see be)
beech, TREE (or see beach)
beedil, beetle
beedul, beetle
beef,fy,finess,fed,fing, FLESHY, MEAT FROM BOVINE, TO COMPLAIN
beek, beak
beeker, beaker
beekin, beacon
beem, beam
been, PAST TENSE FOR THE WORD 'BE' (or see bean)
beeng, being
beer,*, FERMENTED BREW (or see bear)
beerd, beard
beest, beast
beestro, bistro
beet,*, A VEGETABLE (or see beat)
beetle,*, BUG
beetul, beetle
beever, beaver
befall, OCCUR
befol, befall
before, PREVIOUS
befour, before
befrend, befriend
befriend,*,ded, MAKE FRIENDS WITH
befrind, befriend
beg,*,gged,gging, PLEAD (or see big/ beach)
began, PAST TENSE FOR THE WORD 'BEGIN'
begar, beggar
begen, begin
begenir, begin(nner)
beger, beggar
beggar,*,ry,rly,rliness, ONE WHO BEGS
beggir, beggar
beggur, beggar
begil, beagle / bagel
begin,*,nner,nning,gan, TO START
beginer, begin(nner)
begir, beggar
begle, beagle / bagel
begot, bigot
begul, beagle / bagel
begur, beggar
begut, bigot
begutre, bigot(ry)
behaf, behalf

behalf, ON THE PART OF

behave,*,ed,ving,vior, ACT IN A PARTICULAR WAY "prefixes: mis"

behaveor, behavior

behavior,*,ral,rism,rist,ristic, MANNERISMS, ATTITUDE

behavyur, behavior

behind, TO THE BACK

behoof, behoove

behoove,*,ed,ving, TO BE PROPER

behufe, behoove

behuve, behoove

beige, COLOR

being,*, EXISTS

bekame, became

beken, beckon / beacon / bacon

beker, beaker

bekin, beckon / beacon / bacon

bekit, bigot

bekom, become

bekon, beckon / beacon / bacon

bekos, because

bekum, become

bekur, beaker

bekus, because

bekut, bigot

bekuz, because

beladed, belated

beladid, belated

belated,dly, OVERDUE

belatide, belated

beld, build / bill(ed) / built

bele, belly

beleaguer, BLOCK, SIEGE

belegarant, belligerent

beleger, beleaguer

beleon, billion

belerds, billiards

belevuble, believe(vable)

beli, belly

belief,*, FAITH, HOPE "prefixes: dis/ mis/un"

believe,*,ed,ving,vable,vably,vability, FAITH, HOPE "prefixes: dis/mis/un"

believeable, believe(vable)

beligerent, belligerent

belise, police

belittle,*,ed,ling,ement, TO INSULT

belle, belly

belligerent,tly,nce,ncy, WAR-LIKE AGGRESSIVENESS

bellow,*,wed,wing, DEEP ROAR, INSTRUMENT (or see below/billow)

belly,llies, ABDOMEN "prefixes: under"

belo, bellow / below / billow

belonee, bologna / baloney

belong,*,ging,gings, HAVE RIGHTS TO

beloon, balloon

below, BENEATH, LOWER (or see bellow/billow)

belt,*,ted,ting, STRAP TO WEAR AROUND THE WAIST, PUNCH/HIT SOMETHING (or see built) "prefixes: un"

belurds, billiards

belyon, billion

belyunar, billion(aire)

bemt, beam(ed)

ben, been / bin / bean

benafactor, benefactor

benaficial, beneficial

benaficiary, beneficiary

benafishiary, beneficiary

benafishul, beneficial

benafit, benefit

benansa, bonanza

benanu, banana

bench,hes,hed,hing, RELATES TO LAW, GEOLOGY, SPORTS "prefixes: un"

bend,*,ding,nt, CROOK/ANGLE (or see bent/bind) "prefixes: un"

bended, bent

bendid, bent

bene, PREFIX INDICATING 'GOOD/ WELL' MOST OFTEN MODIFIES THE WORD

beneath, UNDER, LOWER

beneeth, beneath

benefactor,*,tion, CONTRIBUTOR

beneficial,lly, HELPFUL "prefixes: un"

beneficiary,ries, ONE WHO BENEFITS FROM

benefishiery, beneficiary

benefishul, beneficial

benefit,*,ted,ting, TO SERVE "prefixes: dis"

benevolance, benevolence

benevolence,nt, BIG HEARTED, KIND

benevolent,ntly, BIG HEARTED, KIND

benevulense, benevolence

benge, binge

benifactor, benefactor

benificial, beneficial

benifisheary, beneficiary

benifishul, beneficial

benifit, benefit

benign,nity,nities,nly, KINDLY

benine, benign

benje, binge

bent, PAST TENSE FOR THE WORD" BEND" "prefixes: un"

bented, bent

benufactor, benefactor

benuficial, beneficial

benuficiary, beneficiary

benufisheary, beneficiary

benufishul, beneficial

benufit, benefit

beond, beyond

ber, burr / bear / bare / beer

berbin, bourbon

berch, birch

berd, bird / beard

berden, burden

berdinsum, burden(some)

bere, berry / bury / bare / bear

bereave,*,ed,ving,ement, ANGUISH OVER LOSS

bereble, bearable

berecade, barricade

bereft, LACKING/ LOSS/ DEPRIVED

berek, barrack

berekade, barricade

berel, barrel

beren, barren

bereng, bearing / bare(ring)

berer, bear(er) / barrier

berestur, barrister

beret,*, CLOTH CAP (or see barrette)

beretone, baritone

bereul, burial

bereur, barrier

bergendy, burgundy

bergler, burglar

bergundy, burgundy

beri, bury / berry

berial, burial

berible, bearable

bericade, barricade

berick, barrack

berier, barrier

berikade, barricade

beril, barrel

berin, barren

bering, bearing / bar(ing) / bar(rring)

berister, barrister

beristur, barrister

beritone, baritone

beriv, bereave

berkler, burglar

berlap, burlap

berlesk, burlesque

berly, burly
berm,*,med, SLOPED SOIL
bern, burn
bernt, burnt
bero, barrow / burrow / burro / borough
berog, barrage
beroj, barrage
berol, barrel
beron, barren
berow, barrow / borrow
berp, burp
berry,rries, FRUIT (or see bury)
bersaverense, persevere(rance)
bersd, burst
bersding, burst(ing)
berserk, VIOLENT FRENZY
berst, burst
berth,*, PLACE TO SETTLE INTO/SLEEP (or see birth)
berthday, birthday
beruble, bearable
berubul, bearable
berukad, barricade
berul, barrel
beruton, baritone
bery, berry / bury
berzd, burst
berzding, burst(ing)
bes, bee(s) / best
besanes, business
besar, bizarre / bazaar
besd, best / beast
bese, busy
beseach, beseech
beseech,her,hingly, IMPLORE
besely, busy(sily)
besenes, business
beserk, berserk
besi, busy
beside,*, ALONGSIDE, AS WELL AS
besines, business
besirk, berserk
besk, bisque
besket, biscuit
besque, bisque
best, PAST TENSE FOR THE WORD 'BETTER' (or see beast)
bestro, bistro
besurk, berserk
besy, busy
bet,*,tted,tting,ttor, PLACE A WAGER WITH HOPE OF WINNING

SOMETHING (or see beet/beat/ bed)
beted, bet(tted) / bed(dded)
beter, better / bid(dder) / bitter / bet(ttor)
betid, bet(tted) / bed(dded)
betir, better / bid(dder) / bitter / bet(ttor)
beton, baton
betor, better / bid(dder) / bitter / bet(ttor)
betray,*,yal,yer, VIOLATION OF TRUST
betrothed, ENGAGEMENT TO SOMEONE
better,red,ring,rment, MORE SUPERIOR (or see bet(ttor))
betud, bet(tted) / bed(dded)
between, IN THE MIDDLE OF HERE AND THERE
beudeful, beautiful
beudiful, beautiful
beudy, beauty
beugl, bugle
beurd, beard
beuro, bureau
beurocrasy, bureaucracy
beurocrat, bureaucrat
beut, butte
beuteshun, beautician
beutiful, beautiful
beuty, beauty
bevarige, beverage
bevel,*,led,ling, INCLINED SURFACE
beverage,*, FLAVORED LIQUID TO DRINK
bevil, bevel
bevir, beaver
bevirage, beverage
bevle, bevel
bevol, bevel
bevrag, beverage
bevrech, beverage
bevrig, beverage
bevul, bevel
bevur, beaver
beware, CAUTION
bewere, beware
bewhere, beware
bewhove, behoove
bewilder,*,red,ring,ringly,rment, CONFUSE
bewt, butte
bewte, beauty
bewteful, beautiful

bewteshin, beautician
bewyon, bouillon
beyeng, being
beyond, OUT OF REACH
beyut, butte
bezar, bizarre / bazaar
bezd, best / beast
beze, busy
bezenes, business
bezerk, berserk
bezi, busy
beznes, business
bezt, best / beast
bezunes, business
bezzar, bizarre / bazaar / buzz(er)
bi, PREFIX INDICATING 'TWO/TWICE' MOST OFTEN MODIFIES THE WORD (or see by/bye/bee)
biadic, biotic
biagrafik, biography(hic)
bialegy, biology
bianeal, biennial / biannual
bianel, biennial / biannual
biannual, TWICE A YEAR (or see biennial)
bianuel, biannual
bianyual, biannual
bias, PREFERENCE TOWARDS/FOR "prefixes: un"
biatic, biotic
biaudec, biotic
biaugrafe, biography
biaulugy, biology
biautec, biotic
bibleografy, bibliography
bibleogrufy, bibliography
biblio, PREFIX INDICATING 'BOOK' MOST OFTEN MODIFIES THE WORD
bibliography,hies,hic,hical, LIST OF PRINTED MATERIAL
bic, bike / beak
bicame, became
bicas, because
bicentenial, bicentennial
bicentennial,*, TWO HUNDRED YEAR MARK
biceps, MUSCLES
bicker,*,red,ring, ARGUE (or see bike(r))
bicom, become
bicon, beacon
bicos, because
bicus, because
bicycle,*,ed,ling,list, TWO-WHEEL TRANSPORTATION

bid,*,dder,dding, TO TELL, BE TOLD, BID FAREWELL, WAGER SOMETHING TO GAIN SOMETHING ELSE (or see bite(r)/bitter/bit/bed/bide/bead) "prefixes: over/under"

bidder, bitter / bid(der) / bite(r)

bide,*,ed,ding, WAIT, WITHSTAND (or see bid/bite) "prefixes: un"

bider, bite(r) / bid(dder) / bitter

bidragled, bedraggled

bidraguled, bedraggled

bidtrothed, betrothed

bieng, buy(ing)

bienial, biennial / biannual

biennial, TWO YEARS (or see biannual)

bifal, befall

bifocals, TWO-PART LENS

bifocul, bifocals

bifokul, bifocals

bifol, befall

bifor, before

bifour, before

bifrend, befriend

big,gger,ggest,ggy, LARGE (or see beg)

bigan, began / begin

bigetry, bigot(ry)

bigot,ted,try, NARROW-MINDED "prefixes: un"

bigutry, bigot(ry)

bihaf, behave / behalf

bihalf, behave / behalf

bihav, behave / behalf

bihind, behind

bikame, became

bike,*,ed,king,er, WHEEL TRANSPORTATION "prefixes: retro"

bikeeny, bikini

bikeim, became

biker,*, RIDES MOTORCYCLE (or see bicker/beaker)

bikini,*, TWO-PIECE BATHING SUIT

bikose, because

bikum, become

bikur, bicker / biker

bikus, because

bikut, bigot

bilak, black

bilanear, bilinear

bilards, billiards

bilateral, BOTH SIDES

bilatirul, bilateral

bild, build / bill(ed) / built

bile, FLUID MADE BY THE LIVER (or see bill)

biled, build / bill(ed) / built

bileef, belief

bileeve, believe

bileger, beleaguer

bilenear, bilinear

bilengual, bilingual

bilengwul, bilingual

bileon, billion

bilerds, billiards

bileve, believe

bilevuble, believe(vable)

biliards, billiards

bilinear, TWO LINES

bilingual, SPEAKS TWO LANGUAGES

bilingwal, bilingual

bilion, billion

bilitol, belittle

bill,*,lled,lling, TOTAL COSTS (or see bile) "prefixes: over/pre"

billiards, POOL GAME

billion,*,nth,naire, ONE THOUSAND MILLION

billow,*,wed,wing, OF WIND(or see below/bellow)

bilo, billow / below / bellow

bilonee, baloney / bologna

bilong, belong

bilow, below / billow / bellow

bilt, built / build

bilurds, billiards

bilyon, billion

bilyunar, billion(aire)

bimonthly, TWICE A MONTH

bimunthly, bimonthly

bin,*,nned,nning, COMPARTMENT FOR STORAGE, PREFIX INDICATING 'TWO/TWICE' MOST OFTEN MODIFIES THE WORD (or see been/bean)

binanu, banana

binanzu, bonanza

binary,ries, UNITS OF TWO

binch, binge / bench

bind,*,bound,ding,dingly,der, HOLD THINGS TOGETHER "prefixes: multi/un"

bineeth, beneath

binefacter, benefactor

binery, binary

binevilance, benevolence

binevulense, benevolence

bing, being / binge

binge,*,ed,ging, SPREE

binign, benign

binine, benign

binith, beneath

binje, binge

binocular,*, DEVICE THAT MAGNIFIES FOR BOTH EYES

binokuler, binocular

binomeal, binomial

binomial,*, HAS TWO NAMES/TERMS

binoquler, binocular

bint, bent

binufakter, benefactor

binufishal, beneficial

binufishary, beneficiary

binufit, benefit

binury, binary

bio, PREFIX INDICATING 'LIFE' MOST OFTEN MODIFIES THE WORD

biocide,dal, CIVILIZATION CHOKING OFF IT'S OWN LIFE SUPPLY

biodagradable, biodegradable

biodec, biotic

biodegradable, ELEMENTS EASILY BREAKS DOWN

biofisics, biophysics

biofizecs, biophysics

biografee, biography

biography,hies,hic,hical, STORY OF PEOPLE'S HISTORY "prefixes: auto"

biogrufee, biography

biology,gical,gically,gist, STUDY OF LIFE "prefixes: exo/pre"

biophisics, biophysics

biophysics, STUDY OF LIFE

biopsy,sies, STUDY OF TISSUE

biorethum, biorhythm

biorhythm, BIOLOGICAL RHYTHM

biorithum, biorhythm

biorythm, biorhythm

bios, bias

biosfeare, biosphere

bioside, biocide

biosphere, ALL THAT SUPPORTS LIFE ON EARTH

biotic,*, ABOUT LIVE ORGANISMS "prefixes: pre/pro/sym"

bipadle, bipedal

bipardesan, bipartisan

bipardisan, bipartisan

bipartisan, TWO SIDES SHARING SAME PURPOSE

bipedal, ANIMAL THAT USES TWO LEGS/ARMS

bipedle, bipedal

bipedul, bipedal

bipetle, bipedal
bir, burr / beer
birben, bourbon
birch, A TREE
bird,*, ANIMAL WITH WINGS/
    FEATHERS (or see beard)
birden, burden
birdensum, burden(some)
birdinsum, burden(some)
biret, barrette / beret
birglur, burglar
birgundy, burgundy
birkler, burglar
birlesk, burlesque
birlup, burlap
birm, berm
birn, burn
birnt, burnt
biro, burro / burrow / borough
birometer, barometer
birp, burp
birsd, burst
birsding, burst(ing)
birst, burst
birth,*,hed,hing, PHYSICAL BODY
    BECOMES VISIBLE (or see berth)
    "prefixes: re"
birthday,*, DATE OF BIRTH
birzd, burst
birzding, burst(ing)
bis, PREFIX INDICATING 'TWO/TWICE'
    MOST OFTEN MODIFIES THE WORD
bisar, bizarre / bazaar
biscuit,*, NORMALLY GOES WITH
    GRAVY, A SOFT ROLL
biscut, biscuit
bise, busy
biseach, beseech
biseech, beseech
bisekul, bicycle
bisenteneal, bicentennial
biseps, biceps
bisi, busy
bisicle, bicycle
biside, beside
bisikul, bicycle
bisintineal, bicentennial
bisk, bisque
biskit, biscuit
biskut, biscuit
bisness, business
bisnis, business
bisnus, business
bisque, OF SPORTS, A SOUP

bistro, NIGHTCLUB
bisurk, berserk
bisy, busy
bit,*, TINY INCREMENTS OF
    SOMETHING, TOOL FOR DRILLING,
    PAST TENSE FOR THE WORD 'BITE'
    (or see bite/bid/bead/beat/beet)
bite,*,ting,ter, USE OF MOUTH AS A
    TOOL(or see bit) "prefixes: non/
    over/under"
biter, bitter / bid(dder) / bite(r)
biton, baton
bitray, betray
bitrothed, betrothed
bitter,*,rer,rest,red,ring,rly,rness,
    UNPLEASANT/HARSH, ALCOHOLIC
    BREW (or see bid(dder)/bite(r))
bitur, bitter / bid(dder) / bite(r)
bitween, between
bius, bias
biusfere, biosphere
biusphere, biosphere
biwar, beware
biwelder, bewilder
biwilder, bewilder
biyopse, biopsy
biyorethum, biorhythm
biyou, bayou
biyu, bayou
biyus, bias
bizar, bizarre / bazaar
bizarre,ely,eness, PECULIAR (or see
    bazaar)
bizee, busy
bizenes, business
bizerk, berserk
biznes, business
bizurk, berserk
bizzar, bizarre / bazaar
black,*,ken,kened,ker,kest, COLOR
bladder, HOLDS URINE/LIQUIDS
blade,*, USED TO SLICE/CUT
bladur, bladder
blaenkit, blanket
blair, blare
blak, black
blam, blame
blame,*,ed,ming,mable,eful,eless,
    elessly,eness, WHAT/WHO IS
    RESPONSIBLE
bland,der,dest,dly,dness, EXPRESSIVELY
    FLAT
blank, NOTHING
blanket,*,ted,ting, COVER

blankit, blanket
blanquet, blanket
blare,*,ed,ring, SOUND LOUDLY
blasa, plaza
blase, blaze
blasem, blossom
blasfemus, blasphemy(mous)
blasfemy, blasphemy
blasma, plasma
blasphemy,mous, SPEAK BADLY OF
    SOMEONE
blast,*,ted,ting, BURSTING FORCE/
    RUSH, PREFIX INDICATING "GERM/
    BUD" MOST OFTEN MODIFIES THE
    WORD, BURSTING FORCE/RUSH
blastek, plastic
blastik, plastic
blasto, PREFIX INDICATING "GERM/
    BUD" MOST OFTEN MODIFIES THE
    WORD, BURSTING FORCE/RUSH
blatebus, platypus
blater, bladder
blatibus, platypus
blaus, blouse
blawse, blouse
blaze,*,ed,zing,er, FLAME, HORSE
    MARK, PROCLAIM, SPORT COAT
blazu, plaza
blea, plea
bleach,es,hed,hing, TO MAKE WHITE
    "prefixes: un"
bleachers, SEATS FOR SPECTATORS
bleak,kish,kly,kness, PALLID, DESOLATE,
    STARK
bled, PAST TENSE FOR THE WORD
    'BLEED'
bleech, bleach
bleechers, bleachers
bleed,*,der,ding, LOOSE BLOOD,
    ALLOW RELEASE OF FLUID
bleef, belief
bleek, bleak
blek, bleak
blemish,hes,hed,hing,her, DEFECT ON A
    SURFACE
blemp, blimp
blend,*,ded,ding,der, MIX
blenk, blink
bler, blur / blare
blerb, blurb
bles, bless / bliss
bless,ssess,ssed,ssing, FAVOR UPON (or
    see bliss) "prefixes: un"
blester, blister

blew, TO DO WITH AIR, PAST TENSE FOR THE WORD 'BLOW' (or see blue)

blezurd, blizzard

blight,*, DESTROYED BY ORGANISM (or see plight)

blimp,*, HELIUM BALLOON

blind,*,ded,ding,ders, WITHOUT SIGHT, WINDOW COVERING (or see blend)

blink,*,ked,king,ker, TO OPEN/CLOSE/ OPEN "prefixes: un"

blinker,*, TURN INDICATORS ON VEHICLES

blir, blur

blirb, blurb

blire, blur(rry)

blis, bliss

blisful, bliss(ful)

bliss,ssful,ssfully,ssfulness, EXTREMELY HAPPY (or see bless)

blister,*,red,ring, SORE

blisurd, blizzard

blite, blight

blizzard,*, VIOLENT STORM

blo, blow / below

bloan, blown

bloat,*,ted,ting, SWELL (or see blot)

block,*,ked,king,kage, IN PATHWAY "prefixes: un"

blockade,*,ed,ding, OBSTRUCT TRAVEL

blod, blood / bloat / blown

blog,*,gged,gging,gger, COMPUTER INTERNET TERM (or see block)

blok, block / blog

blokade, blockade

blon, blown / blonde

blonde,*, A COLOR

blone, blown / blonde

blont, blonde / blown

blood,*,ded,dy,dily,dless,diness, BODY FLUID CARRYING NUTRIENTS

blooish, blue(uish)

bloom,*,med,ming, OPEN UP

blosim, blossom

blossom,*,med,ming, FLOURISH

blosum, blossom

blot,*,tted,tting,tter, SPOT, STAIN (or see bloat/blood)

blouse,es, WOMAN'S SHIRT

blouze, blouse

blow,*,wing,lew,wn, FORCEFUL AIR CURRENT (or see below)

blown, TO DO WITH AIR, PAST TENSE FOR THE WORD 'BLOW' "prefixes: over"

blowse, blouse

blowt, bloat

blu, blue / blew

blubber,*,red,ring,ry,rer, WHALE FAT, SOBBING

blubur, blubber

blud, blood

blue,*,uish,uing, COLOR (or see blew)

bluesh, blue(uish)

bluff,*,ffed,ffing,ffer, A CLIFF, TO PRETEND/FAKE

blume, bloom

blunder,*,red,ring, BUNGLES

blunt,*,tly,tness, DULL

bluper, blubber

blupir, blubber

blur,*,rred,rring,rry, INDISTINCT/FUZZY

blurb,*,bed,bing, SHORT DESCRIPTION

blush,hes,hed,hing, PHYSICAL RESPONSE IN THE CHEEKS, TYPE OF WINE "prefixes: un"

blut, blood

bluty, blood(y)

bo, bough / bow / beau

boar,*, SWINE, PIG (or see bore)

board,*,ded,ding, MILLED WOOD, FURNISH WITH FOOD (or see bore(d)) "prefixes: over/pre"

boast,*,ted,ting,tful,tfully, TO BRAG, COMPLIMENT

boat,*,ting,ter, VESSEL IN WATER

bob,*,bbed,bbing, TO MOVE UP AND DOWN (or see bobbin/bop)

bobbin,*, SEWING TOOL (or see bop(pping))

bobd, bop(pped) / bob(bbed)

boben, bobbin / bob(bbing)

bobin, bobbin / bob(bbing)

bobt, bop(pped) / bob(bbed)

bochulism, botulism

bock, box / bog

bocks, box

bocs, box

bodchulism, botulism

boddle, bottle

bode,*, PAST TENSE FOR THE WORD 'BIDE', TO WAIT (or see body/ bought)

bodeese, bodice / body

bodel, bottle

bodely, body(dily)

bodem, bottom

bodes, body(dies) / bodice

bodice, WOMAN'S GARMENT FOR UPPER TORSO

bodim, bottom

bodis, body(dies) / bodice

bodjulism, botulism

bodle, bottle

bodul, bottle

bodulism, botulism

bodum, bottom

body,dies,dily, THE PHYSICAL FORM WHICH HOUSES A SPIRIT/LIFE (or see bodice) "prefixes: under"

boe, boy / buoy

boee, boy / buoy

boel, boil

boence, bounce(cy) / buoyant(ncy)

boensy, buoyant(ncy)

boent, buoyant

boes, boy(s)

boesdrus, boisterous

boestures, boisterous

boeul, boil

boeunse, buoyant(ncy)

bofalou, buffalo

bofer, buffer

bog,*,gged,gging,ggy,gginess, SOGGY/ SPONGY/WET SOIL AREA/GROUND, SLOW DOWN, A LAVATORY (or see balk/baulk)

boi, boy / buoy

boiant, buoyant

boient, buoyant

boil,*,led,ling,ler, BRING LIQUID TO STEAM TEMPERATURE

boince, buoyant(ncy)

boisdrus, boisterous

boisterous,sly,sness, ROWDY

boiunse, buoyant(ncy)

boiunt, buoyant

bojwaze, bourgeois(ie)

bok, book / poke / bog / baulk / balk

boka, bouquet

bokol, buckle

boks, box

bol, ball / bowl / bawl / bull

bolb, bulb

bolbus, bulb(ous)

bold,der,dest,dly,dness, BRAVE, STANDS OUT (or see bolt) "prefixes: semi"

bolder, boulder / bold(er)

bole, bowl / ball / bawl / bully

bolef, belief
boletin, bulletin
boletle, belittle
boleve, believe
bolidel, belittle
boligerant, belligerent
bolistic, ballistic
bolit, bullet
boliten, bulletin
bolivard, boulevard
bolk, bulk / baulk / balk
boll, bowl / ball / bawl
bollion, bullion / bouillon
bolm, balm
bolme, balmy
bolmy, balmy
bologna, MIXTURE OF MEAT TYPES (or see baloney)
bolonee, baloney / bologna
bolster,*,red,ring, SUPPORT
bolt,*,ted,ting, SECURES, THREADED ROD WITH HEAD (or see bold) "prefixes: un"
bolter, boulder / bold(er)
bolyon, bullion / bouillon
bom, balm / bomb
bomb,*,bed,bing,ber, EXPLOSIVE DEVICE
bomirang, boomerang
bon, bone
bona fide, GENUINE
bonafide, SPELLED AS TWO WORDS "BONA FIDE", GENUINE
bonanza, BONUS DEAL
bond,*,ded,ding,dage,dable,der, TO JOIN/ATTACH TO, TIE UP "prefixes: non"
bondry, boundary
bone,*,ed,ning,ny,nier,niest,niness, SKELETAL
bonefide, bona fide
boneon, bunyon / bunion
bones, bone(s) / bunny(nnies) / bonus
bonifide, bona fide
bonion, bunyon / bunion
bonis, bonus / bunny(nnies)
bonsy, bounce(cy) / buoyant(ncy)
bonufide, bona fide
bonus,ses, EXTRA, ADDITIONAL, MORE
bony, bone(y)
bonyen, bunyon / bunion
bonyon, bunion / bunyon

book,*,ked,king,kish,kishly,kishness,kie, BOUND PAPER WITH A COVER, TO RESERVE A PLACE "prefixes: over"
bookie,*, BOOKS BETS
booky, bookie
boomerang,*,ged,ging, ARTICLE FOR SPORT
boomurang, boomerang
boose, booze / buzz
boost,*,ted,ting,ter, TO LIFT (or see boast/bust)
boosum, bosom
boot,*, OVER ANKLE SHOE (or see butte) "prefixes: re"
booteek, boutique
booth,*, PRIVATE STALL/AREA
bootshur, butcher
booy, buoy
booyon, bouillon / bullion
booze, HARD LIQUOR (or see buzz)
bop,*,pped,pping,pper, TO HIT/WHACK (or see bob)
boped, bop(pped) / bob(bbed)
bopt, bop(pped) / bob(bbed)
boquet, bouquet
bor, boar / bore / bar
borbon, bourbon
borc, bark
bord, board / bore(d)
bordem, boredom
border,*,red,ring, TO LIMIT
bordim, boredom
bordor, border
bordum, boredom
bordur, border
bore,*,ed,ring,ringly, PIERCE/ PUNCTURE/DRILL, LACKS INTEREST, PAST TENSE FOR THE WORD 'BEAR' (or see boar) "prefixes: re"
boredom, DOLDRUMS, LACK OF INTEREST
boren, borne / born
boret, barrette / beret
borin, borne / born
born, BROUGHT INTO EXISTENCE (or see borne/barn) "prefixes: in/re/ un"
borne, SUFFIX MEANING TO BE CARRIED/MOVED BY A PARTICULAR THING (or see born/barn)
boro, PREFIX INDICATING 'BORON' MOST OFTEN MODIFIES THE WORD (or see borrow/borough)
borot, borrow(ed)

borough,*, SELF-GOVERNING TOWN (or see burrow/burro/borrow)
borow, borrow/ burrow/ borough
borrow,*,wed,wing,wer, LOAN (or see burrow)
bort, bore(d) / board
borter, border
bortur, border
bos, boss / bus
bose, bough(s) / bow(s) / bossy
bosed, boss(ed)
boseness, boss(iness)
boserd, buzzard
boshel, bushel
bosiness, boss(iness)
bosom,*,med,my,mier,miest, WOMEN'S BREASTS
boss,sses,ssed,ssing,ssy,ssily,ssiness, COMMAND/ORDER SOMEONE TO DO SOMETHING, ONE IN CHARGE "prefixes: under"
bossom, bosom
bossy,siness, DOMINEERING
bost, boast / boss(ed) / boost
bosy, bossy
bot, but / butt / boat / bought
botany,nic,nical,nist, OF PLANTS
botch,hes,hed,hing, MESS SOMETHING UP, SLANG WORD IN WRESTLING, A BAND
botcher, butcher
botchulism, botulism
bote, boat / bought
boteek, boutique
botel, bottle
botem, bottom
botes, body(dies) / bodice
both, TWO TOGETHER (or see booth)
bother,*,red,ring,rsome, ANNOY "prefixes: un"
botil, bottle
botim, bottom
botiney, botany
botle, bottle
botler, butler / bottle(r)
botn, button
botni, botany
botok, buttock
botom, bottom
boton, button
botshulism, botulism
bottle,*,ed,ling,er, GLASS CONTAINER
bottom,*,med,ming,mless,mlessness, BASE

botul, bottle
botulism, FOOD POISONING
botum, bottom
boty, body
bou, beau / bow
bough,*, BUNCHED FLOWERS, TREE
    BRANCHES, PART OF A SHIP (or see
    bow/beau)
bought, PURCHASED, PAST TENSE FOR
    THE WORD 'BUY' (or see bout)
    "prefixes: over"
bouillon, BROTH (or see bullion)
boulder,*, LARGE ROCK (or see bold)
boulevard,*, AVENUE
boulion, bouillon / bullion
bouls, bowel(s) / bowl(s)
bounce,*,ed,cing,cy,er, REBOUND, UP/
    DOWN ACTION (or see
    buoyant(nce))
bound,*,ded,ding,dless,dlessly,
    dlessness, TO HOLD, JUMP,
    DESTINY "prefixes: in/out/re/un"
boundary,ries, A LIMIT/BORDERLINE
bounse, bounce / buoyant(ncy)
bounsy, bounce(y)
bountiful,lly,lness, PLENTIFUL
bounty,ties,tiful,tifully,tifulness,teous,
    teously,teousness, PAYMENT/
    REWARD FOR CAPTURE, PLENTY,
    ABUNDANCE
bouquet, BUNCH OF FLOWERS
bourbon, WHISKEY
bourgeois,sis, PROPERTY-OWNING
    UPPER MIDDLE CLASS
bout,*, A SPELL OF, TEMPORARY
    EXPERIENCE (or see boat)
boutique,*, WOMEN'S CLOTHING
bouwls, bowel(s)
bouyant, buoyant
bouynce, buoyant(ncy)
bow,*,wed,wing, BEND, HAIR
    ORNAMENT, TOOL USED WITH
    INSTRUMENT/ARROW (or see
    bough/beau) "prefixes: un"
bowel,*, INTESTINES OF ANYTHING
bowkay, bouquet
bowl,*,led,ling,ler, ROUND VESSEL,
    GAME OF BALLS WITH PINS (or see
    ball/bawl)
bowlder, boulder / bold(er)
bownce, bounce / bounce(cy)
bownd, bound
bowndee, bounty
bowndeful, bountiful

bowndery, boundary
bowndury, boundary
bowndy, bounty
bownse, bounce / bound(s)
bownsee, bounce(cy)
bowntee, bounty
bownteful, bountiful
bownts, bounce / bound(s)
bowt, bout
bowteek, boutique
box,xes,xed,xing,xer,xy, SQUARE
    SHAPED CONTAINER, SPORT
    "prefixes: un"
boy,*,yish,yishly, YOUNG MALE (or see
    buoy)
boyanse, buoyant(ncy)
boyant, buoyant
boyent, buoyant
boyint, buoyant
boyle, boil
boysdrus, boisterous
boysterus, boisterous
boyunse, buoyant(ncy)
boyunt, buoyant
bra,*, WOMEN'S UNDERGARMENT
brace,*,ced,cing, SUPPORT (or see
    brass/braise) "prefixes: un"
bracelet,*, WRIST ORNAMENT
bracket,*,ting, FIXTURE TO ATTACH TO,
    TO ENCLOSE WITHIN
bracoli, broccoli
brad,*, VERY SMALL NAILS (or see brat/
    braid)
brael, brail / braille
braen, brain
braes, brace / braise
braf, brave
brag,*,gged,gging,ggart, TO BOAST/
    PRAISE
bragert, braggart
braggart,*, ONE WHO BOASTS
bragirt, braggart
braid,*,ded,ding, TO INTERTWINE
    TOGETHER
brail, OF BOATS, BIRD, FISH (or see
    braille)
braille, TEXT FOR THE BLIND (or see
    brail)
brain,*,nless,nlessly,nlessness,ny,
    THINKING PART/MASS IN THE
    SKULL
braise,*,ed,sing, TO BROWN MEAT
    THEN COVER TO COOK (or see
    brace)

brakale, broccoli
brake,*,ed,king,er, TO STOP, HOLD
    BACK (or see break)
braket, bracket
brakible, breakable
brakit, bracket
brakle, broccoli
brakoli, broccoli
brakuble, breakable
bral, brail / braille / brawl
bran,*, A GRAIN YOU EAT (or see brain/
    brawn/brown/brand)
brand,*,ded,ding, A NAME THAT
    SIGNIFIES OWNERSHIP "prefixes:
    mis/un"
brane, brain
brankeal, bronchial
braquet, bracket
bras, brace / brass / braise / bra(s)
braslet, bracelet
brass,ssy,ssier,ssiest,ssily,ssiness,
    METAL, MILITARY OFFICERS (or see
    brace/braise)
brat,*,tty,ttish, SOMEONE WHO IS
    AGGRAVATING/IRRITATING (or see
    braid/brad)
brathren, brethren
brau, bra / brow
braucoli, broccoli
braud, broad
braukali, broccoli
braukle, broccoli
braun, brown / brawn
braus, browse / brow(s)
brave,*,ed,ving,er,ely,est,ery,eness,
    COURAGEOUS
braw, bra
brawkley, broccoli
brawl,*, LOUD FIGHT
brawn, MUSCLES (or see brown)
brawnkeul, bronchial
brawnkitis, bronchitis
brawnze, bronze
brayed, braid
brayel, brail / braille
braz, braise / brace / bra(s)
breach,hes,hed,hing, BREAK
    CONTRACT/AGREEMENT
bread,ded,ding,dth, BAKED DOUGH (or
    see bred/breed)
breadth, THE EXTENT/DISTANCE/
    BROADNESS (or see breath)
break,*,king,kage,ker,roke, COME
    APART (or see brake)

breakable, CAN COME APART "prefixes: un"

breakuble, breakable

breast,*,ted, BOSOM

breath,hes,hed,hing,hless,hlessly,her, INHALE, EXHALE AIR (or see breadth)

brec, brick

brech, breach

bred, PAST TENSE FOR THE WORD 'BREED', HAVING MATED (or see bread/breed/barrette) "prefixes: in/under"

breed,*,ding,der,red, TO MATE FOR PROCREATION, A CLASSIFICATION/TYPE (or see bred/bread) "prefixes: in/un"

breef, brief

breeng, bring

breenk, brink

breeth, breath

breeve, bereave

breeze,*,ed,zing,zily,zy, GENTLE WIND

bref, brief

brege, bridge

breif, brief

brej, bridge

brek, brick / break

breluns, brilliance

brelyans, brilliance

brem, brim

breng, bring

brenk, brink

brese, breeze

brest, breast

bret, barrette / beret / breed / bread / bred

breth, breath / breadth

brethless, breath(less)

brethlis, breath(less)

brethren, PLURAL FOR BROTHER

brethrin, brethren

brew,*,wed,wing, A DRINK CONCOCTION

breze, breeze

bribe,*,ed,bing,ery, REWARD FOR CORRUPTION

brick,*,ked,king, CLAY BLOCK

brid, bride / bright / bread

bride,*,dal, FEMALE GETTING MARRIED

bridegroom,*, MALE GETTING MARRIED

bridesmaid,*, ATTENDS BRIDE

bridge,*,ed,ging,eable,eless, LINK FOR TRAVEL "prefixes: under"

bridgroom, bridegroom

bridgrum, bridegroom

bridle,*,ed,ling, FOR RESTRAINT (or see brittle) "prefixes: un"

bridmade, bridesmaid

bridol, bridle / brittle

bridsmaid, bridesmaid

bridul, bridle / brittle

brief,*,fed,fing, SHORT/SWEET/TO THE POINT, UNDERWEAR

brig, bridge

bright,*,ter,test,tly,tness, STRONG LIGHT ENERGY

brij, bridge

brik, brick

brileans, brilliance

briliance, brilliance

brilliance,nt, INTENSE LIGHT ENERGY

brilliant,ntly, INTENSE LIGHT ENERGY

brim,*,mmed,mming, THE EDGE/RIM OF SOMETHING

bring,*,ging,rought, BEAR FORTH "prefixes: up"

brink, NEAR THE EDGE

brit, bright / bride

britesmade, bridesmaid

britle, bridle / brittle

brittle,eness, CRISP (or see bridle)

britul, bridle / brittle

brn, burn/ barn

bro,*, SHORT FOR BROTHER (or see bra)

broad,*,dly,den,dness, AS IN WIDTH OR BREADTH

broadcast,*,ted,ting,ter, ANNOUNCE, SCATTER

broccoli , VEGETABLE (same as brocoli)

brochere, brochure

brochure,*, PAMPHLET

brocoli, VEGETABLE (same as broccoli)

brocolli, broccoli

brod, broad / brought / brood

brodkast, broadcast

broeel, broil

broel, broil

broil,*,led,ling,ler, WAY TO COOK

brok, broke

brokali, broccoli

broke,en, PAST TENSE FOR THE WORD 'BREAK', NO MONEY "prefixes: un"

brokle, broccoli

brokley, broccoli

brokule, broccoli

brol, brawl

bron, brawn / brown

brona, prana / piranha

bronceal, bronchial

bronch, PREFIX INDICATING 'BRONCHIAL' MOST OFTEN MODIFIES THE WORD

broncheul, bronchial

bronchi, PREFIX INDICATING 'BRONCHIAL' MOST OFTEN MODIFIES THE WORD

bronchial,lly, OF THE AIR/BREATHING PASSAGES

bronchitis, BREATHING PROBLEM

broncho, PREFIX INDICATING 'BRONCHIAL' MOST OFTEN MODIFIES THE WORD

bronckial, bronchial

bronkeul, bronchial

bronkites, bronchitis

bronse, bronze

bronze,ed,zing, METALLIC

brood,*,ding,dingly, CONCERNING OFFSPRING IN A GROUP, TO GRIEVE, BIRD SITTING ON EGGS

broodel, brutal

brook,*, STREAM

broom,*, FOR SWEEPING

broonet, brunet

brootal, brutal

brootle, brutal

bropane, propane

brosh, brush

brosher, brochure

broshur, brochure

brot, brought / broad

broth, SOUP

brother,*,rly, MALE SIBLING

brought, PAST TENSE FOR THE WORD "BRING"

broun, brown / brawn

brow,*, ABOVE EYES (or see browse)

browl, brawl

brown,*,ned,ning,ner,nest, COLOR (or see brawn)

browse,*,ed,sing,er, GLANCE/PERUSE/CASUALLY GO THROUGH (or see brow(s))

broyl, broil

brud, brood

brudel, brutal

brue, brew

bruise,*,ed,sing,er, A BLOW TO, DAMAGED TISSUE

bruke, brook

brume, broom

brunet, DARK COLOR

brunkitis, bronchitis

brunnet, brunet

bruro, bureau

bruse, bruise

brush,hes,hed,hing, ENCOUNTER, HAIR TOOL, BUSHES "prefixes: under"

brutal,lly,lize,lization,lity, SAVAGE

bruther, brother

brutil, brutal

bruz, bruise

brydgroom, bridegroom

brydle, bridle / brittle

brydsmade, bridesmaid

bryt, bright

buanse, bounce(cy)

bubble,*,ed,ling,er,ly, AIR, GAS GLOBULES

bubil, bubble

buble, bubble

bucame, became

bucher, butcher

buchur, butcher

buck,*,ked,king, UNSEAT RIDER, MALE DEER, DOLLAR

bucket,*, A CONTAINER

buckil, buckle

buckit, bucket

buckle,*,ed,ling, TOOL TO SECURE SOMETHING, TO FOLD UNDER PRESSURE

bud,*,dded,dding, READY TO OPEN, FULL OF FUTURE POTENTIAL (or see butt/butte/but) "prefixes: de/dis"

budder, butter

buddy,ddies,ddied,ddying, SOMEONE YOU BEFRIEND, TRAVEL ALONGSIDE (or see beauty)

bude, buddy / beauty

budeful, beautiful

buden, button

buder, butter

budge,*,ed,ging, TO MOVE

budget,*,ted,ting,ter,tary, RATION A SPECIFIC AMOUNT FOR EXPENDITURES

budi, buddy / beauty

budiful, beautiful

budin, button

budj, budge

budler, butler

budok, buttock

budres, buttress

budris, buttress

budrothed, betrothed

buduk, buttock

budy, buddy / beauty

buee, buoy

bufa, buffet

bufal, befall

bufalo, buffalo

bufer, buffer

buff,*,ffed,ffing,ffer, A COLOR, NUDE, MASCULINE/MUSCULAR, TO POLISH WITH CLOTH "prefixes: re"

buffalo,*, ANIMAL

buffer,*,red,ring, ABSORBS SHOCK, POLISHES

buffet,*, SELF-SERVE RESTAURANT

bufilo, buffalo

bufir, buffer

bufol, befall

bufrend, befriend

bufulo, buffalo

bufur, buffer

bug,*,gged,gging,ggy,ggier,ggiest, gginess,gger, ERROR IN DEVICE, AN INSECT, TO IRRITATE SOMEONE/ SOMETHING, SPY DEVICE (or see budge) "prefixes: de"

buge, budge / buggy

bugel, bugle

bugener, begin(nner)

buget, budget

buggy,ggies, LIGHTWEIGHT CARRIAGE FOR MANY PURPOSES

bugil, bugle

bugin, begin

bugit, budget

bugle,*, INSTRUMENT

bugul, bugle

bugwazee, bourgeois(ie)

bugy, buggy

buhaf, behave

buhind, behind

build,*,der,ding,dable,lt, CONSTRUCT (or see built) "prefixes: over/re/up"

built, PAST TENSE FOR THE WORD 'BUILD'

buj, budge

bujet, budget

bujit, budget

bujwau, bourgeois

bujwazee, bourgeois(ie)

buk, buck / book / bug

bukame, became

bukaus, because

buke, bookie

bukel, buckle

bukene, bikini

buket, bucket

bukie, bookie

bukil, buckle

bukit, bucket

bukos, because

bul, bull

bulated, belated

bulaten, bulletin

bulatide, belated

bulavard, boulevard

bulb,*,bous, OF PLANTS, GLASS GLOBES WITH FILAMENTS

bulbus, bulb(ous)

bulch, bulge

bulck, bulk

bule, bully

buledul, belittle

buleef, belief

buleeve, believe

bulef, belief

buleger, beleaguer

bulegirant, belligerent

buleon, bullion / bouillon

bulese, police

bulet, bullet

buletin, bulletin

bulevard, boulevard

buleve, believe

bulevuble, believe(vable)

bulge,*,ed,ging, SWELL OUT

bulian, bouillon

buligerant, belligerent

bulijurent, belligerent

bulion, bullion / bouillon

bulistic, ballistic

bulit, bullet

bulitel, belittle

buliten, bulletin

bulivard, boulevard

bulje, bulge

bulk,ky,kiness,kier,kiest, MASS OF SOMETHING

bull,*, MALE ANIMAL

bullet,*, PROJECTILE

bulletin,*, DOCUMENT

bullion, OF GOLD (or see bouillon)

bully,llies,llied,llying, INTIMIDATOR

bullyon, bouillon / bullion

bulo, blow / below
bulonee, baloney / bologna
bulong, belong
buloon, balloon
bulow, below / bellow / billow
bulp, bulb
bulune, balloon
buluvard, boulevard
buly, bully
bulyon, bullion / bouillon
bumbelbee, bumblebee
bumblebee,*, BIG BEE
bumer, bummer
bumerang, boomerang
bumir, bummer
bummer, OF QUARRY, NOT HAPPY
bumur, bummer
bumurang, boomerang
bunana, banana
bunansa, bonanza
bunch,hes,hed,hing, MORE THAN A
    FEW IN THE GROUP
bundle,*,ed,ling,er, TO GROUP/BIND
    TOGETHER "prefixes: un"
bune, bunny
buneeth, beneath
buneon, bunion / bunyon
bunes, bunny(nnies) / bonus
buneun, bunyon / bunion
bunevilance, benevolence
bungil, bungle
bungle,*,ed,ling,ler, MESS UP, SPOIL,
    WRECK
bunie, bunny
bunine, benign
bunion,*, SWELLING ON BIG TOE, ALSO
    SPELLED "BUNYON"
bunis, bunny(nnies)
bunny,nies, RABBIT
bunsh, bunch
buny, bunny
bunyon,*, SWELLING ON BIG TOE, ALSO
    SPELLED "BUNION"
bunyun, bunion / bunyon
buond, beyond
buorgeoise, bourgeois(ie)
buownse, bounce(cy)
buoy,*, FLOATING DEVICE
buoyant,ncy, TO FLOAT
bur, burr
bura, barrette / beret
buracracy, bureaucracy
buracrat, bureaucrat
burakracy, bureaucracy

burau, bureau
buraukracy, bureaucracy
burave, brave
burbon, bourbon
burch, birch
burd, bird
burden,*,ned,ning,nsome, HEAVY LOAD
    "prefixes: dis/over/un"
burdensum, burden(some)
burdin, burden
burdinsum, burden(some)
burdon, burden
bureal, burial
bureau,*, A DRESSER, GOVERNMENT
    DEPARTMENT
bureaucracy,cies,at, GOVERNMENT
    ADMINISTRATION
bureaucrat,*, AGENTS OF
    GOVERNMENT ADMINISTRATION
bureeve, bereave
bureft, bereft
buret, barrette / beret
bureve, bereave
burgendy, burgundy
burgeois, bourgeois
burglar,*,ry,ries,rize,rizes,rized,rizing,
    ROBBER/THIEF
burglir, burglar
burgundy, A COLOR, A WINE
burial,*, BURYING DECEASED
burileans, brilliance
buring, bring
burite, bright
burkler, burglar
burlap, WOVEN HEMP/JUTE
burlee, burly
burlesk, burlesque
burlesque,er, MOCKERY
burlip, burlap
burly, BIG MUSCULAR BODY
burm, berm
burn,*,ned,ning,nable,nt, SCORCH
    "prefixes: un"
burnt, BEEN BURNED, PAST TENSE FOR
    THE WORD 'BURN'
buro, burro / burrow / borough /
    bureau
burocrasy, bureaucracy
burocrat, bureaucrat
burog, barrage
burokracy, bureaucracy
burokrat, bureaucrat
buromiter, barometer

burow, burro / burrow / borough /
    bureau
burp,*,ped,ping, BELCH
burr,*,rred,rring, PRICKLY SEED, ROUGH
    EDGES, EXPRESSION FOR BEING
    COLD "prefixes: de"
burro,*, DONKEY (or see burrow/
    borough)
burrow,*,wed,wing, LODGE INTO HOLE
    (or see burro/borough)
bursd, burst
burst,*,ting,ter, ERUPT
burth, berth / birth
burthday, birthday
bury,ries,ried,rying, PUT IN GROUND
    (or see berry) "prefixes: un"
bus,sses,ssed,ssing, LARGE VEHICLE TO
    TRANSPORT MANY PASSENGERS,
    CARRIER OF INFORMATION
busar, bizarre / bazaar
busd, bust / boost / bus(ssed)
busdid, bust(ed) / burst
busech, beseech
buseech, beseech
busel, bustle
busem, bosom
buserd, buzzard
buses, bus(sses)
bushel,*, MEASUREMENT OF AMOUNT
bushil, bushel
bushwaze, bourgeois(ie)
busi, busy
buside, beside
busil, bustle
busim, bosom
business,sses, A SERVICE
busle, bustle
busness, business
busniss, business
bust,*,ted,ting,ty,tier,tiest, HEAD AND
    SHOULDERS, WOMEN'S BREASTS,
    CAUGHT RED-HANDED (or see
    boost/burst/bus(ssed))
busted, burst / bust(ed)
bustle,*,ed,ling, HURRIES ABOUT, FOR
    SKIRTS
busul, bustle
busum, bosom
busurk, berserk
busy,sies,sier,siest, ENGROSSED
but, A PREPOSITION MEANING
    "EXCEPT/ONLY/DIFFERENCE" (or
    see butte/bud/boot)
butcher,*,red,ring, CUT UP

bute, boot / but / butt / butte
buted, butt(ed) / bud(dded)
buteek, boutique
buteful, beautiful
buten, button
butenchul, potential
buter, butter
buth, booth
buti, buddy / beauty
butid, butt(ed) / bud(dded)
butiful, beautiful
butike, boutique
butin, button
butinchul, potential
butir, butter
butishun, beautician
butler,*, MALE SERVANT
butlur, butler
butok, buttock
buton, baton / button
butra, betray
butres, buttress
butris, buttress
butrothed, betrothed
buts, butt(s) / bud(s) / boot(s)
butsher, butcher
butshir, butcher
butt,*,tted,tting, REAR END/BOTTOM
OF SOMETHING, FORCE UPON (or
see bud/but/butte)
butte,*, HILL/MOUNTAIN WITH FLAT
TOP (or see but/butt)
butter,red,ring,ry, CHURNED FROM
MILK
buttock,*, RUMP
button,*,ned,ning, FIXTURE FOR
CLOTHING "prefixes: un"
buttress, TO STRENGTHEN
butuk, buttock
butween, between
buty, buddy / beauty
buvileon, pavilion
buware, beware
buwee, buoy
buwelder, bewilder
buwildre, bewilder
buwro, bureau
buwte, beauty
buy,*,ying,yer,bought, TO PURCHASE
(or see bye/by/bi)
buyent, buoyant
buyint, buoyant
buyond, beyond
buzar, bizarre / bazaar / buzz(er)

buzd, buzz(ed) / bust / bus(ssed)
buzded, bust(ed)
buze, booze / buzz
buzer, buzz(er) / bizarre / bazaar
buzerd, buzzard
buzerk, berserk
buzir, buzz(er) / bizarre / bazaar
buzor, buzz(er) / bizarre / bazaar
buzted, bust(ed) / burst
buzum, bosom
buzurk, berserk
buzz,zzes,zzed,zzing,zzer, A SOUND,
DEVICE WHICH MAKES SOUND
buzzar, bizarre / bazaar / buzz(er)
buzzard,*, CARNIVOROUS BIRD
buzzer, buzz(er) / bizarre / bazaar
by, ALONGSIDE, PREFIX INDICATING
'NEAR/SECONDARY' MOST OFTEN
MODIFIES THE WORD(or see bye/
bi/buy)
bye, AS IN GOOD-BYE (or see by/bi/
buy)
byeneul, biennial / biannual
byker, bike(r)
bysenteneal, bicentennial
byu, bayou
c, see / sea
cabach, cabbage
cabage, cabbage
cabaret, TYPE OF MUSICAL SHOW
cabbage,*, VEGETABLE
cabdive, captive
cabduve, captive
cabech, cabbage
cabel, cable
caben, cabin
caberay, cabaret
cabich, cabbage
cabichulate, capitulate
cabige, cabbage
cabin,*, RUSTIC STRUCTURE
cabinet,*,try, STORAGE WITH DOORS,
POLITICAL ADVISORY
cabiret, cabaret
cabitate, capitate
cabitch, cabbage
cable,*,ed,ling, WIRE ROPE,
CONNECTION
cabnet, cabinet
cabnit, cabinet
caboose, LAST CAR ON A TRAIN
cabsel, capsule
cabshure, capture
cabten, captain

cabture, capture
cabtuve, captive
cabul, cable
cabus, caboose
cac, PREFIX INDICATING 'HARSH/BAD'
MOST OFTEN MODIFIES THE WORD
(or see cake/caulk/cock)
cach, catch / cache / cash
cache,*,ed,hing, PLACE TO HIDE ITEMS
IN (or see cash/catch)
cacher, catcher / cashier
cachup, ketchup / catsup
cachwul, casual
cackle,*,ed,ling, SHRILL SOUND/LAUGH
caco, PREFIX INDICATING 'HARSH/ BAD'
MOST OFTEN MODIFIES THE WORD
cacol, cackle
cacoon, cocoon
cactis, cactus
cactus,ses,ti, DESERT PLANT
cacun, cocoon
cadagory, category
cadal, cattle
cadaver,*,ric, LIFELESS BODY
caddie, caddy
caddy,ddie,ddies, PERSON WHO
CARRIES CLUBS IN GOLF, BOX
cadech, cottage
cadecism, catechism
cadee, caddy
cadegerize, categorize
cadegory, category
cadekism, catechism
cadence, MARCHING RHYTHM
cader, cater
caderact, cataract
cadet,*, TRAINING FOR SERVICE
cadi, caddy
cadigorize, categorize
cadigory, category
cadikism, catechism
cadil, cattle
cadilist, catalyst
cadilog, catalog
cadinse, cadence
cadl, cattle
cadle, cattle
cadol, cattle
cadugorize, categorize
cadugory, category
cadul, cattle
cadulist, catalyst
cadulize, catalyst(yze)
cadulog, catalog

cadur, cater
caduract, cataract
caf, calf / cave / cough
cafa, cafe
cafanated, caffeine(nated)
cafe,*, SMALL RESTAURANT (or see coffee/calf)
cafeene, caffeine
cafene, caffeine
cafeteria,*, SELF-SERVE RESTAURANT
caffeine,nate,nated,nation,nism, ALSO SPELLED 'CAFFEIN', STIMULANT, DIURETIC "prefixes: de/under"
cafin, caffeine
cafiteria, cafeteria
cafs, calves / cave(s)
cafunated, caffeine(nated)
cafutirea, cafeteria
cage,*,ed,ging, FOR CONFINEMENT
cagwal, casual
cahoot,*, IN PARTNERSHIP
cahute, cahoot
cainker, canker / chancre
cairfree, carefree
cairful, careful
caje, cage
cajewul, casual
cajole,*,ed,ling, COAX
cajuol, casual
cajwul, casual
cak, caulk / calk / cake / cock
cakd, cake(d)
cake,*,ed,king,ey, BAKED SWEET DOUGH, RESEMBLES CAKE
cakel, cackle
cakt, cake(d)
caktis, cactus
caktus, cactus
caky, khaki
cal, call / cowl / kale
calaberate, collaborate
calabrate, calibrate
caladeral, collateral
calag, collage / college
calametous, calamity(tous)
calamity,ties,tous,tously, DISASTER
calander, calendar / calender / colander
calanize, colony(nize)
calany, colony
calapse, collapse
calas, callous / callus
calasthenics, calisthenics
calastomy, colostomy
calasul, colossal

calateral, collateral
calaug, collage
calcefy, calcify
calcify,fies,fied,fying,fication,fier, BECOME RIGID, LIME/CALCIUM DEPOSIT "prefixes: de"
calcilate, calculate
calcilus, calculus
calcium, ELEMENT ON EARTH
calcufy, calcify
calculate,*,ed,ting,tingly,tion,tor, TO MENTALLY/MATHEMATICALLY ESTIMATE/FIGURE "prefixes: in/mis/un"
calculus,li,ses, REFERENCE TO MATH, ORGAN STONE "prefixes: pre"
cale, kale
calebrate, calibrate
calech, college
caleflower, cauliflower
caleg, colleague / college
calegen, collision
caleget, collegiate
calek, colic
calendar,*,red,ring,rize,dric,drical, REGISTER OF MONTHS/DAYS OF THE YEAR (or see calender/colander)
calender,*,red,ring,rer, PRESS/ ROLLER FOR PAPER/CLOTH (or see calendar/colander)
calendula, MEDICINAL FLOWER
caler, collar / call(er)
cales, callous / callus
calesthenics, calisthenics
calf,lves,lved,lving, YOUNG BOVINE, BIRTHING OF BOVINE, LOWER PORTION OF LEG
caliber,*,bre, OF MEASUREMENT, DIAMETER (or see caliper) "prefixes: sub"
calibrate,*,ed,ting,tion,tor, SET/ DETERMINE MEASUREMENT/SIZE
calibre, caliber
calide, collide
calidiscope, kaleidoscope
califlower, cauliflower
calig, college
caligen, collision
caligent, collegiate
calinder, calendar / calender / colander
calindula, calendula
caliper,*,lliper, INSTRUMENT FOR MEASURING (or see caliber)

calire, calorie
calis, callous / callus
calision, collision
calisthenics, EXERCISES
calk, DEVICE FOR SHOES (or see caulk)
calkilate, calculate
calkulus, calculus
call,*,lled,lling,ller, ATTEMPT TO CONTACT/INVITE SOMEONE TO ANSWER/RESPOND (or see cowl) "prefixes: mis"
calleague, colleague
callous,llus,ses,sed,sly,sness, HARDENED/ROUGH AREA ON SKIN/ PLANT, INSENSITIVE BEHAVIOR (also spelled callus)
callus,ses,sed,sing,sity,llose, HARDENED/ROUGH AREA ON SKIN/ PLANT, INSENSITIVE BEHAVIOR (also spelled callous)
calm,mes,med,ming,mly,mative,mness, TO SOOTHE (or see come)
calobrate, calibrate
calokweul, colloquial
caloquial, colloquial
calorie,*,ric,rically,rific, UNIT OF MEASUREMENT FOR FOOD
calorize,*,ed,zing, PROCESS USED IN METALLURGY
calos, callous / callus
calostemy, colostomy
calosthenics, calisthenics
calous, callous / callus
calsefy, calcify
calseum, calcium
caluber, caliber
calubrate, calibrate
calunder, colander
caluper, caliper
calur, collar / call(er)
calury, calorie
calus, callous / callus
calusthenics, calisthenics
calves,ed,ving, PLURAL FOR THE WORD 'CALF', YOUNG BOVINE, BIRTHING BOVINE
camb, camp
came, PAST TENSE FOR THE WORD 'COME', CHANNEL USED FOR MANUFACTURING "prefixes: over"
camel,*, ANIMAL
camend, commend
camendible, commendable
camenduble, commendable

camera,*, TAKES PHOTOS
camfor, camphor
camind, commend
caminduble, commendable
camins, commence
camitee, committee
camofloje, camouflage
camouflage,*,ed,ging, DISGUISED
camp,*,ped,ping,per, STAY OVERNIGHT/
    OUTDOORS IN WILDERNESS
    "prefixes: en"
campaign,*,ned,ning,ner, ACTION TO
    INFLUENCE
campane, campaign
camphor,ric, FROM TREES, MEDICINAL
campis, campus
campus,ses, SCHOOL GROUNDS
camra, camera
camuflodge, camouflage
camul, camel
camune, commune
camunicate, communicate
camunity, community
camute, commute
can,*,nned,nning,nner,nnery, ABLE TO,
    TIN VESSEL (or see cane)
can't, CONTRACTION OF THE WORDS
    'CAN NOT' (or see cent/ sand/
    can(nned)/con(nned))
canabis, cannabis
canabol, cannibal
canabus, cannabis
canal,*, WHERE FLUIDS FLOW
canalop, cantaloupe
canan, canon / canyon
canapi, canopy
canare, cannery / canary
canary,ries, A YELLOW BIRD (or see
    cannery)
cancel,*,led,ling,lable,ler,llation,
    DELETE,RENDER NULL/VOID
cancellation,*, DELETE, ELIMINATE,
    INVALIDATE
cancer,rous, DISEASE
cancl, cancel
cancr, cancer
cancur, chancre / canker
candedate, candidate
candid,dly,dness, TO BE FRANK/
    TRUTHFUL
candidate,*,acy,acies, SEEKS OFFICE
candle,*,ed,ling, WAX WITH WICK
candudite, candidate
candul, candle

candy,dies,died, WEET TREAT
cane,*,ned, STICK OF WOOD/SUGAR
canebulize, cannibal(ize)
canelop, cantaloupe
caneon, canyon
canere, cannery / canary
canery, cannery / canary
canesis, kinesis
cangaroo, kangaroo
cangruis, congruous
canibal, cannibal
canibis, cannabis
canikcanik, kinnikinnick
canin, cannon / canine
canine,*, DOG
canion, canyon
canipe, canopy
caniry, cannery / canary
canister,*, CONTAINER
canker,*,rous, DISEASE, SORE (or see
    chancre)
cannabis, A USEFUL PLANT
cannery,ries, PLACE WHICH CANS FOOD
    (or see canary)
cannibal,*,lism,listic,lize, EATS FLESH
    OF ITS OWN SPECIES
cannon,*, WEAPON
canon, cannon
canopy,pies,pied,ying, COVERING FOR
    SHELTER
canosieur, connoisseur
canseld, cancel(lled)
canser, cancer
cansil, cancel
cansilashen, cancellation
cansir, cancer
cansl, cancel
cansr, cancer
cansul, cancel
cansulation, cancellation
cansuld, cancel(lled)
cantaloupe,*,pe,pes, EDIBLE FRUIT
cantankerous,sly,sness, RESISTANT,
    DIFFICULT
canted, candid
canteen,*, CONTAINER FOR LIQUIDS
cantelope, cantaloupe
cantena, cantina
canter,*, SPEED OF HORSE
cantidit, candidate
cantiguis, contiguous
cantilope, cantaloupe
cantina,*, SALOON, BAG FOR SADDLE
cantul, candle

cantulope, cantaloupe
cantur, canter
canty, candy
canubelize, cannibal(ize)
canubil, cannibal
canubis, cannabis
canulop, cantaloupe
canupe, canopy
canuster, canister
canvas,ses, WOVEN HEMP/NATURAL
    FIBERS (or see canvass)
canvass,sser, TO SOLICIT (or see
    canvas)
canves, canvas / canvass
canvis, canvas / canvass
canvus, canvass / canvas
canyon,*, DEEP VALLEY
cap,*,pped,pping,pful, TOP, HAT, TO
    LIMIT (or see cape) "prefixes: re/
    un"
capability,ties, CAPACITY, ABILITY, SKILL
capable,eness,ly,bility,bilities, CAPACITY,
    ABILITY, SKILL "prefixes: in"
capacity,ties, STATUS OF, AMOUNT
    "prefixes: over"
capadol, capital / capitol
capalery, capillary
capasety, capacity
capatol, capital / capitol
capatulism, capitalism
capcher, capture
capchun, caption
capchur, capture
capdivate, captivate
capdof, captive
capduvate, captivate
cape,*,ped, CLOAK, GARMENT, LAND
    FORM (or see cap)
capebilety, capability
capechulate, capitulate
capedal, capital
capedalism, capitalism
capedul, capital / capitol
capedulism, capitalism
capelary, capillary
capetate, capitate
capetul, capital / capitol
capetulate, capitulate
capetulesm, capitalism
capichulate, capitulate
capidal, capital
capidalism, capitalism
capillary,ries, OF THE BODY

capital,*,list,lists,listically,lize,lizable, lizes,lized,lizing,lization,lly,lism, LARGE, MAIN, TOP (or see capitol) "prefixes: under"

capitalism, PRIVATE/FREE ENTERPRISE

capitate,*,ed,ting,tion,tions,tive, COUNTING/TAXING BY HEADS, HEAD OF SOMETHING

capitol, CENTER OF GOVERNMENT (or see capital)

capitulate,*,ed,ting,ant,tion,tions,tor, tory, CONSENT/GIVE IN/YIELD "prefixes: re"

capol, couple

capshun, caption

capshur, capture

capsile, capsule

capsize,*,ed,zing, OVERTURN A BOAT

capsulate,*,ed,ting,tion,tor, MATERIAL BEING CONTAINED "prefixes: de/ en/in"

capsule,*,ed,ling,lar,late,lize,lized,lizing, CONTAINED MATERIAL, COMPACT FORM WITH PROTECTIVE EXTERIOR

captain,*, ONE WHO COMMANDS

captin, captain

caption,*,ned,nless, HEADING OR TITLE

captivate,*,ed,ting, CHARMED, HELD UNWILLFULLY

captive,*,vity,vation,vator, CONTROLLED/HELD AGAINST ONE'S WILL

captun, captain

capture,*,ed,ring,er, TAKE BY FORCE "prefixes: re"

captuvate, captivate

captuve, captive

capubility, capability

capuble, capable

capudul, capital / capitol

capudulesm, capitalism

capulary, capillary

caput, kaput

caputate, capitate

car,*,rful, AUTOMOBILE (or see care)

caracter, character

carakter, character

caramel,*,lize,lizes,lized,lizing,lization, CANDY, HEAT PROCESS

caraoke, karaoke

carat,*, MILLIGRAMS (or see caret/ carrot/karat)

carate, karate

carauti, karate

caravan,*,ned,ning,ner, GROUP OF VEHICLES/TRAVELERS

carbarator, carburetor

carbender, carpenter

carberator, carburetor

carbin, carbon

carbinete, carbonate

carbirater, carburetor

carbon,*,nize,nator, FORMS ORGANIC COMPOUNDS

carbonate,*,ed,ting,tion, SALT OR GAS "prefixes: bi/de"

carbunete, carbonate

carburetor,*, HEART OF COMBUSTIBLE ENGINE

carcass,sses, EXTERNAL REMAINS OF ANYTHING

carcino, PREFIX INDICATING 'CANCER' MOST OFTEN MODIFIES THE WORD

carcinogen,*,nic,nicity,nesis, CANCER CAUSING

carcus, carcass

card,*,ded,ding, STIFF PAPER, ASKED FOR I.D. (or see cart)

cardboard, THICK PAPER

cardeac, cardiac

cardenul, cardinal

cardi, PREFIX INDICATING "HEART" MOST OFTEN MODIFIES THE WORD

cardiac, OF THE HEART

cardilege, cartilage

cardin, carton

cardinal,*, A BIRD, RANK IN CATHOLIC CHURCH

cardio, PREFIX INDICATING 'HEART' MOST OFTEN MODIFIES THE WORD

cardulege, cartilage

care,*,ed,ring,ringly,eful,efully,efulness, eless,elessness, CONCERN OVER (or see carry) "prefixes: multi/un"

careboo, caribou

carebral, cerebral

carebrul, cerebral

carech, carriage

carecter, character

caredge, carriage

caredor, corridor

careen,*,ned,ning, LEAN TO ONE SIDE

career,*, PROFESSION

carefree, WITHOUT CARE

careful,lly,lness, WITH CARE

carege, carriage

carekter, character

careless,ssly,ssness, NOT WITH CARE

caremel, caramel

careoke, karaoke

carer, career

cares, care(s) / caress

caress,sses,ssed,ssing,ssingly,ssive, ssively, PET/STROKE SMOOTHLY/ GENTLY

caret,*, PROOFREADING MARK (or see carrot/carat/karat)

careur, carrier

carful, careful

cargo,oes,os, FREIGHT ON VESSEL

cariage, carriage

carib, carob

caribou, reindeer

caricature,*,ed,ring,rist, EXAGGERATED IMITATION

carich, carriage

caricter, character

carie, carry

carier, carrier

carige, carriage

carikter, character

carioke, karaoke

carir, career

carisma, charisma

carit, carat / caret / carrot / karat

carivan, caravan

carkis, carcass

carkus, carcass

carlis, careless

carma, karma

carmel, caramel

carmil, caramel

carmu, karma

carmul, caramel

carn, care(ring) / carton

carnashun, carnation

carnation,*, FLOWER

carnival,*, TRAVELING AMUSEMENT SHOW

carnivore,*,rous, EATS FLESH

carnuvil, carnival

carnuvore, carnivore

carob, LOCUST BEAN RESEMBLING CHOCOLATE

caroberate, corroborate

carode, corrode

carogan, corrode(osion)

carogate, corrugate(d)

carogen, corrode(osion)

carogin, corrode(osion)

carojen, corrode(osion)

carojin, corrode(osion)

carojun, corrode(osion)

caroke, karaoke

carol,*,led,ling, SONGS

caroner, coroner

carosef, corrode(osive)

carosel, carousel

carosene, kerosene

caroshen, corrode(osion)

carot, carat / caret / carrot / karat

caroty, karate

carouse,*,ed,sing, UNDESIRABLE DRUNKEN BEHAVIOR

carousel,*, MERRY-GO-ROUND

carpenter,*,try, BUILDS WITH WOOD

carpet,*,ted,ting, SOFT FLOOR COVERING

carpinder, carpenter

carpinter, carpenter

carpit, carpet

carriage,*, PULLED FOUR-WHEELED CART, OF CARRYING "prefixes: mis/under"

carrier,*, ONE WHO TRANSPORTS (or see career)

carrot,*, VEGETABLE (or see carat/caret/karat)

carry,rries,rried,rrying,rrier,rriage, rriages, TO TRANSPORT "prefixes: mis"

carsenagen, carcinogen

carsinugen, carcinogen

cart,*,ted,ting, VEHICLE FOR TRANSPORT

cartilage, SOFT BONE IN THE BODY "prefixes: sub"

cartin, carton

cartleg, cartilage

cartn, carton

cartnul, cardinal

carton,*, PAPER BOX

cartoon,*,ning,nist, ANIMATED CARICATURES

cartrege, cartridge

cartridge,*, REFILLABLE/REPLACEABLE CONTAINER

cartrige, cartridge

cartulige, cartilage

cartun, carton / cartoon

carubtion, corrupt(ion)

carubu, caribou

carudge, carriage

carupd, corrupt

carupshen, corrupt(ion)

carupt, corrupt

carusel, carousel

carusen, kerosene

carut, carat / caret / carrot / karat

carve,*,ed,ving,er, TO SHAPE WITH KNIFE

cary, carry

casadilla, quesadilla

casal, castle / cause(sal)

casc, cask

cascade,*,ed,ding, LIKE A WATERFALL

cascara, TREE

case,*,ed,sing, CERTAIN NUMBER OF ITEMS CONTAINED TOGETHER (too many definitions, please see standard dictionary) "prefixes: en/upper"

casedilla, quesadilla

caseng, casing

caseno, casino

caserole, casserole

casete, cassette

cash,hed,hing, MONETARY/MONEY (or see cache)

cashere, cashier

cashew,*, NUT

cashier,*, HANDLES MONEY

cashmere, GOAT WOOL

cashon, caution

cashos, cautious

cashu, cashew

cashual, casual

cashuol, casual

cashwul, casual

casil, castle

casing,*, COVERING OR SUPPORT

casino,*, FOR GAMBLING

casirole, casserole

casiroll, casserole

cask,*, KEG FOR LIQUIDS

caskade, cascade

caskeid, cascade

caskera, cascara

casket,*, COFFIN

caskit, casket

casmic, cosmic

casol, castle

casserole,*, MIXTURE OF FOOD INTO ONE DISH

cassette,*, AUDIO CARTRIDGE

cast,*,ting,ter, TO THROW AWAY FROM (or see caste) "prefixes: mis/over/re/up"

caste,*, A SOCIAL CLASS OF PEOPLE (or see cast)

caster,*, ON/FOR FURNITURE, FISHING, MOLD MAKER, CONDIMENT STAND

castle,*,ed, FORTRESS

castrate,*,ed,ting,tion, REMOVE REPRODUCTIVE ORGANS

castum, costume

casual,lly,lness, BY CHANCE, RELAXED

casudilla, quesadilla

casul, castle

caswal, casual

cat,*, ANIMAL, PREFIX INDICATING "APART/DOWN" MOST OFTEN MODIFIES THE WORD

cata, PREFIX INDICATING "APART/DOWN" MOST OFTEN MODIFIES THE WORD

catal, cattle

catalog,*,ged,ging, LIST IN ORDER

catalyst,*,ysis,ytic,yze,yzes,yzed,yzing, yzer, STIMULUS "prefixes: bio"

catapult,*,ted,ting, TO BE HURLED

cataract,*, EYE DISEASE OR WATERFALL

catastrophe,*,hic, DISASTER

catch,hes,hing,her,aught, CAPTURE (or see cache)

catcher,*, BASEBALL FIELD POSITION

catchup, ketchup / catsup

catech, cottage

catechism, TEACHING OF CHRISTIAN PRINCIPLES

catecism, catechism

categorize,*,ed,zing,zable,zation, ASSIGN TO SPECIFIC AREA/RANGE "prefixes: un/mis"

category,ries,ric,rical,rically,ricalness, rize,rizes,rized,rizing,rizable, rization, SPECIFIC AREA/RANGE "prefixes: mis/un"

catekisom, catechism

catelog, catalog

catepiler, caterpillar

catepult, catapult

cater,*,red,ring, PROVIDE FOR

cateract, cataract

caterpillar,*, WORM

cath, PREFIX INDICATING 'APART/DOWN' MOST OFTEN MODIFIES THE WORD

catichisom, catechism

catigorize, categorize

catigory, category

catikisom, catechism

catilist, catalyst

catilog, catalog

catl, cattle
catle, cattle
catol, cattle
catsup, ketchup
cattle, DOMESTIC BEEF, BOVINE
catugorize, categorize
catugory, category
catukism, catechism
catulist, catalyst
catulize, catalyst(yze)
catulog, catalog
catupiler, caterpillar
catupult, catapult
caturact, cataract
cau, cow
cauc, caulk
cauchis, cautious / caucus
caucus,ses, NOMINATION PARTY
caught, PAST TENSE FOR THE WORD
'CATCH', OBTAINED (or see cot)
caul, call / cowl
caulagen, collision / collagen
caulam, column
cauliflower, VEGETABLE
caulk,*,ked,king, FILL SEAMS/JOINTS (or
see calk)
caulm, calm
caulom, column
caum, calm / come
cauncil, council
caunsel, council
caunt, count
caunter, counter
caunti, county
caunvex, convex
cause,*,ed,sing,sal,sality,salities,sation,
BRING ABOUT "prefixes: retro"
caushes, cautious
caushesly, cautious(ly)
caushus, cautious
causmic, cosmic
caustic,cal,cally,city, CORROSIVE
CHEMICAL "prefixes: en"
caut, caught / cot
caution,*,ned,ning,nary,ous, BEWARE,
BE CAREFUL "prefixes: pre"
cautious,sly,sness, PREPARED FOR
DANGER "prefixes: in"
cava, kava
cavalry,ries, MOUNTED SOLDIERS
cave,*,ed,ving, HOLE IN THE EARTH
cavern,*,nous, HOLLOW IN EARTH
cavety, cavity
cavilry, cavalry

cavirn, cavern
cavitate,*,ed,ting,tion, HOLLOWED OUT
AREAS/BUBBLES
cavity,ties,tate,tation,tational,
HOLLOWED OUT AREA, DECAYED
TOOTH
cavs, calves / cave(s)
cavu, kava
cavulry, cavalry
cavurn, cavern
cawcus, caucus
cawl, call / cowl
cawshesly, cautious(ly)
cawshis, cautious
cawshun, caution
cawt, caught / cot
cawtion, caution
cayan, cayenne
cayenne, HOT PEPPER
cayning, canine
cazual, casual
ce, see / sea
cease,ses,ed,sing,eless,elessly, STOP (or
see sea(s)/seize/see(s)) "prefixes:
sur/un"
cechup, ketchup / catsup
ceel, keel
cegar, cigar
ceiling,*, OVERHEAD IN ROOM (or see
seal)
cel, cell / seal / sell
celabent, celibate
celabet, celibate
celafane, cellophane
celar, cellar / sell(er) / seal(er)
celary, celery
celebrate,*,ed,ting,tion,tive,tory,ant,
REJOICE
celebrity,ties, PERSON WELL EXPOSED
TO THE PUBLIC
celer, cellar / sell(er) / seal(er)
celery, VEGETABLE
celestial,*,lly, SPIRITUAL, NOT PHYSICAL
ON THIS PLANE "prefixes: sub"
celibate,acy,tarian, ABSENT FROM
SEXUAL ACTIVITY "prefixes: un"
celibet, celibate
celibrate, celebrate
celinder, cylinder
celing, ceiling / seal(ing)
celir, cellar / sell(er) / seal(er)
cell,*,llular,llularly,llularity, OF
STRUCTURES/SCIENCE (or see sell/

sail/keel) "prefixes: intra/multi/sub/
uni"
cellar,*, STORAGE UNDERGROUND (or
see sell)
cellophane, PLASTIC WRAP
cellular,rly,rity, OF COMMUNICATIONS
OR SCIENCE "prefixes: intra/multi/
non/sub/uni"
cellulite, FAT POCKETS IN THE BODY
cellulose,sic, CARBOHYDRATE "prefixes:
non"
celofane, cellophane
celophane, cellophane
celseus, celsius
celsius, METHOD OF REPORTING
TEMPERATURE
celt,*,tic, TOOL, GROUP OF PEOPLE,
LANGUAGE
celubasy, celibate(acy)
celubet, celibate
celubit, celibate
celubrate, celebrate
celular, cellular
celulite, cellulite
celulose, cellulose
celur, cellar / sell(er) / seal(er)
cem, seem / seam
cematari, cemetery
cement,ted,ter,tum,tation,tatory,tless,
COMBINATION OF MATERIALS
WHICH HARDENS, CONCRETE
cemest, chemist
cemetery,ries,tarial, GRAVEYARD
cemist, chemist
cemiteri, cemetery
cempothe, sympathy
cems, seem(s) / seam(s)
cemutary, cemetery
cenameter, centimeter
cendral, central
cendrulize, centralize
cenik, cynic
cenikal, cynical
cenima, cinema
cense, since / sense / cent(s) / scent(s)
censeer, sincere
censhury, century
censor,*,red,ring,rship,rable,rious,
riously,riousness,sure, CONTROL
INFORMATION (or see sensor/
censure) "prefixes: pre"
censure,rable,er, SEVERE/OFFICIAL
CRITICISM/STATEMENT (or see
censor/sensor)

census, SURVEY (or see sense(s))

cent,*, PREFIX INDICATING 'HUNDRED/ HUNDREDTH' MOST OFTEN MODIFIES THE WORD, MONETARY (or see scent/sent)

centennial,*,lly, HUNDREDTH YEAR ANNIVERSARY "prefixes: bi"

center,*,red,ring, THE MIDDLE "prefixes: con/re"

centi, PREFIX INDICATING 'HUNDRED/ HUNDREDTH' MOST OFTEN MODIFIES THE WORD

centigrade,*, WAY OF REPORTING TEMPERATURE

centiment, sentiment

centimeter,*, MORE THAN 0.39 OF AN INCH

centinial, centennial

centipede,*, POISONOUS BUG

central,lly,lity,lism,lize, FOCUS BETWEEN TWO OR MORE "prefixes: non"

centralize,*,ed,zing,zation, LOCATE CONVENIENTLY IN THE CENTER/ MIDDLE "prefixes: de/non"

centri, PREFIX INDICATING 'CENTER' MOST OFTEN MODIFIES THE WORD (or see sentry)

centric,cal,cally,city, AT OR NEAR CENTER "prefixes: exo"

centro, PREFIX INDICATING 'CENTER' MOST OFTEN MODIFIES THE WORD

centrul, central

centry, sentry / centri

centugrade, centigrade

centumeter, centimeter

centupede, centipede

century,ries, YEAR MARK

cenverdable, convertible

ceptic, septic

cer, care

ceramic,*, CLAY-FIRING METHOD

cerashen, serrate(tion)

cerat, carat / caret / carrot / karat / serrate

ceration, serrate(tion)

cerb, curb

cercimscribe, circumscribe

cercle, circle

cercol, circle

cerculate, circulate

cercumcise, circumcise

cercumfurens, circumference

cercumscribe, circumscribe

cercumstance, circumstance

cerdafy, certify

cerdenle, certain(ly)

cerdenly, certain(ly)

cerdify, certify

cerdle, curdle

cerdufy, certify

cere, care / carry

cereal, EDIBLE GRAIN (or see surreal)

cerebr, PREFIX INDICATING 'BRAIN' MOST OFTEN MODIFIES THE WORD

cerebral,lly, IN/OF THE BRAIN "prefixes: intra"

cerebro, PREFIX INDICATING 'BRAIN' MOST OFTEN MODIFIES THE WORD

ceremony,nies,nial,nially,nious, FORMAL GROUP GATHERING "prefixes: un"

ceret, carat / caret / carrot / karat

cereul, cereal / surreal

cereur, carrier

cerf, curve / surf

cerfew, curfew

cerfue, curfew

ceri, carry

cerial, cereal / serial

cericewlum, curriculum

cericuture, caricature

cerikachur, caricature

cerikulum, curriculum

cerimony, ceremony

cerin, serene

cerisel, carousel

cerit, carat / caret / carrot / karat

ceriul, cereal / serial

cerivan, caravan

cerkemscribe, circumscribe

cerklar, circular

cerkle, circle

cerkomferinse, circumference

cerkul, circle

cerkumsize, circumcise

cerkus, circus

cerl, curl

cernal, colonel

cernil, colonel / kernel

cerogun, corrode(osion)

cerol, carol

cerosene, kerosene

cerot, carat / caret / carrot / karat

cerpent, serpent

cersanthemum, chrysanthemum

cerse, curse

cersif, cursive

cersog, corsage

certain,nly,nty,nties,nness, KNOW FOR SURE "prefixes: un"

certale, curtail

certan, curtain

certatude, certitude

certeficashen, certificate(tion)

certeficate, certificate

certen, certain

certifi, certify

certificasion, certificate(tion)

certificate,*,ed,ting,tion, VALIDATION FOR LEARNING

certify,fies,fied,fying,fier,fiable,fiably, ficated,fication, MAKE CERTAIN, A LEGAL DOCUMENT "prefixes: de/ re"

certin, certain

certinly, certain(ly)

certitude,*, FEELING THAT SOMETHING IS CERTAIN "prefixes: in"

certsy, curtsy

certufi, certify

certul, curdle

certunle, certain(ly)

certunly, certain(ly)

certutude, certitude

cerunsy, currency

cerunt, currant / current

cerus, cirrus / scirrhus

cerusel, carousel

cerut, carat / caret / carrot / karat

ceruvan, caravan

cerv, curve / serve

cervant, servant

cervis, service

cervitud, servitude

cervix,xes,ical, OF THE NECK

cervuchure, curvature

cery, curry / carry

ces, see(s) / sea(s) / seize / cease

cesami, sesame

ceshel, seashell

ceshon, session

cest, cyst / zest

cesta, siesta

cesturn, cistern

ceven, seven

cevendi, seventy

ceventieth, seventieth

ceventin, seventeen

ceventy, seventy

cevin, seven

cevon, seven

cevontin, seventeen

cevul, civil

cevulization, civil(ization)

cevun, seven

cew, cue

cewth, couth

cez, see(s) / sea(s) / seize / cease

cfood, seafood

cfud, seafood

chacra, chakra

chader, chatter

chado, shadow

chaf, chafe / chaff

chafd, shaft / chafe(d) / chaff(ed)

chafe,*,ed,fing, ANNOYED/IRRITATED, RUBBED UNTIL SORE (or see shaft/chaff)

chaff,*,ffed,ffing,ffer,ffy, TO TEASE/JOKE WITH SOMEONE (or see chafe)

chafs, chafe(s) / chaff(s)

chaft, shaft / chafe(d) / chaff(ed)

chain,*,ned,ning, LINKS PUT/HOOKED TOGETHER "prefixes: en/un"

chair,*,red,ring, FURNITURE, HEAD OF MEETINGS/ORGANIZATION

chak, chalk / choke / shock / chock

chakra,*, CENTERS IN BODY

chalant,tly,nce, OVERLY CONCERNED/ANXIOUS "prefixes: non"

chalenge, challenge

chalinge, challenge

chalk,*,ked,king,ky, LIMESTONE

challenge,*,ed,ging,gable,er, TEST OF SKILLS

chalons, chalant(nce)

chalont, chalant

champagne, EFFERVESCENT WINE

champane, champagne

champeon, champion

champion,*,ned,ning,nship, WINS CONTEST OF SKILL

chanal, channel

chance,*,ed, A GAMBLE

chancre,*,rous, ULCERATION ON THE SKIN (or see canker)

chandelier,*, LAMP WITH MANY ARMS FOR BULBS

chandulere, chandelier

chane, chain

chanel, channel

change,*,ed,ging,gable, TRANSFORM "prefixes: un"

chanil, channel

channel,*,led,ling,ler,lize, AVENUE TO RECEIVE "prefixes: re"

channelize,*,zed,zing,zation, TO CHANNEL/DIRECT "prefixes: de/re"

chanse, chance / chant(s)

chant,*,ted,ting,tingly, RECITE/REPEAT WORDS IN VERBAL RHYTHM (or see chain(ed))

chanul, channel

chaos,otic, APPEARS TO US TO BE DISORGANIZED

chap,*,pped,pping, DRY/ROUGH SKIN, LEATHER PART

chapel,*, FOR RITUALS

chaplain,*, PERFORMS RITUAL SERVICES

chaplan, chaplain

chapter,*, SECTION OF PRINT, COLLEGE OR SCHOOL

chapul, chapel

char,*,rred,rring, TO BURN/BLACKEN, CHORES (or see chair/chore/share)

character,*,ristic,ristically,rize,rization, PERSONALITY/QUALITIES

charade,*, PANTOMINE GAME

charcoal,*,led, ORGANIC SUBSTANCE IN EARTH

charder, charter

chare, chair / cherry / sherry / share

charecter, character

charge,*,ed,er,ging,eable, APPLY TOWARDS CREDIT, CREATE POWER, ENERGIZE, APPLY FORCE "prefixes: dis/over/re/sur/under"

charguble, charge(able)

chari, cherry / sherry

charidy, charity

charisma,atic, INSPIRATIONAL QUALITY

charitable,ly, GIVING

charity,ties,table, GIVING UNCONDITIONALLY

charj, charge

charjuble, charge(able)

charjur, charge(r)

charkol, charcoal

charm,*,med,ming,mingly,mer, ALLUREMENT, LUCKY OBJECT

chart,*,ted,ting, PLOT OUT "prefixes: un"

charter,*,red,ring, CONTRACT, OUTLINE "prefixes: un"

charutable, charitable

chary, cherry / sherry

chas, chase / chaste

chasd, chaste / chase(d)

chase,*,ed,sing,er, PURSUE TO CAPTURE (or see chaste)

chasem, chasm

chasim, chasm

chasm,*,mic, DEEP VOID

chassis, FRAME OF VEHICLE

chaste,er,est,ely,eness, SIMPLE, PLAIN, FAITHFUL (or see chase(d))

chasum, chasm

chasy, chassis

chater, chatter / shatter

chatter,*,red,ring, TALK TOO MUCH ABOUT UNINTERESTING TOPICS

chauffeur,*, DESIGNATED DRIVER

chauk, chalk / choke / shock / chock

chaukra, chakra

chaumein, chowmein

chaurkol, charcoal

chauvinist,*,tic, TERM FOR MEN WHO TREAT WOMEN AS LESSERS/UNEQUAL

chayos, chaos

chazm, chasm

chazum, chasm

cheap,per,pest,ply,pens, LOW COST (or see chip)

cheat,*,ted,ting,ter, DISHONEST ACQUISITION

check,*,ked,king,ker,kers,kered, BANK DRAFT, A MARK, TO MAKE CERTAIN, A GAME "prefixes: re/un"

cheef, chief

cheep, cheap

cheer,*,red,ring,ringly,rer,rful,rfully, rfulness,ry,rily,riness,rless, HAPPY/JOYFUL/ENCOURAGEMENT/SHOUTING/TOASTING

cheese, CURDLED MILK

cheet, cheat

chef,*, HEAD COOK (or see sheaf)

chek, check / cheek

chekan, chicken

chekurs, check(ers)

cheldren, children

chelenge, challenge

chelons, chalant(nce)

chelont, chalant

chelren, children

chemest, chemist

chemical,*, OF CHEMISTRY "prefixes: bio"

chemist,*, SCIENTIST WHO STUDIES PROPERTIES OF MATTER "prefixes: bio"

chemistry, MOTHER OF SCIENCE, STUDY OF MATTER "prefixes: bio"

chemney, chimney

chemotherapy, RADIATION TREATMENT

chemucal, chemical

chemustry, chemistry

chen, chin

chep, cheap / sheep

chepd, chip(pped) / ship(pped)

cheped, chip(pped) / ship(pped)

cher, share / chair / cheer

cherch, church

chere, cherry / sherry / cheer(y)

cheretable, charitable

cherety, charity

cheridy, charity

cheritable, charitable

cherity, charity

cherle, sure(ly)

chern, churn

cherry,rries, LITTLE RED FRUIT (or see sherry)

chery, cherry / sherry

chese, cheese

chest, schist

chevolry, chivalry

chevulry, chivalry

chew,*,wed,wing,wable, GRIND WITH TEETH

chewt, shute / chute

cheys, chase

cheyst, chaste

chic, STYLISH

chick,*, YOUNG BIRD, GIRL

chicken,*, FOWL, BIRD

chicory, HERB

chief,*,tain, HIGHEST AUTHORITY

chif, chief

chik, chick

chiken, chicken

chikury, chicory

child,*,dren,dish,dishly,dishness,dly, dlike,PERSON UNDER AGE 18

children,PEOPLE UNDER AGE 18

chilons, chalant(nce)

chilont, chalant

chilostomy, colostomy

chilren, children

chimest, chemist

chimist, chemist

chimney,*, SMOKE STACK

chimotherapy, chemotherapy

chimukul, chemical

chin,*, POINT OF JAW (or see shin/ shine)

chip,*,pped,pping,pper, THIN SLICE/ WEDGE OF SOMETHING (or see ship/cheap) "prefixes: bio"

chiped, chip(pped) / ship(pped)

chirch, church

chirle, sure(ly)

chiro, PREFIX INDICATING 'HAND' MOST OFTEN MODIFIES THE WORD

chiropractor,tic, REALIGNS BONES OF BODY FOR HEALTH

chirtch, church

chis, cheese

chisel,*,led,ling, TOOL FOR FORMING SHAPES

chist, schist

chivalry,rous, COURTEOUS AND HELPFUL GENTELMAN

chizt, schist

chizul, chisel

chlor, PREFIX INDICATING 'GREEN/ CHLORINE' MOST OFTEN MODIFIES THE WORD

chlorene, chlorine

chlorine,nate,idize, CHEMICAL IRRITANT

chloro, PREFIX INDICATING 'GREEN/ CHLORINE' MOST OFTEN MODIFIES THE WORD

chock,*,ked,king, TO BLOCK/SECURE/ BRACE (or see choke/chalk/shock)

chocklat, chocolate

choclat, chocolate

chocolate,*,ty,tier,tiest, FROM CACAO NUT

choice,*, SELECTION "prefixes: pro-"

choir,*, SINGING GROUP

chok, chalk / choke / shock / chock

choke,*,ed,king,kingly,er, RESTRICTED SUPPLY OF AIR/MOVEMENT(or see chalk/shock/chock)

choklat, chocolate

choklut, chocolate

chokra, chakra

chol, PREFIX INDICATING 'BILE/ GALLBLADDER' MOST OFTEN MODIFIES THE WORD

chole, PREFIX INDICATING 'BILE/ GALLBLADDER' MOST OFTEN MODIFIES THE WORD

cholesterol, NATURALLY PRESENT IN THE BODY

cholk, chalk

cholons, chalant(nce)

cholont, chalant

cholostemy, colostomy

choo, chew / shoe

choose,*,sing,er,sy,sier,siest,sily,siness, hose, PICK ONE OVER THE OTHER (or see chew(s)/chose)

chop,*,pped,pping,pper,ppy,ppier, pppiest,ppily,ppiness, HACK/CUT INTO PIECES, SUDDEN CHANGE IN DIRECTION (or see shop)

chopeng, chop(pping) / shop(pping)

chor, chore / shore / char

choral, OF A CHOIR (or see coral/corral/ chorale)

chorale, A HYMN OF SIMPLE TUNE (or see choral/corral/coral)

chorcol, charcoal

chord,*, OF MUSICAL NOTES (or see cord/short)

chore,*, SMALL TASKS (or see shore)

chorkol, charcoal

chorn, shorn

chorus, A UNION OF PERFORMERS (or see course)

chorz, chore(s) / shard(s)

chose,en, HAVING SELECTED, PAST TENSE FOR THE WORD 'CHOOSE' (or see choose)

choyse, choice

chrapnul, shrapnel

christmas, A RELIGIOUS HOLIDAY

chrom, PREFIX INDICATING 'COLOR/ CHROMIUM' MOST OFTEN MODIFIES THE WORD (or see chrome)

chrome,ed,ming, METALLIC

chromizone, chromosome

chromo, PREFIX INDICATING 'COLOR/ CHROMIUM' MOST OFTEN MODIFIES THE WORD

chromosome,*, DNA STRAND

chronalogical, chronology(gical)

chronic,cally,city, CONTINUOUS

chronicle,*,ed,ling, LIST OF FACTS

chronk, shrunk

chrono, PREFIX INDICATING 'TIME' MOST OFTEN MODIFIES THE WORD

chronology,gical,lgically, ORGANIZE BY DATES

chronulogical, chronology(gical)

chrud, shrewd / truth

chrunk, shrunk

chrys, PREFIX INDICATING 'GOLD' MOST OFTEN MODIFIES THE WORD

chrysanthemum,*, FLOWER

chryso, PREFIX INDICATING 'GOLD' MOST OFTEN MODIFIES THE WORD

chu, chew

chue, chew

chugar, sugar

chugur, sugar

chulons, chalant(nce)

chulont, chalant

churade, charade

chural, choral / coral / corral / chorale

church,hes,hy, FOR RELIGIOUS PURPOSES

churle, sure(ly)

churn,*,ned,ning, FAT, MILK SEPARATION

chus, chew(s) / choose / shoe(s)

chuse, chew(s) / choose / choose(sy) / shoe(s)

chute,*,ed,ting, RAPID/STEEP DESCENT (or see shoot/shut)

cianide, cyanide

ciburnetiks, cybernetics

ciclist, cyclist

cid, kid / kite

cider, STRONG JUICE

cidur, cider

cigar,*, ROLLED TOBACCO

cigarette,*, OF TOBACCO

cilinder, cylinder

cilinoid, solenoid

cilosal, colossal

cimbeosis, symbiosis

cimbol, cymbal / symbol

cimen, semen

ciment, cement

cimist, chemist

cimpathetic, sympathetic

cimpathy, sympathy

cinch,hes,hed,hing, FIRM GRIP ON, EASILY ACHIEVED, FOR CERTAIN (or see singe)

cinda, kind of

cinder,*, CHARRED SUBSTANCE (or see send)

cinduf, kind of

cine, PREFIX INDICATING 'MOTION PICTURE' MOST OFTEN MODIFIES THE WORD

cinema,*,atic, MOTION PICTURE

cinery, canary / cannery

cing, zing / sing

cinima, cinema

cinnamon, SPICE FROM TREE BARK

cinsestently, consistent(ly)

cinsistency, consistence(cy)

cinspirusy, conspiracy

cinstrucshen, construction

cint, can't / cent / scent / sent

cintential, centennial

cinverdable, convertible

cip, zip / sip

circle,*,ed,ling, ROUND FIGURE/SHAPE "prefixes: semi"

circompherence, circumference

circuit,*,try, MAKES THE ROUNDS, GOES AROUND, NETWORK

circular,*, GOES AROUND IN THE SHAPE OF A CIRCLE "prefixes: semi"

circulate,*,ed,ting,tion, FLOWING/ MOVING "prefixes: un"

circum, PREFIX INDICATING 'AROUND' MOST OFTEN MODIFIES THE WORD

circumcise,*,ed,sing,sion,er, REMOVAL OF FORESKIN ON PENIS "prefixes: un"

circumference, DISTANCE/LINE AROUND A CIRCLE

circumscribe,*,ed,bing,bable,er, SET NARROW LIMITS, ENCIRCLE "prefixes: un"

circumstance,*,ntial,ntiate, INCIDENT

circus,ses, ENTERTAINING PERFORMANCE IN TENTS

cireol, cereal / serial

cirial, cereal / serial

cirios, serious

ciris, series

cirius, serious

cirkemscribe, circumscribe

cirkumscribe, circumscribe

cirkumsize, circumcise

cirnel, colonel / kernel

ciroberate, corroborate

cirogun, corrode(osion)

cirrus, CLOUD TYPE/SHAPE (or see scirrhus)

cirsanthemum, chrysanthemum

cirten, certain

cirteus, courteous

cirus, cirrus / scirrhus

cirvature, curvature

cis, PREFIX INDICATING 'ON THIS SIDE' MOST OFTEN MODIFIES THE WORD

cist, COFFIN OF THE STONE AGE (or see cyst/kiss(ed))

citashun, citation

cistern,*,nal, CONTAINER/COLLECTOR FOR LIQUID/WATER

citation,*, A SUMMONS

cite,*,ed,ting,tation,tations, OFFICIALLY CALL FORTH (or see site)

citizen,*,nry,nship, MEMBER OF, WITH PRIVILEDGES

citres, citrus

citric, ACID FROM FRUIT

citrus, FRUIT

citusin, citizen

city,ties, METROPOLIS

ciunide, cyanide

civic, CITIZENSHIP

civil,lly,lize,lizes,lized,lizing,lization, lizations, OF STATE OR COMMUNITY "prefixes: in/un"

civilean, civilian

civilian,*, NOT MILITARY CITIZENS

civul, civil

civulization, civil(ization)

ciyen, cayenne

cla, claw

clad,*,ding, WEARING ON BODY, COVERED WITH "prefixes: un"

clae, clay

claim,*,med,ming,mer,mant,mable, ASSERT POSSESSION OF (or see clamor/climb) "prefixes: re/de"

claimant,*, TAKE POSSESSION OF

clairvoyance,nt, THOSE WHO CHANNEL INFORMATION

clam,*,mmed,mming, SHELLFISH (or see claim)

clamable, claim(able)

clament, claimant

clamor,*,red,ring,rer, SUDDEN/LOUD/ INSISTENT NOISE (or see claim(er))

clamp,*,ped,ping, PINCH TOGETHER

clams, claim(s) / clam(s)

clan, BODIES OF LIKE-MINDED INDIVIDUALS

clandestine,ely,eness, WITH DECEPTION IN MIND

clandustine, clandestine

clap,*,pped,pping,pt, SOUND, GONORRHEA

clarical, clerical

clarify,fies, GIVE SPECIFIC MEANING TO

clarity, MAKE CLEAR

clarvoyants, clairvoyance

claset, closet
clash,hes,hed,hing, COLLIDE, LOUD SOUND
clasha, cliche
clasic, classic
clasify, classify
clasp,*,ped,ping, HOLD "prefixes: en/un"
class,sses,ssed,ssing,ssy, GROUPED TOGETHER DUE TO SIMILARITIES "prefixes: un/under"
classic,*,cal,cally, WITHSTOOD TEST OF TIME "prefixes: neo/semi"
classify,fies,fied,fying,fication,fiable, ABLE TO PLACE INTO A GROUP "prefixes: de/non/un"
clasuc, classic
clauc, clock / cloak
claud, cloud
clauged, clog(gged) / cloak / clock(ed)
clause,*,sal, STIPULATION (or see claw(s))
claustrophobia, FEAR OF COZY/TIGHT PLACES
claustrophobic, FEAR OF COZY/TIGHT PLACES
claw,*,wed,wing, HOOKED, FINGERLIKE (or see clause)
clawn, clown
clawsit, closet
clawzet, closet
clay, SOIL FROM EARTH
clean,*,ned,ning,ner,nly,liness, UNSOILED "prefixes: un"
cleanse,*,sed,sing,er, MAKE CLEAN
cleanser, CHEMICALS USED TO CLEAN
clear,*,red,ring,rance, FREE OF OBSTRUCTION
clearance,*, TO CLEAR OF
cleat,*, FOR TRACTION, STRENGTH
clebtomaniac, kleptomania(c)
clecha, cliche
cleche, cliche
cleck, click / clique
cleen, clean
cleer, clear
cleerance, clearance
cleff, cliff
clek, click / clique
clen, clean
clench,hes,hed,hing, TO HOLD/GRASP TIGHTLY (or see clinch)
cleng, cling
clenik, clinic

clens, cleanse / clean(s)
clenser, cleanser
clenz, cleanse / clean(s)
clenzr, cleanser
clep, clip
cleptomaniac, kleptomania(c)
clepur, clipper
cler, clear
clerady, clarity
clerchi, clergy
clerd, clear(ed)
cleredy, clarity
clereng, clear(ing)
clerense, clearance
clerety, clarity
clergy,gies, ORDAINED BY CHRISTIANS
clerical, OFFICE WORKER
cleridi, clarity
clering, clear(ing)
clerity, clarity
clerk,*,kly, PERFORMS GENERAL DUTIES
clerle, clear(ly)
clert, clear(ed)
clervoyanse, clairvoyance
clesha, cliche
clet, cleat
cletoras, clitoris
clever,rly,rness, INGENIOUS
clew, clue
cliant, client
clibtomaniac, kleptomania(c)
cliche,*, STEREOTYPICAL PHRASE
click,*,ked,king,ker, SNAPPING NOISE, FIT WELL TOGETHER (or see clique)
clics, click(s) / clique(s)
client,*,tele, CUSTOMER
cliff,*, STEEP ROCK FACE
clik, click / clique
clim, climb
climate,*,tic,tize,tized,tizing,tization, WEATHER OR ATMOSPHERIC CONDITION "prefixes: ac/bio"
climax,xes,xed,xing,actic, GREATEST HEIGHT
climb,*,bed,bing,bable, MOMENTUM UPWARDS,GO UP (or see claim)
clims, climb(s)
climute, climate
clinch,hes,hed,hing,her, TO RESOLVE, FASTEN/HOLD (or see clench)
cling,*,clung,ging,gy,gingly,ger, ATTACH TIGHTLY TO

clinic,*,cal,cally, PLACE FOR EXAMINATION "prefixes: sub"
clinser, cleanser
clip,*,pped,pping,pper, CUT OFF OR OUT, A TACKLE
clipper,*, CUTTING TOOL
cliptomaniac, kleptomania(c)
clipur, clipper
clique,*,uish,ey, A SELECT GROUP
clirans, clearance
clirge, clergy
clirk, clerk
clisha, cliche
clishe, cliche
clitoris,ral, POINT FOR FEMININE AROUSAL
cloak,*,ked,king, A GARMET, TO CONCEAL/DIGUISE (or see clock) "prefixes: un"
clob, club
clobber,*,red,ring, TO BEAT UP
clober, clobber
cloc, cloak / clock
cloch, clutch / clock
clock,*,ked,king, KEEP TIME (or see cloak)
cloder, clutter
clodur, clutter
clofe, clove
clofur, clover
clog,*,gged,gging, STOPPED/BACKED UP (or see cloak/clock(ed)) "prefixes: un"
cloger, closure
cloister,*,red,ring, OF BUILDINGS, TO ENCLOSE
clojer, closure
clok, clock / cloak
cloked, clog(gged) / cloak / clock(ed)
clomp, clump
clomsi, clumsy
clone,*,ed,ning, REPLICAS (or see clown/cologne)
clos, clothes / claw(s) / close / clause
closder, cluster
close,*,ed,sing,ely,er,est, SHUT DOWN, NEAR TO (or see clause/clothes) "prefixes: en/ex/re/un"
closet,*,ted,ting, SMALL PRIVATE SPACE
closher, closure
closir, close(r) / closure
closline, clothesline
closter, cluster
closturfobeu, claustrophobia

closur, close(r) / closure

closure,*, CONCEAL, SHUT DOWN (or see close(r))

clot,*,tted,tting, LUMP, MASS OF MATTER

cloted, clot(tted)

cloter, clutter

cloth,*,he,hes,hed,hing, WOVEN FIBERS INTO MATERIAL, USED FORCLOTHING (or see close)

clothes, OUTER/UNDER GARMENTS FOR THE BODY (or see close/ cloth(es)) "prefixes: under"

clothesline,*, LINE FOR HANGING GARMENTS/CLOTHES ON

cloths, clothes / cloth(es)

clothsline, clothesline

clotur, clutter

cloud,*,dy,ded,ding,diness, SMOKE, WATER PARTICLES, OBSCURES VISION "prefixes: over"

cloun, clown / clone / cologne

clout, INFLUENCE, TO STRIKE (or see cloud)

clove,*, OF A PLANT, FORM OF MEASUREMENT

clover,*, HERBAL PLANT

clow, claw

clowd, cloud

clown,*,ned,ning,nish, FUNNY, GOOFY, NOT NORMAL, SOMETIMES RIDICULOUS/OBNOXIOUS

clows, clothes / claw(s) / close / clause

clowsit, closet

clowt, clout

cloyster, cloister

cloz, clothes / claw(s) / close / clause

clozer, close(r) / closure

clozir, close(r) / closure

clozline, clothesline

clozur, close(r) / closure

club,*,bbed,bbing, GROUP MEMBERSHIP, AN INSTRUMENT USED AS A WEAPON

cluch, clutch

cluder, clutter

clue,*,ed,eless,elessness, HINT

clump,*,ped,ping,py, COLLECTION OF/ INTO A MASS

clumsy,sily,siness, AWKWARDLY DONE

clumze, clumsy

clurgy, clergy

cluster,*,red,ring,ry, GROUPINGS TOGETHER "prefixes: non"

clutch,hes,hed,hing, USED TO CHANGE GEARS IN TRANSMISSION, GRASP FIRMLY, GROUP OF EGGS "prefixes: de"

cluter, clutter

clutorus, clitoris

clutter, CONFUSING SIGHT OR NOISE "prefixes: un"

co, PREFIX INDICATING 'WITH/ TOGETHER' MOST OFTEN MODIFIES THE WORD

co-op, COMMUNITY-OWNED BUSINESS, A COOPERATIVE (or see coop/coup)

coach,hes,hed,hing, TO GUIDE OTHERS (or see couch)

coagulate,*,ed,ting,tion, TO THICKEN, FORM CLOTS

coal,*, ORGANIC SUBSTANCE IN THE EARTH

coalition,*,nal,nist, VOLUNTARY GATHERING OF PEOPLE FOR A CAUSE

coar, core / corp

coarse,er,est,ely,eness, HARSH, ABRASIVE, ROUGH (or see course)

coast,*,ted,ting, BETWEEN LAND AND WATER, TO BE MOVING WITHOUT PROPULSION (or see cost) "prefixes: bi/intra"

coaster,*, TO SET DRINKS ON

coat,*,ted,ting, OUTER GARMENT FOR WARMTH "prefixes: over/sur/ under"

coax,xes,xed,xing, TO PERSUADE/ INFLUENCE

cob,*, TUBULAR IN SHAPE

cobalt, CHEMICAL, BLUE COLORING

cobi, cubby

cobolt, cobalt

cobra,*, SNAKE

cobweb,*, SPIDER'S WEB

coc, caulk / cock

cocaine, NARCOTIC DRUG

cocane, cocaine

coch, coach

cocher, kosher

coches, cautious

cochus, cautious

cock,*,ky, A ROOSTER, OF MASCULINE SUGGESTION (or see cook)

cockroach,hes, INFESTATING INSECT

cocktail,*, ALCOHOLIC BEVERAGES

cocoa, FROM THE CACAO SEED

coconut,*, FRUIT

cocoon,*, HOME SPUN BY LARVAE

coctale, cocktail

cocun, cocoon

cocunut, coconut

cocus, caucus

cod,*, FISH, A POD, A PENINSULA (or see code/caught/could/cold)

code,*,ded,ding, LANGUAGE "prefixes: en"

codeine, DRUG FROM OPIUM

coden, cotton / codeine

codich, cottage

codien, codeine

codin, cotton / codeine

codol, cuddle

coduge, cottage

coed,*, BOTH SEXES

coel, coil

coelate, collate

coen, coin

coencident, coincident

coenside, coincide

coensident, coincident

coerce,*,ed,cing,cible,cion,cive,civeness, cively, FORCE INTO COMPLIANCE "prefixes: in/non"

coersment, coerce(ment)

cof, cough / cuff

cofe, cove / coffee / cough

cofen, coffin / cough(ing)

cofert, covert / cover(ed)

coffee, BEVERAGE (or see cove)

coffin,*, BOX FOR TRANSPORT, CASKET

cofi, coffee

cofin, coffin / cough(ing)

cofy, coffee

cognative, cognitive

cogneshun, cognition

cognezant, cognizant

cognisant, cognizant

cognition,nal,ive, PERCEPTIVE/AWARE (or see cognizant) "prefixes: pre/ retro"

cognitive,ely,vism,ion, COME TO KNOW THROUGH PERCEPTION/ REASONING "prefixes: pre/retro"

cognizant,nce,able,ably,nce,ition, PERCEPTIVE/AWARE

cognutev, cognitive

cohabitate,*,ed,ting,tion, DWELL/LIVE TOGETHER

cohabutate, cohabitate

coherent,nce,ncy, WORKS CONSISTENTLY/PREDICTABLY "prefixes: in/non"

coherse, coerce

cohersive, coerce(cive)

cohersment, coerce(ment)

cohesive,ely,eness,ion, BONDS TOGETHER

cohesuf, cohesive

cohort,*, CO-PARTNER

cohurse, coerce

cohursive, coerce(cive)

coil,*,led,ling, SPIRAL SHAPE "prefixes: un"

coin,*,ned,nage, METAL USED FOR MONEY

coincide,*,ed,ding,ence,ent, TO HAPPEN/OCCUPY AT SAME TIME

coincident,nce,tal,tally, CHANCE HAPPENING "prefixes: un"

coircment, coerce(ment)

cok, cook / cock

cokane, cocaine

cokes, coax

cokie, cookie

cokroch, cockroach

coktale, cocktail

col, PREFIX INDICATING 'INTESTINES' MOST OFTEN MODIFIES THE WORD (or see call/cowl/coal)

colaborate, collaborate

colach, collage

coladerul, collateral

colage, collage

colamedy, calamity

colander,*, STRAINER

colani, colony

colanize, colony(nize)

colanoid, solenoid

colaps, collapse

colapse, collapse

colapsuble, collapse(sible)

colar, color / collar / call(er)

colash, collage / college

colastomy, colostomy

colasul, colossal

colate, collate

colcher, culture

cold,der,dest,dly, OPPOSITE OF HOT (or see colt)

coldesak, cul-de-sac

coldslaw, coleslaw

cole, coal / call

coleage, colleague

colech, college

colechat, collegiate

colecshon, collection

colect, collect

colection, colleciton

colector, collect(or)

coleg, colleague / college

colegen, collision / collagen

coleget, collegiate

colegiate, collegiate

colekshin, collection

colem, column

colen, colon

colenise, colonize

colenoid, solenoid

coleny, colony

coler, color / cooler / collar

colesh, college

coleshon, collision / coalition

coleshun, collision / coalition

coleslaw, CABBAGE SALAD

colic, PAIN CAUSED BY ACID IN THE INTESTINES

colich, college

colide, collide

coliflower, cauliflower

colig, college / colleague

coligen, collision / collagen

colijin, collision

colim, column

colinary, culinary

colinoid, solenoid

coliny, colony

colk, calk / caulk

collaborate,*,ed,ting,tion,tive,tively, COOPERATE

collage,*, MIXED MEDIA ART

collagen,*,nic,nous, FIBROUS PROTEIN FOUND IN BONE/TISSUE

collander, colander

collapsable, collapse(sible)

collapse,*,ed,sing,sable, BREAK DOWN

collar,*,red,rless, RIM ON SHIRT, BELT FOR NECK

collard greens, VEGETABLE

collate,*,ed,ting,tion, MERGE, COMPARE

collateral,lly,lize, USED TO GUARANTEE/ SECURE A LOAN

colleague,*, ASSOCIATE

collect,*,ted,ting,tion,tive,tor, GATHER "prefixes: non/re"

collection,*, ACT OF GATHERING THINGS "prefixes: re"

college,*, HIGHER EDUCATION

collegiate, OF COLLEGE AND/OR STUDENTS

collide,*,ed,ding,ision, RUN INTO

collision,*, ACT OF RUNNING INTO

colloquia,al, PLURAL FOR COLLOQUIUM, STYLE/ADVENT OF WRITING OR SPEAKING

colloquial,lity,lly,lness,lism,ium,iums, STYLE/ADVENT OF WRITING OR SPEAKING

colloquium,*, MEETING/CONFERENCE OF SPEAKERS ON SPECIFIC TOPIC

colm, calm

colmenate, culminate

colminate, culminate

colo, PREFIX INDICATING 'INTESTINES' MOST OFTEN MODIFIES THE WORD

coloch, collage / college

colog, collage / college

cologne,*, TOILET WATER (or see colon)

colokweul, colloquial

colon, INTESTINES, PUNCTUATION IN TEXT (or see cologne) "prefixes: semi"

coloneal, colonial

colonel,*, U.S. MILITARY OFFICER (or see kernel)

colonial,list,lism, FIRST EUROPEANS TO AMERICA "prefixes: neo"

colonize,*,ed,zing,zation, FIRST SETTLERS "prefixes: de"

colony,nies,nize, ACCUMULATION OF SIMILAR PEOPLES

color,*,red,ring,rful,rless,rlessly, rlessness,ration,rant,rize,rizes, rized, rizing,rization, HUES OF LIGHT SPECTRUM "prefixes: bi/de/un/uni"

colossal, GREAT MAGNITUDE

colostomy,mies, INVOLVES INTESTINES/ ANUS

colpret, culprit

colsla, coleslaw

colt,*, THE YOUNG OF SOME IN ANIMAL KINGDOM (or see cold)

coltevate, culminate

coltivate, cultivate

coltsfoot, USEFUL HERB

coltuvate, cultivate

coluge, college

column,*,ned,nar,nist, VERTICAL PILLARS OR ROWS, WRITTEN ARTICLE

colun, colon

colunise, colonize
coluny, colony
colurd, collard greens
colvert, culvert
com, PREFIX INDICATING 'WITH/ TOGETHER' MOST OFTEN MODIFIES THE WORD (or see come/comb)
coma,*,atose, UNCONSCIOUSNESS (or see comma) "prefixes: semi"
comand, command
comander, commander
comasery, commissary
comb,*,bed,bing, TOOL FOR HAIR (or see come)
combat,*,ted,ting,tant,tive, OPPOSE
combensashen, compensation
comber, cumber
combersome, cumber(some)
combination,*,tive,able, UNIFY "prefixes: re"
combine,*,ed,ning,nation, BRING TOGETHER, FARM MACHINE
combrahensiv, comprehensive
combunashen, combination
combunation, combination
combustchen, combustion
combustible,*,bility,eness,ion,ive, POTENTIAL TO IGNITE INTO FLAMES
combustion,ive, CHEMICAL REACTION, FIRE/OXYGEN
come,*,ming,came, RESPOND, GO TOWARDS (or see comb/cum) "prefixes: over/up"
comec, comic
comedeun, comedian
comedian,*, AMUSING ENTERTAINER
comedy,dies,dic, HUMOROUS ACCOUNTS
comemorate, commemorate
comence, commence
comend, commend
comendable, commendable
comendation, commendation
comenduble, commendable
comens, commence
comensirate, commensurate
comensurate, commensurate
coment, comment
comentative, commentate(tive)
comentator, commentator
coments, commence / comment(s)
comerbund, cummerbund
comerce, commerce
comercial, commercial

comerse, commerce
comershul, commercial
comesary, commisary
comeshen, commission
comeshener, commissioner
comet,*, SPACE MATTER AND ICE AT HIGH SPEED (or see commit)
comete, committee
cometion, commission
cometioner, commissioner
cometment, commitment
comewn, commune
comfert, comfort
comfort,*,ted,ting,ter, RELIEF, CALM, PLEASANT "prefixes: dis"
comfortable,ly, RELIEF, CALM, PLEASANT "prefixes: un"
comfurter, comfort(er)
comic,*,cal,cally,cality,calness, FUNNY, HUMOROUS
comidian, comedian
comidore, commodore
comidy, comedy
comimurate, commemorate
comin, common
comind, commend
comindation, commendation
cominduble, commendable
comins, commence
cominsirate, commensurate
comint, comment
comintator, commentator
comirse, commerce
comirshul, commercial
comisary, commissary
comishen, commission
comishener, commissioner
comisioner, commissioner
comissary, commissary
comission, commission
comit, comet / commit
comitee, committee
comition, commission
comitioner, commissioner
comitment, commitment
comittee, committee
comity, comedy
comma,*, PUNCTUATION (or see coma)
command,*,ded,ding,der, DOMINATING, DIRECTING
commander,*, DOMINANCE, MILITARY
commemorate,*,ed,ting,tion,tive, HONORING SOMEONE OR SOMETHING OF THE PAST

commence,*,ed,cing,ement, TO BEGIN "prefixes: re"
commend,*,ded,ding,dable,dation, SERIES OF CIRCLES WITH SAME CENTER POINT "prefixes: re"
commendable,*,eness,ly,ation, PRAISEWORTHY
commendation,*, PRAISE "prefixes: re"
commensurable,bility,bly,ate, SHARE THE SAME MEASURABLE QUALITIES "prefixes: in"
commensurate,ely,tion,able, EQUAL/ CORRESPONDS TO "prefixes: in"
comment,*,ted,ting,tate,tary,taries, tative,tation,tator, MAKE REMARKS, GIVE OPINION
commentate,*,ed,ting,tion,tive,tor,ary, aries, TO COMMENT UPON
commentator,*,tate, ONE WHO GIVES OPINIONS/REMARKS
commerce, EXCHANGING WARES OR GOODS
commercial,*,lize,lization, ADVERTISEMENTS, ABOUT TRADE "prefixes: non/un"
commisary, commissary
commision, commission
commissary,ries, MILITARY STORE
commission,*,ned,ning, ALOTTED SUM/ PERCENT, DELEGATE "prefixes: de"
commissioner,*, POSITION OF AUTHORITY
commit,*,tted,ttedly,tting,tment,ttable, tter, RELEGATE, ENTRUST "prefixes: non/over/un"
commitee, committee
commitment,*, OBLIGATED, ENTRUSTED TO SOMEONE OR SOMETHING
committee,*, SELECTED GROUP TO DO WORK "prefixes: sub"
commodity,ties, OBJECT FOR TRADE
commodore,*, MILITARY OFFICER
common,*,nly,ner,nest,nness, FAMILIAR "prefixes: un"
communal,*, OF COMMUNITY
commune,*, COLLECTION OF PEOPLE WITH SIMILAR IDEAS/VALUES
communicable, PASSED ON, ABLE TO COMMUNICATE "prefixes: in"
communicate,*,ed,ting,tion,tive,tively, tiveness,able, EXCHANGE INFORMATION "prefixes: ex/in/ non/un"

communion,*, CHRISTIAN RITUAL
communism, TYPE OF GOVERNMENT
communist,*,tic, ADVOCATE OF COMMUNISM
community,ties, ASSOCIATION OF SIMILAR PEOPLES
commute,*,ed,ting,table, INTERCHANGE, DISTANCE TRAVEL, MATHEMATICAL EXPRESSION, REDUCE/REPLACE "prefixes: in/non"
comodity, commodity
comodore, commodore
comon, common
compact,*,ted,ting,tion, SMALLEST DIMENSION POSSIBLE "prefixes: sub"
compalshen, compulsion
compaltion, compulsion
companeon, companion
companion,*,nship, MATE/PARTNER
company,nies, ASSOCIATION OF INDIVIDUALS "prefixes: intra"
comparable,ly,eness,bility, SIMILAR, ALIKE "prefixes: in"
compare,*,ed,ring,arative,aratively, rable,rably,rison, PARALLEL EXAMINATION "prefixes: in"
comparetive, compare(rative)
comparison,*, ENGAGING EXAMINATION
compartment,*,tal,tally,talize,talized, talizing, SECTIONED SEPARATELY "prefixes: non"
compashinet, compassionate
compasionate, compassionate
compass,ses, DIRECTION FINDER "prefixes: en"
compassion,nate,nless, TAKE PITY ON
compassionate,ely,eness, TAKE PITY ON
compatible,bility,bilities, AGREEABLE "prefixes: bio/in/non"
compedidor, competitor
compeditor, competitor
compel,*,lled,lling,llingly,llingness, DRIVEN TO, AN URGING/DESIRE
compelation, compellation
compellation,*, NAME, DENOMINATION
compensate,*,ed,ting,tion,tory, MAKE UP FOR "prefixes: over"
compensation, MAKE UP FOR "prefixes: de"
compeny, company

comper, compare
comperable, comparable
comperative, compare(rative)
compereson, comparison
comperison, comparison
compersome, cumber(some)
comperuble, comparable
compes, compass
compete,*,ed,ting,tition,titive,titively, titiveness,titor, BE BETTER THAN
competent,nce,ncy, BEING ADEQUATE "prefixes: in"
competishen, competition
competition,*, MATCH FOR SKILL TESTING
competitor,*, ONE WHO COMPETES
compilashun, compellation
compile,*,ed,ling,lation, BRING/ PUT TOGETHER
compinsate, compensate
compitance, competent(nce)
compiut, compute
compiuter, computer
compizishen, composition
complacence,cy,cies,nt,ntly, HAPPY WITH SELF (or see complaisance)
complain,*,ned,ning,nt,ner, FIND FAULT
complaisance,nt, DESIRE TO PLEASE, CIVIL (or see complacence)
complasens, complacence / complaisance
complekate, complicate
compleks, complex
complekshin, complexion
complement,*,tal,tary,tarily,tarity, tarities,tation, WHEN ADDED MAKES COMPLETE (or see compliment)
compleshin, completion
complete,*,ed,ting,tly, CONCLUDE, FINISH "prefixes: in"
completion, CONCLUDE/FINISH
complex,xes,xity, COMBINATION OF INTERCONNECTED PARTS
complexion,*,ned, SKIN PHYSICAL CHARACTERISTIC
compli, comply
compliant,tly,nce,ncy, CONFORM/ AGREE TO "prefixes: in/non"
complicashin, complication
complicate,*,ed,ting,tion, MORE TO CONSIDER "prefixes: un"

complication,*, ADDITIONAL INVOLVEMENT/ CONSIDERATION
complient, compliant
complikashun, complication
complikat, complicate
compliment,*,ted,ting,tary, PRAISE, EXPRESS ADMIRATION (or see complement)
complishon, completion
complokeit, complicate
comploqueit, complicate
complucashun, complication
complukate, complicate
complument, complement / compliment
comply,lies,ying,liance,liant, CONFORM
compolshon, compulsion
compoltion, compulsion
component,*, PHASE/PART OF SOMETHING "prefixes: sub"
compose,*,ed,sing,er, TO FORM "prefixes: de/dis/re"
composite,*, PARTS OF THE WHOLE
composition,*,nal,nally, IDENTIFY/ ARRANGE PARTS OF THE WHOLE
compost,*,ted,ting, RECYCLING ORGANIC MATTER
composure, CENTERED STATE OF MIND
compound,*,ded,ding, ADDITIONAL PARTS, TO ADD TO THE WHOLE
compownd, compound
compoze, compose
comprable, comparable
compramise, compromise
compreble, comparable
comprehend,*,ded,ding,nsion,nsive, nsible, GRASP, UNDERSTAND "prefixes: in"
comprehenshun, comprehension
comprehensible,bility,eness, ABLE TO GRASP/UNDERSTAND "prefixes: in"
comprehension,ive,ible, UNDERSTAND/ GRASP "prefixes: in"
comprehensive,ely, UNDERSTAND/ GRASP "prefixes: in"
comprehinsive, comprehensive
compreshun, compression
compress,ses,sed,sing,sible,sibility,ssive, ssion, COMPACT, CONDENSE "prefixes: de/in"
compression,nal, REDUCING VOLUME
compressor,*, MACHINE THAT CONDENSES/REDUCES
compretion, compression

compromise,*,ed,sing, OUTCOME IMPERFECT, AGREE FOR THE SAKE OF BEING AGREEABLE "prefixes: un"

compruble, comparable

compruhensive, comprehensive

comprumize, compromise

comptroller,*, CONTROLLER OF FINANCES

compuder, computer

compulashun, compellation

compulsary, compulsory

compulsev, compulsive

compulshun, compulsion

compulsion,*,ive, IRRESISTIBLE URGE TO ACT

compulsive,ely,eness,ion,sory, GIVEN TO ACT ON URGES

compulsory,rily, REINFORCED FACT

compultion, compulsion

compusition, composition

computashun, computation

computation,*,nal,ive,ively, TO RECKON/ESTIMATE

compute,*,ed,ting,table, FIGURE DATA, ESTIMATE

computer,*,rize,rized,rization, ELECTRONIC DATA PROCESSOR "prefixes: bio"

computishen, competition

compuzishen, composition

comrade,*,ely,ery,eship, CLOSE ASSOCIATES

comtroler, comptroller

comudoor, commodore

comunal, communal

comune, commune / common

comunecuble, communicable

comunete, community

comunicable, communicable

comunicate, communicate

comunion, communion

comunism, communism

comunist, communist

comunity, community

comurse, commerce

comurshal, commercial

comusery, commissary

comutable, commute(table)

comute, commute

con,*,nned,nning, TO TRICK, PREFIX INDICATING 'WITH/TOGETHER' MOST OFTEN MODIFIES THE WORD (or see cone)

conaseur, connoisseur

conasure, connoisseur

conc, conch / konk

concaf, concave

concaquently, consequent(ly)

concarge, concierge

concave,*,ed,ving,ely,eness,vity,vities, OF INWARD CURVES "prefixes: bi"

conceairg, concierge

conceal,*,led,ling,lment, TO HIDE FROM SIGHT

concede,*,ed,ding, YIELD (or see conceit)

conceit,ted, VAIN (or see concede)

conceivable,bility,eness,ly, ABILITY TO UNDERTAND, IMAGINE "prefixes: in"

conceive,*,ed,ving,vable,vably,vability, vableness, A THOUGHT WHICH BECOMES "prefixes: mis"

concent, consent

concentrate,*,ed,ting,tion, FOCUS, CONDENSE "prefixes: de"

concentric,cally,city, SERIES OF CIRCLES WITH SAME CENTER POINT

concept,*,tive,tively, IDEA/PLAN

conception,nal, MOMENT OF CREATION "prefixes: mis/pre"

conceptual,lism,lize,lly,lization,lizer, THOUGHTS BECOMING

concequence, consequence

concerg, concierge

concern,*,ned,ning,nment, WORRIED ABOUT NEGATIVE OUTCOME, INTEREST IN "prefixes: non/un"

concert,*,ted,ting, PLAN/WORK/ACT TOGETHER IN MUSIC/THEATER "prefixes: pre"

concervashon, conservation

concesion, concession

concession,*, TO PART WITH SOME CONTROL, SELL UNDER AUTHORITY

conch,hes, A SHELL, OF DOME

conchas, conscious

concheinchus, conscientious

conches, conscious / conch(es)

conchis, conscious / conch(es)

conchos, conscious / conch(es)

conchus, conscious / conch(es)

concierge, OVERSEES GATES/ ENTRYWAYS

concint, consent

concise,ely,eness, TO THE POINT WITH FEW WORDS

concistensy, consistent(ncy)

concistent, consistent

conclewsive, conclusive

conclude,*,ed,ding,usion,usive, WRAP-UP, SUMMARIZED ENDING

conclugen, conclusion

conclusion,*, FINALIZE, END

conclusive,ely,eness, FINALIZE, END "prefixes: in"

conclution, conclusion

concoct,*,ted,ting, PUTTING TOGETHER IDEAS

concrete,ely,eness, HARDENED GRAVEL MIXTURE

concussion,*,ssive, INJURY FROM IMPACT

concution, concussion

condemn,*,ned,ning,nation, STEP TOWARDS ELIMINATION

condensashen, condensation

condensation,*, GAS REDUCED TO LIQUID

condense,*,ed,er,sing,sable,sation, REDUCE

condescend,ding,dingly, TALK DOWN TO SOMEONE, TREAT AS AN INFERIOR

condesend, condescend

condewit, conduit

condimeneum, condominium

condiment,*, SPICES, SAUCES

condinsashen, condensation

condinsation, condensation

condisend, condescend

condishen, condition

condition,*,ned,ning,nal, TO FORCE INTO ANOTHER FORM, RESTRUCTURE "prefixes: bi/de/pre/ un"

condolence,*, SYMPATHY FOR SOMEONE'S PAIN

condom,*, COVER FOR PENIS

condomeneum, condominium

condominium,*, FORM OF APARTMENTS

condone,*,ed,ning, FORGIVE

conduct,*,ted,ting,tion,tive,tor, ESCORT, TRANSPORT, BEHAVIOR "prefixes: mis"

conductor,*,rial,rship, TRANSMITS, LEADS, GUIDES "prefixes: semi"

conduit, CHANNEL FOR ENERGY, FLUIDS, ETC.

condukter, conductor

condum, condom
condument, condiment
condunsation, condensation
cone,*, GEOMETRIC SHAPE OF MANY THINGS
conect, connect
conekshen, connection
conesur, connoisseur
conexshon, connection
confadant, confidant / confident
confection,*,nary,nery,ner, A DESSERT
confedant, confidant / confident
confederate,*,acy,tion, UNITED ALLIANCE
confedont, confidant
confeduret, confederate
confedy, confetti
confekshen, confection
conference,*, MEETING FOR DISCUSSION
confermation, confirmation
confesion, confession
confess,sses,ssed,ssing,ssion,ssor, DISCLOSE INFORMATION, ADMIT FACTS
confession,*,nal, ADMIT INVOLVEMENT
confetion, confession
confetti, PARTY MATERIAL
confety, confetti
confidant,*, TRUSTED PERSON (or see confident)
confide,*,ed,ding, SHARE THOUGHTS WITH SOMEONE
confidence,nt,ntial, TRUST
confidenshul, confidential
confident,tly,tial, TRUST
confidential,lly,lity,lness, PRIVATE/ SECRET
confidont, confidant
configerashun, configuration
configuration,*, ARRANGEMENT OF PARTS
confine,*,ed,ning,nment, RESTRICTED, IMPRISONED "prefixes: un"
confinement, BEING RESTRICTED, IMPRISONED
confinment, confinement
confirents, conference
confirm,*,med,ming,mation,mative, TO VALIDATE "prefixes: dis"
confirmation,*,ive, ACT OF VALIDATION
conflict,*,ted,ting, GOES AGAINST
conform,*,med,ming,mer,mist,mity, mism,mance, TO TAKE ON

ANOTHER FORM "prefixes: dis/non/ un"
confrens, conference
confrins, conference
confront,*,ted,ting,tation,tational, FACE, ENCOUNTER
confudant, confidant / confident
confudense, confidence
confujen, confusion
confuranse, conference
confurmashun, confirmation
confuse,*,ed,sing, DISORDER, OFF- CENTER
confusion, STATE OF DISORDER, OFF- CENTER
congectivitis, conjunction(ivitis)
conger, conjure
congest,*,ed,ting,tible,tive,tion, TOO MUCH WITHIN A SMALL SPACE/ PLACE "prefixes: de"
congestun, congest(ion)
conglomerate,*,ed,ting,tion, GATHERED INTO MASS
congradulashen, congratulation
congratulate,*,ed,ting,tion, WISH ONE WELL, COMPLIMENT
congratulation,*, EXPRESS WISHING ONE WELL, COMPLIMENT
congregate,*,ed,ting,tion, GATHERING, ASSEMBLY
congregation,*,nal, TO GATHER, ASSEMBLY
congress,ssional,ssionally, LEGISLATIVE ASSEMBLY TO PROMOTE A GROUPS INTERESTS
congrewedy, congruent(uity)
congrewes, congruous
congrewint, congruent
congrewity, congruent(uity)
congrigate, congregate
congris, congress
congruedy, congruent(uity)
congruent,nce,ncy,ntly,uity,uties, AGREEMENT, CONSISTENCE(CY) "prefixes: in/non"
congrugashun, congregation
congrugate, congregate
congruous,sly,sness, AGREEMENT, CONSISTENCE(CY) "prefixes: in"
conifer,*, TREE GROUP
coning, cunning / con(nning)
conjesten, congest(ion)
conjugal,lity,lly, RELATION WITH PARTNER/MATE

conjugate,*,ed,ting,tion,tive, RELATION WITH PARTNER/MATE
conjunctavitis, conjunction(ivitis)
conjunction,*,nal,nally,ivitis, UNIFICATION, BRING TOGETHER
conjunkshen, conjunction
conjure,*,ed,ring, CREATE/ CONSPIRE
conkaf, concave
conkafety, concave(vity)
conkavudy, concave(vity)
conker, conquer
conklude, conclude
conkrete, concrete
conkur, conquer
conkushen, concussion
conkwest, conquest
connasure, connoisseur
connect,*,ted,ting,tive,tivity,tion, BOND, ASSOCIATE, BRING TOGETHER "prefixes: dis/un"
connection,*, ACT OF BRINGING TOGETHER, LINK, BOND
conniseur, connoisseur
connoisseur,*, SPECIALIZES, TRAINED, WELL-VERSED IN SOMETHING SUCH AS THE FINE ARTS
conoseur, connoisseur
conosieur, connoisseur
conosure, connoisseur
conphert, comfort
conquer,*,red,ring, OBTAIN BY FORCE
conquest,*, WIN BY WILL
consacrashen, consecrate(tion)
consacrate, consecrate
consacration, consecrate(tion)
consalidate, consolidate
consaquently, consequent(ly)
conscientious,sly,sness, WITH UNSELFISH MOTIVES
conscious,sly,sness, AWARE OF PHYSICAL REALITY "prefixes: non/ semi/sub/un"
consdatute, constitute
conseal, conceal
consecrate,*,ed,ting,tive,tor,tory,tion, tive, MAKE SACRED/HOLY "prefixes: de"
consecutive,ely,eness, DIRECTLY FOLLOWING ANOTHER "prefixes: in"
consedarashen, considerate(tion)
conseduration, considerate(tion)
conseed, conceit / concede
conseet, conceit / concede

conseevable, conceivable

conseeve, conceive

conseinshus, conscientious

conseintious, conscientious

consekcutive, consecutive

consekwential, consequent(ial)

consekwently, consequent(ly)

consel, conceal / council / counsel

consemate, consummate

consensus,ual,ually, AGREEMENT, MUTUAL CONSENT

consent,*,ted,ting, YIELD OR COMPLY

consentrate, concentrate

consentric, concentric

consepshun, conception

consept, concept

conseption, conception

conseptual, conceptual

consequence,*,nt, REACTION TO AN ACTION "prefixes: in"

consequent,*,tly,ntial,ntially,ntiality, ntialness,ntialist,ntialism, REACTION TO AN ACTION "prefixes: in"

consern, concern

consert, concert

conservation,nist,nism, TO PRESERVE/ PROTECT

conservative,*,ely,eness,vism, PRACTICES RESTRAINT "prefixes: neo/semi"

conservator,*,ry,ries,rial,rship, PROTECTOR/GUARDIAN

conservatory,ries, A SCHOOL OF MUSIC, GREENHOUSE

conserve,*,ed,ving,vatist,vative,vator, vatize,vation, TO PRESERVE/ PROTECT/RESTRAIN

conseshun, concession

consestintly, consistent(ly)

conset, conceit / concede

consetion, concession

consev, conceive

consevable, conceivable

conseve, conceive

conshas, conscious

conshus, conscious

consider,*,red,ring,rable,rate, ENGAGE IN THOUGHT "prefixes: in/un"

considerate,ely,eness,ation, ENGAGE IN THOUGHT "prefixes: in"

consierge, concierge

consignment,*, GIVING SOMEONE A PERCENT FOR SELLING YOUR WARES

consikwense, consequence

consil, conceal / council

consilation, consolation

consimate, consummate

consinent, consonant

consinment, consignment

consintrate, concentrate

consintric, concentric

consiquence, consequence

consirvation, conservation

consirvator, conservator

consirvatory, conservatory

consirve, conserve

consise, concise

consist,*,ted,ting,tence,tent, COMPOSED OF

consistence,cy,cies, HOW FLUID, VISCOUS "prefixes: in"

consistency, consistence(cy)

consistent,tly, COMPOSED OF "prefixes: in"

consolation,*, TO OFFER SOLACE/ SUPPORT FOR EFFORT (or see constellation)

console,*,ed,ling,lable,latory,er,lingly, SOOTHE, OFFER SUPPORT, CABINET FOR ELECTRONICS (or see counsel/ council) "prefixes: dis/in"

consolidate,*,ed,ting,tion, PUT ALL TOGETHER

consonant,*, LETTERS IN ENGLISH WORDS THAT AREN'T VOWELS

consoom, consume

conspearusy, conspiracy

conspicuous,sly,sness, OBVIOUS, STRIKING "prefixes: in"

conspikuos, conspicuous

conspikyous, conspicuous

conspiracy,cies, A GROUP OF PEOPLE PLOTTING AN EVENT TO USPSET STATUS QUO

constancy, DILIGENT/REPEATEDLY CONSISTENT

constant,*,tly,ncy, UNIFORM, UNCHANGING "prefixes: in"

constatushen, constitution

constatute, constitute

constellation,*, NAME FOR GROUPED CELESTIAL STARS (or see consolation)

constense, constancy

constetute, constitute

constilashen, constellation

constilation, constellation

constint, constant

constipashen, constipation

constipation, RESTRICTED BOWEL MOVEMENT

constitushen, constitution

constitute,*,ed,ting,tion, SET-UP/ CREATE/ESTABLISH "prefix: re"

constitution,*,nal, WRITTEN RULES/ PRINCIPLES/ REGULATIONS "prefixes: un"

constrict,*,ted,ting,tion,tive, PREVENT FROM PROPER MOVEMENT

construct,*,ted,ting,tive,tively,tion, tional,tionally, MOLD/FORM/ CREATE "prefixes: de/re"

construction,nal,nally, BUILDING/ FORMING "prefixes: mis/re"

constulashen, constellation

constulation, constellation

constupashen, constipation

consucrat, consecrate

consukwenshul, consequent(ial)

consukwently, consequent(ly)

consukwinse, consequence

consulashen, consolation

consulation, consolation

consult,*,ted,ting,tant,tation,table, tative,tatively,ter, COMMUNICATE WITH SOMEONE WHO IS SEEKING ADVICE

consultashen, consult(ation)

consumate, consummate

consume,*,ed,er,erism,ming,mable, mption,mptive, DECOMPOSE OR DESTROY, INGEST, MAKE USE OF

consummate,*,ed,ting, COMPLETE, FULFILL

consumpshen, consumption

consumption,ive, USED, DIGESTED, DECOMPOSED

consumshen, consumption

consunent, consonant

consuquential, consequent(ial)

consurt, concert

consurvation, conservation

consurvator, conservator

consurvatory, conservatory

consurve, conserve

contact,*,ted,ting, TOUCHING, ASSOCIATION WITH

contagious,sly,sness, SPREAD TO OTHERS

contain,*,ned,ning,ner,nment, HOLD WITHIN

contaminate,*,ed,ting,ant,tion, SOMETHING INCLUDED WHICH DOESN'T BELONG AT ALL "prefixes: de"

conteguis, contiguous

contemplate,*,ed,ting,tion,tive,tively, tiveness, TO OBSERVE THOROUGHLY

contemporary,ries,riness, REFLECTIVE OF CURRENT TIMES "prefixes: non"

contempt,tible,tibleness,tibly,tuous, tuously, THE STATE OF BEING DISHONORED/DISRESPECTED

contend,*,ded,ding,der, CHOOSE OR FORCED TO DEAL WITH, FACE OFF

content,*,ted,tedly,tedness,tment, THAT WHICH IS CONTAINED WITHIN, SATISFIED "prefixes: dis"

contenual, continue(ual)

contenuense, continuance

contenuisly, continue(uously)

contenule, continue(ual)

contest,*,ted, DISPUTE, FOR SUPERIORITY "prefixes: in"

context,ture, INTERWOVEN MEANING IN TEXT

contiguis, contiguous

contiguous,sly,sness, NEIGHBORING/ SHARING A BORDER

contimplate, contemplate

contimporary, contemporary

continent,*,tal, LAND MASS "prefixes: intra/sub"

continet, continent

contingent,*,nce,ncy,ncies, MAY HAPPEN IF...

contint, content

continuance, POSTPONEMENT TO CONTINUE AT A FUTURE DATE

continuants, continuance

continue,*,ed,uing,ual,ually,uation, uouse,uously,uousness,uity, KEEP GOING "prefixes: dis"

contorshenist, contortionist

contortionist,*, FLEXIBLE ACTS WITH THE BODY

contour,*,red,ring, THE SHAPE/FORM OF OUTLINE

contra, PREFIX INDICATING 'AGAINST' MOST OFTEN MODIFIES THE WORD

contraception,ive, FOR PREVENTION OF PREGNANCY

contract,*,ted,ting,tor,tual,tive,tion, tional,tionary, WRITTEN OBLIGATION OF SERVICE "prefixes: non/sub"

contraction,*,nal,nary, MUSCLES TIGHTENING, COMBINATION OF WORDS

contradict,*,ted,ting,tion,tory, CONTRARY/OPPOSE/DENY

contrak, contract

contrakshen, contraction

contrary,ries,rily,riness,rian,riety,rieties, PROVE OPPOSITE, DENY "prefixes: sub"

contrast,*,ted,ting,tingly,tive,tively, tiveness,table,tably, COMPARING DIFFERENCES

contraversy, controversy

contravert, controvert

contravertible, controvert(ible)

contrebute, contribute

contrery, contrary

contribute,*,ed,ting,tion,tive,tory, GIVE, LEND

contrition, AMENDING SIN WITH PRAYER

contro, PREFIX INDICATING 'AGAINST' MOST OFTEN MODIFIES THE WORD

control,*,lled,lling,ller,llable,llably, llability, ATTEMPT TO GAIN ORDER "prefixes: bio/in/sub/un"

controversy,sies,sial, DIFFERENCE IN OPINION, DEBATE

controvert,*,ted,ting,ter,tible,tibly, DEBATE STRONGLY AGAINST "prefixes: in"

contrudik, contradict

contrusepshun, contraception

contumplate, contemplate

contunent, continent

conture, contour

conufir, conifer

conva, convey

convalescence,nt, RECOVERING HEALTH

convay, convey

convayer, convey(or)

convelesents, convalescence

convene,*,ed,ning, CALL TO APPEAR, MEET

convenient,nce,nces, EASE OF FACILITIES, COMFORT "prefixes: in"

convense, convince

convention,*,nal, PEOPLE GATHERING, AN ASSEMBLY "prefixes: non/un"

convenyant, convenient

convenyut, convenient

conversashen, conversation

conversation,*,nal,nally,nalist, COMMUNICATING THOUGHTS

converse,es,sing,sant, EXCHANGE INFORMATION, MADE OPPOSITE/ REVERSE

conversion,*, CHANGED IN ONE FORM OR ANOTHER "prefixes: bio"

convert,*,ted,ting,ter,rsion, OF CHANGE, TRANSFORM "prefixes: in"

convertible,*,bility, CHANGE FROM ONE FORM TO ANOTHER, VEHICLE WITH REMOVABLE ROOF

convex,xes,xed,xedly,xedness,xing,xly, xity,xities, CURVING OUTWARD "prefixes: bi/sub"

convey,*,yed,ying,yable,yance,yances, yancing,yor, TRANSFER OF PEOPLE/ ITEMS/MEANING/EXPRESSION "prefixe: re"

convicshen, convict(ion)

convict,*,ted,ting,tion, HAVING BEEN FOUND GUILTY/AT FAULT

convilesense, convalescence

convince,*,ed,cing, TO PERSUADE SOMEONE TO YOUR OPINION "prefixes: in"

convinshon, convention

convintion, convention

convirsation, conversation

convirse, converse

convirt, convert

convulesense, convalescence

convulesent, convalescent

convulgin, convulsion

convulshen, convulsion

convulsion,*,sive,sively, INTENSE MUSCLE CONTRACTION

convurgin, conversion

convursashen, conversation

convursation, conversation

convurtable, convertible

coocoo, cuckoo

cood, could

coodent, couldn't

cooger, cougar

cook,*,ked,king, PREPARE FOOD "prefixes: pre"

cookie,*, SWEET CAKE TREAT

cool,*,led,ling,lingly,lly,lness,ler, BETWEEN WARM/COLD TEMPERATURE, EXPRESSION OF APPRECIATION "prefixes: pre/sub/un/under"

cooler,*, COLD CONTAINER FOR FOOD

coop,*,ped, SMALL CAGE FOR SMALL ANIMALS (or see co-op/coup)

cooperate,*,ed,ting,tion,tive, UNITE TO PRODUCE

coordinate,*,ed,ting,ely,eness,tive,tion, tor, ORGANIZE FOR DESIRED RESULTS, LINE SYSTEM "prefixes: in/un"

cooth, couth

cop,*,pped,pping,pper, SLANG FOR "POLICE", RUN OUT OF ENERGY (or see co-op/coup/coop/cope/copy)

copbord, cupboard

cope,*,ed,ping, TO DEAL WITH STRESS, SHAPE/MATCH (or see co-op/coup/coop/copy)

coper, copper

copeur, copy(pier)

copi, copy

copitchulate, capitulate

copler, coupler

copol, couple

copper,*,ry, METAL

copulate,*,ed,ted,tion, PHYSICAL SEXUAL UNITY

copur, copper

coputr, computer

copy,pies,pied,ying, TO REPRODUCE

copyuter, computer

cor, TO TRICK, PREFIX INDICATING 'WITH/TOGETHER' MOST OFTEN MODIFIES THE WORD (or see core/car)

coraborate, corroborate

coragated, corrugate(d)

coral, OCEAN REEF ANIMALS

corc, cork

corchal, cordial

cord,*, STRANDS WOVEN/TWISTED TOGETHER (or see chord/quart(s)/quartz)

cordaroy, corduroy

cordial,lity,lness,lly, GRACIOUS, KIND, A LIQUEUR

cordinate, coordinate

cordunate, coordinate

corduroy, RIBBED MATERIAL

core,*,ed,ring, THE CENTER OF (or see corp)

corect, correct

coredor, corridor

corelate, correlate

cores, core(s) / chorus / caress

corespond, correspond

corgul, cordial

coridor, corridor

corigate, corrugate

corilate, correlate

coriner, coroner

corinery, coronary

coris, chorus / course

corispond, correspond

corjil, cordial

cork,*,ked, BARK FROM A TREE (or see quark) "prefixes: un"

corn,*, GRAIN, ON TOE

cornacopia, cornucopia

cornea,al, PART OF EYE

corner,*,red,ring, WHERE WALLS OR LINES MEET, NO WAY OUT

cornia, cornea

cornikopea, cornucopia

cornol, colonel

cornucopia, HORN OF PLENTY

coroborate, corroborate

corode, corrode

corogan, corrode(osion)

corogen, corrode(osion)

corogin, corrode(osion)

corojin, corrode(osion)

coronary,ries, HEART ARTERIES

coroner,*, INVESTIGATES SUSPICIOUS DEATHS

coropt, corrupt

corosef, corrode(osive)

coroud, corrode

corp,*, NUMBER OF PEOPLE WORKING TOGETHER (or see core)

corparul, corporal

corpirate, corporate

corporal, OF THE PHYSICAL BODY

corporate,tion,ely, UNITE MANY INTO ONE "prefixes: in/non"

corpret, corporate

corpse,*, DEAD BODY

corpural, corporal

corpurate, corporate

corral,*, FENCED ENCLOSURE FOR ANIMALS (or see coral)

correct,*,ted,ting,tly,tion,tional,table, tible,tness,tor, TO SET RIGHT/STRAIGHT "prefixes: in/over"

correlate,*,ed,ting,tion, IF ONE... THEN THE OTHER

correspond,*,ded,ding,dence, SIMILAR/RELATED TO, COMMUNICATE WITH

corridor,*, NARROW PASSAGE

corroborate,*,ed,ting,tion,tive,tively,tor, tory, CAN BACK UP THE TRUTH WITH EVIDENCE

corrode,*,ed,ding,osion,osive,dant, dible,dibility, CHEMICAL EROSION, EATEN AWAY

corrugate,*,ed,ting, ALTERNATING BENDS, FORMS

corrupt,*,ted,ting,tion,tible,tibly,tibility, tibleness,tness, TO NEGATIVELY STEER OFF COURSE "prefixes: in"

cors, course / coarse / core(s)

corsage,*, FLOWERS TO WEAR, BODICE

corse, course / coarse / core(s)

corsog, corsage

corsoge, corsage

cort, cord / court / quart

cort-marshul, court-martial

corteks, cortex

cortex,xes,tices,tical,tically, INTERNAL ORGAN'S PROTECTIVE LAYER "prefixes: sub"

corts, cord(s) / court(s) / quart(s)

corudoor, corridor

corugate, corrugate

corul, choral / coral / corral / chorale

corulate, correlate

corunary, coronary

coruner, coroner

corupt, corrupt

coruspond, correspond

cos, cause / cuss

cosdodian, custodian

cosdum, costume

cosee, cozy

coshen, caution

cosher, kosher

coshis, cautious

coshun, caution

cosin, cousin

cosmic,cally, NOT OF THIS PHYSICAL PLANE

cosmopolitan, BELONGS TO THE WORLD, NO ATTACHMENT

cosmos, UNIVERSAL HARMONY

cospid, cuspid

cost,*,ting,tly, EXPENSE (or see coast/ cause(d))
costard, custard
costem, custom
coster, coaster
costic, caustic
costodian, custodian
costom, custom / costume
costomer, customer
costomize, custom(ize)
costoom, costume
costume,*, GARMENTS TO SUIT A CHARACTER TYPE
cosy, cozy
cot,*, FOLDING BED (or see caught/ coat/cut)
cotage, cottage
cotej, cottage
coten, cotton
cotn, cotton
coton, cotton
cottage,*, SMALL DWELLING
cotton, PLANT WHICH CLOTH IS PRODUCED FROM
cotuge, cottage
couc, caulk
couch,hes,hed,hing, FURNITURE, PUT-DOWN (or see coach)
coud, code / could
coued, coed
couers, coerce
couf, cough / cove
cougar,*, ANIMAL
cough,*,hed,hing, FORCEFULLY EXPEL AIR FROM LUNGS
cought, caught / cot / cough(ed)
could, PAST TENSE FOR THE WORD 'CAN'
could've, CONTRACTION OF THE WORDS 'COULD HAVE'
couldn't, CONTRACTION OF THE WORDS 'COULD NOT'
coulishun, coalition
coun, cone
council,*, A GROUP MEETING TO DISCUSS/MAKE DECISIONS (or see counsel/console)
counsel,*,led,ling,lor, GIVES ADVISE, PROVIDES INFORMATION (or see console/council)
counside, coincide
count,*,ted,ting,table,tless, ADD THE NUMBER OF THINGS "prefixes: dis/ mis/re-/un"

counter,*,red,ring,ract, PREFIX INDICATING 'AGAINST' MOST OFTEN MODIFIES THE WORD, SURFACE FOR SERVING, SOMETHING THAT COUNTS, OPPOSING MOVE "prefixes: en"
country,ries, OUT OF THE CITY, COLLECTION OF STATES, NATION OF PEOPLE "prefixes: up"
county,ties, A GEOGRAPHICAL AREA
coup, QUICK/SUCCESSFUL MOVE (or see coop)
couple,*,ed,ling,er, PARTNERS, BRING TWO TOGETHER "prefixes: un"
coupler,*,ling, DEVICE FOR CONNECTING
coupon,*, REDEEM FOR CASH VALUE
coupurate, cooperate
courage,eous,eously,eousness, BRAVE IN FACING DANGER "prefixes: dis/ en"
courier,*, MESSENGER
cours, course / coerce
course,*, PATH, IDEA, CONCEPT TO FOLLOW (or see coarse) "prefixes: dis/re"
coursive, coerce(cive)
coursment, coerce(ment)
court,*,ted,ting, ENCLOSED AREA, HALL/CHAMBER FOR SPORTS/CIVIC ACTIVITIES FOLLOW (or see quart)
court-martial,led,ling, MILITARY TRIAL
courteous,sly,sness, POLITE
courtesy,sies, POLITE BEHAVIOR "prefixes: dis"
cousin,*, KINSHIP, RELATIVE
cout, caught / cot / coat
couth, SOPHISTICATED "prefixes: un"
cova, kava
cove,*,ed,ving, NOOK, CAVE (or see coffee)
covenant,*, AGREEMENT, CONTRACT TO KEEP PROMISE "prefixes: un"
cover,*,red,ring,rage, TO HIDE/ PROTECT "prefixes: dis/re/un/ under"
coverage, ACT OF HIDING OR BEING PROTECTED
covert,tly,tness, UNDER COVER, DISGUISED, SHELTERED
covet, DESIRE WITHOUT REGARDS TO CONSEQUENCE
covrach, coverage
covunent, covenant

covurt, covert
cow,*, THE FEMININE OF VARIOUS SPECIES, BOVINE
coward,*,dly,dliness,dice, CANNOT BRAVELY FACE DANGER
cowch, couch
cowculus, calculus
cowerd, coward
cowkulate, calculate
cowl,*,ling, A HOOD (or see call)
cownder, counter
cownsul, council / counsel / console
cownt, count
cowntur, counter
cownty, county
cowurd, coward
coxs, coax
coyol, coil
coz, cause
cozmic, cosmic
cozmopoletin, cosmopolitan
cozmos, cosmos
cozy,zies,zily,ziness, COMFORTABLE, CONTENT, SNUG
crab,*, CRUSTACEAN, HARD SHELLED OCEAN ANIMAL
crachin, creation / crash(ing)
crack,*,ked,king, TO SPLIT APART, SLANG FOR A SERIOUSLY ADDICTIVE DRUG, A SOUND
cracker,*, YEASTLESS BISCUIT, FIREWORKS
crackle,*,ed,ling, SOUND, GLAZE ON POTTERY
cracol, crackle
crader, crater / creator
cradible, credible
cradle,*,ed,ling, BED FOR INFANT, HOLD IN ARMS, TOOL
cradul, cradle
crafe, crave
craft,*,ted,ting,ter,tily,tiness, KILL USING HANDS, VESSEL FOR TRAVEL
crain, crane
craink, crank
crak, crack
crakel, crackle
craker, cracker
cral, crawl
cram,*,mmed,mming, FORCE INTO A SPACE
cramp,*,ped,ping, CONFINES, MUSCLE CONTRACTIONS
crampt, cramp(ed)

cranberry,ries, EDIBLE BERRY

crane,*,ed,ning, A MACHINE, TO STRETCH OUT

craneum, cranium

crani, PREFIX INDICATING 'SKULL' MOST OFTEN MODIFIES THE WORD

cranio, PREFIX INDICATING 'SKULL' MOST OFTEN MODIFIES THE WORD

cranium,*,ia,ial, SKULL "prefixes: endo/intra"

crank,*,ked,king,ky, TOOL, SOMEONE IRRITABLE

cranny,nies, CREVICE, NOOK, CRACK

crany, cranny

craon, crayon

crap,*,pped,pping,ppy, GAME OF DICE, TIRED OUT (or see crepe)

crape, crepe / crap(ppy)

crase, crazy

crash,hes,hed,hing, SOUND, TO RUN INTO, OFF OF SOMETHING

crass,sness, COARSE, THICK, DENSE

crate,*,ed,ting, BOX, BOX UP

crater,*,red,ring, BOWL-SHAPED DEPRESSION, CONCAVE (or see creator)

crauch, crouch

craud, crowd

craul, crawl

craun, crown

craunec, chronic

craunekl, chronicle

crave,*,ed,ving, TO YEARN, DESIRE HEAVILY

crawl,*,led,ling, ON HANDS AND KNEES, MOVE SLOWLY, CROUCHED POSITION

crayon,*, WAX PENCIL

crazy,zier,ziest,zily,ziness, INSANE, INFATUATED

creachin, creation

creader, creator

creak,*,ked,king, NOISE (or see creek)

creal, creel

cream,my,mily,miness, FROM MILK, TO WHIP ON SOMEONE (or see creme)

creap, creep

creapy, creep(y)

crease,*,ed,sing, MAKE FOLDED LINES, MARK IN "prefixes: in"

creashun, creation

creasul, creosol

create, *,ed,ting,tive,tively,tiveness,tion, tivity, TO TURN THOUGHT INTO REALITY "prefixes: mis/pro/re"

createf, creative

creation,*,nist, ACT OF CREATING

creative,ely,eness,ion,vity, IMAGINE/ CREATE SOMETHING UNUSUAL "prefixes: un"

creator,*, ONE WHO TURNS THOUGHT INTO PHYSICAL REALITY

creature,*,ely, SOMETHING OTHER THAN HUMAN, ANIMATE, INANIMATE

creb, crib

crebeg, cribbage

crec, creek / creak

crecher, creature

crechor, creature

credable, credible

crededer, creditor

credenchol, credential

credential,*,led, TO VALIDATE CONFIDENCE, ASSURE OF AUTHENTICITY "prefixes: un"

creder, critter

credible,ly,bility,eness, WORTHY/ BELIEVABLE "prefixes: in"

credibul, credible

credider, creditor

credinshul, credential

credisize, criticize

credit,*,ted,ting,table,tor, RECORD OF HANDLING OTHER'S MONEY/ SPENDING/EARNINGS, ACCOUNT TO BORROW AGAINST "prefixes: ac/ dis/un"

creditor,*, ONE WHOM MONEY IS OWED TO

creduble, credible

creducal, critical

creecher, creature

creek,*, SMALL STREAM/TRIBUTARY (or see creak)

creel, FISH BASKET, OF SEWING MACHINES

creen, careen

creenkul, crinkle

creep,*,rept,ping,py,per, SOMETHING WHICH CAUSES FEARFUL SENSATION, TO SNEAK UP

creisote, creosote

creke, creak / creek

crekit, cricket

cremate,*,ed,ting,tion,tor,torium, BURN A BODY TO ASH

creme, LIKE CREAM (or see cream)

cremenul, criminal

cremson, crimson

creng, cringe

crenium, cranium

crenj, cringe

crenkle, crinkle

creosol, BLACK, FROM TAR AND RESIN (or see creosote)

creosote, FROM WOOD TAR USED FOR PRESERVATIVE/ANTISEPTIC (or see creosol)

crep, creep / crepe

crepe,*, THIN PAPER, FABRIC (or see creep)

creple, cripple

crept, PAST TENSE FOR THE WORD "CREEP"

creptic, cryptic

crepy, creep(y)

crescendo,*,di, GRADUAL/GROWING/ INCREASING

crescent,*, SHAPE OF QUARTER MOON

crescross, crisscross

crese, crease

cresendo, crescendo

cresent, crescent / croissant

cresmas, christmas

cresmus, christmas

crest,*,ted,ting, TOP/CROWN/PEAK

cresunt, crescent / croissant

cretable, credible

creteek, critique

creteke, critique

cretible, credible

cretik, critic

cretir, critter / creator

cretisize, criticize

creusol, creosol

creusote, creosote

crevasse,*,ed,sing, FISSURE OF GLACIER/RIVER (or see crevice)

crevice,*, CRACK/FISSURE (or see crevasse)

crevus, crevasse crevice

crew,*, GANG/BODY OF PEOPLE (or see cruise) "prefixes: un"

crewd, crude

crews, cruise / crew(s)

crewsade, crusade

crewshul, crucial

crewsufix, crucifix

crewton, crouton
criasol, creosol
criasot, creosote
crib,*,bbed,bbing,bbage, ENCLOSURE/
CONTAINER, CHEAT SHEET
cribach, cribbage
cribage, cribbage
cribbage, GAME, CARDS
cribd, crib(bbed)
cribeg, cribbage
cric, creek / creak
crichur, creature
cricket,*, INSECT
crid, cried
cridenshols, credential(s)
cridentials, credential(s)
crider, critter
cridik, critic
criducal, critical
cridusize, criticize
cried, PAST TENSE FOR THE WORD
"CRY"
cries, PAST TENSE FOR THE WORD
"CRY"
crik, creek / creak
criket, cricket
crim, crime / cream / creme
crime,*, ACT AGAINST MAN'S LAWS
crimenal, criminal
criminal,*,lly, ONE WHO VIOLATED
MAN'S LAWS
crimson, COLOR
cringe,*,ed,ging, RECOIL IN POSTURE,
RETRACT
crinj, cringe
crinkle,*,ed,ling, NOISE, CRUMPLE
criple, cripple
cripol, cripple
cripple,*,ed,ling,ler, LAME, DISABLE
criptic, cryptic
criquet, cricket / croquet
crisanthemom, chrysanthemum
criscross, crisscross
crisis,ses, TURNING POINT IN LIFE
crismas, christmas
crismus, christmas
crisont, croissant
crisp,ply,piness,py, BRITTLE, FRESH
crisscross,sses,ssed,ssing, TWO LINES
THAT INTERSECT TO FORM AN "X"
cristal, crystal
cristashen, crustacean
cristl, crystal
cristolize, crystal(ize)

criter, critter
critic,*,cal,cize,cism,ique, ONE WHO
PASSES JUDGEMENT
critical,cally,calness, BEING
JUDGEMENTAL "prefixes: sub/un"
criticize,*,ed,zing,ism, TO PROVIDE
PERSONAL JUDGEMENT
critique,*,ed,uing, PROVIDE WRITTEN
OPINION
critir, critter
critter,*, NON-HUMAN CREATURE
criz, cries
croak,*,ked,king, FROG SOUND, TO DIE
croan, crone
croch, crutch
crochet,*,ted,ting, KNIT WITH NEEDLE
crock,*,kery, KETTLE, POT,
DEROGATORY RESPONSE (or see
croak)
crocodile,*, LARGE BROWN REPTILE
crocus, FLOWER
croissant,*, FRENCH PASTRY
crok, crock / croak
crokedile, crocodile
croket, croquet / croquette
crokudile, crocodile
crol, crawl
crom, crumb
crombl, crumble
crompl, crumple
cronalogical, chronology(gical)
cronch, crunch
crone,*, AGED WOMAN WITH WISDOM
cronec, chronic
cronecal, chronicle
cronological, chronology(gical)
cronuc, chronic
cronucl, chronicle
crony,nies, FRIENDS, BUDDIES
crook,*,ked,kedly,kedness,kery,
DISHONORABLE PERSON, A BEND/
HOOK "or see croak"
croose, cruise / crew(s)
crop,*,pped,pping, YIELD IN FIELD,
SUDDEN APPEARANCE "prefixes:
over"
croquet, GAME (or see croquette)
croquette, PREPARED FOOD (or see
croquet)
cros, cross / crow(s)
crosant, croissant
croshay, crochet

cross,sses,ssed,ssing, TWO LINES
PERFORMING INTERSECTION
"prefixes: un"
crost, cross(ed) / crust
crostashen, crustacean
crotch,hless, WHERE LEGS MEET THE
TORSO, FORK OF SOMETHING
crouch,hes,hed,hing, HUDDLE, SQUAT,
CRINGE
croud, crowd
croun, crown / crone
crouton, SMALL TOAST
crow,*,wed,wing, BOAST, ROOSTER
SOUND
crowch, crouch
crowd,*,ded,ding, BODIES CLOSE
TOGETHER "prefixes: over"
crowkus, crocus
crown,*,ned,ning, PEAK, CREST, TOP,
HEAD ADORNMENT "prefixes: un"
crowshay, crochet
crowtch, crouch
cru, crew
cruc, crook
cruch, crutch
crucial, UPMOST IMPORTANCE
crucifix,xion, PERTAINING TO
CHRISTIAN CROSS
crucs, crux
crude,er,est,ely,eness, NEED FURTHER
DEVELOPMENT
crudenshul, credential
crudinshuls, credential(s)
crue, crew
cruise,*,ed,sing,er, MOVE ABOUT IN
CAR/BOAT FOR PLEASURE (or see
crew)
cruke, crook
cruks, crux
crumb,*,ble, TINY BITS OF SOMETHING
crumble,*,ed,ling,ly, FALL APART IN
PIECES
crumple,*,ed,ling, WRINKLE, SQUEEZE
OR FORM CREASES
crunch,hes,hed,hing,hy,hiness, TO
BREAK, WRINKLE
crupt, corrupt
crusade,*,ed,ding,er, MOVEMENT
WITH ASSERTIVE INTENT
cruse, cruise / crew(s)
crusendo, crescendo
crush,hes,hed,hing,her,hable, TO
SMASH
crushul, crucial

crust,*,ty,ted,tal,tless, PASTRY LINING, PLANETARY GEOLOGY "prefixes: en"

crustacean,*,eous, WATER ANIMAL, ANTHROPOD

crutch,hes, TOOL FOR SUPPORT

cruteek, critique

cruteke, critique

cruton, crouton

crux,xes, TROUBLE, CROSS

cry,ries,ried,ying, VERBAL SOUND, EMOTIONAL RELEASE

cryptic,cally,calness, CODES TO CONCEAL OR HIDE

crysis, crisis

crystal,*,llize,llized,llizing,llizability, llizable,llization,llizer,lline, llinity, llite, OF OR LIKE CLEAR QUARTZ ROCK

cshel, seashell

cu, cue

cuadrent, quadrant

cuagmayer, quagmire

cuaint, quaint

cuak, quake

cual, quail

cualify, qualify

cuality, quality

cuam, qualm

cuandry, quandary

cuantify, quantify

cuantity, quantity

cuarel, quarrel

cuarentin, quarantine

cuark, quake

cuasar, quasar

cuasi, quasi

cuazar, quasar

cubby,bies, SMALL, SNUG SPACE

cube,*,ed,bic,bicle,bicles, SHAPE WHERE ALL SIDES ARE THE SAME, MATHEMATICAL EXPRESSION (or see cubby)

cubek, cubic

cubekle, cubicle

cubic, OF A CUBE, MATHEMATICAL EXPRESSION

cubicle,*, AREA SECTIONED OFF, SMALL SPACE

cubird, cupboard

cuburd, cupboard

cubuse, caboose

cuc, cook

cuce, cook / kook(y) / cookie

cuci, kook(y) / cookie

cuckoo,*,oed,oing, BIRD, CRAZY

cucu, cuckoo

cucumber,*, VEGETABLE

cucune, cocoon

cud, WHAT A COW CHEWS (or see could/cue(d)/cute)

cudaver, cadaver

cuddle,*,ed,ling,er,ly, HOLD SNUGGLY

cudent, couldn't

cudet, cadet

cudev, could've

cudint, couldn't

cudle, cuddle

cudov, could've

cudv, could've

cue,*,ed,uing, SIGNAL/SIGN, SOMETHING WHICH DISTINGUISHES "prefixes: mis"

cueic, quake / quick

cueint, quaint

cueisar, quasar

cueizar, quasar

cuek, quake

cuel, quail

cuen, queen

cuepon, coupon

cuerc, quirk

cueshten, question

cuf, cuff

cufer, cover

cuferege, coverage

cuff,*,fed,fing, FIST BLOW, ON SLEEVES, ON CREDIT, RESTRAINT FOR WRISTS/ANKLES

cuger, cougar

cugole, cajole

cuil, quill

cuilt, quilt

cuin, queen

cuintuplet, quintuplet

cuir, queer

cuirk, quirk

cuisine, FINE COOKING

cuit, quit / quite

cuiver, quiver

cuk, cook / cock / kook

cuke, cook / cookie / kook

cuki, kook(y) / cookie

cukoon, cocoon

cuku, cuckoo

cukumber, cucumber

cul, cool

cul-de-sac,*, BULB SHAPE AT END OF STREET WITH EXIT/ENTRANCE BEING THE SAME

culagen, collision / collagen

culamity, calamity

culander, colander

culapse, collapse

culejet, collegiate

culekshun, collection

culekt, collect

culektur, collect(or)

culenary, culinary

culendjula, calendula

culer, color / cooler

culide, collide

culidescope, kaleidoscope

culigen, collision

culinary, ART OF FOOD PREPARATION

culindula, calendula

culishun, collision

culition, collision

cull,*,lled,lling,ller, TO SEPARATE OUT FROM OTHERS, CHOOSE, GLEAN (or see cool)

culmenate, culminate

culminate,*,ed,ting,tion, CLIMAX/ GREAT HEIGHT

culoge, collage

culokweul, colloquial

culone, cologne / colon

culoneul, colonial

culoquial, colloquial

culor, color

culostimy, colostomy

culosul, colossal

culprit,*, ONE WHO COMMITTED AN OFFENSE

culsher, culture

cult, GROUP OF PEOPLE WITH FIRM RELIGIOUS BELIEFS

cultavashen, cultivate(tion)

cultivashen, cultivate(tion)

cultivate,*,ed,ting,tion, DEVELOP/ FACILITATE GROWTH OF SOMETHING

cultsher, culture

culture,*,ral,rally, ESSENCE OF A GROUP/SOCIETY, NURTURING "prefixes: ac/bi/en/sub"

culvert,*, A DRAIN

cum, WITH/TOGETHER, A SECRETION (or see come)

cum laude, METHOD OF COMPARING GRADUATES AGAINST ONE ANOTHER
cumaletive, cumulative
cumand, command
cumander, commander
cumber,*,red,ring,rsome,rsomely, rsomeness, BULKY/AWKWARD TO HANDLE/MANAGE "prefixes: en"
cumberbun, cummerbund
cumbine, combine
cumbuschen, combustion
cumbustible, combustible
cumedean, comedian
cumemorate, commemorate
cumenduble, commendable
cumenserite, commensurate
cuments, commence
cumerbund, cummerbund
cumershal, commercial
cumewtable, commute(table)
cumfert, comfort
cumfertible, comfortable
cuminduble, commendable
cumishen, commission
cumishioner, commissioner
cumitee, committee
cumitment, commitment
cumlota, cum laude
cummerbund,*, BAND FOR WAIST WORN WITH FORMALS
cumnee, company
cumodity, commodity
cumpartment, compartment
cumpashun, compassion
cumpashunet, compassionate
cumpass, compass
cumpatuble, compatible
cumpedidor, competitor
cumpel, compel
cumpeny, company
cumperible, comparable
cumperison, comparison
cumpersome, cumber(some)
cumpete, compete
cumpetitor, competitor
cumpient, compliant
cumpile, compile
cumplane, complain
cumplasens, complacence / complaisance
cumplecshun, complexion
cumpleks, complex
cumpleshun, completion

cumplete, complete
cumplians, compliant(nce)
cumply, comply
cumponent, component
cumpose, compose
cumposier, composure
cumposit, composite
cumpownd, compound
cumpreshun, compression
cumpresor, compressor
cumpress, compress
cumpuder, computer
cumpulsery, compulsory
cumpulshun, compulsion
cumpulsuve, compulsive
cumpute, compute
cumputer, computer
cumulative,ely,eness, ACCUMULATION/ COLLECTS
cumunal, communal
cumunikable, communicable
cumunyon, communion
cumutable, commute(table)
cunal, canal
cunclude, conclude
cunclusive, conclusive
cunclution, conclusion
cuncoct, concoct
cundem, condemn
cundense, condense
cundinse, condense
cundishen, condition
cundition, condition
cundolense, condolence
cundone, condone
cundukt, conduct
cunekshen, connection
cunekt, connect
cunfecshin, confection
cunferm, confirm
cunfeshun, confession
cunfess, confess
cunfetion, confetion
cunfetty, confetti
cunfide, confide
cunfiguration, configuration
cunfine, confine
cunfinment, confinement
cunfirm, confirm
cunflict, conflict
cunform, conform
cunfront, confront
cunfugin, confusion
cunfuse, confuse

cunfusion, confusion
cunglomurete, conglomerate
cungradulashen, congratulation
cungratshulate, congratulate
cungruint, congruent
cungunctavitis, conjunction(ivitis)
cuning, cunning
cunjest, congest
cunjested, congest(ed)
cunjestion, congest(ion)
cunjunctivitis, conjunction(ivitis)
cunjunkshen, conjunction
cunklusev, conclusive
cunklusion, conclusion
cunkokt, concoct
cunkushun, concussion
cunning,gly,gness, CRAFTY, SKILLFUL
cunsederashen, considerate(tion)
cunseed, concede
cunseel, conceal
cunseet, conceit
cunseeve, conceive
cunseevuble, conceivable
cunsent, consent
cunsentric, concentric
cunsepshual, conceptual
cunsepshun, conception
cunseption, conception
cunservutive, conservative
cunsiduration, considerate(tion)
cunsinment, consignment
cunsise, concise
cunsist, consist
cunsistency, consistence(cy)
cunsiter, consider
cunsole, console
cunsoludate, consolidate
cunsoom, consume
cunsoul, console
cunspikuos, conspicuous
cunstrict, constrict
cunstrucshen, construction
cunstruct, construct
cunsult, consult
cunsurn, concern
cuntamunate, contaminate
cuntane, contain
cunteguis, contiguous
cuntemporary, contemporary
cuntemt, contempt
cuntend, contend
cuntent, content
cuntenuense, continuance
cuntest, contest

cuntiguis, contiguous
cuntrakshen, contraction
cuntree, country
cuntrery, contrary
cuntrishen, contrition
cuntrol, control
cunvay, convey
cunvekt, convict
cunvence, convince
cunvene, convene
cunvenshen, convention
cunvenyent, convenient
cunverdable, convertible
cunvergin, conversion
cunvershen, conversion
cunvert, convert
cunvertable, convertible
cunvulgin, convulsion
cunvulshen, convulsion
cuoda, quota
cuonatative, quantitative
cuorum, quorum
cuoshent, quotient
cuot, quote
cuota, quota
cup,*,pped,pping, VESSEL/SHAPE LIKE
SMALL BOWL (or see coop/coup)
cupal, couple
cupasity, capacity
cupboard,*, CABINET IN KITCHEN
cupcake,*, SMALL CAKE
cupe, coop
cupil, couple
cupitchulate, capitulate
cupler, coupler
cupon, coupon
cupul, couple
cupyuter, computer
curabirate, corroborate
curable,bility,eness,ly, CAN BE CURED
"prefixes: in"
curach, courage
curader, curator
curage, courage
cural, corral
curamic, ceramic
curant, currant / current
curator,*, APPOINTED BY COURT,
OVERSEER "prefixes: pro"
curb,*,bed,bing, FOR RESTRAINT, TO
PROTECT SOMETHING
curcle, circle
curcumsize, circumcise

curd,*, USED TO MAKE CHEESE (or see
cure(d))
curdesy, courtesy
curdeus, courteous
curdisy, courtesy
curdle,*,ed,ling, COAGULATING
cure,*,ed,ring,rative,rable, GET BACK
TO EQUILIBRIUM/HEALTHY STATE
(or see curry)
cureen, careen
cureer, career
curege, courage
curekt, correct
curekulum, curriculum
curency, currency
curensy, currency
curent, currant / current
cureosedy, curiosity
cureosity, curiosity
cures, cure(s) / care(s) / caress
curess, caress
cureur, courier
cureus, curious
cureusol, creosol
curf, curve
curfew,*, A TIME TO BE OFF THE
STREETS
curfu, curfew
curi, curry
curiculum, curriculum
curier, courier
curige, courage
curiosity,ties, ACT OF BEING CURIOUS
curious,sly,sness, INQUISITIVE,
QUESTIONING "prefixes: in"
curl,*,led,ling,ler,ly, A TWIST, LOOP,
RINGLET "prefixes: un"
curnol, colonel / kernel
curnul, colonel / kernel
curoberate, corroborate
curoborate, corroborate
curode, corrode
curogen, corrode(osion)
curogun, corrode(osion)
curojin, corrode(osion)
curosef, corrode(osive)
curoshen, corrode(osion)
curotion, corrode(osion)
curoty, karate
curowse, carouse
currant, FRUIT, BERRY (or see current)
currency,cies, MONEY
current,*,tly,tness, AS OF NOW IN TIME,
FLOWING, HOW WATER/AIR

CARRIES ITSELF (or see currant)
"prefixes: in/re/under"
curriculum,*,lar, LEARNING COURSES
curry,rried,rric, SPICE
cursash, corsage
curse,ed,sing,edness, SWEAR
cursive,ely, FLOWING HAND WRITING
curtail,lment, SHORTEN
curtain,*, TEMPORARY DIVIDER, CLOTH
PROTECTION
curtale, curtail
curten, curtain
curtesy, courtesy
curteus, courteous
curtsy,sies,sied,ying, FEMALE BOW TO
AUDIENCE
curtul, curdle
curuge, courage
curvature,*, PROFILE OF SHAPE
curve,*,ed,ving,vature, BEND WITH NO
ANGLES "prefixes: in/up/re"
curvechure, curvature
cury, curry
cus, cuss
cusen, cousin
cuset, cassette
cushen, cushion
cushion,*,ned,ning, PADDING TO
SOFTEN, FORM OF PROTECTION
cusin, cousin
cusp,*,pid,pidate,pidated,pidation,
INTERSECTION OF TWO ARCS/
CURVES/POINTS
cuspid,*,dal,dated, TOOTH "prefixes:
bi"
cuss,sses,ssed,ssing,ssedly,ssedness,
sser, TO CURSE
custard,*, DESSERTS
custedy, custody
custodian,*,al,nship, GUARDIAN
custody,dies,dial,dian, UNDER CARE OF
GUARDIAN, IMPRISONED
custom,*,mable,mize, TRADITION,
HABIT "prefixes: ac"
customary,ries,rily,riness, ROUTINE,
TRADITIONALLY
customer,*, CLIENT, PURCHASER
customize,*,ed,zing,zation, INDIVIDUAL
SHAPE/DESIGN FOR DESIRED
RESULTS
cut,*,tter,tting, CAUSE SEPARATION (or
see cud/cute) "prefixes: in/over/un/
under/upper"
cutastrufe, catastrophe

cute,er,test,tie, APPEALING TO THE EYE, SHREWD

cutev, could've

cuth, couth

cuticle,*, AROUND NAILS AND CELLS

cutlary, cutlery

cutlery, CUTTING TOOL, KNIVES

cutov, could've

cutukle, cuticle

cutv, could've

cuvenent, covenant

cuver, cover

cuvit, covet

cuvridge, coverage

cuwiat, quiet

cuzen, cousin

cuzn, cousin

cwuzene, cuisine

cyanide, ELEMENT FOR POISON/ EXTRACTING GOLD

cybernetics, STUDY OF COMMUNICATIONS SYSTEMS

cyborg,*, HUMAN MODIFIED INTO PARTIAL ROBOT

cycle,*,ed,ling, REPEATING INTERVALS, A COURSE OF EVENTS, REVOLUTIONS "prefixes: bi/en/re"

cyclist,*, THOSE WHO RIDE TWO-WHEELED BIKES

cyclone,*,nic,nal,nically, CONICAL SHAPED WIND STORM

cylanoid, solenoid

cylinder,*,dric,drical,dricality,drically, GEOMETRIC SHAPE WHICH MAY BE MOBILE OR STATIONERY

cymbal,*,list, MUSICAL INSTRUMENT (or see symbol)

cympathetic, sympathetic

cympathy, sympathy

cynic,*,cal,cally,calness,cism, DISBELIEVER

cynical,lly,lness, BEING A DISBELIEVER

cyst,tic, SACK OF FLUID "prefixes: en"

cyt, PREFIX INDICATING 'CELL' MOST OFTEN MODIFIES THE WORD

cyto, PREFIX INDICATING 'CELL' MOST OFTEN MODIFIES THE WORD

czar,*, RULER OF PEOPLE

da, day / they

dab,*,bbed,bbing,bber, BLOT/DIP/ BARELY TOUCH

dabate, debate

dabble,*,ed,ling,er, PARTICIPATE WITHOUT SERIOUS COMMITMENT

dabekable, despicable

dabelatate, debilitate

dabilutate, debilitate

dable, dabble

dabre, debris

dacend, descend / dissent / descent / decent

daciduous, deciduous

dacind, descend / dissent / descent / decent

daclare, declare

dacree, decree

dacrepit, decrepit

dacury, daiquiri

dad,*,ddy,ddies, TERM FOR 'FATHER' (or see that/date/they'd)

dada, data

dadu, data

dadukt, deduct

dadur, daughter

daduse, deduce

dae, day

daedy, deity

dafalt, default

dafeet, defeat

dafenative, definitive

dafensable, defensible

dafense, defense

dafeshansy, deficiency

daffy,ffily,ffiness, BEING SILLY

dafiants, defiance

dafide, divide

dafie, defy / daffy

dafiense, defiance

dafinative, definitive

dafindant, defendant

dafine, define

dafinse, defense

dafinsible, defensible

dafisable, divisible

dafishantsy, deficiency

dafishensy, deficiency

dafishent, deficient

dafisubilety, divisible(bility)

dafoleate, defoliate

daform, deform

dafraust, defrost

dafray, defray

dafrod, defraud

dafumation, defamation

dafunkt, defunct

dafur, defer

dafuze, diffuse

dafy, defy / daffy

dagavoo, dejavu

dager, dagger

dagger,*, SHARP INSTRUMENT

dagree, degree

dai, die / day / dye

daidy, deity

daily,lies, EVERY DAY (or see dally/dale)

dainty,tily,tiness, FRAGILE, DELICATE

daiquiri,*, MIXED RUM DRINK

dair, dare

dairy,ries, WHERE MILK IS

dairyar, derriere

daisy,sies, A FLOWER

daity, deity

dajavu, dejavu

dakary, daiquiri

daklare, declare

dakline, decline

dakorate, decorate(tion)

dakrate, decorate(tion)

dakree, decree

dakrepit, decrepit

dakury, daiquiri

dal, dale / dowel / doll / dole / they'll

dalar, dollar

dalay, delay

dale,*, VALLEY (or see daily/dalles/dell/ dolly)

daleburite, deliberate

dalectable, delectable

dalema, dilemma

dalenkwent, delinquent

dalenquent, delinquent

daler, dollar

dalereus, delirious

daleshus, delicious

dalete, delete

dalfan, dolphin

dali, dolly

daliberate, deliberate

dalima, dilemma

dalinquent, delinquent

dalishus, delicious

dalite, delight / daylight

daliver, deliver

dalles, SHALLOW RIVER ROCK BOTTOM WITH RAPIDS (or see dowel/doll)

dally,llies,llied,llying, TO DABBLE IN, NOT SERIOUS (or see dale/daily/ dolly)

daloot, dilute

dalugen, delusion / dilute(tion)

daluks, deluxe

dalushen, delusion / dilute(tion)

dalute, dilute
daluxe, deluxe
daly, daily / dally / dale
dam,*,mmed,mming, BARRIER
 AGAINST WATER (or see damn)
damage,*,ed,ging, TO HARM/ALTER
 NEGATIVELY
damand, demand
dameg, damage
damenish, diminish
dameno, domino
damenor, demeanor
damenshen, dimension
damented, demented
damention, dimension
damenyen, dominion
damestic, domestic
damig, damage
daminish, diminish
damino, domino
daminyun, dominion
damize, demise
damn,ned,ning,nable,nation,
 EXPRESSION OF FRUSTRATION (or
 see dam)
damolish, demolish
damonik, demon(ic)
damp,per,pest, MOIST "prefixes: un"
dampen,*,ned,ning,ner, TO MOISTEN
damper,*, CONTROLS FLOW
dampin, dampen
dampun, dampen
dampur, damper
damsel,*, YOUNG WOMAN
damsul, damsel
damug, damage
damzul, damsel
dan, then / than
danc, dank
dance,*,ed,cing,er, TO BODILY MOVE
 TO MUSIC
dancher, danger
dandreff, dandruff
dandruff, FLAKEY SKIN ON SCALP
danger,*,rous,rously,rousness, BEWARE
 OF IMMINENT HARM "prefixes: en"
dangle,*,er,ling,ly, TO SWING FREELY
dangul, dangle
danjur, danger
dank,kly,kness, UNPLEASANTLY DAMP
danominashun, denomination
danote, denote
danse, dance
dante, dainty

danty, dainty
daoderant, deoderant
daoderize, deodorize
daparsher, departure
dapart, depart
dapartment, department
daparture, departure
dapend, depend
dapikt, depict
dapind, depend
dapindant, dependant / dependent
dapindence, dependence
dapleshin, depletion
daplete, deplete
daploma, diploma
daplomacy, diplomacy
daplorable, deplorable
daplore, deplore
daport, deport
dapose, depose
daposit, deposit
dapresheate, depreciate
dapreshen, depression
dapress, depress
daprive, deprive
darbe, darby
darbies, HANDCUFFS
darby,bies, PLASTERER'S TOOL
darc, dark
dare,*,ed,ring,ringly,ringness, HAVE
 COURAGE TO CHALLENGE (or see
 dairy)
dareair, derriere
darear, derriere
darect, direct
darection, direction
darectory, directory
darekshun, direction
darektory, directory
darelik, derelict
darevutive, derivative
darier, derriere
darivadev, derivative
darivative, derivative
darive, derive
dark,*,ker,kest,ken,kened,kness,
 OPPOSITE OF LIGHT "prefixes:
 semi"
darling,*,gly,gness, SOMEONE
 ENDEARING/ BELOVED
darn, TO SEW, SHORT FOR "OH, TOO
 BAD..."
dart,*,ted,ting, OF SPORT, MOVE WITH
 QUICK SPEED

darulik, derelict
dary, dairy
das, day(s) / daze / that(s)
dasal, dazzle
dasbikable, despicable
dasbite, despite
dasblay, display
dasburse, disperse / disburse
dascrepshun, description
dasdrakt, distract
dasdruction, destruction
dasdrust, distrust
dase, daisy / daze
dasease, decease / disease
daseet, deceit
daseeve, deceive
dasegin, decision
dasel, dazzle
dasember, december
dasenagrate, disintegrate
dasend, descend / dissent / descent /
 decent
dasendent, descendant
dasenshen, dissension/ descension
dasent, dissent / descent / decent /
 descend
dasentugrate, disintegrate
daservise, disservice
dasesd, decease(d) / disease(d)
dasese, decease / disease
daset, deceit
dasetful, deceit(ful)
daseve, deceive
dash,hes,hed,hing, SMALL AMOUNT OF,
 QUICKLY IN SHORT TIME, TEXT TYPE
dasidewus, deciduous
dasifur, decipher
dasigen, decision
dasijen, decision
dasile, docile
dasimbur, december
dasinagrate, disintegrate
dasind, descend / dissent / descent /
 decent
dasinshen, dissension/ descension
dasinshent, dissent(ient)
dasint, dissent / descent / decent /
 descend
dasipher, decipher
dasiple, disciple
daskreptef, descriptive
daskripshen, description
daskwalefy, disqualify
dasmiss, dismiss

dasosheate, dissociate
daspare, despair
daspekable, despicable
daspense, dispense
daspensible, dispensable
dasperse, disperse / disburse
daspikable, despicable
daspite, despite
daspize, despise
dasplay, display
daspondent, despondent
daspose, dispose
daspute, dispute
dasrebutuble, disreputable
dasrobe, disrobe
dastardly,dliness, COWARDLY
dasteengwish, distinguish
dastengwesh, distinguish
dastenkt, distinct
dastill, distill
dastingwish, distinguish
dastirdly, dastardly
dastort, distort
dastract, distract
dastress, distress
dastroy, destroy
dasturb, disturb
dasturdly, dastardly
dasul, dazzle
dasy, daisy
dat, date / that / dot
data, FACTS, INFORMATION
date,*,ed,ting, TIME REFERENCE, A
    SOCIAL OUTING WITH ANOTHER, A
    FRUIT "prefixes: up"
datective, detective
datekt, detect
datektif, detective
datektor, detector
datenshin, detention
dater, daughter
daterant, deterrent
datereate, deteriorate
daterent, deterrent
datereorate, deteriorate
datergent, detergent
daterminent, determine(nt)
datont, detente
datu, data
daturgent, detergent
daturjent, detergent
daturmen, determine
daturmenashen, determination

daturmenint, determine(nt)
daubt, doubt
dauder, daughter
daug, dog
daughter,*, FEMALE BORN/LEGALLY
    ENDOWED TO MOTHER/FATHER
daul, dowel / doll
daule, dolly
daulfen, dolphin
daulur, dollar
daun, don't / daunt / don(nned) /
    dawn(ed) / down
daunt,*,ted,ting,ter,tingly,tless,tlessly,
    tlessness, MAKE SOMEONE FEEL
    DISCOURAGED/UNSURE (or see
    don't/don(nned)/dawn(ed))
    "prefixes: un"
daus, douse / dowse
dausil, docile
daut, doubt
dauter, daughter
dautful, doubt(ful)
dav, they've
davegen, division
davejin, division
davelop, develop
daversidy, diversity
daversudy, diversity
davert, divert
davesubility, divisible(bility)
davide, divide
davigen, division
davine, divine
davisable, divisible
davision, division
davize, device
davoid, devoid
davorse, divorce
davoshen, devotion
davout, devout
davurt, divert
davurzade, diversity
dawn,*,ned,ning, MORNING DAYBREAK
    (or see don/down)
dawrekt, direct
daws, douse / dowse
day,*, SUNRISE TO SUNRISE (or see
    daze)
dayede, deity
dayity, deity
dayjavue, dejavu
daylight, LIGHT IN THE DAY
daytont, detente

daze,ed, NOT OF CLEAR THINKING,
    CONFUSED (or see daisy/day(s))
dazeese, disease / daisy(s)
dazel, dazzle
dazzle,*,ed,ling, INFLUENCE BY
    UNUSUAL MEASURES
dcline, decline
ddukt, deduct
de, PREFIX INDICATING 'AWAY FROM/
    DOWN FROM/REVERSE/ NEGATIVE'
    MOST OFTEN MODIFIES THE WORD
    (or see the/thee/they)
deacon,*,ness,nry,nries, OFFICIAL OF A
    CHURCH "prefixes: sub"
deactivate,*,ed,ting,tion,tor, STOP
    ACTION, DISSOLVE
deactovate, deactivate
dead,dly,dlier,dliest,den,dens,dened,
    dening,dener, PAST TENSE FOR THE
    WORD 'DIE', NO LONGER ALIVE/
    FUNCTIONAL (or see deed/did)
    "prefixes: un"
deaden,*,ner,ning,ner, TO SEEM DEAD,
    NUMB (or see did(n't))
deadleist, dead(liest)
deaf,fen,fening,feningly,fness,fly, LOSS
    OF THE ABILITY TO HEAR
deakon, deacon
deaktevat, deactivate
deaktuvate, deactivate
deal,*,ler,ling,dealt, ARRANGEMENT
    BETWEEN PEOPLE, DO IN CARD
    GAME (or see dell/dill)
dealed, dealt
dealt, PAST TENSE FOR THE WORD
    "DEAL"
deam, deem
dean,*, HEAD OF FORMAL GROUP (or
    see den)
deanky, dinky
deap, deep
dear,rly,rness,rie, HEARTFELT (or see
    deer)
death,hless,hly, WHEN THE SPIRIT
    LEAVES THE BODY
debach, debauch
debasition, deposition
debate,*,ed,ting, ARGUE FACTS
debauch,hes,hed,hing,hment,hery,
    heries, CORRUPT, CHANGED FROM
    ORIGINAL DIRECTION
debauchury, debauch(ery)
debazishen, deposition
debelatate, debilitate

debelutat, debilitate

debenar, debonair

deber, deburr

debet, debit

debilitate,*,ed,ting,tion,tive, NOT UP TO PAR, WEAKEN

debinar, debonair

debir, deburr

debisition, deposition

debit,*,ted,ting, A DEBT OWING

debizeshen, deposition

debloma, diploma

deblomusy, diplomacy

debo, depot

deboch, debauch

debochury, debauch(ery)

debonair, CHARMING, LIKABLE, AIR OF CLASS

deboner, debonair

debosition, deposition

debotch, debauch

debozeshen, deposition

debozishen, deposition

debre, debris / deburr

debri, debris

debrief,*,fed,fing,fings, REPORT IN AFTER MISSION/EVENT

debris, GARBAGE, RUBBISH

debry, debris

debt,*,tor, IN THE STATE OF OWING TO ANOTHER

debth, depth

debtor, ONE WHO OWES ANOTHER (or see detour/deter)

debude, deputy

debunair, debonair

debunar, debonair

debunk,*,ked,king,ker, MAKE UNTRUE, PROVE FALSE

deburr,*,rred,rring, REMOVE BURRS/ ROUGH EDGES

debut,*,ted,ting, FIRST SHOWING TO THE PUBLIC (or see debit)

debutize, deputize

debuty, deputy

dec, PREFIX INDICATING "TEN" MOST OFTEN MODIFIES THE WORD (or see deck)

deca, PREFIX INDICATING "TEN" MOST OFTEN MODIFIES THE WORD (or see deck)

decade,*, TEN YEARS (or see decay(ed))

decadence,ncy, ON THE DECLINE/ DETERIORATE

decadent,tly, ON THE DECLINE/ DETERIORATE

decal,*, IMAGE OF PICTURE OR WORDS

decanter,*, VESSEL FOR STORAGE

decapitate,*,ed,ting,tion,tor, LOSS OF HEAD

decarate, decorate(tion)

decate, decade / decay(ed)

decay,*,yed,ying, DETERIORATE, CHANGE FROM ONE FORM TO ANOTHER

decease,*,ed, TO PASS AWAY, DEPART FROM THIS PHYSICAL REALITY (or see disease) "prefixes: pre"

decedent,*, PAST TENSE FOR THE WORD 'DECEASED' (or see decadent)

deceit,tful,tfully,tfulness, TO PURPOSELY MISLEAD

deceive,*,ed,ving,vingly,vable,vably, vableness,vability, TO PURPOSELY MISLEAD "prefixes: un"

decelerate,*,ed,ting,tion,tor, TO DECREASE SPEED

december, A MONTH OF THE YEAR (ENGLISH)

decency,cies, WHAT'S PROPER

decend, descend / decent

decension, descension

decent,tly,tness, RESPECTABLE (or see descent/ dissent)

decentralize,*,ed,zing,zation, TAKE FROM A FEW AND GIVE TO MANY, TO SHARE AROUND

deception,*,ive,ively,iveness, THE ACT OF PURPOSELY MISLEADING "prefixes: un"

deceptive,ely,eness, THE ACT OF PURPOSELY MISLEADING

decerate, decorate

dech, ditch

dechevled, dishevel(ed)

dechonary, dictionary

deci, PREFIX INDICATING "TENTH" MOST OFTEN MODIFIES THE WORD

decibel,*, MEASUREMENT OF SOUND WAVES

decide,*,ed,ding,edly,er,ision, FORM A CONCLUSION, PICK AN OPTION "prefixes: un"

deciduous, SHEDS ITS LEAVES IN THE FALL "prefixes: in"

decifur, decipher

decimal,*,lize,lized,lizing, A POINT TO SEPARATE NUMBERS

decimate,*,ed,ting, TO DESTROY, KILL ONE IN TEN

decimber, december

decind, descend / dissent / descent / decent

decint, descent / decent / dissent / descend

decintralize, decentralize

decipher,*,red,ring,rable,rer,rment, TO DECODE "prefixes: in"

decision,*,ive,ively,iveness, FINAL CONCLUSION "prefixes: in"

deck,*,ked,king, OUTDOOR FLOOR

deckorus, decorous

deckrotive, decorative

deckstarety, dexterity

decksterity, dexterity

deckstrus, dexterous

declaration,*,ive,tory, ANNOUNCEMENT, MAKE A STATEMENT

declare,*,ed,ring,rable,edly,ration, rations,rative,rator,ratory, ratorily, TO STATE/ANNOUNCE "prefixes: un"

decleration, declaration

decline,*,ed,ning,nation, DOWNWARD BEND/SLOPE

decode,*,ed,ding,dable,er, DECAY, TO TRANSFORM TO BASIC ELEMENTS

decompose,*,ed,sing,sition, DECAY, TO TRANSFORM TO BASIC ELEMENTS

decon, deacon

decorashun, decoration

decorate,*,ed,ting,tor,tion,tive, ADORN, ORNAMENTAL "prefixes: re"

decoration, ADORNMENT, ORNAMENTAL

decorative,ely,eness, ADORNMENT, ORNAMENTAL

decorous,sly,sness, COMPATIBLE/ APPROPRIATE, DIGNIFIED "prefixes: in"

decorum, COMPATIBLE/APPROPRIATE, MATCHES "prefixes: in"

decoy,*, A FAKE TO FOOL OR MISLEAD

decradive, decorative

decrative, decorative

decrease,*,ed,sing, BECOME LESS THAN THE ORIGINAL "prefixes: non"

decree,*,eed,eeing,eeable, JUDICIAL/ AUTHORITATIVE DECISION

decrepit,tly,tude,tate,tated,tating,
tation,tness, WEAK/WORN/
WASTED

decrese, decrease

decritive, decorative

decrous, decorous

decrutive, decorative

decsterity, dexterity

decudens, decadence

decudent, decedent / decadent

decumpose, decompose

decurate, decorate(tion)

ded, dead / deed / did

dedakashun, dedication

dedakate, dedicate

dedar, debtor

deden, didn't / den / deaden

dedicate,*,ed,ting,tion,tory,tive,
APPROPRIATE, DEVOTE

dedication,*,nal, APPROPRIATE,
DEVOTE

dedin, deaden

dedinate, detonate

dedir, debtor

dedle, dead(ly)

dedleist, dead(liest)

dedleur, dead(lier)

dedly, dead(ly)

dedlyest, dead(liest)

dednate, detonate

dedo, ditto

dedonate, detonate

dedor, debtor

dedriment, detriment

dedrument, detriment

deduce,*,ed,cing, DRAW CONCLUSION
FROM EVIDENCE

deduct,*,ted,ting,tible,tibilty,tion,tive,
SUBTRACT, TAKE AWAY "prefixes:
non"

dedukashun, dedication

dedukate, dedicate

dedun, deaden

deed,*,ded, AN ACT/CONTRACT/
AGREEMENT (or see dead)
"prefixes: mis"

deel, deal

deeled, dealt

deem,*,med, JUDGED/BELIEVED/
THOUGHT

deen, dean / den

deenge, dinghy / dingy

deenky, dinky

deep,per,pest,ply,pen,penly,pened,
pness, BEYOND THE SURFACE,
GREAT IN DIMENSION

deer, ANIMAL (or see dear)

def, deaf / thief

deface,*,ed,cing,eable,ement,er, ALTER
THE FACE/FRONT OF

defakate, defecate

defalt, default

defamation,tory, INTENT TO INJURE
ANOTHER'S CHARACTER

defame,*,ed,ming,mation,matory,er,
INTENT TO INJURE ANOTHER'S
CHARACTER

defanishun, definition

defanit, definite

defasit, deficit

defastate, devastate

default,*,ted,ting,ter, LEGALLY FAILING
TO ANSWER, FAIL AN AGREEMENT

defeat,*,ted,ting,tism,tist, OVERCOME,
OVERTHROW

defecate,*,ed,ting,tion,tor, CLEAR THE
BOWELS

defechant, deficient

defect,*,ted,ting,tion,tor,tive, NOT
USEFUL AS INTENDED, MARRED
"prefixes: in"

defective,ely,eness, NOT USEFUL AS
INTENDED

defector,*, ABANDON NATIVE STATE/
COUNTRY

defecult, difficult

defekate, defecate

defekt, defect

defektive, defective

defektor, defector

defemation, defamation

defend,*,ded,ding, PROTECT

defendant,*, ONE WHO DEFENDS/
PROTECTS AGAINST

defenet, definite

defenetly, definite(ly)

defenishun, definition

defense,*,sive,eless,elessly,elessness,
PROTECT AGAINST ATTACK

defensible,eness,bility,ly, ABLE TO
DEFEND "prefixes: in"

defenutef, definitive

defer,*,rred,rring,rrable,rence,rent,rrer,
rential,rral,rment, DELAY, POST-
PONE, YIELD TO ANOTHER (or see
differ)

deferens, difference

deferensheate, differentiate

deferent, different

deferentiate, differentiate

defesit, deficit

defews, diffuse

defi, defy

defiance,nt,ntly, CHALLENGE, RESIST,
OPPOSE

deficate, defecate

deficiency,cies, SHORT OF
EXPECTATIONS/NEEDS, NOT
ENOUGH

deficient,tly,ncy, LESS THAN EXPECTED/
NEEDED

deficit,*, OWE MORE THAN WHAT'S
AVAILABLE

deficult, difficult

defide, divide

defients, defiance

defikate, defecate

defimation, defamation

defind, defend

defindant, defendant

define,*,ed,ning, SET BOUNDARIES/
RULES/BORDERS "prefixes: in/re"

defineshun, definition

definet, definite

definetion, definition

definetly, definite(ly)

definite,ely,eness,tive, FOR SURE,
ABSOLUTELY

definition,*,nal, STATEMENT
DESCRIBING BOUNDARIES/RULES/
BORDERS

definitive,ely,eness, FOR CERTAIN,
FINAL

definute, definite

defir, defer / differ

defishant, deficient

defishantsy, deficiency

defisit, deficit

defistate, devastate

deflashun, deflate(tion)

deflate,*,ed,ting,tion,tionary,tionist,
REMOVE VOLUME/FULLNESS,
REDUCE

deflect,*,ted,ting,tive,tor,tion,
RICHOCHET OFF/ALTER COURSE/
DIRECTION OF SOMETHING

defoleate, defoliate

defoliate,*,ed,ting,tion,tor, LOSS OF
LEAVES FROM PLANT

deforestation,*, REMOVE TREES FROM
FOREST

deforistashun, deforestation

deform,*,med,ming,mation,medly, medness,mity, OF UNUSUAL/ ABNORMAL FORM

deforustashin, deforestation

defostate, devastate

defraud,*,ded,ding,der,dation,dment, ROB OF RIGHTS/PROPERTY

defraust, defrost

defray,*,yed,ying,yer,yal,yment,yable, MONETARY COMPENSATION/ ARRANGEMENT

defrense, difference

defrent, different

defrint, different

defrod, defraud

defrost,*,ted,ting,ter, REMOVE FROST/ ICE

defruns, difference

defukate, defecate

defumashun, defamation

defunct, NO LONGER IN USE

defuneshun, definition

defunetle, definite(ly)

defunishun, definition

defunit, definite

defur, defer / differ

defurinse, difference

defurns, difference

defuse, diffuse

defusit, deficit

defustate, devastate

defuze, diffuse

defy,fies,fied,ying,fier, TO RESIST/DARE/ CHALLENGE

deg, dig

degekt, deject

degenerate,*,ed,ting,tive,acy,ely,eness, BECOME LESS, OPPOSITE OF GETTING BETTER

deginerate, degenerate

degit, digit

degradashen, degrade(dation)

degrade,*,ed,ding,dable,dability,dation, LOWER/BREAK DOWN IN RANK/ STANDARDS/GRADE "prefixes: bio"

degree,*, MEASUREMENT OF STANDARD/ANGLES, SUM OF

degression,ive, LOWERING, DECREASING (or see digress(ion))

degrudashen, degrade(dation)

dehidrate, dehydrate

dehumanize,*,ed,zing,zation, REMOVE HEALTHY HUMAN CHARACTERISTICS

dehumidify,fies,fied,fying,fier,fication, REMOVE MOISTURE FROM THE AIR

dehydrate,*,ed,ting,tion,tor, REMOVE MOISTURE FROM

deity,ties, SUPREME BEING

dejavu, TWO WORDS (deja vu), SEEN BEFORE

deject,*,ted,ting,tedly,tedness,tion, DISPIRIT, DISCOURAGE

dejenurate, degenerate

dejinurate, degenerate

dejit, digit

dek, deck

deka, PREFIX INDICATING "TEN" MOST OFTEN MODIFIES THE WORD (or see deck)

dekad, decay(ed) / decade

dekadins, decadence

dekadint, decedent / decadent

dekal, decal

dekantur, decanter

dekaputate, decapitate

dekay, decay

deken, deacon

dekerashun, decoration

dekerate, decorate

dekin, deacon

deklare, declare

dekleration, declaration

dekline, decline

deklurashun, declaration

dekodable, decode(dable)

dekode, decode

dekompose, decompose

dekon, deacon

dekorashun, decoration

dekorate, decorate(tion) / decorate

dekorative, decorative

dekorus, decorous

dekoy, decoy

dekradashen, degrade(dation)

dekratev, decorate(tion) / decorative

dekrative, decorative

dekree, decree

dekrepit, decrepit

dekrese, decrease

dekrous, decorous

dekrudev, decorative

dekrus, decorous

dekrutive, decorative

deksderady, dexterity

deksdrus, dexterous

dekshunare, dictionary

deksterudy, dexterity

dekstrus, dexterous

dektion, diction

dekudens, decadence

dekudent, decedent / decadent

dekumpose, decompose

dekun, deacon

dekurashun, decoration

dekurater, decorate(tor)

del, deal / dell / dill

delacatesen, delicatessen

delacit, delicate

delacusy, delicacy

delagation, delegation

delakatesen, delicatessen

delaket, delicate

delay,*,yed,ying,yer, DETAIN, HINDER, PROLONG

deld, dealt

dele, deli

deleburant, deliberate

delecacy, delicacy

delectable,*,eness,bility,ly, HIGHLY PLEASURABLE

deled, dealt

delegate,*,ed,ting,tion,tor,ee,able, APPOINT AS REPRESENTATIVE, ENTRUST "prefixes: non"

delegation,*, TO DELEGATE, ASSEMBLY OF PEOPLE "prefixes: non"

delenkwent, delinquent

delenquent, delinquent

deler, deal(er)

delereus, delirious

delete,*,ed,ting,tion, REMOVE/UNDO "prefixes: un"

deleverens, deliverance

delf, delve

deli,*, A DELICATESSEN, STORE WITH VARIETY OF PREPARED FOODS/ MEATS

deliberate,*,ed,ting,eness,ely,tion, PURPOSEFUL, CAREFULLY THOUGHT OUT "prefixes: un"

deliburate, deliberate

delicacy,cies, OF REFINED QUALITY IN TASTE "prefixes: in"

delicate,*,ely,eness, FRAGILE, FINE QUALITY, CHOICE "prefixes: in"

delicatessen,*, STORE WITH VARIETY OF PREPARED FOODS/MEATS

delicious,sly,sness, EXQUISITE TASTE, HAPPY TO TASTE BUDS

deligation, delegation

delight,*,ted,ting,tful,tedly,tfully, tfulness, PROVIDE GREAT SATISFACTION (or see daylight)

delikatesen, delicatessen

deliket, delicate

delinquent,tly,ncy,ncies, FAILURE TO SATISFY AGREEMENT ON TIME

deliquet, delicate

delir, deal(er)

delirious,sly,sness, IRRATIONAL BEHAVIOR

delishus, delicious

delite, delight / daylight

deliver,*,red,ring,ry,rable,rability,rer, rance, TO SEND/PRESENT ITEMS SUCH AS GOODS/THOUGHTS/ ARTICLES

deliverance,*, TO BE RESCUED, AN ANNOUNCEMENT

dell, A HOLLOW/VALLEY (or see deal/ dill)

deloot, dilute

delor, deal(er)

delt, dealt

delugashun, delegation

delugen, delusion / dilute(tion)

delukatesen, delicatessen

delukit, delicate

deluks, deluxe

delukusy, delicacy

delur, deal(er)

delusion,nal, PAST TENSE FOR THE WORD "DELUDE", BEING MISLED, HAVING FALSE IMPRESSION

delute, dilute

deluxe, FINEST QUALITY

delve,*,ed,ving, TO BURY/DIG INTO

dem, deem / dim / them / they

demacrasy, democracy

demacrat, democrat

demagogue,*,guery,gic,gical, LEADER WHO USES POPULAR EMOTIONS

demagrafy, demography

demakratic, democratic

demalishun, demolition

demand,*,ded,ding, COMMAND/INSIST ON FULFILLMENT OF DESIRES "prefixes: un"

demarcation,*, SETTING BOUNDARIES, ESTABLISHING GUIDELINES

demarkashun, demarcation

demble, dimple

demean,*,ned,ning, HUMILIATE

demeanor, CONCERNING BEHAVIOR/ CONDUCT "prefixes: mis"

demenor, demeanor

demented, CRAZY, UNPOPULAR BEHAVIOR/THOUGHTS

demer, dimmer

demestek, domestic

demi, PREFIX INDICATING "HALF/ PARTLY" MOST OFTEN MODIFIES THE WORD

demigog, demagogue

demikrat, democrat

demilaturise, demilitarize

demilitarize,*,ed,zing,zation, REMOVE MILITARY

demiluturise, demilitarize

demin, demon

deminstrate, demonstrate

demir, dimmer

demise,ed,sing, TRANSFER, PASSED FROM THIS REALITY

demobilize,*,ed,zing,zation, DISARM, DISBAND

democracy,cies, BY AND FOR ALL PEOPLE

democrat,*, ONE IN PARTY WHO WORKS FOR SOCIAL EQUALITY FOR ALL

democratic,ize,ization, PROCESS OF WORKING TOWARDS SOCIAL EQUALITY FOR ALL "prefixes: un"

demography,hic,hical,hically, STATISTICS/RECORDS OF PUBLIC VITAL INFORMATION

demokrasy, democracy

demokrat, democrat

demokratic, democratic

demokruse, democracy

demolish,hes,hed,hing,ition, DESTROY, RUIN

demolition,*,nist, ACT OF DESTROYING/ RUINING

demon,*,nic,niac,niacal,nically,nization, nize,nizes,nized,nizing, nization, nism, MAKE OR APPEAR EVIL

demonek, demon(ic)

demonstrate,*,ed,ting,tion,tive, HOW TO, EXPLAIN CLEARLY/ DELIBERATELY "prefixes: in/un"

demple, dimple

demugog, demagogue

demuleshin, demolition

demun, demon

demunstrashen, demonstrate(tion)

demunstrate, demonstrate

demur, dimmer

den,*, CONCEALED HIDEOUT,COZY/ TUCKED AWAY PLACE (or see then)

denacher, denature

denaturalize,es,ed,zing,zation, REMOVE CITIZENSHIP OR NATURE OF

denature,*,ed,ring,rant,ration, ROB OF NATURAL COMPOSURE

dencher, denture

dendr, PREFIX INDICATING "TREE" MOST OFTEN MODIFIES THE WORD

dendri, PREFIX INDICATING "TREE" MOST OFTEN MODIFIES THE WORD

dendrite,*, PATHWAYS OF NEURONS CARRYING IMPULSES IN THE BRAIN

deng, ding

denge, dingy / dinghy

dengle, dangle

deni, deny

deniable,lity,ly, REFUSE AS TRUTH, DISAVOW

denial,*, REFUSE, DENY

denil, denial

denim,*, HEAVY COTTON FABRIC

denir, dinner

deniul, denial

denje, dingy

denky, dinky

denomenator, denominator

denomination,*,nal,nally,nalism,ive,tor, SPECIES OF THE WHOLE, SEPARATE BUT SAME

denominator,*, OF FRACTIONS

denote,*,ed,ting,tive,table,tation,tive, tative, DESIGNATED, SYMBOLIZES

dense,er,est,ely,eness,sity, THICK/ COMPACT, CLOSE TOGETHER

density,ties, DEGREE OF MASS/ CONCENTRATION

dent,*, AN IMPRESSION OR HOLLOW, PREFIX INDICATING "TOOTH" MOST OFTEN MODIFIES THE WORD (or see didn't)

dental,*, OF TEETH

denti, PREFIX INDICATING "TOOTH" MOST OFTEN MODIFIES THE WORD

dentist,*,try, DOCTOR FOR TEETH

denture,*,rist, ARTICIFIAL TEETH

denum, denim

denur, dinner

deny,nies,nied,ying,nial, NOT ADMIT, WON'T CLAIM "prefixes: un"

deoderant, deodorant

deoderint, deodorant

deoderize, deodorize

deodorant, HIDES ODOR/SMELLS

deodorize,*,ed,zing,zation,er, REMOVE ODOR/SMELL

deoksidize, deoxidize

deoksudize, deoxidize

deoxidize,*,ed,zing, REMOVE OXYGEN

dep, deep / dip

deparcher, depart(ure)

deparjur, depart(ure)

deparsher, depart(ure)

depart,*,ted,ting,ture, GO AWAY FROM

departer, depart(ure)

department,*,tal,talize,talizes,talized, talizing, SECTIONS OF THE WHOLE, A SUBSET

departure,*, TO GO AWAY FROM, LEAVE

depazeshen, deposition

depazishen, deposition

depend,*,ded,ding,dable,dably,dability, dant,dent,dance, RELY ON "prefixes: in/un"

dependant,*, RELATIONSHIP TO OTHER THINGS (or see dependent) "prefixes: in"

dependence,cy,cies, TO NEED/RELY UPON "prefixes: in"

dependent,*,tly,nce, SUPPORTED BY OTHERS "prefixes: in"

deper, dipper

depewtise, deputize

depict,*,ted,ting,tion, SHAPE/FORM/ CREATE IMAGE

depir, dipper

deplete,*,ed,ting,tive,table,tability,tion, USE TO THE END, RUNNING OUT OF

depletion, THE ACT OF RUNNING OUT OF

deploma, diploma

deplomacy, diplomacy

deplomat, diplomat

deplorable,ly,bility,eness, LAMENT

deplore,*,ed,ring,ringly,rable, LAMENT

deploy,*,yed,ying,yable,yer,yment, PREPARE TO BE USED/MAKE USE OF "prefixes: re"

depo, depot

depoortashen, deportation

depor, deep(er)

deporcher, depart(ure)

deport,*,ted,ting,tment,tation,tee,table, BE EXPELLED, SENT FROM COUNTRY

deportation, ACT OF SENDING FROM THE COUNTRY

deportee,*, ONE WHO WAS DEPORTED FROM COUNTRY

depose,*,ed,sing,sal,er,sable,sition, WRITE OR SPEAK UNDER OATH

deposit,*,ted,ting,tor,tory,tories, PLACE SOMETHING OF VALUE INTO SAFEKEEPING "prefixes: non"

deposition,*, STATEMENT UNDER OATH

depot,*, LOADING/UNLOADING STATION FOR TRANSPORT

depravashen, deprivation

depravation, deprivation

depreciate,*,ed,ting,able,tion,tive, tingly, ESTIMATE OF LOWER VALUE

depresheate, depreciate

depreshen, depression

depresion, depression

depress,sses,ssed,ssing,ssion, LOWER IN ELEVATION, LOW IN HOPE/FAITH

depression,*, A LOW POINT

deprivation, LACK OF ACCESS TO

deprive,*,ed,ving,vable,val,vation,er, PREVENT FROM HAVING ACCESS TO

depruvashen, deprivation

depth,*, A MEASURE DOWNWARDS OR INTO

depude, deputy

depudize, deputize

depur, dipper

depusishen, deposition

deputize,*,ed,zing, APPOINT AS DEPUTY

deputy,ties,tize,tizes,tized,tizing, AGENT OF THE LAW

depuzishen, deposition

der, dear / deer / dare / there / they're

derable, durable

deracenate, deracinate

deracinate,*,ed,ting,tion, UPROOT, REMOVE FROM NATIVE LAND/ CULTURE/ENVIRONMENT

deralik, derelict

derasenate, deracinate

derashen, duration

derasinate, deracinate

deration, duration

derdee, dirty

dere, dairy

derear, derriere

derekshen, direction

derektury, directory

derelict,*,tion, SOMEONE/ SOMETHING LEFT WITHOUT A GUIDE

deress, duress

derevative, derivative

derfor, therefore / therefor

deri, dairy

derible, durable

deric, derrick

derier, derriere

derik, derrick

derilect, derelict

dering, during / dare(ring)

derivative,*,ely,ion,ional, ROOT/ ORIGIN OF

derive,*,ed,ving,vable,vative,vatively, vation,vational, FROM THE ORIGINAL, DESCENDED FROM

derma, PREFIX INDICATING "SKIN" MOST OFTEN MODIFIES THE WORD

dermal,atitis,mis, CONCERNS THE SKIN "prefixes: endo/intra/sub"

dermat, PREFIX INDICATING "SKIN" MOST OFTEN MODIFIES THE WORD

dermato, PREFIX INDICATING "SKIN" MOST OFTEN MODIFIES THE WORD

dermes, dermal(mis)

dermititus, dermal(atitis)

dermle, dermal

dermotidus, dermal(atitis)

dermul, dermal

dermus, dermal(mis)

dermutidis, dermal(atitis)

derrick,*, TOWERLIKE EQUIPMENT WITH A CENTRAL POST

derriere,*, REAR END, GLUTEUS MAXIMUS MUSCLES

dert, dirt

derty, dirty

deruble, durable

derulik, derelict

dery, dairy

des, this / these / ditch

desabelity, disability

desable, disable

desacord, disaccord

desacrate, desecrate

desadisfacshen, dissatisfy(faction)

desadvantage, disadvantage

desafect, disaffect

desagre, disagree

desakord, disaccord
desalinate,*,ed,ting,tion,tor,nize,nizes,
    nized,nizing,nization, REMOVE SALT
    FROM
desalow, disallow
desalugen, disillusion
desalunate, desalinate
desapashen, dissipate(tion)
desapate, dissipate
desaplen, discipline
desapoint, disappoint
desaprove, disapprove
desaray, disarray
desarm, disarm
desarmament, disarmament
desaster, disaster
desatisfaction, dissatisfy(faction)
desavantage, disadvantage
desbaleef, disbelief / disbelieve
desband, disband
desbar, disbar / despair
desbaret, desperate
desbatch, dispatch
desbekable, despicable
desberit, desperate
desbicable, despicable
desbikable, despicable
desbiret, desperate
desbite, despite
desblay, display
desbondent, despondent
desboret, desperate
desbot, despot
desbozul, disposal
desbulef, disbelief / disbelieve
desburet, desperate
desburse, disperse / disburse
desbute, dispute
desbuzishun, disposition
desc, desk / disk / disc
descard, discard
descend,*,ded,ding,dible,dable,nt,nsion,
    STEP DOWN FROM, DOWNWARD
    (or see descent/decent) "prefixes:
    con/un"
descendant,*,dent, PREVIOUS/PRIOR
    TO THE CURRENT GENERATION, IN
    RELATION TO
descension,nal, GO DOWN/INTO, SINK/
    FALL (or see dissension)
descent,*,nsion, PAST TENSE FOR THE
    WORD "DESCEND", A STEP DOWN
    (or see decent/descend)
descerech, discourage

descharge, discharge
desclose, disclose
descontenue, discontinue
descord, discord
descors, discourse
descotek, discotheque
descover, discover
descredit, discredit
descremenate, discriminate
descrepensy, discrepancy
descrete, discreet / discrete
descretion, discretion
describe,*,ed,bing,bable,er,iptively,
    iptiveness,iptivist,iptivism, EXPLAIN
    DETAILS OF SOMETHING
descripshen, description
description,*,ive, PROVIDE DETAILS,
    EXPLAIN
descriptive,*,ely,eness,vist,vism,
    PROVIDE DETAILS, EXPLAIN
descumfert, discomfort
descurech, discourage
descushen, discussion
descust, disgust
descuver, discover
desdanation, destination
desdane, disdain
desdany, destiny
desdaste, distaste
desdent, distant
desdeny, destiny
desdination, destination
desdinduble, distend(sible)
desdindubleshen, distend(nsion)
desdindubletion, distend(nsion)
desdint, distant
desdiny, destiny
desditute, destitute
desdort, distort
desdrabute, distribute
desdrakt, distract
desdrot, distraught
desdruckshen, destruction
desdruktion, destruction
desdrust, distrust
desdunashun, destination
desduny, destiny
desdurb, disturb
desdutute, destitute
desease, disease
deseble, decibel
desecragate, desegregate
desecragation, desegregate(tion)

desecrate,*,ed,ting,er,tor,tion, TO
    TREAT WHAT'S SACRED TO OTHERS
    AS UNSACRED
desecrogate, desegregate
desecrogation, desegregate(tion)
desee, dizzy
deseese, decease / disease
deseet, deceit
desefect, disaffect
desegon, decision
desegregate,*,ed,ting,tion,tionist,
    UNDO RACIAL SEGREGATION
desegrigate, desegregate
desegrugate, desegregate
deselarate, decelerate
deselurate, decelerate
desemate, decimate
desember, december
desemul, decimal
desencion, descension
desend, descend / descent / dissent /
    decent
desendent, descendant
desenherit, disinherit
desensee, decency
desent, decent / descent
desenter, dissent(er)
desentient, dissent(ient)
desentralise, decentralize
desepshun, deception
deseption, deception
deseptive, deceptive
desern, discern
desert,*,ted,ting,ter,tification,tion,
    LAND LACKING LUSH VEGETATION,
    TO LEAVE WITHOUT PERMISSION
    (or see dessert) "prefixes: non/
    semi/un"
deserter,*, SOMEONE WHO LEAVES/
    ABANDONS WITHOUT PERMISSION
deserve,*,ed,ving,edly,er, REWARD/
    PUNISHMENT FOR ACT/THOUGHT/
    DEED "prefixes: un"
deservise, disservice
desesd, decease(d) / disease(d)
deset, deceit
desetful, deceit(ful)
deseve, deceive
desfegure, disfigure
desfigure, disfigure
desfunction, dysfunction
desfunkshen, dysfunction
desgard, discard
desgarge, discharge

desgise, disguise
desgoint, disjoint
desgrase, disgrace
desgrechun, discretion
desgretion, discretion
desgruntle, disgruntle
desgruntled, disgruntle(d)
desgurag, discourage
desgus, discus / discuss
desgust, disgust / discuss(ed)
desguys, disguise
desh, dish
desharden, dishearten
desharten, dishearten
deshevel, dishevel
desheveld, dishevel(ed)
deshonest, dishonest
deshonor, dishonor
deshonorable, dishonorable
desibal, decibel
desible, decibel
desicrate, desecrate
desid, decide
desidewus, deciduous
desifer, decipher
design,*,ned,ning,nable,nedly,ner,
    CREATION OF A MODEL, OUTLINE/
    PLAN FOR SOMETHING "prefixes:
    re/un"
designate,*,ed,ting,tion,tive,tory,tor,
    TO ASSIGN/APPOINT "prefixes: re"
designer,*, ONE WHO CREATES
    DESIGNS
desijen, decision
desijues, deciduous
desil, diesel
desilat, desolate
desimal, decimal
desimanate, disseminate
desimate, decimate
desimbark, disembark
desimber, december
desincy, decency
desind, descend
desine, design
desiner, designer
desinfect, disinfect
desingage, disengage
desinsee, decency
desinshen, dissension / descension
desint, decent / descent
desintary, dysentery
desintegrate, disintegrate
desinter, dissent(er) / dissent

desintient, dissent(ient)
desintion, dissension / descension
desintralise, decentralize
desinugrate, disintegrate
desipher, decipher
desipul, disciple
desirable,*,bility,eness,ly, LIKE TO HAVE
desire,*,ed,ring,rous,rously,rousness,
    rable,rability,rableness,rably, A
    WISH/ WANT/COMPULSION FOR
    "prefixes: un"
desirtashen, dissertation
desiruble, desirable
desis, disease / decease
desisd, disease(d) / decease(d)
desisev, decision(ive)
desjoint, disjoint
desk,*, FURNITURE (or see disc/disk)
deskard, discard
deskerdeus, discourteous
deskerege, discourage
desklame, disclaim
deskonekt, disconnect
deskontenue, discontinue
deskord, discord
deskordeus, discourteous
deskors, discourse
deskover, discover
deskredit, discredit
deskremenate, discriminate
deskrepdef, descriptive
deskrepincy, discrepancy
deskribe, describe
deskripshen, description
deskunekt, disconnect
deskurdeus, discourteous
deskurege, discourage
deskus, discus / discuss
deskushun, discussion
deskust, disgust / discuss(ed)
deskuver, discover
deskwalefy, disqualify
desl, diesel
desleksea, dyslexia
deslexia, dyslexia
deslocate, dislocate
desloch, dislodge
deslodge, dislodge
deslog, dislodge
deslokate, dislocate
desmantul, dismantle
desmanul, dismantle
desmay, dismay
desmember, dismember

desmimbur, dismember
desmiss, dismiss
desmount, dismount
desmownt, dismount
desmul, dismal
desobay, disobey
desobedeanse, disobedience
desocheate, dissociate
desociate, dissociate
desolate,ed,ely,eness,tion,er,
    DESERTED, EMPTY OF
desolenate, desalinate
desolushen, dissolute(tion)
desolute, dissolute
desolve, dissolve
deson, disown
desonent, dissonant
desoner, dishonor
desonerible, dishonorable
desonest, dishonest
desonins, dissonant(nce)
desont, decent / descent
desorder, disorder
desorderly, disorderly
desoreint, disorient
desosheate, dissociate
desown, disown
despair,*,red,ring,ringly, DEEPLY
    TROUBLED, HOPELESS
desparashin, desperation
despare, despair
desparedy, disparity
despatch, dispatch
despense, dispense
despensible, dispensable
desperashun, desperation
desperate,ely,eness,ado,tion, OF
    FEELING FRANTIC, GIVEN TO
    HOPELESSNESS
desperation, BEYOND REGARD FOR
    HOPE
desperit, desperate
desperity, disparity
desperse, disperse / disburse
despicable,eness,ly,bility, BEING
    WORTHLESS/ NO GOOD
despikable, despicable
despinse, dispense
despinsuble, dispensable
despise,*,ed,sing,sable,sal,sableness,
    edness,ement,er, VERY LOW
    OPINION OF, STRONG DISLIKE
    "prefixes: un"
despit, despite

despite,ed,ting,eful,efully,eous,eously,
    IN SPITE OF, INSULT, MALICE, ILL
    INTENT
desplas, displace
desplased, displace(d)
desplay, display
desplejur, displease(sure)
desplesed, displease(d)
desplesher, displease(sure)
despond,*,ded,ding,dingly,dency,dent,
    SEVERELY DISPIRITED/DEPRESSED/
    HOPELESS
despondent,ncy,tly, SEVERELY
    DISPIRITED/DEPRESSED
desposal, disposal
desposeshun, disposition
desposition, disposition
despositive, dispositive
desposuble, disposable
despot,*,tic,tical,tically,tism, ABUSIVE/
    TYRANNICAL USE OF POWER
despraporshen, disproportion
desproportion, disproportion
despurashin, desperation
despurit, desperate
despusishun, disposition
despute, dispute
desputuble, dispute(table)
despuzition, disposition
desqualify, disqualify
desqwalefy, disqualify
desregard, disregard
desrepare, disrepair
desreputable, disreputable
desrespect, disrespect
desrespkt, disrespect
desrobe, disrobe
desrobt, disrupt
desropt, disrupt
desrubshen, disruption
desrubt, disrupt
desrupshen, disruption
desrupt, disrupt
desruption, disruption
dessapate, dissipate
dessapation, dissipate(tion)
dessatisfaction, dissatisfy(faction)
dessemble, dissemble
dessenter, dissent(er)
dessert,*, A TASTY SWEET DISH
    FOLLOWING MAIN COURSE (or see
    desert)
dessertation, dissertation
dessimble, dissemble

dessinter, dissent(er)
dessirtashen, dissertation
dessociate, dissociate
dessolute, dissolute
dessolution, dissolute(tion)
destanashin, destination
destanation, destination
destance, distance
destane, disdain
destany, destiny
destaste, distaste
destemper, distemper
desten, distend / destine
destenation, destination
desteni, destiny
destenkt, distinct
destense, distance
destenshen, distend(nsion)
destent, distant
destention, distend(nsion)
desterb, disturb
destill, distill
destimper, distemper
destinachen, destination
destination,*, ARRIVAL POINT
    "prefixes: pre"
destinct, distinct
destinduble, distend(sible)
destine,*,ned,ning,ny,nation, FATE,
    PREORDAINED, SPECIFIC OUTCOME
    (or see destiny) "prefixes: pre"
destint, distant
destiny,nies, FATE, OVERALL ARRIVAL
    POINT
destitute,*,eness,tion, WITHOUT
    POSSESSION OF, HOMELESS
destort, distort
destrabute, distribute
destract, distract
destraught, distraught
destrekt, district
destrikt, district
destrot, distraught
destroy,*,yed,ying,yable,yer,
    OBLITERATE/RUIN/DEMOLISH
destruct,*,ted,ting,tible,tibility,tion,tive,
    tor, DESTROY A MISSILE AFTER
    LAUNCH "prefixes: in/non"
destruction, ACT OF RUINING/
    DEMOLISHING
destructive,ely,eness,vity, OBLITERATE/
    RUIN/DEMOLISH
destrukshen, destruction
destruktive, destructive

destruktof, destructive
destrust, distrust
destulashen, distill(ation)
destunashin, destination
destuny, destiny
destutute, destitute
desuade, dissuade
desubel, decibel
desubilety, disability
desucrate, desecrate
desufect, disaffect
desugree, disagree
desukrate, desecrate
desul, diesel
desulit, desolate
desulooshen, dissolute(tion)
desuloot, dissolute
desulow, disallow
desumal, decimal
desumate, decimate
desumbark, disembark
desunt, decent / descent
desupashen, dissipate(tion)
desupate, dissipate
desupeer, disappear
desupoent, disappoint
desuprove, disapprove
desurn, discern
desurt, desert / dessert
desurtashen, dissertation
desurve, deserve
deswade, dissuade
det, debt
detach,hes,hed,hedly,hedness,hing,
    ment,hable,hably,her, PULL AWAY
    FROM, SEPARATE "prefixes: semi"
detachment,*, DISCONNECTED,
    SEPARATE FROM THE WHOLE
detail,*,led,ling,ler, EXACT
    PARTICULARS
detain,*,ned,ning,nable,nment,nee, TO
    KEEP FROM GOING, HOLD BACK,
    DELAY
detakashun, dedication
detakate, dedicate
detale, detail
detane, detain
detauks, detox
detch, ditch
detect,*,ted,ting,table,tably,tability,tion,
    tor, UNCOVER, SENSE, DISCOVER
detective,*, ONE WHO UNCOVERS
    FACTS, DISCOVERS

detector,*, A DEVICE WHICH SENSES/ DISCOVERS

detekt, detect

detektif, detective

detektur, detector

deten, deaden

detenate, detonate

detenshen, detention

detente,*, CEASE-FIRE, LESSENING OF TENSIONS BETWEEN WARRING PEOPLE

detention,*, FORCED CONFINEMENT

deter,*,rred,rring,rrable,rrability,rment, rrent,rrence, ATTEMPT TO RESTRAIN FROM (or see detour/ debtor)

deterant, deterrent

detereate, deteriorate

deterent, deterrent

detergent,*, CHEMICAL CLEANSER

deteriorate,*,ed,ting,tion,tive, LOOSE FORM/FUNCTION

determenent, determine(nt)

determination,*, DECIDED, DECISION, STRONG DESIRE FOR ACCOMPLISHMENT

determine,*,ed,ning,nism,nist,nistic, nistically,nedly,nedness,ner,nant, nate, nation,native,natively,nable, THINK OUT, PLAN A COURSE OF ACTION "prefixes: in/non/pre"

deterrent,nce, PAST TENSE FOR "DETER", USED TO PREVENT/ RESTRAIN

detest,*,ted,ting,table,tably,tability, tableness,tation,ter, EXTREME DISLIKE, DISAGREE WITH

deteur, detour / debtor / deter

deth, death

deticashun, dedication

deticate, dedicate

detikashun, dedication

detikate, dedicate

detin, deaden

detinate, detonate

detinshun, detention

detir, debtor / detour / deter

detirmenedly, determine(dly)

detirmenent, determine(nt)

detly, dead(ly)

detnate, detonate

deto, ditto

detoks, detox

detoksefy, detoxify

detoksuficashen, detoxify(fication)

detonate,*,ed,ting,table,tion,tive,tor, CAUSE TO EXPLODE

detont, detente

detor, debtor / detour / deter

detour,*,red,ring, STEER FROM PRIMARY PATH/ROAD

detox,xes,xed,xing,xify,xicate,xication, xicant, SLANG FOR "DETOXIFY", ELIMINATE CHEMICALS FROM THE BODY

detoxicate,*,ed,ting,tion, DETOXIFY, REMOVE IMPURITIES

detoxify,fies,fied,fying,fication, REMOVE IMPURITIES FROM BODY

detract,*,ted,ting,tion,tive,tively,tor, TAKES AWAY FROM

detrament, detriment

detriment,*,tal,tally, COULD HARM, NEGATIVE INPUT

detrument, detriment

dets, debt(s)

detukashun, dedication

detukate, dedicate

detunate, detonate

detur, deter / detour / debtor

deture, detour / debtor / deter

deturgent, detergent

deturmen, determine

deturmenashen, determination

deturmenent, determine(nt)

deturmenism, determine(nism)

deturminent, determine(nt)

deuce,*,ed,edly, TWO DOTS ON DICE, GAMBLING EXPRESSION (or see duce)

deva, ENTITY OF GOOD SPIRITS (or see diva)

devadend, dividend

devastate,*,ed,ting,tive,tion,tor, TOTAL DISARRAY/CHAOTIC ARRANGEMENT,UNRECOGNIZABLE

devaulv, devolve

deveanse, deviance

deveant, deviant

deveashen, deviation

deveat, deviate

deveation, deviation

deveents, deviance

devegen, division

devel, devil

develop,*,ped,ping,pment,pmental, pmentally,per, GATHERING OF

THOUGHTS AND PLANS TOGETHER INTO ON "prefixes: re/under"

deverse, diverse

devershen, diversion

devestate, devastate

deveunse, deviance

deveunt, deviant

deviance,cy, UNACCEPTABLE BEHAVIOR

deviant,*,ate, THOSE WHO DISPLAY UNACCEPTABLE BEHAVIOR

deviate,*,ed,ting,tingly,tion,ance,ant, TO STEER OFF THE PATH "prefixes: un"

deviation,*,nism,nist, TO DEVIATE, BE DEVIANT

device, SOMETHING DESIGNED TO BE USED AS A TOOL/AID (or see devise)

devide, divide

devidend, dividend

devil,*,led,ling,lish,lishness,lishly,lment, lry, FOOD PROCESS, MAN'S CREATION OF A BEING TO BE FEARED

devine, divine

devious,sly,sness, NOT TRUTHFUL, EVASIVE IN TRUTH/DIRECTION

devise,*,ed,sing,sable,er, OF WILLS/ PROPERTY, TO CREATE (or see device)

devisible, divisible

devistate, devastate

devize, devise / device

devoid,dness, ABSENCE OF, EMPTY

devol, devil

devolve,*,ed,ving,ement,lution,lutionist, DOWNWARD, DEGENERATE, DETERIORATE

devorse, divorce

devoshen, devotion

devostate, devastate

devote,*,ed,edly,edness,ting,tion,tional, tee, DEDICATED, LOYAL COMMITMENT

devotion,*,nal,nally, DEDICATED, LOYAL

devour,*,red,ring,ringly,rer, EARNEST TO RELIGION

devout,tly,tness, DEEPLY DEVOTED

devoyd, devoid

devu, deva / diva

devudend, dividend

devul, devil

devulg, divulge

devulution, devolve(lution)

devursity, diversity
devurt, divert
devustate, devastate
dew,*,wed,wing,wy, MOISTURE THAT COLLECTS INTO DROPS (or see do/due/doe)
dewal, dual / duel
dewdle, doodle
dewet, duet
dewing, doing
dewl, duel / dual
dewo, duo
dewplecity, duplicity
dewplekate, duplicate
dewplex, duplex
dewse, duce / deuce / due(s)
dewsh, douche
dex, deck(s) / dig(s)
dexshen, diction
dexshunery, dictionary
dexsteridy, dexterity
dexterity,ties, SHARP/QUICK MENTAL/PHYSICAL SKILL
dextero, PREFIX INDICATING "RIGHT" MOST OFTEN MODIFIES THE WORD
dexterous,sly,sness, OF DEXTERITY
dextr, PREFIX INDICATING "RIGHT" MOST OFTEN MODIFIES THE WORD
dextro, PREFIX INDICATING "RIGHT" MOST OFTEN MODIFIES THE WORD
dextrus, dexterous
dez, these
dezal, diesel
dezapashen, dissipate(tion)
dezapate, dissipate
dezapeer, disappear
dezaster, disaster
dezbot, despot
deze, dizzy
dezeez, disease
dezenteant, dissent(ient)
dezert, desert / dessert
dezerve, deserve
dezignate, designate
dezine, design
deziner, designer
dezinteant, dissent(ient)
dezirable, desirable
dezire, desire
dezklose, disclose
dezl, diesel
dezmay, dismay
dezmul, dismal
dezolve, dissolve

dezordurly, disorderly
dezposuble, disposable
dezrepare, disrepair
dezugnate, designate
dezul, diesel
dezurt, desert / dessert
dezurtashen, dissertation
dezurve, deserve
dfraust, defrost
dfrost, defrost
dfroust, defrost
di, PREFIX INDICATING "FROM/AWAY/NEGATIVE" MOST OFTEN MODIFIES THE WORD
dia, PREFIX INDICATING "ACROSS/THROUGH" MOST OFTEN MODIFIES THE WORD
diabalekle, diabolical
diabedik, diabetic
diabetes, IMBALANCE IN GLUCOSE LEVELS
diabetic, SOMEONE WITH GLUCOSE IMBALANCE
diabolic,cal,ize,izes,ized,izing,ism, OF BEING/SEEMING EVIL/CRUEL, OF THE DEVIL
diabolical,lly,lness, OF BEING DIABOLIC, EVIL
diacdavate, deactivate
diactevate, deactivate
diafram, diaphragm
diagenul, diagonal
diagnose,*,ed,sing,sable,sis,stic,stically, stician, TO STUDY THE NATURE OF A PROBLEM
diagnosis, OPINION ON THE NATURE OF A PROBLEM
diagnul, diagonal
diagnule, diagonal(lly)
diagonal,lly, OPPOSITE/CATTY CORNER FROM
diagram,*,mmed,mming,mmatic, mmatical,mmatically,mmable, DRAWING "prefixes: mis/un"
diahrea, diarrhea
dial,*,led,ling,ler, FACE OF WATCH, PLACE A PHONE CALL "prefixes: mis/re"
dialasis, dialysis
dialect,*,tal,tally,tic,tician,ticism,tical, tically, THE WAY THE LANGUAGE IS SPOKEN
dialogue,*,ed,uing,gist,gistic,gize,gizes, gized,gizing, VERBAL

COMMUNICATION BETWEEN ENTITIES
dialysis,ytic,ytically,lyze,lyzes,lyzed, lyzing,lyzable,lyzability,lyzation, CLEANSE THE BLOOD OF WASTES, SEPARATE SUBSTANCES BY DIFFUSION
diameter,*,ric,rical,trically,tral, STRAIGHT LINE THROUGH THE CENTER OF A CIRCULAR SHAPE LEAVING EQUAL PARTS "prefixes: semi"
diamider, diameter
diamond,*, CUT STONE INTO GEM/SHAPE/PATTERN
diaper,*,red, ABSORBENT PANTS FOR FLUIDS
diaphragm,*,matic,matically, A DIVISION BETWEEN TWO THINGS, CONTRACEPTIVE DEVICE
diarea, diarrhea
diaretik, diuretic
diarrhea,al,hoea,hoeic, VERY LIQUID FECAL EXCREMENT
diary,ries,rist,rize,rizes,rized,rizing, LOG/JOURNAL OF THOUGHTS EACH DAY
diatery, dietary
dibach, debauch
dibate, debate
dibauch, debauch
dibelutate, debilitate
diber, dipper / diaper
dibiletate, debilitate
diblomu, diploma
diblomusy, diplomacy
dibochury, debauch(ery)
dibs, SLANG FOR LAYING A CLAIM, SMALL MONETARY PARTICIPATION
dibur, dipper / diaper
dic, thick / dike / dyke
dical, decal
dicanter, decanter
dicapitate, decapitate
dicaudame, dichotomy
dicay, decay
dice,*,ed,cing,ey, PLURAL FOR "DIE", TWO CUBES WITH VARIETY OF DOTS, TO CHOP UP (or see dicey)
dicelerate, decelerate
dicember, december
dicensy, decency
dicentrolize, decentralize
dicet, deceit

diceve, deceive

dicey,cier,eist, IFFY/RISKY WITH ELEMENT OF DANGER

dich, ditch / dish

diches, ditch(es)

dicheveled, dishevel(ed)

dichotomy,mies,mic,mous,mously,mize, mizes,mized,mizing, mization, SEPARATION/DIVISION INTO TWO PARTS

dichroic,cism, DIFFERENT COLORS FROM DIFFERENT ANGLES

dicker,*,red,ring, RALLY TO STRIKE A DEAL

diclain, decline

dicler, declare

dicompos, decompose

dicon, deacon

dicotomy, dichotomy

dicoy, decoy

dicreped, decrepit

dicrepit, decrepit

dicroek, dichroic

dicshen, diction

dicshunairy, dictionary

dictate,*,ed,ting,tor,tory,torial, COMMAND/RULE/GIVE ORDERS

dictation, TO WRITE OR TYPE WHAT SOMEONE IS SAYING

dictatorial,lly,lness, OPPRESSIVE, AUTHORITARIAN

diction, A WAY OF SPEAKING, ENUNCIATION "prefixes: retro"

dictionary,ries, WORDS WITH DEFINITIONS ARRANGED ALPHABETICALLY

did,does, PAST TENSE FOR THE WORD "DO"(or see dead/died) "prefixes: un"

diden, didn't / deaden

didn't, CONTRACTION OF THE WORDS 'DID NOT' (or see dent/deaden)

dido, ditto

didukt, deduct

diduse, deduce

die,*,ed,dying,dead, TO BE DEAD/ CEASE TO BE ALIVE, AN ENGRAVED STAMP, A PUNCHED OUT TEMPLATE, CUBE USED FOR GAMING (or see dye)

died, PAST TENSE FOR THE WORD "DIE" (or see dye(d))

diegnosus, diagnosis

dielekt, dialect

diere, diary

dierrhea, diarrhea

diesel,*,led,ling, TYPE OF ENGINE/FUEL "prefixes: bio"

diet,*,ted,ting,tary,taries,tetic,tetically, tician, SPECIFIC FOOD/BEVERAGE

dietary,ries, A SYSTEM OF FOOD FOR TYPES OF PEOPLE

dif, PREFIX INDICATING "FROM/AWAY/ NEGATIVE" MOST OFTEN MODIFIES THE WORD (or see thief)

difadend, dividend

difalt, default

difase, deface

difault, default

dife, dive

difechant, deficient

difechensi, deficiency

difeet, defeat

difekult, difficult

difend, defend

difenitive, definitive

difense, defense

difensible, defensible

difensive, defense(sive)

difer, defer / differ

diferens, difference

diferense, difference

diferensheate, differentiate

diferent, different

diferentiate, differentiate

diferently, different(ly)

diferintiate, differentiate

difeshensy, deficiency

difet, defeat

difews, diffuse

differ,*,red,ring,rent,rence,rential, TO NOT BE ALIKE

differantly, different(ly)

difference,*, QUALITIES NOT ALIKE "prefixes: in"

different,tly,tness,tial, NOT THE SAME "prefixes: in"

differential,*, RATE DIFFERENCE/ VARIANCE

differentiate,*,ed,ting,tion, TO OUTLINE DIFFERENCES, BIOLOGY TERM "prefixes: un"

difficult,ty,ties, NOT EASY TO PERFORM

diffuse,*,ed,sing,ely,eness,er,sive,sible, sibility, ELIMINATE FOCUS BY SPREADING OUT, TO END PRESSURE

difichant, deficient

difichensy, deficiency

dificult, difficult

difiense, defiance

difikult, difficult

difine, define

difir, defer / differ

difishant, deficient

difishensy, deficiency

diflact, deflect

diflate, deflate

difoleate, defoliate

difor, differ / defer

diforensheate, differentiate

diforent, different

diform, deform

diformed, deform(ed)

difraud, defraud

difraust, defrost

difray, defray

difrense, difference

difrent, different

difrod, defraud

difrost, defrost

difucult, difficult

difukult, difficult

difunkt, defunct

difur, defer / differ

difurense, difference

difursheate, differentiate

difurent, different

difurently, different(ly)

difurinsheate, differentiate

difurintly, different(ly)

difuse, diffuse

dify, defy

dig,*,dug,gging,gger, TO GO BELOW/ BEYOND THE SURFACE

digesgen, digestion

digest,*,ted,ting,tible,tibility,tibleness, tive,tively,tiveness,tion, CONSUME, PROCESS, SUMMARIZATIONS "prefixes: pre/un"

digestev, digest(tive)

digestif, digest(tive)

digestion, CONSUME AND PROCESS

digestuf, digest(tive)

digestyon, digestion

diget, digit

digit,*,tize,tization,tal,tally,talize, talization, COUNTING/MEASURING

dignafid, dignified

dignafied, dignified

dignified, STATELY IN FIGURE OR FORM, HONORABLE

dignify,fies,fied,fying, EXPRESS HONOR FOR

dignity,ties,tary, WORTHY OF RESPECT, HONOR "prefixes: in"

dignosis, diagnosis

dignufied, dignified

digrade, degrade

digree, degree

digress,sses,ssed,ssing,ssion,ssional, ssionary,ssive,ssively,ssiveness, WANDER AWAY FROM, DEPART FROM MAIN TOPIC/SUBJECT (or see degression)

dijest, digest

dijestev, digest(ive)

dijeston, digestion

dijet, digit

dika, decay

dikad, decay(ed)

dikanter, decanter

dikautumy, dichotomy

dikdutoreal, dictatorial

dike,*,ed,king,er, ALSO SPELLED "DYKE", A BARRIER/CAUSEWAY/PASSAGE

diker, dicker

diklar, declare

diklin, decline

dikotumy, dichotomy

dikrepit, decrepit

dikroic, dichroic

dikshen, diction

dikshenare, dictionary

dikshun, diction

dikshunare, dictionary

diksterity, dexterity

diktashen, dictation

diktate, dictate

diktater, dictate(tor)

diktation, dictation

diktatur, dictate(tor)

diktion, diction

diktionery, dictionary

diktutoreal, dictatorial

dil, dial / dill / deal

dilagense, diligence

dilajense, diligence

dilate,*,ed,ting,tion,tability,table,tably, tingly,tive, EXPAND/SWELL/ BROADEN

dilatont, dilettante

dilay, delay

dilectable, delectable

diledaly, dillydally

dilekt, dialect

dilema, dilemma

dilemma,*,atic, NOT A SITUATION OF CHOICE

dilenkwent, delinquent

dilenquent, delinquent

dilereus, delirious

dileshos, delicious

dilete, delete

diletont, dilettante

dilettante,*,tish,tism, A DABBLER FOR AMUSEMENT

dilidaly, dillydally

diligence,nt,ntly, STEADY PERSEVERANCE, CONSTANT

dilikt, dialect

dilinquent, delinquent

dilirious, delirious

dilishos, delicious

diliver, deliver

dill, AN HERB (or see dial/deal)

dilledaly, dillydally

dillydally,llies,yied,ying, SHOULD BE SEPARATED INTO 2 WORDS "DILLY DALLY", TO WASTE TIME

diloot, dilute

diluchen, delusion / dilute(tion)

dilucs, deluxe

dilugen, delusion / dilute(tion)

dilugense, diligence

dilugent, diligence(nt)

dilujents, diligence

diluks, deluxe

dilur, deal(er)

dilushen, delusion/ dilute(tion)

dilute,*,ed,ting,eness,tion,tive,er, WEAKEN THE STRENGTH OF

dilutont, dilettante

diluxe, deluxe

dim,*,mmed,mming,mly,mness,mmer, mmest, BETWEEN BRIGHT AND DARK, NOT CLEAR/BRIGHT (or see dime)

dimagog, demagogue

dimand, demand

dimaughraphy, demography

dimaulesh, demolish

dimble, dimple

dime,*, A COIN (or see dim)

dimean, demean

dimeanor, demeanor

dimen, demean

dimend, diamond

dimenor, demeanor

dimension,*,nless,nal,nally,nality,nless, MORE THAN ONE LAYER "prefixes: multi"

dimentchen, dimension

dimented, demented

dimer, dimmer

dimestek, domestic

diminish,hes,hed,hing,hingly,hment, TO LESSEN/MAKE SMALLER

dimis, demise

dimize, demise

dimmer,*, LESSEN BRIGHTNESS

dimobalize, demobilize

dimocrat, democrat

dimografy, demography

dimokresy, democracy

dimolish, demolish

dimolishin, demolition

dimon, demon / diamond

dimond, diamond

dimonek, demon(ic)

dimple,*,ed,ling,ly, A DEPRESSION INTO SURFACE, INDENTATION

dimukratic, democratic

dimulishun, demolition

dimunstrate, demonstrate

dimur, dimmer

din, den / dine / dean / didn't

dinamek, dynamic

dinamic, dynamic

dinamination, denomination

dinamite, dynamite

dinasor, dinosaur

dinasty, dynasty

dinaumenation, denomination

dincher, denture

dindrite, dendrite

dine,*,ed,ning,er, TO EAT

diner,*, PLACE TO EAT (or see dinner)

dinesor, dinosaur

dinet, dinette

dinette, DINING ROOM/PLACE NEAR KITCHEN TO EAT

ding,*,ged,ging, BELL SOUNDS, INDENTATIONS/MARKS

dingee, dinghy / dingy

dinger,*, HOME RUN BASEBALL

dinghy,hies, SMALL BOAT/VESSEL ON WATER (or see dingy)

dingy,gier,giest,giness,gily, DIM/MURKY, NOT VIBRANT (or see dinghy/dinky)

dinial, denial

dinie, deny

dinil, denial

dinisor, dinosaur
dinje, dingy
dinky,kier,kiest, SMALL/TINY
dinner,*, EVENING MEAL (or see diner)
dinomenashin, denomination
dinomenator, denominator
dinominashan, denomination
dinominator, denominator
dinomite, dynamite
dinostea, dynasty
dinote, denote
dinse, dense
dinsity, density
dint, dent / didn't / dine(d)
dintal, dental
dintist, dentist
dinture, denture
dinumite, dynamite
dinur, diner / dinner
dinusor, dinosaur
dinusty, dynasty
dioderant, deodorant
dioreu, diarrhea
dip,*,pper,pped,pping, SLIGHTLY
　　IMMERSE/DECLINE/GO INTO
diparcher, departure
diparsher, departure
dipart, depart
dipartment, department
diparture, departure
dipect, depict
dipend, depend
dipendant, dependant / dependent
dipendence, dependence
diper, diaper / dipper
diplechen, depletion
diplesihin, depletion
diplete, deplete
diploma,*, DOCUMENT FOR
　　COMPLETION OF COURSE/SCHOOL
diplomacy, SKILLFUL NEGOTIATIONS
diplomat,*,tic,tics,tically,acy,tist,
　　PERSON WHO PERFORMS TACTFUL
　　NEGOTIATIONS "prefixes: non/un"
diplorable, deplorable
diplore, deplore
dipo, depot
diporcher, depart(ure)
diport, deport
diportashon, deportation
diportee, deportee
dipose, depose
diposeshon, deposition

diposit, deposit
dipozishen, deposition
dipper,*, SPOON WITH HANDLE, A BIRD
　　(or see diaper)
dipres, depress
dipresheate, depreciate
dipreshen, depression
dipresion, depression
diprive, deprive
dipur, diaper / dipper
dirashen, duration
dirdee, dirty
dire,ely,eness, EXTREME, DISASTROUS
direct,*,ted,ting,tly,tness,tor,tion,tive,
　　torate,torship,tory, AIM FOR/WITH, OF
　　COMMANDS "prefixes: in/mis/multi/
　　non/re/sub/un"
direction,*,nal,nality,nless, WAVE/
　　SIGNALS IN SPACE "prefixes: in/multi/
　　non/uni"
directive,*,eness, A DIRECTION/
　　INDICATOR/GUIDE
directory,ries, BOOK WITH
　　ALPHABETICAL LISTINGS "prefixes:
　　sub"
direkshen, direction
direktory, directory
direng, during
diress, duress
dirivative, derivative
dirive, derive
dirmal, dermal
dirmas, dermal(mis)
dirmatites, dermal(atitis)
dirmle, dermal
dirmul, dermal
dirmus, dermal(mis)
dirmutidus, dermal(atitis)
dirmutitis, dermal(atitis)
dirt,ty,ties,tied,tying,tier,tiest,tily,tiness,
　　SOILED, SOIL (earth)
dirty,tied,tier,tiest,ying,tily,tiness,
　　UNCLEAN
dis, PREFIX INDICATING "NOT/
　　OPPOSITE/LACK OF" MOST OFTEN
　　MODIFIES THE WORD (or see this/
　　dice/die(s)/dye(s))
disabelity, disability
disability,ties, UNABLE TO PERFORM AT
　　NECESSARY CAPACITY
disable,*,ed,ling,ement,bility, UNABLE
　　TO PERFORM, DISCONNECT
disaccord,*,ded,ding, NOT IN
　　HARMONY/AGGREEMENT

disadisfaction, dissatisfy(faction)
disadvantage,*,ed,ging,eous,eously,
　　eousness, A DIFFICULTY/
　　CHALLENGE IN ACCOMPLISHING
　　SUCCESS/GOAL
disaffect,*,ted,ting,tedly,tion,
　　NEGATIVELY AFFECT SOMEONE
　　CONCERNING ANOTHER
disagree,*,eed,eeing,eement,eeable,
　　eeably,eeability,eeableness, NOT
　　AGREE WITH
disakree, disagree
disalanate, desalinate
disallow,*,wed,wing,wance,wable, NOT
　　ALLOWED
disalow, disallow
disalugen, disillusion
disalusion, disillusion
disalute, dissolute
disalution, dissolute(tion)
disambiguate,*,ed,ting,tion,
　　EXPRESSION OPEN TO
　　MISINTERPRETATION, CONFUSING
disanens, dissonant(nce)
disanent, dissonant
disapate, dissipate
disapation, dissipate(tion)
disaper, disappear
disaplen, discipline
disappear,*,red,ring,rance, VANISH
　　FROM SIGHT
disappoint,*,ted,tedly,ting,tingly,tment,
　　HOPES NOT REALIZED
disapprove,*,ed,ving,vingly,val,
　　DOESN'T CARE FOR/APPROVE OF
disaray, disarray
disarm,*,med,ming,mament,mer,
　　REMOVE POWER/WEAPONS
disarmament,*, ACT OF DISARMING
disarray,*,yed,ying, DISORDERED/
　　JUMBLED
disassociate, dissociate
disaster,*,rous,rously,rousness,
　　MISFORTUNE, CALAMITY,
　　EXTENSIVE DAMAGE
disatation, dissertation
disatisfaction, dissatisfy(faction)
disavantage, disadvantage
disbaleef, disbelief / disbelieve
disband,*,ded,ding,dment, DISMISSED
　　FROM GROUP OR MILITARY
disbar,rred,rring, REMOVED FROM
　　LEGAL COURT OR PRACTICE (or see
　　despair)

disbatch, dispatch
disbecable, despicable
disbekable, despicable
disbelief,*,eve, DOESN'T BELIEVE TO BE TRUE
disbelieve,*,ed,ving,vingly,er, DOESN'T BELIEVE TO BE TRUE
disberse, disperse / disburse
disbicable, despicable
disbikable, despicable
disbileef, disbelief / disbelieve
disbite, despite
disblay, display
disblese, displease
disbolef, disbelief / disbelieve
disbondent, despondent
disbose, dispose
disbozishun, disposition
disbozul, disposal
disbraporshen, disproportion
disbuleef, disbelief / disbelieve
disburse,*,ed,sing,sable,ement,er, FUND, PAY OUT MONEY (or see disperse)
disbusishun, disposition
disbute, dispute
disbuzishun, disposition
disc,*, COMPUTER/MUSIC STORAGE DEVICES, SECTIONS IN THE SPINE, BRAKE PARTS (or see disk)
discard,*,ded,ding, TO RID OF/THROW AWAY
discension, dissension / descension
discerach, discourage
discern,*,ned,ning,nible,nibleness,nibly, nment, PERCEIVE ONE FROM ANOTHER, SEE A DIFFERENCE "prefixes: in"
discharge,*,ed,ging,eable,er, TO RELEASE FROM
discinshen, dissension / descension
disciple,*, ONE WHO FOLLOWS A TEACHER
discipline,*,ed,ning,nable,nary,narian, er,nal, CONTROL/TRAIN TO PERFORM SPECIFICALLY "prefixes: in"
disclaim,*,med,ming,mer, NOT LAY CLAIM TO, DISOWN/DENY RESPONSIBILITY OF
disclose,*,ed,sing,sure,ser, REVEAL/ MAKE KNOWN "prefixes: un"
discombobulate,*,ed,ting,tion, DISTURB, PERPLEX

discomfort,*,ted,ting,tingly,table, UNCOMFORTABLE, UNHAPPY
disconnect,*,ted,ting,tion,tedly,tedness, BE REMOVED FROM CONNECTION WITH
discontinue,*,ed,uing,uation,uity,uities, uance,uous,uously,uousness,uity, unities,er, ABANDON, CEASE, STOP THE USE OF
discord,dance,dancy,dancies,dant, dantly, NOT IN HARMONY WITH, DISAGREE WITH
discotek, discotheque
discotheque,*, NIGHTCLUB WITH MUSIC
discount,*,ted,ting, MAKE LESS, REDUCE PRICE OF
discourage,*,ed,ging,ement,gingly,er, LESSEN HOPES OF ACCOMPLISHING
discourse,*,ed,sing,er, REVEAL/MAKE KNOWN
discourteous,sies,sly,sness, NOT POLITE/COURTEOUS
discover,*,red,ring,rer,ry,ries,rable, TO FIND, REALIZE "prefixes: un"
discownt, discount
discredit,*,ted,ting,table,tably,tor, GIVE NO CREDIT TO, DISBELIEF
discreet,tly,tness, GUARDED, CAREFUL, SUBTLE (or see discrete) "prefixes: in"
discremenate, discriminate
discrepancy,cies,nt,ntly, DIFFERENCE BETWEEN
discrepant,ntly,ncy, DIFFERENCE BETWEEN THINGS
discrepchen, description
discreptef, descriptive
discreption, description
discrete,ely,eness,tion, SEPARATE PARTS, DISTINCT/FINITE (or see discreet) "prefixes: in"
discretion,nary,narily, MAKE YOUR OWN DECISION/JUDGEMENT, BEING DISCREET "prefixes: in"
discribe, describe
discriminate,*,ed,ting,nation,nable, nably,nability,nant,nately, native, nator,natory,natorily, USING DIFFERENCE AGAINST, CHOOSE ONE OVER ANOTHER "prefixes: in"
discripchen, description
discripshen, description
discumbobulate, discombobulate

discumfert, discomfort
discunect, disconnect
discuntenue, discontinue
discurage, discourage
discurech, discourage
discus,ses, USED FOR THROWING (or see discuss)
discuss,sses,ssed,ssing,ssable,ssant,sser, ssion, CONVERSATION TO EXAMINE SUBJECT (or see discus)
discussion,*, ACT OF CONVERSATION TO EXAMINE SUBJECT
discust, disgust
discuver, discover
disdain,*,ned,ning,nful,nfully,nfulness, SCORN, CONTEMPT FOR, REJECT
disdend, distend
disdendible, distend(sible)
disdendshen, distend(nsion)
disdendtion, distend(nsion)
disdent, distant
disderb, disturb
disdinduble, distend(sible)
disdort, distort
disdrabushen, distribute(tion)
disdrabute, distribute
disdrakt, distract
disdrebute, distribute
disdress, distress
disdrot, distraught
disdrubute, distribute
disdruckshen, destruction
disdruktion, destruction
disdrust, distrust
disdulashen, distill(ation)
disdurb, disturb
dise, dice / dizzy / dicey
disease,*,ed,sing, BLOCK OF ENERGY ALLOWING TISSUE BREAKDOWN VIA MINUTE ORGANISMS
disecragate, desegregate
disecragation, desegregate(tion)
disecrogate, desegregate
disecrogation, desegregate(tion)
disect, dissect
diseese, decease / disease
diseet, deceit
diseeve, deceive
disefect, disaffect
disefectant, disinfect(ant)
disegragate, desegregate
disegragation, desegregate(tion)
disegrogate, desegregate
disegrogation, desegregate(tion)

disekt, dissect
diselarate, decelerate
diselooshen, dissolute(tion)
diseloot, dissolute
disembar, december
disembark,*,ked,king,kation,kment,
MOVE FROM SHIP TO SHORE
disemble, dissemble
disembowel,*,led,ling,lment, REMOVE
ORGANS/INTESTINES
disembur, december
diseminate, disseminate
disenagrate, disintegrate
disenchan, descension / dissension
disend, descend / decent / descent /
dissent
disendant, descendant
disenfect, disinfect
disengage,*,ed,ging,ement, SET FREE
FROM BEING ATTACHED
disenherit, disinherit
disenshent, dissent(ient)
disenshin, dissension / descension
disenshun, dissension / descension
disent, dissent / decent / descend /
descent
disentagrate, disintegrate
disentary, dysentery
disenter, dissent(er)
disentient, dissent(ient)
disention, dissension / descension
disentralize, decentralize
disepchen, deception
diseplen, discipline
disepoint, disappoint
diseption, deception
diseray, disarray
disern, discern
disert, dessert / desert
disertation, dissertation
diserv, deserve
diservice, disservice
disesd, decease(d) / disease(d)
diset, deceit
disetful, deceit(ful)
diseve, deceive
disfigure,*,ed,ring,ration,ement,
CAUSING UNSIGHTLY APPEARANCE
disfoncshon, disfunction
disfunction, dysfunction
disfunkshon, dysfunction
disgarge, discharge
disgise, disguise
disgoint, disjoint

disgrace,*,ed,cing,eful,efully,efulness,
er, SHAME, DISHONOR
disgrechen, discretion
disgretion, discretion
disgrundeld, disgruntle(d)
disgruntle,*,ed,ling,ement, NOT
CONTENTED, UNGRATIFIED
disguise,*,ed,sing,sable,er, MASK TRUE
IDENTITY "prefixes: un"
disgurag, discourage
disgus, discuss / discus
disgust,*,ted,ting,tingly,tingness,
REPUGNANT, AWFUL (or see
discuss(ed))
dish,hes,hed,hing, SHALLOW PLATE/
BOWL/VESSEL, TO SERVE IT UP (or
see ditch)
disharten, dishearten
dishaveled, dishevel(ed)
dishearten,*,ned,ning,nment, LOOSE
SPIRIT/HOPE/COURAGE
dishevel,*,led,ling,lment, MESSED UP,
UNTIDY
dishonest,ty,tly,ties, BEING DECEITFUL,
NOT HONEST
dishonor,*,red,ring,rable,rably,
rableness, NOT TREATED
RESPECTFULLY, SHAMEFUL
dishonorable,ly,eness, UNRESPECTABLE,
NOT HONORABLE
disi, dizzy
disidvantege, disadvantage
disifer, decipher
disillusion,ned,nment,ive, NO LONGER
UNDER ILLUSION, KNOWING
disilushen, disillusion
disimanate, disseminate
disimbark, disembark
disimbul, dissemble
disimbur, december
disin, design
disiner, designer
disinfect,*,ted,ting,tant,tion,tor,
CLEANSE AWAY UNWANTED
MICROORGANISMS
disingage, disengage
disinherit,*,ted,ting,tance, REMOVED
FROM A WRITTEN WILL
disint, descend / decent
disintegrate,*,ed,ting,tion,tor,able,tive,
TO FALL APART
disintery, dysentery
disintient, dissent(ient)
disiplen, discipline

disipul, disciple
disir, desire
disirable, desirable
disis, decease
disisev, decision(ive)
disiv, deceive
disjoint,*,ted,ting,tedly,tedness,
DISLOCATE, ALTER UNITY/
MOVEMENT
disk,*, FLAT/CIRCULAR, FLOWER HEAD,
STEEL BLADE (or see disc/desk)
diskard, discard
diskeruge, discourage
disklame, disclaim
disklose, disclose
diskomfurt, discomfort
diskonect, disconnect
diskontenue, discontinue
diskord, discord
diskors, discourse
diskotek, discotheque
diskover, discover
diskownt, discount
diskredit, discredit
diskrepincy, discrepancy
diskreshun, discretion
diskrete, discreet / discrete
diskribe, describe
diskripshen, description
diskumbobulate, discombobulate
diskumfert, discomfort
diskunekt, disconnect
diskuntenue, discontinue
diskurdeus, discourteous
diskurege, discourage
diskus, discus / discuss
diskust, disgust / discuss(ed)
diskuver, discover
diskwalefy, disqualify
diskwolify, disqualify
dislecsea, dyslexia
disleksea, dyslexia
dislexia, dyslexia
dislocate,*,ed,ting,tion, MOVE FROM
ORIGINAL PLACE
disloch, dislodge
dislodge,*,ed,ging,gment, MOVE FROM
FIXED POSITION
dislog, dislodge
dismal,lly,llness, DEPRESSING/GLOOMY
dismanle, dismantle
dismantle,*,ed,ling,ement,er, REMOVE,
TAKE APART
dismanul, dismantle

dismay,*,yed,ying,yingly, DISTRESS, DREAD, DISILLUSIONED

dismbark, disembark

dismember,*,red,ring,rment, DESTROY/ REMOVE ALL PARTS OF THE WHOLE

dismiss,sses,ssed,ssing,ssal,ssion,ssive, ssively,ssiveness,ssible, PERMIT TO LEAVE, REMOVE, DISCHARGE "prefixes: non/pre/re"

dismount,*,ted,ting,table, REMOVE FROM POSITION

dismownt, dismount

dismul, dismal

disoba, disobey

disobdeinse, disobedience

disobedience,nt,ntly, REFUSE TO BE CONTROLLED

disobey,*,yed,ying,edient,ediently, edience, BEYOND CONTROL

disociate, dissociate

disolfe, dissolve

disolve, dissolve

dison, disown

disonance, dissonant(nce)

disonent, dissonant

disoner, dishonor

disonerible, dishonorable

disoninse, dissonant(nce)

disonist, dishonest

disonurable, dishonorable

disorder,*,red,ring,rly,redness, NOT ORGANIZED

disorderly,liness, NOT PROPER ORDER

disoreint, disorient

disorient,*,ted,ting,tate,tates,tated, tating,tation, LOSS OF PERCEPTION, CONFUSED

disosheate, dissociate

disown,*,ned,ning, RELEASE OWNERSHIP OF

dispair, despair

dispar, despair

disparity,ties, GAP BETWEEN, INEQUALITY

disparody, disparity

disparty, disparity

dispatch,hes,hed,hing,her, SEND SOMEONE OUT

dispekable, despicable

dispensable,bility,eness, CAN BE DISCARDED "prefixes: in"

dispense,*,ed,sing,er,sable,sability, sableness,sary, TO DISTRIBUTE "prefixes: un"

disper, despair

disperse,*,ed,sing,sion,sive,sively, siveness,er,sal, SCATTER INTO VARIOUS DIRECTIONS (or see disburse)

disperudy, disparity

dispeutible, dispute(table)

dispewt, dispute

dispikuble, despicable

dispinsable, dispensable

dispite, despite

dispize, despise

displace,*,ed,cing,eable,ement,er, NOT IN PLACE OR POSITION NORMALLY FOUND

display,*,yed,ying, ON SHOW, EXHIBITION

displease,*,ed,sing,sure, NOT TO SOMEONE'S SATISFACTION

displejur, displease(sure)

displese, displease

displesher, displease(sure)

dispondent, despondent

disposable,*,bility,eness, CAN DISCARD/THROW AWAY

disposal,able, PLACE/WAY TO DISCARD ITEMS

dispose,*,ed,sing,sal,sable,er, TO RID OF, ORGANIZE "prefixes: in/pre/un"

disposition,nal, ATTITUDE, INCLINATION "prefixes: in"

dispositive, FINAL SETTLEMENT OF COURT CASE

dispraporshen, disproportion

disproportion,nal,nate,nately,nally, nateness,nation, NOT IN RELATION TO ITSELF OR ITS SURROUNDINGS

disput, dispute

dispute,*,ed,ting,table,tably,tability, tableness,tant, DEBATE "prefixes: in/un"

disputuble, dispute(table)

disqard, discard

disqualify,fies,fied,ying,fication,fiable, fier, DISBAR, REMOVE FROM COMPETITION

disregard,*,ded,ding, PAY NO NOTICE OF OR ATTENTION TO

disrepair, NEED TO BE FIXED

disreputable,eness,bility,ly, OF POOR REPUTATION/CHARACTER

disrespect,*,ted,ting,table,tful,tfully, tfulness, SHOW NO HONOR/ RESPECT

disrobe,*,ed,bing, UNDRESS, REMOVE GARMENTS

disrupt,*,ted,ting,tion,tive,tiveness, tively, INTERRUPT, CAUSE CHAOS

disruption, INTERRUPT, CAUSE CHAOS

dissalute, dissolute

dissalution, dissolute(tion)

dissanence, dissonant(nce)

dissanent, dissonant

dissapate, dissipate

dissapation, dissipate(tion)

dissatation, dissertation

dissatisfy,fies,fied,fying,faction,factory, UNHAPPY WITH OUTCOME

dissect,*,ted,ting,tion,tible,tor, CRITICALLY EXAMINE, TAKE APART

dissemble,*,ed,ling,lingly,lance, HIDING TRUE FEELINGS/FACTS

disseminate,*,ed,ting,tion,tive,tor, TO PASS ON, SPREAD

dissend, descend/ descent/ dissent

dissension,*, INTENSE DIFFERENCE/ DISAGREEMENT IN OPINION (or see descension)

dissent,*,ted,ting,ter,tience,tiency,tient, tiently,nsion, WILL NOT BEND TOWARDS MAJOR AUTHORITY (or see descent)

dissertation,*,nal,nist, WRITTEN/ FORMAL PAPER FOR DEGREE

disservice, UNWANTED SERVICE

dissipate,*,ed,edly,edness,ting,tive,tor, tion, DISAPPEARS, GOES AWAY

dissociate,*,ed,ting,tion,able,tive, STOP ASSOCIATING WITH "prefixes: un"

dissolute,ely,eness,tion, DISMEMBER, DISINTEGRATE, TERMINATE

dissolve,*,ed,ving,vable,ent,er,luble, lubility,lubleness, BREAK AWAY TO NOTHING, DISAPPEAR

dissonance, dissonant(nce)

dissonant,tly,nce,ncies, LACK OF COMPLETION/CONSISTENCY

dissosheate, dissociate

dissuade,*,ed,ding,dable,er,asion,sive, sively,siveness, SWAY SOMEONE AWAY FROM INTENDED IDEA/PATH

distalashen, distill(ation)

distance,*,ed,cing,nt, TIME/SPACE IN BETWEEN

distane, disdain

distanst, distance(d)

distant,tly, REMOVED IN MIND OR BODY FROM THIS PLACE OR TIME distaste,eful,efully,efulness, DOESN'T LIKE THE WAY IT APPEALS TO THE SENSES

disteengwish, distinguish

distemper, CONTAGIOUS DISEASE IN ANIMALS, OF PAINTING

distence, distance

distend,*,ded,ding,nsibility,sible,nsion, SWELLING FROM INTERNAL PRESSURE

distengwish, distinguish

distenkt, distinct

distent, distant

disterb, disturb

distill,*,lled,lling,llation,llate,llable, llatory,ller,llery,lleries, SEPARATION, CONDENSATION OF LIQUID

distimper, distemper

distinct,tly,tness,tion,tive,tively, tiveness, CONTRAST, DISTINGUISHED, DIFFERENT "prefixes: in"

distinguish,hed,hes,hing,hable,hably, her, DIFFERENCE/ UNIQUENESS "prefixes: contra/in/un"

distort,*,ted,ting,tion,tional,tnary,tive, ter, WARP/TWIST/CONFUSE FROM NATURAL/PROPER FORM

distrabushen, distribute(tion)

distrabute, distribute

distract,*,ted,ting,tingly,tion,tive,tibility, tible,tor, DEVIATE FROM ORIGINAL FOCUS/INTENT

distrat, distraught

distraught,tly, EXTREME STRESS

distrekt, district

distress,sses,ssed,ssing,ssingly,ssful, GREAT NEED, PAIN OR GRIEF

distribute,*,ed,ting,tion,tional,tive, tively,tal,tor, TO SPREAD AROUND, PASS ALONG "prefixes: re/un"

district,*, SPECIFIC AREA OF TERRITORY/LAND "prefixes: re/sub"

distrocshen, destruction

distroct, destruct

distroctive, destructive

distrot, distraught

distroy, destroy

distruction, destruction

distructive, destructive

distrukshen, destruction

distruktof, destructive

distrust,*,ted,ting,tful, NOT TRUST OR HAVE CONFIDENCE IN

distulashen, distill(ation)

distunst, distance(d)

disturb,*,bed,bing,bingly,bance,bances, ber, TO MAKE IRREGULAR, INTERRUPT "prefixes: un"

disuade, dissuade

disubiluty, disability

disufectant, disinfect(ant)

disugre, disagree

disugree, disagree

disulow, disallow

disulugen, disillusion

disulushen, dissolute(tion)

disulute, dissolute

disumbark, disembark

disuneins, dissonant(nce)

disunent, dissonant

disupate, dissipate

disupation, dissipate(tion)

disupeer, disappear

disuplen, discipline

disupoint, disappoint

disuprove, disapprove

disuray, disarray

disurn, discern

disurvuse, disservice

diswade, dissuade

dit, died / diet / dye(d) / did

ditach, detach

ditan, detain

ditch,hes,hed,hing, A GULLEY IN THE EARTH, SKIP OUT OF SCHOOL, LEAVE SOMEONE

ditect, detect

ditective, detective

ditector, detector

ditekt, detect

ditektur, detector

ditel, detail

ditenshon, detention

diterent, deterrent

ditereorate, deteriorate

diteriorate, deteriorate

ditermenint, determine(nt)

ditermin, determine

ditermination, determination

ditest, detest

dito, ditto

ditocs, detox

ditox, detox

ditrakt, detract

ditto,*, COPY, DUPLICATE, SAME BACK TO YOU

ditur, deter

diturgent, detergent

diturmenism, determine(nism)

diubolikul, diabolical

diufram, diaphragm

diugnose, diagnose

diugram, diagram

diul, dial

diulekt, dialect

diulog, dialogue

diure, diary

diurea, diarrhea

diuretek, diuretic

diuretic,*, INCREASES THE ELIMINATION OF LIQUID

diureuh, diarrhea

diutery, dietary

diva, GODDESS (or see deva)

divadend, dividend

divaulv, devolve

divaut, devout / devote

dive,*,ving,er,dove, TO PLUNGE HEAD-FIRST INTO ANYTHING

divelop, develop

diverse,ely,sify,sifies,sified,sifying, sifability,sifiable,sification,sion, eness, sifier,rt,sity, A VARIETY, OTHER THAN THE NORM

diversion,*,nal,nary,nist, CHANGE COURSE/DIRECTION

diversity,ties, TO BE DIFFERENT "prefixes: bio"

divert,*,ted,ting,tingly,rse,rsion,rsity, CHANGE COURSE/DIRECTION

divians, deviance

divide,*,ed,ding,ision,isive,er,isor, SEPARATE, CREATE PARTS "prefixes: sub"

dividend,*, A NUMBER THAT CAN BE DIVIDED BY ANOTHER NUMBER

divient, deviant

divine,ely,eness,nity, OF A HIGH DEGREE, SUPREME, ABOVE AVERAGE (or see define) "prefixes: semi"

divise, device / devise

divisible,bility,ly, CAN BE DIVIDED "prefixes: in/multi"

division,*,nal, SEPARATE PARTS WITHIN THE WHOLE "prefixes: multi/sub"

divize, devise

divoed, devoid

divoid, devoid

divolve, devolve

divorce,*,ed,cing,eable,ee, FORMAL DIVISION/SEPARATION FROM
divoshen, devotion
divout, devout
divoution, devotion
divu, diva / deva
divudend, dividend
divulge,*,ed,ging,ence, REVEAL A SECRET/FACT
divurse, diverse
divurshen, diversion
divursity, diversity
divurt, divert
dixtarety, dexterity
diyul, dial
dizalujen, disillusion
dizapashen, dissipate(tion)
dizapate, dissipate
dizastur, disaster
dizatation, dissertation
dizbondent, despondent
dize, dizzy
dizeez, disease
dizembark, disembark
dizemunate, disseminate
dizenteant, dissent(ient)
dizi, dizzy
dizinfect, disinfect
dizmantul, dismantle
dizmul, dismal
dizobay, disobey
dizolve, dissolve
dizorder, disorder
dizordurly, disorderly
dizposuble, disposable
dizrepare, disrepair
dizrespekt, disrespect
dizumbark, disembark
dizupashe, dissipate(tion)
dizupate, dissipate
dizuray, disarray
dizzy,zier,ziest,zily,zied,zying, FUZZY, DISORIENTED, UNFOCUSED
do,oing,oes,one,oable,did, THE ACT OF (or see dew/due/doe/dough) "prefixes: over/un/under"
doal, dual / duel
dob, dub
dobal, double
dobil, double
dobl, double
dobul, double
doc, dock / duck / dose
docd, dock(ed) / duct / duck(ed)

docenchen, descension / dissension
docend, descend / dissent / descent / decent
docent, descend / dissent / descent / decent
doch, dodge
docile,ely,lity, OF RECEPTIVE/ ACCEPTABLE ATTITUDE, ABLE TO CONFORM
docinchen, descension / dissension
docind, descend / dissent / descent / decent
docint, descend / dissent / descent / decent
dock,*,ked,king,ker, TYPE OF HERB BEHAVIOR, LOADING PLATFORM FOR VESSELS, TO REMOVE "prefixes: un"
docma, dogma
docmadek, dogmatic
doct, dock(ed) / duct / duck(ed)
doctor,*,red,ring,rly,ral,rate, ONE WHO REPAIRS BODILY INJURY "prefixes: pre"
doctrenul, doctrine(nal)
doctrine,*,nal,nality,nally,naire, DOGMATIC TEACHING OF BELIEFS/ VALUES "prefixes: in"
document,*,ted,ting,tary,tation,tal, talist,table,ter, PAPERS WHICH STATE EVIDENCE
documentary,ries,rily, FACTS FOR PUBLIC VIEWING "prefixes: semi"
dodad, doodad
dodch, dodge
doder, daughter
doderize, deodorize
dodge,*,ed,ging,er, MOVES ASIDE, SHIFTS FROM PREDICTED POSITION (or see dog)
dodil, doodle
dodul, doodle
dodurent, deodorant
doe,*, FEMALE OF SHEEP/GOAT/DEER/ RABBIT/ ANTELOPE (or see do/ dough)
doel, duel / dual
doeng, doing
does, A TENSE OF THE WORD 'DO', DOING CURRENTLY (or see due(s)/ doe(s)/dose/douse)
doesn't, CONTRACTION OF THE WORDS 'DOES NOT'
doet, duet

dofesubelity, divisible(bility)
dofisable, divisible
dofol, duffle
dog,*,ggy,ggies, IN CANIS ANIMAL FAMILY (or see dodge) "prefixes: under"
doge, dodge / dog
dogma,*,atize,atizes,atized,atizing, atism,atist,atic,atically, PRINCIPLES/ TRUTHS DECIDED BY AUTHORITY
dogmadek, dogmatic
dogmatic,*,cally, BELIEVE YOUR PRINCIPLES ARE THE TRUTH
dogmutized, dogma(tized)
doil, duel / dual
doing,one, CURRENTLY IN THE ACT OF
doje, dodge
dok, dock
dokewment, document
dokma, dogma
dokter, doctor
doktren, doctrine
dokument, document
dol, doll / dole / dual / duel / dull
dolar, dollar
dolcimer, dulcimer
dole,*,ed,ling,eful, DEAL/HAND/GIVE OUT PORTIONS OF SOMETHING (or see dolly)
doler, dollar
dolfen, dolphin
dolfin, dolphin
dolir, dollar
doll,*,lled,lling,lly,llish,llishly,llishness, A TOY, CUTE LOOKING, GET DRESSED UP (or see dole/dodge)
dollar,*, U.S. MONEY/BILL
dolly,lies, OBJECT WITH WHEELS FOR MOVING THINGS, TOOL FOR VARIOUS TRADES, A DOLL
dolphin,*, LIVES IN WATER, CETACEAN
dolsemer, dulcimer
dolsumer, dulcimer
dom, dome / doom / dumb
domain,*,anial, TERRITORY/ PROPERTY WITH BOUNDARIES "prefixes: sub"
domane, domain
domanet, dominant
domasile, domicile
dome,*,ed,ming, HALF CIRCLE/180O (or see dumb/doom) "prefixes: semi"
domenate, dominate
domeneer, domineer
domenint, dominant

domenion, dominion
domeno, domino
domenyen, dominion
domestic,*,cally,cate,cated,cating, cation,cator,cable,city,cities, cize, FORCED TO CONFORM TO HUMAN USE "prefixes: semi"
domi, dummy
domicile,*,ed,ling,liary,liate,liation, HOME/RESIDENCE
dominance,cy, AUTHORITY, RULE "prefixes: pre"
dominant,tly,nce, AUTHORITY, RULE "prefixes: pre"
dominate,*,ed,ting,tion,tive,tor,ant, POWER OVER, OVERRULER "prefixes: pre/sub"
domineer,*,red,ring,ringly, EXCESSIVE RULE OVER OTHERS
dominion,*,ium, CONTROL OVER TERRITORY, OWNERSHIP OF
dominish, diminish
domino,oes, MASQUERADE COSTUME, GAME
domnate, dominate
domonent, dominant
domosile, domicile
domplin, dumpling
domunate, dominate
domunent, dominant
domunet, dominant
domusile, domicile
don,*,nned,nning, TO PUT ON, ADDED TO NAME (or see dawn/done)
don't, CONTRACTION FOR WORDS "DO NOT" (or see daunt/don(nned)/ dawn(ed))
donate,*,ed,ting,tion,tor,tive, A GIFT, PERHAPS WITH STRINGS ATTACHED
donc, dunk
dond, don't / daunt / don(nned) / dawn(ed)
done, PAST TENSE FOR THE WORD "DO", TASK/JOB COMPLETED "prefixes: re/under"
doner, donor
dong, dung
dongari, dungaree
dongen, dungeon
dongeri, dungaree
donjen, dungeon
donk, dunk
donkey,*, AN ANIMAL

donor,*,rship, SOMEONE WHO GIVES SOMETHING AWAY
dont, don't / daunt / don(nned) / dawn(ed)
donur, donor
donut, doughnut
dooal, duel / dual
dood, dude
doodad,*, GADGET, DECORATION
doode, duty
doodle,*,ed,ling,er, IDLY SKETCH, DRAW
doom,*,med,ming,msday, THE END OF
doon, dune
doop, dupe
dooplicity, duplicity
door,*,rless, OBJECT WHICH SEPARATES TWO SIDES WHEN CLOSED
doose, duce / deuce / due(s)
doosh, douche
doote, duty
dooz, due(s)
dope,*,ed,ping,er,ey, SLANG FOR DRUGS, NOT SMART
doplex, duplex
doplicate, duplicate
doplicity, duplicity
dor, door
dorivative, derive(vative)
dorive, derive
dormant,ncy, ASLEEP
dormatory, dormitory
dormet, dormant
dormetory, dormitory
dormit, dormant
dormitory,ries, A LARGE PLACE WITH MANY ROOMS FOR SLEEPING/ LIVING
dormut, dormant
dormutory, dormitory
dorsal,lly, ON THE BACK
dorsil, dorsal
dorsul, dorsal
dos, does / doze / doe(s) / dose / due(s) / dowse / those
dosable, disable
dosach, dosage
dosage,*, AMOUNT OF DRUG
dosbekable, despicable
dosberse, disperse / disburse
dosbikable, despicable
dosblased, displace(d)
dosblay, display

dosbose, dispose
doscremenate, discriminate
doscrete, discreet / discrete
dosderb, disturb
dosdrakt, distract
dosdrebute, distribute
dosdress, distress
dosdrust, distrust
dosdurb, disturb
dose,*,ed,sing,sage,sages, SPECIFIC AMOUNT OF SOMETHING (or see doze/due(s)) "prefixes: over"
dosech, dosage
dosege, dosage
dosej, dosage
dosemanate, disseminate
dosembar, december
dosend, descend / dissent / descent / decent
dosent, doesn't / descend / dissent / descent / decent
dosenugrate, disintegrate
doser, dozer
dosfigyer, disfigure
dosgreshun, discretion
dosgruntle, disgruntle
dosh, douche
dosich, dosage
dosige, dosage
dosij, dosage
dosil, docile
dosimbur, december
dosimer, dulcimer
dosin, dozen
dosind, descend / dissent / descent / decent
dosint, descend / dissent / descent / decent
dosk, dusk
doskrete, discreet / discrete
dospinse, dispense
dosplaced, displace(d)
dosplay, display
dosplease, displease
dospose, dispose
dosposuble, disposable
dospozul, disposal
dosputuble, dispute(table)
dosqualify, disqualify
dosreputuble, disreputable
dosrupshen, disruption
dosrupt, disrupt
dost, dust
dostengwish, distinguish

dosterb, disturb
dostingwish, distinguish
dostract, distract
dostress, distress
dostrust, distrust
dosuj, dosage
dosul, docile
dot,*,tted,tting, ROUND SPOTS (or see dote)
dote,*,ed,ting,tingly, TO WATCH OVER, OVERSEE CLOSELY (or see dot/doubt)
doted, dot(tted) / dote(d)
doter, daughter
dotir, daughter
dotur, daughter
dou, doe / dough
double,*,ed,ling,eness,ly,er, TWICE AS MANY AS THE ORIGINAL "prefixes: re"
doubt,*,ted,ting,table,tingly,tful,tfully, tless,tlessly, NOT COMPLETELY BELIEVABLE "prefixes: re/un"
douche,*,ed,hing, INTRODUCING FLUID INTO CAVITY OF BODY
dough,hy,hier,hiest,hiness, PASTY/ TACKY MIXTURE, MONEY
doughnut,*, ROUND PASTRY WITH HOLE
doul, dual / duel / dowel / dole
douls, dowel(s)
doun, down
doup, dope
dous, dose / douse / those / thus
douse,*,ed,sing,er, SMOTHER, PUT OUT, EXTINQUISH, SEEKS WATER, ALSO SPELLED 'DOUSE' (or see dowse)
dout, doubt / dote
dove,*, PAST TENSE FOR THE WORD "DIVE", A BIRD
dovegin, division
dovesubelity, divisible(bility)
dovesubl, divisible
dovine, divine
dovisability, divisible(bility)
dovorse, divorce
dow, dough / doe
dowel,*,led,ling, USED LIKE A NAIL/PIN/ SCREW
dowen, doing
dowl, dowel
down, OPPOSITE OF UP, FEATHERS OF A FOWL
downut, doughnut

dows, douse / dowse / dowel(s)
dowse,*,ed,sing,er, SMOTHER, PUT OUT, EXTINGUISH, SEEKS WATER, ALSO SPELLED 'DOUSE' (or see douse)
dowt, doubt
dowtful, doubt(full)
doz, doze / does / dose
doze,*,ed,zing,er,zy,zily,ziness, SLEEP LIGHTLY (or see dose)
dozen, TWELVE OF SOMETHING
dozent, doesn't
dozer,*, HEAVY EQUIPMENT WHICH MOVES EARTHEN MATERIAL
drad, dread
draft,*,ted,ting,ter,tier,tiest,ty,tily, tiness, A LIGHT BREEZE, TO PULL/ DRAW FROM "prefixes: in/over/up"
drag,*,gged,gging,ggingly, SLIDE/PULL WITH DIFFICULTY, PULLING WITHOUT LIFTING, MEN IN WOMEN'S CLOTHING
dragen, dragon
dragenfly, dragonfly
dragin, dragon
draginfly, dragonfly
dragon,*,nish, MYTHICAL ANIMAL
dragonfly,lies, INSECT
draid, dried
draier, drier
draiest, driest
draik, drake
drain,*,ned,ning,nage, FLUID/ENERGY FLOWING AWAY FROM, OUTLET "prefixes: under"
drake,*, INSECT FOR BAIT, MALE IN DUCK FAMILY
drama,*,atic,atical,atically,atize,aturgy, atist, GIVEN TO THEATER/PLAYS/ CHARACTER ROLES "prefixes: over/ melo"
dramatize,*,ed,zing,zation, GIVEN TO THEATER/PLAYS/ CHARACTER ROLES "prefixes: over"
dran, drawn / drain
drank, PAST TENSE FOR THE WORD "DRINK"
draot, drought
drape,*,ed,ping,ery,eries, HANGING CLOTH USED TO VEIL SOMETHING FROM SIGHT OR TO ENHANCE
drapir, dropper
drapur, dropper
dras, dress

drastic,cally, SEVERELY
drau, draw
draught, U.K. WORD FOR DRAFT (or see drought)
draul, droll / drawl
draun, drawn / drown
drauper, dropper
drause, drowsy
draut, drought
draw,*,wing,wn,rew,wable, TO BRING FORTH FROM OUT OF SIGHT, BRING TOWARDS "prefixes: over/un"
drawin, drawn
drawl,*,led,ling,ler,lingly, TO DRAG VOWELS OUT SLOWLY IN SPEAKING (or see droll)
drawn, PAST TENSE FOR THE WORD "DRAW" (or see drown) "prefixes: in/over"
drawnd, drown(ed)
drawpur, dropper
drawt, drought
dread,*,ded,ding,dful,dfully,dfulness, COMPLETE APPREHENSION IN FACING A SITUATION
dream,*,med,ming,mless,mlessly, mlessness,mful,mfully, mfulness, mily, my,mt, IMAGINE, THINK, ENVISION "prefixes: un"
dreary,rily,riness, GLOOMY
drebul, dribble
drebuld, dribble(d)
drech, dredge
dred, dread
dredge,*,ed,ging,er, TO GATHER OBJECTS UP FROM THE BOTTOM OF A BODY OF WATER WITH TOOLS/ MACHINERY
dreem, dream
dreft, drift
dreg, dredge
dreid, dried
drej, dredge
drel, drill
drem, dream
drench,hes,hed,hing,her, SOAKING WET
drenk, drink
drenker, drinker
drep, drip
drere, dreary
drery, dreary
dres, dress
dreser, dresser

dress,sses,sser,ssing,ssage, TO PUT ON CLOTHING "prefixes: re/un/under"

dresser, ONE WHO HELPS OTHERS DRESS IN COSTUMES, A CABINET WITH DRAWERS

dresur, dresser

drew, PAST TENSE FOR THE WORD "DRAW" "prefixes: over"

drewl, drool

drewp, droop

drezur, dresser

dri, dry

dribble,*,ed,ling,er, SMALL OR SHORT AMOUNT OF ANYTHING

dribul, dribble

drid, dried

dried, PAST TENSE FOR THE WORD "DRY"

drier, MORE DRY

driest, MOST" DRY

drift,*,ted,ting,tingly,tless,ty,ter, AMBLES ABOUT/AROUND/AWAY WITH EASE

drill,*,lled,lling,llable,ller, TO BORE, MAKE OPENINGS

drinch, drench

drink,*,king,rank,ker,kable,kability,runk, TO TAKE IN LIQUIDS

drinker,*, ONE WHO OVER INDULGES IN ALCOHOL

drip,*,pped,pping,ppy,pless, FALLING DROPS OF FLUID

drire, dreary

dris, dry(ries)

driur, drier / dryer

drive,*,ving,en,rove,er, TO MOVE/ PUSH/RIDE SOMETHING ALONG "prefixes: over"

drizzle,*,ed,ling,ly, VARIETY OF RAINFALL

dro, draw

drofe, drove

drog, drug

drol, drawl / droll

droll,ller,llest,llness,lly, ODDLY HUMOROUS (or see drawl)

droma, drama

dron, drone/ drawn / drown

dronc, drunk

drone,*,ed,ning,ningly,er, SINGLE TONE SOUND, A BEE, INCAPABLE OF FREE WILL/THOUGHT, REMOTE COMBAT VEHICLE

drool,*,led,ling,lingly,ler, SALIVA COMING FROM MOUTH

droop,*,ped,ping,pingly,py, TO LAY FORWARD LAZILY, SLUMP

drop,*,pped,pping,ppings,pper, LIQUID FALLING IN BLOBS, LET SOMETHING GO

droper, dropper

dropir, dropper

dropper,*,rful, AN INSTRUMENT WHICH ALLOWS A DROP AT A TIME

dropur, dropper

drought,*,ty, LONG PERIODS OF TIME WITHOUT WATER (or see draught)

droun, drown / drone

drouse, drowsy

drout, drought

drouze, drowsy

drove,*, PAST TENSE FOR THE WORD "DRIVE", MANY OF SOMETHING

drow, draw

drown,*,ned,ning, INTAKE OF WATER WHICH MAY KILL (or see drawn)

drowsy,sily,siness, NEARING SLEEP

drowt, drought

droz, draw(s)

dru, drew / true

druch, drudge

druchary, drudge(ry)

drudge,*,ed,ging,ery,eries,gingly, MENIAL/DULL WORK

druel, drool

drug,*,gged,gging,ggy, CHEMICALS (or see drudge)

drugd, drug(gged) / drudge(d)

druge, drudge / drug

druj, drudge

drujary, drudge(ry)

druk, drug

drul, drool

drum,*,mmed,mming,mmer, PERCUSSION INSTRUMENT, A LURING SOUND OR ACTION

drumd, drum(mmed)

drumer, drum(mmer)

drunk,*,ken,ker,kest,kard, PAST TENSE FOR THE WORD "DRINK", SOMEONE WHO DRINKS TOO MUCH ALCOHOL

drupe, droop

drus, dress

dry,ries,ried,ying,yable,yer,yest,iest, yable,yness,yly, TO REMOVE MOISTURE "prefixes: semi"

dryd, dried

dryer, APPLIANCE THAT DRIES CLOTHES (or see dry(rier))

dryest, driest

dryur, drier / dryer

du, dew / due / do

duable, do(able) / due(able)

dual,lity,lly,lism, TWO WORKING THE SAME, DOUBLE (or see duel) "prefixes: non"

duarf, dwarf

duarfs, dwarf(rves)

duat, duet

dub,*,bbed,bbing,bber, TITLE/NAME BESTOWED ON YOU BY ANOTHER, SOUND RECORDING

dubate, debate

dubilutate, debilitate

duble, double

dublikate, duplicate

dubol, double

dubry, debris

dubul, double

ducanter, decanter

duce,*, TWO, PEACE, LEAVING, LATER, STREET GANG (or see deuce)

ducenchen, descension / dissension

ducend, descend / dissent / descent / decent

ducent, dissent / descent / decent / descend

duch, douche

ducinchen, descension / dissension

ducind, descend / dissent / descent / decent

ducint, dissent / descent / decent / descend

duck,*,ked,king,ker,ky, TO STOOP/ TUCK/DIVE, FOWL/BIRD (or see duct)

ducline, decline

duct,*,ted,ting,tless,tal, CABLE/ CHANNEL FOR VARIOUS THINGS, TAPE (or see duck(ed))

dud,*, DOESN'T WORK, CLOTHES (or see dude)

dudad, doodad

dude,*, TOURIST ON A RANCH, INFORMAL REFERENCE TO ANOTHER PERSON (or see duty)

dudi, duty

dudil, doodle

dudol, doodle

dudy, duty

due,*, OUTSTANDING DEBT, DATE IT IS PAYABLE UPON (or see dew/do) "prefixes: en/over/un"
dueble, do(able) / due(able)
duel,*,ling,list,ler, DISPUTE/FIGHT BETWEEN TWO PEOPLE/ FACTIONS (or see dual/dwell)
duen, doing
dueng, doing
duet,*,tist, TWO VOICES/INSTRUMENTS PERFORMING TOGETHER
duf, dove
dufalt, default
dufase, deface
dufeet, defeat
dufel, duffel
dufenative, definitive
dufendant, defendant
dufense, defense
dufensible, defensible
duffel, CANVAS/WOOL MATERIAL
duffil, duffel
duffle, duffel
dufianse, defiance
dufide, divide
dufil, duffel
dufinative, definitive
dufine, define
dufishant, deficient
dufishensy, deficiency
dufle, duffel
dufol, duffel
dufray, defray
dufrost, defrost
duful, duffel
dufunkt, defunct
dufy, defy
dugrade, degrade
dugree, degree
duible, do(able) / due(able)
duil, dual / duel
duin, doing
duing, doing
duk, duck / duke / duct
duka, decay
dukanter, decanter
dukd, duck(ed) / duct / duke(d)
duke,*,edom, FISTS, POSITION UNDER THAT OF PRINCE (or see duck/duct)
dukline, decline
dukrepit, decrepit
dukt, duck(ed) / duct / duke(d)
dul, dual / duel / dull
dulay, delay

dulcimer,*, STRINGED INSTRUMENT
dulectable, delectable
dulema, dilemma
dulereus, delirious
dulete, delete
dulever, deliver
duliburate, deliberate
dulicacy, delicacy
dulimu, dilemma
dulishus, delicious
dulite, delight / daylight
duliver, deliver
dull,*,lled,lling,ller,llest,llish,llness,lly, llard, WITHOUT SHINE/ ATTRACTIVENESS, BORING (or see duel/dual)
dulsemur, dulcimer
dulsimer, dulcimer
dulujen, delusion / dilute(tion)
duluxe, deluxe
dum, doom / dumb
dumand, demand
dumb,*,ber,best,bing,bly,bness,mmy, CANNOT SPEAK, NOT TOO BRIGHT, MANNEQUIN
dumbling, dumpling
dume, dummy / doom
dumean, demean
dumeener, demeanor
dumenish, diminish
dumenshen, dimension
dumention, dimension
dumenyen, dominion
dumer, dumb(er)
dumes, dummy(mies)
dumesdek, domestic
dumest, dumb(est)
dumestic, domestic
dumie, dummy
duminish, diminish
duminted, demented
dumir, dumb(er)
dumist, dumb(est)
dumize, demise
dummy,mmies,mmied,mmying, ONE BEING MANIPULATED INTO ACTION/MOTION, A MANNEQUIN/ PUPPET
dumonik, demon(ic)
dumor, dumb(er)
dump,*,ped,ping,per,py,pily,piness,pier, piest, TO HEAVILY FALL, BE DROPPED

dumpling,*, DOUGHBALLS EATEN IN SAUCE
dumur, dumb(er)
dumy, dummy
dun, done / dune
dunce,*, DERAGATORY TERM FOR SLOW LEARNER
dune,*, MOUND/HILL OF SAND
dung,*,ged,ging,gy, MANURE (or see dunk)
dungaree,*, HEAVY COTTON CLOTHING
dungeon,*, PRISON CELL, CASTLE BASEMENT
dungeree, dungaree
dunguree, dungaree
dunie, deny
dunjen, dungeon
dunk,*,ked,king, TO DIP INTO (or see dung)
dunomenator, denominator
dunomunashin, denomination
dunote, denote
duns, dunce / dune(s)
duo,uet, A PAIR
duol, dual / duel
duorf, dwarf
duorfs, dwarf(rves)
duparsher, departure
dupart, depart
dupartment, department
duparture, departure
dupe,*,ed,ping, TO TRICK/DECEIVE
dupend, depend
dupendant, dependant / dependent
dupendence, dependence
dupikt, depict
dupind, depend
duplacate, duplicate
dupleshin, depletion
duplete, deplete
duplex,xes,xity, TWO WORKING IDENTICALLY, SIDE-BY-SIDE
duplicate,*,ed,ting,tion,tor,able,ability, tely,tive, COPY OF THE ORIGINAL "prefixes: in/re"
duplicity,tous, TWO-FACED, MISLEADING
duplokate, duplicate
duploma, diploma
duplomusy, diplomacy
duplorable, deplorable
duplore, deplore
dupose, depose
dupozishen, deposition

dupozit, deposit
dupresheate, depreciate
duprive, deprive
durable,*,bility,eness,ly, USEFUL MANY TIMES "prefixes: non"
durachon, duration
durashen, duration
duration, FROM NOW UNTIL...
durdee, dirty
durebul, durable
durect, direct
durection, direction
durectory, directory
durekshun, direction
durekt, direct
durektory, directory
dureng, during
dureshon, duration
duress, UNDER STRESS, RESTRAINED FROM FREEDOM
duretion, duration
durible, durable
during, AT THE SAME TIME
durivadive, derivative
durivative, derivative
durive, derive
durmatites, dermal(atitis)
durt, dirt
durty, dirty
dus, does / due(s) / deuce
dusabiludy, disability
dusable, disable
dusaster, disaster
dusbite, despite
dusblay, display
dusbose, dispose
dusbute, dispute
duscrete, discreet / discrete
duscretion, discretion
duscuss, discuss
dusdane, disdain
dusdent, distend
dusdention, distend(nsion)
dusdentshen, distend(nsion)
dusderb, disturb
dusdort, distort
dusdrakt, distract
dusdrebute, distribute
duse, does / due(s) / deuce
duseese, decease / disease
duseft, deceive(d)
dusember, december
dusemble, dissemble
dusembul, dissemble

dusemunate, disseminate
dusenagrate, disintegrate
dusenchen, descension / dissension
dusend, descend / dissent / descent / decent
dusendent, descendant
dusenshen, dissension / descension
dusent, dissent / descent / decent / descend
duses, decease / disease / deuce(s)
dusest, decease(d) / disease(d)
duset, deceit
dusetful, deceit(ful)
dusev, deceive
dusevd, deceive(d)
duseze, disease
dusfegure, disfigure
dusgard, discard
dusgise, disguise
dusgrase, disgrace
dush, douche
dushevul, dishevel
dusidewus, deciduous
dusimanate, disseminate
dusimbul, dissemble
dusimbur, december
dusin, dozen
dusinagrate, disintegrate
dusindent, descendant
dusinshun, dissension/ descension
dusint, doesn't
dusipul, disciple
dusk,ky,kily,kiness, END OF DAY BEFORE NIGHTFALL
duskremanate, discriminate
duskrepensy, discrepancy
duskrete, discreet / discrete
duskribe, describe
duskripshen, description
duskust, disgust
duskuver, discover
duskwolify, disqualify
duslocate, dislocate
dusloge, dislodge
dusmanul, dismantle
dusmay, dismay
dusmiss, dismiss
dusmownt, dismount
dusolfe, dissolve
dusoreant, disorient
duspensible, dispensable
duspeut, dispute
duspinse, dispense
duspite, despite

dusplay, display
dusplease, displease
duspose, dispose
dusposil, disposal
dusposuble, disposable
dusregard, disregard
dusrobe, disrobe
dust,*,ted,ting,ty,tless,tily,tiness,ter, TINY PARTICLES OF MATTER
dustane, disdain
duste, dust(y)
dusteengwish, distinguish
dustendible, distend(sible)
dustenkt, distinct
dusterb, disturb
dustill, distill
dustingwish, distinguish
dustintible, distend(sible)
dustort, distort
dustract, distract
dustress, distress
dustroy, destroy
dustrukshen, destruction
duswrubshen, disruption
duswrubt, disrupt
dute, duty
dutektur, detector
dutenshin, detention
dutereate, deteriorate
dutereorate, deteriorate
duterint, deterrent
dutermin, determine
duterminashen, determination
duti, duty
duturgent, detergent
duty,ties,tiful,tifully,tifulness,teous, OBLIGATION, RESPONSIBILITY, NECESSARY "prefixes: un"
duv, dove
duvejin, division
duvelup, develop
duversity, diversity
duvesubelity, divisible(bility)
duvide, divide
duvigen, division
duvigin, division
duvijen, division
duvine, divine
duvise, device
duvisubil, divisible
duvize, device
duvoid, devoid
duvorse, divorce
duvoshen, devotion

duvursedy, diversity
duwen, doing
dux, duck(s) / duct / duke(s)
duz, due(s) / does
duzaster, disaster
duzen, dozen
duzent, doesn't
duzeze, disease
duzin, dozen
duzint, doesn't
duzolve, dissolve
duzoreint, disorient
dwarf,*,fed,fing,fish,fishly,fishness,fism, rves, STUNTED FROM FULL GROWTH "prefixes: semi"
dwarves, MORE THAN ONE DWARF (or see dwarf)
dwell,*,lled,lling,ller,lt, DELAY, LINGER
dwendle, dwindle
dwindle,*,ed,ling,er, SHRINK, DEGENERATE, SHRIVEL
dworf, dwarf
dyagnol, diagonal
dyagnose, diagnose
dyalekt, dialect
dyameter, diameter
dyatery, dietary
dye,*,ed,eing,er,yable, STAIN/COLOR/ PIGMENTS TO APPLY (or see die/di) "prefixes: over"
dyet, diet
dyetery, dietary
dyignose, diagnose
dying, TOWARDS DEATH, TRANSFORMATION "prefixes: un"
dyke,*, MASCULINE LESBIAN (or see dike)
dylate, dilate
dynamic,*,ism,ist,istic,cal,cally, MOTION OF HIGH ENERGY "prefixes: bio"
dynamite,tic,er, EXPLOSIVES
dynasty,ties, STRING OF HEREDITARY RULERS
dypur, diaper / dipper
dyre, dire
dys, PREFIX INDICATING "BAD" MOST OFTEN MODIFIES THE WORD (or see die(s)/dice)
dysekt, dissect
dysentery,ric, INFECTIOUS DISEASE
dysfunction,*,nal, NOT ACTING WITHIN IDEAL LIMITS

dyslexia,ic, TIMING IN CORRPUS CALLOSUM NEURON SIGNALS WHICH AFFECTS COMMUNICATION BETWEEN BRAIN HEMISPHERES
dyufram, diaphragm
dyul, dial
dyulog, dialogue
dyureuh, diarrhea
each, ONE APIECE, TREATED INDIVIDUALLY
eager,rly,rness, MOTIVATED, VERY INTERESTED
eagle,*, BIRD
ear,*, GROWTH ON HEAD TO HEAR WITH
earing, earring
early,lier,liest,liness, PRIOR TO ORIGINAL TIME
earn,*,ned,ner,ning, REWARD FOR SERVICE/LABOR (or see urn) "prefixes: non/un"
earnest,*,tly,tness, SINCERE FEELINGS, EFFORT, MONEY TRANSACTION TO HOLD CONTRACT
earring,*, EAR ADORNMENT
earth,*,hed,hing,hen,hly,hlier,hliest, OUR PLANET "prefixes: un"
ease,*,ed,sing,eful,efully,efulness,sy, ABLE TO PERFORM WITHOUT STRAIN (or see easy) "prefixes: dis/ un"
easel,*, TRIPOD TO HOLD WORKBOARDS, ETC.
easement,*, LEGAL USE/RIGHTS TO SOMETHING, TO HELP MAKE EASIER
easily, NO DIFFICULTY
east,tern,ternly,tward,terly,terlies, terner,ting,tings, COMPASS DIRECTION
easy,sier,siest,sily,siness, NOT DIFFICULT/HARD (or see ease) "prefixes: un"
eat,*,ting,ten,tery,table,tables,ter, edible, TO INGEST "prefixes: over"
eaves, OVERHANG OF A BUILDING
eaze, ease / easy
eb, ebb
ebademik, epidemic
ebasode, episode
ebb,*,bbed,bbing, TO FALL/SINK/ RECEDE
ebdikate, abdicate
ebdumin, abdomen

ebedemek, epidemic
eberigenie, aborigine
ebide, abide
ebirijeny, aborigine
ebiss, abyss
ebnormul, abnormal
ebolish, abolish
ebomenable, abominable
ebominable, abominable
ebony, BLACK WOOD
ebord, aboard / abort
ebort, abort / aboard
ebowt, about
ebreveate, abbreviate
ebrod, abroad
ebsolv, absolve
ebstain, abstain
ebundinse, abundance
ebune, ebony
ebuve, above
ecademic, academic
eccentric,*,cally,city,cities, ODD, NOT OF THE NORM
ech, each / etch / edge / itch
echd, itch(ed) / etch(ed)
echo,oes,oed,oing,oingly, REPETITIVE SOUNDS BOUNCING BACK TOWARDS ORIGINATOR "prefixes: re"
echu, issue
echud, issue(d)
eckbrest, express(ed)
ecksderminate, exterminate
ecksdensible, extensible
eckdravert, extrovert
ecksdreem, extreme
eckspedeant, expedient
ecksplikuble, explicable
ecksploit, exploit
eckstensev, extensive
eckstensibly, extensible(ly)
ecksterminate, exterminate
ecksturminate, exterminate
eckuivocal, equivocal
eckwalibreum, equilibrium
eckwunimity, equanimity
eclectic,cally,cism, COMPILATION OF OTHERS WORK/VARIOUS SOURCES
eclektic, eclectic
eclepse, eclipse
eclipse,*,ed,sing,ptic, SHADOW CAST BY PLANETARY BODIES BLOCKING ANOTHER PLANETARY BODY
ecnolege, acknowledge

eco, PREFIX INDICATING "ECOLOGY" MOST OFTEN MODIFIES THE WORD (or see echo)

ecoli, A BACTERIA, PROPERLY SPELLED 'E COLI'

ecology,gical,gically,gist, SCIENCE ON ORGANISMS IN THE ENVIRONMENT

ecolugy, ecology

ecosfere, ecosphere

ecosistem, ecosystem

ecosphere, BREATHABLE AREA FOR LIFE

ecosystem,*, ORGANISMS INTERACTING TO CREATE ENVIRONMENT

ecquit, acquit

ecsclimashin, exclamation

ecsebt, except / accept

ecselerate, accelerate

ecsempt, exempt

ecsepshen, except(ion)

ecsite, excite

ecsklumashen, exclamation

ecspekt, expect

ecstasy,sies,atic,atically, JUBILANT, IN BLISS

ecsteengwish, extinguish

ecstradite, extradite

ecstrakt, extract

ecstuse, ecstasy

ecto, PREFIX INDICATING "OUTSIDE" MOST OFTEN MODIFIES THE WORD

ecute, acute

ecwanemity, equanimity

ecwashin, equation

ecwatic, aquatic

ecwilebreum, equilibrium

eczema,atous, SKIN IRRITATION FROM BACTERIA

eczima, eczema

ed, eat / eight / ate

edable, edible

edabt, adapt

edakit, etiquette

edapd, adapt

edapt, adapt

edatur, editor

edch, etch / edge / itch

eddy,ddies,ddied,ying, CIRCULAR MOVING CURRENT IN WATER/AIR

ede, eddy

edel, it'll

edelescense, adolescence

edelt, adult

edendum, addendum

edeology, ideology

edeosy, idiocy

edept, adept

edeshen, edition / add(ition)

edet, edit

edetur, editor

edeusy, idiocy

edeut, idiot

edge,*,ed,ging,gy,gier,giest,giness,er, POINT OF ANGLE WHERE ONE ANGLE DROPS OFF AT

edgust, adjust

edhere, adhere

edible,*,lity,eness, CAN BE SAFELY EATEN "prefixes: in"

edikit, etiquette

edikshen, addict(ion)

edil, it'll

edindum, addendum

ediosy, idiocy

edishen, edition / add(ition)

edit,*,ted,ting,tor,tion, MAKE READY FOR PUBLICATION "prefixes: in/un"

edition,*, ONE OUT OF A SET OF A PUBLISHED VOLUME (or see add(ition))

editor,*,rial,rially,rialist,rialize,rializes, rialized,rializing, DIRECTOR/ PREPARER OF WRITTEN MATERIAL

editur, editor

edj, etch / edge / itch

edjust, adjust

edmechen, admission

edmichen, admission

edmire, admire

edmishun, admission

edmit, admit

edmonish, admonish

edobt, adopt

edolt, adult

edoo, adieu

edopt, adopt

edore, adore

edorn, adorn

edrenulin, adrenaline

edres, address

edroit, adroit

edsedura, etcetera

edself, itself

edsh, etch / edge / itch

edu, adieu

eduble, edible

educate,*,ed,ting,tion,tional,tive,tor, INSTRUCT "prefixes: in/un"

edukit, etiquette

edul, it'll

edulescense, adolescence

edult, adult

edut, edit

edvantij, advantage

edverse, adverse

edvirse, adverse

edvise, advise / advice

edvurse, adverse

edy, eddy

edzetera, etcetera

eel,*, OCEAN FISH

eet, eat / yet

ef, if / eve

efact, effect / affect

efadent, evident

efaire, affair

efakt, effect / affect

efal, evil

efalushin, evolution

efan, even

efar, ever

efare, affair

efect, effect / affect

efegy, effigy

efekt, effect / affect

efektive, effect(ive) / affect(ive)

efeminate, effeminate

efeminit, effeminate

efen, even

efening, evening

efenity, affinity

efer, ever / affair

efert, effort

eferves, effervesce

efervesant, effervescent

efervescent, effervescent

efeus, effuse

efews, effuse

effect,*,ted,ting,tive,tively,tiveness,tual, tually,tualness,tuate, tuation, RESULT, FULFILLMENT ACCOMPLISHMENT (or see affect) "prefixes: in"

effeminate,acy,acies,ely,eness, OF FEMININE PERSUASION

effervesce,*,ed,cing,ence,ent,ently, GASEOUS BUBBLES, HAPPY FEELINGS

effervescent,tly,nce, GASEOUS BUBBLES, STRONG FEELINGS

efficacy,city,cious,ciously,ciousness, TO BE EFFECTIVE "prefixes: in"

efficiency,cies,nt, PRODUCE WELL IN SHORT PERIOD OF TIME, TYPE OF LIVING QUARTERS

efficient,tly,ncy, PRODUCE EFFECTIVELY IN SHORT PERIOD OF TIME "prefixes: in"

effigy,gies, SOMETHING CONSTRUCTED IN HUMAN LIKENESS

effort,*,tless,tlessly,tlessness, ATTEMPT TO PRODUCE, SHOW SKILLS/ TALENTS

effuse,*,ed,sing,sion,sive,sively,siveness, EXPRESS/FLOW/SPREAD FREELY

efichent, efficient

eficiency, efficiency

efident, evident

efigy, effigy

efil, evil

efilushen, evolution

efin, even

efinity, affinity

efir, ever

efirves, effervesce

efirvesant, effervescent

efishensy, efficiency

efishent, efficient

efisiancy, efficiency

efl, evil

eflikt, afflict

eflot, afloat

efluinse, affluence

efning, evening

efodent, evident

efogy, effigy

efol, evil

efolushin, evolution

efolve, evolve

efon, even

efoot, afoot

efor, ever

eford, afford

efort, effort

efrad, afraid

efrebote, every(body)

efreda, every(day)

efree, every

efrething, every(thing)

efrewer, every(where)

efrewun, every(one)

efriwun, every(one)

efront, affront

efrunt, affront

efryday, every(day)

efudent, evident

efugy, effigy

eful, evil

efulushun, evolution

efur, ever

efurt, effort

efurves, effervesce

efurvesant, effervescent

efuse, effuse

efut, afoot

eg, edge / egg / etch / itch

egajurate, exaggerate

egalatarian, egalitarian

egalitarian,*,nism, EQUALITY OF ALL PEOPLES

egalutarean, egalitarian

egekt, eject

egemplify, exemplify

egenst, against

eger, eager

egern, adjourn

egg,*,gged,gging,ggy, PRODUCED BY FOWL/BIRD/REPTILES

eginst, against

egle, eagle

egneranse, ignorant(nce)

egneshin, ignition

egneus, igneous

egnide, ignite

egnishin, ignition

egnite, ignite

egnor, ignore

egnorants, ignorant(nce)

egnurant, ignorant

ego,*,oism,oist,otistic,oistical,oistically, otist,otism,ocentric, PART OF US THAT IS SELF-SERVING/FEARFUL (or see echo)

egotist,tic,tical,tically, CENTERED ON SELF

egotistic,cal,cally, CENTERED ON ONESELF

egre, agree

egresiv, aggressive

egsabishen, exhibit(ion)

egsadera, etcetera

egsagurate, exaggerate

egsajurate, exaggerate

egsakt, exact

egsam, exam

egsample, example

egsaspurate, exasperate

egsastshin, exhaust(ion)

egsbarenshal, experiential

egsbereanse, experience

egsberenshal, experiential

egsberimentashen, experiment(ation)

egsbire, expire

egsblan, explain

egsblekuble, explicable

egsblod, explode

egsblor, explore

egsbloshen, explosion

egsbort, export

egsboz, expose

egsbres, express

egsburenshal, experiential

egsburt, expert

egscavate, excavate

egsclusive, exclusive

egsdensible, extensible

egsdra, extra

egsdradite, extradite

egsdrakt, extract

egsdreem, extreme

egsdrordinare, extraordinaire

egsdrordinary, extraordinary

egsduse, ecstasy

egsebit, exhibit

egsebt, except / accept

egsecutive, executive

egsedira, etcetera

egseed, exceed

egsemplify, exemplify

egsempt, exempt

egsemshen, exempt(ion)

egsepshen, except(ion)

egsept, except / accept

egsersize, exercise / exorcise

egsert, exert

egsesif, excess(ive) / access(ive)

egsest, exist

egsetara, etcetera

egsglumashen, exclamation

egshale, exhale

egsibeshen, exhibit(ion)

egsibit, exhibit

egsilarate, exhilarate / accelerate

egsile, exile

egsima, eczema

egsimplify, exemplify

egsimt, exempt

egsist, exist

egsistens, exist(ence)

egsit, exit

egskershun, excursion
egskurshen, excursion
egskuvate, excavate
egsorsize, exercise / exorcise
egsost, exhaust
egsostshen, exhaust(ion)
egsotic, exotic
egspadishen, expedition
egspand, expand
egspans, expanse / expense
egspect, expect
egspedient, expedient
egspeedeint, expedient
egspel, expel
egspense, expense
egsperament, experiment
egspereanse, experience
egspinse, expense
egspirashen, expire(ration)
egspire, expire
egsplanashen, explanation
egsplanatory, explanatory
egsplane, explain
egsplecable, explicable
egsplesit, explicit
egsplod, explode
egsplor, explore
egsplorashen, explore(ration)
egsploratory, explore(ratory)
egsploshen, explosion
egsplosive, explosive
egsplunashen, explanation
egsport, export
egsportashen, export(ation)
egspos, expose
egspres, express
egspurashen, expire(ration)
egspurt, expert
egsqwizit, exquisite
egstend, extend
egstengwish, extinguish
egstenkt, extinct
egstensev, extensive
egstenshen, extension
egstenuate, extenuate
egstereor, exterior
egsternul, external
egstinkt, extinct
egstinsev, extensive
egstra, extra
egstradite, extradite
egstrakt, extract
egstravert, extrovert
egstrem, extreme

egstremly, extreme(ly)
egstrordinare, extraordinaire
egstrordinary, extraordinary
egsturnal, external
egsubishen, exhibit(ion)
egsulent, excellent
egsurshen, exert(ion)
egsurt, exert
egszemt, exempt
egukate, educate
egul, eagle
egur, eager
egzajurate, exaggerate
egzakt, exact
egzam, exam
egzample, example
egzema, eczema
egzershin, exert(ion)
egzile, exile
egzilurate, exhilarate / accelerate
egzima, eczema
egzimpt, exempt
egzimt, exempt
egzist, exist
egzit, exit
egzotek, exotic
egzurshen, exert(ion)
egzursize, exercise / exorcise
egzurtion, exert(ion)
ehed, ahead
eight,*,teen,teenth,tieth,ty, ENGLISH
    NUMBER (or see ate)
eighteen,nth,nths, ENGLISH NUMBER
eil, aisle
eir, air / heir / err
eit, eight / ate
ej, edge / etch / itch
ejakt, eject
eject,*,ted,ting,tion,table,tive,tor,tors,
    FORCED TO LEAVE/BE EXPELLED
ejekt, eject
ejenda, agenda
ejern, adjourn
ejorn, adjourn
ejrenalin, adrenaline
ejukate, educate
ejusduble, adjust(able)
ejust, adjust
ekademe, academy
ekadume, academy
ekaunemity, equanimity
ekcept, accept / except
ekcesori, accessory
ekchange, exchange

eklektic, eclectic
eklipse, eclipse
ekliptik, eclipse(ptic)
eknolege, acknowledge
eknor, ignore
eknurint, ignorant
eko, echo / ego
ekod, echo(ed)
ekology, ecology
ekolugy, ecology
ekonimy, economy
ekonume, economy
ekosestum, ecosystem
ekosfere, ecosphere
ekosistem, ecosystem
ekosphere, ecosphere
eksadra, etcetera
eksagerashen, exaggerate(tion)
eksajurashen, exaggerate(tion)
eksakute, execute
eksalant, excellent
eksalins, excel(llence)
eksam, exam
eksamen, examine
eksamenashen, examine(nation)
eksamin, examine
eksaminashen, examine(nation)
eksample, example
eksapurashen, exasperate(tion)
eksaqute, execute
eksated, exit(ed)
eksbarenshal, experiential
eksbedeant, expedient
eksberament, experiment
eksberenshal, experiential
eksbire, expire
eksbirenshal, experiential
eksblan, explain
eksblanashen, explanation
eksblanatory, explanatory
eksbleckable, explicable
eksblinashen, explanation
eksblod, explode
eksblor, explore
eksblorashen, explore(ration)
eksbloshen, explosion
eksbloytashen, exploit(ation)
eksbortashen, export(ation)
eksbos, expose
eksbres, express
eksburashen, expire(ration)
eksburenshal, experiential
eksburt, expert
ekscalate, escalate / escalade

ekscerjen, excursion
ekschange, exchange
eksclemashin, exclamation
eksclusive, exclusive
ekscurshin, excursion
ekscuse, excuse
eksdansev, extensive
eksdensible, extensible
eksderminate, exterminate
eksdra, extra
eksdradite, extradite
eksdrakt, extract
eksdravert, extrovert
eksdreem, extreme
eksdrem, extreme
eksdremly, extreme(ly)
eksdrivurt, extrovert
eksdrordinare, extraordinaire /
    extraordinary
eksdurminate, exterminate
eksebit, exhibit
eksebt, except / accept
eksecutive, executive
eksedra, etcetera
eksekute, execute
eksel, excel / accel
ekselarashen, accelerate(tion)
ekseld, excel(lled) / accel(lled)
ekselense, excellent
ekselerashen, accelerate(tion)
ekselerate, accelerate
ekselurashen, accelerate(tion)
ekseluratur, accelerate(tor)
eksemplify, exemplify
eksentrek, eccentric
eksentrik, eccentric
eksepshen, except(ion)
ekseptense, accept(ance)
ekserpt, excerpt
eksert, exert
ekses, excess / access
eksesif, excess(ive) / access(ive)
eksesis, excess(es) / access(es)
eksesori, accessory
eksetera, etcetera
eksfoleate, exfoliate
eksglud, exclude
eksglumashen, exclamation
eksglut, exclude
ekshale, exhale
eksibishen, exhibit(ion)
eksibit, exhibit
eksilarat, exhilarate / accelerate
eksile, exile

eksilens, excel(llence)
eksimplify, exemplify
eksimpt, exempt
eksimshen, exempt(ion)
eksinshuate, accentuate
eksintrik, eccentric
eksirpt, excerpt
eksistens, exist(ence)
eksit, exit / excite
eksitment, excite(ment)
ekskalate, escalate / escalade
eksklumashen, exclamation
ekskurshen, excursion
ekskuse, excuse
ekskuvaded, excavate(d)
ekskuvashen, excavate(tion)
ekskuvate, excavate
ekskwisit, exquisite
ekslusef, exclusive
eksolent, excellent
eksorbeint, exorbitant
eksorbident, exorbitant
eksorsize, exercise / exorcise
ekspadishen, expedition
ekspand, expand
ekspans, expanse / expense
ekspedishen, expedition
ekspekt, expect
ekspektashen, expect(tation)
ekspektent, expect(ant)
ekspel, expel
ekspend, expend
ekspense, expense
ekspensef, expense(sive)
eksperament, experiment
ekspereanse, experience
eksperenshal, experiential
ekspert, expert
ekspinse, expense
ekspire, expire
ekspirenshal, experiential
eksplan, explain
eksplanashen, explanation
eksplanatory, explanatory
eksplecable, explicable
eksplicit, explicit
eksplisit, explicit
eksplisitly, explicit(ly)
eksplod, explode
eksploet, exploit
eksploit, exploit
eksplor, explore
eksplorashen, explore(ration)
eksploratory, explore(ratory)

eksploshen, explosion
eksplosive, explosive
eksployt, exploit
eksplunashen, explanation
eksport, export
eksportashen, export(ation)
ekspos, expose
eksprenshal, experiential
ekspres, express
ekspurenshal, experiential
eksqus, excuse
ekstansive, extensive
ekstend, extend
ekstengwish, extinguish
ekstensebly, extensible(ly)
ekstensev, extensive
ekstenshen, extension
ekstenuate, extenuate
ekstenzable, extensible
ekstereur, exterior
ekstind, extend
ekstinkt, extinct
ekstinsebly, extensible(ly)
ekstinsev, extensive
ekstra, extra
ekstradite, extradite
ekstrakt, extract
ekstravert, extrovert
ekstrem, extreme
ekstremly, extreme(ly)
ekstrivurt, extrovert
ekstrordinare, extraordinaire
ekstrordinary, extraordinary
ekstruvert, extrovert
eksturnal, external
ekstuse, ecstasy
eksubishen, exhibit(ion)
eksulant, excellent
eksulashen, exhale(lation)
eksulins, excellent(nce)
eksuqushen, execute(tion)
eksurpt, excerpt
eksurshen, exert(ion)
eksursize, exercise / exorcise
eksurt, exert
eksuvashen, excavate(tion)
ekuate, equate
ekute, acute
ekwabil, equable
ekwable, equable
ekwade, equity
ekwader, equator
ekwal, equal
ekwalebreum, equilibrium

ekwalete, equality
ekwaliz, equal(ize)
ekwanimety, equanimity
ekwanimity, equanimity
ekwashun, equation
ekwate, equate / equity
ekwatur, equator
ekwaul, equal
ekwauzition, acquisition
ekwebul, equable
ekwel, equal
ekwelebreum, equilibrium
ekwenox, equinox
ekwevalent, equivalent
ekwevokul, equivocal
ekwil, equal
ekwinoks, equinox
ekwip, equip
ekwipment, equipment
ekwit, acquit
ekwity, equity
ekwivokate, equivocate
ekwivulent, equivalent
ekwolity, equality
ekwoliz, equal(ize)
ekwotek, aquatic
ekwuble, equable
ekwude, equity
ekwul, equal
ekwulebrium, equilibrium
ekwuliz, equal(ize)
ekwunimity, equanimity
ekwunox, equinox
ekwuzition, acquisition
el, eel / ail / ill / ale
elagint, elegant
elakwens, eloquence
elakwense, eloquence
elakwent, eloquent
elamentary, elementary
elaquence, eloquence
elaquens, eloquence
elaquent, eloquent
elarm, alarm
elastic,*,cally,city,cize,cizes,cized,cizing,
STRETCHES OUT/ SHRINKS BACK
"prefixes: in"
elastrate, illustrate
elate,*,ed,ting,tion, RAISED MOOD/
SPIRIT
elavashen, elevate(tion)
elavater, elevate(r)
elbow,*,wed,wing, JOINT IN THE ARM
elbum, album

elchuhol, alcohol
elder,*,est,rly,liness,rship, ONE WHO
HAS LIVED MORE YEARS THAN
OTHERS (or see alder)
eldur, elder
ele, alley
elect,*,ted,ting,tion,tions,table,tive,
tively,tiveness,tor,toral, torally,
torate,tioneer,tioneers,tioneered,
tioneering, TO MAKE A CHOICE
"prefixes: un"
elective,*,ely,eness, OPTION TO
CHOOSE
elector,*,ral,rally,rate, VOTERS
electric,cal,cals,cally,city,ify,ro,cian,
FREQUENCY/ENERGY EXISTING IN
ALL PARTICLES "prefixes: bio"
electrician,*, PEOPLE WHO WORK
WITH WIRES/ELECTRICITY
electrishun, electrician
electro, PREFIX INDICATING "ELECTRIC"
MOST OFTEN MODIFIES THE WORD
electron,*,nic,nics,nically, A CHARGED
PARTICLE
eledge, allege
elefint, elephant
elegable, eligible
elegance, BEAUTIFUL/CLASSY "prefixes:
in"
eleganse, allegiance / elegance
elegant,tly,nce, BEAUTIFUL/CLASSY
"prefixes: in"
elege, allege
elegible, eligible
elegul, illegal
elejense, allegiance / elegance
elekt, elect
elektev, elective
elektric, electric
elektrician, electrician
elektrishen, electrician
elekul, illegal
elekwens, eloquence
elekwent, eloquent
elemanate, eliminate
element,*,tal,tally,tary, BASIC,
FUNDAMENTAL "prefixes: retro"
elementary,rily,riness, FIRST AND BASIC
elephant,*, AN ANIMAL
eleptic, elliptic
elere, allure
elergik, allergic
elert, alert
elet, elite

eletist, elite(tist)
elevashen, elevate(tion)
elevate,*,ed,ting,tion,tional,tor, RAISE
HORIZONTAL LEVEL
eleveate, alleviate
eleven,nth,nths, AN ENGLISH NUMBER
elevin, eleven
elevinth, eleven(th)
elf,elves,fin,fish, IMAGINARY ENTITIES
elfs, elf(lves)
elgebra, algebra
elianse, alliance
elicit,*,ted,ting,tation,tor, PROVOKE/
DRAW RESPONSE (or see illicit)
eliderate, illiterate
elifent, elephant
eligable, eligible
eligent, elegant
eligible,*,bly,bility,bilities, POTENTIAL
TO BE CHOSEN "prefixes: in"
elikwens, eloquence
elikwent, eloquent
elimenate, eliminate
eliminate,*,ed,ting,tion,tive,tor,tory,
GET RID OF, DISPOSE
elimony, alimony
eline, align
elipse, ellipse
elipsus, ellipsis
eliptic, elliptic
eliquence, eloquence
eliquent, eloquent
eliset, elicit / illicit
elisit, elicit / illicit
elistrate, illustrate
elite,*,tist,tism, GROUP OF THOSE WHO
BELIEVE THEY ARE THE BEST OF
THEIR KIND/CATEGORY
eliturate, illiterate
elivashen, elevate(tion)
elive, alive
elk, IN THE DEER FAMILY
ellipse,sis, GEOMETRIC SHAPE
ellipsis, SYMBOL USED IN PLACE OF A
WORD (...)
elliptic,cal,cally,city,cities, OVAL SHAPE,
TO BE CONCISE "prefixes: semi"
ellsit, elicit / illicit
elliterate, illiterate
ellustrious, illustrious
elnes, ill(ness)
elogekul, illogical
elogicul, illogical

elongate,*,ed,ting,tion, TO LENGTHEN, MAKE LONGER

elood, elude

eloor, allure

eloosuf, allusive / elusive / illusive

eloot, elude

elope,*,ed,ping, GO AWAY TO BE WED WITHOUT NOTIFICATION

eloquence,*, TASTEFULLY/ PERSUASIVELY COMMUNICATED

eloquent,tly,tness,nce, STRIKING/ MOVING EXPRESSION "prefixes: in"

elorm, alarm

elostrious, illustrious

elovate, elevate

eloy, alloy

else,*, NOT WHO/WHAT/WHERE INTENDED OR EXPECTED

elsewhere, SOMEWHERE OTHER THAN WHERE EXPECTED TO BE

elso, also

eltetude, altitude

eltitude, altitude

elucidate,*,ed,ting,tion,tive,tor,tory, useness,usion, MAKE CLEAR/ UNDERSTANDABLE, EXPLAIN

elude,*,ed,ding,usive,usion, GET AWAY, NOT BE PERCEIVED/DEFINED (or see allude)

elufint, elephant

elugable, eligible

elugant, elegant

elugens, elegant(nce) / elegance

elugent, elegant

elugint, elegant

elukwens, eloquence

elukwent, eloquent

elumenade, illuminate

elumentary, elementary

elumenum, aluminum

eluminate, illuminate

elumintry, elementary

eluminum, aluminum

elumony, alimony

eluquence, eloquence

eluquent, eloquent

elure, allure

elurgik, allergic

elurjik, allergic

elurt, alert

elushun, illusion / allusion

elusive,ely,eness,sory, GET AWAY, NOT BE PERCEIVED (or see allusive/ illusive)

elustrate, illustrate

elustrious, illustrious

eluvashen, elevate(tion)

eluvate, elevate

em, PREFIX INDICATING "INTO/ON/PUT INTO" MOST OFTEN MODIFIES THE WORD (or see am/them)

emachure, amateur

emaculet, immaculate

emage, image

emagenashen, imagine(ation)

emagrant, immigrant / emigrant

emagrashen, immigrate(tion)

emagrate, immigrate

emagrunt, immigrant / emigrant

emagunashen, imagine(ation)

emaj, image

emajinashen, imagine(nation)

emakewlit, immaculate

emakulit, immaculate

emanate,*,ed,ting,tion,tional,tionist, tive, EMITS, GIVES OFF, SENDS OUT

emancipate,*,ed,ting,tion, FREE FROM BONDAGE

emanens, eminence / imminence / immanence

emanent, eminent / imminent / immanent

emanit, eminent / imminent / immanent

emansepade, emancipate

emansipate, emancipate

ematashin, imitate(tion)

ematate, imitate

ematation, imitate(tion)

ematerial, immaterial

emature, immature

embankment,*, A BURM/MOUND

embargo,oes, RESTRICT FROM PORTS

embaris, embarrass

embark,*,ked,king, PREPARING TO TAKE A JOURNEY "prefixes: dis"

embarrass,sses,ssed,ssing,ssingly, ssment, UNDESIRABLY EXPOSED "prefixes: dis"

embassy,sies, SAFE PLACE WITHIN ANOTHER COUNTRY

embaudes, embody(dies)

embed,*,dded,dding, SINK INTO UNTIL FLUSH

ember,*, SPARK/COAL FROM FIREWOOD

emberis, embarrass

embilukil, umbilical

embishun, ambition

emblem,*, A SYMBOL OR FIGURE

emblie, imply

emblum, emblem

embody,dies,died,dying,diment, diments, OF A VISIBLE FORM, TANGIBLE, PARTS INTO A WHOLE "prefixes: dis"

emboss,sses,ssed,ssing,sser,ssment, IMPRINT INTO

embostur, imposter

emboudes, embody(dies)

embrace,*,ed,cing,eable,ement,er, TO HOLD DEAR

embrase, embrace

embreo, embryo

embroeder, embroider

embroider,*,red,ring,rer,ry,ries, STITCH WITH NEEDLE/THREAD

embrufe, improve

embrufment, improve(ment)

embryo,*,onic,onical,onically,ology, ologist,otic, SOMETHING GROWING INSIDE BEFORE IT EMERGES "prefixes: pre"

embtee, empty

embulense, ambulance

embur, ember

embush, ambush

embuzishun, impose(sition)

emcompruble, incomparable

emcumblete, incomplete

emeable, amiable

emedeat, immediate

emej, image

emenate, emanate

emend, amend

emense, immense

emensurable, immensurable

emerald, A COLOR, A GEMSTONE

emerchen, immerse(sion)

emerge,*,ed,ging,ence,ent,ency,encies, COME FROM WITHIN, ERUPT, COME INTO BEING

emergency,cies, TO BE DEALT WITH IMMEDIATELY

emerjensee, emergency

emersable, immersible

emersed, PLANT PARTS ABOVE WATER (or see immerse(d))

emershen, immerse(sion)

emeshen, emission / omission

emeterial, immaterial

emfadek, emphatic

emfasis, emphasis / emphasize
emfusis, emphasis / emphasize
emigrant,*, FOREIGNER FROM ANOTHER COUNTRY (or see immigrant)
emigrate,*,ed,ting,tion, LEAVE A COUNTRY TO GO TO ANOTHER (or see immigrate)
emigrunt, immigrant / emigrant
emij, image
eminate, emanate
emind, amend
eminence,cy, FORMAL RANK/POSITION (or see imminence/immanence)
eminens, eminence / imminence / immanence
eminent,tly,nce, SOMEONE WHO ACHIEVES BEYOND OTHERS (or see eminence/imminence/immanence) "prefixes: pre"
eminse, immense
eminsurable, immensurable
emirchen, immerse(sion)
emirge, emerge
emirsable, immersible
emirshen, immerse(sion)
emission,*, SOMETHING DISCHARGED, PUT INTO CIRCULATION (or see omission)
emit,*,tted,tting,tter, DISCHARGE, PUT OUT A FREQUENCY (or see omit)
emitate, imitate
emitation, imitate(tion)
emiterial, immaterial
emmagrate, immigrate / emigrate
emmensurable, immensurable
emmershen, immerse(sion)
emminsurable, immensurable
emmirsible, immersible
emmobile, immobile
emmpresion, impression
emmpressive, impressive
emmurshen, immerse(sion)
emobile, immobile
emochun, emotion
emograte, immigrate / emigrate
emonate, emanate
emonens, eminence / imminence / immanence
emonent, eminent / imminent / immanent
emonia, ammonia
emople, immobile
emoral, immoral

emordul, immortal
emortal, immortal
emortalety, immortal(ity)
emorul, immoral
emoshin, emotion
emoterial, immaterial
emotion,*,nal,nally,nality,nless,nalize, nalizes,nalized,nalizing,ive,ivism, REACTION CAUSED BY CHEMICALS RELEASED BY WHAT WE ARE THINKING "prefixes: non/un"
emownt, amount
empachuis, impetuous
empact, impact
empairm, empower
empar, empower
emparasist, empirical(cist)
empare, impair
emparetive, imperative
emparical, empirical
emparment, empower(ment)
emparor, emperor
empathy, ABILITY TO UNDERSTAND/ FEEL ANOTHER PERSON'S EXPERIENCE/FEELINGS
empaurment, empower(ment)
empeach, impeach
empecable, impeccable
empechuis, impetuous
empede, impede
empeed, impede
empekuble, impeccable
emperative, imperative
emperfect, imperfect
emperor,*, RULER OF PEOPLE/LAND
empersenate, impersonate
empersonal, impersonal
empersonashen, impersonate(tion)
empersonate, impersonate
empetchuis, impetuous
emphasis,ize, PLACE GREAT IMPORTANCE IN/UPON "prefixes: de-/over"
emphasize,*,ed,zing,is, PLACE GREAT IMPORTANCE IN/UPON "prefixes: de-/over"
emphatic,cally, PLACE GREAT IMPORTANCE IN/UPON
emphisis, emphasis / emphasize
empire,*, REGION OF PEOPLE/LAND RULED BY AN EMPEROR
empirer, emperor
empirfect, imperfect

empirical,lly,cism,cist,cists,rics, RELIES ONLY ON OBSERVATION/ EXPERIMENT
empirsonal, impersonal
emplament, implement
emplant, implant
emplicate, implicate
emplication, implicate(tion)
emploe, employee / employ
emploer, employer
employ,*,yed,ying,yable,yability,yer, yee,yeement, USE SOMETHING/ SOMEONE TO COMPLETE A TASK WHICH MAY/MAY NOT INVOLVE MONEY (or see employee) "prefixes: sub/un"
employee,*, SOMEONE WHO IS LEGALLY HIRED AND WORKS FOR PAY (or see employ) "prefixes: non/ under"
employer,*, SOMEONE WHO PAYS SOMEONE ELSE TO WORK "prefixes: non"
employment,*, BEING HIRED TO WORK "prefixes: un"
emplucashen, implicate(tion)
emplucate, implicate
emplument, implement
emply, imply
empofuresh, impoverish
empolite, impolite
empolse, impulse
emport, import
emportant, important
emportashen, import(ation)
emportins, important(nce)
empose, impose
emposible, impossible
emposter, imposter
emposuble, impossible
empound, impound
empour, empower
empourtens, important(nce)
empourtent, important
empoverish, impoverish
empower,*,red,ring,ment, TEACH/ PROVIDE SOMEONE WITH ABILITY TO DO THINGS FOR THEMSELVES "prefixes: dis"
empoze, impose
empraktecul, impractical
emprapuble, improbable
emprasev, impressive
emprashen, impression

emprasise, imprecise
empravize, improvise
emprechen, impression
emprecise, imprecise
empregnable, impregnable
empregnate, impregnate
empregnuble, impregnable
emprent, imprint
empres, empress / impress
empresef, impressive
empreshen, impression
empresif, impressive
empresise, imprecise
empresive, impressive
empresont, imprison(ed)
empress,sses, FEMALE RULER OF
EMPIRE (or see impress)
empretion, impression
emprint, imprint
emprison, imprison
emprobable, improbable
empromptu, impromptu
empromtu, impromptu
empropable, improbable
emproper, improper
emprove, improve
emprovement, improve(ment)
emprovisation, improvise(sation)
emprovize, improvise
emprovusashen, improvise(sation)
emprufe, improve
emprus, empress / impress
empruve, improve
empruvize, improvise
emptee, empty
empty,ties,tied,tying,tier,tiest,tily,tiness,
REMOVE CONTENTS FROM
SOMETHING "prefixes: non"
empulite, impolite
empulse, impulse
empulsef, impulse(sive)
empulsive, impulse(sive)
empurfect, imperfect
empurfekt, imperfect
empuror, emperor
empursenate, impersonate
empursonal, impersonal
emput, input
emputate, amputate
empuzishen, impose(sition)
emruld, emerald
emte, empty
emug, image
emugrant, immigrant / emigrant

emugrashen, immigrate(tion) /
emigrate(tion)
emugrate, immigrate
emuj, image
emulate,*,ed,ting,tion,tive,tively,tor,
lous,lously,lousness, STRIVE TO LIVE
UP TO
emune, immune
emunens, eminence / imminence/
immanence
emunety, immune(nity)
emunezashen, immunize(zation)
emunise, immunize
emurg, emerge
emurgensee, emergency
emursable, immersible
emurse, immerse / emersed
emutashin, imitate(tion)
emutate, imitate
emuterial, immaterial
emuze, amuse
en, PREFIX INDICATING "INTO/ON/PUT
INTO" MOST OFTEN MODIFIES THE
WORD (or see prefix in/un/inn)
enabiledy, inability
enability, inability
enabishen, inhibit(ion)
enable,*,ed,ling,ement,er, EMPOWER/
AID SOMEONE/SOMETHING TO
PERFORM MORE EFFICIENTLY (or
see unable) "prefixes: dis"
enabul, enable / unable
enaccessible, inaccessible
enact,*,ted,ting,tment,table,tor,tive,
TO PERFORM/MAKE INTO (or see
inactive)
enaction, inaction
enacuracy, inaccurate(acy)
enacurate, inaccurate
enadekwit, inadequate
enadequate, inadequate
enadikwit, inadequate
enadmisable, inadmissible
enadukwit, inadequate
enadverdent, inadvertent
enadvirdent, inadvertent
enadvisable, inadvisable
enagerashen, inaugurate(tion)
enaksesible, inaccessible
enakshen, inaction
enakt, enact
enaktif, inactive / enact(ive)
enakurite, inaccurate
enalegy, analogy

enalesis, analysis
enaleuble, inalienable
enalienable, inalienable
enaligy, analogy
enaliuble, inalienable
enalugy, analogy
enamel,*,led,ling,ler,list, PAINT, A
PROTECTIVE COATING
enamoly, anomaly
enanemit, inanimate
enanimate, inanimate
enapal, enable / unable
enappreciative, inappreciative
enapproachable, inapproachable
enappropriate, inappropriate
enaprochible, inapproachable
enapropriate, inappropriate
enapul, enable / unable
enaquerisy, inaccurate(acy)
enaqulashen, inoculate(tion)
enaqulate, inoculate
enaqurite, inaccurate
enarferins, interfere(nce)
enarkey, anarchy
enarup, interrupt
enasinse, innocence
enate, innate
enatequit, inadequate
enatible, inaudible
enatmisable, inadmissible
enatvirdent, inadvertent
enatvisable, inadvisable
enatvurtent, inadvertent
enaudible, inaudible
enauf, enough
enaugurate, inaugurate
enaukulate, inoculate
enaumily, anomaly
enavadif, innovate(tive)
enbankment, embankment
enbark, embark
enbasee, embassy
enbed, embed
enberis, embarrass
enblem, emblem
enboard, inboard
enbord, inboard
enboss, emboss
enbrase, embrace
enbroder, embroider
encamp,*,ped,ping,pment, BE IN/ OF A
CAMP
encandescent, incandescent
encantashen, incantation

encantation, incantation
encapable, incapable
encapacitate, incapacitate
encapacity, incapacity
encapsulate,*,ed,ting,tion, SURROUND, ENCLOSE
encapuble, incapable
encarnate, incarnate
encarsurate, incarcerate
encase,*,ed,sing,ement, ENCLOSE/ SURROUND WITH A COVER
encast, encase(d)
encendiary, incendiary
encenerate, incinerate
encentive, incentive
enception, incept(ion)
encereg, encourage / anchor(age)
encesant, incessant
encesint, incessant
encesunt, incessant
ench, inch
enchant,*,ted,ting,tment, DELIGHT, FASCINATE "prefixes: dis"
enchenyewus, ingenuous
enchor, anchor
enchur, ensure / insure
encindeary, incendiary
encircle,*,ed,ling,ement, SURROUND WITH A CIRCLE
encisor, incise(sor)
encite, incite / inside
encitment, incite(ment)
encize, incise
enclanation, incline(nation)
encline, incline
enclood, include
enclose,*,ed,sing,sable,sure, SURROUND/KEEP IN
encloser, enclose(sure)
enclosment, enclose(ment)
enclude, include
enclunashen, incline(nation)
enclusef, inclusive
enclusion, inclusion
encogneto, incognito
encoherent, incoherent
encokneto, incognito
encombatent, incompetent
encomber, encumber
encome, income
encommodious, incommode(dious)
encomode, incommode
encomodious, incommode(dious)
encomoteous, incommode(dious)

encomparable, incomparable
encompass,sses,ssed,ssing, ITEMS WITHIN A CIRCLE
encompatible, incompatible
encompetent, incompetent
encomplete, incomplete
encompruble, incomparable
enconclusef, inconclusive
enconclusive, inconclusive
enconsiderate, inconsiderate
enconsistent, inconsistent
enconvenient, inconvenient
encoragable, incorrigible
encore,*,ed,ring, ASKED TO PERFORM MORE BY AN AUDIENCE
encorect, incorrect
encorij, encourage / anchor(age)
encorporate, incorporate
encorrect, incorrect
encounter,*,red,ring, TO EMBARK UPON SOMETHING/SOMEONE
encourage,*,ed,ging,gingly,ement, INSTILL FAITH/HOPE
encrease, increase
encredible, incredible
encremenate, incriminate
encrement, increment
encriminate, incriminate
encroach,hes,hed,hing,hingly,hment, her, NEARLY TRESPASSING
encrust,*,ted,ting,tation, FORM A THICK COVER/EXTERIOR
encubate, incubate
encumbent, incumbent
encumber,*,red,ring,brance,brances, brancer, TO BE A WEIGHT/BURDEN, TO HAMPER
encumode, incommode
encumpatable, incompatible
encumplete, incomplete
encunklusif, inconclusive
encunsestant, inconsistent
encunveneunt, inconvenient
encupasitate, incapacitate
encupasity, incapacitate
encur, incur
encurable, incurable
encuragable, incorrigible
encurej, encourage / anchor(age)
encurekt, incorrect
encurig, encourage / anchor(age)
encyclopedia,*, REFERENCE SOURCE THAT DEFINES/EXPLAINS THINGS THAT ARE NOUNS

encyst,*,ted,ting,tation,tment, WITHIN A CYST (or see insist)
end,*,ded,ding, NO MORE, OVER (or see and) "prefixes: un/up"
endakashen, indicate(tion)
endaluble, indelible
endanger,*,red,ring,rment, IN HARM'S WAY, NEEDS PROTECTION
endangurment, endanger(ment)
endanjer, endanger
endapendense, independent(nce)
endasishen, indecision
endau, endow
endaument, endow(ment)
endavigual, individual
endear,*,red,ring,ringly,rment, VERY FOND OF
endeavor,*,red,ring,rer, SET ABOUT THE TASK TO DO SOMETHING
endebted, indebted
endecashen, indicate(tion)
endecision, indecision
endecisive, indecisive
endecks, index
endeed, indeed
endefanete, indefinite
endefinite, indefinite
endefir, endeavor
endefur, endeavor
endefurent, indifferent
endego, indigo
endelible, indelible
endelluble, indelible
endemafy, indemnify
endemic,*,cally,city,ism, CONFINED/ LIVING IN ONE GROUP/AREA
endemnafy, indemnify
endent, indent
endentashen, indent(ation)
endependense, independent(nce)
endependent, independent
ender, inter / enter
enderfere, interfere
endermetant, intermittent
endesent, indecent
endeted, indebted
endever, endeavor
endex, index
endicashen, indicate(tion)
endicate, indicate
endifrent, indifferent
endigo, indigo
endirmedent, intermittent
endirmetant, intermittent

endisisuf, indecisive
endite, indict
endless,ssly,ssness, WILL NEVER STOP
endlis, endless
endo, PREFIX INDICATING "INSIDE"
    MOST OFTEN MODIFIES THE WORD
endocrine,nology,nologic,nological,
    nologist, OF THE GLANDS IN THE
    BODY
endoer, endure
endoose, induce
endormetant, intermittent
endors, indoor(s)
endorse,*,ed,sing,ement, TO SUPPORT/
    AFFIRM IN WRITING (or see
    indoor(s))
endostry, industry
endoument, endow(ment)
endow,*,wed,wing,wment, PROVIDE
    SOMEONE SOMETHING THEY
    WANT/NEED "prefixes: dis"
endrukit, intricate
enduce, induce
enduckshen, induct(ion)
enducktor, induct(or)
enduction, induct(ion)
endukren, endocrine
endukshen, induct(ion)
endukt, induct
enduktor, induct(or)
endulge, indulge
endulgense, indulge(nce)
endupendent, independent
endur, inter / enter / endure
endure,*,ed,ring,rance,rable,rably, PUT
    UP WITH/TOLERATE "prefixes: un"
endurmedeate, intermediate
enduse, induce
enduseshin, indecision
endustreul, industrial
endustry, industry
enduztreal, industrial
ene, any
enebody, anybody
eneckwitable, inequitable
eneduble, inedible
eneg, inning
enegma, enigma / enema
enekwetable, inequitable
enekwity, inequity
enema,*, RECTAL CLEANSING (or see
    anemia/enigma)
enemik, anemic
enemut, intimate

enemy,mies, A FOE, NOT FRIENDS
    WITH
eneng, inning
enept, inept
enequitable, inequitable
enequity, inequity
ener, inner
eneract, interact
enerchange, interchange
enercom, intercom
enerconnect, interconnect
enercors, intercourse
enerelate, interrelate
energetic,cally, TO HAVE LOTS OF
    ENERGY "prefixes: bio"
energy,gies,gize,gizes,gizing,gizer,
    gization,getic,getically, HAVING
    ENOUGH POWER TO DO
    SOMETHING "prefixes: de-"
enerject, interject
enerjetek, energetic
enerkorse, intercourse
enerlude, interlude
enermedeary, intermediary
enermingle, intermingle
enermission, intermission
enermost, innermost
enernashenul, international
enernet, internet
enersculastic, interscholastic
enersect, intersect
enersection, intersection
enersekshen, intersection
enersperse, intersperse
enerstate, interstate
enert, inert
enervene, intervene
enervue, interview
enervul, interval
enerwoven, interwoven
enescapable, inescapable
enesense, innocence
enesheation, initiate(tion)
enesthezia, anesthesia
eneviduble, inevitable
enevitable, inevitable
enexpensive, inexpensive
enexperience, inexperience
enfachuashen, infatuate(tion)
enfachuate, infatuate
enfadik, emphatic
enfallible, infallible
enfaltrate, infiltrate
enfaluble, infallible

enfansy, infant(ncy)
enfant, infant
enfantry, infantry
enfasiz, emphasis / emphasize
enfatchuashen, infatuate(tion)
enfatik, emphatic
enfatuate, infatuate
enfecshus, infect(ious)
enfect, infect
enfekshen, infect(ion)
enfekt, infect
enfeltrate, infiltrate
enfenativly, infinite(tively)
enfentre, infantry
enfereorety, inferior(ity)
enferior, inferior
enfermashen, information
enfermation, information
enfesiz, emphasis / emphasize
enfestructure, infrastructure
enfeureate, infuriate
enfiltrate, infiltrate
enfinetly, infinite(ly)
enfinite, infinite
enfirmary, infirmary
enfirmashen, information
enfirmation, inform(ation)
enfisiz, emphasis / emphasize
enfistructure, infrastructure
enfite, invite
enfitengly, invite(ingly)
enflagingly, unflagging(ly)
enflame, inflame
enflamitory, inflame(mmatory)
enflammation, inflammation
enflammatory, inflame(mmatory)
enflamutory, inflame(mmatory)
enflapable, unflappable
enflashen, inflate(tion)
enflate, inflate
enflection, inflection
enfleksuble, inflexible
enflemashen, inflammation
enflewanse, influence
enflexchen, inflection
enflexible, inflexible
enflextion, inflection
enflicked, inflict
enflict, inflict
enflimation, inflammation
enfluence, influence
enfluensable, influence(able)
enflumation, inflammation

enforce,*,ed,cing,ement,eable,cability,
    er, SUPPORT, TO BACK "prefixes:
    un"
enform, inform
enformal, informal
enformant, informant
enformation, inform(ation)
enfraction, infraction
enfrakshen, infraction
enfrared, infrared
enfrastructure, infrastructure
enfrekwent, infrequent
enfrenj, infringe
enfrequent, infrequent
enfringe, infringe
enfrured, infrared
enfugen, infuse(sion)
enfujen, infuse(sion)
enfultrate, infiltrate
enfunsy, infant(ncy)
enfunt, infant
enfuntre, infantry
enfuriate, infuriate
enfurmashen, inform(ation)
enfurmery, infirmary
enfuse, infuse
enfushen, infuse(sion)
enfusiz, emphasis / emphasize
enfustrukture, infrastructure
engage,*,ed,ging,gingly,ement,er, TO
    PUT INTO MOTION, DIRECT
    ATTENTION "prefixes: dis"
enganly, ungainly
enge, inch
engect, inject
engection, inject(ion)
engekshen, inject(ion)
engelate, ungulate
engen, engine
engeneer, engineer
engenious, ingenious
engenuity, ingenuity
engenuous, ingenuous
engenyus, ingenious
enger, injure / anger
engest, ingest
enget, ingot
engilate, ungulate
engine,*, MACHINE/DEVICE USED FOR
    POWER/PROPELLING
engineer,*,red,ring, PUT ITEMS
    TOGETHER TO BECOME
    SOMETHING ELSE "prefixes: bio"
enginuety, ingenuity

engoement, enjoy(ment)
engoeuble, enjoy(able)
engoiment, enjoy(ment)
engolf, engulf
engot, ingot
engoy, enjoy
engoyuble, enjoy(able)
engrain, ingrain
engrave,*,ed,ving,er, TO MARK/CARVE
    TEXT/SYMBOLS INTO SOMETHING
engredient, ingredient
enguish, anguish
engulate, ungulate
engulf,*,fed,fing, TAKE IN, OVERCOME
engun, engine
enguneer, engineer
engury, injure(ry)
engustes, injustice
engut, ingot
enhabetent, inhabit(ant)
enhabit, inhabit
enhabitency, inhabit(ancy)
enhalant, inhalant
enhalation, inhale(lation)
enhale, inhale
enhance,*,ed,cing,ement,cive,er, MAKE
    MORE APPEALING
enharent, inherent
enharet, inherit
enharitance, inherit(ance)
enharmonic,*,ed,cing,ement,cive,er,
    MUSICAL NOTATION/FREQUENCY
    (or see inharmonic)
enhebit, inhibit
enhelashen, inhale(lation)
enherent, inherent
enherit, inherit
enheritance, inherit(ance)
enhewmane, inhumane
enhibishen, inhibit(ion)
enhibit, inhibit
enhosbatalety, inhospitable(ality)
enhosbitable, inhospitable
enhubishen, inhibit(ion)
enhulashen, inhale(lation)
enhumane, inhumane
eni, any
enialate, annihilate
enibishen, inhibit(ion)
enibode, anybody
enielate, annihilate
enig, inning

enigma,*,atic,atical,atically, NOT
    EXPLAINABLE, NOT UNDERSTOOD
    (or see enema/anemia)
enigrate, integrate
enima, enema / anemia
enime, enemy
enimut, intimate
enindashen, inundate(tion)
enindate, inundate
ening, inning
enipropreut, inappropriate
eniquality, inequality
enir, inner / inter
enircom, intercom
enircors, intercourse
enirelate, interrelate
enirgetek, energetic
enirgy, energy
enirlude, interlude
enirmission, intermission
enirnet, internet
enirsculastic, interscholastic
enirsection, intersection
enirtwine, intertwine
enirupt, interrupt
enirvene, intervene
enirview, interview
enirvue, interview
enishiashen, initiate(tion)
enishul, initial
enisthezia, anesthesia
enitial, initial
enitiate, initiate
enitiation, initiate(tion)
eniulate, annihilate
enje, inch
enjecshen, inject(ion)
enjekt, inject
enjelate, ungulate
enjen, engine
enjeneer, engineer
enjenuedy, ingenuity
enjenuity, ingenuity
enjenuous, ingenuous
enjenyewus, ingenuous
enjest, ingest
enjin, engine
enjineer, engineer
enjoement, enjoy(ment)
enjoy,*,yed,ying,yment,yable,yably,
    yableness, APPRECIATE "prefixes:
    pre"
enjoyuble, enjoy(able)
enjulate, ungulate

enjuner, engineer
enjure, injure
enjustice, injustice
enk, ink
enkabuble, incapable
enkamped, encamp(ed)
enkampment, encamp(ment)
enkapacity, incapacity
enkapasitate, incapacitate
enkapasity, incapacitate
enkapuble, incapable
enkarserade, incarcerate
enkase, encase
enker, anchor / incur
enkerej, encourage / anchor(age)
enkewbate, incubate
enkipacity, incapacity
enklin, incline
enkling, inkling
enklood, include
enklose, enclose
enkloshur, enclose(sure)
enkloze, enclose
enklud, include
enklunashen, incline(nation)
enklusev, inclusive
enklushen, inclusion
enkogneto, incognito
enkomber, encumber
enkomodeus, incommode(dious)
enkompus, encompass
enkomputent, incompetent
enkonsistent, inconsistent
enkore, encore
enkoreg, encourage / anchor(age)
enkoreguble, incorrigible
enkorpurate, incorporate
enkownter, encounter
enkreduble, incredible
enkredulus, incredulous
enkreese, increase
enkremunate, incriminate
enkroch, encroach
enkrument, increment
enkrust, encrust
enkum, income
enkumbent, incumbent
enkumber, encumber
enkumodeus, incommode(dious)
enkumpatuble, incompatible
enkumpus, encompass
enkunsiduret, inconsiderate
enkunsistent, inconsistent
enkunvenyunt, inconvenient

enkupacity, incapacity
enkupasedy, incapacity
enkupasitate, incapacitate
enkurable, incurable
enkurekt, incorrect
enkwesishun, inquisition
enkwire, inquire / inquire(ry)
enkwisative, inquisitive
enkwisition, inquisition
enland, inland
enlarge,*,ed,ging,ement,er, MAKE
    BIGGER/ GREATER
enlargment, enlarge(ment)
enlarje, enlarge
enlaw, in-law
enles, unless
enlest, enlist
enlet, inlet
enlighten,*,ned,ning,nment, ACHIEVE
    GREATER KNOWLEDGE
enlist,*,ted,ting,tment,ter, SIGN-UP,
    JOIN SOMETHING
enliten, enlighten
enlund, inland
enmachure, immature
enmade, inmate
enmate, inmate
enmature, immature
ennacurate, inaccurate
enner, inner
ennuendo, innuendo
enoardinent, inordinate
enoberative, inoperable(ative)
enocence, innocence
enocreate, inaugurate
enoculate, inoculate
enoculation, inoculate(tion)
enodible, inaudible
enof, enough
enogreashen, inaugurate(tion)
enogreate, inaugurate
enogurate, inaugurate
enokewlate, inoculate
enokulation, inoculate(tion)
enomoly, anomaly
enonimus, anonymous
enonseade, enunciate
enoperable, inoperable
enopertune, inopportune
enopurative, inoperable(ative)
enopurtunity, inopportune(nity)
enoqulent, inoculate(ant)
enorcors, intercourse
enordenate, inordinate

enordunet, inordinate
enorgetek, energetic
enorgy, energy
enormis, enormous
enormous,sly,sness, GIGANTIC/
    BIGGEST
enormus, enormous
enorpherans, interfere(nce)
enorsect, intersect
enosent, innocence(nt)
enotable, inaudible
enouf, enough
enough, TIME TO STOP
enovadef, innovate(tive)
enovate, innovate
enovative, innovate(tive)
enowe, annoy
enownse, announce
enoy, annoy
enoyens, annoy(ance)
enpare, impair
enpatient, inpatient
enpecable, impeccable
enpech, impeach
enpersonate, impersonate
enpli, imply
enpolite, impolite
enpolse, impulse
enportant, important
enpose, impose
enposibul, impossible
enposter, imposter
enposuble, impossible
enpound, impound
enpoverish, impoverish
enpownd, impound
enpractical, impractical
enprasise, imprecise
enpration, impression
enpravize, improvise
enprecise, imprecise
enpregnable, impregnable
enpregnate, impregnate
enpres, impress
enpreshen, impression
enpresidented, (un)precedent(ed)
enpresise, imprecise
enpresive, impressive
enpreson, imprison
enpressed, impress(sed)
enprint, imprint
enprison, imprison
enprobuble, improbable
enpromptu, impromptu

enpromtu, impromptu
enpropable, improbable
enproper, improper
enprove, improve
enprovement, improve(ment)
enprovisation, improvise(sation)
enprovise, improvise
enprovusashen, improvise(sation)
enprufe, improve
enpruve, improve
enpruvize, improvise
enpulite, impolite
enpulse, impulse
enpulsef, impulse(sive)
enpulsive, impulse(sive)
enput, input
enqubate, incubate
enquesidev, inquisitive
enquire, SEE WORD "INQUIRE"
enquisadev, inquisitive
enquisition, inquisition
enquisitive, inquisitive
enquizeshen, inquisition
enrage,*,ed,ging,ement, GREAT
    ANGER/ RAGE
enraj, enrage
enrech, enrich
enrich,hes,hed,hing,hment, MAKE
    BETTER/FINER
enrjekshen, interject(ion)
enrol, enroll
enroll,*,led,ling,lment,llee, JOIN, ENLIST
enrolment, enroll(ment)
enroot, enroute
enroute, OR "EN ROUTE", IN THE
    PROCESS OF TRAVELING TO/
    TOWARDS
enrut, enroute
ensabordinate, insubordinate
ensadent, incident
ensafishent, insufficient
ensakure, insecure
ensakuredy, insecure(rity)
ensakurity, insecure(rity)
ensalate, insulate
ensane, insane
ensanetashen, insanitary(ation)
ensanety, insane(nity)
ensanidy, insane(nity)
ensanitary, insanitary
ensanitashen, insanitary(ation)
ensasheat, insatiate
ensasheuble, insatiable
ensatiable, insatiable

ensatiate, insatiate
ensaulvent, insolvent
ensbarashen, inspire(ration)
ensbekable, unspeakable
ensboken, unspoken
enscribe, inscribe
enscription, inscription
enseam, inseam
ensebordinate, insubordinate
ensect, insect
ensecticide, insecticide
ensecure, insecure
ensedent, incident
ensedius, insidious
ensegnea, insignia
ensegnifukent, insignificant
ensejen, incision
ensekt, insect
ensektaside, insecticide
enselashen, insulate(tion)
ensem, inseam
ensemanation, inseminate(tion)
enseminate, inseminate
ensen, ensign
ensenarate, incinerate
ensendiary, incendiary
ensense, incense
ensenseer, insincere
ensensible, insensible
ensensitive, insensitive
ensentive, incentive
ensentuf, incentive
ensenuashen, insinuate(tion)
ensenuate, insinuate
ensepshen, incept(ion)
ensept, incept
enserekshen, insurrection
ensermowntible, insurmountable
ensershen, insert(ion)
ensert, insert
ensesint, incessant
ensest, incest / insist / encyst
ensh, inch
ensher, ensure / insure
enshiranse, insure(rance)
enshree, entry / entree
enshure, insure
enshurence, insure(rance)
enside, inside / insight / incite
ensident, incident
ensidious, insidious
ensidnea, insignia
ensigen, incision
ensight, insight / incite / inside

ensightation, incite(tation)
ensightment, incite(ment)
ensign,*, MILITARY RANK
ensignia, insignia
ensignificant, insignificant
ensiklopedia, encyclopedia
ensikure, insecure
ensikuredy, insecure(rity)
ensilate, insulate
ensilin, insulin
ensim, enzyme / inseam
ensimanashen, inseminate(tion)
ensimanate, inseminate
ensin, ensign
ensinarate, incinerate
ensincere, insincere
ensinsative, insensitive
ensinse, incense
ensinsuble, insensible
ensinuashen, insinuate(tion)
ensinuate, insinuate
ensirection, insurrection
ensishen, incision
ensisor, incise(sor)
ensist, insist
ensistent, insist(ent)
ensitation, incite(tation)
ensite, inside / insight / incite
ensiteful, insight(ful)
ensitement, incite(ment)
ensiteus, insidious
ensition, incision
ensize, incise
enskribe, inscribe
enskripshen, inscription
ensoluble, insoluble
ensolvable, insolvable
ensolvent, insolvent
ensomnia, insomnia
ensovent, insolvent
ensoyuble, insoluble
ensparashen, inspire(ration)
enspecshen, inspect(ion)
enspect, inspect
enspection, inspect(ion)
enspekable, unspeakable
enspekshen, inspect(ion)
enspekt, inspect
enspire, inspire
enspoken, unspoken
enspuration, inspire(ration)
enstall, install
enstalment, install(ment)
enstance, instance

enstant, instant
enstantaneous, instantaneous
enstatute, institute
enstatution, institute(tion)
enstaulment, install(ment)
ensted, instead
enstenked, instinct
enstense, instance
enstetushen, institute(tion)
enstigate, instigate
enstill, instill
enstinct, instinct
enstinse, instance
enstintaneusly, instantaneous(ly)
enstitute, institute
enstol, install
enstolashen, install(ation)
enstolment, install(ment)
enstrament, instrument
enstriment, instrument
enstrucshen, instruct(ion)
enstruct, instruct
enstruction, instruct(ion)
enstrukt, instruct
enstrument, instrument
enstrumental, instrument(al)
enstugate, instigate
enstunt, instant
enstuntly, instant(ly)
ensubordinate, insubordinate
ensucure, insecure
ensue,*,ed,uing, CLOSELY FOLLOW
ensufishent, insufficient
ensugnifakent, insignificant
ensulate, insulate
ensulation, insulate(tion)
ensulin, insulin
ensult, insult
ensunseer, insincere
ensure,*,ed,ring, GUARANTEE/
    PROMISE (or see insure)
ensurkle, encircle
ensurmountable, insurmountable
ensurrection, insurrection
ensurshen, insert(ion)
ensurt, insert
ensyklopedia, encyclopedia
ensym, enzyme
ent, end / and
entacate, indicate
entact, intact
entaferance, interfere(rance)
entager, integer
entagral, integral

entagrate, integrate
entail,*,led,ling,lment, RESTRICTIONS
    TO OWNERSHIP "prefixes: dis"
entak, intact / intake
entale, entail
entalect, intellect
entalectual, intellect(ual)
entamet, intimate
entangible, intangible
entangle,*,ed,ling,ement, GET MIXED
    UP IN "prefixes: dis/un"
entanjuble, intangible
entareor, anterior / interior
entarmedeate, intermediate
entatee, entity
enteger, integer
entegral, integral
entegrate, integrate
entegrity, integrity
entegrude, integrity
entekashen, indicate(tion)
entelagents, intelligent(nce)
entelijuble, intelligible
entellect, intellect
entelugeble, intelligible
entelugint, intelligent
entenation, intonate(tion)
entend, intend
entense, intense
entenshin, intent(ion)
entensity, intense(sity)
entensuve, intense(sive)
entent, intent
enter,*,red,ring,rable,rance, GO INTO,
    PREFIX INDICATING "INTESTINE"
    MOST OFTEN MODIFIES THE WORD
    "prefixes: re"
enteract, interact
entercede, intercede
entercept, intercept
enterchange, interchange
entercom, intercom
enterconnect, interconnect
entercourse, intercourse
enterd, enter(ed)
entereor, anterior / interior
enterferans, interfere(nce)
enterfere, interfere
enterference, interfere(rance)
entergekshen, interject(ion)
enterim, interim
enterior, anterior / interior
enterject, interject
enterlock, interlock

enterlude, interlude
entermediary, intermediary
entermediate, intermediate
entermetant, intermittent
entermingle, intermingle
entermission, intermission
entern, intern
enternal, internal
enternational, international
enternet, internet
entero, PREFIX INDICATING
    "INTESTINE" MOST OFTEN
    MODIFIES THE WORD
enterog, entourage
enterogate, interrogate
enterpreneur, entrepreneur
enterpret, interpret
enterpretation, interpretation
enterprise,*,sing,singly, USE AMBITION
    TO TAKE ON RISKS
enterrelate, interrelate
enterrogate, interrogate
enterrupt, interrupt
enterscholastic, interscholastic
entersept, intercept
entersperse, intersperse
enterstate, interstate
entertain,*,ned,ning,nment,ner,
    AMUSE/ENGAGE SOMEONE
entertaner, entertain(er)
entertanment, entertain(ment)
entertwine, intertwine
enterupt, interrupt
enterval, interval
entervene, intervene
enterview, interview
enterwoven, interwoven
entestine, intestine
entety, entity
entever, endeavor
enthooseastik, enthuse(siastic)
enthrall,*,led,ling, OVERWHELMED
    WITH AWE
enthrol, enthrall
enthuse,ed,siasm,siastic,siastically,
    HAVE INTEREST/ENERGY FOR
    "prefixes: over/un"
enthuseastek, enthuse(siastic)
enthuziazm, enthuse(siasm)
entice,*,ed,cing,ement,er, APPEAL TO,
    ALLURE, SUCCUMB TO
entid, end(ed)
entidle, entitle
entiger, integer

entigo, indigo
entigral, integral
entigration, integrate(tion)
entil, until
entilect, intellect
entimadate, intimidate
entimate, intimate
entimidate, intimidate
entina, antenna
entinse, intense
entinsive, intense(sive)
entint, intent
entintion, intent(ion)
entire,ely,ety, COMPLETE, THE WHOLE
    THING
entirest, interest
entirferans, interfere(nce)
entirle, entire(ly)
entirmediate, intermediate
entirmitant, intermittent
entirnet, internet
entirpreneur, entrepreneur
entirprize, enterprise
entirprutashen, interpretation
entirty, entire(ty)
entisepate, anticipate
entitle,*,ed,ling,ement, RIGHTS,
    AUTHORITY TO
entity,ties, A BEING WITH HUMAN
    FORM "prefixes: non"
entlis, endless
ento, into
entoishen, intuit(ion)
entolerable, intolerable
entonate, intonate
entor, enter
entouet, intuit(ive)
entourage,*, GROUP WHO TRAVELS
    WITH IMPORTANT/FAMOUS
    PEOPLE
entowment, endow(ment)
entoxicate, intoxicate
entra, entree
entraduction, introduce(ction)
entraduse, introduce
entrakit, intricate
entramural, intramural
entrance,ed,cing, PLACE/WAY TO GET
    IN
entranet, intranet
entrapreneur, entrepreneur
entraspect, introspect
entravenous, intravenous
entray, entree

entree,*, A MEAL, FOOD SERVING (or
    see entry)
entrege, intrigue
entrense, entrance
entrensic, intrinsic
entrepreneur,*,rial,rialism,rism,rship,
    ONE WHO RISKS FINANCING A NEW
    BUSINESS/ ENTERPRISE
entres, entry(ries) / entree(s)
entrest, interest
entri, entry / entree
entricate, intricate
entrigue, intrigue
entrinsic, intrinsic
entroduce, introduce
entrospect, introspect
entrost, interest / entrust
entrovert, introvert
entrude, intrude
entrudukshen, introduce(ction)
entruduse, introduce
entrugen, instrusion
entrumural, intramural
entrunse, entrance
entrupreneur, entrepreneur
entrusef, intrusive
entrushen, intrusion
entrust,*,ted,ting, LEAVE THE CARE OF
    SOMETHING/ SOMEONE TO
    ANOTHER (or see interest)
entry,ries,rant, OPENING GOING IN,
    ENTER INTO (or see entree)
    "prefixes: re/sub"
entuative, intuit(ive)
entueshen, intuit(ion)
entuetion, intuit(ion)
entufere, interfere
entuger, integer
entugrate, integrate
entuishen, intuit(ion)
entuit, intuit(ive) / intuit
entuition, intuit(ion)
entunate, intonate
entur, enter
enturact, interact
enturauj, entourage
enturem, interim
enturlock, interlock
enturmediate, intermediate
enturmetant, intermittent
enturn, intern
enturnal, internal
enturnalize, internal(ize)
enturpreneur, entrepreneur

enturpret, interpret
enturprise, enterprise
entursept, intercept
enturtane, entertain
enturtaner, entertain(er)
enturtanment, entertain(ment)
entutes, entity(ties)
entwoishen, intuit(ion)
entwoit, intuit(ive)
entyre, entire
enubelidy, inability
enubishen, inhibit(ion)
enuendo, innuendo
enuf, enough
enuindo, innuendo
enume, enemy
enunciate,*,ed,ting,tion,tive,tively,tor,
    SPEAK CLEARLY/SPECIFICALLY
enundate, inundate
enunseate, enunciate
enupresheative, inappreciative
enuprochible, inapproachable
enupropreut, inappropriate
enur, inner
enuract, interact
enurcom, intercom
enurelate, interrelate
enurferins, interfere(nce)
enurgee, energy
enurgekshen, interject(ion)
enurim, interim
enurjetek, energetic
enurlude, interlude
enurmediary, intermediary
enurmingle, intermingle
enurmission, intermission
enurmost, innermost
enurnet, internet
enursculastic, interscholastic
enursecshen, intersection
enursperse, intersperse
enurt, inert
enurupt, interrupt
enurval, interval
enurvene, intervene
enurview, interview
enurvue, interview
enurwoven, interwoven
enuscapuble, inescapable
enusense, innocence
enusent, innocence(nt)
enuther, another
enuvate, innovate
envachinate, invaginate

envade, invade
envaginate, invaginate
envagination, invaginate(tion)
envajunate, invaginate
envalid, invalid
envalope, envelope
envaluable, invaluable
envasef, invasive
envashen, invasion
envashenation, invaginate(tion)
envasion, invasion
envatashen, invitation
envate, invade
envaulve, involve
enve, envy
enved, envy(vied)
envelope,*,ed,ping,ement, ENCLOSE/
  WRAP TO PROTECT SOMETHING
envensable, invincible
envenshen, invent(ion)
envent, invent
enventory, inventory
enverdebrae, invertebrate
envereably, invariable(ly)
enverse, inverse
enversion, inversion
enversive, inverse(sive)
envert, invert
envertebrate, invertebrate
enves, envy(vies)
envest, invest
envestagashen, investigate(tion)
envestigate, investigate
envestmant, invest(ment)
envetashen, invitation
enveuble, enviable
enveus, envious
enviable,ly, SOMEONE WISHING THEY
  HAD
enviding, invite(ingly)
envigorate, invigorate
envilope, envelope
envincible, invincible
envintory, inventory
enviornmental, environment(al)
envious,sly,sness, BEING JEALOUS
envirdebrate, invertebrate
environment,*,tal,tally,talist,talism,
  EXTERIOR SURROUNDINGS
envirs, inverse
envirsion, inversion
envirsive, inverse(sive)
envirtebrate, invertebrate
envisability, invisible(bility)

envisible, invisible
envitashen, invitation
envitation, invitation
envitingly, invite(ingly)
envizable, invisible
envoice, invoice
envoluntary, involuntary
envolve, involve
envoyse, invoice
envulid, invalid
envurdabrae, invertebrate
envurt, invert
envy,vies,vied,vying,vyingly,vious,
  viously,viousness,viable, WANT
  SOMETHING THAT SOMEONE ELSE
  HAS "prefixes: un"
enward, inward
enword, inward
enwrech, enrich
enwrich, enrich
enwroll, enroll
eny, any
enzerkle, encircle
enzide, inside
enzyme,*,matic,mic,mically,mology,
  CHEMICAL ACTION CREATED BY
  CELLS "prefixes: endo/exo/non/
  pro"
ep, PREFIX INDICATING "OVER/NEAR"
  MOST OFTEN MODIFIES THE WORD
epademic, epidemic
epareshin, apparition
eparition, apparition
epart, apart
epartmint, apartment
epasenter, epicenter
epasode, episode
epazode, episode
epeal, appeal
epeel, appeal
eperatus, apparatus
eperinse, appearance
eperint, apparent
eperul, apparel
epi, PREFIX INDICATING "OVER/NEAR"
  MOST OFTEN MODIFIES THE WORD
epicenter,*, CENTRAL SPOT OF
  EARTHQUAKE
epidemic,*, MANY LIVES AT RISK IN AN
  AREA
episode,*, PARTS OF AN ONGOING
  SHOW
epizode, episode
epliense, appliance

eplod, applaud
eply, apply
epodemec, epidemic
epoint, appoint
epointment, appointment
epoynt, appoint
epoyntment, appointment
eprasal, appraisal
epreciate, appreciate
eprentis, apprentice
epresheate, appreciate
eprintise, apprentice
epruvel, approve(val)
epsolv, absolve
epsorb, absorb
epstane, abstain
epsurd, absurd
eptikate, abdicate
epusode, episode
epzolv, absolve
epzorb, absorb
epzurd, absurd
eqaul, equal
eqaulity, equality
eqaunimity, equanimity
eqauzition, acquisition
eqivocate, equivocate
equable,ly,bility,eness, IS EQUAL TO,
  SAME IN VALUE, UNIFORM
  "prefixes: in"
equal,*,led,ling,lly,able,lize,lizes,lized,
  lizing,lizer,lization, SAME AS,
  EQUIVALENT, UNIFORM "prefixes:
  un"
equalibrium, equilibrium
equality,ties,tarian,tarianism, OF BEING
  THE SAME, EQUIVALENT "prefixes:
  in"
equanemity, equanimity
equanimity,ties,mous, OF EVEN
  TEMPERAMENT
equate,*,ed,ting,tion,table,tability,
  COMPARE/BALANCE/MAKE
  UNIFORM "prefixes: un"
equation,*,nal,nally, BALANCE OF BOTH
  SIDES
equator,*,rial,rially, ONE OF TWO
  HALVES OF A PLANET/STAR
  "prefixes: sub"
equel, equal
equelebreum, equilibrium
equevocal, equivocal
equi, PREFIX INDICATING "EQUAL"
  MOST OFTEN MODIFIES THE WORD

equifocal, equivocal
equifocate, equivocate
equil, equal
equilibrium,*, BALANCE, STABILITY
"prefixes: dis/non"
equinox,xes, WHEN DAY/NIGHT ARE IN
EQUAL PARTS
equip,*,pped,pping,pper,pment, TO
MAKE READY FOR A TASK, EVENT
equipment, ARTICLES/IMPLEMENTS TO
PERFORM WORK
equity,ties,tize,tizes,tized,tizing,tization,
HOW MUCH YOU OWN, JUSTICE/
RIGHTS "prefixes: in"
equivalent,tly,nce,ncy, THE SAME AS,
EQUAL "prefixes: non"
equivilense, equivalent(ncy)
equivocal,lity,lly,lness,ate, EQUAL
ENOUGH TO LEAD TO
MISINTERPRETATION, SUSPICION,
DOUBT "prefixes: un"
equivocate,*,ed,ting,tingly,tor,tory,tion,
tions, EQUAL ENOUGH TO LEAD TO
MISINTERPRETATION, SUSPICION,
DOUBT
eqwanemity, equanimity
eqwanimity, equanimity
eqwareum, aquarium
eqwashin, equation
eqwel, equal
eqwerium, aquarium
er, PREFIX INDICATING EMPHASIS ON
THE ACTIVITY/DOING OF A VERB (or
see ear/err/air/heir)
erabrochuble, irreproachable
eracer, eraser
eradeate, irradiate
eradesent, iridescent
eradiate, irradiate
eradic, erratic / erotic
eradicate,*,ed,ting,tion,tive,able,ably,
tor, ELIMINATE, DISPOSE "prefixes:
in/un"
eradukashen, eradicate(tion)
eragardles, irregardless
eragashen, irrigate(tion)
eragate, irrigate
eragation, irrigate(tion)
eraguardless, irregardless
erain, arraign
erakned, arachnid
eran, arraign
erand, errand
erange, arrange

erangment, arrange(ment)
eranment, arraign(ment)
erant, errant
eraplasible, irreplaceable
eraprochuble, irreproachable
erasbonsuble, irresponsible
erasbonzible, irresponsible
erase,*,ed,sing,er,sable, ELIMINATE
COMPLETELY
eraser,*, RUBBER/FELT PAD FOR
REMOVING INK
erashinul, irrational
erashunal, irrational
erasistible, irresistible
erasol, aerosol
eraspective, irrespective
eraspektif, irrespective
erasponsuble, irresponsible
erasponzuble, irresponsible
eratant, irritant
eratashen, irritate(tion)
eratate, irritate
eratible, irritable
eratic, erratic / erotic
erational, irrational
eratrevible, irretrievable
eraudik, erotic
eravokable, irrevocable
eray, array
erayn, arraign
erazestuble, irresistible
erazistuble, irresistible
erb, herb
erbal, herb(al)
erbashis, herb(aceous)
erbel, herb(al)
erbivore, herbivore
erborne, airborne
erbul, herb(al)
erbulism, herb(alism)
erbulist, herb(alist)
erchen, urchin
erchin, urchin
erea, area
erebrochuble, irreproachable
erect,*,ted,ting,tion,tile,table,tly,tness,
tor, SET STRAIGHT UP, RAISE
ered, arid
eredesent, iridescent
ereer, arrear
eregardles, irregardless
eregashen, irrigate(tion)
eregate, irrigate
eregation, irrigate(tion)

eregeno, oregano
eregewler, irregular
eregler, irregular
erekshen, erect(ion)
erelavense, irrelevant(nce)
erelavent, irrelevant
ereluvense, irrelevant(nce)
ereluvint, irrelevant
erena, arena
ereng, earring
erent, errant
ereperuble, irreparable
erepirable, irreparable
ereprochible, irreproachable
erepruble, irreparable
erepurable, irreparable
erer, error
eresistible, irresistible
erespective, irrespective
erest, arrest
erestokrat, aristocrat
eretant, irritant
eretashen, irritate(tion)
eretat, irritate
eretibul, irritable
eretrevible, irretrievable
eretrievable, irretrievable
ereu, area
ereul, aerial
erevocable, irrevocable
erg, urge
ergense, urge(ncy)
ergent, urge(nt)
erginsy, urge(ncy)
ergint, urge(nt)
eri, awry
eribrochuble, irreproachable
erid, arid
eridesent, iridescent
erift, arrive(d)
eriful, arrival
erigardles, irregardless
erigashen, irrigate(tion)
erigate, irrigate
erigation, irrigate(tion)
eriguardless, irregardless
erind, errand
ering, earring / err(ing)
eriplasible, irreplaceable
eriproachable, irreproachable
erir, error
erisbonsuble, irresponsible
erisistible, irresistible
erisol, aerosol

erispective, irrespective
erispektif, irrespective
erisponsuble, irresponsible
eristocrat, aristocrat
eritant, irritant
eritate, irritate
erithmatic, arithmetic
eritrevuble, irretrievable
erive, arrive
erivokuble, irrevocable
erivul, arrival
erizisduble, irresistible
erj, urge
erjense, urge(nce) / urge(ncy)
erjinse, urge(nce) / urge(ncy)
erjint, urge(nt)
erk, irk
erle, early
erloom, heirloom
erly, early
ern, earn / urn
ernest, earnest
ero, arrow
erobik, aerobic
erochun, erosion
erode,*,ed,ding,osion,osive,dible, dibility,osible, WEAR, WASH AWAY "prefixes: non/un"
erodik, erotic
erodynamic, aerodynamic
eroganse, arrogance
erogate, irrigate
erogint, arrogance(nt)
eroma, aroma
eromadek, aroma(tic)
erond, errand
eronic, ironic
eror, error
erosbonsuble, irresponsible
erosef, erosive
erosion,nal,nally, WEARING, WASHING AWAY
erosive,eness,vity, WEARS/WASHES AWAY
erosponsuble, irresponsible
erote, erode
erotic,ca,cally,cize,cism,tology,tological, tologist, SEXUAL AROUSAL/ SENSATION
erport, airport
err,*,rred,rring,rrancy, SHORT FOR ERROR, TO MAKE A MISTAKE (or see ear/air/heir) "prefixes: un"
erradiate, irradiate

errand,*, TRAVEL TO PERFORM A TASK
errant,tly,try, TO WANDER "prefixes: in"
erratate, irritate
erratic,cally,cism, SUDDEN/ UNPREDICTABLE MOVEMENTS OR THOUGHTS
errogate, irrigate
error,*, NOT CORRECT
ershen, urchin
ertearial, arterial
erth, earth
erubt, erupt / irrupt
erubtif, erupt(ive) / irrupt(ive)
erubtion, erupt(ion) / irrupt(ion)
erugardles, irregardless
erugashen, irrigate(tion)
erugate, irrigate
erugation, irrigate(tion)
eruguardless, irregardless
erunt, errant
eruplasuble, irreplaceable
eruprochuble, irreproachable
erupshen, erupt(ion) / irrupt(ion)
erupt,*,ted,ting,tion,tive,tively,tible, FORMING BULGE WHICH OPENS/ BURSTS (or see irrupt)
eruptif, erupt(ive) / irrupt(ive)
erur, error
erusbonsuble, irresponsible
erusistible, irresistible
erusol, aerosol
eruspective, irrespective
eruspektif, irrespective
erusponsuble, irresponsible
erutant, irritant
erutashen, irritate(tion)
erutate, irritate
erutible, irritable
erutrevible, irretrievable
erutuble, irritable
eruvokuble, irrevocable
eruzistuble, irresistible
es, is / ease
esa, essay
esael, assail
esail, assail
esalt, assault
esanse, essence
esasen, assassin
esault, assault
esay, essay
esbeshulee, especially

escalade,*,er, TO SCALE WALL WITH LADDERS (or see escalator)
escalate,*,ed,ting,tor,tory,tion, TO RISE (or see escalade) "prefixes: de-"
escalator,*, A CONVEYOR WHICH CARRIES/MOVES ITEMS/PEOPLE
escapade,*, AN ADVENTURE WITHOUT PERMISSION
escape,*,ed,ping,pable,er,pist,pism,pee, pees,pology,pologist, TO GET AWAY FROM WITHOUT PERMISSION "prefixes: in"
escort,*,ted,ting, SOMEONE WHO ACCOMPANIES TO ASSIST
escrow,*,wed,wing, MONEY RETAINED BY THIRD PARTY
esculator, escalator
esdeem, esteem
ese, ease / easy
esedik, acetic / acidic / ascetic
esemble, assemble
esemulate, assimilate
esence, essence
esend, ascend / isn't
esenshul, essential
esent, ascend / ascent / assent / isn't
esential, essential
esert, assert
esesmint, assessment
esfikseat, asphyxiate
esfixeat, asphyxiate
eshamed, ashamed
esherance, assure(rance)
eshew, issue
eshu, issue
eshurance, assure(rance)
eside, aside
esidik, acetic / acidic / ascetic
esidjewus, assiduous
esiguous, assiduous
esil, easel
esilum, asylum
esily, easily
esimble, assemble
esimelate, assimilate
esimetric, asymmetric
esind, ascend
esindant, ascendant
esine, assign
esinment, assignment
esinse, essence
esinshul, essential
esint, isn't / ascend / ascent / assent
esirt, assert

esist, assist
eskapade, escapade
eskape, escape
eskort, escort
eskplinashen, explanation
eskrow, escrow
eskulate, escalate / escalade
eskulater, escalator
eskupade, escapade
esm, ism
esment, easement
esmint, easement
esnt, isn't
esofigus, esophagus
esolt, assault
esophagus,gi,geal, TUBE IN THE THROAT
esordment, assortment
esorted, assorted
esortment, assortment
esosheate, associate
esoshiate, associate
esoteric,ca,cally,cism, KNOWLEDGE GAINED BY A FEW
especially, PARTICULARLY, MOST CERTAINLY
esperugus, asparagus
espeshulee, especially
espir, aspire
essay,*,yed,ying,yist,yistic, WRITE ABOUT A SPECIFIC POINT/THING
essence,*, THE AMBIANCE OR BASIC SENSE OF THE OVERALL
essential,*,lly,tiality,tialness, MUST HAVE, MOST IMPORTANT "prefixes: in/non/un"
est, east
estableshment, establish(ment)
establish,es,ed,hing,hment,her, hmentarian, TO CREATE A BASIS, BEGINNING "prefixes: dis/non"
estamashen, estimate(tion)
esteem,*,med,ming, BEST REGARDS FOR, ADMIRE "prefixes: dis"
esteengwish, extinguish
estem, esteem
estemut, estimate
estern, east(ern)
estimashen, estimate(tion)
estimate,*,ed,ting,tion,able,ably, ableness,tive,tor, TO APPROXIMATE BASED ON KNOWLEDGE "prefixes: in/over/under"
estirle, east(erly)

estonesh, astonish
estragen, estrogen
estrawlegy, astrology
estrengent, astringent
estringent, astringent
estris, estrus
estrogen, A HORMONE CREATED BY FEMALES BEGINNING AT PUBERTY
estrolugy, astrology
estronume, astronomy
estrugen, estrogen
estrus,rum,ual, WHEN CONCEPTION IS POSSIBLE
estumashen, estimate(tion)
estumit, estimate
esturle, east(erly)
esue, issue
esuense, issue(uance)
esuinse, issue(uance)
esul, easel
esume, assume
esunse, essence
esunt, isn't
esylum, asylum
et, eat / eight/ ate
etable, edible
etach, attach
etack, attack
etaen, attain
etak, attack
etalek, italic
etane, attain
etatch, attach
etcetera, MORE OF THE SAME
etch,hes,hed,hing,her, CARVE INTO (or see edge/itch)
ete, eddy
etempt, attempt
etemt, attempt
etenchin, attention
etend, attend
etenshin, attention
etenshun, attention
eternal,lly,nity,nities,lity,lize,lizes,lized, lizing, FOREVER
eteusy, idiocy
eteut, idiot
ether,ric, ALL THINGS AROUND AND BEYOND THE EARTH
ethic,*,cal,cally,cality,calness,cist, JUDGEMENT OF CONDUCT/ BEHAVIOR "prefixes: bio/un"
ethnac, ethnic

ethnic,*,cally,city,cities,nology,nologist, nologic,nologically, GROUP OF PEOPLE WITH THE SAME LANGUAGE, TRAITS
ethnuk, ethnic
ethrik, ether(ic)
ethuk, ethic
etikit, etiquette
etimt, attempt
etinchon, attention
etinshun, attention
etiquette, RULES OF PROPER BEHAVIOR
etire, attire
etmonish, admonish
etrakshun, attraction
etrakt, attract
etroshus, atrocious
ets, it's / eat(s)
etself, itself
etsetara, etcetera
etsulf, itself
eturnal, eternal
eturney, attorney
eu, PREFIX INDICATING "GOOD" MOST OFTEN MODIFIES THE WORD
eucalyptus, A TREE
euforia, euphoria
eul, eel
eunaform, uniform
euphoria,ant,ic,ically, FEELS JOYFUL/ UNREAL
euraneum, uranium
eurinery, urinary
eutopea, utopia
evacuate,*,ed,ting,tion,tive,tor, TO EMPTY FROM A PLACE
evade,*,ed,ding,asion,evasive,er, TO NOT BE/THINK/BEHAVE AS EXPECTED
evadins, evidence
evakuashen, evacuate(tion)
evakuate, evacuate
evale, evil(lly)
evaluashen, evaluate(tion)
evaluate,*,ed,ting,tion,tive, TO STUDY/ REVIEW FOR FINAL OPINION/ JUDGEMENT
evalushen, evolution
evalutionery, evolution(ary)
evan, even
evanly, even(ly)
evaperate, evaporate
evaperation, evaporate(tion)

evaporate,*,ed,ting,tion, LIQUID/SOLID CONVERTED INTO GAS

evapurashen, evaporate(tion)

evapurate, evaporate

evarewer, every(where)

evasef, evasive

evashen, evasive

evasion, TO NOT BE/THINK/BEHAVE AS EXPECTED

evasive,ely,eness, TO NOT BE/THINK/ BEHAVE AS EXPECTED

evate, evade

eve, THE EVENING, A PERIOD OF TIME BEFORE AN EVENT

evedins, evidence

evekshin, evict(ion)

evekt, evict

even,*,ed,ning,nly,nness, LEVEL WITH "prefixes: un"

evendful, eventful

evening,*, AFTER 6 O'CLOCK P.M.

evenshuele, event(ually)

event,*,tual,tually,tful,tfully,tfullness, SOMETHING OUT OF THE ORDINARY, WILL HAPPEN IN THE FUTURE "prefixes: un"

eventful,lly,lness, SOMETHING OUT OF THE ORDINARY

eventualy, event(ually)

ever,rmore, AT ANY TIME "prefixes: for"

everewar, every(where)

everves, effervesce

evervesent, effervescent

every,ybody,yday,yone,ything,ywhere, ALL

eves, eaves

evict,*,ted,ting,tion,tee, TO FORCIBLY REMOVE

evidence,*,ed,cing,nt, PROOF OF TRUTH "prefixes: in"

evidens, evidence

evident,tly,tial,tially,tiality,tiary,tialism, nce, PROOF OF BEING SEEN, UNDERSTOOD, TRUTH "prefixes: in"

evikshen, evict(ion)

eviktion, evict(ion)

evil,*,lly,lness, OPPOSITE OF LOVE, THREATENING

evilutionary, evolution(ary)

evin, even

evindful, eventful

evinly, even(ly)

evinshuale, event(ually)

evint, event

---

evintualy, event(ually)

evir, ever

evl, evil

evneng, evening

evning, evening

evoke,*,ed,king,ocable,ocator,er, MAKE HAPPEN, CREATE REACTION

evol, evil

evolushenary, evolution(ary)

evolution,*,nal,nally,nary,narily,nist, nism, THE ACT OF EVOLVING

evolvd, evolve(d)

evolve,*,ed,ving,lution, ADAPT, GAIN WISDOM, TRANSFORM

evon, even

evoneng, evening

evor, ever

evow, avow

evre, every

evrebode, every(body)

evreda, every(day)

evretheng, every(thing)

evrewer, every(where)

evrewun, every(one)

evriwun, every(one)

evry, every

evryday, every(day)

evrywere, every(where)

evs, eaves

evudens, evidence

evudins, evidence

evudintly, evident(ly)

evul, evil

evule, evil(lly)

evulushin, evolution

evuneng, evening

evunle, even(ly)

ew, ewe / you / yew

eway, away

ewe,*, FEMALE SHEEP (or see you/yew)

ewrekt, erect

ex, PREFIX INDICATING "FORMER/ OUTSIDE/EXTERNAL" MOST OFTEN MODIFIES THE WORD

exact,ted,ting,tingly,tingness,tly,tness, table,tor, SPECIFIC "prefixes: in"

exagerate, exaggerate

exageration, exaggerate(tion)

exaggerate,*,ted,tedly,ting,tingly,tive, tion,tor, STRETCH/ELONGATE THE TRUE FORM

exajurashen, exaggerate(tion)

exakude, execute

exakushen, execute(tion)

---

exale, exhale

exam,*,mine, A TEST/EVALUATION

examenashen, examine(nation)

examine,*,ed,ning,nation,nable,ee,er, CLOSELY/CAREFULLY OBSERVE

example,*,ed,ling, SIMILAR TO, USED TO DESCRIBE "prefixes: un"

exampul, example

examunashen, examine(nation)

exaqushen, execute(tion)

exasperate,*,ed,edly,ting,tingly,tion, GREATLY ANNOY/IRRITATE

exaspiration, exasperate(tion)

exaspurate, exasperate

exaustshen, exhaust(ion)

exbarenshal, experiential

exbedeant, expedient

exberenshal, experiential

exbirenshal, experiential

exblanashen, explanation

exblanatory, explanatory

exblikuble, explicable

exblode, explode

exbloetashen, exploit(ation)

exblor, explore

exbloshen, explosion

exbloshun, explosion

exblosive, explosive

exblunashen, explanation

exborashen, expire(ration)

exbort, export

exbortashen, export(ation)

exbos, expose

exbress, express

exburashen, expire(ration)

exburenshal, experiential

excalate, escalate / escalade

excavate,*,ed,ting,tion,tor, DIG FOR SOMETHING "prefixes: un"

exceed,*,ded,ding,dingly,dance, EXCEL, DO MORE THAN EXPECTED

excel,*,lled,lling,llence,llency,llent, PERFORM BETTER THAN NORMAL/ AVERAGE (or see accel) "prefixes: un"

excelaration, accelerate(tion)

excellent,tly, OUTSTANDING

excelurashen, accelerate(tion)

exceluration, accelerate(tion)

excenshuate, accentuate

excentuate, accentuate

excepshen, except(ion)

except,*,ted,ting,tion,tional,tionalism, tionality,tionalities,tionalness, tionable, tive, THIS BUT NOT THAT, EXTRACT FROM (or see accept) "prefixes: un"

excerpt,*,ted,ting,tible,tion,tor, A SMALL PART OF THE WRITTEN WHOLE

excesorize, accessory(rize)

excesory, accessory

excess,sses,ssive,ssively,ssiveness, MORE THAN ENOUGH (or see access)

exchange,*,ed,ging,eable,eability,er, TO TRADE

excinshuate, accentuate

excite,*,ed,ting,ement,table,tability, tableness, AROUSE, FEEL TINGLY INSIDE "prefixes: un"

excksbedeant, expedient

exclamation,*,nal, DISPLAY OF FORCE/ ENTHUSIASM/WILLFULLNESS, PUNCTUATION, EXCLAMATION POINT

excloot, exclude

exclude,*,ded,ding,usive,usively, usiveness,usivity,usion,usions, usionary, NOT INCLUDED AS PART OF SOMETHING OR GROUP

exclusive,ely,eness, SPECIAL, UNLIKE ANY OTHER

excrow, escrow

excuisit, exquisite

exculate, escalate / escalade

excursion,*,nist,ive,ively,iveness, A SHORT TRIP, CHEAP FARE

excuse,*,ed,sing,sable,sably,sableness, er, REASONS FOR A PROBLEM BEING "prefixes: in/un"

excuvashen, excavate(tion)

excuvation, excavate(tion)

exdansev, extensive

exdensible, extensible

exdensive, extensive

exdensubly, extensible(ly)

exderminate, exterminate

exdinsev, extensive

exdravert, extrovert

exdruvirt, extrovert

exdurminate, exterminate

execute,*,ed,ting,tion,tor, CARRY OUT/ ENFORCE/ENACT A PLAN, TO KILL FOR RELIGIOUS/POLITICAL REASONS

executive,*,ely, PERSON WITH POSITION/POWER TO CREATE/ ENACT WITHIN AN ORGANIZATION

exelarate, exhilarate / accelerate

exema, eczema

exemplify,fies,fied,fying,fiable,fication, fier, MAKE CLEAR OR CONVINCING

exempt,ted,ting,tion,tible, SET FREE, EXCUSE FROM DUTY/TAXES/RULES/ LEGAL HOLDINGS

exemshen, exempt(ion)

exepshen, except(ion)

exequtef, executive

exercise,*,ed,sing,sable,er, MENTAL/ PHYSICAL ACTIVITY FOR IMPROVEMENT (or see exorcise)

exert,*,ted,ting,tion, PUT FORTH POWER/ENERGY

exest, exist

exfoliate,*,ed,ting,tion,tive,ant,tor, LAYERS LIFTING OFF

exglusef, exclusive

exhale,*,ed,ling,lation, TO BREATH OUT

exhaust,*,ted,ting,tion,tive,tively, tiveness,ter,tible,tibility, RUN OUT OF, DISCHARGE, FUMES FROM A MOTOR "prefixes: in"

exhaustein, exhaust(ion)

exhibit,*,ted,ting,tion,tioner,tory,tor, tive,tively,tionist,tionism, ON SHOW

exhilarate,*,ed,ting,tingly,tion,tive,tor, REFRESHING, EXCITING (or see accelerate)

exhilation, exhale(lation)

exhostion, exhaust(ion)

exhostshen, exhaust(ion)

exhulation, exhale(lation)

exibit, exhibit

exicute, execute

exicution, execute(tion)

exikude, execute

exikushen, execute(tion)

exikut, execute

exile,*,ed,ling,lic, TO REMOVE/BE REMOVED FROM YOUR COUNTRY

exilurate, exhilarate

exima, eczema

eximplify, exemplify

exirsize, exercise / exorcise

exirtion, exert(ion)

exist,*,ted,ting,tence,tent,tential, tentially,tialism, OF FORM, AN ENTITY "prefixes: in/pre"

exit,*,ted,ting, TO LEAVE FROM

exitment, excite(ment)

exkalate, escalate / escalade

exkergen, excursion

exkerjen, excursion

exkeus, excuse

exklumashen, exclamation

exkro, escrow

exkulate, escalate / escalade

exkurgen, excursion

exkurshun, excursion

exkuze, excuse

exlant, excellent

exo, PREFIX INDICATING "OUTSIDE/ EXTERNAL" MOST OFTEN MODIFIES THE WORD

exorbeant, exorbitant

exorbetant, exorbitant

exorbiant, exorbitant

exorbitant,tly, WAY TOO MUCH, RIDICULOUS AMOUNT

exorcise,*,ed,sing,ism,ist, BANISH/ EXPEL SPIRITS (or see exercise)

exost, exhaust

exostshen, exhaust(ion)

exotic,*,cally, MYSTERIOUS/DIFFERENT/ STRANGE

expadishen, expedition

expadition, expedition

expand,*,ded,ding,der,dable,dability, nse, TO EXTEND BEYOND WHAT IS

expanse,*,sive,sively,siveness,sivity, sion,sionary,sible,sionism, EXTEND BEYOND WHAT IS (or see expense)

exparential, experiential

expect,*,ted,tedly,ting,tation,tant, tantly,table,tably,tedness,tancy, tancies, WANT/WISH SOMETHING TO HAPPEN "prefixes: un"

expedient,*,tly,ncy,ncies, HASTEN THE PROCESS BUT MAY COMPROMISE INTEGRITY "prefixes: in"

expedition,*,nary,ous,ously,ousness, JOURNEY TO GATHER INFORMATION

expel,*,lled,lling,llable,llant,llee,ller, FORCE OUT/AWAY FROM

expend,*,ded,ding,dable,dability,diture, PAY OUT

expense,*,ed,sing,sive,sively,siveness, REQUIRES TIME AND/OR MONEY (or see expanse) "prefixes: in"

experential, experiential

experience,*,ed,cing,ntial,ntially, SKILL/ KNOWLEDGE ABOUT "prefixes: in/ un"

experiential,lly, GAIN KNOWLEDGE/ WISDOM THROUGH EXPERIENCE

experiment,*,ted,ting,tation,tal,tally, talism,ter, TRY SOMETHING NEW

expert,*,tly,tness,tise, SPECIALIZES IN, GREAT DEAL OF EXPERIENCE "prefixes: in"

expire,*,ed,ring,ration,ratory,ry, DETERIORATE, RUN OUT OF TIME

expirential, experiential

explain,*,ned,ning,anation,nable,ner, anatory,anatorily, LIST THE FACTS ABOUT SOMETHING

explanation, PROVIDE DETAILS/ REASONS FOR/ABOUT

explanatory,rily, AIDS/SERVES TO EXPLAIN SOMETHING "prefixes: un"

explenashen, explanation

explicable,ly, CAN BE EXPLAINED "prefixes: in"

explicit,*,tly,tness, SPECIFIC, EXACT, FACTUAL "prefixes: in"

explikable, explicable

explinashen, explanation

explode,*,ed,ding,osion,osive, SUDDEN POWERFUL FORCE OUT "prefixes: un"

exploit,*,ted,ting,tate,tation,tative, TAKE UNFAIR ADVANTAGE OF FOR SELFISH GAIN "prefixes: non/under"

explore,*,ed,ring,ration,ratory, SEARCH BEYOND WHAT IS KNOWN

explosion, INTENSE FORCE/BLAST

explosive,ely,eness, INTENSIVE ACTION/REACTION "prefixes: un"

exploytation, exploit(ation)

explunashen, explanation

expodeshen, expedition

exporashen, expire(ration)

export,*,ted,ting,tation,table,tability, ter, SHIP GOODS OUT OF THE COUNTRY "prefixes: re"

expose,*,ed,sing,sure,sal,sition,sitive, sitory,sition,sitor,er, LET IT OUT/BE SEEN "prefixes: non/over/under"

exposhur, expose(sure)

expreshun, express(ion)

express,sses,ssed,ssing,ssion,ssional, ssionless,ssible,ssive,ssively, ssiveness, ssivity,ssionism,sser, TO VERBALIZE/ACT OUT WHAT ONE

THINKS, GET THERE FASTER "prefixes: in/un"

expurashen, expire(ration)

expuration, expire(ration)

expurential, experiential

exquisite,ely,eness, PERFECTLY BEAUTIFUL

exqwisit, exquisite

exsalins, excel(llence)

exsdensive, extensive

exseed, exceed

exsel, excel / accel

exselarashen, accelerate(tion)

exselaratur, accelerate(tor)

exseld, excel(lled) / accel(lled)

exselens, excel(llence)

exselent, excellent

exselerashen, accelerate(tion)

exselurashen, accelerate(tion)

exselurate, accelerate

exseluratur, accelerate(tor)

exsenshuate, accentuate

exsentrik, eccentric

exserpd, excerpt

exsersize, exercise / exorcise

exses, excess / access

exsesif, excess(ive) / access(ive)

exsesis, excess(es) / access(es)

exsesory, accessory

exshange, exchange

exsibition, exhibit(ion)

exsilent, excellent

exsilurate, exhilarate / accelerate

exsintrik, eccentric

exsirped, excerpt

exsistens, exist(ence)

exsitment, excite(ment)

exskalate, escalate / escalade

exskavate, excavate

exskuvashen, excavate(tion)

exsost, exhaust

exspedient, expedient

exspektashen, expect(ation)

exspektent, expect(ant)

exspel, expel

exspense, expense

exsplod, explode

exsploshen, explosion

exsplosive, explosive

exstase, ecstasy

exstend, extend

exstengwish, extinguish

exstenshen, extension

exstinsibly, extensible(ly)

exstract, extract

exstradite, extradite

exstrakt, extract

exstravert, extrovert

exstrem, extreme

exstremly, extreme(ly)

exstrivurt, extrovert

exstrordenary, extraordinary

exstusee, ecstasy

exsubishen, exhibit(ion)

exsulens, excel(llence)

exsulent, excellent

exsuqushen, execute(tion)

exsurpt, excerpt

exteenkt, extinct

extend,*,ded,ding,nsion,nsive,nsively, nsiveness,dable,dability,dible,nsible, STRETCH/ADD BEYOND WHAT EXISTS "prefixes: over/pre"

extenquish, extinguish

extensible,bility,bly, ABLE TO STRETCH BEYOND WHAT EXISTS "prefixes: in"

extension,*,ive, STRETCH/ADD BEYOND WHAT EXISTS

extensive,ely,eness,ible, STRETCH/ADD BEYOND WHAT EXISTS

extenuate,*,ed,ting,tingly,tion,tive,tor, tory, LESSEN A MISTAKE BY PROVIDING GOOD EXCUSE

exterior,*,rity,rize,rizes,rized,rizing, rization, OUTSIDE LAYER

exterminate,*,ed,ting,tion,tive,tor,tory, able, COMPLETELY GET RID OF

external,lly,lism,lity,lize,lizes,lized,lizing, lization, OUTSIDE OF SOMETHING OR SOMEONE

extinct,tion,tive, DOES NOT EXIST ANY LONGER

extinguish,hes,hed,hing,hable,hment, her, TO PUT OUT, END "prefixes: in"

extra,*, PREFIX INDICATING "OUTSIDE/ BEYOND" MOST OFTEN MODIFIES THE WORD, MORE OF THE SAME

extract,*,ted,ting,tion,table,tive,tively, tor, TAKE/DRAW FROM

extradite,*,ed,ting,tion, RELEASE FROM ONE LEGAL AUTHORITY TO ANOTHER

extraneous,sly,sness, EXTRA, FROM OUTSIDE OF, NOT NECESSARY

extraordinaire,*,ry, OVER AND ABOVE, EXCELLENT

extraordinary,rily,riness, OVER AND ABOVE, EXCELLENT

extravurt, extrovert

extreme,*,ely,eness,mity,mities,mism, OF THE GREATEST/MOST

extro, PREFIX INDICATING "OUTSIDE/ BEYOND" MOST OFTEN MODIFIES THE WORD

extrovert,*,ted,tly, OUTGOING, GREGARIOUS

exturminate, exterminate

exuated, acuate(d)

exukushen, execute(tion)

exuqushen, execute(tion)

exuqute, execute

exursize, exercise / exorcise

exurt, exert

exurtion, exert(ion)

exzamen, examine

exzema, eczema

eye,*,ed,ying, ORGAN OF SIGHT (or see I)

eyebrow,*, HAIR AROUND TOP OF EYES

eyelash,hes, HAIR ON EYELIDS

ez, ease / easy

ezale, easily

ezay, essay

ezbeshulee, especially

ezdragen, estrogen

eze, easy / ease

ezel, easel

ezinshil, essential

ezkort, escort

ezment, easement

ezoteric, esoteric

ezperagus, asparagus

ezsperugus, asparagus

eztablush, establish

ezteem, esteem

eztimate, estimate

eztonish, astonish

eztrawlegy, astrology

eztrogin, estrogen

eztrus, estrus

ezul, easel

ezule, easily

fabewlus, fabulous

fabewlusly, fabulous(ly)

fable,*, MYTH/LEGEND/STORY

fabrecation, fabricate(tion)

fabrek, fabric

fabrekashin, fabricate(tion)

fabrekate, fabricate

fabric,*,cate,cation,cator, THREADS WOVEN TOGETHER "prefixes: bio"

fabricate,*,ed,ting,tion,tor, TO CREATE, CHANGE FROM ONE MATERIAL FORM TO ANOTHER "prefixes: pre"

fabrukashen, fabricate(tion)

fabrukate, fabricate

fabuare, february

fabul, fable

fabules, fabulous / fable(s)

fabulis, fabulous

fabulous,sly,sness, EXCELLENT, WONDERFUL

fabulus, fabulous

fabulusly, fabulous(ly)

fac, face / fake / phase / faze

facade,*, FALSE FRONT, PHONY

facalty, faculty

face,*,ed,cing,cial,cially,cable,eable, EXTERIOR FRONT, ON FRONT OF HEAD (or see phase) "prefixes: re/ sur"

facechus, facetious

facelity, facility

facelty, faculty

facen, fasten / face(cing) / fake(king)

faceshus, facetious

facest, fascist

facet,*,tious, ONE PLANE/FACE/SIDE AMONG MANY (or see faucet) "prefixes: multi"

facetious,sly,sness, NOT SERIOUS, BEING AMUSING

facha, fascia

fachel, facial

fachen, fashion

fachest, fascist

fachinuble, fashion(able)

fachism, fascism

fachist, fascist

fachul, facial

fachun, fashion

fachunible, fashion(able)

facial,*,lly,list, HAVING TO DO WITH THE FACE

facilitate,*,ed,ting,tion,tive,tor, HELP/ ENABLE SUCCESS

facility,ties, PLACE PROVIDING SERVICES

facin, fasten / face(cing) / fake(king)

facinate, fascinate

facishus, facetious

facism, fascism

facit, facet / faucet

facitious, facetious

facshun, faction

fact,*,tual,tually,tuality,tualness, tualism, FOR REAL, TRUE (or see fake(d)/ fax/face(d)) "prefixes: contra"

faction,*,nal,nally,nalism, OF MATH, PART OF A LARGER GROUP

faculty,ties,tative,tatively, SKILL OR ABILITY, TEACHING STAFF

fad,*, CURRENT STYLE (or see fade/ fate)

fadar, father / fodder

fadaret, federate

fade,*,ed,ding,eless, LOSS OF COLOR/ MEMORY/SUBSTANCE (or see fate) "prefixes: pre"

fadel, fatal

fadelity, fidelity

fadul, fatal

faen, feign

faer, fair / fire

faes, phase

fafret, favorite

fag,*,gged,ggot,ggoting, BUNDLE OF STICKS, CIGARETTE, DERAGATORY REMARK

fagism, fascism

fahrenheit, OF THERMOMETERS/ TEMPERATURE

fail,*,led,ling,lingly,lure, NOT SUCCEED(or see fall) "prefixes: un"

fain, feign / vain / vein / vane / fine

faint,*,ted,ting,tly,tness,ter, LOOSE OXYGEN TO BRAIN CAUSING COLLAPSE, NOT CLEAR

fair,*,red,ring,rly,rness, PLACE OF ACTIVITY, IN BETWEEN GOOD AND BAD (or see fare) "prefixes: un"

fairenhite, fahrenheit

fairwel, farewell

fairy,ries, TINY ENTITIES WITH WINGS SEEN ONLY TO A FEW (or see ferry)

fais, phase

faith,*,hful,hfully,hless,hlessly, hlessness, HAVING A BELIEF OR HOPE "prefixes: multi/un"

faiz, phase

fajism, fascism

fak, fake

fakchinul, faction(al)

fakd, fact / fake(d)

fake,*,ed,king,er, PHONY OR ILLUSION

fakelty, faculty

fakilty, faculty

fakshen, faction

fakshunil, faction(al)
fakt, fact / fake(d)
faktionul, faction(al)
fakulty, faculty
fal, fail / fall / fowl / foul
falacy, fallacy
falanthropist, philanthropy(pist)
fald, fault / fail(ed)
falek, phalli(c)
falese, fallacy
falfill, fulfill
falic, phalli(c)
falicity, felicity
falise, fallacy
fall,*,llen,lling,fell, A SEASON,COME
DOWN (or see fail)
fallacy,cies, NOT TRUE, UNFOUNDED
fallow,wness, AGRICULTURE
EXPRESSION, NOT ACTIVE (or see
follow)
fallsefy, falsify
fallsify, falsify
falo, follow / fallow
faloer, follow(er)
falose, fallacy
falosify, philosophy
falou, follow / fallow
falow, follow / fallow
falowir, follow(er)
false,ely,eness,sies,sify,sity,sifier,shood,
NOT TRUE
falsify,fies,fied,fying,fiable,fiability,
fication,fier, PRETEND/FEIGN TO BE
TRUTHFUL
falt, fault / fail(ed)
falter,*,red,ring,ringly,rer, LOOSE
FOOTING/CONFIDENCE (or see
fault) "prefixes: un"
faluse, fallacy
faly, folly
fam, fame
famas, famous
famaslee, famous(ly)
famblee, family
fame,*,ed,ming,mous, REKNOWN,
RECOGNIZED, PUBLIC REPUTATION
"prefixes: de/in"
famelur, familiar
famen, famine
fames, famous
fameslee, famous(ly)
familiar,rly,rity, EXPERIENCE WITH, A
KNOWING "prefixes: over/un"

family,lies,lial, GROUP OF PEOPLE
RELATED IN SOME WAY "prefixes:
multi/sub"
famine,*,ish, SEVERE LACK OF FOOD
OVER TIME
famis, famous
famislee, famous(ly)
famlee, family
famous,sly,sness, WIDELY KNOWN
"prefixes: in"
famus, famous
famuslee, famous(ly)
fan,*,nned,nning,nner,nny, MOTION TO
CREATE BREEZE/LIFT, SPREAD OUT
(or see feign)
fana, fauna
fanadek, phonetic / fanatic
fanatic,*,cal,cally,cism, EXTREME/
IRRATIONAL ENTHUSIASM, HIGHLY
MOTIVATED IN BELIEF/BEHAVIOR
(or see phonetic)
fancy,cier,ciest,ciful,cifully,cifulness,
DECORATIVE, PLAYFUL, LIGHT
fane, feign / fan(ny)
fanedik, phonetic / fanatic
fanesh, finish
fanetic, phonetic / fanatic
fang,*,ged,ging, TOOTH IN SNAKE/
CANINE/SPIDER "prefixes: de"
fangeprint, fingerprint
fangernail, fingernail
fangur, finger
fanic, phonic
fanomanen, phenomenon
fanomena, phenomenon
fanomenul, phenomenal
fanominul, phenomenal
fansee, fancy
fant, faint
fantastic,cal,cally,cality,calness,
ABSOLUTELY GREAT
fantastikul, fantastic(al)
fantasy,sies,sia,size,sizes,sized,sizing,
sist, DREAMY IDEA OF A FUTURE
EVENT
fantem, phantom
fantesy, fantasy
fantisy, fantasy
fantum, phantom
fantusy, fantasy
faond, found
faprecate, fabricate
faprek, fabric

faprekashin, fabricate(tion)
faprukashen, fabricate(tion)
fapulus, fabulous
far,rther,rthest, QUITE A DISTANCE
AWAY (or see for/fare/fair/fire)
farce, SATIRE, NON-FACTUAL, COMICAL
fare,*,ed,ring, COST FOR
TRANSPORTATION, PRESENT
CONDITION (or see fair/fire/fairy)
farenhite, fahrenheit
fares, ferry(ries) / fairy(ries)
farest, far(thest)
farewell,*, GOOD-BYE
farit, ferret
farm,*,med,ming,mable,mer, LAND
WHERE ANIMALS/CROPS ARE
RAISED/GROWN "prefixes: un"
farmaceutical, pharmaceutic(al)
farmasist, pharmacist
farmasutical, pharmaceutic(al)
farmir, farm(er)
farmisist, pharmacist
farmosutekul, pharmaceutic(al)
farmusutekul, pharmaceutic(al)
faro, pharaoh
farotious, ferocious
fars, farce / fair(s)
farsighted,dness, ABLE TO SEE FARTHER
AWAY BETTER THAN CLOSE UP
farsited, farsighted
farther,hest,rmost, EXCEEDS CURRENT
PHYSICAL DIMENSION/DEPTH (or
see further)
farthist, farther(hist)
farthur, farther
farwell, farewell
fary, ferry / fairy
fas, phase / face / faze
fasa, fascia
fascanate, fascinate
fascia,ae,as,al, ROOFLINE ADDENDUM,
BIOLOGY/ANATOMY TERM
fascinate,*,ed,edly,ting,tingly,tion,tor,
CAPTIVATES INTEREST/ATTENTION
fascism,st,stic, CENTRALIZED
OPPRESSIVE CONTROL
fascist,*,tic,sm, PERSON WHO
SUPPORTS OPPRESSIVE/
AUTHORITARIAN CONTROL
fasd, face(d) / fast / phase(d) / faze(d)
fasea, fascia
fasechus, facetious
fasecian, physician
fased, face(d) / fast / phase(d)

fasek, physique / physic
fasel, fossil
faselisd, fossil(ized)
faselitashen, facilitate(tion)
faselitation, facilitate(tion)
faselity, facility
faselutate, facilitate
fasen, fasten / face(cing)
fasenate, fascinate
fasener, fastener
faseque, physique
faseshan, physician
faseshis, facetious
faseshus, facetious
fasesm, fascism
faset, facet / faucet
fasetious, facetious
fasfate, phosphate
fasha, fascia
fashel, facial
fashen, fashion
fashenuble, fashion(able)
fashest, fascist
fashil, facial
fashin, fashion
fashinuble, fashion(able)
fashion,*,ned,ning,nable,nably,nability,
  nableness,ner, CLOTHING STYLES
  WITHIN A CERTAIN TIMEFRAME
  "prefixes: un"
fashism, fascism
fashist, fascist
fashul, facial
fashun, fashion
fashunebul, fashion(able)
fasia, fascia
fasichus, facetious
fasician, physician
fasik, physic / physique
fasil, fossil
fasilatashen, facilitate(tion)
fasilatat, facilitate
fasilatation, facilitate(tion)
fasilety, facility
fasilitate, facilitate
fasility, facility
fasin, fasten / face(cing)
fasinate, fascinate
fasiner, fastener
fasing, face(cing) / phase(ing)
fasique, physique
fasishus, facetious
fasism, fascism
fasit, facet / faucet

fasitious, facetious
fasner, fastener
fasnir, fastener
fasnor, fastener
fasnur, fastener
fast,*,ted,ting,ter,test,tness,tnesses,
  RATE OF SPEED, TO NOT EAT FOOD,
  REMAIN FIXED/SECURE
fasten,*,ned,ning,ner, ADHERE, CLOSE,
  SECURE "prefixes: un"
fastener,*, BUTTONS, ZIPPERS, SNAPS,
  CLOSURE
fasul, fossil
fasunate, fascinate
fat,*,tter,ttest,tten,ttening,tteningly,tty,
  tness,tso, LAYER OF FOOD STORE IN
  MOST LIVING THINGS (or see fad/
  fade/fate/fought) "prefixes: non"
fatal,*,lly,lity,lities,list,lism, LIFE
  THREATENING
fate,*,ed,eful,efully,efulness, THE
  BELIEF THAT EVENTS ARE PRE-
  PLANNED
fateg, fatigue
fatek, fatigue
fath, faith
father,*, MALE PARENT, NAME FOR A
  PRIEST
fathom,*,med,ming,mless,mable,
  MEASUREMENT FOR THE OCEAN
  DEPTH, DEEP TO UNDERSTAND
  "prefixes: un"
fathur, feather / father
fatia, fascia
fatig, fatigue
fatigue,*,ed,uing,gable, EXHAUSTION,
  WEARY, MILITARY CLOTHING
  "prefixes: inde"
faucet,*, PLUMBING DEVICE FOR
  WATER/LIQUIDS
fauculize, focal(ize)
faukalize, focal(ize)
faul, foul / fowl / fall
faulsefy, falsify
faulsify, falsify
fault,*,ted,ting,tier,tiest,ty,tless,tlessly,
  tily,tiness, SOMETHING/SOMEONE
  TO BLAME, A PROBLEM, TECTONIC
  EXPRESSION (or see falter)
faulter, falter
faun,*, HALF GOAT HALF HUMAN (or
  see fawn)
fauna, ANIMALS OF A REGION
faund, found

faundashen, foundation
faundation, foundation
faundry, foundry
faunic, phonic
faunt, found
fauntry, foundry
fausefy, falsify
fausel, fossil
fausfate, phosphate
fausify, falsify
fausit, faucet
fausphate, phosphate
fauster, foster
fausul, fossil
faut, fought
faux, FALSE/IMITATION/FAKE/
  ARTIFICIAL
fauxpas, ALSO FAUX PAS, A BLUNDER
faveret, favorite
favor,*,red,ring,rable,rably,rableness,
  rite,rer, PREFERENCE FOR "prefixes:
  dis/un"
favorite,*,tism, PREFERENCE FOR
fawcet, faucet
fawdur, fodder
fawel, foul / fowl
fawl, foul / fowl
fawlust, foul(est)
fawn,*, BABY DEER (or see faun)
fawnd, fond / found
fawndashen, foundation
fawnt, font / found
fawntry, foundry
fawsefy, falsify
fawsel, fossil
fawsify, falsify
fawsilized, fossil(ized)
fawsul, fossil
fawt, fought
fawul, foul / fowl
fax,xes,xed,xing, SEND A LETTER BY
  PHONE (or see fact(s))
faze,*,ed,zing, SEND A LETTER BY
  PHONE (or see phase)
fazek, physique
fazeshan, physician
fe, fee
feable, feeble
fear,*,red,ring,rful,rfully,rfulness,rless,
  rlessly,rlessness,rsome,rsomely,
  rsomeness, AFRAID, POWERLESS
feasent, pheasant

feasible,eness,ly,bility, QUESTION/ STUDY ABILITY TO ACCOMPLISH/ ACHIEVE "prefixes: de/inde/un"

feast,*,ted,ting, GREAT AMOUNT OF FOOD

feasta, fiesta

feasubilety, feasible(bility)

feasuble, feasible

feat,*, PERFORM WITH UNUSUAL ABILITY (or see feet)

feather,*,red,ring,ry, BIRD CLOTHES, A DECORATIVE EFFECT

feature,*,ed,ring,eless, SPECIAL "prefixes: dis/multi/un"

feb, fib

febal, feeble

february, A MONTH OF THE YEAR (ENGLISH)

febuare, february

febul, feeble

febwuare, february

fecechus, facetious

fecer, figure

feces, EXCREMENT, WASTE PRODUCT, BODILY DISCHARGE (or see face(s))

feceshis, facetious

fecetious, facetious

fech, fetch

fecher, feature

fechet, fidget

fecility, facility

feckle, fickle

fecsher, fixture

fecster, fixture

fed, PAST TENSE FOR THE WORD "FEED"

fedality, fidelity

fedar, fetter / feed(er) / feather

fedarashen, federation

fedaration, federation

fedarul, federal

fedder, fetter / feed(er)

feder, fetter / feed(er) / feather

federal,*,lly,list,lize,lizes,lized,lizing,lism, ation,ative, NATIONAL GOVERNMENT "prefixes: con"

federate,*,ed,ting,tion,tive, GROUPS JOINED UNDER ONE UNIT/ UMBRELLA

federation,*,ive, GROUP OF PEOPLE FORMING IN UNION, UNITED

fedir, fetter / feed(er) / feather

fedirate, federate

fediration, federation

fedish, fetish

fedle, fiddle

fedler, fiddle(r)

fedral, federal

fedrol, federal

fedul, fiddle

fedulize, fertile(lize)

fedur, fetter / feed(er) / feather

fedurashen, federation

fedurate, federate

fee,*, COST FOR/TO DO SOMETHING

feeble,er,est,eness,ly, WEAK, LACKS STRENGTH "prefixes: en"

feebul, feeble

feecher, feature

feed,*,ding,der,fed, GIVE FOOD TO (or see feet) "prefixes: under"

feel,*,ling,lings,felt,ler, USE OF TOUCH/ EMOTIONS TO SENSE ENVIRONMENT "prefixes: un"

feeld, field

feer, fear

feest, feast

feesta, fiesta

feet, MORE THAN ONE FOOT (or see feat)

fefer, fever

feferish, fever(ish)

fefir, fever

fefiresh, fever(ish)

fefor, fever

feftee, fifty

fefteen, fifteen

feften, fifteen

fefth, fifth

feftinth, fifteen(th)

feftis, fifty(ties)

fefty, fifty

fefur, fever

fefurish, fever(ish)

feg, fig

fegen, fission / fusion

feger, figure

fegit, fidget

fegmint, figment

feianse, fiance'

feign,*,ned,ning, TO PRETEND/COPY

feild, field

fein, feign

feis, phase

feiz, phase

fejin, fission / fusion

fejit, fidget

fejon, fission / fusion

fekle, fickle

fekment, figment

feks, fix

feksher, fixture

fekshun, fiction

fekst, fix(ed)

fekster, fixture

feksus, fix(es)

fekul, fickle

fekur, figure

fel, feel / fell / fill / full

felade, fillet

feladendron, philodendron

felanthrepy, philanthropy

felanthropist, philanthropy(pist)

felay, fillet

feld, felt / field / fill(ed) / fell(ed)

feldration, filtrate(ion)

feldur, filter / field(er)

fele, fillet / filly

felicity,ties,tous,tously,tousness,tate, tates,tated,tation,tator, HAPPINES WITH PERFECTION "prefixes: in"

feline,*,ely,eness,nity, OF CATS

fell,lled,lling,ller, PAST TENSE FOR THE WORD "FALL", CUT DOWN TREE (or see fill/feel)

felm, film

felosofy, philosophy

felt, PAST TENSE FOR THE WORD "FEEL", CRUSHED WOOL/COTTON (or see field)

felter, filter

felth, filth

felthe, filthy

feltration, filtrate(ion)

feludindron, philodendron

felurmonek, philharmonic

female,*,eness, THE FEMININE, LIFE GIVER

femanen, feminine

femanist, feminist

femelear, familiar

feminine,nity,ely,eness,nism,ist,ize,izes, ized,izing,ization,mme, THE COMPLIMENT OF MASCULINE "prefixes: de"

feminist,*,tic, A PERSON WHO SUPPORTS WOMEN'S EQUALITY WITH MEN

femunin, feminine

femunist, feminist

fen, fin

fence,*,ed,cing,eless,er, OUTSIDE BARRIER/WALL, A SPORT
fench, finch
fender,*, PART OF A BICYCLE/VEHICLE, A SCREEN, A GUITAR
fenedic, phonetic / fanatic
fenesh, finish
fenetick, phonetic / fanatic
fenger, finger
fengernail, fingernail
fengerprint, fingerprint
fengur, finger
fenish, finish
fenker, finger
fenkerprint, fingerprint
fenkur, finger
fennel, EDIBLE HERB
fenomanen, phenomenon
fenomena, phenomenon
fenominul, phenomenal
fense, fence
fensh, finch
fentur, fender
feonsa, fiance'
fepel, feeble
fepol, feeble
fepuary, february
fepul, feeble
fepuwary, february
fer, fear / for / fir / fur / far / fair / fare
ferbed, forbid
ferbedin, forbid(dden)
ferbid, forbid
ferdelize, fertile(lize)
ferdul, fertile
ferdulizashen, fertile(lization)
fere, ferry / fairy / furry
ferefur, forever
ferenhite, fahrenheit
feres, ferry(ries) / fairy(ries)
feret, ferret
ferever, forever
fergave, forgave
fergetful, forget(ful)
fergif, forgive
fergifness, forgive(ness)
fergit, forget
fergitful, forget(ful)
fergive, forgive
fergivnes, forgive(ness)
fergot, forgot
fergoten, forgot(tten)
feriner, foreign(er)
ferius, furious

ferkets, forget(s)
ferkiv, forgive
ferlough, furlough
ferlow, furlough
ferm, firm
fermaledy, formal(ity)
fermality, formal(ity)
fermashen, formation
fermation, formation
ferment,*,ted,ting,table,tability,tation, tative, MOVING TOWARDS FERMENTATION
fermentation,nal, ENZYMATIC/ CELLULAR REACTION
fern,*, A PLANT
fernachur, furniture
fernecher, furniture
fernes, furnace
fernis, furnace
fernish, furnish
ferniture, furniture
fernus, furnace
fernush, furnish
fero, pharaoh / furrow
ferochusle, ferocious(ly)
ferocious,sly,sness, FIERCE, INTENSE
feroshusle, ferocious(ly)
ferotious, ferocious
ferow, furrow / pharaoh
ferr, PREFIX INDICATING "IRON" MOST OFTEN MODIFIES THE WORD
ferret,*, MEMBER OF THE WEASEL FAMILY
ferri, PREFIX INDICATING "IRON" MOST OFTEN MODIFIES THE WORD
ferro, PREFIX INDICATING "IRON" MOST OFTEN MODIFIES THE WORD
ferroso, PREFIX INDICATING "IRON" MOST OFTEN MODIFIES THE WORD
ferry,rries,rried,rrying, BOAT THAT CROSSES WATER CARRYING THINGS (or see fairy/furry)
fers, fierce / fear(s) / first
fersake, forsake
fersakin, forsake(n)
fersd, first
ferse, fierce
fersest, fierce(st)
fersly, fierce(ly)
fersnis, fierce(ness)
ferst, first
ferther, farther / further
ferthur, farther / further

fertile,lity,ely,eness,lize, ABLE/READY TO PRODUCE, PREPARE FOR PRODUCTION "prefixes: in/inter"
fertilize,*,ed,er,zing,zation, USED TO ENHANCE PRODUCTION
fertulize, fertilize
ferut, ferret
ferwal, farewell
ferwel, farewell
fery, ferry / fairy / furry
ferys, ferry(ries) / fairy(ries)
ferzd, first
ferzt, first
fesabilety, feasible(bility)
fesable, feasible
fesasist, physicist
fescal, fiscal
fesdev, festive
feseble, feasible
fesechus, facetious
fesekl, physical
fesekly, physical(lly)
feseks, physics
fesent, pheasant
feseologe, physiology
feseshus, facetious
fesetious, facetious
fesh, fish
feshen, fission / fusion
fesible, feasible
fesical, physical
fesichus, facetious
fesics, physics
fesik, physique
fesikle, physical
fesilatashen, facilitate(tion)
fesilaty, facility
fesint, pheasant
fesiologe, physiology
fesiology, physiology
fesishen, physician
fesishus, facetious
fesitious, facetious
feskal, fiscal
fesode, facade
fest, fist
festaful, festive(val)
festive,ely,eness,val,vity,vities, A CELEBRATION
festofil, festive(val)
fesubility, feasible(bility)
fesuble, feasible
fesunt, pheasant
fesusist, physics(cist)

fet, feet / feat / feed / fed
fetarashen, federation
fetaration, federation
fetch,hes,hed,hing, TO GET AND BRING BACK
feteg, fatigue
feter, fetter / feed(er)
feth, fifth
fethar, feather
fethur, feather
fetir, fetter / feed(er)
fetirashen, federation
fetish,hes,hism,hist, OBSESSION FOR SOMETHING
fetler, fiddle(r)
fetter,*,red,ring, TO SHACKLE/RESTRAIN "prefixes: un"
feturation, federation
feture, feature
feu, few
feucher, future
feud,*,ding,dal,dalism,dality,dalize, datory, A LONGSTANDING QUARREL/FIGHT
feugen, fusion / fission
feul, fuel
feuld, field
feum, fume
feumegat, fumigate
feumigate, fumigate
feumugation, fumigate(tion)
feuree, fury / furry
feurius, furious
feus, fuse
feushen, fusion / fission
feut, feud
fever,*,red,ring,rish, BODY TEMPERATURE TOO HIGH
fevir, fever
fevirish, fever(ish)
fevur, fever
fevurish, fever(ish)
few, MORE THAN TWO
fewchur, future
fewd, feud
fewgen, fusion / fission
fewgitive, fugitive
fewmigashen, fumigate(tion)
fewmigate, fumigate
fewmigation, fumigate(tion)
fewnarul, funeral
fewreus, furious
fews, fuse
fewton, futon

fewul, fuel
fex, fix
fext, fix(ed)
feyuree, fury
fezability, feasible(bility)
fezable, feasible
fezacul, physical
fezakle, physical
fezakul, physical
fezalogical, physiology(gical)
fezasest, physics(cist)
fezek, physique
fezekle, physical
fezeks, physics
fezent, pheasant
fezeology, physiology
fezeshan, physician
fezik, physique
fezikol, physical
feziks, physics
fezint, pheasant
fezubelity, feasible(bility)
fezuble, feasible
fezucul, physical
fezuks, physics
fezukul, physical
fezulogically, physiology(gically)
fezunt, pheasant
fezusist, physics(cist)
fi, fee
fiance', HUMAN TO BE MARRIED
fiar, fire
fib,*,bber,bbing, TO TELL A LIE
fiber,*,brous, PLANT MATERIAL (or see fib(bber)/fever) "prefixes: multi"
fibre, fiber
fibrous,sly,sness, TEXTURE IS THREAD-LIKE "prefixes: multi"
fibur, fiber
fichar, feature
fichen, fish(ing) / fusion / fission
ficher, feature
fichet, fidget
fichur, feature
fickle,er,est,eness, WILL LIKELY CHANGE PERSPECTIVE/PREFERENCE
ficshan, fiction
ficshen, fiction
ficsher, fixture
ficshon, fiction
ficster, fixture
fiction,nal,nalize,nalizes,nalized,nalizing, nalization,tious,tiously,tiousness, ive,ively, STORIES/BOOKS ABOUT

MADE UP CHARACTERS "prefixes: non"
fiddle,*,er,ling, AN INSTRUMENT
fidelity, FAITHFUL "prefixes: in"
fider, fight(er) / fit(tter)
fidget,*,ted,ting,tingly,ty,tiness, AN INSTRUMENT
fidir, fight(er) / fit(tter)
fidle, fiddle
fidlur, fiddle(r)
fidol, fiddle
fidor, fight(er) / fit(tter)
fidul, fiddle
fidur, fight(er) / fit(tter)
field,*,der,ding, LAND WITH FEW IF NO TREES "prefixes: in/sub/up"
fierce,er,est,ely,eness, DANGEROUS, THREATENING
fiesta,*, CELEBRATION
fife, five
fiflth, filth
fifteen,nth, NUMBER
fiftees, fifty(ties)
fiften, fifteen
fiftenth, fifteen(th)
fiftes, fifty(ties)
fifth,*, ONE-FIFTH OF FIVE PARTS
fifty,ties,tieth, A NUMBER
fig,*, A FRUIT
figen, fission
figer, figure
figerene, figurine
figet, fidget
fight,*,ter,ting,fought, STRUGGLE, BATTLE BETWEEN "prefixes: in"
figit, fidget
figment,*, IMAGINARY
figure,*,ed,ring,ral,rant,ration,rative, ratively,rativeness,rine, SHAPE/FORM OF SOMETHING, NUMBERS "prefixes: con/dis/pre"
figurine,*, SHAPE/FORM OF SOMETHING
fijen, fission / fusion
fijet, fidget
fijon, fission / fusion
fikchen, fiction
fiker, figure
fikle, fickle
fikment, figment
fiks, fix / fig(s)
fikshin, fiction
fikshur, fixture
fikster, fixture

fiksus, fix(es)
fikt, fix(ed)
fikul, fickle
fikur, figure
fil, fill / fell / file / feel
fila, fillet
filadendron, philodendron
filanthrepy, philanthropy
filanthropist, philanthropy(pist)
filarmonek, philharmonic
filasofical, philosophy(hical)
fild, file(d) / field / fill(ed)
fildration, filtrate(ion)
fildur, filter
file,*,ed,ling,er, TO ORGANIZE, TOOL
    TO GRIND, FORM A LINE (or see fill/
    fillet/filly) "prefixes: inter/pre"
filermonek, philharmonic
filet, fillet
filhermonic, philharmonic
filings, file(lings) / feel(ings)
fill,*,lled,lling,ller, MAKE OPPOSITE OF
    EMPTY (or see file/fell)
fillet,*,ted,ting, ALSO FILET, BONES
    REMOVED FROM FISH/ANIMALS
filly,llies, YOUNG FEMALE HORSE
film,*,med,ming,mation,my,mily,
    miness,mer, A COATING, A MOVING
    PICTURE "prefixes: bio"
filodendron, philodendron
filosofy, philosophy
filosophy, philosophy
filt, file(d) / field / fill(ed)
filter,*,red,ring,rless,rable,trable,trate,
    rer, USED TO SEPARATE/SORT
    "prefixes: bio"
filth,hy, DIRTIEST OF THE DIRTY, NASTY
filthy,hier,hiest, DIRTIEST OF THE DIRTY,
    NASTY
filtrate,*,ed,ting,tation, TO SEPARATE/
    STRAIN
filudendron, philodendron
filurmonic, philharmonic
fily, filly
fimanist, feminist
fimilear, familiar
fin,*,nned,nning, EXTRUSION FOR
    WEAVING THROUGH AIR/WATER
    (or see fine)
final,*,lly,le,list,lize,lizes,lized,lizing,
    lization,lizer, THE END, THE LAST
    "prefixes: semi"
finance,*,ed,cing,cial,cials,cially,eable,
    cier, ABOUT MONEY

finants, finance
finch,hes, A BIRD
find,*,der,ding,found, REVEAL THE
    UNSEEN/UNKNOWN
findur, fender / find(er)
fine,*,er,est,ed,ning,ely,eness, THIN,
    VERY NICE, MONETARY
    PUNISHMENT (or see fin)
finedik, phonetic / fanatic
finel, final / fennel
finely, fine(ly) / final(lly)
fines, finesse / fine(s) / fine(st)
finesh, finish
finesse,*, HANDLE WITH SKILL/
    CONTROL/DELICATELY (or see
    fine(st))
finetic, phonetic / fanatic
finger,*,red,ring, ON THE HAND, USE
    THE HAND, EXTRUSION
fingernail,*, ON THE FINGER
fingerprint,*,ted,ting, ON THE FINGER
finight, finite
finish,es,hed,hing,her, TO COMPLETE
    "prefixes: semi/un "
finite,ely,eness, LIMITED
finker, finger
finkerprint, fingerprint
finle, final / fennel
finol, final / fennel
finomanen, phenomenon
finomena, phenomenon
finominul, phenomenal
finse, fence
finsh, finch
fintur, fender
finul, final / fennel
finuly, final(lly)
fionsa, fiance'
fiper, fiber
fipur, fiber
fir,*, AN EVERGREEN TREE (or see fire/
    fur/for/fear)
firbed, forbid
firbedin, forbid(dden)
firbiten, forbid(dden)
firdul, fertile
firdulize, fertilize
fire,*,ed,ring,er, CHEMICAL REACTION
    THAT BURNS, TAKE JOB AWAY,
    EMOTIONAL (or see far/furry)
    "prefixes: mis/retro"
firefur, forever
firevur, forever
firgave, forgave

firgefnis, forgive(ness)
firget, forget
firgetful, forget(ful)
firgitful, forget(ful)
firgive, forgive
firgot, forgot
firgoten, forgot(tten)
firketing, forget(tting)
firkets, forget(s)
firkiteng, forget(tting)
firkiv, forgive
firlow, furlough
firm,*,med,ming,mly,mness,mer,mest,
    BETWEEN SOFT/HARD, CAPITALIST
    GROUP
firmaledy, formal(ity)
firmality, formal(ity)
firmashen, formation
firmation, formation
firment, ferment
firn, fern
firnus, furnace
firochusle, ferocious(ly)
firoshis, ferocious
firoshusle, ferocious(ly)
firow, furrow
firs, fir(s) / fire(s) / first / fierce
firsaken, forsake(n)
first,*,tly, BEFORE ALL
firtalize, fertilize
firtul, fertile
firy, furry
firzd, first
fisasist, physicist
fiscal,lly, REFERRING TO MONEY
fisealugist, physiology(gist)
fisecal, physical
fisek, physic / physique
fiseks, physics
fiselity, facility
fiseolagekul, physiology(gical)
fiseolochi, physiology
fiseologist, physiology(gist)
fiseology, physiology
fiseshan, physician
fisesist, physicist
fish,hed,hing,hy,her,hery,heries,
    VERTEBRATE IN WATER, CATCH
    FISH IN WATER
fishun, fission / fish(ing) / fusion
fisic, physic / physique
fisical, physical
fisician, physician
fisics, physics

fisicul, physical
fisik, physique
fisiolochi, physiology
fisiologest, physiology(gist)
fision, fission / fusion
fisique, physique
fisisest, physicist
fisishan, physician
fisishen, physician
fiskul, fiscal
fisode, facade
fisokul, physical
fisologically, physiology(gically)
fisots, facade(s)
fission,nable, USE HEAT TO SPLIT AN
    ATOMS NUCLEUS (or see fusion)
fist,*,ted,ting, CLOSED HAND, AN
    EXPRESSION (or see feast)
fit,*,tted,tting,ttingly,ttingness,tter,
    ttest,tful,tfully,tfulness,tness,
    SOMETHING THAT WEARS WELL,
    EMOTIONAL OUTBURST (or see
    fight/feat/feet) "prefixes: mis/
    retro/un"
fite, fight
fiteg, fatigue
fiter, fight(er) / fit(tter)
fith, fifth
fitlur, fiddle(r)
fitur, fight(er) / fit(tter) / feature
fiud, feud
five,*,er, AN ENGLISH NUMBER
fiver, fever
fix,xes,xed,xer,xing,xate,xates,xated,
    xating,xation,xative,xatives, xable,
    INTENSE FOCUS, TO REPAIR
    "prefixes: un"
fixture,*, PERMANENTLY FASTENED
fizalogical, physiology(gical)
fizasist, physicist
fizek, physique
fizeolagekul, physiology(gical)
fizeolagist, physiology(gist)
fizeological, physiology(gical)
fizeology, physiology
fizeshan, physician
fizesist, physicist
fizicol, physical
fizik, physique
fiziks, physics
fiziologest, physiology(gist)
fiziological, physiology(gical)
fizisest, physics(cist)
fizocol, physical

fizological, physiology(gical)
fizukle, physical
fizulogically, physiology(gically)
flabides, phlebitis
flabites, phlebitis
flabodumy, phlebotomy
flabotimest, phlebotomy(mist)
flack, flake
flader, flatter / fillet
fladery, flatter(y)
flafur, flavor
flag,*,gged,gging,gger, MATERIAL WITH
    A SYMBOL, WAVE SOMEONE OVER,
    TAG SOMEONE "prefixes: re"
flail,*,led,ling, THRASH ABOUT, A TOOL
    FOR THRASHING GRAIN
flain, flat(tten)
flair,*, APTITUDE/KNACK FOR,
    DEMEANOR(or see flare)
flake,*,ed,king,er,ky,kier,kiest,kily,
    kiness, THIN LAYER, NOT RELIABLE
flal, flail
flamable, flammable
flame,*,ed,ming,mer, TIP OF FIRE,
    SUDDEN ERUPTION
flamingo,*, A BIRD, DANCE
flammable,*,bility, CAN CATCH ON FIRE
    "prefixes: in"
flanel, flannel
flank,*,ked,king,ker, THE REAR, SIDES
flannel,*, COTTON MATERIAL
flap,*,pped,pping,pper,ppy, WAVE
    ABOUT, REMOVABLE COVER
flare,*,ed,ring, SHOOTING LIGHT, TO
    SPREAD OUT (or see flair)
flash,hes,hed,hing,her, LIGHTS FOR A
    BRIEF MOMENT, TATTOO LINGO
flat,*,tten,tter,tters,ttest,ttens,ttened,
    ttening,ttener, THIN, HORIZONTAL,
    OFF KEY
flatter,*,ry, PRAISE THAT'S NOT
    SINCERE/SERIOUS "prefixes: un"
flatur, flat(tter) / flatter
flau, flaw / flow
flaunder, flounder
flaur, flower / flour / floor
flaus, floss / flaw(s)
flavor,*,red,ring,rful,rless, PERCEIVED
    BY TASTEBUDS ON THE TONGUE
flaw,*,wed,wless,wlessly,wlessness,
    NOT RIGHT (or see flow)
flawer, flour / flower
flawnder, flounder
fle, flea / flee

flea,*, A TINY BUG (or see flee)
flebant, flippant
flebidis, phlebitis
flebitis, phlebitis
flebodumy, phlebotomy
fleck,*,ked,king, BITS/PIECES/FLAKES
    OF SOMETHING (or see flex)
flecks, fleck(s) / flex
flecs, flex / fleck(s)
fled, PAST TENSE FOR THE WORD
    "FLEE" (or see fleet/flee(d))
flee,*,eed,eeing,led,eer, RUN AWAY (or
    see flea)
fleece,es,ed,cing,cy,er, SHEEP COAT,
    COAT MATERIAL
fleet,*,ted,ter,ting,tingly,ter,test,
    tingness,tly,tness, GROUP OF
    BOATS, MOVE SWIFTLY, QUICKLY
flegm, phlegm
fleks, flex / fleck(s)
flem, phlegm
flemingo, flamingo
flemsy, flimsy
flench, flinch
fleng, fling
flent, flint
flep, flip
flepant, flippant
fleper, flipper
fler, flare / flair
flert, flirt
flery, flurry
flese, fleece / flea(s)
flesh,hy,hier,hiest,hiness,hly,hlier,hliest,
    hliness, SOFT/FIRM PARTS OF
    FRUIT/ANIMALS
flete, fleet
flew, PAST TENSE FOR THE WORD "FLY"
    (or see flu/flue) "prefixes: over"
flewent, fluent
flewid, fluid
flex,xes,xed,xing,xible,xibly,xibility,
    xibleness, TO BEND, TEMPORARILY
    BEND (or see fleck(s)) "prefixes: re/
    retro"
fli, fly / flea / flee
fliar, flier / fly(er)
flibent, flippant
flibidis, phlebitis
flibitis, phlebitis
flibodumy, phlebotomy
flibotimest, phlebotomy(mist)
flick,*,ker,king,kered,kering,keringly,
    SNAP, CANDLE FLAME ACTION

flid, flew / flight

flier,*, A PIECE OF PAPER WITH INFORMATION TO BE CIRCULATED (or see fly(er))

flight,*,ty,tless, TO TRAVEL THROUGH THE AIR "prefixes: over"

flik, flick

flim, phlegm

flimengo, flamingo

flimsy,sier,siest,siness, LIGHTWEIGHT, DELICATE

flinch,hes,hed,hing,hingly,her, TO JERK "prefixes: un"

fling,*,ging,lung,ger, THROW/CAST AWAY, A CAREFREE TIME

flint,*,ty,tiness, USED TO START FIRE

flip,*,pped,pping,pper, ALTERNATING SIDES WHILE IN THE AIR

fliper, flipper

flippant,tly,tness, NOT TREAT SERIOUSLY

flipper,*, MOVEABLE EXTRUSION ON ANIMALS FOR MOVEMENT, MANMADE FOOT PADDLES

flirt,*,ted,ting,tation,tatious,tatiously, tatiousness,ty,tier,tiest,tily,tiness, TEASING/TOYING WITH

flit,*,tted,tting,tter,tters,ttered,ttering, DART IN/OUT (or see flight)

fliur, flier / fly(er)

flo, flow

float,*,ted,ting,ter,table,tability, STAYS ON TOP OF LIQUID/AIR, BUOYANT

flock,*,ked,king, GROUP TOGETHER

flod, flood / float

floder, flutter / float(er)

floent, fluent

flof, fluff

flok, flock

flone, flown

flong, flung

flood,*,ded,ding,dable,der, TOO MUCH WATER

flooint, fluent

flook, fluke

floor,*,red,ring,rage, A SURFACE TO WALK ON "prefixes: sub/under"

flooride, fluoride

floot, flute

flop,*,pped,pping,ppy,ppier,ppiest,ppily, ppiness, FALL FLAT DOWN, LOOSE

flor, floor / flour / flower

floral,*,lly, FLOWERS

florescent,nce, FLOWERING (or see fluorescent) "prefixes: in"

floresh, flourish

florid, fluoride

florish, flourish

florist,*, WORKS WITH FLOWERS

flosh, flush

floss,sses,ssed,ssing,sser, WAY TO CLEAN BETWEEN TEETH

floster, fluster

flot, float / flood

floter, flutter / float(er)

flounder,*,red,ring, FISH, STRUGGLE FOR PROPER STANCE

flour,red,ring,ry,rier,riest, GRINDING GRAIN TO POWDER (or see flower)

flourescent, fluorescent / florescent

flouride, fluoride

flourish,hes,hed,hing, GROW HEALTHY AND STRONG

flow,*,wed,wing,wingly, STEADILY MOVING ALONG, MOVEMENT "prefixes: in/over/under"

flower,*,red,ring,ry,rer,orescent, orescence, PLANT, PART OF PLANT WHICH PREPARES THE SEED (or see flour) "prefixes: de"

flown, PAST TENSE FOR THE WORD "FLY"

flownder, flounder

flu, A VIRUS (or see flew/flue)

flubotemist, phlebotomy(mist)

flubotemy, phlebotomy

fluc, fluke

flucks, flux

flucshuate, fluctuate

fluctuate,*,ed,ting,tion,ant, MOVE BACK AND FORTH IN DEGREES

flud, flood

fludder, flutter

fluder, flutter

flue,*, CHIMNEY PIPE (or see flew/flu)

flued, fluid

fluent,tly,ncy, CONSISTENTLY CORRECT

fluff,*,fed,fing,fy,ffier,ffiest,ffily,ffiness, LIGHTEN UP BY SHAKING

fluid,*,dal,dally,dity,dly,dness,dic,dize, dizes,dized,dizing,dization,dizer, LIQUID STATE "prefixes: semi"

fluke,*,ky,kily,kiness, UNUSUAL OCCURANCE, PART OF A FISH, PART OF ANCHOR

fluks, flux

flumengo, flamingo

flung, PAST TENSE FOR THE WORD "FLING" (or see flunk)

flunk,*,ked,king,ker, TO FAIL

flunt, fluent

fluo, PREFIX INDICATING "FLOURINE" MOST OFTEN MODIFIES THE WORD

fluor, PREFIX INDICATING "FLOURINE" MOST OFTEN MODIFIES THE WORD

fluorescent,nce, ILLUMINATING LIGHT (or see florescent)

fluoride,date,dates,dated,dating,dation, GAS, CHEMICAL ADDED TO WATER CONSIDERED POISONOUS

fluoro, PREFIX INDICATING "FLOURINE" MOST OFTEN MODIFIES THE WORD

fluresent, florescent / fluorescent

fluresh, flourish

flurid, flouride

flurish, flourish

flurry,rries,rried,rrying, SPORADIC, FAST SNOW/BEHAVIOR

flurt, flirt

flury, flurry

flush,hes,hed,hing,hable,her, RID OF SOMETHING

fluster,*,red,ring, CONFUSED, NERVOUS

flute,*,ed,ting,tist, AN INSTRUMENT/ DESIGN

fluter, flutter

flutter,*,red,ring, BACK AND FORTH OR UP AND DOWN VIGOROUSLY

flux,xes,xed,xing,xion, OF/PROMOTES FLUIDITY/FLOW "prefixes: re"

fly,lies,lew,ying,yer, AIRBORNE, INSECT (or see flier) "prefixes: over"

fo, foe / faux / for

foal,*,led,ling, YOUNG ANIMAL

foalt, foal(ed)

foam,*,med,ming,my, ENCASED POCKETS OF AIR

fobea, phobia

fobia, phobia

focal,lly,lize,lizes,lized,lizing,lization, KEEP ON FOCUS WITH EYES/ MENTALLY/ EMOTIONALLY "prefixes: bi"

foceshes, facetious

foceshis, facetious

foch, fudge

focis, focus

focks, fox

focle, focal

foculize, focal(ize) / focal

focus,ses,sed,sing,sable,ser, CONCENTRATE ONLY ON ONE THING OR THOUGHT, HAVE NO THOUGHTS "prefixes: re/un"

fod, food
fodagraf, photo(graph)
fodar, fodder
fodasenthesis, photosynthesis
fodasinthesis, photosynthesis
fodch, fudge
fodder,*, FOOD FOR CATTLE
fodegraf, photo(graph)
foder, fodder
fodigraf, photo(graph)
fodir, fodder
fodisinthasis, photosynthesis
fodo, photo
fodograf, photo(graph)
fodon, photon / futon
fodosinthesis, photosynthesis
fodugraf, photo(graph)
fodur, fodder
fodusinthesis, photosynthesis
foe,*, AN ADVERSARY (or see faux)
foel, foil / foal
foeul, foil
fog,*,gged,gger,gging,ggy, A MISTY CLOUD "prefixes: de"
foil,*,led,ling,ler, THIN SHEETS OF METAL, TRICKED
fok, folk / fog
fokes, focus
fokis, focus
fokle, focal
foklize, focal(ize)
foks, folk(s) / fox
fokul, focal
fokulize, focal(ize)
fokus, focus
fol, foal / fool / full / fall
folanthrapy, philanthropy
fold,*,ded,der,ding,dable, BEND/ CREASE OVER (or see foal(ed)/ fool(ed)/fault) "prefixes: en/inter/ over/multi/un"
folder,*, FOLDED SHEET TO HOLD PAPERS
foldur, folder
foleashun, foliate(tion)
foleate, foliate
folecity, felicity
foleg, foliage
folesee, fallacy
folesh, fool(ish)

folfill, fulfill
foliage,ed,aceous,ate,ation, ABOUT PLANTS
foliate,*,ed,ting,tion, THIN SHEETS, CONCERNS LEAVES "prefixes: bi/de/ multi/uni"
folicity, felicity
folig, foliage
folish, fool(ish)
folk,*,ksy, STYLE OF MUSIC, THE PARENTS/PEOPLE
folksee, folk(sy)
follow,*,wed,wing,wer, ONE BEHIND ANOTHER (or see fallow)
folly,llies, FOOLISH
folo, follow / fallow
foloer, follow(er)
folowir, follow(er)
fols, false / foal(s) / fall(s)
folsefy, falsify
folsify, falsify
folt, foal(ed) / fold
folter, folder
foltur, folder
foly, folly
folze, false
fombal, fumble
fombl, fumble
fombul, fumble
fome, foam / foam(y)
fomileur, familiar
fomy, foam(y)
fon, fun / phone / fawn / faun
fona, fauna
fonadik, phonetic / fanatic
fonagraf, phonograph
fonatek, phonetic / fanatic
foncshin, function
fond,der,dest,dly,ness, ATTRACTED TO (or see font/phone(d))
fondamental, fundamental
fondle,*,ed,ling, AFFECTIONATE TOUCHING WITH HANDS
fondumentle, fundamental
fone, phone / funny / phony
fonec, phonic
fonedik, phonetic / fanatic
fonegraf, phonograph
fonek, phonic
fonel, funnel
fonemic, phoneme(mic)
fonetic, phonetic / fanatic
fongas, fungus
fongus, fungus

foni, funny / phony
fonic, phonic
fonigraf, phonograph
fonik, phonic
fonil, funnel
fonimic, phoneme(mic)
fonkshen, function
font,*,tal, SIZE/STYLE OF LETTERS, BASIN (or see fond)
fontementul, fundamental
fonugraf, phonograph
fonul, funnel
food,*, WHAT IS CHEWED/ SWALLOWED FOR SUSTENANCE
fool,*,led,ling,lingly,lish,lishly,lishness, lery, DOESN'T COMPREHEND THE SITUATION
foome, fume
foonrul, funeral
foot,ting,tings,tage,tless,tling,ter, ATTACHED TO LEG, FIRM SPOT, U.S. MEASUREMENT OF LENGTH "prefixes: under"
footon, futon
fophade, phosphate
for, PREFIX INDICATING "AWAY/OFF/ EXTREMELY" MOST OFTEN MODIFIES THE WORD, ALSO MEANS, GIVE TOWARDS, BELONGS TO (or see fore/four/far)
forach, forage
forage,*,ed,ging,er, TO SEARCH FOR
foram, forum
foran, foreign
foraner, foreign(er)
forasdry, forest(ry)
forast, forest
forastir, forest(er)
forbedin, forbid(dden)
forbet, forbid
forbetin, forbid(dden)
forbid,*,dden,dding,ddingly,ddingness, ddance,dder,bade, NOT ALLOWED
forbiten, forbid(dden)
force,*,ed,cing,eless,eful,efully,efulness, cible,cibly,cibility, cibleness,er, A PUSH OR PULL WITH INTENSE ENERGY "prefixes: en/un"
forceps, MEDICAL INSTRUMENT
forchanet, fortunate
forchen, fortune
forchun, fortune
forchunet, fortunate
forchunitly, fortunate(ly)

fordafid, fortify(fied)
forde, forty
fordeath, fortieth
fordeen, fourteen
fordefication, fortification
fordefid, fortify(fied)
fordefy, fortify
fordeith, forty(tieth)
fordi, forty
fordifid, fortify(fied)
fordify, fortify
fordle, fertile
fordufecashen, fortification
fordufid, fortify(fied)
fordufy, fortify
fordulizashen, fertilize(zation)
fordulize, fertilize
fordyeth, fortieth
fore, PREFIX INDICATING "BEFORE/IN
   FRONT" MOST OFTEN MODIFIES
   THE WORD, FRONT OF A VESSEL (or
   see four/for)
foreg, forage
forego,es,one,oing,oer, PRECEDE, GO
   BEFORE
foregone, PAST TENSE FOR THE WORD
   "FOREGO"
foreign,ner,ners, NOT FAMILIAR, FROM
   ANOTHER PLACE
forein, foreign
forem, forum
foren, foreign
forenir, foreign(er)
foresaw, PAST TENSE FOR THE WORD
   WORD 'FORESEE'
foresdashen, forest(ation)
foresdry, forest(ry)
foresee,*,saw,een,eeing,eeable,eeably,
   eer, TO KNOW BEFORE IT HAPPENS/
   YOU SEE IT
foresent, florescent / fluorescent
foreside, LAND ALONG THE OCEAN,
   THE FRONT OF SOMETHING (or see
   foresight)
foresight,*,ted,tedly,tedness, KNOW/
   THINK BEFOREHAND (or see
   farsighted)
foresite, foresight
forest,*,ted,tal,tial,tation,ter,try, LAND
   MADE UP OF WILD ANIMALS/
   PLANTS, LARGE/HEAVILY WOODED/
   TREED AREA "prefixes: dis/re"
forestashen, forest(ation)
foresteul, forest(ial)

forestur, forest(er)
foretuety, fortuity
forever, ON AND ON WITHOUT END
foreword,*, INTRODUCTORY WRITING
   (or see forward)
forfat, forfeit
forfeit,*,ted,ting,ture, FORCED TO LET
   GO OF
forfut, forfeit
forg, fork / forge / forage
forgave, PAST TENSE FOR THE WORD
   "FORGIVE"
forge,*,ed,ging,eable,eability,er,ery,
   eries, FAKE COPY, SOFTEN METAL
   BY FIRE (or see forage)
forget,*,tting,got,gotten,tter,tful,tfully,
   tfulness,ttable, CHOOSE TO OR
   CANNOT REMEMBER "prefixes: un"
forgifnes, forgive(ness)
forgit, forget
forgitful, forget(ful)
forgive,*,en,ving,eness,gave,vable,
   vably,er, GIVEN MERCY, PARDON,
   EXCUSED "prefixes: un"
forgo, forego / foregone
forgon, foregone
forgot,tten, PAST TENSE FOR THE
   WORD "FORGET"
forgoten, forgot(tten)
forige, forage / forge
forim, forum
forin, foreign
foriner, foreign(er)
forisdashen, forest(ation)
forisdry, forest(ry)
forist, forest
foristation, forest(ation)
foristir, forest(er)
foristry, forest(ry)
forje, forge / forage
fork,*,ked,king, TOOL FOR EATING/
   WORKING, SPLIT IN THE PATH
forketing, forget(tting)
forkit, forget
forkiv, forgive
forlow, furlough
form,*,med,ming,mation,mational,
   mative,matively,mable,mless,mer,
   SHAPED BY FORCE OR INTENT
   "prefixes: con/multi/pre/re/-re/un"
formad, format
formaded, format(tted)
formader, format(tter)

formal,*,lly,lity,lities,lize,lization,lizer,
   PROPER, DONE WITH CERTAIN
   RULES,DRESS-UP OCCASION
   "prefixes: in/semi"
formalesation, formal(ization)
formalidy, formal(ity)
formalise, formal(ize)
formaluzashen, formal(ization)
formaly, formal(lly) / former(ly)
formashen, formation
format,*,tted,tting,tter,tion,tive,tively,
   SPECIFIC PROTOCOL/DESIGN/
   SHAPE/ STRUCTURE MOST OFTEN
   USED "prefixes: un"
formated, format(tted)
formatef,format(ive)
formater, format(tter)
formatif,format(ive)
formation,*,nal, MADE/ENCOURAGED
   INTO A SHAPE "prefixes: re"
formativly, format(ively)
formd, form(ed)
formel, formal
formelize, formal(ize)
formely, formal(lly)
former,*,rly, PREVIOUSLY, USED TO BE
formetive,format(ive)
formewla, formula
formewlashen, formula(tion)
formil, formal
formily, formal(lly) / former(ly)
formir, former
formirly, former(ly) / formal(lly)
formitevly, format(ively)
formitive,format(ive)
formle, formal
formolezashen, formal(ization)
formolize, formal(ize)
formotev,format(ive)
formotivly, format(ively)
formt, form(ed)
formul, formal
formula,*,ate,ates,ated,ating,ation,aic,
   aically,arize,arizes,arized,arizing,
   arizer, lism, SPECIFIC MIXTURE OF
   MOLECULES
formulashen, formula(tion)
formule, formal(lly)
formulisashen, formal(ization)
formulise, formal(ize)
formulu, formula
formuluzashen, formal(ization)
formuly, formal(lly)
formur, former

formurly, former(ly)
formutef, format(ive)
formutivly, format(ively)
forogt, forage(d)
foroshus, ferocious
fors, force / four(s) / farce
forsake,*,en,king,sook, ABANDON,
QUIT
forsakin, forsake(n)
forsau, foresaw
forsaw, foresaw
forseable, foresee(able)
forsee, foresee
forseps, forceps
forseuble, foresee(able)
forshen, fortune
forside, foreside / foresight
forsite, foresight / foreside
fort,*,tify,tress, A STRUCTURE OR AREA
TO BE PROTECTED
fortafid, fortify(fied)
fortchunetly, fortunate(ly)
forte, forty
forteen, fourteen
forteenth, fourteenth
forteeth, forty(tieth)
forteficashen, fortification
fortefid, fortify(fied)
fortefy, fortify
fortens, fourteen(s)
forteuth, forty(tieth)
fortewnit, fortunate
forth,hright, MOVEMENT FORWARD (or
see fourth)
fortieth,*, AN ENGLISH NUMBER
fortification,*, PROTECTING AN AREA/
STRUCTURE, TO STRENGTHEN/
IMPROVE UPON
fortifid, fortify(fied)
fortify,fies,fied,fying,fyingly,fiable,fier,
fication, STRENGTHEN/ADD/
IMPROVE UPON "prefixes: un"
fortifyed, fortify(fied)
fortinth, fourteenth
fortoety, fortuity
fortufecation, fortification
fortufid, fortify(fied)
fortufy, fortify
fortuity,ties,tous,tously,tousness, SELF-
CREATED OPPORTUNITY
fortunate,ely,eness, SELF-CREATED
OPPORTUNITY
fortune,*, GREAT WEALTH "prefixes:
mis"

fortunetly, fortunate(ly)
fortunit, fortunate
fortunitly, fortunate(ly)
forty,ties,tieth,tyish, AN ENGLISH
NUMBER
fortyeth, forty(tieth)
foruge, forage
forujt, forage(d)
forum,*, GROUP OF PEOPLE IN
DISCUSSION
forun, foreign
foruner, foreign(er)
forusdashen, forest(ation)
forusdry, forest(ry)
forust, forest
forustashen, forest(ation)
foruster, forest(er)
forustre, forest(ry)
forward,*,ded,ding,dly,dness, GO
AHEAD, BE FRANK (or see
foreword)
forwurd, forward / foreword
fos, foe(s) / faux / fuss
fosal, fossil
fosder, foster
fosdur, foster
fosechus, facetious
fosefy, falsify
fosel, fossil
foselisd, fossil(ized)
foset, faucet
fosfade, phosphate
fosfate, phosphate
fosiches, facetious
fosify, falsify
fosil, fossil
fosilisd, fossil(ized)
fosphate, phosphate
fossil,*,lize,lized,lizing,lizable,lization,
ssorial, CARBON MATTER TURNED
TO STONE "prefixes: sub"
foster,*,red,ring,rage, PLACEBO
PARENT
fosul, fossil
fosulisd, fossil(ized)
fosulzd, fossil(ized)
fosut, faucet
fot, foot / food / fought
fotagraf, photo(graph)
fotar, fodder
fotasinthesis, photosynthesis
fotegraf, photo(graph)
foter, fodder
fother, father

fotigraf, photo(graph)
fotigue, fatigue
fotir, fodder
foto, photo
fotograf, photo(graph)
foton, photon / futon
fotosinthesis, photosynthesis
fotugraf, photo(graph)
fotur, fodder
fotusinthesis, photosynthesis
fought, PAST TENSE FOR THE WORD
"FIGHT"
foul,*,led,ling,ler,lest,lly,lness,
OFFENSIVE, OUTSIDE OF THE RULES
(or see fowl)
found,ded,der,ding, PAST TENSE FOR
THE WORD "FIND", ONE WHO
DISCOVERED/LOCATED FIRST,
INITIAL DATE OF DISCOVERY
"prefixes: un"
foundashen, foundation
foundation,*,nal,nally,nalist,nalism,
BASE/BASIS FOR A BUILDING/
CORPORATION/ BUSINESS/
FRIENDSHIP
foundry,ries, WHERE METAL IS MELTED
fountain,*, STATUE OR STRUCTURE
SHOOTING WATER
fountin, fountain
four,*,rth,rteen, AN ENGLISH NUMBER
(or see fore/for)
fourest, forest
fourever, forever
fourfit, forfeit
fourgave, forgave
fourget, forget
fourgive, forgive
fourgot, forgot
fourmadur, format(tter)
fourmalize, formal(ize)
fourmashin, formation
fourmer, former
fourmul, formal
fours, force / four(s)
foursau, foresaw
foursaw, foresaw
fourseable, foresee(able)
foursee, foresee
fourteen,*,nth, AN ENGLISH NUMBER
fourteenth,*, AN ENGLISH NUMBER,
ONE OF 14
fourth,*,hly, AN ENGLISH NUMBER,
ONE TO FOUR PARTS (or see forth)
fourtinth, fourteenth

fourtuety, fortuity
fourwurd, forward
fow, foe / faux
fowel, foul / fowl
fowks, fox
fowl,*,ler,ling, WILD BIRD (or see foul/
  foal)
fowlest, foul(est)
fowlust, foul(est)
fownd, found
fowndashun, foundation
fowndation, foundation
fowndre, foundry
fownt, found
fowntin, fountain
fowt, fought
fowul, foul / fowl
fox,xes,xed,xing,xy,xier,xiest,xiness, A
  FURRY ANIMAL
foyel, foil
foyl, foil
foz, fuzz / foe(s)
fozdur, foster
fozel, fossil
fozter, foster
fra, fray
fracshan, fraction
fracshenal, fraction(al)
fracsher, fracture
fracshun, fraction
fracshur, fracture
fraction,*,nal,nally,nalize,nalizes,
  nalized,nalizing,nalization,nary,nate,
  nates, nated,nating,nation,nator,
  nary, PART OF THE WHOLE (or see
  friction/fracture)
fractioneal, fraction(al)
fracture,*,ed,ring,rable, A BREAK,
  BROKEN (or see fraction)
frad, afraid / fray(ed) / freight
fraded, freight(ed)
frader, freighter
fradewlent, fraud(ulent)
fradewlently, fraud(ulently)
frael, frail
fraeltee, frail(ty)
fragelidy, fragile(lity)
fraghted, freight(ed)
fragile,ely,lity, DELICATE
fragise, franchise
fragment,*,ted,ting,tal,tary,tarily,tize,
  tizes,tized,tizing,tation, PIECE OF
  THE WHOLE
fragmint, fragment

fragmintashen, fragment(ation)
fragmintul, fragment(al)
fragrance,*,cy,nt, A SMELL, AROMA
fragrant,*,tly,nce,nces, A SMELL,
  AROMA
fragrinse, fragrance
fragrint, fragrant
fragul, fragile
fraight, freight
fraighter, freighter
frail,ler,lest,lty,lties, VERY DELICATE
frailtee, frail(ty)
frait, freight
frajilety, fragile(lity)
frajiludy, fragile(lity)
frajul, fragile
frakchen, fraction
frakment, fragment
frakmentashen, fragment(ation)
frakmentul, fragment(al)
frakmint, fragment
frakmintul, fragment(al)
frakshenul, fraction(al)
frakshin, fraction
frakshur, fracture
fraktionul, fraction(al)
frakul, freckle
frale, frail
fralest, frail(est)
fralic, frolic
fraluc, frolic
frame,*,ed,ming,mable,er, STRUCTURE
  TO ENCASE SOMETHING, CRIMINAL
  ACT "prefixes: sub/under"
framur, frame(r)
franc,*, FRENCH MONEY (or see frank)
franchise,*,ee,ement,er, MEMBERSHIP
  OF SPORTS TEAMS/ BUSINESS
  "prefixes: disen/en"
frandikly, frantic(ally)
frank,*,ker,kest,kly,kness, HONEST,
  OPEN EXPRESSION, HOT DOGS (or
  see franc)
frankist, frank(est)
frankle, frank(ly)
franshise, franchise
frantek, frantic
frantekly, frantic(ally)
frantic,cally, ANXIOUS, DISORDER,
  WILDLY RUNNING ABOUT
frantikly, frantic(ally)
frash, fresh
frate, freight / fray(ed)
frater, freighter

fraternal,*,lly,lism, BROTHERS, MALE
  FRIENDSHIP
fraternity,ties, MEN'S SOCIAL/SOCIETY
  "prefixes: con"
fraternize,*,ed,zing,zation,er,
  INAPPROPRIATE RELATIONSHIP
  "prefixes: non"
fratid, freight(ed)
fraud,*,dly,dulent,dulently,dulence,
  TRICKING/CHEATING
fraul, frail
frauler, frail(er)
fraulist, frail(est)
fraultee, frail(ty)
fraun, frown
frauns, frown(s)
frawd, fraud
frawdly, fraud(ly)
frawn, frown
fraxshen, fraction
fray,*,yed,ying, MATERIAL THAT
  UNRAVELS, A BRAWL, SITUATION
  THAT IS STRESSFUL OR EXCITING
fre, free / fray
freak,*,ked,king,ky,kier,kiest,kily,kiness,
  kish, SHOCKING/ODD, UNUSUAL
freaze, freeze
frech, fridge
freched, frigid
frechen, fresh(en)
frecher, fresh(er)
frechnur, fresh(ener)
frechun, fresh(en)
freckle,*,ed,ling,ly, BEAUTY SPOT ON
  SKIN
frecol, freckle
frection, friction
fred, free(d) / fret / afraid
fredom, freedom
fredum, freedom
free,*,eed,eeing,eer,eest,eely,eeness,
  eedom, LIBERTY
freedom,*, TO HAVE LIBERTY
freekwensee, frequency
freekwint, frequent
freekwintly, frequent(ly)
freeky, freak(y)
freese, freeze
freetim, freedom
freetum, freedom
freeze,*,roze,zing,er,zable, LIQUID TO
  SOLID, WATER AT 32˚ F, 0˚ C
  "prefixes: re/sub/un"
freg, fridge

freged, frigid
freghted, freight(ed)
fregit, frigid
freight,*,ted,ting,ter, GOODS BEING
    TRANSPORTED
freighter,*, SHIP CARRYING CARGO
freigter, freighter
freiht, freight
freit, freight / fright
freitor, freight
frej, fridge
frejid, frigid
frek, freak
frekal, freckle
frekol, freckle
frekqint, frequent
frekqintly, frequent(ly)
frekshen, friction
frekul, freckle
frekwensee, frequency
frekwent, frequent
frekwently, frequent(ly)
freky, freak(y)
frel, frail
frely, free(ly)
fren, french / fringe
french, A NATIONALITY (or see fringe)
frend, friend
frendle, friend(ly)
frendleist, friend(liest)
frendlenes, friend(liness)
frendleur, friend(lier)
frenge, french / fringe
frense, frenzy
frent, friend
frentleist, friend(liest)
frentleur, friend(lier)
frently, friend(ly)
frenzy,zies,zied, CHAOTIC EXCITEMENT
frequency,cies,nt, DISTANCE/NUMBER
    OF TIMES BETWEEN WAVE PEAKS,
    NUMBER OF OCCURENCES
frequent,*,ted,ting,tly,tness,ntation,ter,
    ncy, HOW OFTEN "prefixes: un"
freqwensee, frequency
freqwint, frequent
freqwintly, frequent(ly)
fres, freeze / free(s) / frizz
frese, freeze / frizz(y)
fresh,her,hest,hen,hens,hened,hening,
    hener,hly,hness, PEAK CONDITION
    "prefixes: re"
freshenur, fresh(ener)
freshin, fresh(en)

freshir, fresh(er)
freshnur, fresh(ener)
freshon, fresh(en)
freshur, fresh(er)
frestrate, frustrate
fret,*,tted,tting,tless, PART OF A
    CLOCK/STRINGED INSTRUMENT, TO
    WORRY, BE ERODED/CORRODED
    (or see afraid/free(d))
fretem, freedom
freter, freighter
fretum, freedom
frevalus, frivolous
frevolus, frivolous
frewgul, frugal
frewktose, fructose
frez, freeze / frizz / free(s)
freze, frizz(y) / freeze / free(s)
fri, fry / free
frich, fridge
friched, frigid
frichid, frigid
fricshen, friction
friction,nal,nless, RESISTANCE
    BETWEEN TWO THINGS (or see
    fraction)
frid, fried / fright
frida, friday
friday,*, A DAY OF THE WEEK (ENGLISH)
friden, frighten
fridgarator, refrigerate(tor)
fridge,*, SLANG FOR REFRIGERATOR
fridy, friday
fried, PAST TENSE FOR THE WORD
    "FRY", COOK IN SKILLET "prefixes:
    re"
friend,*,dly,dlier,dliest,dliness,
    FRIENDSHIP, MUTUAL INTEREST/
    ADMIRATION "prefixes: un"
frier, fry(er)
fries,ed, COOK IN SKILLET, GET TOO
    HOT, POTATOES DEEP FRIED
frig, fridge
frigarador, refrigerate(tor)
friged, frigid
frigerator, refrigerate(tor)
friget, frigid
fright,ten,tener,tens,tened,tening,tful,
    tfully,tfulness, SUDDEN FEAR
frighten,*,ned,ning, TO SUDDENLY
    SCARE SOMEONE
frigid,dly,dness,dity, STIFF/COLD
frigirator, refrigerate(tor)
frigit, frigid

frij, fridge
frijik, frigid
frikshen, friction
frikshenles, friction(less)
frikshenul, friction(al)
friktion, friction
friktional, friction(al)
frin, friend
frinch, french / fringe
frind, friend
frindleist, friend(liest)
frindlenes, friend(liness)
frindleur, friend(lier)
frindly, friend(ly)
fringe,*,ed,ging, DECORATIVE EDGE, ON
    THE OUTSIDE EDGE (or see french)
frinsy, frenzy
frint, friend
frintleist, friend(liest)
frintleur, friend(lier)
frintly, friend(ly)
frinzy, frenzy
fris, fries / frizz
frisy, frizz(y)
frit, fried / fright
friten, frighten
frivalus, frivolous
frivolous,sly,sness,lity, SILLY, NOT
    SERIOUS
frivulus, frivolous
friz, frizz / freeze / fries
frize, frizz(y) / fries
frizy, frizz(y)
frizz,zzes,zzed,zzing,zzier,zziest,zzy,
    zziness,zzily,zzliness,zzle, KINKY/
    WAVY (or see freeze/fries)
frock, frog
frod, fraud
frodewlint, fraud(ulent)
frodewlintly, fraud(ulently)
frodth, froth
frodulent, fraud(ulent)
frodulently, fraud(ulently)
frog,*,gged,ggy, AN AMPHIBIAN
frogle, frugal
frogy, frog(ggy)
frojewlint, fraud(ulent)
frojewlintly, fraud(ulently)
frojiledy, fragile(lity)
frojulent, fraud(ulent)
frojulently, fraud(ulently)
frok, frog
frolek, frolic

frolic,*,cked,cking, PLAY LIGHTHEARTED, ROMP HAPPILY
froluc, frolic
from, WHERE IT WAS BEFORE
frond, front
frondeer, frontier
front,*,ted,ting, OUTSIDE FACING, GIVE IN ADVANCE
frontal,lly, IN/AT THE FRONT OF "prefix: pre"
fronteer, frontier
frontid, front(ed)
frontier,*, FRINGE OR EDGE OF A PLACE OR IN INFORMATION
frontle, frontal
froogle, frugal
frooishen, fruition
froot, fruit
fros, froze
frosd, frost / froze
frosdee, frost(y)
frosen, froze(n)
frosin, froze(n)
frost,*,ted,ting,ty,tier,tiest,tless,tily, tiness, COATING OF SOMETHING ON OBJECT, ICE, ICING ON CAKES (or see froze)
froth,*,hed,hing,hy,hier,hiest,hily, hiness, FOAM
frous, froze
frousen, frozen
frouzen, frozen
frowd, fraud
frown,*,ned,ning,ningly,ner, MOUTH TURNED DOWN, DOESN'T APPROVE
frozd, frost / froze
froze,en, PAST TENSE FOR THE WORD "FREEZE"
frozen, PAST TENSE FOR THE WORD "FREEZE" "prefixes: un"
fructose, NATURAL SUGAR
frude, fruit
frueshin, fruition
frug, frog
frugal,lly,lity,lities,lness, VERY LITTLE WASTE
frugelidy, fragile(lity)
frugiledy, fragile(lity)
frugle, frugal
fruishin, fruition
fruit,*,ted,ting,ty,tiness,tful,tfully, tfulness,tless, SEED BEARING PART PRODUCED BY FEMALE PLANTS "prefixes: un"

fruition, A REALIZATION/REWARD FOR EFFORT/ACCOMPLISHMENT
frujilety, fragile(lity)
frujiludy, fragile(lity)
fruktose, fructose
frum, from
frund, front
frundeer, frontier
frundle, frontal
frunt, front
frunteer, frontier
fruntle, frontal
frushtrate, frustrate
frustrate,*,ed,ting,tingly,ter,tion,tive, SHAKEN BY LACK OF KNOWLEDGE OR INFORMATION "prefixes: re"
frut, fruit
frute, fruit(y)
fry,ries,ried,ying,yer, COOK IN SKILLET, GET TOO HOT, GET IN TROUBLE
fryd, friday / fried
fryday, friday
fu, few
fuceshes, facetious
fuch, fudge
fucher, future
fucishas, facetious
fud, feud / food / foot
fudaledy, fidelity
fudch, fudge
fudelity, fidelity
fudge,*,ed,ging, CHOCOLATE DESSERT, EXAGGERATE THE TRUTH
fudon, futon
fued, feud
fuel,*,led,ling,ler, USED TO POWER THINGS "prefixes: bio/re"
fug, fudge
fugative, fugitive
fugitive,*, RUNAWAY, ROAMS
fugt, fudge(d)
fuil, fuel
fuj, fudge
fujative, fugitive
ful, fool / full / fuel
fula, fillet
fulanthrapist, philanthropy(pist)
fulanthrapy, philanthropy
fulate, fillet
fulay, fillet
fuld, fool(ed) / fuel(ed)
fule, fuel / fool / full / full(lly)
fuled, fool(ed) / fuel(ed)
fuler, full(er)

fulesh, fool(ish)
fulesity, felicity
fulest, full(est)
fulfill,*,lled,lling,llment,ller, CONTENT, HAVE WHAT WAS WANTED "prefixes: un"
fulir, full(er)
fulish, fool(ish)
fulisity, felicity
fulist, full(est)
full,ler,lest,lly,llness, HOLDING THE MOST IT CAN HOLD
fulor, full(er)
fulosofy, philosophy
fulur, full(er)
fulust, full(est)
fuly, full(y)
fum, fume
fumbel, fumble
fumbil, fumble
fumble,*,ed,ling,er, DROP SOMETHING ACCIDENTALLY, DROP A BALL DURING PLAY
fumbol, fumble
fume,*,ed,ming,mingly,my,migate, EMIT STEAM/GAS/SMOKE, SMELL
fumegashen, fumigate(tion)
fumegate, fumigate
fumegation, fumigate(tion)
fumelear, familiar
fumigashen, fumigate(tion)
fumigate,*,ed,ting,tion,ant, TO FLOOD/ OVERWHELM WITH SMOKE/GAS
fumpl, fumble
fumugation, fumigate(tion)
fun,nny,nnier,nniest, HAPPINESS, PLAYFUL (or see fund(s))
funal, funnel
funarul, funeral
funcshenul, function(al)
funcshin, function
function,*,ned,ning,nal,nally,nalist, nality,nalities,nalism,nary,nalize, nalizes,nalization, SERVE, HAVE OPERATIONAL, PERFORM "prefixes: inter/multi/neo/over/pre"
functionul, function(al)
functshen, function
fund,*,ded,ding,der, PUT MONEY TOWARDS, HOLDS MONEY FOR PURPOSE "prefixes: re/un"
fundamental,*,lly,lism, NECESSARY
fundemintol, fundamental
fundumintel, fundamental

fundur, fund(er)
fune, funny
funedic, phonetic / fanatic
funeir, fun(nnier)
funeist, fun(nniest)
funel, funnel
funeor, fun(nnier)
funeral,*, EVENT HONORING THE DEAD
funes, finesse / fun(nnies)
funetic, phonetic / fanatic
funeur, fun(nnier)
fungis, fungus
fungus, NOT A PLANT BUT IS LIVING
  AND GROWS
funie, funny
funies, fun(nnies)
funiest, fun(nniest)
funil, funnel
funior, fun(nnier)
funiral, funeral
funkshenul, function(al)
funkshin, function
funkshunal, function(al)
funkus, fungus
funle, funnel
funnel,*,led,ling, CONE SHAPE WITH
  HOLE IN MIDDLE
funnil, funnel
funny,nnies,nnier,nniest,nniness,
  CREATES SMILE/LAUGHTER,
  HUMOR "prefixes: un"
funol, funnel
funomenal, phenomenal
funominul, phenomenal
funrul, funeral
funs, fund(s)
funt, fund
funtamental, fundamental
funy, funny
funyer, fun(nnier)
funyest, fun(nniest)
funyur, fun(nnier)
fur,*,rred,rring,rry,rless, HAIR ON
  ANIMAL (or see for/fury) "prefixes:
  under"
furbed, forbid
furbedin, forbid(dden)
furbet, forbid
furbid, forbid
furbiten, forbid(dden)
furdal, fertile
furdalize, fertilize
furdil, fertile
furdulizashen, fertilize(zation)

furdulize, fertilize
fure, fury / furry
furefir, forever
furefur, forever
furesteul, forest(ial)
fureus, furious
furever, forever
furgave, forgave
furgefnis, forgive(ness)
furget, forget
furgetful, forget(ful)
furgitful, forget(ful)
furgive, forgive
furgivnes, forgive(ness)
furgot, forgot
furgotin, forgot(tten)
furious,sly,sness, BEYOND ANGRY
furket, forget
furketing, forget(tting)
furkiv, forgive
furlough,*, A LEAVE OF ABSENCE
furlow, furlough
furm, firm
furmaledy, formal(ity)
furmality, formal(ity)
furmashen, formation
furment, ferment
furn, fern
furnace,*, HEATER
furnacher, furniture
furnature, furniture
furnish,hes,hed,hing,hings, PLACE
  FURNITURE INTO A ROOM
  "prefixes: un"
furniture, OBJECTS/ARTICLES PLACED
  IN A ROOM FOR COMFORT
furnusher, furniture
furochusle, ferocious(ly)
furod, furrow(ed)
furoshus, ferocious
furoshusle, ferocious(ly)
furot, furrow(ed)
furotious, ferocious
furow, furrow
furrow,*,wed,wing, A TRENCH IN THE
  SOIL, WRINKLE IN BROW
furry,rrier,rriest, HAIRY (or see fury)
fursake, forsake
fursaken, forsake(n)
furst, first
furtal, fertile
further,red,ring,est, MORE THAN FAR
  (or see farther)
furtile, fertile

furtulize, fertile(lize)
fury,ries,rious, RAGE (or see furry)
furzd, first
fuse,*,ed,sing,sible, ITEM WHICH
  PROTECTS FROM FIRE HAZARD,
  USED TO IGNITE EXPLOSIVES, MELT
  ITEMS TOGETHER (or see fuss/fuzz)
  "prefixes: inter"
fusechus, facetious
fuseir, fuss(ier) / fuzz(ier)
fuseist, fuss(iest) / fuzz(iest)
fusek, physique
fuselitate, facilitate
fuselitation, facilitate(tion)
fuselity, facility
fuseur, fuss(ier) / fuzz(ier)
fushen, fusion / fission
fusher, future
fusiches, facetious
fusilatate, facilitate
fusilatation, facilitate(tion)
fusines, fuss(iness) / fuzz(iness)
fusion,nism, BLEND/COMBINE,
  SCIENTIFIC TERM (or see fission)
  "prefixes: in"
fusod, facade
fuss,sses,ssed,ssing,ssy,ssily,ssiness, TO
  FOCUS ON MINOR DETAILS (or see
  fuse/fuzz)
fusy, fuss(y) / fuzz(y)
fut, food / foot / feud
futaledy, fidelity
futch, fudge
futeg, fatigue
futon,*, A CUSHION/MATTRESS WITH
  HEAVY COTTON BATTING (or see
  photon)
futsher, future
future,*,rity,ristic,ristically,rless,
  rlessness,rism, A TIME AFTER NOW
fuz, fuzz / fuse / fuss
fuzd, fuse(d) / fuss(ed)
fuze, fuse/ fuss(y) / fuzz(y)
fuzed, fuse(d) / fuss(ed)
fuzeir, fuss(ier) / fuzz(ier)
fuzek, physique
fuzines, fuss(iness) / fuzz(iness)
fuzt, fuse(d) / fuss(ed)
fuzyest, fuss(iest) / fuzz(iest)
fuzynes, fuss(iness) / fuzz(iness)
fuzz,zzy,zzes,zzed,zzing,zzies,zzier,zziest,
  zziness, FUR/ OTHER MATERIAL,
  BLURRY TO THE EYES (or see fuse/
  fuss)

fuzzyness, fuss(ines) / fuzz(iness)

fynite, finite

gab,*,bbed,bbing,bby,bbier,bbiest,
TALKING JUST TO BE TALKING (or
see jab)

gabe, gab(bby)

gaber, jabber

gach, gauge

gack, jack

gad, jade / gate

gader, gather / gaiter

gadget,*, AN ITEM USED AS A TOOL

gaend, gain(ed)

gaf, golf / gave

gafel, gavel

gaful, gavel

gag,*,gged,gging, NEARLY CHOKE, TO
KEEP SOMEONE FROM SPEAKING
(or see gauge/jag)

gagd, gag(gged) / guage(d) / jag(gged)

gagels, goggles

gaget, gadget

gail, jail / gale

gain,*,ned,ning,nful,nfully, BENEFIT,
IMPROVE

gait,*, DISTANCE BETWEEN FOOTSTEPS
(or see gate)

gaiter,*, WRAP FOR LEGS BELOW THE
KNEE, SLANG FOR ALLIGATOR

gaje, gauge

gajit, gadget

gak, jack

gakass, jackass

gakd, jack(ed)

gal,*, REFERENCE TO A FEMALE (or see
gall/gale/jail)

galactic,cally, THE MILKY WAY, GALAXY
"prefixes: inter"

galan, gallon

galant, gallant

galashes, galoshes

galaxy,xies, PLANETS/STARS WITHIN A
SYSTEM

gale,*, STRONG WINDS (or see gal/
galley/jail)

galeksy, galaxy

galen, gallon

galent, gallant

galep, gallop

galery, gallery

galexy, galaxy

galey, galley / jelly

galf, golf

gali, galley / jelly

galin, gallon

galip, gallop

galiry, gallery

gall,*,lled,lling, TO UNNERVE/IRRITATE/
ANNOY/RUB SOMEONE/
SOMETHING THE WRONG WAY, A
GROWTH (or see gal)

gallant,*,ted,ting,tly,try, COURAGEOUS,
STATELY, AMOROUS, IN REFERENCE
TO MALES

gallen, gallon

gallery,ries,ria, SHOWPLACE FOR ART

galley,*, KITCHEN IN A VESSEL,
ANCIENT BOAT

gallon,*, U.S.MEASURE FOR LIQUID

gallop,*,ped,ping, GAIT OF A HORSE OR
ANIMAL BEING RIDDEN

gallows, STRUCTURE FROM WHICH
PEOPLE WERE HUNG TO DEATH

gallun, gallon

galon, gallon

galop, gallop

galory, gallery

galoshes, RUBBER BOOTS

galows, gallows

galre, gallery

galun, gallon

galup, gallop

galury, gallery

galy, july / jelly

gam, jam / jamb / game

gamble,*,ed,ling,er, BET MONEY ON
NUMBERS

game,*,ming,er, COMPETITION TO WIN

gamet, gamut

gamut, FULL SCALE OF MUSICAL NOTES,
THE WHOLE RANGE OF THINGS

gander,*, MALE GOOSE

gane, gain

ganedic, genetic

ganeury, may

gang,*,ged,ging, GROUP OF PEOPLE/
THINGS WITH COMMONALITY

ganitor, janitor

gant, gain(ed) / chant

gantlet, gauntlet

ganuary, january

gap,*,pped,pping,ppy,pper, A SPACE,
BREAK IN CONTINUITY (or see
gape/gob)

gape,ped,ping,pingly, NORMALLY
CONCERNS THE MOUTH OPENING
WIDE (or see gap/gob)

gar, jar

garage,*,ed,ging, STRUCTURE
INTENDED FOR VEHICLES

garantee, guarantee

garbage, TRASH

gard, guard

garden,*,ned,ning,ner, GROWING
PLANTS

gardeun, guardian

gardian, guardian

garela, gorilla / guerilla

garentee, guarantee

gargen, jargon

gargle,*,ed,ling, RINSE THE THROAT
WITH LIQUID

gargoele, gargoyle

gargoyle,*, CARVED GOTHIC FIGURES

garila, gorilla / guerilla

garland,*, PLANT ITEMS WOVEN
TOGETHER

garlic,cky, EDIBLE BULB FROM PLANT

garment,*, CLOTHING "prefixes: under"

garner,*,red,ring,nish, GATHER/GAIN
SOMETHING

garnish,hes,hed,hing,hment,hee,iture,
DECORATION FOR FOOD/DRINK, TO
PORTION OUT

gart, guard

garteun, guardian

gas,ses,ssed,ssing,seous,seousness,sify,
sifies,sified,sifying,sification, NOT
LIQUID OR SOLID, PETROLEUM
PRODUCT

gasoline, USED TO POWER MOTORS

gasp,*,ped,ping, STRUGGLE FOR AIR

gastr, PREFIX INDICATING "STOMACH"
MOST OFTEN MODIFIES THE WORD

gastro, PREFIX INDICATING "STOMACH"
MOST OFTEN MODIFIES THE WORD

gasture, gesture

gasuntite, gesundheit

gate,*,ted,ting, CLOSURE TO MONITOR
EXIT/ENTRANCE

gater, alligator / gaiter

gather,*,red,ring, COLLECT TOGETHER

gator, alligator / gaiter

gaudy,dier,diest,dily,diness,
OUTRAGEOUS STYLE NAMED AFTER
FAMOUS ARCHITECT IN
BARCELONA

gauge,*,ed,ging,eable,eably,er,
INSTRUMENT FOR MEASURING
THINGS SUCH AS PRESSURE
"prefixes: en/mis/multi/re" (or see
gouge)

gauly, jolly / golly

gaunt,tly,tness, HAGGARD/THIN, LACKING AVERAGE VOLUME/SIZE (or see jaunt)

gauntlet,*, CHALLENGE

gaurantee, guarantee

gaus, gauze

gauze,zily,zy, CLOTH FOR BANDAGES

gava, java

gave, PAST TENSE FOR THE WORD "GIVE"

gavel,*, WOODEN HAMMER USED IN COURTROOMS

gaw, jaw

gawalk, jaywalk

gawn, gown

gawok, jaywalk

gawul, jowl

gay,*,yly, BRIGHT, HAPPY, HOMOSEXUAL (or see guy)

gaywalk, jaywalk

gaywok, jaywalk

gaz, jazz / gaze / guaze

gaze,*,ed,zing,er, A LONG LOOK AT (or see gauze)

gazuntite, gesundheit

ge, PREFIX INDICATING "EARTH" MOST OFTEN MODIFIES THE WORD

geagrafee, geography

gear,*,red,ring, INTERLOCKING NOTCHED RINGS WHICH DRIVE MACHINES

geburish, gibber(ish)

ged, get

gedo, ghetto

geeneol, genial

geens, jean(s) / gene(s)

geese, MORE THAN ONE GOOSE

gef, give

geffy, jiffy

geft, gift

geg, gig / jig

gegle, giggle / jiggle

geit, gait / gate

gel,*,lled,lling,llable, SEMI-SOFT/FIRM SUBSTANCE (or see jello/jail/gal)

gelatin,*,nous, LIKE JELLO

geld, guild / guilt / jell(ed)

gele, jelly

geletin, gelatin

geli, july / jelly

gelt, guilt / jilt / jell(ed) / guild

gelty, guilt(y)

gelus, jealous

gelutin, gelatin

gely, july / jelly

gem,*, STONE, JEWEL (or see gym)

gemek, gimmick

gemik, gimmick

gemmy, jimmy

gemnaseum, gymnasium

gemnast, gymnast

gen, gene / jean

genacide, genocide

genarate, generate

genaration, generation

genarulize, general(ize)

genarus, generous

genasis, genesis

gender,*,rless, CLASSIFICATION BY SEX "prefixes: en"

gendr, gender

gene,*, STRING OF CHROMOSOMES (or see jean)

genedic, genetic

genepig, guineapig

general,*,lly,lity,lities,lize,lizes,lized, lizing,lizable,lizability,lization, ENCOMPASSES MANY THINGS, A MILITARY OFFICER "prefixes: over"

generate,*,ed,ting,tion,tive,tively, tiveness,tor, CREATE, PRODUCE

generation,*,nal, PEOPLE BORN IN GROUPS AT SAME TIME "prefixes: inter/multi"

generator,*, MACHINE THAT CREATES AC ENERGY

generic,*,cally, GENERAL NAME BRAND/CLASSIFICATION

generous,sly,sness,osity,osities, GIVE AWAY WHAT CAN BE SPARED "prefixes: multi"

genesis, BEGINNING OF TIME/ EVENT "prefixes: bio"

genetic,*,cal,cally,cist,trix, STUDY OF GENES AND ASSOCIATED PARTICLES "prefixes: bio"

geneul, genial

geneus, genius

genial,lly,lity,lness, WELCOMING, DOESN'T APPEAR JUDGEMENTAL

genie,*, MAGIC ENTITY IN A BOTTLE

geniral, general

genirus, generous

genises, genesis

genital,*,lia,lly, EXTERNAL REPRODUCTIVE ORGANS

genius,ses,sness, CAPABLE OF DEEP THINKING

genjur, ginger

genle, gentle

genocide,dal,dally, KILLING CERTAIN PEOPLES SYSTEMATICALLY

genome,*,mic, STUDY OF HUMAN GENES AND ALL ASSOCIATED INTERACTIONS

genre',*, DIFFERENT STYLES/MEDIUM, EXPRESSION FOR ART, MUSIC "prefixes: sub"

genrul, general

gentle,er,est,tility,eness, KIND IN BEHAVIOR/DISPOSITION, NON-THREATENING

gentul, gentle

genucide, genocide

genuine,ely,eness, TRUTHFUL, REAL

genurul, general

genurus, generous

genus,nera, METHOD TO ORGANIZE PLANTS AND ANIMALS "prefixes: sub"

genyus, genius

geo, PREFIX INDICATING "EARTH" MOST OFTEN MODIFIES THE WORD

geography,hies,hic,hical,hically, ophysicist, THE STUDY OF EVERYTHING ON THE SURFACE OF THE EARTH "prefixes: bio"

geology,gies,gic,gical,gist,ophysicist, STUDY OF THE EARTH'S CRUST

geometry,ries,ric,rical,rically,rize,rizes, rized,rizing,rization,rician, VARIOUS SHAPES/SYMBOLS/ LINES/ANGLES

gep, gyp

gepardy, jeopardy

gepsee, gypsy

gepsum, gypsum

gerantee, guarantee

gerbil,*, A SMALL RODENT

gere, gear / jury

geresdikshen, jurisdiction

gergul, gurgle

gerila, gorilla / guerilla

gerk, jerk

gerky, jerky

gerl, girl

gerlfrend, girlfriend

germ,*,minate, BACTERIA

germinate,*,ed,ting,tion,tive,tor, SEED BEGINNING TO GROW

gernal, journal

gernalist, journal(ist)

gerne, journey / gurney

gernulest, journal(ist)

gerny, gurney / journey

gerter, girder

gerth, girth

gerunte, guarantee

gerur, juror

gery, jury

gesd, guest / guess(ed) / jest

gese, geese / guess

gesoontite, gesundheit

gess, guess

gest, jest / just / guest / guess(ed)

gesture,*,ed,ring, BODILY MOTIONS

gesundheit, WISHING GOOD HEALTH TO SOMEONE WHO SNEEZED (German)

gesuntite, gesundheit

get,*,got,tta,tten,tter,tting, TO TAKE IN, HAVE IT (or see jet)

gete, jetty

geter, jitter

geto, ghetto

getsam, jetsam

gety, jetty

gev, give

gewdeshal, judicial

gewdishes, judicious

gewel, jewel

gewly, july

gewn, june / goon

gews, juice

geyser,*, WATER WHICH SHOOTS UP FROM A HOLE IN THE EARTH

ghetto,*, A SECTION OF LAND WHERE OVERCROWDING IS A RESULT OF DISCRIMINATION

ghost,*,tly, SPIRITS WHICH PROVE TO EXIST BUT ARE INVISIBLE TO US

gi, guy

giant,*, HUGE, ENORMOUS

gib, jib / jibe

gibber,*,red,ring,rish,rer, LANGUAGE/ WORDS THAT DO NOT MAKE SENSE (or see jibe)

gibe,*,ed,bing,bingly, COMMENT MADE TO PROVOKE NEGATIVE FEELINGS IN ANOTHER (or see jibe)

giberish, gibber(ish)

gid, get / guide

giddy,ddier,ddiest,ddily,ddiness, JOYFUL, EXTREMELY EXCITED, FRIVOLOUS (or see jibe)

gide, guide

gidense, guidance

gif, give

giffy, jiffy

gift,*,ted,ting, TO GIVE SOMETHING WITHOUT EXPECTATIONS OF RETURN

gig,*, ARRANGEMENT FOR MUSICAL PERFORMANCE (or see jig)

giga, PREFIX INDICATING "ONE BILLIONTH" MOST OFTEN MODIFIES THE WORD

gigantic,cally,ism, INCREDIBLY HUGE, ENORMOUS

gigger, jigger

giggle,*,ed,ling,lly,er, STYLE OF LAUGHING (or see jiggle)

gigle, giggle

gigol, giggle

gigsaw, jigsaw

gilatnus, gelatin(ous)

gild, guild / guilt / jell(ed)

gildy, guilt(y)

giloshes, galoshes

gilt, guild / guilt / jell(ed)

gilty, guilt(y)

gily, july / jelly

gim, gem / gym

gimik, gimmick

gimmick,*,ky, TRICK, ATTENTION GETTER

gimmy, jimmy

gimnaseum, gymnasium

gimnast, gymnast

ginacologist, gynecology(gist)

ginarashin, generation

ginarate, generate

ginarator, generator

ginarulize, general(ize)

ginarus, generous

ginasis, genesis

gindur, gender

gine pig, guineapig

ginecologist, gynecology(gist)

ginerik, generic

ginetic, genetic(s)

ginger,*,red,ring,ry,rly, EDIBLE PLANT, TO BE CAUTIOUS

gingle, jingle

ginks, jinx

ginokologist, gynecology(gist)

ginrul, general

ginter, gender

ginucalugist, gynecology(gist)

ginucide, genocide

ginucologist, gynecology(gist)

ginuen, genuine

ginul, gentle

ginurulize, general(ize)

ginus, genus

ginuses, genesis

giologee, geology

giometry, geometry

gip, gyp

gipsee, gypsy

gipsum, gypsum

girate, gyrate

girble, gerbil

gird,*,ded,ding,der, PHYSICALLY PROTECT YOURSELF, PHYSICAL PROTECTION BY GIRDLE/BELT/ STRAPS "prefixes: under"

girder,*, BEAM USED FOR HORIZONTAL BRACING IN BUILDINGS

girgul, gurgle

girl,*,ly, YOUNG FEMALE PERSON

girlfriend,*, A GIRL WHO IS ALSO A FRIEND

girm, germ

girmanate, germinate

girnalist, journal(ist)

girney, gurney / journey

girnul, journal

girth,*, WIDTH OF SOMETHING ACROSS, CIRCUMFERENCE

giry, jury

giser, geyser

gisuntite, gesundheit

git, get

gito, ghetto

gitter, jitter

give,*,ving,gave,en, PROVIDE/GIFT/ PRESENT SOMETHING (or see jive) "prefixes: mis"

gizer, geyser

gizuntite, gesundheit

glachal, glacial

glachel, glacial

glachil, glacial

glachol, glacial

glacial,*,ally,ate,ates,ated,ating,ation, ICE, FROZEN WATER, FROM THE WORD 'GLACIER' "prefixes: en/ inter/sub"

glacier,*,red,ial, ICE, FROZEN WATER AROUND MOUNTAIN

glad,dder,ddest,dly, PLEASED

glair, glare

glamour,rous,rously,rousness,orize, orizes,orized,orizing,orization,orizer, ALLURING, BEWITCHING

glance,*,ed,cing, A QUICK LOOK

gland,*,dule,dular,dulous,dulously,dless, ORGANS IN THE BODY "prefixes: multi"

glare,*,ed,ring,ringly,ringness, A SHARP LOOK WITH THE EYES, INTENSE LIGHT

glas, glass / glaze

glaser, glacier / glaze(r)

glashal, glacial

glashel, glacial

glasher, glacier

glashil, glacial

glashol, glacial

glass,sses,ssed,ssy,ssful,ssier,ssiest,ssily, ssiness, HARD/FLAT/FRAGILE SUBSTANCE MADE WITH MIXTURE OF MINERALS/CHEMICALS

glaze,*,ed,zing,er, A COATING OF SUBSTANCE ON SOMETHING "prefixes: multi/over/under"

glazr, glaze(r)

gleam,*,med,ming,my,mier,miest, A BRIEF MOMENT IN APPEARANCE

glech, glitch

gleder, glitter

gledur, glitter

glee,*,eful,efully,efulness, WITH JOY, EXUBERANCE "prefixes: un"

gleful, glee(ful)

glemmer, glimmer

glempse, glimpse

glent, glint

glesen, glisten

glesten, glisten

gletch, glitch

gleu, glue

glew, glue

glich, glitch

glide,*,ed,ding,er, TO MOVE SMOOTHLY WITHOUT RESISTANCE

glider, glide(r) / glitter

glimer, glimmer

glimmer,*,red,ring, A DIM LIGHT

glimpse,*,ed,sing, SLIGHT GLANCE, SEE BRIEFLY

glint,*,ted,ting, A TWINKLE, SPARKLE

glisen, glisten

glisten,*,ned,ning, TO REFLECT LIGHT, SHINY

glitch,hes,hy, MONKEYWRENCH IN THE PLANS, PROBLEM IN THE OPERATION OF

glite, glide

gliter, glitter / glide(r)

glitter,*,red,ring,ringly,ry, SHINY SPECKS, FLECKS OF LIGHT (or see glider)

gliture, glitter / glide(r)

glo, glow

gloat,*,ted,ting,tingly,ter, OVERLY PROUD OF AN ACCOMPLISHMENT

global,lly,lize,lizes,lized,lizing,lization, lism,lizer, INCORPORATES THE GLOBE, INCLUDES THE WORLD

globe,*,ed,bing,boid, THE SHAPE AND PICTURE OF THE WORLD

globel, global

globul, global

glof, glove

glofs, glove(s)

glomp,*,ped,ping, MANY THINGS WHICH GRAB/STICK, AFFECTIONATE POUNCE/HUG

gloo, glue

gloom,*,med,ming,my,mily,miness, DULL SENSE OF FEAR

glorify,fies,fied,fying,fication,fier,ious, WORSHIP

glorufy, glorify

glory,ries,rify,rious,riously,riousness, IN HONOR, PRAISE "prefixes: in"

glosery, glossary

gloss,sses,ssed,ssing,ssy,ssier,ssiest,ssily, ssiness, SHINE UP "prefixes: semi"

glossary,ries, AREA IN SOME BOOKS WITH DEFINITIONS

glote, gloat / glow(ed)

glove,*,ed,ving,eless, COVERING FOR HANDS

glow,*,wed,wing,wingly,wer, TO BE LITE FROM WITHIN, INTERNAL LIGHT

gluco, PREFIX INDICATING "SUGAR" MOST OFTEN MODIFIES THE WORD

glucose, SUGAR, SYRUP

glue,*,ed,uing,ey,uily,uiness, TYPE OF LIQUID USED TO STICK THINGS TOGETHER, STUCK TO SOMETHING "prefixes: un"

gluecose, glucose

glufs, glove(s)

glukose, glucose

glum,mly,mness,mmer,mmest, DISAPPOINT, NEGATIVE PERSPECTIVE, APPEARS TO BE NO SOLUTION, SULLEN (or see gloom)

glumy, glum(mmy) / gloom(y)

glutinous,sly, STICKS TOGETHER, LIKE GLUE

gluvs, glove(s)

glyco, PREFIX INDICATING "SUGAR" MOST OFTEN MODIFIES THE WORD

gnat,*,tty,tier,tiest, TINY FLY

gnaw,*,wed,wing, MOUTH OR CHEW ON SOMETHING GENTLY

gnome,*, A SMALL HUMAN ENTITY WHICH ONLY SOME PEOPLE CAN SEE

go,oes,oing,one, READY, SET, MOVE/ MOBILIZE TO ANOTHER PLACE "prefixes: in/under"

goad,*,ded,ding, TO PROD/POKE/ FORCE SOMETHING/SOMEONE TO REACT (or see goat)

goal,*,lie, SOMETHING TO ACHIEVE/GO FOR, ATTEMPT TO REACH

goalie,*, SOMEONE WHO DEFENDS AGAINST SOMEONE WHO WANTS TO MAKE POINTS IN A GAME

goat,*, AN ANIMAL

goatee,*, A BEARD SHAVED TO A POINT

gob,*,ed, A CLUMP/LUMP OF WAY TOO MUCH OF SOMETHING

gobble,*,ed,ling,er, TO EAT VERY QUICKLY

goble, gobble

goblet,*, A DRINKING VESSEL

goblin,*, AN ENTITY ONLY SOME PEOPLE CAN SEE

gobul, gobble

god,*, REFERENCE TO A SUPREME BEING (or see good/got/goad) "prefixes: un"

goddess,sses, FEMALE ENTITY WHO CO-CREATES

gode, gaudy

goden, gotten

goen, join

goent, joint / join(ed)

goes, FORM OF "GO", IS MOVING TO ANOTHER SPACE/ATTITUDE/LEVEL

goest, joist

gof, golf

gofener, governor

gofer, gopher / golf(er)

gofeul, jovial

gofur, gopher
gog, jog
gogels, goggles
goger, jog(gger)
goggles, SAFETY EYE PROTECTION
gogils, goggles
gogir, jog(gger)
goguls, goggles
gogur, jog(gger)
goin, join
goint, joint / join(ed)
goke, joke / jockey
goky, jockey
gol, goal
golaktik, galactic
gold,den, A PRECIOUS METAL
golden,nly,nness, THE COLOR OF GOLD
goldun, golden
gole, goal / goalie / golly / jolly
golf,*,fed,fing,fer, A SPORT
golie, goal / goalie / golly / jolly
golly, VERBAL EXPRESSION OF
    SURPRISE (or see goalie/jolly)
goloshes, galoshes
golt, jolt / gold
golten, golden
goly, jolly / golly / goalie
gon, gone / going
gondes, jaundice
gone,er, PAST TENSE FOR THE WORD
    "GO", ALREADY LEFT
goner,*, SOMEONE WHO IS GONE OR
    IN TROUBLE
gong,*, A MUSICAL INSTRUMENT
gonir, gone(r)
gont, jaunt / gaunt / join(ed)
gontlet, gauntlet
gonur, gone(r)
good,*,dy,dly,dness, ACCEPTABLE
good-bye,*, FAREWELL, EXPRESSION
    FOR LEAVING
goods, STUFF, STUFF FOR SALE
gooly, july
goon,*, THUG, A DERAGATORY NAME
    FOR SOMEONE
goose,geese, A FEMALE BIRD, SQUEEZE
    SOMEONE (or see juice)
goot, jute
gopher,*, A RODENT, SOMEONE WHO
    GOES TO PICK UP SOMETHING
gor, jar
gord, gourd / guard
gorela, gorilla / guerilla

gorge,*,ed,ging,er, TO STUFF,
    GEOLOGICAL FORMATION
    "prefixes: dis/en"
gorgeous,sly,sness, SOMETHING VERY
    ATTRACTIV
gorgis, gorgeous
gorgus, gorgeous
gorilla,*, A MAMMAL (or see guerilla)
gorj, gorge
gorjus, gorgeous
gorlend, garland
gorlic, garlic
gorma, gourmet
gorment, garment
gorner, garner
gornish, garnish
gos, goes / gauze
gosep, gossip
gosepd, gossip(ed)
gosip, gossip
gospel,*, PARTS OF THE BIBLE
gossip,*,ped,ping,per,pry,py, WORDS
    SAID ABOUT SOMEONE WHO ISN'T
    AROUND TO HEAR
gost, ghost
gosup, gossip
got,tten, PAST TENSE FOR THE WORD
    "GET", ACQUIRED SOMETHING
    DIDN'T HAVE BEFORE (or see goat/
    god/jot)
gote, goat / goatee / gaudy
goten, gotten
goth,hic,hically,hicism, DARK FORM OF
    SELF EXPRESSION, MEDIEVAL
    THEME
gothec, goth(ic)
gotin, gotten
gotten, PAST TENSE FOR THE WORD
    "GET/GOT"
goty, gaudy
gouge,*,ed,ging, MAKE HOLES OR
    GROOVES INTO
goun, gown
gourd,*, FRUIT FROM A PLANT
gourmet,*, ONE WHO UNDERSTANDS
    FINE FOODS
goverment, government
govern,*,ned,ning,nable,nance,ness,
    nment,nor, CONTROLLING ENTITIES
    WHO UPHOLD, CREATE RULES
    "prefixes: un"
government,*,tal,tally,talize, GROUP
    OF PEOPLE WHO RULE, UPHOLDS

    RULES FOR A PEOPLE "prefixes:
    inter"
governor,*,ness,rate, STATE ELECTED
    POLITICIAN
goveul, jovial
govirment, government
govnur, governor
gowge, gouge
gown,*, FULL LENGTH DRESS, ROBE
gownse, jounce
gowul, jowl
goy, joy
goyful, joy(ful)
goyn, join
goynd, joint / join(ed)
goynt, joint / join(ed)
goyus, joy(us)
goz, goes / gauze / jaw(s)
gra, gray
grab,*,bbed,bbing,bby,bbable,bber,
    TAKE ROUGHLY/QUICKLY
grabel, gravel / grapple
grabetate, gravitate
grable, grapple / gravel
grabuling, gravel(ing) / grapple(ling)
grace,*,ed,cing,eful,efully,efulness,
    cious,ciously,ciousness, ELEGANCE
    (or see graze) "prefixes: dis/un"
grachuashen, graduate(tion)
grachus, gracious
gracious,sly,sness, PERFORM
    ELEGANTLY "prefixes: un"
grad,*, SHORT FOR 'GRADUATE' (or see
    grade/grate/great) "prefixes:
    under"
grade,*,ed,ding,er,dient, LEVEL IN
    LEARNING, DEGREES, STEPS (or see
    grate/great/grad) "prefixes: de/
    inter/multi/retro/sub/up"
gradeant, grade(dient)
gradetude, gratitude
gradful, grateful
gradguashen, graduate(tion)
gradiant, grade(dient)
gradify, gratify
graditude, gratitude
gradjual, gradual
gradjuate, graduate
gradle, great(ly)
gradly, great(ly)
gradual,lly,lness,lism, MOVEMENT A
    BIT AT A TIME
graduate,*,ed,ting,tion, CEREMONY
    CELEBRATING COMPLETION, MOVE

UP TO THE NEXT LEVEL "prefixes: under"

graf, graph

grafe, grave

grafek, graphic

graffiti,to, PICTURES/WORDS PLACED/ PAINTED IN PUBLIC PLACES WITHOUT PERMISSION

grafic, graphic

grafite, graphite / graffiti / gravity

grafity, gravity / graffiti

graft,*,ted,ting,ter, TO ATTACH PART OF A LIVE THING TO PART OF ANOTHER LIVE THING "prefixes: en"

grafudy, gravity

grafux, graphic

gragereus, gregarious

graguashen, graduate(tion)

graguate, graduate

grain,*,ned,ner,nless,ny,nery,anul, EDIBLE PLANT/SEED, WOOD TEXTURE, BASIC CHARACTERISTIC "prefixes: en/multi"

grainery,ries, GRAIN STOREHOUSE

grainual, granule

grajeashen, graduate(tion)

grajual, gradual

grajuashen, graduate(tion)

grajuate, graduate

gram,*, MEASURE OF WEIGHT "prefixes: deca"

gramatical, grammatical

grammar,*,atical,rian,atology, WORDS AND THE WAY THEY ARE USED BY PEOPLE

grammatical,lly,lity,lness, WORDS AND THE WAY THEY ARE USED BY PEOPLE "prefixes: un"

gran, grain

grand,der,dest,dly,dness,deur,diose, OF GREAT STATURE, IMMENSE, BEST THERE IS (or see grant)

grandeos, grandiose

grandiose,ely,eness,sity, IMPRESSIVE STATURE

grandure, grand(eur) / grand(er)

granery, grainery

granet, granite

granite, IGNEOUS ROCK

granola, DRIED GRAIN AND FRUIT MIXED TOGETHER

grant,*,ted,ting,tee,tor, GIVE WHAT WAS ASKED FOR

granual, granule

granule,*,lar,larity,larly,late,lates,lated, lating,lation,lative,lator, VERY SMALL MASS OF SOMETHING "prefixes: multi"

granut, granite

grape,*, FRUIT OF THE VINE

grapefruit,*, CITRUS FRUIT

grapevine,*, VINE OF A FRUIT

grapfruit, grapefruit

grapfrut, grapefruit

graph,*,hed,hing,her,hic, TO PLOT ON, SHOWS CHANGES IN NUMBERS

graphic,*,cal,cally,cness,cacy, VISUAL ART BY PEOPLE OR COMPUTER

graphite, TYPE OF ROCK

grapple,*,ed,ling,er, TO STRUGGLE/ WRESTLE WITH

grapul, grapple / gravel

grapvine, grapevine

grase, grace / graze

grashis, gracious

grasp,*,ped,ping,pable, GET A FIRM HOLD OF SOMETHING "prefixes: un"

grass,sses,ssed,ssing,ssy,ssier,ssiest, ssiness, PLANT

grat, great / grate / grade

grate,*,ed,ting,er, FABRICATED METAL/ STEEL, KITCHEN DEVICE, SOMETHING IRRITATING(or see great/grade)

grateant, grade(dient)

grateful,lly,llness, APPRECIATE "prefixes: un"

gratetude, gratitude

gratiant, grade(dient)

gratify,fies,fied,fying,fication,itude,tuity, FULFILLING, PLEASURABLE

gratitude,*, APPRECIATION "prefixes: in"

gratle, great(ly)

gratly, great(ly)

gratshuation, graduate(tion)

gratuate, graduate

gratuity,ties,tous,tously,tousness, TIP/ MONEY FOR SERVICE

graul, growl

grave,*,er,est,ely,eness,en, WHERE SOMETHING IS BURIED, SERIOUS SITUATION

gravedy, gravity

gravel,*,led,ling,lly, SMALL ROCKS

gravitate,*,ed,ting,tive,tion, BEING DRAWN BY A FORCE

gravitation,nal,nally, THE ACT OF BEING AFFECTED BY GRAVITY

gravity,tate,tative,tation, POWERFUL FORCE KEEPING THINGS FROM FLOATING INTO SPACE

gravul, gravel

gravy,vies, THICK SAUCE

grawl, growl

grawnd, ground

gray,*,yer,ying, COLOR, FROM AGING

graze,*,ed,zing,er, HOW HERD ANIMALS EAT (or see grace)

grease,*,ed,sing,er,sy,sier,siest,eless, sily,siness, FROM ANIMAL FAT, LUBRICANT FOR MOVING MACHINE PARTS

great,*,ter,test,tly,tness, HIGH ON THE SCALE OF IMPRESSIVE (or see grate)

greater, great(er) / grate(r)

greatful, grateful

gred, grid / greed

gredy, grit(tty) / greed(y)

greed,dy,dier,diest,dily,diness, TAKE MORE THAN NEED

greef, grief

green,*,ner,nest, COLOR, PLANTS

greese, grease

greet,*,ted,ting, TO WELCOME

greeve, grieve

greeze, grease

grefiti, graffiti

gregarious,sly,sness, PREFERS TO LIVE IN SOCIAL ENVIRONMENT WITH LIKE KIND

grell, grill

grem, grim / grime

grematical, grammatical

gren, grin / green

grenola, granola

grep, grip

greshus, gracious

gret, grit / greet / greed

grety, grit(tty) / greed(y)

grew, PAST TENSE FOR THE WORD "GROW"

grewsome, gruesome

greze, grease

grid,*, PERPENDICULAR LINES

griddle,*,ed,ling,er, FLAT COOKING UTENSIL

gride, grit(tty)

gridul, griddle

grief,eve, DEEP SADNESS (or see grieve)

grieve,*,ed,ving,vant,vance,vances, gous,gously,gousness, MOURNING A LOSS

grifete, graffiti

grigarious, gregarious

grill,*,lled,lling,ller, COOK ON METAL GRID OVER COALS

grim,mmer,mmest,mly,mness, STUBBORN, VIRTUALLY UNCHANGABLE (or see grime)

grime,*,ed,ming,my, DIRT/GREASE/ SOOT (or see grimy)

grimy,mier,miest,mily,miness, DIRT/ GREASE/SOOT

grin,*,ned,ning, SMILE BROADLY (or see green)

grind,*,ded,ding,round,der, TO MILL/ CHOP/SMASH/PULVERIZE (or see grin(nned))

grinola, granola

grip,*,pped,pping,pper, FIRMLY GRASP, HAND HOLD (or see gripe)

gripe,*,ed,ping,er, VERBALLY COMPLAINING TO SOME OTHER THAN THE INTENDED RECIPIENT (or see grip)

grit,*,tted,tting,tty,ttier,ttiest,ttily, ttiness, TINY GRANULES OF VARIETY OF MATERIAL, GROUND CORN

grital, griddle

gritle, griddle

grity, grit(tty)

gro, grow

groan,*,ned,ning, MOAN FROM PAIN

grocery,ries, FOOD, NON-FOODS BOUGHT FROM STORE

grof, gruff / grove

groggy,gier,giest,ggily,gginess, NOT QUITE AWAKE, STUPOR

grone, groan

groof, groove

groom,*,med,ming,mer, MALE GETTING MARRIED, TO CLEAN THE BODY

groove,*,ed,ving,vy,vier,viest,vily,viness, LONG INDENTATION IN SOMETHING, GET IN-STEP TO BE COOL

grope,*,ed,ping,per, TO AIMLESSLY ATTEMPT TO GRASP WITH HAND (or see group)

grosery, grocery

grosry, grocery

gross,sses,ssed,ssing,sser,ssest,ssly, ssness, SUM BEFORE EXPENDITURES, MEASUREMENT OF WEIGHT, DISTASTEFUL, REPULSIVE "prefixes: en"

grotesk, grotesque

grotesque,ely,eness, UGLY, DESPICABLE

groth, growth

grouch,hes,hy,hier,hiest,hily,hiness, UNREASONABLY IRRITATED

groul, growl

groun, groan / grown

ground,*,ded,ding,der,dless,dlessly, dlessness, THE EARTH, FEET PLANTED SOLIDLY, BE ON THE EARTH'S SURFACE "prefixes: over/ under"

group,*,ped,ping,per,pable,pie, TO PUT SIMILAR OBJECT, THINGS, PEOPLE TOGETHER "prefixes: re/semi/sub/ un"

grouse,*, GAME BIRD (or see gross)

grout,*,ted,ting,ter, MORTAR FOR STONE/TILE

grove,*, A FIELD WHERE TREES WITH EDIBLE FRUIT IS GROWN

grow,*,wing,rew,wn,wth, GET BIGGER/ TALLER "prefixes: in/over/under"

growch, grouch

growl,*,led,ling,ler, VERBAL WARNING COMING FROM DEEP IN THE THROAT

grown, PAST TENSE FOR THE WORD "GROW" (or see groan) "prefixes: in/over/under"

grownd, ground

grows, grow(s) / grouse / gross

growth,*, COMPARE SIZE OR AMOUNT OF SOMETHING GROWING "prefixes: in/inter/over/up"

groz, gross / grow(s) / grouse

grub,*,bbed,bbing,bber,bby,bbier, bbiest,bbily,bbiness, SLANG FOR FOOD, DIRTY AND MESSY

grudge,*,ed,ging,gingly,eless,er, WILL NOT FORGIVE SOMEONE "prefixes: un"

gruel,*,ling, RUNNY/SLOPPY BOWL OF FOOD

grueling,gly, HARD AND TEDIOUS

gruesome,ely,eness, AWFUL

gruf, groove

grufede, graffiti

gruff,ffer,ffest,ffly,ffiness, RUDE AND ROUGH

grufiti, graffiti

grug, grudge

grugarious, gregarious

gruj, grudge

grumatical, grammatical

grumble,*,ed,ling, LOW/IRRITABLE MUMBLING, STOMACH SOUNDS WHEN HUNGRY

grundled, grunt(led)

grunola, granola

grunt,*,ted,ting,tingly,tled, ANNOYED VERBAL RESPONSE, LOW-RANK WORKER "prefixes: dis"

grupe, group

grusome, gruesome

guady, gaudy

guage, gauge

guantlet, gauntlet

guarantee,*,eed,eeing,tor, BACK UP A CLAIM, WITHOUT A DOUBT

guard,*,ded,ding,dian, PROTECT AGAINST INVADER "prefixes: un"

guardian,*,nship, PROTECTOR

guaze, gauze

gubalee, jubilee

gubelashen, jubilant(ation)

gubilation, jubilant(ation)

gud, good / gut

gud-by, good-bye

guder, gutter

guderal, guttural

gudge, judge

gudishal, judicial

gudishes, judicious

gudo, judo

guds, goods / gut(s)

guel, jewel

guerilla,*, PEOPLE WHO HIDE WHEN FIGHTING (or see gorilla)

guess,sses,ssed,ssing,sser, TAKE A GAMBLE AT THE PROPER ANSWER, DON'T KNOW ANSWER

guest,*, STAYING TEMPORARILY AT A PLACE THAT IS NOT YOURS (or see guess(ed))

gufener, governor

gufner, governor

gug, jug / judge

guggle, juggle

gugul, juggle

guidance, RECEIVE DIRECTION

guide,*,ded,ding,dance, SHOW THE WAY "prefixes: mis"

guil, jewel

guild,*, COOPERATIVE GROUP OF PEOPLE WITH A PARTICULAR INTEREST

guilt,ty,tier,tiest,tily,tiness, BEING OR FEELING RESPONSIBLE FOR AN ACTION

guineapig,*, TWO WORDS 'GUINEA PIG', A RODENT

gul, gull / jewel / joule

gulactic, galactic

gulaktek, galactic

gulatnus, gelatin(ous)

guleble, gull(ible)

gull,*,llery,lled,lling,llible,llibility,llibly, TYPE OF BIRD, TO BE TRICKED/ DECEIVED

guloshes, galoshes

gulp,*,ped,ping,pingly,per, TAKE IN A LARGE MOUTHFUL

guly, july

gum,*,mmed,mming,my,mmier,mmiest, mmily,miness, SOMETHING CHEWABLE, RUBBERY, FROM A TREE

gumble, jumble

gump, jump

gun,*,nned,nning,nner, A FIRING WEAPON, TO STEP ON THE ACCELERATOR, TO SHOOT SOMEONE (or see goon/june)

gune, june / goon

gungle, jungle

gungul, jungle

guniur, junior

gunk, junk

gunker, junk(er)

gunkie, junkie

gunkshen, junction

gunksher, juncture

gunyer, junior

guppy,ppies, FISH

gurbel, gerbil

gurder, girder

gure, jury

gurer, juror

guresdiction, jurisdiction

gurgle,*,ed,ling, SOUNDS COMING FROM THE THROAT, BUBBLING SOUND

guri, jury

gurilla, guerilla / gorilla

gurk, jerk

gurl, girl

gurlfrend, girlfriend

gurm, germ

gurmenate, germinate

gurnelist, journal(ist)

gurney,*, A COT/STRETCHER TO CARRY BODIES (or see journey)

gurnol, journal

gurter, girder

gurth, girth

gus, goose / juice

gusd, gust / just

gusdefecation, justify(fication)

gusdefiable, justifiable

gusdes, justice

gusdify, justify

guse, goose / juice

gusee, juicy

gush,hes,hed,hing, SPEW FORTH IN SUDDEN BURST

gusle, guzzle

gust,*,ted,ting,ty,tier,tiest,tily,tiness, BIG BLOWS IN BURSTS, ERRATIC/ HIGH WINDS (or see just)

gustefy, justify

gustes, justice

gustification, justify(fication)

gut,*,tted,tting, INSIDES OF LIVING THINGS, TO REMOVE INSIDES (or see good/jewt/jut)

gute, jute

gutir, gutter

guto, judo

gutter,*,red,ring,ral, ALONG ROOFS FOR RAIN COLLECTION

guttural,*,lly,lity,lism,lness,lizes,lized, lizing,lization, TYPE OF SOUND MADE IN THE THROAT

guverment, government

guviner, governor

guvinile, juvenile

guy,*, MALES, WIRE OR ROPE USED TO SUPPORT OR STEADY SOMETHING

guynacologist, gynecology(gist)

guzzle,*,ed,ling,er, RAPIDLY DRINK

gy, guy

gym,*,mnast,mnasium, A PLACE TO WORK-OUT (or see gem) "prefixes: multi"

gymnasium,*, A BUILDING WHERE PEOPLE DO PHYSICAL ACTIVITIES

gymnast,*,tics, ONE WHO PRACTICES THE ART OF MANIPULATING THEIR BODIES

gyn, PREFIX INDICATING "FEMALE" MOST OFTEN MODIFIES THE WORD

gyne, PREFIX INDICATING "FEMALE" MOST OFTEN MODIFIES THE WORD

gynecology,gical,gist, THE SCIENCE OF, ONE WHO STUDIES WOMEN'S ORGANS

gyno, PREFIX INDICATING "FEMALE" MOST OFTEN MODIFIES THE WORD

gyp,*,ped,ping, TO CHEAT/STEAL

gypsum, CHALKY ROCK

gypsy,sies, PEOPLE WHO CHOOSE TO BE ON THE FRINGE OF SOCIETY FOR WHATEVER REASON

gyrate,*,ed,ting,tion, TO SPIRAL "prefixes: multi"

ha, hay / hey

habachi, hibachi

habe, happy

haben, happen

habin, happen

habit,*,ted,ting,table,tability,tableness, tably,tant,tat,tation,tual, tuate, tuates,tuated,tuating,tuation,tude, tudinal,tus, DOING THE SAME THING OVER AND OVER

habitat,*,tation,tational,tor, NATURAL HOME FOR LIVING THINGS "prefixes: inter/non"

habitual,*,lly,lness,ate, SOMEONE WHO DEALS WITH MANY HABITS

habochi, hibachi

haby, happy

hach, hatch / hash / hack

hachet, hatchet

hachit, hatchet

hack,*,ked,king,kies,ker,ktivate,ktivism, ktivist, TO ILLEGALLY ACCESS PRIVATE DATA ON COMPUTERS, CHOP AT

hactare, hectare

had, PAST TENSE FOR THE WORD "HAVE" (or see hat)

hade, hate

haden't, hadn't

hadint, hadn't

hadn't, CONTRACTION OF THE WORDS 'HAD NOT'

hadur, hot(tter)

hael, howl

haf, half / have / halve

hafen, haven / heaven
hafhasert, haphazard
hafhazard, haphazard
hafhazurdle, haphazard(ly)
hafint, haven't
hafnt, haven't
hafun, haven / heaven / have(ving)
hagerd, haggard
haggard,*,dly,dness, ROUGH, WORN
haggle,*,ed,ling,er, DEBATING OVER PRICE/CONTRACT
hagio, PREFIX INDICATING " HOLY " MOST OFTEN MODIFIES THE WORD
hagurd, haggard
haiku,*, FORM OF JAPANESE POETRY
hail,*,led,ling,ler, RAIN IN THE FORM OF ICE, LOUD VOCAL WELCOME (or see hale)
hainger, hanger
hainkerchef, handkerchief
hair,ry,rier,riest,riness, STRANDS OF WHICH GROW FROM THE SKIN (or see hare/heir/harry)
hak, hawk / hack
hakd, hack(ed)
haker, hack(er)
haktare, hectare'
hal, PREFIX INDICATING "SALT/ HALOGEN" MOST OFTEN MODIFIES THE WORD (or see hall/hale/hail/ haul/howl)
halagen, halogen
halagenic, halogen(ic)
halareus, hilarious
hale,*,ed,ling,er,est,eness, TO COMPLY, PULL/DRAG SOMEONE/ SOMETHING (or see hall/haul/hail/ holly)
halegram, hologram
halekopter, helicopter
haleluya, hallelujah
half,lve,lves, WHOLE MADE INTO TWO PARTS (or see have/halve)
halfhasard, haphazard
halfhasurdly, haphazard(ly)
halibut, A FISH
haligen, halogen
haligenic, halogen(ic)
hall,*, NARROW CORRIDOR WITH DOORS INSIDE A BUILDING (or see hale/haul/hail)
hallelujah,*, REJOICE
halloween,*, A HOLIDAY
halm, helm

halo,*,lation, REFLECTS LITE COMING FROM WITHIN SOMEONE, PREFIX INDICATING "SALT/HALOGEN" MOST OFTEN MODIFIES THE WORD (or see hollow/hello)
halogen,*,nate,nates,nating,nation,nic, NONMETALLIC/ REACTIVE CHEMICALS, TYPE OF LIGHT SOURCE
halokost, holocaust
halow, hollow / halo
halowen, halloween
halp, help
halpful, helpful
halt,*,ted,ting,ter, STOP NOW (or see haul(ed))
halter,*, GEAR FOR A HORSE, A SHIRT
halubet, halibut
halugram, hologram
halve,*,ed,ving, TO SEPARATE ONE INTO TWO PARTS (or see have)
haly, holly
ham,*,mmed,mming, PORK, TO BE GOOFY
hamak, hammock
hambergur, hamburger
hamburger,*, BEEF GROUND UP
hamer, hammer
hamileate, humiliate
hammer,*,red,ring,rer, FORCE SOMETHING IN, HANDTOOL
hammock,*, WOVEN FABRIC STRETCHED BETWEEN TWO POINTS TO SIT OR LIE IN
hamogenize, homogenize
hamper,*,red,ring, PUT CLOTHES INTO, GET IN THE WAY OF PROGRESS
hamster,*, A RODENT
hamuk, hammock
hamur, hammer
hand,*,ded,ding,dful,dy, AT THE END OF THE ARM WITH FINGERS ON IT "prefixes: over/un/under"
hande, handy
handeist, handy(diest)
handel, handle
handeur, handy(dier)
handicap,*,pped,pping,pper, UNABLE TO FUNCTION AT FULL CAPACITY, CHALLENGED "prefixes: multi"
handil, handle
handkerchief,*, SQUARE CLOTH
handle,*,ed,ling,er, FOR HANDS OR WITH HANDS "prefixes: mis"

handmade, MADE BY HAND NOT BY MACHINE
handout,*, GIVE SOMETHING TO SOMEONE IN NEED
handsome,ely,eness, GOOD LOOKING, SIZEABLE AMOUNT/BENEFITS
handul, handle
handy,dier,diest, SOMETHING EASILY AVAILABLE
hang,*,ged,ging,ger, SECURE SOMETHING ABOVE THE FLOOR ALLOWING FOR A VERTICAL POSITION "prefixes: over"
hangar,*, PLACE FOR LARGE TRANSPORTATION VESSELS (or see hanger)
hanger,*, FOR SUSPENSION OFF THE GROUND (or see hangar)
hank, hang
hankerchif, handkerchief
hansome, handsome
hant, hand
hantecap, handicap
hantel, handle
hantil, handle
hantmade, handmade
hantowt, handout
hantul, handle
hanty, handy
hapale, happy(pily)
hape, happy
hapeir, happy(pier)
hapeist, happy(piest)
hapele, happy(pily)
hapen, happen
hapenes, happy(piness)
hapeur, happy(pier)
haphazard,dly,dness, DO THINGS UNSAFELY, DISORGANIZED
hapie, happy
hapile, happy(pily)
hapin, happen
hapines, happy(piness)
happen,*,ned,ning, AN EVENT THAT HAS OCCURRED
happy,ppier,ppiest,ppily,ppiness, BEING JOYFUL IN LIFE "prefixes: un"
hapule, happy(pily)
hapun, happen
hapy, happy
hapyer, happy(pier)
hapyest, happy(piest)
hapynes, happy(piness)
har, hair / heir / hare

harass,sses,ssed,ssing,ssment, AGGRAVATE BEYOND NORMAL

haray, hurrah

harbor,*,red,ring,rer,rless,rage, WHERE BOATS DOCK, HOLD ONTO

hard,der,dest,den,dener,dy, CHALLENGING, DENSE, SOLID (or see heart) "prefixes: semi"

hardily, heart(ily)

hardin, hard(en)

hardles, heartless

hardly, BARELY, NOT QUITE

hardship,*, TOUGH TIMES

hardware,*, TOOLS, USE TO BUILD WITH, REPAIR MATERIAL

hardy,dier,diest,dily,diness, STRONG AND CAPABLE

hardyness, hardy(diness)

hare,*, A WILD RABBIT (or see hair(y)/ harry/here)

haredetary, hereditary

haredity, heredity

harefy, horrify

harendus, horrendous

harer, horror

haretitary, hereditary

haretity, heredity

hareur, hair(ier)

hareust, hair(iest)

harfest, harvest

harifik, horrify(fic)

harindus, horrendous

harison, horizon

harm,*,med,ming,mful,mfully,mfulness, mless,mlessly,mlessness, TO INJURE "prefixes: un"

harmeny, harmony

harmfel, harm(ful)

harmlis, harm(less)

harmonica,*, MUSICAL INSTRUMENT

harmonize,*,ed,zing,er,zation, SYNCHRONIZE SOUNDS

harmony,nies,nic,nically,nious,niously, niousness,nist,nium,nize,nizes,nized, nizing,nizable,nization,nizer, VARIETY OF DIFFERENT SOUNDS VIBRATING AT A COMPATIBLE FREQUENCY "prefixes: dis/en/in/re/ sub/un"

harmuny, harmony

harness,sses,ssed,ssing,sser, HOLD ONTO, GET HOLD OF "prefixes: un"

haroen, heroin / hero(ine)

haroik, hero(ic)

haroin, heroin / hero(ine)

haron, heron / heroin / hero(ine)

harp,*,ped,ping,per,pist, MUSICAL INSTRUMENT, TO NAG

harpoon,*,ned,ning,ner, TO STAB WITH A LONG METAL POLE WITH BARB ON THE END

harpsichord,*, A MUSICAL INSTRUMENT

harry,rries,rried,rrying, WAR PILLAGE/ RAID, STRESS/DISTRESS (or see hair(y)/hare)

harsh,her,hest,hly,hness, STERN AND ROUGH

hart,*, MALE DEER (or see hard/heart)

harteist, heart(iest) / hard(iest)

harteur, heart(ier) / hard(ier)

harth, hearth

hartily, heart(ily)

hartiness, hardy(diness)

hartles, heartless

hartly, hardly

hartship, hardship

hartware, hardware

harty, heart(y) / hardy

haruble, horrible

harvest,*,ted,ting,ter, BRING IN RIPENED FOOD

hary, hair(y) / harry

has, ACQUIRED (or see have)

hasard, hazard

hase, haze / haze(y)

hasel, hassle / hazel

hasen, hasten

hash,hes,hed,hing,hish, A FOOD, TO TALK IT OVER

hasil, hassle

hasn't, CONTRACTION OF THE WORDS 'HAS NOT'

haspitality, hospitality

hassle,*,ed,ling, TO AGITATE

haste,*,ed,ting,en,ened,ening,ty,tier, tiest,tily,tiness, DO IT QUICKLY

hasten,ned,ning, TO SPEED UP

hasul, hassle / hazel

hat,*, COVERING FOR HEAD (or see had/hate)

hatch,hes,hed,hing,hling, COVER OF STORAGE AREA, LIVE THINGS COMING FROM EGGS

hatchet,*, SMALL AX

hate,*,ed,ting,eful,efully,efulness,eable, er,tred, MOST OPPOSITE FROM LOVE (or see haughty/hot)

haud, hod / hot / haul(ed)

haude, hod(ddie) / haughty / hood(y) / hot(ttie)

hauder, hot(tter)

hauefur, however

haughty,tier,tiest,tily,tiness, ACTING AS IF BETTER THAN OTHERS

hauk, hawk / hock

haul,*,led,ling,ler,lage, TRANSPORT A LOAD (or see hall) "prefixes: in/ over"

hauleluea, hallelujah

haulo, hollow / wallow

haulter, halter / alter

haultur, halter

haunch,hes,hed,hless, REAR LEGS ON ANIMALS, ARCH

haund, hound

haunt,*,ted,ting,tingly,ter, TO SPOOK

haups, hops

haured, horrid

haurur, horror

haus, house

hausd, house(d)

hauspus, hospice

haustej, hostage

haustel, hostel / hostile

haustig, hostage

haut, hot / hod

haute, haughty / hod(ddie) / hood(y) / hot(ttie)

hauty, haughty / hod(ddie) / hood(y) / hot(ttie)

hauvel, hovel

hauztul, hostel / hostile

hav, halve / have / half

havd, halve(d)

have, TO POSSESS, ACQUIRE (or see half/halve)

haven,*, A SAFE PLACE (or see heaven/ have(ving))

haven't, CONTRACTION OF THE WORDS 'HAVE NOT'

havin, haven / heaven

havint, haven't

havs, halve(s)

havun, haven / heaven

haw, how

hawever, however

hawk,*, A BIRD (or see hock)

hawl, howl / haul

hawle, holly

hawnd, hound

hawnt, hound

hawvul, hovel

hay,*,yed,ying, DRY GRASS, ALFALFA, WORKING WITH HAY (or see hey)

haz, has / haze

hazard,*,ded,ding,dous,dously, dousness, DANGEROUS "prefixes: bio"

haze,*,ed,zing,zy,zier,ziest,zily,ziness, SMOKE, MIST, DUST, BLURRY

hazel, A PLANT, A COLOR (or see hassle)

haznt, hasn't

hazurd, hazard

he, A MALE

he'd, CONTRACTION OF THE WORDS 'HE COULD, HE SHOULD, HE WOULD, HE HAD'

he'll, CONTRACTION OF THE WORDS 'HE WILL' (or see hell/heal/heel)

he's, CONTRACTION OF THE WORDS 'HE IS'

head,*,ded,ding,der,dy,dsier,diest,dily, diness, BODY PART ON TOP OF SHOULDERS, ON TOP OF, LEADING "prefixes: multi/over/sub"

heal,*,led,ling,ler,lable, TO CURE, SOMEONE WHO CURES, MEND (or see heel/he'll)

health,hy,hier,hiest,hily,hiness,hful, hfully,hfulness, OF SOUND BODY/ MIND "prefixes: un"

heap,*,ped,ping, TO MOUND UP

hear,*,ring,rd, SOUND IN EARS (or see here) "prefixes: over"

heard, PAST TENSE FOR "HEAR "(or see herd) "prefixes: un"

hearsay, GOSSIP

hearse, A VEHICLE FOR MOVING CASKETS

hearst, hearse

heart,*,ty,tier,tiest,tily,tiness,tless, tlessly,tlessness, AN ORGAN IN A BODY (or see hard) "prefixes: dis"

hearth,*, SURROUNDING A FIREPLACE "prefixes: multi"

heartless,ssly,ssness, CRUEL

heat,*,ted,tedly,tedness,ting,er,tless, WARM, FOR MAKING WARM (or see heed/he'd) "prefixes: over/un"

heave,*,ed,ving, TO THRUST SOMETHING HEAVY USING FORCE

heaven,*,nly,nlier,nliest,nliness, A EUPHORIC STATE OF MIND, DIVINE

heavy,vier,viest,vily,viness, OF GREAT WEIGHT

hebachi, hibachi

hebapotamus, hippopotamus

hebnutize, hypnotize

heckle,*,ed,ling,er, ANNOYING NOISES/ WORDS AIMED AT A SPEAKER

hecksugon, hexagon

heckup, hiccup

hectare,*, METRIC MEASUREMENT, 2.5 ACRES

hectic,cally, CONFUSING RUSH

hecto, PREFIX INDICATING "ONE HUNDRED" MOST OFTEN MODIFIES THE WORD

hed, head / hit / he'd / heat / heed

hedch, hitch / hedge

hedeus, hideous

hedge,*,ed,ging, BUSHES, TO TRIM BY CUTTING

hedid, heed(ed) / heat(ed) / head(ed)

hedud, heed(ed) / heat(ed) / head(ed)

heed,*,ded,ding, PAY ATTENTION, TAKE NOTICE OF (or see heat/he'd/heat) "prefixes: un"

heef, heave

heel,*,led,ling, PART OF THE FOOT (or see heal/he'll)

heep, heap

heet, heat

hefen, heaven

hefer, heifer

hefon, heaven

hefur, heifer

hefy, heavy

heg, hedge

heifer,*, IMMATURE COW

height,*,ten,tens,tened,tening,tener, MEASURE TOP TO BOTTOM, MAKE TALLER

heigth, height

heimlek, heimlich

heimlich, A MANEUVER WHICH CLEARS WINDPIPE FOR BREATHING

heir,*,rless,rship,ress, ONE WHO RECEIVES MONEY/PROPERTY BEQUEATHED TO THEM UPON SOMEONES DEATH (or see hair/air/ err)

heirarchy, hierarch(y)

heirloom,*, SOMETHING PRECIOUS HANDED DOWN TO FOLLOWING GENERATIONS

heiroglyph, hieroglyph

heist,*,ted,ting,ter, THEFT, ROBBERY

heiten, height(en)

heith, height

heithen, height(en)

hej, hedge

heks, hex

heksigon, hexagon

heksugon, hexagon

hektare, hectare'

hektik, hectic

hekul, heckle

hekup, hiccup

hel, heel / hell / heal / he'll / hill

helakopter, helicopter

helareus, hilarious

held, PAST TENSE FOR THE WORD "HOLD"

heleom, helium

helicopter,*, FLYING MACHINE

helio, PREFIX INDICATING "SUN" MOST OFTEN MODIFIES THE WORD

helium, A GAS

hell,*,lled,lling,llish,llishly,llishness,llion, AN IMAGINARY PLACE OF GREAT DISCOMFORT (or see he'll/heal/ heel)

hello,*, AMERICAN GREETING

helm,*, STEERING PART OF A BOAT

helmet,*,ted, A PROTECTIVE COVER FOR THE HEAD

helo, hello

help,*,ped,ping,pings,pful,per,pless, SOMEONE/SOMETHING BEING AIDED

helpd, help(ed)

helpful,lly,lness, THOSE WHO AID OTHERS "prefixes: un"

helpfulnes, helpful(ness)

helpless,ssly,ssness, UNABLE TO AID ONESELF

helpt, help(ed)

helt, held / hilt

helth, health

hem,*,mmed,mming, HAVING TO DO WITH BORDERS ON THINGS (or see him/hymn)

hema, PREFIX INDICATING "BLOOD" MOST OFTEN MODIFIES THE WORD

hemarag, hemorrhage

hemaroid, hemorrhoids

hemat, PREFIX INDICATING "BLOOD" MOST OFTEN MODIFIES THE WORD

hemato, PREFIX INDICATING "BLOOD" MOST OFTEN MODIFIES THE WORD

hemerag, hemorrhage

hemeroid, hemorrhoids

hemi, BRAND NAME, PREFIX INDICATING "HALF" MOST OFTEN MODIFIES THE WORD

hemirag, hemorrhage

hemisphere,*,ric,rical,rically, ONE HALF OF EARTH

hemmaroid, hemorrhoids

hemmoroid, hemorrhoids

hemo, PREFIX INDICATING "BLOOD" MOST OFTEN MODIFIES THE WORD

hemorag, hemorrhage

hemoroid, hemorrhoids

hemorrhage,*,ed,ging,gic, VALUABLE/ UNCONTROLLABLE LOSS

hemorrhoids,dal,dectomy, VARICOSE VEINS IN ANUS

hemosfere, hemisphere

hemp,*, A PLANT USEFUL FOR CLOTHING/MATERIAL/ROPE/PAPER

hemself, himself

hemurag, hemorrhage

hemuroid, hemorrhoids

hen,*, FEMALE CHICKEN

hena, henna

hence,*, THEREFORE, AND SO

hender, hinder

hendrance, hindrance

henge, hinge

henje, hinge

henna, PLANT FOR DYING HAIR/FABRIC, FOR TEMPORARY TATTOOS

hens, hen(s) / hence

hent, hint

hep, heap / hip

hepabotamus, hippopotamus

hepacrite, hypocrite

hepakrete, hypocrite

hepatitis, ILLNESS CAUSED BY VIRUS

hepnosis, hypnosis

hepnutize, hypnotize

hepobotamus, hippopotamus

hepokrite, hypocrite

hepopotamus, hippopotamus

hepothesis, hypothesis

hept, PREFIX INDICATING "SEVEN" MOST OFTEN MODIFIES THE WORD

hepta, PREFIX INDICATING "SEVEN" MOST OFTEN MODIFIES THE WORD

hepy, hip(py)

her,*, IN REFERRING TO A FEMALE (or see hear/here/hair/hare/heir)

heracane, hurricane

herass, harass

herb,*,bed,bal,balism,balist,baceous, baceously,bage,bivore, PLANTS FOR HEALING/COOKING WITH (THE "H" IS SILENT)

herbavor, herbivore

herbivore,*,rous, PLANT EATING ANIMAL (THE "H" IS SILENT)

herbulist, herb(alist)

herd,*,ded,ding,der, ANIMALS GATHERED INTO A GROUP FOR MOVING (or see heard/hurt)

herdle, hurdle / hurtle

herdul, hurdle / hurtle

here,*, IN THIS VICINITY, WHERE YOU ARE (or see hear/hair(y)/hare/ harry)

hered, hurry(ried)

hereditary,rily,riness, ABLE TO BE PASSED ON FROM ONE GENERATION TO ANOTHER

heredity,table,tability,tament,tarian, tarianism,tary,tarily,tariness, PASSED DOWN THROUGH GENERATIONS

hereist, hair(iest)

herendus, horrendous

heresay, hearsay

hereur, hair(ier)

hericane, hurricane

herison, horizon

herizun, horizon

herl, hurle

hermetic,cal,cally, PROTECTED/ AIRTIGHT ENVIRONMENT

hermit,*,tic,tical,tically, A RECLUSE, CRUSTACEAN

hernia,*,al, ABDOMINAL MUSCLE PROBLEM

hero,oes,oic,oics,oical,oically,oicalness, oine,oines,oism, BRAVE ACT TO SAVE SOMETHING FROM PERIL OR DEATH

heroek, hero(ic)

heroin, MANMADE DRUG TO EASE PAIN, ADDICTIVE (or see hero(ine))

heron,*, A BIRD (or see heroin/ hero(ine))

hers, hearse / her(s) / here(s) / hear(s)

herself, SHE ALONE, FEMALE SELF

herst, hearse

hert, hurt / heard / herd

hertful, hurt(ful)

herth, hearth

hertle, hurdle / hurtle

hertul, hurdle / hurtle

hery, hair(y) / hurry / harry

herz, hearse / her(s) / here(s) / hear(s)

hes, his / hiss / he's

hesatashen, hesitate(tion)

hesatation, hesitate(tion)

hesderical, hysterical

hesdorean, historian

hesdorik, historic

hesdory, history

hesdurekteme, hysterectomy

hesetashen, hesitate(tion)

hesetation, hesitate(tion)

hesitant,tly,nce,ncy,tate,tation, PAUSE TO CONSIDER BEFORE CONTINUING, CONSIDERING BEFORE STARTING

hesitashen, hesitate(tion)

hesitate,*,ted,ting,tingly,tant,tantly, tation,tive,er, TAKE A PAUSE BEFORE CONTINUING "prefixes: un"

hesterektomy, hysterectomy

hesterical, hysterical

hestorian, historian

hestorical, historic(al)

hestorik, historic

hestory, history

hesutashen, hesitate(tion)

hesutation, hesitate(tion)

het, head / hit / he'd / heat / heed

hetch, hitch

hetero, PREFIX INDICATING "OTHER/ DIFFERENT" MOST OFTEN MODIFIES THE WORD

heteus, hideous

hetid, heed(ed) / heat(ed) / head(ed)

hetud, heed(ed) / heat(ed) / head(ed)

heu, hue / who

heug, huge

heuj, huge

heumen, human

heve, heave / heavy

hevin, heaven

hevy, heavy

hew, hue / who

hewman, human / humane

hewmer, humor

hewmid, humid

hewmileate, humiliate

hex,xes,xed,xing,xer,xagon, CURSE, A COMPUTATION, PREFIX INDICATING "SIX" MOST OFTEN MODIFIES THE WORD

hexagon,*,nal, SIX-SIDED FIGURE/ SHAPE

hey, AN EXCLAMATION FOR GREETING/ FOR SURPRISE, WAY OF GREETING (or see hay)

hezetante, hesitant

hezitate, hesitate

hezutashen, hesitate(tion)

hi, A WELCOME GREETING (or see high)

hiarchy, hierarch(y)

hibachi,*, ROUND COOKING GRILL

hiberacteve, hyperactive

hibernate,*,ed,ting,tion,tor, SLEEP OVER THE WINTER

hibochi, hibachi

hibopotamus, hippopotamus

hibred, hybrid

hibrud, hybrid

hiccup,*,pped,pping, THROAT MUSCLE IN TEMPORARY SPASM

hid,dden, IN HIDING, PAST TENSE FOR THE WORD "HIDE", STORED FROM EYESIGHT (or see hide/height/hit)

hidch, hitch / hedge

hide,*,ding, STORE/PLACE OUT OF SIGHT, SKIN OFF OF ANIMAL (or see hid/height/hit)

hiden, hid(dden)

hideous,sly,sness, FRIGHTFULLY UGLY

hideout,*, WHERE SOMEONE GOES TO HIDE

hidout, hideout

hidrant, hydrant

hidrashen, hydrate(tion)

hidrat, hydrate

hidration, hydrate(tion)

hidrent, hydrant

hidroelectric, hydroelectric

hidrophonic, hydroponic

hidroponic, hydroponic

hidrugen, hydrogen

hierarch,*,hy,hies,hic,hical,hically,hize, hizes,hized,hizing,hization, OF FORMAL RANK

hieroglyph,*,hic, CARVED, PAINTED SYMBOLS FROM PAST PEOPLES

hiest, heist

hif, hive

hifen, hyphen

hifenate, hyphen(ate)

hifer, heifer

hifin, hyphen

higene, hygiene

higenist, hygiene(nist)

high,*,her,hest,hly,hness, ALTITUDE BETWEEN THE GROUND AND

SPACE, A EUPHORIC SENSE UNDER THE INFLUENCE OF A HALLUCINOGEN (or see hi)

hight, height

hijack,*,ked,king,ker, TAKE VEHICLE/ VESSEL BY FORCE

hijene, hygiene

hike,*,ked,king,ker, TO WALK ON ROUGH/NATURAL TERRAIN

hikoo, haiku

hiku, haiku

hikup, hiccup

hilarious,sly,sness,ity, ABSOLUTELY FUNNY

hill,*,lled,lling,ller,lly, MOUNDS ON THE EARTH (or see he'll) "prefixes: up"

hilt,*, SWORD OR DAGGER HANDLE, COMPLETELY AND ABSOLUTELY

him, REFERENCE TO MALE OVER THERE, MALE/THIRD PERSON (or see hem/ hymn)

himarag, hemorrhage

himaroid, hemorrhoids

hime, hemi

himeroid, hemorrhoids

himesfere, hemisphere

himesphere, hemisphere

himiroid, hemorrhoids

himlek, heimlich

himluk, heimlich

himoroid, hemorrhoids

himp, hemp

himself, HIS OWN SELF

himuroid, hemorrhoids

hin, hen

hince, hence

hind, THE REAR PORTION OF AN ANIMAL

hinder,*,red,ring,rer,drance, IN THE WAY OF PROGRESS OR SUCCESS "prefixes: un"

hindrance,*, IN THE WAY OF PROGRESS/SUCCESS

hinge,*,ed,ging,eless, SWINGS BY WAY OF A PIN ENCASED IN A HINGE "prefixes: un"

hinje, hinge

hinse, hence

hint,*,ted,ting,tingly, TINY PORTION OF THE FULL FACT

hip,*,pper,ppest,pply,pness,ppy,ppier, ppiest, THE PELVIC AREA ON PEOPLE/ ANIMALS, TO BE COOL/ INDIFFERENT TO SOCIAL PRESSURE

hipadrete, hypocrite

hipapotamus, hippopotamus

hipatidus, hepatitis

hipauthusis, hypothesis

hipawthusis, hypothesis

hipe, hype / hip

hiperactive, hyperactive

hiperactuve, hyperactive

hipernate, hibernate

hipnosis, hypnosis

hipnosus, hypnosis

hipnutise, hypnotize

hipocrite, hypocrite

hipokrit, hypocrite

hipopotamus, hippopotamus

hipotenuse, hypotenuse

hipothurmeu, hypothermia

hipothusis, hypothesis

hippopotamus,*, LARGE/HEAVY HERBIVORE

hir, her / hire / here

hiracane, hurricane

hirarchy, hierarch(y)

hirass, harass

hird, heard / herd / hurt / hire(d)

hirdul, hurdle / hurtle

hire,*,ed,ring,rable,er, PAID TO WORK (or see high(er))

hirison, horizon

hirl, hurle

hirmet, hermit

hirmetic, hermetic

hiro, hero

hiroek, hero(ic)

hiroglif, hieroglyph

hiroin, hero(ine) / heroin

hirs, hearse / her(s) / hire(s)

hirself, herself

hirst, hearse

hirt, hurt / heard / herd

hirtul, hurdle / hurtle

hirz, her(s) / hearse / hire(s)

his, BELONGS TO HIM (or see hiss)

hisdarecal, hysterical

hisderektomy, hysterectomy

hisdorean, historian

hisdoric, historic

hisdurekteme, hysterectomy

hiself, himself

hiss,sses,ssed,ssing,ssy,sser, SOUND A SNAKE/STEAM MAKES (or see his)

hisself, himself

hist, PREFIX INDICATING "LIVING TISSUE" MOST OFTEN MODIFIES THE WORD

histare, history

histarical, hysterical

histere, history

histerical, hysterical

histo, PREFIX INDICATING "LIVING TISSUE" MOST OFTEN MODIFIES THE WORD

historian,*, PEOPLE WELL STUDIED IN HISTORY

historic,cal,calness,cally,city,cize,cizes, cized,cizing,ize,izes,ized,izing,izingly, ry,izedly,iographer,ization,iography, EVENT ABOUT THE PAST "prefixes: pre"

history,ries,ric,ricism,rize,ricization, riography, ABOUT THE PAST "prefixes: pre"

histrektomy, hysterectomy

histure, history

histurektemy, hysterectomy

hit,*,tting,ttable,tter, STRIKE A BLOW (or see height/hid/hide) "prefixes: over"

hitch,hes,hed,hing, JOIN TWO THINGS TOGETHER BY WAY OF (or see hedge) "prefixes: un"

hite, height / hide

hiten, height(en) / hid(dden)

hiteout, hideout

hiteus, hideous

hith, height

hithen, height(en)

hitout, hideout

hitrashen, hydrate(tion)

hitrate, hydrate

hitun, height(en)

hive,*, BUMPS ON A PERSON, HOME OF BEES OR WASPS

ho, hoe / who / hue

hoard,*,ded,ding,der, TO STOCKPILE MORE GOODS THAN NECESSARY (or see horde)

hoarse,er,est,ely,eness,en,ens,ened, ening, VOICE/THROAT IS RASPY/ ROUGH (or see horse)

hoax,xes, A TRICK IN DECEPTION

hobble,*,ed,ling, WALK WITH A LIMP

hobby,bies, A PASTTIME

hobe, hope / hobby

hobful, hope(ful)

hobil, hobble

hobless, hope(less)

hobt, hop(pped) / hope(d)

hobul, hobble

hoby, hobby

hock,*,ked,king, CUT OF MEAT/LEG, TO PAWN ITEMS (or see hawk/hog/ hokey)

hockey, A SKATING SPORT (or see hokey)

hocky, hokey / hockey

hod,*,ddie, HOLDER FOR MORTAR (or see hot/hold/hood)

hode, haughty / hod(ddie) / hood(y)

hodel, hotel

hoder, hot(tter)

hodir, hot(tter)

hody, haughty

hoe,*,ed,oing, A HAND TOOL (or see whole/whore)

hoest, hoist

hof, huff

hofel, hovel

hofer, hover

hoful, hovel

hofur, hover

hog,*,gged,gging, A PIG, SOMEONE WHO EATS LIKE A PIG

hoist,*,ted,ting, LIFT OR RAISE UP

hok, hawk / hock / hog

hokey,kier,kiest,yness,kily, CORNY, NOT REALISTIC (or see hockey)

hoks, hoax / hock(s)

hoky, hockey / hokey

hol, hole / whole / haul / hall

hold,*,ding,dings,held,der, KEEP FROM MOVING/FALLING, TO GRASP, KEEP STILL (or see haul(ed)) "prefixes: in/ up"

holder,*, SOMETHING THAT HOLDS THINGS

hole,*,ed,ling, AN OPENING/ SPACE/ ORIFICE/GAP (or see holy/holly/ whole(y)/wholly)

holegram, hologram

holeist, holy(liest)

holer, holler / haul(er) / hollow

holeur, holy(lier)

holey, wholly / whole(y) / holy

holi, holy / holly / whole(y) / wholly

holiday,*, A DAY OF REMEMBERANCE/ HONORING SOMEONE/EVENT

holigram, hologram

holl, hall / haul / whole / hole

holler,*,red,ring, YELLING/CALLING LOUDLY

hollow,*,wed,wing,wly,wness, TO DIG/ CARVE OUT SO INSIDE IS EMPTY (or see halo/haul(er))

holly,lies, PLANT (or see holy/hole/ whole/wholly)

holo, PREFIX INDICATING "WHOLE" MOST OFTEN MODIFIES THE WORD (or see hollow/hello)

holocaust,*, DEVASTATING DESTRUCTION OF PEOPLE/PLACES

hologram,*, A THREE DIMENSIONAL ILLUSION, VISUAL REFLECTED BY LASERS

holow, hollow

holoween, halloween

holsal, wholesale

holsel, wholesale

holsem, wholesome

holsome, wholesome

holster,*, HOLDER FOR A PISTOL

holsum, wholesome

holt, hold / halt / haul(ed)

holter, halter / hold(er)

holuday, holiday

holugram, hologram

holur, holler

holy,lier,liest,liness,lism,listic,listically, SACRED (or see hole/holly/wholly/ hole(y)/whole(y)) "prefixes: un"

hom, whom / home

homade, homemade

home,*,ey,ely,elier,eliest,eliness,eless, elessness, STRUCTURE WHERE SOMEONE LIVES

homeless,ssness, HAVING NO HOME

homely, PERSON WHO IS WITHDRAWN/ SHY

homemade, NOT MADE BY A MACHINE IN A FACTORY

homeny, hominy

homeo, PREFIX INDICATING "THE SAME" MOST OFTEN MODIFIES THE WORD

homer,*, HOME RUN IN BASEBALL

homevur, whomever

homey, HOME BOY

hominy, GROUND CORN

homir, homer

homless, homeless

homly, homely

homo, PREFIX INDICATING "THE SAME" MOST OFTEN MODIFIES THE WORD

homogenize,*,ed,zing,zation,er, CREAM/MILK MIXED TOGETHER

homogenous,sly,sness, SIMILAR/ UNIFORM TO, THE SAME AS

homur, homer

homy, homey

honch, haunch / hunch

hond, hone(d) / haunt / hound

hondred, hundred

hone,*,ed,ning,er, TO SHARPEN (or see honey)

honemoon, honeymoon

honemun, honeymoon

honer, honor

honerary, honorary

honest,ty,ties,tly,tness, TRUTHFUL ("H" IS SILENT) "prefixes: dis"

honey,*,yed,ying, A LIQUID FROM NECTAR MADE BY BEES

honeymoon,*,ned,ning,ners, WHAT A COUPLE HAS AFTER THEIR WEDDING

honimoon, honeymoon

honimun, honeymoon

honist, honest

honk,*,ked,king, A HORN SOUND, SOUND A GOOSE MAKES

honker, hunk(er) / honk

honor,*,red,ring,rer,rless,rable,rably, rableness,rarium,rary,ree, rific, RESPECT, STRONG MORAL INTEGRITY "prefixes: dis/re"

honorary, AWARD OF HONOR

hont, haunt / hone(d) / hunt

hontred, hundred

honur, honor

honymoon, honeymoon

hoo, hue / who

hood,*,ded,ding,dless,dy, JACKET/HAT COMBINATION, ENGINE COVER ON CAR, IN THE NEIGHBORHOOD (or see hoot/who'd)

hooever, whoever

hoof,*,fed,fing,fer,oves,oved, FEET OF SOME ANIMALS

hook,*,ked,king, A CURVED TOOL WITH SHARP TIP FOR GRABBING "prefixes: un"

hoomever, whomever

hoop,*,ped,ping, THINGS THAT ARE A CIRCLE USED AS A TOOL/TOY (or see hop)

hooray, hurrah

hoos, who's / whose / hue(s)

hoot,*,ted,ting,ter, SOUND OWL MAKES, FOND EXPRESSION TOWARDS SOMEONE (or see hood/ who'd)

hoove,*,ed, MORE THAN ONE HOOF

hop,*,pped,pping,ppy, JUMP UP AND DOWN LIKE A RABBIT, A PLANT (or see hope)

hopd, hop(pped) / hope(d)

hope,*,ed,ping,er,eful,efully,efulness, eless,elessly,elessness, WISH FOR SOMETHING (or see hop/hops/ hobby)

hopful, hope(ful)

hopless, hope(less)

hops, A PLANT (or see hope(s))

hopscotch, GAME

hopskoch, hopscotch

hor, hour / horror / whore

horable, horrible

horafid, horrify(fied)

horascope, horoscope

hord, hoard / hard / horde / horrid

horde,*,ed,ding, MANY THINGS/ PEOPLE ALL TOGETHER AT ONCE, SWARMS OF (or see hoard/hard/ hardy/horrid)

hordervs, horsd'oevres

hordurves, horsd'oevres

horeble, horrible

hored, hoard / horrid / horde

horefik, horrify(fic)

horefy, horrify

horendous, horrendous

horer, horror

horescope, horoscope

horesontul, horizontal

horible, horrible

horify, horrify

horindus, horrendous

horir, horror

horiscope, horoscope

horizon,*,nal,ntal, WHERE THE SUN/ MOON RISES/SETS

horizontal,*,lly,lness,lity, POSITION SITUATED LINEAR WITH THE HORIZON

hormeny, harmony

hormful, harm(ful)

hormles, harm(less)

hormone,*,nal,nally, HEMICALS MANUFACTURED BY THE BODY (pineal gland) "prefixes: pro"

hormuny, harmony

horn,*,ned,ning,ny, INSTRUMENT PLAYED BY BLOWING, USED FOR SOUND ON VEHICLES AND VESSELS

horne, horny

hornet,*, LARGE VOLATILE WASP

horny, MADE OF HORN, SLANG FOR CERTAIN DESIRES

horoscope,*,pic, USING THE STARS TO GUESS THE FUTURE

horrendous,sness,sly, TERRIBLE, DREADFUL

horrible,ly,eness, AWFUL, UGLY, HORRENDOUS

horrid,dly,dness, HORROR, DREADFUL, OFFENSIVE

horrify,fies,fied,fying,fyingly,fication,fic, ror, VERY FRIGHTENING, BEYOND SCARY

horror,*, OVERPOWERING/ UNIMAGINABLE FEAR

horsd'oevres, TWO WORDS 'hors d'oevres', APPETIZERS

horse,*,ed,sing, ANIMAL(or see hoarse/ horror) "prefixes: un"

hort, horde / hard

horte, horde / hardy

horuble, horrible

horufid, horrify(fied)

horufy, horrify

horur, horror

horuscope, horoscope

horusontel, horizontal

hos, hoe(s) / hose / who's / hue(s) / whose

hosbedul, hospital

hosbetality, hospitality

hosbidul, hospital

hosbitality, hospitality

hosbituble, hospitable

hosbitul, hospital

hosdege, hostage

hosdej, hostage

hosdel, hostel / hostile

hosdij, hostage

hosdul, hostel / hostile

hose,*,ed,sing, RUBBER TUBE(or see whose/who's)

hospetable, hospitable

hospetality, hospitality

hospetul, hospital

hospice,*, LODGING FOR TRAVELERS, PROGRAM FOR PATIENTS

hospitable,ly,leness, KIND/FRIENDLY TO GUESTS

hospital,*,lize,lized,lizing,lization, PLACE FOR SICK/INJURED PEOPLE "prefixes: multi/post"

hospitality,ties, KINDNESS TO GUESTS

host,*,ted,ting,tess, TO SPONSOR, ONE WHO ENTERTAINS/IS IN CHARGE

hostage,*, PERSON HELD AGAINST THEIR WILL

hostel,*,ler,ling,lry, SHELTERS AROUND THE WORLD WHERE TRAVELING PEOPLE MAY STAY CHEAPLY (or see hostile)

hoster, holster

hostes, host(ess)

hostige, hostage

hostile,lity,lities, ACTS AGGRESSIVE/ ANGRY (or see hostel)

hostis, host(ess)

hostle, hostile / hostel

hostul, hostel / hostile

hostus, host(ess)

hot,tter,ttest,ttie, CAN BURN, WARMER THAN WARM, IN REFERENCE TO SOMEONE VERY ATTRACTIVE (or see hod/hold/hood/hoot/who'd)

hote, haughty / hod(ddie) / hold / hood(y)

hotel,*, BUILDINGS WITH ROOMS FOR TRAVELERS TO STAY THE NIGHT

hoter, hot(tter)

hotur, hot(tter)

hoty, haughty / hod(ddie) / hood(y) / hot(ttie)

houefur, however

houl, howl / haul

hound,*,ded,ding, TO AGITATE SOMEONE, BE PERSISTENT LIKE A HOUND DOG ON A SCENT, A DOG

hour,*,rly, SECONDS (or see our)

house,*,ed,sing, STRUCTURE/ DWELLING TO LIVE IN

hovel,*, A TINY DWELLING, SMALL OPEN STRUCTURE

hover,*,red,ring, TO FLOAT ABOVE FOR A PERIOD OF TIME WITHOUT MOVING, TO FLOAT ABOVE

hovil, hovel

hovul, hovel

hovur, hover

how, EXPLAIN THE WAY SOMETHING IS SAID OR DONE, QUESTION THE WAY SOMETHING HAPPENS

however, IN ANY EVENT, ON THE OTHER HAND, STILL

howl,*,led,ling,lingly,ler, SOUND DOG MAKES, A LOUD SOUND

hownd, hound

hownt, hound

howse, house

hox, hoax / hock(s)

hoz, hose / hoe(s) / who's / whose

hozbetuble, hospitable

hozdul, hostel / hostile

hozpetality, hospitality

hozpitable, hospitable

hozt, host

hoztus, host(ess)

hu, hue / who

hub,*, THE CENTER OF SOMETHING WHICH HOLDS IT ALL TOGETHER, KEEPS IT MOVING

hubcap,*, COVER FOR WHEELS, COVERS THE HUB

huch, hutch / huge / hush

huckleberry,ries, AN EDIBLE BERRY

hud, hood / hoot / who'd / hut

huddle,*,ed,ling, FORM/HUNCH INTO A TIGHT GROUP

hude, hood / hoot / who'd

hudel, huddle

hue,*, SHADES, DEGREES OF THE SAME COLOR (or see who) "prefixes: multi/un"

huever, whoever

huf, hoof / huff / hoove

hufd, huff(ed) / hoove(d)

hufed, huff(ed) / hoove(d)

huff,*,ffed,ffing,ffy, DEEP GASPS FOR AIR, DEEP BREATH OUT

hug,*,gged,gging,ggable,ggably,gger, WRAP ARMS AROUND SOMEONE/ SOMETHING WITH GOOD INTENT (or see huge)

hugable, hug(ggable)

hugd, hug(gged)

huge,er,est,eness,ely, ENORMOUS IN BULK, TAKES UP ALOT OF SPACE (or see hutch)

hugible, hug(ggable)

hugt, hug(gged)

huguble, hug(ggable)

huj, huge / hutch

huk, hook / hug

hukd, hug(gged)

hukeble, hug(ggable)

huklbery, huckleberry

hukt, hook(ed) / hug(gged)

hul, hull / who'll

hulareus, hilarious

hull,*, MAINFRAME/COVER (or see who'll) "prefixes: multi"

hum,*,mmed,mming,mmer, A SOUND MADE WITH LIPS PURSED (or see whom)

human,*,ne,nness,nism,nist,nistic, nistically,nitarian,nitarianism, nity, nities,nize,nizes,nized,nizing, nization,nly, HOMO SAPIEN BEING (or see humane) "prefixes: in/neo/ sub"

humane,ely,eness, BE FAIR, CIVILIZED, REFINED (or see human) "prefixes: in"

humble,*,ed,ling,er,est,ly,eness, NOT SELF-RIGHTEOUS, ISN'T FLAGRANTLY PROUD OR OPINIONATED

humbul, humble

humdinger, OUTSTANDING

humed, humid

humeleate, humiliate

humen, human

humenbird, hummingbird

humengbird, hummingbird

humer, humor / hummer

humerus, humor(ous)

humes, hummus / humus

humever, whomever

humid,dity,dify,difies,dified,difier, difying,dification,dly, MOISTURE IN THE AIR

humiliate,*,ed,ting,tion,ity, BELITTLED, ATTACK ON SELF-ESTEEM, HARSH JUDGEMENT

humility, RESPECTFUL/MODEST

humin, human

huminbird, hummingbird

humis, hummus / humus

hummer,*, TYPE OF TRUCK

hummingbird,*, TINY BIRD

hummus, CHICKPEA, GARBONZO MIXTURE FOR AN EDIBLE SPREAD (or see humus)

humongous,sly, HUGE, ENORMOUS

humor,*,red,ring,rous,rously,rousness, rless,rlessly,rlessness,rist,resque, FUNNY (or see hummer)

hump,*,ped,ping, A BUMP, WHAT A MALE DOG DOES

humple, humble

humud, humid

humur, humor / hummer

humus, ORGANIC RICH SOIL (or see hummus)

hunch,hes,hed,hing, BENT OVER, HAVE AN IDEA

hundred,*,dth, A NUMBER USED IN THE U.S.

hunemoon, honeymoon

hung, PAST TENSE FOR THE WORD "HANG" "prefixes: over"

hunger,*,red,ring,gry,grily,griness, TO NEED/WANT SOMETHING DESPERATELY (or see hunker)

hungry,rier,riest,rily,riness, NEED FOOD

hunk,*,ker,ky, CHUNK OF SOMETHING (or see hung/honk)

hunker, hunk(er)

hunsh, hunch

hunt,*,ted,ting,ter, PURSUE TO LOCATE

huntch, hunch

huntret, hundred

huntrid, hundred

huntur, hunt(er)

huny, honey

hunymoon, honeymoon

hup, hoop / hub

hupcap, hubcap

hur, her

huracane, hurricane

hurass, harass

hurb, herb

hurbavore, herbivore

hurd, heard / herd / hurt

hurdid, herd(ed) / hurt(ed)

hurdle,*,ed,ling,er, JUMP OVER OBSTACLES (or see hurtle)

hure, hurry

huredetary, hereditary

hureditare, hereditary

huredity, heredity

huricane, hurricane

hurifek, horrify(fic)

hurisun, horizon

hurle,*,ed,ling,er, PITCH/SWING SOMETHING

hurmetic, hermetic

hurmit, hermit

huroik, hero(ic)

hurrah,*, YELL FOR JOY

hurricane,*, HIGH WINDS FROM THE SEAS

hurried, hurry(ried)

hurry,ries,ried,rying, TO GO FASTER THAN NORMAL "prefixes: un"

hurs, hearse / her(s)

hurself, herself

hurst, hearse

hurt,*,ting,tful,tfully,tfulness, PAIN, CAUSES PAIN (or see herd/heard) "prefixes: un"

hurtle,*,ed,ling, TO THROW/FLING VIOLENTLY WITH GREAT FORCE (or see hurdle)

hury, hurry

hurz, her(s) / hearse

hus, hue(s) / who's / whose

husband,*,dman,ubby, PARTNER OF A WIFE, MARRIED TERM

husbend, husband

husbind, husband

husderical, hysterical

hush,hes,hed,hing, BEING TOLD TO BE QUIET WITH A SOUND, GET SILENT

husk,*,ked,king,ker,ky, PROTECTIVE SHELLS ON THE FRUIT FROM PLANTS, TO REMOVE HUSKS

husky,kies,kier,kiest,kily,kiness, A DOG, SOMEONE WHO IS LARGER IN SIZE AND MUSCLE THAN PEERS

husle, hustle

husler, hustle(r)

huspend, husband

hustle,*,ed,ling,er, GET A MOVE ON IT, SOMEONE WHO GAMBLES AT POOL

hut,*, RAMSHACKLE STRUCTURE, WORD USED IN FOOTBALL (or see hoot)

hutch,hes, CAGE FOR ANIMALS, TO HOLD DISHES

hutel, huddle

hutul, huddle

huv, hoove

huz, who's / whose / hue(s)

huzbend, husband

huze, hue(s) / who's / whose

huzpend, husband

hybernate, hibernate

hybred, hybrid

hybrid,*,dism,dist,dity,dize,dizes,dized, dizing,dizable,dization, dizer, OFFSPRING FROM TWO ANIMALS OR PLANTS

hydr, PREFIX INDICATING "WATER/ LIQUID" MOST OFTEN MODIFIES THE WORD

hydrant,*, CAP FOR ACCESS TO STORED WATER

hydrate,*,ed,ting,tion,tor, ADD WATER "prefixes: de/re"

hydraulic,*, USE OF LIQUID UNDER PRESSURE TO MAKE PARTS MOVE

hydrint, hydrant

hydro, PREFIX INDICATING "WATER/ LIQUID" MOST OFTEN MODIFIES THE WORD

hydroelectric,cal,cally, USED TO RUN MACHINES VIA WATER PRESSURE THROUGH GENERATORS

hydrogen,nate,nates,nated,nating, nation,nator,nize,nizes,nized,nizing, nization,nous,eology,graphy, A COMMON/PLENTIFUL GAS

hydroponic,*,cally,cist,ist, USE OF WATER WITH ADDED VITAMINS/ MINERALS TO FEED ROOT PLANTS INSTEAD OF SOIL

hyfen, hyphen

hygene, hygiene

hygiene,nist,nics,nics,nically, CARE FOR THE EXTERIOR OF THE BODY "prefixes: un"

hygro, PREFIX INDICATING "MOISTURE" MOST OFTEN MODIFIES THE WORD

hyjack, hijack

hyke, hike

hymn,*,ned,ning,nal,nist, RELIGIOUS SONG (or see him/hem)

hymorag, hemorrhage

hypawthusis, hypothesis

hype, EXAGGERATING (or see hip)

hyper, PREFIX INDICATING "ABOVE/ OVER" MOST OFTEN MODIFIES THE WORD

hyperactive,vity, UNFOCUSED ENERGY

hypernate, hibernate

hypertherimia, hypothermia

hypethermia, hypothermia

hyphen,*,nate,nates,nated,nating, nation, A MARK WHICH SHOWS CONNECTION BETWEEN TWO WORDS

hyphenate, hyphen(ate)

hypnosis, SLIP TO A PLACE IN THE SUBCONSCIOUS MIND

hypnotic,cally,ize,ism, PUT INTO A SUBCONSCIOUS STATE OF MIND, MAGNETICALLY DRAWN TO SOMETHING

hypnotize,*,ed,zing,osis,ism, TALKED INTO A SUBCONSCIOUS STATE OF MIND

hypo, PREFIX INDICATING "BELOW/UNDER" MOST OFTEN MODIFIES THE WORD

hypocrite,*,tical,tically,isy,isies, SOMEONE WHO SAYS ONE THING BUT DOES ANOTHER, LYING

hypotenuse, LONGEST SIDE OF TRIANGLE, USUALLY THE BASE

hypothermia, BODY BELOW NORMAL TEMPERATURE

hypothesis,ses, A THEORY FORMED DUE TO LACK OF INFORMATION OR TIME

hypothusis, hypothesis

hysdurekteme, hysterectomy

hysterectomy,mies, REMOVAL OF FEMALE ORGANS/UTERUS

hysterical,lly,lness, EXTREME EMOTION

hytrashen, hydrate(tion)

hytrat, hydrate

I, REFERS TO SELF (or see eye)

I'd, CONTRACTION OF THE WORDS 'I WOULD, I COULD, I SHOULD, I HAD'

I'll, CONTRACTION OF THE WORDS 'I WILL' (or see ill)

I'm, CONTRACTION OF THE WORDS 'I AM'

I've, CONTRACTION OF THE WORDS 'I HAVE'

ial, aisle

ibrau, eyebrow

ibreveate, abbreviate

ibreviate, abbreviate

ibrow, eyebrow

ice,*,ed,cing,cy,cily, FROZEN WATER

ich, itch / each

ichu, issue

ichuense, issue(uance)

ichuinse, issue(uance)

icicle,*, FROZEN ICE SHAPED LIKE DAGGERS

icing, TOPPING FOR BAKED GOODS

ickstensev, extensive

icon,*,nic,nical,nically,noclasm,noclast, noclastic,noclastically,nography, nographer,nographic,nographical, nolater,nology,nological,nologist, nomatic,nomaticism, SYMBOLS OR IMAGES THEY REPRESENT, PREFIX INDICATING "IMAGE" MOST OFTEN MODIFIES THE WORD

icono, PREFIX INDICATING "IMAGE" MOST OFTEN MODIFIES THE WORD

icselerate, accelerate

icy,cier,ciest,cily, FROZEN WATER

id, BASED ON FREUD'S EGO THEORY (or see eye(d)/I'd)

idalegy, ideology

idapt, adapt

idch, itch

idea,*,al,ally,alism,alist,alistic,alistically, ality,alize,alizes,alized,alizing,alizer, ally,ate,ates,ated,ating,ation,ational, ationally,ative, THE FORM/ THOUGHT OF SOMETHING "prefixes: un"

idel, it'll / idle / idol

idelogical, ideological

idem, item

idemize, item(ize)

idenify, identify

idenity, identity

identical,lly,lness, EXACTLY THE SAME

identification,*, PICTURE/LEGAL DOCUMENT PROVING WHO A PERSON IS (I.D.)

identify,fies,fied,fying,fication,fier, fiable,fiably, fiability,ity, TO RECOGNIZE "prefixes: un"

identity,ties, A CHARACTERISTIC WHICH IDENTIFIES ONE FROM ANOTHER

idenufi, identify

ideo, PREFIX INDICATING "IDEA" MOST OFTEN MODIFIES THE WORD (or see idio)

ideology,gic,gical, OF IDEAS/THOUGHTS "prefixes: un"

ideosy, idiocy

ideut, idiot

idilogical, ideological

idim, item

idimise, item(ize)

idinefy, identify

idinety, identity

idintekul, identical

idintufecation, identification

idio, PREFIX INDICATING "PRIVATE/INDIVIDUAL/PROPER" MOST OFTEN MODIFIES THE WORD (or see ideo)

idiocy,cies, LACKS INTELLIGENCE

idiology, ideology

idiot,*,tic,tically,tness, ACTS LIKE A FOOL

idl, it'll / idle

idle,*,er,ling, RUN IN NEUTRAL, SITTING WITHOUT MOVING (or see idol/it'll)

idmire, admire

idmit, admit

idmyre, admire

idol,*,lator,latry,latrous,lize,lizes,lized, lizing,lization, ADMIRED, WORSHIPPED (or see idle)

idolegy, ideology

idological, ideological

idology, ideology

idolt, adult

idoo, adieu

idself, itself

idsetura, etcetera

idsulf, itself

idu, adieu

idul, idol / idle / it'll

idult, adult

idum, item

idvanse, advance

idvantige, advantage

idvize, advise / advice

ie, eye

iel, I'll / yell

ieng, eye(ying)

if, THEN THIS IF NOT THAT, IT COULD BE THIS OR THAT BASED ON WHETHER

ife, ivy / iffy

ifekt, effect / affect

iffy,fier,fiest,finess, PROBABILITY IT WILL/WILL NOT HAPPEN

ifre, ivory

ifree, every

ifry, ivory

ify, ivy / iffy

ig, PREFIX INDICATING "NOT" MOST OFTEN MODIFIES THE WORD

igalatarian, egalitarian

igalutarean, egalitarian

igloo,*, DOME DWELLING BUILT OF ICE BLOCKS

iglu, igloo

ignarent, ignorant

igneous, OLD ROCK FORMED BY HIGH HEAT

ignerants, ignorant(nce)

ignerent, ignorant

igneus, igneous

ignide, ignite

ignishin, ignition

ignite,*,ed,ting,tion,ter, SPARK TO MAKE IT START, START A FIRE "prefixes: pre"

ignition,*, ELECTRICAL SPARK TO START AN ENGINE "prefixes: pre"

ignor, ignore

ignorant,ntly,ance, LACKING INFORMATION

ignore,*,ed,ring,rant, PURPOSELY NOT PAY ATTENTION

ignurent, ignorant
igree, agree
igsajurate, exaggerate
igsakt, exact
igsample, example
igsberament, experiment
igsblanatory, explanatory
igsblod, explode
igsbozishen, expose(sition)
igsebshen, except(ion)
igsebt, except / accept
igsecutive, executive
igsempt, exempt
igsept, except / accept
igsert, exert
igsglude, exclude
igsilarate, exhilarate / accelerate
igsklute, exclude
igsotik, exotic
igspand, expand
igspans, expanse / expense
igspect, expect
igsperument, experiment
igspir, expire
igsplan, explain
igsplisit, explicit
igsplod, explode
igsplorashen, explore(ration)
igsploshen, explosion
igsplosive, explosive
igspoz, expose
igstend, extend
igstensev, extensive
igstenshen, extension
igstenuate, extenuate
igstereur, exterior
igstinkt, extinct
igstrakt, extract
igsturnel, external
igsurt, exert
igzajerate, exaggerate
igzakt, exact
igzample, example
igzasperate, exasperate
igzile, exile
igzist, exist
igzost, exhaust
igzurt, exert
ijusduble, adjust(able)
iknauleg, acknowledge

iknolege, acknowledge
iknor, ignore
iknurent, ignorant
ikon, icon
iksagerashen, exaggerate(tion)
iksajerashen, exaggerate(tion)
iksam, exam
iksamen, examine
iksamenashen, examine(nation)
iksampl, example
iksamunashen, examine(nation)
iksblan, explain
iksblod, explode
iksblor, explore
iksbloshen, explosion
iksblosive, explosive
iksboz, expose
ikschange, exchange
ikscuse, excuse
iksebt, except / accept
ikselirate, accelerate
ikseluratur, accelerate(tor)
iksepshen, except(ion)
iksept, except / accept
iksert, exert
iksglud, exclude
iksit, excite
iksitment, excite(ment)
ikskwisit, exquisite
iksost, exhaust
ikspans, expanse / expense
ikspant, expand
ikspektent, expect(ant)
ikspensef, expense(sive)
ikspereanse, experience
iksperement, experiment
ikspire, expire
iksplan, explain
iksplanatory, explanatory
iksplisitly, explicit(ly)
iksplod, explode
iksplor, explore
iksplorutory, explore(ratory)
iksploshen, explosion
iksplosive, explosive
ikspoz, expose
ikspreshen, express(ion)
ikspress, express
ikstend, extend
ikstengwish, extinguish
ikstensev, extensive
ikstenshen, extension
ikstenuate, extenuate
ikstereor, exterior

iksternul, external
ikstradite, extradite
ikstrem, extreme
ikstrordenair, extraordinaire
ikstrordinery, extraordinary
iksturmenate, exterminate
ikuate, equate
ikwalibreum, equilibrium
ikwalite, equality
ikwanimity, equanimity
ikwashun, equation
ikwate, equate
ikwater, equator
ikwaunimity, equanimity
ikwefalent, equivalent
ikwelbreum, equilibrium
ikwenox, equinox
ikwip, equip
ikwivalent, equivalent
ikwunimity, equanimity
ikzam, exam
ikzamen, examine
il, PREFIX INDICATING "NOT IN/INTO/ ON" MOST OFTEN MODIFIES THE WORD (or see ill/aisle/i'll/eel)
iland, island
ilarm, alarm
ilash, eyelash
ilasteck, elastic
ilastick, elastic
ilastrate, illustrate
ilbow, elbow
ile, i'll
ilect, elect
ilectiv, elective
ilectrician, electrician
iledaret, illiterate
ilegal, illegal
ileganse, allegiance
ilegul, illegal
ilekul, illegal
ilend, island
ilent, island
ileptic, elliptic
ilesit, elicit / illicit
ilestrate, illustrate
ileterate, illiterate
iletest, elite(tist)
ileventh, eleven(th)
ileviate, alleviate
ilicit, elicit / illicit
iliderate, illiterate
iliderit, illiterate
iliiptical, elliptic(al)

iliktrishen, electrician
ilind, island
ilipsus, ellipsis
ilisit, elicit / illicit
iliterate, illiterate
ilive, alive
ill,lness, NOT WELL
illegal,lly,lity,lities,lize,lizes,lized,lizing, lization, AGAINST THE LAW, NOT LEGAL
illeterate, illiterate
illicit,tly,tness, PROHIBITED BY LAW, NOT ALLOWED (or see elicit)
illiptic, elliptic
illisit, elicit / illicit
illiterate, HARDLY ABLE TO READ AND WRITE, NOT EDUCATED
illogical,lly,lity,lities, NOT LOGICAL, NOT REALISTIC
illuminate,*,ed,ting,tingly,tion,ance,ant, OF BEING ENLIGHTENED/ INFORMED "prefixes: retro"
illumine,*,ed,ning,nance,nant,nate, nism, OF BEING ENLIGHTENED/ INFORMED
illusion,*,nal,nary,nist,nism, SENSE SOMETHING AS IF IT WERE PHYSICAL/REAL (or see allusion) "prefixes: dis"
illusive,ely,eness, SENSE SOMETHING AS IF IT WERE PHYSICAL/REAL (or see allusive)
illustrate,*,ed,ting,tive,tively,tion,tional, tor, DRAW A PICTURE, ONE WHO DRAWS
illustrious,sly,sness, FAMOUS FOR ACHIEVEMENT
ilness, ill(ness)
ilnus, ill(ness)
ilogikul, illogical
ilongate, elongate
ilop, elope
ilorm, alarm
ilostrious, illustrious
ilud, elude
ilujen, illusion / allusion
ilumenade, illuminate
iluminate, illuminate
ilund, island
ilur, allure
ilusdreus, illustrious
ilushen, illusion / allusion
ilusion, illusion / allusion
ilusive, illusive / allusive / elusive

ilustrate, illustrate
ilustrious, illustrious
ilute, elude
im, PREFIX INDICATING "NOT/IN/INTO/ ON" MOST OFTEN MODIFIES THE WORD (or see them/him)
imaculet, immaculate
image,*,ed,ery,er,ging,gine,gism, A PICTURE REAL OR IN THE MIND
imagenashen, imagine(nation)
imaginashen, imagine(nation)
imagine,*,ed,ning,nable,ary,native, nativeness,natively,nation, A PICTURE/THOUGHT IN THE MIND "prefixes: un"
imagrant, immigrant / emigrant
imagrate, immigrate / emigrate
imagrent, emigrant / immigrant
imagrints, emigrant(s) / immigrant(s)
imagrits, emigrant(s) / immigrant(s)
imagunashen, imagine(nation)
imaj, image
imajenashen, imagine(nation)
imanate, emanate
imanens, eminence / imminence/ immanence
imanint, eminent / imminent / immanent
imanserable, immensurable
imansopate, emancipate
imatashin, imitate(tion)
imatate, imitate
imaterial, immaterial
imature, immature
imbankment, embankment
imbargo, embargo
imbark, embark
imbasee, embassy
imbaudes, embody(dies)
imbeded, embed(dded)
imbelikul, umbilical
imberis, embarrass
imbet, embed
imbilakul, umbilical
imblim, emblem
imbodys, embody(dies)
imboss, emboss
imbotys, embody(dies)
imboudes, embody(dies)
imbrase, embrace
imbreo, embryo
imbrorder, embroider
imbrufment, improve(ment)
imbtee, empty

imbur, ember
imbuse, embassy
imediate, immediate
imeduetly, immediate(ly)
imenate, emanate
imenent, eminent / imminent / immanent
imense, immense
imensurable, immensurable
imerch, emerge
imerg, emerge
imergensi, emergency
imerj, emerge
imersable, immersible
imerse, immerse / emersed
imersion, immerse(sion)
imertality, immortal(ity)
imetashen, imitate(tion)
imeterial, immaterial
imeteut, immediate
imfasis, emphasis / emphasize
imfusis, emphasis / emphasize
imigrant, immigrant / emigrant
imigrashen, immigrate(tion) / emigrate(tion)
imigrate, immigrate / emigrate
imigration, immigrate(tion) / emigrate(tion)
imigrunt, immigrant / emigrant
iminate, emanate
iminens, eminence / imminence/ immanence
iminent, eminent / imminent / immanent
iminse, immense
iminsurable, immensurable
imirsable, immersible
imirsed, immerse(d) / emersed
imirshen, immerse(sion)
imirsion, immerse(sion)
imitate,*,ed,ting,tion,tional,tive,tively, tiveness, COPIES/REPRODUCTIONS OF THE REAL THING
imiterial, immaterial
imkombutent, incompetent
immaculate,ely,eness, NO SPOTS/ STAINS/MARS/FLAWS
immagrate, immigrate/ emigrant
immanence,cy,nt, WITHIN, INTRINSIC (or see eminence/imminence)
immanent,tly, WITHIN, INTRINSIC (or see eminent/imminent)

immaterial,lly,lity,lism,lize,lizes,lized, lizing, NO IMPORTANT/ USEFUL FOR THE SITUATION

immature,ely,eness,rity, NOT OLD ENOUGH/MATURE/GROWN, FOOLISH

immeasurable,ly,bility, NOT ABLE TO MEASURE

immediate,ely,eness, RIGHT NOW

immense,ely,eness, GREAT IN SIZE, HUGE, VAST

immensurable,ely,bility,eness, IMPOSSIBLE TO MEASURE HOW VAST IT IS

immerchen, immerse(sion)

immerse,es,ed,sing,sion,sionist,sionism, sible, SINK INTO LIQUID/THOUGHT/ ACTIVITY (or see emerse)

immershen, immerse(sion)

immersible, CAN BE SUBMERGED INTO LIQUID

immeterial, immaterial

immigrant,*, LEFT YOUR COUNTRY PERMANENTLY TO LIVE IN ANOTHER COUNTRY (or see emigrant) "prefixes: non"

immigrate,*,ed,ting,ant,tion,tioner, GOING TO ANOTHER COUNTRY (or see emigrate)

imminence,cy,nt,ntly, COULD POTENTIALLY HAPPEN (or see eminence/immanence)

imminent,tly,ncy, IT WILL HAPPEN NO MATTER HOW LONG IT TAKES, INEVITABLE (or see eminent/ immanent)

immobile,lize,lizes,lized,lizing,lization, lizer,lity,lism, NOT ABLE TO MOVE/ BE MOVED

immoral,lly,lity,lities,list, NOT PROPER/ MORAL/ DECENT

immortal,lly,lity,lize,lizes,lized,lizing, lization, EXISTS FROM NOW ON, NEVER ENDING

immpresion, impression

immpresive, impressive

immune,nity,nities,nize, FREE FROM, EXEMPT, HEALTHY

immunize,*,ed,zing,er,zation, PHARMACEUTICALS INTRODUCED INTO THE BODY TO FIGHT MICRO ORGANISMS WHICH MAY/MAY NOT INVADE BODY

immurshen, immerse(sion)

immursion, immerse(sion)

imobile, immobile

imochen, emotion

imochun, emotion

imonate, emanate

imople, immobile

imoral, immoral

imorchen, immerse(sion)

imordle, immortal

imorshen, immerse(sion)

imortaledy, immortal(ity)

imortality, immortal(ity)

imorul, immoral

imoterial, immaterial

imownt, amount

impact,*,ted,ting,tion,tive, TWO BODIES OF MASS COLLIDING INTO ONE ANOTHER, SIZEABLE EFFECT

impair,*,red,ring,rer,rment, MAKE WORSE "prefixes: un"

impar, empower

imparer, emperor

imparical, empirical

imparment, empower(ment)

imparutev, imperative

impashent, impatient

impatient,tly,nce, NOT PATIENT, UNABLE TO RELAX

impaurment, empower(ment)

impeach,hes,hed,hing,her,hable,hment, CHARGE WITH CRIME/ MISDEMEANOR "prefixes: un"

impeachuis, impetuous

impeccable,ly,bility, NO FLAWS/ MISTAKES

impech, impeach

impechuous, impetuous

impede,*,ed,ding,er, DELAY/OBSTRUCT "prefixes: un"

impeed, impede

imper, impair

imperative,*,val,ely,eness, ABSOLUTELY ESSENTIAL, NECESSARY

imperfect,tly,tness,tion,tive,tiveness, NOT AS GOOD AS COULD BE

imperor, emperor

impersonal,lly,lity,lize,lizes,lized,lizing, ate, NOT ATTACHED IN A PERSONAL WAY, ABSENCE OF PERSONAL FEELINGS

impersonate,*,ed,ting,tion,tor,al, ACT/ BEHAVE LIKE SOMEONE ELSE

impetuous,sly,sness,osity,osities, ACT/ BEHAVE ON THE SPUR OF THE MOMENT

imphasis, emphasis / emphasize

impire, empire

impirical, empirical

implamint, implement

implant,*,ted,ting,tation, TO INSTILL IDEAS OR THOUGHTS, REPLACE BODY ORGAN WITH ANOTHER ONE

implecate, implicate

implement,*,ted,ting,tal,ter,tation, SOMETHING USED AS A TOOL, TO INCORPORATE INTO

implicate,*,ed,ting,tion,tional,tive,tively, BE TANGLED/INVOLVED IN, SUSPECTED PARTICIPATION

imploe, employee / employ

imploer, employer

imploy, employ / employee

imployer, employer

implucate, implicate

implucation, implicate(tion)

implument, implement

imply,lies,lied,ying,lication, SUGGEST SOMETHING/SOMEONE IS RESPONSIBLE

impolite,ely,eness, RUDE/FRANK/ IMPERSONAL/HONEST

impols, impulse

impolsive, impulse(sive)

import,*,ted,ting,tation,table,tability, BRING INTO THE COUNTRY FROM ANOTHER COUNTRY

important,tly,nce, PRIORITY, MUST BE TENDED TO "prefixes: un"

impose,*,ed,sing,sition, TO INTERRUPT, SUGGESTED REFERENCE, UNWELCOME INCLUSION

imposebul, impossible

impossible,ly,bility, NOT POSSIBLE, COULD NEVER HAPPEN

imposter,*, UNWELCOME INCLUSION, BE WHERE ONE IS NOT WANTED, ILLEGITIMATE

impound,*,ded,ding, TAKE AWAY/ CONFISCATE/HOLD LAWFULLY

impour, empower

impourment, empower(ment)

impourtens, important(nce)

impourtent, important

impoverish,hed,her,hment, MARGINALIZED, UNABLE TO ADEQUATELY SUPPORT ONESELF impovuresh, impoverish

impowerment, empower(ment)

impoze, impose

impractical,able,ability,ableness, NOT PRACTICAL/LOGICAL FOR SITUATION

impraktecle, impractical

imprasev, impressive

imprashen, impression

imprechen, impression

imprecise,ely,eness,sion, NOT PRECISE/ FACTUAL

impregnable,bility,ly, NOT ABLE TO PENETRATE/GET INTO MOVE

impregnate,*,ed,ting,tion,tor,able, TO INTRODUCE/INJECT INTO, MAKE PREGNANT, INFUSE

impregnuble, impregnable

imprent, imprint

impresef, impressive

impreshen, impression

impresif, impressive

impresion, impression

impress,sses,ssed,ssing,ssion,ssive, ssivley,ssible,ssibly,ssibility, ssibilities,ssibleness,ssment, FAVORABLY AFFECTED "prefixes: over/re/un"

impression,*,nable,nability,nableness, nist,nistic,nism,ive, FAVORABLY AFFECTED, PRESSED/ MOLDED/ EMBOSSED INTO "prefixes: re/un"

impressive,ely,eness, FAVORABLY AFFECTED "prefixes: re/un"

impretion, impression

imprint,*,ted,ting,ter, PRINT/STAMP INTO, TO LODGE/INSTILL INTO MEMORY

imprison,*,ned,ning,nment, PLACE INTO PRISON, CONFINE, INCARCERATE

improbable,ly,bility, HIGHLY UNLIKELY, NOT NORMALLY POSSIBLE, MOST LIKELY NOT

improbabol, improbable

improf, improve

impromptu, OFF THE TOP OF YOUR HEAD, SPUR OF THE MOMENT IDEA

impropar, improper

improper,rly,rness, NOT PROPER/ ACCEPTABLE

impropuble, improbable

improve,*,ed,ving,er,ement,vable, vability, MAKE BETTER THAN

BEFORE, TOWARDS PERFECTION "prefixes: over/un"

improvise,*,ed,sing,er,sation,sational, sator,satorial, MAKE IT UP AS YOU GO, IMPROMPTU

improvusashen, improvise(sation)

impruf, improve

impte, empty

impulite, impolite

impulse,*,sion,sive,sively,siveness, SUDDEN ACT/MOVEMENT WITHOUT APPARENT THOUGHT

impurer, emperor

impurfekt, imperfect

impursenate, impersonate

impursonal, impersonal

impursonation, impersonate(tion)

impuseshen, impose(sition)

imput, input

imruld, emerald

imte, empty

imug, image

imugrant, immigrant / emigrant

imugrashen, immigrate(tion) / emigrate(tion)

imugrate, immigrate

imugrent, immigrant / emigrant

imuj, image

imun, immune

imunent, eminent / imminent / immanent

imunezashen, immunize(zation)

imunezation, immunize(zation)

imunise, immunize

imunity, immune(nity)

imunize, immunize

imurchen, immerse(sion)

imurgency, emergency

imursable, immersible

imurse, immerse / emersed

imurshen, immerse(sion)

imurtalety, immortal(ity)

imutashin, imitate(tion)

imutation, imitate(tion)

imuterial, immaterial

in, CONTAINED/BELONGS WITHIN, CONFINED,ENTER, PREFIX INDICATING "NOT" MOST OFTEN MODIFIES THE WORD (or see inn/ en)

in-law,*, PEOPLE RELATED BY MARRIAGE

inabel, enable / unable

inability,ties, UNABLE, NOT ABLE TO, WITHOUT CAPACITY TO

inabishen, inhibit(ion)

inable, enable / unable

inabler, enable(r)

inabul, enable / unable

inaccessible,bility,eness,ly, CANNOT BE OBTAINED, UNREACHABLE, NO ACCESS

inaccurate,ely,eness,acy,acies, NOT CORRECT/FACTUAL/ACCURATE

inacsesable, inaccessible

inact, enact

inaction,*, NO ACTION, IDLE

inactive,ely,eness,vity,vate, NO ACTION, IDLE (or see enact(ive))

inaculation, inoculate(tion)

inacurate, inaccurate

inadequate,ely,eness,acy,acies, NOT ENOUGH, INADEQUATE, LACKING

inadmissible,bility,bly, NOT ALLOWED TO ENTER, NOT ADMISSABLE

inadvertent,tly,nce,ncy,ncies, NOT PAYING ATTENTION, NOT DIRECT/ STRAIGHTFORWARD

inadvisable,bility, ADVISE/ RECOMMEND AGAINST, BEST NOT TO DO/SAY SOMETHING

inakd, enact

inakshen, inaction

inaktif, enact(ive) / inactive

inakulation, inoculate(tion)

inaleable, inalienable

inaleuble, inalienable

inalienable,ly,bility, CANNOT TAKE AWAY

inalisis, analysis

inamel, enamel

inamet, intimate

inamul, enamel

inanimate,ely,eness, NOT ANIMATE, USUALLY AN OBJECT WHICH DOESN'T ACT/MOVE

inaple, enable / unable

inappreciative,able,ably, NOT APPRECIATED, ACTIONS NOT REGARDED AS USEFUL/NECESSARY (also unappreciative)

inapproachable, NOT ACCESSIBLE/ APPROACHABLE, UNREACHABLE

inappropriate,ely,eness, NOT PROPER/ APPROPRIATE/ACCEPTABLE AT THE MOMENT

inapul, enable / unable

inaqulate, inoculate

inaqurite, inaccurate

inarferins, interfere(nce)

inasinse, innocence

inate, innate

inatequit, inadequate

inatible, inaudible

inatly, innate(ly)

inatmisable, inadmissible

inatvertense, inadvertent

inatvizable, inadvisable

inatvurtent, inadvertent

inaudible,ly,bility, NOT ABLE TO HEAR, NOT AUDIBLE, CAN'T BE HEARD

inaugurate,*,ed,ting,tion,tor,al, FORMALLY INSTALL/BEGIN, ADDRESS TO THE PUBLIC

inaukulate, inoculate

inbankment, embankment

inbaris, embarrass

inbark, embark

inbasee, embassy

inbed, embed

inberis, embarrass

inbet, embed

inblem, emblem

inblum, emblem

inboard,*, BOAT WITH MOTOR/ENGINE INSIDE

inbord, inboard

inbosd, emboss(ed)

inboss, emboss

inbrase, embrace

inbreo, embryo

inbrorder, embroider

incadesent, incandescent

incamped, encamp(ed)

incampment, encamp(ment)

incandescent,tly,nce, A BULB TYPE WITH A FILAMENT THAT HEATS UP, BRIGHT/SHINING LITE

incantashen, incantation

incantation,*,nal,tory, SPELLS/CHANTS FOR MAGIC

incapable,ly,eness,bility, NOT CAPABLE/ ABLE TO, DON'T HAVE WHAT IT TAKES TO ACCOMPLISH

incapacitate,*,ed,ting,tion, OUT OF ORDER, UNABLE TO FUNCTION AS USUAL, LACKING POWER TO

incapacity,ties, NOT ABLE EITHER PHYSICALLY/MENTALLY TO PERFORM TASKS WELL

incarcerate,*,ed,ting,tion, SENTENCED TO CONFINEMENT

incarnate,*,ed,ting,tion, TAKE ON PHYSICAL FORM "prefixes: re"

incarserate, incarcerate

incase, encase

incast, encase(d)

incendiary,ries, ABLE TO CREATE FIRE, CIVIL UNREST

incense,ed,sing, AROMATIC PRESSED POWDER FOR BURNING

incentive,*,vize,vizes,vized,vizing, A MOTIVATION FOR PERFORMING A TASK "prefixes: dis"

incenurate, incinerate

incepshen, incept(ion)

incept,tor,tion,tive,tively, FROM THE BEGINNING, MOMENT OF CREATION

incercl, encircle

incerense, insure(rance)

incerkl, encircle

incesant, incessant

incessant,ncy,tly, CONTINUE WITHOUT STOPPING

incest,tuous,tuously,tuousness, SEX AMONGST THE FAMILY IF RELATED BY BLOOD

inch,hes,hed,hing, A U.S. MEASUREMENT

inchant, enchant

inchantmint, enchant(ment)

incher, ensure / insure / injure

inchoy, enjoy

inchur, ensure / insure / injure

incide, incite/ inside

incident,*,nce,ntal,ntally, HAPPENING ATTACHED TO A LARGER EVENT, DISTINCT BUT SEEMINGLY MINOR

incindiary, incendiary

incinerate,*,ed,ting,tor,tion, TO BURN, COOKS TO ASHES WITH FIRE

incircle, encircle

incise,*,ed,sing,sor,sion, CUT/CARVE INTO

incision,*,nal,ned, MAKE A CUT INTO

incist, insist

incite,*,ed,ting,tation,ement,er, TO ROUSE/SPUR/PROVOKE TO ACT/ REBEL (or see inside/insight)

incline,*,ed,ning,nation, A GRADUALLY ELEVATED PLANE, TO GO UP, MOST LIKELY TO "prefixes: dis"

inclood, include

inclose, enclose

incloser, enclose(sure)

inclosment, enclose(ment)

inclozur, enclose(sure)

include,*,ed,ding,usion,usive,usively, usiveness,dible,dable, ADD/ INVOLVE SOMETHING INTO GROUP OF OTHER THINGS

inclusef, inclusive

inclushen, include(usion)

inclusion,*,ive, ADD/INVOLVE SOMETHING INTO GROUP OF OTHER THINGS

inclusive,ely,eness, ADD/INVOLVE SOMETHING INTO GROUP OF OTHER THINGS

incognedo, incognito

incognito,*, DISGUISED TO BE UNRECOGNIZABLE

incoherent,tly,nce,ncy,ncies, UNABLE TO COMPREHEND UNDERSTAND, CANNOT COMMUNICATE LOGICALLY/ UNDERSTANDABLE

incokneto, incognito

incomber, encumber

incombutent, incompetent

income,*,ming, MONEY COMING IN

incommode,*,ed,ding,dious,diously, DISTURB SOMEONE BY HAVING THEM CATER TO YOUR NEEDS UNNECESSARILY

incomode, incommode

incomodious, incommode(dious)

incomparable,bility,bly, NOTHING TO COMPARE TO

incompas, encompass

incompatible,bility,eness,ly, NOT ABLE TO GET ALONG WITH, TOO MANY DIFFERENCES

incompetent,tly,nce,ncy, NOT ABLE TO COMPETE/KEEP UP, LACKS QUALIFICATIONS

incomplete,*,ely,eness,etion, NOT COMPLETE, NEEDS MORE TO FINISH

incompruble, incomparable

inconclusive,ely,eness, NO FINAL RESULTS, NO CERTAIN ANSWERS

inconsiderate,ely,eness,tion,ably, ableness, NOT CONCERNED WITH SOMEONE'S EMOTIONAL REACTION OR WELL BEING

inconsistent,tly,ncy,ncies, DOESN'T PERFORM STEADILY/PREDICTABLY

incontinent,nce,tly, NOT ABLE TO CONTAIN/CONTROL ONESELF

inconvenient,tly,nce,ncy,ncies, DOESN'T FIT INTO THE PLAN CAUSING DELAY OF FINISHING, NOT ON THE WAY THERE, UNPLANNED

incorect, incorrect

incoriguble, incorrigible

incorporate,*,ed,ting,tion,tive,tor,able, TO INCLUDE INTO THE WORKINGS OF, BROUGHT INTO A LARGER BODY, UNITE, COMBINE "prefixes: dis/un"

incorrect,tly,tness, NOT EXACT/ FACTUAL/SUITABLE

incorrigible,ly,bility,eness, NOT ABLE TO BE CORRECTED/REFORMED TO MEET EXPECTED STANDARDS

incorugible, incorrigible

incounter, encounter

incownter, encounter

increase,*,ed,sing,singly,sable, TO MAKE MORE THAN THERE WAS, ADD MORE

incredible,ly,lity,eness, ASTONISHING, BEYOND EXPECTATION

incredulous,sly,sness, CROSS BETWEEN INCREDIBLE AND RIDICULOUS

incremenate, incriminate

increment,*,tal,tally, MOVE EXACT AMOUNT IN ONE DIRECTION, INCREASE

incriminate,*,ed,ting,tion, TO ACCUSE OR LEND SUSPICION, CHARGE WITH A CRIME

incroach, encroach

incrochment, encroach(ment)

incruments, increment(s)

incrust, encrust

incubate,*,ed,ting,tion,tional,tive,tor, TO PROTECT AN EGG IN PERFECT ENVIRONMENT FOR EMBRYO TO GROW INTO FULL FORM

incumbent,*,ntly,ncy,ncies, FILL A POST OR OFFICE

incumber, encumber

incumode, incommode

incumpatuble, incompatible

incunklusef, inconclusive

incunsideret, inconsiderate

incunsistent, inconsistent

incupasitate, incapacitate

incur,*,rred,rring,rrable, LIABLE FOR, ADDED DEBT IN ORIGINAL LOAN

incurable,ly,bility,eness, SEEMINGLY UNABLE TO CURE, EXTREMELY DIFFICULT TO HEAL

incureg, encourage / anchor(age)

incurekt, incorrect

incurig, encourage / anchor(age)

ind, and / end

indanger, endanger

indangurment, endanger(ment)

indanjer, endanger

indapendense, independent(nce)

indasishen, indecision

indau, endow

indaument, endow(ment)

indaveguel, individual

indavishual, individual

indebted,dness, OWE SOMETHING TO SOMEONE

indecent,ncy,ncies,ntly, NOT ACCEPTABLE BY SOCIETY'S STANDARDS

indecision, NOT ABLE TO BE FIRM IN MAKING A CHOICE

indecisive,eness,ely, NOT ABLE TO MAKE A FIRM CHOICE

inded, end(ed)

indeded, indebted

indedud, indebted

indeed, CERTAINLY, CONFIRMATION

indefer, endeavor

indeferent, indifferent

indefinite,ely,eness, WITH NO END OR FINAL GOAL, NOT DEFINED

indefur, endeavor

indefurent, indifferent

indego, indigo

indekat, indicate

indeks, index

indeleble, indelible

indelible,bility,ly, HARD TO REMOVE, NEARLY PERMANENT

indemafy, indemnify

indemic, endemic

indemnify,fies,fied,fying,fication,fier, COMPENSATE/REIMBURSE FOR LOSS

indent,*,ted,ting,tation, A DENT IN SOMETHING, DIFFERENT DEPTH FROM REST OF THE SURFACE

independent,*,tly,nce,ncy,ncies, ABLE TO STAND PRIMARILY ON ITS OWN, NOT DEPENDENT

inder, inter / enter

indermetant, intermittent

indesent, indecent

indeted, indebted

indever, endeavor

index,xes,dices,xed,xing,xical, TO CATEGORIZE, DIVIDE INTO GROUPS, PROVIDE A NAME FOR EASY RETRIEVAL "prefixes: sub"

indicate,*,ed,ting,tion,tive,tively,tor, tory, GIVE A SIGN TOWARDS A DIRECTION, PROVIDES INFORMATION, HELPS IN FIGURING ANSWER "prefixes: contra"

indicater, indicate(tor)

indict,*,ted,ting,table,ter,tor,tment, CHARGE WITH A CRIME ("C" IS SILENT)

indifferent,tly,nce, NOT PARTIAL OR CONCERNED WITH CHOICES/ACT/ EVENT

indifrent, indifferent

indigenous, ORIGINAL TO THE LAND, NATIVE

indigo,*, DEEP BLUE COLOR, COLOR FROM A PLANT

indikate, indicate

indimec, endemic

indintashen, indent(ation)

indirmetant, intermittent

indite, indict

individual,*,lly,lism,lity,lize,lities,ization, ate, ON ITS OWN, DOESN'T BELONG TO A GROUP

indlis, endless

indoctrinate,*,ed,ting,tion,tor, FORCED TEACHING PRINCIPLES/IDEOLOGY TO ELIMINATE CREATIVE THINKING

indoer, endure

indoor,*, INSIDE A STRUCTURE/ DWELLING

indoose, induce

indor, endure / indoor

indormetant, intermittent

indorse, endorse / indoor(s)

indorsment, endorse(ment)

indostry, industry

indou, endow

indoument, endow(ment)

indow, endow

indowment, endow(ment)

indrakit, intricate

indubitable,ly,bility, BEYOHND A DOUBT

inducate, indicate

induce,*,ed,cing,ement,er,cible, BRING ON, START/MAKE HAPPEN
induckshen, induct(ion)
inducktor, induct(or)
induct,*,ted,ting,tee,tance,tion,tional, tive,tively,tiveness,tor, ELECTRIC CURRENT CHANGE, BE ENLISTED, TERM IN PHYSICS/MILITARY/ EMBRYOLOGY/CHEMISTRY/ MATHEMATICS
indukshen, induct(ion)
induktor, induct(or)
indulge,*,ed,ging,gingly,ger,gence, gencies,gent,gently, TO AFFORD ONESELF A DESIRE, SATISFY AN IMPULSE "prefixes: over"
indur, inter / enter / endure
indurmitant, intermittent
induseshin, indecision
industrial,lly,list,lness,lism,lize,lized, lizing,lization, PRODUCTIVE, MANUFACTURES "prefixes: re"
industry,ries,rious,riously,rial, MACHINE/TECHNOLOGY/ MANUFACTURING "prefixes: re"
induvijual, individual
inebriate,*,ed,ting,tion,iety, DRUNK/ INTOXICATED
ineckwitable, inequitable
inecwity, inequity
inedible,ly, CANNOT OR SHOULD NOT EAT
inegma, enigma / enema
inekspensef, inexpensive
inekwality, inequality
inekwitable, inequitable
inekwity, inequity
inema, enema / anemia
inemut, intimate
inendashen, inundate(tion)
inendate, inundate
inengs, inning(s)
inept,tly,tness,titude, UNABLE, INCOMPETENT
inequality,ties, NOT EQUAL, DIFFERENCES EXIST
inequitable,ly,ty, NOT EQUAL, DIFFERENCES EXIST
inequity,ties, NOT FAIR/JUST/EQUAL
iner, inner / inter / enter
ineract, interact
inerchange, interchange
inercom, intercom
inerconnect, interconnect

inercors, intercourse
inerem, interim
inerferins, interfere(nce)
inerge, energy
inergetek, energetic
inerject, interject
inerjetek, energetic
inerkorse, intercourse
inerlock, interlock
inerlude, interlude
inermedeary, intermediary
inermingle, intermingle
inermishen, intermission
inermission, intermission
inermost, innermost
inernashenul, international
inernational, international
inernet, internet
inerrelate, interrelate
inersculastic, interscholastic
inersect, intersect
inersection, intersection
inerseksehn, intersection
inersperse, intersperse
inert,tly,tness, VISIBLY INACTIVE, NO APPARENT ACTION/MOVEMENT
inertwine, intertwine
inerupt, interrupt
inervene, intervene
inerview, interview
inervol, interval
inervue, interview
inervul, interval
inerwoven, interwoven
inescapable,ly,bility,bilities, CANNOT ESCAPE
inesent, innocence(nt)
inesheashen, initiate(tion)
ineshul, initial
inesince, innocence
inesthesia, anesthesia
inetiale, initial(lly)
inetuble, inedible
inetvizable, inadvisable
inevitable,bility,eness,ly, CANNOT AVOID
inexcesable, inaccessible
inexpensive,ely,eness, FAIR PRICE, NOT EXPENSIVE
inexperience,ed, DOESN'T HAVE SKILLS TO PERFORM
infachuashen, infatuate(tion)
infachuate, infatuate
infadek, emphatic

infallible,lity,eness,ly, FOR CERTAIN
infaluble, infallible
infant,*,ncy,ncies,thood,tlike, BABIES UP TO ONE YEAR OLD
infantry,ries,ymen, FOOT SOLDIERS
infasis, emphasis / emphasize
infatashen, invitation
infatik, emphatic
infatuate,ed,tion,edly, INSTANTLY ATTRACTED FOR BRIEF PERIOD OF TIME
infect,*,ted,ting,tion,tive,tor,tious, TO POLLUTE AN AREA "prefixes: dis/ retro"
infekshus, infect(ious)
infenatively, infinite(tively)
infent, infant
infentry, infantry
inferior,rity,rly,rity, LESSER THAN ANOTHER, NOT SUPERIOR
infermashen, inform(ation)
infermation, information
infermury, infirmary
infest,*,ed,ting,tation, THREATENINGLY OVERWHELM "prefixes: re"
infeureate, infuriate
infiltrate,*,ed,ting,tion,tive, PASS BEYOND BORDERS OF A SPACE WHERE UNINVITED
infinite,ely,eness,tude,tive,tival,tively,ty, ties, GOES ON AND ON PERHAPS FOREVER
infirmary,ries, SITE FOR MEDICAL CARE
infirmashen, information
infistructure, infrastructure
infite, invite
inflagingly, unflagging(ly)
inflame,*,ed,ming,er,mmable, mmability,mmation,mmatory, mmatorily, TO PROVOKE/INTENSIFY ANGER/STRONG EMOTIONS, SWOLLEN TISSUE
inflammation,*, SWOLLEN TISSUE
inflapable, unflappable
inflashen, inflate(tion)
inflate,*,ed,ting,tion,tionism,tionist, table, TO AIR UP, RAISE, EXPAND/ INCREASE "prefixes: dis"
inflection,*,nal,nally,nless, CHANGE IN FORM/SOUND/SHAPE
inflekshen, inflection
infleksuble, inflexible
inflemashen, inflammation
inflewance, influence

inflexible,bility,eness,ly, WON'T BEND, STUBBORN, NOT FLEXIBLE

inflextion, inflection

inflict,*,ted,ting,tion,tor,tive, TO CAUSE PAIN, TO BRING ABOUT PUNISHMENT

inflimation, inflammation

influence,*,ed,cing,eable,er,ntial,ntially, TO IMPRESS/EXERT UPON, ONE WHO IMPRESSES OTHERS, AUTHORITY, POSITION OF POWER

inform,*,med,ming,mation,mer,mative, matively,mativeness, matory,mant, OFFER ADVICE/FACTS "prefixes: dis/un"

informal,lly,lity, NOT FORMAL, RELAXED/UNRESTRICTED

informant,*, SOMEONE WHO PROVIDES INFORMATION TO HIGHER AUTHORITY

information,nal, COLLECTION OF DATA "prefixes: dis/mis"

inforse, enforce

infotation, invitation

infra, PREFIX INDICATING "BENEATH" MOST OFTEN MODIFIES THE WORD

infraction,*, BREAK A RULE/LAW/ CONTRACT

infrared, A LASER TYPE, A LEVEL OF FREQUENCY NEAR THE COLOR RED

infrastructure, SKELETAL/FOUNDATION OF

infrenge, infringe

infrenj, infringe

infrequent,tly,ncy, OCCASIONALLY

infringe,*,ed,ging,er,ement, UNLAWFULLY OCCUPY/ DISREGARD SOMEONE'S BOUNDARIES

infugen, infuse(sion)

infultrate, infiltrate

infunently, infinite(ly)

infunit, infinite

infunsy, infant(ncy)

infunt, infant

infuntry, infantry

infuriate,*,ed,ting,tingly,tion,ely, ENRAGE, FURIOUSLY ANGRY

infurmation, inform(ation)

infurmery, infirmary

infuse,*,ed,sing,sibility,sible,sive,er, LIQUID INTRODUCED/INJECTED INTO ANOTHER LIQUID

infustashen, infest(ation)

infustrukture, infrastructure

infutashen, invitation

ingage, engage

ingaje, engage

ingalate, ungulate

inganuity, ingenuity

ingection, inject(ion)

ingen, engine

ingeneer, engineer

ingenious,sly,sness, ESPECIALLY CREATIVE IN PERSPECTIVE/IDEAS (or see ingenuous) "prefixes: dis"

ingenuity,ties, ABLE TO USE CREATIVE IMAGINATION "prefixes: dis"

ingenuous,sly,sness, GENUINELY HONEST/DIRECT/NAIVE/ TRUSTING (or see ingenious) "prefixes: dis"

inger, injure

ingery, injure(ry)

ingest,*,ted,ting,tive,tion, TO SWALLOW, SWALLOWED THROUGH THE MOUTH

inginuity, ingenuity

ingoeuble, enjoy(able)

ingolf, engulf

ingot,*, MASS OR CHUNK OF METAL

ingoy, enjoy

ingrafe, engrave

ingrain,*,ned,ning, ROUTED INTO, CARVED INTO, DEEPLY IMPRESSED WITHIN

ingrave, engrave

ingredient,*, VARIETY OF ELEMENTS COMBINED TO MAKE SOMETHING ELSE

ingulate, ungulate

ingulf, engulf

ingun, engine

inguneer, engineer

ingury, injure(ry)

ingustes, injustice

inhabetent, inhabit(ant)

inhabit,*,ted,ting,tation,table,tant, tancy,tancies, TO OCCUPY, LIVE IN "prefixes: un"

inhalant,*, A DEVICE FOR BREATHING IN MEDICINE

inhalashin, inhale(lation)

inhale,*,ed,ling,lation,lational,er,lator, BREATH IN

inhanse, enhance

inharent, inherent

inharet, inherit

inharitance, inherit(ance)

inharmonic,ious,iously,iousness,icity, icities,ny, TONES NOT PEAKING TOGETHER, FREQUENCY NOT SYNCHRONIZED or see enharmonic)

inherent,tly, BELONGS AS PART OF THE WHOLE, INSEPARABLE

inherit,*,ted,ting,tor,tress,table,tability, tableness,tance, GOODS AND MONEY RECEIVED WHEN SOMEONE DIES "prefixes: dis"

inhewmane, inhumane

inhibit,*,ted,ting,tor,tory,tive,ter,tion, KEEP BACK/RESTRAINED, TIMID/ SLOW TO ACT "prefixes: dis/un"

inhormonic, inharmonic / enharmonic

inhosbitable, inhospitable

inhospitable,eness,ly,ality,alities, NOT TREATED WARMLY/ FRIENDLY/ GENEROUSLY

inhubeshen, inhibit(ion)

inhulashen, inhale(lation)

inhumane,ely, CRUEL

inigma, enigma / enema

inima, enema / anemia

inime, enemy / enema

inimet, intimate

inimutle, intimate(ly)

ining, inning

iniquity,ties,tous,tously,tousness, COMPLETELY LACKS MORALITY/ JUSTICE/FAIRNESS

inisheation, initiate(tion)

inishul, initial

initial,*,led,ling,lly,lize,lizes,lized,lizing, lizer,lism, ORIGINALLY, THE BEGINNING, THE FIRST

initiate,*,ed,ting,tion,tive,tor,tory, BREAK INTO NEW KNOWLEDGE, BEGIN SOMETHING NEW "prefixes: un"

inje, inch

inject,*,ted,ting,tion,table,tive,tor, INSERT SOMETHING INTO SOMETHING ELSE

injekshen, inject(ion)

injelate, ungulate

injen, engine

injeneer, engineer

injeneus, ingenious

injenuidy, ingenuity

injenuous, ingenuous

injenyus, ingenuous

injest, ingest

injin, engine

injineer, engineer
injoy, enjoy
injoymint, enjoy(ment)
injoyuble, enjoy(able)
injulate, ungulate
injun, engine
injunction,*, COURT ORDER TO ACT
injure,*,ed,ring,ry,rious,riously,
   riousness,rer, DAMAGE, OFFEND,
   VIOLATE ANOTHER'S RIGHTS
   "prefixes: un"
injustice,*, NOT PLAYING FAIRLY,
   SOMEONE'S RIGHTS VIOLATED
ink,*,king,ky,kier,kiest, FLUID USED IN A
   PEN
inkabuble, incapable
inkadesent, incandescent
inkamped, encamp(ed)
inkampment, encamp(ment)
inkantashen, incantation
inkantation, incantation
inkarsurate, incarcerate
inkase, encase
inkast, encase(d)
inker, incur
inkerej, encourage / anchor(age)
inkewbate, incubate
inkline, incline
inkling, A FEELING/HINT/IDEA
inklood, include
inkloshur, enclose(sure)
inkloze, enclose
inklud, include
inklusev, inclusive
inkognito, incognito
inkomber, encumber
inkomodeus, incommode(dious)
inkompruble, incomparable
inkompus, encompass
inkonsistent, inconsistent
inkoreg, encourage / anchor(age)
inkoreguble, incorrigible
inkorpurate, incorporate
inkownter, encounter
inkreduble, incredible
inkredulus, incredulous
inkreese, increase
inkroach, encroach
inkrochment, encroach(ment)
inkrument, increment
inkrust, encrust
inkum, income
inkumbent, incumbent
inkumber, encumber

inkumblete, incomplete
inkumodeus, incommode(dious)
inkumpatuble, incompatible
inkumplete, incomplete
inkumpus, encompass
inkunsiduret, inconsiderate
inkunvenyunt, inconvenient
inkupacity, incapacity
inkurect, incorrect
inkwesishun, inquisition
inkwesutev, inquisitive
inkwire, inquire(ry)
inkwisative, inquisitive
inland,der, AWAY FROM THE SEA
inlarge, enlarge
inlargmint, enlarge(ment)
inlarje, enlarge
inles, unless
inlest, enlist
inlet,*,ting, RECESS BETWEEN LAND/
   WATER, INSERTED
inlist, enlist
inliten, enlighten
inlund, inland
inmachure, immature
inmate,*, ONE CONFINED TO PRISON/
   JAIL
inmature, immature
inmertaledy, immortal(ity)
inmortalidy, immortal(ity)
inn,*, A DWELLING TO SLEEP FOR THE
   NIGHT
innacurate, inaccurate
innate,ely,eness, BELONGS WITH THE
   BODY
inner,rly, TOWARDS THE CENTER (or
   see inter)
innerchange, interchange
innerlock, interlock
innerlude, interlude
innermingle, intermingle
innermission, intermission
innermost, DIRECTLY IN THE CENTER
innernational, international
innernet, internet
innerscolastic, interscholastic
innertwine, intertwine
innervene, intervene
inning,*, A SECTION OF PLAY IN A
   GAME OF SPORTS
innocence,cy,cies,nt, FREE FROM
   ULTERIOR MOTIVES
innocent,tly, FREE FROM ULTERIOR
   MOTIVES

innovate,tive,tion,tor,tory, IMPROVE
   SYSTEM WITH NEW CREATIVE IDEA
   INSTILLING CHANGE
innuendo,*, UNOBVIOUS/INDIRECT
   HINT OR MEANING
inoberable, inoperable
inoburatef, inoperable(ative)
inocent, innocence(nt)
inocreate, inaugurate
inoculate,*,ed,ting,able,ability,ation,
   ative,ator,lum,ant, TO INJECT A
   PATHOGEN
inoduble, inaudible
inof, enough
inogerashen, inaugurate(tion)
inogerate, inaugurate
inogeration, inaugurate(tion)
inogurate, inaugurate
inokewlate, inoculate
inokewlent, inoculate(ant)
inokulation, inoculate(tion)
inonemus, anonymous
inonseate, enunciate
inoperable,bly,bility,bleness,ative,
   ativeness, WILL NOT OPERATE
inopportune,ely,eness,nity, NOT THE
   BEST TIME TO ENSURE SUCCESS
inopurtune, inopportune
inoqulashen, inoculate(tion)
inoqulent, inoculate(ant)
inordinate,acy,ely,eness, EXCESSIVE
   WITHOUT RESTRAINT/CONTROL
inordunet, inordinate
inorge, energy
inorgetek, energetic
inormis, enormous
inormus, enormous
inorsect, intersect
inosense, innocence
inotable, inaudible
inougeration, inaugurate(tion)
inovadef, innovate(tive)
inovative, innovate(tive)
inownse, announce
inpar, impair
inpashent, impatient
inpatient,*, VISITS HOSPITAL FOR
   TREATEMENT (or see impatient)
inpech, impeach
inpecuble, impeccable
inpersonashen, impersonate(tion)
inpersonate, impersonate
inplie, imply
inpolite, impolite

inpolse, impulse
inport, import
inportant, important
inpose, impose
inposebul, impossible
inposition, impose(sition)
inpossible, impossible
inposter, imposter
inpound, impound
inpoverish, impoverish
inpownd, impound
inpractical, impractical
inpragnuble, impregnable
inprasise, imprecise
inpravize, improvise
inprecise, imprecise
inpregnable, impregnable
inpregnate, impregnate
inpregnuble, impregnable
inprent, imprint
inpres, impress / empress
inpresion, impression
inpresive, impressive
inpreson, imprison
inprint, imprint
inprison, imprison
inprobuble, improbable
inpromptu, impromptu
inpromtu, impromptu
inpropable, improbable
inproper, improper
inprove, improve
inprovement, improve(ment)
inprovisation, improvise(sation)
inprovise, improvise
inprufment, improve(ment)
inpruve, improve
inpruvize, improvise
inpulse, impulse
inpulsive, impulse(sive)
input,*,tted,tting, ADD TO EXISTING
    INFORMATION
inquazishen, inquisition
inqubate, incubate
inquire,*,ed,ring,ringly,ry,ries,er, TO
    ASK OF, SEEK FURTHER
    INFORMATION
inquisition,nal,nist,tor, TAKE PEOPLE IN
    AGAINST THEIR WILL TO
    INTERROGATE THEM
inquisitive,ely,eness,tor, TO SEEK
    ANSWERS/KNOWLEDGE
inquisitor,rial,rially, TO INTERROGATE
inquizadive, inquisitive

inquizeshen, inquisition
inrage, enrage
inraj, enrage
inrech, enrich
inrich, enrich
inrol, enroll
inrolmint, enroll(ment)
inroot, enroute
inroute, enroute
inrut, enroute
insabordinate, insubordinate
insacure, insecure
insadent, incident
insafishent, insufficient
insakuredy, insecure(rity)
insalate, insulate
insalin, insulin
insane,ely,eness,nity,nities, THINK IN
    UNPOPULAR MODALITY, MENTAL
    HEALTH IN DOUBT
insanetation, insanitary(ation)
insanifekent, insignificant
insanitary,ation, UNCLEAN/
    UNACCEPTABLE
insarektion, insurrection
insatiable,ly,bility,eness,ate, APPETITE
    FOR SOMETHING THAT CANNOT BE
    SATIATED/SATISFIED
insatiate,ely,eness, APPETITE FOR
    SOMETHING THAT CANNOT BE
    SATIATED/SATISFIED
insawyuble, insoluble
insayuble, insoluble
insbarashen, inspire(ration)
insbekable, unspeakable
insboken, unspoken
insburashen, inspire(ration)
inscribe,*,ed,bing,bable,ber, LEAVE A
    MARK BY ANY METHOD
inscription,*,nal,nless,ive,ively,
    LEAVING A MARK BY MANY
    METHODS
inseam,*, SEAM ON THE INSIDE OF
    PANTLEGS
insebordinate, insubordinate
insect,*, BUGS (or see incest)
insecticide,*,dal, CHEMICALS TO KILL
    BUGS
insecure,ely,rity,rities,eness, ILL AT
    EASE, NOT SECURE/COMFORTABLE
    WITH ENVIRONMENT
insedent, incident
insedius, insidious
insefficient, insufficient

insegnea, insignia
insegnifakent, insignificant
insejen, incision
insekt, insect
insektaside, insecticide
insekurety, insecure(rity)
inselate, insulate
inselation, insulate(tion)
inseminate,*,ed,ting,tion, INJECT
    SEMEN INTO
insen, ensign
insenarade, incinerate
insendiary, incendiary
insenea, insignia
insense, incense
insenseer, insincere
insensible,ly,eness,bility,bilities, NOT
    MAKING SENSE TO PERCEIVER,
    MISUNDERSTOOD
insensitive,eness,vity,ely, DOESN'T
    EASILY REACT TO SENSORY INPUT
insentive, incentive
insentuf, incentive
insenuashen, insinuate(tion)
insenuate, insinuate
inseparable,bility,bly, WILL NOT BE
    DISJOINTED OR TAKEN APART
insepshen, incept(ion)
insept, incept
inseption, incept(ion)
inserekshen, insurrection
inserkle, encircle
insermountable, insurmountable
insert,*,ted,ting,ter,tion,tional, PLACE
    INTO ALREADY EXISTING FORM OR
    METHODOLOGY
inseshun, incision
insest, insist / incest / encyst
insestent, insist(ent)
insh, inch
insher, ensure / insure
insherance, insure(rance)
inshree, entry / entree
inshurans, insure(rance)
inshure, insure
insice, incise
insicor, incise(sor)
insicure, insecure
inside,*,er, INTERIOR OF A FORM (or
    see insight/incite)
insident, incident
insidious,sly,sness, ILL INTENT
    DETECTABLE, MANIPULATE TO

HARM WITHOUT BEING PERCEIVED AS SO

insidnea, insignia

insificient, insufficient

insigen, incision

insight,*,tful,tfully,tfulness, ABILITY TO PERCEIVE FUTURE OUTCOMES OF CURRENT EVENT (or see inside/incite)

insightation, incite(tation)

insightment, incite(ment)

insignia,*, BADGES/MEDALS OF HONOR/AUTHORITY IN MILITARY

insignificant,tly,nce, NOT SIGNIFICANT/WORTHY TO CALCULATE IN, NOT IMPORTANT

insiklopedea, encyclopedia

insimanation, inseminate(tion)

insime, enzyme

insin, ensign

insinarate, incinerate

insincere,ely,rity,rities, NOT SINCERE/TRUTHFUL

insinsative, insensitive

insinseer, insincere

insinsuble, insensible

insintuf, incentive

insinuate,*,ed,ting,tion,tive,tingly,tor, LEADING TOWARDS ACCUSATION, INDIRECTLY IMPLYING

insishen, incision

insisor, incise(sor)

insist,*,ted,ting,tingly,tent,tently,tence,tency, MUST HAVE/BE, ABSOLUTE (or see encyst)

insitation, incite(tation)

insite, inside / insight / incite

insiteful, insight(ful)

insitement, incite(ment)

insiteus, insidious

insition, incision

insize, incise

inskribe, inscribe

inskripshen, inscription

insoluble,bility,eness,bly, WILL NOT DISSOLVE IN LIQUID

insolvable, NOT ABLE TO BE SOLVED, NO ANSWER

insolvent,*,ncy, NOT ENOUGH FLUID CAPITAL TO GET OUT OF DEBT, CANNOT BE LIQUIDATED

insomnia,ac, PROBLEM SLEEPING

insovable, insolvable

insparation, inspire(ration)

inspect,*,ted,ting,tion,tive,tor,torate,toral,torial,torship, EXAMINE FOR FLAWS

inspekable, unspeakable

insperation, inspire(ration)

inspire,*,ed,ring,ringly,er,ration,rational,rator, EMPOWER, INSTILL FAITH/HOPE "prefixes: un"

inspoken, unspoken

instagate, instigate

install,*,lled,lling,llation,ller,llment, PUT SOMETHING/SOMEONE INTO A PLACE TO PERFORM A FUNCTION, MAKE A PAYMENT (or see instill) "prefixes: un"

instance,*,ed,cing, AN EXAMPLE/MOMENT

instant,tly,taneous, IN A WINK, RIGHT AWAY

instantaneous,sly,sness, HAPPENED SO QUICKLY THAT TIME COULDN'T BE MEASURED

instatushen, institute(tion)

instatute, institute

instaul, install

instaulment, install(ment)

instead, IN PLACE OF, A SUBSTITUTE

instegate, instigate

instenked, instinct

instense, instance

instentaneusly, instantaneous(ly)

instetution, institute(tion)

instigate,*,ed,ting,tion,tive,tor, PROVOKE, STIR UP, INITIATE AN ACTION

instill,*,lled,lling,llation, INTRODUCE GRADUALLY (or see install)

instinct,*,tual,tive,tively,tiveness, KNOWINGNESS WE'RE ALL BORN WITH

instinse, instance

instintaneusly, instantaneous(ly)

institute,*,ed,ting,er,tion,tive, ESTABLISH TO WORK AS A GROUP, FORMAL PLACE OF LEARNING

institution,*,nal,nalism,nalist,nally,nalize,nalizes,nalized,nalizing,nalization, FORMAL PLACE OF LEARNING

instol, install

instolashen, install(ation)

instolment, install(ment)

instrament, instrument

instriment, instrument

instruct,*,ted,ting,tor,tion,tional,tive,tively,tiveness, PROVIDE KNOWLEDGE TO/FOR OTHERS "prefixes: un"

instrument,*,tal,tally,talist,talism,tality,tation, AN ITEM WHICH MEASURES OR FUNCTIONS AS A DEVICE TO HELP WITH WORK, MUSICAL DEVICE "prefixes: bio"

instugate, instigate

instulation, install(ation) / instill(ation)

instunle, instant(ly)

instunlty, instant(ly)

instunt, instant

insubordinate,*,ely,tion, DOESN'T SUBMIT TO AUTHORITY

insucure, insecure

insue, ensue

insufficient,tly,ncy,ncies, NOT SUFFICIENT, NOT ENOUGH

insugnifakent, insignificant

insukurety, insecure(rity)

insulate,*,ed,ting,tion,tor, LAYER/COAT OF SOMETHING FOR PROTECTION/BARRIER

insulin, SECRETED BY A HORMONE IN THE BODY, A MANMADE CHEMICAL TO TREAT DIABETES "prefixes: pro"

insult,*,ted,ting,tingly,ter, AN ATTEMPT TO LOWER ANOTHER'S SELF ESTEEM

insunseer, insincere

insurcle, encircle

insure,*,ed,ring,er,rable,rability,rance, PROTECT AGAINST MONETARY/PROPERTY/JOB LOSS (or see ensure/assure) "prefixes: re/un/under"

insurekshen, insurrection

insurens, insure(rance)

insurkle, encircle

insurmountable,ly, CANNOT BE ACHIEVED/OVERCOME

insurrection,nary,naries,nism,nal,nally, REVOLT AGAINST FIGURES OF AUTHORITY

insurshen, insert(ion)

insurt, insert

insyklopedia, encyclopedia

insyme, enzyme

intact,tness, NOT AFFECTED BY A POTENTIALLY DAMAGING EVENT

intaferance, interfere(rance)

intagral, integral

intagrate, integrate

intagration, integrate(tion)

intail, entail

intak, intact / intake

intake, A TUBE/DEVICE WHICH TAKES IN FLUID/AIR FOR MECHANICS (or see intact)

intale, entail

intalect, intellect

intalectual, intellect(ual)

intamit, intimate

intangible,*,bility,eness,ly, NOT REAL/ PHYSICAL

intarier, interior / anterior

intatee, entity

intecate, indicate

integer,*, TERM IN MUSIC AND MATH

integral,*,lly,lity, IMPORTANT PART OF THE WHOLE

integrate,*,ed,ting,ability,tion,tionist, tive,tor, INCLUDE INTO THE WHOLE, MAKE A PART OF A WHOLE "prefixes: dis"

integrity,ties, SOUND PRINCIPLES, HONORABLE

inteligible, intelligible

intellect,*,tion,tive,tual,tually,tuality, tualism,tualize, ABILITY FOR MENTAL COMPREHENSION

intelligent,tly,nce,er, LEVEL OF ABILITY TO PERFORM COMPLEX REASONING "prefixes: un"

intelligible,bility,ly, NOT UNDERSTANDABLE "prefixes: un"

intelugeble, intelligible

intenation, intonate(tion)

intend,*,ded,ding,der,dment, APPARENT GOAL (or see intent)

intense,ely,eness,sity,sities,sive,sively, sify,sifier,sification, FIRM/ FORWARD/ KEEN/VIGOROUS/ EXTREME

intenshin, intent(ion)

intent,*,tly,tness,tion,tional,tionally, tioned,tionality, THOUGHTFULLY PLAN COURSE OF ACTION "prefixes: un"

inter,*,rred,rring, TO BURY, PREFIX INDICATING "BETWEEN/AMONG" MOST OFTEN MODIFIES THE WORD (or see enter/intra)

interact,*,ted,ting,tion,tions,tional, tionism,tionist,tionists,tive,tively,

tivity, EXCHANGE BETWEEN TWO/ MORE THINGS (or see enter)

interagate, interrogate

intercede,*,ed,ding,er, MEDIATE/ FACILITATE

intercept,*,ted,ting,ter,tion,tive, PASS BETWEEN/THROUGH A LINE/ OBSTRUCT A LINEAR ACTION

interchange,*,ed,ging,eability,eable, eableness,eably, EXCHANGE/ ALTERNATE BETWEEN/WITH

intercom, INTERCOMMUNICATION SYSTEM/COMMUNICATE BY MICROPHONE

interconnect,*,ted,ting,tion,tedness, tible, TO CONNECT BETWEEN TWO SOURCES

intercourse, INTERCHANGE OF FEELINGS/THOUGHTS, COPULATION

interdisciplinary,rity,rian, WHEN ALL FIELDS/SYSTEMS ARE INTERCONNECTED/ COMMUNICATING

interest,*,ted,tedly,ting,tingly, ATTENTIVENESS TO LEARN SOMETHING NEW, LENDERS COLLECT THIS "prefixes: dis/un"

interfere,*,ed,ring,ringly,er,ence,ential, TO INTERCEPT BETWEEN ONGOING EXCHANGE, PRESENCE OF SLOWS PROGRESS

interim, A TEMPORARY PAUSE IN AN ONGOING PROJECT

interior,*,rity,rly,rize,rizes,rized,rizing, rization, INSIDE A STRUCTURE (or see anterior)

interject,*,ted,ting,tion,tory,torily, INTERRUPT WITH INFORMATION

interlock,*,ked,king,ker, CHAINLIKE, ONE ENMESHED WITH ANOTHER, PART OF ONE MECHANISM EMBEDDED INTO THE OTHER

interlude,*,dial, PAUSE DURING A PERFORMANCE/ACTIVITY

intermediary,ries, FACILITATOR/ AMBASSADOR/AGENT WHO AIDS COMMUNICATION BETWEEN GROUPS

intermediate,*,ed,ting,tion,tor,ary, HELPS WITH COMMUNICATION BETWEEN PEOPLE/GROUPS "prefixes: dis"

intermetant, intermittent

intermingle,*,ed,ling,ement, MINGLE TOGETHER, INTERTWINED

intermission,*,ive, A BREAK BETWEEN EVENTS/ACTIVITY/PERFORMANCE

intermittent,nce,tly, STOPPING/ STARTING WITH PAUSES IN BETWEEN

intern,*,nship,nist,nment, A STUDENT PRACTICING UNDER SUPERVISION, SOMETHING CONFINED DURING WAR

internal,lly,lize,lization,lity, INSIDE A FORM/BODY

international,lity,lly,lism,list,lize,lization, OUTSIDE NATIONAL BOUNDARIES

internet, A COMPUTER WEB WHICH NETS BETWEEN COMPUTERS ALL OVER THE WORLD

interoj, entourage

interpherens, interfere(nce)

interpret,*,ted,ting,tability,table,ter, tive,tively,tation, REVIEW FACTS FOR FURTHER CLARIFICATION, BRING ABOUT THE MEANING OF

interpretation,nal, ACT OF REVIEWING FACTS FOR FURTHER CLARIFICATION

interprise, enterprise

interrelate,tion,tionship, TO RELATE THINGS TOGETHER, SECURE COMMON GROUND BETWEEN TWO THINGS

interrogate,*,ed,ting,tion,tional,tive, tively,tor,tory,tories, TRANSMIT A SIGNAL FOR SETTING OFF AN APPROPRIATE RESPONSE, INTENSE QUESTIONING BY AUTHORITIES

interrupt,*,ted,ting,tion,ter,tive, HINDER THE PROGRESS OF MOMENTARILY "prefixes: un"

interscholastic,*, ACTIVITIES BETWEEN SCHOOLS

intersect,*,ted,ting,tion,tive, POINT WHERE TWO LINE CRISSCROSS, PLACE WHERE OPPOSING LINES CROSS

intersection,*,nal, POINT WHERE TWO LINE CRISSCROSS, PLACE WHERE OPPOSING LINES CROSS

intersperse,*,ed,edly,sing,sion, TO SCATTER, BEING SCATTERED ABOUT

interstate,*, HIWAYS BETWEEN STATES, ROADS CONNECTING STATES

intertane, entertain

intertanment, entertain(ment)

intertwine,*,ed,ning,ningly,ement, WEAVE TOGETHER

interupt, interrupt

interval,*, A PAUSE OR GAP BETWEEN

intervene,*,ed,ning,ner,ntion,ntionist, ntionism, TO INTERFERE, GET BETWEEN

interview,*,wed,wing,wer,wee, QUESTIONING PERSON FOR QUALIFICATIONS OR ANSWERS

interwoven, INTERTWINED, BRAIDED TOGETHER

intestine,*,nal,nally, ORGAN INSIDE BODY WHERE FOOD IS PROCESSED

intety, entity

intever, endeavor

inthooseastik, enthuse(siastic)

inthooziazm, enthuse(siasm)

inthrall, enthrall

inthroll, enthrall

inthuseastek, enthuse(siastic)

inthusiasm, enthuse(siasm)

inticate, indicate

intication, indicate(tion)

intidle, entitle

intiger, integer

intigo, indigo

intil, until

intimadate, intimidate

intimate,ely,er,tion, CLOSE/BONDING, MAKE KNOWN

intimidate,*,ed,ting,tion,tor, ATTEMPT TO LOWER SOMEONE'S SELF ESTEEM/CONFIDENCE BY APPEARING GREATER THAN THEM

intinse, intense

intinshen, intent(ion)

intire, entire

intirle, entire(ly)

intirlee, entire(ly)

intirmediate, intermediate

intirmitant, intermittent

intirsept, intercept

intirty, entire(ty)

intise, entice

intite, entity

intitle, entitle

intlis, endless

into, ENTER TO THE INSIDE

intoishen, intuit(ion)

intolerable,eness,ly,bility,ance,ant,antly, WILL NOT TOLERATE, NOT ABLE TO DEAL WITH

intonate,*,ed,ting,tion,tional,er, ACCENT ON CERTAIN WORDS WHICH AFFECT MEANING

intormident, intermittent

intorse, endorse / indoor(s)

intortane, entertain

intourage, entourage

intoxicate,*,ed,edly,ting,tingly,ant,tion, DRUNK FROM ALCOHOL, INEBRIATED, HIGH WITH EXCITEMENT "prefixes: dis"

intra, PREFIX INDICATING "INSIDE/ WITHIN" MOST OFTEN MODIFIES THE WORD (or see inter)

intradukshen, introduce(ction)

intraduse, introduce

intrakit, intricate

intramural,lly, EVENTS HAPPENING WITHIN, SCHOOL SPORTS

intrance, entrance

intranet,*, A WEB OF NETWORKING WITHIN A CLOSED/RESTRICTED COMPUTER SYSTEM

intraspect, introspect

intravenous,sly, INJECTING FLUID INTO VEINS

intrees, entry(ries) / entree

intrege, intrigue

intrense, entrance

intrensic, intrinsic

intres, entry(ries) / entree

intrest, interest / entrust

intricate,ely,eness,acy,acies, OF THE TINIEST DETAIL

intridukshen, introduce(ction)

intrigue,*,ed,uing,uingly,er, DEEPLY INTERESTED, CAPTIVATED

intrinsic,cal,cally,calness, ABSOLUTELY IMPORTANT, ESSENTIAL, CANNOT DO WITHOUT IT

intro, PREFIX INDICATING "INSIDE/ WITHIN" MOST OFTEN MODIFIES THE WORD (or see inter)

introduce,*,ed,cing,er,ction,ctory,ctive, ctorily, ACQUAINTING PEOPLE TOGETHER, PRESENT SOMETHING

introduse, introduce

introspect,tion,tional,tive,tively, tiveness, TO GO WITHIN FOR KNOWLEDGE AND ANSWERS

introst, interest / entrust

introvert,*,ted,rsion, SOMEONE WHO SPENDS MOST OF THEIR TIME WITH THEMSELVES, DOESN'T SEEK THE OUTSIDE WORLD FOR ANSWERS

intrude,*,ed,ding,er,usion,usive, ENTER WITHOUT INVITATION, FISSURES FILLED WITH MOLTEN LAVA

intrukit, intricate

intrumural, intramural

intrunse, entrance

intrusion, ENTER WITHOUT INVITATION, ROCK FORM

intrusive,ely,eness, ENTER WITHOUT INVITATION

intrust, entrust / interest

intry, entry / entree

intuative, intuit(ive)

intueshen, intuit(ion)

intufer, interfere

intuger, integer

intugrate, integrate

intuishen, intuit(ion)

intuit,tion,tional,tionism,tionalism, tionist,tive,tively,tiveness, A KNOWINGNESS WE ARE ALL BORN WITH, CAN SEE OUR OWN FUTURE

intunate, intonate

intur, enter / inter

inturage, entourage

inturauj, entourage

inturmedeate, intermediate

inturmetant, intermittent

inturn, intern

inturnalize, internal(ize)

inturnil, internal

inturoj, entourage

inturpret, interpret

inturpretation, interpretation

inturprise, enterprise

intursede, intercede

intursept, intercept

inturtane, entertain

inturtaner, entertain(er)

inturtanment, entertain(ment)

intutes, entity(ties)

intwoet, intuit(ive)

intyre, entire

inubelidy, inability

inubishen, inhibit(tion)

inucent, innocence(nt)

inuendo, innuendo

inuf, enough

inuindo, innuendo

inume, enemy

inunciate, enunciate

inundate,*,ed,ting,tion, OVERWHELMED, OVERFLOWING, OVER ABUNDANCE
inunseade, enunciate
inupresheative, inappreciative
inuprochible, inapproachable
inupropreut, inappropriate
inur, inner
inuract, interact
inurcom, intercom
inurelate, interrelate
inurem, interim
inurge, energy
inurjetek, energetic
inurlock, interlock
inurlude, interlude
inurmediary, intermediary
inurmingle, intermingle
inurmission, intermission
inurmost, innermost
inurnashenul, international
inurnet, internet
inursculastic, interscholastic
inursection, intersection
inursperse, intersperse
inurt, inert
inurtwine, intertwine
inurupt, interrupt
inurval, interval
inurvene, intervene
inurvue, interview
inurwoven, interwoven
inuscapable, inescapable
inusense, innocence
inuvate, innovate
invade,*,ed,ding,er,asion,asive, OVERWHELM A TERRITORY OR PEOPLES BY UNWELCOME OCCUPATION, ENEMY WHO ENTERS TO OCCUPY A SYSTEM
invaginate,*,ed,ting,tion,tions, MEDICAL TERM INVOLVING FOLDING
invajenation, invaginate(tion)
invalid,dly,dity,date,dation,dator,dism, NOT VALID/LEGAL, VOIDED, A PERSON INCAPABLE OF FUNCTIONING NORMALLY
invalope, envelope
invaluable,ly,eness, WORTH MORE THAN CAN BE BOUGHT FOR, MOST VALUABLE
invariable,ly,bility,eness, CONSTANT, NEVER CHANGING

invashen, invasion
invashenate, invaginate
invasion,*,nary, ATTEMPT TO CONQUER IN A HOSTILE MANNER, HOSTILE OVERTHROW
invasive,ely,eness, HOSTILE TAKEOVER
invatation, invitation
invate, invade
inved, envy(vied)
invee, envy
invegorate, invigorate
invelop, envelope
invensable, invincible
invenshen, invent(ion)
invent,*,ted,ting,tion,tor,tible,tive, tively,tiveness, CREATION FROM THOUGHT "prefixes: dis/re"
inventory,ries,ried,rying, A CATALOG/ LIST OF GOODS
inverdebrate, invertebrate
inveriably, invariable(ly)
inverse,*,ely,sion,sive,rt, SWITCH AROUND, MAKE OPPOSITE, INSIDE OUT
inversion,*,ive, SWITCH AROUND, MAKE OPPOSITE, INSIDE OUT
invert,*,ed,tibility,tible,ter,rsion,rsive, SWITCH AROUND, MAKE OPPOSITE, INSIDE OUT
invertebrate,*, HAS NO SPINE/ BACKBONE
inves, envy(vies)
invesible, invisible
invest,*,ted,ting,tment, PUT TIME/ MONEY INTO SOMETHING/ PROJECT "prefixes: dis/re"
investigate,*,ed,ting,tion,tive,tor,tory, SEARCH FOR CLUES/ANSWERS/ SIGNS
investmunt, invest(ment)
invetation, invitation
inveuble, enviable
inveus, envious
invezible, invisible
invigorate,*,ed,ting,tingly,tion,tive, tively,ant,er, BRING EXCITEMENT TO, RENEW
invilope, envelope
invincible,eness,ly,bility, NOT ABLE TO CONQUER/PENETRATE
invintory, inventory
invious, envious
invirenment, environment
invirunmental, environment(al)

invisability, invisible(bility)
invisible,ly,eness,bility, NOT PERCEIVABLE, CANNOT SEE/FEEL
invitation,*,nal, ASKED TO COME TO AN EVENT, WELCOME TO VISIT
invite,*,ed,ting,tingly,tingness,ee,tor, tation,tatory, ASKED TO COME TO AN EVENT, WELCOME TO VISIT, OFFER PLEASURE "prefixes: dis/un"
invoice,*,ed,cing, A DETAILED BILL DUE AND OWING
involope, envelope
involuntary,rily,riness, DID NOT VOLUNTEER
involve,*,ed,ving,ement,er, BE CAUGHT UP IN, INTERACTING WITH, OBLIGATE TIME/THOUGHT "prefixes: un"
invotashen, invitation
invoyce, invoice
invulid, invalid
invurdabrae, invertebrate
invurt, invert
invy, envy
inward,*,dly,dness, FACING TOWARDS THE INSIDE, ON IN SIDE
inword, inward
inwrech, enrich
inwroll, enroll
inzyme, enzyme
iodine, A CHEMICAL ELEMENT
ion,*,nize,nizes,nized,nizing,nizer, nization,nizable, ATOM/PARTICLE WITH A CHARGE "prefixes: inter"
ionesfer, ionosphere
ionesphere, ionosphere
ionisfere, ionosphere
ionosphere,ric, A PROTECTIVE LAYER SURROUNDING THE EARTH ABOVE 43 MILES, HOLES MADE IN IT WITH ROCKETS CREATE OZONE DEPLETION
iquevocate, equivocate
iquivocate, equivocate
iqwantense, acquaintance
ir, PREFIX INDICATING "NOT" MOST OFTEN MODIFIES THE WORD
irabrochuble, irreproachable
iradebul, irritable
iradek, erratic / erotic
iradekate, eradicate
iradesent, iridescent
iradiate, irradiate
iradic, erratic / erotic

iradubel, irritable
iradukashen, eradicate(tion)
iragardles, irregardless
iragashen, irrigate(tion)
iragate, irrigate
iraguardless, irregardless
iraknid, arachnid
iranment, arraign(ment)
irant, errant
iraplasible, irreplaceable
iraproachable, irreproachable
irasbonsuble, irresponsible
irase, erase
iraser, eraser
irashenul, irrational
irasistible, irresistible
iraspective, irrespective
iraspektif, irrespective
irasponsuble, irresponsible
iratable, irritable
iratant, irritant
iratashen, irritate(tion)
iratate, irritate
iratation, irritate(tion)
irate,ely,eness, ANGRY
iratent, irritant
iratic, erratic / erotic
irational, irrational
iratrevible, irretrievable
iratuble, irritable
iraudik, erratic / erotic
iravokuble, irrevocable
iraze, erase
irazer, eraser
irazistuble, irresistible
irchin, urchin
irebrochuble, irreproachable
iredescent, iridescent
iredesent, iridescent
iredubel, irritable
iregardless, irregardless
iregashen, irrigate(tion)
iregate, irrigate
iregation, irrigate(tion)
iregeuler, irregular
iregeuleredy, irregular(ity)
iregewler, irregular
ireglur, irregular
ireguardless, irregardless
iregular, irregular
ireguleredy, irregular(ity)
irekshen, erect(ion)
irekt, erect
irelavense, irrelevant(nce)

irelevant, irrelevant
irelevense, irrelevant(nce)
ireluvense, irrelevant(nce)
ireluvint, irrelevant
iren, iron
ireny, irony
ireperuble, irreparable
irepirable, irreparable
ireproachable, irreproachable
ireprochible, irreproachable
irepruble, irreparable
irepurable, irreparable
ires, iris
iresbonsuble, irresponsible
iresistible, irresistible
irespective, irrespective
irespektif, irrespective
iresponsuble, irresponsible
iretant, irritant
iretashen, irritate(tion)
iretate, irritate
iretibul, irritable
iretreavible, irretrievable
iretrievable, irretrievable
irevocable, irrevocable
irg, urge
irgint, urge(nt)
iribrochuble, irreproachable
irid, PREFIX INDICATING "IRIS/
    RAINBOW" MOST OFTEN MODIFIES
    THE WORD
iridescent,tly,nce, A LIGHT REFLECTION
    WITH RAINBOW COLORS
irifd, arrive(d)
iriful, arrive(val)
irigardles, irregardless
irigashen, irrigate(tion)
irigate, irrigate
irigation, irrigate(tion)
iriplasible, irreplaceable
iris, PART OF THE EYE, A FLOWER
irisbonsuble, irresponsible
irisistible, irresistible
irispective, irrespective
irispektif, irrespective
irisponsuble, irresponsible
iritable, irritable
iritashen, irritate(tion)
iritate, irritate
iritation, irritate(tion)
iritrevible, irretrievable
irivokuble, irrevocable
irizisduble, irresistible
irj, urge

irk,*,ked,king, ANNOYING
irn, earn / urn / iron
irnd, earn(ed) / iron(ed)
irnest, earnest
irochun, erosion
irode, erode
irodinamic, aerodynamic
irodynamic, aerodynamic
irogate, irrigate
iron,*,ned,ning, A METAL, A TOOL FOR
    TAKING WRINKLES OUT OF
    CLOTHES/ TOOL FOR GOLF/
    SMOOTH OUT WRINKLES
irone, irony
ironic,cal,cally,ny,calness, OPPOSITE TO
    WHAT YOU WOULD EXPECT
irony,nies, ODDLY COINCIDENTAL
irosbonsuble, irresponsible
irosef, erosive
iroshin, erosion
irosif, erosive
irosponsuble, irresponsible
irote, erode
irovokuble, irrevocable
irowze, arouse
irradescent, iridescent
irradiate,*,ed,ting,tion,tor,ant,
    ILLUMINATE, EXPOSE TO
    RADIATION
irragate, irrigate
irragation, irrigate(tion)
irrant, errant
irraplasible, irreplaceable
irraproachable, irreproachable
irratable, irritable
irratant, irritant
irratate, irritate
irrate, irate
irratic, erratic
irrational,lity,lness,lly,lism,list,listic,
    NOT RATIONAL, NOT ABLE TO
    PROVE RATIONALE
irredescent, iridescent
irregardless, NOT REGARDED, ASIDE
    FROM THAT
irregate, irrigate
irregation, irrigate(tion)
irregular,*,rly,rity, NOT REGULAR
irrelavent, irrelevant
irrelevant,ntly,nce,ncy, NOT RELEVANT,
    DOES NOT PERTAIN TO
irrepairable, irreparable
irreparable,ly,eness,bility, CANNOT BE
    REPAIRED

irreplaceable,ly,eness,bility, NOT ABLE TO BE REPLACED

irreproachable,ly,eness,bility, NOT ABLE TO BE APPROACHED, UNBLEMISHED

irresistible,ly,eness,bility, NOT ABLE TO RESIST

irrespective,ely, NOT TO BE CONSIDERED IN THE EQUATION/CIRCUMSTANCE/EVENT

irresponsible,ly,eness,bility, NOT RESPONSIBLE

irretrievable,ly,eness,bility, NOT ABLE TO BE

irrevocable,ly,eness,bility, NOT REVERSIBLE, CANNOT BE UNDONE/CHANGED

irridescent, iridescent

irrigate,*,ed,ting,tion,tional,tive,tor, METHOD OF PROVIDING WATER TO "prefixes: sub"

irriplasible, irreplaceable

irritable,ly,eness,bility, ANNOY/AGGRAVATE/STIMULATE, INFLAMMED TISSUE

irritant,*,ncy,ncies, SOMETHING THAT IRRITATES

irritate,*,ed,ting,tion,tive,tingly,tor, ANNOY/AGGRAVATE/STIMULATE, INFLAMMED TISSUE

irrogate, irrigate

irrugation, irrigate(tion)

irruplacable, irreplaceable

irrupt,*,ted,ting,tion,tive,tively, SUDDENLY/FORCIBLY INVADE/ENTER (or see erupt)

irth, earth

irubshen, erupt(ion) / irrupt(ion)

irubt, erupt / irrupt

irubtif, erupt(ive) / irrupt(ive)

irudebul, irritable

irudibul, irritable

irugardles, irregardless

irugashen, irrigate(tion)

irugate, irrigate

irugation, irrigate(tion)

iruguardless, irregardless

irune, irony

iruplaseble, irreplaceable

iruprochuble, irreproachable

irupshen, erupt(ion) / irrupt(ion)

irupt, erupt / irrupt

iruptif, erupt(ive) / irrupt(ive)

iruption, erupt(ion) / irrupt(ion)

irus, iris

irusbonsuble, irresponsible

irusistible, irresistible

iruspective, irrespective

iruspektif, irrespective

irusponsuble, irresponsible

irutashen, irritate(tion)

irutate, irritate

irutation, irritate(tion)

irutrevible, irretrievable

irutrievable, irretrievable

irutuble, irritable

iruvokuble, irrevocable

iruzistuble, irresistible

is, THIRD PERSON SINGULAR, PRESENT IN TIME, PREFIX INDICATING "EQUAL" MOST OFTEN MODIFIES THE WORD (or see ease/eye(s))

isalashen, isolate(tion)

isalation, isolate(tion)

isay, essay

isbeshalee, especially

isbeshulee, especially

iscape, escape

isdeem, esteem

ise, ice / icy / eye(s)

iselate, isolate

iselation, isolate(tion)

isense, essence

isenshil, essential

isential, essential

ishew, issue

ishu, issue

ishuense, issue(uance)

isier, icy(cier)

isikle, icicle

isilate, isolate

isilation, isolate(tion)

ising, icing

isinshul, essential

iskape, escape

iskort, escort

island,*,der, BODY OF LAND SURROUNDED BY WATER, ONE WHO LIVES ON AN ISLAND "prefixes: inter"

ism,*, A SUFFIX WHICH MEANS A SYSTEM OF PRINCIPLES, A PRACTICE

isn't, CONTRACTION OF THE WORDS 'IS NOT'

iso, PREFIX INDICATING "EQUAL" MOST OFTEN MODIFIES THE WORD

isofigus, esophagus

isolashen, isolate(tion)

isolate,*,ed,ting,tion,tionism,tionist, TO PREVENT HAVING CONTACT WITH ANOTHER THING

isoteric, esoteric

ispeshalee, especially

ispeshulee, especially

issuanse, issue(uance)

issue,*,ed,uing,er,uance,uable, DISTRIBUTE/HAND OUT INFORMATION, POINT OF MATTER "prefixes: un"

issuence, issue(uance)

istablish, establish

istablush, establish

isteem, esteem

istrologe, astrology

isuance, issue(uance)

isue, issue

isuinse, issue(uance)

isulashen, isolate(tion)

isulate, isolate

isulation, isolate(tion)

it,*, PRONOUN REFERRING TO PERSON/PLACE/THING/TIME/EVENT (or see eat/ate/eight)

it'll, CONTRACTION OF THE WORDS 'IT WILL'

it's, CONTRACTION OF THE WORDS 'IT IS'

itach, attach

itak, attack

italic,*,cize,cized,cizing,cization, SLANTED STYLE OF PRINT TO ATTRACT ATTENTION

italisize, italic(ize)

itch,hes,hed,hing,hy,hiness, DESIRE TO SCRATCH, A NEED TO SATISFY (or see etch)

item,*,mize,mizer,mization, ARTICLE/UNIT IN A COLLECTION, AN OBJECT

itenarary, itinerary

itenerate, itinerate

iteosy, idiocy

iternul, eternal

iteut, idiot

itinerary,ries,ate,ation, LIST OF DETAILS PERTAINING TO A TRIP

itinerate,*,ed,ting,ration,ary, LIST OF DETAILS PERTAINING TO A TRIP

itl, it'll / idle / idol

its, it's

itself, ONE ON ITS OWN

itsetera, etcetera

itul, idol / idle / it'll

itum, item
itumize, item(ize)
iturnal, eternal
iu, ewe / you / yew
iudine, iodine
iul, i'll
iun, ion
iunizur, ion(izer)
iurn, iron
ivacuate, evacuate
ivade, evade
ivakuashen, evacuate(tion)
ivakuate, evacuate
ivaluashen, evaluate(tion)
ivaluate, evaluate
ivant, event
ivaparate, evaporate
ivaporate, evaporate
ive, ivy
ivent, event
ivoke, evoke
ivolution, evolution
ivolve, evolve
ivory, A BONE OR HORN FROM
MAMMALS
ivow, avow
ivry, ivory
ivy,vies,vied, A PLANT
ixagerate, exaggerate
ixajurate, exaggerate
ixamunashen, examine(nation)
ixblanatory, explanatory
ixempt, exempt
ixemshen, exempt(ion)
ixequtif, executive
ixitment, excite(ment)
ixkershen, excursion
ixklude, exclude
ixklute, exclude
ixkurjen, excursion
ixkus, excuse
ixost, exhaust
ixperiense, experience
ixpire, expire
ixplanatory, explanatory
ixplisitly, explicit(ly)
ixploet, exploit
ixseluratur, accelerate(tor)
izbeshulee, especially
izenshil, essential
izkape, escape
izkort, escort
izoteric, esoteric
iztablish, establish

izteem, esteem
jab,*,bbed,bbing, TO POKE, PUNCH (or
see gab)
jabber,*,red,ring,ry, TALKS VERY FAST
jaber, jabber
jac, jack
jack,*,ked,king,ker, TO STEAL, TO
RAISE/LIFT, A GAME, PREFIX
INDICATING "MALE/LARGE/HEAVY"
MOST OFTEN MODIFIES THE WORD
jackass,sses, MALE DONKEY
jacket,*,ted,tless, A COVERING,
PROTECTIVE COAT
jacks,ses, TOOLS FOR HOLDING UP
CARS, A GAME FOR KIDS
jacs, jacks
jad, jade
jade,*,ed,edly,edness, LACK OF
ENTHUSIASM/INTEREST RESULTING
FROM TOO MUCH OF SOMETHING,
A PRECIOUS STONE
jag,*,gged,gging,gger,gless, UNEVEN
CUTS, POKE/STAB/SPREE
jail,*, BUILDING WHERE PEOPLE WHO
BREAK LAWS ARE CONFINED
jak, jack
jaket, jacket
jaks, jacks
jale, jail / jelly
jaly, july / jelly
jam,*, FRUIT SPREAD, BEING STUCK (or
see jamb)
jamb,*, HOLDS A STABLE OPENING FOR
A DOOR (or see jam)
janedic, genetic
janewery, january
janitor,*,tial, A CUSTODIAN, SOMEONE
WHO SEES TO CLEANING/
MAINTENANCE OF PUBLIC
BUILDING
january, A MONTH OF THE YEAR
(ENGLISH)
januery, january
janyuery, january
jar,*,rred,rring, STARTLE SOMEONE,
GLASS CONTAINER WITH A LID
jargon,*, A DIALECT, THE WAY A
LANGUAGE IS SPOKEN
jas, jazz
jasture, gesture
jau, jaw
jaundice,ed, AN UNHEALTHY BODY
CONDITION
jauns, jounce

jaunt,*, SPONTANEOUS/BRIEF
JOURNEY
jaus, joust / jaw(s)
jaust, joust
java, COMPUTER SOFTWARE, COFFEE
BEVERAGE
jaw,*, PART OF THE MOUTH
jawalk, jaywalk
jawolk, jaywalk
jaywalk,*,ked,king,ker, CROSSING A
STREET AT AN INAPPROPRIATE
PLACE
jazz,zes,zed,zing,zy, TYPE OF MUSIC, TO
MODERNIZE
jealous,sy,sness,sly,sies, EMOTION
WHICH ERUPTS WHEN ONE IS
INSECURE/FEARFUL
jean,*, THICK FABRIC USED FOR PANTS
(or see gene)
jeaneul, genial
jeauluge, geology
jeb, gibe / jib / jibe
jebalashen, jubilant(ation)
jeburish, gibber(ish)
jech, jig / gig
jeens, jean(s) / gene(s)
jefe, jiffy
jegle, jiggle
jegsaw, jigsaw
jelatin, gelatin
jelatnus, gelatin(ous)
jele, jelly
jeli, july / jelly
jelis, jealous
jeliten, gelatin
jell,*,led,ling,ly,lify, CONSISTENCY
BETWEEN LIQUID AND SOLID, A
GELATIN (or see gel)
jello, A BRAND NAME FOR 'GEL', A
GELATIN
jelly,llies,llied,llying,llify,llifying,llified,
FRUIT SPREAD, SEMI SOLID
SUBSTANCE
jeluten, gelatin
jely, july / jelly
jem, gem / gym
jemmy, jimmy
jemnaseum, gymnasium
jemnast, gymnast
jen, gene / jean
jenarashin, generation
jenarate, generate
jenarator, generator
jenarus, generous

jenaside, genocide
jendur, gender
jene, genie
jeneal, genial
jeneol, genial
jenerik, generic
jenerul, general
jenerus, generous
jenetic, genetics
jeneus, genius
jengle, jingle
jengur, ginger
jenicide, genocide
jenks, jinx
jenome, genome
jenrul, general
jens, jean(s) / gene(s)
jenter, gender
jentul, gentle
jentur, gender
jenuen, genuine
jenul, gentle
jenurulize, general(ize)
jenus, genus
jenyus, genius
jeografy, geography
jeological, geology(gical)
jeometry, geometry
jeopardy,dize,dizes,dized,dizing, GREAT RISK OF DANGER IF NOT SKILLFUL ENOUGH
jep, gyp
jepardy, jeopardy
jeperdize, jeopardy(dize)
jepsee, gypsy
jepsum, gypsum
jerbul, gerbil
jeresdikshen, jurisdiction
jerk,*,ked,king,kily,kiness,ky, QUICK MOTION/JOLT
jerky, DRIED MEAT
jermanate, germinate
jernal, journal
jernalist, journal(ist)
jerney, journey
jeror, juror
jery, jury
jest,ter,ting,tingly, IN FUN, TO MAKE LIGHT OF
jesture, gesture
jet,*,ted,ting,ty, A PLANE, A ROCK, TYPE OF STREAM ACTION (or see get)
jete, jetty
jeti, jetty

jetsam, WASTE/ITEMS ELIMINATED FROM A JET
jetty,ties, PIER/STRUCTURE AT AN OCEAN SHORE
jety, jetty
jeulogical, geology(gical)
jewbalee, jubilee
jewdeshul, judicial
jewdishes, judicious
jewel,*,lry,ler, DECORATIVE ORNAMENTS FOR THE BODY (or see joule)
jewly, july
jewn, june
jewse, juice
jewt, jute
jewvinile, juvenile
jib,*,bed,bing,ber, SAIL OF A BOAT, ARM OF A CRANE (or see jibe/gibe)
jibe,*,ed,bing, SAILING TERM, CONFORM, SHIFT (or see gibe)
jife, jiffy
jiffy, DONE FAST
jifi, jiffy
jig,*,ged,ging,ger, A DANCE, FISHING/ TOOLING DEVICE, TEMPLATE (or see gig) "prefixes: re"
jigantic, gigantic
jigger, A TOOL, THING THAT DOESN'T HAVE A NAME "A THING AMA JIGGER", MEASURING DEVICE
jiggle,*,ed,ling,ly, ACTION LIKE JELLO IN MOTION, DANCE MOVEMENT (or see giggle)
jigsaw,*,wed,wing, A CUTTING TOOL, A PUZZLE
jilatnus, gelatin(ous)
jilt,*,ted,ting,ter, REJECT SOMEONE'S AFFECTION
jily, july / jelly
jim, gem / gym / him
jimmy,mies,mied,ying, FORCE A LOCK TO OPEN
jimnaseum, gymnasium
jimnast, gymnast
jinarashin, generation
jinarate, generate
jinarator, generator
jinarulize, general(ize)
jinarus, generous
jinch, hinge
jind, hint / hind
jinder, gender / hinder
jindrens, hindrance

jindur, gender / hinder
jinerik, generic
jinetic, genetics
jinger, ginger
jingle,*,ed,ling,ly, BELL SOUNDS, BRIEF, CATCHY TUNE
jinks, jinx
jinocide, genocide
jinrul, general
jint, hint
jinter, gender
jintul, gentle
jinuen, genuine
jinurulize, general(ize)
jinus, genus
jinuside, genocide
jinusist, genesis
jinx,xes,xed, SOMETHING THAT CAUSES BAD LUCK
jiolugee, geology
jiometry, geometry
jip, gyp
jipse, gypsy
jipsum, gypsum
jirate, gyrate
jirble, gerbil
jirm, germ
jirmanate, germinate
jirney, journey
jirnul, journal
jirnulist, journal(ist)
jirur, juror
jiry, jury
jitter,*,red,ring,ry, BRIEF BURSTS OF SHAKING OR JIGGLING, A DANCE, FEARFUL REACTION
jive,*,ed,ving, A RHYTHM STYLE OF MUSIC AND ALL ASSOCIATED WITH IT, MISLEADING/PHONY
job,*,bless,blessness, WORKING CONSISTENTLY FOR INCOME
jock,*, SOMEONE WHO FOCUSES PRIMARILY ON SPORTS IN SCHOOL
jockey,*,yed,ying, RIDER IN HORSE RACING, METAPHOR FOR GETTING INTO POSITION TO WIN
joe, joy
joen, join
joent, joint / join(ed) / jaunt
joest, joist
jofeul, jovial
jog,*,ged,ging,ger, TYPE OF RUNNING
jogur, jog(gger)

join,*,ned,ning,nable,ner, BRING TWO OR MORE INDEPENDENT THINGS/ GROUPS TOGETHER IN UNION "prefixes: con/dis/en/re/sub/un"

joint,*,ted,ting, WHERE PARTS INTERSECT, JUNCTION "prefixes: con/dis/un"

joist,*, HORIZONTAL/PARALLEL BOARDS IN A STRUCTURE/ FOUNDATION

jok, jock / joke

joke,*,ed,king,kingly,er,ester, COMMENT/STORY INTENDED TO GENERATE LAUGHTER (or see jock)

joky, jockey

jol, joule / jewel

jole, jolly

jolly,lier,liest,lity, MERRY, LIVELY, GAY

jolt,*,ted,ting,ty, A SUDDEN HARSH ACTION

joly, jolly

jonc, junk

jonci, junkie

jondis, jaundice

jongal, jungle

jongul, jungle

jonk, junk

jonke, junkie

jonki, junkie

jont, jaunt / join(ed) / joint

jooly, july

joon, june

joot, jute

jop, job

jore, jury

jori, jury

jornul, journal

josel, jostle

josh,hing,her, TEASING WITH GOOD HUMOR

jostle,*,ed,ling,ement,er, TO PUSH/ JUMBLE/SHOVE/ BUMP/COLLIDE IN A CROWDED SITUATION

josul, jostle

jot,*,ted,ting, QUICKLY WRITE SOMETHING DOWN, WRITE A QUICK NOTE

jouel, jowl / joule

joule,*, A METHOD OF MEASURING (or see jewel)

jounce,*,ed,cing, TO BOUNCE AROUND

journal,*,lize,lizes,lized,lizing,lizer,lism, lization,list, AN ITEMIZED ACCOUNT OF AN EVENT OR SPAN OF TIME

journalist,*,tic,tically,ize,ism, ONE WHO DOCUMENTS/RECOUNTS AN EVENT OR SPAN OF TIME

journey,*,yed,ying, TO TRAVEL OR TAKE A TRIP

joust,*,ted,ting,ter, MEDIEVAL COMBAT

jovial,lity,lness,lly, JOLLY, GOOD CHEER/ HUMOR

jow, jaw

jowl,*,led, THE JAW, FISH HEAD (or see joule)

jownse, jounce

joy,yful,yfully,yfulness,yous,yously, yousness, A PLEASURABLE STATE OF BEING, HARMONIC "prefixes: en/over"

joyes, joy(ous)

joyesly, joy(ously)

joyfil, joy(ful)

joyis, joy(ous)

joyn, join

joynd, joint / join(ed)

joynt, joint / join(ed)

joyst, joist

joyusness, joy(ousness)

jubalashen, jubilant(ation)

jubilant,tly,lance,lancy,ation,ate,atory, EXHULTANT/TRIUMPHANT/FESTIVE

jubilee,*, A ROWDY/FESTIVE CELEBRATION NORMALLY HONORING A TIMESPAN

juce, juice / juicy

judeshal, judicial

judeshus, judicious

judge,*,ed,ging,gment,gmental, gmentally, MAKING A DECISION BASED ON KNOWN INFORMATION "prefixes: mis/pre"

judicial,lly,ary, ACTS/ADMINISTRATION OF JUDGING

judicious,sly,sness, BEHAVING IN A JUDGEMENTAL FASHION

judo, SELF-DEFENSE SPORT

juel, joule / jewel

jug,*,gged,gging,gful, A LARGE CONTAINER FOR FLUIDS/LIQUID (or see judge)

juge, jug / judge

juggle,*,ed,ling,er, KEEP OBJECTS AFLOAT IN THE AIR SIMULTANEOUSLY

jugil, juggle

jugment, judge(ment)

juice,*,ed,er,cy,cier,ciest,eless, LIQUID FROM FRUIT

juicy,cier,ciest, EDIBLE FOOD LADEN WITH MOISTURE

juj, judge

jujment, judge(ment)

jul, joule / jewel

july, A MONTH OF THE YEAR (ENGLISH)

jumble,*,ed,ling, TO MIX TOGETHER WITHOUT ORDER

jump,*,ped,ping,py,piness,per, TO TAKE TO THE AIR FOR NANOSECONDS TO DEFY GRAVITY

junc, junk

juncer, junk(er)

junction,*,nal, PLACE WHERE THINGS MEET, TIME/PLACE INTERCHANGE "prefixes: dis/sub"

juncture,*, ONE POINT WHERE THINGS OR THOUGHTS MEET, PLACE FOR EXCHANGE

june, A MONTH OF THE YEAR (ENGLISH)

jungle,*,led,ly, PLACE WHERE PLANTS/ ANIMALS ARE ABUNDANT/FREE FROM HUMAN RESTRAINT

junior,*, A CLASS LEVEL IN SCHOOL, THE MALE OFFSPRING OF A FATHER

junk,ked,king,ky,ker,kie, OBJECTS CONSIDERED TO BE OF NO VALUE

junke, junkie

junkie,*, PERSON WITH HABITUAL DRUG PROBLEM

junkshen, junction

junksher, juncture

junky, junkie

junyer, junior

juol, jewel / joule

juometree, geometry

jurasdiction, jurisdiction

jurbel, gerbil

jure, jury

juresdiction, jurisdiction

jurisdiction,nal,nally, AN AREA/RANGE CONTROLLED BY PARTICULAR ENTITIES

jurk, jerk

jurky, jerky

jurm, germ

jurmenate, germinate

jurnal, journal

jurney, journey

jurni, journey

jurnil, journal

jurnilist, journal(ist)

jurnul, journal

juror,*, MEMBER OF A GROUP WHO SITS IN COURT AND JUDGES A DEFENDANT

jurusdikshen, jurisdiction

jury,ries,ried,ror,rist, A GROUP WHO SIT IN COURT AND JUDGES A DEFENDANT

jusd, just

jusdes, justice

jusdifiable, justifiable

jusdify, justify

jusdufecation, justify(fication)

juse, juice / juicy

juser, juice(r)

just,tly,tness, WHAT IS RIGHT BY SOCIAL NORMS "prefixes: un"

justefiable, justifiable

justefication, justify(fication)

justes, justice

justice,*,eless,elike,ciable,ciability, ONE WHO IS EMPLOYED BY THE GOVERNMNENT TO MAKE LAWFUL DECISIONS "prefixes: in"

justifiable,bility,bleness,ly, DEFENDS THAT THE ACTION REFLECTS THE CAUSE "prefixes: un"

justify,fies,fied,fying,fyingly,fier,fication, ficative,ficatory, DEFEND REACTIONS, ARGUE IN DEFENSE OF ACTION/ THOUGHT "prefixes: un"

jusy, juice(cy)

jut,*,tted,tting, STICKS OUT (or see jute)

jute, PLANT FIBER FOR WEAVING AND BRAIDING

juto, judo

juvenile,*,lism,lity, A YOUTH, IMMATURE

juxta, PREFIX INDICATING "NEAR/ CLOSE" MOST OFTEN MODIFIES THE WORD

kabduve, captive

kaben, cabin

kabenet, cabinet

kaberay, cabaret

kabich, cabbage

kabige, cabbage

kabin, cabin

kabinet, cabinet

kable, cable

kabnet, cabinet

kabnit, cabinet

kaboose, caboose

kabsher, capture

kabsul, capsule

kabten, captain

kabture, capture

kabul, cable

kabunet, cabinet

kabuse, caboose

kacdus, cactus

kach, catch / cache / cash

kacher, catcher / cashier

kackel, cackle

kacl, cackle

kactus, cactus

kadagore, category

kadagorize, categorize

kadagory, category

kadagurize, categorize

kadal, cattle

kadalize, catalyst(yze)

kadavir, cadaver

kade, caddy

kadecism, catechism

kadegore, category

kadegurize, categorize

kadekism, catechism

kadence, cadence

kadet, cadet

kadigore, category

kadigurize, categorize

kadikism, catechism

kadil, cattle

kadilist, catalyst

kadilog, catalog

kadinse, cadence

kadl, cattle

kadugore, category

kadugorize, categorize

kadugory, category

kadugurize, categorize

kadul, cattle

kadulist, catalyst

kadulize, catalyst(yze)

kadulog, catalog

kadur, cater

kaduract, cataract

kady, caddy

kaf, calf / cave

kafa, cafe

kafanated, caffeine(nated)

kafatirea, cafeteria

kafe, cafe / coffee

kafene, caffeine

kafetirea, cafeteria

kafi, coffee

kafinated, caffeine(nated)

kafine, caffeine

kafiterea, cafeteria

kafiteria, cafeteria

kafs, calves / cave(s)

kafunated, caffeine(nated)

kage, cage

kagol, cajole

kahoot, cahoot

kahute, cahoot

kail, kale

kainker, chancre / canker

kairful, careful

kaje, cage

kajole, cajole

kajuol, casual

kajwul, casual

kak, caulk / calk / cake / cock

kakd, cake(d)

kake, cake / khaki

kakil, cackle

kakoon, cocoon

kakt, cake(d)

kaktis, cactus

kakul, cackle

kakulashun, calculate(tion)

kakulation, calculate(tion)

kaky, khaki

kal, kale / call

kalamity, calamity

kalcefy, calcify

kalceum, calcium

kalculashun, calculate(tion)

kalculate, calculate

kalculus, calculus

kale, AN EDIBLE PLANT

kalebrate, calibrate

kaleidoscope,*,pic,pical,pically, COLORFUL VIEWING OBJECT

kalek, colic

kalender, calendar / calender / colander

kalentur, calendar / calender / colander

kalepur, caliper / caliber

kaler, collar / call(er)

kales, callous / callus

kalesdenics, calisthenics

kalesterol, cholesterol

kalesthenics, calisthenics

kaliber, caliber

kalibrate, calibrate

kalide, collide

kalidoscope, kaleidoscope

kaliflower, cauliflower

kalindula, calendula
kalindur, calendar / calender / colander
kalintur, calendar
kalipur, caliper
kalir, collar / call(er)
kalire, calorie
kalis, callous / callus
kalisdenics, calisthenics
kalisthenics, calisthenics
kalk, calk / caulk
kalkewlashun, calculate(tion)
kalkewlate, calculate
kalkewlus, calculus
kalkilate, calculate
kalkulate, calculate
kalkulus, calculus
kalobrate, calibrate
kalokweul, colloquial
kalon, cologne / colon
kaloneil, colonial
kaloquial, colloquial
kalore, calorie
kalostemy, colostomy
kalqulus, calculus
kalsafy, calcify
kalseum, calcium
kalsufy, calcify
kaluber, caliber
kalubrate, calibrate
kaluper, caliper
kalury, calorie
kalus, callous / callus
kalusdenics, calisthenics
kalusthinics, calisthenics
kalvs, calves
kam, came
kamb, camp
kamend, commend
kamenduble, commendable
kamfer, camphor
kamil, camel
kaminduble, commendable
kamofloje, camouflage
kamp, camp
kampane, campaign
kampus, campus
kamru, camera
kamu, comma
kamul, camel
kamunecate, communicate
kamunety, community
kamute, commute
kancer, cancer / chancre / canker
kanded, candid

kandidat, candidate
kandil, candle
kandy, candy
kane, cane
kanebul, cannibal
kanebulize, cannibal(ize)
kaneon, canyon
kanepy, canopy
kanery, canary / cannery
kanesiology, kinesis(iology)
kanesis, kinesis
kangaroo,*, LARGE MARSUPIAL
   ANIMAL
kangrues, congruous
kanibul, cannibal
kanibus, cannabis
kanikanik, kinnikinnick
kanin, cannon / canine
kaniry, cannery / canary
kanister, canister
kanker, chancre / canker
kanon, cannon
kanopy, canopy
kanselashin, cancellation
kanseld, cancel(lled)
kansilashun, cancellation
kansild, cancel(lled)
kansir, cancer
kansul, cancel
kansulashen, cancellation
kansult, cancel(lled)
kant, can't
kantalope, cantaloupe
kantankerus, cantankerous
kanted, candid
kanteen, canteen
kantelope, cantaloupe
kantiguis, contiguous
kantina, cantina
kantir, canter
kantrovert, controvert
kantulope, cantaloupe
kantur, canter
kanubelize, cannibal(ize)
kanubis, cannabis
kanuster, canister
kanves, canvas / canvass
kanvus, canvas / canvass
kanyun, canyon
kaos, chaos
kap, cap / cape
kapabul, capable
kapasety, capacity
kapdivate, captivate

kape, cap / cape
kapechulate, capitulate
kapedul, capital / capitol
kapedulism, capitalism
kapelary, capillary
kapetate, capitate
kapetul, capital / capitol
kapetulesm, capitalism
kapibilety, capability
kapibul, capable
kapilary, capillary
kapitulate, capitulate
kapoot, kaput
kapshun, caption
kapsil, capsule
kapsize, capsize
kapsul, capsule
kaptin, captain
kaption, caption
kaptuf, captive
kaptun, captain
kaptuvate, captivate
kapubilety, capability
kapubul, capable
kapulery, capillary
kaput, DIED, PASSED OUT, FELL OVER
   DEAD
kaputate, capitate
kapzize, capsize
kar, car
karacter, character
karaoke, GAME WHERE SONGS
   WITHOUT WORDS ARE SUNG TO
karat,*, A MEASUREMENT FOR GEMS
   AND GOLD (or see karate/carrot/
   carat/caret)
karate, MARTIAL ART FORM (or see
   karat)
karbin, carbon
karbinete, carbonate
karbon, carbon
karburator, carburetor
kard, card / care(d) / cart
kardboard, cardboard
kardeac, cardiac
kardenul, cardinal
kardilege, cartilage
kardnul, cardinal
kare, carry / care
karebu, caribou
karecatshure, caricature
karecter, character
kareer, career
karefree, carefree

karekteriz, character(ize)
kareless, careless
kareng, care(ring)
kareoke, karaoke
karer, career
kares, care(s) / caress
karet, carat /caret / carrot / karat
kareur, carrier
karevan, caravan
karf, carve
karfl, careful
karfre, carefree
karful, careful
kargo, cargo
karib, carob
kariboo, caribou
karisma, charisma
karit, carat / caret / carrot / karat
karkes, carcass
karkus, carcass
karlis, careless
karma, A BELIEF
karmil, caramel
karmu, karma
karmul, caramel
karnashun, carnation
karnevul, carnival
karnivore, carnivore
karob, carob
karoburate, corroborate
karode, corrode
karogen, corrode(osion)
karoke, karaoke
karosef, corrode(osive)
karosene, kerosene
karote, karate
karouse, carouse
karows, carouse
karpenter, carpenter
karpet, carpet
karpinder, carpenter
karpit, carpet
kars, care(s) / car(s)
karsenugen, carcinogen
karsinugin, carcinogen
kart, cart
kartoon, cartoon
kartreg, cartridge
kartrig, cartridge
kartuleg, cartilage
kartune, cartoon
karudge, carriage
karukter, character
karul, carol

karusen, kerosene
karv, carve
kary, carry
kasadilla, quesadilla
kascade, cascade
kase, case
kasedeya, quesadilla
kaseno, casino
kaset, cassette
kash, cash / cache
kashen, caution
kasher, cashier
kashes(ly), cautious(ly)
kashmer, cashmere
kashosly, cautious(ly)
kashu, cashew
kashual, casual
kasine, casino
kasing, casing
kasiroll, casserole
kask, cask
kaskera, cascara
kasket, casket
kast, cast / caste
kastrate, castrate
kasudilla, quesadilla
kasul, castle
kat, cat
kata, PREFIX INDICATING "APART/
    DOWN" MOST OFTEN MODIFIES
    THE WORD
katagorize, categorize
katagory, category
katalize, catalyst(yze)
katch, cache / cash / catch
katecism, catechism
kategore, category
kategurize, categorize
katekisom, catechism
katel, cattle
katelog, catalog
katepiler, caterpillar
katepult, catapult
kater, cater
kateract, cataract
katigore, category
katigurize, categorize
katikism, catechism
katl, cattle
katugory, category
katukism, catechism
katul, cattle
katulist, catalyst
katulize, catalyst(yze)

katulog, catalog
katupiler, caterpillar
katupult, catapult
katurakt, cataract
kau, cow
kauchen, caution
kaudej, cottage
kaufe, coffee / cough
kaugorize, categorize
kauk, caulk / calk / cake / cock
kaul, call / cowl
kauleg, college
kaumu, comma
kaunasure, connoisseur
kauncekwently, consequent(ly)
kaunsaquently, consequent(ly)
kaunsuquenshul, consequent(ial)
kaunvex, convex
kausd, cause(d) / cost
kaushas, cautious
kaushen, caution
kaushon, caution
kaushos, cautious
kaut, caught / cot
kav, cave
kava, BEVERAGE FROM PLANT
kavety, cavity
kavilry, cavalry
kavirn, cavern
kavity, cavity
kavs, calves / cave(s)
kavude, cavity
kavulree, cavalry
kavurn, cavern
kawcus, caucus
kawshun, caution
kawshus, cautious
kawt, caught / cot
kayak,*,ker,king, CANOE-LIKE BOAT
kayen, cayenne
kaynine, canine
kayos, chaos
kaysadilla, quesadilla
kazadilla, quesadilla
kazual, casual
kazudilla, quesadilla
ke, key
kech, catch
kechen, kitchen
kechup, ketchup / catsup
ked, key(ed) / kid
kednapur, kidnap(pper)
kedny, kidney
kedul, kettle

kedy, kitty

keel,*,led,ling,less, FALL OVER, STRUCTURAL PART OF A BOAT

keen,nly,nness,ner, SHARP IN SENSES, VERY AWARE

keep,*,per,ping,pable, HOLD ONTO, WITHHOLD FROM SOMEONE, POSSESS "prefixes: up"

kek, kick

kel, kill / keel / kale

keld, kill(ed) / kelt

kell, kill

keln, kiln

kelo, kilo

kelokweul, colloquial

keloquial, colloquial

kelowatt, kilowatt

kelp, WATER PLANT

kelt, celt / kilt / kill(ed)

kelur, kill(er)

kemakol, chemical

kemecol, chemical

kemest, chemist

kemestri, chemistry

kemicol, chemical

kemist, chemist

kemistri, chemistry

kemokol, chemical

kemostry, chemistry

kemotherupy, chemotherapy

kemukol, chemical

kemustri, chemistry

ken, kin / keen / can

kendergarden, kindergarten

kendling, kindle(ling)

kendom, kingdom

kendred, kind(red)

kendul, kindle

kendurgarden, kindergarten

kenel, kennel

kenesiology, kinesis(iology)

kenesis, kinesis

keng, king / kink

kengdom, kingdom

kenikkanik, kinnikinnick

kenk, king / kink

kenly, keen(ly)

kennel,*,led,ling, FENCING/HOUSING FOR ANIMALS "prefixes: un"

kenol, kennel

kensum, consume

kentend, contend

kentenual, continue(ual)

kentling, kindle(ling)

kentred, kind(red)

kenturgarden, kindergarten

kenul, kennel

keosk, kiosk

keper, kipper

kepsize, capsize

kepur, kipper

ker, care

kerab, carob

keracter, character

keral, choral / coral / corral / chorale

keraoky, karaoke

kerat, carat / caret / carrot / karat

keravan, caravan

kerb, curb

kerd, curd

kerdeus, courteous

kerdul, curdle

kere, care / carry

kereb, carob

kerekt, correct

kerekturiz, character(ize)

kereoke, karaoke

keret, carat / caret / carrot / karat

kerf, curve

kerfle, careful / careful(lly)

kerfri, carefree

kerfue, curfew

kerful, careful

kerfule, careful(lly)

keri, carry

kerib, carob

kericuture, caricature

kerier, carrier

kerige, carriage / courage

kerikulum, curriculum

kerioke, karaoke

kerisel, carousel

kerisen, kerosene

kerit, carat / caret / carrot / karat

kerivan, caravan

kerl, curl

kerles, careless

kernal, colonel / kernel

kernel,*,ly, SMALL BITS/SECTIONS OF CORN COB/NUTS/SEEDS (or see colonel)

kernul, colonel / kernel

kerob, carob

keroberate, corroborate

kerol, carol

kerosell, carousel

kerosene, TYPE OF FUEL

kerot, carat / caret / carrot / karat

keroty, karate

kerp, curb

kersanthimum, chrysanthemum

kersash, corsage

kerse, curse / care(s)

kersive, cursive

kersoch, corsage

kersoje, corsage

kersuf, cursive

kertale, curtail

kertin, curtain

kertsy, curtsy

kertul, curdle

keruge, courage

kerunsy, currency

kerunt, currant / current

kerupt, corrupt

kerusel, carousel

kerusen, kerosene

kerut, caret / carrot / karat

keruvan, caravan

kerve, curve

kervicher, curvature

kervuchure, curvature

kery, curry / carry

kes, kiss

kesng, kiss(ing)

kest, kiss(ed) / cist

ket, kid / kit / kite

ketal, kettle

ketch, catch

ketchen, kitchen

ketcher, catcher

ketchup, TOMATO BASED CONDIMENT (also catsup)

keten, kitten

ketny, kidney

kets, kid(s) / kit(s) / kite(s)

kettle,*, LARGE IRON POT, METAL VESSEL WITH ROUNDED BOTTOM AND WIDE TOP

ketul, kettle

kety, kitty

keurader, curator

kew, cue

kewdos, kudos

kewe, kiwi

kewk, cook

kewth, couth

key,*,yed,ying, TOOL TO UNLOCK SOMETHING, IMPORTANT INFORMATION TO UNLOCK A MYSTERY

keylo, kilo

keyosk, kiosk
keysadilla, quesadilla
keysudeya, quesadilla
khaki,*, A TYPE OF COTTON PANT, A COLOR
ki, key
kiak, kayak
kian, cayenne
kibuse, caboose
kic, kick
kichen, kitchen
kick,*,ked,king,ker, STRIKE SOMETHING WITH FRONT OF FOOT
kid,*,ddy,dder,dding,ddingly,ddishness, dlike, YOUNG CHILD/ANIMAL, JOKING(or see kite/kit)
kiddy, kitty
kiden, kitten
kidnap,*,pped,pping,pper, ONE WHO STEALS AWAY WITH SOMEONE
kidnaper, kidnap(pper)
kidney,*, ORGANS IN THE BODY
kidny, kidney
kidur, kid(dder)
kidy, kid(ddy) / kitty
kigole, cajole
kijole, cajole
kik, kick
kil, kill / keel
kild, kill(ed) / kilt / keel(ed)
kiler, kill(er)
kill,*,led,ler,ling, TAKE LIFE AWAY FROM "prefixes: over"
kiln,*, A SPECIAL OVEN WHICH EXCEEDS 1,000°
kilo, PREFIX INDICATING "THOUSAND" MOST OFTEN MODIFIES THE WORD
kiloge, collage
kilokweul, colloquial
kiloneul, colonial
kiloquial, colloquial
kilor, kill(er)
kilosil, colossal
kilostomy, colostomy
kilowatt, ELECTRICAL MEASUREMENT
kilt,*, SKIRT OF SCOTTISH DESCENT (or see kill(ed))
kilur, kill(er)
kimast, chemist
kimecul, chemical
kimest, chemist
kimestry, chemistry
kimist, chemist
kimponent, component

kimustry, chemistry
kin,*,nsmen,nfolk, RELATIVES (or see can)
kinal, canal
kincdom, kingdom
kind,dred,dly,dest,dness,der, WHAT TYPE, BEING NICE WITHOUT ULTERIOR MOTIVES "prefixes: un"
kind of, SORT OF, SOMEWHAT
kinda, kind of
kindergarten,ner, A CLASS LEVEL IN SCHOOL
kindhearted,dly,dness, A GENTLE SPIRIT
kindle,*,ed,ling, MATERIAL USED AS A FIRE STARTER "prefixes: en/re"
kindolense, condolence
kindom, kingdom
kinducter, conductor
kinduf, kind of
kindukt, conduct
kindurgarden, kindergarten
kinery, canary / cannery
kinesis,iology, STUDY OF HEALTH/ MUSCLES OF THE BODY, HEALING USING KINERGETIC STUDY
kinet, PREFIX INDICATING "MOTION" MOST OFTEN MODIFIES THE WORD
kinfedy, confetti
kinfes, confess
kinfeshun, confession
kinfetion, confession
king,*,gdom, RULER IN A MONARCH
kingdom,*, AREA RULED BY MONARCHY "prefixes: sub"
kingradulashun, congratulation
kinikkanik, kinnikinnick
kink,*,ked,king,ky, SOMETHING THAT KNOT'S UP, A BEND/HOOK IN A LINEAR SYSTEM (or see king) "prefixes: un"
kinkdom, kingdom
kinnikinnick, A PLANT
kinol, kennel
kinsestincy, consistence(cy)
kinsistently, consistent(ly)
kinsole, console
kinspirusy, conspiracy
kinstrucshen, construction
kinstruct, construct
kinsult, consult
kinsumpshen, consumption
kint, kind / can't / couldn't
kinta, kind of
kintaminate, contaminate

kintergarden, kindergarten
kintred, kind(red)
kinul, kennel
kinverdable, convertible
kiosk,*, INFORMATION STATION
kiper, kipper
kipper,*, FISH AND RELATED
kiral, choral / coral / corral / chorale
kirnel, colonel / kernel
kiroberate, corroborate
kirogen, corrode(osion)
kiropraktor, chiropractor
kiroshen, corrode(osion)
kirote, karate
kirsanthemum, chrysanthemum
kirsoch, corsage
kirten, curtain
kirteus, courteous
kiruge, courage
kirupraktor, chiropractor
kirvucher, curvature
kis, kiss
kiset, cassette
kiss,sses,ssed,ssing,sser,ssable, TOUCH WITH THE LIPS
kist, cist / kiss(ed)
kit,*, ACCUMULATION OF ITEMS IN A CONTAINER TO USE FOR A SPECIFIC TASK (or see kite)
kitastrufy, catastrophe
kitchen,*, PLACE TO PREPARE FOOD
kite,*, FRAME WITH COVERING THAT SAILS IN THE WIND BY A STRING (or see kit)
kiten, kitten
kitny, kidney
kitten,*, IMMATURE CAT
kitty,tties,tten, IMMATURE CAT, GAMBLING TERM
kity, kitty
kiwi,*, FRUIT, BIRD
kiyak, kayak
kiyan, cayenne
kiyen, cayenne
klad, clad
klairvoyants, clairvoyance
klam, clam / claim
klamable, claim(able)
klament, claimant
klamp, clamp
klan, clan
klandistine, clandestine
klap, clap
klapse, collapse

klarecul, clerical
klaricul, clerical
klarity, clarity
klarvoyuns, clairvoyance
klaset, closet
klash, clash
klasha, cliche
klasic, classic
klasify, classify
klasp, clasp
klass, class
klasuc, classic
klasufy, classify
klauged, clog(gged) / cloak / clock(ed)
klaun, clown
klausterfobic, claustrophobic
klaw, claw
klawsit, closet
klawzet, closet
klay, clay
klebtomaniac, kleptomania(c)
klecter, collect(or)
kleerense, clearance
kleet, cleat
kleff, cliff
klen, clean
klench, clench / clinch
kleng, cling
klenik, clinic
klenikul, clinic(al)
klense, cleanse
klensh, clench / clinch
klenz, cleanse
klenzer, cleanser
klep, clip
kleptomania,ac,acs,acal, OBSESSION
    WITH STEALING
klepur, clipper
kler, clear
klerense, clearance
klerge, clergy
klerical, clerical
klerify, clarify
klerity, clarity
klerk, clerk
klervoyents, clairvoyance
klet, cleat
kletorus, clitoris
klevur, clever
klew, clue
kliant, client
klicha, cliche
klick, click / clique
kliff, cliff

klik, click / clique
klim, climb
klimax, climax
klimet, climate
klimut, climate
klinch, clench / clinch
kling, cling
klinik, clinic
klinsh, clench / clinch
klinzr, cleanser
klip, clip
klipur, clipper
klirk, clerk
klisha, cliche
klitorus, clitoris
kliunt, client
kloak, cloak
klober, clobber
kloester, cloister
klofe, clove
klofur, clover
kloger, closure
klojure, closure
klok, clock / cloak
klokd, clog(gged) / cloak / clock(ed)
klon, clown / clone / cologne
klorene, chlorine
klos, clothes / claw(s) / close / clause
kloser, close(r) / closure
klosher, closure
klosir, close(r) / closure
klosline, clothesline
klosterfobic, claustrophobic
klosturfobia, claustrophobia
klosur, close(r) / closure
klot, clot
kloth, cloth
kloud, cloud
kloun, clown
klout, clout
klove, clove
klovur, clover
klowd, cloud
klown, clown
klowsit, closet
klowt, clout
klowth, cloth / cloth(e)
klowz, clothes / claw(s) / close / clause
kloyster, cloister
kloz, clothes / claw(s) / close / clause
klozer, close(r) / closure
klozit, closet
klozline, clothesline
klu, clue

klub, club
kluch, clutch
kludch, clutch
kluder, clutter
klue, clue
klump, clump
klumze, clumsy
klurge, clergy
kluster, cluster
klutch, clutch
kluter, clutter
klutorus, clitoris
knack, HAVE A NATURAL SKILL/TALENT
    FOR
knap,*,pped,pping,pper,ppy, HAIR
    AFFECTATION
knead,*,ded,ding, PREPARING DOUGH
    FOR BAKING (or see knee(d)/need))
kned, knee(d) / knead
knee,*,ed,eing, BENDABLE JOINT
    HALFWAY DOWN LEG (or see need/
    knead)
kneel,*,led,ling,ler, TO SIT ON YOUR
    KNEES
knel, kneel / knell
knell,*,led,ling, SOUND OF A BELL
    NORMALLY HEARD AT FUNERALS, A
    SOLEMN SOUND (or see kneel)
knes, knee(s) / niece
knew, PAST TENSE FOR THE WORD
    "KNOW" (or see new)
knewmerable, numerable
knick knack,*, SMALL COLLECTIBLES,
    TRINKETS (or see nick)
knife,ed,fing,ives, SHARP, METAL
    BLADE WITH HANDLE FOR CUTTING
knight,*,ted,ting,tly, MEDIEVAL
    SOLDIER
knit,*,tted,tting,tter, USING NEEDLES/
    YARN "prefixes: inter/un"
knitch, niche
knob,*, HANDLES FOR DOORS AND
    DRAWERS
knock,*,ked,king,ker, SOUND MADE ON
    DOOR WITH FIST, USING THE FIST
knoll,*, SMALL ROUND HILL
knot,*,tted,tting,tty, ROPE/STRING TIED
    WITH LOOPING CONFIGURATION,
    SPOT WHERE LIMBS GREW FROM
    (or see not/naught)
know,*,wing,wn,wable,wer,wledge,
    HAVE IT IN YOUR MEMORY, ACCESS
    BY MEMORY (or see noun)
    "prefixes: un"

knowledge,gable,gableness,gably, HAVING A MEMORY BASE

known,*,PAST TENSE FOR THE WORD 'KNOW', INFORMED/AWARE OF

knuckle,*,ed,ling, FINGER JOINT BONE, TO FIST UP HAND TO DISPLAY BONE JOINTS

koagewlate, coagulate
koagulate, coagulate
koal, coal / cool
koalition, coalition
koap, co-op
koar, core / corp
koarse, course / coarse
koaster, coaster
koat, coat
kob, cob
kobalt, cobalt
kobolt, cobalt
kobra, cobra
kobweb, cobweb
kocane, cocaine
koch, coach
kochen, caution
kocher, kosher
koches, cautious
kock, cook / cock
kockroach, cockroach
kod, cod / code / could / cold / caught
kodage, cottage
kode, code
kodej, cottage
kodene, codeine
kodin, cotton
kodo, kudos
koduge, cottage
koed, coed
koel, coil
koen, coin
koenside, coincide
koensudent, coincident
koersment, coerce(ment)
kof, cough
kofe, cove / coffee / cough
kofen, coffin / cough(ing)
kofert, covert
kofin, coffin / cough(ing)
kofy, coffee
kognativ, cognitive
kognisant, cognizant
kognishun, cognition
kognition, cognition
kognutiv, cognitive
kohabutate, cohabitate

kohearent, coherent
koherent, coherent
kohersive, coerce(cive)
kohesuf, cohesive
kohesuve, cohesive
kohort, cohort
kohurse, coerce
koil, coil
koin, coin
koinside, coincide
koinsudent, coincident
kok, cock / cook
kokain, cocaine
kokane, cocaine
koke, kook(y)
koko, cocoa
kokonut, coconut
kokroch, cockroach
koks, coax
koktale, cocktail
kokunut, coconut
kol, call / cowl
koladerul, collateral
kolamedy, calamity
kolander, colander
kolaps, collapse
kolapsubl, collapse(sible)
kolasal, colossal
kolate, collate
kold, cold
koldsfoot, coltsfoot
kole, coal / call
koleage, colleague
koleague, colleague
kolecshin, collection
kolecter, collect(or)
koledg, college
koleg, college
kolegent, collegiate
kolekt, collect
kolem, column
kolen, colon
kolenary, culinary
kolendur, colander
koleng, call(ing) / cowl(ing)
kolenize, colonize
koleny, colony
koler, collar / call(er) / cooler
kolerd, collar(ed) / collard greens
kolesterol, cholesterol
kolic, colic
kolid, collide
koliflower, cauliflower
kolige, college

kolijin, collision
kolim, column
koliny, colony
kolishen, coalition
kolk, calk / caulk
kolm, calm
kolmenate, culminate
koloj, collage
kolostemy, colostomy
kolpret, culprit
kolsla, coleslaw
kolslow, coleslaw
kolt, cold / colt
koltivate, cultivate
koltsfoot, coltsfoot
koluge, college
kolum, column
kolun, colon
kolundir, colander
kolune, colony
kolunise, colonize
kolur, cooler / color / collar / call(er)
kolvurt, culvert
kom, calm / come / comb
koma, coma / comma
komand, command
komander, commander
kombat, combat
kombenation, combination
komber, cumber
kombinashun, combination
kombine, combine
kombinsashen, compensation
kombrahensiv, comprehensive
kombunashen, combination
kombustible, combustible
kombustion, combustion
komec, comic
komedian, comedian
komedy, comedy
komemerate, commemorate
komendable, commendable
komendation, commendation
komenduble, commendable
komense, commence
koment, comment
komentatur, commentator
koments, commence
komerse, commerce
komershul, commercial
komet, commit / comet
komfert, comfort
komfertible, comfortable
komfurter, comfort(er)

komic, comic	kompost, compost	kondem, condemn
komidy, comedy	komposyer, composure	kondensashen, condensation
komimurate, commemorate	kompound, compound	kondense, condense
komin, common	kompownd, compound	kondesend, condescend
komindation, commendation	komprahensive, comprehensive	kondewit, conduit
kominduble, commendable	kompramise, compromise	kondimeneum, condominium
kominsurate, commensurate	komprehend, comprehend	kondiment, condiment
komint, comment	komprehenshun, comprehension	kondinsashun, condensation
komintator, commentator	komprehinsef, comprehensive	kondisend, condescend
komirse, commerce	kompreshun, compression	kondishen, condition
komirshul, commercial	kompresor, compressor	kondition, condition
komisary, commissary	kompress, compress	kondolense, condolence
komishner, commissioner	kompretion, compression	kondomeneum, condominium
komit, comet / commit	kompruble, comparable	kondone, condone
komitee, committee	komprumize, compromise	konduct, conduct
komitment, commitment	komptroler, comptroller	konducter, conductor
komity, comedy	kompulsery, compulsory	konduit, conduit
komodety, commodity	kompulshun, compulsion	kondukt, conduct
kompact, compact	kompulsuve, compulsive	kondum, condom
kompar, compare	kompultion, compulsion	kondument, condiment
komparebul, comparable	komputashun, computation	kone, cone
kompartment, compartment	kompute, compute	konekshen, connection
kompashun, compassion	komputer, computer	konekt, connect
kompashunet, compassionate	komputishen, competition	konesur, connoisseur
kompass, compass	kompuzishen, composition	konfederit, confederate
kompatibility, compatible(bility)	komrad, comrade	konfedont, confidant
kompeditor, competitor	komtroler, comptroller	konfeduret, confederate
kompel, compel	komudoor, commodore	konfedy, confetti
kompensashen, compensation	komun, common / commune	konfekshun, confection
komper, compare	komune, commune	konferanse, conference
kompete, compete	komunest, communist	konferm, confirm
kompetior, competitor	komunety, community	konfermashun, confirmation
kompile, compile	komunicate, communicate	konfes, confess
kompinsate, compensate	komunism, communism	konfeshun, confession
kompitance, competent(nce)	komunul, communal	konfesion, confession
kompizizhen, composition	komutable, commute(table)	konfetty, confetti
komplane, complain	kon, con / cone	konfide, confide
komplasins, complacence /	konasur, connoisseur	konfidense, confidence
complaisance	koncaf, concave	konfidenshul, confidential
komplecshun, complexion	koncafety, concave(vity)	konfidential, confidential
kompleks, complex	koncakwently, consequent(ly)	konfidont, confidant
kompleshun, completion	koncavity, concave(vity)	konfigurashun, configuration
komplete, complete	koncavudy, concave(vity)	konfine, confine
komplians, compliant(nce)	koncesion, concession	konfinment, confinement
kompliant, compliant	konch, conch	konfirents, conference
komplukashun, complication	koncheinchus, conscientious	konfirm, confirm
komplukate, complicate	konchuse, conscious	konfirmashun, confirmation
komplumint, complement /	konclewsef, conclusive	konfirmation, confirmation
compliment	konclude, conclude	konflict, conflict
komply, comply	konclujen, conclusion	konform, conform
komponent, component	konclusef, conclusive	konfrunt, confront
kompose, compose	konclusion, conclusion	konfudense, confidence
komposier, composure	koncucrat, consecrate	konfudenshul, confidential
komposit, composite	koncution, concussion	konfudont, confidant

konfujen, confusion
konfuranse, conference
konfuse, confuse
konfusion, confusion
konger, conjure
kongested, congest(ed)
konglomurete, conglomerate
kongradulashun, congratulation
kongratshulate, congratulate
kongregashun, congregation
kongres, congress
kongrewint, congruent
kongrewity, congruent(uity)
kongrigate, congregate
kongris, congress
kongruedy, congruent(uity)
kongrues, congruous
kongrugate, congregate
kongrugation, congregation
kongruint, congruent
kongunctivitis, conjunction(ivitis)
konifur, conifer
konisur, connoisseur
konjer, conjure
konjest, congest
konjestion, congest(ion)
konjewgul, conjugal
konjugul, conjugal
konjunction, conjunction
konjunctivitis, conjunction(ivitis)
konjunkshen, conjunction
konjure, conjure
konk, conch
konkaf, concave
konkavety, concave(vity)
konker, conquer
konklusive, conclusive
konkokt, concoct
konkrete, concrete
konkwest, conquest
konquest, conquest
konsacrat, consecrate
konsalidate, consolidate
konscientious, conscientious
konsecrashen, consecrate(tion)
konsecrat, consecrate
konsecutive, consecutive
konsedarashen, considerate(tion)
konseduration, considerate(tion)
konseed, concede
konseet, conceit
konseeve, conceive
konseevuble, conceivable
konsekwently, consequent(ly)

konsel, council / counsel / console
konsemate, consummate
konsent, consent
konsentrate, concentrate
konsentric, concentric
konsepshual, conceptual
konsepshun, conception
konsept, concept
konsequenshal, consequent(ial)
konserge, concierge
konsern, concern
konservation, conservation
konservator, conservator
konservatory, conservatory
konserve, conserve
konservutive, conservative
konseshun, concession
konsestenly, consistent(ly)
konsetion, concession
konseve, conceive
konshenshis, conscientious
konsider, consider
konsierge, concierge
konsikwense, consequence
konsimate, consummate
konsinet, consonant
konsinment, consignment
konsintrate, concentrate
konsiquence, consequence
konsirv, conserve
konsirvation, conservation
konsirvator, conservator
konsirvatory, conservatory
konsirvutive, conservative
konsise, concise
konsist, consist
konsistency, consistence(cy)
konsiter, consider
konsolashen, consolation
konsole, console
konsolidate, consolidate
konsoul, console
konspearusy, conspiracy
konspikuos, conspicuous
konspikyewus, conspicuous
konspirusy, conspiracy
konstancy, constancy
konstant, constant
konstatushen, constitution
konstilashen, constellation
konstinse, constancy
konstint, constant
konstipashen, constipation
konstitushen, constitution

konstrict, constrict
konstrucshen, construction
konstruct, construct
konstulashen, constellation
konstupashen, constipation
konstutushen, constitution
konsucrat, consecrate
konsucrating, consecrate(ing)
konsukration, consecrate(tion)
konsukwinse, consequence
konsulashun, consolation
konsult, consult
konsumate, consummate
konsume, consume
konsumshen, consumption
konsunet, consonant
konsurt, concert
konsurvation, conservation
konsurvator, conservator
konsurvatory, conservatory
konsurve, conserve
konsurvutive, conservative
kontagus, contagious
kontain, contain
kontakt, contact
kontamenate, contaminate
kontane, contain
konteguis, contiguous
kontekst, context
kontemporary, contemporary
kontemt, contempt
kontend, contend
kontent, content
kontenuel, continue(ual)
kontest, contest
kontiguis, contiguous
kontimplate, contemplate
kontimporary, contemporary
kontinet, continent
konting, content
kontinuance, continuance
kontorshenist, contortionist
kontradik, contradict
kontrak, contract
kontrasepshun, contraception
kontrast, contrast
kontraversy, controversy
kontravertible, controvert(ible)
kontrebute, contribute
kontrery, contrary
kontrishen, contrition
kontrol, control
kontrovert, controvert
kontrovertible, controvert(ible)

kontrudik, contradict
kontrusepshun, contraception
kontumplate, contemplate
kontunent, continent
konture, contour
konufir, conifer
konusur, connoisseur
konvay, convey
konvayor, convey(or)
konvene, convene
konvenyut, convenient
konversashen, conversation
konvershen, conversion
konvert, convert
konvex, convex
konvict, convict
konvinse, convince
konvinshen, convention
konvulesents, convalescence
konvulgin, convulsion
konvulshen, convulsion
konvursashen, conversation
konvursation, conversation
konvurtable, convertible
kood, could
koodos, kudos
kooger, cougar
kook,*,ky,kier,kiest,kily,kiness, NEW
   SNOWBOARDER, ODD/ECCENTRIC
   BEHAVIOR
kookoo, cuckoo
kooky, cookie
kool, cool
koop, coop / co-op
kooperate, cooperate
kooshin, cushion
kooth, couth
kope, cope / copy
kopeir, copy(pier)
koper, copper
kopier, copy(pier)
kopulate, copulate
kopur, copper
kopy, copy
kor, car
koral, choral / coral / corral / chorale
kord, cord / chord / court
kordaroy, corduroy
kordinate, coordinate
kords, cord(s) / chord(s) / court(s) /
   quart(s) / quartz
kordunate, coordinate
korduroy, corduroy
kore, core / corp

korekt, correct
kores, chorus / course / core(s) / caress
korespond, correspond
korgil, cordial
korgul, cordial
koridoor, corridor
korigate, corrugate
korilate, correlate
koriner, coroner
korinery, coronary
koris, chorus / course
korispond, correspond
korjil, cordial
kork, cork / quark
korn, corn
korner, corner / coroner
korneu, cornea
kornikopea, cornucopia
kornukopea, cornucopia
kornur, corner / coroner
korode, corrode
koroshen, corrode(osion)
korparul, corporal
korpirate, corporate
korps, corpse
korpural, corporal
korpurate, corporate
kors, course / coarse
korsd, coarse(d)
korsoge, corsage
kort, cord / court / quart
kort-marshul, court-martial
korteks, cortex
kortex, cortex
korts, quartz / court(s) / quart(s) /
   cord(s) /chord(s) / car(ts)
korudoor, corridor
korugate, corrugate
korul, choral / coral / corral / chorale
korulate, correlate
koruner, coroner
korunery, coronary
korupt, corrupt
korus, chorus / course
koruspond, correspond
korve, carve
kos, cause
kosd, cause(d) / cost / coast /
kosee, cozy
koshen, caution
kosher,*,red,ring, RESTRICTION IN
   FOOD PREPARATION, LEGITIMATE/
   FIT FOR OCCASION
koshes, cautious

koshin, caution
koshus, cautious
kosmik, cosmic
kosmopolutin, cosmopolitan
kosmos, cosmos
kost, cost / cause(d) / coast
koster, coaster
kostic, caustic
kostum, costume
kostyume, costume
kosy, cozy
kot, caught / cot / coat
kotage, cottage
kotch, coach
koten, cotton
kotuge, cottage
kouch, couch
koulishun, coalition
kounsil, council / counsel / console
kount, count
koursif, coerce(cive)
koursment, coerce(ment)
kova, kava
kove, cove
kovenant, covenant
kover, cover
kovit, covet
kovu, kava
kovurt, covert
kow, cow
kowch, couch
kowculus, calculus
kowerd, coward
kowersev, coerce(cive)
kowkulate, calculate
kowl, call / cowl
kownder, counter
kownsul, council / counsel / console
kownt, count
kowntur, counter
kownty, county
kowurd, coward
kowursif, coerce(cive)
kowursment, coerce(ment)
koyel, coil
koyn, coin
koz, cause
kozd, cause(d) / cost
kozmik, cosmic
kozmopoletin, cosmopolitan
kozmos, cosmos
kozy, cozy
krab, crab
krader, crater / creator

kradul, cradle
kradur, crater / creator
krafe, crave
kraft, craft
krain, crane
kraink, crank
krak, crack
krakel, crackle
kraker, cracker
kral, crawl / corral
kram, cram
kramp, cramp
kranbery, cranberry
krane, crane
kraneum, cranium
krank, crank
krany, cranny
kraon, crayon
krap, crap / crepe
krape, crepe / crap(ppy)
krasee, crazy
krash, crash
krass, crass
krate, crate
krater, crater / creator
kraul, crawl
kraut, PICKLED CABBAGE
krave, crave
krawnik, chronic
krayon, crayon
krazy, crazy
kreader, creator
kreal, creel
kream, cream / creme
kreap, creep
kreapy, creep(y)
krease, crease
kreashun, creation
kreasul, creosol
kreate, create
kreatef, create(ive)
kreative, creative
kreator, creator
kreb, crib
krebd, crib(bbed)
krebeg, cribbage
krecher, creature
kredable, credible
krededer, creditor
kreder, critter
kredet, credit
kredible, credible
kredibul, credible
kredider, creditor

kredik, critic
kredisize, criticize
kredit, credit
kreditor, creditor
kreduble, credible
kreecher, creature
kreel, creel
kreen, careen
kreenkul, crinkle
kreep, creep
kreepy, creep(y)
kreer, career
kreisote, creosote
kreke, creak / creek
krekit, cricket
krel, creel
kremate, cremate
kreme, cream / creme
kremenul, criminal
kreminal, criminal
kremsun, crimson
kreng, cringe
krenj, cringe
krenkle, crinkle
krep, creep / crepe
kreple, cripple
kreptic, cryptic
krepy, creep(y)
krescross, crisscross
krese, crease
kresendo, crescendo
kresent, crescent
kresont, croissant
kresp, crisp
kress, caress
krest, crest
kretable, credible
kreteek, critique
kretik, critic
kretikul, critical
kreusol, creosol
kreusote, creosote
krevas, crevasse / crevice
krevus, crevasse / crevice
krew, crew
krewd, crude
krewshul, crucial
krewsufix, crucifix
krewton, crouton
kri, cry
krib, crib
kribage, cribbage
krid, cried
kridecal, critical

kridenshul, credential
krider, critter
kridesize, criticize
krien, cry(ing)
kriket, cricket
krime, crime
krimenal, criminal
krimson, crimson
kring, cringe
krinj, cringe
kriptic, cryptic
kripul, cripple
krisade, crusade
kriscross, crisscross
krisis, crisis
krismus, christmas
krisont, croissant
krisp, crisp
kristal, crystal
kristashen, crustacean
kritesize, criticize
kritik, critic
kritur, critter
kriz, cries
kroak, croak
kroan, crone
krok, crock / croak
krokedile, crocodile
kroket, croquet / croquette
krokudile, crocodile
krokus, crocus
krol, crawl
krom, chrome / crumb
kromizone, chromosome
kronac, chronic
kronacle, chronicle
kronalogical, chronology(gical)
krone, crone / crony
krones, crony(s)
kronic, chronic
kronicle, chronicle
kronilogical, chronology(gical)
kronlogical, chronology(gical)
kronucle, chronicle
kronulogikul, chronology(gical)
krony, crony
krook, crook
kroose, cruise / crew(s)
krop, crop
kroshay, crochet
kross, cross
krotch, crotch
krouch, crouch
krout, kraut

krow, crow	kudel, cuddle	kultavashen, cultivate(tion)
krowch, crouch	kudent, couldn't	kultivashen, cultivate(tion)
krowd, crowd	kudet, cadet	kultivate, cultivate
krown, crown	kudint, couldn't	kultsher, culture
krows, crow(s) / carouse	**kudos**, BONUS, CREDIT	kulture, culture
krowshay, crochet	kufer, cover	kultuvashen, cultivate(tion)
krowt, kraut	kuferege, coverage	kulvert, culvert
kru, crew	kuff, cuff	kum, come / cum
kruch, crutch	kufredge, coverage	kumand, command
krude, crude	kuger, cougar	kumander, commander
krudenshul, credential	kugole, cajole	kumbarsome, cumber(some)
krue, crew	kuhoot, cahoot	kumber, cumber
kruke, crook	kuhute, cahoot	kumberbun, cummerbund
kruks, crux	kuk, kook / cook	kumbine, combine
krum, crumb	kuke, cook / cookie / kook(y)	kumbirsome, cumber(some)
krumble, crumble / crumple	kukoon, cocoon	kumbur, cumber
krumple, crumble / crumple	kuku, cuckoo	kumbuschen, combustion
krunch, crunch	kukumber, cucumber	kumbustuble, combustible
krupt, corrupt	kukune, cocoon	kumedeun, comedian
krusade, crusade	kul, cool / cull	kumemerate, commemorate
kruse, cruise / crew(s)	kulamity, calamity	kumenduble, commendable
krusefix, crucifix	kulandur, colander	kumensirit, commensurate
krusendo, crescendo	kulaps, collapse	kuments, commence
krush, crush	kulapsebul, collapse(sible)	kumfert, comfort
krushul, crucial	kulcher, culture	kumferter, comfort(er)
krusont, croissant	kuldesac, cul-de-sac	kumfertible, comfortable
krust, crust	kuleckshun, collection	kuminduble, commendable
krustashen, crustacean	kulecter, collect(or)	kumit, commit
krutch, crutch	kulejet, collegiate	kumitment, commitment
kruteke, critique	kulekt, collect	kumity, committee
kruton, crouton	kulenary, culinary	kumodety, commodity
krux, crux	kulendula, calendula	kumpar, compare
kry, cry	kuler, color / cooler / collar	kumpareson, comparison
kryeng, cry(ing)	kulesterol, cholesterol	kumpartment, compartment
kryptic, cryptic	kulid, collide	kumpashun, compassion
krystal, crystal	kulidescope, kaleidoscope	kumpashunate, compassionate
krysus, crisis	kulijin, collision	kumpeny, company
ku, cue	kulishun, collision	kumpile, compile
kuack, quack	kulition, collision	kumplane, complain
kuagmire, quagmire	kulmenate, culminate	kumpleks, complex
kubby, cubby	kulminate, culminate	kumplete, complete
kube, cubby / cube	kuloge, collage	kumplians, compliant(nce)
kubek, cubic	kuloje, collage	kumplient, compliant
kubekle, cubicle	kulokweul, colloquial	kumply, comply
kuberd, cupboard	kulon, cologne / colon	kumponint, component
kubic, cubic	kuloneal, colonial	kumposier, composure
kubicul, cubicle	kuloquial, colloquial	kumposit, composite
kuburd, cupboard	kulor, color / cooler	kumpoze, compose
kubuse, caboose	kulosel, colossal	kumpozer, composure
kuchen, cushion	kulosil, colossal	kumpreshun, compression
kucky, cookie	kulown, cologne / colon	kumpresor, compressor
kucumber, cucumber	kulpret, culprit	kumpress, compress
kud, cud / could / cue(d)	kulsher, culture	kumpuder, computer
kudaver, cadaver	kult, cult	kumpulsery, compulsory

kumpulshun, compulsion
kumpuss, compass
kumpute, compute
kumputer, computer
kumulative, cumulative
kumunal, communal
kumuneon, communion
kumutable, commute(table)
kumutble, commute(table)
kumyewtable, commute(table)
kunal, canal
kuncideration, considerate(tion)
kunclusev, conclusive
kundem, condemn
kundinse, condense
kundishen, condition
kundition, condition
kundolense, condolence
kundone, condone
kundukt, conduct
kundukter, conductor
kunekshen, connection
kunekt, connect
kunfekshun, confection
kunferm, confirm
kunfermashun, confirmation
kunfes, confess
kunfeshun, confession
kunfety, confetti
kunfide, confide
kunfigerashun, configuration
kunfine, confine
kunfinment, confinement
kunflict, conflict
kunform, conform
kunfrunt, confront
kunfujen, confusion
kunfuze, confuse
kunglomurete, conglomerate
kungradulashun, congratulation
kungratshulate, congratulate
kungruedy, congruent(uity)
kungruint, congruent
kungruity, congruent(uity)
kungunctavitis, conjunction(ivitis)
kunikkunik, kinnikinnick
kuning, cunning
kunjest, congest
kunjested, congest(ed)
kunjunction, conjunction
kunklude, conclude
kunklujen, conclusion
kunklusef, conclusive
kunkokt, concoct

kunkushen, concussion
kunning, cunning
kunsecutive, consecutive
kunsedurashen, considerate(tion)
kunseed, concede
kunseel, conceal
kunseet, conceit
kunseevable, conceivable
kunseeve, conceive
kunsent, consent
kunsentric, concentric
kunsepshual, conceptual
kunsepshun, conception
kunsern, concern
kunservator, conservator
kunservatory, conservatory
kunserve, conserve
kunseshun, concession
kunsestently, consistent(ly)
kunsevable, conceivable
kunsider, consider
kunsinment, consignment
kunsirvator, conservator
kunsirvatory, conservatory
kunsirvutive, conservative
kunsise, concise
kunsist, consist
kunsistency, consistence(cy)
kunsiter, consider
kunsole, console
kunsoludate, consolidate
kunsoom, consume
kunsoul, console
kunspearucy, conspiracy
kunspikyus, conspicuous
kunstrict, constrict
kunstrucshen, construction
kunstruct, construct
kunsult, consult
kunsume, consume
kunsumshen, consumption
kunsurvatory, conservatory
kunsurve, conserve
kunsurvutive, conservative
kunsuvator, conservator
kuntagus, contagious
kuntain, contain
kuntamunate, contaminate
kuntane, contain
kunteguis, contiguous
kuntemporary, contemporary
kuntemt, contempt
kuntend, contend
kuntent, content

kuntenual, continue(ual)
kuntenuense, continuance
kuntenule, continue(ual)
kuntest, contest
kuntiguis, contiguous
kuntimporary, contemporary
kuntorshenist, contortionist
kuntrakshen, contraction
kuntree, country
kuntrery, contrary
kuntribute, contribute
kuntrishen, contrition
kuntrol, control
kunveenyut, convenient
kunvene, convene
kunvense, convince
kunvenshen, convention
kunvenyant, convenient
kunvergin, conversion
kunvershen, conversion
kunvert, convert
kunvertable, convertible
kunvict, convict
kunvulgin, convulsion
kunvulshen, convulsion
kup, cup / coop
kupasity, capacity
kupcake, cupcake
kupe, coop
kupil, couple
kupler, coupler
kupon, coupon
kupoot, kaput
kupul, couple
kuput, kaput
kurable, curable
kurader, curator
kural, choral / coral / corral / chorale
kurb, curb
kurd, curd
kurdesy, courtesy
kurdeus, courteous
kurdisy, courtesy
kurdle, curdle
kure, cure
kurect, correct
kureen, careen
kureer, career
kurege, courage
kureje, courage
kurekt, correct
kurekulum, curriculum
kuren, careen / cure(ring)
kurensy, currency

kurent, currant / current	kustemary, customary	kwantum, quanta(tum)
kureosety, curiosity	kustemize, customize	kward, quart
kureosudy, curiosity	kusterd, custard	kwarder, quarter
kures, care(s) / caress / cure(s)	kustimer, customer	kwarderly, quarter(ly)
kureur, courier	kustodeun, custodian	kwards, quartz / quart(s)
kureus, curious	kustomary, customary	kwardur, quarter
kureusol, creosol	kustomer, customer	kwardurly, quarter(ly)
kurf, curve	kustomize, customize	kwardz, quartz / quart(s)
kurfew, curfew	kut, cut / cat	kware, quarry
kurfue, curfew	kutastrufee, catastrophe	kwarel, quarrel
kuri, curry	kute, cute	kwarentene, quarantine
kurige, courage	kutecle, cuticle	kwaril, quarrel
kurin, curtain	kuth, couth	kwarintene, quarantine
kurinsy, currency	kutlury, cutlery	kwark, quark
kurint, current	kutukle, cuticle	kwarol, quarrel
kuriosity, curiosity	kuvenant, covenant	kwart, quart
kurisma, charisma	kuver, cover	kwarter, quarter
kurl, curl	kuvit, covet	kwarterly, quarter(ly)
kurnel, colonel / kernel	kuvridge, coverage	kwarts, quartz / quart(s)
kuroburate, corroborate	kuvunent, covenant	kwarul, quarrel
kurode, corrode	kuzn, cousin	kwary, quarry / query
kuroky, karaoke	kwack, quack / quake	kwasar, quasar
kurosef, corrode(osive)	kwad, quad	kwasy, quasi
kurote, karate	kwadrant, quadrant	kwaundre, quandary
kurotion, corrode(osion)	kwagmire, quagmire	kwaure, quarry
kuroty, karate	kwaik, quake	kwawrel, quarrel
kurowse, carouse	kwail, quail	kwawrul, quarrel
kursanthimum, chrysanthemum	kwaint, quaint	kwawry, quarry
kursathimum, chrysanthemum	kwak, quack / quake	kwaysar, quasar
kurse, curse	kwale, quail	kwazar, quasar
kursif, cursive	kwaledy, quality	kwazee, quasi
kursive, cursive	kwalefication, qualify(fication)	kwazene, cuisine
kursoge, corsage	kwalefikashen, qualify(fication)	kween, queen
kurtale, curtail	kwalefiuble, qualify(fiable)	kweer, queer, career
kurten, curtain	kwalefiur, qualify(fier)	kwefir, quiver
kurtesy, courtesy	kwaletatif, quality(tative)	kwefur, quiver
kurteus, courteous	kwalety, quality	kwek, quick
kurtin, curtain	kwalifekashen, qualify(fication)	kwekest, quick(est)
kurtle, curdle	kwalify, qualify	kwekly, quick(ly)
kurtse, curtsy	kwalitatif, quality(tative)	kweky, quick(ie)
kurupt, corrupt	kwalitee, quality	kwel, quill
kurvachure, curvature	kwalm, qualm	kwelt, quilt
kurve, curve	kwandery, quandary	kwench, quench
kury, curry	kwandree, quandary	kwentuplet, quintuplet
kus, cuss	kwant, quaint	kwer, queer, career
kusen, cousin	kwantefy, quantify	kwerk, quirk
kuset, cassette	kwantem, quanta(tum)	kwerky, quirk(y)
kushen, cushion	kwantetative, quantitative	kwery, query
kusin, cousin	kwantety, quantity	kwes, quiz
kusp, cusp	kwantify, quantify	kwesden, question
kusped, cuspid	kwantifyer, quantify(fier)	kwesekal, quiz(zzical)
kuss, cuss	kwantim, quanta(tum)	kweshten, question
kustedy, custody	kwantity, quantity	kwest, quest
kustem, custom	kwantry, quandary	kwestenair, question(nnaire)

kwesteun, question
kwestshunar, question(nnaire)
kwestun, question
kwet, quit / quite
kweter, quit(tter) / quiet(er)
kwever, quiver
kwez, quiz
kwezekal, quiz(zzical)
kwezene, cuisine
kwezt, quest
kwiet, quiet
kwietly, quiet(ly)
kwifir, quiver
kwifor, quiver
kwik, quick
kwikest, quick(est)
kwikly, quick(ly)
kwiky, quick(ie)
kwil, quill
kwilt, quilt
kwinch, quench
kwintuplet, quintuplet
kwire, choir
kwirk, quirk
kwiry, query
kwisekal, quiz(zzical)
kwisine, cuisine
kwit, quit / quite
kwiter, quit(tter) / quiet(er)
kwiut, quiet
kwiutly, quiet(ly)
kwiver, quiver
kwiyet, quiet
kwiz, quiz
kwizekal, quiz(zzical)
kwochent, quotient
kwod, quad
kwoda, quota
kwodabul, quote(table)
kwodashen, quote(tation)
kwode, quote
kwodrent, quadrant
kwodu, quota
kwoledy, quality
kwolefikashen, qualify(fication)
kwolefy, qualify
kwoletatif, quality(tative)
kwoletative, quality(tative)
kwolety, quality
kwolification, qualify(fication)
kwolifikashen, qualify(fication)
kwolifiuble, qualify(fiable)
kwolifiur, qualify(fier)
kwolitatif, quality(tative)

kwolitative, quality(tative)
kwolitee, quality
kwolm, qualm
kwolufy, qualify
kwondery, quandary
kwontefy, quantify
kwontefyer, quantify(fier)
kwontem, quanta(tum)
kwontetative, quantitative
kwontety, quantity
kwontify, quantify
kwontifyer, quantify(fier)
kwontim, quanta(tum)
kwontity, quantity
kwontre, quandary
kwontum, quanta(tum)
kworam, quorum
kword, quart
kworder, quarter
kworderly, quarter(ly)
kwords, quartz / quart(s)
kwordur, quarter
kwordurly, quarter(ly)
kwordz, quartz / quart(s)
kwore, quarry
kworel, quarrel
kworem, quorum
kworentene, quarantine
kworil, quarrel
kworim, quorum
kworintene, quarantine
kwork, quark
kworol, quarrel
kworom, quorum
kwort, quart
kworter, quarter
kworterly, quarter(ly)
kwortir, quarter
kworts, quartz / quart(s)
kwortur, quarter
kwortz, quartz / quart(s)
kworul, quarrel
kworum, quorum
kworuntene, quarantine
kwoshent, quotient
kwosy, quasi
kwota, quota
kwotabul, quote(table)
kwotashen, quote(tation)
kwotation, quote(tation)
kwote, quote
kwotu, quota
kwozy, quasi
kwurentene, quarantine

kwurintene, quarantine
kwurk, quirk
kwurky, quirk(y)
kwyit, quiet
kwyre, choir
kyak, kayak
la, law / lay
labarenth, labyrinth
labedo, libido
label,*,led,ling, A WAY TO REMEMBER/
    SAVE/RETRIEVE/CATEGORIZE
    THINGS "prefixes: un"
laber, labor
laberatory, laboratory
labeul, labial
labi, PREFIX INDICATING "LIP" MOST
    OFTEN MODIFIES THE WORD
labial,lly,lize,lization, SOUND, OF THE
    LIPS, ORGAN PIPE "prefixes: bi"
labido, libido
labil, label
labio, PREFIX INDICATING "LIP" MOST
    OFTEN MODIFIES THE WORD
labl, label
lable, label
labor,*,red,ring,rious,riously,riousness,
    rism,rist,rer, PHYSICALLY WORKING
    "prefixes: un"
laboratory,ries, PLACE FOR STUDY/
    EXPERIMENTS AND OBSERVATION
laborenth, labyrinth
labratory, laboratory
labrinth, labyrinth
labrutory, laboratory
labul, label
labur, labor
labyrinth,*, A MAZE, CHAOTIC
    CIRCUMSTANCES
lace,*,ed,cing,cy,cier,ciest,ciness,
    SECURE SHOES WITH, WOVEN
    STRING "prefixes: en/un"
lacerate,*,ed,ting,tion, GASH/RIP
    SOMETHING BY PENETRATION
lach, latch / lodge / lash
lack,*,ked,king, BELIEF THAT ONE DOES
    NOT HAVE ENOUGH OF
    SOMETHING (or see lake)
lackative, laxative
lacker, lacquer / lager
lacks, lax / lake(s) / lack(s)
lacktat, lactate
lacquer,*, VARNISH
lacrosse, ORIGINALLY A NATIVE
    AMERICAN SPORTS GAME

lacs, lax

lacsetive, laxative

lact, PREFIX INDICATING "MILK" MOST OFTEN MODIFIES THE WORD

lactate,*,ed,ting,tion, MILK BEING PRODUCED IN MAMMALS

lacti, PREFIX INDICATING "MILK" MOST OFTEN MODIFIES THE WORD

lacto, PREFIX INDICATING "MILK" MOST OFTEN MODIFIES THE WORD

lactose, SUGAR FROM COW MILK

lad,*, YOUNG MEN (or see laid/late)

ladder,*, TWO POLES WITH RUNGS FOR CLIMBING (or see later)

lade, laid / lady / late

ladel, ladle

laden, BURDENED DOWN, HEAVY LOAD

lader, ladder / later / latter

laderal, lateral

laderuly, lateral(ly)

ladery, lottery

lades, lattice / lady(dies) / lettuce

ladetude, latitude

ladir, latter / ladder / later

ladis, lattice / lady(dies) / lettuce

laditude, latitude

ladle,*,ed,ling, LONG HANDLE SPOON TO SERVE FOOD

ladul, ladle

ladur, later / ladder / latter

ladural, lateral

ladutude, latitude

lady,dies, A WOMAN

lae, lay

laed, laid / late

laeng, lay(ing)

laer, layer

laevo, PREFIX INDICATING "COUNTER-CLOCKWISE" MOST OFTEN MODIFIES THE WORD

laf, laugh

lafdur, laughter

lafender, lavender

laff, laugh

lafter, laughter

lag,*,gged,gging, BE SLOWER THAN THE OTHERS, SHAPE OR CASING, DELAY (or see log/lodge/lack/leg/lake)

lager, BEER (or see logger/lacquer)

lageslat, legislate

lagestics, logistic(s)

lagetamate, legitimate

lagicul, logic(al)

lagir, logger / lacquer

lagislat, legislate

lagistics, logistic(s)

lagitamate, legitimate

lagoon,*, ENCLOSED/NEARLY ENCLOSED SMALL BODY OF WATER NEAR LARGER BODY OF WATER

lagor, logger / lacquer

lagoslat, legislate

lagur, lacquer / lager / logger

laguslat, legislate

lai, lay

laid, PAST TENSE FOR THE WORD "LAY" (or see late)

lain, PAST TENSE FOR THE WORD "LAID" (or see lane/line)

laing, lay(ing) / lying

laingwege, language

lair,*,red,ring, ANIMALS DEN (or see lyre/layer)

laj, lodge

lajekul, logic(al)

lajeslat, legislate

lajislat, legislate

lajistics, logistic(s)

lajoslat, legislate

lajuslat, legislate

lake,*, LARGE BODY OF WATER FED BY SPRINGS (or see lack)

laker, lacquer / lager / logger

lakross, lacrosse

laks, lax / lake(s) / lack(s)

laksetif, laxative

laksutef, laxative

laktate, lactate

laktose, lactose

lam, RUNNING FROM TROUBLE (or see lamb/lame)

lama, llama

lamb,*, YOUNG SHEEP (or see lam/lame)

lame,ly,eness, PERMANENTLY INJURED LIMB/LIMBS THAT DON'T WORK (or see lam/lamb)

lamenate, laminate

lament,*,ted,ting,tingly,table,tably, tableness,tation,ter, MOURN THE LOSS OF SOMEONE, SPEND TIME IN THE PAST ON REGRETS

laminate,*,ed,ting,tion,tor,able, GLUE LAYERS TOGETHER "prefixes: inter/ multi/non"

lamp,*, A LIGHT WITH A SHADE/COVER OVER THE BULB

lamunate, laminate

lance,*,ed,cing,er, MEDIEVAL WEAPON

lanch, launch

land,*,ded,ding,dless, EARTH, SETTLE ONTO, DIVIDING THE GROUND

landern, lantern

landers, launder(s)

landlord,*, OWNER WHO RENTS/ LEASES PROPERTY

landscape,*,ed,ping,er, FOLIAGE/ FAUNA/TERRAIN OF WHAT THE EYE SEES

landslide,*, WHEN LAND BREAKS AWAY FROM OTHER LAND DUE TO WATER

lane,*, PASSAGEWAYS/ROADS FOR VEHICLES, PATHS IN BOWLING (or see lain)

lanelin, lanolin

language,*, WORDS/MEANS OF COMMUNICATION IN DIFFERENT REGIONS "prefixes: inter"

langweg, language

lankwij, language

lanky,kily,kiness, TALL AND THIN

lanlord, landlord

lanolin, OIL FROM WOOL

lanqueg, language

lans, lance / lane(s) / land(s)

lanskap, landscape

lanskapur, landscape(r)

lant, land

lantern,*, FUELED FLAME WITHIN CONTAINER

lantlord, landlord

lantscape, landscape

lantslide, landslide

lanulin, lanolin

lap,*,pped,pping, TO GO AROUND, HOW ANIMALS DRINK, CREATED IN SITTING POSITION "prefixes: over"

lapadary, lapidary

lapel,*, COLLARS

lapidary,ries,rian, CUT/POLISH/ ENGRAVE STONES

laprutory, laboratory

laps, lapse / lap(s)

lapse,*,ed,sing, SLIPPING INTO, LOOSE A MOMENT IN TIME, PAUSE (or see lap(s)) "prefixes: pro"

lapudary, lapidary

lar, lair / layer

larch, large

lard, FAT FROM DEAD PIGS

larel, laurel

larengitis, laryngitis

lareut, laureate

large,er,est,ely,eness, BIG "prefixes: en"

larges, largess / large(st)

largess, GENEROUS GIFT/DONATION EXPECTING NOTHING IN RETURN

largist, large(st)

largly, large(ly)

lariet, laureate

lariette, laureate

larinex, larynx

larj, large

larjes, largess

lark,*, BIRD, PRANT, ON AN IMPULSE FOR FUN

larniks, larynx

larol, laurel

larva,al, BABY INSECT THAT RESEMBLES A WORM BEFORE IT BECOMES AN ADULT

larying, PREFIX INDICATING "LARYNX/ VOCAL ORGAN" MOST OFTEN MODIFIES THE WORD

laryngitis,ic, THROAT INFLAMMATION

larynx, THROAT

lasarate, lacerate

lasd, last / lace(d)

lase, lace / lace(y) / lazy

lasench, lozenge

laser,*, A LIGHT FREQUENCY

laserashen, lacerate(tion)

laserate, lacerate

laseration, lacerate(tion)

lash,hes,hed,hing,her, HAIRS ON THE EYE, USE SOMETHING SUCH AS ROPE TO STRIKE/TIE UP SOMETHING, THRUST OUT WITH ILL INTENT "prefixes: un"

lasinch, lozenge

lasirashen, lacerate(tion)

lasirate, lacerate

lasiration, lacerate(tion)

lass,ssie, GIRL

lasso,oes, SLIDING HOOP MADE OF ROPE

last,*,ted,ting,tly, NOT THE FIRST, WON'T GO AWAY FOR QUITE AWHILE (or see lace(d))

lasuit, lawsuit

lasurashen, lacerate(tion)

lasurat, lacerate

lasuration, lacerate(tion)

lasute, lawsuit

latch,hes,hed, CLOSURE FOR A DOOR/ LID

late,er,ely,eness,tish, NOT ON TIME, OF A PARTICULAR TIME (or see lady/ ladder/latter)

laten, laden

latent,tly,ncy, A TIME LAPSE BETWEEN WHEN IT HAPPENED AND THE REACTION

later, FURTHER ALONG IN TIME (or see late/ladder/latter)

lateral,lly, EXTENDS FROM THE SIDE, A MOVEMENT IN A SIDEWAYS DIRECTION "prefixes: bi/contra/ multi/uni"

latex,xes,tices, FORM OF MANMADE RUBBER/PLASTIC USED FOR GLOVES, PAINT, ETC.

lath,*, NARROW STRIPS OF WOOD USED TO BUILD WITH (or see lathe)

lathargic, lethargic

lathe,*,ed,hing, WOOD SHAPING MACHINE (or see lath)

lather,*,red,ring,ry,rer, SOAPY/FOAMY BUBBLES (or see leather)

latil, ladle

latincy, latent(ncy)

latise, lattice

latitude,*,dinal,dinally, LINES THAT RUN NORTH/ SOUTH

latle, ladle

latrine,*, MILITARY WORD FOR TOILET

latter,rly, MORE TOWARDS THE LAST (or see ladder)

lattice,ed, WOOD STRIPS CRISSCROSSED TOGETHER FOR DECORATION

latur, later / ladder / latter

latural, lateral

latury, lottery

laty, lady

lau, law

laud, loud

lauger, lager / logger

laugh,hes,hed,hing,hable,hably,hter, DISPLAY/EXPRESS GLEE/ ENJOYMENT IN VOCAL BURSTS

laughter, VOCAL EXPRESSION OF HAPPINESS/GLEE

lauk, lock / log

laukd, lock(ed)

laun, lawn

launch,hes,hed,hing,her, PROPEL/ SHOOT SOMETHING (or see lounge)

launder,*,rer,ry, WASH AND IRON CLOTHING

laundry, CLEANING/CARING OF CLOTHES

laung, lounge / long

laur, layer

laurch, large

laureate,eship, HONORED/ DISTINGUISHED POET

laurel, A TREE, REST ON PREVIOUS AWARDS

lausut, lawsuit

lauyer, lawyer

lava, MOLTEN ROCK

laven, leaven(ed)

lavender, A PLANT

lavesh, lavish

lavinder, lavender

lavish,hes,her,hly,hness,hment, TO BESTOW UPON SOMEONE GIFTS AND OTHER THINGS

lavun, leaven(ed)

lavunder, lavender

law,*,wful,wfully,wfulness,wless, wlessly, RULES SUPPORTED BY A GOVERNMENT "prefixes: un"

lawn,*, GRASSY AREAS

lawnch, launch

lawsuit,*, A CASE BROUGHT BEFORE A JUDGE CONCERNING THE LAW

lawyer,*, PAID PEOPLE TO HELP YOU WITH THE LAWS

lax,xly,xness,xity,xative, RELAXED, NO HURRY (or see lake(s)/lack(s))

laxative,*, PLANT/CHEMICALS FOR RELAXING THE BOWELS

laxsatif, laxative

laxsutif, laxative

laxutif, laxative

lay,*,aid,ying,yer, SET ASIDE/DOWN AN OBJECT, TO INSTALL, SOMEONE WHO IS TRAINING TO BE AN UPPER RANK, RECLINE (or see lie) "prefixes: in/inter/mis/over/re-/un/ under"

layeng, lay(ing) / lying

layer,*,red,ring, THICKNESS OF SOMETHING OVER TOP OF ANOTHER, ONE LEVEL OVER ANOTHER "prefixes: bi/multi"

laytex, latex

layur, layer / lawyer

lazarashen, lacerate(tion)

laze, lazy

lazeng, lozenge

lazer, laser

lazeur, lazy(zier)

lazing, lozenge / laze(zing)

lazy,zier,ziest,zily,ziness, NO AMBITION TO DO ANYTHING (or see lace(y))

lbo, elbow

leach,hes,hed,hing, SEEPING/ PERCOLATING LIQUID (or see leech)

lead,*,ded,dless,der,derless,ding,den, denly,denness, A HEAVY METAL, SOMEONE WHO TAKES CHARGE OF A SITUATION "prefixes: mis/un"

leader,*,rless,rship, ONE WHO TAKES CHARGE (or see letter/liter)

leaf,aves,fy,fier,fiest,finess, GROWS ON A TREE/BUSH "prefixes: inter"

league,*,er, GROUPS PARTICIPATING IN A SIMILAR ACTIVITY DIVIDED INTO REGIONS/ABILITIES "prefixes: pro"

leak,*,ked,king,kage,ky,kiness, WHEN LIQUID/INFORMATION SEEPS OUT (or see leek)

lean,*,nly,nness,ner,nest, VERY LITTLE FAT, VERTICAL POSITION LEANING TOWARDS A HORIZONTAL STATE (or see lien)

leap,*,ped,ping,pt, TO BOUND/JUMP

lear, leer

learn,*,ned,ning,nable,ner,nedly, nedness, TAKE IN INFORMATION AS KNOWLEDGE "prefixes: un"

leary, leery

lease,*,ed,sing,sable,ssee,er, BORROW/ USE FOR AWHILE IN EXCHANGE FOR MONEY (or see lees) "prefixes: re-/sub"

leash,es,hed,hing, RESTRAINT FOR ANIMALS "prefixes: un"

leason, liaison

least,twise, SMALLEST AMOUNT, GREATER THAN "LESS" (or see lease(ed))

leasy, lessee

leather,*,red,ring, DRIED SKIN FROM ANIMALS

leave,*,ving,eft, TO GO AWAY, PAST TENSE FOR THE WORD "LEAF/ LEAVE" (or see leaf/leaven) "prefixes: inter"

leaven,*,ned,ning, USED TO FERMENT DOUGH, TO RAISE MOODS/SPIRITS (or see leave(ving)) "prefixes: un"

leazon, liaison

lebarul, liberal

lebirate, liberate

lebrul, liberal

lebural, liberal

leburate, liberate

leburty, liberty

lecar, liquor / liqueur / lick(er)

lech, leech / leach / ledge

lechibol, legible

lecshur, lecture

lecture,*,ed,ring,er, TO SPEAK AT GREAT LENGTH ABOUT SOMETHING TO A GROUP OF PEOPLE

lecur, liquor / liqueur / lick(er)

led, PAST TENSE FOR THE WORD "LEAD" (or see lid/lead/let)

ledagation, litigate(tion)

ledal, little

ledaret, literate

leder, liter / litter / letter / leader

lederachure, literature

lederary, literary

lederul, literal

ledge,*,er, A FLAT LANDING ATOP A WALL/SECTION, A BOOK WHICH KEEPS ACCOUNTING RECORDS, AN OVERHANG

ledigation, litigate(tion)

ledir, leader / letter / liter / litter

ledis, lettuce

leds, let(s) / lead(s)

ledur, liter / litter / letter / leader

ledurasy, literacy

ledus, lettuce

leech,hes, BLOOD SUCKING BUG (or see leach)

leed, lead

leef, leaf / leave

leeg, league

leek, A VEGETABLE (or see leak)

leen, lean / lien

leenyency, leniency

leep, leap

leer,*,red,ring,ry, A LONG GLANCE WITH MALICIOUS INTENT

leery, SUSPICIOUS/WARY OF

lees, SEDIMENTS OF WINE/LIQUOR (or see lease)

leese, lease

leesh, leash

leest, least / lease(d)

leet, lead

leeward, AWAY FROM THE WIND

lef, leaf / live / leave / left

lefd, lift / left / leaf(ed) / live(d)

lefee, levee / levy / leaf(y)

lefol, level

left,*,ty, LEFT VS. RIGHT, PAST TENSE FOR THE WORD "LEAVE", APPEARS TO BE GONE (or see lift/live(d))

leful, level

leg,*,gged,gging,ggings, EXTREMITY ON THE LOWER END OF THE TORSO, SUPPORT FOR TABLE/CHAIRS, AN EXTENSION, COVER FOR LEGS (or see league/ledge)

legacy,cies, SOMETHING HANDED DOWN FROM PREDECESSORS

legal,ly,lity,lities,lize,lization,lism, RULES AS DECIDED BY THE SUPREME COURT "prefixes: il"

legament, ligament

leganse, allegiance / elegance

legasy, legacy

lege, ledge / league

legebul, legible

legecy, legacy

legend,*,dary,daries, A STORY HANDED DOWN THROUGH HISTORY

leger, leisure / ledge(r)

legeslat, legislate

legesy, legacy

legible,ly,bility, WRITING CAPABLE OF BEING READ "prefixes: il"

legibul, legible

legido, libido

legind, legend

legion,*,nary,naries, LARGE GROUP ASSOCIATED WITH THE MILITARY

legislat, legislate

legislate,*,ed,ting,tion,tive,tor,ture, RELATED TO LAWMAKING

legislation, PASSING AND CREATING LAWS

legislative,ely, RELATED TO LAWMAKING

legislature, LAWMAKING BRANCH

legistics, logistic(s)

legisy, legacy

legitimate,*,ed,ting,ely,eness,tize,acy, tion,mist,mize,mized,mizing,azation, mizer, LEGALLY RECOGNIZED "prefixes: il"

legium, legume

legoslat, legislate

leguble, legible

legue, league

legul, legal

legulize, legal(ize)

legume,*, SPECIES OF PLANT
legun, lesion / legion
leguse, legacy
leguslashen, legislation
leguslat, legislate
leguslative, legislative
leguslature, legislature
legusy, legacy
lei, lay
leier, layer
lein, lain / lane
leis, lace
leisure,ed,eless,ely,reliness,eness,
    RELAXED, UNHURRIED
lej, ledge / leech
lejable, legible
lejanse, allegiance
lejebul, legible
lejen, lesion / legion
lejend, legend
lejer, leisure / ledge(r)
lejeslat, legislate
lejibul, legible
lejin, legion / lesion
lejislashen, legislation
lejislat, legislate
lejislative, legislative
lejislature, legislature
lejitamet, legitimate
lejoslat, legislate
lejun, legion / lesion
lejuslat, legislate
lek, lick / leak / leek / league
leked, lick(ed) / leak(ed)
lekemia, leukemia
leker, liquor / liqueur / lick(er)
lekoresh, licorice
leksher, lecture
lekture, lecture
lekume, legume
lekur, liquor / liqueur / lick(er)
lekwefide, liquify(fied)
lekwid, liquid
lekwidate, liquid(ate)
lekwify, liquify
lem, limb
lemazene, limousine
lemb, limb
lember, limber
lembo, limbo
lemet, limit
lemfatic, lymph(atic)
lemintation, lament(tation)
lemit, limit

lemitation, limit(ation)
lemon,*,ny,nade, CITRUS FRUIT, JUICE
lemp, limp
lemphatic, lymph(atic)
lemune, lemon(y)
lemusine, limousine
lemutation, limit(ation)
lemuzene, limousine
len, lean / lien
lenament, liniment
lend,*,ding,nt,der, LET SOMEONE
    BORROW SOMETHING (or see lint/
    lean(ed))
leneanse, leniency
lenear, linear
lenen, linen
leneuge, lineage
leneul, lineal
lenger, linger
lengo, lingo
length,*,hen,hener,hiness,hy, HOW
    LONG SOMETHING IS
lengual, lingual
lenguist, linguist
lenguistic, linguistic
lenguistics, linguistic(s)
lengwestic, linguistic
lengwist, linguist
lengwistics, linguistic(s)
lengwul, lingual
leniansy, leniency
leniency,cies,ce,nt,ntly, NOT RIGID OR
    TOO STRICT
lenin, linen / lean(ing)
leniuge, lineage
leniur, linear
lenk, link
lenkage, link(age)
lenker, linger
lenkth, length
lenkwol, lingual
lenoleum, linoleum
lenon, linen / lean(ing)
lens, PART OF THE EYE, USED IN
    GLASSES
lenseed, linseed
lent, PAST TENSE FOR THE WORD
    "LEND", LET SOMEONE BORROW, A
    RELIGIOUS EVENT (or see lint/lend/
    lean(ed))
lenth, length
lentil,*, PLANT IN THE LEGUME FAMILY
lentul, lentil
lenument, liniment

lenyensy, leniency
leotard,*, HEAVYWEIGHT PANTYHOSE
lep, lip / leap
lepel, lapel
leqer, liquor / liqueur
lequid, liquid
lequidate, liquid(ate)
lequifide, liquify(fied)
lequify, liquify
leranex, larynx
lerch, lurch
lere, leery
lerengitis, laryngitis
leric, lyric
lerinex, larynx
leringitis, laryngitis
lerk, lurk
lern, learn
lernicks, larynx
lery, leery
les, less / lease
lesard, lizard
lesbian,*, WOMAN WHO PREFERS
    INTIMATE COMPANIONSHIP WITH
    ANOTHER WOMAN
lese, lessee
lesee, lessee
lesen, lessen / lesson / listen
leser, lesser / lessor
lesh, leash
leshun, lesion
lesi, lessee
lesin, lessen / lesson / listen
lesion,*, AN INJURED SPOT ON HUMAN
    TISSUE
lesir, lesser / lessor
lesless, listless
leson, lessen / lesson / listen
lesp, lisp
less,sser, NOT AS MUCH AS BEFORE OR
    AS EXPECTED
lessee,*, ONE WHO IS LEASING
lessen, TAKE SOME AWAY, REMOVE
    SOME (or see lesson)
lesser, NOT AS MUCH AS BEFORE, LESS
    THAN (or see lessor)
lesson,*, A TEACHING/LEARNING
    SECTION/SESSION (or see lessen)
lessor,*, ONE WHO LEASES OUT
    PROPERTY TO OTHERS (or see
    lesser)
lest, list / least
lesten, listen
lestless, listless

lesun, lessen / lesson / listen

lesur, lesser / lessor

let,*,tting, PERMIT, ALLOW (or see led/ lead)

let's, CONTRACTION OF THE WORDS 'LET US'

leter, liter / litter / letter / leader

leteracy, literacy

leteral, literal

leterally, literal(ly)

leterary, literary

leterate, literate

leterature, literature

letes, lettuce

lethal,lly,lity, DEADLY "prefixes: non/ semi"

lethargic,cally,gy, SLEEPY, NO ENERGY, SLUMPED

lethargy,gic, SLEEPY, HARD TO MOVE, NO ENERGY

lether, leather

lethergy, lethargy

lethul, lethal

letir, liter / litter / letter / leader

letiracher, literature

letis, lettuce

letmus, litmus

letrine, latrine

letter,*,red,ring, SYMBOLS OF THE ALPHABET, PAPER WITH WRITING TO SOMEONE, MAKE LETTER SHAPES (or see leader) "prefixes: un"

lettuce, AN EDIBLE PLANT

letur, liter / litter / letter / leader

leturacher, literature

letus, lettuce

leuc, PREFIX INDICATING 'WHITE/ COLORLESS' MOST OFTEN MODIFIES THE WORD

leuco, PREFIX INDICATING 'WHITE/ COLORLESS' MOST OFTEN MODIFIES THE WORD

leukemia,ic, A FATAL DISEASE

leuko, PREFIX INDICATING 'WHITE/ COLORLESS' MOST OFTEN MODIFIES THE WORD

leutard, leotard

lev, PREFIX INDICATING 'COUNTERCLOCKWISE' MOST OFTEN MODIFIES THE WORD

levabul, live(vable)

leval, level

levatate, levitate

leve, leave / levy / levee

levee,*, TRENCH/EMBANKMENT FOR CONTROLLING WATER (or see levy)

level,*,led,ling,lly,lness,ler, STRAIGHT UP OR HORIZONTAL, TRUTHFUL WITH SOMEONE "prefixes: multi/un"

leven, leaven(ed)

lever,*,rage, APPLY PHYSICS/ HARDWARE TO LIFT "prefixes: un"

levi, levee / levy

levid, livid

levil, level

levitate,*,ed,ting,tion,ty, DEFY GRAVITY

levo, PREFIX INDICATING "COUNTERCLOCKWISE" MOST OFTEN MODIFIES THE WORD

levol, level

levor, lever / liver

levs, leave(s)

levuble, live(vable)

levul, level

levun, leaven(ed)

levur, liver / lever

levury, livery

levutate, levitate

levy,vies,vied,vying,viable,vier, USED TO COLLECT MONEY, WAGE WAR (or see levee)

lew, lieu

lewb, lube

lewbrecashen, lubricate(tion)

lewbrecate, lubricate

lewbrikate, lubricate

lewcid, lucid

lewcratef, lucrative

lewd,dly,dness, OBSCENE, GIVEN TO LUST AND INDECENCY (or see loot)

lewdakris, ludicrous

lewducris, ludicrous

lewkrative, lucrative

lewkwarm, lukewarm

lewlu, lulu

lewmenary, luminary

lewmenesense, luminescence

lewmenosity, luminosity

lewmenus, luminous

lewmin, lumen

lewner, lunar

leword, leeward

lewpine, lupine

lewse, loose / lose

lewsid, lucid

lewsun, loose(n)

lewt, loot / lute / lewd

leyor, layer

lezard, lizard

lezbeun, lesbian

li, lie / lye / lay

liabelity, liable(bility)

liable,bility,bilities, SOMEONE TO BE BLAMED

liaison,*, FORMATION OF DEEP CONNECTION BETWEEN PEOPLE FOR MANEUVERING, BONDING

liar,*, SOMEONE WHO DOESN'T TELL THE TRUTH (or see lyre)

liatard, leotard

libary, library

libel,llant,lee,lous,lously, WRITE MALICIOUS WORDS ABOUT SOMEONE ELSE FOR PUBLIC VIEWING (or see liable)

liberal,*,lly,lness,lism,lity,lities,listic,list, MODERATE, TOLERANT, PROVIDE FREELY "prefixes: neo"

liberate,*,ed,ting,tion,tor, TO SET FREE

liberde, liberty

liberty,ties, THE ACT OF FREEDOM

libery, library

libido,dinal,dinally, THOUGHTS WHICH DRIVE THE SEXUAL IMPULSES

lible, libel / liable

libol, libel

liboral, liberal

liborashun, liberate(tion)

liborate, liberate

liboration, liberate(tion)

liborte, liberty

liborul, liberal

library,ries,rian, A PLACE WHICH COLLECTS AND DISSEMINATES WRITTEN HISTORY "prefixes: inter"

librul, liberal

libul, libel / liable

libural, liberal

licd, lick(ed) / like(d)

lice, PLURAL WORD FOR LOUSE, PARASITIC INSECT (or see like/lick/ lie(s)/lay(s))

license,*,ed,sing,sable,see,er, A PERMIT TO OPERATE "prefixes: sub/un"

lich, leach / leech

lichen,*, MOSS, A FORM OF PLANT WITH HEALING QUALITIES (or see liken)

lichon, legion / lesion / lichen

licinse, license

lick,*,ked,king,ker, USING THE TONGUE (or see like) "prefixes: un"

licorice, A PLANT EXTRACT, A CANDY

lict, lick(ed) / like(d)

lid,*,dded,dless, TOP FOR A CONTAINER, A COVERING (or see lie(d)/light/lit)

lidagachon, litigate(tion)

lidagation, litigate(tion)

lidegashen, litigate(tion)

lidegate, litigate

lidel, little

lider, liter / litter / light(er) / leader

liderachure, literature

lideral, literal

liderally, literal(ly)

liderary, literary

liderasy, literacy

liderate, literate

liderature, literature

liderit, literate

lidigachen, litigate(tion)

lidigate, litigate

lidigation, litigate(tion)

lidirachure, literature

lidirary, literary

lidol, little

lidor, litter / leader / liter / letter

lidul, little

liduracher, literature

lidurally, literal(ly)

lidurare, literary

lie,*,ed,lying, TO NOT TELL THE TRUTH, BODY IN A RECLINED/FLAT POSITION, INACTIVE POSITION (or see lay/lye) "prefixes: under"

lien,*, SOMEONE WHO TAKES AWAY PROPERTY FOR MONEY DUE (or see lion)

lieng, lying

lier, liar / lyre

lieu, INSTEAD OF, IN PLACE OF

lieutenant,*, A MILITARY OFFICER

lif, life / live / leaf / leave

lifd, lift / live(d)

life,er,ive, ANIMATE MATTER/ ORGANISM "prefixes: pro-"

lifeble, live(vable)

lifle, live(ly)

liflehood, livelihood

liflehud, livelihood

lift,*,ted,ting,ter, PICK/HOIST UP (or see live(d)/left) "prefixes: up"

ligal, legal

ligale, legal(lly)

ligality, legal(ity)

ligament,*,tous,tal,tary, FIBROUS TISSUE IN THE BODY

ligan, legion / lesion / lichen

light,*,ted,ting,tly,it,ten,tens,tened, tening,tless,tness, VISIBLE WAVE/ PARTICLES, NOT HEAVY "prefixes: en"

lightening, ILLUMINATED ELECTRICAL BOLTS IN SKY

lightness, NOT HEAVY, FEATHER WEIGHT, DEGREE OF ILLUMINATION

ligol, legal

ligole, legal(lly)

ligoly, legal(lly)

ligon, legion / lesion / lichen

ligoon, lagoon

ligument, ligament

lik, lick / like / leak / leek

likd, lick(ed) / like(d)

like,*,ed,kable,eness,ely,elier,eliest, SIMILAR TO SOMETHING/ SOMEONE ELSE, ENJOY SOMETHING, ATTRACTED TO SOMETHING (or see lick) "prefixes: dis/un"

liken,*, SIMILAR TO, RESEMBLING (or see lichen/lick(ing))

likeness, SIMILAR TO, RESEMBLING

liker, liquor / liquer / lick(er)

likerish, licorice

likewise, SIMILARLY, ALSO

likness, likeness

likor, liquor / liqueur

likoresh, licorice

likt, like(d) / lick(ed)

likuble, like(kable)

likued, liquid

likuefi, liquify

likun, liken

likwed, liquid

likwid, liquid

likwidate, liquid(ate)

likwifide, liquify(fied)

likwify, liquify

likwise, likewise

lilac,*, AROMATIC PLANT

liluc, lilac

limasen, limousine

limazene, limousine

limb,*,bed,bing, BRANCHES OF TREES/ SHRUBS, TO REMOVE BRANCHES/

EXTRUSIONS FROM THE BODY TORSO

limber,*,red,ring,rly,rness, ABLE TO MOVE BODY SMOOTHLY, WITH DEXTERITY "prefixes: un"

limbo, PLACE BETWEEN HERE AND THERE, WITH UNCERTAINTY, A PHYSICAL GAME

lime,*, A CITRUS FRUIT, MINERAL FOR SETTING BRICKS/STONE

limelight,*, BEING IN THE SPOTLIGHT

limen, lemon

limesine, limousine

limet, limit

limetation, limit(ation)

limfatic, lymph(atic)

limit,*,ted,ting,tation,tless,tative,ter, tary, ONLY GO SO FAR, A FIXED VALUE "prefixes: il/sub/un"

limlite, limelight

limon, lemon

limosen, limousine

limousine,*, LONG AUTOMOBILE FOR TRANSPORTING PEOPLE

limozen, limousine

limp,*,ped,ping,ply,per, NOT STIFF/ RIGID, LOSS OF FUNCTION, LACK OF WILLFUL CONTROL OVER THE BODY

limphatic, lymph(atic)

limpt, limp(ed)

limusine, limousine

limuzene, limousine

lin, line / lean / lend

linament, liniment

lind, lend / lint / line(d)

line,*,ed,ning,er,eless,eable,eal,ear, eate, BETWEEN TWO POINTS, FOR FISHING "prefixes: inter/multi/un/ under"

lineage,*, OUR ANCESTORS, FAMILY TREE, WHERE WE COME FROM

lineal,lly, HEREDITY FOLLOWING A DIRECT PATH "prefixes: bi/inter/ multi/uni"

lineansi, leniency

linear,rly,rize,rizes,rized,rizing,rization, rity, PATH STRAIGHT AHEAD WITH NO DEVIATION "prefixes: bi/inter/ multi/non/uni"

linen,*, TAN COTTON FABRIC (or see linin/lining) "prefixes: under"

lineng, lining

liner,*, COATING INSIDE A VESSEL FOR PROTECTION

lineur, linear

linger,*,red,ring,ringly,er, STAY AROUND LONGER, LOITER, WAITING

lingo,oes, WAY TO SAY SOMETHING, UNIQUE METHOD OF COMMUNICATION

lingual,lly, OF THE TONGUE/LANGUAGE "prefixes: bi/intra/multi/sub"

linguist,*,tic, ONE WHO SPECIALIZED IN LANGUAGES

linguistic,*,tical,tically, STUDY OF LANGUAGES AND SPEECH

lingwestic, linguistic

lingwist, linguist

lingwistics, linguistic(s)

lingwul, lingual

liniansi, leniency

liniment,*, HEALING OINTMENTS

linin, IN CELL NUCLEUS (or see linen/lining)

lining,*, LAYER INSIDE OF EXTERIOR LINING (or see linin/linen)

liniul, lineal

link,*,ked,king,kage,ker, TWO THINGS JOINED TOGETHER "prefixes: inter/up"

links, lynx / link(s)

linkth, length

linkuge, link(age)

linkwol, lingual

linoleum, FLOOR COVERING

lins, lens / line(s)

linseed, OIL

lint,*,ty,tless, FUZZ FROM MATERIAL (or see lent/line(d))

linth, length

lintul, lentil

linument, liniment

linur, liner

linx, lynx

linz, lens / line(s)

lion,*,ness, A WILD ANIMAL (or see lien)

lior, liar

liotard, leotard

lip,*,pped,pping,ppy,pless, PREFIX INDICATING "FATTY" MOST OFTEN MODIFIES THE WORD, FLESHY FOLDS WORKING TOGETHER, A RIM, PART OF THE MOUTH "prefixes: under"

lipo, PREFIX INDICATING "FATTY" MOST OFTEN MODIFIES THE WORD

liprul, liberal

liqer, liquor / liqueur

liqoresh, licorice

liqueur,*, A SWEETENED/FLAVORED ALCOHOLIC LIQUID (or see liquor)

liquid,*,date,dated,dating,dation,dize, dity,ify,uefy, FLUID

liquify,fiable,fier,fies,fied,fying,faction, factive,fier,uifiable,uifier,uifies, uified, uifying,uifaction,uifactive, uifier, ALSO SPELLED 'LIQUEFY', TURN TO LIQUID/FLUID

liquifying, liquify(ing)

liquor,*, FERMENTED ALCOHOLIC LIQUID (or see liqueur)

lir, leer / liar

lirch, lurch

lire, leery/ leer

lirec, lyric

liric, lyric

lirn, learn

lis, lie(s) / lease / list / lice

lisard, lizard

lisen, listen

lisense, license

liserd, lizard

lishan, legion / lesion

lisles, listless

lison, listen

lisp,*,pingly, PRONUNCIATION IS CHALLENGED BY SHAPE OF TEETH/JAW MUSCLE FORMATION

list,*,ted,ting, IDENTIFY OBJECTS BY ITEMIZING, ORGANIZING TECHNIQUE "prefixes: en/un"

listen,*,ned,ning, TO HEAR AND PAY ATTENTION

listless,ssly,ssness, NO ENERGY, LACKS INTEREST

lisun, listen

lisuns, license

lisurt, lizard

lit, PAST TENSE FOR THE WORD "LIGHT" (or see lite/lid/light/lie(d)) "prefixes: un"

lite, SHORT SPELLING OF "LIGHT", LOW IN SOMETHING (or see lid/lit/light/lie(d))

litegation, litigate(tion)

litel, little

litening, lightening

liter,*, METRIC MEASUREMENT (or see litter/light(er)) "prefixes: deca"

literacy, ABILITY TO WRITE AND READ "prefixes: il"

literal,lly,lity,lize,list,listic,lism, QUITE SO, PERFECT INTERPRETATION "prefixes: uni"

literale, literal(lly)

literary,rily,riness,ate, OF WRITTEN TEXT, LEARNED, EDUCATED "prefixes: sub"

literate,*,ely,acy,ture, EDUCATED, SKILLFUL "prefixes: il/pre/semi/sub"

literature, WRITINGS ABOUT EVERYTHING, TEXT "prefixes: sub"

lithal, lethal

lithargic, lethargic

lithargy, lethargy

lithol, lethal

litigate,*,ed,ting,tor,tion,gious, giousness, BRING DISPUTE INTO LAWFUL JUDGEMENT, TAKE TO COURT

litigation,*, A LAWSUIT

litle, little

litly, light(ly)

litmas, litmus

litmos, litmus

litmus, AN ACID TEST

litneng, lightening

litness, lightness

litning, lightening

litor, light(er) / litter / liter / leader

litr, light(er) / litter / liter / leader

litter,*,red,ring, TRASH/GARBAGE WHERE IT DOESN'T BELONG, GROUP OF INFANT ANIMALS IN A CERTAIN SPECIES (or see liter/light(er))

little, SMALL SIZE IN COMPARISON

litul, little

litur, litter / liter / light(er) / leader

liturally, literal(ly)

liu, lieu

liubility, liable(bility)

liur, liar / lyre

liv, live / life / alive

livad, livid

livapul, live(vable)

live,*,ed,ving,ely,vable,vability, PLACE WHERE YOU DWELL, NOT DEAD, ACTIVE/VITAL "prefixes: en/re/un"

liveable, live(vable)

livebul, live(vable)

livelihood,*, OCCUPATION

livelyhood, livelihood
liver,*, AN ORGAN IN THE BODY
livery,ries, UNIFORM, CARE OF HORSES
livid,dly,dness,ditity, FURIOUS, BRUISED
    FLESH COLOR
livle, live(ly)
livlihood, livelihood
livly, live(ly)
livur, liver
livury, livery
lizard,*, A REPTILE
llama,*, A WOOLY MAMMAL
lo, low
load,*,ded,ding,der, BURDEN, WEIGHT,
    HEAP/PILE INTO A VESSEL, ADD
    AMMUNITION "prefixes: un/up"
loaf,*,fed,fing,fer,aves, OF BREAD,
    SOMEONE WHO LIES AROUND
    DOING NOTHING, A SHOE, FOOD
    SHAPE
loafer,*, SOMEONE WHO IS LAZY, A
    SHOE
loam,my, A RICH/ORGANIC SOIL
loan,*,ned,ning,lent, ALLOW SOMEONE
    TO BORROW SOMETHING (or see
    lone)
loathe,*,ed,hing,er,hsome,hsomely,
    hsomeness, DESPISES, STRONGLY
    DISLIKES
lob,*,bbed,bbing,bber, A HIGH,
    ROUNDED ARCH BY A BALL IN A
    SPORT (or see lobe/lop)
lobby,bbies,bbied,ying,yist,yism,
    WAITING/RESTING ROOM, TO
    COERCE POLITICAL LAWMAKERS
    FOR VOTES
lobd, lob(bbed)
lobe,*,ed,bule, BULBOUS PART OF THE
    EAR/A PLANT, ROUND SHAPE (or
    see lobby)
lobster,*, AN EDIBLE CRUSTACEAN
loby, lobby
loc, lock
locader, locate(tor)
local,*,lly,le,lism,lity,lities,lize, IN THE
    AREA, WITHIN DESIGNATED
    REGION
localety, local(ity)
localize,ed,zation, TO BE LOCATED IN A
    SPECIFIC REGION, IN THE AREA
locashen, locate(tion)
locate,*,ed,ting,tion,tive,tor, TO
    IDENTIFY A SPECIFIC PLACE
    "prefixes: dis/re"

locemoshen, locomotive
locer, locker
locest, locust
loch, lodge / lock
lock,*,ked,king,kage,kable,kless,ker,
    MECHANISM WHICH REQUIRES A
    KEY, SECURE, BE INEXCUSABLY
    INVOLVED, EXCLUDED "prefixes:
    inter/un"
locker,*, A CONTAINER WITH A LOCK
locksmith,*, ONE WHO WORKS WITH
    LOCKS
loco, CRAZY
locomotion, THE ACT OF MOVING,
    LOCATING FROM ONE PLACE TO
    ANOTHER
locomotive,*, THE BODILY OR PHYSICAL
    ACT OF MOVEMENT FROM ONE
    PLACE TO ANOTHER
locsmith, locksmith
locul, local
loculizashen, localize(zation)
loculize, localize
loculy, local(ly)
locumoshen, locomotion
locumotive, locomotive
locur, locker
locust,*, A BUG ("T" IS SILENT)
lod, load
lodery, lottery
lodge,*,ed,ging,gment, SOMETHING
    JAMMED INTO A TIGHT SPACE,
    HABITATION FOR VISITORS WHO
    OCCASIONALLY COME FOR THE
    NIGHT, BRING FORTH ACTION ("D"
    IS SILENT) "prefixes: dis"
lodis, lotus
lodury, lottery
lodus, lotus
loeder, loiter
loen, loin
loer, lower / lawyer
loest, low(est)
loeul, loyal
lof, loaf
lofa, lava
lofer, loafer
lofly, lovely
loft,*,ted,ting,ty,tily, SMALL LANDING
    ABOVE THE MAIN FLOOR, PROPEL
    SOMETHING INTO THE AIR
lofur, loafer
log,*,gged,gging,gger, MAKE A
    WRITTEN NOTE OF, REMOVED

SECTION OF LIMB/TREE, TO
    REMOVE TIMBER, MEASURE
    VELOCITY (or see lodge)
logarithm,*,mic,mically, A MATH
    FUNCTION "prefixes: semi"
loge, lodge
logec, logic
logecul, logic(al)
loger, logger
logestics, logistic(s)
logger,*, SOMEONE WHO CUTS TREES
    (or see lager)
logic,*,cal,cally,cality,calness, TO MAKE
    SENSE OF, BE REASONABLE
    "prefixes: il"
logicul, logic(al)
logir, logger
logistic,*,cal,cally,cian, ARRANGING
    ACTIONS TO BENEFIT AN
    ADDITIONAL ACTION,
    CALCULATING
logo,*, A THEME OR SYMBOL WHICH
    IDENTIFIES
logrethm, logarithm
logrythm, logarithm
logur, logger
loider, loiter
loin,*, SECTION OF A BODY
loir, lower
loiter,*,red,ring, TO STAND AROUND,
    HANGING OUT
lojecul, logic(al)
lojek, logic
lojical, logic(al)
lojik, logic
lok, look / lock
lokality, local(ity)
lokashen, locate(tion)
lokate, locate
lokator, locate(tor)
lokel, local
lokelizashen, localize(zation)
lokelize, localize
lokely, local(ly)
lokemotive, locomotive
loker, locker / look(er) / logger
lokes, locust / look(s) / lock(s)
lokimoshen, locomotive
lokimotev, locomotive
lokir, locker / look(er) / logger
lokist, locust
loko, loco
loksmeth, locksmith
lokt, lock(ed) / look(ed)

lokul, local
lokule, local(ly)
lokulization, localize(zation)
lokulize, localize
lokumoshen, locomotion
lokumotef, locomotive
lokumotive, locomotive
lokur, locker / look(er) / logger
lokus, locust
lolegag, lollygag
lolepop, lollipop
loligag, lollygag
lollipop,*, CANDY
lollygag,*,gged,gging, TO LOITER/HANG AROUND DOING NOTHING
loly, low(ly)
lolypop, lollipop
lom, loam / loom
loma, llama
lomanesense, luminescence
lombur, lumber / lumbar
lome, loam
lomp, lump
lomunesense, luminescence
lomy, loam(y)
lon, lone / loan / lawn
lonch, launch / lunch
londer, launder
londry, laundry
londurer, launder(er)
lone,er,ely,eliness,esome,esomely, esomeness, BY ITSELF, SINGLED OUT, JUST ONE (or see loan)
long,ger,gest, THE LENGTH/DURATION OF SOMETHING, MEASURE OF TIME
longatude, longitude
longetudenul, longitude(dinal)
longir, long(er)
longist, long(est)
longitude,*,dinal,dinally, INVISIBLE LINE ON EARTH THAT RUNS EAST, WEST
lonir, lone(r)
lonjatude, longitude
lonjetudenul, longitude(dinal)
lonjitude, longitude
lonk, long
lonker, long(er)
lonkist, long(est)
lonly, lone(ly)
lons, lawn(s) / loan(s)
lonsem, lone(some)
lonsum, lone(some)
lonter, launder
lontre, laundry

lonur, lone(r)
loob, lube
loobrucate, lubricate
lood, lewd / load
loodekres, ludicrous
look,*,ked,king,ker, TO VIEW WITH THE EYES
lookwarm, lukewarm
looloo, lulu
loom,*,med,ming, INTO THE FUTURE, LATER IN TIME, A MACHINE FOR WEAVING YARN/THREAD (or see loam)
loomanocity, luminosity
loomenesent, luminescence(nt)
loomenocity, luminosity
loominesinse, luminescence
loominocity, luminosity
loominus, luminous
loomy, loam(y)
loon,*,ny, A BIRD, BEHAVING GOOFY (or see lune)
looner, lunar
loop,*,ped,ping,py, A SEMI-CIRCULAR SHAPE, WRAP/GO AROUND, BEHAVING ODDLY
loopen, lupine
loose,*,sing,en,ens,ened,ening, MISPLACE/FORGET SOMETHING, RELAX HOLD ON, UNTIGHTEN, SLOPPY, GET RID OF (or see lose) "prefixes: un"
loosid, lucid
loot,*,ted,ting,ter, MONEY/GOODS, ONE WHO STEALS THINGS (or see lute/lewd)
looze, loose / lose
lop,*,pped,pping, ACT OF REMOVING, ROUGHLY (or see lobe/lope)
lope,*,er,ed,ping, EASY STRIDES WITH BOUNCE (or see lop)
lor, lore / low(er)
lorch, large
lord,*,ded,ding, MASTER, ONE WHO TAKES OWNERSHIP
lore,*, BELIEF IN THE FORM OF A STORY OF THE PAST
loreate, laureate
lorg, large
loriette, laureate
lorj, large
lort, lord
lorul, laurel
losd, lost

lose,*,er,sing,st, PAST TENSE FOR THE WORD "LOST", HAVING LOST (or see loose)
losenge, lozenge
losh, lush
loshen, lotion
loshin, lotion
losinge, lozenge
losinje, lozenge
losir, lose(r) / loose(r)
loss,ses, TAKEN AWAY, REMOVED
lost, PAST TENSE FOR THE WORD "LOOSE", CANNOT BE FOUND (or see lust)
loster, luster
losuit, lawsuit
losur, lose(r) / loose(r)
losute, lawsuit
lot,*,tted,tting, WHOLE BUNCH, A SPECIFIC SIZE OF SOMETHING, A SECTION AMONG MANY
lotery, lottery
lotes, lotus
lothe, loathe
lotion,*, CREAMY LIQUID TO APPLY TO THE BODY
lotis, lotus
lottery,ries, GAMBLING
lotury, lottery
lotus, A FLOWER, A POSITION, A PLANT
loud,dly,dness,der,dest, SOUND THAT IS BEYOND A COMFORTABLE HEARING RANGE
loul, loyal
lounch, lounge
lounge,*,ed,ging,er, TO LIE AROUND, RECLINED POSITION, ROOM WHERE PEOPLE REST/RELAX
lour, lower
louver,*, SHUTTERS
lova, lava
love,*,ed,ving,vable,vableness,vably, vability,er,eless, A SPECIAL/DEEP AFFECTION FOR
lovely,lier,liest,liness, PERFECTLY ATTRACTIVE "prefixes: un"
lovle, lovely
lovte, loft(y)
lovu, lava
low,wer,west,wly, CLOSE TO THE BOTTOM OR THE GROUND, LACK OF ENERGY
lowd, loud
lowder, loud(er)

lowdest, loud(est)

lowen, loin

lower,*,red,ring, ACT OF LETTING DOWN, CLOSE TO THE BOTTOM OR GROUND, LESSEN

lownch, lounge

lownge, lounge

lows, low(s) / loathe(s)

lowt, loud / load

lowtest, loud(est)

lowyer, lawyer

lowyul, loyal

loyal,list,lly,lty,lties, FAITHFUL "prefixes: dis"

loyer, lawyer

loyn, loin

loyulty, loyal(ty)

loyure, lawyer

lozenge,*, THROAT MEDICINE

lu, lieu

lub, lube

lube,*,ed,bing,bricate, GREASE

lubracashen, lubricate(tion)

lubracate, lubricate

lubricate,*,ed,ting,tion,ant, TO GREASE/ OIL UP

luc, look / luck

lucgireate, luxury(riate)

lucgiry, luxury

lucheus, luscious

luchious, luscious

luchness, lush(ness)

lucid,dity,dness,dly, A STATE OF BEING BETWEEN HERE AND THERE

lucjireate, luxury(riate)

lucjiry, luxury

luck,ky,kily,kier,kiest,kless, GOOD FORTUNE "prefixes: un"

lucke, luck(y)

luckgerious, luxurious

luckjiry, luxury

lucrative,ely,eness, COULD YIELD PROFIT OR GAIN

lucwarm, lukewarm

ludakris, ludicrous

lude, lewd / lute / loot

ludecris, ludicrous

luder, loot(er)

ludicrous,sly,sness, RIDICULOUS

luf, love

lufable, love(vable)

lufer, louver / love(r)

lufless, love(less)

lufly, lovely

lug,*,gged,gging, CARRY AROUND A HEAVY LOAD, ON A WHEEL, PULL (or see luck/look)

lugach, luggage

lugd, lug(gged)

lugege, luggage

luggage, TRAVELING BAGS

lugich, luggage

lugije, luggage

lugjureus, luxurious

lugshureant, luxuriant

lugshureous, luxurious

lugshury, luxury

lugt, lug(gged)

luk, look / luck / lug

lukchury, luxury

luke, luck / luck(y) / look

lukege, luggage

lukemea, leukemia

lukewarm, BETWEEN WARM AND HOT

lukgery, luxury

lukgureus, luxurious

lukiest, luck(iest)

lukige, luggage

lukjereus, luxurious

lukrative, lucrative

luks, look(s) / luck(s)

lukshereant, luxuriant

lukshury, luxury

luksuryant, luxuriant

lukwarm, lukewarm

luky, luck(y)

lull,*,led,ling, A PAUSE, GENTLY COAX, CAUSE TO RELAX

lulu,*, REAL WINNER

lum, loom

lumanesense, luminescence

lumbar,*, AREA IN LOWER BACK (or see lumber)

lumber,rer,rman,ring, BOARDS CUT FROM TIMBER (or see lumbar)

lumbir, lumber / lumbar

lumbur, lumber / lumbar

lume, loom

lumen,*,mina,minal,minous, OF LIGHT, GIVING OFF LIGHT, UNIT OF MEASURE "prefixes: il"

lumenary, luminary

lumenesense, luminescence

lumenesent, luminescence(nt)

lumenosidty, luminosity

lument, lament

lumentation, lament(ation)

lumenus, luminous

lumenusly, luminous(ly)

luminary,ria,ries, GIVING OFF LIGHT

luminescence,nt, GIVING OFF LIGHT "prefixes: bio"

luminosity,ties, INTENSITY OF LIGHT

luminous,sly,sness, AMOUNT OF LIGHT, OF LIGHT

luminus, lumen(ous)

lump,*,ped,ping,py, MASS OR AGGREGATE OF SOMETHING

lumunesense, luminescence

lun, loon / lune

lunar,ate,rian, OF THE MOON "prefixes: inter/semi/sub"

lunch,hes,hed,hing,heon, AFTERNOON MEAL (or see lunge)

lune,nula, MOON WHEN IT'S NOT FULL (or see loon)

luney, loon(y) / lune

lung,*, ORGAN OF THE BODY (or see lunge)

lunge,*,ed,ging, LEAP FORWARD TOWARDS SOMETHING, PULL QUICKLY/ HARD AGAINST RESTRAINTS

lunir, lunar

lunje, lunge

lunur, lunar

lup, loop

lupe, loop / loop(y)

lupel, lapel

lupen, lupine

lupine,*, A WOLF, A PLANT

lurch,hes,hed,hing,her, HANG ABOUT SUSPICIOUSLY, DRUNKEN STAGGER, LEAP INTO ACTION

lurk,*,ked,king,ker, STALK, SECRETLY WAIT TO AMBUSH

lus, loose / lose

luscious,sly,sness, GLORIOUS SENSORY EXPERIENCE OF SOMETHING USING TASTE/SMELL/SIGHT/TOUCH

lusd, lust

lusder, luster

lusdruss, lust(rous)

luse, loose / lose

lused, lucid

lusen, loose(n)

lush,hly,hness, ABUNDANT, OPULENT FLORAL AND FAUNA, RICH IN FOLIAGE, AN ALCOHOLIC

lusheous, luscious

lushus, luscious

lusid, lucid

lusin, loose(n)

lust,*,ted,ting,tful,tfully,tfulness,trous, TEMPORARY INTENSE DESIRE

luster,*,red,ring,rless, GLISTENING, WAY LIGHT REFLECTS, AS IF GLOWING, SHINY REFLECTION

lustious, luscious

lusty,tily,tiness, HEARTY AND JOVIAL, ROBUST

lut, lute / loot / lewd

lute,*, A MUSICAL INSTRUMENT (or see loot/lewd)

lutenant, lieutenant

luter, loot(er)

lutinant, lieutenant

lutrene, latrine

luv, love

luvabul, love(vable)

luver, louver / love(r)

luvle, lovely

luvless, love(less)

luxuriant,nce,ncy,tly, VERY HEALTHY, RICHLY ABUNDANT, PROFUSE

luxurious,sly,sness, EXPENSIVE COMFORT

luxury,ries,riate,riated,riating,rious, GREAT RICHNESS, OPULENT, OVERLY ABUNDANT

luz, loose / lose

ly, lye / lie

lye, WOOD ASH FOR SOAP (or see lie)

lying, NOT TELLING THE TRUTH, PAST TENSE FOR THE WORD "LIE" (or see lay(ing))

lymfatic, lymph(atic)

lymph,hatic, FLUID WITH WHITE BLOOD CELLS, OF THE BODY, PREFIX INDICATING "LYMPH/YELLOWISH" MOST OFTEN MODIFIES THE WORD

lympho, PREFIX INDICATING "LYMPH/ YELLOWISH" MOST OFTEN MODIFIES THE WORD

lynx,xes, A WILD ANIMAL

lyo, PREFIX INDICATING "DISSOLVED/ DISPERSED" MOST OFTEN MODIFIES THE WORD

lyre,*, AN INSTRUMENT (or see liar)

lyric,*,cal,cally,cism,cist, WORDS SANG IN A SONG

lys, PREFIX INDICATING "DISSOLVED/ DISPERSED"MOST OFTEN MODIFIES THE WORD

lyso, PREFIX INDICATING "DISSOLVED/ DISPERSED"MOST OFTEN MODIFIES THE WORD

m, am

ma, may

mab, mob

mabe, maybe

mabilety, mobile(lity)

mac, mach / make / mock / mace

macaroni,ies, CHEESY NOODLES

macaroon,*, A COOKIE

macasen, moccasin

macaw,*, A TROPICAL BIRD

mace,ed, SPICE, MEDIEVAL WEAPON, CHEMICAL SPRAY (or see make/ maize/ maze/mach)

mach, AMOUNT OF SPEED (or see make/match/mock/mash)

machenery, machine(ry)

macheng, match(ing) / mash(ing)

macherel, mackerel

macherly, mature(ly)

maches, match(es) / mash(es)

machestral, magistral

machestrate, magistrate

machete,*, A CHOPPING HAND TOOL

machine,*,nability,nable,nate,nation, nator,ery,eries,nist, DEVICE WITH MOVING PARTS THAT PERFORMS WORK

machis, match(es) / mash(es)

machistral, magistral

machistrate, magistrate

machurashen, mature(ration)

machure, mature

machuredy, mature(rity)

machuril, mackerel

machus, match(es) / mash(es)

mack, make / mach / mock

mackerel,*, EDIBLE FISH

macks, max / make(s)

macrame, LACED/WOVEN ROPE

macro, PREFIX INDICATING "DISSOLVED/DISPERSED" MOST OFTEN MODIFIES THE WORD

macrocosm,*,mic,mically, THE BIG PICTURE, INCORPORATES EVERYTHING BIG AND SMALL

macruma, macrame

macs, max / make(s)

macsimul, maximal

macuroni, macaroni

macuroon, macaroon

macusen, moccasin

mad,dder,ddest,dden,ddening, ddeningly,dness, NOT HAPPY, MORE THAN IRRITATED, ANGRY (or see made/maid/matte/mat/mate)

madch, match

made, PAST TENSE FOR THE WORD "MAKE", HAVING CREATED (or see maid/mate) "prefixes: re/un"

madekulus, meticulous

madel, modal /model / mottle

madena, matinee

mader, matter / mad(dder)

maderde, maitre d'

madereulise, materialize

madernize, modern(ize)

madernulistic, maternal(istic)

madesenul, medicine(nal)

madina, matinee

madir, mad(dder) / matter

madirde, maitre d'

madisenul, medicine(nal)

madist, mad(ddest)

madna, matinee

madnes, mad(dness)

mado, motto

madramony, matrimony

madreark, matriarch

madrearkul, matriarch(al)

madremony, matrimony

madren, matron

madress, mattress

madrexs, matrix

madricks, matrix

madrimony, matrimony

madris, mattress

madron, matron

madur, matter / mad(der)

madurde, maitre d'

mae, may

maer, mayor

maestro,*, MASTER OF ANY MEDIUM RELATED TO ART

mafe, mauve

maferick, maverick

mafrek, maverick

magacul, magic(al)

magazine,*, COMPILED PAGES OF WRITTEN ARTICLES, HAVING TO DO WITH WEAPONS

mager, major

magesine, magazine

magestral, magistral

magestrate, magistrate

magesty, majesty

maggot,*, LARVA OF AN INSECT

magic,cal,cally,cian, DIDN'T VISIBLY WITNESS THE CHANGE OF EVENTS WHICH LED TO AN EVENT

magir, major

magirete, major(ette)

magistral,lly,lity,ature,terial,terially, terialness,terium,ate, LOCAL OFFICIAL OFFICE

magistrate,*,acy,acies,ture,al, LOCAL OFFICIAL OFFICE

magisty, majesty

magit, maggot

magizene, magazine

magma,*,ata,atic, MOLTEN ROCK

magnate,*, PROMINENT INDUSTRIALIST (or see magnet))

magnatise, magnetize

magnatisum, magnet(ism)

magnatude, magnitude

magnedic, magnet(ic)

magnefacashen, magnify(fication)

magnefasent, magnificent

magnefesently, magnificent(ly)

magnefiable, magnify(iable)

magnefy, magnify

magnet,*,tic,tically,tism,tize, DRAWN TO, ORE FROM THE EARTH, TOWARD THE NORTH/SOUTH ENDS, PREFIX INDICATING "MAGNET" MOST OFTEN MODIFIES THE WORD (or see magnate) "prefixes: bio"

magnetize,*,ed,zing,zable,zation,zer, BE DRAWN TO, MAKE POLAR

magneto, PREFIX INDICATING "MAGNET" MOST OFTEN MODIFIES THE WORD

magnetude, magnitude

magnifesent, magnificent

magnificent,tly,nce, SPLENDID

magnify,fies,fied,ying,fiable,fier,fication, TO ENLARGE, GET CLOSER TO, MAKE BIGGER "prefixes: bio"

magnit, magnet / magnate

magnitise, magnetize

magnitude,*,dinous, THE SIZE OR EXTENT OF, THE DEGREE OF

magnufecashen, magnify(fication)

magnufy, magnify

magnutise, magnetize

magnutisum, magnet(ism)

magnutude, magnitude

magoredy, major(ity)

magorete, major(ette)

magority, major(ity)

magot, maggot

maguk, magic

magul, module

maguler, module(lar)

magur, major

magurete, major(ette)

magustrate, magistrate

maguzene, magazine

mai, may / my

maid,*,den, ONE WHO CLEANS BEHIND OTHERS FOR A LIVING (or see made/mate)

mail,*,led,ling,ler, SEND A PHYSICAL THING AWAY TO SOMEONE (or see male/mile)

maim,*,med,ming, TO MUTILATE/ DESTROY (or see mime)

main,*,nly, THE MOST IMPORTANT ONE, THE ONE THAT STANDS OUT (or see mane/mine)

maingy, mangy

maintain,*,ned,ning,nable,tenance, UPKEEP, KEEP IN GOOD REPAIR

maintenance, TO KEEP IN WORKING ORDER, TO FIX, SUPPORT, UPKEEP

maitre d',*, HEADWAITER/HOTEL MANAGER

maize,*, CORN (or see maze)

maj, image

majek, magic

majen, imagine

majer, major

majestral, magistral

majestrate, magistrate

majesty,tic,tically, OF AUTHORITY/ GRANDEUR, GREAT IMPRESSION

majewlate, modulate

majir, major

majistral, magistral

majistrate, magistrate

major,*,red,ring,rity,rities,rette, GREATEST NUMBER OF, A MILITARY RANK, FEMALE MARCHER, HIGHEST NUMBER OF

majoredy, major(ity)

majul, module

majulate, modulate

majur, major

majustrate, magistrate

mak, mach / make / mock

makanek, mechanic

makanekul, mechanic(al)

makanize, mechanize

makaril, mackerel

makarony, macaroni

makaroon, macaroon

makaw, macaw

make,*,ade,king,er, TO CREATE, BRING TO REALITY (or see mach/mock) "prefixes: re/un"

maked, made / mock(ed)

makerony, macaroni

makinate, machine(nate)

makir, make(r)

makirony, macaroni

makremay, macrame

makrocosim, macrocosm

makrumay, macrame

maks, max / make(s) / mock(s)

maksamis, maximize

maksemal, maximal

maksemize, maximize

maksimul, maximal

maksimum, maximum

maksumum, maximum

makuril, mackerel

makurone, macaroni

makusen, moccasin

makzemize, maximize

mal, PREFIX INDICATING "BAD" MOST OFTEN MODIFIES THE WORD (or see mall/maul/male/mail)

malable, malleable

maladek, melody(dic)

maladjusted,tment, NOT SITUATED AS SHOULD BE, IMPROPER ORIENTATION

malado, mulato

malady,dies, A DISORDER OR CONFLICT BETWEEN THE BODY AND MIND, ABNORMAL ARRANGEMENT

malajusted, maladjusted

malanosis, melanosis

malaria, DISEASE TRANSPORTED TO HUMANS BY SOME MOSQUITOES

malarkey, DOESN'T APPEAR TO BE THE TRUTH, CALLING A BLUFF

malas, malice

malases, molasses

mald, maul(ed) / mail(ed) / malt

male,*,eness, THE MASCULINE GENDER, THE INSERTION END (or see mail)

maleable, malleable

maleble, malleable

maledy, malady

malegnent, malignant

malegusted, maladjusted

malegustment, maladjusted(tment)

malejusted, maladjusted

malekule, molecule

malekuler, molecule(lar)

maleneum, millennium

malenoma, melanoma

malenosis, melanosis

malerd, mallard

malese, malice

malesha, militia

maleshes, malicious

malest, molest

malet, mallet

maleuble, malleable

malevolent,tly,nce, MALICIOUS, HATEFUL

malfunction,*,ned,ning, DOESN'T WORK AS IT WAS INTENDED

malfunkshen, malfunction

malible, malleable

malice,cious, DIRECT HATE TOWARDS ANOTHER, EMOTION OF FEAR/ INSECURITY

malicious,ciously,ciousness, DIRECT HATE TOWARDS ANOTHER, EMOTION OF FEAR/INSECURITY

malignant,tly,ncy, ACT OF BEING MALICIOUS, DANGEROUS GROWTH "prefixes: pre"

maligusted, maladjusted

malineum, millennium

malinoma, melanoma

malinosis, melanosis

malisha, militia

malishes, malicious

malit, mallet

malitia, militia

mality, malady

maliuble, malleable

mall,*, LARGE BUILDING WITH SMALL STORES INSIDE (or see mail/male/ maul)

mallard,*, WILD DUCK

malleable,billity,eness, SEEMINGLY STIFF MATERIAL/METAL THAT'S EASILY WORKED/MOLDED

mallet,*, HAMMER TYPE TOOL

malluble, malleable

malnerished, malnourished

malnewtrishen, malnutrition

malnourished, NOT ENOUGH NUTRITIONAL FOOD

malnureshed, malnourished

malnutrition, SUFFERING LACK OF NUTRITIOUS FOOD

malodic, melody(dic)

malos, malice

malpractice,*,cioner, DR. WHO PRODUCED A FATAL/SERIOUS INJURY WHILE PRACTICING MEDICINE

malpraktes, malpractice

malt,*,ted,ty, A FROTHY COLD DRINK (or see maul(ed)/molt)

maluble, malleable

maludy, malady

malugusted, maladjusted

malujustment, maladjusted(tment)

malunosis, melanosis

malurd, mallard

malus, malice

malut, mallet

mam, maim

mama, A MOTHER (or see mamma)

mamal, mammal

mamalean, mammal(ian)

mamary gland, mammary gland

mamel, mammal

mamento, memento

mamery gland, mammary gland

mameth, mammoth

mamil, mammal

maminto, memento

mamiry gland, mammary gland

mamith, mammoth

mamma, MILK SECRETING BREASTS/ TEATS/ORGAN

mammal,*,lian, WARM BLOODED ANIMAL THAT GIVES BIRTH TO ITS YOUNG

mammary gland,*, GLANDS IN THE BREAST THAT SECRETES MILK

mammoth, ICE AGE ELEPHANT

mamory gland, mammary gland

mamoth, mammoth

mamt, maim(ed)

mamul, mammal

mamury gland, mammary gland

man, ADULT MALE (or see mane/main) "prefixes: un"

manacle,*, WRIST RESTRAINTS

manage,*,ed,ging,ement,eable,eably, eableness,er,erial, ABILITY TO DEAL WITH AND ORCHESTRATE AFFAIRS SMOOTHLY "prefixes: mis/un"

manakin,*, BIRD (or see mannikin/ manikin/mannequin)

manakure, manicure

manark, monarch

manarkeul, monarch(ial)

manarky, monarch(y)

manase, mayonnaise

manchen, mansion

mandala,*, A SYMBOL OF SPIRITUAL SIGNIFICANCE

mandalin, mandolin

mandarin,*, FRUIT

mandate,*,ed,ting,tory, A COMMAND, RULE

mandatory,ries,rily, COMMANDE, ORDERED

mandel, mantel / mantle

mandelin, mandolin

manderin, mandarin

mandetory, mandatory

manditory, mandatory

mandle, mantel / mantle

mandola, mandala

mandolin,*, A STRINGED INSTRUMENT

mandrake, AN HERB

mandrel,*, A DEVICE TO AID IN CUTTING A SOLID MATERIAL

mandril, mandrel

mandrul, mandrel

mandul, mantel / mantle

manduren, mandarin

mandutory, mandatory

mane, HAIR ABOUT THE NECK OF AN ANIMAL (or see main/many)

manea, mania

maneac, maniac

manecure, manicure

manee, many

manefest, manifest

manefesto, manifest(o)

manefold, manifold

manege, manage

manegment, manage(ment)

maneje, manage

manekin, manikin / manakin / mannequin

manekul, manacle

manense, maintenance

maner, manner / manor / manure

manerism, manner(ism)

manerlee, manner(ly)

maneuver,*,red,ring,rable,rability,rer, SKILLFUL DISPLAY OF MOVEMENT

manevest, manifest

mang, mange

mange, A SKIN CONDITION

manger, TROUGH FOR ANIMALS

mangle,*,ed,ling,er, TO SHRED/TEAR UP, A LARGE IRON

mango,*, A FRUIT

mangul, mangle

mangy,gily,giness, SHABBY, ILL-KEPT

mania, NTENSE EMOTION

maniac,*,cal,cally, SOMEONE UNCONTROLLABLE ON A CONTINUOUS BASIS

manicle, manacle

manicure,*,ed,ring,rist, CARING OF FINGERNAILS

manifest,*,ted,ting,ter,tly,tation,tant, ter,to, DESIRED RESULT ACHIEVED WITH LITTLE EFFORT

manifold,*,ded,ding,der,dly,dness, ON A MOTOR, A COPY, TO MULTIPLY

manige, manage

manigment, manage(ment)

manikin, A MOLD OF A BODY FOR CLOTHING DISPLAY (or see manakin/mannequin)

manila, BUFF-COLORED HEMP PAPER

manipulate,*,ed,ting,tion,able,ability, table,tor,tory,tive,tively,tiveness, CONTROL ENVIRONMENT/EVENTS

manir, manner / manor / manure

manirism, manner(ism)

manirlee, manner(ly)

manj, mange

manjur, manger

manle, main(ly) / man(ly)

mannequin,*, LITTLE/DWARFED HUMAN, MODEL OF PART OF THE BODY OR ENTIRE TORSO, SOMEONE WHO MODELS CLOTHING, ALSO SPELLED 'MANNIKIN OR MANIKIN' (or see manakin/manikin)

manner,*,red,rless,rism,rist,ristic,rly, TO HANDLE ONESELF PROPERLY, BE POLITE (or see manor) "prefixes: un"

manofestation, manifest(ation)

manogumy, monogamy

manolith, monolith

manopuly, monopoly

manor,*, HOME OF MEDIEVAL TIMES (or see manure/manner)

manotny, monotony

manotone, monotone

manotunus, monotony(nous)

manshen, mansion

mansion,*, A VERY LARGE HOME

mantane, maintain

mantanuble, maintain(able)

mantel,*, FIREPLACE SHELF (or see mantle)

mantenanse, maintenance

mantil, mantel / mantle

mantle,*, A CLOAK, A CLOTH SLEEVE FOR A GAS LANTERN (or see mantel)

mantul, mantel / mantle

mantunense, maintenance

manual,*,lly, DIRECTIONS ON HOW TO USE SOMETHING, TO DO BY HAND

manucle, manacle

manuel, manual

manuely, manual(ly)

manufacture,*,ed,ring,rer,rable,ral, CREATE SOMETHING FROM RAW MATERIALS

manufaksher, manufacture

manufestation, manifest(ation)

manufold, manifold

manuge, manage

manugment, manage(ment)

manuil, manual

manukin, manakin

manul, mantel / mantle

manur, manner / manor / manure

manure,rial,er, WASTE FROM ANIMALS (or see manor/manner)

manurism, manner(ism)

manurly, manner(ly)

manuscript,*, STORY SOMEONE WRITES THAT MAY BECOME A BOOK/MOVIE

manuskrept, manuscript

manustery, monastery

manuver, maneuver

many, MORE THAN A FEW (or see mini)

manyewfaksher, manufacture

manyual, manual

manyuskrept, manuscript

maonase, mayonnaise

maor, mayor

map,*,pped,pping, DIRECTIONS/GUIDE TO A SPECIFIC AREA (or see mop)

mapal, maple

mapd, map(pped) / mop(pped)

mape, maybe

mapel, maple

maple,*, A TREE, SYRUP FROM TREE

mapul, maple

mar,*,rred,rring, TO RUIN/DETRACT FROM (or see mare/mayor)

maraje, mirage

marakulus, miracle(culous)

maranade, marinade / marinate

maranate, marinade / marinate

marange, meringue

marathon,*,ner, A LONG DISTANCE EVENT

marbel, marble

marble,*,ed,ling,ly,er, A LITTLE GLASS BALL, TYPE OF ROCK, A VISUAL EFFECT

marbul, marble

marc, mark

marcetable, market(able)

march,hes,hed,hing,her, BRISK FORM OF WALKING, MONTH OF THE YEAR

marchel, martial / marshal

marchel law, martial law

marchen, martian / march(ing) / margin(s)

marchenulize, marginalize

marchoram, marjoram

marchul, martial / marshal

marchul law, martial law

marden, martin

mardene, martini

mardengale, martingale

marder, martyr

mardin, martin

mardine, martini

mardingale, martingale

mardir, martyr

mardur, martyr

mare,*, FEMALE HORSE (or see marry/mayor)

mared, married / mar(rred)

maredean, meridian

mareg, marriage

maregold, marigold

marej, marriage

marejuana, marijuana

marena, marina

marenad, marinade / marinate

marene, marine

mareonette, marionette

maret, merit

maretime, maritime

maretul, marital

mareunette, marionette

marewana, marijuana

marfilus, marvelous

margarine, A FAKE BUTTER

margen, margin

margenul, margin(al)

margenulize, marginalize
margerem, marjoram
margin,*,nal,nally,nality,nalize,nate,
nates,nated,nating,nation, SPACE
OUTSIDE OF THE TEXT/ BORDER
AREA "prefixes: sub"
marginalize,*,ed,zing,zation,nate,
BLOCK SOMEONE FROM
SOMETHING THEY NEED/ WANT
margorem, marjoram
margurim, marjoram
mari, marry
marid, married
maridian, meridian
marig, marriage
marigold,*, A FLOWER
marij, marriage
marijuana, ALSO MARIHUANA,
MEDICINAL PLANT (or see hemp)
marily, merry(rily)
marina,*, FOR BOAT MOORING
marinade,*,ate, SAUCE WITH SPICES
THAT FISH/MEAT IS SOAKED IN (or
see marinate)
marinate,*,ted,ting,tion,ade, THE ACT
OF SOAKING FISH/MEAT IN A
SAUCE (or see marinade)
marine,*,er, CONCERNED WITH THE
OCEAN/ SEA
marionette,*, A PUPPET ON STRINGS
marit, merit
marital,lly, INVOLVES MARRIAGE
"prefixes: pre"
marithon, marathon
maritime, OF THE OCEAN OR SEA
mariwana, marijuana
marjaren, margarine
marjen, margin
marjenalize, marginalize
marjenul, margin(al)
marjeren, margarine
marjin, margin
marjinul, margin(al)
marjinulize, marginalize
marjoram,*, HERBAL PLANT
mark,*,ked,king,ker,kedly, A GOUGE/
LINE/ SCRATCH/ IMPRESSION
"prefixes: un"
markee, marquee / marquis
marker,*, A LINE OF MARKATION, A
TOOL OR INSTRUMENT THAT
MARKS

market,*,ted,ting,table,tability,ter,
ABOUT SELLING GOODS "prefixes:
sub"
marki, marquee / marquis
markit, market
markt, mark(ed)
markur, marker
marmalade, A FRUIT PRESERVE
marmulade, marmalade
marn, martin / marten
maroon,*,ned,ning, BE LEFT
ABANDONED, STRANDED, A COLOR
marose, morose
marow, marrow
marquee, A BANNER, TENT, SIGN OVER
ENTRANCEWAY (or see marquis)
marquis,ses,sate, BRITISH RANK (or see
marquee)
marriage,*,eable,eability,eableness,
TWO PEOPLE WHO LEGALLY BOND
IN MATRIMONY "prefixes: inter"
married, PAST TENSE FOR THE WORD
"MARRY"
marrow, INNER BONE, PARTNER, MATE
marry,ries,ried,ying,riage, TWO PEOPLE
LEGALLY BONDING (or see merry)
"prefixes: inter/un"
marsh,hes,hy, WETLAND
marshal,*,led,ling,lcy,lship, EUROPEAN
OFFICER, SIMILAR TO A SHERIFF, TO
LEAD, USHER (or see martial)
marshal law, martial law
marshen, martian / march(ing)
marshil, marshal / martial
marshin, martian / march(ing)
marshmallow, A SUGAR SWEET , AN
HERBAL PLANT
marshmelow, marshmallow
marshul, marshal / martial
marsoopeal, marsupial
marsupeul, marsupial
marsupial, AN ANIMAL THAT SLEEPS
DURING THE DAY
martch, march
marten, MEMBER OF THE WEASEL
FAMILY (or see martin)
martengale, martingale
marteny, martini
marter, martyr
martial,lism,list,lly,lness, OF WAR (or
see marshal)
martial law, PERMANENT MILITARY
RULE IN THE U.S.
martian,*, PLANET MARS INHABITANTS

martin,*, A BIRD
martingale,*, A BIRD
martini,*, ALCOHOLIC DRINK
martir, martyr
martur, martyr
martyr,*,red,ring,rize,rdom, SOMEONE
WHO RISKS THEIR LIVES FOR A
CAUSE OF THEIR CHOOSING
marune, maroon
marut, merit
marutime, maritime
marvel,*,led,ling,lous,lously,lousness,
GREATLY IMPRESSIVE, ATTENTION
GETTER
marvelous,lously,lousness, VERY
IMPRESSIVE
marvelus, marvelous
marvil, marvel
marvilus, marvelous
marvul, marvel
mary, marry / merry
maryonette, marionette
mas, mace / mass / moss / maize
masa, mesa
masach, massage
masacistic, masochism
masacur, massacre
masage, massage
masakistic, masochism(stic)
masakisum, masochism
masakur, massacre
masanine, mezzanine
masc, mask
mascara, A DYE PUT ON EYELASHES
mascarade, masquerade
mascot,*, A THING OF LUCK
masculine,ely,eness,nity,nize,nized,
nizing, MALE
masd, mast
masdebashen, masturbate(tion)
masdek, mastic
masder, master
masderbade, masturbate
masdereus, mysterious
masdides, mastitis
masdik, mastic
masdir, master
masditis, mastitis
masdurful, master(full)
mase, mace / maize / maze
masectame, mastectomy
masectome, mastectomy
masecur, massacre
masef, massive

masekur, massacre
masen, mason
masenger, messenger
masenry, mason(ry)
maseurse, masseuse
maseve, massive
masgot, mascot
mash,hes,hed,hing,her, TO SHRED/ PULVERIZE/SQUISH, TURN TO PASTE (or see match)
mashene, machine
mashenery, machine(ry)
mashenest, machine(nist)
mashes, mash(es) / match(es)
mashety, machete
mashin, machine / mash(ing)
mashinury, machine(ry)
mashis, mash(es) / match(es)
mashus, mash(es) / match(es)
masif, massive
masiker, massacre
masin, mason
masive, massive
mask,*,ked,king, COVER UP "prefixes: un"
maskalen, masculine
maskarade, masquerade
maskarate, masquerade
maskeet, mesquite
maskera, mascara
maskerate, masquerade
masketo, mosquito
maskewlen, masculine
maskot, mascot
maskulin, masculine
maskurade, masquerade
maskurate, masquerade
masochism,st, PATHOLOGICAL SELF- DESTRUCTION
masochist,tic,tically,sm, PATHOLOGICAL SELF-DESTRUCTION
masof, massive
masoge, massage
masoje, massage
masokism, masochism
masokistic, masochism(stic)
masokizum, masochism
mason,*,nry,nries,nic, WORKS WITH STONE
masoose, masseuse
masquerade,*,ed,ding,er, USE A MASK OR DISGUISE TO COVER IDENTITY
masquite, mesquite

mass,ses,sed,sing,sive, MEASURE OF VOLUME, WEIGHT, ACCUMULATION OF SIGNIFICANT AMOUNT "prefixes: bio"
massacre,*,ed,ring, KILLING OF SIGNIFICANT AMOUNT AT ONCE
massage,*,ed,ging, MANIPULATE/RUB SKIN TO AFFECT INTERNAL TISSUE (or see message)
masseur,*,use, MALE WHO GIVES MASSAGE
masseuse,*,ur, FEMALE WHO GIVES MASSAGE
massiuse, masseuse
massive,ely,eness, OF GREAT QUANTITY, SIZE
massuer, masseur
massuse, masseuse
mast, PART OF SAIL ON VESSEL, HOG FEED (or see mace(d))
mastectomy,mies, BREAST REMOVAL
mastek, mastic
master,*,red,ring,ry,rful,rfully,rfulness, rliness,rly,rhood, ONE WHO IS HIGHLY SKILLFUL/WISE "prefixes: over/re"
masterbashen, masturbate(tion)
masterbate, masturbate
mastereus, mysterious
mastic,*, RESIN OR SEALANT FOR PROTECTIVE COAT
mastidis, mastitis
mastique, mystique
mastir, master
mastirbashen, masturbate(tion)
mastirful, master(full)
mastitis,ic, INFLAMMED BREAST OR UDDER
masturbate,*,ed,ting,tion, TO STIMULATE ONE'S OWN SEXUAL ORGANS TO AROUSAL/ORGASM
masturly, master(ly)
mastytis, mastitis
masuese, masseuse
masukestik, masochism
masukistic, masochism(stic)
masure, masseur
masuse, masseuse
mat,*,tted,tting, FLAT ITEM FOR DOORSTEPS, FOR DISPLAYING VISUAL IMAGES, A FLAT MESH OF SOME MATERIAL (or see mad/ made/mate/matte)
matabulism, metabolism

match,hes,hed,hing, PAIR UP, PUT SUITABLES TOGETHER, CHEMICALLY TREATED ITEM USED TO CREATE FLAME "prefixes: mis/over/re/un"
matcherashen, mature(ration)
matchure, mature
mate,*,ed,ting, TO JOIN TOGETHER, METHOD OF PROPOGATION, A CALL IN THE GAME OF CHESS (or see made/maid/matte) "prefixes: un"
matekulus, meticulous
matena, matinee
matenens, maintenance
mater, matter / mad(dder)
materde, maitre d'
materealise, materialize
matereul, material
material,*,lly,lism,list,listic,listically,lity, lities,lness,lize, NON-VIRTUAL, OF THE PHYSICAL PLANE, OF MASS, OF THE PHYSICAL "prefixes: bio/im/ non"
materialize,*,ed,zing,zation,er, TO PHYSICALLY APPEAR "prefixes: im"
maternal,lly,listic,lism, MOTHERING, NURTURING
maternity,ties, A HUMAN STATE OF BEING PREGNANT
mateure, mature
math, LANGUAGE OF NUMBERS
mathematic,*,cal,cally,cian, SCIENCE AND LANGUAGE DEALING WITH NUMBERS "prefixes: bio"
mathology, mythology
matikulus, meticulous
matina, matinee
matinee,*, SPECIFIC AREA OF TIME WHEN A MOVIE IS SHOWN IN A THEATER
matir, mad(dder) / matter
matirde, maitre d'
matireal, material
matirnol, maternal
matirnulistic, maternal(istic)
matist, mad(ddest)
matna, matinee
matne, matinee
matness, mad(ness)
mato, motto
matramony, matrimony
matrearch, matriarch
matrearchal, matriarch(al)
matreark, matriarch

matreks, matrix
matremony, matrimony
matren, matron
matress, mattress
matrex, matrix
matriarch,*,hal,halism,hate,hy,hies, MOTHER IS LEADING ROLE
matricks, matrix
matriculate,*,ed,ting,tion, REGISTERED/ ENROLLED
matrimony,nies,nial,nially, OF MARRIAGE
matrin, matron
matris, mattress
matrix,xes,ices, MYSTERY/LABYRINTH/ RIDDLE
matron,*,nage,nly,nal,nage,nize, A FEMALE CHAPERONE/GUARDIAN/ ATTENDANT
matropolis, metropolis
matte, METAL STYLE, NON-GLOSSY SURFACE
matter,*,red, OF IMPORTANCE/ SUBSTANCE/PHYSICAL MATERIAL
mattress,ses, BED OF STUFFING FOR SLEEPING ON
matunens, maintenance
matur, matter / mad(der)
maturde, maitre d'
mature,*,ed,ring,rate,ration,rational, rative,ely,eness,rity, GROWN TO PHYSICAL PEAK "prefixes: im/pre"
maturnedy, maternity
maturnity, maternity
mauf, mauve
maugul, module
maujul, module
maul,*,led,ling, A TOOL, TO PHYSICALLY BATTER, REDUCE TO LESSER STATE (or see mall/mole)
mauld, maul(ed) / malt
maunaz, mayonnaise
maunten, mountain
mauntenus, mountain(ous)
mauroon, maroon
mausoleum, GRANDIOSE TOMB
mauve, A COLOR
mave, mauve
maverick,*, RADICALS, ONE'S WHO DON'T FOLLOW TRADITIONAL BELIEFS/ VALUES
mavrik, maverick
mavurek, maverick
mawntin, mountain

max,xes,xed,xing,ximal,ximize,ximum, SHORT FOR MAXIMUM
maximal,lly, THE MOST POSSIBLE
maximize,*,ed,zing,er,mum, THE MOST POSSIBLE
maximum,*, THE MOST POSSIBLE
may, ALLOWED TO, A MONTH IN THE YEAR (ENGLISH)
maybe, PERHAPS
maydreark, matriarch
mayenase, mayonnaise
mayer, mayor
mayonnaise, SPREAD OR SALAD DRESSING FOR FOOD
mayor,*,ral,ralty,ralties, POLITICAL POSITION
mazanine, mezzanine
mazdek, mastic
mazderful, master(full)
mazdik, mastic
mazdur, master
maze,*,ed,zing,zy, INABILITY TO MOVE/ THINK ALONG A CONTINUOUS PATH (or see mace/maize)
mazef, massive
mazeker, massacre
mazektomy, mastectomy
mazenine, mezzanine
mazif, massive
maziker, massacre
mazonry, mason(ry)
mazt, mast
mazturbate, masturbate
mazzanine, mezzanine
meadow,*, A FIELD GENERALLY WITHOUT TREES
meager,rly,rness, SMALL PORTION/ AMOUNT
meal,*,ly,lier,liest,liness, FOOD, FOOD EATEN AT CERTAIN TIME
mean,*,ning,ningful,ningfully, ningfulness,ningless,nt, ILL INTENT, EXPRESS THOUGHTS OF HARMFUL INTENT, METHOD OF ACHIEVING A GOAL, INTENT TO REFER/CONVEY SOMETHING "prefixes: un"
meant, PAST TENSE FOR THE WORD "MEAN", ATTEMPT TO EXPRESS THOUGHTS
mear, mere
measles, A VIRUS
measure,*,ed,ring,rable,rably,rability, rableness,ement, USE NUMBERS/

WORDS TO EXPLAIN SIZE/AMOUNT/ DISTANCE "prefixes: un"
meat,*,ty,tier,tiest,tiness, MUSCLE FIBER IN LIVING THINGS, EDIBLE PARTS (or see meet)
mecaneks, mechanic(s)
mechanic,*,cal,cally,calness,ist,istic, istically,ize,ism, WORKS WITH PARTS WHICH MAKES OBJECTS MOVE, SYSTEM OF APPROACH "prefixes: bio/un"
mechanize,*,ed,zing,zation,ist,istic, istically,er,ism, USE MACHINE TO PERFORM A TASK
mechen, mission
mechenary, mission(ary)
med, mid / meet
meda, meta
medabulism, metabolism
medacate, medicate
medafesic, metaphysic
medafisical, metaphysic(al)
medafore, metaphor
medagashen, mitigate(tion)
medagate, mitigate
medal,*,llic,llist,llion, A BADGE/OBJECT FOR AWARD (or see metal/mettle/ meddle/middle)
medamorfasis, metamorphosis
medaphore, metaphor
medaphysic, metaphysic
medaphysical, metaphysic(al)
medasen, medicine
medatashen, meditate(tion)
meddle,*,ed,ling,er,esome,esomeness, INTERFERE WITH OTHER'S THINGS/ AFFAIRS, (or see medal/metal/ mettle/middle) "prefixes: inter"
medea, media
medeader, mediate(tor)
medean, median
medeashen, mediate(tion)
medeat, mediate
medeator, mediate(tor)
medec, medic
medecal, medical
medefisic, metaphysic
medefl, medieval
medefol, medieval
medefore, metaphor
medek, medic
medekal, medical
medekulus, meticulous

medel, medal / metal / mettle / meddle / middle
medemorfasis, metamorphosis
medeokrity, mediocre(rity)
medeokur, mediocre
medeor, meteor
medeorite, meteorite
medeorology, meteorology
medephore, metaphor
meder, meter
medernedy, maternity
mederology, meteorology
medesin, medicine
medetashen, meditate(tion)
medeum, medium
medeur, meteor
medevul, medieval
medget, midget
media,*, AUDIO/VIDEO MEANS OF COMMUNICATION "prefixes: multi/ retro"
median,*,nly, OF THE MIDDLE, SEPARATION
mediate,*,ed,ting,tion,tive,tize,tor, tization, TO FACILITATE/DIFFUSE BETWEEN TWO OPPOSING PARTIES OR OBJECTS
medic,*, ONE'S WHO WORK WITH INJURIES, MEDICINE
medicable,ly, RESPONSIVE TO MEDICAL TREATMENT "prefixes: im/non/un"
medical,*,lly,cine,ate, OF MEDICINE, EXAMINATION "prefixes: bio/pre"
medicate,*,ed,ting,tion, GIVE MAN- MADE DRUGS TO "prefixes: pre"
medicine,*,nal,nally, MAN-MADE CHEMICALS TAKEN INTO THE BODY "prefixes: bio"
medieval,lism,list,lly, OF THE MIDDLE AGES
medifal, medieval
medifiseks, metaphysic(s)
medifl, medieval
medik, medic
medikulus, meticulous
medil, medal / metal / mettle / meddle / middle
mediocre,rity,rities, BETWEEN POOR AND GOOD QUALITY, IN-BETWEEN
mediocur, mediocre(rity)
medir, meter
medirology, meteorology
medisine, medicine

meditate,*,ed,ting,tion,tative,tatively, tor,tiveness, BE SILENT/STILL, ELIMINATE THOUGHT "prefixes: pre"
medium,*,mistic, COMMUNICATION USING THE VIRTUAL FIELD, TRANSLATE INFORMATION FROM ONE FORM OF MEDIA TO ANOTHER
medjet, midget
medl, medal / meddle / metal / mettle / middle
medle, medal / metal / mettle / meddle / middle
medo, meadow
medol, medal / metal / mettle / meddle / middle
medow, meadow
medrapolitan, metropolitan
medrek, metric
medric, metric
medropoletan, metropolitan
medst, midst
medtrik, metric
medufore, metaphor
medugation, mitigate(tion)
medukul, medical
medul, medal / metal / mettle / meddle / middle
medulsom, meddle(some)
medumorfasis, metamorphosis
medur, meter
medurology, meteorology
medusin, medicine
medutashen, meditate(tion)
medwife, midwife
meek,kly,kness, GENTLE/MILD TEMPERAMENT
meel, meal
meen, mean
meet,*,met,ting, COME TOGETHER, ARRIVE AT SAME DESTINATION AND TIME (or see meat)
mega, PREFIX INDICATING "MILLION/ VERY LARGE" MOST OFTEN MODIFIES THE WORD
megalo, PREFIX INDICATING "MILLION/ VERY LARGE" MOST OFTEN MODIFIES THE WORD
meger, meager / measure
megir, measure / major
megu, mega
megur, measure / meager
meiosis, CELLULAR PROCESS, UNDERSTATEMENT
mejer, measure / major

mejur, measure / major
mejut, midget
mek, meek
mekanek, mechanic
mekanekul, mechanic(al)
mekanise, mechanize
mekcher, mixture
mekenize, mechanize
meker, meager
mekschur, mixture
mekster, mixture
mekunize, mechanize
mekur, meager
mel, meal / mail / male
melado, mulato
meladramatic, melodrama(tic)
melady, melody
melameter, milli(meter)
melan, melon
melancholy,lies,lily,liness,lic, DESPONDENT, DEPRESSED, CONTEMPLATIVE
melancoli, melancholy
melanoma,*,ata,osis,nism, TUMOR, CELLS WITH DARK PIGMENT
melanosis,oma,nism, OVER PRODUCTION OF PIGMENT MELANIN IN SKIN/TISSUE
melasecond, millisecond
melatent, militant
melateristic, military(ristic)
melato, mulato
melaturize, military(rize)
meld,*,ded,ding, AS IF TO MELT TOGETHER, BLEND INTO ONE (or see melt/mill(ed))
meldoo, mildew
meldu, mildew
meledy, melody
melen, melon
melencholy, melancholy
melenium, millennium
melenkaly, melancholy
melenoma, melanoma
melenosis, melanosis
meleonaire, million(aire)
melet, millet
meletary, military
melin, melon
melincholy, melancholy
melinium, millennium
melinkoly, melancholy
melinoma, melanoma
melinosis, melanosis

melisha, militia
melit, millet
melitia, militia
melk, milk
mell, mill / meal
mellapede, millipede
mellinium, millennium
mellow,wly,wness, BECOME SOFTENED/RELAXED WITHOUT FEAR
melnutrishen, malnutrition
melo, mellow
melodrama,*,atic,atically,atist, EXAGERRATED ACT/EVENT, OVER EMPHASIS
melody,dies,dic,dically,dious,diousness, A SERIES OF SOUNDS/FREQUENCY, TUNES IN HARMONY
melogram, milli(gram)
melon,*, EDIBLE FRUIT
melonkoly, melancholy
melonosis, melanosis
melow, mellow
melt,*,ted,ting,table,tability,ter, TO CHANGE FROM SOLID TO LIQUID, CHANGE FORM (or see meld)
meltary, military
meludrumatek, melodrama(tic)
melugram, milli(gram)
meluleter, milli(liter)
melun, melon
meluncholy, melancholy
melunoma, melanoma
melunosis, melanosis
melupete, millipede
melusekund, millisecond
melutare, military
melutint, militant
melyonaire, million(aire)
melyun, million
memacree, mimic(ry)
memakry, mimic(ry)
member,*,rship, PART/PERSON WHICH BELONGS TO LARGER ORGANISM/ ORGANIZATION
membrane,*,nal,nous, LAYER OF THIN TISSUE "prefixes: non/semi"
memek, mimic
memento,*, ARTICLE/OBJECT REMINDER OF THE PAST
memerabelia, memorabilia
memerable, memorable
memerize, memorize
memic, mimic

memoir,*,rist, PRINTED REMINDER OF THE PAST
memok, mimic
memorabilia, REMINDERS OF THE PAST
memorable,ly,eness,bility,bilia, WORTHY OF REMEMBERING
memorais, memorize
memorial,*,list,lly,lize,lizes,lized,lizing, lization,lizer, AN OBJECT PLACED IN MEMORY OF THOSE WHO DIED "prefixes: im"
memorize,*,ed,zing,zable,er, STORE INTO MEMORY
memory,ries,rize, COLLECTION OF STORED INFORMATION
memrable, memorable
memrize, memorize
memruble, memorable
memry, memory
memuk, mimic
memurabilea, memorabilia
memurise, memorize
memwar, memoir
men,*, HUMAN ADULT MALE (or see mean)
menace,*,ced,cing, HARMFUL/ THREATENING, A NUISANCE
menacher, miniature
menamize, minimize
menamul, minimal
menamuly, minimal(y)
menamum, minimum
menapos, menopause
menarolization, mineral(ization)
menarul, mineral
menarulize, mineral(ize)
menas, menace
menasher, miniature
menaskewul, minuscule
menastrony, minestrone
menastry, minister(y)
mences, menses
menchen, mention
mend,*,ded,ding,dable, TO FIX/REPAIR (or see mint/meant)
mene, mean / mini / many
meneacher, miniature
menemize, minimize
menengidos, meningitis
menenjidus, meningitis
menerable, memorable
menerul, mineral
menes, menace
menestrony, minestrone

menestry, minister(y)
menet, minute
meneul, menial
mengul, mingle
meni, mini / many
menial,lly, REQUIRES LITTLE THOUGHT
meniature, miniature
menila, manila
meningitis,ic, VIRUS OF THE BODY
menipause, menopause
menipulate, manipulate
menis, menace
menk, mink
menmerable, memorable
mennow, minnow
meno, minnow
menogamy, monogamy
menokside, monoxide
menopause,sal, STOP HAVING MONTHLY ESTRUS CYCLES, ESTROGEN CHANGES IN FEMALES
menopuly, monopoly
menoscule, minuscule
menotnus, monotony(nous)
menotny, monotony
menoxide, monoxide
menruble, memorable
mens, men(s) / mean(s) / mince
menses, MENSTRUATION
menshen, mention
mensteration, menstruation
menstral, menstrual / minstrel
menstrashen, menstruation
menstration, menstruation
menstrual,uous,ate,uum,ation, MENSTRUATION (or see minstrel) "prefixes: pre"
menstruation, FEMALE MONTHLY UTERUS LINING DISCHARGE, A PERIOD
ment, mint / mend / meant
mental,lly,lity, THOUGHT, OF THE MIND
menthol, OIL
mention,*,ned,ning,nable,ner, CALLING BRIEF ATTENTION TO SOMETHING "prefixes: un/under"
mentle, mental
mentol, mental
mentor,*, A COACH, GUIDE
mentur, mentor
menu,*, LIST OF RESTAURANT MEALS
menuet, minuet
menumem, minimum
menumly, minimal(y)

menupause, menopause
menure, manure
menus, menace
menustrony, minestrone
menyew, menu
menyewet, minuet
menyon, mignon
meol, meal
mer, mere / mirror / mare
meracle, miracle
meraculus, miracle(culous)
merage, mirage
meragolt, marigold
meraje, mirage
merakle, miracle
merakulus, miracle(culous)
meral, morale / mural
meraly, merry(rily)
meranade, marinade / marinate
merange, meringue
merathon, marathon
mercantile,lism,list, COMMERCE,
    TRADE
mercenary,ries,rily,riness, HIRED TO
    KILL
merch, merge
merchandise,ed,sing,er,sable,sability,
    ize,izes,ized,izing,izer, GOODS FOR
    RETAIL SALE
merchant,*,table,ndise, ONE WHO
    DEALS IN GOODS FOR RETAIL
mercury,rial,rialism,rialize,rializes,
    rialized,rializing,rialization,ric, A
    PLANET, BEHAVIOR AS IF RULED BY
    THE PLANET, METALLIC ELEMENT
    USED IN THERMOMETERS
mercy,cies,ciful,cifully,ciless,cilessly,
    cilessness, PROVIDE COMPASSION/
    BENEVOLENCE AT A CRUCIAL TIME
    "prefixes: un"
merder, murder
merdurer, murder(er)
mere,ely, SIMPLY FOR THE REASON OF,
    SMALL IN MATTER (or see marry/
    merry/mirror)
merech, marriage
mered, married
meredian, meridian
mereg, marriage
meregold, marigold
mereinette, marionette
merej, marriage
merekul, miracle
meren, marine

merenate, marinade / marinate
mereod, myriad
mereonett, marionette
meret, merit
meretal, marital
merethon, marathon
meretime, maritime
meretul, marital
mereunett, marionette
merewana, marijuana
merg, merge
merge,*,ed,ging,er,ence, COME
    TOGETHER AS ONE "prefixes: sub/
    un"
meri, marry / merry
meriad, myriad
merich, marriage
merid, married
meridg, marriage
meridian,*,nal,nally, INVISIBLE CIRCLE
    RUNNING AROUND EARTH
    THROUGH NORTH/SOUTH POLES
merigold, marigold
merijuana, marijuana
merily, merry(rily)
merin, marine
merina, marina
merinad, marinade / marinate
merinat, marinade / marinate
meringue, WHIPPED EGGS
merit,*,ted,tedly,tless,torious, WORTHY
    OF HONOR OR NOTE "prefixes: un"
merital, marital
merithon, marathon
meritime, maritime
meritol, marital
meriwana, marijuana
merje, merge
merk, murky
merkanteel, mercantile
merkury, mercury
merky, murky
merlen, merlin
merlin, BIRD
mermaid,*, ILLUSIONARY FISH WOMAN
mermer, murmur
mermur, murmur
mero, marrow
meroge, mirage
meroj, mirage
meror, mirror
merose, morose
merow, marrow

merry,rriment,rrily,rriness, CHEERY,
    HAPPY
mersenary, mercenary
mershandise, merchandise
mersinary, mercenary
mersy, mercy
merukul, miracle
merur, mirror
mery, marry / merry
mes, PREFIX INDICATING "MIDDLE"
    MOST OFTEN MODIFIES THE WORD
mesa,*, LAND PLATEAU
mesach, message / massage
mesage, message / massage
mesalaneus, miscellaneous
mesals, measles / missile(s)
mesanine, mezzanine
mesbahave, misbehave
mesbaleef, misbelief
mesbaleve, misbelieve
mesbok, misspoke
mesbokin, misspoke(n)
mescalculate, miscalculate
meschef, mischief
mesconstrue, misconstrue
mesdake, mistake
mesdamener, misdemeanor
mesderius, mysterious
mesdress, mistress
mesdriul, mistrial
mesdufy, mystify
mesdur, mister
mesdury, mystery
meseg, message
mesej, message
mesel, missile
meseness, mess(iness)
mesenger, messenger
mesenine, mezzanine
mesenturpet, misinterpret
meseur, mess(ier) / masseur
meseust, mess(iest)
mesfet, misfit
mesfire, misfire
mesforshen, misfortune
mesfortune, misfortune
mesgeving, misgiving
mesguge, misjudge
mesh,hes,hed,hing, INTERWOVEN
    METAL STRANDS TO CREATE A
    BLANKET/ NET "prefixes: en"
meshandle, mishandle
meshap, mishap
meshen, mission

meshenary, mission(ary)
meshur, measure
mesige, message
mesije, message
mesil, missile
mesils, measles / missile(s)
mesinene, mezzanine
mesinform, misinform
mesinger, messenger
mesinturpret, misinterpret
mesjef, mischief
mesjug, misjudge
meskalaneus, miscellaneous
meskarege, miscarriage
meskedo, mosquito
meskeet, mesquite
meskenstrew, misconstrue
meskownt, miscount
meskwote, misquote
mesled, misled
mesleed, mislead
mesmach, mismatch
mesmerize,*,ed,zing,ism,ic,ically,ist,er, zation, INTENSELY ATTENTIVE TO THE POINT OF EXCLUDING ALL OTHER THINGS
mesmurize, mesmerize
mesnomer, misnomer
meso, PREFIX INDICATING "MIDDLE" MOST OFTEN MODIFIES THE WORD
mesoje, massage
mesonderstand, misunderstand
mesonderstood, misunderstood
mesonine, mezzanine
mespell, misspell
mesplase, misplace
mespok, misspoke
mespokin, misspoke(n)
mesprent, misprint
mesprunounce, mispronounce
mesquite, LAND TYPE, A TREE, SHRUB
mesquote, misquote
mesred, misread
mesrepresent, misrepresent
mesruble, miserable
mess,ses,sed,sing,sy,sily,siness,sier,siest, SLOPPY, DISHEVELED, DISARRAY
message,*,ed,ging, SHORT NOTE OF VOICE/TEXT
messanine, mezzanine
messenger,*,red,ring, ONE WHO DELIVERS A NOTE
messusege, misuse(sage)
mest, mist / midst / miss(ed) / mess(ed)

mestake, mistake
mestakin, mistake(n)
mestamener, misdemeanor
meste, mist(y)
mesteek, mystique
mestefy, mystify
mesteik, mystic / mystique / mistake
mester, mister
mestereus, mysterious
mestic, mystic
mestides, mastitis
mestify, mystify
mestikul, mystic(cal)
mestireus, mysterious
mestook, mistook
mestreat, mistreat
mestress, mistress
mestrete, mistreat
mestris, mistress
mestriul, mistrial
mestufy, mystify
mestuk, mistook
mestumener, misdemeanor
mestury, mystery
mesuge, message
mesuje, message
mesulaneus, miscellaneous
mesuls, measles / missile(s)
mesultoe, mistletoe
mesunderstand, misunderstand
mesunine, mezzanine
mesure, measure
mesurible, miserable
mesuse, masseuse / misuse
mesuseje, misuse(sage)
mesuze, misuse / masseuse
mesyews, misuse
met, PAST TENSE FOR THE WORD "MEET", (or see mitt/mite/meet/ meat) "prefixes: un"
meta, PREFIX INDICATING "BEYOND/ CHANGE" MOST OFTEN MODIFIES THE WORD
metabolism,*,ize,ic,ically, THE CONVERSION OF ENERGY IN A LIVING ORGANISM, FUNCTION OF LIFE
metabolize,*,ed,zing,zable, CONCERNED WITH METABOLISM
metabulism, metabolism
metacate, medicate
metafisical, metaphysic(al)
metagate, mitigate

metal,*,led,ling,llic,llically,llurgy, CHEMICAL ELEMENTS FOUND IN THE EARTH (or see mettle/meddle/ medal/middle) "prefixes: bi/non/ semi/un"
metamorphosis, MAJOR TRANSFORMATION AS A CATERPILLAR TO A BUTTERFLY
metaphor,*,ric,rical,rically, EXPRESSING THOUGHT USING UNCONVENTIONAL COMPARISONS
metaphysic,*,cal,cally, STUDY OF THE SUPERNATURAL, INVISIBLE
metapolize, metabolize
metasen, medicine
metatashen, meditate(tion)
mete, meat(y)
metea, media
metean, median
meteashen, mediate(tion)
meteate, mediate
meteator, mediate(tor)
metefisical, metaphysic(al)
metek, medic
metekal, medical
metekulus, meticulous
metel, medal / metal / mettle / meddle / middle
metemorfusis, metamorphosis
meten, mitten
meteokrety, mediocre(rity)
meteokur, mediocre
meteor,*,ric,rite,rology, COMPACTED SAND AND ICE TRAVELING AT HIGH VELOCITY THROUGH SPACE
meteorite,*, METEOR THAT SURVIVES ENTRY THROUGH EARTH'S ATMOSPHERE
meteorology,gic,gical,gically,gist, STUDY OF THE ATMOSPHERE SUCH AS WEATHER/CLIMATE
metephysical, metaphysic(al)
meter,*,red,ring, FORM/INSTRUMENT OF MEASUREMENT "prefixes: deca/ un"
metesen, medicine
metetashen, meditate(tion)
meteum, medium
meteurology, meteorology
metevul, medieval
meteyorite, meteorite
meth, SHORT FOR METHAMPHETAMINE
methad, method

methadology, methodolgy
methadone, MAN-MADE DRUG, DOWNER, HIGHLY ADDICTIVE
methakul, myth(ical)
methalogic, mythologic
methamphetamine,*, ABBREVIATION FOR METH, MANMADE CHEMICAL STIMULANT
methane, A GAS
methanfetamene, methamphetamine
methanol, TOXIC LIQUID
methanphetamine, methamphetamine
methasize, myth(icize)
methecul, myth(ical)
methed, method
methedology, methodology
methedone, methadone
methemfetamine, methamphetamine
methenphetamine, methamphetamine
methid, method
methidology, methodology
method,*,dize,dizes,dized,dizing,dizer, dical,dically,dicalness, dology, A SYSTEM/PROCEDURE/TECHNIQUE
methodology,gies,gical,gically,gist, A SYSTEM/ PROCEDURE/TECHNIQUE
metholugy, mythology
methonol, methanol
methud, method
methudology, methodology
methudone, methadone
methunol, methanol
metia, media
metic, medic
metical, medical
meticulous,sly,sness, EXCESSIVE ATTENTION TO DETAIL/ CLEANLINESS/ EXACTING
metil, medal / metal / mettle / meddle / middle
metin, mitten
meting, meet(ing)
metir, meter
metirology, meteorology
metisine, medicine
metitate, meditate
metle, medal / metal / mettle / meddle / middle
meto, meadow
metr, PREFIX INDICATING "WOMB/ MOTHER" MOST OFTEN MODIFIES THE WORD
metrapolitan, metropolitan

metric,*,cal,cally,cate,cates,cated, cating,cation,cist,cize,cizes, cized, cizing, A MEASUREMENT SYSTEM "prefixes: bio"
metro, REFERRING TO TRANSIT SYSTEM IN CITY, SHORT FOR "METROPOLITAN"
metropolis,ses, CENTRAL CITY
metropolitan,nism, HUB OF CITY AND THOSE WHO DWELL THERE "prefixes: non"
metruk, metric
metst, midst
mettle,*,ed,esome, COURAGEOUS, SPIRITED (or see medal/metal/ meddle/middle)
metukul, medical
metul, medal / metal / mettle / meddle / middle
metur, meter
meturnedy, maternity
meturnul, maternal
meturology, meteorology
metutashen, meditate(tion)
meuchuel, mutual
meudilate, mutilate
meukus, mucus
meul, meal / mule
meurol, mural
meus, muse
meusikul, music(al)
meut, mute
meutashen, mutate(tion)
meutat, mutate
meutene, mutiny
meutilate, mutilate
meutulashen, mutilate(tation)
meuzeim, museum
meuzek, music
meuzeshen, musician
mewfee, movie
mewfuble, move(vable)
mewkus, mucus
mewl, mule
mewn, moon
mewnisapaledy, municipal(ity)
mewnisepal, municipal
mewral, mural
mewse, muse/ moose/ mousse
mewseum, museum
mewsik, music
mewt, moot / mute
mewtashen, mutate(tion)
mewtelate, mutilate

mewteny, mutiny
mewtint, mutate(ant)
mewvee, movie
mewvuble, move(vable)
mewzishen, musician
mexcher, mixture
mexter, mixture
mez, mess
mezandul, mishandle
mezanine, mezzanine
mezdamener, misdemeanor
mezder, mister
mezdery, mystery
mezdumener, misdemeanor
mezenine, mezzanine
mezfet, misfit
mezfire, misfire
mezforchen, misfortune
mezhap, mishap
mezinform, misinform
mezinine, mezzanine
mezkwote, misquote
mezled, misled
mezleet, mislead
mezmach, mismatch
mezmurize, mesmerize
meznomer, misnomer
mezonine, mezzanine
mezpell, misspell
mezplase, misplace
mezprent, misprint
mezred, misread
mezreprezent, misrepresent
mezruble, miserable
meztake, mistake
meztamener, misdemeanor
meztek, mystic
mezter, mister
meztereus, mysterious
meztreat, mistreat
meztress, mistress
meztriul, mistrial
mezuls, measles
mezunine, mezzanine
mezury, misery
mezzanine,*, LOW UPPER FLOOR OR THEATER BALCONY
mfusiz, emphasize
mi, my
mibuleve, misbelieve
mic, meek
mica, ORGANIC, SILICATE
michanek, mechanic
michanekul, mechanic(al)

michen, mission

michenary, mission(ary)

micks, mix

micrawave, microwave

micro, VERY SMALL, PREFIX INDICATING "SMALL" MOST OFTEN MODIFIES THE WORD

microbe,*,bial,bian,bic, ORGANISMS SEEN ONLY UNDER A MICROSCOPE

micrometer, SYSTEM OF MEASUREMENT

micron,*,ra,nation, MICROMETER "prefixes: sub"

microphone,*, TRANSMITS SOUND

microscope,*,pic,pically,py,pist, INSTRUMENT WHICH ENLARGES OBJECTS FOR VIEWING WITH THE EYES "prefixes: sub"

microwave,*, ELECTROMAGNETIC WAVELENGTH, AN APPLIANCE

micu, mica

mid, PREFIX INDICATING "HALF/ MIDDLE" MOST OFTEN MODIFIES THE WORD (or see mitt)

midachondria, mitochondria

midagashen, mitigate(tion)

midagate, mitigate

middle, IN BETWEEN (or see medal/ metal/mettle/meddle)

midegate, mitigate

midegation, mitigate(tion)

mider, miter

midevil, medieval

midget,*, UNUSUALLY SMALL PERSON

midia, media

midian, median

midieit, mediate

midigashen, mitigate(tion)

midioker, mediocre

midium, medium

midival, medieval

midjet, midget

midle, middle

midochondria, mitochondria

midokondrea, mitochondria

midol, middle

midoses, mitosis

midst, LOCATED IN THE MIDDLE, AMONG

miduchondria, mitochondria

midul, medal / metal / mettle / meddle / middle

midur, miter

midwife,eves,ery, ASSISTS MOTHER THROUGH BIRTHING A CHILD

miff,*,fed,fing,fy, BE OFFENDED

miget, midget

might,ty,tier,tiest,tily,tiness, STRENGTH, POWER, PERHAPS, MAYBE (or see mite)

mignon,*, SMALL, DELICATE

migraine,*, A SERIOUS HEADACHE

migrant,*, ONE WHO IS CONTINUOUSLY MOVING

migrashen, migrate(tion)

migrate,*,ed,ting,tion,ant,tor,tory, TO MOVE LOCATION OF HOME BASED UPON THE SEASONS

migro, micro

migrunt, migrant

migrutory, migrate(tory)

mijet, midget

mika, mica

mikanek, mechanic

mikanekul, mechanic(al)

mikaw, macaw

mikcher, mixture

mikount, miscount

mikrafone, microphone

mikrascope, microscope

mikrawave, microwave

mikro, micro

mikrobe, microbe

mikrofone, microphone

mikrometer, micrometer

mikron, micron

mikrowave, microwave

mikshter, mixture

mikster, mixture

miku, mica

mil, mile / meal

milado, mulato

milage, mile(age)

milagram, milli(gram)

milaleter, milli(liter)

milameter, milli(meter)

milapede, millipede

milarea, malaria

milasecond, millisecond

milasus, molasses

milatent, militant

milato, mulato

milaturestic, military(ristic)

milaturise, military(rize)

mild,der,dest,dly,dness, PLEASANT (or see mill(ed))

mildew,*,wed,wing,wy, FUNGI

mildu, mildew

mile,*,eage, U.S. MEASUREMENT FOR DISTANCE

milegram, milli(gram)

milekuler, molecule(lar)

milemeder, milli(meter)

milenium, millennium

mileonaire, million(aire)

milepete, millipede

miler, mill(er)

milesekent, millisecond

milest, molest

milet, millet

miletary, military

mileturezation, military(rization)

miligram, milli(gram)

milileter, milli(liter)

milimeter, milli(meter)

milinium, millennium

milion, million

milionair, million(aire)

milipede, millipede

militant,tly,tness,ncy, ORDERLY, BY STRICT RULES

military,ries,rily,rism,rist,rize,rizes,rized, rizing,rization,ristic,ristically, GROUP OF PEOPLE BEING LED WITH STRICT RULES, AN ORDERLY GROUP

militia,*, GROUP ORGANIZED/TRAINED TO FIGHT

milk,ker,ky,kiness, WHITE LIFE-GIVING FLUID EXCRETED BY MOTHERS OF MAMMALS, ANY RESEMBLANCE TO MILK

mill,*,lled,lling,ller, GRINDS GRAIN/ REMOVAL OF HULL (or see mile)

millaliter, milli(liter)

millameter, milli(meter)

millenium, millennium

millennia,ial,ium, MEASUREMENT BY 1,000 "prefixes: pre"

millennium,*,ia, MEASUREMENT BY 1,000

millet, EDIBLE GRAIN, GRASS

milli,igram,iliter,imeter, LATIN THOUSAND/THOUSANDTH, PREFIX INDICATING "ONE THOUSANDTH" MOST OFTEN MODIFIES THE WORD

millinium, millennium

million,*,naire, U.S. NUMBER TO IDENTIFY QUANTITY "prefixes: multi"

millipede,*, INSECT

millisecond,*, METRIC NUMBER

miltary, military
miluge, mile(age)
milugram, milli(gram)
milumeter, milli(meter)
milupede, millipede
milutant, militant
milutare, military
milyen, million
milyonaire, million(aire)
mimakry, mimic(ry)
mimbrane, membrane
mimbur, member
mime,*,ed,ming, ACTOR WHO USES THE BODY TO ACT, COMMUNICATE WITHOUT USING WORDS
mimic,*,cking,cry,cries, TO COPY, IMITATE ANOTHER PERSON
mimorabilia, memorabilia
mimorabul, memorable
mimorealzation, memorial(ization)
mimoreul, memorial
mimorise, memorize
mimory, memory
mimuck, mimic
mimurabilia, memorabilia
mimwar, memoir
min, mine / mean
minacher, miniature
minamize, minimize
minamul, minimal
minamum, minimum
minapos, menopause
minaralize, mineral(ize)
minarul, mineral
minasher, miniature
minaskule, minuscule
minaster, minister
minastrony, minestrone
mince,*,ed,cing, CHOP SOMETHING INTO SMALL PIECES
minchen, mention
mind,*,ded,ding,dful,dfully,dfulness, dless,dlessly,dlessness, TO OBEY, PLACE WHERE THOUGHTS ARE GENERATED (or see mend/mint)
mine,*,ed,ning,er, PAST TENSE FOR THE WORD "MY", CLAIMING OWNERSHIP, A FORMED TUNNEL INTO THE GROUND WHICH BEARS PRECIOUS ROCKS/METALS, SUBSURFACE BOMB (or see mind/ main)
mineature, miniature
minemal, minimal

minemize, minimize
minemum, minimum
minengidus, meningitis
mineon, mignon
miner, mine(r) / minor
mineral,*,lize,lizes,lized,lizing,lizable, lization,lizer,logy, ORGANIC SUBSTANCES "prefixes: bio"
mines, minus / mine(s) / mince / menace
mineskule, minuscule
minester, minister
minestrone, SOUP
minet, minute
mingle,*,ed,ling, TO BE AMONG, ASSOCIATE WITH "prefixes: inter"
mini, LATIN FOR SMALL, SHORT, BRIEF, PREFIX INDICATING "SMALL" MOST OFTEN MODIFIES THE WORD (or see many)
miniature,*,rist,rize,rizes,rized,rizing, rization, SMALL FORM OF ORIGINAL SIZE "prefixes: sub"
minimal,ly,lism, THE LEAST POSSIBLE
minimize,*,ed,zing, MAKE SMALLER, LESS
minimum,*, THE LEAST POSSIBLE "prefixes: sub"
miniscule, minuscule
minister,*,ry,ries,rial,rially, PREACHING ABOUT RELIGION
miniucher, miniature
mink,*, A RODENT
minnow,*,wed,wing, A VERY SMALL FISH
mino, minnow
minogumy, monogamy
minokside, monoxide
minon, mignon
minopos, menopause
minopuly, monopoly
minor,*, BELOW MAJOR, SMALLER THAN, MUSICAL CHORD (or see miner)
minority,ties, SMALLER NUMBER WHEN COMPARED TO PREDOMINANT GROUP
minos, minus / minnow(s)
minotnus, monotony(nous)
minotny, monotony
minow, minnow
minoxite, monoxide
minse, mince
minses, menses

minshen, mention
minsteration, menstruation
minstral, menstrual / minstrel
minstrel,*, ONE WHO ENTERTAINS WITH POETRY/SONG (or see menstrual)
mint,*,ted,ting, AN HERB, PLACE WHERE COINS ARE MADE (or see meant/mend)
mintalety, mental(ity)
mintel, mental
minter, mentor
minthol, menthol
mintle, mental
mintor, mentor
mintul, mental
minu, menu
minuet,*, SLOW RYTHM IN MUSIC, DANCE
minural, mineral
minure, manure
minus, MATH EXPRESSION, TAKE AWAY/SUBTRACT FROM (or see menace)
minuscule, OF LITTLE IMPORTANCE, TINY
minuskule, minuscule
minustrony, minestrone
minute,*,ely, MEASURE OF TIME, RECORD A MEETING, SLIGHT/ SMALL
minuver, maneuver
minyew, menu
minyewet, minuet
minyon, mignon
miosis, meiosis
mir, mere / mire
miracle,*,culous,culously, EVENT PRECEDED BY MYSTERIOUS ACTIONS, SEEMINGLY IMPOSSIBLE OCCURRENCE
miraculus, miracle(culous)
mirage,*, AN OPTICAL ILLUSION
mirakle, miracle
miral, morale / mural
mirange, meringue
mircantile, mercantile
mirchandise, merchandise
mirchant, merchant
mire,*,ed,ing,ry, DIFFICULT, MUDDY
miread, myriad
mirekul, miracle
mireod, myriad
mirer, mirror

mirje, merge
mirkanteel, mercantile
mirky, murky
mirlin, merlin
mirmer, murmur
mirmur, murmur
miroge, mirage
miror, mirror
mirose, morose
mirquery, mercury
mirror,*,red,ring, REFLECTION
mirseful, mercy(ciful)
mirsy, mercy
mirukul, miracle
mirur, mirror
mirurd, mirror(ed)
mis, PREFIX INDICATING "BAD/WRONG/ WRONGLY" MOST OFTEN MODIFIES THE WORD (or see miss/mice)
misalaneus, miscellaneous
misandul, mishandle
misap, mishap
misapprehension,*, NOT CORRECT UNDERSTANDING/IMPRESSION
misbaleef, misbelief
misbaleve, misbelieve
misbehave,*,ed,ving,vior, TO NOT BEHAVE
misbehavior, NOT BEHAVE
misbelief, DO NOT BELIEVE
misbelieve,*,ed,ving, PAST TENSE FOR THE WORD "MISBELIEF"
misbok, misspoke
misbokin, misspoke(n)
misbuleef, misbelief
miscalculate,*,ed,ting,tion, NOT PROPER CALCULATION
miscarriage,*,ed,ging, LOSS IN CARRYING A FETUS TO FULL TERM
miscellaneous, VARIETY OF ELEMENTS/ THINGS WHICH HAVE NO RELEVANCE TO ONE ANOTHER
mischef, mischief
mischief,evous,evously,evousness, ACTION/BEHAVIOR THAT CREATES AGITATION FOR OTHERS
misconstrue,*,ed,uing, MISINTERPRET, INCORRECT UNDERSTANDING OF INFORMATION
miscount,*,ted,ting, COUNT DIDN'T COME OUT CORRECTLY
miscownt, miscount
misd, miss(ed) / mist
misdacism, mystic(icism)

misdaken, mistake(n)
misdamener, misdemeanor
misdemeanor,*, CITED FOR NOT OBEYING SET RULES
misdereus, mysterious
misdirection,*, WRONG DIRECTIONS/ INFORMATION
misdireus, mysterious
misdress, mistress
misdriul, mistrial
misdrus, mistress
misdufy, mystify
misdur, mister
misdury, mystery
mised, miss(ed) / mist
misel, missile
miself, my(self)
miseltoe, mistletoe
misenform, misinform
misenterpret, misinterpret
miser,rly,rliness, ONE WHO IS OVERLY FEARFUL ABOUT USING, SPENDING THEIR MONEY
miserable,ly,eness, EXTREMELY UNCOMFORTABLE, FEELING BEYOND CAPACITY
misery,ries, DREADFUL EMOTIONAL OR PHYSICAL STATE OF BEING
misfire,*,ed,ring, DIDN'T HIT THE TARGET
misfit,*, DOESN'T QUITE FIT IN WITH THE OTHERS
misfortune,*, UNPLANNED DISTURBING EVENT
misgef, mischief
misgiving,*, GIVEN TO DOUBT OR APPREHENSION IN MAKING A JUDGEMENT
misguge, misjudge
mishandle,*,ed,ling, TO NOT TREAT CAREFULLY
mishap,*, EVENT WHICH RENDERS UNCONTROLLABLE REACTIONS
mishen, mission
mishenary, mission(ary)
misinform,*,med,ming,mant,mer, mation, NOT CORRECT INFORMATION
misinterpret,*,ted,ting,tation, DOESN'T REPRESENT THE FACTS
mision, mission
misionary, mission(ary)
misjif, mischief

misjudge,*,ed,ging,ement, MAKE DECISION WITHOUT TAKING ALL FACTS INTO CONSIDERATION
misjuge, misjudge
miskalaneus, miscellaneous
miskalkulate, miscalculate
miskedo, mosquito
miskeet, mesquite
miskerage, miscarriage
miskeruge, miscarriage
miskonstrue, misconstrue
miskownt, miscount
miskunstrew, misconstrue
misle, missile
mislead,*,ed,ding, MANIPULATE INTO UNDESIRABLE DIRECTION
misled, PAST TENSE FOR THE WORD MISLEAD
misletoe, mistletoe
mismach, mismatch
mismatch,hes,hed,hing, DO NOT MATCH UP TOGETHER
misnomer,*, INCORRECT NAME FOR
misoge, massage
misoje, massage
misonderstand, misunderstand
misonderstood, misunderstood
mispell, misspell
misplace,*,ed,cing,ement, NOT PLACED WHERE IT NORMALLY BELONGS
mispoke, misspoke
mispokin, misspoke(n)
misprint,*,ted,ting, PRINTED INCORRECT INFORMATION
mispronounce,*,ed,cing,nunciation, WORD NOT SPOKEN CORRECTLY
misprunownse, mispronounce
misquote,*,ed,ting,tation, DIDN'T ACCURATELY REFLECT WHAT WAS ACTUALLY SAID
misread,*, TO NOT READ CORRECTLY
misred, misread
misrepresent,*,ted,ting,tation,tative, ter, DOESN'T ACCURATELY REPRESENT
misruble, miserable
miss,sses,ssed,ssing, NOT IN USUAL/ PREFERRED PLACE, IN REFERENCE TO YOUNG UNMARRIED WOMAN
missile,*,ery, A THROWN OR SHOT PROJECTILE WITH INTENT TO INJURE

mission,*,nary,naries, SET OUT TO COMPLETE A TASK AS IF WITH AUTHORITY

misslede, mislead

misspell,*,lled,lling, TO SPELL INCORRECTLY

misspoke,en, DID NOT SAY WHAT WAS MEANT TO BE SAID, SPOKEN INCORRECTLY

missusage, misuse(sage)

missuse, misuse

mist,*,ted,ting,ty,tily,tiness, VERY LIGHT SPRAY OF WATER, A HAZE (or see midst/miss(ed))

mistacism, mystic(icism)

mistake,*,en,enly,enness,kable, THINK IT IS SOMETHING IT IS NOT, INCORRECT "prefixes: un"

mistakuble, mistake(kable)

mistamener, misdemeanor

misteek, mystique

mistefy, mystify

mistek, mystic / mystique / mistake

mistektamy, mastectomy

mister, MR.(ABBREVIATION), REFERENCE TO A MAN

mistereus, mysterious

mistic, mystic

misticul, mystic(cal)

mistique, mystique

mistireus, mysterious

mistletoe, PARASITIC PLANT ON A TREE

mistook, PAST TENSE FOR THE WORD 'MISTAKE'

mistreat,*,ted,ting,tment, TREAT SOMETHING/SOMEONE IMPROPERLY

mistress,sses, WOMAN IN POSITION OF COMMAND/RULE

mistret, mistreat

mistrial,*, UNABLE TO MAKE A JUDGEMENT IN A TRIAL DUE TO VARIOUS REASONS

mistro, maestro

mistufy, mystify

mistuk, mistook

misul, missile

misulaneus, miscellaneous

misulf, my(self)

misultoe, mistletoe

misunderstand,*,ding,tood, NOT ABLE TO COMPREHEND/UNDERSTAND

misunderstood, PAST TENSE FOR THE WORD "MISUNDERSTAND"

misur, miser

misuruble, miserable

misury, misery

misus, miss(es)

misuse,*,ed,sing,er,sage, NOT USING PROPERLY

misuze, misuse

mit, mitt / mite / might / meat / meet / met

mitabolize, metabolize

mitachondria, mitochondria

mitagashen, mitigate(tion)

mitagate, mitigate

mitapolize, metabolize

mite,*, TINY INSECT, ANIMAL, SOMETHING TINY (or see might/ mitt/might(y))

miten, mitten

miter,*,red,ring, REFERENCE TO ANGLES (or see meter)

mitereul, material

miteur, might(ier)

mitevul, medieval

mith, myth

mithakul, myth(ical)

mithalogic, mythologic

mithasize, myth(icize)

mithecul, myth(ical)

mitholagize, mythologic(ize)

mithology, mythology

mitiest, might(iest)

mitigate,*,able,tion,tive,tor,tory, TO LESSEN A BURDEN OR SEVERITY "prefixes: un"

mitir, meter / miter

mitochondria,al,ion, ORGANELLES WITHIN A CELL WHICH ASSIST IN METABOLISM

mitoesis, mitosis

mitosis,ic, CELL DIVISION FROM ORIGINAL CELL "prefixes: endo"

mitropolis, metropolis

mitst, midst

mitt,*,ten, A COVERING FOR THE HAND (or see mite/might)

mitten,*, HAND COVERING TO PROTECT SKIN FROM GREAT TEMPERATURE DIFFERENCES

mitul, medal / metal / mettle / meddle / middle

mityest, might(iest)

mix,xes,xed,xing,xer, TO BLEND/STIR VARIOUS ELEMENTS/ARTICLES/ INGREDIENTS TOGETHER

ELIMINATING ORDER "prefixes: inter"

mixchur, mixture

mixture,*, COMBINE DIFFERENT THINGS TOGETHER TO CREATE SOMETHING ENTIRELY DIFFERENT "prefix: inter"

mizconstsrue, misconstrue

mizdakin, mistake(n)

mizdamener, misdemeanor

mizdereus, mysterious

mizdress, mistress

mizdrus, mistress

mizdur, mister

mizdury, mystery

mizenformation, misinform(ation)

mizenturpret, misinterpret

mizer, miser

mizeruble, miserable

mizfet, misfit

mizfire, misfire

mizforchen, misfortune

mizgeving, misgiving

mizhandul, mishandle

mizhap, mishap

mizinform, misinform

mizkunstrew, misconstrue

mizkwote, misquote

mizled, misled

mizleed, mislead

mizmach, mismatch

miznomer, misnomer

mizpell, misspell

mizplase, misplace

mizpronounce, mispronounce

mizread, misread

mizreprezent, misrepresent

miztake, mistake

miztakuble, mistake(kable)

miztamener, misdemeanor

mizteek, mystique

miztek, mystic

mizter, mister

miztereus, mysterious

miztress, mistress

miztret, mistreat

miztrial, mistrial

mizunderstand, misunderstand

mizur, miser

mizury, misery

mizuse, misuse

mo, mow

moan,*,ned,ning, A LOW, GUTTERAL SOUND COMING FROM THE THROAT

moat,*, DUG OUT TRENCH AROUND A STRUCTURE WHICH IS NORMALLY FILLED WITH WATER (or see mote)

mob,*,bbed,bbing, GATHERING OF LARGE GROUP OF PEOPLE

mobal, mobile

mobalezation, mobile(lization)

mobalize, mobile(lize)

mobelity, mobile(lity)

mobeluzation, mobile(lization)

mobile,lity,lize,lizes,lized,lizing,lization, ABILITY TO BE PHYSICALLY ON THE MOVE, TEMPORARY "prefixes: im"

moble, mobile

mobt, mop(ped) / mope(d)

mobul, mobile

mobulization, mobile(lization)

mobulize, mobile(lize)

moc, mach / make / mock

moca, mocha

mocasin, moccasin

moccasin,*, SOFT LEATHER SHOE/BOOT

mocha, COLOR, TYPE OF COFFEE

mochen, motion

mochenist, machine(nist)

mochure, mature

mock,*,ked,king,kery,keries,kingly,ker, DISRESPECTFULLY MIMIC/IMITATE SOMEONE (or see mach)

mocksy, moxie

mocusen, moccasin

mod, mode / mud / mood

modafekashen, modify(fication)

modafy, modify

modal,*,lly,lity,lities, OF MODE/ MANNER/FORM "prefixes: bi/inter"

modavashen, motive(vation)

modavate, motive(vate)

mode,*, POSITION/TYPE/USAGE/WAY/ FORM

modeef, motif

modef, motive

modefekashen, modify(fication)

modefy, modify

model,*,led,ling,ler, ABOUT SHAPE/ STYLE/FORM (or see modal/mottle/ motel/muddle)

moder, motor / mutter

moderate,*,ed,ting,tion,tor, BETWEEN EXTREMES OF HIGH/LOW, IN BETWEEN "prefixes: im"

moderet, moderate

modern,nism,nist,nistic,nize,nizes,nized, nizing,nizer,nization, CURRENT IN STYLE/FASHION, TRENDY

modest,tly,ty,ties, MODERATE IN DEMEANOR, NOT EXTREME "prefixes: im"

modevashen, motive(vation)

modevate, motive(vate)

modeve, motive

modewlashen, modulate(tion)

modgual, module

modgul, module

modi, mood(y) / muddy

modify,fies,fied,fying,fication,ficative, ficatory,fiable,fier, CHANGE/ALTER THE MODE/CONFIGURATION OR OPERATION OF

modil, modal / model / mottle

modir, motor

modirn, modern

modisly, modest(ly)

modist, modest

modisty, modest(y)

modivashen, motive(vation)

modivate, motive(vate)

modive, motive

modjual, module

modjulashen, modulate(tion)

modjule, module

modle, modal / model / mottle

modo, motto

moduf, motive

moduficashen, modify(fication)

modul, modal / model / module / mottle

modulate,*,ed,ting,tion,tor,tory, ABILITY TO ADJUST TO ACCEPTABLE FREQUENCY "prefixes: inter"

module,*,lar,larity,lus,li, A STANDARDIZED SIZE/SHAPE/ DIMENSION, PRE-MADE

modur, motor

modurashen, moderate(tion)

moduret, moderate

modurise, motor(ize)

modurn, modern

modurnasation, modern(ization)

moduvashen, motive(vation)

moduvate, motive(vate)

mody, mood(y)

moer, mow(er)

moest, moist

mof, mauve / move

mofment, move(ment)

mogma, magma

mogulate, modulate

mogule, module

moguler, module(lar)

mohair,*, HAIR OF ANGORA GOAT

mohare, mohair

moir, mow(er)

moist,ten,tens,tened,tening,ture,turize, turizes,turized,turizing, turizer,tness, BETWEEN DRY/ WET, MORE THAN DAMP

mojul, module

mojulate, modulate

mojulir, module(lar)

mok, mach / make / mock

moka, mocha

mokasen, moccasin

mokery, mock(ery)

mokesin, moccasin

moksy, moxie

moku, mocha

mol, mall / maul / mole

molakul, molecule

molakuler, molecule(lar)

molar,*,rity, A TOOTH, CHEMISTRY AMOUNT "prefixes: pre"

molarky, malarkey

molasis, molasses

molasses, RICH/DARK SYRUP

mold,*,ded,ding,dy,diness,dable, FUNGI, CONTAINER USED TO MAKE A FORM, USED FOR FRAMING/ FINISHING WORK (or see molt/ maul(ed)) "prefixes: un"

moldibul, mold(able)

molduble, mold(able)

mole,*, A CHEMISTRY MEASUREMENT OF WEIGHT, A RODENT, A BEAUTY MARK, GROWTH ON SKIN

molecule,*,lar,larly,larity, TINY PARTICLES SUSPECTED TO EXIST BUT CANNOT BE SEEN "prefixes: bi/ bio/inter/intra"

molekuler, molecule(lar)

moler, molar

moleshes, malicious

molest,*,ted,ting,ter,tation, TO PHYSICALLY FORCE SOMEONE INTO AN UNACCEPTABLE SITUATION

molicious, malicious

molikule, molecule

moll, mall / maul / mole

mollusk,*, INVERTEBRAE GENERALLY WITH SHELLS AND NO SEGMENTS

molt,*,ted,ting,ter, TO SHED OUTER LAYER SUCH AS SKIN (or see mold/malt/maul(ed))

molur, molar

molusk, mollusk

mom,*,mma,mmy, PARENT WHO PERFORMED THE BIRTHING

moma, mamma

momendus, moment(ous)

moment,*,tary,tarily,tariness,tly,tous, tously,tousness,tum, VERY BRIEF MEASURE/AMOUNT OF TIME

momento, memento

momentus, moment(ous)

mominshus, moment(ious)

momint, moment

mominterily, moment(arily)

mominto, memento

momintum, moment(um)

momintus, moment(ous)

mon, PREFIX INDICATING "ALONG/ONLY/SINGLE" MOST OFTEN MODIFIES THE WORD (or see moan/moon)

monafilament, monofilament

monagram, monogram

monalith, monolith

monalithic, monolith(ic)

monalogue, monologue

monanukleosis, mononucleosis

monarale, monorail

monarch,*,hal,hial,hally,hical,hically, hism,hist,histic,hy,hies, LARGE BUTTERFLY, POWERFUL POSITION, SOLE RULER

monark, monarch

monarkial, monarch(ial)

monastery,ries,rial,tic,tical,ticism, PLACE OF ISOLATION

monater, monitor

monatone, monotone

mondane, mundane

monday,*, A DAY OF THE WEEK (ENGLISH)

mone, moan / money

monee, money

monegram, monogram

monelogue, monologue

monenukleosis, mononucleosis

monerale, monorail

monestasism, monastery(tacism)

monestery, monastery

monetary,rily,tize,tization,rist, OF MONEY

monetone, monotone

monetor, monitor

monewment, monument

money,nies, MINTED COIN AND PAPER USED FOR EXCHANGE OF ITEMS OR SERVICES

mongrel,*,ly,lism,lize,lizes,lized,lizing, lization, MIXED BREED OF DOG

mongril, mongrel

mongrul, mongrel

monie, money

monigram, monogram

monilogue, monologue

moninukleosis, mononucleosis

monirale, monorail

monistery, monastery

monitary, monetary

monitone, monotone

monitor,*,red,ring,ry,rship, ENFORCER OF RULES, A MACHINE THAT READS VITAL LIFE SIGNS "prefixes: bio"

monk,*,khood,kish,kishly,kishness,kery, keries, ONE WHO PRACTICES TO OVERCOME EGO

monkey,kies,ying, ANIMAL, MAMMAL, TO ACT LIKE A MONKEY

mono, SHORT FOR MONONUCLEOSIS, PREFIX INDICATING "ALONG/ONLY/SINGLE" MOST OFTEN MODIFIES THE WORD

monocular,*, ITEM WHERE ONE EYE CAN SEE MAGNIFICATION

monofilament,*, ONE FILAMENT IN A BULB

monogamy,mous,mic,mist,mistic, mously,mousness, ADULT WHO ACCEPTS ONLY ONE PARTNER

monogram,*,med,ming,matic, LETTER/CHARACTER REPRESENTING A NAME

monolith,hic,hically, SINGLE SKIN, STONE

monologue,*,gic,gist,gize, ONE PERSON WHO SPEAKS

mononucleosis, ONE-NUCLEUS BLOOD CELLS RESULTANT FROM A VIRUS

monopoly,lies, ONE COMPANY DOMINATES LEAVING NO CHOICE

monorail,*, A SINGLE RAIL FOR TRAVEL

monotary, monetary

monotone,*,nosity, ONE TONE

monotony,nous,nously,nousness, REPETITION, SAME THING OVER AND OVER AGAIN

monoxide, ONE OXYGEN ATOM IN A MOLECULE

monsoon,*, GREAT RUSH OF RAIN IN A CERTAIN SEASON WHICH LASTS FOR MONTHS

monster,*,red,ring,trance,trous,trosity, USED TO DESCRIBE SOMETHING UNUSUAL/FRIGHTENING, RELIGIOUS VESSEL, DRUNK

monstrasute, monstrosity

monstrausete, monstrosity

monstres, monstrous

monstrocity, monstrosity

monstrosete, monstrosity

monstrosity,sities,ous, USED TO DESCRIBE SOMETHING UNUSUAL/FRIGHTENING/ABNORMAL

monstrous,sly,sness,osity, USED TO DESCRIBE SOMETHING UNUSUAL/FRIGHTENING

monstrus, monstrous

monstur, monster

monsune, monsoon

monten, mountain

month,*,hly,hlies, A MEASURE OF TIME WHICH DIVIDES DAYS OF THE YEAR INTO SECTIONS "prefixes: bi/semi"

montin, mountain

monuer, manure

monugram, monogram

monulithic, monolith(ic)

monulogue, monologue

monument,*,tal,tally,talize, A MARKER/STONE/ARTICLE/STRUCTURE IN HONOR OF SOMEONE/SOMETHING

monumint, monument

monurale, monorail

monure, manure

monustery, monastery

monutary, monetary

monutone, monotone

mony, money

monyument, monument

monzoon, monsoon

monzter, monster

mood,*,dy,dier,diest,dily,diness, AN EMOTIONAL STATE OF MIND (or see moot/mute)

moodyness, mood(iness)

moof, move

moofuble, move(vable)

moon,*,ned,ning,nish,nishly,ny, LARGEST PLANET SEEN AT NIGHT, A PRANK

moor,*,red,ring,rage, A BOG, A PLACE TO DOCK A BOAT, ACT OF DOCKING A SHIP (or see more) "prefixes: un"

moose, A LARGE MEMBER OF THE DEER FAMILY (or see mouse/mousse)

moot,tness, UP FOR DISCUSSION WITHOUT DECISION, ARGUABLE, DEBATABLE (or see mute/mood)

mootiness, mood(iness)

mooty, mood(y)

moove, move

mop,*,pped,pping, AN ITEM USED WET TO CLEAN FLOORS (or see mob/map)

mope,*,ed,ping,per,pey, TO BE DISINTERESTED DUE TO SADNESS/ BEING BORED, TO HAVE LOW SPIRITS (or see mop)

moped, mop(ped) / mope(d)

mopt, mop(ped) / mope(d)

mor, mar / more / moor / mow(er)

moral,*,lly,lism,list,listic,lize,lizes,lized, lizing,lization,lizer, ABILITY TO JUDGE/ BEHAVE RIGHT FROM WRONG (or see morale/morel) "prefixes: im/un"

morale,*,lity,lities, CONDITION/STATE OF ONE'S ABILITY TO JUDGE/ACT ON THOSE JUDGEMENTS (or see mural/moral/morel)

moralestic, moral(istic)

moraly, moral(ly)

moratorium,*,ry, A PURPOSELY IMPOSED DELAY FOR AN UNDETERMINED AMOUNT OF TIME

morbed, morbid

morbedly, morbid(ly)

morbel, marble

morbet, morbid

morbid,dly,dness,dity, AKIN TO DEATH/ DARKNESS

morbidety, morbid(ity)

morbil, marble

morbit, morbid

morbul, marble

morch, march

morchoery, mortuary

morchuery, mortuary

mordar, mortar

mordel, mortal

mordir, mortar

mordul, mortal

morduly, mortal(ly)

mordur, mortar

more, OF A GREATER NUMBER WHEN COMPARING, GREATER (or see moor/mow(er))

morege, moor(age)

morel,*, EDIBLE MUSHROOM (or see moral/morale)

morelise, moral(ize)

morelistic, moral(istic)

mores, SOCIAL ACCEPTANCE

moretoreum, moratorium

morgage, mortgage

morge, morgue

morgedge, mortgage

morgeje, mortgage

morgen, margin

morgenulize, marginalize

morgerin, margarine

morgije, mortgage

morgue,*, PLACE WHERE BODIES WITHOUT SPIRITS ARE TEMPORARILY HELD

morige, moor(age)

moril, moral / morel

morily, moral(ly)

moritoreum, moratorium

morjaren, margarine

morjenulize, marginalize

mork, morgue

morn, mourn / morning

mornen, morning / mourn(ing)

morneng, mourn(ing) / morning

mornful, mourn(ful)

mornin, morning / mourn(ing)

morning,*, MORN, FIRST PART OF THE DAY BEFORE 12 NOON (or see mourn(ing))

moroon, maroon

morose,ely,eness,sity, GLOOMY OR DARK THOUGHTS, IDEAS, BEHAVIOR

morotoreum, moratorium

morph, PREFIX INDICATING "SHAPE/ FORM/STRUCTURE" MOST OFTEN MODIFIES THE WORD

mors, mores

morshuery, mortuary

mortal,*,lly,lity,lities, RELATED TO DEATH/KILLING/DYING "prefixes: im"

mortaledy, mortal(ity)

mortalidy, mortal(ity)

mortar,*, MIXTURE USED FOR JOINTS TO HOLD BRICK, VESSEL SHAPE WITH A PESTLE

mortel, mortal

morter, mortar

mortgage,*,ed,ging,ger,gor, TITLE/ DEED OF PROPERTY HELD BY SOMEONE WHICH REQUIRES MONEY TO OWN/HAVE

mortil, mortal

mortir, mortar

mortuary,ries, A FUNERAL HOME

mortul, mortal

mortur, mortar

morul, moral

morulesm, moral(ism)

morulestic, moral(istic)

morulise, moral(ize)

moruly, moral(ly)

mos, moss / most

mosaic,*,cally,cist, MANY PIECES PLACED TOGETHER TO FORM A PICTURE

mosayic, mosaic

mosdereus, mysterious

mosdly, most(ly)

mose, moose / mousse

moseik, mosaic

mosektimy, mastectomy

moshen, motion

moshenist, machine(nist)

moshun, motion

mosk, mosque

moskeet, mesquite

mosketo, mosquito

moskewlur, muscle(cular)

mosly, most(ly)

mosoleum, mausoleum

mosoose, masseuse

mosque,*, A BUILDING WHERE MUSLIMS PRAY

mosquito,oes,oey, AN INSECT WHO SEEKS BLOOD

mosquler, muscle(cular)

moss,sses,ssy,ssier,ssiest,ssiness, A PLANT GROWTH

most,tly, PAST TENSE FOR THE WORD MORE, THE GREATEST AMOUNT IN COMPARISON TO ANOTHER AMOUNT (or see must) "prefixes: under/up/upper"

mostache, mustache / moustache

mostash, mustache / moustache

mostectemy, mastectomy

moster, monster / muster
mostereus, mysterious
mostique, mystique
mosuleum, mausoleum
mosuse, masseuse
mot, moat / mutt / mode / mote
motabolize, metabolize
motafikashen, modify(fication)
motapolize, metabolize
motavashen, motive(vation)
motchewlate, modulate
motchulashen, modulate(tion)
motchulate, modulate
mote, SPECK, PARTICLE (or see moat/ mode)
moteef, motif
motef, motif / motive
motel,*, LODGING WHERE YOU CAN PARK YOUR VEHICLE NEAR THE DOOR (or see mottle)
moter, motor / mutter
moterashen, moderate(tion)
moteret, moderate
motereul, material
moterise, motor(ize)
motern, modern
moternul, maternal
motevashen, motive(vation)
moth,*, A NOCTURNAL INSECT
mother,*,red,ring,rly,rless,rlessness, ONE WHO HAS GIVEN BIRTH, BACTERIAL COATING ON FERMENTING LIQUIDS, ORGINATOR OF LIFE
motif, RECURRING THEME IN VISUAL PRESENTATION (or see motive)
motil, modal / model / mottle
motion,*,nal,ned,ning,nless,nlessness, ACTIVITY, MOVEMENT
motir, motor
motirn, modern
motivashen, motive(vation)
motive,*,vate,vates,vated,vating,vation, vational,vative,vity, ENCOURAGE TO PERFORM ALONG IN A PLANNED DIRECTION (or see motif)
motle, mottle / modal / model
motled, mottle(d) / model(ed)
moto, motto
motor,*,red,ring,rist,rize,rized,rizing, rization, AN ENGINE/DEVICE USED TO CREATE MOTION
mottle,ed,er,ling, SPLOTCHY IN COLOR, PATCHES OF IRREGULAR SHAPES

motto,*, A CONCISE DESCRIPTION OF PRINCIPLE OR PURPOSE
motul, modal / model / mottle
motur, motor
moturashen, moderate(tion)
moturet, moderate
moturise, motor(ize)
moturn, modern
moturnize, modern(ize)
motuv, motive
motuvashen, motive(vation)
motuvate, motive(vate)
moucus, mucus
moud, mood / mode
mound,*,ded,ding, A SMALL HILL/PILE/ HEAP (or see mount)
mount,*,ted,ting, TO SIT ATOP OF, SHORT FOR MOUNTAIN, AFFIX SOMETHING, GET ON TOP OF "prefixes: dis/re/sur"
mountain,*,neer,nous,nously,nousness, GREAT HILLS OF ORGANIC MATTER, LARGE JUTTING EXTRUSIONS OF EARTH "prefixes: inter"
mounteneer, mountain(eer)
mountenus, mountain(ous)
mountin, mountain
mour, mow(er)
mourn,*,ned,ning,ningly,nful,nfully, nfulness,ner, EMOTIONALLY EXPERIENCE LOSS OF SOMETHING (or see morning)
mouse,er,sing,ey,mice, SMALL RODENT (or see moose/mousse)
mousse, DESSERT (or see mouse/ moose)
moustache, FACIAL HAIR GROWING ABOVE THE LIP (also spelled mustache)
moutenus, mountain(ous)
mouth,*,hed,hing,her,hful,hfuls,hy, ORIFICE ON THE FACE WHICH MAKES SOUNDS/INGESTS
mov, mauve / move
movd, move(d)
move,*,ed,ving,vingly,er,vable, vableness,vably,vability,eless, elessly,elessness,ement, CHANGE/ RELOCATE FROM ONE PLACE/ LOCATION TO ANOTHER, BE IN MOTION "prefixes: im/non/re/un"
movie,*, PICTURES IN MOTION
movment, move(ment)

mow,*,wed,wing,wer, CUT GRASS/ BRUSH WITH A TOOL/MACHINE, REMOVE/LOWER IN WIDE SWATHES
mowder, motor
mowenus, mountain(ous)
mownd, mound
mownden, mountain
mownt, mound / mount
mownten, mountain
mowse, mouse
mowten, mountain
mowteneer, mountain(eer)
mowtenus, mountain(ous)
mowth, mouth
mowtin, mountain
mowtinus, mountain(ous)
moxie, COURAGE, ASSERTIVE
moxy, moxie
moyeast, moist
moyster, moist(ure)
moysturize, moist(urize)
mozaek, mosaic
mozayic, mosaic
mozed, most
mozly, most(ly)
mozoleum, mausoleum
mozt, most
mozuleim, mausoleum
mozuleim, mausoleum
mperical, empirical
mpethy, empathy
mpithy, empathy
mportant, important
mportens, important(nce)
mportent, important
mpress, impress
mpurfikt, imperfect
mputhy, empathy
mr, mister
mrk, mark
mt, empty
mubiledy, mobile(lity)
mubility, mobile(lity)
mucaw, macaw
much, AMOUNT OF SOMETHING, SIZEABLE QUANTITY
muchanek, mechanic
muchanekul, mechanic(al))
muchene, machine
muchenist, machine(nist)
muchety, machete
muchual, mutual
muchure, mature
muchuredy, mature(rity)

muchurle, mature(ly)
muchyual, mutual
mucus,coid,citis,sity,cous, SLIPPERY SECRETED SUBSTANCE FOR PROTECTION OF SKIN
mud,*,dded,dding,ddy, DIRT MIXED WITH WATER (or see mood/mutt)
mudalate, mutilate
muddle,*,ed,ling, TO CONFUSE, MAKE UNCLEAR, MAKE A MESS, CREATE DISORDER
muddy,ddies,ddier,ddiest,ddying,ddily, ddiness, WATER MIXED WITH DIRT
mude, mood / mute / muddy
mudel, muddle
mudelate, mutilate
muden, mutton
mudeness, mood(iness)
muder, mutter
mudereul, material
mudereulise, materialize
mudernol, maternal
mudiest, muddy(diest)
mudil, muddle
mudilate, mutilate
mudir, mutter
mudle, muddle
mudon, mutton
mudul, muddle
mudur, mutter
mudy, muddy / mood(y)
mudyest, muddy(diest)
muer, moor
muerege, moor(age)
muf, move / muff
mufan, muffin / move(ving)
mufd, move(d) / muff(ed)
mufee, movie
mufen, muffin / move(ving)
muff,*,ffed,ffing, BE CLUMSY, BUNGLE SOMETHING, HAND WARMER, TUFT ON BIRDS /FOWL
muffen, muffin
muffin,*, BAKED DESSERT
muffler,*, KEEPS LOUD NOISES QUIET
mufin, muffin
mufler, muffler
mufment, move(ment)
muft, move(d)
mufuble, move(vable)
mug,*,gged,gging,gger,ggy, DRINKING VESSEL, SOMEONE WHO ASSAULTS WITH INTENT TO ROB, A FACE, WARM/DAMP/STILL AIR

mugd, mug(gged)
muge, muggy
mugeness, muggy(giness)
mugestekal, majesty(tical)
mugestik, majesty(tic)
muggie, muggy
muggy,ggily,gginess, WARM AND HUMID
mugi, muggy
mugishen, magic(ian)
mugority, major(ity)
mugy, muggy
mugynes, muggy(giness)
muir, moor
muj, much
mujestical, majesty(tical)
mujishen, magic(ian)
mukanek, mechanic
mukanekul, mechanic(al)
mukaw, macaw
mukus, mucus
mul, mull / mule / mole / mall
mulado, mulato
mularea, malaria
mularky, malarkey
mulasis, molasses
mulato,oes, MIXTURE OF RACES OR BREEDS
mulch,hes,hed,hing, TO TILL UP GROUND, ADD ORGANIC MATERIAL TO SOIL
muldaplekashen, multiplication
muldaplikation, multiplication
muldiply, multiply
mule,*,lish, HYBRID MAMMAL/PLANT, STUBBORN PERSON, SHOE WITHOUT A BACK (or see mull)
mulecious, malicious
mulekuler, molecule(lar)
muleneum, millennium
muleshes, malicious
mulest, molest
mulevolens, malevolent(nce)
mulevolent, malevolent
mulicious, malicious
mulignant, malignant
mulinium, millennium
mulk, milk
mull,*, A FABRIC, TO STUDY/THINK ABOUT, MUSLIN, HUMUS (or see mule)
mullenium, millennium
multaplekashen, multiplication
multaply, multiply

multch, mulch
multeply, multiply
multi, PREFIX INDICATING "MUCH/ MANY" MOST OFTEN MODIFIES THE WORD
multiple,*,ly,lies,lied,lying,lier,licity, lication, DUPLICATES, A NUMBER THAT CAN BE DIVIDED WITH NO REMAINDERS "prefixes: sub"
multiplekashen, multiplication
multiplication,tive,tively, THE ACT OF WORKING NUMBERS TIMES NUMBERS
multiply,lies,lied,lying,lier,licity, TO INCREASE NUMBERS BY REPRODUCTION, ADDING NUMBERS TIMES NUMBERS, MATH
mumble,*,ed,ling,er,lingly, TO SPEAK WITHOUT ANNUNCIATING OR BE UNINTELLIGIBLE,SPOKEN WORDS NOT UNDERSTANDABLE
mumbul, mumble
mume, mummy
mummy,mmies,mmify,mmification, A DRIED UP CORPSE, WORD FOR MOM IN ENGLAND
mumps, A VIRUS WHICH ATTACTS THE THROAT
mumy, mummy
mun, moon
munarkikul, monarch(ical)
munarky, monarch(y)
munda, monday
mundane,ely,eness, DULL ROUTINE
munday, monday
mune, moon / money
munepulate, manipulate
munesipality, municipal(ity)
munesipul, municipal
municipal,*,lity,lities,lly,lize,lization, TOWN/CITY GOVERNED BY/WITH ITS OWN LAWS
munie, money
munila, manila
munipulate, manipulate
munisepal, municipal
munisepality, municipal(ity)
munisipal, municipal
munk, monk
munkee, monkey
munky, monkey
munodnes, monotony(nous)
munogemy, monogamy
munogimy, monogamy

munokside, monoxide
munokuler, monocular
munopuly, monopoly
munorkeul, monarch(ial)
munotny, monotony
munotunus, monotony(nous)
munoxide, monoxide
munsoon, monsoon
munstrocity, monstrocity
munstrosedy, monstrocity
munsune, monsoon
munth, month
munthly, month(ly)
munure, manure
munuver, maneuver
muny, money
muraculus, miracle(culous)
muraje, mirage
murakulus, miracle(culous)
mural,*, LARGE PAINTING APPLIED
    ONTO A WALL
muraledy, morale(lity)
murality, morale(lity)
murange, meringue
murchandise, merchandise
murchant, merchant
murder,*,red,ring,rer,rous,rousness,
    KILL SOMEONE UNLAWFULLY
murdir, murder
murdur, murder
murege, moor(age)
murel, mural
murena, marina
murene, marine
murge, merge
murgur, merge(r)
muridean, meridian
muril, mural
murina, marina
murine, marine
murje, merge
murk, murky
murkanteel, mercantile
murkery, mercury
murky,kily,kiness, DARK, SILTY OR
    THICK LIQUID/AIR, GLOOMY
murlin, merlin
murmade, mermaid
murmer, murmur
murmir, murmur
murmur,*,rer,ring,ringly,rous,rously, A
    LOW STEADY STREAM OF SOUND,
    MUFFLED SOUND
muroge, mirage

muroje, mirage
murose, morose
mursenary, mercenary
mursinary, mercenary
mursy, mercy
mursyful, mercy(ciful)
murul, mural
murun, maroon
mus, mouse / mousse / moose
musal, mussel / muscle / muzzle
muscle,*,ed,ling,cular,cularity,cularly,
    THICK TISSUE WHICH MOVES
    BONES (or see mussel/muzzle)
    "prefixes: intra/non"
musdach, moustache
musdake, mistake
musdakin, mistake(n)
musderd, mustard
musdurd, mustard
muse,*,ed,sing,singly,er, WHAT
    INSPIRES AN ARTIST, A DEEP THINK/
    CONTEMPLATION (or see moose/
    mouse/mousse)
musec, music
musecal, music(al)
musecian, musician
musecul, music(al)
musek, music
musektome, mastectomy
musekul, music(al)
musel, mussel / muscle / muzzle
museshen, musician
museum,*, A STRUCTURE FOR EXHIBITS
    OF INTERESTING ITEMS
mushedy, machete
mushene, machine
mushenest, machine(nist)
mushete, machete
mushinary, machine(ry)
mushroom,*,med,ming, FUNGI WITH
    BELL SHAPED HEAD ON A STEM
mushrum, mushroom
mushual, mutual
music,cal,cally,cality,calness,cian,
    TONES, SOUNDS PLAYED IN
    HARMONY ON INSTRUMENTS,
    PLEASING SOUND TO EARS
    "prefixes: un"
musician,*,nly,nship, PROFESSIONALLY
    INVOLVED IN CREATING MUSIC
musik, music
musil, mussel / muscle / muzzle
musishen, musician
muskedo, mosquito

muskeet, mesquite
muskera, mascara
musketo, mosquito
muskuler, muscle(cular)
musle, mussel / muscle / muzzle
muslen, muslin
muslin,*, MEDIUM WEIGHT COTTON
    CLOTH
musoge, massage
musoje, massage
musol, muscle / mussel / muzzle
musoose, masseuse
musquedo, mosquito
musquler, muscle(cular)
mussel,*, EDIBLE MARINE MOLLUSK
    WITH SHELL (or see muscle/muzzle)
mussle, mussel / muscle / muzzle
must, HAS TO BE, IMPERATIVE
mustache,*, HAIR ON TOP OF THE
    UPPER LIP ON ADULT MALES (also
    spelled moustache)
mustake, mistake
mustakin, mistake(n)
mustang,*, WILD HORSES
mustard, AN HERB USED AS A
    CONDIMENT
muster,*,red,ring, TO GATHER/
    COLLECT/ASSEMBLE
musterd, mustard
mustereus, mysterious
mustir, muster
mustird, mustard
mustireus, mysterious
musturd, mustard
musuese, masseuse
musul, muscle / mussel / muzzle
mususe, masseuse
mut, mutt / mute / mud / moot
mutabolize, metabolize
mutalate, mutilate
mutapolize, metabolize
mutashen, mutate(tion)
mutate,*,ed,ting,tive,tion,ant,
    ENDURED CHROMOSOME
    ALTERATION
mutch, much
mutchuel, mutual
mute,*,ed,ting,ely,eness,tism, NO
    SPEECH, UNABLE TO SPEAK (or see
    mutt/moot)
mutelate, mutilate
muten, mutton / mutate(ant)
mutent, mutate(ant)
muteny, mutiny

muter, mutter
mutereolise, materialize
mutereul, material
muternedy, maternity
muternol, maternal
muternulistek, maternal(istic)
muther, mother
muthor, mother
mutil, muddle
mutilashen, mutilate(tation)
mutilate,*,ed,ting,tion,tor, TO SHRED, RIP, TEAR BEYOND RECOGNITION
mutin, mutton
mutint, mutate(ant)
mutiny,nous, RESISTANCE TO AUTHORITY BY MORE THAN ONE ENTITY
mutir, mutter
mutireul, material
mutirnil, maternal
mutle, muddle
muton, mutton
mutony, mutiny
mutt,*, MIXED BREED (or see mute)
mutter,*,red,ring,ringly, TO MURMUR, SPEAK LOW AND UNINTELLIGIBLY, UNDECIPHERABLE SPEECH
mutton,*, SHEEP MEAT
mutual,*,lly,lism,list,listic,lity,lize, lization, CONSENT TO SHARE/ AGREE
mutul, muddle
mutulashen, mutilate(tation)
mutune, mutiny
mutur, mature / mutter
muty, muddy / mood(y)
muvd, move(d)
muve, move / movie
muvee, movie
muvi, movie
muvuble, move(vable)
muzdake, mistake
muzeim, museum
muzektame, mastectomy
muzekul, music(al)
muzel, muzzle
muzeshen, musician
muzeum, museum
muzik, music
muzikul, music(al)
muzishen, musician
muzlen, muslin
muzlin, muslin
muzt, must

muztake, mistake
muzter, muster
muztereus, mysterious
muzul, muzzle
muzzle,*,ed,ling,er, DEVICE TO RESTRAIN ANIMALS FROM BITING (or see muscle) "prefixes: un"
my, MYSELF, DENOTES OWNERSHIP, PREFIX INDICATING "MUSCLE" MOST OFTEN MODIFIES THE WORD
myc, PREFIX INDICATING "FUNGUS" MOST OFTEN MODIFIES THE WORD
mycrascope, microscope
mycrobeul, microbe(bial)
mycron, micron
mycrophone, microphone
myder, miter
mydokondrea, mitochondria
mydukondrea, mitochondria
mygrane, migraine
mygrashen, migrate(tion)
mygrate, migrate
mygratory, migrate(tory)
mykrafone, microphone
mykraskope, microscope
mykro, micro
mykrobe, microbe
mykrofone, microphone
mykrometer, micrometer
mykron, micron
mykrowave, microwave
myld, mild
myluge, mile(age)
myme, mime
myn, mine
mynd, mind / mend
myne, mine
myreod, myriad
myriad, MANY, MORE THAN TEN THOUSAND
mysdacism, mystic(icism)
mystecal, mystic(cal)
mysteek, mystique
mystek, mystique / mystic
mystereus, mysterious
mysterious,sly,sness, OF THE UNKNOWN, NOT ENOUGH FACTS TO UNDERSTAND
mystery,ries,rious, NOT ENOUGH FACTS TO UNDERSTAND, THE UNKNOWN
mystic,*,cal,cally,calness,cism,ify, A MYSTERY, THE UNSEEN/ UNEXPLAINED (or see mystique)

mystify,fies,fied,fying,fyingly,fication, PURPOSELY MISLEAD/BE VAGUE
mystique, BELIEF/AURA OF MYSTERIOUS POWER (or see mystic)
mystirious, mysterious
mystukul, mystic(cal)
mystury, mystery
mysulf, my(self)
myt, mitt / mite / might
myter, miter
myth,*,hic,hical,hically,hicize,hicizes, hicized,hicizing,hicization,hicizer, hography,hology, A STORY SURVIVING HISTORY THAT ISN'T SUPPORTED BY FACT
mythologic,cal,cally, OF MYTHS, LEGENDS, FOLKLORE
mythology,gies,gize,gizes,gized,gizing, gization,gize,gic, OF THE UNKNOWN, ATTEMPT TO EXPLAIN THE UNKNOWN
mytochondrea, mitochondria
mytokondrea, mitochondria
mytosis, mitosis
n, in / inn
nab,*,bbed,bbing,bber, TO GRAB/SEIZE/ CATCH UNEXPECTEDLY
naber, neighbor
naberhood, neighbor(hood)
nabir, neighbor
nabken, napkin
nabkin, napkin
nabor, neighbor
naborhud, neighbor(hood)
nabt, nab(bed) / nap(ped)
nabur, neighbor
naburhood, neighbor(hood)
nacessity, necessity
nach, notch
nacheirpath, naturopath
nachen, nation
nachenaluty, nation(ality)
nachenul, nation(al)
nacher, nature
nacheralist, natural(ist)
nacheropethy, naturopath(y)
nacherul, natural
nacheruly, natural(ly)
naches, nauseous
nachinal, nation(al)
nachir, nature
nachon, nation
nachral, natural

nachrul, natural
nachur, nature
nachuril, natural
nachurily, natural(ly)
nachuropath, naturopath
nachuropathy, naturopath(y)
nachus, nauseous
nadal, natal
nadef, native
nadefly, native(ly)
nadical, nautical
nadilus, nautilus
nadive, native
nadle, natal
nadol, natal
naduf, native
nady, naughty / knot(ty)
naefe, naive
naem, name
naevet, naive(te)
naevly, naive(ly)
nafee, navy
nafegashen, navigate(tion)
nafegubul, navigable
nafel, naval/ navel/ novel
nafigate, navigate
nafigubul, navigable
nafil, naval / navel / novel
nafol, naval / navel / novel
nafugate, navigate
nafuguble, navigable
naful, naval / navel / novel
nafulty, novelty
nafy, navy
nag,*,gged,gging,ggingly, AN ACT
    PERFORMED REPEATEDLY,
    IRRITATED BY REPETITION, YOUNG/
    OLD HORSE
naglekt, neglect
nagosheate, negotiate
nagoshubul, negotiable
nagotiate, negotiate
nagutev, negative
naif, naive / knife
naighbor, neighbor
nail,*,led,ling,ler, SLENDER STEEL WITH
    POINT/HEAD FOR HAMMERING,
    PROTECTIVE GROWTH ON FINGERS/
    TOES
naim, name
nait, night / knight
naive,ely,eness,ete,ety, LACKS
    INFORMATION, CLUELESS
nak, knack

naked,dly,dness, WITHOUT CLOTHES
    OR COVERING
nakit, naked
nale, nail
nalege, knowledge
namadik, pneumatic / nomad(ic)
name,*,ed,ming,ely,eless,elessly,
    elessness, LEGAL/PROPER TITLE,
    WHAT TO CALL SOMETHING/
    SOMEONE "prefixes: mis/sur/un"
namles, name(less)
namly, name(ly)
nane, nanny
nanny,nies, SOMEONE WHO IS HIRED
    BY A FAMILY TO TAKE CARE OF THE
    CHILDREN, A FEMALE GOAT
nano, PREFIX INDICATING "ONE
    BILLIONTH/EXTREMELY SMALL"
    MOST OFTEN MODIFIES THE WORD
nany, nanny
nap,*,pped,pping,pper, SLEEP BRIEFLY,
    PILE/CLOTH/ SUBSTANCE/FUZZ (or
    see knap/nape)
nape, BACK OF NECK (or see nap/knap/
    knap(ppy))
naped, nab(bed) / nap(pped)
napken, napkin
napkin,*, CLOTH/PAPER USED AT
    MEALTIME FOR FACE/HANDS
nappy, knap(ppy)
napt, nab(bed) / nap(ped)
narashen, narrate(tion)
narate, narrate
narative, narrate(tive)
narator, narrate(tor)
narcisim, narcissism
narcism, narcissism
narcissi,ssus,ssuses,ist,istic,istically,ism,
    EXCESSIVE SELF-LOVE
narcissism,st,stic,stically, EXCESSIVE
    SELF-LOVE
narcistic, narcissi(tic)
narcistik, narcissi(tic)
narco, PREFIX INDICATING "NARCOTIC/
    STUPOR/SLEEP" MOST OFTEN
    MODIFIES THE WORD
narcotic,*,cally,ize,izes,ized,izing,ization,
    CHEMICAL WHICH ALTERS BODY
    METABOLISM
nare, nary
narely, narrow(ly)
nari, nary
narkotek, narcotic
naro, narrow

naroly, narrow(ly)
narou, narrow
narowd, narrow(ed)
narrate,*,ed,ting,tion,tional,tive,tively,
    tor, TO RECOUNT/TELL/RELATE A
    STORY
narrow,*,wed,wing,wer,west,wly,
    wness, NOT AS WIDE AS USUAL/
    NORMAL, THIN STRIP, MAKE
    SMALLER
narsesm, narcissism
narsistic, narcissi(tic)
nary, NEVER, NOT
nasal,lity,lism,lly,lize,lization,
    INVOLVING THE NOSE AND ITS
    PASSAGEWAYS "prefixes: intra"
nasdeor, nasty(tier)
nasdursheum, nasturtium
nasdy, nasty
nasel, nasal
nasely, nasal(ly)
nasesidy, necessity
nasesitate, necessitate
nashen, nation
nashenaledy, nation(ality)
nashenul, nation(al)
nashinality, nation(ality)
nashonul, nation(al)
nashos, nauseous
nashunaludy, nation(ality)
nashuropathy, naturopath(y)
nasia, nausea
nasius, nauseous
nastee, nasty
nastershem, nasturtium
nastershum, nasturtium
nasti, nasty
nasturtium,*, A FLOWERING PLANT
nasty,tier,tiest,tily,tiness, UNDESIRABLE,
    OBJECTIONABLE, UNACCEPTABLE ,
    NOT PROPER
nat, not / naught / knot / gnat
natal, OF/RELATING TO BIRTH
    "prefixes: neo"
natcheroputhy, naturopath(y)
natcherul, natural
natchural, natural
natchurely, natural(ly)
natecal, nautical
natef, native
nateuropath, naturopath
nateve, native
natical, nautical
natif, native

natilus, nautilus

nation,*,nal,nally,nalize,nalization, nhood,nless,nalism,nalist,nality, nalities, nalizer, DEVOTED/LOYAL TO A PEOPLE/COUNTRY "prefixes: bi/inter/intra/multi"

natiunality, nation(ality)

native,*,ely,eness,vism,vist,vistic,vity, vities, BORN/BELONG TO CERTAIN LAND/ AREA, RACE OF PEOPLES, NOT AN IMMIGRANT

natle, natal

natol, natal

natoreus, notorius

natorius, notorious

natsher, nature

natsheropethy, naturopath(y)

natshur, nature

natuf, native

natufly, native(ly)

natul, natal

natural,*,lly,lness,lism,list,listic,listically, lize,lization, NOT REFINED/ MODIFIED/ REARRANGED/ CHANGED/MOLDED OR MANIPULATED "prefixes: un"

naturapathy, naturopath(y)

nature,*,ral, BASIC ESSENCE OF THINGS, CHARACTER, COMBINATION OF QUALITIES

naturel, natural

naturilist, natural(ist)

naturopath,*,hy,hic, TREATS ILLNES/ INJURIES WITH NATURAL REMEDIES

natuv, native

nau, gnaw / know / now

naude, naughty / knot(ty)

naudical, nautical

nauev, naive

naught, NOTHING, NOT, DON'T NEED ANYTHING (or see not/knot)

naughty,tier,tiest,tily,tiness, IMPROPER BEHAVIOR, MISCHIEVOUS (or see knot(ty))

naumenol, nominal

nauminoly, nominal(lly)

naumune, nominee

naun, noun

nausdalgea, nostalgia

nausdalgik, nostalgic

nausdrel, nostril

nausea,ate,ating,atingly, FEELING ILL IN STOMACH

nauseous,sly,sness, STOMACH FEELING ILL

naushus, nauseous

nausious, nauseous

naustalgea, nostalgia

naustalgik, nostalgic

naustrel, nostril

naut, not / naught / knot

nautch, notch

nautical,ally, OCEAN NAVIGATION

nautilus,ses,li, SPIRAL OCEAN SHELL

nauves, novice

nauvulest, novel(ist)

nauvulte, novelty

navagate, navigate

navagation, navigate(tion)

naval, SHIPS, OF A NAVY (or see navel/ novel)

navee, navy

navegable, navigable

navegashen, navigate(tion)

navegate, navigate

navegation, navigate(tion)

navel,*, SPOT ON THE BELLY WHERE THE UMBILICAL CORD WAS SEVERED, MIDDLE/CENTRAL PLACE (or see naval/novel)

navember, november

navigable,bility,eness,ly, ABLE TO MANEUVER/GUIDE

navigate,*,ed,ting,tion,tional,tionally, tor, STEER OR MANEUVER, ONE WHO STEERS/MANEUVERS/GUIDES

navil, naval / navel / novel

navimber, november

navol, naval / navel / novel

navugashen, navigate(tion)

navugate, navigate

navugation, navigate(tion)

navuguble, navigable

navul, naval / navel / novel

navuldy, novelty

navy,vies,val, COLLECTION OF SHIPS BELONGING TO A NATION

naw, gnaw / now

nawleg, knowledge

nawstrel, nostril

nayber, neighbor

nazdeur, nasty(tier)

nazdursheum, nasturtium

nazdy, nasty

nazel, nasal

nazely, nasal(ly)

nazil, nasal

nazily, nasal(ly)

naztersheum, nasturtium

nazty, nasty

ne, knee

near,*,rer,rest,rly,rness, CLOSE TO

neat,ter,test,tly,tness, ORDERLY/ ORGANIZED, APPEALING (or see need/knead/ knee(d))

nebal, nibble

neber, neighbor

nebir, neighbor

neble, nibble

nebor, neighbor

nebul, nibble

nebur, neighbor

nec, niece / neck

necasery, necessary

necatene, nicotine

neccesary, necessary

neccesitate, necessitate

neccesity, necessity

neccessary, necessary

necdur, nectar

nece, niece

necesadi, necessity

necesary, necessary

necesitate, necessitate

necesite, necessity

necessary,rily,riness, MUST BE/HAVE, REQUIRED "prefixes: un"

necessatate, necessitate

necessitate,*,ed,ting,tion,tive, REQUIRED, ESSENTIAL

necessity,ties,tous,tously,tousness, REQUIRED, MUST HAVE

necesudi, necessity

neche, niche

nechel, nickel

necisary, necessary

neck,*,ked,king, PART OF THE BODY BETWEEN HEAD AND SHOULDERS, PART OF THE SPINE

necklace,*, ORNAMENT/ADORNMENT FOR THE NECK

necklajay, negligee

neckleshay, negligee

neclas, necklace

neclasha, negligee

neclos, necklace

neclus, necklace

necotine, nicotine

necramancer, necromancer

necrimancer, necromancer

necromancer,*,cy,ntic, PERSON OR OCCURENCE WHICH REFLECTS OUR GREATEST FEAR, THE DARK/ UNAPPEALING SIDE OF OUR NATURE

nectar,*, SWEET JUICE OF A FLOWER

nectarine,*, CROSS BETWEEN PEACH/ PLUM

necterene, nectarine

nectir, nectar

nectirene, nectarine

nectur, nectar

necturene, nectarine

ned, need / neat / knead / knee(d)

nede, need(y)

neded, need(ed) / knead(ded)

nedel, needle / nettle

nedil, needle / nettle

nedle, needle / nettle

nedly, neat(ly)

nedul, needle / nettle

nedwurk, network

nedy, need(y)

nee, knee

need,*,ded,ding,diness,dy,dful,dfully, dfulness,dless,dlessly,dlessness, REQUIRED, ESSENTIAL, MANDATORY (or see knead/ knee(d)/neat)

needle,*,ed,ling, SLENDER METAL PIN WITH A SHARP POINT AT ONE END AND HOLE AT THE OTHER END, FOR SEWING (or see nettle)

needly, neat(ly)

neel, kneel

neer, near

neerer, near(er)

neerest, near(est)

neerly, near(ly)

nees, niece / knee(s)

nefew, nephew

nefir, never

nefiu, nephew

nefu, nephew

nefur, never

negative,*,ely,eness,vity,vism,vistic, MINUS,IN THE RED,OPPOSITE OF POSITIVE,FILM UNPROCESSED "prefixes: non"

negetiv, negative

neghbor, neighbor

neghborhood, neighbor(hood)

negitif, negative

negitive, negative

neglagay, negligee

neglagense, negligence

neglagent, negligence(nt)

neglagible, negligence(gible)

neglagint, negligence(nt)

neglaja, negligee

neglect,*,ted,ting,tful,tfully,tfulness,tor, NOT BE RESPONSIBLE/TAKE CARE OF

neglegable, negligence(gible)

neglegense, negligence

negligee,*, WOMEN'S UNDERGARMENTS

negligence,*,nt,ntly,gible,gibly,gibility, gibleness, NOT TAKE CARE OF OR BE RESPONSIBLE FOR

neglijay, negligee

neglijents, negligence

neglisha, negligee

neglugense, negligence

negodev, negative

negosheate, negotiate

negosheuble, negotiable

negoshubul, negotiable

negotef, negative

negotiable,bility, ABLE TO COME TO AGREEMENT

negotiate,*,ed,ting,tion,tor,able, COME TO AGREEMENT BY COMMUNICATING

negudev, negative

negutif, negative

negutive, negative

neibor, neighbor

neice, niece

neighbor,*,rly,rhood, PEOPLE WHO DWELL NEAR YOU, THOSE WHO LIVE CLOSE TO YOU

neither, NOT ONE OR THE OTHER, NOT THIS ONE OR THAT ONE

nek, neck / nick

nekatene, nicotine

nekdur, nectar

nekil, nickel

neklagent, negligence(nt)

neklajense, negligence

neklegent, negligence(nt)

nekles, necklace

neklesha, negligee

neklijent, negligence(nt)

neklis, necklace

neklisha, negligee

neklus, necklace

nekotene, nicotine

nekrumanser, necromancer

nekst, next

nektarine, nectarine

nekter, nectar

nekturene, nectarine

nekul, nickel

nekzd, next

nel, nil / kneel / nail

nemf, nymph

nemfomanea, nymphomania

nemonia, pneumonia

nemph, nymph

nemphomanea, nymphomania

neo, PREFIX INDICATING "NEW" MOST OFTEN MODIFIES THE WORD

neon, A NOBLE/INERT GAS, USED IN LAMPS

nep, nip

nepd, nip(pped)

nepe, nip(ppy)

nephew,*, FAMILY RELATION

nephu, nephew

nepil, nipple

nept, nip(pped)

nepul, nipple

nerador, narrrate(tor)

nerashen, narrate(tion)

nerate, narrate

neratek, neurotic

nerative, narrate(tive)

nerator, narrate(tor)

nercher, nurture

nere, near / nary

neresh, nourish

nereshen, narrate(tion)

nerf, nerve

nerfona, nirvana

nerfus, nervous

neri, nary

nerly, near(ly)

nero, narrow

nerodic, neurotic

neroly, narrow(ly)

neron, neuron

nerosis, neurosis

nerotic, neurotic

nerow, narrow

ners, nurse / near(s)

nerture, nurture

nerv, nerve

nervana, nirvana

nervas, nervous

nerve,*,ed,ving,eless,vous, SOFT TISSUE IN THE BODY WHICH RELATES BODY

TO BRAIN BY ELECTRICAL IMPULSES, BODY'S FORM OF COMMUNICATION "prefixes: un"

nervous,sly,sness, UNGROUNDED, WORRIED, STRESSED, UNSURE, DOUBTFUL, FEARFUL

nervus, nervous

nery, nary

nes, knee(s) / niece

nesasary, necessary

nesd, nest

nesdalgik, nostalgic

nese, niece

nesesary, necessary

nesesitate, necessitate

nesesudy, necessity

nesil, nestle

nesisary, necessary

nesol, nestle

nesold, nestle(d)

nest,*,ted,ting,ter, A BIRD'S HOME

nestalgek, nostalgic

nestle,*,ed,ling,ler, COZY/SNUGGLE UP AGAINST

nestursheum, nasturtium

nesul, nestle

net,*,tted,tting,table,tlike, A WEB, WEAVING OF SOMETHING, COLLECTION OF (or see neat/knit) "prefixes: inter/intra"

netal, needle / nettle

nete, neat / need(y)

nethur, neither

netil, needle / nettle

netly, neat(ly)

netol, needle / nettle

netorius, notorius

netpiky, nitpick(y)

netrishu, nutricious

netrishun, nutrition

netsh, niche

nettle,*, AN HERB (or see needle)

netul, needle / nettle

network,*,ked,king,ker, JOIN/CONNECT TOGETHER "prefixes: inter"

netwurk, network

nety, need(y)

neuder, neuter

neur, PREFIX INDICATING "NERVE" MOST OFTEN MODIFIES THE WORD

neural,lly, OF THE NERVOUS SYSTEM

neuresh, nourish

neurish, nourish

neurodic, neurotic

neuron,*,nal,nally,osis,oses, OF THE NERVOUS SYSTEM "prefixes: inter"

neurosis, DISORDER OF NERVES/ EMOTIONS

neurotic,cally,cism,osis, DISORDER AFFECTING EMOTIONS AS IT RELATES TO THE NERVOUS SYSTEM

neuter,*,red,ring, A LIVING THING WITHOUT ABILITY TO REPRODUCE

neutral,lity,lly,lism,list,listic,lize,lizes, lized,lizing,lization,lizer, BETWEEN EXTREMES/OPPOSITES, IN THE MIDDLE

neutreshen, nutrition

neutreshus, nutritious

neutretive, nutritive

neutricious, nutritious

neutrino,*, TINY UNCHARGED PARTICLE

neutron,*,nic, UNCHARGED PARTICLE IN ATOM

nevember, november

never, NOT EVER

nevimber, november

nevor, never

new,*,wer,west,wish,wly,wness, JUST CAME INTO BEING, JUST CREATED (or see knew) "prefixes: re"

newborn,*, JUST BORN

newcleate, nuclear(ate)

newcleur, nuclear

newdul, noodle

newdur, neuter

newkleate, nuclear(ate)

newkleus, nucleus

newlewed, newlywed

newlywed,*, COUPLES IN FIRST YEAR OF MARRIAGE

newmadik, pneumatic / nomad(ic)

newmarible, numerable

newmaril, numeral

newmatek, pneumatic

newmerology, numerology

newmerus, numerous

newmirary, numerary

newmonia, pneumonia

newmresy, numeracy

newmurable, numerable

newmurader, numerate(tor)

newmurary, numerary

newmurecy, numeracy

newmurology, numerology

newmurus, numerous

newron, neuron

newsans, nuisance

newspaper,*, PAPER WITH PRINTED TEXT CIRCULATED AS NEWS

newsuns, nuisance

newter, neuter

newtral, neutral

newtrative, nutritive

newtreant, nutrient

newtreno, neutrino

newtril, neutral

newtrishen, nutrition

newtrishus, nutritious

newtrol, neutral

newtron, neutron

next, FOLLOWS AFTER, COMING UP

nezt, nest

ngoy, enjoy

ni, knee

nibble,*,ed,ling, TINY BITE/MORSEL TO EAT

nibul, nibble

nicatene, nicotine

nice,er,est,ely,ety, KIND, THOUGHTFUL, CONSIDERATE, APPEALING, PLEASANT

nicesity, necessity

niche,*, A CORNER OF, A LITTLE PLACE CARVED/ETCHED OUT OF SOMETHING

nichel, nickel

nicity, nice(ty)

nick,*,ked,king, SHALLOW MARK/CUT/ NOTCH, AT THE LAST MINUTE

nickel,*,led, U.S. COIN

nicotine,nic,nism, A CHEMICAL SUBSTANCE NATURALLY FOUND IN TOBACCO

nid, night / need / knead

nidal, needle

nider, neither

nidl, needle

nidol, needle

nidul, needle

niece,*, A RELATIVE BY BLOOD FAMILY

niese, niece

nif, knife

night,*,tly,tless, THE DARK PART OF A 24 HOUR PERIOD, WITHOUT THE SUN (or see knight) "prefixes: over"

niglekt, neglect

niglekted, neglect(ed)

nigosheate, negotiate

nigosheuble, negotiable

nigotiable, negotiable

nigotiate, negotiate

nik, nick
nikatene, nicotine
nikel, nickel
niknak, knick knack
nikotene, nicotine
nikul, nickel
nikutene, nicotine
nil, NOTHING, NONE (or see kneel)
nilon, nylon
nimf, nymph
nimfomanea, nymphomania
nimfomaneac, nymphomania(c)
nimonea, pneumonia
nimph, nymph
nimphomania, nymphomania
nindeith, nine(tieth)
nindes, nine(ties)
nindy, nine(ty)
nine,*,er,ety,eties,nth,neteenth,netieth, ENGLISH NUMBER BETWEEN EIGHT AND TEN
ninfomaneac, nymphomania(c)
ninphomania, nymphomania
nintenth, nine(teenth)
ninthe, nine(nth)
ninty, nine(ty)
nintys, nine(ties)
nio, neo
niol, kneel
nion, neon
nip,*,pped,pping,pper,ppy, TAKE A LITTLE BITE, TAKE IN JUST A LITTLE
niped, nip(pped)
niple, nipple
nipple,*, FORMED TIP EXTRUSIONS ON THE CHEST CAVITY, TIP WITH ORIFICE
nipul, nipple
nipy, nip(ppy)
nircher, nurture
nireshment, nourish(ment)
nirfona, nirvana
nirfus, nervous
niron, neuron
nirosis, neurosis
nirse, nurse
nirvana, A STATE OF BLISS WHERE ONE IS TRANSFORMED FROM THE MATERIAL PLANE
nirves, nervous / nerve(s)
nirvus, nervous
nis, nice / niece
nise, nice / niece
nisedy, nice(ty)

niser, nice(r)
nisesity, necessity
nisest, nice(st)
nistalgek, nostalgic
nit,*, PARASITIC LARVAE (or see night/ knit/net/knight)
nitch, niche
nite, night / knight / knit
nited, knit(tted) / knight(ed)
nither, neither
nitorius, notorious
nitpeky, nitpick(y)
nitpick,*,ky, BE OVERLY CONCERNED ABOUT MINISCULE DETAILS
nitpiky, nitpick(y)
nitr, PREFIX INDICATING "NITROGEN" MOST OFTEN MODIFIES THE WORD
nitragen, nitrogen
nitral, nitrile
nitregen, nitrogen
nitrel, nitrile
nitrigen, nitrogen
nitrile, CHEMICAL CLASSIFICATION
nitro, PREFIX INDICATING "NITROGEN" MOST OFTEN MODIFIES THE WORD
nitrogen,nous, A GAS
nitrul, nitrile
nitsh, niche
niu, new / knew
niw, new / knew
njoy, enjoy
no, NEGATORY (or see know)
nob,*,bby, BUMPS/EXTRUSIONS (or see knob)
nobel, noble
nobelity, nobility
nobil, noble
nobility,ties, SUPERIOR, REPUTABLE, OF QUALITY
noble,*,er,est,esse,eman,bility, OF RANK/REPUTATION, CHEMICALLY INERT "prefixes: en"
nobody, NO BODY, NO PERSON
noboty, nobody
nobul, noble
noc, nock / knock / nook
noch, notch / nudge
nochin, notion
nochus, nauseous
nock,*,ked,king, SETTING AN ARROW INTO PLACE ON BOW STRING, PART OF ARROW (or see knock)
nocol, knuckle
nocshos, noxious

noct, PREFIX INDICATING "NIGHT" MOST OFTEN MODIFIES THE WORD
nocturnal,lity,lly,ne, ACTIVE AT NIGHT
nod,*,dded,dding, UP AND DOWN HEAD MOVEMENT (or see not/ node)
nodafekashen, notify(fication)
nodariety, notorius(iety)
nodary, notary
nodch, notch
node,*,dal,dality, STUMP/BULGE (too many definitions please see standard dictionary) (or see note/ naughty/knot(tty)) "prefixes: inter"
nodefication, notify(fication)
nodefy, notify
nodekul, nautical
nodelus, nautilus
noderiety, notorius(iety)
noderize, notary(rize)
nodery, notary
nodes, notice / node(s)
nodical, nautical
nodier, naughty(tier)
nodiest, naughty(tiest)
nodify, notify
nodikal, nautical
nodiriety, notorius(iety)
nodirize, notary(rize)
nodiry, notary
nodis, notice
nodle, noodle
nodufikashen, notify(fication)
nodufy, notify
nodukul, nautical
nodure, notary
noduriety, notorius(iety)
nodurise, notary(rize)
nodus, notice
nody, naughty / knot(ty)
noefe, naive
noese, noise / noise(sy) / nosy
noeve, naive
noevet, naive(te)
nofa, nova
nofel, novel
nofelty, novelty
nofember, november
nofil, novel
nofilty, novelty
nofu, nova
noget, nugget
noglekted, neglect(ed)
nois, noise

noise,*,eless,elessly,elessness,sy,sily, siness, DISHARMONIC SOUND, AN ALARMING/OFFENSIVE SOUND

noisey, noise(y)

nok, nock / knock / nook

nokel, knuckle

nokshus, noxious

nokternul, nocturnal

nokturnal, nocturnal

nol, knoll / null

nole, knoll

nolech, knowledge

noleg, knowledge

nolige, knowledge

noll, knoll

nom, gnome / numb

nomad,*,dic,dically,dism, A WANDERER, WITHOUT A PERMANENT HOME (or see pneumatic) "prefixes: semi"

nomadek, pneumatic / nomad(ic)

nomanaded, nominate(d)

nomanate, nominate

nomanee, nominee

nomat, nomad

nomatic, nomad(ic) / pneumatic

nomenashen, nominate(tion)

nomenate, nominate

nomene, nominee

nomenoly, nominal(lly)

nominal,lly,lism,lize,lizes,lized,lizing, lization, LOW COST, OF A NAME, BANKING TERM, NOUN FORM "prefixes: pre/pro"

nominate,*,ted,ting,tion,tive,tor, SELECT PEOPLE WHO WILL BE IN AN ELECTION "prefixes: de"

nominee,*, SOMEONE SELECTED TO BE VOTED FOR, ONE WHOM IS SELECTED FOR ELECTION

nomunashin, nominate(tion)

nomunate, nominate

nomunee, nominee

non, PREFIX INDICATING "NOT" MOST OFTEN MODIFIES THE WORD (or see known/none/nun/noon)

noncense, nonsense

nonchalant,tly,nce, CASUAL, UNCONCERNED

nonchelot, nonchalant

nonchulot, nonchalant

none, WITHOUT ANY, ABSENT FROM (or see nun/noun/known)

nonfiction,nal, FACTUAL

nonsense,sical,sically,sicalness, ABSURB, GOOFY, NOT POSSIBLE, IRRATIONAL

nonsents, nonsense

nonshelont, nonchalant

nonshulot, nonchalant

nonsinse, nonsense

noo, new / knew

noocleate, nuclear(ate)

noodle,*, PASTA

noodul, noodle

nook,*, A CORNER/CREVICE/RECESSED AREA

noon, O'CLOCK P.M. (or see nun)

noos, noose / new(s)

noose, SLIPKNOT ROPE WITH A LOOPED END FOR HOLDING SOMETHING (or see new(s))

nooz, noose / new(s)

noozpaper, newspaper

nop, nob/ knob/ nope

nope, NO

nor, ANOTHER WORD FOR 'NEITHER'

norishment, nourish(ment)

norm,*,mal, SLANG FOR WHAT'S NORMAL

normal,lly,lity,lcy,lize,lizes,lized,lizing, lization, MIDDLE OF THE ROAD BEHAVIOR/THOUGHT/ACTION, IN BETWEEN, AVERAGE "prefixes: re/ sub/un"

normul, normal

normuly, normal(lly)

nors, nurse

norsism, narcissism

norsistik, narcissi(tic)

north,hen,hener,hern,hernmost,her, herly,herlies,herliness, ONE OF FOUR COMPASS/MAGNETIC DIRECTIONS

northirn, north(ern)

northurly, north(erly)

nos, nose / know(s)

nosdalgek, nostalgic

nosdalgia, nostalgia

nosdrul, nostril

nose,*,ed,sing,eless,sy, PROBOSCUS, FACIAL FEATURE REQUIRED FOR SMELLING AND BREATHING (or see know(s))

nosel, nozzle

noseus, nauseous

noshen, notion

noshes, nauseous

noshus, nauseous

nosil, nozzle

nosle, nozzle

nost, nose(d)

nostalgea, nostalgia

nostalgia,ic, REMINISCE/REFER TO THE PAST

nostalgic,cally, REMINISCE/REFER TO THE PAST

nostrel, nostril

nostril,*, ORIFICES ON NOSE WHICH EMPLOYS AIR MOVEMENT

nostrul, nostril

nosul, nozzle

nosy,sier,siest,sily,siness, FOLLOW THE NOSE, PRY/SNOOP AROUND IN ANOTHERS BUSINESS, ALSO SPELLED 'NOSEY'

not, THIS ONE/THAT ONE, NO (or see note/knot/naught)

notariety, notorius(iety)

notary,ries,rize,rizes,rized,rizing,rization, AN OFFICIAL WHO PREPARES LEGAL DOCUMENTS

notch,hes,hed,hing, TO CUT/KNOCK OUT A WEDGE IN SOMETHING, TO CARVE OUT OF

note,*,ed,ting,tice, WRITE TEXT ON PAPER, KEEP IN MIND, OBSERVE/ REMEMBER (or see node/knot/ naught)

notee, naughty / knot(ty)

notefication, notify(fication)

notefikashen, notify(fication)

notefy, notify

notekul, nautical

notelus, nautilus

noterize, notary(rize)

notery, notary

notes, notice / note(s)

notheng, nothing

nothing, NOT A THING

notice,*,ed,cing, TO TAKE NOTE OF, OBSERVE A DISCREPANCY "prefixes: un"

notiest, naughty(tiest)

notifacation, notify(fication)

notify,fies,fied,fying,fication, TO INFORM, COMMUNICATE TO SOMEONE BY VARIOUS MEANS

notikal, nautical

notilus, nautilus

notion,*, AN INKLING/VIEW/OPINION "prefixes: pre"

notiriety, notorius(iety)

notiry, notary
notis, notice
notorious,sly,sness,iety,ieties, WIDELY KNOWN BUT WITHOUT POSITIVE REGARD
notufikashen, notify(fication)
notufy, notify
notukul, nautical
noturiety, notorius(iety)
noturize, notary(rize)
notury, notary
notus, notice
noty, naughty / knot(ty)
noun,*, A WORD REFERRING TO PEOPLE PLACE/THING/TIME/ PROPER NAME (or see known)
nourish,hes,hed,hing,her,hment, TO PROVIDE NECESSARY NUTRIENTS "prefixes: under"
nouse, noose
nova,*, STAR FLARE-UPS/BURSTS, NEW STAR
novel,*,list,listic,ette,lize,lization,lla,lty, FICTITIOUS WRITING, IMAGINED PLOT AND CHARACTERS, A CREATIVE IDEA OR DESIGN
novela, novel(lla)
novelty,ties, UNUSUAL AND CREATIVE
november, A MONTH OF THE YEAR (ENGLISH)
noves, novice
novice,*, A BEGINNER
novil, novel
novildy, novelty
novimber, november
novis, novice
novle, novel
novlety, novelty
novu, nova
novul, novel
novulest, novel(ist)
novulty, novelty
novus, novice
now, IN THE MOMENT/PRESENT
nowar, nowhere
noweesy, noise(sy)
nowere, nowhere
nowese, noise
nowhere, NO WHERE, NOT HERE NOW
nowleg, knowledge
nown, noun / known
noxious,sly,sness, HARMFUL TO HEALTH(or see nauseous)
noxus, noxious

noyse, noise
noze, nose / know(s)
nozeate, nausea(te)
nozel, nozzle
nozy, nosy
nozzle,*, AN APERTURE FOR SPRAYING
nu, new / knew
nuborn, newborn
nubshuel, nuptial
nuc, nook
nucle, PREFIX INDICATING "NUCLEUS/ NUCLEAR" MOST OFTEN MODIFIES THE WORD
nuclear,ate,ates,ated,ating,ation, HAVING TO DO WITH A NUCLEUS "prefixes: bi/inter/intra/pro/sub"
nucleus,ei,eic,ein, CENTRAL HUB, PRIMARY CONTROL "prefixes: pro"
nud, nude
nuddy, nut(ty) / nude(ies)
nude,*,ely,eness,dism,dity,dities, WITHOUT COVERINGS "prefixes: semi"
nudel, noodle
nuder, neuter
nudesm, nude(dism)
nudety, nude(dity)
nudge,*,ed,ging, GENTLY POKE/PUSH
nudil, noodle
nudl, noodle
nudmeg, nutmeg
nudol, noodle
nudril, neutral
nudul, noodle
nudy, nut(ty)
nue, new / knew
nuendo, innuendo
nuer, new(er)
nufember, november
nuge, nudge
nuget, nugget
nugget,*, A SMALL CHUNK OF SOMETHING
nugit, nugget
nuglekt, neglect
nuglere, nuclear
nugleus, nucleus
nugosheate, negotiate
nugoshiable, negotiable
nugotiable, negotiable
nugotiate, negotiate
nuindo, innuendo
nuisance, ANNOYING, OBNOXIOUS, CONTINUOUS IRRITATION

nuist, new(est)
nujt, nudge(d)
nuk, nook
nukle, knuckle
nukleate, nuclear(ate)
nukleir, nuclear
nukleus, nucleus
nukul, knuckle
nul, null
nulefy, nullify
nulewed, newlywed
nulify, nullify
null,llity,llities,llify, OF NO VALUE
nullify,fies,fied,fying,fier,fication,ity, RENDER NOT VALUABLE/ NECESSARY
nuly, new(l)
nulywed, newlywed
num, numb
numadik, pneumatic / nomad(ic)
numarader, numerate(tor)
numarery, numerary
numaril, numeral
numatic, pneumatic / nomad(ic)
numb,*,bed,bing,bness, VOID OF FEELING, INABILITY TO FEEL ANYTHING
number,*,red,ring,ral, A UNIT/SYMBOL WHICH REPRESENTS AN AMOUNT "prefixes: un"
numberible, numerable
numbroble, numerable
numerable, CAN BE COUNTED, COUNTABLE "prefixes: in"
numeracy, COMMON MATH "prefixes: in"
numeral,*,lly,ate,ary,ric,ator, ONE NUMBER/DIGIT, OF A DIGIT, ADD/ SUBTRACT
numerary, ABOUT NUMBERS
numerate,*,ed,ting,tion,tor,tors, BASIC MATH "prefixes: en/in"
numeric,*,rical,rically,rous, USE OF NUMBERS
numerology, SCIENCE OF NUMBERS/ FREQUENCY
numeros, numerous
numerous,sly,sness, MANY IN NUMBER "prefixes: in"
numirator, numerate(tor)
numirology, numerology
numirus, numerous
numonia, pneumonia
numorator, numerate(tor)

numper, number
numpir, number
numral, numeral
numrecy, numeracy
numrisy, numeracy
numrul, numeral
numurery, numerary
numurologe, numerology
numurus, numerous
nun,*, RELIGIOUS WOMAN WHO VOWS TO OBEY RULES AS A NUN (or see non/none/known/noun/noon)
nundo, innuendo
nune, noon
nupshuel, nuptial
nuptial,lly, CONCERNS WEDDING/ RITUAL
nuradic, neurotic
nurcher, nurture
nuresh, nourish
nurfus, nervous
nurish, nourish
nurishment, nourish(ment)
nurodic, neurotic
nuron, neuron
nurosis, neurosis
nurotic, neurotic
nurs, nurse
nurse,*,ed,sing,er,ery,eries, TO NURTURE AND/OR PROTECT VULNERABLE THINGS/PEOPLE
nurture,*, PROVIDE NECESSARY NOURISHMENT TO
nurve, nerve
nurvis, nervous
nurvus, nervous
nus, new(s) / noose
nusans, nuisance
nusdalgik, nostalgic
nuse, noose / new(s)
nusel, nuzzle
nusense, nuisance
nusesidy, necessity
nusesitate, necessitate
nusil, nuzzle
nusinse, nuisance
nusle, nuzzle
nuspaper, newspaper
nustalgek, nostalgic
nusul, nuzzle
nut,*,tty, HIGH PROTEIN WOODY FRUIT, SOMEONE WHO DOESN'T BEHAVE LOGICALLY
nute, nude

nutedy, nude(dity)
nutel, noodle
nuter, neuter
nutesm, nude(dism)
nuthen, nothing
nuthing, nothing
nutil, noodle
nutle, noodle
nutmeg, A SPICE
nutoreus, notorius
nutral, neutral
nutrality, neutral(ity)
nutralize, neutral(ize)
nutreant, nutrient
nutreno, neutrino
nutreshen, nutrition
nutreshus, nutritious
nutrichas, nutritious
nutrient, FOOD THAT NOURISHES LIVING THINGS
nutril, neutral
nutrino, neutrino
nutrishen, nutrition
nutrishenal, nutrition(al)
nutrition,nal,nally,nist,ous,ive, GIVES/ PROVIDES NOURISHMENT
nutritious,sly,sness, PROVIDES NOURISHMENT
nutritive,ely,eness, PROVIDES NOURISHMENT
nutron, neutron
nuty, nut(ty)
nuvember, november
nuvimber, november
nuwkleus, nucleus
nuwlewed, newlywed
nuz, new(s)
nuzle, nuzzle
nuzpaper, newspaper
nuzzle,*,ed,ling, TO SNUGGLE/DIG IN/ THRUST GENTLY INTO
nve, envy
nylon, A MANMADE CHEMICAL FIBER
nymph,*, ENTITIES, DEITIES, A STAGE IN THE DEVELOPMENT OF AN INSECT
nymphomania,ac, CONTINUAL/ INTENSE FOCUS ON SEXUAL ACTIVITY
nyn, nine
nyte, night / knight / knit
nzime, enzyme
o, oh
o'clock, SHORT FOR "ON THE CLOCK"

oak,*, A DECIDUOUS TREE WITH ACORNS
oar,*,red, USED TO ROW A BOAT (or see or)
oarthodox, orthodox
oases, oasis
oasis, SPOT OF TREES/WATER IN THE DESERT, COMFORT AMIDST AN UNCOMFORTABLE ENVIRONMENT
oat,*, A GRAIN (or see ode)
oath,*, PLEDGE/OBLIGATE TO CERTAIN RULES/LAWS
oatmeal, EDIBLE OAT GRAIN
ob, PREFIX INDICATING "AGAINST/ TOWARDS/IN THE WAY OF" MOST OFTEN MODIFIES THE WORD
obay, obey
obazit, opposite
obecity, obese(sity)
obedeinse, obedience
obedeint, obedient
obedience,*,nt, TO COMPLY/OBEY "prefixes: dis"
obedient,ly,nce, TO COMPLY/OBEY "prefixes: dis"
obees, obese
obese,ely,seness,sity, OVERLY HEAVY, EXCESSIVELY OVERWEIGHT
obetchuery, obituary
obeteinse, obedience
obey,*,yed,ying,edient, COMPLY, FOLLOW RULES AND LAWS "prefixes: dis"
obfeus, obvious
obgectif, object(ive)
obgectivity, object(ivity)
obgekshen, object(ion)
obgektif, object(ive)
obichuery, obituary
obideinse, obedience
obituary,ries, LIST OF PEOPLE WHO HAVE TRANSPIRED FROM THIS PHYSICAL PLANE
object,*,ted,ting,tion,tive,tively,tivism, tion,tionable,tionably,tionability, PHYSICAL/TANGIBLE THINGS, ARGUE IN DEFENSE OF, NEUTRAL POSITION
oblagation, obligate(tion)
oblederate, obliterate
oblefeus, oblivious
oblegate, obligate
obleterate, obliterate
obleveus, oblivious

oblevion, oblivion

oblifeus, oblivious

oblig, oblige(d)

obligate,*,ed,ting,tion,tory,torily, toriness, ACCEPT TERMS/ RESPONSIBILITY TO PERFORM

oblige,*,ed,ging,gingly, WILLING TO HELP "prefixes: dis"

oblij, oblige(d)

obliterate,*,ed,ting,tion,tive,tor, TO DESTROY COMPLETELY

oblivion,ous, COMPLETELY FORGET

oblivious,ously,ousness,on, COMPLETELY FORGET

oblong, LONGER LENGTH THAN SIDES, LONG/ROUND

oblugashen, obligate(tion)

oblugate, obligate

obnoksheus, obnoxious

obnoxious,sly,sness, OFFENSIVE, ROUGH FREQUENCY, DISHARMONIC IN NATURE

obozit, opposite

obreble, operable

obruble, operable

obsalesens, obsolescent(nce)

obsalesent, obsolescent

obscene,ely,eness,nity,nities, VERY UNDESIRABLE, INDECENT

obscure,*,ed,ring,ely,eness,ration,er, est,rity,rities, VAGUE, UNFOCUSED, DIFFICULT TO EXPLAIN/ UNDERSTAND

obselesens, obsolescent(nce)

obselesent, obsolescent

obselete, obsolete

obsene, obscene

observe,*,ed,ving,vingly,vance,vant, vantly, TO WATCH/SEE AND STUDY "prefixes: in"

obseshen, obsess(ion)

obsesive, obsess(ive)

obsess,sses,ssed,ssive,ssively,ssion, ssional,ssionally, TO BECOME OVERWHELMED WITH THOUGHT ABOUT ONE THING, COMPULSIVE

obshen, option

obsilesens, obsolescent(nce)

obsilete, obsolete

obsinety, obscene(nity)

obsolescent,nce,tly, NOT MODERN, OUT OF DATE

obsolesens, obsolescent(nce)

obsolete,ely,eness, NO LONGER MODERN

obsquire, obscure

obssesed, obsess(ed)

obssesion, obsess(ion)

obstacle,*, OBSTRUCTION, SOMETHING IN THE PATH

obstatrician, obstetrician

obstatrishen, obstetrician

obstetric,*,cal,cally,cian, SCIENCE INVOLVING WOMEN IN CHILDBEARING PROCESS (or see obstetrician)

obstetrician,*, PERSON PRACTICING MEDICINE ON WOMEN IN THE CHILDBEARING PROCESS

obstikul, obstacle

obstinate,ely,eness,acy,acies, RESOLVED IN PURPOSE/OPINION, UNABLE TO ARGUE WITH, STUBBORN

obstruct,*,ted,ting,tion,tionist,tive, tively,tiveness,tor, GET INTO THE PATH OF, PREVENT FROM TRAVELING FURTHER

obstukel, obstacle

obstunint, obstinate

obsulesens, obsolescent(nce)

obsulesense, obsolescent

obsulete, obsolete

obsurvashen, observe(vation)

obt, opt

obtain,*,ned,ning,nment,nable, ACQUIRE, COME INTO POSSESSION OF

obtametry, optometry

obtamist, optimist

obtamize, optimize

obtane, obtain

obtek, optic

obtekul, optic(al)

obtemal, optimal

obtemist, optimist

obtemize, optimize

obtemum, optimum

obteshen, optician

obtience, obedience

obtik, optic

obtikul, optic(al)

obtimesum, optimism

obtimum, optimum

obtishen, optician

obtometrist, optometry(rist)

obtometry, optometry

obtomitrist, optometry(rist)

obtreshen, optician

obtroosive, obtrusive

obtrude,*,ed,ding,usion,usive,er, STICKS OUT, FORCED PRESENCE IN UNWELCOME WAY

obtrusive,ely,eness,ion, INTRUDES ON OTHERS, NOT WELCOME, THRUSTS OUT "prefixes: un"

obtumal, optimal

obtumem, optimum

obtumist, optimist

obtumistek, optimist(ic)

obtumize, optimize

obtumizum, optimism

obulent, opulent

obulint, opulent

obusev, abuse(sive)

obusif, abuse(sive)

obuzit, opposite

obveus, obvious

obvious,sly,sness, MOST APPARENT, PLAIN TO SEE/INTERPRET

obzurvashen, observe(vation)

oc, PREFIX INDICATING "AGAINST/ TOWARDS/IN THE WAY OF" MOST OFTEN MODIFIES THE WORD

ocashen, occasion

ocasional, occasion(al)

occasion,*,ned,nal,nally,nalism, NOT FREQUENT/OFTEN

occularist, ocular(ist)

occult,*,tism, A SCHOOL OF THOUGHT OUTSIDE OF SOCIETAL NORMS, KNOWLEDGE CONCERNING THE ESOTERIC SCIENCES

occupancy,cies, SPECIFIC NUMBER OF SPACES SET ASIDE FOR PEOPLE TO OCCUPY

occupation,*,nal, JOB/ACTIVITY, BE IN A CERTAIN SPACE IN TIME "prefixe: non/pre"

occupy,pies,pied,pying,pation,piable, pier, TO FILL A SPACE "prefixes: pre/ un"

occur,*,rred,rring,rrence,rrences,rrent, TO TAKE PLACE/HAPPEN

occurinse, occur(rrence)

ocean,*,nic, LARGEST BODIES OF WATER "prefixes: inter/sub"

ocen, ocean

ocerents, occur(rrence)

ocra, A COLOR (or see okra)

oct, PREFIX INDICATING "EIGHT" MOST OFTEN MODIFIES THE WORD

octa, PREFIX INDICATING "EIGHT" MOST OFTEN MODIFIES THE WORD

octagon, SIDED SHAPE WITH ANGLES

octahedron,*,ra,ral, FACED SOLID

octane,*, METHANE HYDROCARBON

octave,*, SECTION OF 8 TONES

octif, octave

octihedron, octahedron

octo, PREFIX INDICATING "EIGHT" MOST OFTEN MODIFIES THE WORD

october, A MONTH OF THE YEAR (ENGLISH)

octopus,pi, SEA CREATURE WITH 8 ARMS

octuf, octave

octugon, octagon

octuhedron, octahedron

octupus, octopus

ocular,rist,rly,ulist, OF THE EYE AND EYESIGHT "prefixes: intra"

ocult, occult

ocupancy, occupancy

ocupashen, occupation

ocupation, occupation

ocupied, occupy(pied)

ocupy, occupy

ocurence, occur(rrence)

ocurinse, occur(rrence)

od, odd / ode / ought

odamin, ottoman

odamotive, automotive

odd,*,ddly,ddish,ddness,ddity, NOT EVEN/NORMAL (or see ode/ought)

oddesy, odyssey

ode, POEM (or see odd/ought)

odeanse, audience

odeble, audible

odeinse, audience

odem, autumn

odeo, audio

oder, odor / otter / outer / utter / udder / other / odd(er)

odeshen, audition

odesy, odyssey

odet, audit

odete, odd(ity)

odetion, audition

odetoreum, auditorium

odety, odd(ity)

odible, audible

odim, autumn

odio, audio

odir, odor / otter / outer / utter / udder / other / odd(er)

odishun, audition

odissy, odyssey

odisy, odyssey

odit, audit

odite, odd(ity)

odition, audition

oditorium, auditorium

odity, odd(ity)

odle, odd(ly)

odly, odd(ly)

odmeal, oatmeal

odnes, odd(ness)

odobiaugrufe, autobiography

odograf, autograph

odomashen, automatic(ion)

odomatik, automatic

odomen, ottoman

odometer,*, INSTRUMENT THAT MEASURES NUMBER OF REVOLUTIONS OF A WHEEL AND DISTANCE

odomobeel, automobile

odomotive, automotive

odor,*,rous,rless, SMELL (or see otter/ udder) "prefixes: in"

oduble, audible

odum, autumn

odumin, ottoman

odur, odor / otter / outer / utter / udder / other / odd(er)

odyssey,*, A JOURNEY

oel, oil

oeng, owe(wing)

oer, or / oar / over

oestur, oyster

oeul, oil

oeuly, oil(y)

of, A WORD WHICH HELPS TO PULL SENTENCE STRUCTURE TOGETHER (or see off)

ofarall, overall

ofary, ovary

ofashen, ovation

ofation, ovation

ofecial, official

ofel, awful / oval

ofem, ovum

ofen, oven / often

ofend, offend

ofense, offense

ofensive, offense(sive)

ofer, offer / over

oferbering, overbearing

ofercast, overcast

ofercot, overcoat

ofercum, overcome

oferien, ovary(rian)

oferkame, overcame

oferkast, overcast

oferkot, overcoat

oferkum, overcome

oferlay, overlay

oferly, over(ly) / overly

oferot, overwrought

ofert, overt / avert

oferture, overture

oferwelming, overwhelm(ing)

ofery, ovary

ofes, office

ofeser, office(r)

ofeshul, official

ofewlate, ovulate

off, NOT OPERATING, NOT ON (or see of)

offend,*,ded,ding,nse, TO IRRITATE/ ANNOY, BREAK RULES

offense,*,eless,sive,sively,siveness, INITIATE, MAKE THE FIRST MOVE "prefixes: in"

offer,*,red,ring, TO GRANT/GIVE

offes, office

office,*,er, A PLACE/PERSON CONDUCTING BUSINESS "prefixes: inter"

official,*,lly,lism, ASSIGNED BY DUTY, CONFIRMED BY AUTHORITY "prefixes: semi/un"

offurt, overt/ avert

ofice, office

oficer, office(r)

oficial, official

ofil, awful / oval

ofim, ovum

ofin, oven / often

ofind, offend

ofinse, offense

ofinsuf, offense(sive)

ofir, offer / over

ofirbering, overbearing

ofircame, overcame

ofircast, overcast

ofircot, overcoat

ofircum, overcome

ofirkame, overcame

ofirkast, overcast

ofirkot, overcoat

ofirkum, overcome
ofirly, over(ly)
ofirot, overwrought
ofirwelming, overwhelm(ing)
ofiry, ovary
ofis, office
ofiser, office(r)
ofishul, official
ofishuly, official(lly)
ofol, oval
often, FREQUENTLY, DO SOMETHING
   MORE THAN NOT
oftin, often
oful, awful / oval
ofulashen, ovulate(tion)
ofulate, ovulate
ofulation, ovulate(tion)
ofum, ovum
ofur, offer / over
ofurall, overall
ofurbering, overbearing
ofurcame, overcame
ofurcast, overcast
ofurla, overlay
ofurly, over(ly) / overly
ofurot, overwrought
ofurt, overt / avert
ofurture, overture
ofurwelming, overwhelm(ing)
ofury, ovary
ofus, office
ofuser, office(r)
ofvir, over
ofvur, over
ogast, august
oger, auger / ogre
ogern, adjourn
ogest, august
ogir, ogre / auger
ogirn, adjourn
ogist, august
ogli, ugly
ogly, ugly
ogment, augment
ogmint, augment
ogorn, adjourn
ogre,*, UGLY AND MEAN (or see auger)
ogua, aqua
ogur, ogre / auger
ogust, august
ogwa, aqua
ogwu, aqua
ogzelery, auxiliary
ogzilery, auxiliary

oh, AN EXCLAMATION OF SURPRISE OR
   SUDDENNESS
oil,*,led,ler,ling,ly,lier,liest, SLIPPERY/
   LUBRICATING SUBSTANCE
oing, owe(wing)
ointment,*, A SALVE/LOTION APPLIED
   TO THE SKIN FOR HEALING
oister, oyster
ojern, adjourn
ojorn, adjourn
ok, okay / oak
okashenul, occasion(al)
okashiun, occasion
okay, O.K./YES/FINE
okerinse, occur(rrence)
okest, august
okewpansy, occupancy
okewpie, occupy
okist, august
oklok, o'clock
okra, A VEGETABLE (or see ocra)
oks, ox
oksadashen, oxide(dation)
oksadate, oxidant
oksagen, oxygen
oksedation, oxide(dation)
oksejin, oxygen
oksen, ox(en)
oksid, oxide
oksidashen, oxide(dation)
oksidation, oxide(dation)
oksigen, oxygen
oksijen, oxygen
oksilery, auxiliary
oksin, ox(en)
oksudashen, oxide(dation)
oksudation, oxide(dation)
oksugen, oxygen
oktahedron, octahedron
oktane, octane
oktegon, octagon
oktehedron, octahedron
oktev, octave
oktif, octave
oktihedron, octahedron
oktober, october
oktopus, octopus
oktuf, octave
oktugon, octagon
okularest, ocular(ist)
okult, occult
okupashen, occupation
okupensy, occupancy

okupit, occupy(pied)
okupy, occupy
okur, occur
okurinse, occur(rrence)
okust, august
okwa, aqua
okwadukt, aqueduct
okwafer, aquifer
okward, awkward
okwefer, aquifer
okword, awkward
okwu, aqua
okwurd, awkward
okzilary, auxiliary
ol, owl / all / awl / old
olastick, elastic
olau, allow
olaw, allow
olcer, ulcer
old,der,dest, PAST ITS PRIME, OF THE
   PAST
ole, old / all / awl
olef, olive
olempek, olympic
olempic, olympic
olesit, elicit / illicit
oleve, olive
olfebet, alphabet
olif, olive
olimpic, olympic
olisit, elicit / illicit
olive,*, A FRUIT FROM A TREE
oll, all
olmenak, almanac
olmost, almost
olone, alone
olser, ulcer
olso, also
olt, old
oltegether, altogether
olter, altar / alder / alter
olternativ, alternative
olternutev, alternative
oltigether, altogether
oltirnutev, alternative
oltugethur, altogether
oltur, altar / alder / alter
olturnativ, alternative
olturnutev, alternative
oluf, aloof / olive
oluv, olive
olwaz, always
olympic,*, RELATING TO GAMES/
   COUNTRY/MOUNTAIN

om, home / them
omaga, omega
omed, omit / emit
omeded, omit(tted) / emit(tted)
omega, LAST, AT THE END
omeka, omega
omenus, ominous
omesable, omit(issible)
omeshin, omission / emission
omet, omit / emit
ometion, omission / emission
ominous,sly,sness, A SIGN, THREATENING DUE TO LACK OF UNDERSTANDING, FOREBODING
ominus, ominous
omishen, omission / emission
omissible, LEAVE SOMETHING OUT
omission,*,ible, THE ACT OF LEAVING SOMETHING OUT (or see emission)
omit,*,tted,tting,issible,ission, LEAVE SOMETHING OUT (or see emit))
omition, omission / emission
omne, omni
omnefurus, omnivore(ous)
omnevore, omnivore
omnevorus, omnivore(ous)
omni, ALL AS ONE, HAVING IT ALL, ALL OF IT, PREFIX INDICATING "ALL" MOST OFTEN MODIFIES THE WORD
omniferus, omnivore(ous)
omniverus, omnivore(ous)
omnivore,*,rous,rously, EATS ANYTHING DIGESTIBLE
omnuvore, omnivore
on, OPERATING, FUNCTIONING, PERFORMING (or see own/one)
onarary, honorary
once, ONLY ONE TIME, FORMER (or see want(s)/ounce)
oncore, encore
ond, own(ed)
one,*,eness, SINGLE, NUMERAL MEANING LESS THAN TWO BUT MORE THAN ZERO (or see won/ own)
onebreated, inebriate(d)
oneng, awning / own(ing)
oner, honor / owner
onerable, honor(able)
onest, honest
onibreated, inebriate(d)
oning, awning / own(ing)
onion,*, A VEGETABLE
onir, honor / owner

onirable, honor(able)
onist, honest
onkore, encore
onle, only
only, NO EXCEPTIONS, EXCLUSIVELY, MERELY
onomaly, anomaly
onor, honor / owner
onoruble, honor(able)
onry, ornery / honorary
ons, own(s) / ounce
onsbekable, unspeakable
onsboken, unspoken
onse, once / one(s) / own(s) / ounce
ont, own(ed)
onto, ON/TO, ABOUT/TOWARDS (or see unto)
ontra, entree
ontrapreneur, entrepreneur
ontre, entree
ontrupreneur, entrepreneur
ontu, onto
onurary, honorary
onvasef, invasive
onward,*, FORWARD
onwry, ornery / honorary
onwurd, onward
onyen, onion
onyun, onion
oos, ooze
ooserp, usurp
oosurp, usurp
ooze,*,ed,zing, GENTLE FLOW, GENERAL OVERALL APPEARANCE OF EXCESSIVE, HEAVY MOISTURE
op, PREFIX INDICATING "AGAINST/ TOWARDS/IN THE WAY OF" MOST OFTEN MODIFIES THE WORD
opake, opaque
opal,*, AN IRRIDESCENT STONE
opalescence,nt, HAVING A COATING/ APPEARANCE OF RAINBOW COLORED/ IRREDESCENT LIGHT, FILMY/COLORFUL
opaque,*,ely, NON-TRANSPARENT, DULL, DENSE
oparade, operate
oparate, operate
opaset, opposite
opasit, opposite
opazeshen, oppose(sition)
opazit, opposite
opeate, opiate

open,*,ned,ning,nness,ner, INVITING, ALLOWING, PENETRABLE, ACCEPTING "prefixes: re"
openeun, opinion
openyun, opinion
opera,*,retta, PLAY/DRAMA WITH MUSIC/SINGING
operable,bility,ly, CAN BE OPERATED ON "prefixes: in/inter"
operade, operate
operader, operate(tor)
operashen, operate(tion)
operate,*,ed,ting,tion,tional,tive,tivity, tively,tor, MAKE FUNCTIONAL, PUT INTO EFFECT, MAKE ACTIVE, REMEDY WITH ACTION "prefixes: in/post/pre"
operater, operate(tor)
opertune, opportune
opertunedy, opportune(nity)
opertunest, opportune(st)
opertunity, opportune(nity)
opesishen, oppose(sition)
opesit, opposite
opeum, opium
opeute, opiate
opewlent, opulent
opezit, opposite
opfeis, obvious
opfeus, obvious
ophil, awful
ophul, awful
opiate,*, DRUG/NARCOTIC USED TO DULL PAIN AND INDUCE SLEEP
opilesent, opalescence(nt)
opilesinse, opalescence
opilessence, opalescence
opin, open
opinion,*,ned,nated, A JUDGEMENT/ THOUGHT
opirashen, operate(tion)
opirate, operate
opirtune, opportune
opirtunedy, opportune(nity)
opirtunist, opportune(st)
opirtunity, opportune(nity)
opiruble, operable
opisit, opposite
opium, JUICE FROM FLOWERING POPPY FRUIT
opizit, opposite
oplagashen, obligate(tion)
opleveus, oblivious
opligate, obligate

oplige, oblige(d)
oplij, oblige(d)
opliveus, oblivious
oplivion, oblivion
oplong, oblong
oplugashen, obligate(tion)
oplugate, obligate
opnokshes, obnoxious
oponent, opponent
oponit, opponent
oporashin, operate(tion)
oporate, operate
oportune, opportune
opose, oppose
oposet, opposite
opossum, A MARSUPIAL ANIMAL
opostrufe, apostrophe
opozishen, oppose(sition)
oppasite, opposite
oppazit, opposite
oppezit, opposite
opponent,*, THE OTHER SIDE IN COMPETITION, ONE OF TWO SIDES COMPETING
opportune,ely,eness,nism,nist,nistic, nistically,nity,nities, FAVORABLE MOMENT TO ACT/MAKE A CHANGE "prefixes: in"
oppose,*,ed,sing,site,sitely,siteness, sition, ADVERSE/ CONTRARY/ CONTRASTING "prefixes: un"
opposishen, oppose(sition)
opposite,*,ely,eness,tion, ADVERSE/ CONTRARY/CONTRASTING
oppposum, opossum
oppreshen, oppress(ion)
oppress,sses,ssed,ssing,ssion,ssive, ssively,ssiveness,ssor, CONTROL OTHER'S FREEWILL BEYOND REASONABLE EXTENT, TYRANNIZE, CRUEL/UNUSUAL PUNISHMENT
opptimism, optimism
opptomistic, optimist(ic)
oppusite, opposite
opra, opera
oprasef, opress(ive) / abrasive
oprasuf, opress(ive) / abrasive
oprater, operate(tor)
opres, oppress
opreshen, oppress(ion)
opror, uproar
opru, opera
oprut, uproot
opsalesens, obsolescent(nce)

opsalesent, obsolescent
opscure, obscure
opseen, obscene
opselesens, obsolescent(nce)
opselete, obsolete
opsenity, obscene(nity)
opserve, observe
opshin, option
opsilesens, obsolescent(nce)
opsilesent, obsolescent
opsilete, obsolete
opsirvashen, observe(vation)
opskure, obscure
opsolesens, obsolescent(nce)
opsolete, obsolete
opstatrishen, obstetrician
opstekul, obstacle
opstenit, obstinate
opstikul, obstacle
opstinesy, obstinate(acy)
opstitrishen, obstetrician
opstruksen, obstruct(ion)
opstrukt, obstruct
opstukel, obstacle
opstunint, obstinate
opstutrishen, obstetrician
opsulesens, obsolescent(nce)
opsulesense, obsolescent
opsulete, obsolete
opsurvashen, observe(vation)
opt,ted,ting,tion, THE ACT OF MAKING A CHOICE, PREFIX INDICATING "EYE/ VISION" MOST OFTEN MODIFIES THE WORD
optametry, optometry
optamism, optimism
optamist, optimist
optamistek, optimist(ic)
optamisum, optimism
optamize, optimize
optane, obtain
optek, optic
optemal, optimal
optemistic, optimist(ic)
optemisum, optimism
optemum, optimum
opteshen, optician
optic,*,cal,cally, CONCERNING THE EYE
optician,*, DOCTOR WHO WORKS WITH EYES
optico, PREFIX INDICATING "EYE/ VISION" MOST OFTEN MODIFIES THE WORD

optimal,lly,lity, BEST THAT CAN BE ACHIEVED
optimesm, optimism
optimism,stic, BELIEF BASED ON HOPE/ FAITH, LOOKS ON THE BRIGHT SIDE
optimist,tic,tically,sm,ize,ization, BASED ON HOPE/FAITH, HOPE FOR A BRIGHTER FUTURE
optimize,*,ed,zing,zation,mum, TO MAXIMIZE, REAP GREATEST BENEFIT FROM
optimum,*, OPTIMAL, HOPE FOR THE BEST
option,*,ned,nal,nally, A CHOICE
optishen, optician
opto, PREFIX INDICATING "EYE/VISION" MOST OFTEN MODIFIES THE WORD
optometry,rist,ric,rical, DOCTOR OF THE EYES
optrood, obtrude
optrude, obtrude
optrusive, obtrusive
optumem, optimum
optumist, optimist
optumistek, optimist(ic)
optumle, optimal
opul, opal
opulent,tly,nce, OVER ACCUMULATION OF WEALTH AND/OR POWER
opulesense, opalescence
opulesent, opalescence(nt)
opulessence, opalescence
opulint, opulent
opun, open
opura, opera
opurader, operate(tor)
opurashen, operate(tion)
opurate, operate
opurtune, opportune
opurtunedy, opportune(nity)
opurtunest, opportune(st)
opurtunity, opportune(nity)
opusishen, oppose(sition)
opusit, opposite
opuzet, opposite
opuzishen, oppose(sition)
opuzit, opposite
opveus, obvious
opzerve, observe
oqua, aqua
oquelarist, ocular(ist)
oquepy, occupy
oquepnsy, occupancy
oqupied, occupy(pied)

oqupy, occupy

oqwa, aqua

or, WORD USED AS A CONJUNCTION, OTHERWISE (or see oar/ore/over/are)

oracle,*,lar,larity,larly, PERSON/THING WHO HOLDS GREAT/SECRET WISDOM (or see auricle)

orador, orator

orafes, orifice

orafus, orifice

oragen, origin

orageno, oregano

oragin, origin

orajin, origin

orajinate, originate

orakul, oracle / auricle

oral,lly, OF/FROM THE MOUTH

orange,*, COLOR, FRUIT

orashen, orator(tion)

orator,tion,tor,torical,torically,ry,ries, SPOKEN FROM THE MOUTH, PUBLIC SPEAKING

orb,*,bit,bited,biting,bital,biter,bitary, bicular,bicularly,bicularity,biculate, biculately,biteer,biteering, SPHERE, GLOBE, CIRCULAR "prefixes: sub"

orbut, orb(it)

orbutrate, arbitrate

orcanek, organic

orcanekly, organic(ally)

orcasem, orgasm

orced, orchid

orcestra, orchestra

orchard,*, FIELD OF FRUIT TREES

orchart, orchard

orchastra, orchestra

orchen, organ

orcherd, orchard

orchestra,*,al,ally,ate,ated,ating,ator, ation, GROUPS OF PEOPLE WITH INSTRUMENTS PERFORMING MUSIC TOGETHER IN SYNCHRONICITY

orchid,*, A FLOWER

orchird, orchard

orchistra, orchestra

orchurt, orchard

orcid, orchid

ordain,*,ned,ning,ner,nment, APPOINT "prefixes: pre"

ordane, ordain

ordanery, ordinary

ordaninse, ordinance

ordeal,*, MORE DRAMA THAN NECESSARY

ordel, ordeal

ordenary, ordinary

ordenate, ordinate

ordenense, ordinance

order,*,red,ring,rly,rliness, ORGANIZED, PROPER PLACEMENT, FOLLOWING SET OF RULES/LAWS "prefixes: dis/sub"

ordervs, horsd'oevres

ordinance,*, A LAW

ordinary,*, COMMON, EVERYDAY, AVERAGE "prefixes: sub"

ordinate,*, VERTICAL PLACEMENT/POSITION "prefixes: sub"

ordinence, ordinance

ordinery, ordinary

ordir, order

ordirves, horsd'oevres

ordninse, ordinance

ordunery, ordinary

ordur, order

ordurvs, horsd'oevres

ore,*, ROCK CONTAINING METAL (or see oar)

orefis, orifice

orefus, orifice

oregano, AN HERB/SPICE

oregen, origin

oregenate, originate

oregeno, oregano

oregin, origin

oreginate, originate

oregino, oregano

oreint, orient

oreintul, orient(al)

orejen, origin

orejenal, origin(al)

orejenashen, originate(tion)

orejenat, origin(ate)

orejin, origin

orejinul, origin(al)

orel, oral

orenge, orange

orenj, orange

oretor, orator

oreundashen, orient(ation)

oreunt, orient

oreuntashen, orient(ation)

orfan, orphan

orfun, orphan

organ,*,nist, MUSICAL INSTRUMENT, A MAJOR INTERNAL BODY PART

organek, organic

organic,*,cally,city,cism, ALL NATURAL SUBSTANCE, FROM THE EARTH "prefixes: bio/in"

organism,*,mic,mically, A LIFE FORM

organization,*,nal,nally, SYSTEM/METHOD OF OPERATION WHICH KEEPS A BODY/HOST ALIVE, COLLECTION OF WORKING PARTS WHICH MAKE UP THE WHOLE "prefixes: dis"

organize,*,ed,zing,zable,er,zation, TO CREATE/USE A METHOD/SYSTEM WHICH CREATES ORDER/FUNCTION BETWEEN MOVING PARTS "prefixes: dis/re/un"

orgasm,*,mic,mically, THE ELEVATED POINT/HEIGHT OF AN EMOTIONAL/PHYSICAL EXPERIENCE/EVENT

orgazem, orgasm

orge, orgy

orgen, organ

orgenise, organize

orgenism, organism

orgenuzashen, organization

orgin, organ / origin

orginazation, organization

orginesm, organism

orginise, organize

orginuzashen, organization

orgon, organ

orgunise, organize

orgunism, organism

orgy,gies, COMBINING NUMBERS OF BODIES WHO EXCESSIVELY INDULGE THEMSELVES

oriendul, orient(al)

orient,*,ted,ting,tates,tation,tational, tive, DEFINITE POSITION/BEARING IN REFERENCE TO SPECIFIC POINTS, OF THE EAST "prefixes: dis"

oriental,*,lly,lism,list,lize, EASTERN PLACE IN RELATION TO THE REST OF THE WORLD

orifice,*, OPENINGS

origen, origin

origin,*,nal,nally,nality,nalities,nate, BEGINNING OF CREATION, FIRST THOUGHT, THE BEGINNING

originate,*,ed,ting,tion,tor,tive,tively, tion, FROM WHERE IT BEGAN, FIRST THOUGHT

orijenal, origin(al)

orijenate, originate

orijinal, origin(al)
orikul, oracle / auricle
oril, oral
oringe, orange
orinj, orange
orivul, arrive(val)
orjy, orgy
orkan, organ
orkanek, organic
orkanekly, organic(ally)
orkanik, organic
orkanism, organism
orkanize, organize
orkanusashen, organization
orkastra, orchestra
orkasum, orgasm
orked, orchid
orken, organ
orkenasashen, organization
orkenism, organism
orkenize, organize
orkenuzashen, organization
orkestra, orchestra
orkestrete, orchestra(ate)
orket, orchid
orkid, orchid
orkin, organ
orkinasation, organization
orkinazashen, organization
orkinism, organism
orkinize, organize
orkistra, orchestra
orkit, orchid
orkunise, organize
orkunism, organism
orkustra, orchestra
ormer, armor
ormur, armor
ornade, ornate
ornament,*,tal,tally,tation,
    DECORATIONS, ACCESSORIZE,
    BEAUTIFY
ornamintal, ornament(al)
ornate,ely,eness, ARTISTICALLY
    DETAILED, EMBELLISHED
ornement, ornament
ornemintal, ornament(al)
ornery,riness, STUBBORN/ADVERSE
    DISPOSITION OR ATTITUDE
ornge, orange
ornry, ornery
ornument, ornament
ornumentul, ornament(al)
orocle, oracle

orofes, orifice
orp, orb
orpet, orb(it)
orphan,*,nage,nhood, ONE LEFT
    WITHOUT PARENTS, PLACE FOR
    THOSE WITHOUT PARENTS
orphen, orphan
orpit, orb(it)
orput, orb(it)
orsherd, orchard
orshurd, orchard
ortanery, ordinary
ortenanse, ordinance
ortenary, ordinary
orter, order
orth, PREFIX INDICATING "MAKE
    NORMAL/CORRECTION" MOST
    OFTEN MODIFIES THE WORD
orthodontic,*,ia,ist, TEETH/DENTISTRY
orthodox,xes,xly,xy,xies, OF SOCIAL
    CUSTOM/PRACTICE "prefixes: un"
orthopedic,*,cally,ist, TEETH/
    DENTISTRY
orthridus, arthritis
orthudox, orthodox
ortinanse, ordinance
ortinary, ordinary
ortir, order
ortnense, ordinance
ortunense, ordinance
ortur, order
orufis, orifice
orugin, origin
orujin, origin
orukle, oracle / auricle
orukul, oracle / auricle
orul, oral
orunj, orange
orupt, erupt / irrupt
oryent, orient
oryentashen, orient(ation)
oryentul, orient(al)
oryindashen, orient(ation)
os, us / owe(s)
osalate, osculate / oscillate
osanefurus, ozone(niferous)
oscillate,*,ed,ting,tion,tor,tory,
    VOLUME OF MOVEMENT/
    VIBRATION IN BETWEEN, MOVE TO/
    FRO (or see osculate)
osculate,*,ed,ting,tion,tor,tory, KISS,
    COME IN CONTACT, TWO OR MORE
    COINCIDENT POINTS (or see
    oscillate) "prefixes: inter"

osdrege, ostrich
osdrich, ostrich
osdrije, ostrich
ose, owe(s)
oselate, osculate / oscillate
osheanic, ocean(ic)
osher, usher
oshin, ocean
osilate, osculate / oscillate
osmose,ed,sing,sis,otic,otically,
    PENETRATION OF A BARRIER
    WHERE TWO SHARE THE SAME AS
    ONE, SHARING OF INFORMATION
    BETWEEN TWO "prefixes: end"
osmoses, osmose(sis)
osone, ozone
osonic, ozone(nic)
osonusfere, ozone(nosphere)
ost, PREFIX INDICATING "BONE" MOST
    OFTEN MODIFIES THE WORD
ostracize,*,ed,zing,ism, TO EXPEL OR
    EXCLUDE FROM A GROUP
ostrech, ostrich
ostreje, ostrich
ostresize, ostracize
ostrich,hes, A LARGE BIRD
ostrisize, ostracize
ostrusize, ostracize
osulashen, oscillate(tion)
osulate, osculate / oscillate
osum, awesome / assume
osuniferus, ozone(niferous)
ot, PREFIX INDICATING "EAR" MOST
    OFTEN MODIFIES THE WORD (or
    see oat/ odd/ought/ode)
otamate, automate
otamotive, automotive
otej, outage
otem, autumn
otemin, ottoman
oteo, audio
oter, odor / otter / outer / utter / udder
otesm, autism
otest, attest
otesy, odyssey
otezum, autism
oth, oath
othentik, authentic
other,*, THAT ONE NOT THIS ONE, THE
    FURTHER ONE, THE ALTERNATIVE
    (or see author)
othintik, authentic
othir, author
othoretarean, authoritarian

othorety, authority
othoritarean, authoritarian
othority, authority
othoruterein, authoritarian
otim, autumn
otiman, ottoman
otimobil, automobile
otimotive, automotive
otir, odor / otter / outer / utter / udder
otism, autism
otisum, autism
otisy, odyssey
otitoreum, auditorium
otizum, autism
otle, odd(ly)
otluk, outlook
otmel, oatmeal
otmost, utmost
oto, PREFIX INDICATING "EAR" MOST OFTEN MODIFIES THE WORD
otobiografe, autobiography
otograf, autograph
otomadik, automatic
otoman, ottoman
otomashen, automatic(ion)
otomate, automate
otomobel, automobile
otomotive, automotive
otoneme, autonomy
otonume, autonomy
otopse, autopsy
otor, odor / otter / outer / utter / udder
otter,*, WATER MAMMAL
ottoman,*, FOOTSTOOL/COUCH WITHOUT BACK/ARMS
otur, odor / otter / outer / utter / udder
ou, oh / owe
ouch, SOUND ASSOCIATED WITH PAIN/ GETTING HURT
oud, out / ode
oudacity, audacity
oudasedy, audacity
ouder, outer / odor
ouding, outing
oudsmart, outsmart
oudstand, outstand
oudwerd, outward
oudwet, outwit
oughn, own
ought, SHOULD/WOULD/COULD TAKE ACTION/DO SOMETHING
ounce,*, MEASUREMENT FOR DRY PRODUCTS (or see once)
ouns, ounce / own(s)

our,*, BELONGS IN THE GROUP, OWNERSHIP (or see hour/oar)
ourle, hour(ly)
out,tting,tage,ter, NOT IN, EXIT, NOT THERE ANYLONGER, BEYOND THE MAIN/ OBJECT, DOESN'T EXIST AS IT ONCE DID (or see ought)
outage,*, QUIT WORKING, LACKING WITHOUT
outer, BEYOND THE MAIN AREA OR BODY, NOT PART OF THE WHOLE ANY LONGER, EXTERIOR
outfit,*,tted,tting,tter, EXTERNAL GEAR/ CLOTHING
outgo,oes,oing, AWAY FROM THE CENTER, LEAVING THE AREA, REMOVED FROM THE PREVIOUS PLACE
outij, outage
outing,*, TAKE A SMALL EXCURSION AWAY, GO AWAY BRIEFLY
outlaw,*, PEOPLE WHO PERFORM ACTS OUTSIDE OF THE LAW
outlet,*, A WAY TO GET OUT
outline,*,ed,ning, BOUNDARIES OF, DEFINING PRINCIPLES, SKETCH OR WORDS DESCRIBING THE INSIDE
outlook, PERSPECTIVE OF THE OBSERVER, WAY OF PERCEPTION
outluk, outlook
outlying, ON THE OUTSKIRTS, OUTSIDE OF, BEYOND
outpost,*, A STATION OR POST OUTSIDE OF THE MAIN CONFINES, A REMOTE SETTLEMENT
output, THE RESULT OF MANUFACTURING, WHAT IS PRODUCED
outrage,*,ed,ging,eous,eously,eousness, EXCESSIVE EMOTIONAL REACTION, SUDDEN OUTBURST
outright, WITHOUT CONCEALMENT OR RESTRAINT, OPEN, STRAIGHT OUT
outset, AT THE BEGINNING
outside,er, NOT IN THE MAIN PORTION, REMOTE FROM THE CENTER
outskirt,*, AT THE EDGES OF TOWN, BORDER DISTRICTS
outskurt, outskirt
outsmart,*,ted,ting, OUTWIT
outstand,ding, STANDS OUT, PROTRUDES, APART FROM THE REST, LEAVE PORT

outward,*,dly,dness, AWAY FROM CENTER, TOWARDS THE EXTERIOR, ON THE OUTSIDE
outwit,*,tted,tting, OUTSMART, THINK FASTER THAN
oval,*,lly,lness, ELONGATED CIRCLE, SHAPE OF EGG
ovalable, available
ovart, overt / avert
ovarwelming, overwhelm(ing)
ovary,ries,rian,rial,ritis,riotomy, riectomy, REPRODUCTIVE GLANDS
ovashen, ovation
ovashin, ovation
ovation,*, ENTHUSIASTIC APPLAUSE
ovau, avow
ovekt, evict
ovel, oval
ovem, ovum
oven,*,nable, CONTAINER BUILT FOR HIGH HEAT TO COOK/BAKE THINGS
ovent, event
oventful, eventful
over,rly, ABOVE AND BEYOND, MORE THAN NORMAL, PREFIX INDICATING "EXCESSIVELY/COMPLETELY/ UPPER/ABOVE/OUTER" MOST OFTEN MODIFIES THE WORD
overall, SUMMARY, WITH ALL THINGS TAKEN INTO ACCOUNT
overbearing,gly, DOMINATING, OPPRESSING, TYRANNICAL, FORCEFUL
overbering, overbearing
overcame, PAST TENSE FOR THE WORD "OVERCOME"
overcast,ting, SHADOWING, GLOOMS OVER, SEWING ROUGH EDGES
overcoat,*, TO APPLY A COAT OVER ANOTHER
overcome,ming,came, TO RISE ABOVE AN OBSTACLE, TO MANAGE THROUGH A PROBLEM, RISE ABOVE OPPOSITION
overcum, overcome
overhang,*,ging, LEDGE/OUTCROP WHICH JUTS OUT/OVER, OVER AN UDERCUT, HANGS UNDER
overien, ovary(rian)
overkame, overcame
overkast, overcast
overkot, overcoat
overkum, overcome

overlap,*,pped,pping, LAYER THAT PARTIALLY COVERS/LAPS THE EDGE OF ANOTHER LAYER

overlay,*,aid,ain,ying, A COAT/COVER AS TOP FOR PROTECTION

overly, TOO MUCH, TOO EXTREME

overot, overwrought

overt,tly,tness, NO ATTEMPT TO CONCEAL/HIDE (or see avert)

overter, overture

overture,*, INTRODUCTION/ BEGINNING TO

overwelming, overwhelm(ing)

overwhelm,*,med,ming,mingly, OVERLOAD, OVERPOWERING, RESISTANCE IS FUTILE

overwrot, overwrought

overwrought, EMOTIONAL DISTRESS, TOO MUCH TO HANDLE GRACEFULLY

overy, ovary

oveulate, ovulate

ovewlate, ovulate

ovil, oval

ovim, ovum

ovin, oven

ovint, event

ovintful, eventful

ovios, obvious

ovir, over

ovirall, overall

ovirbering, overbearing

ovircast, overcast

ovircot, overcoat

ovircum, overcome

ovirkast, overcast

ovirkot, overcoat

ovirkum, overcome

ovirla, overlay

ovirle, overly

ovirly, over(ly)

ovirot, overwrought

ovirshur, overture

ovirture, overture

ovirwelming, overwhelm(ing)

oviry, ovary

ovow, avow

ovul, oval

ovulashen, ovulate(tion)

ovulate,*,ed,ting,tion, TO RELEASE AN EGG (OVUM) FROM THE OVARY "prefixes: pre"

ovum,*, AN EGG

ovur, over

ovurall, overall

ovurbering, overbearing

ovurcast, overcast

ovurcoat, overcoat

ovurcum, overcome

ovure, ovary

ovurkame, overcame

ovurkast, overcast

ovurkot, overcoat

ovurkum, overcome

ovurla, overlay

ovurly, over(ly)

ovurot, overwrought

ovurt, overt / avert

ovurwelming, overwhelm(ing)

ovury, ovary

ow, owe

owch, ouch

owd, out / ought / owe(d)

owdacity, audacity

owdamotive, automotive

owdasedyy, audacity

owdege, outage

owdemotive, automotive

owdeng, outing

owdfit, outfit

owdimotive, automotive

owdir, outer

owdishun, audition

owdition, audition

owdline, outline

owdpost, outpost

owdrage, outrage

owdrit, outright

owdskirt, outskirt

owdsmart, outsmart

owdstand, outstand

owe,*,ed,wing, TO BE INDEBTED FOR

owl,*, NOCTURNAL BIRD (or see oil)

own,*,ned,ning,ner, HAVE FULL RIGHTS TO TITLE/PROPERTY (or see one/ on) "prefixes: dis"

owner,*, ONE WHO HOLDS RIGHTS/ TITLE TO PROPERTY

owns, ounce/ own(s)

owperable, operable

owr, are / hour / our

owra, aura

owrie, awry

owrit, outright

owrle, hour(ly)

owry, awry

owsh, ouch

owson, ozone

owt, out / ought

owtege, outage

owtej, outage

owtfit, outfit

owtige, outage

owting, outing

owtir, outer

owtlaw, outlaw

owtlet, outlet

owtlieng, outlying

owtline, outline

owtlook, outlook

owtluk, outlook

owtpost, outpost

owtput, output

owtragus, outrage(ous)

owtraj, outrage

owtrite, outright

owtset, outset

owtside, outside

owtskirt, outskirt

owtsmart, outsmart

owtstand, outstand

owtwet, outwit

owtwit, outwit

owtwurd, outward

owur, hour / our

ox,xen,xes, TYPE OF BOVINE (CATTLE)

oxa, PREFIX INDICATING "OXYGEN/ ADDITIONAL OXYGEN" MOST OFTEN MODIFIES THE WORD

oxajen, oxygen

oxedate, oxidant

oxedation, oxide(dation)

oxejen, oxygen

oxejin, oxygen

oxidant,*,ation,ative, OXYGEN ACTIVELY PARTICIPATING WITH OTHER ELEMENTS

oxidashen, oxide(dation)

oxidate, oxidant

oxide,*,dic,dize,dizes,dized,dizing,dizer, dizable,dation,dant, INTERACTION BETWEEN OXYGEN AND OTHER ELEMENTS "prefixes: sub"

oxijen, oxygen

oxilery, auxiliary

oxin, ox(en)

oxo, PREFIX INDICATING "OXYGEN/ ADDITIONAL OXYGEN" MOST OFTEN MODIFIES THE WORD

oxsadashen, oxide(dation)

oxsagen, oxygen

oxsigen, oxygen

oxsudashen, oxide(dation)
oxudiz, oxide(dize)
oxugen, oxygen
oxujin, oxygen
oxy, PREFIX INDICATING "OXYGEN/ ADDITIONAL OXYGEN" MOST OFTEN MODIFIES THE WORD
oxydate, oxidant
oxygen,nic,nicity,nate,nation, A GAS, GAS USED FOR RESPIRATION OF ALL LIVING THINGS
oyle, oil / oil(y)
oyntment, ointment
oyster,*, MARINE SHELLFISH, MOLLUSK
oystur, oyster
ozmosis, osmose(sis)
ozone,*,nic,niferous,nous,nide,nize, nized,nizing,nizer,nosphere, PURE AIR, FORM OF OXYGEN, LAYER AROUND THE EARTH
p, pea
pa, paw / pay
paber, paper / papier mache'
pabreka, paprika
pabur, paper / papier mache'
pace,*,ed,cing,er, RATE OF PROGRESS/ MOVEMENT, A GAIT/STEP
pach, patch
pachen, passion
pachendly, patient(ly)
pachense, patience / patient(s)
pachin, passion
pachindly, patient(ly)
pachints, patience / patient(s)
pacht, patch(ed)
pacific, PEACEFUL, THE PACIFIC OCEAN
pacify,fies,fied,fying,fication,ficatory, fier,fism, TO CODDLE/APPEASE/ SETTLE/ SOOTHE
pack,*,ked,king,kage,kaged,kaging,ker, ket, PREPARE FOR TRANSPORT "prefixes: pre/retro/un"
packet,*, SMALL COLLECTION OF DATA/ MATERIAL PROVIDING INFORMATION
packit, packet
pact,*, AN AGREEMENT (or see pack(ed))
pacterul, pectoral
pad,*,dded,dding,ddy, LAYER OF MATERIAL OF VARYING THICKNESS FOR PROTECTION, A RESIDENCE, BOTTOM OF PAW (or see pat/paid)
pada, pate'

paddle,*,ed,ling,er, TO USE OARS/FEET FOR MOBILIZATION, ITEM USED FOR ROWING, A SPANKING
paddock,*, SMALL AREA TO CONFINE ANIMALS/VEHICLES TEMPORARILY
paddy,dies, HAVING TO DO WITH RICE (or see patty)
pade, paid / paddy / patty / pate'
paded, pad(dded) / pat(tted)
padel, paddle
paden, patent
padeo, patio
padern, pattern
padestrein, pedestrian
padid, pad(dded) / pat(tted)
padik, paddock
padil, paddle
padin, patent
padio, patio
padirn, pattern
padled, paddle(d)
padlock,*, LOCK WITH KEY OR COMBINATION DIAL
padok, paddock
padreark, patriarch
padrearkul, patriarch(al)
padreit, patriot / patriate
padren, patron
padrenize, patron(ize)
padreodic, patriot(ic)
padreut, patriot / patriate
padriarch, patriarch
padrin, patron
padrinize, patron(ize)
padrun, patron
padrunize, patron(ize)
padryet, patriot / patriate
padsee, patsy
padthulogical, pathology(gical)
padtult, paddle(d)
paduk, paddock
paduled, paddle(d)
padurn, pattern
pady, paddy / patty
pae, pay / pay(ee)
pael, pail / pale
paer, pay(er)
paet, paid
paf, pave
pafd, pave(d)
pafeleon, pavilion
paferty, poverty
pafileon, pavilion
pafmint, pave(ment)

paft, pave(d)
pafurted, pervert(ed)
pagamus, pajamas
pagan,*,nish,nism,nize,nizes,nized, nizing,nizer, PEOPLE WHO SUPPORT NATURE AS THEIR DEITY
page,*,ed,ging,ginate,gination,er, SHEET IN A BOOK, TO CALL FOR "prefixes: un"
pageant,*,try,tries, A SHOWY DISPLAY
pagen, pagan
pagenashen, page(gination)
pagenate, page(ginate)
pagense, patience / patient(s)
pagent, pageant
pagentre, pageant(ry)
pagin, pagan
paginashen, page(gination)
pagint, pageant
pagonism, pagan(ism)
pagun, pagan
pai, pay / pie / pi
paibul, pay(yable)
paid, PAST TENSE FOR THE WORD "PAY" (or see pad) "prefixes: pre/ re/un"
pail,*, BUCKET TYPE VESSEL (or see pal/ pale/pall)
pain,*,ned,nful,nfully,nfulness,nless, nlessly,nlessness, INTERPRETATION BY THE BRAIN FROM NERVE ENDINGS SENSING HARM/THREAT (or see pane/pine)
paint,*,ted,ting,table,ter, MANMADE OR NATURAL BASED COLORANT, VIVID DESCRIPTION "prefixes: re/ under"
pair,*,red,ring, TWO IDENTICAL/ SIMILAR ITEMS TOGETHER (or see par/parr/pare/pear) "prefixes: un"
pairadox, paradox
pairalise, paralyze
pairudox, paradox
pait, paid
paj, page
pajamas, SLEEPING GARMENTS
pajenashen, page(gination)
pajenate, page(ginate)
pajense, patience / patient(s)
pajent, pageant
pajinashen, page(gination)
pajint, pageant
pakd, pact / pack(ed)
pakeg, pack(age)

paket, packet

pakij, pack(age)

pakt, pact / pack(ed)

pakut, packet

pal,*,lled,lling, A FRIEND, SOMEONE YOU ENJOY HANGING OUT WITH (or see pail/pale/pall)

palace,*, DWELLING OF ROYALTY

palas, palace

palate,table,tableness,tability,tably,tal, tally,tize, ROOF OF THE MOUTH AS A SENSOR (or see pallet/palette/ pallid) "prefixes: un"

pale,*,ed,ling,lish,ely,eness,llid,llidly, llidity, DIM/WAN, STAKE WITH SHARP END, SPACE WITHIN A FIXED BOUNDARY (or see pail/pal/pall)

paled, pale(d) / palate / palette / pallet / pallid

paleduble, palate(table)

paleintology, paleontology

palenate, pollinate

paleo, PREFIX INDICATING "EARLY/ ANCIENT/PREHISTORIC" MOST OFTEN MODIFIES THE WORD

paleontology,gies, SCIENCE CONCERNED WITH ALL LIFE IN THE PAST

paleredy, polar(ity)

palerity, polar(ity)

pales, palace / police / pale(s)

palesh, polish

palesy, policy

palet, palate / palette / pallet / pallid

paletical, politic(al)

palette,*, PAINTER'S BOARD, VARIETY OF COLORS/TECHNIQUES (or see pallet/palate)

paleuntology, paleontology

palid, pallid / palate / palette / pallet

paliduble, palate(table)

paligamus, polygamy(mous)

paligemy, polygamy

paligine, polygyny

palin, pollen

palinize, pollen(ize)

palip, polyp

palise, palace

palish, polish

palisy, policy

palit, palate / palette / pallet / polite / pallid

palitasize, politic(ize)

palite, palate / palette / pallet / polite / pallid

palitecal, politic(al)

palituble, palate(table)

pall,*, EVOKES A DULL/OPPRESSIVE ATMOSPHERE, COVERING FOR A COFFIN (or see palor pale/pail)

pallet,*,tize,tized,tizing, PLATFORM TO HOLD GOODS, A TOOL, IN A CLOCK/ WATCH, POTTER'S TOOL (or see palette/palate/pallid)

pallid,dly,dness, LACKS COLOR (or see palette/palate/pallet)

palm,*, THE HAND, A PLANT

palpitate,*,ed,ting,tion, PULSATE, TREMBLE

palt, pale(d)

palud, pallid

paluduble, palate(table)

paluse, palace

palushen, pollute(tion)

palut, palate / palette / pallet / pollute

palutent, pollute(tant)

palutics, politic(s)

palution, pollute(tion)

palygamus, polygamy(mous)

palyginy, polygyny

palyintology, paleontology

pam, palm

pamendo, pimento

pament, pay(ment)

pamento, pimento

pamflet, pamphlet

pamint, pay(ment)

pamphlet,*, PUBLICATION CONSISTING OF FOLDED PIECES OF PAPER WITH TEXT

pamplet, pamphlet

pamunt, pay(ment)

pan,*,nned,nning, FLAT METAL ITEM WITH SIDES, A COOKING UTENSIL, PREFIX INDICATING 'ALL' MOST OFTEN MODIFIES THE WORD (or see pane/pain)

pancho, poncho

pancreas,atic,atin, PART OF THE STOMACH

pancreus, pancreas

pand, pond / pant

panda,*, A BLACK/WHITE BEAR

pandees, pant(ies)

pander, ponder

pandilunes, pantaloon(s)

pandre, pantry

pandulunes, pantaloon(s)

pane,*, FRAME TO PLACE GLASS/ PHOTOGRAPHS, DIAMOND FACE (or see pain)

panek, panic

panel,*,led,ling,list, FLAT SHEET USED FOR COVER/DECORATION, PEOPLE WORKING AS A GROUP TO MAKE A DECISION

panemine, pantomime

panensula, peninsula

paneramic, panorama(mic)

panic,*,cked,cking,cky, SUDDEN OVERWHELMING FEAR WHICH CAUSES REACTION

panik, panic

panil, panel

panimine, pantomime

paninsula, peninsula

paniramic, panorama(mic)

pankreus, pancreas

panol, panel

panomine, pantomime

panorama,*,mic,mically, ABILITY TO VIEW/OBSERVE ENTIRE EVENT/ SCENE WITHOUT OBSTRUCTION

panoramic, panorama(mic)

pant,*,ted,ting,ties, BREATH/GASP HEAVILY, ARTICLE OF CLOTHING FOR LEGS/ LOWER TORSO, UNDERWEAR (or see paint/ pan(nned)) "prefixes: under"

pantaloon,*, LOOSE FITTING PANTS

pantees, pant(ies)

panteloons, pantaloon(s)

pantemime, pantomime

panther,*, LARGE WILD CAT

panthur, panther

pantilunes, pantaloon(s)

pantimime, pantomime

pantomime,*,ed,ming,mist,mic, COMMUNICATE WITH GESTURES, NON SPEAKING PERFORMANCE

pantre, pantry

pantry,ries, A FOOD STORAGE CLOSET/ ROOM

pantu, panda

pantulunes, pantaloon(s)

pantumime, pantomime

pantys, pant(ies)

panul, panel

panulist, panel(ist)

panumine, pantomime

paode, peyote

paodur, powder
paond, pound
paonse, pounce
paont, pound
paote, peyote
papaya,*, A FRUIT
papcorn, popcorn
paper,*,red,ring,rer,riness,ry,rless, USABLE SHEET OF MATERIAL FOR INK/PAINT, MADE OF WOOD/HEMP PULP, TO APPLY PAPER
papier mache', DIFFERENT TYPES OF PAPER PUT TOGETHER, COLLAGE OF PAPER (or see paper)
papir, paper / papier mache'
papreka, paprika
paprika, *, A SPICE
papur, paper / papier mache'
papyu, papaya
par,rred,rring,rity, AN AVERAGE OR NORMAL, BALANCE EQUALLY, A PREFIX, SPORTS TERM (or see parr/ pear/pair/pare) "prefixes: sub"
para, PREFIX INDICATING "BESIDE/ BEYOND" MOST OFTEN MODIFIES THE WORD
parable,*,list, SHORT STORY/ SENTENCES WHICH REFLECTS HUMAN EMOTIONAL WISDOMS (or see parabola)
parabola,*,lic, BOWL SHAPE (or see parable)
parachute,*,ed,ting,tist, DEVICE FOR DROPPING FROM GREAT HEIGHT/ PLANES
parade,*,ed,ding, AN ORGANIZED CEREMONIAL MARCH DOWN STREETS OF A CITY
paradigm,*,matic, MAKING RELATIVE COMPARISONS, CATEGORIZING INTO A DEFINED SET
paradox,xes,xical,xically, A CONTRADICTION OF TERMS, WORDS/ACTIONS WHICH CANCEL EACH OTHER OUT
paraffin,nic, MELTABLE/WAXY SUBSTANCE
paragraph,*, SEVERAL SENTENCES TOGETHER SUPPORTING A THEME
parakeet,*, A TROPICAL BIRD
paralasis, paralysis
paralel, parallel

parallel,*,led,ling, EACH GOING THE SAME DIRECTION, SIDE BY SIDE, BELONG TOGETHER "prefixes: un"
parallyzed, paralyze(d)
paralusis, paralysis
paralysis,ytic,yze, LOOSE ABILITY TO MOVE VOLUNTARILY
paralyze,*,ed,zing,ysis,ytic,ytically, LOOSE ABILITY TO MOVE VOLUNTARILY
paramater, parameter / perimeter
paramedic,*,cal, MEDICAL PROFESSIONAL WHO TRAVELS TO GATHER INJURED/SICK PEOPLE
parameter,*,tric,trical, A DEFINED BOUNDARY WHICH BELONGS AS A UNIT, A MATH EXPRESSION
parametic, paramedic
paramiter, parameter / perimeter
paramount,tly,tcy, UPMOST IN IMPORTANCE, AT THE TOP, SUPERIOR TO ANYTHING ELSE
paranoia,id,ic, FEAR WITHOUT APPARENT REASON
paranoyd, paranoia(id)
paraplegia,ic, PARALYSIS OF LOWER TORSO, LOWER HALF OF BODY CANNOT BE MOVED VOLUNTARILY
parasite,*,tic,tical,tically,ticide,ticidal, tism,tize,tology,tosis, TAKES NOURISHMENT FROM ANOTHER WITHOUT PERMISSION/ WILLINGNESS FROM HOST "prefixes: endo"
parate, parade
paratrooper,*, ONE WHO JUMPS FROM PLANE WITH A PARACHUTE
parcel,*,led,ling, A SMALL PACKAGE, BOXED ITEMS, SMALL SECTION OF LAND, TO SECTION OFF
parch,hed,hment, DRY, NEEDS MOISTURE
parcht, parch(ed)
parcle, parcel
pard, part / pair(ed) / pare(d)
pardake, partake
parde, party
pardekul, particle
pardes, party(ties)
pardesapate, participate
pardesubate, participate
pardezan, partisan
pardikul, particle
pardisubant, participate(ant)

pardisupate, participate
pardizan, partisan
pardner, partner
pardnur, partner
pardon,*,ned,ning,nable,nably, FORGIVE "prefixes: un"
pardukle, particle
pardun, pardon
parduzen, partisan
pardy, party
pare,*,ed,ring, TRIM, CUT-OFF (or see par/parr/pair/pear)
parebolic, parabola(lic) / parable(lic)
paredime, paradigm
paredoks, paradox
parefen, paraffin
pareferul, peripheral
paregraf, paragraph
paregraph, paragraph
pareid, parade
parekeet, parakeet
parel, peril
parelel, parallel
parelize, paralyze
paremedic, paramedic
paremeter, perimeter / parameter
paremider, perimeter / parameter
paremount, paramount
parend, parent
parendul, parent(al)
pareneul, perennial
parenial, perennial
parenoid, paranoia(id)
parense, parent(s)
parent,*,ted,ting,tal,tage, PROVIDER OF DNA TO BIRTHED OFFSPRING "prefixes: bi"
parenthesis,es,etic,tical,tically,ize,izes, ized,izing, TWO MARKS (SHAPED LIKE CRESCENT MOONS) ON EITHER SIDE OF WORDS INSERTED INTO A SENTENCE
parepheral, peripheral
pareplegic, paraplegia(ic)
parescope, periscope
paresh, parish / perish
paretruper, paratrooper
parews, peruse
parfa, parfait
parfae, parfait
parfait, DESSERT
pari, PREFIX INDICATING "EQUAL" MOST OFTEN MODIFIES THE WORD
paribolic, parabola(lic) / parable(lic)

paride, parity / parody / parrot(y)

paridime, paradigm

paridokical, paradox(ical)

paridoks, paradox

parifen, paraffin

parifuril, peripheral

parigraf, paragraph

parikeet, parakeet

parilel, parallel

parilize, paralyze

parimiter, perimeter / parameter

parimount, paramount

parind, parent

parinoid, paranoia(id)

parinse, parent(s)

parint, parent

parintal, parent(al)

parinthases, parenthesis

paripheral, peripheral

pariplegic, paraplegia(ic)

pariscope, periscope

parish,hes,hioner, CHURCH CONGREGATION (or see perish)

parishute, parachute

parisite, parasite

paritrooper, paratrooper

parituper, paratrooper

parity, THE ACT OF CUTTING/DIVIDING (or see parody/parrot(y))

park,*,ked,king,ker, LAND FOR PUBLIC REST/RECREATION, SITUATE A VEHICLE WHERE IT WILL BE IMMOBILE FOR A PERIOD OF TIME

parka,*, HEAVY COAT WITH FUR

parkay, parquet

parkeet, parakeet

parket, parquet

parkt, park(ed)

parku, parka

parodoks, paradox

parody,dies,died,dying,dic,dical,dically, dist, A STORY MAKING LIGHT OF A SERIOUS DRAMA/SITUATION (or see parity/parrot(y))

parogative, prerogative

parokside, peroxide

parole,ed,ling, UNDER COURT SUPERVISION

parona, piranha

paroose, peruse

parot, parrot

paroxside, peroxide

parportional, proportion(al)

parquet,*,try, TYPE OF WOOD FLOORING

parr, YOUNG FISH (or see par/pare/ pear/pair)

parrot,*,ted,ting,ter,ty, A TROPICAL BIRD, TO REPEAT LIKE THE BIRD (or see parody)

parsel, parcel

parsen, parson

parshal, partial

parshul, partial

parsil, parcel

parsin, parson

parsle, parcel

parsley, AN EDIBLE HERB

parsly, parsley

parsnip,*, VEGETABLE

parson,*,nage,nic,nical, IN CHARGE OF CHURCH PARISH

parsul, parcel

parsun, parson

part,*,ted,ting,tition,titioned,titioning, SELECT PART OF THE WHOLE, LET GO OF "prefixes: under"

partake,*,king,took, TAKE PART, BE INVOLVED IN AN ASPECT OF

partekul, particle

partekularly, particular(ly)

parten, pardon

partequler, particular

partequlurly, particular(ly)

partesan, partisan

partesapate, participate

parteshen, partition

partial,*,led,lling,lly,lity,lities,lness, PORTION/SECTION FROM THE WHOLE, FOCUS ON ONE

participate,*,ed,ting,tion,ant,tive,tor, tory, WORK/PLAY WITH A GROUP, BE A PART OF

particle,*, OF SMALL PIECE/FRAGMENT IN SCIENTIFIC TERMS, PERTAINS TO ENGLISH GRAMMAR

particular,rate,rity,rities,rism,rist,ristic, rize,rization,rly,ate, REFERRING SPECIFICALLY TO A SMALL PIECE/ FRAGMENT/ PART

partiel, partial

partikquler, particular

partikul, particle

partikularly, particular(ly)

partin, pardon

partiquler, particular

partisan,*, SUPPORTS A SPECIFIC POLITICAL DOGMA

partisapate, participate

partisapunt, participate(ant)

partishen, partition

partisupent, participate(ant)

partition,*,ned,ning,ner,nment, SEGMENT OFF, DIVIDE UP INTO PARTS "prefixes: re"

partner,*,red,ring, ASSOCIATE, RELATIONS BETWEEN TWO PEOPLE/ GROUPS, ONE OF TWO PEOPLE

partook, PAST TENSE FOR THE WORD "PARTAKE", BE INVOLVED IN

partreg, partridge

partridge,*, A GAME BIRD

partrij, partridge

partucle, particle

partuk, partook

partukle, particle

partun, pardon

partusen, partisan

party,ties,tied,tying,yer, PEOPLE GATHERING FOR FUN/SPORT/ LAUGHTER/SPECIFIC REASON "prefixes: intra"

paruchute, parachute

parudime, paradigm

parudoks, paradox

parugraf, paragraph

parukeet, parakeet

parul, peril

parulel, parallel

parulize, paralyze

parumont, paramount

parunt, parent

paruplegic, paraplegia(ic)

paruse, peruse

parushute, parachute

parusite, parasite

paruskope, periscope

parutruper, paratrooper

paruze, peruse

parzly, parsley

parznip, parsnip

pas, pass / pause / pase

pasable, pass(able)

pasage, passage

pascripshen, prescript(ion)

pasd, past / paste / pass(ed)

pasdasheo, pistachio

pasdel, pastel

pasder, pastor / pasture

pasderize, pasteurize

pasdirize, pasteurize
pasdor, pastor / pasture
pasdrame, pastrami
pasdre, pastry
pasdree, pastry
pasdrome, pastrami
pasdur, pastor / pasture
pasduresashen, pasteurize(zation)
pasdurize, pasteurize
pase, pace
paseble, pass(able)
pasedge, passage
pasef, passive
pasefikashen, pacify(fication)
pasefy, pacify
paseg, passage
pasej, passage
pasenger, passenger
pases, possess / pass(es) / pause(s)
paseshen, position / possess(ion)
pasesuf, possess(ive)
pasev, passive
pashen, passion
pashendly, patient(ly)
pashenit, passion(ate)
pashens, patience / patient(s)
pashin, passion
pashindly, patient(ly)
pashins, patience / patient(s)
pashinute, passion(ate)
pashun, passion
pashunit, passion(ate)
pasif, passive
pasific, pacific
pasification, pacify(fication)
pasify, pacify
pasig, passage
pasij, passage
pasinger, passenger
pasinjur, passenger
pasion, passion
pasionate, passion(ate)
pasishen, position
pasition, position
pasive, passive
paskrepshen, prescript(ion)
paskripshen, prescript(ion)
paskription, prescript(ion)
pass,sses,ssed,ssing,ssable,ssably, SKIP
    FROM ONE TO THE NEXT, MOVE
    ALONG WITHOUT STOPPING, TO
    GO AROUND WITHOUT STOPPING
    "prefixes: over/sur"

passage,*,ged,ging,eway, A NARROW
    WAY THROUGH, INTERCHANGE,
    CORRIDOR
passenger,*, PEOPLE RIDING ON/IN A
    VEHICLE/VESSEL TO SOME
    DESTINATION
passion,*,nate,nately,nal,nality,nless,
    DEEPLY DEVOTED DESIRE FOR
    SOMETHING "prefixes: dis"
passive,ely,eness,vity, HAS NO
    REACTION TO ACTION, DOESN'T
    GENERATE ACTION
past, PAST TENSE FOR THE WORD
    "PASS", YESTERDAY AND BEYOND,
    BACK THERE (or see pass(ed)/paste)
pasta, PASTE USED TO MAKE NOODLES
pastachio, pistachio
pastasheo, pistachio
paste,*,ed,ting,ty, A THICK/VISCOUS
    LIQUID TEXTURE MADE OF A
    VARIETY OF MATERIAL (or see past)
pastel,*,list, PALE IN COLOR, TYPE OF
    PAINTING
paster, pastor / pasture
pasteurize,*,ed,zing,zation,zer, HIGH
    TEMPERATURE OVER PERIOD OF
    TIME TO KILL BACTERIA
pastirize, pasteurize
pastor,*,rship, ONE IN CHARGE OF A
    CHURCH CONGREGATION (or see
    pasture)
pastrami, PICKLED BEEF
pastrome, pastrami
pastry,ries, DESSERT, BAKED GOODS
pasture,*,ed,ring,rage,rer, GRASS FIELD
    USED FOR GRAZING ANIMALS (or
    see pastor)
pasturesashen, pasteurize(zation)
pasturize, pasteurize
pasuble, pass(able)
pasuf, passive
pasufi, pacify
pasuges, passage(s)
pasuj, passage
pasuve, passive
pat,*,tted,tting, TO LIGHTLY/GENTLY
    SLAP/STROKE USING THE HANDS/
    FEET (or see paid/pate')
pata, pate'
patado, potato
pataseum, potassium
patato, potato

patch,hes,hed,hing,hy, COVER A HOLE
    WITH SOMETHING, PROTECTION
    FOR OPENING
pate',*, A PASTE (or see paid/pat(tty))
pateet, petite
patel, paddle
paten, patent
patenchul, potential
patenshil, potential
patent,*,ted,ting,ncy,tly,tability,table,
    tor, LEGAL OWNERSHIP OF A
    PROPERTY/IDEA/INVENTION
patential, potential
pateo, patio
paterbed, perturb(ed)
patern, pattern
paternal,lly,lism,list,listic,nity, MALE
    PARENT
pateshen, petition
patet, petite
path,*,hway, A DEFINED TRAIL
pathalogical, pathology(gical)
pathetic,cally, MISERY, INHUMANE
    QUALITY, UNAGREEABLE
    CONDITION
patho, PREFIX INDICATING "DISEASE"
    MOST OFTEN MODIFIES THE WORD
pathology,gies,gic,gical,gically, SCIENCE
    FIELD WHICH STUDIES DISEASE
patience, RELAX AND ALLOW A
    NATURAL COURSE (or see
    patient(s))
patient,*,tly, PAST TENSE FOR THE
    WORD "PATIENCE", PERSON
    UNDERGOING MEDICAL CARE (or
    see patience) "prefixes: im/in"
patil, paddle
patina,*, CHEMICAL APPLICATION FOR
    METAL
patinchul, potential
patint, patent
patintial, potential
patio,*, OUTSIDE AREA NEAR DOOR
    INTO DWELLING
patirn, pattern
patirnal, paternal
patishen, petition
patite, petite
patition, petition
patle, paddle
patlok, padlock
patluc, potluck
patreark, patriarch
patrearkul, patriarch(al)

patreit, patriot / patriate
patren, patron
patrenize, patron(ize)
patreotic, patriot(ic)
patreut, patriot / patriate
patriarch,hal,hy,hies, MALE WHO IS HEAD OF HOUSEHOLD, DOMINANT MALE
patriate,*,ed,ting, TAKE CONTROL OF COUNTRY UNDER FORMER COLONIAL POWER (or see patriot)
patrinize, patron(ize)
patriot,*,tic,tically,tism, SOMEONE WITH STRONG EMOTIONAL TIES TO THEIR COUNTRY (or see patriate)
patrol,*,lled,lling, ONE WHO COVERS PRESCRIBED/DESIGNATED AREA FOR SECURITY, TO PATROL
patroleum, petrol(eum)
patron,*,nal,nage,nize,nized,nizing, nizingly, SOMEONE WHO PROVIDES SUPPORT FOR GROUPS OF PEOPLE IN NEED, CLIENT
patronise, patron(ize)
patrude, protrude
patrun, patron
patrunize, patron(ize)
patrushen, protrude(usion)
patryarkle, patriarch(al)
patse, patsy
patsy,sies, THE SCAPEGOAT, TAKES THE BLAME
pattern,*,ned,ning, A SHAPE MADE TO REPRESENT AN ORIGINAL TO BE REPRODUCED, ORIGINAL TO BE REPRODUCED
patty,tties, FLAT/ROUND SHAPE (or see paddy)
patunia, petunia
patunya, petunia
paturbed, perturb(ed)
paturn, pattern
paturnal, paternal
paty, patty / paddy
pauble, pay(yable)
pauch, pouch
pauder, powder
pauer, power
paulanize, pollen(ize)
paulen, pollen
paulenize, pollen(ize)
pauletics, politic(s)
paulip, polyp
paum, palm

paun, pawn
paund, pound / pawn(ed) / pond
paunder, pound(er) / ponder
pauns, pounce / pound(s) / pawn(s)
paur, pay(er) / power
paus, pause / paw(s)
pauschur, posture
pausder, posture
pausdur, posture
pause,*,ed,sing,sal, A BRIEF MOMENT OF SILENCE BETWEEN, BRIEF HESITATION (or see paw(s))
paustr, posture
pausture, posture
paut, pout
pauvurde, poverty
pauwer, power
pauwr, power
pauzder, posture
pave,*,ed,ving,ement, TO LAY/PREPARE A TRAIL/ROAD/PATH FOR SMOOTHER TRAVEL, APPLY A COMPOSITE ON TOP OF THE GROUND
paverdy, poverty
pavershen, pervert(rsion)
pavilion,*, SMALL ADDITION TO A LARGER BUILDING WHICH IS NORMALLY EXPOSED TO THE ELEMENTS
pavillion, pavilion
pavmint, pave(ment)
pavt, pave(d)
pavurted, pervert(ed)
paw,*,wed,wing, ANIMAL FOOT
pawer, power
pawir, power
pawlen, pollen
pawn,*,ned,ning, BORROW MONEY AGAINST AN ARTICLE FOR LATER RETRIEVAL, TO PLEDGE
pawur, power
paxs, pack(s)
pay,es,aid,ying,yment,yable,yee,yer, TO GIVE MONEY IN EXCHANGE FOR GOODS/SERVICES (or see pad/paid/ pie) "prefixes: pre/re"
payd, paid
payleontology, paleontology
payn, pain / pane / pine
paynt, paint / pane(d) / pain(ed)
payode, peyote
payote, peyote
payst, paste

payt, paid
pazd, past / paste / pass(ed)
pazdel, pastel
pazdry, pastry
pazefy, pacify
pazenjer, passenger
pazinger, passenger
pazishen, position
pazt, past / paste / pass(ed)
pe, pee / pay
pea,*, LEGUME/FOOD (or see pee/ peace/piece)
peace,eful,efully,efulness,eable, eableness,eably, ATTITUDE/AIRE OF CALM/ QUIET (or see piece)
peach,hes,hy, A FRUIT
peacock,*, A COLORFUL BIRD
peak,*,ked,king,kedness, THE CLIMAX/ HIGHEST POINT OF A WAVE/ OBJECT, MAXIMUM POINT (or see peek/pique)
peakok, peacock
peal, SOUNDS/RINGS (or see peel)
peano, piano
peanut,*, A LEGUME, SMALL NUT
pear,*, A FRUIT (or see pare/pair)
pearl,*,ly,lized, PRODUCED BY OYSTER, HAVING THE QUALITIES OF A PEARL
peasant,*,try, SIMPLE PERSON WHO LIVES OFF THE LAND (or see pheasant)
peasful, peace(ful)
peat,ty, DRIED PLANTS PARTIALLY DECAYED (or see pit)
peave, peeve
pebble,*, TINY ROCKS/STONES
pebel, pebble
peber, pepper
pebil, pebble
pebir, pepper
pebl, pebble
pebol, pebble
pebul, pebble
pebur, pepper
pec, peck / pick / pig / pique / peak / peek
pecalo, piccolo
pecan,*, AN EDIBLE NUT
pecd, pick(ed) / peck(ed) / peak(ed)
pecdorul, pectoral / pictorial
pech, peach / pitch
peched, pitch(ed)
pecher, pitcher / picture
pechr, pitcher / picture

peck,*,ked,king,ker, BIRDS USING THEIR BILLS TO STAB/JAB, A MEASUREMENT OF WEIGHT (or see pick/pig/pique/peak/peek)

pecnic, picnic

pecok, peacock

pecon, pecan

pecs, SHORT FOR PECTORAL MUSCLES(or see peck(s))

pecsher, picture / pitcher

pect, pick(ed) / peck(ed) / peak(ed)

pecten,*, A SCIENTIFIC PROCESS (or see pectin)

pectin, WAXY SUBSTANCE COLLECTED FROM WALLS OF PLANTS, USED TO STIFFEN (or see pecten)

pecton, pectin / pecten

pectoral,*, OF THE CHEST/BREAST, FINS ON FISH

pectorial, pectoral / pictorial

pectun, pectin / pecten

pecturul, pectoral

peculiar,rly,rity,rities, STRANGE, UNUSUAL

ped, PREFIX INDICATING "FOOT/CHILD" MOST OFTEN MODIFIES THE WORD

pedagogy,gies,gogue,gic,gical,gically, gics, ART/SCIENCE OF TEACHING, AN EDUCATOR

pedagree, pedigree

pedakure, pedicure

pedal,*,led,ling, USE FOOT/LEVER TO CREATE MOVEMENT/ACTION (or see petal/peddle)

peddle,*,ed,ling,er, MOVING/GOING ABOUT SELLING WARES/GOODS (or see petal/pedal)

pede, petty / pity

pedeatrician, pediatrician

pedeatrics, pediatrics

pedeatrishen, pediatrician

pedecoat, petticoat

pedegogy, pedagogy

pedegree, pedigree

pedekote, petticoat

pedekure, pedicure

pedel, pedal / petal / peddle

peder, peter

pedestal,*,led,ling, A BASE/STAND/ PODIUM

pedestle, pedestal

pedestrian,*, ONE WHO TRAVELS BY FOOT/ON THEIR FEET, SOMEONE WHO IS WALKING

pedeutrishen, pediatrician

pedi, PREFIX INDICATING "FOOT/ CHILD" MOST OFTEN MODIFIES THE WORD

pediatrician,*, DOCTOR FOR CHILDREN

pediatrics, SCIENCE THAT WORKS WITH CHILDREN

pediatrishen, pediatrician

pedicoat, petticoat

pedicure,*,rist, WORKING WITH THE FEET

pedid, pet(tted)

pedigogy, pedagogy

pedigree,*,eed, HAS LEGAL PAPERS SHOWING ANCESTRY

pedikote, petticoat

pedil, pedal / petal / peddle

pedir, peter

pedistal, pedestal

pedle, pedal / petal / peddle

pedo, PREFIX INDICATING "FOOT/ CHILD" MOST OFTEN MODIFIES THE WORD

pedol, pedal / petal / peddle

pedrafication, petrify(fication)

pedrify, petrify

pedrol, petrol

pedroleim, petrol(eum)

pedrufy, petrify

peds, pet(s)

pedugogy, pedagogy

pedugree, pedigree

pedul, pedal / petal / peddle

pedur, peter

pedustal, pedestal

pedy, petty / pity

pee,*,eed,eeing, TO URINATE (or see pea)

peech, peach

peed, peat / pee(d)

peek,*,ked,king,ker, TO GET A QUICK GLIMPSE OF, TO LOOK QUICKLY (or see peak)

peekt, peek(ed)

peel,*,led,ling,ler, TO REMOVE OUTER LAYER/SKIN

peenk, pink

peep,*,ped,ping,per, LOOK/GLIMPSE INTO

peeple, people

peer,*,rless,rlessly,rlessness, OF THE SAME AGE/RANK/STATUS, TO FOCUS YOUR GAZE FARAWAY,

LOOK INTO (or see pyre/pierce/ pier(s))

peeroet, pirouette

peers, pier(s) / peer(s) / pierce

pees, pea(s) / peace / piece / pee(s)

peeve,*,vish,vishly,vishness, IRRITATE/ AGGRAVATE

pef, peeve

pefs, peeve(s)

peg,*,gged,gging, A SPIKE OF ANY MATERIAL USED TO HOLD UP/ DOWN SOMETHING "prefixes: un"

pegamus, pajamas

pegated, picket(ed)

pegen, pigeon

peget, picket

pegul, pickle

pegy, pig(ggy) / pick(y)

pein, pain / pane

peiny, peony

peiper, paper

peiper mache, paper mache

peir, pier / peer / pyre

peirce, pierce

peirse, pierce / pier(s) / peer(s)

pejamus, pajamas

pejen, pigeon

pek, peck / pick / pig / pique / peak / peek

pekalo, piccolo

pekan, pecan

pekel, pickle

peker, pick(er) / peck(er)

pekewler, peculiar

pekit, picket

peknik, picnic

pekok, peacock

pekol, pickle

pekon, pecan

peksher, picture / pitcher

pektin, pectin / pecten

pektoral, pectoral / pictorial

pektun, pectin / pecten

pekture, picture / pitcher

pekul, pickle

pekuler, peculiar

pekuleur, peculiar

pekur, pick(er) / peck(er)

peky, pick(y)

pel, peel / peal / pill / pale

pelacan, pelican

pelaf, pilaf

pelage, pillage

pelakan, pelican

pelar, pillar
pelaredy, polar(ity)
pelej, pillage
pelekan, pelican
peler, pillar
pelese, police
pelet, pellet
peletical, politic(al)
pelgrem, pilgrim
pelgremege, pilgrim(age)
pelgrim, pilgrim
pelican,*, A LARGE BIRD WHO EATS
    FISH
peligamus, polygamy(mous)
peligamy, polygamy
pelit, pellet / polite
pelitecal, politic(al)
pellet,*, ANYTHING SMALL/ROUND/
    HARD
pellow, pillow
pelminary, pulmonary
pelof, pilaf
pelot, pellet
pelow, pillow
pelt,*,ted,ting, ANYTHING SMALL/
    ROUND/HARD HITTING
    SOMETHING, THE HIDE/HAIR FROM
    SMALL ANIMAL
peluch, pillage
peludge, pillage
peluge, pillage
pelukin, pelican
pelushen, pollute(tion)
pelut, pellet / pollute
pelutent, pollute(tant)
pelution, pollute(tion)
pelvek, pelvic
pelves, pelvis
pelvic, LARGE BONE ON LOWER TORSO
    WHERE LEGS ARE ATTACHED
pelvis,es,ic, LARGE BONE ON LOWER
    TORSO WHERE LEGS ARE
    ATTACHED
pelygamus, polygamy(mous)
pelygamy, polygamy
peminto, pimento
pemp, pimp
pempul, pimple
pemt, pimp(ed)
pen,*,nned,nning, INSTRUMENT WITH
    INK FOR WRITING, HAVING BEEN
    WRITTEN/COMPOSED, FEMALE
    SWAN, CAGE FOR PIGS (or see pin/
    pent)

penacle, pentacle / pinnacle
penada, pinata
penagon, pentagon
penagram, pentagram
penakle, pinnacle / pentacle
penal,lize,lizes,lized,lizing,lization,lly,lty,
    lties, PUNISHMENT
penasilen, penicillin
penatentiary, penitentiary
penatinchory, penitentiary
penatrable, penetrable
penatrashen, penetrate(tion)
penatrate, penetrate
penc, pink
pench, pinch
penchant, DESIRE MOSTLY, STRONG
    LIKING FOR, BIAS
penchers, pinch(ers) / pincers
pencil,*,led,ling, WOODEN/GRAPHITE
    WRITING INSTRUMENT, TO USE TO
    WRITE
pendalum, pendulum
pendant,dent,*, ITEM HANGING FROM
    SOMETHING, SUSPENDED ITEM
pendelum, pendulum
pending, ACTION IN PROCESS AIMED
    FOR COMPLETION
pendlum, pendulum
pendo, pinto
pendulum,*,lar, SUSPENDED FROM A
    FIXED POINT, ENDS FREE TO SEEK
    BALANCE/EQUILIBRIUM
peneal gland, pineal gland
penecilin, penicillin
penecle, pinnacle / pentacle
penegram, pentagram
penensula, peninsula
peneol gland, pineal gland
penes, penis
penesilin, penicillin
penetrable,bility,eness,ly, EXPOSED,
    ACCEPT/EXPERIENCE INCOMING
    PENETRATION, BOUNDARIES
    ALLOWING FOR INFILTRATION
penetrate,*,ed,ting,tion,ant,tive,tively,
    tiveness, ENTER/PIERCE/AFFECT
    "prefixes: inter"
pengalum, pendulum
pengilum, pendulum
penguin,*, BIRD OF THE ANTARCTIC
pengwen, penguin
peni, penny
penial gland, pineal gland

penicillin,ium,ia, ANTIBIOTIC DERIVED
    FROM A MOLD, USED FOR KILLING
    BACTERIA
penikul, pentacle / pinnacle
peninsula,*,ar, FINGER/PORTION OF
    LAND JUTTING FROM THE
    MAINLAND, SURROUNDED BY
    WATER
penis, MALE ORGAN USED FOR
    COPULATION/URINATION (or see
    penny(nies))
penitenchery, penitentiary
penitentiary,ries, PRISON, ROMAN
    CATHOLIC TERM
penitintiary, penitentiary
penjalum, pendulum
penjulem, pendulum
penk, pink
penkwen, penguin
penky, pink(y)
pennicilin, penicillin
penny,nnies, A U.S. COIN
pennyul gland, pineal gland
pensel, pencil
pensers, pincers / pinch(ers)
penshen, pension
penshent, penchant
pensil, pencil
pension,*,nable,nary,naries,ner, A
    REGULARLY ALLOTTED ALOWANCE
pensul, pencil
pent, CLOSED OFF, SHUT IN (or see
    pen(ned)/pint)
pentacle,*, A FIVE POINT STAR
pentagon,nal,nally, U.S. OFFICE OF
    DEFENSE
pentagram,*, A PENTACLE, FIVE POINT
    STAR
pentalum, pendulum
pentegram, pentagram
pentigon, pentagon
pentilum, pendulum
penting, pending
pento, pinto
pentucle, pentacle / pinnacle
pentugon, pentagon
pentulem, pendulum
penud, peanut
penugon, pentagon
penugram, pentagram
penukel, pentacle / pinnacle
penulize, penal(ize)
penulty, penal(ty)
penus, penis

penusilen, penicillin
penut, peanut
penutrashen, penetrate(tion)
penutruble, penetrable
peny, penny
penyada, pinata
penyoda, pinata
peode, peyote
peol, pail / pale / peel
peony,nies, A FLOWER
people,*, HUMANS
peote, peyote
pep,*,pped,pping,ppy, VIGOR/ENERGY,
    ENERGETIC (or see peep)
pepal, people
pepe, pep(ppy)
peper, pepper
pepil, people
pepir, pepper
pepiu, papaya
pepl, pebble / people
peple, people
peporshenal, proportion(al)
pepper,*,red,ring,ry, A SPICE/
    VEGETABLE, TO BE SPRINKLED/
    PELTED BY
pepul, people
pepur, pepper
pepy, pep(ppy)
pequleur, peculiar
per, BY/THROUGH/EACH, PREFIX
    INDICATING "COMPLETELY/
    THOROUGHLY" MOST OFTEN
    MODIFIES THE WORD (or see peer/
    purr/pear/pier/pair/pare)
perabolic, parabola(lic) / parable(lic)
perabul, parable
perade, parade
peradime, paradigm
peradox, paradox
perafen, paraffin
peragative, prerogative
peragraf, paragraph
perakeet, parakeet
peralasis, paralysis
peralel, parallel
peralises, paralysis
peralusis, paralysis
peramaunt, paramount
peramedur, parameter / perimeter
perametic, paramedic
perametur, parameter / perimeter
peramid, pyramid
peramitur, parameter / perimeter

peramount, paramount
peranoid, paranoia(id)
peranoyd, paranoia(id)
perant, parent
peraplegic, paraplegia(ic)
perascope, periscope
perashute, parachute
perasite, parasite
perate, parade
peratruper, paratrooper
peraty, parody / parity / parrot(y)
perbendikuler, perpendicular
perceive,*,ed,ving,er, SEE/
    UNDERSTAND/KNOW
percent,*,tage,tages,tile,tum, PORTION
    OF THE WHOLE AMOUNT
percept,tion,tional,tive,tively,tiveness,
    tivity,tual,tually, TO KNOW/
    PERCEIVE WITH THE SENSES
perceptible,bility,bly, KNOW/PERCEIVE
    WITH SENSES
perceve, perceive
perch,hes,hed,hing, A FISH, WHERE
    BIRDS ROOST, TINY BUILDING
    OUTCROP (or see purge)
perchus, purchase / perch(es)
percieve, perceive
percintage, percent(age)
percipatation, precipitate(tion)
percivere, persevere
percrastination, procrastinate
percushen, percussion
percussion,*,nist,ive,ively,iveness,
    IMPACT BETWEEN TWO BODIES OF
    MATTER, MUSICAL INSTRUMENT
    GROUP
pereadontek, periodontic
pereadontist, periodontist
pereatic, periodic
pereaudic, periodic
perebolic, parabola(lic) / parable(lic)
perebul, parable
perechute, parachute
peredime, paradigm
peredox, paradox
peredy, parody / parity / parrot(y)
pereferul, peripheral
perefin, paraffin
peregraf, paragraph
perekeet, parakeet
perel, peril
perelel, parallel
perelize, paralyze
peremedic, paramedic

peremont, paramount
peremownt, paramount
perend, parent
perenial, perennial
perennial,*,lly, EXISTS/GROWS ALL
    YEAR LONG
perenoya, paranoia
perens, parent(s)
perent, parent
pereod, period
pereodic, periodic / periotic
pereot, period
pereotecul, periodic(al)
pereotic, periodic / periotic
pereotical, periodic(al)
perepheral, peripheral
pereple, parable
pereplegic, paraplegia(ic)
perescope, periscope
peresh, parish / perish
pereshute, parachute
peresite, parasite
peret, parrot
peretruper, paratrooper
pereud, period
pereudonteks, periodontic(s)
pereudontest, periodontist
perfect,*,ted,ting,tion,tness,tible,
    tionism,tionist,tive,tiveness, tivity,
    tly,to, GREAT AT THE MOMENT,
    SYNCHRONOUS, HARMONIC
perfekshen, perfect(ion)
perferted, pervert(ed)
perfeum, perfume
perfikt, perfect
perfium, perfume
perform,*,med,ming,mance,mances,
    mable,mer, ACT/PLAY OUT/
    MOTION/ FUNCTIONABLE "prefixes:
    over/under"
performence, perform(ance)
perfume,*,ed,ming,ery,eries, SCENT/
    SMELL WHICH COMES NATURALLY
    OR IS APPLIED
pergatory, purgatory
perge, purge
perger, perjure
pergery, perjure(ry)
pergitory, purgatory
pergury, perjure(ry)
pergutory, purgatory
perhaps, COULD BE, LIKELY, POSSIBLE

peri, PREFIX INDICATING "AROUND/ ABOUT" MOST OFTEN MODIFIES THE WORD

periadontist, periodontist

peribolic, parabola(lic) / parable(lic)

peribul, parable

perichute, parachute

peridime, paradigm

peridox, paradox

peridy, parody / parity / parrot(y)

perifen, paraffin

perifuril, peripheral

perigraf, paragraph

perikeet, parakeet

peril,*,led,ling,lous,lously,lousness, CAUTION, GREAT DANGER, HAZARDOUS (or see pearl)

perilel, parallel

perilize, paralyze

perimed, pyramid

perimedic, paramedic

perimeter,*,tric,trical,trically,try, AROUND A PARTICULAR AREA, CIRCUMFERENCE, BOUNDARY/ SIDES (or see parameter)

perimetic, paramedic

perimider, perimeter / parameter

perimiter, perimeter / parameter

perimount, paramount

perind, parent

perinoid, paranoia(id)

perinoya, paranoia

perinse, parent(s)

perint, parent

period,*, A PUNCTUATION MARK, SPAN OF TIME, MENSTRUATION

periodic,cal,cally,city, RECURRING, PREDICTABLE PATTERN (or see periotic)

periodontic,*,tal,ia,ium, SCIENCE/ STUDY OF TEETH/GUMS

periodontist, DENTIST/DOCTOR, OF TEETH

periotic, OF THE EAR (or see periodic)

peripheral,ric,rally,ry,ries, GENERAL EXTERIOR AREA AROUND A NUCLEUS/ CENTER/TOWN, CIRCUMFERENCE

periple, parable

periplegic, paraplegia(ic)

periscope,*,pic,pical, USED IN SUBMARINES/TANKS FOR VIEWING ABOVE THE VESSEL/WATER

perish,hes,hed,hing,hable,hably,hability, hableness, STOP BEING ALIVE, END OF GROWING/BREATHING, BEGIN TO ROT (or see parish)

perisite, parasite

perit, parrot

peritruper, paratrooper

perity, parody / parity / parrot(y)

perje, purge

perjure,*,ed,ring,er,ry,ries,rious,riously, KNOWINGLY MAKE A FALSE STATEMENT UNDER OATH

perkeet, parakeet

perkrastination, procrastinate

perkushen, percussion

perkusion, percussion

perl, pearl

permanence,cy,cies,nt, THE STATE OF BEING PERMANENT/FIXED

permanent,tly,tness,nce, CHEMICAL TREATMENT TO HAIR, FIXED POSITION, NONMOVING "prefixes: semi"

permanins, permanence

permeable,ly,bility, FILTERS/SPREADS/ ABSORBS, FILLS SPACE IN BETWEEN "prefixes: semi"

permeate,*,ed,ting,tion,tive,ance,able, ableness,ably,ability, FILTERS/ SPREADS/ ABSORBS, FILLS SPACE IN BETWEEN

permenant, permanent

permenence, permanence

permeuble, permeable

permiable, permeable

permiate, permeate

permichen, permission

perminet, permanent

permisable, permissible

permisen, permission

permishen, permission

permisive, permissive

permissible,ly,bility, HAVE APPROVAL FOR/OF, ALLOWABLE "prefixes: non"

permission,ible,ive, HAVE APPROVAL FOR/OF

permissive,ely,eness,ion,ible, MORE ALLOWABLE THAN THE NORM

permisuble, permissible

permisuf, permissive

permit,*,tted,tting,tter, RECEIPT/ LICENSE/ALLOWING APPROVAL (or see pyramid)

permited, permit(tted)

permition, permission

permunins, permanence

permunint, permanent

perodox, paradox

perody, parody / parity / parrot(y)

peroet, pirouette

perogative, prerogative

perograf, paragraph

perokside, peroxide

perole, parole

perona, piranha

peront, parent

peroose, peruse

perosity, porosity

peroty, parody / parity / parrot(y)

peroxide,ed,ding, A CHEMICAL

perpel, purple

perpendicular,rity,rly, RIGHT ANGLE TO A PLANE

perpes, purpose

perpesly, purpose(ly)

perpetrate,*,ed,ting,tion,tor, EXECUTE, COMMIT

perpetshuate, perpetual(ate)

perpetual,lly,ate,able,ation,ator,uity, ONGOING, FOREVER, CONTINUOUS

perpetuity,uties, FOREVER, ONGOING, CONTINUOUS

perpil, purple

perpindicular, perpendicular

perpis, purpose

perpisly, purpose(ly)

perpitrate, perpetrate

perpituity, perpetuity

perple, purple

perplex,xes,xed,xing,xingly,xity,xities, NOT UNDERSTANDING, CONFUSED

perpol, purple

perporshenal, proportion(al)

perportional, proportion(al)

perpos, purpose

perposly, purpose(ly)

perposterus, preposterous

perpul, purple

perpus, purpose

perpusle, purpose(ly)

perputrate, perpetrate

perrenial, perennial

pers, pierce / purse / pier(s) / peer(s)

persacute, persecute

persafere, persevere

persanu, person(a)

persarverance, persevere(rance)

persavere, persevere

persbektif, perspective
persbiration, perspiration
persbire, perspire
perscripshen, prescript(ion)
perse, pierce / purse / pier(s) / peer(s)
persebduble, perceptible
persebtef, percept(ive)
persecute,*,ed,ting,tion,tive,tor,
AGGRAVATE/HARASS/PUNISH (or
see prosecute)
persede, precede / proceed
persenality, personality
persenaly, personal(lly)
persenel, personnel
persent, percent
persentige, percent(age)
persentil, percent(ile)
persenuble, person(able)
persenulize, personal(ize)
persepatashen, precipitate(tion)
persepshen, percept(ion)
perseptable, perceptible
perseptef, percept(ive)
perseption, percept(ion)
perseptive, percept(ive)
perserverance, persevere(rance)
perservere, persevere
persesshen, precision / procession /
precession
persest, persist
persestince, persist(ence)
persev, perceive
perseve, perceive
persevere,*,ed,ring,ringly,rance, TO
PERSIST, CONTINUE ON DESPITE
ODDS/ OBSTACLES
persh, perch / purge
pershis, purchase / perch(es)
persikute, persecute
persin, person
persinaledy, personality
persinel, personnel
persint, percent
persinuble, person(able)
persinul, personal
persinulize, personal(ize)
persinuly, personal(lly)
persipetashen, precipitate(tion)
persipitation, precipitate(tion)
persirverance, persevere(rance)
persishen, precision
persist,*,ted,ting,tence,tency,tent,
tently, CONSISTENT IN FOCUS,
TENACIOUS

persition, precision
persiv, perceive
persivere, persevere
persiverense, persevere(rance)
perskripshen, prescript(ion)
persokut, persecute
person,*,na,nable,nably,nability,
nableness,nage,nal,nate,nality,
nation,nator, nify,nnel,nhood, ONE
HUMAN BEING "prefixes: un"
personal,*,ly,lism,lity,lize, AURA/
ESSENCE/ATTITUDE/BEHAVIOR OF
A PERSON, CAN RELATE TO OTHERS
"prefixes: im/inter/intra/un/uni"
personality,ties, A PERSON'S ATTITUDE/
BEHAVIOR
personefication, person(ification)
personel, personnel / personal
personify,fies,fied,fying,fication,fier, TO
REPRESENT AS HUMAN, ACT LIKE,
ACT AS IF
personnel, GROUP/BODY OF PEOPLE,
DEPARTMENT WHICH HANDLES
EMPLOY OF PEOPLE
persoo, pursue
perspective,*,ely, FROM A CERTAIN
POINT OF VIEW
persperashen, perspiration
perspiration, TO SWEAT, RELEASE
WATER FROM THE PORES TO COOL
OFF
perspire,*,ed,ring,ration,ratory, TO
SWEAT, RELEASE WATER FROM THE
PORES TO COOL OFF
persu, pursue
persuade,*,ed,ding,asion,dable,asive,
asively,asiveness,asion, COERCE/
SWAY/ IMPRESS SOMEONE/
SOMETHING TO COMMIT TO YOUR
IDEALS "prefixes: over"
persuasion,ive, COERCE/SWAY/
IMPRESS SOMEONE
persude, pursue(d)
persun, person
persunal, personal
persunality, personality
persunaly, personal(lly)
persunel, personnel
persute, pursue(uit)
persuvere, persevere
perswade, persuade
perswaseve, persuade(asive)
perswashen, persuade(asion)
perswasif, persuade(asive)

pert,tly,tness, BRIGHT, LIVELY
pertain,*,ned,ning, ASSOCIATED WITH,
BELONGS TO
pertane, pertain
pertishen, partition
pertrayal, portray(al)
pertrude, protrude
perturb,*,bed,bing,bable,bation,
bational, BOTHERED BY, DISTURBED
"prefixes: un"
peruble, parable
perudime, paradigm
perudox, paradox
perufin, paraffin
perugraf, paragraph
perukeet, parakeet
perul, peril
perulel, parallel
perulised, paralyze(d)
perulize, paralyze
perumedic, paramedic
perumid, pyramid
perumount, paramount
perund, parent
perunoid, paranoia(id)
perunoya, paranoia
perunt, parent
peruphen, paraffin
peruplegic, paraplegia(ic)
perupul, parable
peruse,*,ed,sing,sal, TO READ/
EXAMINE CAREFULLY
perushute, parachute
perusite, parasite
peruskope, periscope
perut, parrot
perutruper, paratrooper
pervade,*,ed,ding,er,asion,asive,asively,
asiveness, PERMEATE, SPREAD
THROUGHOUT
pervashen, pervade(asion)
pervasif, pervade(asion)
perversef, pervert(rsive)
pervert,*,ted,tedly,tedness,ter,tible,rse,
rsely,rseness,rsion,rsity, rsities,rsive,
rsively,rsiveness, DEVIANT BY
SOCIETAL NORMS
pervirsive, pervert(rsive)
perzakute, persecute
perzaverinse, persevere(rance)
pes, peace / piece / pee(s) / pea(s)
pesa, pizza
pesamist, pessimism(st)
pesamistic, pessimism(stic)

pesamisum, pessimism
pesant, peasant
pesd, pest
pesdalense, pestilence
pesdasheo, pistachio
pesdaside, pesticide
pesdrome, pastrami
pesdulinse, pestilence
pesebly, peace(ably)
pesel, pestle
pesemisum, pessimism
pesent, peasant
peses, possess
pesesuf, possess(ive)
pesful, peace(ful)
pesher, pitcher / picture
pesibly, peace(ably)
pesific, pacific
pesil, pestle
pesimesum, pessimism
pesimist, pessimism(st)
pesimistic, pessimism(stic)
pesint, peasant
pesishen, position
pesition, position
peskripshen, prescript(ion)
pesol, pestle
pesont, peasant
pessimism,st,stic, CONTRARY TO, THE
   DOWNSIDE
pessimistic,cally, CONTRARY TO, THE
   DOWNSIDE
pest,*,ty, ANNOYANCE, BOTHERSOME
pestachio, pistachio
pestal, pestle / pistol / pistil
pestalinse, pestilence
pestasheo, pistachio
pestaside, pesticide
pestel, pistil / pistol / pestle
pestelinse, pestilence
pesten, piston
pesticide,*,dal, HARMFUL/POISONOUS
   CHEMICALS USED TO KILL INSECTS/
   ANIMALS/PLANTS
pestil, pistil / pistol / pestle
pestilence, DISEASE WHICH SPREADS
   THROUGHOUT
pestin, piston
pestle,*,ed,ling, GRIND/PULVERIZE/
   CRUSH/SMASH AGAINST A
   SURFACE WITH THIS AS A TOOL,
   NORMALLY ASSOCIATED WITH
   MORTAR/PESTLE
pestrome, pastrami

pestul, pistil / pistol / pestle
pestuled, pestle(d)
pestun, piston
pestuside, pesticide
pesuble, peace(able)
pesubly, peace(ably)
pesul, pestle
pesumisem, pessimism
pesumistic, pessimism(stic)
pesunt, peasant
pet,*,tted,tting, AN ANIMAL KEPT
   CONFINED AND FED BY HUMANS,
   TO STROKE (or see peat)
peta, PREFIX INDICATING "FIVE" MOST
   OFTEN MODIFIES THE WORD
petado, potato
petagogy, pedagogy
petagojik, pedagogy(gic)
petagree, pedigree
petakure, pedicure
petal,*,led, PART OF FLOWER(or see
   pedal/peddle)
petaseum, potassium
petasium, potassium
petato, potato
petch, pitch
petcher, pitcher / picture
petchir, pitcher/ picture
pete, petty / pity
peteatriks, pediatrics
peteatrishen, pediatrician
petecoat, petticoat
peted, pet(tted)
petegree, pedigree
petekote, petticoat
petekure, pedicure
petel, pedal / petal / peddle
petena, patina
peteness, petty(ttiness)
peter,*,red,ring, TO GET TIRED, RUN
   OUT OF ENERGY
petestul, pedestal
peteutrishen, pediatrician
pethetic, pathetic
peti, petty
petiatrics, pediatrics
peticoat, petticoat
peticure, pedicure
petier, petty(ttier)
petiest, petty(ttiest)
petigree, pedigree
petikote, petticoat
petikure, pedicure
petil, pedal / petal / peddle

petina, patina
petinchul, potential
petiness, petty(ttiness)
petinshul, potential
petir, peter
petistul, pedestal
petite,eness, SMALL WITH NORMAL
   PROPORTIONS
petition,*,ned,ning, SOLICIT/
   APPROACH/REQUEST SOMETHING
petle, pedal / petal / peddle
petnik, picnic
petr, PREFIX INDICATING "STONE/
   PETROLEUM" MOST OFTEN
   MODIFIES THE WORD
petrafikashen, petrify(fication)
petrafy, petrify
petrefication, petrify(fication)
petrefy, petrify
petrewd, protrude
petrify,fies,fied,fying,fication,factive,
   faction, FROZEN WITH HORROR,
   TURNED TO STONE
petro, PREFIX INDICATING "STONE/
   PETROLEUM" MOST OFTEN
   MODIFIES THE WORD
petrol,*,leum, HYDROCARBON/OIL/
   FUEL
petrolium, petrol(eum)
petrude, protrude
petrushen, protrude(usion)
petsa, pizza
petticoat,*, UNDERGARMENT, LAYERED
   SLIP
petty,ttier,ttiest,ttily,ttiness, SMALL/
   RESTRICTIVE/HABITUAL OUTLOOK
   LOOK FOR FLAWS
petugogy, pedagogy
petugree, pedigree
petul, pedal / petal / peddle
petunia,*, A FLOWER
petur, peter
peturbed, perturb(ed)
peturnol, paternal
petustel, pedestal
pety, petty / pity
peu, pew
peub, pube
peuberdy, puberty
peubesent, pubescent
peubik, pube(bic)
peuburdy, puberty
peuk, puke
peunatef, punitive

peune, peony / puny
peunutive, punitive
peuny, peony / puny
peupul, pupil
peur, pier / peer / pyre / pure
peuraficashen, purify(fication)
peure, puree'
peurefide, purify(fied)
peurefy, purify
peurly, pure(ly)
peury, puree'
peutrid, putrid
pev, peeve
pevurted, pervert(ed)
pew,*, BENCH SEATS IN CHURCH
pewbesent, pubescent
pewder, pewter
pewding, pudding / putt(ing)
pewdur, pewter
pewne, puny
pewpul, pupil
pewt, put
pewter,rer, MOLDABLE METAL MADE
    WITH LEAD, USED AS DISHES/
    VESSELS
pewtrid, putrid
pex, pick(s) / peck(s)
peyer, pure
peyeree, puree'
peyerify, purify
peyerly, pure(ly)
peyir, pure
peyote,*,tle, CACTUS, PRODUCES
    MESCALINE
peyur, pure
peyuree, puree'
peyurefide, purify(fied)
peyurify, purify
peyurly, pure(ly)
pez, pea(s) / peace / piece
peza, pizza
pezamistic, pessimism(stic)
pezd, pest
pezdalense, pestilence
pezdaside, pesticide
pezent, peasant
pezes, possess
pezful, peace(ful)
pezt, pest
pezubly, peace(ably)
pezunt, peasant
phalanthropy, philanthropy
phalek, philli(c)
phalicity, felicity

phalli,ic,icism,ism,icist,lluses, OF THE
    PENIS
phalosify, philosophy
phanetik, phonetic / fanatic
phanik, phonic
phanomena, phenomena
phanomenal, phenomenal
phantem, phantom
phantom,*, AN ILLUSIVE/SURREAL
    APPARITION, NOT PHYSICAL
pharaoh,*,onic,onical, EGYPTIAN KINGS
pharmac, PREFIX INDICATING "DRUGS/
    MEDICINES" MOST OFTEN
    MODIFIES THE WORD
pharmaceutic,*,cal,cally, DISPENSING
    OF MANMADE CHEMICALS/DRUGS
    "prefixes: bio"
pharmacist,*, ONE WHO DISPENSES
    MANMADE CHEMICALS/DRUGS/
    MEDICINE
pharmasutical, pharmaceutic(al)
pharmicist, pharmacist
pharmusutical, pharmaceutic(al)
pharoh, pharaoh
phase,*,ed,sing, AN ASPECT/PORTION
    OF AN OVERALL PROJECT/DESIGN,
    CHANGES/MOVEMENT (or see faze)
    "prefixes: in/inter/multi"
phasek, physique
phaselity, facility
phasic, physique
phasility, facility
phasishen, physician
phasphate, phosphate
phausfate, phosphate
phaze, phase / faze
pheasant,*, GAME BIRD
pheladendron, philodendron
phelanthrapist, philanthropy(pist)
phelanthropek, philanthropy(pic)
phelarmonic, philharmonic
phelicity, felicity
phelodendron, philodendron
phelosofy, philosophy
pheludindron, philodendron
phenaminan, phenomenon
phenomena,al, OF THE INCREDIBLE,
    EXTRAORDINARY
phenomenal,ly,lism,list,listic,listically,
    INCREDIBLE, EXTRAORDINARy
phenomenon,*, STRANGE/
    UNCHARACTERISTIC BEHAVIOR/
    EVENT, GIVEN TO THE INVISIBLE
phenominon, phenomenon

pheroh, pharaoh
phesant, pheasant
phesasist, physicist
phesek, physique / physic
pheselity, facility
phesent, pheasant
pheseology, physiology
phesesist, physicist
phesic, physic / physique
phesility, facility
phesint, pheasant
phesod, facade
phesunt, pheasant
phil, PREFIX INDICATING "LOVE" MOST
    OFTEN MODIFIES THE WORD
philadendron, philodendron
philanthrapist, philanthropy(pist)
philanthropek, philanthropy(pic)
philanthropy,pies,pic,pical,pically,pist,
    GIVE TO MANKIND VIA A KIND ACT/
    MONEY, A BENEFACTOR
philarmonic, philharmonic
philasofical, philosophy(hical)
philasophical, philosophy(hical)
philermonic, philharmonic
philharmonic,*, LOVE OF HARMONICS,
    ENJOYMENT OF HARMONIC
    MUSICAL INSTRUMENTS
philodendron,*, A TROPICAL PLANT
philosofy, philosophy
philosophy,hies,her,hic,hical,hically,
    hize,hizer, ACQUISITION/
    ACCUMULATION OF WISDOM
    WHETHER PHYSICAL OR
    METAPHYSICAL
philudindron, philodendron
philurmonic, philharmonic
phinaminan, phenomenon
phinaumena, phenomena
phinetik, phonetic / fanatic
phinite, finite
phinomenal, phenomenal
phinominan, phenomenon
phisasist, physicist
phisecal, physical
phisek, physique / physic
phiseks, physics
phiseologikul, physiology(gical)
phiseology, physiology
phisesist, physicist
phishen, fission
phisic, physic / physique
phisical, physical
phisiks, physics

phisiology, physiology
phisisist, physicist
phisyological, physiology(gical)
phisyologist, physiology(gist)
phlabadumist, phlebotomy(mist)
phlabitis, phlebitis
phlabodumist, phlebotomy(mist)
phlabotomy, phlebotomy
phlebitis,ic, VEIN INFLAMMATION/
SWELLING
phlebodomist, phlebotomy(mist)
phlebotomy,mic,mist,mize, OPENING
VEINS TO RELIEVE PRESSURE
phlegm,my, MUCUS
phlem, phlegm
phlibites, phlebitis
phlibodumist, phlebotomy(mist)
phlibotomy, phlebotomy
phlim, phlegm
phlubotomy, phlebotomy
phnegraf, phonograph
phobea, phobia
phobia,*,bic, UNFOUNDED FEAR, NO
APPARENT REASON FOR FEAR/
DREAD
phodagraf, photo(graph)
phodasinthesis, photosynthesis
phodegraf, photo(graph)
phodesinthesis, photosynthesis
phodo, photo
phodograf, photo(graph)
phodon, photon
phodosynthesis, photosynthesis
phodugraf, photo(graph)
phon, PREFIX INDICATING "SOUND"
MOST OFTEN MODIFIES THE WORD
(or see phone/fawn)
phone,*,ed,ning, SPEAKING/HEARING
COMMUNICATION DEVICE
"prefixes: inter"
phonegraph, phonograph
phoneme,*,mic,mics, DISTINCT
SOUNDS OF LETTERS
phonetic,*,cal,cally, HOW WORDS ARE
HEARD/SPOKEN/TRANSMITTED,
THE SOUND/AUDIO CONCERNING
WORDS "prefixes: un"
phonic,*, IDENTIFYING/SPELLING
WORDS ACCORDING TO THEIR
SOUNDS
phonigraf, phonograph
phonimic, phoneme(mic)
phonograph,*,hic,hical,hically, RECORD
PLAYER

phony,ney,nies,nier,niest,nily,niness,
FAKE, NOT REAL (also spelled
phoney)
phosfade, phosphate
phosfate, phosphate
phosphate,*, A CHEMICAL/SALT
phot, PREFIX INDICATING "LIGHT"
MOST OFTEN MODIFIES THE WORD
photagraf, photo(graph)
photasinthesis, photosynthesis
photigraf, photo(graph)
photo,*,ograph,ographable,ographer,
ography,ographic,ogenic, ogenically,
PICTURE CREATED IN A PROCESS
USING LIGHT "prefixes: un"
photograf, photo(graph)
photon,*,nic, A QUANTUM PARTICLE
WITH NO MASS/CHARGE
photosinthesis, photosynthesis
photosynthesis,ize,etic,etically,
PROCESS WHERE PLANTS TURN
LIGHT INTO ENERGY
photugraf, photo(graph)
phsycist, physicist
phulanthrapy, philanthropy
phulicity, felicity
phulosefy, philosophy
phunamina, phenomenon
phunomenal, phenomenal
phusility, facility
phuzek, physique
phycisian, physician
phycisist, physicist
physasist, physicist
physecal, physical
physek, physique / physic
physeks, physics
physekul, physical
physeological, physiology(gical)
physeology, physiology
physeshan, physician
physesist, physicist
physi, PREFIX INDICATING "PHYSICAL/
NATURAL" MOST OFTEN MODIFIES
THE WORD
physic,*,cist, OF NATURE (or see
physique/physics)
physical,*,lly,lity,lities, CAN BE SEEN/
SENSED WITH THE EYE, AN EXAM
physician,*, LICENSED TO PRACTICE
MEDICINE
physicist,*, ONE WHO STUDIES PHYSICS

physico, PREFIX INDICATING
"PHYSICAL/NATURAL" MOST OFTEN
MODIFIES THE WORD
physics,cist, THE STUDY OF SUBATOMIC
PARTICLES, A SCIENCE (or see
physic/physique) "prefixes: bio"
physik, physique / physic
physiology,gist,gical,gically,gist,
CONCERNING PLANTS/ANIMALS,
SCIENCE OF NATURE
physique, PHYSICAL BODY/STRUCTURE
physisist, physicist
phyt, PREFIX INDICATING "PLANT"
MOST OFTEN MODIFIES THE WORD
pi, GREEK LETTER WHICH STANDS FOR
MATHEMATICAL RATIO 3.141592
(or see pie/pea/pee)
pial, pile
pianeer, pioneer
piano,*, USING KEYS TO STRIKE
STRINGS OF THIS INSTRUMENT
HOUSED IN A LARGE WOODEN BOX
pibe, pipe
pic,*, SMALL/TRIANGULAR/FLAT/RIGID
ITEM USED TO STRUM STRINGS OF
A MUSICAL INSTRUMENT (or see
pick/pig/pique/peak/peek/pike)
picalo, piccolo
piccolo,*,list, INSTRUMENT/FLUTE
picdorul, pectoral / pictorial
pich, pitch / peach
pichen, pigeon
picher, pitcher / picture
pichon, pigeon
pichur, pitcher / picture
pichy, pitch(y)
pick,*,ked,king,kier,kiest,ky,ker,
CHOOSE/SELECT FROM AMONGST
OTHERS, ACQUIRE (or see pic/pig/
pique/peak/ peek/pike) "prefixes:
un"
pickalo, piccolo
picket,*,ter,ted,ting, WOODEN POST
WITH SHARPENED END, BARRIER/
FENCE AS IN A UNION STRIKE, POST
GUARD
pickle,*,ed,ling, TO SOAK/MARINATE
FOOD IN A BRINE/SALT SOLUTION
picknic, picnic
pickul, pickle
picnic,*, A LUNCH OUTDOORS
picol, pickle
picon, pecan
picsher, picture / pitcher

pict, pick(ed) / pig(gged)

picter, picture / pitcher

pictorial,*,lly,lism,lness, VISION/ ENVISIONED AS A PICTURE

picture,*,ed,ring, A VISUAL REPRESENTATION OF A SCENE

piculear, peculiar

pid, pit

pide, pity

pidestreun, pedestrian

pidi, pity

pidiatrics, pediatrics

pidiatrishan, pediatrician

pidy, pity

pie,*, FOOD ITEM INCORPORATING A CRUST AND FILLING (or see pi)

piece,*,ed,cing,er, ONE PART OF THE WHOLE, ONE AMONGST MANY (or see peace)

piel, pile

pieneer, pioneer

pieni, peony

pieno, piano

pier,*, MANMADE OUTCROP ON THE WATER FOR DOCKING BOATS/ FISHING (or see peer/pierce/pyre)

pierce,*,ed,cing,cingly, TO PENETRATE/ PUNCTURE (or see peer(s)/pier(s))

pies, pious

piethon, python

pif, peeve

pig,*,gged,gging,ggish,ggy, DOMESTICATED SWINE/BOAR (or see peg/pick/pic)

pigal, pickle

pigamus, pajamas

pigated, picket(ed)

pigen, pigeon

pigeon,*, A CITY BIRD, OF THE DOVE FAMILY

piget, picket

pigeted, picket(ed)

pigil, pickle

pigin, pigeon

pigit, picket

pigle, pickle

pigme, pygmy

pigmi, pygmy

pigul, pickle

pigy, pig(ggy)

pijamus, pajamas

pijen, pigeon

pik, pic / pick / pike / pig

pikal, pickle

pikalo, piccolo

pikcher, picture / pitcher

pikchir, picture / pitcher

pikchor, picture / pitcher

pikchr, picture / pitcher

pikchur, picture / pitcher

pikd, pick(ed) / pique(d)

pike,*,ed,king, A FISH, STAFF WITH POINTED TIP USED AS WEAPON/ TOOL, A POINT, TURNPIKE (or see pick/pig/ pique/peak/peek)

pikel, pickle

piker, pick(er)

piket, picket

pikeust, pick(iest)

piki, pick(y)

pikiest, pick(kiest)

pikir, pick(er)

pikit, picket

pikl, pickle

pikle, pickle

piknik, picnic

pikol, pickle

pikon, pecan

piksher, picture / pitcher

pikshor, picture / pitcher

pikshr, picture / pitcher

pikt, pick(ed) / pique(d)

piktorul, pectoral / pictorial

pikture, picture / pitcher

pikul, pickle

pikuleur, peculiar

pikur, pick(er)

piky, pig(ggy) / pick(y)

pil, pill / pile / peel

pilach, pillage

pilaf, ASIAN STYLE OF RICE

pilage, pillage

pilar, pillar

pilaredy, polar(ity)

pile,*,ed,ling,lings, MOUND/ ACCUMULATION OF SOMETHING, A POST/ TIMBER/PILLAR WITH POINTED END, NAP OF FABRIC, HEMORRHOIDS (or see peel/pill)

pilech, pillage

pileg, pillage

pilej, pillage

pilengs, pile(lings)

piler, pillar

pilerity, polar(ity)

pilese, police

pilet, pilot

pilgrim,*,mage, ORIGINAL SETTLERS IN AMERICA FROM EUROPE, THOSE WHO TRAVEL TO UNSEEN PLACES

pilich, pillage

pilig, pillage

pilij, pillage

pilite, polite / pilot

pill,*, TABLET/CAPSULES

pillach, pillage

pillage,*,ed,ging, TO GO THROUGH OTHER PEOPLES STUFF, TO PLUNDER/ TAKE AWAY/STEAL

pillar,*, A POST/MONUMENT/SUPPORT

pillow,*, A CUSHION, HEAD SUPPORT WHEN LYING DOWN, CUSHION TO PROTECT FROM HARM

pilo, pillow

pilot,*,ted,ting,tage,tless, ONE WHO NAVIGATES/OPERATES A VESSEL, ONE THAT STEERS, FLAME ON A GAS APPLIANCE

pilow, pillow

pils, pill(s) / pile(s) / peel(s)

piluch, pillage

piludge, pillage

piluge, pillage

pilur, pillar

pilushen, pollute(tion)

pilut, pilot / pollute

pilutent, pollute(tant)

pilution, pollute(tion)

pimento,*, A SWEET PEPPER

pimp,*,ped,ping, VIOLENT/ABUSIVE PERSON WHO CAPITALIZES OFF OF WOMEN, INSIGNIFICANT, PETTY, COOL

pimpel, pimple

pimple,*, INFLAMED SKIN PORES

pimpul, pimple

pin,*,nned,nning,nner, TO FASTEN, SHARP TIPPED THIN OBJECT (or see pen/pent/pine) "prefixes: un"

pinacle, pentacle / pinnacle

pinada, pinata

pinagon, pentagon

pinagram, pentagram

pinakle, pinnacle / pentacle

pinalty, penal(ty)

pinaple, pineapple

pinapple, pineapple

pinasilun, penicillin

pinata,*, A PAPIER MACHE PARTY DECORATION FILLED WITH GOODIES FOR CHILDREN

pinatentiary, penitentiary
pinatrate, penetrate
pinatruble, penetrable
pinc, pink
pincers, USED FOR GRIPPING,
    CLAWLIKE (or see pinch(ers))
pinch,hes,hed,hing,her, SQUEEZE
    TOGETHER FOR HOLDING
    SOMETHING, TWO SIDES COMING
    TOGETHER (or see pincers)
pinchent, penchant
pinchers, pinch(ers) / pincers
pind, pine(d) / pin(nned)
pindalem, pendulum
pindent, pendant / pendent
pinding, pending
pindlum, pendulum
pindo, pinto
pindulum, pendulum
pine,*,ed,ning, EVERGREEN TREE,
    PAINFULLY LONG FOR SOMEONE/
    SOMETHING (or see pain/pane)
pineal gland, PINE CONE SHAPED
    ORGAN IN THE BODY WHICH
    SECRETES MELATONIN
pineapple,*, A TROPICAL FRUIT
pinecillin, penicillin
pinecle, pinnacle / pentacle
pineer, pioneer
pinegon, pentagon
pineng, pine(ning) / pin(nning)
pines, pine(s) / penis
pinetentiary, penitentiary
pinetrate, penetrate
pingalum, pendulum
pinguin, penguin
pingwen, penguin
pinial gland, pineal gland
piniselin, penicillin
pinitenchery, penitentiary
pinjalum, pendulum
pinjulim, pendulum
pink,*,ky, A COLOR, THE LITTLE FINGER
    ON THE HAND
pinkwen, penguin
pinnacle,*, PEAK/POINT/CREST/CONE
    (or see pentacle)
pinol, penal
pinos, penis
pinot, peanut
pinotrashen, penetrate(tion)
pinotrate, penetrate
pinsel, pencil
pinsers, pincers / pinch(ers)

pinshen, pension
pinshent, penchant
pinsil, pencil
pinsion, pension
pinsul, pencil
pint,*, A U.S. FORM OF MEASUREMENT
    FOR LIQUIDS (or see paint/pine(d)/
    pent/pin(nned))
pintacle, pentacle / pinnacle
pintagon, pentagon
pintagram, pentagram
pintalum, pendulum
pintegon, pentagon
pinting, pending
pinto,*, SPOTTED HORSE/BEAN
pintucle, pentacle / pinnacle
pintulem, pendulum
pinugram, pentagram
pinukle, pinnacle / pentacle
pinulize, penal(ize)
pinulty, penal(ty)
pinusilun, penicillin
pinut, peanut
pinutentiary, penitentiary
pinutrashen, penetrate(tion)
pinutrate, penetrate
pinutruble, penetrable
piny, penny / pine(y)
pinyada, pinata
pioneer,*,red,ring, ONE WHO
    DISCOVERS NEW TERRITORY/THE
    UNKNOWN
pious,sly,sness, HOLIER THAN THOU,
    INTENSELY MOTIVATED ABOUT
    THEIR GOD, REVERENCE FOR
pipe,*,ed,ping, TUBULAR/HOLLOW
    FORM
piporshenal, proportion(al)
pique,*,ed,uing, HEIGHTEN/STIMULATE,
    RIBBED/RAISED EFFECT (or see
    peak/peek)
piquleur, peculiar
pir, per / purr / peer / pier
pirade, parade / pirate
piraet, pirouette
piralusis, paralysis
piramid, pyramid
pirana, piranha
piranha,*, FLESH EATING FRESH WATER
    FISH (or see prana)
pirat, parade / pirate
pirate,*,ed,ting,acy, ONE WHO
    TRAVERSES THE SEAS STEALING
    FROM OTHERS, TAKE FROM

OTHERS WITHOUT PERMISSION
    "prefixes: bio"
pirbendikuler, perpendicular
pirceive, perceive
pircent, percent
pirceptible, perceptible
pirch, perch / purge
pirchus, purchase / perch(es)
pircushen, percussion
pircusion, percussion
pirdly, pert(ly)
piremid, pyramid
pireneal, perennial
pireod, period
pireodic, periodic / periotic
pireodontic, periodontic
pireodontist, periodontist
pireot, period
pireoticul, periodic(al)
piret, pirate
pireud, period
pireut, period
pirews, peruse
pirfect, perfect
pirfekd, perfect
pirferted, pervert(ed)
pirfeum, perfume
pirfikt, perfect
pirfium, perfume
pirform, perform
pirformence, perform(ance)
pirfume, perfume
pirgatory, purgatory
pirge, purge
pirger, perjure
pirgery, perjure(ry)
pirgetory, purgatory
pirgury, perjure(ry)
pirgutory, purgatory
pirhaps, perhaps
piright, pyrite
piriodontic, periodontic
piriodontist, periodontist
pirit, pirate / pyrite
pirje, purge
pirjury, perjure(ry)
pirkrastination, procrastinate
pirkushen, percussion
pirmanence, permanence
pirmanent, permanent
pirmeate, permeate
pirmenant, permanent
pirmesabul, permissible
pirmet, permit

pirmeuble, permeable
pirmishen, permission
pirmisive, permissive
pirmisuf, permissive
pirmit, permit
pirmition, permission
pirmnent, permanent
piro, pyro
piroet, pirouette
pirogative, prerogative
pirokside, peroxide
pirole, parole
pirona, piranha
pirosedy, porosity
pirosity, porosity
pirot, pirate
pirouette,*, TO TWIRL ABOUT ON THE
    TIPS OF TOES
piroxside, peroxide
pirpechuel, perpetual
pirpendicular, perpendicular
pirpes, purpose
pirpeshual, perpetual
pirpesly, purpose(ly)
pirpetrate, perpetrate
pirpetshuate, perpetual(ate)
pirpetual, perpetual
pirpetuate, perpetual(ate)
pirpetuity, perpetuity
pirpis, purpose
pirpisly, purpose(ly)
pirple, purple
pirpleksity, perplex(ity)
pirplexity, perplex(ity)
pirporshenal, proportion(al)
pirportional, proportion(al)
pirpos, purpose
pirposful, purpose(ful)
pirposly, purpose(ly)
pirpus, purpose
pirpusly, purpose(ly)
pirputrate, perpetrate
pirs, purse / pierce / peer(s) / pier(s)
pirsacute, persecute
pirsavere, persevere
pirsbektif, perspective
pirsbiration, perspiration
pirsbire, perspire
pirscripshen, prescript(ion)
pirscription, prescript(ion)
pirsebtef, percept(ive)
pirsecute, persecute
pirsen, person
pirsenal, personal

pirsenaledy, personality
pirsenality, personality
pirsenaly, personal(lly)
pirsenel, personnel
pirsent, percent
pirsentage, percent(age)
pirsenuble, person(able)
pirsenulize, personal(ize)
pirseptable, perceptible
pirseptive, percept(ive)
pirseshen, precision
pirsest, persist
pirsestans, persist(ence)
pirseve, perceive
pirseverense, persevere(rance)
pirsh, perch / purge
pirshes, purchase / perch(es)
pirsikute, persecute
pirsinuble, person(able)
pirsinulize, personal(ize)
pirsistence, persist(ence)
pirskripshen, prescript(ion)
pirson, person
pirsona, person(a)
pirsonality, personality
pirsonefication, person(ification)
pirsonel, personnel / personal
pirsonification, person(ification)
pirsonifikashen, person(ification)
pirsonify, personify
pirsonuble, person(able)
pirsoo, pursue
pirspective, perspective
pirspektif, perspective
pirspiration, perspiration
pirspire, perspire
pirsu, pursue
pirsuade, persuade
pirsuasion, persuade(asion)
pirsuasive, persuade(asive)
pirsude, pursue(d)
pirsunal, personal / personnel
pirsunel, personnel / personal
pirsute, pursue(uit)
pirsuvere, persevere
pirswade, persuade
pirswashen, persuade(asion)
pirswasif, persuade(asive)
pirt, pert
pirtain, pertain
pirtane, pertain
pirtly, pert(ly)
pirtray, portray
pirtrayal, portray(al)

pirturb, perturb
pirumid, pyramid
piruse, peruse
pirut, pirate
pirvade, pervade
pirvashen, pervade(asion) / provision
pirvasif, pervade(asion)
pirvershen, pervert(rsion)
pirversive, pervert(rsive)
pirvert, pervert
pirvirsev, pervert(rsive)
piryte, pyrite
pirzukewt, persecute
pis, peace / piece / pie(s) / pea(s)
pisa, pizza
pisdachio, pistachio
pisdasheo, pistachio
pisdrome, pastrami
pises, possess
piseshen, position
pisesif, possess(ive)
pisher, pitcher / picture
piskrepshin, prescript(ion)
pistachio,*, AN EDIBLE NUT
pistasheo, pistachio
pisten, piston
pistil,*,llate, PART OF A FLOWER (or see
    pistol)
pistol,*,led,ling, HANDGUN/FIREARM
    (or see pistil)
piston,*, PART OF AN ENGINE
pistrome, pastrami
pistul, pistil / pistol / pestle
pistun, piston
pit,*,tted,tting, THE SEED OF A FRUIT, A
    HOLLOWED DEPRESSION (or see
    pet/peat)
pitado, potato
pitaseum, potassium
pitasium, potassium
pitato, potato
pitch,hes,hed,hing,hy, TAR, BASEBALL
    MANEUVER "prefixes: over/un"
pitcher,*, POSITION IN THE GAME OF
    BASEBALL, A VESSEL FOR HOLDING
    LIQUIDS (or see picture)
pite, pity
pitena, patina
pitenchul, potential
pitenshil, potential
pithon, python
piti, pity
pitifol, pity(tiful)
pitina, patina

pitinshil, potential
pitnik, picnic
pitrol, patrol
pitroleum, petrol(eum)
pitrood, protrude
pitrude, protrude
pitrushen, protrude(usion)
pitsa, pizza
pituitary,ries, PERTAINING TO A GLAND
PRODUCING HORMONES
pitunia, petunia
piturbed, perturb(ed)
pity,ties,tied,tying,tier,tiful,tifully,
tifulness,tiless,tilessly,tilessness,
ying,tiable, tiably,tiableness, FEEL
SYMPATHY/GRIEF/COMPASSION
FOR SOMEONE
piu, pew
piuder, pewter
piul, pile
piuneer, pioneer
piuny, puny
pius, pious
piuter, pewter
piutrid, putrid
piv, peeve
pivurted, pervert(ed)
piwrite, pyrite
piwro, pyro
pix, pick(s) / pic(s)
piyuree, puree'
pizdromy, pastrami
pizes, possess
piztacheo, pistachio
pizza,*, A FLAT BREAD WITH OTHER
FOODS COOKED ON TOP OF IT
pla, play
placard,*, FLAT CARD DISPLAYING
INFORMATION
placate,*,ed,ting,er,tion,tive,tory, TO
PACIFY/APPEASE/LET THEM HAVE
THEIR WAY
place,*,ed,cing,ement, POSITION/AREA
"prefixes: dis/mis/re/un"
placebo,*, AN IMITATION/FAKE,
PRETENDING TO BE THE REAL
THING
placed, placid / place(d)
placenta,*,al,ary,ation, LINING OF A
MAMMALS WOMB/UTERUS WHICH
HOLDS THE FETUS
placerd, placard
placid,dity,dness,dly, CALM/GENTLE/
QUIET

plack, plaque
placment, place(ment)
placurd, placard
plad, plaid / plait / play(ed) / plate
pladenum, platinum
plader, platter
pladform, platform
pladinum, platinum
pladir, platter
pladnum, platinum
pladur, platter
plaeng, play(ing)
plag, plague
plagarism, plagiarism
plager, please(sure)
plagerism, plagiarism
plagiarism,st,stic,ize,izes,ized,izing,izer,
COPY SOMEONE ELSES WORK
WITHOUT PERMISSION
plagiresm, plagiarism
plague,*,ed,uing, A SPREADING
DISEASE WHICH CAUSES HARM, A
NUISANCE (or see plaque)
plagur, please(sure)
plagurism, plagiarism
plai, play / ply
plaid,*,ded, A CROSS WEAVING
PATTERN (or see plait/play(ed))
plaigerism, plagiarism
plain,*,nly,nness, WITHOUT ACCENTS/
ORNAMENTS, NO OUTSTANDING
FEATURES (or see plane)
plait,*,ted,ting,ter, BRAID/ FOLD OVER/
INTERWOVEN (or see plate/plaid)
plajer, please(sure)
plajerism, plagiarism
plajir, please(sure)
plajur, please(sure)
plajurism, plagiarism
plak, plaque
plakard, placard
plakate, placate
plakurd, placard
plan,*,nned,nning,nner, TO CONTRIVE/
DREAM/CONJURE/DESIGN (or see
plane/plain) "prefixes: un"
planaterium, planetary(rium)
plancton, plankton
plane,*,ed,ning,er,nar,narity, FLAT/
LEVEL SURFACE, FLYING VESSEL (or
see plan/plain) "prefixes: bi/de/en/
uni"
planet,*, A SPHERICAL BODY IN SPACE

planetary,rium,riums, OF/CONCERNING
BODIES OF MATTER IN SPACE
planit, planet
planitareum, planetary(rium)
plank,*,ked,king, FLAT/WIDE BOARD
plankton,nic, TINY WATER ORGANISMS
plant,*,ted,ting,ter, ORGANISM WHICH
TRANSFORMS LIGHT ENERGY AND
HAS NO NERVOUS SYSTEM, TO
TAKE A STAND, TAKE ROOT
"prefixes: re"
plantain,*, ANTI-BACTERIAL/
INFLAMMATORY/VIRAL/HEALING
PLANT
plantane, plantain
plantashen, plantation
plantation,*, ESTATE WHICH GROWS
LARGE FIELDS OF CROPS
planter,*, VESSEL/CONTAINER WHICH
HOLDS PLANTS/DIRT
planut, planet
plaque,*, A COATING OF SOMETHING,
A FLAT BOARD WITH TEXT
COMMEMORATING SOMEONE
plasa, plaza
plasdur, plaster
plasebo, placebo
plased, placid
plashur, please(sure)
plasible, plausible
plasinta, placenta
plasit, placid
plasma,mic, CONCERNS THE BLOOD
"prefixes: endo"
plasment, place(ment)
plastek, plastic
plaster,*,red,ring,ry, A GYSUM OR
OTHER PASTE MATERIAL THAT
SPREADS, TO COAT WITH
plastic,*, MOLDABLE/VERSATILE
SUBSTANCE
plasu, plaza
plasuble, plausible
plat,*,tted,tting, MAP/CHART/PLOT, A
BRAID (or see plate/plait/play(ed))
platau, plateau
plate,*,ed,ting, FLAT/ROUND VESSEL
(or see plat/plait/play(ed))
"prefixes: retro"
plateau,*, ELEVATED AREA OF LAND
WITH A FLAT TOP
platepus, platypus
plater, platter

platform,*, ELEVATED FORM WITH A FLAT TOP/AREA
platibus, platypus
platinum,*, A METAL
platipus, platypus
platir, platter
platnem, platinum
platnum, platinum
plato, plateau
platonic,ism,ist,istic,ize, LOVE/ FRIENDSHIP WITHOUT SEX, SPIRITUAL, OF PLATO
platoon,*, A GROUP/UNIT IN MILITARY
platter,*, A FLAT PLATE/VESSEL
platur, platter
platypus,ses,pi, UNDERWATER MAMMAL WITH BIRD-LIKE QUALITIES
plauding, plod(dding) / plot(tting)
plausible,bility,eness,ly,ive, POSSIBLE/ CONVINCING
plauteng, plod(dding) / plot(tting)
plaw, plow
play,*,yed,ying,yer,yful,yfully,yfulness, BEHAVE CHEERFULLY/JOYFULLY/ HAPPY "prefixes: inter/over/re/ under"
playkate, placate
plaza, A SQUARE CITY CENTER/TOWN
plazma, plasma
plaztek, plastic
plea,*,ad, BEG/DECLARE/ARGUE FOR (or see pleat)
plead,*,ded,ding,dable,der, BEG/ DECLARE/ARGUE FOR (or see pleat) "prefixes: inter/mis"
pleasant,try,tly,tness,try,tries, AMIABLE/ENJOYABLE/ UNDRAMATIC EXPERIENCE "prefixes: un"
please,*,ed,sing,singly,singness,surable, surableness,surably,sure,sures, sured, SATISFY/QUENCH/APPEASE/ PROVIDE COMFORT "prefixes: dis"
pleat,*,ted,ter, FOLDS/CREASES (or see plead)
plecebo, placebo
plecenta, placenta
plech, pledge
plecher, please(sure)
plecht, pledge(d)
plechur, please(sure)
plecksiglass, plexiglass
plecseglas, plexiglass

plecsiglas, plexiglass
pleded, plea(ded)
pledge,*,ed,ging,ger, OFFER A PROMISE/GUARANTEE
pledonic, platonic
pleduble, plea(dble)
pleed, plead
plees, please / plea(s)
pleet, pleat / plead
plege, pledge
pleger, please(sure)
plegeurism, plagiarism
plegir, please(sure)
plegt, pledge(d)
plegur, please(sure)
pleig, plague
plein, plain / plane
pleit, plait / plate
pleje, pledge
plejer, please(sure)
plejir, please(sure)
plejor, please(sure)
plejur, please(sure)
pleksaglass, plexiglass
pleksiglass, plexiglass
plendiful, plenty(tiful)
plendy, plenty
plentaful, plenty(tiful)
plenty,tiful,tifully,tifulness,teous, teously,teousness, ENOUGH/ AMPLE AMOUNT
pleral, plural
pleril, plural
ples, please / plea(s)
plesant, pleasant
plesebo, placebo
plesent, pleasant
pleser, pleas(sure) / please(r)
plesher, please(sure)
pleshur, please(sure)
plesinta, placenta
plesunt, pleasant
plesure, please(r)
plet, pleat / plead
pleted, plea(ded)
pleto, plateau
pletonic, platonic
pletoon, platoon
pletune, platoon
plewm, plume
plewrel, plural
plewtonium, plutonium
plexaglass, plexiglass
plexiglass, CLEAR SHEET OF PLASTIC

plez, please / plea(s)
plezent, pleasant
plezint, pleasant
pli, ply / plea
pliable,bility,eness,ly, BENDABLE/ FLEXIBLE
plicebo, placebo
plieble, pliable
plight,*, SITUATION/CONDITION (or see polite)
plintaful, plenty(tiful)
plinty, plenty
plirul, plural
plis, please / ply(lies)
plisebo, placebo
plisenta, placenta
plit, plight / polite / pleat
plito, plateau
plitonic, platonic
plitune, platoon
pliuble, pliable
pliwood, plywood
pliwute, plywood
ploc, pluck
plod,*,dded,dding,ddingly,dder, MOVE ABOUT WITHOUT ENTHUSIASM, IN THE DOLDRUMS, HEAVY/SLOW WALKING (or see plot)
ploded, plod(dded)/ plot(tted)
plodeng, plod(dding)/ plot(tting)
ploding, plod(dding) / plot(tting)
ploe, ploy
plog, plug
ploi, ploy
plom, plum / plumb / plume / plump
plomber, plumb(er)
plomer, plumb(er)
plomet, plummet
plomp, plump
plomr, plumb(er)
ploom, plume
plop,*,pped,pping, SOUND/ MOVEMENT RESEMBLING DROPPING SOMETHING HEAVY/ FLAT
ploped, plop(pped)
plopt, plop(pped)
plos, plus
ploseble, plausible
plosh, plush
plosible, plausible
plot,*,tted,tting,tter,ttage, MAP/PLAN/ CHART OUT (or see plod) "prefixes: sub/under"

ploted, plot(tted)
ploteng, plod(dding) / plot(tting)
ploter, plot(tter)
plotoon, platoon
plotune, platoon
plow,*,wed,wing,wable,wer, PHYSICALLY CAUSE TO TURN OVER/ ROLL/REARRANGE "prefixes: un"
plowee, ploy
ploy,*, A TRICK
plozible, plausible
pluc, pluck
plucenta, placenta
pluck,*,ked,ker,king,ky,kily,kiness, PULL STRINGS ON INSTRUMENT, REMOVE FEATHERS
pludonic, Platonic
plug,*,gged,gging, AN OBJECT WHICH FILLS/FITS INTO HOLES, SHOOT, BULLET (or see pluck) "prefixes: un"
pluk, pluck / plug
plum,*, A FRUIT (or see plumb/plume)
plumb,*,bed,ber,bing, USE PIPES TO TRANSPORT LIQUIDS/GAS, TO SQUARE/ MAKE LEVEL (or see plum) "prefixes: un"
plume,*,ed,ming,my, BILLOWY CLOUD OF MATTER FROM VOLCANO, BIRD'S FEATHERS (or see plum/ plumb)
plumer, plumb(er)
plumit, plummet
plummet,*,ted,ting, FALL STRAIGHT DOWN, USED TO TEST FOR PERPENDICULAR LEVEL
plump,ply,pish, ROUND/FULL/CHUBBY, HEAVY FALLING SOUND (or see plumb)
plunch, plunge
plunder,*,red,ring,rer,rable,rous,rage, TO FORCIBLY ROB
plunge,*,ed,ging,er, DIVE/DELVE/ THRUST INTO
plunje, plunge
plunter, plunder
plural,lly,lism,list,listic,lity,lities,lize, lized,lizing,lization, MORE THAN ONE
plus,ses, TO ADD/GAIN/POSITIVE "prefixes: non"
plusebo, placebo
plusenta, placenta
plush,hier,hiest,hy,hly, THICK/SOFT/ LUXURIOUS

plusinta, placenta
pluto, plateau
plutonic, platonic
plutonium, A CHEMICAL ELEMENT
plutoon, platoon
plutune, platoon
pluwrel, plural
ply,lies,lied,ying,liable, TO DO/ FURNISH/WORK AT, OF LAYERS
plyible, pliable
plys, ply(lies) / please
plyt, plight / polite
plyuble, pliable
plywood, FORMED SHEET CONSISTING OF LAYERS OF WOOD/COMPOSITE
plywude, plywood
plywute, plywood
pneumatic,*,cally, USING COMPRESSION TO OPERATE TOOLS, AIR/GAS SCIENCE
pneumonia,ic, LUNG INFLAMMATION
pnewmatic, pneumatic
pnumatic, pneumatic
pnumonia, pneumonia
poach,hes,hed,hing,her, WAY TO COOK EGGS, UNLAWFULLY TAKE/KILL ANIMALS/FISH (or see pouch)
poatry, poetry
pob, pub
poblec, public
poblecher, publish(er)
poblecis, publicize
poblecist, publicist
poblek, public
poblesh, publish
poblesist, publicist
poblesiz, publicize
poblic, public
poblicis, publicize
poblicist, publicist
poblisest, publicist
poblisher, publish(er)
poblisist, publicist
poblisiz, publicize
poc, poke / pock
pocediv, positive
poces, possess
poceshen, possess(ion)
pocetion, possess(ion)
pocetiv, positive
poch, poach
pocht, poach(ed)
pock, SCAR/PIT/ERUPTION ON THE SKIN (or see poke)

pocker, poker
pocket,*,ted,ting,tful, A FOLD IN CLOTHING WHICH HOLDS THINGS, STORAGE PLACE IN CLOTHING
pocks, pox
pocreate, procreate
pod,*,dded,dding, THAT WHICH ENVELOPES SOME OF MANY (or see pot) "prefixes: uni"
podable, potable
podary, potter(y)
pode, potty
podebul, potable
poded, pot(tted) / pod(dded)
podel, puddle / poodle
podend, potent
podeng, pudding
podensy, potent(ncy)
podent, potent
poder, potter
podery, potter(y)
podestrein, pedestrian
podeum, podium
podibul, potable
podid, pot(tted) / pod(dded)
podind, potent
poding, pudding
podinsy, potent(ncy)
podir, potter
podiry, potter(y)
podium,*, A PLATFORM FOR SPEAKERS, PEDESTAL
podl, puddle
podlach, potlatch
podlage, potlatch
podluk, potluck
podol, puddle
podpory, potpourri
poduble, potable
podunsy, potent(ncy)
podur, potter
podury, potter(y)
pody, potty
poed, poet
poedik, poet(ic)
poem,*, TEXT/WRITINGS WHICH DEPICT A STORY/THOUGHT/ EMOTION
poenseda, poinsettia
poenseta, poinsettia
poent, point
poenyent, poignant
poenzeda, poinsettia
poes, poise / pose

poesin, poison
poet,*,tic,tical,tically,ticize,ticized,
    ticizing, SOMEONE WHO WRITES/IS
    GIVEN TO POETRY
poetry, LITERARY VERSE PROJECTING
    EMOTIONS/EVENT/IDEA
poez, poise
poezun, poison
pof, puff
poferdy, poverty
pofirty, poverty
pofurdee, poverty
poger, poker
poid, poet
poignant,tly,ncy, TO THE POINT,
    PRECISE, EXACT
poim, poem
poinant, poignant
poinseda, poinsettia
poinsettia,*, A SEASONAL FLOWERING
    PLANT
point,*,ted,ter,ting,ty,tless,tlessly,
    tlessness, THE TIP, DIRECT, AIM,
    SHOW, PRIMARY THEME/ISSUE
poinyent, poignant
poinzeta, poinsettia
poise,ed, IN POSITION TO, SUSPENDED
    ACTION, IN EQUILIBRIUM
poison,*,ned,ning,nous,nously, TOO
    HIGH A DOSE OF THIS WILL KILL,
    ABILITY TO HARM
poit, poet
poitry, poetry
poizen, poison
pok, poke / pock
pokd, poke(d)
poke,*,ed,king,ey, USE SOMETHING TO
    PRY/PUSH/MOVE, TO BE SLOW (or
    see pock)
poker, A CARD GAME, A TOOL
poket, pocket
pokit, pocket
pokreate, procreate
poks, pox
pokut, pocket
poky, poke(y)
pol, pole / poll / pool / pall
polar,rity,rities,rize,rization, OPPOSITE
    ELECTRICAL IMPULSE/ STREAM
    "prefixes: bi/de/re/sub/uni"
polaredy, polar(ity)
polarization, OF CELL ELECTRICAL
    SIGNALS "prefixes: re"

polarize,*,ed,zing,zation,zable,er,
    OPPOSITE FREQUENCY/PULSE/
    POLES
polatics, politic(s)
pold, poll(ed)
poldes, poultice
poldis, poultice
poldre, poultry
poldus, poultice
pole,*, ROD, STAFF, (too many
    definitions please see standard
    dictionary) (or see poll)
polegimy, polygamy
polegon, polygon
polegraf, polygraph
polegraph, polygraph
polehedron, polyhedron
polemur, polymer
polen, pollen
polenade, pollinate
polenate, pollinate
polenation, pollinate(tion)
polenize, pollen(ize)
poleo, polio
polep, polyp
poler, polar
polerize, polarize
polese, police
polesh, polish
polester, polyester
polesy, policy
polet, pullet
poletics, politic(s)
poleticul, politic(al)
poletishen, politic(ian)
poley, pulley
poli, pulley
police,*,ed,cing, KEEP WATCH OVER A
    DESIGNATED AREA, ONE WHO
    KEEPS WATCH
policy,cies, RULES ESTABLISHED BY
    PRINCIPLES WHICH GUIDE
    BUSINESS AFFAIRS
polie, pulley
poliester, polyester
poligamus, polygamy(mous)
poligamy, polygamy
poligine, polygyny
poligon, polygon
poligraf, polygraph
poligraph, polygraph
polihedren, polyhedron
polimer, polymer
polin, pollen

polinate, pollinate
polination, pollinate(tion)
polinize, pollen(ize)
polio, POLIOMYELITIS, A CRIPPLING
    DISEASE
polip, polyp
polir, polar
polirize, polarize
polis, police
polish,hes,hed,hing,her, USE
    CHEMICAL/FRICTION TO REMOVE
    OXYDATION, A NATIONALITY
polit, pullet
polite,ely,eness, CONSIDERATE,
    RESPECTFUL
politecal, politic(al)
politecize, politic(ize)
politeshen, politic(ian)
politic,*,cal,cally,cian,cize,cized,cizing,
    CONCERNING GOVERNMENT
    "prefixes: de"
politicize,*,ed,zing,zation, MAKE
    AWARE OF/ABOUT POLITICS
    "prefixes: de"
poll,*,lled,lling,ller, USED TO TAX/
    SURVEY/VOTE, PART OF HEAD
    WITH HAIR (or see pole) "prefixes:
    un"
pollen,*,nize,nizes,nized,nizer,nizing,
    nate,nia,nium, MICROSCOPIC
    SPORES PRODUCED BY PLANTS
pollenate, pollinate
pollinate,*,ed,ting,tion,tor,niferous,
    nize,nizes,nizer,nizing, POLLEN
    TRANSMITTED FROM ONE PLANT
    TO ANOTHER
pollute,*,ed,er,tant,ting,tion, HARMFUL
    (BYPRODUCTS) RELEASED INTO THE
    ENVIRONMENT "prefixes: de"
polm, palm
polomer, polymer
polre, polar
pols, poll(s) / pole(s) / pulse
polt, poll(ed)
poltes, poultice
poltice, poultice
poltis, poultice
poltree, poultry
poltry, poultry
poltus, poultice
polun, pollen
polunize, pollen(ize)
polup, polyp
polur, polar

polurize, polarize
polusee, policy
polushen, pollute(tion)
polusy, policy
polut, pullet / pollute
polutent, pollute(tant)
poluteshen, politic(ian)
polutics, politic(s)
polution, pollute(tion)
poly, PREFIX INDICATING "MANY" MOST OFTEN MODIFIES THE WORD
polyester,rification, CHEMICAL CHAIN WHICH IS USED TO MAKE PRODUCTS
polygamus, polygamy(mous)
polygamy,mist,mous, MAN/WOMAN HAVING MORE THAN ONE LEGAL PARTNER/SPOUSE AT A TIME (or see polygyny)
polyginy, polygyny
polygon,*,nal,nally, THREE OR MORE STRAIGHT SIDES
polygraph,*,hic, VERSATILE INSTRUMENT FOR REPLICATING/ RECORDING
polygyny,nous, HAVING MORE THAN ONE WIFE AT A TIME (or see polygamy)
polyhedren, polyhedron
polyhedron,*,ra,ral, A SOLID SURROUNDED BY MANY PLANED SURFACES
polymer,*,ric,rism,rization,rize, COMPOUNDS OF TWO OR MORE WITH A SIMILAR RELATIONSHIP
polymir, polymer
polyp,*,pous,pary, MANY GROWTHS/ TUMORS
pom, palm / poem
pomagranate, pomegranate
pombus, pompous
pomegranate,*, A FRUIT
pomel, pummel
pomigranate, pomegranate
pomil, pummel
pomkin, pumpkin
pomp, pump
pompis, pompous
pompkin, pumpkin
pompous,sly,sness, EXAGGERATED EXPRESSION TO SHOW SELFIMPORTANCE
pompus, pompous
pomugranate, pomegranate

pomul, pummel
pon, pawn
ponc, punk
ponchent, pungent
poncho,*, BLANKET/COAT
poncsher, puncture
poncshual, punctual
poncshuate, punctuate
ponctshur, puncture
pond,*, SMALL BODY OF WATER (or see pawn(ed))
ponder,*,rance,red,ring,rable,rer,rous, rously,rousness, TAKE TIME TO CONTEMPLATE SOMETHING "prefixes: pre"
pondificate, pontificate
pondir, ponder
pondoon, pontoon
pondune, pontoon
pondur, ponder
pone, pony
ponk, punk
ponsho, poncho
pont, pond / pawn(ed) / punt
pontcho, poncho
ponteficate, pontificate
ponter, ponder
pontificate,*,ed,ting,tion,tor, HAVE DOGMATIC CHARACTERISTICS, RELIGIOUS EXPRESSION
pontoon,*, FLOATS ON A PLANE IN PLACE OF WHEELS, A TYPE OF BOAT
pontune, pontoon
pontur, ponder
pony,nies, YOUNG/SMALL HORSE
pooch,hes, DOG
pood, put
pooding, pudding / putt(ing)
poodle,*, A BREED OF DOG (or see puddle)
pool,*,led,ling, PLACE TO SWIM, GAME USING BALLS/STICKS, COLLECTION/ ACCUMULATION OF LIQUID
poold, pull(ed) / pool(ed)
poolt, pull(ed) / pool(ed)
poor,rish,rly,rness, LACKING BASIC NECESSITIES (or see pore/pour)
poos, puss
poosh, push
pooshis, push(es)
pooshy, push(y)
poosy, puss(y)
poot, put
pootal, poodle

pooting, pudding / putt(ing)
pootle, poodle
pop,*,pped,pping,pper, A SOUND, A SOFT DRINK, SOMETHING BURSTING (or see pup)
popalashen, populate(tion)
popaler, popular
popcorn,*, COOKED CORN KERNEL
pope, pup(ppy) / poppy
popelashen, populate(tion)
popelur, popular
popery, potpourri
popet, puppet
popewlashen, populate(tion)
popewler, popular
popi, pup(ppy) / poppy
popilashen, populate(tion)
popiler, popular
poping, pop(pping)
popiry, potpourri
popit, puppet
popiuleit, populate
popkorn, popcorn
poplar,*, A TREE (or see popular)
poplashen, populate(tion)
poplur, poplar / popular
poporshenal, proportion(al)
poppy,ppies, A FLOWER
popree, potpourri
popt, pop(pped)
populachen, populate(tion)
popular,ly,rity,rize,rization,rizer, DESIRABLE BY MANY (or see poplar) "prefixes: un"
populashen, populate(tion)
populate,*,ed,ting,tion,list,lous,lously, lousness, TWO OR MORE THINGS THRIVING TOGETHER "prefixes: de/ over/sub"
populus, populate(lous)
popury, potpourri
popy, poppy
popya, papaya
por, poor / pour / pore
porc, pork / park
porcalin, porcelain
porcelain, FINE/TRANSLUCENT CERAMIC "prefixes: semi"
porcepine, porcupine
porch,hes, A PLATFORM/STOOP/ LANDING ADDED TO THE OUTSIDE OF A STRUCTURE
porchen, portion
porchun, portion

porcipine, porcupine
porcupine,*, LARGE RODENT WITH
    EXTERIOR QUILLS
pord, port / pour(ed)
pordable, portable
pordal, portal
pordeble, portable
pordel, portal
porder, porter
pordfolio, portfolio
pordible, portable
pordol, portal
porduble, portable
pordul, portal
pordur, porter
pore,*,ed,ring,rous, ONE OF MANY
    LOCATION ON THE SKIN/SURFACE
    FOR RESPIRATION, LOOK/EXAMINE
    WITH PERSERVERANCE (or see
    poor/pour)
pores, porous / pore(s)
porform, perform
poris, porous
pork,ky,ker, MEAT/OF PIGS/BOAR
porkepine, porcupine
porkewpine, porcupine
porkipine, porcupine
porkupine, porcupine
porogative, prerogative
porole, parole
porosity,sities, NUMBER/AMOUNT OF
    OPENINGS/PORES
porous,sly,sness, MANY OPENINGS/
    PORES
porpis, porpoise
porpoise,*, LARGE FISH THAT LOOKS
    LIKE A DOLPHIN, A CETACEAN
porpus, porpoise
porqupine, porcupine
porsalin, porcelain
porselan, porcelain
porsh, porch
porshin, portion
porsilan, porcelain
porsion, portion
porslin, porcelain
port,*,ted,ting,tly,table, A PLACE ON
    LAND WHERE VESSELS DOCK, TYPE
    OF WINE
portable,*,bility,bly, ABLE TO BE
    MOVED ABOUT EASILY
portal,*, OPENING ALLOWING ABILITY
    TO MOVE FROM ONE PLACE TO
    ANOTHER, PART OF THE LIVER

portch, porch
porteble, portable
porteon, portion
porter,*, AN ATTENDANT ON RAILCARS
portfolio,*, A DELIBERATE COLLECTION
    OF SPECIFIC PAPERS FOR
    PRESENTATION
portible, portable
portil, portal
portion,*,ned,ning, PART OF THE
    WHOLE "prefixes: pro"
portir, porter
portle, portal
portrait,*,tist, PAINTING/PHOTO OF A
    PERSON
portrat, portrait
portray,*,yed,ying,yal,yer, ATTEMPT TO
    PERSONIFY/DESCRIBE
portret, portrait
portuble, portable
portul, portal
portur, porter
porus, porous / peruse
porusness, porous(ness)
pos, pause / paw(s) / pose
posabiledy, possible(bility)
posability, possible(bility)
posative, positive
posatron, positron
posbone, postpone
poscher, posture
posd, post / pose(d)
posda, pasta
posdal, postal
posdchur, posture
posdel, postal
posder, poster / posture
posderety, posterior(ity)
posderior, posterior
posderity, posterior(ity)
posdil, postal
posdir, poster / posture
posdireor, posterior
posdle, postal
posdmark, postmark
posdpardum, postpartum
posdr, posture / poster
posdu, pasta
posdul, postal
posdulate, postulate
posdur, poster / posture
pose,*,ed,sing,er, STRIKE/HOLD AN
    ATTITUDE/POSTURE (or see posse/
    posy)

posebiledy, possible(bility)
posebly, possible(ly)
posebul, possible
posechon, position
posee, posy / posse
posem, opossum
poses, possess / pose(s) / posy / posse
poseshon, position
posesuf, possess(ive)
posetef, positive
posetive, positive
posetron, positron
posey, posse / posy
poshin, potion
poshon, potion
posibiledy, possible(bility)
posibly, possible(ly)
posibul, possible
posichen, position
posichon, position
posie, posse / posy
posim, opossum
posishen, position
positef, positive
position,*,ned,ning,nal,ner, POSTURE/
    ATTITUDE/STANCE/PLACEMENT
    "prefixes: contra/dis/inter/pre/pro"
positive,*,ely,eness,vism,vist,vistic,
    TYPE OF CHARGE, ON THE UP SIDE,
    OPTIMISTIC "prefixes: contra/dis/
    pre"
positron,*, PARTICLE OF POSITIVE
    CHARGE
posl, puzzle
posmordum, postmortem
posmortem, postmortem
posol, puzzle
posom, opossum
posotive, positive
pospartum, postpartum
pospone, postpone
posse, A GROUP OUT TO COLLECT
    JUSTICE
possess,sses,ssed,ssing,ssion,ssive,
    ssively,ssiveness, OWN/HAVE
    "prefixes: dis/pre"
possesuf, possess(ive)
possible,bility,bilities,ly, MOST LIKELY
    COULD BE DONE/PERFORMED
    "prefixes: im"
possum, opossum
post,*,ted,ting,ter,terize, MAKE
    INFORMATION PUBLIC, VERTICAL

SUPPORT TO ATTACH SOMETHING TO (or see pose(d))

posta, pasta

postage,al, PRICE TO SHIP/FREIGHT SOMETHING TO A MAILBOX/ LOCATION

postaj, postage

postal,age, MAIL BY POST, PAY TO MAIL "prefixes: semi"

postasheo, pistachio

postcher, posture

postege, postage

postej, postage

postel, postal

poster,*, LARGE/BLOWN-UP PICTURE/ DIGITAL IMAGE (or see posture)

posterety, posterior(ity)

posterior,rly, THE REAR, FOLLOWS

posterity, CONCERNING THE FUTURE

postige, postage

postij, postage

postil, postal

postir, poster / posture

postireor, posterior

postle, postal

postmark,*,ked,king, AN INKED STAMP SHOWING DATE SOMETHING WAS MAILED

postmordem, postmortem

postmortem, A BODY ONCE THE SPIRIT IS REMOVED, AFTER DEATH

postpartum, AFTER GIVING BIRTH

postpone,*,ed,ning,nable,ement,er, PUT OFF UNTIL ANOTHER TIME

postr, posture / poster

postu, pasta

postuge, postage

postulate,*,ed,ting,tion,tor, TO CLAIM/ PETITION, ASSUME WITHOUT TRUTH

postur, poster / posture

posture,*,ed,ring, STANCE/PHYSICAL ATTITUDE

posubel, possible

posubility, possible(bility)

posubly, possible(ly)

posum, opossum

posutron, positron

posy,sies, A FLOWER (or see posse)

pot,*,tted,tting,table,tability,tableness, FLAT BOTTOM CONTAINER FOR COOKING/PLANTS (or see pod)

potable,bility,eness, WATER YOU CAN DRINK

potary, potter(y)

potaseum, potassium

potassium,ic, METALLIC CHEMICAL ELEMENT

potato,oes, A STARCHY VEGETABLE

pote, putty / potty

poteble, potable

poted, pot(tted) / pod(dded)

potee, potty

poten, potent

potenchul, potential

potend, potent

potenshul, potential

potensy, potent(ncy)

potent,ncy,ncies,tly, AMOUNT/DEGREE OF STRENGTH "prefixes: pre/sub/ uni"

potential,*,lly,lity,lities, STRONG POSSIBILITY "prefixes: bi"

poter, potter

potery, potter(y)

poteum, podium

poti, putty / potty

potible, potable

potid, pot(tted) / pod(dded)

potin, potent

potinchul, potential

potind, potent

potinshul, potential

potinsy, potent(ncy)

potint, potent

potintial, potential

potintiale, potential(lly)

potintialy, potential(lly)

potion,*, LIQUID WITH SPIRITUAL POWERS

potir, potter

potiry, potter(y)

potium, podium

potlach, potlatch

potlatch,hes, FESTIVAL/PARTY EXCHANGING GIFTS/GOODS

potlege, potlatch

potluck,*, A GATHERING OF PEOPLE WHERE EACH BRINGS A DISH OF FOOD TO SHARE

potluk, potluck

potpery, potpourri

potpourri,*, DRIED PLANTS COMBINED FOR THEIR AROMATHERAPY

potrude, protrude

potrushen, protrude(usion)

potter,*, ONE WHO WORKS WITH CLAY

pottery,ries, THINGS MADE OF CLAY THEN FIRED IN A KILN

potty,tties, A TOILET

potuble, potable

potun, potent

potunsy, potent(ncy)

potury, potter(y)

poty, potty

pouch,hes,hed, BAG/SACK/CAVITY FOR HOLDING THINGS (or see poach)

poud, pout

pouder, powder

poudir, powder

pouer, power

poultes, poultice

poultice,*,ed,cing, CRUSHED PLANTS/ HERBS MIXED WITH A BASE FOR APPLICATION

poultry,ries, EDIBLE BIRDS/FOWL

poum, poem

pounce,*,ed,cing, JUMP/LEAP TOWARDS AS IF TO GRAB/ATTACK, A POWDER

pound,*,ded,ding, U.S. MEASUREMENT FOR SOLIDS, TO HAMMER/STRIKE, BRITISH MONEY, AN AREA OF CONFINEMENT/HOLDING

pounse, pounce

pount, pound

pouperi, potpourri

pour,*,red,ring, WHEN TRANSFERRING LIQUID, A STREAMING FROM ONE PLACE TO ANOTHER (or see pore/ poor/power) "prefixes: in"

pourus, porous

pous, pose

pout,*,ted,ting,ter, TO SULK, BE SULLEN, A FISH (or see poet)

pouwir, power

pouwur, power

poverdy, poverty

poverty, WITHOUT BASIC NEEDS BEING FULFILLED

povileon, pavilion

povirty, poverty

povurty, poverty

powar, power

powch, pouch

powd, pout

powder,*,red,ring,rer,ry, FINELY CRUSHED MINERAL/PLANT, PULVERIZED

powdir, powder

powdur, powder

power,*,red,ring,rful,rfully,rfulness,
    rless,rlessly,rlessness, A CHARGE,
    RAISING FREQUENCY, EUPHORIC
    SENSE OF SUPREMACY/MASTERY
    (or see poor/pour) "prefixes: over"
powir, power
powlar, polar
powlur, polar
pownd, pound
pownse, pounce
pownt, pound
powr, power
powt, pout
powtch, pouch
powtur, powder
powur, power
pox, INDICATION THAT ONE IS
    DISTURBED BY A VIRUS IN THE
    BODY
poynt, point
poynyent, poignant
poyse, poise
poysin, poison
poz, pause / paw(s) / pose
pozd, pose(d) / pause(d)
pozda, pasta
pozderedy, posterior(ity)
pozdmark, postmark
pozdmordum, postmortem
pozdr, posture
pozdu, pasta
pozdul, postal
poze, pose / pause / posy / paw(s)
pozeble, possible
pozebly, possible(ly)
pozee, posy
pozetron, positron
pozible, possible
pozishen, position
pozitef, positive
pozol, puzzle
pozpardum, postpartum
pozpone, postpone
pozt, post / pose(d) / pause(d)
pozta, pasta
poztaj, postage
poztal, postal
pozteg, postage
poztej, postage
poztel, postal
pozter, poster / posture
poztereur, posterior
pozterior, posterior
poztij, postage

poztil, postal
poztir, poster / posture
poztmordum, postmortem
poztpardim, postpartum
poztu, pasta
poztul, postal
poztur, poster / posture
pozuble, possible
pozubly, possible(ly)
pozutif, positive
pozy, posy
pra, pray / prey
prababelity, probable(bility)
prabable, probable / probable(ly)
prabared, prepare(d)
prabebly, probably
praberty, property
prabibly, probably
prabirty, property
prablem, problem
prablum, problem
prabobelity, probable(bility)
prabozkus, proboscis
prabubilety, probable(bility)
prabubly, probably
prabugate, propagate
prabur, proper
praburly, proper(ly)
praburty, property
pracareus, precarious
pracaushen, precaution
pracawshen, precaution
pracedure, procedure
praceedure, procedure
pracepitous, precipitous
pracess, process
pracipitashen, precipitate(tion)
pracipitous, precipitous
pracise, precise
pracisly, precise(ly)
pracktus, practice
praclame, proclaim
praclemashen, proclamation
praclevity, proclivity
praclimation, proclamation
praclivedy, proclivity
praclivity, proclivity
praclution, preclusion
pracoshus, precocious
pracrastination, procrastinate(tion)
pracrastunate, procrastinate
practekul, practical
practes, practice
practeshener, practitioner

practical,lly,lity,lness, BEING LOGICAL,
    EASE OF USE/ OPERATION/
    FUNCTION "prefixes: im/un"
practice,*,ed,cing,cal, PERFORM
    REPEATEDLY TO ACHIEVE MASTERY
    "prefixes: un"
practishener, practitioner
practitioner,*, ONE WHO PRACTICES
practus, practice
prad, parade / prod / pray(ed) /
    prey(ed)
pradasheus, predacious
pradatious, predacious
pradecament, predicament
pradector, predict(or)
pradegul, prodigal
pradegy, prodigy
pradekament, predicament
pradekshen, predict(ion)
pradekt, predict
pradektability, predict(ability)
pradektable, predict(able)
pradicament, predicament
pradict, predict
pradiction, predict(ion)
pradictor, predict(or)
pradigul, prodigal
pradigy, prodigy
pradikament, predicament
pradikshen, predict(ion)
pradiktability, predict(ability)
pradiktable, predict(able)
pradomenate, predominate
pradomenatly, predominate(ly)
pradominate, predominate
pradukshen, product(ion)
praduktion, product(ion)
prae, pray / prey
praer, pray(er)
prafale, prevail
prafanedy, profane(nity)
prafanity, profane(nity)
prafedik, prophet(ic)
prafes, profess
prafeser, professor
prafeshenul, profession(al)
prafeshinul, profession(al)
prafesy, prophecy / prophesy
prafet, profit / prophet
prafetable, profit(able)
prafetek, prophet(ic)
prafetible, profit(able)
prafetik, prophet(ic)
prafide, provide

prafiduble, provide(dable)
prafishent, proficient
prafit, profit / prophet
prafiteer, profit(eer)
prafoundly, profound(ly)
prafusy, prophecy / prophesy
prageks, project(s)
pragekshin, project(ion)
pragektile, project(ile)
pragektor, project(or)
pragesterone, progesterone
pragmadik, pragmatic
pragmatic,*,cal,cally,ism,ist,istic,
 BUSINESSLIKE, OFFICIAL ACTIVITY,
 OF PRACTICALITY/TRUTH
pragmatism, pragmatic(ism)
pragmitist, pragmatic(ist)
pragmutism, pragmatic(ism)
pragmutist, pragmatic(ist)
pragreshen, progress(ion)
pragresive, progress(ive)
pragress, progress
pragretion, progress(ion)
prahebatif, prohibit(ive)
prahebit, prohibit
prahibative, prohibit(ive)
prahibetory, prohibit(ory)
prahibit, prohibit
praid, parade / pride
praink, prank
prair, pray(er)
prairie,*, LARGE AREA OF LAND
 MOSTLY VOID OF TREES
praise,*,ed,sing, TO CONDONE/
 COMPLIMENT SOMEONE/
 SOMETHING (or see price)
 "prefixes: dis"
prajection, project(ion)
prajeks, project(s)
prajekshun, project(ion)
prajektile, project(ile)
prajektor, project(or)
prajesterone, progesterone
prakawshen, precaution
praklaim, proclaim
praklemashen, proclamation
praklemation, proclamation
praklevity, proclivity
praklimation, proclamation
praklivity, proclivity
praklude, preclude
praklumation, proclamation
praklusion, preclusion
praklusive, preclusive

prakoshen, precaution
prakoshious, precocious
prakotius, precocious
prakrastenate, procrastinate
prakrastination, procrastinate(tion)
praktekul, practical
praktes, practice
prakteshener, practitioner
praktetioner, practitioner
praktical, practical
praktikul, practical
praktis, practice
praktishener, practitioner
praktitioner, practitioner
praktus, practice
praleminary, preliminary
pralene, praline
pralimenary, preliminary
praline,*, CANDY
pralong, prolong
pralongate, prolong(ate)
pralood, prelude
pralude, prelude
pramenant, prominent
pramenit, prominent
pramere, premier
prames, promise
prameskuis, promiscuity(uous)
pramesuble, permissible
praminade, prom(enade)
praminent, prominent
pramis, promise
pramisable, permissible
pramiskuis, promiscuity(uous)
pramisquety, promiscuity
pramisquos, promiscuity(uous)
pramoder, promote(r)
pramonishen, premonition
pramoshen, promote(tion)
pramoter, promote(r)
pramotion, promote(tion)
prana, LIFE/ENERGY OF THE BREATH (or
 see piranha)
pranaunse, pronounce
prance,*,ed,cing,er, TO LIGHTLY DANCE
 ABOUT, TO WALK A GAIT WITH A
 PROUD/BOLD POSTURE
prank,*,kish,kster, TO PULL A TRICK ON
 SOMEONE, A SHOWFUL TRICK
pranounce, pronounce
pranownse, pronounce
pranse, prance / prawn(s)
pranunseashen, pronunciate(tion)
pranunsiate, pronunciate

pranunsiation, pronunciate(tion)
prapablee, probably
prapare, prepare
praparidness, prepare(dness)
prapegate, propagate
prapel, propel
prapeler, propel(ller)
prapelint, propel(llant)
praper, proper / prepare
praperedness, prepare(ness)
praperly, proper(ly)
praperty, property
praphat, prophet / profit
praphisy, prophecy / prophesy
praphut, prophet / profit
prapigate, propagate
prapir, proper
prapirty, property
praplum, problem
prapogate, propagate
praponint, proponent
praporshen, proportion
praportion, proportion
praposal, propose(sal)
prapose, propose
praposition, proposition
praposterus, preposterous
praposturis, preposterous
prapoze, propose
prapozishen, proposition
praprietor, proprietor
prapubly, probably
prapuganda, propaganda
prapugashen, propagate(tion)
prapugate, propagate
prapur, proper
prapurty, property
prare, prairie
prarogative, prerogative
prary, prairie
prascribe, prescribe / proscribe
prascription, prescript(ion)
prascriptive, prescript(ive)
prasdeje, prestige
prasdrate, prostrate / prostate
prase, praise
prasechen, precision / procession /
 precession
prasecute, prosecute
prasede, precede / proceed
prasedger, procedure
praseet, precede
prasejur, procedure
prasekushen, prosecute(tion)

prasekute, prosecute
prasentuble, present(able)
praserve, preserve
prases, process / precess
praseshen, precision / procession / precession
prasetchur, procedure
prasetion, precision / procession / precession
prasetyur, procedure
prasicute, prosecute
praside, preside
prasidger, procedure
prasijer, procedure
prasikushen, prosecute(tion)
prasintable, present(able)
prasipatate, precipitate
prasise, precise
prasishen, precision / procession / precession
prasisly, precise(ly)
prasited, preside(d)
praskrepshen, prescript(ion)
praskribe, prescribe / proscribe
praskribshen, prescript(ion)
praskript, prescript / prescribe(d)
prasomtif, presume(mptive)
praspect, prospect
praspective, prospect(ive)
praspekt, prospect
praspektif, prospect(ive)
prasperus, prosper(ous)
praspur, prosper
prastate, prostate / prostrate
prastegis, prestige(gious)
prasteje, prestige
prastejus, prestige(gious)
prastetute, prostitute
prasthesis, prosthesis
prasthesus, prosthesis
prastrate, prostrate / prostate
prasukushen, prosecute(tion)
prasum, presume
prasumptive, presume(mptive)
prasumshen, presume(mption)
prasumtif, presume(mptive)
prasumtion, presume(mption)
prasumtuis, presume(mptuous)
prasurve, preserve
pratect, protect
pratection, protect(ion)
pratekshen, protect(ion)
pratekt, protect
pratektuf, protect(ive)

pratend, pretend
pratended, pretend(ed)
pratind, pretend
pratrude, protrude
pratrugin, protrude(usion)
pratrusef, protrude(usive)
pratrusion, protrude(usion)
praublem, problem
praud, proud
praudly, proud(ly)
praufet, prophet / profit
praufut, prophet / profit
praukse, proxy
praul, prowl
praun, prawn
prauphet, prophet / profit
prauses, process
praustat, prostate / prostrate
praut, proud
prautly, proud(ly)
pravale, prevail
pravalent, prevalent
pravelent, prevalent
pravense, province
pravenshen, prevent(ion)
pravent, prevent
praventable, prevent(able)
praventive, prevent(ive)
praverb, proverb
praverbeul, proverb(ial)
pravide, provide
praviduble, provide(dable)
pravilent, prevalent
pravinse, province
pravinshen, prevent(ion)
pravinshul, province(cial)
pravint, prevent
pravintable, prevent(able)
pravirb, proverb
pravirbeal, proverb(ial)
pravocative, provocative
pravock, provoke
pravokative, provocative
pravoke, provoke
pravulent, prevalent
pravurb, proverb
pravurbeul, proverb(ial)
prawdly, proud(ly)
prawess, prowess
prawl, prowl
prawn,*, LARGE SHRIMP
prawt, proud
prawtly, proud(ly)

pray,*,yed,ying,yer, TO FOCUS ON A THOUGHT OR A DESIRE YOU WISH TO PHYSICALLY MANIFEST IN THE MOMENT OR THE FUTURE (or see praise/prey)
praylene, praline
prayr, pray(er)
prayree, prairie
praze, praise / pray(s)
prazens, presence / present(s)
prazent, present
prazentuble, present(able)
prazerve, preserve
prazint, present
prazumtues, presume(mptuous)
prazurve, preserve
pre, PREFIX INDICATING "BEFORE" MOST OFTEN MODIFIES THE WORD
preach,hes,hed,hing,hingly,her,hify, hified,hifying,hy, VOCALLY TEACH A LESSON
preamble, BRIEF INTRODUCTION, PREFACE
preample, preamble
preampt, preempt
prebozkus, proboscis
precadent, precedent / president
precarious,sly,sness, UNCERTAIN ABOUT STABILITY OR FIRM POSITION, NOT SECURE
precastinate, procrastinate
precaushen, precaution
precaution,*,nary,nal,ous, TAKE STEPS TO PREPARE TO AVERT DANGER/ HARM
precede,*,ed,ding,ence,ency,ent, GOING/BEING BEFORE, SETS GUIDELINES FOR ALL THAT FOLLOWS (or see proceed)
precedent,*,tly,tial,tially, GOING/BEING BEFORE, SETS GUIDELINES FOR ALL THAT FOLLOWS (or see proceed) "prefixes: un"
precens, presence / present(s)
precent, present
precentashen, presentation
precepitate, precipitate
precepitous, precipitous
precersory, precursor(y)
precess,ssion, FIRST IN ORDER/RANK/ TIME, BEHAVIOR OF PLANETS/AXIS/ MOTION
precession,ssional, FIRST IN ORDER/ RANK/TIME, BEHAVIOR OF

PLANETS/ AXIS/MOTION (or see
procession/precision)

prech, preach

precher, preach(er)

precidense, precede(nce) / president(s)

precident, precede(nt) / president /
precedent

precinct,*, AREAS DIVIDED FOR
VOTING/CONTROL

precious,ly,ness, HIGHLY CHERISHED,
VALUABLE "prefixes: semi"

precipitate,*,ed,ting,able,ely,eness,tive,
tor,tion,ant,ancy,antly, FALLING
MOISTURE, BRING ABOUT

precipitous,sly,sness, BRING ABOUT
QUICKLY WITHOUT MUCH
THOUGHT, STEEP HEIGHT

precise,ely,eness,sion, EXACT/CLOSE TO
PERFECT, CAREFUL ATTENTION TO
DETAIL

precishen, precision / procession /
precession

precision,nist, EXACT/CLOSE TO
PERFECT, CAREFUL ATTENTION TO
DETAIL (or see procession/
precession)

precius, precious

preclame, proclaim

preclude,*,ed,ding,usion,usive,
PREVENT OR EXCLUDE SOMEONE/
SOMETHING

preclushen, preclusion

preclusion, PREVENT/EXCLUDE
SOMEONE/SOMETHING

preclusive,ely,ion, PREVENT/EXCLUDE
SOMEONE/SOMETHING

preclution, preclusion

precochusly, precocious(ly)

precocious,sly,sness,sity, MATURING
EARLY/QUICKLY

precognative, precognitive

precognishen, precognition

precognition,ive, ABLE TO SENSE/
KNOW THE FUTURE

precognitive, ABILITY TO SENSE/KNOW
THE FUTURE

precoshen, precaution

precoshus, precocious

precotion, precaution

precotious, precocious

precrastination, procrastinate

precugnishen, precognition

precursor,ry,sive, COMES BEFORE

predacious,sness,sity,ation,
PREDATORY/PREYS, ATTACKING/
KILLING/HUNTING

predacity, predacious(ity)

predasesor, predecessor

predasheus, predacious

predater, predator

predatious, predacious

predator,*,rial,rily,ry, ATTACKING/
KILLING/HUNTING

predatoreul, predator(ial)

prede, pretty

predecesor, predecessor

predecessor,*, WHO LIVED/CAME
BEFORE, ANCESTOR

predekshen, predict(ion)

predekt, predict

predesesor, predecessor

predespasition, predispose(sition)

predespazishen, predispose(sition)

predespose, predispose

predetor, predator

predetorial, predator(ial)

predeur, pretty(ttier)

prediar, pretty(ttier)

predicament,*,tal, TO BE IN AN
AWKWARD/CHALLENGING/
DIFFICULT POSITION

predicesor, predecessor

predict,*,ted,ting,table,tably,tability,
tion,tive,tively,tiveness,tor, TO
FORETELL THE FUTURE "prefixes:
un"

predier, pretty(ttier)

prediest, pretty(ttiest)

predikament, predicament

prediktable, predict(able)

predisesor, predecessor

predispazishen, predispose(sition)

predispose,*,ed,sing,sition, TENDENCY
TOWARDS BEFOREHAND

preditor, predator

preditorial, predator(ial)

predomenashen, predominate(tion)

predominate,ely,tion,nant,nantly,ance,
ancy, DOMINATE/AUTHORITY/
CONTROL OVER

predsul, pretzel

prediction, product(ion)

predukshen, product(ion)

predusesor, predecessor

predutor, predator

predutoreul, predator(ial)

predutory, predator(y)

predy, pretty

predyest, pretty(ttiest)

preech, preach

preechy, preach(y)

preempt,tor,ption,ptive,ptively, TO
OCCUPY/SEIZE/ACQUIRE BEFORE
ANYONE ELSE CAN ACQUIRE
OWNERSHIP

preemshen, preempt(ion)

preemt, preempt

preface,ed,cing, REMARKS/
INTRODUCTION BEFORE A BOOK/
LITERARY WORK

prefale, prevail

prefanedy, profane(nity)

prefanity, profane(nity)

prefeks, prefix

prefer,*,rred,rring,rence,rences,rable,
rableness,rability,rably,rential,
rentialist, rentialism,rentiality,
rentially,rment, CHOOSE OVER
OTHERS, MOST DESIRABLE

preferinse, prefer(ence)

preferuble, prefer(able)

prefese, preface

prefeshenul, profession(al)

prefesur, professor

prefex, prefix

preficks, prefix

prefide, provide

prefiduble, provide(dable)

prefiks, prefix

prefir, prefer

prefirability, prefer(ability)

prefirable, prefer(able)

prefirense, prefer(ence)

prefirenshul, prefer(ential)

prefirential, prefer(ential)

prefis, preface

prefix,xes,xal,xally,xation,xion, LETTERS
BEFORE A BASE WORD THAT
MODIFIES IT'S MEANING, EXISTS
PRIOR TO

preforenshul, prefer(ential)

prefound, profound

prefoundly, profound(ly)

prefur, prefer

prefurabiledy, prefer(ability)

prefurable, prefer(able)

prefurenshul, prefer(ential)

prefurential, prefer(ential)

prefurinse, prefer(ence)

prefuse, preface

prefy, privy

pregadis, prejudice
pregedis, prejudice
pregekshin, project(ion)
pregesterone, progesterone
pregidis, prejudice
pregnant,tly,ncy,ncies,able,ability,
    BODY CARRYING AN EMBRYO
pregnensy, pregnant(ncy)
pregnet, pregnant
pregnint, pregnant
pregnonsy, pregnant(ncy)
pregnunt, pregnant
pregnut, pregnant
pregodis, prejudice
pregreshen, progress(ion)
pregretion, progress(ion)
pregudis, prejudice
prei, prey / pray
preimshen, preempt(ion)
preimt, preempt
preimtif, preempt(ive)
preimtive, preempt(ive)
preis, prey(s) / pray(s) / praise
prejadis, prejudice
prejekshin, project(ion)
prejidis, prejudice
prejodis, prejudice
prejudice,*,ed,cing,cial,cially, AN
    OPINION/ATTITUDE ABOUT
    SOMETHING/ SOMEONE WITHOUT
    BASIS OF FULL KNOWLEDGE
prek, prick
prekareus, precarious
prekarius, precarious
prekastinate, procrastinate
prekaution, precaution
prekawshen, precaution
preked, prick(ed)
prekersery, precursor(y)
prekirsor, precursor
prekirsory, precursor(y)
preklame, proclaim
preklewd, preclude
preklude, preclude
preklushen, preclusion
preklusive, preclusive
preklution, preclusion
preknet, pregnant
preknit, pregnant
preknut, pregnant
prekognative, precognitive
prekognishen, precognition
prekognition, precognition
prekoshen, precaution

prekoshious, precocious
prekoshus, precocious
prekotius, precocious
prekrastination, procrastinate
prekursor, precursor
prekursory, precursor(y)
preleminary, preliminary
prelene, praline
prelewt, prelude
preliminary,ries,rily, INTRODUCTION
    TO THE MAIN
prelong, prolong
prelongate, prolong(ate)
prelood, prelude
prelude,*,ded,ding,er,usive,usively,
    usorily,usory, LEADING UP/
    INTRODUCTORY TO
prelute, prelude
prem, prim
premachure, premature
premanishen, premonition
premanition, premonition
prematif, primitive
prematively, primitive(ly)
premature,ely,eness,rity, BEFORE RIPE/
    MATURE/FULLY FORMED
premear, premier
premechure, premature
premedatate, premeditate
premeditate,*,ed,ting,tion,tive, PLAN
    OUT BEFORE THE ACT OF "prefixes:
    un"
premeim, premium
premeneshen, premonition
premenishen, premonition
premenstrual,lly, PRIOR TO/BEFORE
    MENSTRUATION
premenzdrul, premenstrual
premere, premier
premese, premise
premetetate, premeditate
premetitate, premeditate
premeum, premium
premichure, premature
premier,*, PLAY/OPERA/MOVIE FIRST
    PUBLIC EXPOSURE
preminishen, premonition
preminstral, premenstrual
preminstrul, premenstrual
premiom, premium
premir, premier
premisabul, permissible

premise,*, ASSUMPTION, BEFOREHAND,
    LAND WITH TENANTS, BEGINNING
    OF, PROPOSITION
premiskues, promiscuity(uous)
premitive, primitive
premiture, premature
premium,*, BONUS, ADDITIONALLY
premoder, promote(r)
premoneshen, premonition
premonition,*, SENSE/FEELING BEFORE
    AN EVENT
premose, premise
premoshen, promote(tion)
premote, promote
premotion, promote(tion)
premoture, premature
premp, primp
prempt, primp(ed)
premuchure, premature
premunishen, premonition
premunition, premonition
premuse, premise
premutif, primitive
premuture, premature
prence, prince / print(s)
prenceses, princess(es)
prencess, princess
prenciple, principle / principal
prend, print
prendable, print(able)
prender, print(er)
prendible, print(able)
prenduble, print(able)
prenoense, pronounce
prenounce, pronounce
prensabul, principle / principal
prensaple, principle / principal
prense, prince / print(s)
prenses, princess / prince(s)
prensibul, principle / principal
prensipul, principle / principal
prensis, princess / prince(s)
prensuple, principle / principal
prent, print
prentabul, print(able)
prenter, print(er)
prentible, print(able)
prentr, print(er)
prentur, print(er)
prenunseate, pronunciate
prenunsiation, pronunciate(tion)
prenus, apprentice
prep,*,pped,pping,pper,ppy, PREPARE/
    MAKE READY FOR

prepare,*,ed,edness,ring,ration,rative, rationally,rator,ratory,rer, EQUIP/ COMPOSE/ASSEMBLE/ MANUFACTURE/CONDITION SOMETHING/ SOMEONE FOR ACTIVITY/EVENT "prefixes: un"

prepaseshen, preposition / proposition / prepossess(ion)

prepazishen, preposition / proposition / prepossess(ion)

preperashen, prepare(ration)

preperatory, prepare(ratory)

preperidness, prepare(ness)

prepiration, prepare(ration)

prepiratory, prepare(ratory)

prepiseshen, preposition / proposition / prepossess(ion)

preponent, proponent

preporashen, prepare(ration)

preporshen, proportion

preportion, proportion

preposal, propose(sal)

prepose, propose

preposeshun, prepossess

preposesing, prepossessing

preposishen, preposition / proposition / prepossess(ion)

preposition,*,ned,ning,nal,nally, ENGLISH LANGUAGE TERM (or see proposition)

prepossess,ssing,ssion, POSSESS BEFORE SOMEONE ELSE DOES, TO IMPRESS

prepossessing,gly,gness,ion, TO IMPRESS/CHARM FAVORABLY "prefixes: un"

preposterous,sly,sness, BEYOND RATIONAL, GOES AGAINST COMMON SENSE

preposturis, preposterous

prepoze, propose

prepozes, prepossess

prepozishen, preposition / proposition / prepossess(ion)

prepozle, propose(sal)

prepriator, proprietor

prepurashen, prepare(ration)

prepuration, prepare(ration)

prepusition, proposition

prepuzishen, preposition / proposition / prepossess(ion)

prer, pray(er)

prere, prairie

prerogative,*, PRIVILEGED

prery, prairie

pres, press

presadense, precede(nce) / president(s)

presadenshul, president(ial)

presadent, precedent/ president

presadinse, precede(nce) / president(s)

presadint, precede(nt) / president

prescrebshin, prescript(ion)

prescribe,*,ed,bing,er, RULE/COURSE/ ACTION TO BE FOLLOWED (or see prescript/proscribe)

prescripshen, prescript(ion)

prescript,tible,tion,tive,tively,tiveness, tivism, CLAIM/CUSTOM/RULE/ RIGHT/ TITLE TO (or see prescribe)

prescrishen, prescript(ion)

presd, press(ed)

presdeje, prestige

presdo, presto

presede, precede / proceed

presedent, precede(nt) / president

presedential, president(ial)

presedger, procedure

presedintial, president(ial)

presedyur, procedure

presee, prissy

preseet, precede

preseger, procedure

presejur, procedure

presence, OF BEING PRESENT, IN IMMEDIATE VICINITY OF (or see present)

presenked, precinct

presenkt, precinct

presens, presence / present(s)

present,*,ted,ter,ting,tly,tness,table, tableness,tability,tably,tment,tation, nce, GIVEN FREELY, ACCEPTABLE, TO OFFER SOMETHING, IN IMMEDIATE VICINITY OF, MAKE VISIBLE (or see presence) "prefixes: re,-re"

presentation,*,nal,ive, PRESENT/ OFFER/EXHIBIT SOMETHING "prefixes: re,-re"

presepitous, precipitous

preser, pressure / press(er)

preservashen, preserve(vation)

preserve,*,ed,er,vable,vation,ving, PROTECT FROM, PREVENT CONDITION FROM BEING ALTERED/ EXPLOITED/CHANGED

preses, precess

preseshen, precision / procession / precession

presetgur, procedure

presetion, precision / procession / precession

presh, preach

presher, pressure

presherize, pressure(rize)

preshes, precious

preshir, pressure

preshis, precious

preshorize, pressure(rize)

preshur, pressure

preshurize, pressure(rize)

preshus, precious

preside,*,ed,ding,er, ONE IN A HIERARCHAL POSITION OVER, THE AUTHORITY OF THE GROUP, OVERSEEING

presidense, precede(nce) / president(s)

presidenshul, president(ial)

president,*,ncy,ncies,tial, LEADERSHIP POSITION (or see precedent)

presiger, procedure

presijur, procedure

presim, prism

presin, prison

presinct, precinct

presiner, prison(er)

presinked, precinct

presinkt, precinct

presinse, presence

presint, present

presintable, present(able)

presintashen, presentation

presintation, presentation

presintly, present(ly)

presints, present(s) / presence

presipatate, precipitate

presipatation, precipitate(tion)

presipitate, precipitate

presipitous, precipitous

presiputashen, precipitate(tion)

presir, pressure / press(er)

presirvation, preserve(vation)

presis, precise / press(es)

presishen, precision / procession / precession

presisly, precise(ly)

presited, preside(d)

presition, precision/procession

preskrepshen, prescript(ion)

preskribe, prescribe / proscribe

preskribshen, prescript(ion)

presm, prism
presmadik, prism(atic)
presodent, precede(nt) / president
presomtif, presume(mptive)
preson, prison
press,sses,ssed,ssing,sser, APPLY/EXERT
FORCE, SQUEEZE, COMPACT
"prefixes: re,-re"
pressure,*,ed,ring,rize,rizer,rizing,
rization, THE APPLICATION/
EXERTION OF FORCE, SQUEEZE,
COMPACT, REMOVE AIR "prefixes:
over"
prest, priest / press(ed)
prestege, prestige
prestegus, prestige(gious)
prestej, prestige
prestene, pristine
prestess, priest(ess)
presthesus, prosthesis
presthood, priest(hood)
prestige,gious,giousness,giously, OF
DISTINCTION RANK/QUALITY
prestigous, prestige(gious)
prestine, pristine
prestly, priest(ly)
presto, INSTANT/AUTOMATIC/
SUDDEN/QUICK
presudent, precede(nt) / president /
precedent
presum, prism / presume
presume,*,ed,ming,er,mption,mptive,
mptively,tuous,tuously, tuousness,
MOST PROBABLE WITHOUT PROOF,
CONCLUSION/SUPPOSING
WITHOUT FACTS
presumshen, presume(mption)
presumtif, presume(mptive)
presumtion, presume(mption)
presumtuis, presume(mptuous)
presumtuous, presume(mptuous)
presun, prison
presur, pressure / press(er)
presurf, preserve
presurvashen, preserve(vation)
presurve, preserve
presus, press(es)
presy, prissy
prete, pretty
pretekt, protect
pretektif, protect(ive)
pretektive, protect(ive)

pretend,*,ded,ding,der,nse, ACT AS IF
REAL, MAKE BELIEVE, DECEPTIVE
"prefixes: un"
pretense,*,sion,sionless,sive,ntious,
ACT AS IF REAL, MAKE BELIEVE,
DECEPTIVE
pretenshen, pretense(sion)
pretentious,sly,sness, FIRMLY
CONFIDENT, OVERSTEPS OTHERS'
BOUNDARIES "prefixes: un"
preteur, pretty(ttier)
pretiest, pretty(ttiest)
pretind, pretend
pretinse, pretense
pretinshen, pretense(sion)
pretrude, protrude
pretrusion, protrude(usion)
pretsul, pretzel
pretty,ttier,ttiest,tties,ttiness,ttily,ttyish,
ttify,ttifier,ttifying,ttification,
ATTRACTIVE/VISUALLY PLEASING
prety, pretty
pretzel,*,led, DOUGHY FOOD TWISTED
INTO A KNOT
prevade, pervade
prevail,*,led,ling, WILL ENDURE,
ONGOING, WILL NOT BE
OVERCOME
prevale, prevail
prevaleg, privilege
prevalense, prevalent(nce)
prevalent,tly,nce, WILL PREVAIL, MOST
COMMON/POPULAR
prevalige, privilege
prevalijes, privilege(s)
prevalinse, prevalent(nce)
prevalint, prevalent
prevalt, prevail(ed)
preveis, previous
preveisly, previous(ly)
prevelent, prevalent
prevelinse, prevalent(nce)
prevelint, prevalent
prevenshen, prevent(ion)
prevent,*,ted,ting,tion,tability,table,ter,
tive,tively,tiveness,tative, STOP/
PREPARE/KEEP FROM HAPPENING
preveos, previous
preveosly, previous(ly)
preveus, previous
preveusly, previous(ly)
previde, provide
previduble, provide(dable)
privilege, privilege

previlense, prevalent(nce)
previlent, prevalent
previnshun, prevent(ion)
previntion, prevent(ion)
previntive, prevent(ive)
previous,sly, HAPPENED/OCCURRED
BEFORE
previus, previous
previusly, previous(ly)
prevlej, privilege
prevlig, privilege
prevocative, provocative
prevok, provoke
prevokative, provocative
prevokt, provoke
prevulense, prevalent(nce)
prevulent, prevalent
prevulinse, prevalent(nce)
prevy, privy
prey,*,yed,ying,yer, STALK/HUNT
DOWN SOMEONE/SOMETHING
FOR SATISFACTION/NOURISHMENT
(or see pray)
prezadinshul, president(ial)
prezadint, precede(nt) / president
prezedinshul, president(ial)
prezedint, precede(nt) / president
prezent, present
prezentashen, presentation
prezents, presence / present(s)
prezervashen, preserve(vation)
prezerve, preserve
prezident, precede(nt) / president
preziner, prison(er)
prezint, present
prezintly, present(ly)
prezints, presence / present(s)
prezodent, precede(nt) / president
prezomtuis, presume(mptuous)
prezt, priest
prezudenshul, president(ial)
prezudent, precede(nt) / president
prezum, prism
prezumtues, presume(mptuous)
prezunt, present
prhaps, perhaps
pri, pry / pre
priboskus, proboscis
pric, prick / price
pricarius, precarious
pricashen, precaution
pricastinate, procrastinate
pricaushen, precaution
pricaution, precaution

price,*,ed,cing,ey,eless, COST OF/FOR SOMETHING (or see prick) "prefixes: under"

pricechen, precession / procession / precision

pricede, precede / proceed

pricersor, precursor

prices, price(s) / precess

priceshen, precession / procession / precision

pricise, precise

pricisely, precise(ly)

pricishen, precession / procession / precision

pricision, precession / procession / precision

prick,*,ked,king,kley,klier,kliest,kliness, PIERCE/PUNCTURE WITH SHARP POINT, SLANG FOR MALE ORGAN

priclame, proclaim

priclude, preclude

priclushen, preclusion

priclution, preclusion

pricochen, precaution

pricognative, precognitive

pricogneshen, precognition

pricognition, precognition

pricoshus, precocious

pricotion, precaution

pricotious, precocious

pricursor, precursor

pricy, price(y)

pridachus, predacious

pridacity, predacious(ity)

pridashius, predacious

pridatious, predacious

pride,*,ded,ding,eful,efully,efulness, roud, EGO PROTECTING ITS SELF-ESTEEM, BOASTFUL, ARROGANT

pridear, pretty(ttier)

pridecament, predicament

pridect, predict

pridekter, predict(or)

pridespose, predispose

prideur, pretty(ttier)

pridful, pride(ful)

pridfulness, pride(fulness)

pridfuly, pride(fully)

pridi, pretty

pridicament, predicament

pridictable, predict(able)

pridiction, predict(ion)

pridiest, pretty(ttiest)

pridikament, predicament

pridikshen, predict(ion)

pridikt, predict

pridispose, predispose

pridominate, predominate

pridukshen, product(ion)

priduktion, product(ion)

pridy, pretty

pridyest, pretty(ttiest)

priempt, preempt

priemt, preempt

prieng, pry(ing)

prier, prior

prieredy, prior(ity)

priest,*,tly,tliness,thood,tess, ASSIGNED PERSON TO REPRESENT A RELIGIOUS BELIEF

prifale, prevail

prifasee, private(acy)

prifatize, private(tize)

prifatlee, private(ly)

prifee, privy

prifer, prefer

prifes, profess

prifeshen, profession

prifeshinol, profession(al)

prifesor, professor

prifesy, private(acy)

prifet, private

prifetize, private(tize)

prifetlee, private(ly)

prifex, prefix

prifide, provide

prifir, prefer

prifisee, private(acy)

prifit, private

prifitize, private(tize)

prifitlee, private(ly)

prifix, prefix

prifot, private

prifotize, private(tize)

prifound, profound

prifur, prefer

prifusy, private(acy)

prifut, private

prifutize, private(tize)

prifutlee, private(ly)

prify, privy

prigekshen, project(ion)

prignostik, prognostic

prigreshen, progress(ion)

prijekshen, project(ion)

prijektile, project(ile)

prijidus, prejudice

prik, prick

prikareus, precarious

prikashen, precaution

prikastinate, procrastinate

prikaushen, precaution

prikd, prick(ed)

priked, prick(ed)

prikereous, precarious

priklame, proclaim

prikle, prick(ly)

priklusion, preclusion

priklusive, preclusive

prikognishen, precognition

prikoshen, precaution

prikoshus, precocious

prikotion, precaution

prikotius, precocious

prikrastination, procrastinate

prikt, prick(ed)

prilemenary, preliminary

prilimenary, preliminary

prilong, prolong

prilongate, prolong(ate)

prim,mmer,mmest,mly,mness, FORMAL/PROPER (or see prime)

primachur, premature

primade, primate

primal, PRIMITIVE, BASE, FUNDAMENTAL

primary,ries,rily, MAIN ONE, CENTRAL, MOST IMPORTANT, FUNDAMENTAL

primate,*,eship,tial, MAMMALS, MAN/MONKEYS/APES

primatif, primitive

primative, primitive

primativly, primitive(ly)

prime,ed,ming,eness,er, AT ITS PEAK, READY, PREPARED FOR AN EVENT, TYPE OF NUMBER "prefixes: un"

primechur, premature

primedidate, premeditate

primel, primal

primenstral, premenstrual

primer, premier / prime(r)

primerily, primary(rily)

primery, primary

primir, prime(r) / premier

primise, premise

primitive,*,ely,eness,vism,vist,vistic, SIMPLE, EARLIEST EXPRESSION, CRUDE, GEOMETRIC EXPRESSION

primle, primal

primly, prim(mmly) / prime(ly)

primoder, promote(r)

primol, primal

primoshen, promote(tion)
primote, promote
primoter, promote(r)
primotion, promote(tion)
primp,*,ped,ping, TO ADORN/GROOM/ DRESS UP
primul, primal
primur, prime(r) / prim(mmer)
primutif, primitive
prinaunse, pronounce
princabol, principal/ principle
prince,*,edom, MALE POSITION OF ROYALTY
princepol, principal/ principle
princess,sses, FEMALE POSITION OF ROYALTY
principal,*,lly,lship,lity,lities,lly, PRIMARY/FIRST IN POSITION/ IMPORTANCE, TERM HAVING TO DO WITH MONEY/LAW (or see principle) "prefixes: sub"
principle,*,ed, MAIN POINT, GENERAL TRUTH, ADOPTED METHOD/RULE/ LAW (or see principal) "prefixes: un"
principol, principal / principle
prind, print
prinounce, pronounce
prinownse, pronounce
prins, prince / print(s)
prinsabul, principle / principal
prinse, prince / print(s)
prinsepul, principle / principal
prinses, princess / prince(s)
prinseses, princess(es)
prinsipul, principle / principal
prinsuple, principle / principal
print,*,ted,ting,table,tability,ter,tery, tless, USE OF TEXT TO COMMUNICATE "prefixes: mis/ over/pre/un"
printuble, print(able)
printur, print(er)
prinunseashen, pronunciate(tion)
prinunseate, pronunciate
prinunsiation, pronunciate(tion)
prior,rly,rship,rate,rity,rities, FIRST, BEFORE, EARLIER, RELIGIOUS RANK
priorety, prior(ity)
prioridy, prior(ity)
pripare, prepare
pripeler, propel(ller)
priper, prepare
priponent, proponent

priporshen, proportion
priportion, proportion
priposal, propose(sal)
pripose, propose
priposteros, preposterous
pripozle, propose(sal)
pripriator, proprietor
prirogative, prerogative
pris, price / prize
priscraib, prescribe
priscribe, prescribe / proscribe
priscript, prescript
prisdeje, prestige
prise, price / price(y) / prize
prisechen, precision / procession / precession
prised, precede / proceed / price(d)
prisedger, procedure
prisee, prissy / price(y)
priseet, precede / proceed
prisejur, procedure
prisem, prism
prisen, prison
prisener, prison(er)
prisentable, present(able)
prisentashin, presentation
prisentation, presentation
priserv, preserve
priservation, preservation
priserve, preserve
prises, price(s)/ precess
priseshen, precision / procession / precession
prisetgur, procedure
prisetion, precision / procession / precession
priside, preside / precede
prisigur, procedure
prisim, prism
prisin, prison
prisipatate, precipitate
prisipatation, precipitate(tion)
prisise, precise
prisisly, precise(ly)
priskrepshen, prescript(ion)
priskribe, prescribe / proscribe
prisless, price(less)
prislis, price(less)
prism,*,matic,matically, GEOMETRICAL SHAPE, OPTICAL/CRYSTAL/ RAINBOW EFFECT
prismadik, prism(atic)
prisom, prism
prisomtif, presume(mptive)

prison,*,ner, BUILDING USED TO CONFINE/HOLD, A FEELING OF INVOLUNTARY RESTRAINT
prisontation, presentation
prissy,ssily,ssiness, ARROGANTLY PRIM, GIRLY GIRL
prist, priest / price(d)
pristege, prestige
pristegus, prestige(gious)
pristeje, prestige
pristene, pristine
pristine,ely, UNCONTAMINATED, PURE
prisum, prism / presume
prisumptive, presume(mptive)
prisumtion, presume(mption)
prisumtuis, presume(mptuous)
prisun, prison
prisuner, prison(er)
prisurf, preserve
prisurve, preserve
prisy, prissy / price(y)
prit, pride
pritear, pretty(ttier)
pritect, protect
pritection, protect(ion)
prited, pride(d)
pritekshen, protect(ion)
pritekt, protect
pritektif, protect(ive)
pritenchus, pretentious
pritend, pretend
pritenshen, pretense(sion)
pritenshus, pretentious
pritentious, pretentious
priteur, pretty(ttier)
pritful, pride(ful)
priti, pretty
pritiest, pretty(ttiest)
pritinchos, pretentious
pritinshus, pretentious
pritintious, pretentious
pritrude, protrude
pritrushen, protrude(usion)
pritrusion, protrude(usion)
prity, pretty
priur, prior
prival, prevail
privaledged, privilege(d)
privalent, prevalent
privalije, privilege
privalt, prevail(ed)
privasee, private(acy)
private,*,ely,acy,tness,tize,tized,tizing, tization,tion,tist,tism, MUST GAIN

PERMISSION TO ACCESS, SECLUDED, U.S.MILITARY RANK, NON-GOVERNMENTAL "prefixes: semi"

privatisation, private(tization)

privatly, private(ly)

privecy, private(acy)

privee, privy

priveisly, previous(ly)

priveledged, privilege(d)

privelent, prevalent

privelige, privilege

privenshen, prevent(ion)

privent, prevent

priventable, prevent(able)

priventive, prevent(ive)

priverbeul, proverb(ial)

privese, private(acy)

privet, private

privetisation, private(tization)

privetly, private(ly)

priveus, previous

priveusly, previous(ly)

privicy, private(acy)

prividuble, provide(dable)

privilege,*,ed,ging, SPECIAL, HONORARY, FAVORED, CHOSEN "prefixes: under"

privilent, prevalent

privilige, privilege

privios, previous

privit, private

privitly, private(ly)

priviusly, previous(ly)

privocative, provocative

privock, provoke

privokative, provocative

privoke, provoke

privokt, provoke(d)

privolent, prevalent

privulej, privilege

privusee, private(acy)

privut, private

privutization, private(tization)

privutly, private(ly)

privvy, privy

privy,vies,vier,viest, OUTDOOR TOILET, IN ON A PRIVATE MATTER/SECRET

privyed, privy(vied)

prize,*,ed,zing, GIFT/REWARD/AWARD FOR ACCOMPLISHMENT/WINNING (or see price/pry(s))

prizen, prison

prizener, prison(er)

prizent, present

prizerve, preserve

prizin, prison

prizis, prize(s) / price(s)

prizm, prism

prizmadik, prism(atic)

prizmatic, prism(atic)

prizomtuis, presume(mptuous)

prizoner, prison(er)

prizum, prism

prizumshen, presume(mption)

prizumtues, presume(mptuous)

prizun, prison

prizuner, prison(er)

prizus, prize(s) / price(s)

pro,*, SHORT FOR PROFESSIONAL (or see prose) "prefixes: semi"

prob, prop / probe

probabil, probable

probable,ly,bilism,bilist,bilistic,bility, bilities, MOST LIKELY, CHANCE TO OCCUR/HAPPEN "prefixes: im"

probably, MOST LIKELY TO OCCUR/HAPPEN

probade, probate

probaganda, propaganda

probagashen, propagate(tion)

probagate, propagate

probagation, propagate(tion)

probane, propane

probashen, probate(tion)

probashinul, probate(tional)

probate,*,ed,ting,tion,tional,tionary, tionally,tioner,tive,tory, EXAMINATION/ INVESTIGATE THE TRUTH/VALIDITY/GENUINENESS/ AUTHENTICITY "prefixes: re"

probatid, probate(d)

probe,*,ed,bing,er, DEEPLY INVESTIGATE/OBSERVE, INSTRUMENT/ACT FOR RELAYING FACTUAL INFORMATION (or see prop)

probebly, probably

probebul, probable

probeganda, propaganda

probegashen, propagate(tion)

probegate, propagate

prober, proper

proberte, property

probibly, probably

probibul, probable

probiganda, propaganda

probigashen, propagate(tion)

probigate, propagate

probirty, property

problem,*,matic,matical,matically, CHALLENGING SITUATION/ INFORMATION WHICH REQUIRES RESOLUTION/ANSWERS/RESULTS

problum, problem

probobul, probable

proboganda, propaganda

probogation, propagate(tion)

proboscis,ses,ides, SNOUT/NOSE/ TRUNK

probs, probe(s) / prop(s)

probubilety, probable(bility)

probuble, probable

probuganda, propaganda

probugashen, propagate(tion)

probugate, propagate

probur, proper

proburty, property

procede, proceed

procedure,*,ral,rally, NORMAL/PROPER ACTION/METHOD/PROCESS

proceed,*,ded,ding, GO AHEAD/ VENTURE FORTH, PROFIT/REVENUE FROM EVENT (or see precede)

proceedure, procedure

proces, process

proceshen, precision / procession / precession

procesion, precision / procession / precession

process,sses,ssed,ssing,ssor,ssion, ssional,ssionally, STEPS TO ACHIEVE A GOAL, INCREMENTAL/GRADUAL CHANGES "prefixes: bio"

procession,nal,nally, MOVING ALONG AS A GROUP (or see precession/ precision)

procetion, precision / procession / precession

prockreashen, procreate(tion)

proclaim,*,med,ming,mer, MAKE VERBAL ANNOUNCEMENT WITH AUTHORITY

proclamashen, proclamation

proclamation,*, ANNOUNCE/DECLARE TO THE PUBLIC

proclimashen, proclamation

proclimation, proclamation

proclivity,ties, A TENDENCY TOWARDS

proclumashen, proclamation

proclumation, proclamation

procram, program

procrastinate,*,ed,ting,tion,tor, REPEATEDELY PUT OFF UNTIL LATER

procreashen, procreate(tion)

procreate,*,ed,ting,tion,tive,tor, TO REPRODUCE/PRODUCE

prod,*,dded,dding,dder, POKE/JAB, POLE/STICK WITH POINTED END

prodakol, protocol

prodatipe, prototype

prodegul, prodigal

prodegy, prodigy

prodekol, protocol

prodest, protest

prodetipe, prototype

prodews, produce

prodicol, protocol

prodigal,lity,lly, ONE WHO SPENDS/ WASTES TOO MUCH MONEY

prodigul, prodigal

prodigy,gies, YOUTH WITH REMARKABLE TALENTS/SKILLS/ APTITUDE

prodikol, protocol

prodikt, predict

proditipe, prototype

prodon, proton

prodotype, prototype

produce,*,ed,cing,cible,er, CREATE/ MANUFACTURE/BRING FORTH, FRUIT/ VEGETABLE "prefixes: re"

producol, protocol

producshen, product(ion)

product,*,tion,tive, SOMETHING PRODUCED/MANUFACTURED/ DEVELOPED AS SALEABLE GOOD, ACT OF CREATING GOODS "prefixes: pre/re"

productive,ely,eness,vity,ion, SOMETHING PRODUCED/ DEVELOPED/ MANUFACTURED AS SALEABLE GOOD, ACT OF CREATING GOODS "prefixes: re/un"

produgee, prodigy

produgil, prodigal

produkol, protocol

produkshen, product(ion)

produktion, product(ion)

produse, produce

produtipe, prototype

prof, proof / prove

profable, prove(vable)

profail, prevail / profile

profalaktik, prophylactic

profale, prevail

profane,ely,eness,er,nity,nities, TO MISUSE WORDS, VULGAR LANGUAGE

profanedy, profane(nity)

profat, profit / prophet

profedik, prophet(ic)

profelaktik, prophylactic

profeser, professor

profeshen, profession

profeshenul, profession(al)

profesional, profession(al)

profesor, professor

profess,sses,ssed,ssedly,ssing, TO VOW, CLAIM ALLEGIANCE/ACCEPTANCE

profession,*,nal,nally,nalism,nalize, LOYAL TO A VOCATION, ADEPT IN THEIR FIELD "prefixes: semi/sub/ un"

professor,*,rial,rially,rate,riate,rship, TEACHER ON COLLEGE/UNIVERSITY STAFF

profesy, prophecy / prophesy

profet, profit / prophet

profetable, profit(able)

profeteer, profit(eer)

profetible, profit(able)

profetik, prophet(ic)

proficient,tly,ncy, SKILLED/ KNOWLEDGEABLE

profide, provide

profiduble, provide(dable)

profilaktik, prophylactic

profile,*,ed,ling, SIDE VIEW OF FACE, OUTLINE/CONTOUR, BIOGRAPHICAL OUTLINE

profishent, proficient

profisy, prophecy / prophesy

profit,*,ted,ting,tless,table,tably,tability, tableness,teer, GAIN ON THE SALE OF SOMETHING (or see prophet) "prefixes: un"

profituble, profit(able)

profolaktik, prophylactic

profound,dly,dness, DEEP/SIGNIFICANT IN KNOWLEDGE/INSIGHT

profownd, profound

profowndly, profound(ly)

profownt, profound

profulaktik, prophylactic

profusy, prophecy / prophesy

progeks, project(s)

progekshin, project(ion)

progekt, project

progektile, project(ile)

progesterone, CHEMICAL PRODUCED BY FEMALES HUMANS/MAMMALS

prognastic, prognostic

prognosis,ses, A MEDICAL OPINION

prognostic,*,cate,cative,cator,cation, PREDICT A MEDICAL CONDITION'S OUTCOME

program,*,mmed,mming,mmer,mmatic, mmatically, OUTLINE OF EVENTS/ ACTIONS/SCHEDULES "prefixes: de/ pre/sub"

programt, program(mmed)

progreshen, progress(ion)

progresive, progress(ive)

progress,sses,ssed,ssing,ssion,ssional, ssionist,ssive, FORWARD MOVEMENT, ADVANCEMENT, EVOLUTION

progressive,ely,eness, ADVANCEMENT/ EVOLUTION/FORWARD MOVEMENT

progretion, progress(ion)

progris, progress

prohabeshin, prohibit(ion)

prohebatory, prohibit(ory)

prohebit, prohibit

prohebition, prohibit(ion)

prohibatif, prohibit(ive)

prohibetory, prohibit(ory)

prohibit,*,ted,ting,tive,tively,tion, tionist,tory, NOT ALLOWED TO DO, FORBID, PREVENT

project,*,ted,ting,table,tile,tion,tional, tionist,tive,tively,tivity,tor, PLAN/ OBJECTIVE/UNDERTAKING TO BE CARRIED OUT, JUT OUT, PROTRUDE, PRESENT

projekshin, project(ion)

projeksion, project(ion)

projektile, project(ile)

projesterone, progesterone

projestirone, progesterone

prokastinate, procrastinate

proklaim, proclaim

proklame, proclaim

proklemashen, proclamation

proklevidy, proclivity

proklimation, proclamation

proklumation, proclamation

proklusion, preclusion

proklusive, preclusive

proknosis, prognosis

prokram, program

prokrastinate, procrastinate
prokrastination, procrastinate(tion)
prokreashen, procreate(tion)
prokreate, procreate
prokreation, procreate(tion)
prokriate, procreate
prokse, proxy
proksemate, proximate
proksimety, proximate(mity)
proksumit, proximate
proleminary, preliminary
prolimenary, preliminary
prolog, prologue
prologue,*,ed,uing,uize,uized,uizing,
INTRO/PREFACE/SPEECH BEFORE A
BOOK/PLAY/POEM/NOVEL
prolok, prologue
prolong,*,ged,ging,gate,gates,gated,
gating,gation, EXTEND/LENGTHEN/
ELONGATE TIME
prolongade, prolong(ate)
prolonk, prolong
prom,*,menade,menaded,menading,
menader, FORMAL DANCE
promanent, prominent
promanintly, prominent(ly)
promanitly, prominent(ly)
promd, prompt
promded, prompt(ed)
promdly, prompt(ly)
promenant, prominent
promenintly, prominent(ly)
promes, promise
promeskuis, promiscuity(uous)
promesquis, promiscuity(uous)
promesquity, promiscuity
prominade, prom(enade) / prominent
prominate, prom(enade) / prominent
prominent,tly,ncy, PRONOUNCED/
DISTINCT/JUTS OUT/STANDS OUT/
NOTICEABLE
prominet, prominent
promiscuity,uous,uously,uousness,
GIVEN TO CONDUCTING SEXUAL/
RANDOM/INDISCRIMINATE
ACTIVITY WITH MANY
promise,*,ed,sing,ser,see,sor,sory,
PLEDGE, AGREE, LOYAL TO FOLLOW
THROUGH AS STATED "prefixes: un"
promiskuis, promiscuity(uous)
promisquis, promiscuity(uous)
promisquity, promiscuity
promist, promise(d)

promote,*,ed,ting,tion,tional,tive,
tiveness,er, ADVERTISE/PRESENT/
ENGAGE TO FURTHER A PROJECT/
EVENT/SALE
prompnes, prompt(ness)
prompt,*,ted,ting,tly,tness,ter,titude,
TIMELY/EXACT/TO REMIND/
PUNCTUAL "prefixes: un"
promt, prompt
promted, prompt(ed)
promtlee, prompt(ly)
promunetly, prominent(ly)
promus, promise
prona, prana / piranha
pronaun, pronoun
pronaunse, pronounce
prondo, pronto
prone,eness, GIVEN/INCLINED TO,
HAVE AN AFFILIATION FOR
prones, prone(ness) / prawn(s)
pronnis, prone(ness)
pronoun, CLASS OF WORDS IN ENGLISH
GRAMMAR
pronounce,*,ed,edly,cing,eable,er,
ement, ARTICULATE/ANNUNCIATE
SPEAKING, DEFINE, SPEAK WITH
CONFIDENCE/AUTHORITY "prefixes:
mis/un"
pronown, pronoun
pronto, QUICKLY/IMMEDIATELY
pronu, prana / piranha
pronunciate,*,ed,ting,tion, ARTICULATE,
BE SPECIFIC IN SPEECH/SPEAKING
pronunseashen, pronunciate(tion)
pronunseate, pronunciate
pronunsiation, pronunciate(tion)
prood, prude
proodish, prude(dish)
proof,*,fed,fing,fer, FACTUAL EVIDENCE,
SUPPORT THE TRUTH, TESTED (or
see prove) "prefixes: dis/over/re"
proon, prune
proot, prude
proove, prove
prop,*,pped,pping, THEATER STAGE SET
TERM, A SUPPORT, AIRPLANE
PROPELLER (or see probe)
"prefixes: under"
propabel, probable
propabelity, probable(bility)
propable, probable / probably
propabul, probable
propagade, propagate

propaganda,dist,distic,distically,dism,
dize, MISINFORMATION,
PURPOSEFUL HALF-TRUTHS
propagashen, propagate(tion)
propagate,*,ed,ting,tion,tional,tive,tor,
BREED/REPRODUCE/MAKE MORE
OF
propain, propane
propane, A GAS
propasishen, preposition / proposition /
prepossess(ion)
propasterus, preposterous
propazishen, preposition / proposition /
prepossess(ion)
propd, prop(pped) / robe(d)
propebly, probably
proped, prop(pped) / probe(d)
propeganda, propaganda
propegashen, propagate(tion)
propegate, propagate
propegation, propagate(tion)
propel,*,lled,lling,llant,ller, EXERT/GIVE
MOMENTUM/START INTO ACTION,
MOVING PART ON A PLANE,
ELEMENT USED TO CREATE
MOVEMENT "prefixes: bi"
propeler, propel(ller)
propelint, propel(llant)
proper,rly,rness, CORRECT/ACCURATE
properedness, prepare(dness)
properidness, prepare(dness)
property,ties,tied,tyless, SOMETHING
TANGIBLE/PHYSICAL TO BE OWNED
BY SOMEONE
prophalaktik, prophylactic
prophecy,cies, PREDICTION OF A DIRE/
UNDESIRABLE FUTURE (or see
prophesy)
prophelaktik, prophylactic
prophesy,sies,sied,sying,siable,sier,
PREDICTION OF THE FUTURE (or
see prophecy)
prophet,*,tic,ecy,esy, ONE WHO IS
BELIEVED TO HAVE CONNECTION
TO THE UNKNOWN SOURCE FOR
PREDICTIONS/ANSWERS (or see
profit)
prophilaktik, prophylactic
prophile, profile
prophisy, prophecy / prophesy
prophit, prophet / profit
propholaktik, prophylactic
prophylactic,*,cally, ITEM USED FOR
CONTRACEPTION

propibly, probably
propigade, propagate
propiganda, propaganda
propigashen, propagate(tion)
propigate, propagate
propigation, propagate(tion)
propiseshen, preposition / proposition / prepossess(ion)
proplem, problem
proplum, problem
propogate, propagate
proponent,*, ONE WHO MAKES A PROPOSAL
proporshen, proportion
proportion,*,ned,ning,nal,nally,nable, nality,nate,nately,nateness, PARTS EQUAL/RELATIVE IN PERSPECTIVE/ SIZE "prefixes: dis/over"
propose,*,ed,er,sing,sal,sition, OFFER/ PRESENT AN IDEA (or see preposition)
proposishen, preposition / proposition / prepossess(ion)
proposition,nal,nally, OFFER/PRESENT AN IDEA/SUGGESTION
proposterus, preposterous
propozishen, preposition / proposition / prepossess(ion)
propriater, proprietor
proprietor,rship,ty,ties,tary, LEGAL OWNER/TITLE HOLDER
propriuter, proprietor
propseshen, preposition / proposition / prepossess(ion)
propt, prop(pped) / probe(d)
propubil, probable
propubiledy, probable(bility)
propubly, probably
propuganda, propaganda
propugashen, propagate(tion)
propugate, propagate
propugation, propagate(tion)
propur, proper
propurle, proper(ly)
propuzishen, preposition / proposition / prepossess(ion)
pros, prose / pro(s)
prosberity, prosper(ity)
proscribe,*,ed,bing,er, OUTLAW/ PROHIBIT (or see prescribe)
prosdatoot, prostitute
prosdetushen, prostitute(tion)
prosditute, prostitute
prosdituion, prostitute(tion)

prosdrate, prostrate / prostate
prose, MORE LIKE NORMAL WRITTEN LANGUAGE THAN POETRY (or see pro(s))
prosechin, precision / procession / precession
prosecute,*,ed,ting,tion,tor, FOLLOW THROUGH, FINAL DETERMINATION, ENFORCE THE LAW, INITIATE A LAWSUIT (or see persecute)
prosed, proceed
proseds, proceed(s)
proseets, proceed(s)
proseetsher, procedure
proseger, procedure
prosejur, procedure
prosekewt, prosecute
prosekushen, prosecute(tion)
prosekution, prosecute(tion)
proses, process
proseshen, precision / procession / precession
prosetion, precision / procession / precession
prosicute, prosecute
prosidger, procedure
prosijur, procedure
prosikushen, prosecute(tion)
prosikute, prosecute
prosis, process
prosparidy, prosper(ity)
prospect,*,ted,ting,tor,tive,tively,tus, EXPECTING/FUTURE/POSSIBLE EVENT/ SITUATION, MINING FOR SOMETHING "prefixes: bio"
prospectif, prospect(ive)
prospekt, prospect
prospektif, prospect(ive)
prosper,*,red,ring,rity,rities,rous,rously, rousness, BENEFIT GREATLY, BE SUCCESSFUL
prosperidy, prosper(ity)
prospir, prosper
prospirus, prosper(ous)
prospures, prosper(s) / prosper(ous)
prostate,ectomy,ectomies,tism, PERTAINS TO A GLAND AROUND THE MALE URETHRA (or see prostrate)
prostatution, prostitute(tion)
prostetute, prostitute
prostetution, prostitute(tion)
prosthesis,etic,etically, ARTIFICIAL REPLACEMENT OF A BODY PART

prosthesus, prosthesis
prostitute,*,tion,tor, PERSON WHO TRADES SEXUAL FAVORS FOR MONEY/GOODS
prostrade, prostrate / prostate
prostrate,*,ed,ting,tion,tor, TO PLACE ONE'S BODY INTO A SUBMISSIVE POSITION/POSTURE, ASSUME A HUMILIATED/HELPLESS/ POWERLESS POSITION (or see prostate)
prosukushen, prosecute(tion)
prot, prod
protacol, protocol
protaga, protege'
protagenist, protagonist
protaginest, protagonist
protagonist,*, LEADING/PRINCIPAL CHARACTER
protajay, protege'
protakol, protocol
protatype, prototype
protean, protein
protecol, protocol
protect,*,ted,ting,tion,tionism,tionist, tive,tor, GUARD/SHIELD/PREVENT FROM DANGER/HARM/ DESTRUCTION "prefixes: un"
protectif, protect(ive)
protega, protege'
protege',*, YOUNG PERSON UNDER CARE/PROTECTION OF AN ELDER/ MASTER (or see prodigy)
protein,*, CHEMICAL COMPOUNDS
protejay, protege'
protekol, protocol
protekshen, protect(ion)
protekt, protect
protektuf, protect(ive)
protene, protein
protes, protest
protest,*,ted,ting,ter, TAKE ACTION AGAINST A PERCEIVED INJUSTICE TO AFFECT CHANGE
protestur, protest(er)
protetipe, prototype
protetype, prototype
proticol, protocol
protiga, protege'
protijay, protege'
protikol, protocol
protitype, prototype
protocol,*,led,ling, GENERAL RULE WHETHER FORMALIZED OR NOT

proton,*,nic, A MOLECULAR PARTICLE OF POSITIVE CHARGE
protonek, proton(ic)
prototipe, prototype
prototype,*,pal,pic, A MODEL/ REPLICATE OF ORIGINAL, FIRST MODEL
protract,tion,tive,ted,tor, DRAW OUT/ LENGTHEN TIME/SPACE/DISTANCE, A TOOL FOR DRAWING
protrakt, protract
protrakter, protract(or)
protrude,*,ed,ding,ent,usible,usion, usile,usive,usively,usiveness, EXTENDS/PROJECTS OUT
protrugin, protrude(usion)
protrushen, protrude(usion)
protrusuf, protrude(usive)
protukol, protocol
protutipe, prototype
proud,dly,dness, PAST TENSE FOR THE WORD" PRIDE", HAPPY ABOUT AN ACCOMPLISHMENT
proues, prowess
prouis, prowess
proul, prowl
provacation, provocative(ion)
provakashen, provocative(ion)
prove,*,ed,ving,vable,vably, BRING FORTH FACTS, MAKE TRUTH KNOWN (or see proof) "prefixes: dis/re"
proveable, prove(vable)
proveble, prove(vable)
provecation, provocative(ion)
provekation, provocative(ion)
provence, province
provencial, province(cial)
provensial, province(cial)
provent, prevent
provents, province / prevent(s)
proverb,*,bial,bially, POPULAR/WISE SAYING
proverbeil, proverb(ial)
proverbeul, proverb(ial)
proveshen, provision
provible, prove(vable)
provication, provocative(ion)
provide,*,ed,ding,er,dable, MAKE AVAILABLE/GIVE/EXPOSE "prefixes: un"
provikation, provocative(ion)
province,*,cial,cially,ciality,cialize, cialities,cialist,cialize,cialism,

DESIGNATED AREA OUTSIDE OF MAINSTREAM GIVEN TO A SPECIFIC ORDER/RULE
provinshul, province(cial)
provint, prevent
provints, province
provirb, proverb
provirbeul, proverb(ial)
provision,*,ned,ning,ner, SUPPLIES, ALLOWANCES, PROVIDE FOR
provocative,ely,eness,ion, STIMULATE/ ENTICE TO REACT
provokative, provocative
provoke,*,ed,king,kingly,ocation, ENTICE/LURE/MANIPULATE TO REACT
provost,tship, CHURCH/EDUCATIONAL SUPERIOR
provuble, prove(vable)
provukashen, provocative(ion)
provukation, provocative(ion)
provurb, proverb
provurbeul, proverb(ial)
provurbial, proverb(ial)
prowd, proud
prowdly, proud(ly)
prowess, EXCEPTIONAL BRAVERY/SKILL
prowis, prowess
prowl,*,led,ling,ler, SOMEONE SNEAKING AROUND IN SEARCH OF SOMETHING/SOMEONE
prowt, proud
prowtly, proud(ly)
proxamit, proximate
proxemidy, proximate(mity)
proximate,ely,eness,mity,al, NEXT/ NEAR IN TIME/SPACE, CLOSE TO (or see approximate)
proxsemity, proximate(mity)
proxumit, proximate
proxy,xies, AUTHORIZED/LEGAL TO SUBSTITUTE FOR
prozdatute, prostitute
prozdetushen, prostitute(tion)
prozditushin, prostitute(tion)
prozdrate, prostrate / prostate
proztate, prostate / prostrate
prubaskis, proboscis
prubozkis, proboscis
prucede, precede / proceed
prucedure, procedure
prucepitous, precipitous
pruclivity, proclivity
pruclusion, preclusion

pruclusive, preclusive
prude,ery,eries,dish,dishness, SOMEONE UNCOMFORTABLE WITH SEX RELATED ISSUES
prudence,nt,ntly,ntial,ntially, PRACTICING CAUTION/GOOD JUDGEMENT
prudense, prudence
prudesh, prude(dish)
prudikament, predicament
prudinse, prudence
prudunt, prudence(nt)
pruf, proof / prove
prufanedy, profane(nity)
prufanity, profane(nity)
prufedik, prophet(ic)
prufeshen, profession
prufeshinul, profession(al)
prufesional, profession
prufible, prove(vable)
prufide, provide
prufiduble, provide(dable)
prufuble, prove(vable)
prugektile, project(ile)
prugnostik, prognostic
prugnoztek, prognostic
prugreshen, progress(ion)
prugresif, progress(ive)
prugresive, progress(ive)
prugretion, progress(ion)
pruhebit, prohibit
pruhibatif, prohibit(ive)
pruhibet, prohibit
prujektile, project(ile)
pruklivedy, proclivity
pruklivity, proclivity
pruklusion, preclusion
pruklusive, preclusive
pruleminary, preliminary
prulimenary, preliminary
prumere, premier
prumiskues, promiscuity(uous)
prumoder, promote(r)
prumoshen, promote(tion)
prumote, promote
prumoter, promote(r)
prumotion, promote(tion)
prune,*,ed,ning, DRIED PLUM, TRIM A SHRUB/TREE
prunownse, pronounce
prupare, prepare
prupel, propel
prupeler, propel(ller)
prupelint, propel(llant)

prupelir, propel(ller)
prupelt, propel(lled)
pruponent, proponent
pruporshen, proportion
pruporshenate, proportion(al)
pruportion, proportion
prupose, propose
pruposition, proposition
pruposle, propose(sal)
prupoze, propose
prupozel, propose(sal)
prupozishen, proposition
prupriater, proprietor
pruprietor, proprietor
prusdej, prestige
prusdejus, prestige(gious)
prusechen, precision / procession / precession
prusede, precede / proceed
prusejur, procedure
prusepitous, precipitous
pruseshin, precision / procession / precession
prusetgur, procedure
prusetion, precision / procession / precession
prusipitous, precipitous
prusiputashen, precipitate(tion)
prusishen, precision
prusisly, precise(ly)
prusition, precision / procession / precession
pruskribe, prescribe / proscribe
prusteg, prestige
prustegis, prestige(gious)
prustejus, prestige(gious)
prute, prude
prutective, protect(ive)
prutekshen, protect(ion)
prutektuf, protect(ive)
prutish, prude(dish)
prutrude, protrude
prutrushen, protrude(usion)
prutrusion, protrude(usion)
pruv, prove
pruvale, prevail
pruvencial, province(cial)
pruvenshen, prevent(ion)
pruvenshul, province(cial)
pruvent, prevent
pruventable, prevent(able)
pruventive, prevent(ive)
pruverbeul, proverb(ial)
pruvide, provide

pruviduble, provide(dable)
pruvinshul, province(cial)
pruvint, prevent
pruvintable, prevent(able)
pruvokative, provocative
pruzentuble, present(able)
pruzumshen, presume(mption)
pry,ries,ried,ying,yingly,rier, PEEP IN, METHOD OF OPENING SOMETHING THAT'S TIGHTLY CLOSED
pryer, prior
prymate, primate
psalm,*, BIBLICAL SONG
psariasis, psoriasis
pseudo, PREFIX INDICATING 'FALSE/ PRETEND/IMITATION' MOST OFTEN MODIFIES THE WORD
pseudonym,*, USING ANOTHER NAME
psicheatric, psychiatric
psichopathologist, psychopath(ologist)
psikeatric, psychiatric
psikik, psychic
psikilegekul, psychology(gical)
psikilegy, psychology
psikologekul, psychology(gical)
psikologest, psychology(gist)
psikology, psychology
psikopath, psychopath
psikopathic, psychopath(ic)
psikopatholagist, psychopath(ologist)
psikosis, psychosis
psikotic, psychotic
psoriasis,atic, SKIN PROBLEM
psudo, pseudo
psuriesis, psoriasis
psych, PREFIX INDICATING "MIND/ MENTAL" MOST OFTEN MODIFIES THE WORD
psychadelic, psychedelic
psyche,edelic, OVERALL ESSENCE OF THE HUMAN BEING, SOUL/BODY/ MIND/ SPIRIT (or see sic/sick)
psycheatric, psychiatric
psychedelic,*, HALLUCINATION/ DELUSION/MIND ALTERING
psychiatric,*,cally, FIELD OF SCIENCE WHICH STUDIES THE MIND/ EMOTIONS
psychiatry,rist, PHYSICIAN WHO STUDIES THE MIND, STUDY OF THE MIND/ EMOTIONS
psychic,*,cal,cally, USE OF THE MORPHOGENIC FIELD TO SEE PAST/ PRESENT/ FUTURE EVENTS, EXTRA-

SENSORY PERCEPTION "prefixes: intra"
psychidelic, psychedelic
psychietrist, psychiatry(rist)
psychietry, psychiatry
psychiotrist, psychiatry(rist)
psycho,*, SLANG FOR SOMEONE WHO IS BEING LUDICROUS/CRAZY
psychodelic, psychedelic
psycholagy, psychology
psycholgekul, psychology(gical)
psychology,gies,gical,gically,gism,gist, gize, FIELD OF SCIENCE RELATED TO STUDYING THE MIND/MENTAL "prefixes: bio"
psychopath,*,hic,hically,hy,hology, hylogical,hologist, SOMEONE WHO HAS OR WORKS WITH A PERSONALITY DISORDER
psychopathic, psychopath(ic)
psychopatholagist, psychopath(ologist)
psychosis, A MENTAL DISORDER WHICH RENDERS A PERSON DISATTACHED FROM NORMAL REALITY
psychotic,cally, MENTAL DISORDER THAT RENDERS A PERSON DISATTACHED FROM NORMAL REALITY "prefixes: non"
psychudelic, psychedelic
psycik, psychic
psykadelic, psychedelic
psykapathic, psychopath(ic)
psykeatric, psychiatric
psykedelic, psychedelic
psykek, psychic
psykepathic, psychopath(ic)
psykiatric, psychiatric
psykiatrist, psychiatry(rist)
psykiatry, psychiatry
psykidelic, psychedelic
psykik, psychic
psykipathic, psychopath(ic)
psykiutry, psychiatry
psyko, psycho
psykolegy, psychology
psykoligekul, psychology(gical)
psykoligy, psychology
psykologekul, psychology(gical)
psykologest, psychology(gist)
psykology, psychology
psykopath, psychopath
psykopathic, psychopath(ic)
psykopatholagist, psychopath(ologist)
psykosis, psychosis

psykotic, psychotic
psykudelic, psychedelic
psykyatric, psychiatric
pu, pew
pub,*, A TAVERN (or see pube)
pube,*,bic,escent,escence,escency,
    HAIR ON GENITALS WHICH APPEAR
    DURING PUBERTY, THE DOWN ON
    PLANTS
pubek, pube(bic)
puberdy, puberty
puberty, BECOMING OF AGE FOR
    REPRODUCTION
pubescent,nce,ncy, GOING THROUGH
    PUBERTY "prefixes: pre"
pubirty, puberty
publacation, publication
publacist, publicist
publakashen, publication
publakation, publication
publash, publish
publasher, publish(er)
publasist, publicist
publasize, publicity(ize)
publecation, publication
publecist, publicist
publecity, publicity(ity)
publek, public
publekashin, publication
publekation, publication
publesher, publish(er)
publeshuble, publish(able)
publesist, publicist
publesity, publicity(ity)
publesize, publicity(ize)
public,cly,cness, NOT PRIVATE
publicashen, publication
publication,*, ISSUE PRINTED
    MATERIAL FOR PUBLIC
publicist,ity,ize,cation, INVOLVED IN
    THE PRODUCTION/DISSEMINATION
    OF WRITTEN TEXT
publicity, USING MEDIA TO GAIN
    PUBLIC ATTENTION
publicize,*,ed,zing, ADVERTISE, MAKE
    PUBLICLY KNOWN
publikashen, publication
publikation, publication
publisaty, publicist(ity)
publisety, publicity(ity)
publish,hes,hed,hing,hable,her,
    INVOLVED IN PRODUCTION/
    DISSEMINATION OF WRITTEN TEXT/
    INFORMATION "prefixes: un"

publishuble, publish(able)
publisist, publicist
publisity, publicist(ity)
publisize, publicity(ize)
publokashen, publication
publosher, publish(er)
publosist, publicist
publosize, publicity(ize)
publucation, publication
publucist, publicist
publukation, publication
publush, publish
publushable, publish(able)
publusher, publish(er)
publusist, publicist
publusize, publicity(ize)
puburdy, puberty
puc, puck / puke
puch, pooch / push
puck,*, A DISC USED IN HOCKEY (or see
    puke)
pud, put
pudado, potato
pudal, puddle / poodle
puddil, puddle / poodle
pudding, A CREAMY DESSERT (or see
    putt(ing))
puddle,*,ed,ling, SMALL POOL OF
    LIQUID (or see poodle)
puddul, puddle / poodle
pude, put / putty
pudel, puddle / poodle
pudeng, pudding / putt(ing)
puder, pewter / putt(er)
pudestrein, pedestrian
pudgie, pudgy
pudgy, A BIT OVERWEIGHT
pudil, puddle / poodle
puding, pudding / putt(ing)
pudir, pewter / putt(er)
pudje, pudgy
pudl, puddle / poodle
pudul, puddle / poodle
pudur, pewter / putt(er)
pudy, putty
puer, poor / pour / pore
puf, puff
pufeleon, pavilion
pufer, puff(er)
puff,*,ffed,ffing,ffer, SHORT/SUDDEN
    BURST OF AIR/SMOKE, TO INHALE/
    EXHALE SMOKE
pufileon, pavilion
pufs, puff(s)

puft, puff(ed)
pugamus, pajamas
puge, pudgy
puir, poor / pour / pore
puit, put
pujamus, pajamas
puje, pudgy
pujomus, pajamas
puk, puck / puke
puke,*,ed,king, TO VOMIT/THROW-UP
    (or see puck)
pukon, pecan
pukuleur, peculiar
pul, pull / pool
pularity, polar(ity)
puld, pull(ed) / pool(ed)
pule, pool / pulley
puled, pull(ed) / pool(ed)
pulegimy, polygamy
puleridy, polar(ity)
pules, police / pulley(s)
pulet, pullet
pulewshen, pollute(tion)
puley, pulley
pulferise, pulverize
pulfurise, pulverize
puli, pulley
pulies, pulley(s)
puligamus, polygamy(mous)
puligemy, polygamy
puligine, polygyny
puling, pull(ing) / pool(ing)
pulit, pullet / polite
pull,*,lled,lling,ller,lley, TO DRAW/
    BRING TOWARDS, TUG
    SOMETHING/SOMEONE (or see
    pool)
pullet,*, YOUNG DOMESTICATED HEN
pulley,*, TOOL USED WITH ROPE FOR
    LIFTING/PULLING
pullit, pullet
pulmanery, pulmonary
pulmonary, PERTAINING TO THE LUNGS
pulmunery, pulmonary
pulp,piness,py, FIBROUS/THICK
    SUBSTANCE LEFT BEHIND WHEN
    VEGETABLE/ FRUIT/PLANTS ARE
    COOKED/ SMASHED
pulpet, pulpit
pulpit, CHURCH PLATFORM
pulsashen, pulsate(tion)
pulsate,*,ed,ting,tile,tion,tor,tory,
    PULSE/THROB

pulse,*,ed,sing, THROB/BEAT
RYTHMICALLY
pult, pull(ed) / pool(ed)
pulushen, pollute(tion)
pulut, pollute / pullet
pulutent, pollute(tant)
pulution, pollute(tion)
pulverize,*,ed,zing,er, REDUCE TO
POWDER/PULP
pulvirise, pulverize
pulvorise, pulverize
puly, pulley
pulygamus, polygamy(mous)
pulygamy, polygamy
pulyginy, polygyny
pulzate, pulsate
pumal, pummel
pumas, pumice
pumb, pump
pumbt, pump(ed)
pumcan, pumpkin
pumel, pummel
pumes, pumice
pumice,eous, VOLCANIC STONE USED
FOR SANDING
pumil, pummel
pumis, pumice
pumkan, pumpkin
pumkun, pumpkin
pumle, pummel
pummel,*,led,ling, POMMEL/HIT
REPEATEDLY CAUSING DAMAGE
pumol, pummel
pumos, pumice
pump,*,ped,ping,per, FORCE LIQUID/
OBJECT TO MOVE INTO A
DESIGNATED DIRECTION
pumpken, pumpkin
pumpkin,*, A LARGE SQUASH
pumpt, pump(ed)
pumul, pummel
pumus, pumice
pun,*,nned,nning, TO USE WORDS
SIMILAR BUT DIFFERENT FOR
HUMOROUS INTENT
punatef, punitive
punative, punitive
punch,hes,hed,hing,her, STRIKE
AGAINST SOMETHING WITH FORCE,
TO PIERCE, DRINK MIXTURE
puncherd, puncture(d)
puncht, punch(ed)
punchuate, punctuate
puncsher, puncture

puncshuate, punctuate
puncshuel, punctual
punctewashen, punctuate(tion)
punctual,lity,lly, ARRIVE ON TIME
punctuashen, punctuate(tion)
punctuate,*,ed,ting,tion,tor, USE
MARKS/SYMBOLS IN TEXT FOR
CLARIFICATION
puncture,*,ed,ring,rable, PIERCE/
PERFORATE/PRICK THROUGH
SOMETHING
pund, punt / pun(nned)
punech, punish
puneched, punish(ed)
punechmint, punish(ment)
punensula, peninsula
punesh, punish
puneshmint, punish(ment)
punesht, punish(ed)
punetive, punitive
pungensy, pungent(ncy)
pungent,tly,ncy, STRONG/SHARP SMELL
OR TASTE
punginsy, pungent(ncy)
pungunt, pungent
punich, punish
punichment, punish(ment)
puninsula, peninsula
punish,hes,hed,hing,her,hable,hment,
APPLY MEASURES TO CORRECT
INTOLERABLE ACT
punishmint, punish(ment)
punisht, punish(ed)
punitive,ely,eness, INFLICT/IMPOSE
PUNISHMENT
punjensy, pungent(ncy)
punjinsy, pungent(ncy)
punjunt, pungent
punk,*,ker, STICK USED FOR STARTING
FIREWORKS, DERAGATORY WORD
FOR BAD BEHAVIOR
punkchashen, punctuate(tion)
punkcher, puncture
punkchewashen, punctuate(tion)
punkchewate, punctuate
punkchir, puncture
punkchuate, punctuate
punkchuation, punctuate(tion)
punkchur, puncture
punkir, punk(er)
punksher, puncture
punkshewal, punctual
punkshewashen, punctuate(tion)
punkshewate, punctuate

punkshewul, punctual
punkshir, puncture
punkshooate, punctuate
punkshooation, punctuate(tion)
punkshooel, punctual
punkshor, puncture
punkshual, punctual
punkshuashen, punctuate(tion)
punkshuate, punctuate
punkshuation, punctuate(tion)
punkshuol, punctual
punkshur, puncture
punktual, punctual
punktuate, punctuate
punotif, punitive
punsh, punch
punshur, puncture / punch(er)
punt,*,ted,ting,ter, DROP/KICK A BALL,
PROPEL, OF A POINTED NATURE,
GAMBLE (or see pun(ed))
punuched, punish(ed)
punuchment, punish(ment)
punudeve, punitive
punudive, punitive
punushed, punish(ed)
punushment, punish(ment)
punutive, punitive
puny,nier,niest, INSIGNIFICANT, SMALL,
WEAK IN SIZE/STRENGTH
pup,*,ppy,ppies, A NEWBORN DOG/
SEAL (or see pop)
pupal, pupil
pupater, puppet(eer)
pupatree, puppet(ry)
pupe, pup(ppy)
pupel, pupil
pupet, puppet
pupeteer, puppet(eer)
pupetry, puppet(ry)
pupil,*,llary, PART OF THE EYE,
STUDENT UNDER TUTELAGE OF
INSTRUCTOR/GUARDIAN "prefixes:
inter"
pupit, puppet
pupiteer, puppet(eer)
pupitry, puppet(ry)
pupiya, papaya
puplasher, publish(er)
puplasist, publicist
puplasize, publicity(ize)
puple, pupil
puplek, public
puplekashin, publication
puplesh, publish

puplesist, publicist
puplik, public
puplikashen, publication
puplish, publish
puplisher, publish(er)
puplisist, publicist
puplisize, publicity(ize)
puplosher, publish(er)
puplosist, publicist
puplukashin, publication
puplusher, publish(er)
puplusize, publicity(ize)
pupol, pupil
puporshenal, proportion(al)
puportion, proportion
puppateer, puppet(eer)
puppet,*,try,teer, A DOLL/FIGURE/
    MARIONETTE RESEMBLING
    ANIMAL/HUMAN
puppiteer, puppet(eer)
pupput, puppet
pupputeer, puppet(eer)
pupul, pupil
puput, puppet
puputer, puppet(eer)
puputry, puppet(ry)
pupy, pup(ppy)
pupyu, papaya
pur, purr / per / pure / pour / poor
purabula, parabola
purade, parade
purafecashen, purify(fication)
purafication, purify(fication)
puragative, prerogative
puralasis, paralysis
puralises, paralysis
puramedur, parameter / perimeter
puramiter, parameter / perimeter
purapula, parable
purate, parade
purbendikuler, perpendicular
purceptible, perceptible
purch, perch / purge
purchase,*,ed,sing,er,sable, ACQUIRE/
    SECURE OWNERSHIP OF
purchis, purchase / perch(es)
purcivere, persevere
purdly, pert(ly)
pure,ely,er,est,eness, NOT MIXED, FREE
    OF IMPURITIES/CONTAMINANTS
puree', FOOD BOILED INTO A PULP AND
    RUN THROUGH A STRAINER/SIEVE
purefacation, purify(fication)
pureferul, peripheral

pureficashen, purify(fication)
purefide, purify(fied)
purendal, parent(al)
pureneul, perennial
purental, parent(al)
purenthases, parenthesis
purfect, perfect
purfekshen, perfect(ion)
purfektion, perfect(ion)
purfert, pervert
purferted, pervert(ed)
purfikt, perfect
purform, perform
purformence, perform(ance)
purfume, perfume
purgatory,ries,tive, THEORETICAL
    PLACE WHERE A PERSON MAY
    SPEND TIME AFTER DEATH
purge,*,ed,ging,ger, PURIFY/CLEANSE/
    GET RID OF/FREE/REMOVE
purger, perjure
purgery, perjure(ry)
purgetory, purgatory
purgury, perjure(ry)
purgutory, purgatory
purhaps, perhaps
purifecation, purify(fication)
puriferul, peripheral
purificashen, purify(fication)
purifide, purify(fied)
purify,fies,fied,ying,ficator,fication, ACT
    OF CLEANSING/RIDDING/FREEING/
    REMOVING
purineal, perennial
purintal, parent(al)
purinthusees, parenthesis
purje, purge
purjury, perjure(ry)
purkushen, percussion
purl, pearl
purly, pure(ly)
purmanence, permanence
purmanent, permanent
purmanins, permanence
purmeate, permeate
purmenint, permanent
purmeuble, permeable
purmishen, permission
purmisive, permissive
purmit, permit
purmited, permit(tted)
purmition, permission
purmnent, permanent
purogative, prerogative

purokside, peroxide
purole, parole
purona, piranha
purooze, peruse
purosedy, porosity
purosity, porosity
puroxside, peroxide
purpel, purple
purpendicular, perpendicular
purpes, purpose
purpeshual, perpetual
purpesly, purpose(ly)
purpetrate, perpetrate
purpetshual, perpetual
purpetshuate, perpetual(ate)
purpetual, perpetual
purpetuate, perpetual(ate)
purpetuity, perpetuity
purpil, purple
purpindicular, perpendicular
purpis, purpose
purpisly, purpose(ly)
purpitrate, perpetrate
purple,lish, A COLOR
purpleksity, perplex(ity)
purplex, perplex
purplexity, perplex(ity)
purporshenal, proportion(al)
purportional, proportion(al)
purpose,*,ed,sing,eful,efully,efulness,
    eless,ely,sive,sively,siveness,
    elessness, REASON FOR/MISSION/
    GOAL, DESIGN FOR "prefixes: multi"
purposly, purpose(ly)
purpul, purple
purpus, purpose
purpusly, purpose(ly)
purr,*,rred,rring, GUTTURAL SOUND
    COMING FROM A CATS THROAT
    WHEN PLEASED
pursacute, persecute
pursavere, persevere
pursbektif, perspective
pursbiration, perspiration
pursbire, perspire
purscription, prescript(ion)
purse,*,ed,sing, HAND BAG, PRIZE
    MONEY, SQUEEZE TIGHTLY
    TOGETHER
pursebduble, perceptible
pursebtef, percept(ive)
pursecute, persecute
pursen, person
pursenality, personality

pursenaly, personal(lly)
pursenel, personnel
pursent, percent
pursentige, percent(age)
pursentil, percent(ile)
pursenuble, person(able)
pursenul, personal
pursenulize, personal(ize)
pursepdable, perceptible
pursepshen, percept(ion)
purseptef, percept(ive)
purseption, percept(ion)
purseptive, percept(ive)
purseshen, precision
pursest, persist
purseve, perceive
purseverense, persevere(rance)
purshis, purchase / perch(es)
pursikute, persecute
pursin, person
pursinaledy, personality
pursinel, personnel
pursint, percent
pursinuble, person(able)
pursinulize, personal(ize)
pursinuly, personal(lly)
pursipatation, precipitate(tion)
pursishen, precision
pursist, persist
pursistence, persist(ence)
purskripshen, prescript(ion)
purson, person
pursona, person(a)
pursonality, personality
pursonefication, person(ification)
pursonifekashen, person(ification)
pursonify, personify
pursoo, pursue
pursparashen, perspiration
purspective, perspective
pursperashen, perspiration
purspiration, perspiration
purspire, perspire
pursuade, persuade
pursuasion, persuade(asion)
pursuasive, persuade(asive)
pursude, pursue(d)
pursue,*,ed,uing,er,uant,uit, SEEKING/
    STRIVING TO OVERCOME/
    OVERTAKE
pursute, pursue(uit)
pursuvere, persevere
purswade, persuade
purswashen, persuade(asion)

purswasif, persuade(asive)
purt, pert
purtain, pertain
purtane, pertain
purterb, perturb
purterbt, perturb(ed)
purteshen, partition
purtishen, partition
purtrayal, portray(al)
purtrayed, portray(ed)
puruficashun, purify(fication)
purufied, purify(fied)
puruse, peruse
purvade, pervade
purvashen, pervade(asion)/provision
purvasif, pervade(asion)
purversev, pervert(rsive)
purvert, pervert
purvirsev, pervert(rsive)
purvurshen, pervert(rsion)
pury, puree'
purzakute, persecute
pus, FLUID/INFLAMMATION PRESENT
    AS THE RESULT OF AN INFECTION
    (or see puss)
pusdasheo, pistachio
pusdromy, pastrami
pusefic, pacific
pusel, puzzle
puseld, puzzle(d)
puses, possess
push,hes,hed,hing,hier,hiest,her,hy,hily,
    hiness, FORCE/EXERT MOVEMENT
pushenis, push(iness)
pushir, push(er)
pusie, puss(y)
pusific, pacific
pusil, puzzle
pusiled, puzzle(d)
pusishen, position
puskrepshen, prescript(ion)
pusl, puzzle
puss,ssy,ssies, A CAT, THE FACE WHERE
    THE MOUTH IS, SLANDER FOR A
    WHIMP (or see pus)
pustasheo, pistachio
pustrome, pastrami
pusul, puzzle
pusy, puss(y)
put,*,tted,tting,tter, TO PLACE (or see
    putt)
putado, potato
putal, puddle / poodle
putato, potato

pute, putty / putt
putees, putty(tties)
putel, puddle / poodle
putena, patina
putenchul, potential
puteng, pudding / putt(ing) / put(tting)
putenshul, potential
putential, potential
puter, pewter / putt(er)
puterbd, perturb(ed)
puternol, paternal
putestrein, pedestrian
puthetic, pathetic
putil, puddle / poodle
putina, patina
putinchul, potential
puting, pudding / putt(ing) / put(tting)
putintial, potential
putir, pewter / putt(er)
putishen, petition / beautician
putition, petition
putle, puddle / poodle
putol, puddle / poodle
putoto, potato
putrid,dity,dness,dly, ROTTEN,
    CORRUPT, VILE
putrol, patrol
putrood, protrude
putrude, protrude
putt,*,tting,tter, A GOLF STROKE (or see
    put)
puttle, puddle / poodle
putty,tties,ttied,ttying, TACKY/PASTY
    SUBSTANCE
putul, puddle / poodle
puty, putty
puveleon, pavilion
puvileon, pavilion
puvirted, pervert(ed)
puwding, pudding / putt(ing) /
    put(tting)
puzel, puzzle
puzeld, puzzle(d)
puzes, possess
puzil, puzzle
puzl, puzzle
puzled, puzzle(d)
puzzle,*,ed,ling,er,ement, PROBLEM
    WITH ONLY ONE SOLUTION, MANY
    PARTS MAKE UP THE BIG PICTURE
pygme, pygmy
pygmy,mies, VERY SMALL/DWARFED IN
    COMPARISON TO OTHERS IN ITS
    SPECIES

pyis, pious

pyke, pike

pyle, pile

pype, pipe

pyramid,*, FOUR-SIDED/TRIANGULAR STRUCTURE

pyrana, piranha

pyranna, piranha

pyre,*, MOUND OF COMBUSTIBLE MATERIAL WHERE AN EXPIRED BODY IS PLACED FOR CEREMONIAL CREMATION (or see pier/peer/pierce)

pyrite,*,tic, YELLOW COLORED METAL

pyro,*, SLANG FOR SOMEONE WHO PLAYS WITH FIRE, PREFIX INDICATING "FIRE/HEAT" MOST OFTEN MODIFIES THE WORD

pyrona, piranha

python,*, A VENOMOUS SNAKE

q, cue

qkumber, cucumber

qkwant, quaint

qords, quartz / quart(s)

qork, quark / cork

qorts, quartz / quart(s)

qu, cue

quack,*,ked,king, SOUND A DUCK MAKES, SLANG FOR A 'NO GOOD DOCTOR' (or see quake)

quad,*, SHORT FOR QUADRANT, FOUR, QUADRANGLE, QUADRUPLET

quadrant,*,tal, ONE QUARTER OF A CIRCLE

quadrint, quadrant

quael, quail

quaent, quaint

quagmire,*, BOG, SOFT EARTH HEAVY WITH MOISTURE

quail,*, A GAME BIRD

quaint,tly,tness, PLEASING/COMFORTABLE/PICTURESQUE

quak, quack

quake,*,ed,king, A TREMBLING/SHAKING (or see quack)

quakmire, quagmire

qual, quail

qualedy, quality

qualefy, qualify

qualefyable, qualify(fiable)

qualetatif, quality(tative)

qualetative, quality(tative)

qualety, quality

qualidy, quality

qualify,fies,fied,fying,fiedly,fier,fiable, fying,fication, IS ELIGIBLE/CAPABLE/SKILLFUL ENOUGH "prefixes: dis/over/un"

qualifyable, qualify(fiable)

qualifyer, qualify(fier)

qualitatif, quality(tative)

quality,ties,tative,tatively, A MEASURE/GUAGE OF RESULTS IN THE OUTCOME OF AN EFFORT, A SCALE WHICH RATES THE BEST/WORST

qualm,*,mish,mishly,mishness, FEELING OF DOUBT/TWINGE/UNEASINESS

qualufecashen, qualify(fication)

qualufi, qualify

quandary,ries, DIFFICULTY/HESITANCY/PERPLEXING

quandery, quandary

quandre, quandary

quanetative, quantitative

quanitative, quantitative

quanotative, quantitative

quant, quaint

quanta,tum, SMALLEST AMOUNT OF ENERGY CAPABLE OF EXISTING ON ITS OWN, QUALITY/EXTENT

quantefy, quantify

quantefyer, quantify(fier)

quantem, quanta(tum)

quantery, quandary

quantetative, quantitative

quantety, quantity

quantify,fies,fied,fying,fiable,fication, fier, MEASURE/DETERMINE THE AMOUNT OF

quantim, quanta(tum)

quantitative,ely, MEASURE BY QUALITY RATHER THAN QUANTITY

quantity,ties, MEASURE OF THE AMOUNT/FREQUENCY OF OCCURENCE

quantom, quanta(tum)

quantry, quandary

quarantine,*,ed,ning,nable, SECTION OFF/ISOLATE FROM EVERYTHING ELSE

quarder, quarter

quarderly, quarter(ly)

quardur, quarter

quardurly, quarter(ly)

quare, quarry / query

quarel, quarrel

quarentene, quarantine

quari, query

quaril, quarrel

quarinteen, quarantine

quark,*, BASIC/ELEMENTARY PARTICLE (or see cork)

quarol, quarrel

quarontene, quarantine

quarrel,*,led,ling,lsome,lsomely, lsomeness, BICKER, ARGUE, BE AT ODDS WITH, ENHARMONIC, SQUARE SHAPED HEAD, A TOOL

quarry,rries,rried,ying,rrier, DIG A PIT INTO THE EARTH FOR STONE/DIRT, PURSUED GAME

quart,*, U.S. MEASUREMENT OF LIQUID (or see quartz)

quarter,*,red,ring,rage,rly,rlies, ONE-FOURTH OF THE WHOLE, U.S. COIN

quartirly, quarter(ly)

quartur, quarter

quarturly, quarter(ly)

quartz,zite,zose,zous, MINERAL/ROCK (or see quart(s))

quarunteen, quarantine

quasadilla, quesadilla

quasar,*, ASTRONOMICAL OBJECT WITH HIGH ENERGY OUTPUT

quasi, SORT OF, SIMILAR, NOT CERTAIN

quawry, quarry

quazar, quasar

qucumber, cucumber

quean, queen

queck, quick

queckest, quick(est)

queen,*,ned,nliness,nly, A FEMALE OF ROYALTY

queer,*,rly,rness, STRANGE/ODD, HOMOSEXUAL

quefer, quiver

queint, quaint

quek, quick

queke, quick(ie)

quekest, quick(est)

quekly, quick(ly)

quel, quill / quail / kale

quelt, quilt

quemulutive, cumulative

quench,hes,hed,hing,hable,her,hless, TO SATISFY, PUT AWAY, EXTINGUISH

quentuplet, quintuplet

querable, curable

queri, query

querk, quirk

querky, quirk(y)

query,ries,ried,rying,rist, ASK OF, QUESTION, INQUIRE

quesadilla,*, FLOUR TORTILLAS WITH FILLING

quesdun, question

quest,*,ted,ting,ter, ON A JOURNEY/ ADVENTURE SEEKING SOMETHING "prefixes: in"

questen, question

question,*,ned,ning,nable,nably, nability,nary,naries,nnaire, ASK/ INQUIRE, HAVE DOUBT, NEED INFORMATION ON MATTER/ SUBJECT "prefixes: un"

questshunar, question(nnaire)

questun, question

quet, quit / quite

queter, quit(tter) / quiet(er)

quevor, quiver

quevur, quiver

quez, quiz

quezene, cuisine

quezt, quest

quick,kly,ker,kest,kness,ken,kie,kener, FAST, WITHOUT DELAY, BRIEF, SKIN UNDER NAILS

quiet,ter,test,tly,tness,tism,tude, SILENT, CALM, STILL, TRANQUIL (or see quit/quite) "prefixes: dis/un"

quifur, quiver

quik, quick

quikest, quick(est)

quikly, quick(ly)

quiky, quick(ie)

quil, quill / kill / keel

quill,*, WING/TAIL FEATHER OF LARGE BIRD

quilt,*,ted,ting,ter, HANDMADE/ STITCHED BLANKET, THICKLY BLANKETED (or see kilt)

quin, keen / kin / queen

quinch, quench

quinsh, quench

quintuplet,*, FIVE OF ANYTHING

quirk,*,ky,kily,kiness, GIVEN TO ERRATIC MOVEMENT, JERKING, SUDDEN CHANGES

quiry, query

quisadilla, quesadilla

quisen, cuisine

quisine, cuisine

quit,*,tted,tting,tter, STOP (or see quite)

quite, COMPLETELY CERTAIN/CLEAR (or see quit/quiet)

quiut, quiet

quiutly, quiet(ly)

quiver,*,red,ring, CASE TO CARRY ARROWS, TREMBLE/SHAKE/ TREMOR

quivor, quiver

quiz,zzes,zzed,zzing,zzical,zzically, zzicality,zzer, TO TEST/WONDER, BE CONFUSED

qukumber, cucumber

qumulotive, cumulative

quochent, quotient

quochiunt, quotient

quoda, quota

quode, quote

quodrant, quadrant

quodrunt, quadrant

quodu, quota

quoledy, quality

quolm, qualm

quondery, quandary

quondry, quandary

quontefy, quantify

quontefyer, quantify(fier)

quontem, quanta(tum)

quontery, quandary

quontety, quantity

quontify, quantify

quontim, quanta(tum)

quontity, quantity

quontre, quandary

quontum, quanta(tum)

quord, quart

quorderly, quarter(ly)

quordir, quarter

quordorly, quarter(ly)

quords, quartz / quart(s)

quordurly, quarter(ly)

quordz, quartz / quart(s)

quore, quarry

quorel, quarrel

quorem, quorum

quorentene, quarantine

quoril, quarrel

quorim, quorum

quorintene, quarantine

quork, quark

quorol, quarrel

quorom, quorum

quort, quart

quorter, quarter

quorterly, quarter(ly)

quortir, quarter

quortirly, quarter(ly)

quorts, quartz / quart(s)

quorturly, quarter(ly)

quortz, quartz / quart(s)

quorum, THE MAJORITY OF A SELECTED GROUP

quoruntene, quarantine

quory, quarry

quoshent, quotient

quoshunt, quotient

quota,*, A PERMITTED NUMBER/ QUANTITY

quotashen, quote(tation)

quote,*,ted,ting,tation,table,tability,ta, tient, IDENTIFY/CITE/REPEAT EXACTLY WHAT WAS HEARD, STATE FACTS, USE MARKS AROUND WORDS SPOKEN "prefixes: un/ under"

quotient,*, A MATHEMATICAL RESULT

quowry, quarry

qurader, curator

qureus, curious

qutikle, cuticle

qwack, quack

qwad, quad

qwadrent, quadrant

qwagmire, quagmire

qwaint, quaint

qwak, quack / quake

qwakmire, quagmire

qwale, quail

qwaledy, quality

qwalefieur, qualify(fier)

qwalefiuble, qualify(fiable)

qwaletatif, quality(tative)

qwalety, quality

qwalidy, quality

qwalifecation, qualify(fication)

qwalifikashen, qualify(fication)

qwalitative, quality(tative)

qwalitee, quality

qwalm, qualm

qwant, quaint

qwantefy, quantify

qwantefyer, quantify(fier)

qwantem, quanta(tum)

qwantety, quantity

qwantify, quantify

qwantifyer, quantify(fier)

qwantim, quanta(tum)

qwantity, quantity

qwantum, quanta(tum)

qwarder, quarter
qwards, quartz / quart(s)
qwardur, quarter
qwarel, quarrel
qwarentene, quarantine
qwaril, quarrel
qwarintene, quarantine
qwark, quark
qwarol, quarrel
qwarter, quarter
qwarts, quartz / quart(s)
qwartur, quarter
qwarul, quarrel
qwary, query
qwasar, quasar
qwasy, quasi
qwazar, quasar
qwazy, quasi
qwear, queer
qween, queen
qweer, queer
qwek, quick
qwekest, quick(est)
qwekly, quick(ly)
qweky, quick(ie)
qwel, quill
qwelt, quilt
qwench, quench
qwensh, quench
qwentuplet, quintuplet
qwerk, quirk
qwerky, quirk(y)
qwery, query
qwes, quiz
qwesden, question
qwesekal, quiz(zzical)
qweshten, question
qwest, quest
qwestchenair, question(nnaire)
qwestshun, question
qwestunair, question(nnaire)
qwet, quit / quite
qweter, quit(tter) / quiet(er)
qwevir, quiver
qwevur, quiver
qwez, quiz
qwezekal, quiz(zzical)
qwik, quick
qwikest, quick(est)
qwikly, quick(ly)
qwiky, quick(ie)
qwil, quill
qwilt, quilt
qwinch, quench

qwinsh, quench
qwintuplet, quintuplet
qwirk, quirk
qwirky, quirk(y)
qwiry, query
qwis, quiz
qwit, quit / quite
qwiter, quit(tter) / quiet(er)
qwivur, quiver
qwiz, quiz
qwizekal, quiz(zzical)
qwochent, quotient
qwod, quad
qwoda, quota
qwodashen, quote(tation)
qwodation, quote(tation)
qwode, quote
qwodrent, quadrant
qwodrunt, quadrant
qwodu, quota
qwoduble, quote(table)
qwoledy, quality
qwolefikashen, qualify(fication)
qwolefiuble, qualify(fiable)
qwolefiur, qualify(fier)
qwoletatif, quality(tative)
qwolety, quality
qwolifekation, qualify(fication)
qwolm, qualm
qwomtum, quanta(tum)
qwondry, quandary
qwontefy, quantify
qwontefyer, quantify(fier)
qwontem, quanta(tum)
qwontery, quandary
qwontety, quantity
qwontify, quantify
qwontifyer, quantify(fier)
qwontim, quanta(tum)
qwontity, quantity
qworam, quorum
qworder, quarter
qwords, quartz / quart(s)
qwordur, quarter
qworel, quarrel
qworem, quorum
qworentene, quarantine
qworil, quarrel
qworim, quorum
qworintene, quarantine
qwork, quark
qworol, quarrel
qworom, quorum
qworter, quarter

qworts, quartz / quart(s)
qwortur, quarter
qworul, quarrel
qworum, quorum
qwoshent, quotient
qwosy, quasi
qwota, quota
qwotashen, quote(tation)
qwotation, quote(tation)
qwote, quote
qwotuble, quote(table)
qwozy, quasi
qwurentene, quarantine
qwurintene, quarantine
qwurk, quirk
qwurky, quirk(y)
r, are
ra, ray / raw
rabbi,*, JEWISH RELIGIOUS TITLE
rabbit,*, LONG-EARED RODENT
rabcity, rhapsody
rabed, rabbit / rabid / rapid
rabees, rabid(ies)
rabel, rebel
rabeleon, rebel(llion)
rabeleus, rebel(llious)
rabelius, rebel(llious)
rabet, rabbit/rabid/rapid
rabi, rabbi
rabid,dity,dly,dness,ies, MADNESS/
    FURIOUSNESS/UNREASONABLE,
    DISEASE (or see rapid)
rabit, rabbit / rabid / rapid
rablie, reply
rabodek, robot(ic)
rabot, rabbit / rabid / rapid
rabotik, robot(ic)
rabsady, rhapsody
rabsudy, rhapsody
rabt, rape(d) / wrap(pped) / rap(pped)
rabud, rabbit / rabid / rapid
rabut, rabbit / rabid / rapid / rebut
rabutal, rebut(ttal)
rac, rack / rake / wrack / rock
racat, racket / racquet
racateer, racketeer
raccoon,*, PLANTIGRADE
    CARNIVOROUS MAMMAL
raccune, raccoon
race,*,ed,cing,er,cy, COMPETITION
    WITH MORE THAN ONE, GAME
    WITH A BEGINNING/END,
    CATEGORY FOR HUMAN TYPES (or
    see raise) "prefixes: de"

racede, recede
raceptecle, receptacle
racepter, receptor
racepticle, receptacle
raception, reception
raceptucle, receptacle
racet, racket / racquet
raceteer, racketeer
rach, rash
rachal, racial
rachen, ration
racheo, ratio
rachet, ratchet
rachil, racial
rachin, ration
rachio, ratio
rachit, ratchet
rachon, ration
rachul, racial
rachun, ration
rachunil, rational
rachut, ratchet
racial,lly,lism,list,listic,ism,ist,
    CHARACTERISTICS/DIFFERENCES IN
    RACES/PEOPLE "prefixes: bi/inter"
racipeint, recipient
raciprocation, reciprocate(tion)
racism,*, HUMAN FEAR/IGNORANCE
    TOWARDS PEOPLE OF A DIFFERENT
    COLOR/RACE
racist,*, HUMAN FEAR/IGNORANCE
    TOWARDS PEOPLE OF A DIFFERENT
    COLOR/RACE
racit, racket / racquet / recite
raciteer, racketeer
rack,*,ked,king,ker,ket, APPARATUS
    USED FOR HANGING/STRETCHING
    THINGS (or see rake/wrack/rock)
racket,*,teer, NOISY SOUND, USED IN
    SPORTS TO HIT A BALL (or see
    racquet)
racketeer,*,ring, SLANG FOR SOMEONE
    ENGAGED IN ILLEGAL ACTIVITY
rackit, racket / racquet
rackiteer, racketeer
rackoteer, racketeer
rackut, racket / racquet
rackuteer, racketeer
raconasinse, reconnaissance
raconstitushen, reconstitute(tion)
raconstitute, reconstitute
racoon, raccoon
racquet,*, STRINGED TOOL FOR SPORT
    (or see racket)

racrute, recruit
racruter, recruit(er)
racumbent, recumbent
racut, racket / racquet
racuteer, racketeer
rad, raid / rate
radar,*, A RADIO WAVE FREQUENCY
raddle, rattle
rade, raid
radeal, radial
radeans, radiance
radeant, radiant
radeashen, radiate(tion)
radeate, radiate
radeater, radiate(tor)
radeation, radiate(tion)
radecal, radical
radech, radish
radechulus, ridiculous
radeemible, redeem(able)
radefy, ratify
radeil, radial
radeim, radium
radeinse, radiance
radeint, radiant
radeints, radiance
radekly, radical(lly)
radekul, radical
radel, rattle
rademe, redeem
rademption, redemption
rademshin, redemption
rademtif, redemption(ive)
rademtion, redemption
rademtive, redemption(ive)
rademuble, redeem(able)
radeo, radio
radeol, radial
radeom, radium
radeos, radius / radio(es)
radequelus, ridiculous
radesh, radish
radeul, radial
radeum, radium
radeunse, radiance
radeunt, radiant
radeus, radius
radial,*,lly, CENTER WITH SPOKES/RAYS
    GOING OUT FROM THE CENTER,
    TYPE OF TIRE "prefixes: bi/inter"
radiance,cy,cies,nt,ntly, BRIGHT/
    SHINING LIKE A STAR, GLOWING
    BRIGHT
radians, radiance

radiant,ntly,nce, TYPE OF HEAT/WAVE/
    LIGHT, TO GLOW "prefixes: ir"
radiashen, radiate(tion)
radiate,*,ed,ting,tion,tional,tive,tor,
    EMIT/GIVE FORTH/EXUDE
    "prefixes: ir/re"
radiater, radiate(tor)
radical,*,lly,lness,lism, FAR-SWEEPING
    CHANGE/ACT/ATTITUDE FROM THE
    EXISTING IDEALISM
radicaly, radical(lly)
radich, radish
radicle, radical
radicly, radical(lly)
radiel, radial
radiem, radium
radient, radiant
radify, ratify
radikle, radical
radikly, radical(lly)
radikul, radical
radil, rattle
radio,*,oed,oing, WIRELESS AUDIO
    TRANSMITTING/RECEIVING DEVICE,
    PREFIX INDICATING "RADIO/
    RADIATION" MOST OFTEN
    MODIFIES THE WORD, FROM
    ANCIENT WORD "RADIUS" (RAY)
radiol, radial
radiquelus, ridiculous
radish,hes, A VEGETABLE
radiul, radial
radium, A METALLIC ELEMENT WHICH
    IS RADIOACTIVE
radiunse, radiance
radius,ii,ses, AREA WITHIN A CIRCLE,
    RAY EXTENDING FROM CENTER OF
    CIRCLE, BONE DESCRIPTIONS
radol, rattle
radon, A CHEMICAL ELEMENT
rador, radar
raduction, reduce(ction)
radufy, ratify
radukle, radical
radukly, radical(lly)
radukshen, reduce(ction)
radul, rattle
radundense, redundant(ncy)
radundent, redundant
radundunse, redundant(ncy)
radusable, reduce(cible)
raduse, reduce
radush, radish
raelm, realm

raelrod, railroad
raen, rain / reign / rein
raenbo, rainbow
raenj, range
raer, rare
raesesem, racism
raf, rave
rafal, raffle / ravel
rafalee, reveille
rafan, raven
rafash, ravish
rafd, raft / waft
rafded, raft(ed)
rafdur, raft(er)
rafe, rave
rafel, raffle / ravel / reveal
rafelashen, revelation
rafen, raven / ravine
rafenge, revenge
rafenje, revenge
rafenus, raven(ous)
rafeole, ravioli
rafer, revere / refer
rafers, reverse / refer(s)
rafesh, ravish
rafeusil, refuse(sal)
rafewsel, refuse(sal)
raffle,*,ed,ling, A GAME
rafiew, review / revue
rafif, revive
rafiful, revival
rafil, raffle / ravel
rafilee, reveille
rafin, raven / refine
rafinable, refine(nable)
rafinery, refine(ry)
rafinje, revenge
rafinment, refine(ment)
rafinuble, refine(nable)
rafinury, refine(ry)
rafinus, raven(ous)
rafioly, ravioli
rafirse, reverse
rafish, ravish
raflashen, revelation
rafle, raffle / ravel
raflect, reflect
raflection, reflect(ion)
raflective, reflect(ive)
raflekshen, reflect(ion)
raflektor, reflect(or)
rafol, raffle
rafolee, reveille
raformutory, reform(atory)

rafractory, refract(ory)
rafrain, refrain
rafraktory, refract(ory)
rafrane, refrain
rafregirant, refrigerate(ant)
rafregirator, refrigerate(tor)
rafresh, refresh
rafreshment, refresh(ment)
rafrigerant, refrigerate(ant)
rafrigerator, refrigerate(tor)
raft,*,ted,ting,ter, A SMALL BOAT
     MADE WITH A MATERIAL FILLED
     WITH AIR (or see rave(d))
raftur, raft(er) / waft(er)
rafue, review / revue
raful, raffle / ravel
rafulashen, revelation
rafulation, revelation
rafulee, reveille
rafun, raven
rafunus, raven(ous)
rafurbish, refurbish
rafurse, reverse
rafusel, refuse(sal)
rafute, refute
rag,*,gged,ggedness,ggedly,ggedy,
     TATTERED/TORN/WORN OUT
     MATERIAL/CLOTH (or see rack/
     rage)
ragalia, regal(ia)
ragardless, regard(less)
ragd, rage(d) / rag(gged)
rage,*,ed,ging,gingly, INTENSE/VIOLENT
     ANGER, OF INTENSE/GREAT FORCE
     "prefixes: en"
raged, rag(gged) / racket
ragedy, rag(ggedy)
ragektion, reject(ion)
rager, roger
raget, rag(gged) / racket
ragid, rag(gged) / racket
ragidy, rag(ggedy)
ragir, roger
ragit, rag(gged) / racket
ragity, rag(ggedy)
ragret, regret
ragreted, regret(tted)
ragretful, regret(ful)
ragretfuly, regret(fully)
ragt, rage(d) / rake(d) / rack(ed) /
     wrack(ed)
ragud, rag(gged) / racket
ragudy, rag(ggedy)
ragut, rag(gged) / racket

raid,*,ded,ding,der, A SUDDEN ENTRY/
     ATTACK/SALE (or see rate/ride)
rail,*,led,ling,ler, METAL/WOOD BARS/
     POSTS, TO PUNISH/SCOLD, A BIRD
     (or see rale) "prefixes: de"
railroad,*,ded,ding,der, ROAD MADE
     OF RAILS, BRING A FALSE CHARGE
     AGAINST SOMEONE, OF
     LOCOMOTIVES
rain,*,ned,ning,ny, WATER RELEASED
     FROM CLOUDS (or see reign/rein)
rainbow,*, AN ARC/BOW OF COLORS
     NORMALLY CAUSED BY RAIN
rainder, reindeer
raing, range
rair, rare
rairly, rare(ly)
rais, rise / raise / ray(s)
raise,es,ed,sing,er, TO LIFT/BRING/TAKE
     UP (or see ray(s)/razor) "prefixes:
     un/up"
raisin,*, A DRIED PLUM
rait, rate / right / rite / write / wright
raive, rave
raj, rage
rajd, rage(d)
rajekshen, reject(ion)
rajekt, reject
rajektion, reject(ion)
rajer, roger
rajur, roger
rak, rack / rake / wrack / rag
rakat, racket / racquet
rakateer, racketeer
rake,*,ed,king, TOOL/IMPLEMENT TO
     MOVE ORGANIC MATERIAL
     AROUND (or see rack/wrack)
raket, racket / racquet
raketeer, racketeer
rakit, racket / racquet
rakiteer, racketeer
rakonesinse, reconnaissance
rakonstitute, reconstitute
rakonusents, reconnaissance
rakoon, raccoon
rakord, record
rakorder, record(er)
rakot, racket / racquet
rakoteer, racketeer
rakrute, recruit
rakruter, recruit(er)
rakt, rake(d) / rack(ed) / wrack(ed)
rakumbent, recumbent
rakune, raccoon

rakut, racket / racquet
rakuteer, racketeer
rakwest, request
rakwire, require
rakwirment, require(ment)
rakwit, requite
rakwitable, requite(table)
rakwrute, recruit
ralaks, relax
ralax, relax
rale, A BREATHING SOUND (or see rail/ rally)
raleenkwish, relinquish
ralef, relief
ralejis, religion(ous)
ralek, rollick
ralenkwish, relinquish
ralenqwish, relinquish
ralent, relent
ralentless, relentless
ralerode, railroad
ralese, release
raleve, relieve
ralevens, relevance
ralevent, relevant
ralevir, relieve(r)
rali, rely / rally
raliable, reliable
raliant, reliance(nt)
ralick, rollick
ralie, rally
raliense, reliance
raligeon, religion
raligis, religion(ous)
ralijus, religion(ous)
ralik, rollick
ralinkwish, relinquish
ralinquish, relinquish
ralintless, relentless
ralish, relish
raliubility, reliable(bility)
raliuble, reliable
raliunts, reliance
ralivens, relevance
ralivent, relevant
rally,llies,llied,ying,llier, BRING/CALL SUMMON FORTH SPIRIT/ACTION/ ENTHUSIASM
ralm, realm
ralrod, railroad
ralrot, railroad
ralrus, walrus
raluctant, reluctant
raluctinse, reluctant(nce)

raluktint, reluctant
raluvence, relevance
raluvent, relevant
ralwrod, railroad
raly, rally / rely
ram,*,mmed,mming,mmer, MALE SHEEP, DEVICE USED TO STRIKE/ FORCE/ CRUSH/POUND
ramadik, rheumatic
ramafication, ramification
ramafikashen, ramification
ramain, remain / romaine
ramander, remain(der)
ramane, remain / romaine
ramantek, romantic
ramantic, romantic
ramantisize, romantic(ize)
ramarkible, remark(able)
ramatik, rheumatic
rambal, ramble
rambant, rampant
rambint, rampant
ramble,*,ed,ling,er, WANDER/ MEANDER, STYLE OF HOME
rambul, ramble
rambunctious,sly,sness, NOISY/ BOISTEROUS/LOUD
rambunktious, rambunctious
rambunt, rampant
ramd, ram(mmed)
ramedeul, remedy(dial)
ramediashen, remedy(diation)
ramediation, remedy(diation)
ramefekashen, ramification
ramefekation, ramification
ramember, remember
ramembranxe, remember(ance)
ramesable, remissible
rameshen, remission
ramet, remit
rameteul, remedy(dial)
ramidal, remit(ttal)
ramifekashen, ramification
ramification,*, THE RESULT/RESPONSE OF AN ACTION
ramifikation, ramification
ramindur, remind(er)
ramint, remind
ramintur, remind(er)
ramishen, remission
ramisible, remissible
ramision, remission
ramit, remit
ramital, remit(ttal)

ramition, remission
ramituble, remit(ttable)
ramofer, remove(r)
ramorse, remorse
ramorsless, remorse(less)
ramote, remote
ramotly, remote(ly)
ramover, remove(r)
ramp,*,ped,ping,part, DEVICE TO CREATE INCLINE/SLOPE FOR MOVING/RAISING FROM ONE LEVEL TO ANOTHER
rampage,*,ed,ging,eous,eously, BOISTEROUS/VIOLENT/PASSIONATE BEHAVIOR
rampaje, rampage
rampant,tly,ncy, RUN AMUCK/WILD/ UNPREDICTABLY
rampel, ramble
rampent, rampant
rampint, rampant
rample, ramble
rampt, ramp(ed)
rampunkshes, rambunctious
rampunt, rampant
ramsum, ransom
ramt, ram(mmed)
ramuf, remove
ramufecation, ramification
ramufekashen, ramification
ramufel, remove(val)
ramufible, remove(vable)
ramufication, ramification
ramufikashen, ramification
ramufil, remove(val)
ramufucation, ramification
ramuneration, remunerate(tion)
ramuvable, remove(vable)
ramuval, remove(val)
ran, PAST TENSE FOR THE WORD "RUN" (or see rain/rein/reign) "prefixes: re"
ranbo, rainbow
ranbow, rainbow
ranced, rancid
ranch,hes,hed,hing,her, WHERE HORSES/CATTLE ARE RAISED/ BOARDED, A TYPE OF DRESSING
ranchi, raunch(y)
ranchur, ranch(er)
rancid,dity,dness, SMELL/TASTE OF FOOD THAT IS SPOILED/ROTTEN
rancud, rancid
rand, rant / rain(ed)

randam, random
rander, reindeer
randim, random
random,mly,mness, WITHOUT AN APPARENT/RECOGNIZABLE ORDER "prefixes: non/un"
rane, rain / reign / rein
ranege, renege
range,*,ed,ging,er, DEFINED/SPECIFIC AREA WHICH HOLDS DATA/ INFORMATION/ANIMALS (or see ranch) "prefixes: de"
rangel, wrangle
ranglur, wrangle(r)
rangt, range(d)
rangul, wrangle
rangur, range(r)
ranige, renege
ranik, renege
ranj, range / ranch
rank,*,ked,king,ker,kest,kly,kness, CHRONOLOGICAL/LINEAR ORDER, A BAD/ OFFENSIVE SMELL/ODOR
ranone, renown
ranoserus, rhinoceros
ranosirus, rhinoceros
ranouncement, renounce(ment)
ranounse, renounce
ranown, renown
ranownsment, renounce(ment)
ransack,*,ked,king,ker, PLUNDER/ SEARCH THROUGH PEOPLE'S BELONGINGS
ransak, ransack
ransam, ransom
ransed, rancid
ransem, ransom
ransh, ranch
ransher, ranch(er)
ransid, rancid
ransim, ransom
ransit, rancid
ransom,*,mer, FORCE SOMEONE TO PAY FOR THE RETURN OF GOODS/ PEOPLE
ransud, rancid
ransum, ransom
ransut, rancid
rant,*,ted,ting,tingly,ter, TALK/UTTER LOUD AGITATED OR AGGRESSIVE WORDS
rantsum, ransom
rantum, random
ranumerate, remunerate

ranzak, ransack
ranzum, ransom
raon, rayon
rap,*,pped,pping,pper, TYPE OF MUSIC AND THAT ASSOCIATED WITH IT, TYPE OF SOUND, BLAME/ PUNISHMENT/FOR AN ILLEGAL ACT NOT RESPONSIBLE FOR (or see wrap/rape)
rapad, rapid
rapar, repair
rapcher, rapture
rapcherus, rapture(rous)
rapchur, rapture
rapcity, rhapsody
rape,*,ed,ping,pist, VIOLENTLY/ FORCEFULLY/PHYSICALLY PENETRATE A PERSON AGAINST THEIR WILL (or see rap/wrap)
rapeal, repeal
rapeat, repeat
raped, rape(d) / rapid / rabid
rapededly, repeat(edly)
rapedly, rapid(ly)
rapedutif, repetitive
rapeel, repeal
rapel, rappel / repeal / repel
rapelein, rebel(llion)
rapelent, repellent
rapeleon, rebel(llion)
rapelinsy, repellent(ncy)
rapelint, repellent
rapenins, repent(ance)
rapent, repent
rapentinse, repent(ance)
raper, rap(pper) / rape(r) / wrap(pper)
rapest, rape(pist)
rapete, repeat
rapetedly, repeat(edly)
rapid,*,dly,dness,dity, QUICK (or see rabid)
rapinens, repent(ance)
rapint, repent
rapintense, repent(ance)
rapir, rap(pper) / rape(r) / wrap(pper)
raplacment, replace(ment)
raplase, replace
raplasmint, replace(ment)
raplenish, replenish
raplenishment, replenish(ment)
raplid, reply(lied)
raplinesh, replenish
rapor, rapport
raporder, report(er)

raport, rapport / report
raporter, report(er)
rapository, repository
rapour, rapport
rapozitory, repository
rappel,*,lled,lling, DESCEND FROM A HEIGHT WITH A ROPE (or see repel)
rapport, HARMONY/AFFILIATION WITH
rapreshen, repress(ion)
rapresion, repress(ion)
rapress, repress
rapresuve, repress(ive)
raproch, reproach
raprochuble, reproach(able)
rapsety, rhapsody
rapshur, rapture
rapsuty, rhapsody
rapt, rape(d) / wrap(pped) / rap(pped)
raptcher, rapture
raptor,*, BIRD OF PREY (or see rapture)
raptur, raptor / rapture
rapture,*,ed,ring,rous,rously,rousness, EXTREME DELIGHT/JOY/PLEASURE (or see raptor) "prefixes: en"
rapublek, republic
rapublekan, republic(an)
rapublikan, republic(an)
rapud, rapid
rapugnense, repugnant(nce)
rapugnent, repugnant
rapulshen, repulse(ion)
rapulsif, repulse(sive)
rapulsion, repulse(ion)
rapuplekan, republic(an)
rapur, rap(pper) / rap(er) / wrap(pper)
rapust, rape(pist)
rapute, repute
raqet, racket / racquet
raqeteer, racketeer
raqrute, recruit
raquire, require
raquirment, require(ment)
raquitable, requite(table)
raquite, requite
raqut, racket / racquet
raquteer, racketeer
raqwest, request
raqwire, require
raqwirment, require(ment)
rar, rare
rare,ely,er,est,eness,rity,rities,efy,efies, efied,efying,efiable, MOST UNCOMMON, UNUSUAL, SCARCE, MEAT BARELY COOKED

rarety, rare(rity)
rarist, rare(rist)
rarity, rare(rity)
rarly, rare(ly)
rarudy, rare(rity)
raruty, rare(rity)
ras, race / raise / ray(s)
rasbery, raspberry
rascal,*,lly,lity,lities, MISCHIEVOUS/
    PLAYFUL/ROQUISH BEHAVIOR
rascul, rascal
rasd, race(d) / raise(d)
raseat, receipt
rasebshenist, receptionist
rasebshin, reception
rasebter, receptor
rasebtif, receptive
rasebtive, receptive
raseed, recede
rasefe, receive
rasefible, receive(vable)
rasemblinse, resemble(lance).
rasembul, resemble
rasen, raisin / race(cing) / raise(sing)
rasentful, resent(ful)
rasentment, resent(ment)
rasepdekle, receptacle
rasepe, recipe
rasepeunt, recipient
raseprikul, reciprocal
raseprocation, reciprocate(tion)
raseprokashen, reciprocate(tion)
raseprokate, reciprocate
rasepshenist, receptionist
rasepshun, reception
raseptacle, receptacle
raseptef, receptive
raseptikle, receptacle
raseptionest, receptionist
raseptive, receptive
raseptor, receptor
raseptukle, receptacle
raser, razor / raise(r) / race(r)
raserekshen, resurrect(ion)
raservation, reservation
raservist, reserve(vist)
rasesem, racism
raseshun, recess(ion)
rasesif, recess(ive)
rasesion, recess(ion)
rasesive, recess(ive)
rasession, recess(ion)
rasest, racist
rasestef, resist(ive)

rasestif, resist(ive)
rasestinse, resist(ance)
rasestint, resist(ant)
rasestive, resist(ive)
rasesum, racism
rasete, receipt
rasetion, recess(ion)
raseve, receive
rasevuble, receive(vable)
rash,hes, A SKIN FORMATION
rashal, racial
rashel, racial
rashen, ration
rashenaledy, rational(ity)
rashenality, rational(ity)
rashenalization, rational(ization)
rashent, ration(ed)
rashenul, rational
rasheo, ratio
rasheonalization, rational(ization)
rasheunolezashen, rational(ization)
rashil, racial
rashin, ration
rashinal, rational
rashinaledy, rational(ity)
rashinality, rational(ity)
rashint, ration(ed)
rashinul, rational
rashinulization, rational(ization)
rashio, ratio
rashon, ration
rashonality, rational(ity)
rashonalization, rational(ization)
rashonel, rational
rashs, rash(es)
rashul, racial
rashun, ration
rashunal, ration(al)
rashunaledy, rational(ity)
rashunality, rational(ity)
rashunalization, rational(ization)
rashund, ration(ed)
rashunil, rational
raside, reside
rasiduel, residue(ual)
rasign, resign
rasiliency, resilient(ncy)
rasilient, resilient
rasimblanse, resemble(lance)
rasimble, resemble
rasin, raisin / race(cing) / raise(sing)
rasintful, resent(ful)
rasipeant, recipient
rasipeint, recipient

rasiprikul, reciprocal
rasiprocation, reciprocate(tion)
rasiprokashen, reciprocate(tion)
rasiprokate, reciprocate
rasiprokle, reciprocal
rasiprokul, reciprocal
rasir, razor / raise(r) / race(r)
rasirekshen, resurrect(ion)
rasirvation, reservation
rasirvist, reserve(vist)
rasis, race(s) / raise(s) / racist
rasisem, racism
rasism, racism
rasist, racist / resist
rasistef, resist(ive)
rasistense, resist(ance)
rasistent, resist(ant)
rasister, resist(or)
rasistive, resist(ive)
rasisum, racism
rasite, recite
rasitle, recite(tal)
rasitul, recite(tal)
rasizm, racism
rasizum, racism
raskel, rascal
raskle, rascal
rasn, raisin / raise(sing) / race(cing)
rasodo, risotto
rasolve, resolve
rasolvuble, resolve(vable)
rasor, razor / raise(r) / race(r)
rasort, resort
rasoto, risotto
rasotto, risotto
rasp,*,per,pingly,py, A TOOL WHICH
    ROUGHS/SCRAPES/SANDS, A
    ROUGH SOUND
raspberry,rries, AN EDIBLE BERRY
raspect, respect
raspectful, respect(ful)
raspective, respect(ive)
raspectuble, respect(able)
raspekt, respect
raspektful, respect(ful)
raspektif, respect(ive)
raspektuble, respect(able)
raspite, respite
raspond, respond
rasponder, respond(er)
rasponse, response
rasponsef, response(sive)
rasponsive, response(sive)
rasponsuble, response(sible)

rast, race(d) / raise(d)
rastore, restore
rastrant, restrain(t)
rastrektif, restrict(ive)
rastrektion, restrict(ion)
rastrikshen, restrict(ion)
rastrikt, restrict
rastriktive, restrict(ive)
rasume, resume
rasun, raisin / raise(sing) / race(cing)
rasur, razor / raise(r) / race(r)
rasurekshen, resurrect(ion)
rasus, racist / race(s)
rasusatate, resuscitate
rasuscitate, resuscitate
rasusitashen, resuscitate(tion)
rasusitate, resuscitate
rasusitator, resuscitate(tor)
rasust, racist
rasy, race(y)
rat,*,tted,tting,tty, RODENT, SOMEONE
    WHO REVEALS OTHERS PRIVATE
    INFORMATION WITHOUT
    PERMISSION, TANGLED HAIR (or
    see rate/raid)
ratainer, retain(er)
rataleashen, retaliate(tion)
rataleate, retaliate
rataleation, retaliate(tion)
ratane, retain
rataner, retain(er)
ratar, radar
ratash, radish
ratchat, ratchet
ratchet,*,ted,ting, A DEVICE/TOOL
ratchut, ratchet
rate,*,ed,ting,table, RANK, QUALIFY,
    QUANTIFY, PROVIDE A VALUE FOR
    (or see raid) "prefixes: de/over/pro/
    under"
rateal, radial
rateant, radiant
rateashen, radiate(tion)
rateate, radiate
rateater, radiate(tor)
rateation, radiate(tion)
ratecal, radical
ratech, radish
rated, rate(d) / rat(tted) / rot(tted)
ratefy, ratify
rateil, radial
rateim, radium
rateinse, radiance
rateint, radiant

rateints, radiance
rateis, radius
ratekly, radical(lly)
ratekul, radical
ratel, rattle
ratenshun, retention
ratentif, retentive
ratention, retention
ratentive, retentive
rateo, ratio / radio
rateod, radio(ed)
rateol, radial
rateom, radium
ratesh, radish
rateul, radial
rateum, radium
rateunse, radiance
rateunt, radiant
rateus, radius
rath, wrath
rather, THIS OVER THAT, PREFERENCE
rathful, wrath(ful)
rathur, rather
ratiate, radiate
ratiater, radiate(tor)
ratical, radical
ratich, radish
raticly, radical(lly)
ratid, rat(tted) / rate(d)
ratiel, radial
ratiem, radium
ratient, radiant
ratify,fies,fied,fying,fication,fier,
    APPROVE/CONFIRM/MAKE
    FORMAL
ratikly, radical(lly)
ratikul, radical
ratikuly, radical(lly)
ratil, rattle
ratinshun, retention
ratintion, retention
ratio,*, COMPARISON OF AMOUNTS
ratiol, radial
ration,*,ned,ning, A SPECIFIC/LIMITED
    AMOUNT
rational,le,lly,lness,lism,list,listic,
    listically,lity,lities,lize,lizer,lization,
    FACTUAL/ LEVEL-HEADED/NON
    EMOTIONAL THOUGHT "prefixes:
    ir"
rationalezation, rational(ization)
rationulization, rational(ization)
ratire, retire
ratirment, retire(ment)

ratisery, rotisserie
ratish, radish
ratisury, rotisserie
ratiul, radial
ratium, radium
ratiunse, radiance
ratius, radius
ratl, rattle
ratol, rattle
raton, radon
ratorical, rhetoric(al)
ratrakshen, retract(ion)
ratrakted, retract(ed)
ratrefe, retrieve
ratrefer, retrieve(r)
ratreful, retrieve(val)
ratreve, retrieve
ratrevul, retrieve(val)
ratrevur, retrieve(r)
rattle,*,ed,ling,er,ly,lier,liest,
    INSTRUMENT/TOY WITH BEADS
    INSIDE TO CREATE SOUND
ratufy, ratify
ratukle, radical
ratukly, radical(lly)
ratul, rattle
ratush, radish
raty, rat(tty)
raudy, rowdy
rauk, rock
raunch,hy,hier,hiest, INDECENT/FOUL
raund, round
raunyin, reunion
raunyun, reunion
raust, roust
raut, wrought / route
rauty, rowdy
rav, rave
ravage,*,ed,ging, TO VIOLENTLY
    DAMAGE/DESTROY/DEVASTATE
ravaje, ravage
raval, ravel
ravalashen, revelation
ravalee, reveille
ravalve, revolve
ravan, raven
ravash, ravish / ravage
rave,*,ed,ving,er, DELIRIOUS/WILD/
    EXCESSIVE, CARRYING ON,
    INCESSANT ABOUT
ravech, ravish / ravage
raveel, reveal
raveer, revere
ravege, ravage

ravegen, revise(sion)
raveje, ravage
ravejen, revise(sion)
ravel,*,led,ling,ler,lment, BECOME
    FRAYED/ENTANGLED (or see reveal)
    "prefixes: un"
ravelation, revelation
ravelee, reveille
ravelt, reveal(ed)
raven,*,ner,ning,ningly,nous,nously,
    nousness,ner, BIRD, PLUNDER/
    DEVOUR GREEDILY, VORACIOUS
    APPETITE (or see ravine/rave(ving))
ravench, revenge
ravene, ravine
ravenge, revenge
ravengful, revenge(ful)
ravenje, revenge
ravenjful, revenge(ful)
ravenus, raven(ous)
raveoly, ravioli
raverberate, reverberate
raverbirate, reverberate
ravere, revere
raversuble, reverse(sible)
ravert, revert
ravesh, ravish / ravage
raveshen, revise(sion)
ravesion, revise(sion)
raview, review / revue
ravige, ravage
ravigen, revise(sion)
ravije, ravage
ravijen, revise(sion)
ravil, ravel
ravilashen, revelation
ravilation, revelation
ravilee, reveille / ravel
ravin, raven / ravine
ravinch, revenge
ravine,*, A DEEP GORGE/DRIED RIVER
    BED WORN AWAY BY WATER (or
    see raven)
ravinge, revenge
ravingful, revenge(ful)
ravinje, revenge
ravinjful, revenge(ful)
ravinous, raven(ous)
ravinus, raven(ous)
ravioli,*, STUFFED PASTA/NOODLE
ravirberate, reverberate
ravirse, reverse
ravirsuble, reverse(sible)
ravirt, revert

ravise, revise
ravish,hes,hed,hing,her,hment, CARRY
    AWAY/TRANSPORT/TAKE BY FORCE,
    OVERWHELM EMOTIONALLY
ravishen, revise(sion)
ravision, revise(sion)
ravival, revival
ravive, revive
ravivle, revival
ravivuble, revive(vable)
ravize, revise
ravl, ravel
ravocable, revocable
ravokable, revocable
ravoke, revoke
ravokt, revoke(d)
ravol, ravel
ravolashen, revelation
ravolation, revelation
ravolee, reveille
ravolfe, revolve
ravolfer, revolve(r)
ravolt, revolt
ravolushen, revolution
ravolutioniz, revolution(ize)
ravolve, revolve
ravolver, revolve(r)
ravon, raven / rave(ving)
ravonous, raven(ous)
ravu, review / revue
ravuge, ravage
ravuje, ravage
ravul, ravel
ravulashen, revelation
ravulation, revelation
ravulee, reveille
ravurbarate, reverberate
ravurse, reverse
ravurt, revert
raw,wly,wness,wish, UNFINISHED,
    UNCOOKED, UNADULTERATED, IN
    ITS NATURAL STATE
raward, reward
rawdy, rowdy
rawlik, rollick
rawnd, round
rawnt, round
raword, reward
rawst, roust
rawty, rowdy
ray,*, STREAM OF LIGHT/HOPE/
    ENERGY (or see rye)
raybees, rabid(ies)
raydar, radar

raydeans, radiance
raydon, radon
rayl, rail / rale
rayn, rain / reign / rein
raynbo, rainbow
rayon, SYNTHETIC FIBER
raysd, raise(d) / race(d)
rayunyon, reunion
razberee, raspberry
razd, race(d) / raise(d)
raze, raise / ray(s) / race
razeleant, resilient
razemble, resemble
razemblinse, resemble(lance)
razen, raisin / raise(sing) / race(cing)
razent, resent
razentment, resent(ment)
razer, razor
razervation, reservation
razervist, reserve(vist)
razesd, racist
razesm, racism
razest, racist / resist
razide, reside
raziduel, residue(ual)
razilyent, resilient
razimble, resemble
razimbul, resemble
razin, raisin / raise(sing) / race(cing) /
    resign
razir, razor
razirvation, reservation
razisd, racist
razism, racism
razist, racist / resist
razistef, resist(ive)
razistense, resist(ance)
razistent, resist(ant)
razistur, resist(or)
razite, recite
razizum, racism
razkel, rascal
razkul, rascal
razodo, risotto
razolve, resolve
razon, raisin / raise(sing) / race(cing)
razoom, resume
razor,*, SHARP BLADE INSTRUMENT
    FOR CUTTING HAIR
razort, resort
razoto, risotto
razt, raise(d) / race(d)
razume, resume
razun, raisin / raise(sing) / race(cing)

razur, razor
razust, racist
re, PREFIX INDICATING "BACK/AGAIN/ IN RESPONSE" MOST OFTEN MODIFIES THE WORD
reach,hes,hed,hing, STRETCH FURTHER THAN NORMAL TO ACHIEVE/ GRASP/ ACQUIRE "prefixes: over"
reacshen, react(ion)
react,*,ted,ting,tion,tional,tionary, tionaries,tionist,tive,tance,tor, RESPOND/ ACT/MOVE IN RESPONSE TO STIMULUS "prefixes: bio/over/un"
reacter, react(or)
reactur, react(or)
read,*,ding,dable,dability,dableness, dably,der, ABLE TO VIEW/SEE/ DECIPHER TEXT/LETTERS/ NUMBERS/SYMBOLS (or see red) "prefixes: mis/un"
ready,died,dying,dily,diness, PREPARED TO ACT/PERFORM/RESPOND (or see read) "prefixes: un"
reaf, reef
reak, wreak / reek / wreck
reaked, wreck(ed) / wreak(ed) / reek(ed)
reaks, react(s) / reek(s) / wreak(s)
reakshen, react(ion)
reakshun, react(ion)
reakt, react
reakted, react(ed)
reaktef, react(ive)
reakter, react(or)
reaktif, react(ive)
reaktion, react(ion)
reaktir, react(or)
reaktive, react(ive)
reaktor, react(or)
reaktuf, react(ive)
reaktur, react(or)
real,lness,lism,list,listic,listically,lly,lize, lizes,lized,lizing,lity, PHYSICAL/ TRUTHFUL/FACTUAL (or see reel/ realty) "prefixes: ir/neo/sur"
realdy, realty
realedy, reality
realestic, real(istic)
realety, reality
realidy, reality
reality,ties, PHYSICAL, TRUTHFUL, FACTUAL (or see reel/realty) "prefixes: un"

really, TRULY, ACTUALLY, INDEED
realm,*, AREA OF SCOPE/INTEREST
realty,ties,tor, OF REAL ESTATE/ PROPERTY
ream,*,med,ming,mer, BUNDLED PAPER, ENLARGE/BORE/BEVEL/ ENLARGE/ SQUEEZE WITH A TOOL
reanlistment, reenlist(ment)
reap,*,ped,ping,per, ACCEPT, RECEIVE, HARVEST FOR YOUR EFFORTS
rear,*,red,ring, THE END/LAST/ BOTTOM OF SOMETHING, TO RISE UP ON HINDQUARTERS "prefixes: up"
reary, weary
reason,*,ned,ning,nable,nably, nableness, WEIGH LOGIC AGAINST EMOTIONS IN MAKING DECISIONS, USE MODERATE JUDGEMENT "prefixes: un"
reastat, rheostat
reath, wreath / wreathe
reatret, retreat
reaultee, realty
reax, react(s)
reb, rib
rebade, rebate
rebaflavin, riboflavin
rebal, rebel
reban, ribbon
rebate,*,er, TO RETURN BACK
rebatishen, repetition
rebeit, rebate
rebel,*,lled,lling,llion,llious,lliously, lliousness, RISE UP/GO AGAINST THE MAINSTREAM OF RULE/ THOUGHT
rebelion, rebel(llion)
rebelyus, rebel(llious)
reben, ribbon
reberkushen, repercussion
reberkution, repercussion
rebertwa, repertoire
rebertwor, repertoire
rebetishen, repetition
rebeut, rebut / reboot
rebeutashen, repute(tation)
rebeutel, rebut(ttal)
rebewk, rebuke
rebewt, rebut / reboot
rebewtel, rebut(ttal)
rebil, rebel
rebin, ribbon
rebirkushen, repercussion

rebirkution, repercussion
rebirtwa, repertoire
rebirtwor, repertoire
reble, rebel
rebled, rebel(lled)
rebleka, replica
reblekashen, replica(tion)
reblika, replica
reblikate, replica(te)
reblikation, replica(tion)
rebluka, replica
reblukashen, replica(tion)
reblukate, replica(te)
reblukation, replica(tion)
rebof, rebuff
reboflavin, riboflavin
rebol, rebel
rebon, ribbon
reboot,*,ted,ting, RESTART A COMPUTER/MEMORY/ACTION (or see rebut)
reborkushen, repercussion
rebotek, robot(ic)
rebound,ded,ding, REPERCUSSION/ REACTION TO A COLLISION WITH EMOTIONS/ATTITUDES/ SOMETHING PHYSICAL
rebownd, rebound
rebownt, rebound
rebrahensible, reprehensible
rebrkushen, repercussion
rebt, rib(bbed) / rip(pped)
rebtile, reptile
rebtileun, reptile(lian)
rebudal, rebut(ttal)
rebudle, rebut(ttal)
rebuf, rebuff
rebuff,*,ffed,ffing, REFUSE/REJECT
rebuflavin, riboflavin
rebuke,*,ed,king,er, SEVERE/SHARP REJECT/REFUSE
rebul, rebel
rebuled, rebel(lled)
rebun, ribbon
reburkushen, repercussion
reburkution, repercussion
reburtwa, repertoire
reburtwor, repertoire
rebut,*,tted,tting,ttable,ttal, ARGUE/ REFUTE/OPPOSE/THRUST BACK (or see reboot) "prefixes: sur"
rebutal, rebut(ttal)
rebutashen, repute(tation)
rebute, reboot

rebutishen, repetition
rebutle, rebut(ttal)
rec, wreck
recal, recall
recall,*,lled,lling,llable, CALL/SOLICITE SOMETHING BACK TO THE SOURCE/ CREATOR
recamend, recommend
recansile, reconcile
recant,*,ted,ting, CONTRADICT/ RETRACT WHAT WAS JUST SAID
recap,*,pped,pping, SUMMARIZE/ RECOAT/RESURFACE
recaul, recall
reccomend, recommend
reccomendable, recommend(able)
reccomendation, recommend(ation)
reccomended, recommend(ed)
reccomenduble, recommend(able)
recd, wreck(ed) / wreak(ed) / reek(ed)
recede,*,ed,ding, RETREAT/ WITHDRAW/YIELD TO PREVIOUS/ PRIOR
receipt,*, ACKNOWLEDGEMENT/ INVOICE FOR HAVING RECEIVED SERVICES/ GOODS
receive,*,ed,ving,vable,vables,er,ership, ACCEPT/ACQUIRE/ACCUMULATE
recensile, reconcile
recent,tly,tness,ncy, HAVING OCCURED NEAR/CLOSE TO THE PRESENT TIME (or see resent)
recepe, recipe
receprocate, reciprocate
receprokul, reciprocal
recepshen, reception
recepshenist, receptionist
recepshin, reception
receptacle,*, A PLACE TO DELIVER, A RECEIVING PLACE, ELECTRICAL SOURCE
recepticle, receptacle
reception,*, AN EVENT/CEREMONY/ DEVICE WHICH RECEIVES/ ACKNOWLEDGE/ACCEPTS INCOMING
receptionist,*, SOMEONE WHO ACCEPTS INCOMING CALLS/ VISITORS/CUSTOMERS
receptive,ely,eness,vity,tor, ABLE TO TAKE IN/RECEIVE
receptor,*, THAT WHICH RECEIVES
receptucle, receptacle
recer, recur

reces, recess
recess,sses,ssed,ssing,ssion,ssional, ssionary,sive,sively,siveness, TO TAKE A BREAK, RECEDE
receve, receive
rech, wreck / wreak / reek / reach / wretch / rich
rechd, wreck(ed) / wreak(ed) / reek(ed) / reach(ed)
reched, reach(ed) / wreck(ed) / wreak(ed) / reek(ed)
rechem, regime
rechim, regime
rechis, reach(es) / rich(es)
rechister, register
rechistrashen, registration
rechly, rich(ly)
recht, wreck(ed) / wreak(ed) / reek(ed) / reach(ed)
rechual, ritual
rechuol, ritual
recicle, recycle
recieve, receive
recipe,*, DIRECTIONS FOR COOKING
recipient,*, THOSE WHO RECEIVE/IN RECEIPT OF
recipracate, reciprocate
reciprocal,lity,lly, GIVE AND TAKE, BACK AND FORTH, MUTUALLY RESPONSIVE
reciprocate,*,ted,ting,tion,tive,tor, MOVES BACK AND FORTH, MUTUALLY RESPONSIVE
reciproqueit, reciprocate
recir, recur
recite,*,ed,ting,tal,tation,tative, REPEAT/RELATE GIVE ACCOUNT FROM MEMOR
reck, wreck / wreak / reek
reckamendation, recommend(ation)
recken, wreck(ing) / reek(ing)
reckensile, reconcile
reckety, rickety
reckin, wreck(ing) / reek(ing)
reckinsile, reconcile
reckits, rickets
recklaim, reclaim / reclame
recklamashen, reclamation
recklame, reclaim / reclame
reckless,ssly,ssness, BE UNAWARE/ CARELESS OF SURROUNDING ENVIRONMENT POSING POTENTIAL DANGER/PAIN
reckline, recline
recklus, recluse / reckless

reckognition, recognition
reckomend, recommend
reckon,*,ned,ning, SUPPOSE, TO BE CONSIDERED "prefixes: un"
reckonsile, reconcile
reckumend, recommend
reckumendation, recommend(ation)
reckun, reckon
reckunsile, reconcile
reclaim,*,med,ming,mer,mable,mant, mation, TAKE BACK, MAKE PURE/ USABLE AGAIN (or see reclame) "prefixes: ir"
reclaimable,*,bility, TAKE BACK, MAKE PURE/USABLE AGAIN "prefixes: ir"
reclamashen, reclamation
reclamation,*, TAKE BACK, MAKE PURE/ USABLE
reclame,*, ADVERTISE ONESELF, PUBLIC ATTENTION/NOTORIETY (or see reclaim)
reclamer, reclaim(er)
recles, reckless
recline,*,ed,ning,er, RECUMBENT POSITION/LIE BACK
reclumashen, reclamation
reclumation, reclamation
recluse,*,sion,sive,sively,siveness, SHUT ONESELF OFF/AWAY FROM SOCIETY/ SOCIAL ENVIRONMENT
reclushen, recluse(sion)
recochet, ricochet
recogneshen, recognition
recognetion, recognition
recognition,ive,tory, TO FIND FAMILIAR, FRIENDLY ATTENTION "prefixes: non"
recognize,*,ed,zing,zable,zability,zance, FIND FAMILIAR, KNOW, ACKNOWLEDGE "prefixes: de"
recognizuble, recognize(zable)
recoil,*,led,ling,lless, SUDDEN JERK/ DRAW BACK/SHRINKING FROM
recol, recoil / recall
recold, recall(ed)
recolt, recall(ed)
recomendable, recommend(able)
recomendashen, recommend(ation)
recomindation, recommend(ation)
recommend,*,ded,ding,dation,dable, datory, ADVISE/SUGGEST FAVORABLY
recommendashen, recommend(ation)
reconaisanse, reconnaissance

reconasinse, reconnaissance

reconcile,*,ed,ling,lable,lability, lableness,lably,ement,liation, liatory, REBUILD FRIENDSHIP, RESTORE UNION, ADJUST TO DIFFERENCES "prefixes: ir"

reconnaissance, EXAMINE PARAMETER/ TERRITORY

reconsile, reconcile

reconsileashen, reconcile(liation)

reconsileation, reconcile(liation)

reconstatute, reconstitute

reconstetushen, reconstitute(tion)

reconstetute, reconstitute

reconstitute,*,ed,ting,tion, RECONSTRUCT FROM A CONDENSED/DRIED STATE

reconstruct,*,ted,ting,tion,tive,tible,tor, TO CONSTRUCT AGAIN, RESTORE "prefixes: un"

recoop, recoup

recooped, recoup(ed)

recooperashen, recuperate(tion)

recooperate, recuperate

record,*,ded,ding,dable,der, DOCUMENT/TAPE/WRITE/DEFINE AN EVENT FOR POSTERITY, PRESERVE EVIDENCE "prefixes: pre"

recorse, recourse

recoup,*,ped,ping,pable,pment, TO REGAIN, BE COMPENSATED

recourse, RETURN FOR BACK-UP HELP, ONLY OPTION

recover,*,red,ring,rable,ry, TO GET BACK TO NORMAL/HEALTHY, BECOME OPERABLE AGAIN "prefixes: ir"

recreashen, recreation

recreate,*,ed,ting,tion,tive,tor, AMUSEMENT/DIVERSION/PLAY

recreation,nal,ive, AMUSEMENT/ DIVERSION/PLAY

recreminate, recriminate

recriminate,*,ed,ting,tion,tive,tor,tory, TO ACCUSE THE ONE WHO ACCUSED ORIGINALLY

recruit,*,ted,ting,ter,tment, ORGANIZE/ ENLIST/ENTICE PEOPLE TO JOIN

recrut, recruit

recruter, recruit(er)

rect, wreck(ed) / wreak(ed) / reek(ed)

rectafy, rectify

rectal,lly,tum,ta, INVOLVES/ PERTAINING TO THE RECTUM

rectatude, rectitude

rectem, rectum

rectifie, rectify

rectify,fies,fied,fying,fiable,fication, itude, AMEND/CORRECT/MAKE RIGHT

rectil, rectal

rectim, rectum

rectitude,dinous, RIGHTEOUS IN FORM/ INTEGRITY

rectol, rectal

rectom, rectum

rectul, rectal

rectum,*,ta, THE LOWER LARGE INTESTINE

rectutude, rectitude

recufer, recover

recufry, recover(y)

recuisit, requisite

recumbent,tly,ncy, RECLINING/LYING POSITION

recumendashen, recommend(ation)

recunsdrucdev, reconstruct(ive)

recunsile, reconcile

recunstruct, reconstruct

recupe, recoup

recuped, recoup(ed)

recuperashen, recuperate(tion)

recuperate,*,ed,ting,tion,tive,tory, RECOVER/REGAIN FROM ILLNESS/ FINANCIAL STRESS

recur,*,rred,rring,rrent,rrently,rrence, REPEATEDLY HAPPENING

recurd, record

recuver, recover

recuvry, recover(y)

recwuzit, requisite

recycle,*,ed,ling,er,lable,lables,lability, REUSE, USE AGAIN

red,*,dder,ddest,dding,dness,dden, A COLOR, PERTAINING TO THE COLOR (or see read)

redabel, read(able)

redabul, read(able)

redal, riddle

redard, retard

redasent, reticent

redasint, reticent

rede, ready

redeam, redeem

redeble, read(able)

reded, ready(died) / read

redeem,*,med,ming,mer,mable, CLEAR PAYMENT, RECOVER, FULFILL PLEDGE "prefixes: ir"

redeemible, redeem(able)

redempshun, redemption

redemption,*,nal,ner,ive,tory, TO BE/ ACT OF BEING REDEEMED

redemshen, redemption

redemtion, redemption

redemtive, redemption(ive)

redemuble, redeem(able)

redents, rid(ddance)

reder, red(dder) / read(er)

redern, return

redge, ridge

redi, ready

redible, read(able)

redicint, reticent

redicule, ridicule

rediculus, ridiculous

redimtive, redemption(ive)

redin, red(dden)

redio, radio

redir, red(dder) / read(er)

redisent, reticent

redium, radium

redle, riddle

redna, retina

redniss, red(ness)

redo,oes,did,oing,one, DO AGAIN/OVER

redoo, redo

redoose, reduce

redor, read(er) / red(dder)

redroactive, retroactive

redroaktif, retroactive

redrograte, retrograde

redrospection, retrospect(ion)

redrospekshin, retrospect(ion)

redubel, read(able)

redubol, read(able)

reduce,*,ed,cing,er,cible,cibly,cibility, ction,ctional,ctive, TO LOWER/ DIMUTION/DIVIDE "prefixes: ir"

reducshen, reduce(ction)

reduing, redo(ing)

redukshen, reduce(ction)

reduktion, reduce(ction)

redul, riddle

redun, red(dden)

redundant,tly,ncy,ncies, OVER AND OVER, REPEATEDLY/REPETITION/ UNNECESSARY

redundensy, redundant(ncy)

redur, red(dder) / read(er)

redurn, return
redusable, reduce(cible)
reduse, reduce
redusent, reticent
redusint, reticent
redy, ready
reech, reach
reed,*,ding,dy, A PLANT, CONVEX
    MOLDING, RIDGES (or see read)
reederate, reiterate
reef,*,fer, OCEAN LEDGE, PART OF A
    SAIL, SLANG FOR ROLLED
    MARIJUANA, REFRIGERATOR
reek,*,ked,king,ker,kingly,ky,
    OFFENSIVE/STRONG/AWFUL ODOR
    (or see wreak/wreck)
reel,*,led,ling,ler,lable, TO WIND/PULL
    IN, A DANCE, WOUND UP,
    REVOLVING TOOL (or see real)
    "prefixes: un"
reem, ream
reemberse, reimburse
reembersment, reimburse(ment)
reemburse, reimburse
reembursment, reimburse(ment)
reenact,*,ted,ting,tment, REPLICATE A
    PERFORMANCE/EVENT
reenaktment, reenact(ment)
reenforse, reinforce
reenforsment, reinforce(ment)
reenlestment, reenlist(ment)
reenlist,*,ted,ting,tment, TO ENLIST
    AGAIN
reep, reap
reept, reap(ed)
reer, rear
reeth, wreath / wreathe
reeturate, reiterate
ref, reef / referee
refal, revel
refalashen, revelation
refalation, revelation
refald, revel(lled)
refalee, reveille
refar, river
refarmashen, reform(ation)
refarmation, reform(ation)
refeel, reveal
refel, revel / refill
refelable, refill(able)
refelashen, revelation
refelation, revelation
refeld, revel(lled) / refill(ed)
refelee, reveille

refeloble, refill(able)
refer,*,rred,rring,rable,rral,
    RECOMMEND/HAND OVER/
    REQUEST/ASSIGN SOMEONE ELSE,
    SLANG FOR REFRIGERATOR (or see
    reef(er)/river)
referal, refer(rral)
referbash, refurbish
referbish, refurbish
referbishment, refurbish(ment)
referd, refer(rred)
refere, referee
referee,*,eed,eeing, ASSIGNED TO
    SETTLE DISPUTES/MAKE
    JUDGEMENT CALLS
reference,*,ed,cing, DIRECTION,
    ALLUSION, GUIDE
referendum,*,da, MEASURE PUT
    BEFORE PUBLIC FOR VOTE
referil, refer(rral)
referindum, referendum
referinse, reference
refermashen, reform(ation)
refermation, reform(ation)
referse, reverse
refeuge, refuge
refeugy, refugee
refeuje, refuge
refeuse, refuse
refeusil, refuse(sal)
refeuze, refuse
refewge, refuge / refugee
refewje, refuge
refews, refuse
refewsel, refuse(sal)
refiew, review / revue
refiful, revival
refil, refill
refilable, refill(able)
refilashen, revelation
refilation, revelation
refild, revel(lled)
refilee, reveille
refill,*,lled,lling,llable, FILL AGAIN
refine,*,ed,ning,ery,nable,ement,
    REMOVE IMPURITIES/ALLOYS,
    MAKE FINE "prefixes: un"
refinment, refine(ment)
refinury, refine(ry)
refir, refer / reef(er) / river
refiral, refer(rral)
refirans, reference
refirbash, refurbish
refirbish, refurbish

refird, refer(rred)
refired, refer(rred)
refiree, referee
refirence, reference
refirendum, referendum
refirense, reference
refirmashen, reform(ation)
refirmation, reform(ation)
refirse, reverse
reflashen, revelation
reflecks, reflex / reflect(s)
reflecksef, reflex(ive)
reflect,*,ted,ting,tion,tive,tively,
    tiveness,tor,torize, MIRROR/CAST
    BACK/ REPRODUCE AN IMAGE (or
    see reflex) "prefixes: retro/un"
reflectif, reflect(ive)
refleks, reflex / reflect(s)
reflekshen, reflect(ion)
refleksif, reflex(ive)
reflekt, reflect / reflex(ed)
reflektif, reflect(ive)
reflektion, reflect(ion)
reflektor, reflect(or)
reflex,xes,xed,xing,xly,xive,xively,
    xiveness,xivity, REACTION/
    RESPONSE (or see reflect) "prefixes:
    ir"
reflexsif, reflex(ive)
reflext, reflex(ed)
refol, revel
refolashen, revelation
refolation, revelation
refold, revel(lled)
refolee, reveille
refor, river / refer / reef(er)
reform,*,med,ming,mer,mation,mable,
    matory,matories,mative, CHANGE/
    MODIFY/RETRAIN/REARRANGE/
    RESTORE "prefixes: ir"
reformashen, reform(ation)
reformd, reform(ed)
reformitory, reform(atory)
reformutory, reform(atory)
refract,*,ted,ting,tion,tive,tory,
    DEFLECT/REFLECT INTO A
    DIFFERENT DIRECTION/DENSITY
refrain,*,ned,ning,nment, REPETITIVE
    BREAK/INTERRUPTION, TO
    REPRESS/ ABSTAIN
refrakt, refract
refraktory, refract(ory)
refrane, refrain
refrans, reference / refrain(s)

refred, referee(d)
refree, referee
refregirant, refrigerate(ant)
refregirator, refrigerate(tor)
refrendum, referendum
refrense, reference
refresh,hes,hed,hing,her,hment, TO
MAKE FRESH AGAIN/ INVIGORATE
refrigerate,*,ed,ting,tion,ant, USED TO
KEEP THINGS COOL/ COLD
refrigerator, refrigerate(tor)
refrigerent, refrigerate(ant)
refrindum, referendum
refrinse, reference
refry, referee
reft, rift
refuch, refuge
refuchi, refugee
refue, review / revue
refuge,*, SANCTUARY/SHELTER, SAFE
PROTECTION
refugee,*, ONE ESCAPING
PERSECUTION FROM A FOREIGN
COUNTRY
refugy, refugee
refuje, refuge
reful, revel
refulashen, revelation
refulation, revelation
refulee, reveille
refund,*,ded,ding,dable, RETURN/
COMPENSATE/GIVE BACK
refundible, refund(able)
refunduble, refund(able)
refunt, refund
refur, refer / reef(er) / river
refurbeshment, refurbish(ment)
refurbish,hes,hed,hing,hment,
RENOVATE/MAKE FRESH AGAIN
refurd, refer(rred)
refured, refer(rred)
refuree, referee
refurendum, referendum
refurense, reference
refuril, refer(rral)
refurindum, referendum
refurmashen, reform(ation)
refurse, reverse
refus, raffle / refuse
refuse,*,ed,sing,sal,er, NOT ACCEPT,
DENY/REJECT, TO DISCARD
UNUSABLES/ TRASH
refusel, refuse(sal)

refute,*,ed,ting,tability,table,tably,
tation, CHANGE/MODIFY/RETRAIN/
REARRANGE/RESTORE "prefixes: ir"
refuze, refuse
reg, rig / ridge
regal,lly,lia,le,led,ling,lity,lities,
PERTAINING TO LAVISH FEASTS/
ROYALTY
regalea, regal(ia)
regaledy, regal(ity)
regamen, regime(n)
regamentashen, regime(ntation)
regamentation, regime(ntation)
regamin, regime(n)
regamint, regime(nt)
regan, region
regard,*,ded,ding,dful,dfully,dfullness,
dless,dlessly,dlessness, TO
CONSIDER, SHOW CONCERN/
ATTENTION/RESPECT "prefixes: dis/
ir"
regart, regard
regaster, register
regastrashen, registration
regastration, registration
regect, reject
regekshen, reject(ion)
regekt, reject
regektion, reject(ion)
regel, regal
regementation, regime(ntation)
regemin, regime(n)
regemint, regime(nt)
regemintation, regime(ntation)
regen, region
regenal, region(al)
regenerate,*,ed,ting,able,acy,tely,tion,
tive,tively,tor, RENEW, RESTORE,
REPLACE, REVITALIZE "prefixes: un"
regenuradive, regenerate(tive)
reger, rigor
regergetate, regurgitate
regerjutate, regurgitate
regestir, register
regestrashen, registration
regestration, registration
reget, rigid
regeuler, regular
regeulerly, regular(ly)
regewlashen, regulate(tion)
regewlate, regulate
regewlation, regulate(tion)
regewlerly, regular(ly)
regewvinate, rejuvenate

regid, rigid
regil, regal
regime,*,en,ent,ental,entally,entation,
MODE/SYSTEM OF RULE/
MANAGEMENT
regimentashen, regime(ntation)
regimin, regime(min)
regimint, regime(nt)
regimintation, regime(ntation)
regin, region
reginal, region(al)
reginuradive, regenerate(tive)
reginurate, regenerate
reginurative, regenerate(tive)
region,*,nal,nally,nalism,nalist,nalistic,
AN AREA/PART/SECTION OF
"prefixes: inter/sub"
regirus, rigor(ous)
register,*,red,ring,tration, SIGN UP/
ENROLL TO PARTICIPATE "prefixes:
de"
registrashen, registration
registration,*, SIGN UP/ENROLL TO
PARTICIPATE
regit, rigid
regiular, regular
reglar, regular
reglate, regulate
regle, regal
reglerly, regular(ly)
reglir, regular
reglurly, regular(ly)
regoise, rejoice
regon, region
regonal, region(al)
regoyse, rejoice
regres, regress
regresif, regress(ive)
regresive, regress(ive)
regress,sses,ssed,ssing,ssion,ssive,
ssively,ssiveness,ssor, GOING BACK/
REVERSION
regresuf, regress(ive)
regret,*,tted,tting,tful,tfully,tfulness,
ttable,ttably,tter, SENSE OF LOSS/
SORROW, SORRY
regreted, regret(tted)
regretfuly, regret(fully)
reguard, regard
reguardless, regard(less)
regul, regal
regular,*,rly,rity,rize, NORMAL/
AVERAGE/TYPICAL "prefixes: ir"
regulashen, regulate(tion)

regulate,*,ed,ting,tion,tive,tor,tory, NORMALIZE, KEEP WITHIN LIMITS/ STANDARDS "prefixes: de"
reguler, regular
regulerly, regular(ly)
regulur, regular
regument, regime(nt)
regumentashen, regime(ntation)
regumentation, regime(ntation)
regumin, regime(n)
regumint, regime(nt)
regunal, region(al)
regurgitate,*,ed,ting,tion, RUSH/SURGE BACK AND FORTH
regurjitate, regurgitate
regurs, rigor(s)
regurus, rigor(ous)
regustir, register
regustrashen, registration
regustration, registration
reguvanashen, rejuvenate(tion)
reguvanate, rejuvenate
reguvanation, rejuvenate(tion)
reguvinate, rejuvenate
reguvination, rejuvenate(tion)
reguvunate, rejuvenate
regwasit, requisite
regwazit, requisite
rehab,*,bber,bilitate, SLANG FOR REHABILITATION
rehabeletashen, rehabilitate(tion)
rehabeletate, rehabilitate
rehabilitate,*,ed,ting,tion,tive, RESTORE/REINSTATE/REESTABLISH
rehap, rehab
rehearse,*,ed,sing,sal, TO PRACTICE REPEATEDLY FOR A PERFORMANCE
rehebilatation, rehabilitate(tion)
rehersal, rehearse(sal)
reherse, rehearse
rehersul, rehearse(sal)
rehirsul, rehearse(sal)
rehubelatashen, rehabilitate(tion)
rehubilatate, rehabilitate
rehubiletation, rehabilitate(tion)
rehurse, rehearse
rehursil, rehearse(sal)
reiderate, reiterate
reidurate, reiterate
reign,*,ned,ning, HAVE RULE/POWER/ SOVEREIGNITY (or see rain/rein)
reil, real / reel / rale / rail
reilistec, real(istic)
reiltee, realty

reilty, realty
reimberse, reimburse
reimbirsment, reimburse(ment)
reimburse,*,ed,sing,sable,ement,er, PAY BACK/REFUND/COMPENSATE
rein,*,ned,ning,nless, RESTRAINT/ CURB/CONTROL (or see rain/reign)
reinacment, reenact(ment)
reinacted, reenact(ed)
reinakt, reenact
reinaktment, reenact(ment)
reindeer,*, IN THE DEER FAMILY
reinforce,*,ed,cing,ement, INCREASE/ STRENGTHEN
reinforse, reinforce
reinforsment, reinforce(ment)
reinlest, reenlist
reinlisment, reenlist(ment)
reinlist, reenlist
reinlistment, reenlist(ment)
reip, rape / ripe / reap
reis, race / rise / raise
reiterate,*,ed,ting,tion,tive,tively, TO REPEAT/SAY AGAIN
reiturate, reiterate
rej, ridge / reach
rejament, regime(nt)
rejamin, regime(n)
rejamintashen, regime(ntation)
rejamintation, regime(ntation)
rejan, region
rejaster, register
reject,*,ted,ting,tion,ter,tive, REFUSE TO RECEIVE/RECOGNIZE/ ACKNOWLEDGE/ACCEPT
rejekshen, reject(ion)
rejekt, reject
rejektion, reject(ion)
rejen, region
rejenaradive, regenerate(tive)
rejenarative, regenerate(tive)
rejenul, region(al)
rejenurate, regenerate
rejestir, register
rejestrashen, registration
rejestration, registration
rejet, rigid
rejewvinate, rejuvenate
rejid, rigid
rejimen, regime(n)
rejiment, regime(nt)
rejin, region
rejinarate, regenerate
rejinul, region(al)

rejinuradive, regenerate(tive)
rejister, register
rejistrashen, registration
rejistration, registration
rejit, rigid
rejoese, rejoice
rejoice,*,ed,cing,er,cingly, TO DISPLAY JOY/GLADNESS
rejon, region
rejonal, region(al)
rejoyse, rejoice
rejumen, regime(n)
rejument, regime(nt)
rejumentashen, regime(ntation)
rejumentation, regime(ntation)
rejumin, regime(n)
rejumint, regime(nt)
rejumintashen, regime(ntation)
rejumintation, regime(ntation)
rejun, region
rejunal, region(al)
rejustir, register
rejustrashen, registration
rejustration, registration
rejuvanashen, rejuvenate(tion)
rejuvenate,*,ed,ting,tion,tor,nize, nescence, MAKE YOUTHFUL AGAIN
rejuvinashen, rejuvenate(tion)
rejuvinate, rejuvenate
rejuvination, rejuvenate(tion)
rek, wreck / wreak / reek
rekal, recall
rekamend, recommend
rekamendation, recommend(ation)
rekamenduble, recommend(able)
rekamented, recommend(ed)
rekanize, recognize
rekansile, reconcile
rekansileashun, reconcile(liation)
rekant, recant
rekap, recap
rekapt, recap(pped)
rekashay, ricochet
rekd, reek(ed) / wreck(ed) / wreak(ed)
rekedy, rickety
rekegnise, recognize
reken, reckon
rekendil, rekindle
rekendul, rekindle
rekenize, recognize
rekensile, reconcile
rekensileashun, reconcile(liation)
reker, recur / wrecker
rekerd, record

rekety, rickety
rekeulir, regular
rekewlashen, regulate(tion)
rekewpt, recoup(ed)
rekewpurate, recuperate
rekidy, rickety
rekimented, recommend(ed)
rekin, reckon
rekindle,*,ed,ling, RENEW
rekindul, rekindle
rekinise, recognize
rekinsile, reconcile
rekir, recur / wrecker
rekird, record
rekits, rickets
rekity, rickety
reklaimuble, reclaimable
reklamashen, reclamation
reklamation, reclamation
reklame, reclaim / reclame
reklamshen, reclamation
reklamuble, reclaimable
reklas, reckless
reklemashen, reclamation
rekless, reckless
reklimashen, reclamation
reklimation, reclamation
rekline, recline
reklinur, recline(r)
reklir, regular
reklis, reckless
rekloos, recluse
reklumation, reclamation
reklus, reckless
rekluse, recluse
rekochet, ricochet
rekofry, recover(y)
rekogneshen, recognition
rekognise, recognize
rekognition, recognition
rekognize, recognize
rekognizuble, recognize(zable)
rekoil, recoil
rekol, recall
rekold, recall(ed)
rekole, recoil / recall
rekolt, recall(ed)
rekomend, recommend
rekomendashen, recommend(ation)
rekomented, recommend(ed)
rekon, reckon
rekonasents, reconnaissance
rekonisense, reconnaissance
rekonize, recognize

rekonsdructive, reconstruct(ive)
rekonsile, reconcile
rekonsileat, reconcile(ate)
rekonsileation, reconcile(liation)
rekonstatute, reconstitute
rekonstetushen, reconstitute(tion)
rekonstetute, reconstitute
rekonstitution, reconstitute(tion)
rekonstruct, reconstruct
rekonusinse, reconnaissance
rekoop, recoup
rekooperate, recuperate
rekor, wrecker
rekord, record
rekorder, record(er)
rekorse, recourse
rekover, recover
rekoyl, recoil
rekreashen, recreation
rekreate, recreate
rekreation, recreation
rekreative, recreate(tive)
rekreminate, recriminate
rekrimenate, recriminate
rekroot, recruit
rekrute, recruit
rekruter, recruit(er)
reks, reek(s) / wreck(s) / wreak(s)
rekt, reek(ed) / wreck(ed) / wreak(ed)
rektafy, rectify
rektal, rectal
rektatude, rectitude
rektel, rectal
rektem, rectum
rektify, rectify
rektitude, rectitude
rektol, rectal
rektom, rectum
rektufy, rectify
rektul, rectal
rektum, rectum
rekuasit, requisite
rekufer, recover
rekufry, recover(y)
rekugnise, recognize
rekugnishen, recognition
rekugnize, recognize
rekugnizuble, recognize(zable)
rekulade, regulate
rekular, regular
rekulashen, regulate(tion)
rekulate, regulate
rekulation, regulate(tion)
rekumbent, recumbent

rekumend, recommend
rekumendashen, recommend(ation)
rekumenduble, recommend(able)
rekumented, recommend(ed)
rekumind, recommend
rekun, reckon
rekunize, recognize
rekunsile, reconcile
rekunsileashen, reconcile(liation)
rekunsileation, reconcile(liation)
rekunstruct, reconstruct
rekunstrukdive, reconstruct(ive)
rekupe, recoup
rekuperate, recuperate
rekuperation, recuperate(tion)
rekupirate, recuperate
rekupt, recoup(ed)
rekupurashen, recuperate(tion)
rekur, recur / wrecker
rekurd, record
rekushet, ricochet
rekuver, recover
rekuvry, recover(y)
rekwasit, requisite
rekwest, request
rekwire, require
rekwirment, require(ment)
rekwrute, recruit
rekwuzit, requisite
rel, real / reel / rill / rail / rale
rela, relay
relabs, relapse
relagashen, relegate(tion)
relagate, relegate
relagation, relegate(tion)
relaks, relax
relantless, relent(less)
relaps, relapse
relapse,*,ed,sing,er, TO BACKSLIDE/
    FALL BACK
relashen, relate(tion)
relashunship, relate(tionship)
relate,*,ed,ting,tion,tional,table,
    tionship,edness, BE ALLIED/
    ASSOCIATED/CONNECTED WITH,
    TO TELL/NARRATE "prefixes: inter"
relatevity, relativity
relatif, relative
relative,*,ely,eness,vism,vist,vistic,vity,
    ASSOCIATED/SIMILAR/CLOSE/
    CONNECTION "prefixes: ir"
relativity,vities, THAT WHICH IS
    RELATIVE
relativly, relative(ly)

relavance, relevant(nce)
relavant, relevant
relavence, relevance
relavent, relevant
relax,xes,xed,xing,xation,xedly,xedness, xer,xant, BECOME CALM/LOOSE/ SLACK "prefixes: un"
relay,*,yed,ying, USE OF MACHINERY/ ELECTRICITY/PEOPLE/ TECHNOLOGY/ANIMALS TO SEND/ TRANSMIT/RETRIEVE
rele, really / reel / real
release,*,ed,sing,er,sable, TO FREE
relef, relief
relegate,*,ed,ting,tion, SEND AWAY
releive, relieve
relek, relic
relent,*,ted,ting,tless, INTENSELY PERSISTENT/DEMANDING/ PUNISHING "prefixes: un"
relentless,ssly,ssness, MERCILESS/ HARSH
relese, release
relesh, relish
reletif, relative
reletivity, relativity
reletivly, relative(ly)
relevance, relevant(nce)
relevant,tly,nce,ncy, PERTAINS/ APPLICABLE TO, IMPORTANT/ SUPPORTIVE "prefixes: ir"
releve, relieve
relevence, relevance
relevent, relevant
relever, relieve(r)
relevur, relieve(r)
reli, really / rely
reliable,bility,leness,ly, CONFIDENCE/ TRUST IN, DEPEND ON "prefixes: un"
reliance,cy,nt,ntly, CONFIDENCE/ TRUST/DEPENDENT
reliaple, reliable
relic,*, MEMENTOS/PRESERVED/KEEP SAKES
relichon, religion
relidy, reality
relief,eve, EASE/REMOVAL/ ALLEVIATION FROM PAIN
relieve,*,ed,ving,er,vable, EASED/ REMOVED/ALLEVIATED FROM PAIN (or see relief)
religashen, relegate(tion)
religate, relegate

religation, relegate(tion)
religeon, religion
religion,*,ous,ously,ousness, BELIEF IN A GOD IN A SPECIFIC/PARTICULAR WAY "prefixes: inter/ir"
religon, religion
religus, religion(ous)
relik, relic
relinkwish, relinquish
relinquish,hes,hed,hing,hment,her, GIVE UP POSSESSION OF
relintless, relent(less) / relentless
relish,hes,hed,hing,hable, APPETIZER, PICKLED CONDIMENT, BE GRATIFIED/ PLEASED/LIKE/SAVOR SOMETHING
relity, reality
reliubility, reliable(bility)
reliuble, reliable
reliunse, reliance
reliunt, reliance(nt)
relivance, relevant(nce)
relivant, relevant
relivence, relevance
relivent, relevant
reliver, relieve(r)
relm, realm
reloctant, reluctant
relogate, relegate
relogation, relegate(tion)
reltifly, relative(ly)
relty, realty
reluctant,tly,nce, APPREHENSIVE/ RESISTANT/UNWILLING
reluctinse, reluctant(nce)
reluctint, reluctant
relugashen, relegate(tion)
relugate, relegate
relugation, relegate(tion)
reluktant, reluctant
reluktense, reluctant(nce)
reluktint, reluctant
relur, regular
relush, relish
relutif, relative
relutivly, relative(ly)
reluvence, relevance
reluvent, relevant
rely,lies,lied,lying,liable,liability, liableness,liably, TRUSTWORTHY/ SUPPORTIVE/DEPENDABLE (or see really)
rem, ream / realm / rim
remade, remedy

remadik, rheumatic
remain,*,ned,ning,nder, STAY BEHIND/ LEFT OVER (or see romaine)
reman, remain / romaine
remanis, reminisce
remanisent, reminisce(nt)
remantisize, romantic(ize)
remar, ream(er)
remark,*,ked,king,kable,kably, kableness, WORTHY OF COMMENT/ OBSERVATION/NOTICE "prefixes: un"
remarkuble, remark(able)
rematik, rheumatic
rematy, remedy
rembunctious, rambunctious
rembunkshes, rambunctious
reme, ream
remede, remedy
remediashen, remedy(diation)
remedy,dies,died,dying,diable, diableness,diably,diless,dial, diation, FIX/IMPROVE DAMAGE, RELIEVE DISORDER "prefixes: ir"
remember,*,red,ring,brance,brancer, ACKNOWLEDGE/THINK OF/ RECOLLECT THE PAST "prefixes: dis"
remembrinse, remember(ance)
remembur, remember
remenis, reminisce
remenisent, reminisce(nt)
remer, ream(er)
remeshen, remission
remet, remit
remety, remedy
remidal, remit(ttal)
remidy, remedy
remind,*,ded,ding,der,dful, CAUSE TO RECOLLECT/REMEMBER
remindur, remind(er)
reminis, reminisce
reminisce,*,ed,cing,ent,ently, LONGINGLY REMEMBER/THINK OF THE PAST
reminisent, reminisce(nt)
remintur, remind(er)
remir, ream(er)
remishen, remission
remision, remission
remissible,bility, CAN BE FORGIVEN "prefixes: ir"
remission, ABATEMENT, TEMPORARY REDUCTION/DISAPPEARANCE

remit,*,tted,tting,tment,ttable,tter, ttance,ttent,ttently,ttal, TRANSMIT/ SEND/GIVE BACK "prefixes: un"

remital, remit(ttal)

remited, remit(tted)

remition, remission

remituble, remit(ttable)

remity, remedy

remnant,*, LEFT OVERS/REMAINS/ SCRAPS

remnet, remnant

remnint, remnant

remofer, remove(r)

remonis, reminisce

remoof, remove

remooval, remove(val)

remoovil, remove(val)

remorse,eful,efully,efulness,eless, elessly,elessness, PAIN/GUILT WHEN LOOKING TO SOMETHING IN THE PAST

remorsful, remorse(ful)

remorsless, remorse(ful)

remote,*,ely,eness, REMOVED FROM SOCIAL CENTERS, FAR OFF IN DISTANCE/TIME

remotly, remote(ly)

remove,*,ed,ving,vable,vability, vableness,vably,val,ver, TAKE AWAY/ERASE "prefixes: ir"

remudy, remedy

remufe, remove

remufer, remove(r)

remufible, remove(vable)

remufil, remove(val)

remunerashen, remunerate(tion)

remunerate,*,ed,ting,able,ability,tion, tive,tively, PAY FOR LOSS/REPAY/ COMPENSATE/REWARD

remuneration, remunerate(tion)

remunirate, remunerate

remuniration, remunerate(tion)

remunis, reminisce

remur, ream(er)

remutoed, rheumatic(toid)

remuty, remedy

remuvable, remove(vable)

remuve, remove

remuvel, remove(val)

remuvul, remove(val)

ren, wren

renagade, renegade

renaisance, renaissance

renaissance, PERIOD OF TIME IN EUROPE

renasance, renaissance

renasons, renaissance

renauserus, rhinoceros

renavashen, renovate(tion)

renavate, renovate

renavation, renovate(tion)

renawserus, rhinoceros

rench, wrench

rendal, rent(al)

render,*,red,ring,rable,rer, RETURN/ GIVE IN/SUBMIT/FURNISH/ SURRENDER/CAUSE (or see rent(er))

rendezvous, ARRANGE TO MEET, MEET UP WITH

rendur, render

renegade,*,do, ONE WHO DESERTS, A TRAITOR

renege,*,ed,ging,er, TO FAIL/GO BACK ON WORD, VIOLATE CARD GAME RULE

renevashen, renovate(tion)

renevate, renovate

renevation, renovate(tion)

renew,*,wed,wing,wable,wably, wability,wal,wer, REFRESH/MAKE LIKE NEW/REFURBISH/UPDATE

reng, ring / rink / wring

renger, ring(er) / ranger

renig, renege

renigade, renegade

renik, renege

renisance, renaissance

renissance, renaissance

renk, ring / rink / wring

renkle, wrinkle

renkul, wrinkle

renlistment, reenlist(ment)

renone, renown

renoserus, rhinoceros

renosirus, rhinoceros

renosonse, renaissance

renounce,*,ed,cing,eable,ement,er, DISOWN/REJECT/CAST OFF

renounse, renounce

renounsment, renounce(ment)

renovaded, renovate(d)

renovashen, renovate(tion)

renovate,*,ed,ting,tion,tor, REPAIR TO LIKE NEW CONDITION

renown,ned, ACHIEVEMENTS/ REPUTATION KNOWN FAR AND WIDE

renownse, renounce

renownsment, renounce(ment)

rens, rinse / wren(s) / rent(s)

rensd, rinse(d)

rensur, rinse(r)

rent,*,tal,ted,ting,table,ter,tor, PAY SOMEONE TO BORROW THE USE OF PROPERTY

rentel, rent(al)

renter, render / rent(er)

rentible, rent(able)

rentil, rent(al)

rentuble, rent(able)

rentul, rent(al)

renu, renew

renuable, renew(able)

renuel, renew(al)

renugade, renegade

renuil, renew(al)

renumerate, remunerate

renumeration, remunerate(tion)

renusans, renaissance

renusons, renaissance

renussance, renaissance

renuvadid, renovate(d)

renuvashen, renovate(tion)

renuvate, renovate

renuvation, renovate(tion)

renuzons, renaissance

reol, real / reel / rail / rale

reolistic, real(istic)

reoltee, realty

reolty, realty

reostat, rheostat

rep, rip / ripe / reep

repair,*,red,ring,rer,arable,aration, TO FIX/RESTORE TO A USABLE CONDITION "prefixes: dis"

repal, rebel / ripple

reparable,ly,bility,ative,ation, ABLE TO BE REPAIRED "prefixes: ir"

reparashen, reparation

reparation,*, ABLE TO BE REPAIRED

reparcushen, repercussion

repare, repair

reparkushen, repercussion

repateshen, repetition

repatishus, repetition(ous)

repatition, repetition

repatitious, repetition(ous)

repd, rip(pped) / reep(ed)

repeal,*,led,ling,lable, TO END/
ABOLISH A LAW (or see repel/
rappel) "prefixes: ir"

repeat,*,ted,ting,ter,tedly,table,tability,
TO SAY/DO/HAPPEN AGAIN, MORE
THAN ONCE "prefixes: un"

reped, rip(pped) / reep(ed)

repedatif, repetitive

repededly, repeat(edly)

repedutif, repetitive

repeel, repeal

repeet, repeat

repel,*,lled,lling,ller,llency,llent, KEEP
SOMETHING AWAY/OFF OF,
REJECTS/RESISTS (or see rappel/
repeal/ripple)

repelent, repellent

repelinsy, repellent(ncy)

repellent,*,tly,ncy, REJECT/RESIST,
KEEP OFF OF

repellinsy, repellent(ncy)

repense, repent(s)

repent,*,ted,ting,tance,tant,ter,
REALIZE/REMEDY WRONGDOING

repentinse, repent(ance)

reperable, reparable

reperashen, reparation

reperation, reparation

repercushen, repercussion

repercussion,*,ive, THE EFFECTS/
DEVELOPMENT ACHIEVED/
RESULTING FROM AN ACTION

reperkushen, repercussion

reperkution, repercussion

repertoire,*, LIST OF DRAMAS/
PERFORMANCES/TALENTS/
AVAILABLE RESOURCES

repertor, repertoire

repertwa, repertoire

repertwor, repertoire

repete, repeat

repetedly, repeat(edly)

repetishen, repetition

repetishus, repetition(ous)

repetition,*,ous,ously,ousness,ive,
REPEAT/SAY/DO SOMETHING OVER
AND OVER, ROUTINE

repetitive,ely,eness,ion, REPEAT OVER
AND OVER

repetitous, repetition(ous)

repeutashen, repute(tation)

repeutation, repute(tation)

repeutuble, repute(table)

rephund, refund

repil, rebel / ripple

repint, repent

repintense, repent(ance)

repirable, reparable

repirashen, reparation

repiration, reparation

repircushen, repercussion

repirkution, repercussion

repirtoire, repertoire

repirtwor, repertoire

repitishen, repetition

repitishus, repetition(ous)

repitition, repetition

repititious, repetition(ous)

repl, repel / ripple / rebel

replacation, replica(tion)

replace,*,ed,cing,ement,eable,er, PUT
SOMETHING IN PLACE OF
SOMETHING ELSE "prefixes: ir"

replacment, replace(ment)

replakation, replica(tion)

replasmint, replace(ment)

reple, rebel / ripple

repleca, replica

replecation, replica(tion)

repleka, replica

replekate, replica(te)

replekation, replica(tion)

repleneshment, replenish(ment)

replenish,hes,hed,hing,her,hment, TO
RESTOCK/REFILL

replica,*,ate,ated,ating,ation, MAKE AN
EXACT COPY OF

replika, replica

replikate, replica(te)

replucation, replica(tion)

repluka, replica

replukate, replica(te)

replukation, replica(tion)

reply,lies,lied,lying,lier, TO ANSWER
BACK/RESPOND

repoflavin, riboflavin

repoire, rapport

repol, rebel / ripple

repor, rapport

reporashen, reparation

reporation, reparation

reporder, report(er)

reporkushen, repercussion

report,*,ted,tedly,ting,ter,table,tage,
torial,torially, GIVE ACCOUNT OF
AN EVENT/OCCURRENCE "prefixes:
mis/under"

repository,ries, A PLACE/SHELTER/
DWELLING WHICH STORES/
PRESERVES/ SAFEKEEPS

reposutory, repository

repoteshen, repetition

repour, rapport

repozitory, repository

reprable, reparable

repraduction, reproduce(ction)

repradukshen, reproduce(ction)

repraduse, reproduce

reprahensible, reprehensible

repramand, reprimand

reprasent, represent

reprazintation, represent(ation)

repreble, reparable

repreduction, reproduce(ction)

reprehensible,bility,bly,
UNACCEPTABLE/TO BE CENSURED,
SUPPORTIVE/IMPORTANT
"prefixes: ir"

reprehinsible, reprehensible

repremand, reprimand

represent,*,ted,ting,table,ter,tation,
tational,tative,tatively, tativeness,
TO ACT ON BEHALF OF SOMEONE/
SOMETHING ELSE "prefixes: mis/
under"

represhin, repress(ion)

represif, repress(ive)

represion, repress(ion)

represive, repress(ive)

repress,sses,ssed,ssing,ssion,sser,
PREVENT/SUPPRESS/BLOCK
NATURAL EXPRESSION (or see
oppress) "prefixes: de/ir"

represuve, repress(ive)

reprible, reparable

reprimand,*,ded,ding, TO BE
REPRESSED/REPROVED/FORMALLY
REBUKED

reprisent, represent

reprkushen, repercussion

reproach,hes,hed,hing,hingly,hable,
hableness,hably,her, BLAMED/
CRITICIZED FOR WRONGDOING
"prefixes: ir"

reproch, reproach

reprochuble, reproach(able)

reproduce,*,ed,cing,cible,cibility,er,
ction,ctive,ctively,ctiveness,
PRODUCE ANEW, DUPLICATE/
REPEAT/REMEMBER "prefixes: ir"

reprodukshen, reproduce(ction)

reproduse, reproduce
repruble, reparable
repruduction, reproduce(ction)
reprudukshen, reproduce(ction)
reprumand, reprimand
reprusent, represent
repruzentation, represent(ation)
rept, reap(ed) / rip(pped) / reep(ed)
repteleun, reptile(lian)
reptile,*,lian, COLD BLOODED
VERTEBRATE
reptilein, reptile(lian)
reptishus, repetition(ous)
republek, republic
republekin, republic(an)
republic,*,can, A TYPE OF POLITICAL
SYSTEM "prefixes: pre"
republikan, republic(an)
repugnant,tly,nce,ncy, STRONG
OPPOSITION/DISLIKE/AVERSION
repugnense, repugnant(nce)
repugnent, repugnant
repul, ripple / rebel
repuld, ripple(d)
repulse,*,ed,sing,sion,sive,sively,
siveness, REPEL/AVERT/REBUFF/
FORBID
repulshen, repulse(ion)
repulsif, repulse(sive)
repult, ripple(d)
repurable, reparable
repurashen, reparation
repuration, reparation
repurcushen, repercussion
repurkution, repercussion
repurtoire, repertoire
repurtwa, repertoire
repurtwor, repertoire
reputashen, repute(tation)
repute,ed,edly,table,tably,tability,
tation, TYPE OF CHARACTER
"prefixes: dis"
reputeshen, repetition
reputishus, repetition(ous)
reputition, repetition
reputitious, repetition(ous)
reqrute, recruit
request,*,ted,ting, ASK/PETITION/
SOLICIT FOR
require,*,ed,ring,ement, ESSENTIAL/
NECESSARY
requisite,*,ely,eness, REQUIRED/
NECESSARY "prefixes: de/pre"

requisition,*,ned,ning,nary, REQUEST
TO OBTAIN, FORMAL DEMAND
"prefixes: de"
requite,*,ed,ting,table,tably,tal,ement,
er, ASK/PETITION/SOLICIT FOR
"prefixes: un"
requpe, recoup
reqwasit, requisite
reqwest, request
reqwire, require
reqwirement, require(ment)
rer, rear / rare
rerd, rear(ed)
rere, weary
reridy, rare(rity)
rerity, rare(rity)
resadenshul, reside(ntial)
resadensy, reside(ncy)
resadential, reside(ntial)
resadinshul, reside(ntial)
resadinsy, reside(ncy)
resadue, residue
resal, wrestle
resalushen, resolute(tion)
resan, reason / resin / rise(n)
resanate, resonate / resinate
resandly, recent(ly)
resanense, resonance
resanent, resonance(nt)
resaninse, resonance
resanuble, reason(able)
resape, recipe
resarektion, resurrect(ion)
resatashen, recite(tion)
resauluble, resoluble
rescue,*,ed,uing,er, SAVE/SPARE FROM
DANGER/HARM
resdrane, restrain
research,hes,hed,hing,her, TO STUDY/
OBSERVE/DERIVE FROM FACTS
resebshen, reception
resebshinist, receptionist
resebter, receptor
resebtif, receptive
resebtive, receptive
resede, recede
reseded, recede(d)
resedenshul, reside(ntial)
resedential, reside(ntial)
resedinse, reside(ncy)
resedue, residue
reseed, recede
reseef, receive
reseet, receipt

reseeve, receive
resefe, receive
resefuble, receive(vable)
resegnation, resign(ation)
reselute, resolute
resemble,*,ed,ling,lance, SIMILAR/
LIKENESS
resemblinse, resemble(lance)
resen, reason / resin / rise(n)
resenate, resonate / resinate
resenation, resonate(tion)
resenator, resonate(tor)
resendly, recent(ly)
reseninse, resonance
resent,*,ted,ting,tful,tfully,tfulness,
tment, FEEL SORRY FOR ONESELF,
DOESN'T FEEL APPRECIATED FOR A
DEED DONE (or see recent)
resenuble, reason(able)
resepdekle, receptacle
resepe, recipe
resepeunt, recipient
reseprocal, reciprocal
reseprocation, reciprocate(tion)
reseprokashen, reciprocate(tion)
resepshen, reception
resepshenist, receptionist
resepshun, reception
reseptacle, receptacle
resepticle, receptacle
reseptif, receptive
reseption, reception
reseptionest, receptionist
reseptive, receptive
reseptor, receptor
reseptukle, receptacle
reserch, research
reserect, resurrect
reserection, resurrect(ion)
reserf, reserve
reserfd, reserve(d)
reserginse, resurge(nce)
resergint, resurgent
reservation,*,nist, RESERVE/KEEP
BACK/WITHHOLD SOMETHING,
TERRITORY MANAGED BY NATIVE
TRIBES
reserve,*,ed,ving,edly,edness,vist,
vation, HAVE EXTRA/SPARE/
STORED UP "prefixes: un"
reservoir,*, WHERE WATER IS
COLLECTED/STORED
reservor, reservoir
reses, recess

reseshun, recess(ion)
resesif, recess(ive)
resesion, recess(ion)
resesive, recess(ive)
resession, recess(ion)
reset, receipt
resetion, recess(ion)
reseve, receive
resevuble, receive(vable)
reside,*,ed,ding,er,ence,ency,encies,
    ent,ential,entially,entiary,entiaries,
    PLACE/AREA WHERE PEOPLE
    DWELL/LIVE/OCCUPY "prefixes:
    non"
residenshul, reside(ntial)
residensy, reside(ncy)
residinsy, reside(ncy)
residue,*,ual,ually,uary, WHAT'S LEFT
    OVER/REMAINING AFTER A
    SEPARATION PROCESS
residuel, residue(ual)
resign,*,ned,ning,nation,nedness,ner,
    GIVE UP/RELINQUISH A POSITION/
    AUTHORITY
resignashin, resign(ation)
resikle, recycle
resil, wrestle
resiliensy, resilient(ncy)
resilient,tly,nce,ncy, ABILITY TO SPRING
    BACK/BE FLEXIBLE/ELASTIC
resilute, resolute
resimblanse, resemble(lance)
resimble, resemble
resin,*,nous,nate, ORGANIC/
    INORGANIC CHEMICAL USED FOR
    VARNISH/ PLASTIC/MANY USES (or
    see reason/rise(n))
resinate,*,ed,ting, TO IMMERSE IN
    RESIN (or see resonate)
resination, resonate(tion)
resinator, resonate(tor)
resindly, recent(ly)
resinense, resonance
resinent, resonance(nt)
resint, recent
resintly, recent(ly)
resinuble, reason(able)
resipe, recipe
resipeant, recipient
resipeint, recipient
resipient, recipient
resiprekul, reciprocal
resiprocal, reciprocal
resiprocation, reciprocate(tion)

resiprokashen, reciprocate(tion)
resiprokate, reciprocate
resirch, research
resirect, resurrect
resirection, resurrect(ion)
resirf, reserve
resirgense, resurge(nce)
resirgent, resurgent
resirgint, resurgent
resirvation, reservation
resirvd, reserve(d)
resirve, reserve
resirvist, reserve(vist)
resirvor, reservoir
resist,*,ted,ting,tance,tant,ter,tible,
    tibility,tibly,tive,tively,tivity, tless,
    tor, DEFEND/PROTECT AGAINST
    "prefixes: ir"
resitashen, recite(tion)
resitation, recite(tion)
resite, recite
resitle, recite(tal)
resitul, recite(tal)
resk, risk
resked, risk(ed)
reskeu, rescue
reskiu, rescue
reskt, risk(ed)
resku, rescue
reskud, rescue(d)
resl, wrestle
resnibul, reason(able)
resnuble, reason(able)
resodo, risotto
resol, wrestle
resoluble,bility,eness, CAN BE SOLVED/
    RESOLVED, DISSOLVED TWICE
    "prefixes: ir"
resolushin, resolute(tion)
resolute,*,ely,eness,tion, HAVE FIRM
    DETERMINATION/RESOLVE, FIXED
    PURPOSE/DECISION "prefixes: ir"
resolve,*,ed,ving,vable,er,ent, FINAL
    DETERMINATION/SETTLEMENT
    "prefixes: ir/un"
resolvuble, resolve(vable)
reson, reason / resin / rise(n)
resonance,nt,ntly, A SYMPATHETIC
    VIBRATION/SYNCHRONIZED WAVES
resonate,*,ed,ting,tion,tor, RESOUND/
    ECHO/EXTENDED EFFECT/BE
    FAMILIAR (or see resinate)
resondly, recent(ly)
resonense, resonance

resonent, resonance(nt)
resoninse, resonance
resontly, recent(ly)
resope, recipe
resorse, resource
resorsful, resource(ful)
resort,*,ted,ting,ter, RECOURSE/
    REVERBERATE, PLACE TO RELAX,
    FALL BACK ON
resorvor, reservoir
resoto, risotto
resotto, risotto
resource,*,eful,efully,efulness,
    AVAILABLE MEANS/MEASURE/
    PROPERTY/ SOURCES
resparater, respiration(tor)
respect,*,ted,ting,tful,tfully,tfulness,ter,
    table,tably,tableness,tability,
    tabilities, tive,tively,tiveness, TO
    HONOR/PAY TRIBUTE/RELATE/
    REGARD/HOLD IN HIGH ESTEEM
    "prefixes: dis/ir"
respectif, respect(ive)
respektful, respect(ful)
respektif, respect(ive)
resperashen, respiration
resperater, respiration(tor)
resperation, respiration
respirashen, respiration
respirater, respiration(tor)
respiration,nal,tor,tory, INHALE/
    EXHALE OF THE BREATH IN PLANTS/
    ANIMALS
respite, REST/RELIEF FROM LABOR/
    SUFFERING/FEAR
respond,*,ded,ding,dent,der, ANSWER/
    REPLY/CORRESPOND
respondint, respond(ent)
response,*,sible,sibility,sibilities,
    sibleness,sibly,sive,sively, siveness,
    ANSWER/ REPLY/CORRESPOND
    "prefixes: ir/non/un"
responsef, response(sive)
responsive, response(sive)
responsuble, response(sible)
respont, respond
respurashen, respiration
respurater, respiration(tor)
respuration, respiration
resque, rescue
resqwu, rescue
resrektion, resurrect(ion)
rest,*,ted,ting,tful,tfully,tfulness, TIME/
    TRANQUILITY/PEACE BETWEEN

MOMENTS OF MENTAL/PHYSICAL
EXERTION (or see wrest/wrist)
"prefixes: un"

restaraunt, restaurant
restaront, restaurant
restatushen, restitution
restatution, restitution
restatutive, restitution(ive)
restaurant,*, A PUBLIC EATERY
restauront, restaurant
resterashen, restore(ration)
resteration, restore(ration)
restetushen, restitution
restetution, restitutions
restfuly, rest(fully)
restid, rest(ed) / wrest(ed)
restirashen, restore(ration)
restiration, restore(ration)
restitushen, restitution
restitution,*,tive,itory,
COMPENSATING/GIVING BACK FOR
A LOSS
restorant, restaurant
restorashen, restore(ration)
restoraunt, restaurant
restore,*,ed,ring,er,ration,rative,
REFURBISH/REFINISH BACK TO
NEAR ORIGINAL
restrain,*,ned,ning,nt,nable, STOP/
CONTROL SOMETHING/SOMEONE
FROM DOING SOMETHING
"prefixes: un"
restrane, restrain
restrant, restaurant / restrain(t)
restrektif, restrict(ive)
restrict,*,ted,ting,tion,tive,tively,
tiveness, CONTROL/LIMIT THE
FLOW OF "prefixes: de/un"
restrikshen, restrict(ion)
restrikt, restrict
restriktion, restrict(ion)
restriktive, restrict(ive)
restront, restaurant
resturashen, restore(ration)
resturation, restore(ration)
restutushen, restitution
restutution, restitution
resucitate, resuscitate
resudenshul, reside(ntial)
resudensy, reside(ncy)
resudent, reside(nt)
resudential, reside(ntial)
resudinshul, reside(ntial)
resudinsy, reside(ncy)

resudue, residue
resugnashin, resign(ation)
resugnation, resign(ation)
resul, wrestle
result,*,ted,ting,tant, THE OUTCOME/
REACTION/CONDITION OF AN
ACTION
resulushin, resolute(tion)
resulute, resolute
resuma, resume
resume,*,ed,ming,mable, CONTINUE/
CARRY ON, SUMMARY OF
SOMEONE'S WORK HISTORY
resun, reason / resin / rise(n)
resunate, resonate / resinate
resunation, resonate(tion)
resunator, resonate(tor)
resundly, recent(ly)
resunense, resonance
resunent, resonance(nt)
resuninse, resonance
resuntly, recent(ly)
resunuble, reason(able)
resupe, recipe
resurch, research
resurect, resurrect
resurection, resurrect(ion)
resurfs, reserve(s)
resurge,*,ed,ging,ent,ence, RISE UP/
STRENGTHEN AGAIN
resurgense, resurge(nce)
resurgent,*,nce, RISE UP/STRENGTHEN
AGAIN
resurginse, resurge(nce)
resurgint, resurgent
resurrect,*,ted,ting,tion,tional,tionist,
tionism, RAISE FROM THE DEAD, TO
REINSTATE/RESTORE
resurvd, reserve(d)
resurve, reserve
resurvor, reservoir
resusatashen, resuscitate(tion)
resusatator, resuscitate(tor)
resuscitate,*,ed,ting,tion,tive,tor,
RESTORE LIFE TO BREATHING
AGAIN
resusitate, resuscitate
resusitator, resuscitate(tor)
resycle, recycle
ret, red / read
retabul, read(able)
retail,*,led,ling,ler, SALE OF GOODS IN
SMALL QUANTITIES TO
CONSUMERS

retain,*,ned,ning,ner,nable,nability,
nment, TO CONTINUE/HOLD/KEEP
IN POSSESSION
retal, retail
retaleashen, retaliate(tion)
retaleate, retaliate
retaleation, retaliate(tion)
retaler, retail(er)
retaliate,*,ed,ting,tion, TO RETURN A
PUNISHMENT, DELIBERATE HARM
IN REVENGE
retan, retain
retaner, retain(er)
retanse, rid(ddance)
retard,*,ded,ding,dant,dation,dative,
date,der, DEVELOPMENT/GROWTH
IS SLOWED DOWN/CURBED/
DELAYED
retardashen, retard(ation)
retardat, retard(ate)
retardint, retard(ant)
retardir, retard(er)
retardunt, retard(ant)
retaric, rhetoric
retasense, reticent(nce)
retasent, reticent
retashin, rotate(tion)
retasint, reticent
retch, rich / wretch
reted, ready(died) / read
retee, ready
retenshun, retention
retentif, retentive
retention,ive,ivity, ABLE TO HOLD/
MAINTAIN/REMEMBER
retentive,vity,vities, ABLE TO HOLD/
MAINTAIN/REMEMBER
reter, red(dder) / read(er)
retern, return
reternd, return(ed)
reth, wreath / wreathe
rethem, rhythm
rethum, rhythm
reti, ready
reticent,tly,nce, RESERVED/
APPREHENSIVE IN SPEAKING
FREELY
reticint, reticent
retina,*,al,nitis, ASSOCIATED WITH THE
EYE
retinse, rid(ddance)
retinshun, retention
retintion, retention
retir, read(er) / retire

retire,*,ed,ring,ringly,ringness,rement, REMOVE/RETREAT/WITHDRAW FROM SOME FORM OF ACTIVITY/ CIRCULATION/WORK "prefixes: semi"

retirec, rhetoric

retirment, retire(ment)

retirn, return

retirndt, return(ed)

retisense, reticent(nce)

retisent, reticent

retisint, reticent

retna, retina

retnu, retina

retor, read(er)

retorec, rhetoric

retoric, rhetoric

retorical, rhetoric(al)

retract,*,ted,ting,tion,tability,table, tation,tile,tive, WITHDRAW/ REMOVE/TAKE BACK "prefixes: un"

retraction, retract(ion)

retrad, retread

retrakshen, retract(ion)

retrakted, retract(ed)

retread,*,ded,ding, RESURFACE/RECAP/ GO OVER AGAIN

retreat,*,ted,ting,ter,tal,tive,tful,tant, tism,tist, WITHDRAW/FALL BACK/ REFUGE/ASYLUM/DO AGAIN

retred, retread

retreded, retreat(ed)

retredid, retread(ed)

retrefe, retrieve

retrefer, retrieve(r)

retreful, retrieve(val)

retret, retreat

retreted, retreat(ed)

retrevul, retrieve(val)

retrevur, retrieve(r)

retrieve,*,ed,ving,val,er, RESTORE/ REMEDY/SAVE/GET SOMETHING BACK, A TYPE OF DOG "prefixes: ir"

retrive, retrieve

retro, PREFIX INDICATING "BACKWARDS" MOST OFTEN MODIFIES THE WORD

retroactif, retroactive

retroactive,ely, BACK TO SOME POINT IN THE PAST

retroaktif, retroactive

retroaktive, retroactive

retrograde,*,ed,ding,dation,ely, MOVING CONTRARY/BACKWARDS/ REVERSE/INVERSE

retrogratashen, retrograde(dation)

retrogreat, retrograde

retrosbekt, retrospect

retrospect,tion,tive,tives,tively, RECOLLECTION/REVIEW OF THE PAST

retrospekt, retrospect

retrospektion, retrospect(ion)

retsee, ritzy

retsy, ritzy

retual, ritual

retubil, read(able)

retuble, read(able)

retul, riddle

retur, red(dder) / read(er)

returec, rhetoric

returic, rhetoric

return,*,ned,ning,ner,nable, GO BACK TO THE PLACE OF THE ORIGINATION/BEGINNING/ MOMENT

returndt, return(ed)

retusense, reticent(nce)

retusent, reticent

retusint, reticent

rety, ready

retzy, ritzy

reul, real / reel

reuldee, realty

reuldy, realty

reulestic, real(istic)

reulistic, real(istic)

reulty, realty

reum, realm

reunacmment, reenact(ment)

reunactment, reenact(ment)

reunakt, reenact

reunaktment, reenact(ment)

reunforse, reinforce

reunforsment, reinforce(ment)

reunion,*, GATHERING, COMING TOGETHER

reunyun, reunion

reustat, rheostat

reval, revel

revalation, revelation

revalee, reveille

revaler, revel(er)

revalushen, revolution

revalution, revolution

revalutioniz, revolution(ize)

revalve, revolve

revaly, reveille

revar, river

revarent, reverent

reveal,*,led,ling,ler,lingly, EXPOSE/ MAKE KNOWN/UNCOVER, BE FRANK (or see revel)

reveelt, reveal(ed)

reveer, revere

reveille,*, MILITARY WAKE-UP CALL/ SIGNAL

revejen, revise(sion)

revel,*,led,ling,ler, PLEASURE/ ENJOYMENT IN SOMETHING (or see reveal/reveille)

revelashen, revelation

revelation,*,nal,tory, SUDDEN REALIZATION/UNDERSTANDING OF VALUABLE/ SURPRISING INFORMATION

reveld, revel(lled) / reveal(ed)

revelee, reveille

revelir, revel(er)

revelushen, revolution

revelutioniz, revolution(ize)

revely, reveille

revench, revenge

revene, ravine / raven

revenge,eful,efully,er, BE RETALIATORY/ HARMFUL WITH INTENT

revengful, revenge(ful)

rever, revere / river

reverberate,*,ed,ting,ant,tion,tive,tor, AN ECHO,REFLECTION OF WAVES OFF A SURFACE

reverbirate, reverberate

revere,*,ed,ring, DEEPLY ADMIRE/ RESPECT SOMEONE

reverent,tly,nce,tial,tially, EXPRESS AWE/RESPECT "prefixes: ir"

reverse,*,ed,sing,sal,sely,er,sible,sibly, sibility, CHANGE TO OPPOSITE, INSIDE OUT/BACKWARD "prefixes: ir"

reversuble, reverse(sible)

revert,*,ted,ting,ter,tible, GO BACK TO PREVIOUS/FORMER/ORIGINAL

reveshen, revise(sion)

revesion, revise(sion)

revew, review / revue

review,*,wed,wing,wable,wer, EXAMINE/INSPECT/CRITIQUE/ SURVEY/ASSESS (or see revue)

revigen, revise(sion)

revil, revel / reveal
revilashen, revelation
revilation, revelation
revild, revel(lled)
revilee, reveille
reviler, revel(er)
revilushen, revolution
revilutioniz, revolution(ize)
revily, reveille
revinch, revenge
revine, ravine
revingful, revenge(ful)
revir, river
revirberate, reverberate
revirent, reverent
revirse, reverse
revirsuble, reverse(sible)
revirt, revert
revise,*,ed,sing,sion,sable,er,sory,
    ADJUST/UPDATE/ALTER/IMPROVE
    UPON
revishen, revise(sion)
revision, revise(sion)
revival,*, RENEWAL/RECOVERY/
    REESTABLISHMENT OF
revive,*,ed,ving,vable,er,val, BECOME
    CONSCIOUS/FLOURISH/VIGOROUS
    AGAIN
revivle, revival
revivuble, revive(vable)
revlashen, revelation
revocable,ly,bility, ABILITY TO BE
    CANCELLED/CALLED BACK IN
    "prefixes: ir"
revokability, revocable(bility)
revokable, revocable
revoke,*,ed,king,er,ocable, MAKE NULL
    AND VOID, CANCEL, SUMMON
    SOMEONE/SOMETHING BACK
revol, revel
revolashen, revelation
revolation, revelation
revold, revolt / revel(lled)
revolee, reveille
revolfe, revolve
revolt,*,ted,ting, REBEL/DEFY
    AUTHORITY, REPULSED
revoltid, revolt(ed)
revolution,*,nary,naries,nize,nizes,
    nized,nizing,nism,nist,nists, REBEL/
    DEFY POWERS THAT BE, OF
    CIRCULAR SHAPE/ MOTION

revolve,*,ed,ving,er,vable, RECURRING
    CIRCULAR MOVEMENT, A TYPE OF
    GUN
revorent, reverent
revue,*, MUSICAL EVENT (or see
    review)
revul, revel
revulashen, revelation
revulation, revelation
revuled, revel(lled)
revulee, reveille
revuler, revel(er)
revulushen, revolution
revulutioniz, revolution(ize)
revuly, reveille
revur, river
revurbarate, reverberate
revurent, reverent
revurse, reverse
revursuble, reverse(sible)
revurt, revert
rew, rue / roux
reward,*,ded,ding, SOMETHING
    RECEIVED FOR HAVING DONE
    SOMETHING COMMENDABLE
rewbe, ruby
rewd, rude
rewdest, rude(st)
rewf, roof
rewge, rouge
rewje, rouge
rewl, rule
rewlet, roulette
rewm, room
rewmer, rumor
rewmur, rumor
reword, reward
rewral, rural
rewralee, rural(lly)
rewrul, rural
rewrulee, rural(lly)
rewsdir, rooster
rewsdur, rooster
rewse, ruse
rewstur, rooster
rewt, route / root / rude
rewteen, routine
rewthles, ruthless
rewtlee, rude(ly)
rey, ray
reyewnyin, reunion
reyunyon, reunion
rezadenshul, reside(ntial)
rezadensy, reside(ncy)

rezadinsy, reside(ncy)
rezadue, residue
rezalushen, resolute(tion)
rezalute, resolute
rezalution, resolute(tion)
rezan, reason / resin / rise(n)
rezand, recent
rezandly, recent(ly)
rezanense, resonance
rezanent, resonance(nt)
rezant, recent
rezanuble, reason(able)
rezarection, resurrect(ion)
rezarektion, resurrect(ion)
rezedue, residue
rezegnation, resign(ation)
rezelute, resolute
rezen, reason / resin / rise(n)
rezenate, resinate / resonate
rezenator, resonate(tor)
rezend, recent
rezendly, recent(ly)
rezent, recent / resent
rezenuble, reason(able)
rezerect, resurrect
rezerf, reserve
rezervation, reservation
rezervor, reservoir
rezide, reside
rezidensy, reside(ncy)
rezidinsy, reside(ncy)
rezidual, residue(ual)
rezidue, residue
rezignashin, resign(ation)
rezilute, resolute
rezin, reason / resin / rise(n)
rezinate, resonate / resinate
rezinator, resonate(tor)
rezind, recent
rezindly, recent(ly)
rezine, resign
rezinent, resonance(nt)
rezint, recent / resent
rezinuble, reason(able)
rezirect, resurrect
rezirvation, reservation
rezirvor, reservoir
rezist, resist
rezistense, resist(ance)
rezistent, resist(ant)
rezistif, resist(ive)
rezistor, resist(or)
reznuble, reason(able)
rezodo, risotto

rezolushin, resolute(tion)
rezolute, resolute
rezolve, resolve
rezom, resume
rezon, reason / resin / rise(n)
rezonate, resonate / resinate
rezondly, recent(ly)
rezonense, resonance
rezontle, recent(ly)
rezoom, resume
rezort, resort
rezorvor, reservoir
rezoto, risotto
rezrekshen, resurrect(ion)
rezt, rest / wrist / wrest
rezudensy, reside(ncy)
rezudinsy, reside(ncy)
rezudue, residue
rezult, result
rezultent, result(ant)
rezultunt, result(ant)
rezulushen, resolute(tion)
rezulute, resolute
rezulution, resolute(tion)
rezume, resume
rezun, reason / resin / rise(n)
rezunate, resonate / resinate
rezunation, resonate(tion)
rezund, recent
rezundly, recent(ly)
rezunense, resonance
rezunent, resonance(nt)
rezunt, recent
rezunuble, reason(able)
rezurect, resurrect
rezurection, resurrect(ion)
rezurekshen, resurrect(ion)
rezurf, reserve
rezurve, reserve
rezurvor, reservoir
rezuvor, reservoir
rhain, rain / reign / rein
rhanoceros, rhinoceros
rhanosirus, rhinoceros
rhapsady, rhapsody
rhapsedy, rhapsody
rhapsody,dies, IRREGULAR/INTENSE
    IMPROVISATION IN REGARD TO
    MUSIC/EXPRESSION/LITERATURE
rhapsuty, rhapsody
rhatorecal, rhetoric(al)
rhatorical, rhetoric(al)
rhedaric, rhetoric
rheduric, rhetoric

rhein, rain / reign / rein
rheindeer, reindeer
rhen, rain / reign / rein
rhenoceros, rhinoceros
rhenosirus, rhinoceros
rheostat,*,tic, ELECTRONIC DEVICE
rhetarec, rhetoric
rheteric, rhetoric
rhethm, rhythm
rhethym, rhythm
rhetoric,*,cal,cally, THE ART OF
    SPEAKING/WRITING EFFECTIVELY/
    PERSUASIVELY
rheturec, rhetoric
rheumatic,*,ism,toid,toidal,
    ASSOCIATED WITH STIFF JOINTS/
    MUSCLES IN THE BODY
rhime, rhyme
rhinasurus, rhinoceros
rhinauserus, rhinoceros
rhinestone,*, FAKE GEMS
rhino,*, SHORT FOR RHINOCEROS
rhinoceros,ses, A MAMMAL/ANIMAL
rhinosurus, rhinoceros
rhinstone, rhinestone
rhisome, rhizome
rhithm, rhythm
rhithum, rhythm
rhitorecal, rhetoric(al)
rhitorical, rhetoric(al)
rhiz, PREFIX INDICATING "ROOT" MOST
    OFTEN MODIFIES THE WORD
rhizome,*, TYPE OF PLANT ROOT
rhod, PREFIX INDICATING "RED" MOST
    OFTEN MODIFIES THE WORD
rhodadendron, rhododendron
rhodidendron, rhododendron
rhodo, PREFIX INDICATING "RED" MOST
    OFTEN MODIFIES THE WORD
rhododendron,*,rum, CAN BE SPELLED
    EITHER WAY, FLOWERING PLANT/
    BUSH
rhodudindron, rhododendron
rhotorical, rhetoric(al)
rhubarb, AN EDIBLE PLANT
rhunoceros, rhinoceros
rhunosirus, rhinoceros
rhutorecal, rhetoric(al)
rhutorical, rhetoric(al)
rhyme,*,ed,ming,er, PUT WORDS
    TOGETHER IN SPEECH WHICH
    SOUND LIKE EACH OTHER
rhysome, rhizome

rhythm,*,mic,mical,mically,
    REPETITIOUS BEAT/FREQUENCY/
    PATTERN "prefixes: bio"
rhyzome, rhizome
ri, rye / wry
riact, react
rial, real / rile
rib,*,bbed,bbing, BONES IN TORSO
ribaflavin, riboflavin
riban, ribbon
ribaund, rebound
ribbin, ribbon
ribbon,*,ny, THIN STRIP OF
    SOMETHING, A DECORATION USED
    AS AN AWARD
ribbun, ribbon
ribeled, rebel(lled)
ribeleon, rebel(llion)
ribeleus, rebel(llious)
riben, ribbon
ribin, ribbon
riblase, replace
riblie, reply
ribodek, robot(ic)
ribof, rebuff
riboflavin,*, A CHEMICAL COMPOUND/
    VITAMIN
ribon, ribbon / rib(bbing)
ribt, rib(bbed) / rip(pped)
ribuf, rebuff
ribulican, republic(an)
ribun, ribbon / rib(bbing)
ribut, rebut / reboot
ributle, rebut(ttal)
ric, reek / rice
ricachet, ricochet
ricant, recant
ricap, recap
ricashay, ricochet
rice, A GRAIN (or see rise)
ricebder, receptor
ricebdif, receptive
riced, recede
ricent, recent
ricepter, receptor
ricerch, research
rices, recess
rich,hes,her,hest,hly,hness,
    ABUNDANT/PLENTIFUL/FERTILE/
    PRODUCTIVE (or see reach/ridge/
    wretch) "prefixes: en"
richas, right(eous) / rich(es)
richecshen, reject(ion)
richect, reject

riched, rigid
richem, regime
riches, right(eous) / rich(es)
richewul, ritual
richid, rigid
richoal, ritual
richon, region
richos, right(eous) / rich(es)
richuol, ritual
richus, right(eous) / rich(es)
ricid, reside / recede
ricipient, recipient
ricis, recess
ricit, receipt / recite
riciv, receive
rickets, VITAMIN DEFICIENCY DISEASE
rickety, UNSTABLE CONDITION
rickidy, rickety
rickits, rickets
rickity, rickety
rickliner, recline(r)
rickonusinse, reconnaissance
riclusion, recluse(sion)
ricochet,*,ted,ting, THE ACTION OF
    REBOUNDING/BOUNCING OFF AN
    OBJECT
ricoil, recoil
ricomben, recumbent
riconisans, reconnaissance
riconsile, reconcile
riconstitushen, reconstitute(tion)
riconstitute, reconstitute
ricord, record
ricors, recourse
ricoshay, ricochet
ricover, recover
ricrut, recruit
ricuest, request
ricumbent, recumbent
ricup, recoop
ricuperate, recuperate
ricushay, ricochet
rid,*,dded,dding,ddance, BE DISPOSED
    OF/DONE AWAY WITH (or see ride/
    red/read/reed/right)
ridakeul, ridicule
ridakule, ridicule
ridal, riddle
ridanse, rid(ddance)
ridar, ride(r) / write(r)
ridch, ridge
riddle,*,ed,ling,er, PUZZLE OF WORDS
    "prefixes: un"

ride,*,ding,rode,er, BE CARRIED/
    MOVED ALONG IN/ON SOMETHING
    (or see write/right) "prefixes: over"
ridecule, ridicule
rideculus, ridiculous
rideemible, redeem(able)
ridekule, ridicule
ridekulus, ridiculous
ridem, redeem
ridempshun, redemption
ridemtion, redemption
ridemuble, redeem(able)
ridense, rid(ddance)
ridents, rid(ddance)
ridge,*,ed, RAISED AREA
ridicule,*,ed,ling,er,lous, TO MAKE FUN
    OF
ridiculous,sly,sness, NOT POSSIBLE/
    ACCEPTABLE
ridikule, ridicule
ridikulus, ridiculous
ridim, redeem
ridinse, rid(ddance)
ridle, riddle
ridol, riddle
ridondent, redundant
ridoose, reduce
ridu, redo
riduction, reduce(ction)
ridukeul, ridicule
ridukshen, reduce(ction)
riduktion, reduce(ction)
ridul, riddle
ridundensy, redundant(ncy)
ridundent, redundant
ridundinsy, redundant(ncy)
ridundint, redundant
ridus, reduce
ridusable, reduce(cible)
rie, rye / wry
riel, rile
riemburs, reimburse
rienact, reenact
rienlist, reenlist
riestat, rheostat
riet, riot
rieterate, reiterate
rif, reef / rift
rifal, rifle
rifar, river / refer
rifeel, reveal
rifeelt, reveal(ed)
rifel, rival / rifle
rifenge, revenge

rifenje, revenge
rifer, river / refer
riferbishment, refurbish(ment)
riferse, reverse
rifeusil, refuse(sal)
rifewsel, refuse(sal)
rififul, revival
rifil, rival / rifle
rifin, refine
rifinable, refine(nable)
rifine, refine
rifinery, refine(ry)
rifinje, revenge
rifinment, refine(ment)
rifinury, refine(ry)
rifle,*,ed,ling, A GUN, SWIFTLY GO
    THROUGH, LOOK THROUGH STUFF
    TO STEAL "prefixes: un"
riflecs, reflect(s) / reflex
riflect, reflect
riflection, reflect(ion)
riflective, reflect(ive)
riflector, reflect(or)
riflekshen, reflect(ion)
riflekt, reflect
riflektif, reflect(ive)
riflektor, reflect(or)
rifletive, reflect(ive)
rifol, rifle
rifond, refund
rifor, river / refer
riformitory, reform(atory)
rifract, refract
rifractory, refract(ory)
rifrain, refrain
rifrakt, refract
rifraktory, refract(ory)
rifrane, refrain
rifresh, refresh
rifresher, refresh(er)
rifreshment, refresh(ment)
rifrigerator, refrigerate(tor)
rift,*,ted,ting, SLOWLY SPREAD APART,
    GROWING CHASM
riful, rival / rifle
rifur, river / refer
rifural, refer(rral)
rifurbishment, refurbish(ment)
rifurse, reverse
rifusel, refuse(sal)
rig,*,gged,gging,gger, ASSEMBLE
    DEVICES TOGETHER (or see ridge)
rigal, wriggle / regal
rigaledy, regal(ity)

rigalia, regal(ia)
rigality, regal(ity)
rigard, regard
rigardless, regard(less)
rige, ridge
rigect, reject
riged, rigid
rigekshen, reject(ion)
rigekt, reject
rigektion, reject(ion)
riger, rigor
riget, rigid
right,*,ted,ting,table,ter,tness,teous,
　　teously,teousness,tful,tfully,tfulness,
　　tism,tist,tly,ty, BE CORRECT,
　　SPECIFIC DIRECTION/ORIENTATION,
　　OTHER SIDE OF LEFT (or see rite/
　　write/ wright/writ) "prefixes: un/
　　up"
rigid,dly,dness,dity,dizer,dify,ification,
　　STIFF/UNYIELDING "prefixes: semi"
rigirs, rigor(s)
rigit, rigid
rigle, wriggle
rigol, wriggle
rigor,*,rous,rously,rousness,
　　CONDITIONS INVOLVING
　　HARDSHIP/SEVERITY/TOUGH
　　DEMANDS
rigres, rigor(ous) / regress
rigreshen, regress(ssion)
rigresif, regress(ive)
rigresive, regress(ive)
rigress, regress
rigret, regret
rigreted, regret(tted)
rigretful, regret(ful)
rigretfuly, regret(fully)
rigrus, rigor(ous)
rigul, wriggle
rigurs, rigor(s)
rigurus, rigor(ous)
rij, ridge
rijed, rigid
rijekshen, reject(ion)
rijekt, reject
rijektion, reject(ion)
rijet, rigid
rijid, rigid
rijit, rigid
rikachet, ricochet
rikashay, ricochet
rikedy, rickety
rikendal, rekindle

rikerus, rigor(ous)
rikeshay, ricochet
rikete, rickety
rikets, rickets
rikidy, rickety
rikishay, ricochet
rikity, rickety
rikliner, recline(r)
rikochet, ricochet
rikonasinse, reconnaissance
rikonstitute, reconstitute
rikonusins, reconnaissance
rikord, record
rikorder, record(er)
rikrute, recruit
rikruter, recruit(er)
rikumbent, recumbent
rikurus, rigor(ous)
rikwest, request
rikwire, require
rikwirment, require(ment)
ril, real / reel / rile / rill
rilacs, relax
rilaps, relapse
rilat, relate
rilax, relax
rile,*,ed,ling, PROVOKE INTO ACTION
　　(or see rill/really)
rilef, relief
rilegeon, religion
rilegon, religion
rilegous, religion(ous)
rilenquish, relinquish
rilentles, relentless
rilese, release
rilevar, relieve(r)
rileve, relieve
rilevir, relieve(r)
rili, rely / really
rilians, reliance
riliaple, reliable
rilichon, religion
rilients, reliance
rilif, relief
riligen, religion
rilis, release
riliubility, reliable(bility)
riliuble, reliable
riliunse, reliance
riliunt, reliance(nt)
riliv, relieve
rill,*, NARROW VALLEY/CHANNEL (or
　　see real/reel/rile)
rilly, really

rilm, realm
rilte, realty
riluctanse, reluctant(nce)
riluctant, reluctant
riluktense, reluctant(nce)
riluktint, reluctant
rily, really / rely
rim,*,mmed,mming, CURVED/
　　CIRCULAR OUTER EDGE (or see
　　ream/rhyme)
rimadik, rheumatic
rimander, remain(der)
rimane, remain / romaine
rimanis, reminisce
rimanisent, reminisce(nt)
rimantek, romantic
rimantisize, romantic(ize)
rimark, remark
rimarkible, remark(able)
rimarkt, remark(ed)
rimarkuble, remark(able)
rimatik, rheumatic
rimaty, remedy
rimbunctious, rambunctious
rimbunkshes, rambunctious
rime, rhyme
rimedeul, remedy(dial)
rimedial, remedy(dial)
rimediäshen, remedy(diation)
rimediation, remedy(diation)
rimembranse, remember(ance)
rimembur, remember
rimeng, rhyme(ming)
rimenis, reminisce
rimenisent, reminisce(nt)
rimet, remit
rimeted, remit(tted)
rimetuble, remit(ttable)
rimety, remedy
rimidy, remedy
rimind, remind
rimindur, remind(er)
riming, rhyme(ming)
rimintur, remind(er)
rimishen, remission
rimission, remission
rimit, remit
rimital, remit(ttal)
rimition, remission
rimity, remedy
rimnent, remnant
rimnet, remnant
rimnint, remnant
rimofer, remove(r)

rimonis, reminisce
rimonisent, reminisce(nt)
rimors, remorse
rimorsful, remorse(ful)
rimorsless, remorse(less)
rimot, remote
rimotly, remote(ly)
rimover, remove(r)
rimudy, remedy
rimufel, remove(val)
rimufer, remove(r)
rimufible, remove(vable)
rimunerashen, remunerate(tion)
rimunerate, remunerate
rimunirate, remunerate
rimuniration, remunerate(tion)
rimunis, reminisce
rimunisent, reminisce(nt)
rimuty, remedy
rimuv, remove
rimuvable, remove(vable)
rin, wren
rinagade, renegade
rinasonse, renaissance
rinasonts, renaissance
rinasurus, rhinoceros
rinaun, renown
rinauns, renounce
rinauserus, rhinoceros
rinavashen, renovate(tion)
rinavate, renovate
rinavation, renovate(tion)
rinawserus, rhinoceros
rinch, wrench
rind,*, THE EXTERIOR COVERING/SKIN
    OF SOME FRUIT/TREES/CHEESE
rinder, render
rindur, render
rineg, renege
rinegade, renegade
rinesonse, renaissance
rinestone, rhinestone
rinevashen, renovate(tion)
rinevate, renovate
rinevation, renovate(tion)
ring,*,ged,ging,ger,rung, A SOUND,
    ARTICLE OF JEWELRY, CIRCULAR
    SHAPE (or see wring/rink)
ringur, ring(er) / ranger
rinige, renege
rink,*, PLACE FOR SKATING (or see ring)
rinkle, wrinkle
rinkul, wrinkle
rino, rhino

rinone, renown
rinoserus, rhinoceros
rinosonse, renaissance
rinosurus, rhinoceros
rinounce, renounce
rinouncement, renounce(ment)
rinovadid, renovate(d)
rinovashen, renovate(tion)
rinovate, renovate
rinovation, renovate(tion)
rinown, renown
rinownse, renounce
rinownsment, renounce(ment)
rinoz, rhino(s)
rins, rinse / rind(s) / wren(s)
rinsd, rinse(d)
rinse,*,ed,sing,er, TO WASH/CLEAN
    WITH A LIQUID
rinstone, rhinestone
rinsur, rinse(r)
rint, rind / rent
rinter, render / rent(er)
rintible, rent(able)
rintuble, rent(able)
rinu, renew
rinuable, renew(able)
rinual, renew(al)
rinuel, renew(al)
rinugade, renegade
rinumerate, remunerate
rinusonts, renaissance
rinuvadid, renovate(d)
rinuvashen, renovate(tion)
rinuvat, renovate
rinztone, rhinestone
riol, rile / real / reel
riole, really
riostat, rheostat
riot,*,ted,ting,ter, ANGRY CROWD/
    MOB OF PEOPLE WHO MAY OR
    MAY NOT BE VIOLENT
rip,*,pped,pping,pper, TO TEAR/SLICE
    SOMETHING OPEN/APART (or see
    ripe/reap) "prefixes: un"
ripaflavin, riboflavin
ripair, repair
ripal, ripple
ripar, repair
ripd, rip(pped)
ripe,en,ened,er,est,ening,eness, FULLY
    MATURE/PRIME IN DEVELOPMENT
    (or see rip) "prefixes: over/un"
ripeal, repeal
ripeat, repeat

riped, rip(pped)
ripededly, repeat(edly)
ripeel, repeal
ripeet, repeat
ripel, rappel / repeal / repel
ripelent, repellent
ripeleon, rebel(llion)
ripelinsy, repellent(ncy)
ripelint, repellent
ripellinsy, repellent(ncy)
ripend, ripe(ned)
ripenins, repent(ance)
ripense, repent(s)
ripent, repent
riper, repair / rip(pper)
ripercoshon, repercussion
ripetative, repetitive
ripete, repeat
ripetedly, repeat(edly)
ripil, repeal
ripin, ripe(n) / rip(pping)
ripit, repeat
riplace, replace
riplacement, replace(ment)
riplase, replace
riplasmint, replace(ment)
riple, ripple
riplenesh, replenish
riplenish, replenish
riplenishment, replenish(ment)
riplid, reply(lied)
riplied, reply(lied)
riply, reply
ripnes, ripe(ness)
ripoblic, republic
ripoflavin, riboflavin
ripognant, repugnant
ripoire, rapport
ripol, ripple
ripold, ripple(d)
ripols, repulse
ripolsev, repulse(sive)
ripon, ribbon / ripe(n)
ripor, rapport / rip(pper)
riporder, report(er)
riport, report
riporter, report(er)
ripository, repository
riposutory, repository
ripozitory, repository
ripple,*,ed,ling, A SMALL WAVE
ripreshen, repress(ion)
ripresif, repress(ive)
ripresion, repress(ion)

ripresive, repress(ive)
ripress, repress
ripresuve, repress(ive)
riproch, reproach
riprochuble, reproach(able)
riproductive, reproduce(ctive)
riprodus, reproduce
riprouch, reproach
ripublek, republic
ripublekan, republic(an)
ripublic, republic
ripublican, republic(an)
ripugnense, repugnant(nce)
ripugnent, repugnant
ripul, ripple / rebel
ripuld, ripple(d)
ripuls, repulse
ripulshen, repulse(ion)
ripulsif, repulse(sive)
ripulsion, repulse(ion)
ripult, ripple(d)
ripun, ripe(n)
ripund, ripe(ned)
ripunt, ripe(ned)
ripuplecan, republic(an)
ripuplican, republic(an)
ripur, ripe(r)
ripust, ripe(st)
riqrute, recruit
riquest, request
riqueti, rickety
riquire, require
riquirment, require(ment)
riquite, requite
riqwire, require
riqwirment, require(ment)
rir, rear / we're / were / whirr
risbond, respond
risbons, response
risdrane, restrain
rise,*,sing,en,er,rose, ASSOCIATED
    WITH UPWARDS/MOVING UP/
    UPWARD BOUND (or see rice)
    "prefixes: up"
riseat, receipt
risebdef, receptive
risebtif, receptive
risebtive, receptive
riseed, recede
riseef, receive
riseet, receipt
risefe, receive
riseleant, resilient
risemblanse, resemble(lance)

risent, recent / resent
risentful, resent(ful)
risentment, resent(ment)
risepdekle, receptacle
risepdikul, receptacle
risepeant, recipient
risepeunt, recipient
risepshun, reception
riseptacle, receptacle
riseptef, receptive
riseptekle, receptacle
risepter, receptor
riseption, reception
riseptive, receptive
riseptukle, receptacle
riserch, research
riserv, reserve
riservist, reserve(vist)
riseshun, recess(ion)
risesif, recess(ive)
risesion, recess(ion)
risesive, recess(ive)
risession, recess(ion)
risestanse, resist(ance)
risestor, resist(or)
risete, receipt
risetion, recess(ion)
risevuble, receive(vable)
rishis, right(eous) / rich(es)
rishuel, ritual
rishus, right(eous) / rich(es)
riside, reside / recede
risign, resign
risileant, resilient
risilyent, resilient
risipeunt, recipient
risir, rise(r)
risit, receipt / recite
risitle, recite(tal)
risitul, recite(tal)
risiv, receive
risk,*,ked,king,ky, TAKE A CHANCE/
    GAMBLE
riskt, risk(ed)
risodo, risotto
risolt, result
risoltant, result(ant)
risolv, resolve
risolvuble, resolve(vable)
risome, rhizome
rison, reason / rise(n) / rhizome
risor, rise(r)
risors, resource
risort, resort

risoto, risotto
risotto, TYPE OF EDIBLE DISH/FOOD
rispect, respect
rispectful, respect(ful)
rispective, respect(ive)
rispectuble, respect(able)
rispekt, respect
rispektful, respect(ful)
rispektif, respect(ive)
rispektuble, respect(able)
rispite, respite
rispond, respond
rispondent, respond(ent)
risponder, respond(er)
risponse, response
risponsive, response(sive)
risponsuble, response(sible)
rispont, respond
rist, wrist
ristor, restore
ristrain, restrain
ristraint, restrain(t)
ristrane, restrain
ristrant, restrain(t)
ristrect, restrict
ristrikt, restrict
ristriktive, restrict(ive)
risuma, resume
risume, resume
risurgent, resurgent
risurs, rise(rs)
risusatator, resuscitate(tor)
risusetate, resuscitate
risusitashen, resuscitate(tion)
rit, rite / write / wright / writ / right /
    rid
ritacule, ridicule
ritainer, retain(er)
ritakule, ridicule
rital, riddle
ritaleashen, retaliate(tion)
ritaleate, retaliate
ritaleation, retaliate(tion)
ritaliation, retaliate(tion)
ritane, retain
ritaner, retain(er)
ritanse, rid(ddance)
ritard, retard
ritashen, rotate(tion)
ritch, rich / wretch
ritches, right(eous) / rich(es)
ritchly, rich(ly)
ritchuil, ritual
ritchus, right(eous) / rich(es)

rite,*, A CEREMONY/OBSERVANCE (or
    see right/write/white/writ/wright)
ritein, retain
ritel, retail
ritense, rid(ddance)
ritenshun, retention
ritentif, retentive
rith, writhe
rithem, rhythm
rithm, rhythm
rithum, rhythm
ritinshun, retention
ritire, retire
ritirment, retire(ment)
ritle, riddle
ritorical, rhetoric(al)
ritous, right(eous) / rich(es)
ritracted, retract(ed)
ritraction, retract(ion)
ritrakshen, retract(ion)
ritrakted, retract(ed)
ritrefe, retrieve
ritrefer, retrieve(r)
ritreful, retrieve(val)
ritreve, retrieve
ritrevul, retrieve(val)
ritrevur, retrieve(r)
ritsee, ritzy
ritsy, ritzy
ritual,*,lly,lism,list,listic,listically,lize,
    lization, CEREMONY
rituil, ritual
ritukeul, ridicule
ritul, riddle
riturn, return
ritzy,zier,ziest, SWANKY/ELEGANT
riul, rile
riunyen, reunion
riunyun, reunion
riuse, ruse
riut, riot
riuted, riot(ed)
riuter, riot(er)
rivais, revise
rival,*,led,ling,lry,lries, COMPETITOR
    "prefixes: un"
rivalfe, revolve
rivalree, rival(ry)
rivalve, revolve
riveel, reveal
riveelt, reveal(ed)
riveer, revere
rivegen, revise(sion)
rivejen, revise(sion)

rivel, rival / arrival
rivench, revenge
rivenge, revenge
rivengful, revenge(ful)
rivenje, revenge
river,*, TRIBUTARY/CHANNEL OF
    WATER, SOMETHING FLOWING
    "prefixes: up"
riverberate, reverberate
rivere, revere
rivers, river(s) / reverse
riversuble, reverse(sible)
rivert, revert
riview, review / revue
rivigen, revise(sion)
rivijen, revise(sion)
rivil, revel
riving, revenge
rivingful, revenge(ful)
rivinje, revenge
rivir, revere
rivirbarate, reverberate
rivirs, reverse
rivirt, revert
rivise, revise
rivishen, revise(sion)
rivision, revise(sion)
riviu, review
rivival, revival
rivive, revive
rivivuble, revive(vable)
rivivul, revive(val)
rivize, revise
rivlree, rival(ry)
rivocability, revocable(bility)
rivocable, revocable
rivokability, revocable(bility)
rivokable, revocable
rivoke, revoke
rivokt, revoke(d)
rivol, rival / arrival
rivolfe, revolve
rivolfer, revolve(r)
rivolree, rival(ry)
rivolt, revolt
rivolv, revolve
rivolver, revolve(r)
rivul, rival / arrival
rivulree, rival(ry)
rivurbarate, reverberate
rivurse, reverse
rivurt, revert
riward, reward
riword, reward

riyewnyen, reunion
riyunyun, reunion
rizalfe, resolve
rize, rise / rice
rizelyent, resilient
rizemblanse, resemble(lance)
rizemble, resemble
rizent, resent
rizentful, resent(ful)
rizentment, resent(ment)
rizer, rise(r)
rizid, reside
rizilyent, resilient
rizine, resign
rizist, resist
rizite, recite
rizodo, risotto
rizolve, resolve
rizolvuble, resolve(vable)
rizom, resume
rizome, rhizome
rizoom, resume
rizort, resort
rizoto, risotto
rizulent, result(ant)
rizultunt, result(ant)
rizum, resume
rizuma, esume / resume'
rizume, resume / resume'
rizur, rise(r)
ro, row / raw
roach,hes, AN INSECT, BUTT END OF
    HERB CIGARETTE
road,*,dy, A PATH/PASSAGE/WIDE
    TRAIL TO TRAVEL ON (or see rode/
    wrote) "prefixes: in"
roam,*,med,ming,mer, TO WANDER/
    MOVE ABOUT AIMLESSLY (or see
    room)
roar,*,red,ring, LOUD/DEEP SOUND/
    EXPRESSION COMING FROM THE
    THROAT (or see row(er)) "prefixes:
    up"
roast,*,ted,ting,ter, SLOWLY COOK IN
    AN OVEN, BAKE WITHOUT A FLAME
rob,*,bbed,bbing,bber, STEAL/TAKE
    AWAY FROM WITHOUT
    PERMISSION (or see robe/rope)
robd, robe(d) / rob(bbed) / rope(d)
robe,*,ed,bing, LONG/LOOSE SLEEVED
    GARMENT (or see rob/rope)
    "prefixes: dis/en"
robed, robe(d) / rob(bbed) / rope(d)
robeled, rebel(lled)

robeleus, rebel(llious)
roben, robin / rob(bing)
rober, rob(bber)
robin,*, A TYPE OF BIRD (or see
    rob(bbing))
robodezashen, robot(ization)
robodik, robot(ic)
robost, robust
robot,*,tic,tism,tize,tization, A
    MACHINE WHICH WORKS FOR
    PEOPLE
robotisashen, robot(ization)
robotizashen, robot(ization)
robt, rob(bbed) / rope(d) / robe(d)
robudezashin, robot(ization)
robun, robin / rob(bing)
robushus, robust(ious)
robust,tly,tness,tious,tiously,tiousness,
    FULL/HEALTHY/STRONG
robustus, robust(ious)
robutesation, robot(ization)
robuzd, robust
roch, roach
rocher, roger
roches, roach(es)
rochir, roger
rochur, roger
rock,*,ked,king,ker,ky, HARD MINERAL,
    BACK AND FORTH MOTION
rockateer, rocket(eer)
rocket,*,try,teer, A FUELED CYLINDER
    WITH POINTED TIP
rod,*,dded,dding,dless, THIN ROUND/
    CYLINDRICAL STAFF/POLE/STICK
    SHAPE (or see rotor/road/rode/
    wrote)
rodadendron, rhododendron
rodadindron, rhododendron
rodant, rodent
rodar, rotor
rodaree, rotary
rodary, rotary
rodatelir, rototiller
rodatilur, rototiller
rode, PAST TENSE FOR THE WORD
    "RIDE" (or see road/wrote)
    "prefixes: over"
rodedendron, rhododendron
rodedindron, rhododendron
rodent,*, A SMALL MAMMAL
rodeo,*,oed,oing, GAME IN ARENA
    USING HORSES/COWS/ROPES
roder, rotor
rodery, rotary

rodetilur, rototiller
rodidendron, rhododendron
rodidindron, rhododendron
rodint, rodent
rodio, rodeo
rodiquelus, ridiculous
rodir, rotor
roditelur, rototiller
rododendrem, rhododendron
rodotiler, rototiller
rodudindron, rhododendron
rodunt, rodent
rodur, rotor
roduree, rotary
rodury, rotary
rodutiler, rototiller
roeal, royal
roeul, royal
roeyul, royal
rof, rove / rough
rofeelt, reveal(ed)
rofer, revere / refer / rove(r)
roferse, reverse
rofeusil, refuse(sal)
rofiew, review / revue
rofiful, revival
rofir, rove(r) / rough(er)
rofirst, reverse
rofol, ruffle
rofue, review / revue
rofur, rove(r) / rough(er)
rofurse, reverse
rofute, refute
rog, rogue / rouge
roged, rugged
roger, RADIO COMMUNICATION
    WHICH MEANS "OKAY",
    SOMEONE'S NAME
rogir, roger
rogue,*,uish,uishly,uishness,ery,eries,
    SWINDLER/TRICKY/DEVIANT
    BEHAVIOR (or see rouge)
rogur, roger
roiel, royal
roiul, royal
rojer, roger
rojur, roger
rok, rock / rogue
rokateer, rocket(eer)
roket, rocket
roketeer, rocket(eer)
rokut, rocket
rokuteer, rocket(eer)
rokwit, requite

rokwitable, requite(table)
rol, roll / role
rolar, roll(er)
role,*, A PART/CHARACTER IN A PLAY
    (or see roll)
rolec, rollick
roled, roll(ed)
rolek, rollick
rolent, relent
roler, roll(er)
rolic, rollick
rolik, rollick
rolir, roll(er)
roll,*,lled,lling,ller, A BREAD SHAPE,
    MOVES/GOES AROUND IN
    CIRCULAR FASHION (or see role)
    "prefixes: un"
rollick,*,ked,king, TO PLAYFULLY ROLL/
    TUMBLE/JUMP/SKIP AROUND
rolor, roll(er)
rolres, walrus
rolrus, walrus
rolur, roll(er)
rom, roam / room / rum
romach, rummage
romadik, rheumatic
romaine, TYPE OF LETTUCE (or see
    remain)
romance,*,ed,cing,er,ntic, FANCIFUL/
    WHIMSICAL/EXTRAVAGANT
    EXPERIENCE WITH INFATUATION/
    LOVE BETWEEN TWO PEOPLE
romane, romaine / remain
romanek, romantic
romanse, romance
romantic,cally,cism,cist,cize,cization,
    INVOLVES ROMANCE
romantisize, romantic(ize)
romark, remark
romatik, rheumatic
romatoyd, rheumatic(toid)
romb, romp
rombed, romp(ed) / roam(ed)
rombl, rumble / rumple
rombol, rumble / rumple
romediashen, remedy(diation)
romediation, remedy(diation)
romeshen, remission
rometeul, remedy(dial)
romidal, remit(ttal)
romind, remind
romindur, remind(er)
romintur, remind(er)
romishen, remission

romision, remission
romission, remission
romital, remit(ttal)
romited, remit(tted)
romition, remission
romituble, remit(ttable)
romp,*,ped,ping,per, PLAYFULLY
FROLIC/JUMP/BOUNCE AROUND
(or see rump)
rompt, romp(ed)
roms, room(s) / roam(s)
romufel, remove(val)
romufible, remove(vable)
romufil, remove(val)
romunerate, remunerate
romunirashen, remunerate(tion)
romunirate, remunerate
romuvable, remove(vable)
romuver, remove(r)
romy, room(y)
ron, run
ronchee, raunch(y)
ronchy, raunch(y)
rondavous, rendezvous
rondavu, rendezvous
ronduvu, rendezvous
ronege, renege
rong, wrong / rung / wrung
rongle, wrong(ly)
ronige, renege
ronk, wrong
ronouncement, renounce(ment)
ronounse, renounce
ronownse, renounce
ronownsment, renounce(ment)
ronshy, raunch(y)
ront, runt
rontavu, rendezvous
rontchy, raunch(y)
rontivu, rendezvous
roobarb, rhubarb
rood, rude / root
roodly, rude(ly)
rooen, ruin
rooenus, ruin(ous)
roof,*,fed,fing,fer, TOP/COVER OF A
DWELLING/STRUCTURE
rooin, ruin
rooinus, ruin(ous)
rook,*, A BIRD, CHEAT MONEY OUT OF
SOMEONE, GAME PIECE IN CHESS
roold, rule(d)
rooler, rule(r)
roolet, roulette

roolir, rule(r)
roolt, rule(d)
roolur, rule(r)
room,*,med,ming,mer,mful,my,miness,
mily, CUBICLE/SPACE/PLACE WITH
WALLS WITHIN A LARGER
DWELLING/STRUCTURE (or see
roam)
rooman, rumen
roomanu, rumina
roomatoyd, rheumatic(toid)
roomen, rumen
roomena, rumina
roomenate, rumina(te)
roomenator, rumina(tor)
roomin, rumen
roominate, rumina(te)
roominator, rumina(tor)
roomon, rumen
roon, rune
roonashen, ruin(ation)
roonation, ruin(ation)
roose, ruse
roost,*,ted,ting,ter, SIT ATOP
SOMETHING TO REST/SLEEP,
NORMALLY HOW BIRDS SLEEP (or
see roast/rust/roust)
rooster,*, A MALE CHICKEN
root,*,ted,ting,ter,tage,tless,ty, PART
OF PLANT THAT'S UNDERGROUND
"prefixes: up"
rop, rope / rob
ropair, repair
ropare, repair
ropcher, rupture
rope,*,ed,ping,er, MANY STRANDS
WOVEN TOGETHER INTO ONE (or
see robe)
ropeel, repeal
ropeet, repeat
ropel, rappel / repeal / repel
ropelinsy, repellent(ncy)
ropent, repent
ropete, repeat
roplenish, replenish
roposutory, repository
roquitable, requite(table)
roquite, requite
ror, roar / row(er)
ros, rose / row(s)
rosaree, rosary
rosary,ries, STRAND OF BEADS WITH A
CROSS ON IT
rosdrane, restrain

rose,*,eate,eately,ette,etta, A FLOWER,
COLOR, PAST TENSE FOR "RISE" (or
see row(s))
rosebshin, reception
rosebshinist, receptionist
rosebtif, receptive
rosefe, receive
rosefible, receive(vable)
rosen, rosin
rosepdekle, receptacle
rosepdikul, receptacle
rosepeunt, recipient
roseprikul, reciprocal
rosepshen, reception
rosepshenist, receptionist
roseptekle, receptacle
roseptif, receptive
roseptionest, receptionist
roseptive, receptive
roseree, rosary
roseshun, recess(ion)
rosesive, recess(ive)
rosetion, recess(ion)
roseve, receive
rosevuble, receive(vable)
rosh, rush
rosin,*,ned,ny, OIL FROM TURPENTINE
rosipeant, recipient
rosipeint, recipient
rosiprekul, reciprocal
rosiree, rosary
rosodo, risotto
rosoto, risotto
rospective, respect(ive)
rospektif, respect(ive)
rost, roast / rust
rostar, roster / roast(er) / rooster
roster,*, LIST OF NAMES/EVENTS (or
see roast(er)/rooster)
rostic, rustic
rostir, roster / roast(er) / rooster
rostore, restore
rostrain, restrain
rostrane, restrain
rostrektif, restrict(ive)
rostrikshen, restrict(ion)
rostrikt, restrict
rostriktion, restrict(ion)
rostriktive, restrict(ive)
rostur, roster / roast(er) / rooster
rosun, rosin
rosuree, rosary

rot,*,tted,tting, DETERIORATE, DISINTEGRATE (or see rod/rode/ wrote/rote/ wrought)
rotade, rotate
rotaleation, retaliate(tion)
rotaliation, retaliate(tion)
rotan, rotten
rotaree, rotary
rotary,ries, A SPINNING/ROTATION ON AN AXIS/HUB
rotashen, rotate(tion)
rotashenul, rotate(tional)
rotashun, rotate(tion)
rotate,*,ed,ting,table,tion,tional,tive, tor,tory, TAKE TURNS, REVOLVE/ ALTERNATE
rotatelur, rototiller
rotatiller, rototiller
rote, REPETITION, OVER AND OVER (or see wrote/rotor/road/rode)
roten, rotten
roteo, rodeo
roter, rotor
rotery, rotary
rotesaree, rotisserie
rotesuree, rotisserie
rotetiller, rototiller
rotin, rotten
rotio, rodeo
rotir, rotor / retire
rotiry, rotary
rotisaree, rotisserie
rotisserie,*, A FOOD COOKER
rotisuree, rotisserie
rotitelir, rototiller
rotor,*, TO DO WITH ROTATION/HUB
rototiler, rototiller
rototiller,*, MACHINE TO TILL GROUND
rotten, PAST TENSE FOR "ROT"
rotun, rotten
rotur, rotor
rotury, rotary
rou, row
roub, robe
roudy, rowdy
rouf, rough / roof
roug, rogue / rouge
rouge, RED MAKE-UP FOR FACE (or see rogue)
rough,*,hed,hing,hen,her,hest,hly, hness,hage,hen,hish, ABRASIVE/ FIBROUS/ UNREFINED/UNEVEN
roulette, GAME WITH SPINNING DISK/ BALL

rounation, ruin(ation)
round,*,ded,ding,der,dest,dish,dly, dness, CIRCULAR SHAPE, AROUND, MAKE MORE EVEN/SMOOTH TO SHAPE "prefixes: un"
rount, round
roust,*,ted,ting, WAKEN/AROUSE, FORCE TO ACTION (or see roost)
rout, route / rote / wrote
route,*,ed,ting,er, SPECIFIC/ PARTICULAR PATH/NETWORK/ LINES (or see root)
routeen, routine
routine,*,ely,nize,nized,nizing, PERFORM SPECIFIC FUNCTION ON CONTINUOUS BASIS "prefixes: sub"
routy, rowdy
roux, A PASTE FOR SAUCE/GRAVY (or see rue)
rovalfe, revolve
rove,*,ed,ving,er, TO WANDER/MOVE AIMLESSLY SEEKING FOR SOMETHING "prefixes: un"
roveel, reveal
roveelt, reveal(ed)
rovegen, revise(sion)
rovejen, revise(sion)
rovench, revenge
rovene, ravine
rovenge, revenge
rovengful, revenge(ful)
rovenjful, revenge(ful)
roverberate, reverberate
roverbirate, reverberate
rovere, revere
roverse, reverse
rovert, revert
roveshen, revise(sion)
rovesion, revise(sion)
roview, review / revue
rovigen, revise(sion)
rovijen, revise(sion)
rovinch, revenge
rovinjful, revenge(ful)
rovir, rove(r)
rovirbarate, reverberate
rovirberate, reverberate
rovirse, reverse
rovirsuble, reverse(sible)
rovirt, revert
rovise, revise
rovishen, revise(sion)
rovision, revise(sion)
rovival, revival

rovive, revive
rovivle, revival
rovivuble, revive(vable)
rovize, revise
rovocability, revocable(bility)
rovolfe, revolve
rovolfer, revolve(r)
rovolve, revolve
rovue, review / revue
rovur, rove(r)
rovurse, reverse
rovurt, revert
row,wed,wer,wing, USE OF OARS/ PADDLES TO NAVIGATE THROUGH WATER
roward, reward
rowbot, robot
rowch, roach
rowdy,dier,diest, TALK LOUD, BE ROUGH/RAMBUNCTIOUS
rowmane, romaine
rowmanse, romance
rownd, round
rownt, round
roword, reward
rowp, rope
rowr, row(er) / roar
rowst, roust
rowtee, rowdy
rowty, rowdy
royal,lty,lties,lly,lism,list, OF KINGS/ QUEENS, A SOVEREIGN POWER/ RIGHT, PERCENTAGE AS GAIN
royel, royal
royul, royal
roz, rose / row(s)
rozaree, rosary
roze, rose / row(s)
rozen, rosin
rozeree, rosary
rozin, rosin
roziree, rosary
rozodo, risotto
rozt, roast
rozter, roster
roztur, roster
rozun, rosin
rozuree, rosary
rub,*,bbed,bbing,bber, USE MOTION/ MASSAGE TO WORK AN AREA
rubal, rubble
rubar, rubber
rubarb, rhubarb
rubash, rubbish

rubber,*,rize,rizes,rized,rizing,ry, MATERIAL DERIVED FROM PETROLEUM/TREES

rubbish, GARBAGE/TRASH, WORTH REJECTING/ELIMINATING

rubble, ROCKS/DEBRIS LAYING AROUND

rube, ruby
rubed, rub(bbed)
rubee, ruby
rubel, rubble
rubeled, rebel(lled)
rubelein, rebel(llion)
rubeleus, rebel(llious)
rubelyon, rebel(llion)
ruber, rubber
ruberize, rubber(ize)
rubesh, rubbish
rubil, rubble
rubir, rubber
rubirize, rubber(ize)
rubish, rubbish
rublase, replace
ruble, rubble
rublie, reply
rubodek, robot(ic)
rubodizashen, robot(ization)
ruborb, rhubarb
rubotek, robot(ic)
rubotiks, robot(ics)
rubt, rub(bbed)
rubul, rubble
rubur, rubber

ruby,bies, A GEMSTONE

rucede, recede
rucepter, receptor
ruch, rush
ruciprocation, reciprocate(tion)
ruck, rug
ruclaimuble, reclaimable
rucumbent, recumbent

rudder,*,rless, A BLADE ON A BOAT WHICH STEERS

rude,er,est,dly,eness, TO OFFEND SOMEONE WITH BEHAVIOR/ WORDS, UNREFINED/RAW

rudeculus, ridiculous
rudeemible, redeem(able)
rudeme, redeem
rudemption, redemption
rudemshen, redemption
ruder, rudder
rudikulus, ridiculous
rudir, rudder

rudist, rude(st)
rudur, rudder
ruduse, reduce
rudusible, reduce(cible)

rue,*, AN HERB (or see roux)

ruebarb, rhubarb
ruel, rule
ruelur, rule(r)
ruen, ruin
ruenashen, ruin(ation)
ruenation, ruin(ation)
ruenus, ruin(ous)
ruf, roof / rough / ruff
rufag, rough(age)
rufal, ruffle
rufeel, reveal
rufeelt, reveal(ed)
rufeer, revere
rufeg, rough(age)
rufej, rough(age)
rufel, ruffle
rufen, ravine / rough(en)
rufenge, revenge
rufenje, revenge
rufer, roof(er) / rough(er) / refer
rufere, revere / refer
ruferse, reverse / refer(s)
rufest, rough(est)

ruff,*,ffed, ELABORATE COLLAR, CARD GAME TERM (or see rough/roof)

ruffle,*,ed,ling, TO MESS UP/DISTURB "prefixes: un"

rufiew, review revue
rufiful, revival
rufig, rough(age)
rufij, rough(age)
rufil, ruffle
rufinable, refine(nable)
rufine, refine
rufinery, refine(ry)
rufinje, revenge
rufinment, refine(ment)
rufinuble, refine(nable)
rufinury, refine(ry)
rufir, rough(er) / roof(er) / refer
rufirse, reverse
rufist, rough(est)
rufle, ruffle
ruflection, reflect(ion)
ruflee, rough(ly)
ruflekshen, reflect(ion)
ruflekt, reflect
ruflektion, reflect(ion)
ruflektor, reflect(or)

rufly, rough(ly)
rufol, ruffle
rufor, rough(er) / roof(er) / refer
rufractory, refract(ory)
rufrain, refrain
rufraktory, refract(ory)
rufrane, refrain
rufregirant, refrigerate(ant)
rufregirator, refrigerate(tor)
rufresher, refresh(er)
rufreshment, refresh(ment)
rufrigerant, refrigerate(ant)
rufrigerator, refrigerate(tor)
rufs, roof(s) / ruff(s)
ruft, roof(ed) / rough(ed)
rufue, review / revue
ruful, ruffle
rufur, rough(er) / roof(er) / refer
rufurse, reverse
rufursuble, reverse(sible)
rufust, rough(est)
rufute, refute

rug,*, REMOVABLE FLOOR COVERING

rugard, regard
ruge, rouge
ruged, rugged

rugged,dly,dness, ROUGH/COARSE/ UNREFINED/IRREGULAR "prefixes: semi"

rugit, rugged
rugresif, regress(ive)
rugresive, regress(ive)
rugret, regret
rugreted, regret(tted)
rugretful, regret(ful)
rugretfuly, regret(fully)
rugud, rugged
rugut, rugged
ruil, rule

ruin,*,ned,ning,nation,nous, BREAK/ DESTROY, COMPLETE FAILURE/ DECAY

ruj, rouge
ruk, rug / rook
ruklamuble, reclaimable
rukliner, recline(r)
rukord, record
rukorder, record(er)
rukumbent, recumbent
rukwest, request
rukwire, require
rukwirment, require(ment)
rukwit, requite
rul, rule

rulaks, relax
rular, rule(r)
rulax, relax
ruld, rule(d)
rule,*,ed,ling,er, LAW/COMMAND/
    METHOD, PERIOD OF GOVERNING,
    DEVICE TO MEASURE "prefixes: mis/
    over"
rulegis, religion(ous)
rulejis, religion(ous)
rulenquish, relinquish
rulent, relent
rulentless, relentless
rulese, release
rulet, roulette
rulette, roulette
ruleve, relieve
rulever, relieve(r)
ruli, rely
ruliability, reliable(bility)
rulianse, reliance
ruliense, reliance
ruligeon, religion
ruligous, religion(ous)
rulijes, religion(ous)
rulinkwish, relinquish
rulinqish, relinquish
rulintless, relentless
rulir, rule(r)
rult, rule(d)
ruluktense, reluctant(nce)
ruluktint, reluctant
rulur, rule(r)
ruly, rely
rum,*,mmer,mmy, LIQUOR, UNUSUAL
rumach, rummage
rumadik, rheumatic
rumadoed, rheumatic(toid)
rumage, rummage
rumain, remain / romaine
rumaje, rummage
rumanater, rumina(tor)
rumander, remain(der)
rumane, remain / romaine
rumanek, romantic
rumantek, romantic
rumanticize, romantic(ize)
rumantisize, romantic(ize)
rumanu, rumina
rumar, rumor
rumared, rumor(ed)
rumark, remark
rumarkt, remark(ed)
rumarkuble, remark(able)

rumatezum, rheumatic(ism)
rumatik, rheumatic
rumatism, rheumatic(ism)
rumatizum, rheumatic(ism)
rumatoed, rheumatic(toid)
rumb, rump
rumbal, rumble / rumple
rumble,*,ed,ling,er,ly, DEEP/ROLLING
    SOUND, A FIGHT (or see rumple)
rumbul, rumble / rumple
rume, room
rumech, rummage
rumedeal, remedy(dial)
rumedge, rummage
rumedial, remedy(dial)
rumediashen, remedy(diation)
rumediation, remedy(diation)
rumedoed, rheumatic(toid)
rumege, rummage
rumeje, rummage
rumember, remember
rumen,*,mina, STOMACH IN
    RUMINANT ANIMALS (many
    stomachs)
rumena, rumina
rumenate, rumina(te)
rumenator, rumina(tor)
rumer, rumor / room(er)
rumered, rumor(ed)
rumert, rumor(ed)
rumes, room(s)
rumeshen, remission
rumet, remit
rumetisem, rheumatic(ism)
rumetism, rheumatic(ism)
rumetoid, rheumatic(toid)
rumich, rummage
rumidal, remit(ttal)
rumidoed, rheumatic(toid)
rumige, rummage
rumije, rummage
rumina,al,ant,antly,ate,ation,ative,
    atively,ator, PERTAINING TO
    CHEWING OF CUD, FIRST STOMACH
rumind, remind
rumindur, remind(er)
rumintur, remind(er)
rumir, rumor / room(er)
rumired, rumor(ed)
rumishen, remission
rumission, remission
rumit, remit
rumitable, remit(ttable)
rumited, remit(tted)

rumitezum, rheumatic(ism)
rumition, remission
rumitizum, rheumatic(ism)
rumitoed, rheumatic(toid)
rumitoid, rheumatic(toid)
rummage,*,ed,ging, GO THROUGH/
    SEARCH/RANSACK
rummige, rummage
rumofer, remove(r)
rumor,*,red, GOSSIP/HEARSAY/
    GENERAL TALK
rumorse, remorse
rumorsful, remorse(ful)
rumorsless, remorse(ful)
rumote, remote
rumotisem, rheumatic(ism)
rumotism, rheumatic(ism)
rumotly, remote(ly)
rumovable, remove(vable)
rumover, remove(r)
rump,*, REAR/TAIL END, BUTTOCKS
rumple,*,ed,ling, CREASE/FOLD/
    WRINKLE (or see rumble)
rums, room(s)
rumuch, rummage
rumufer, remove(r)
rumufible, remove(vable)
rumuge, rummage
rumun, rumen
rumunerashen, remunerate(tion)
rumunerate, remunerate
rumuneration, remunerate(tion)
rumunirashen, remunerate(tion)
rumunirate, remunerate
rumur, rumor
rumurt, rumor(ed)
rumutezim, rheumatic(ism)
rumutizem, rheumatic(ism)
rumy, room(y)
run,*,nning,nner,nny,ran, MOVE
    QUICKLY USING LEGS, MOVING
    LIQUID (or see rune) "prefixes:
    over/re/under"
runar, run(nner)
rund, runt
rune,*,nic, SYMBOLS/ALPHABET (or see
    run/ruin/run(nny))
runege, renege
runer, run(nner)
rung,*, PAST TENSE FOR THE WORD
    "RING", STEPS/LEVELS OF A LADDER,
    STEERING FOR SHIP (or see wrung)
runige, renege
runik, renege

runir, run(nner)
runone, renown
runoserus, rhinoceros
runosirus, rhinoceros
runounsment, renounce(ment)
runown, renown
runownse, renounce
runownsment, renounce(ment)
runre, run(nner)
runt,*,tier,tiest,tiness,ty, SMALLEST OF
    A GROUP/LITTER/ SPECIES
runumerate, remunerate
runur, run(nner)
rup, rip / ripe / rub
rupair, repair
rupal, rubble
rupare, repair
rupcher, rupture
rupchur, rupture
rupeal, repeal
rupeat, repeat
rupedidly, repeat(edly)
rupedutif, repetitive
rupee, ruby
rupeel, repeal
rupeet, repeat
rupel, rappel / repeal / repel / rubble
rupelein, rebel(llion)
rupelent, repellent
rupelinsy, repellent(ncy)
rupelint, repellent
rupense, repent(s)
rupent, repent
rupentinse, repent(ance)
ruper, rubber
rupesh, rubbish
rupete, repeat
rupetedly, repeat(edly)
rupil, rubble
rupinens, repent(ance)
rupint, repent
rupintense, repent(ance)
rupir, rubber
rupish, rubbish
ruplace, replace
ruplasmint, replace(ment)
ruple, rubble
ruplenesh, replenish
ruplenish, replenish
ruplid, reply(lied)
ruplied, reply(lied)
ruply, reply
rupor, rapport
ruporder, report(er)

ruport, report
ruporter, report(er)
rupository, repository
rupozitory, repository
rupreshen, repress(ion)
rupresif, repress(ive)
rupress, repress
rupresuve, repress(ive)
ruproch, reproach
ruprochuble, reproach(able)
rupshar, rupture
rupsheruble, rupture(rable)
rupshir, rupture
rupshiruble, rupture(rable)
rupshur, rupture
rupshuruble, rupture(rable)
rupt, rub(bbed)
rupture,*,ed,ring,rable, BURST/BREACH
    CONTAINER
rupublekan, republic(an)
rupublican, republic(an)
rupugnenst, repugnant(nce)
rupugnint, repugnant
rupul, rubble
rupulshin, repulse(ion)
rupulsion, repulse(ion)
rupur, rubber
ruquire, require
ruquirment, require(ment)
ruquitable, requite(table)
ruquite, requite
ruqwest, request
ruqwire, require
ruqwirment, require(ment)
rur, roar
rural,lly,lity,lism,list,lize,lization, CITY
    OUTSKIRTS "prefixes: semi"
ruril, rural
rurilee, rural(lly)
rurul, rural
rurulee, rural(lly)
rus, ruse
rusde, rust(y)
rusder, rooster
rusdrane, restrain
rusdur, rooster
ruse, A TRICK
ruseat, receipt
rusebshin, reception
rusebshinist, receptionist
rusebtif, receptive
rusebtive, receptive
ruseed, recede
ruseef, receive

ruseet, receipt
rusefible, receive(vable)
ruseliensy, resilient(ncy)
rusemblinse, resemble(lance)
rusentful, resent(ful)
rusentment, resent(ment)
rusepdekle, receptacle
rusepdikul, receptacle
rusepeunt, recipient
ruseprocation, reciprocate(tion)
ruseprocul, reciprocal
rusepshen, reception
rusepshenist, receptionist
ruseptef, receptive
ruseptekle, receptacle
rusepter, receptor
ruseptickle, receptacle
ruseption, reception
ruseptionest, receptionist
ruseptive, receptive
ruserved, reserve(d)
ruseshun, recess(ion)
rusesif, recess(ive)
rusesion, recess(ion)
rusesive, recess(ive)
rusession, recess(ion)
rusestinse, resist(ance)
rusestive, resist(ive)
rusete, receipt
rusetion, recess(ion)
ruseve, receive
rusevuble, receive(vable)
rush,hes,hed,hing,hy, UNEXPECTEDLY/
    FORCEFULLY MOVE FORWARD,
    HURRY ALONG "prefixes: in"
rushd, rush(ed)
ruside, reside
rusiduil, residue(ual)
rusileant, resilient
rusilient, resilient
rusimblense, resemble(lance)
rusimbul, resemble
rusine, resign
rusintment, resent(ment)
rusipeint, recipient
rusiprocation, reciprocate(tion)
rusiprocul, reciprocal
rusiprokate, reciprocate
rusiprokle, reciprocal
rusirfed, reserve(d)
rusist, resist
rusistanse, resist(ance)
rusistense, resist(ance)
rusistent, resist(ant)

rusister, resist(or)
rusistive, resist(ive)
rusitil, recite(tal)
rusitle, recite(tal)
rusodo, risotto
rusolve, resolve
rusort, resort
rusoto, risotto
rusotto, risotto
ruspect, respect
ruspectful, respect(ful)
ruspective, respect(ive)
ruspectuble, respect(able)
ruspekt, respect
ruspektful, respect(ful)
ruspektif, respect(ive)
ruspektuble, respect(able)
ruspite, respite
ruspond, respond
ruspondent, respond(ent)
rusponder, respond(er)
rusponse, response
rusponsef, response(sive)
rusponsive, response(sive)
rusponsuble, response(sible)
ruspont, respond
rust,*,ted,ting,ty,tier,tiest, OXIDATION
    OF METAL (or see roost)
rustek, rustic
ruster, rooster
rustic,*,cally,cate,cates,cated,cating,
    cation,cator,city,cities, COUNTRY
    STYLE, SIMPLE
rustid, roost(ed)
rustik, rustic
rustir, rooster
rustore, restore
rustrain, restrain
rustraint, restrain(t)
rustrane, restrain
rustrant, restrain(t)
rustrekt, restrict
rustrektif, restrict(ive)
rustrikshen, restrict(ion)
rustrikt, restrict
rustriktion, restrict(ion)
rustriktive, restrict(ive)
rustuk, rustic
rustur, rooster
rusurfed, reserve(d)
rususcitate, resuscitate
rususetate, resuscitate
rususitashen, resuscitate(tion)
rususitate, resuscitate

rususitator, resuscitate(tor)
rut,*,tted,tting, NOISE DEER MAKES, A
    TRENCH/GROOVE/FURROW (or see
    route/root/rude/wrought)
rutainer, retain(er)
rutaleashen, retaliate(tion)
rutaleate, retaliate
rutaleation, retaliate(tion)
rutaliation, retaliate(tion)
rutane, retain
rutaner, retain(er)
rutashen, rotate(tion)
rute, rude / root / route
ruted, rut(tted)
ruteen, routine
rutenshun, retention
rutentif, retentive
rutention, retention
rutentive, retentive
ruter, rudder
rutesary, rotisserie
rutest, rude(st)
ruthlesnes, ruthless(ness)
ruthless,ssly,ssness, SPEAKING/ACTING
    WITHOUT MERCY
ruthlis, ruthless
rutine, routine
rutinshun, retention
rutintion, retention
rutir, rudder
rutire, retire
rutirment, retire(ment)
rutisary, rotisserie
rutisury, rotisserie
rutlee, rude(ly)
rutorekle, rhetoric(al)
rutorikle, rhetoric(al)
rutracted, retract(ed)
rutraction, retract(ion)
rutrakshen, retract(ion)
rutrakted, retract(ed)
rutre, rudder
rutref, retrieve
rutrefer, retrieve(r)
rutreful, retrieve(val)
rutreve, retrieve
rutrevur, retrieve(r)
rutur, rudder
ruvalfe, revolve
ruvalve, revolve
ruveel, reveal
ruveelingly, reveal(ingly)
ruveelt, reveal(ed)
ruveer, revere

ruvegen, revise(sion)
ruvejen, revise(sion)
ruvench, revenge
ruvene, ravine
ruvenge, revenge
ruvengful, revenge(ful)
ruvenje, revenge
ruvenjful, revenge(ful)
ruverbarate, reverberate
ruverbirate, reverberate
ruvere, revere
ruversuble, reverse(sible)
ruvert, revert
ruveshen, revise(sion)
ruvesion, revise(sion)
ruview, review / revue
ruvigen, revise(sion)
ruvijen, revise(sion)
ruvinch, revenge
ruvine, ravine
ruving, revenge
ruvingful, revenge(ful)
ruvinje, revenge
ruvinjful, revenge(ful)
ruvirberate, reverberate
ruvirse, reverse
ruvirsuble, reverse(sible)
ruvirt, revert
ruvise, revise
ruvishen, revise(sion)
ruvision, revise(sion)
ruvival, revival
ruvive, revive
ruvivle, revival
ruvivuble, revive(vable)
ruvize, revise
ruvocability, revocable(bility)
ruvocable, revocable
ruvokability, revocable(bility)
ruvokable, revocable
ruvoke, revoke
ruvokt, revoke(d)
ruvolfe, revolve
ruvolfer, revolve(r)
ruvolt, revolt
ruvoltid, revolt(ed)
ruvolve, revolve
ruvolver, revolve(r)
ruvue, review / revue
ruvurse, reverse
ruvurt, revert
ruward, reward
ruwidable, requite(table)
ruword, reward

ruwul, rural
ruzemblinse, resemble(lance)
ruzentful, resent(ful)
ruzentment, resent(ment)
ruzerved, reserve(d)
ruzestif, resist(ive)
ruzestir, resist(or)
ruzide, reside
ruziduil, residue(ual)
ruzileant, resilient
ruzilient, resilient
ruzimble, resemble
ruzimblense, resemble(lance)
ruzine, resign
ruzintful, resent(ful)
ruzintment, resent(ment)
ruzist, resist
ruzistanse, resist(ance)
ruzistant, resist(ant)
ruzistef, resist(ive)
ruzistense, resist(ance)
ruzistent, resist(ant)
ruzister, resist(or)
ruzodo, risotto
ruzolfe, resolve
ruzolve, resolve
ruzort, resort
ruzoto, risotto
ruzt, rust / roost
ruztek, rustic
ruztid, rust(ed)
ruztuk, rustic
ruzty, rust(y)
ruzurfs, reserve(s)
ry, rye / wry
rye, A GRAIN (or see wry)
ryle, rile
ryme, rhyme
ryno, rhino
rynstone, rhinestone
rysome, rhizome
ryth, writhe
rythem, rhythm
rythom, rhythm
ryut, riot
ryzome, rhizome
sa, saw / say
sabal, sable
sabateur, saboteur
sabatoj, sabotage
sabature, saboteur
saber,*,red,ring, BROADSWORD,
    LIGHTWEIGHT SWORD WITH BLUNT
    TIP

sabereoredy, superior(ity)
sabereority, superior(ity)
sabereur, superior
sabetaje, sabotage
sabetoge, sabotage
sabeture, saboteur
sabil, sable
sabir, saber
sabitaje, sabotage
sabiteur, saboteur
sabitoge, sabotage
sabitoj, sabotage
sabiture, saboteur
sable,*, CARNIVOROUS ANIMAL
sableng, sapling
sabling, sapling
sabol, sable
sabor, saber
sabotage,*,ed,ging,teur, HINDER/
    DAMAGE SOMEONE'S ATTEMPTS/
    POSSESSIONS/EFFORTS
sabotaje, sabotage
saboteur,*, ONE WHO COMMITS
    SABOTAGE
saboture, saboteur
sabre, saber
sabul, sable
sabur, saber
sabutaje, sabotage
sabuteur, saboteur
sabutoge, sabotage
sabutoj, sabotage
saccaren, saccharin
saccerin, saccharin
saccharin,ne,nely,nity, MANMADE
    SUGAR
saccuren, saccharin
sacede, secede
sacha, sachet
sachal, satchel
sacharate, saturate
sacharation, saturate(tion)
sachatory, statutory
sachay, sashay / sachet
sache, sachet
sacheable, sate(tiable)
sacheatid, sate(tiated)
sachel, satchel
sacherashen, saturate(tion)
sacherate, saturate
sacheration, saturate(tion)
sacherin, saccharin
sachet,*, SMALL/AROMATIC BAG (or
    see sashay)

sachetory, statutory
sacheuble, sate(tiable)
sachil, satchel
sachirashen, saturate(tion)
sachirate, saturate
sachiration, saturate(tion)
sachiren, saccharin
sachol, satchel
sachul, satchel
sachurate, saturate
sachuration, saturate(tion)
sachutory, statutory
sack,*,ked,king,ker,kful, BAG MADE OF
    VARIOUS MATERIALS USED TO
    CONTAIN/HOLD SOMETHING, TO
    BAG/TACKLE (or see sax)
sackarin, saccharin
sackralegus, sacrilege(gious)
sackralijes, sacrilege(gious)
sackrament, sacrament
sackrul, sacral
sackrument, sacrament
sackuren, saccharin
saclusion, seclusion
saclusive, seclusive
sacrafise, sacrifice
sacral, ASSOCIATED WITH RITES
    "prefixes: de"
sacraleje, sacrilege
sacraligous, sacrilege(gious)
sacrament,*,tal,tally,tality,talism,talist,
    tarian,tarianism, THAT WHICH IS
    SACRED
sacrasankt, sacrosanct
sacred,dly,dness, OF REVERENCE/
    WORSHIPPED
sacrefise, sacrifice
sacrel, sacrum(ral)
sacreleje, sacrilege
sacreligus, sacrilege(gious)
sacrem, sacrum
sacremint, sacrament
sacresanct, sacrosanct
sacreshen, secrete(tion)
sacresion, secrete(tion)
sacrete, secrete / sacred
sacretion, secrete(tion)
sacrid, sacred
sacrifice,*,ed,cing,er,cial,cially, GIVE UP
    WITHOUT PROFIT/RETURN, DENY
    ONESELF
sacril, sacrum(ral)
sacrilege,gious,giously,giousness,
    VIOLATION OF SACRED

sacrim, sacrum

sacrosanct,tity,tness, TOO HOLY TO BE CRITICIZED/SLANDERED

sacrud, sacred

sacrufise, sacrifice

sacrul, sacrum(ral)

sacruleje, sacrilege

sacruligus, sacrilege(gious)

sacrum,ral, LUMBAR VERTEBRAE ON THE SPINE

sacrument, sacrament

sacumb, succumb

sacure, secure

sad,dly,dness,dden,dder,ddest, SORROWFUL/MOURNFUL, UNHAPPY WITH RESULTS (or see sat)

sadalight, satellite

sadalite, satellite

sadarday, saturday

sadasfaction, satisfy(faction)

sadasfakshen, satisfy(faction)

sadasfy, satisfy

sadashen, sedate(tion)

sadasion, sedate(tion)

sadate, sedate

sadation, sedate(tion)

saddle,*,ed,ling,er, DEVICE/SEAT USED TO RIDE ON A FOUR LEGGED ANIMAL "prefixes: un"

sadel, saddle

sadelite, satellite

sademize, sodomy(mize)

saden, sad(dden) / satin

sadentary, sedentary

sadeny, satin(y)

saderday, saturday

sadesfaction, satisfy(faction)

sadesfakshen, satisfy(faction)

sadesfy, satisfy

sadesum, sadism

sadews, seduce

sadil, saddle

sadilight, satellite

sadilite, satellite

sadimize, sodomy(mize)

sadin, sad(dden) / satin

sadintary, sedentary

sadiny, satin(y)

sadirday, saturday

sadisfaction, satisfy(faction)

sadisfakshen, satisfy(faction)

sadisfy, satisfy

sadism,stic,st,stically, SEXUALLY AROUSED BY PAIN/TORTURE

sadisum, sadism

sadle, saddle

sadnes, sad(ness)

sadnis, sad(ness)

sadolite, satellite

sadomasakisum, sadomasochism

sadomasochism,st,stic, ASSOCIATED WITH SADISM

sadomasukezim, sadomasochism

sadoose, seduce

sadosfaction, satisfy(faction)

sadosfakshen, satisfy(faction)

saducshen, seduce(ction)

saductive, seduce(ctive)

saduktion, seduce(ction)

saduktive, seduce(ctive)

sadul, saddle

saduld, saddle(d)

sadulite, satellite

sadun, sad(dden) / satin

sadurday, saturday

saduse, seduce

sadusfakshen, satisfy(faction)

sadusfy, satisfy

sae, say

saed, said / set

saen, sane / sain

saend, sound

saent, saint

safari,*, HUNTING EXPEDITION

safd, save(d)

safe,ely,er,est,eness,ety, PROTECT FROM HARM (or see salve)

safekate, suffocate

safekation, suffocate(tion)

safeks, suffix

safestikashen, sophisticate(tion)

safestikated, sophisticate(d)

safestikation, sophisticate(tion)

safex, suffix

safflower, FLOWERS WHICH PRODUCED OIL

saffron, A FLOWER/COLOR

saficashen, suffocate(tion)

saficate, suffocate

safication, suffocate(tion)

safichent, sufficient

saficient, sufficient

safikashen, suffocate(tion)

safikate, suffocate

safikation, suffocate(tion)

safiks, suffix

safinth, seventh

safir, safe(r) / savor / sapphire

safire, sapphire

safise, suffice

safishent, sufficient

safishently, sufficient(ly)

safishunt, sufficient

safist, safe(st)

safistakashen, sophisticate(tion)

safistakated, sophisticate(d)

safistakation, sophisticate(tion)

safix, suffix

saflawur, safflower

saflee, safe(ly)

saflour, safflower

saflower, safflower

safly, safe(ly)

safmore, sophomore

safocashen, suffocate(tion)

safocate, suffocate

safocation, suffocate(tion)

safron, saffron

safrun, saffron / sovereign

saftee, safe(ty)

safucashen, suffocate(tion)

safucate, suffocate

safucation, suffocate(tion)

safukashen, suffocate(tion)

safukate, suffocate

safur, safe(r) / savor

safy, savvy

safyur, savior

sag,*,gged,gging,ggy, TO BOW/BEND IN A CERTAIN AREA (or see sack/sage)

sagd, sag(ged) / sage(d)

sage,*,ed,ging,ely,eness, AN HERB/PLANT, SOMEONE WISE

saged, sag(gged) / sage(d)

sagee, sag(ggy)

sagis, sage(s)

saguaro,*, A CACTUS

sagus, sage(s)

sagy, sag(ggy)

said, PAST TENSE FOR THE WORD "SAY" (or see set) "prefixes: un"

sail,*,led,ling,lor, OF/GIVEN TO A BOAT WITH SAILS, USE OF WIND TO NAVIGATE BOAT/VESSEL (or see sale/sailor))

sailor,*, PEOPLE WHO OPERATE SEAGOING VESSELS (or see sail(er))

saim, same

sain, MAKE THE SIGN OF THE CROSS (or see sane/say(ing))

sainkshuary, sanctuary
saint,*,ted,ting,tly,tdom,thood, OFFICALLY RECOGNIZED IN DYING FOR A HOLY CAUSE, A VERY KIND PERSON
saje, sage
sajed, sage(d)
sak, sack / sake / sag / sax
sakaren, saccharin
sakarin, saccharin
sakd, sack(ed)
sake, PURPOSE/BENEFIT OF, JAPANESE ALCOHOL BEVERAGE (or see sack)
saker, soccer / sack(er)
sakeren, saccharin
sakerin, saccharin
sakeuridy, secure(rity)
sakewr, secure
sakewrity, secure(rity)
sakful, sack(ful)
sakir, soccer / sack(er)
sakiuredy, secure(rity)
sakiutrest, psychiatry(rist)
saklooded, seclude(d)
saklude, seclude
sakluded, seclude(d)
saklusive, seclusive
saklution, seclusion
sakrafise, sacrifice
sakraleje, sacrilege
sakralige, sacrilege
sakraligus, sacrilege(gious)
sakrament, sacrament
sakramintal, sacrament(al)
sakrasinkt, sacrosanct
sakred, sacred
sakrefise, sacrifice
sakrel, sacral
sakrem, sacrum
sakrement, sacrament
sakren, saccharin
sakreshen, secrete(tion)
sakresion, secrete(tion)
sakret, sacred
sakrete, secrete
sakrid, sacred
sakrifice, sacrifice
sakril, sacral
sakrilege, sacrilege
sakrim, sacrum
sakriment, sacrament
sakrimental, sacrament(al)
sakrin, saccharin
sakrit, sacred

sakrom, sacrum
sakrosankt, sacrosanct
sakrud, sacred
sakrufise, sacrifice
sakrufishul, sacrifice(cial)
sakrul, sacral
sakruleje, sacrilege
sakruligus, sacrilege(gious)
sakrum, sacrum
sakrument, sacrament
sakrun, saccharin
sakrusankt, sacrosanct
sakrut, sacred
saks, sack(s) / sag(s) / sax
saksafone, saxophone
saksaphone, saxophone
saksufone, saxophone
saksuphone, saxophone
sakt, sack(ed)
sakum, succumb
sakur, soccer / sack(er)
sakure, secure
sakuren, saccharin
sakurin, saccharin
sakurity, secure(rity)
sakwenshul, sequence(ntial)
sakwential, sequence(ntial)
sakwoia, sequoia
sal, sale / sail / saw
salad,*, COLD MIXED FOOD DISH, TOSSED GREENS
saladerity, solidarity
salal, plant
salamander,*, AMPHIBIOUS LIZARD
salami, A SAUSAGE
salar, sail(er) / sailor
salaree, salary / celery
salary,ries,ried, STEADY PAY IN COMPENSATION FOR WORK PERFORMED
salatood, solitude
salatude, solitude
sald, salt / sail(ed)
salder, solder(ed)
saldered, solder(ed)
sale,*,eable,sell, SELL GOODS/SERVICES (or see sail) "prefixes: pre/re"
salebrity, celebrity
salective, select(ive)
saled, sail(ed) / salad
saledarity, solidarity
saledify, solid(ify)
saleen, saline
saleks, select(s)

salekshen, select(ion)
salekt, select
salektif, select(ive)
salektion, select(ion)
salektive, select(ive)
salelaquy, soliloquy
salem, solemn
salemandur, salamander
salemantur, salamander
salemly, solemn(ly)
salen, saline
salenity, saline(nity)
salenium, selenium
salenoid, solenoid
saler, sail(er) / sailor
saleree, salary celery
salesteal, celestial
salet, salad
saleutation, salute(tation)
salevate, saliva(te)
salewtashen, salute(tation)
salfent, solvent
salfint, solvent
salicit, solicit
salicitation, solicit(ation)
saliciter, solicit(er)
salid, salad / solid
salidarity, solidarity
salidefy, solid(ify)
salidness, solid(ness)
salilakwy, soliloquy
salilaqwy, soliloquy
salim, solemn
salimandur, salamander
salimly, solemn(ly)
saline,na,nity,nization, PERTAINS TO SALT "prefixes: de"
salinidy, saline(nity)
salinoid, solenoid
salir, sail(er) / sailor
saliry, salary / celery
salis, solace
saliset, solicit
saliseter, solicit(er)
salisit, solicit
salisitation, solicit(ation)
salisiter, solicit(er)
salit, salad
salitefy, solid(ify)
saliva,ary,ate,ation, FLUID SECRETED BY GLANDS IN THE MOUTH "prefixes: in"
salm, psalm
salmin, salmon

salmon, a fish
salmonela, salmonella
salmonella, BACTERIA WHICH POISONS FOOD
salmun, salmon
salod, salad
salomander, salamander
salomantur, salamander
salomee, salami
salon,*, CUTS/STYLES HAIR
saloon,*, TYPE OF DRINKING ESTABLISHMENT
saloot, salute
salt,*,ted,ting,ty,tier,tiest,ter, SODIUM/CHEMICAL COMPOUND (or see sail(ed)) "prefixes: de"
salud, salad
saludid, salute(d)
saludness, solid(ness)
salum, solemn
salumandur, salamander
salumly, solemn(ly)
salune, saloon
salunization, saline(nization)
salunoid, solenoid
salur, sail(er) / sailor
saluree, salary / celery
salus, solace
salushen, solution
salut, salad
salutashen, salute(tation)
salute,*,ed,ting,tary,tarily,tariness, tation,tational,tatorian,tor,tories, ter, METHOD OF GREETING
salutid, salute(d)
salution, solution
saluvate, saliva(te)
salvage,*,ed,ging,eable,er, THOUGH DAMAGED, IS STILL WORTHY OF SAVING
salvashen, salvation
salvation,nal,nism, PRESERVE/PROTECT FROM DANGER/HARM
salve,*,ed,ving, AN OINTMENT/BALM USED FOR HEALING SORES (or see solve)
salvech, salvage
salved, solve(d)
salvige, salvage
salvije, salvage
salvuble, solve(vable)
salvug, salvage
salyewble, soluble(ize)
salyutashen, salute(tation)

saman, salmon
samanela, salmonella
samantics, semantics
same,eness, ALIKE/SIMILAR
samen, salmon
samenela, salmonella
samesdur, semester
samester, semester
sametrek, symmetry(ric)
sametric, symmetry(ric)
samin, salmon
saminela, salmonella
samonela, salmonella
sampal, sample
sample,*,ed,ling,er, A SMALL AMOUNT/TASTE OF SOMETHING "prefixes: re/sub"
samplir, sample(r)
sampul, sample
samun, salmon
samunela, salmonella
san, sane / sain / sand
sanada, sonata
sanareo, scenario
sanatarium, sanitorium
sanatate, sanitate
sanatesation, sanitize(zation)
sanatezashen, sanitize(zation)
sanatization, sanitize(zation)
sanatize, sanitize
sanatoreum, sanitorium
sanatu, sonata
sancshen, sanction
sancshin, sanction
sancshuary, sanctuary
sancshun, sanction
sanctafie, sanctify
sanctify,fies,fied,fying,fication,fier, MAKE HOLY
sanction,*,ned,ning,ner,nable, FORMAL/BINDING PERMISSION
sanctofie, sanctify
sanctuary,ries, REPRIEVE FROM PROBLEMS, PLACE OF IMMUNITY
sanctuery, sanctuary
sanctufy, sanctify
sand,*,ded,ding,dy,der, TINY ROCKS, SMOOTH A SURFACE BY SANDING
sandal,*, TYPE OF SHOE
sandee, sand(y)
sandel, sandal
sandul, sandal
sandur, sand(er)
sandwech, sandwich

sandwich,hes,hed,hing, MEAT/VEGETABLES BETWEEN TWO PIECES OF BREAD, PHYSICALLY BE BETWEEN TWO THINGS
sandwitch, sandwich
sane,ely,eness,nity,nities, OF SOUND MIND/JUDGEMENT (or see sain/sand)
sanedy, sanity
sanek, sonic
sanelity, senile(lity)
sanereo, scenario
sanerist, scenario(ist)
sanetareum, sanitorium
sanetary, sanitary
sanetate, sanitate
sanetery, sanitary
sanetize, sanitize
sanetoreum, sanitorium
sanetorium, sanitorium
sanety, sanity
sanidy, sanity
sanility, senile(lity)
sanitareum, sanitorium
sanitarium, sanitorium
sanitary,rian,rily,riness, CLEAN/FREE OF MOST HARMFUL BACTERIA "prefixes: in"
sanitate,*,ed,ting,tion, CLEAN/RID OF HARMFUL BACTERIA
sanitery, sanitary
sanitezation, sanitize(zation)
sanitised, sanitize(d)
sanitize,*,ed,zing,zation,er, CLEAN/RID OF HARMFUL BACTERIA
sanitizer, sanitize(r)
sanitorium,*, RESORT/FACILITY FOR LONG-TERM CARE OF ILLNESS/HEALTH
sanity,ties, RELATED TO A SOUND MIND/JUDGEMENT
sankchuery, sanctuary
sankdefide, sanctify(fied)
sankdefy, sanctify
sankdify, sanctify
sankdufide, sanctify(fied)
sankdufy, sanctify
sankshen, sanction
sankshin, sanction
sankshuery, sanctuary
sankshun, sanction
sanktafi, sanctify
sanktify, sanctify
sanktion, sanction

sanktofie, sanctify
sanktuary, sanctuary
sanktuery, sanctuary
sanktufie, sanctify
sanoda, sonata
sanografee, scenography
sanopsis, synopsis
sanota, sonata
sant, saint
sante, sand(y)
santels, sandal(s)
santly, saint(ly)
santuls, sandal(s)
santur, sand(er)
santwech, sandwich
santwitch, sandwich
sanuc, sonic
sanudy, sanity
sanuk, sonic
sanut, sonnet
sanutareum, sanitorium
sanutary, sanitary
sanutate, sanitate
sanutery, sanitary
sanutezashen, sanitize(zation)
sanutisation, sanitize(zation)
sanutised, sanitize(d)
sanutize, sanitize
sanutizer, sanitize(r)
sanuty, sanity
sanwech, sandwich
saons, se'ance
sap,*,pped,pping,ppy, THE LIFEBLOOD
    OF PLANTS
saped, sap(pped)
sapena, subpoena
sapenid, subpoena(ed)
sapenud, subpoena(ed)
saperb, superb
saperblee, superb(ly)
sapereor, superior
sapereoredy, superior(ity)
sapereority, superior(ity)
saperlative, superlative
saperlutif, superlative
saphire, sapphire
saphmore, sophomore
sapinud, subpoena(ed)
sapirb, superb
sapirblee, superb(ly)
sapireor, superior
sapireority, superior(ity)
sapirlutif, superlative
sapleminul, subliminal

sapleng, sapling
sapli, supply
saplier, supply(lier)
sapling,*, YOUNG TREES
sapliur, supply(lier)
saply, supply
saport, support
saportef, support(ive)
saportive, support(ive)
sapose, suppose
sapository, suppository
saposubly, suppose(dly)
sapoze, suppose
sapozetory, suppository
sapozitory, suppository
sapozubly, suppose(dly)
sapphire,*, A GEM STONE
sappresion, suppress(ion)
saprechen, suppress(ion)
sapreem, supreme
sapremacy, supremacy
sapreme, supreme
sapremusist, supremacy(cist)
sapremusy, supremacy
sapreno, soprano
sapres, suppress
sapreshen, suppress(ion)
sapretion, suppress(ion)
saprimosy, supremacy
saprino, soprano
sapt, sap(pped)
sapurb, superb
sapurblee, superb(ly)
sapurlative, superlative
sapurlitef, superlative
sapurlutif, superlative
sapy, sap(ppy)
saquential, sequence(ntial)
saquer, secure
saquir, secure
saquoia, sequoia
sar, czar
saran, A THIN PLASTIC
sarandipity, serendipity
sarape, serape
sarcafagus, sarcophagus
sarcasm,*,stic, REMARKS MEANT TO BE
    DEMEANING/MOCKERY TO
    ANOTHER
sarcastecly, sarcastic(ally)
sarcastek, sarcastic
sarcastekly, sarcastic(ally)

sarcastic,cally, REMARKS MEANT TO BE
    DEMEANING/MOCKERY TO
    ANOTHER
sarcastikly, sarcastic(ally)
sarcastuk, sarcastic
sarcazum, sarcasm
sarcophagus,ses,gi, STONE COFFIN
sardeen, sardine
sardene, sardine
sardine,*, TINY EDIBLE FISH
sardo, sourdough
sarebrul, cerebral
sarel, sorrel / surreal
sarench, syringe
sarender, surrender
sarendipity, serendipity
sarene, serene
sarenge, syringe
sarenity, serene(nity)
sarenje, syringe
sarenk, saw(ing)
sargeant, sergeant / surgent
sargent, sergeant / surgent
sargint, sergeant / surgent
sari, saury / sorry
saribrol, cerebral
sarinch, syringe
sarinder, surrender
sarindipity, serendipity
saring, saw(ing)
saringe, syringe
sarinje, syringe
sarink, saw(ing)
sariosis, psoriasis
sariusis, psoriasis
sarjent, sergeant
sarjint, sergeant
sarkafigus, sarcophagus
sarkasem, sarcasm
sarkasim, sarcasm
sarkastek, sarcastic
sarkastiklee, sarcastic(ally)
sarkastuk, sarcastic
sarkawfegus, sarcophagus
sarkazum, sarcasm
sarkofigus, sarcophagus
sarkofugus, sarcophagus
sarkophagus, sarcophagus
sarkrowt, sauerkraut
saro, sorrow
saroful, sorrow(ful)
sarong,*, MATERIAL/CLOTH USED TO
    WRAP AROUND THE LOWER TORSO
sarope, serape

saroredy, sorority
sarority, sorority
saround, surround
sarow, sorrow
sarowful, sorrow(ful)
sarownd, surround
sarrated, serrate(d)
sarration, serrate(tion)
sarro, sorrow
sarundipity, serendipity
sarundipudy, serendipity
sary, saury / sorry
sas, sass / say(s)
sasafras, sassafras
sascha, sashay / sachet
sased, sass(ed) / secede
sasede, secede
sasefras, sassafras
saseg, sausage
sasej, sausage
sasenked, succinct
sasenkt, succinct
sasenktly, succinct(ly)
saseptible, susceptible
saseptif, susceptive
saseptive, susceptive
saseptuble, susceptible
saseptuf, susceptive
saser, saucer
saseshen, secession
sasesion, secession
saset, secede
sasetion, secession
sasha, sachet
sashay,*, WISPILY WALK AS IF DANCING (or see sachet)
sasheable, sate(tiable)
sasheated, sate(tiated)
sashet, sashay / sachet
sasheuble, sate(tiable)
sasifras, sassafras
sasig, sausage
sasij, sausage
sasinked, succinct
sasinkt, succinct
sasinktly, succinct(ly)
sasir, saucer
sasofras, sassafras
sasor, saucer
saspekt, suspect
saspend, suspend
saspender, suspender
saspeshus, suspicious
saspishus, suspicious

sass,sses,ssing,ssy, SPEAK IMPUDENTLY, SMART BACK AT
sassafras, USEFUL TREE ROOTBARK
sasufras, sassafras
sasur, saucer
sasy, saucy / sass(y)
sat, PAST TENSE WORD FOR 'SIT' (or see sate/sad)
sata, saute / sate
satalite, satellite
satanek, satanic
satanic,cal,cally,ism,ist, MOCKERY OF CHRISTIAN RITUAL
satanuk, satanic
satanukel, satanic(al)
satarate, saturate
satarday, saturday
satasfaction, satisfy(faction)
satasfakshen, satisfy(faction)
satasfy, satisfy
satay, saute / sate
satchal, satchel
satcharashen, saturate(tion)
satcharate, saturate
satchatory, statutory
satchel,*, BAG/CARRYING CASE
satcherashen, saturate(tion)
satcherate, saturate
satchetory, statutory
satchil, satchel
satchirashen, saturate(tion)
satchirate, saturate
satchitory, statutory
satchul, satchel
satchurashen, saturate(tion)
satchurate, saturate
satchutory, statutory
sate,ed,ting,tiable,tiably,tiability,tiate, tiates,tiated,tiating,tiation,tiety, TO BE COMPLETELY SATISFIED (or see saute) "prefixes: in"
sateable, sate(tiable)
satel, saddle
satelite, satellite
satellite,*, A PLANET OR MANMADE DEVICE WHICH ORBITS THE EARTH "prefixes: bio"
satemize, sodomy(mize)
saten, sad(dden) / satin
satentary, sedentary
sateny, satin(y)
saterate, saturate
saterday, saturday
saterikul, satire(rical)

satesfaction, satisfy(faction)
satesfakshen, satisfy(faction)
satesfy, satisfy
satesm, sadism
satiaty, sate(tiety)
satilite, satellite
satimize, sodomy(mize)
satin,ny, A SOFT FABRIC
satintary, sedentary
satirate, saturate
satirday, saturday
satire,*,ric,rical,rically,rist,rize,rizes, rized,rizing,rization,rizer, EMPLOY IRONY/WIT/SARCASM (or see satyr)
satirest, satire(rist)
satisfakshen, satisfy(faction)
satisfy,fies,fied,fying,fiable,fier,fyingly, faction,factory,factorily, NEEDS/ DEMANDS/EXPECTATIONS FULFILLED "prefixes: dis/un"
satisum, sadism
satle, saddle
satlee, sad(ly)
satnis, sad(ness)
satolite, satellite
satomasakisum, sadomasochism
satomasochism, sadomasochism
satosfaction, satisfy(faction)
satosfakshen, satisfy(faction)
satshetory, statutory
satul, saddle
satulite, satellite
saturate,*,ed,ting,tion,tor, UNABLE TO ABSORB ANYMORE LIQUID "prefixes: de/un/under"
saturday,*, A DAY OF THE WEEK (ENGLISH)
satusfakshen, satisfy(faction)
satusfy, satisfy
satutory, statutory
satyerashen, saturate(tion)
satyirate, saturate
satyr,*,ric,rical, MYTHOLOGICAL CREATURE (or see satire)
satyurate, saturate
satyuration, saturate(tion)
sau, saw
sauble, say(able)
sauce,*,ed,cing,cy, A THICK LIQUID WITH SPICES/HERBS/ FLAVORINGS ADDED
saucer,*, A SMALL PLATE, SHAPE OF A PLATE
sauciur, saucy(cier)

saucy,cier,ciest,cily,ciness, BEING IMPUDENT/FLIPPANT TOWARD SUPERIORS

saud, sod / sold / saw

sauder, solder

sauderd, solder(ed)

saudumize, sodomy(mize)

saudumy, sodomy

sauer, sour

sauerdo, sourdough

sauerkraut, FERMENTED CABBAGE

saufari, safari

saufen, soft(en)

saufet, soffit

saufiner, soft(ener)

saufit, soffit

saufmore, sophomore

saufunir, soft(ener)

saugee, soggy

saught, saute / sought

sauir, sour

sauirdo, sourdough

sauirkrowt, sauerkraut

saulanoid, solenoid

saulder, solder

saulesmint, solace(ment)

saulid, solid

saulis, solace

saulisment, solace(ment)

saulitare, solitaire / solitary

sauluderity, solidarity

saulus, solace

saulutare, solitaire / solitary

saulutude, solitude

saulyewble, soluble(ize)

sauna,*, ROOM WITH MOIST HEAT/ STEAM

saund, sound

saunek, sonic

saunet, sonnet

saunik, sonic

saunit, sonnet

saunt, sound

saunter,*,red,ring, A LEISURLY WALK/ STROLL

saunu, sauna

saunut, sonnet

saur, sour

saurdo, sourdough

sauree, sorry / saury

sauro, sorrow

saury,ries, A FISH (or see sorry)

saus, sauce

sausage,*, MINCED MEAT WITH FLAVORINGS

sauseur, saucy(cier)

sausier, saucy(cier)

saut, sought

saute,*,eed,eing, QUICKLY FRY IN A PAN/WOK (or see sate)

sauter, solder

sautered, solder(ed)

sauvren, sovereign

sauvter, soft(er)

sauvuble, solve(vable)

sauyubil, soluble

sav, save / salve / solve

savach, savage

savage,*,ely,eness,ery,eries, BEASTLY/ RUDE/BARBARIAN

savagly, savage(ly)

savana, savanna

savanna, MEADOW/PLAIN WITH SHRUBS/TREES

savant,*, A WISE/LEARNED PERSON

savar, savor / save(r)

savaren, sovereign

savd, save(d)

save,*,ed,ving,er, RESCUE FROM DANGER/HARM/ALTERCATION (or see safe/savvy/salve)

savech, savage

savechry, savage(ry)

savee, savvy

savege, savage

savegly, savage(ly)

savegry, savage(ry)

saveje, savage

saver, save(r) / savor

saveridy, severe(rity)

saverin, sovereign

saverity, severe(rity)

savich, savage

savichry, savage(ry)

savier, savvy(vvier) / savior

savigly, savage(ly)

savigry, savage(ry)

savije, savage

savinth, seventh

savior,*, ONE CHOSEN BY PEOPLE TO LEAD THEM FROM IGNORANCE INTO ENLIGHTENMENT

savir, savor / save(r) / savior

savird, savor(ed)

saviren, sovereign

savlawur, safflower

savlee, safe(ly)

savont, savant

savor,*,red,ring,rer,ry, FOOD WITH MOST PALATABLE FLAVOR/SMELL/ TASTE (or see savior) "prefixes: un"

savree, savor(y)

savren, sovereign

savron, saffron / sovereign

savrun, sovereign

savry, savor(y)

savtee, safe(ty)

savuch, savage

savugly, savage(ly)

savugry, savage(ry)

savuje, savage

savur, savor / save(r) / savior

savurd, savor(ed)

savuren, sovereign

savurin, sovereign

savvy,vvies,vvied,vvying,vviest, INTELLIGENT/SHREWD UNDERSTANDING

savy, savvy

savyer, savior

savyur, savior

saw,*,wed,wing,wer, PAST TENSE FOR THE WORD "SEE", BLADE WITH TEETH THAT CUTS (or see sauce) "prefixes: over"

sawardo, sourdough

sawarkrowt, sauerkraut

sawaro, saguaro

sawdemise, sodomy(mize)

sawdemy, sodomy

sawder, solder

sawdered, solder(ed)

sawdimy, sodomy

sawdumize, sodomy(mize)

sawdur, solder

sawer, sour

sawerdo, sourdough

sawerkraut, sauerkraut

sawfenir, soft(ener)

sawfet, soffit

sawfin, soft(en)

sawfinur, soft(ener)

sawfit, soffit

sawfmore, sophomore

sawfun, soft(en)

sawfuner, soft(ener)

sawgee, soggy

sawir, sour

sawirdo, sourdough

sawirkraut, sauerkraut

sawirkrowt, sauerkraut

sawker, soccer
sawled, solid
sawlesmint, solace(ment)
sawletare, solitaire / solitary
sawlf, solve
sawlid, solid
sawlidness, solid(ness)
sawlis, solace
sawlisment, solace(ment)
sawlitness, solid(ness)
sawlud, solid
sawludness, solid(ness)
sawlutare, solitaire / solitary
sawlutude, solitude
sawnd, sound
sawnek, sonic
sawnet, sonnet
sawnik, sonic
sawnut, sonnet
sawor, sour
saworo, saguaro
sawp, sop / sob
sawpee, sop(ppy)
sawree, saury / sorry
sawrely, sorry(rily)
sawrench, syringe
sawri, sorry / saury
sawro, saguaro / sorrow
sawrong, sarong
sawry, sorry / saury
saws, saw(s) / sauce / souse
sawsege, sausage
sawseje, sausage
sawser, saucer
sawsige, sausage
sawsor, saucer
sawst, souse(d)
sawsuge, sausage
sawsuje, sausage
sawsur, saucer
sawsy, saucy
sawt, saw(ed)
sawtay, saute / sate
sawte, saute / sate
sawtemy, sodomy
sawtered, solder(ed)
sawtimise, sodomy(mize)
sawtumy, sodomy
sawuble, soluble(ize)
sawur, sour
sawurdo, sourdough
sawurkraut, sauerkraut
sawurkrowt, sauerkraut
sawvuble, solve(vable)

sawyebul, soluble
sawyubil, soluble
sawzy, saucy
sax, SLANG FOR SAXOPHONE (or see sack(s))
saxophone,*,nic,nist, HORN INSTRUMENT
saxsifone, saxophone
saxsuphone, saxophone
say,*,yer,ying,aid, WHAT HAS BEEN SPOKEN, TO SPEAK VERBALLY "prefixes: un"
sayabil, soluble
sayans, se'ance
sayn, sain / sane / say(ing)
sayons, se'ance
sayulose, cellulose
sbase, space / space(y)
sbaser, space(r)
sbast, space(d)
sbasur, space(r)
sbasy, space(y)
sbegut, spigot
sbekit, spigot
sbekot, spigot
sbidel, spittle
sbidul, spittle
sbiget, spigot
sbikit, spigot
sbikot, spigot
sbital, spittle
sbitul, spittle
sblash, splash
sblat, splat
sblendur, splinter / splendor
sblent, splint
sblerge, splurge
sblerje, splurge
sblet, split
sbletur, split(tter)
sblices, splice(s)
sblin, spline / spleen
sblindur, splinter / splendor
sblint, splint
sblirge, splurge
sblirje, splurge
sblis, splice
sbliser, splice(r)
sblist, splice(d)
sblisur, splice(r)
sblit, split
sbliter, split(tter)
sblitur, split(tter)
sbloch, splotch

sblochy, splotch(y)
sblotch, splotch
sblotchee, splotch(y)
sblurje, splurge
sboel, spoil
sboeld, spoil(ed) / spoilt
sboeleg, spoil(age)
sboil, spoil
sboild, spoil(ed) / spoilt
sboiled, spoil(ed) / spoilt
sboileg, spoil(age)
sboke, spoke
sbon, spoon
sboon, spoon
sbore, spore
sboyl, spoil
sbra, spray
sbraket, sprocket
sbran, sprain
sbrauket, sprocket
sbraul, sprawl
sbre, spree
sbreg, sprig
sbrews, spruce
sbrig, sprig
sbrocket, sprocket
sbroket, sprocket
sbroose, spruce
sbruse, spruce
sbun, spun / spoon
sburd, spur(rred)
sburt, spur(rred)
scab,*,bbed,bbing,bby, CRUST FORMED ON SKIN OVER OPEN WOUND, TERM FOR STRIKE WORKERS
scabard, scabbard
scabbard,*, SWORD SHEATH/ SHEATHE
scabburd, scabbard
scabed, scab(bbed)
scabees, scabies
scaberd, scabbard
scabies,etic,ious, SKIN DISEASE
scaburd, scabbard
scaby, scab(bby)
scad,*, EDIBLE FISH, LARGE NUMBER/ QUANTITY
scader, skate(r) / scatter
scadered, scatter(ed)
scadir, skate(r) / scatter
scadured, scatter(ed)
scaffold,*,ding, TEMPORARY FRAMEWORK WITH PLANKS USED TO BUILD
scafold, scaffold

scair, scare
scairslee, scarce(ly)
scairsness, scarce(ness)
scalar, A PHYSICS EXPRESSION, OF
    MASS AND TIME
scald,*,ded,ding, SURFACE BURN
scale,*,ed,ling,eless,eliness,lable,ly,
    INSTRUMENT FOR MEASURING
    WEIGHT, MUSICAL LADDER, TO
    CLIMB (or see scaly) "prefixes: de/
    over/re/up"
scaleness, scaly(liness)
scaleon, scallion
scalep, scallop
scaleun, scallion
scaley, scaly
scalion, scallion
scalip, scallop
scallion,*, TYPE OF ONION
scallop,*,per, SHELLFISH, TYPE OF DISH/
    SHAPE
scalop, scallop
scalor, scalar
scalp,*,ped,ping, SKIN ON HUMAN
    SKULL, WAY OF SELLING TICKETS (or
    see scallop)
scalpal, scalpel
scalpel,*, A SURGICAL KNIFE
scalpul, scalpel
scalup, scallop
scaly,liness,leless, SIMILAR/SAME AS
    SCALES ON A FISH
scalyin, scallion
scalyun, scallion
scamatic, scheme(matic)
scan,*,nned,nning,nner, A MACHINE
    WHICH COPIES/TAKES DIGITAL
    IMAGES "prefixes: over"
scandal,*,lize,lous,lously,lousness,
    EVENT WHICH DEGRADES/
    OFFENDS A SOCIAL VALUE/IDEA
scandel, scandal
scandelus, scandal(ous)
scandil, scandal
scandolus, scandal(ous)
scandul, scandal
scandulus, scandal(ous)
scaner, scan(nner)
scanerio, scenario
scanir, scan(nner)
scanography, scenography
scant,tily,tness, LIMITED RESOURCE
scantuly, scant(ily)
scanur, scan(nner)

scapala, scapula
scapel, scalpel
scapeula, scapula
scapewla, scapula
scapil, scalpel
scapila, scapula
scapul, scalpel
scapula,*, SHOULDER BLADE
scar,*,rred,rring, A PHYSICAL MARK
    LEFT AFTER A BODILY INJURY HAS
    HEALED (or see scare)
scarce,ely,city,eness, IN DEMAND, RARE
scarcedy, scarce(city)
scare,*,ed,ring,ry, FRIGHTEN/ALARM
scared, scare(d) / scar(rred)
scarf,fes,fed,fing,rves, A LIGHTWEIGHT
    MATERIAL WORN ON THE HEAD,
    TO WOLF DOWN FOOD/DRINK
scarfd, scarf(ed)
scarfs, scarf(rves)
scarft, scarf(ed)
scarlet, A COLOR
scarlut, scarlet
scarse, scarce
scarsedy, scarce(city)
scarsity, scarce(city)
scarsly, scarce(ly)
scarsness, scarce(ness)
scarsudy, scarce(city)
scart, scar(rred) / scare(d)
scary, scare(y)
scat,*,tted,tting, SINGING
    IMPROVISATION, TO HURRY AWAY,
    FISH, ANIMAL FECAL (or see skat/
    skate)
scater, scatter
scathe,*,ed,hing,hingly, TO INJURE/
    HARM "prefixes: un"
scatir, scatter
scatter,*,red,ring,rable, DISPERSED
    ABOUT IRREGULARLY (or see
    skate(r))
scatur, scatter
scauler, scholar
scaulerly, scholar(ly)
scavage, scavenge
scavager, scavenge(r)
scavenge,*,ed,ging,er, SEARCH/SEEK
    FOR USABLE ITEMS
scavuge, scavenge
scavunjer, scavenge(r)
scawler, scholar
scawlerly, scholar(ly)
scem, scheme / skim

scenac, scene(nic)
scenario,*,ist, TO OUTLINE SCENES/
    CHARACTERS FOR PLAY/MOVIE
scenary, scene(ry)
scene,*,ery,eries,nic,nerio,nography,
    VISUAL PRESENTATION OF A PLACE/
    EVENT
scenic, scene(nic)
sceniry, scene(ry)
scenography,hic,her, RULES IN
    CREATING PERSPECTIVE
scent,*,ted,tless,tlessness, ODOR/
    FRAGRANCE
scenur, skinner
sceptacism, skeptic(ism)
sceptasisum, skeptic(ism)
scepter,*,red,ring, ROD OF AUTHORITY/
    ROYALTY
scepticism, skeptic(ism)
sceptik, skeptic
sceptir, scepter
sceptisitum, skeptic(ism)
sceptor, scepter
sceptuk, skeptic
sceptur, scepter
sceptusisum, skeptic(ism)
scer, scare
scerfy, scurvy
sceris, scirrhus / cirrus
scersity, scarce(city)
scersly, scarce(ly)
scersudy, scarce(city)
scerus, scirrhus / cirrus
scery, scurry
scesurs, scissor(s)
scewbu, scuba
scewp, scoop
scewper, scoop(er)
schalastic, scholastic
schaler, scholar
schalerly, scholar(ly)
schamatic, scheme(matic)
schaulerly, scholar(ly)
schedewl, schedule
schedule,*,ed,ling, AN ITEMIZED LIST
    CONCERNING TIME AND
    APPOINTMENTS "prefixes: re"
scheem, scheme
schelastic, scholastic
scheme,*,ed,ming,er,ma,mata,matic,
    matically,matism,matist,matize,
    matization,matizer, PLAN/PLOT/
    PROJECT
schemir, skim(mmer) / scheme(r)

schemur, skim(mmer) / scheme(r)

schilastic, scholastic

schimatic, scheme(matic)

schist,tose,tous, ROCK TYPE DETERMINED BY THE WAY IT EXFOLIATES

schitzophrenia, schizophrenia

schizofrenia, schizophrenia

schizoid, PERTAINING TO SCHIZOPHRENIA

schizophrenia,ic, MENTAL PROBLEM

schizoyd, schizoid

scholar,*,rly,rliness, ONE WHO HAS STUDIED/LEARNED A GREAT DEAL

scholastic,*,cal,cally,cate,cism, RELATED/CONCERNING SCHOOL "prefixes: inter"

scholer, scholar

scholerly, scholar(ly)

school,*,led,ling,ler, A PLACE TO LEARN "prefixes: pre/un"

schooner,*, TYPE OF SAILING VESSEL

schuel, school

schulastic, scholastic

schule, school

schumatic, scheme(matic)

schuner, schooner

sciadeca, sciatic(a)

sciadica, sciatic(a)

scianse, science

sciantifek, scientific

sciantifekaly, scientific(ally)

sciantificly, scientific(ally)

sciatek, sciatic

sciatic,ca,cally, MAJOR NERVES IN THE BODY NEAR THE HIPS

sciatik, sciatic

science,*,ntific,ntist, FIELDS OF GENERAL LAWS CONCERNING EVERYTHING IN OUR REALITY "prefixes: bio"

scientest, scientist

scientifek, scientific

scientific,cally, OF FIELDS OF SCIENCE "prefixes: un"

scientifik, scientific

scientifikaly, scientific(ally)

scientist,*,sm, MAJORS IN THE FIELD OF SCIENCE "prefixes: bio"

scif, skiff

scikyatrus, psychiatry(rist)

scimatic, scheme(matic)

scinario, scenario

scinerio, scenario

scinography, scenography

scint, scent

scinur, skinner

scirfy, scurvy

scirhus, scirrhus / cirrus

scirrhus,hoid,hous, CONCERNING TUMORS IN THE BODY (or see cirrus)

scirus, scirrhus / cirrus

sciry, scurry

scisers, scissor(s)

scissor,*, TOOL TO CUT/SEVER

scisurs, scissor(s)

scith, scythe

sciuntefikaly, scientific(ally)

sciuntist, scientist

scizurs, scissor(s)

scof, scoff

scofed, scoff(ed)

scoff,*,ffed,ffing,ffingly,ffer, SHOW MOCKERY/DISTASTE, RIDUCULE

scold,*,ded,ding, TO FIND FAULT/ REPRIMAND SOMEONE FOR THEIR BEHAVIOR (or see scald)

scoleosis, scoliosis

scoliosis,ic, CURVATURE OF THE SPINE

scolt, scold / scald

sconce,*,ed,cing, LIGHTS ON THE WALL, FORT, SKULL

scone,*, A BREAD CAKE

scons, scone(s) / sconce

sconts, sconce

scooba, scuba

scooder, scoot(er)

scoop,*,ped,ping,per,pful, GATHER UP QUANTITY OF SOMETHING ALL AT ONCE

scoopir, scoop(er)

scoot,*,ted,ting,ter, GO/SEND HASTILY ALONG, SLIDE OVER (or see scute)

scorch,hes,hed,hing,her, LIGHTLY BURN

score,*,ed,ring,er,eless, MARK BY GOUGING/SCRATCHING, POINTS IN COMPETITION "prefixes: over/re/ under"

scorlis, score(less)

scorn,*,ned,ning,ningly,nful,nfully, nfulness, EXPRESS DISTATE/ CONTEMPT

scornfuly, scorn(fully)

scorpeon, scorpion

scorpion,*, AN ARACHNOID

scoul, scowl

scouled, scowl(ed)

scoundrel,*,lly, MEAN PERSON WHO HAS NO HONOR FOR OTHERS

scoundril, scoundrel

scoundrle, scoundrel

scour,*,red,ring,rer, SCRUB CLEAN, GO OVER, PURGE

scourd, scour(ed)

scourge,*,ed,ging,er, TORMENT/ TORTURE/SEVERLY PUNISH

scout,*,ted,ting,ter, TO HUNT/SEARCH FOR

scouwl, scowl

scower, scour

scowl,*,led,ling, WEARING A LOOK OF ANGER

scowndrel, scoundrel

scowr, scour

scowt, scout

scowurd, scour(ed)

scrach, scratch

scrag,*,gged,gging,ggy,gily,gginess,ggly, JAGGED/SKINNY/DISHEVELED/ BONEY/SCRAWNY/LEAN

scraggly,lies,lier,liest,ggily,gginess, UNEVEN/IRREGULAR/DISHEVELED/ MESSY

scragleur, scraggly(lier)

scragliest, scraggly(liest)

scragly, scrag(ily) / scraggly

scrakly, scrag(ily) / scraggly

scram,*,mmed,mming, GO AWAY QUICKLY

scrambal, scramble

scrambil, scramble

scramble,*,ed,ling,er, MIX UP TOGETHER, CLUMSILY TAKE ACTION "prefixes: de/un"

scrambul, scramble

scrap,*,pped,pping,pper,ppage, SMALL PARTICLE/PIECE/FRAGMENT, LEFTOVERS, PICK A FIGHT (or see scrape)

scrape,*,ed,ping,er,pable, RASP/GRATE/ DAMAGE, NOISE BY DRAGGING SOMETHING/MARKS (or see scrap)

scrapt, scrap(pped) / scrape(d)

scrapuble, scrap(able)

scratch,hes,hed,hing,her,hy, MARK/ CUT/CROSS OUT

scrawl,*,led,ling,ly,ler, AWKWARD/ IRREGULAR MARKS AS IF DONE HASTILY

screach, screech

scream,*,med,ming,mer,mingly, A LOUD/SHRILL OUTCRY FROM THE THROAT

screan, screen

screanable, screen(able)

screbul, scribble

screch, screech

scred, screed

screech,hes,hed,hing, SHARP/SHRILL/ LOUD SOUND

screed,*,ded,ding, SEPARATE PARTICLES FROM ONE ANOTHER, PLASTER/ MORTAR TECHNIQUE

screem, scream

screen,*,ned,ning,ner,nable, MATERIAL FOR WINDOWS, TO SORT/SIFT THROUGH

scremp, scrimp

scremshaw, scrimshaw

scren, screen

screped, script

screpsher, scripture

scrept, script

screpture, scripture

screw,*,wed,wing,wer,wy, SMALL CYLINDRICAL OBJECT WITH POINTED TIP/SLOTTED HEAD "prefixes: un"

screwdnee, scrutiny

screwge, scrooge

screwje, scrooge

screwpul, scruple

screwpulus, scrupulous

screwtney, scrutiny

scribble,*,ed,ling,er, SCRAWL, UNDECIPHERABLE MARKS

scribd, scribe(d) / script

scribe,*,ed,bing,er,bal, A WRITER

scrible, scribble

scribul, scribble

scrimage, scrimmage

scrimmage,*,ed,ging, PHYSICAL ROUGH ABOUT WITH OTHERS IN A GAME

scrimp,*,ped,ping,py, TIGHT BUDGET/ SPENDING HABIT

scrimshaw, IVORY CARVING

scrimuge, scrimmage

scrimuje, scrimmage

scripshur, scripture

script,*,ted,ting, THE CHARACTERS/ TEXT OF A PLAY/MOVIE/ BROADCAST/ PROGRAM "prefixes: re/un"

scripture,*,ral,rally,ralness, RELIGIOUS WRITING "prefixes: un"

scroge, scrooge

scroje, scrooge

scrol, scrawl / scroll

scroll,*,lled,lling, PARCHMENT/PAPER ROLLED UP

scrooge, A MISER, TIGHTWAD

scrooje, scrooge

scrooteny, scrutiny

scrounge,*,ed,ging,gy,gier,giest, FORAGE AROUND, A DISHEVELED/ UNKEPT LOOK

scroungy, scrounge(y)

scrowl, scrawl

scrowngy, scrounge(y)

scrownje, scrounge / scrounge(y)

scru, screw

scrub,*,bbed,bbing,bber,bby, RUB/ SCOURGE BRISKLY, LOW GROWTH TREE/SHRUBS

scrudnee, scrutiny

scruf, scruff

scruff,ffy, BACK/NAPE OF NECK

scrufy, scruff(y)

scruge, scrooge

scruje, scrooge

scruny, scrutiny

scrup, scrub

scrupel, scruple

scrupewlus, scrupulous

scruple,*,ed,ling, REMAIN CONSCIOUSLY AWARE/ALERT

scrupol, scruple

scrupulous,osity,sness,sly, BEING CAREFUL CONCERNING WHAT IS RIGHT/PROPER "prefixes: un"

scrut, screw(ed)

scruteny, scrutiny

scrutiny,nize,nizes,nized,nizing,nization, nizer, CLOSELY EXAMINE/EVALUATE

scruwy, screw(y)

scruy, screw(y)

scuba,*, UNDERWATER DEVICE FOR BREATHING

scuder, scoot(er)

scuf, scuff

scufel, scuffle

scuff,*,ffed,ffing, LEAVE MARKS BY WEARING/USAGE/WALKING

scuffle,*,ed,ling, DISORDERLY PHYSICAL STRUGGLE/FIGHT

scufil, scuffle

scuful, scuffle

scul, school / skull

sculbed, sculpt

sculbshir, sculpt(ure)

sculpshir, sculpt(ure)

sculpt,*,ted,ting,tor,ture,tural,turally, FORM BY HUMAN/NATURAL PROCESS TO CREATE 3D IMAGES

sculpter, sculpt(ure)

scum,*,mmed,mming,mmy, NASTY/ VILE/WORTHLESS, RESIDUE LEFT BEHIND

scumatic, scheme(matic)

scumy, scum(mmy)

scunario, scenario

scuner, schooner

scup, scoop

scupd, scoop(ed)

scupt, scoop(ed)

scurfy, scurvy

scurry,rries,rried,rrying, TO SCAMPER/ HURRY

scurvy,vies,vier,viest,vily,viness, A DISEASE

scury, scurry

scute,*, BONY PLATE/SHIELD (or see scoot)

scuter, scoot(er)

scwaled, squalid

scwolid, squalid

scythe,*,ed,hing, A TOOL WITH LONG BLADE USED IN SWEEPING MOTIONS TO CUT GRASS/GRAIN

sdabul, stable

sdaroyd, steroid

sdash, stash

sdemulashen, stimulate(tion)

sdemulate, stimulate

sdemulation, stimulate(tion)

sderdy, sturdy

sdergen, sturgeon

sderjon, sturgeon

sderoed, steroid

sderoet, steroid

sderoyd, steroid

sderty, sturdy

sdewdeo, studio

sdewdeus, studious

sdewpendus, stupendous

sdewper, stupor

sdewpid, stupid

sdewpir, stupor

sdewpur, stupor

sdifel, stifle

sdiful, stifle

sdil, style / still
sdilesh, style(lish)
sdilest, style(list)
sdilist, style(list)
sdilush, style(lish)
sdime, stymie
sdimulashen, stimulate(tion)
sdimulate, stimulate
sdimulation, stimulate(tion)
sdirafom, styrofoam
sdirdy, sturdy
sdirefom, styrofoam
sdirty, sturdy
sdirufom, styrofoam
sdo, stow / store
sdoe, stow
sdoek, stoic
sdogee, stogy
sdogy, stogy
sdoik, stoic
sdok, stuck
sdol, stole
sdolen, stole(n)
sdolun, stole(n)
sdon, stun
sdools, stool(s)
sdooped, stupid
sdoopid, stupid
sdoopidudy, stupid(ity)
sdoopiduty, stupid(ity)
sdoopir, stupor
sdoopufid, stupefy(fied)
sdoopur, stupor
sdopid, stupid
sdored, story(ried)
sdoree, story
sdoreg, storage
sdorej, storage
sdores, story(ries)
sdorig, storage
sdorij, storage
sdorm, storm
sdormee, storm(y)
sdow, stow
sdowek, stoic
sdowik, stoic
sdra, straw / stray
sdradagee, strategy
sdradajist, strategy(gist)
sdrade, stray(ed) / straight
sdrades, stratus
sdradis, stratus
sdradugee, strategy
sdradugist, strategy(gist)

sdradus, stratus
sdrae, stray
sdrain, strain
sdrand, strain(ed) / strand
sdrane, strain
sdrap, strap
sdras, stress
sdratagee, strategy
sdrategek, strategic
sdrategekly, strategic(ally)
sdrategist, strategy(gist)
sdrategy, strategy
sdratejik, strategic
sdratejikly, strategic(ally)
sdratejist, strategy(gist)
sdrates, stratus
sdratesfere, stratosphere
sdratesphere, stratosphere
sdratigek, strategic
sdratigekly, strategic(ally)
sdratis, stratus
sdratosfere, stratosphere
sdratosphere, stratosphere
sdratugee, strategy
sdratugist, strategy(gist)
sdratus, stratus
sdratusfere, stratosphere
sdratusphere, stratosphere
sdraw, straw
sdrayd, stray(ed) / straight
sdreakee, streak(y)
sdrech, stretch
sdrecher, stretch(er)
sdrechr, stretch(er)
sdrechur, stretch(er)
sdreek, streak
sdreem, stream
sdreet, street
sdrek, streak
sdrekd, strict / streak(ed)
sdreke, streak(y)
sdreknine, strychnine
sdrekun, stricken
sdreky, streak(y)
sdrem, stream
sdremer, stream(er)
sdremur, stream(er)
sdreneus, strenuous
sdrenewus, strenuous
sdreng, string
sdrengee, string(y)
sdrengint, stringent
sdrenjint, stringent
sdrenkth, strength

sdrenth, strength
sdrenues, strenuous
sdrep, strep/ strip /stripe
sdrepd, stripe(d) / strip(pped)
sdreped, stripe(d) / strip(pped)
sdreper, stripe(r) / strip(pper)
sdrepur, stripe(r) / strip(pper)
sdres, stress
sdresh, stretch
sdret, street
sdreun, strewn
sdrew, strew
sdriashen, striate(tion)
sdriate, striate
sdriation, striate(tion)
sdrife, strife / strive
sdrik, strike
sdrikd, strict
sdriked, strict
sdriken, stricken
sdriknin, strychnine
sdrikun, stricken
sdrinewus, strenuous
sdring, string
sdringee, string(y)
sdrinjint, stringent
sdrinkth, strength
sdrinth, strength
sdrinues, strenuous
sdrip, strep/ strip /stripe
sdriped, stripe(d) / strip(pped)
sdripur, stripe(r) / strip(pper)
sdrivd, strive(d)
sdrive, strive / strife
sdro, straw
sdrobe, strobe
sdroganoff, stroganoff
sdroginof, stroganoff
sdroke, stroke
sdrol, stroll
sdroler, stroll(er)
sdrolur, stroll(er)
sdrong, strong
sdrongist, strong(est)
sdrongur, strong(er)
sdroodel, strudel
sdroodul, strudel
sdroon, strewn
sdrope, strobe
sdru, strew
sdruc, struck
sdud, stood / stud
sdrudel, strudel
sdrudid, strut(tted)

sdrudil, strudel
sdrudul, strudel
sdrueng, strew(ing)
sdrugel, struggle
sdrugul, struggle
sdruk, struck
sdrukchur, structure
sdrukshur, structure
sdrukul, struggle
sdrum, strum
sdrumer, strum(mmer)
sdrun, strewn
sdrung, strung
sdrut, strut
sdrutegek, strategic
sdrutegekly, strategic(ally)
sdrutejik, strategic
sdrutigekly, strategic(ally)
sdruz, strew(s)
sdryate, striate
sdubee, stub(bby)
sdubel, stubble
sdubern, stubborn
sduble, stubble
sduborn, stubborn
sdubul, stubble
sduburn, stubborn
sduby, stub(bby)
sduded, study(died) / stud(dded)
sdudee, study
sdudeo, studio
sduder, stutter
sdudes, study(dies)
sdudeus, studious
sdudio, studio
sdudir, stutter
sdudius, studious
sdudur, stutter
sdudy, study
sduel, stool
sdufee, stuff(y)
sduil, stool
sduk, stuck
sduko, stucco
sdule, stool
sdump, stump
sdumpee, stump(y)
sdun, stun
sdunk, stunk
sdunt, stunt / stun(nned)
sduol, stool
sdupafid, stupefy(fied)
sduped, stub(bbed) / stupid
sdupedudy, stupid(ity)

sdupeduty, stupid(ity)
sdupefy, stupefy
sdupel, stubble
sdupendus, stupendous
sduper, stupor
sdupidudy, stupid(ity)
sdupiduty, stupid(ity)
sdupify, stupefy
sdupil, stubble
sdupindus, stupendous
sdupir, stupor
sduple, stubble
sdupt, stub(bbed)
sdupud, stupid
sdupufie, stupefy
sdupul, stubble
sdupur, stupor
sdurdy, sturdy
sdurgen, sturgeon
sdurjon, sturgeon
sduter, stutter
sduty, study
sdwaple, squabble
sdylesh, style(lish)
sdyme, stymie
sdyrafom, styrofoam
se'ance, A COMMUNICATION WITH
SPIRITS BEYOND THE PHYSICAL
PLANE
sea,*, LARGE SALTWATER BODY/OCEAN
(or see see) "prefixes: over/under"
seable, see(able)
seabul, see(able)
sead, seed / said
seaesta, siesta
seafood,*, EDIBLE SHELLFISH/AQUATIC
ANIMALS
seal,*,led,ling,ler,lery,leries, AQUATIC
MAMMAL, CLOSE SOMETHING
TIGHTLY "prefixes: un/under"
sealeng, seal(ing) / ceiling
seam,*,med,ming,mer,mless,mlessly,
mlessness,my, A LINE/ PLACE
WHERE TWO PIECES OF MATERIAL
ARE JOINED (or see seem)
"prefixes: in/un"
seamen, semen
seamin, semen
seamly, seem(ly)
seamstress,ter, ONE WHO SEWS
sean, scene / seen
sear,*,red,ring, SCORCH/BURN/GRAZE
A SURFACE (or see seer)
seara, sierra

search,hes,hed,hing,her,hable,hingly,
hingness, TO LOOK/SEEK FOR
SOMETHING "prefixes: un"
searchuble, search(able)
searus, scirrhus / cirrus
seas, cease / sea(s) / see(s) / seize
seasan, season
seashell,*, SHELL OF A MOLLUSK
seasin, season
season,*,ned,ning,nal,nally,ner,nable,
nably,nableness, TIME OF THE YEAR,
MIXTURE OF HERBS/SPICES FOR
FOOD, EXPERIENCED/SKILLED
"prefixes: un"
seasun, season
seat,*,ted,ting,ter, A PLACE/CHAIR/
BENCH TO SIT, SOMETHING FIRMLY
FIT INTO PLACE, VACANCY FOR A
PERSON "prefixes: re/un"
seath, seethe
seaz, seize
sebconchus, subconscious
sebkonshes, subconscious
sebkontrakt, subcontract
sebling, sibling
sebtek, septic
sebtember, september
sebtik, septic
sebtimbur, september
seburat, separate
sec, sic / sick
secandery, second(ary)
secandly, second(ly)
secant,*, MATHEMATICAL EXPRESSION,
DIVIDE INTO TWO PARTS (or see
second/secund)
secede,*,ed,ding,er, POLITICAL
WITHDRAWAL
secendly, second(ly)
secesion, secession
secession,nal,nism,nist, TO SECEDE/
WITHDRAW
secewler, secular
sech, sedge
sechewashen, situate(tion)
sechewation, situate(tion)
sechuate, situate
sechuation, situate(tion)
secindery, second(ary)
seckal, sickle
secks, sex
seckstee, sixty

seclude,ed,ding,usion,usive, BECOME PRIVATE/ISOLATED/SHELTERED FROM

seclushen, seclusion

seclusion,ive, BECOME SECLUDED

seclusive,ely,eness, BECOME SECLUDED

seclution, seclusion

second,*,ded,dly,dary,darily,der, AFTER THE FIRST, NOT PRIMARY, MEASURE OF TIME (or see secant/ secund)

secondery, second(ary)

secoority, secure(rity)

secragate, segregate

secrat, secret

secratary, secretary

secratereul, secretary(rial)

secratery, secretary

secrative, secret(ive)

secreshen, secrete(tion)

secret,*,tly,tness,ecy,tive,tively,tiveness, PRIVATE KNOWLEDGE ONLY FEW SHARE, HIDE FROM OTHERS (or see secrete) "prefixes: post/semi"

secretareul, secretary(rial)

secretary,ries,rial, ONE WHO MAINTAINS PRIMARY OPERATIONS OF AN OFFICE "prefixes: under"

secrete,*,ed,ting,tion,tionary,tor,tory, FLUIDS THAT EXCRETE/DISCHARGE FROM ANIMALS/PLANTS/HUMANS

secretion, secrete(tion)

secrit, secret

secritary, secretary

secritereul, secretary(rial)

secritery, secretary

secritive, secret(ive)

secritly, secret(ly)

secrut, secret

secrutary, secretary

secrutereul, secretary(rial)

secrutery, secretary

secrutive, secret(ive)

secrutly, secret(ly)

secshen, section

secshenul, section(al)

secshun, section

secshunal, section(al)

sect,*,tarian,tarianism,tarianize, tarianizes,tarianized,tarianizing,tary, tile,tility, tion, SEGMENT/SECTION OF SOMETHING "prefixes: bi"

secter, sector

section,*,ned,ning,nal,nally,nalize, nalizes,nalized,nalizing,nalization, nalism, ONE PART OF THE WHOLE "prefixes: inter/re/sub"

sectir, sector

sector,*,rial, A PART/DIVISION OF THE WHOLE "prefixes: bi"

sectur, sector

secular,rly,rism,rist,ristic,rity,rities,rize, rizer, UNBIND FROM RELIGIOUS BELIEF

seculir, secular

secumb, succumb

secund,dly, BOTANICAL TERM (or see second/secant)

secundery, second(ary)

secundly, second(ly)

secure,*,ed,ring,rable,ely,eness,ement, er,rity,rities, PROTECT FROM CERTAIN ELEMENTS, KEEP FIRMLY IN PLACE "prefixes: bio/in/un"

securety, secure(rity)

securidy, secure(rity)

sed, said / set / seed

sedalment, settle(ment)

sedam, sedum

sedamentary, sediment(ary)

sedamint, sediment

sedan,*, TYPE OF VEHICLE

sedantary, sedentary

sedashen, sedate(tion)

sedasion, sedate(tion)

sedate,*,ed,ting,ely,eness,tion,tive, APPEASE/SUBSIDE/CALM

sedelment, settle(ment)

sedem, sedum

sedemint, sediment

sedentary,riness, NOT MUCH MOVEMENT/STILL

sedews, seduce

sedge,*,gy, A SWAMP GRASS WITH EDGES

sedil, settle

sedilment, settle(ment)

sedim, sedum

sediment,*,tary,tal,tation,tology,tologic, tologist, ACCUMULATION OF MATTER CARRIED BY LIQUID

sedle, settle

sedlers, settle(rs)

sedling, seedling / settle(ling)

sedlment, settle(ment)

sedol, settle

sedom, sedum

sedoose, seduce

seduce,*,ed,cing,er,cible,ction,ctive, ement,ctively,ctiveness, COERCED/ ENTICED AWAY FROM NORMAL PATTERN OF BEHAVIOR

seducshen, seduce(ction)

seductif, seduce(ctive)

seduktion, seduce(ction)

seduktive, seduce(ctive)

sedul, settle

sedulers, settle(rs)

sedulment, settle(ment)

sedum,*, A PLANT

sedumentary, sediment(ary)

sedumint, sediment

seduntary, sedentary

seduse, seduce

sedy, seed(y)

see,*,eeable,eeing,een,eeing,eer,saw, USE OF THE EYES, VISUAL IMAGING (or see sea/seize) "prefixes: over"

seed,*,ded,ding,dless,dful,der,dy,dling, PLANT POD THAT HOLDS THE FUTURE, DNA BLUEPRINTS "prefixes: re/un"

seedling,*, GROWTH BURSTING FROM A SEED

seefood, seafood

seefud, seafood

seeg, siege

seej, siege

seek,*,ked,king,ker, TO SEARCH FOR

seekratif, secret(ive)

seekrutif, secret(ive)

seel, seal

seeld, seal(ed)

seem,*,med,ming,mingly,mingness,mly, mliness, APPEARS TO BE FACTUAL/ TRUTHFUL/REAL, COULD BE (or see seam) "prefixes: un"

seemstras, seamstress

seemstrus, seamstress

seen, PAST TENSE FOR THE WORD "SEE" (or see scene/seine) "prefixes: un"

seena, sienna

seengle, single

seengul, single

seengulerety, singular(ity)

seep,*,ped,ping,py,page, THE OOZING OF LIQUID THROUGH A BARRIER (or see sipe/ sip)

seepige, seep(age)

seepuge, seep(age)

seer,*, ONE WHO SEES/HAS SPIRITUAL INSIGHT/PREDICTOR OF THE FUTURE (or see sear)
seera, sierra
sees, see(s) / sea(s) / seize / cease / say(s)
seesan, season
seeshell, seashell
seesin, season
seesta, siesta
seesun, season
seethe,*,ed,hing,hingly, STATE OF AGITATION/EMOTION THAT IS BARELY CONTAINED
seety, seed(y)
seez, seize / cease / sea(s) / see(s)
sef, sieve
sefal, civil
sefalezation, civil(ization)
sefalis, syphilis
seful, civil
sefulization, civil(ization)
sefan, seven
sefanteen, seventeen
sefanth, seventh
sefaree, safari
sefenteith, seventieth
sefestikashen, sophisticate(tion)
sefestikation, sophisticate(tion)
sefichent, sufficient
sefichunt, sufficient
sefin, seven
sefinteen, seventeen
sefinteith, seventieth
sefinth, seventh
sefise, suffice
sefishent, sufficient
sefishunt, sufficient
sefistukashen, sophisticate(tion)
sefistukation, sophisticate(tion)
seflus, syphilis
sefon, seven
sefonteen, seventeen
sefood, seafood
sefral, several
sefrense, severance
sefril, several
sefrinse, severance
sefrul, several
sefrunse, severance
sefud, seafood
seful, civil
sefules, syphilis
sefulezation, civil(ization)

sefulization, civil(ization)
sefun, seven
sefunteen, seventeen
sefunteith, seventieth
sefunth, seventh
seg, siege / sedge
segar, cigar
segaret, cigarette
sege, sedge / siege
seged, siege(d)
seger, seize(zure)
seges, sedge(s) / siege(s)
segir, seize(zure)
segis, sedge(s)
segjest, suggest
segjestion, suggest(ion)
segjestshen, suggest(ion)
segma, sigma
segment,*,ted,ting,tary,tal,tally,tation, ONE PORTION/SECTION OF THE WHOLE
segmentul, segment(al)
segmintul, segment(al)
segmu, sigma
segnafiable, signify(fiable)
segnafier, signify(fier)
segnature, signature
segnifukent, significant
segnucher, signature
segnul, signal
segnushure, signature
segragashen, segregate(tion)
segragate, segregate
segregate,*,ed,ting,tion,tionist,tive,tor, able,ant, SET APART, SEPARATE/ DIVIDE FROM THE WHOLE
segrigate, segregate
segrugashen, segregate(tion)
segrugate, segregate
segur, seize(zure)
seguret, cigarette
segus, sedge(s)
seible, see(able)
seige, siege / sage
seine, A NET (or see seen/scene)
seing, see(ing)
seir, sear / seer
seira, sierra
seism,mic,mical,mically,micity,micities, mism,mogram,mograph,mology, mologist, FREQUENCY/WAVES OF THE EARTH, EARTHQUAKE
seista, siesta

seize,*,ed,zing,zure,zer, TO GRAB/ CONFISCATE QUICKLY/ FORECEFULLY (or see cease) "prefixes: dis"
sej, sedge / siege
sejd, siege(d)
sejer, seize(zure)
sejes, sedge(s)
sejt, siege(d)
sejur, seize(zure)
sejus, sedge(s)
sek, sic / sick / seek
sekal, sickle
sekamore, sycamore
sekand, secant / second / secund
sekandery, second(ary)
sekandly, second(ly)
sekendly, second(ly)
sekent, secant / second / secund
sekently, second(ly)
sekeuridy, secure(rity)
sekewlir, secular
sekewlur, secular
sekewr, secure
sekewrity, secure(rity)
sekiatrist, psychiatry(rist)
sekiatry, psychiatry
sekil, sickle
sekind, secant / second / secund
sekindery, second(ary)
sekindly, second(ly)
sekintly, second(ly)
sekir, seek(er)
sekle, sickle
seklushen, seclusion
seklusion, seclusion
seklusive, seclusive
sekma, sigma
sekment, segment
sekmentul, segment(al)
sekmint, segment
seknafiur, signify(fier)
seknafy, signify
seknashure, signature
seknifukent, significant
seknishure, signature
seknol, signal
seknucher, signature
seknul, signal
sekol, sickle
sekondery, second(ary)
sekragashen, segregate(tion)
sekragate, segregate
sekragation, segregate(tion)

sekrat, secret
sekratary, secretary
sekratereul, secretary(rial)
sekratery, secretary
sekratif, secret(ive)
sekrative, secret(ive)
sekregation, segregate(tion)
sekreshen, secrete(tion)
sekresion, secrete(tion)
sekret, secret / secrete
sekretive, secret(ive)
sekretly, secret(ly)
sekrigashen, segregate(tion)
sekrigate, segregate
sekrigation, segregate(tion)
sekrit, secret
sekritary, secretary
sekritereul, secretary(rial)
sekritery, secretary
sekritive, secret(ive)
sekritly, secret(ly)
sekrogate, segregate
sekrtly, secret(ly)
sekrugashen, segregate(tion)
sekrugate, segregate
sekrugation, segregate(tion)
sekrut, secret
sekrutary, secretary
sekrutef, secret(ive)
sekrutereul, secretary(rial)
sekrutery, secretary
sekrutive, secret(ive)
sekrutly, secret(ly)
seks, seek(s) / sex
sekshen, section
sekshenul, section(al)
sekshin, section
sekshinul, section(al)
sekshuel, sexual
sekshuil, sexual
sekshun, section
sekshunal, section(al)
sekshwal, sexual
seksion, section
seksis, sex(es)
seksless, sex(less)
sekst, sex(ed)
sekstant, sextant
sekste, sixty
seksteen, sixteen
seksteenth, sixteen(th)
sekstent, sextant
sekstet, sextet
seksteuth, sixtieth

seksth, sixth
sekstile, sextile
sekstileon, sextillion
sekstillion, sextillion
sekstiuth, sixtieth
sekstuple, sextuple
sekstuplet, sextuplet
sekstupul, sextuple
seksty, sixty
seksualedy, sexual(ity)
seksuality, sexual(ity)
seksus, sex(es)
seksy, sex(y)
sekt, sect / seek(ed)
sekter, sector
sekth, sixth
sektion, section
sektional, section(al)
sektir, sector
sektur, sector
sekul, sickle
sekular, secular
sekulir, secular
sekum, succumb
sekund, secant / second / secund
sekundery, second(ary)
sekundly, second(ly)
sekuntly, second(ly)
sekure, secure
sekuredy, secure(rity)
sekurity, secure(rity)
sekurly, secure(ly)
sekwal, sequel
sekwel, sequel
sekwen, sequin
sekwense, sequence
sekwenshul, sequence(ntial)
sekwential, sequence(ntial)
sekwents, sequence
sekwil, sequel
sekwin, sequin
sekwinse, sequence
sekwoia, sequoia
sekwoya, sequoia
sekwul, sequel
sekwunts, sequence
sel, seal / sell / sale / cell / sail
selabet, celibate
selabil, syllable
selable, syllable
selabrate, celebrate
selabus, syllabus
selafane, cellophane
selakit, silica(te)

selal, salal
selami, salami
selanoid, solenoid
selaphane, cellophane
selar, cellar / sell(er) / seal(er)
selareum, solarium
selary, celery
selawet, silhouette
seld, seal(ed) / sold
seldem, seldom
seldemly, seldom(ly)
seldom,mly,mness, RARELY/
    INFREQUENTLY
seldumly, seldom(ly)
selebrety, celebrity
selebusy, celibate(acy)
select,*,ted,ting,tion,tionist,tness,tor,
    tee,tive,tively,tiveness, tivity,
    CHOOSE ONE AMONG MANY
    "prefixes: de"
selee, silly
selekshen, select(ion)
selekt, select
selektif, select(ive)
selektion, select(ion)
selektive, select(ive)
seleng, ceiling / seal(ing)
selenic,ide,iferous,ious,ite,ium,
    CHEMICAL ELEMENT
selenium,iferous, NONMETALLIC
    ELEMENT
selenoid, solenoid
seler, cellar / seal(er) / sell(er)
selery, celery
self,lves,fless,flessly,flessness,fish,
    FIRST PERSON
selfer, silver
selferware, silverware
selfesh, selfish
selfeshly, selfish(ly)
selfir, silver
selfish,hly,hness, LESS THOUGHT FOR
    OTHERS THAN FOR SELF "prefixes:
    un"
selfishlis, selfish(less)
selflis, self(less)
selflisness, self(lessness)
selfs, self(lves)
selfurware, silverware
selfury, silver(y)
selfush, selfish
seli, silly
selibet, celibate
selibrate, celebrate

selibuse, celibate(acy)
selicon, silicon / silicone
selifane, cellophane
selilaquy, soliloquy
selines, silly(lliness)
seling, ceiling / sell(ing) / seal(ing)
selinoid, solenoid
selir, cellar / seal(er) / sell(er)
seliset, solicit
selisetation, solicit(ation)
seliseter, solicit(er)
selivu, saliva
selk, silk
selkun, silk(en)
selky, silk(y)
sell,*,lling,ller,sale,sold, TRADE GOODS/
    SERVICES FOR MONEY (or see sail/
    sale/sill/seal) "prefixes: over/un/
    under"
seller, cellar / sell(er)
sellfish, selfish
selluler, cellular
sellur, cellar / sell(er) / seal(er)
seloet, silhouette
selofane, cellophane
selomee, salami
selon, salon
selonoid, solenoid
seloon, saloon
seloot, salute
selor, cellar / seal(er) / sell(er)
sels, sell(s) / seal(s) / sail(s)
selseus, celsius
selt, seal(ed) / sold / silt / sail(ed)
seltashen, silt(ation)
seltation, silt(ation)
seltem, seldom
seltum, seldom
selty, silt(y)
selubasy, celibate(acy)
selubel, syllable
selubet, celibate
selubrate, celebrate
selubus, syllabus
selufane, cellophane
selukon, silicon / silicone
selular, cellular
selulite, cellulite
selulose, cellulose
selune, saloon
selunoid, solenoid
selur, cellar / sell(er) / seal(er)
selure, celery
selushen, solution

selute, salute
selution, solution
selverware, silverware
selvir, silver
selvurware, silverware
selvury, silver(y)
sely, silly
semalarity, similar(ity)
semaler, similar
semalerly, similar(ly)
semanar, seminar
semantics,cal,cally,cist, STUDY OF
    LANGUAGE/WORDS
semar, simmer
semashen, sum(mmation)
semation, sum(mmation)
sematry, symmetry
sembal, symbol
sembalism, symbol(ism)
sembathetik, sympathetic
sembathy, sympathy
sembeodik, symbiotic
sembeosis, symbiosis
sembeotek, symbiotic
sembilism, symbol(ism)
sembiosis, symbiosis
semblance,*, SIMILARITY/
    RESEMBLANCE
semble, symbol
semblents, semblance
semblinse, semblance
sembolek, symbol(ic)
sembolik, symbol(ic)
sembul, cymbal / symbol
sembulism, symbol(ism)
sembuthetik, sympathetic
sembuthy, sympathy
semdum, symptom
semecolon, semicolon
semekolun, semicolon
semelur, similar
semelurly, similar(ly)
semen,miniferous,minal, SUBSTANCE
    CONTAINING MALE SPERM
semenal, seminal
semenar, seminar
sement, cement
semenul, seminal
semesder, semester
semester,*,tral,trial, SIX MONTH
    PERIOD OF TIME
semetary, cemetery
semetric, symmetry(ric)
semetry, symmetry

semeulate, simulate
semewlation, simulate(tion)
semfeny, symphony
semfonic, symphony(nic)
semfune, symphony
semi, PREFIX INDICATING "HALF/
    PARTLY" MOST OFTEN MODIFIES
    THE WORD
semicolon,*, A PUNCTUATION MARK
semikolin, semicolon
semilarity, similar(ity)
semiler, similar
semilerly, similar(ly)
semin, semen
seminal,lly,niferous, CAPABLE OF
    CREATING LIFE/FUTURE
    DEVELOPMENT
seminar,*,rian,ries,ry, A GROUP OF
    PEOPLE CONVERGING TOGETHER
    TO LEARN ONE THING IN
    PARTICULAR
semingly, seem(ingly)
semir, simmer
semitary, cemetery
semliness, seem(liness)
semly, seem(ly)
semon, semen
semonal, seminal
semonar, seminar
semoolader, simulate(tor)
sempal, simple
sempalest, simple(st)
sempaly, simple(ly)
sempathee, sympathy
sempathetic, sympathetic
sempathize, sympathy(hize)
sempathy, sympathy
sempdum, symptom
sempel, simple
sempelist, simple(st)
sempethy, sympathy
semphonek, symphony(nic)
semphonic, symphony(nic)
semphuny, symphony
sempithize, sympathy(hize)
sempithy, sympathy
semple, simple
sempler, simple(r)
semplest, simple(st)
semplisity, simple(licity)
semplistec, simple(listic)
semply, simple(ly)
sempol, simple
sempoler, simple(r)

sempolest, simple(st)
semposeum, symposium
sempozeum, symposium
semptem, symptom
semptum, symptom
sempul, simple
sempuler, simple(r)
sempulest, simple(st)
sempuly, simple(ly)
semputhee, sympathy
semputhetic, sympathetic
semputhize, sympathy(hize)
semstras, seamstress
semstrus, seamstress
semtem, symptom
semtum, symptom
semulader, simulate(tor)
semularly, similar(ly)
semulashen, simulate(tion)
semulate, simulate
semulation, simulate(tion)
semulator, simulate(tor)
semuler, similar
semulerly, similar(ly)
semullarety, similar(ity)
semun, semen
semunal, seminal
semunar, seminar
semur, simmer
semutare, cemetery
semutree, symmetry
semwat, somewhat
semwere, somewhere
semwhat, somewhat
semwhere, somewhere
semwot, somewhat
sen, seen / scene / seine / sin
senada, sonata
senak, scene(nic)
senamon, cinnamon
senanem, synonym
senapse, synapse
senapsis, synapsis
senaptek, synaptic
senaptic, synaptic
senareo, scenario
senary, scene(ry)
senaster, sinister
senate,tor, A BODY/HOUSE OF U.S.
    GOVERNMENT
senator,*,rial,rially,rship, ELECTED
    MEMBER OF THE U.S.
    GOVERNMENT
senatoriel, senator(ial)

senatu, sonata
senc, sync / sink / since
sench, cinch
senched, singe(d) / cinch(ed)
senchro, synchro
senchronus, synchrony(nous)
sencht, singe(d) / cinch(ed)
senchual, sensual
sencro, synchro
sencronize, synchrony(nize)
sencrony, synchrony
send,*,ding,der,nt, PUSH/ENCOURAGE
    SOMETHING TO LEAVE YOUR
    VICINITY, HAVE DELIVERED
sendamental, sentiment(al)
sendamintal, sentiment(al)
sender, cinder / send(er)
sendicate, syndicate
sendication, syndicate(tion)
sendikation, syndicate(tion)
sendiket, syndicate
sendral, central
sendrem, syndrome
sendrum, syndrome
sendukit, syndicate
sendumentil, sentiment(al)
sendumeter, centimeter
sene, scene / seen
sened, sin(nned)
senek, scene(nic)
senema, cinema
seneority, senior(ity)
sener, sin(nner)
senerist, scenario(ist)
senery, scene(ry)
senete, senate
senetor, senator
senew, sinew
senful, sin(ful)
senfuly, sin(fully)
seng, sing / sink / singe / cinch
sengal, single
senge, singe / cinch
senged, singe(d) / cinch(ed)
sengel, single
senger, sing(er)
sengewler, singular
sengle, single
sengs, sing(s) / sink(s)
sengt, singe(d) / cinch(ed)
sengul, single
sengularedy, singular(ity)
sengularly, singular(ly)
senguled, single(d)

senguler, singular
senguleridy, singular(ity)
senguly, single(ly)
senical, cynical
senik, cynic / scene(nic)
senile,lity, WHEN THE MIND CEASES TO
    STAY SHARP/ALERT DUE TO AGING
senilidy, senile(lity)
senior,*,rity, UPPER RANK, OLDER
    THAN MOST, HIGHER IN CLASS
senir, sin(nner)
senirgy, synergy
seniry, scene(ry)
senistur, sinister
senite, senate
senitor, senator
senitoreul, senator(ial)
senj, singe / cinch
senjt, singe(d) / cinch(ed)
senk, sync / sink
senker, sink(er) / sing(er)
senkewler, singular
senkil, single
senkir, sink(er) / sing(er)
senkle, single(ly)
senkranes, synchrony(nous)
senkro, synchro
senkrone, synchrony
senkronize, synchrony(nize)
senkrunus, synchrony(nous)
senkt, sink(ed)
senkul, single
senkularedy, singular(ity)
senkularly, singular(ly)
senkuler, singular
senkur, sink(er) / sing(er)
senles, sin(less)
senoda, sonata
senodu, sonata
senografee, scenography
senography, scenography
senonemus, synonym(ous)
senonim, synonym
senonimus, synonym(ous)
senonym, synonym
senopsis, synopsis
senota, sonata
senotor, senator
sens, sense / since / cent(s) / sin(s) /
    scene(s)
sensability, sensible(bility)
sensable, sensible
sensaridy, sincere(rity)
sensarity, sincere(rity)

sensashen, sensation

sensation,*,nal,nally,nalism,nalist, nalistic, A FEELING/SENSE/ KNOWINGNESS OF AN AFFECT

sensative, sensitive

sensatize, sensitize

sensd, sense(d)

sense,*,ed,sing,eless,sor,sors,sorial, sorially,sorium,sory, FEEL/KNOW THE SIX SENSES; SOUND/SIGHT/ SMELL/TASTE/ TOUCH/FEEL (or see sent/cent(s)/scene(s)) "prefixes: non"

sensebility, sensible(bility)

senseble, sensible

senser, sincere / censor

sensere, sincere / censor

senseredy, sincere(rity)

senserity, sincere(rity)

senserly, sincere(ly)

sensetize, sensitize

senshewality, sensual(ity)

senshewus, sensuous

senshual, sensual

senshuality, sensual(ity)

senshues, sensuous

senshuil, sensual

senshury, century

sensible,eness,ly,bility,bilities, BE NORMAL/PREDICTABLE TO OTHERS "prefixes: in"

sensir, sensor / censor / censure

sensitive,ely,eness,vity,vities,ize,ization, izer, READILY RESPONDS TO STIMULUS "prefixes: de/in/pre"

sensitivity, sensitive(vity)

sensitize,*,ed,zing,zation,er, BECOME VERY SENSITIVE TO STIMULUS "prefixes: de"

sensless, sense(less)

sensor,*,red,ring,rial,rially,rium,ry, ABLE TO RESPOND TO A PARTICULAR STIMULUS/IMPULSE (or see censor/censure) "prefixes: bio"

sensoreal, sensor(ial)

sensual,lity,lly,lism,list,listic,lize,lization, uous, OPEN TO THE BODY'S EXPRESSION/DESIRE/FEELINGS, UNINHIBITED

sensuble, sensible

sensuous,sly,sness, OF BEING SENSUAL

sensur, sensor / censor / censure

sensus, census / sense(s)

sensutive, sensitive

sensutivity, sensitive(vity)

sensutize, sensitize

sent, PAST TENSE FOR THE WORD 'SEND' (or see scent/sin(nned))

sentaks, syntax

sentamental, sentiment(al)

sentax, syntax

sentchuous, sensuous

sented, scent(ed)

senteince, sentient(ncy)

senteint, sentient

sentekit, syndicate

sentement, sentiment

sentemental, sentiment(al)

sentence,*,ed,cing,ntial,ntially, COMPLETE THOUGHT GRAMMATICALLY, FORMAL JUDGEMENT/DECISION

senteneul, centennial

sentennial, centennial

sentense, sentence

senter, center

senthasis, synthesis

senthasize, synthesize

senthedik, synthetic

senthesis, synthesis

senthetic, synthetic

senthusis, synthesis

sentient,tly,nce,ncy, ABILITY/FACULTY TO PERCEIVE CONSCIOUSLY "prefixes: in/pre"

sentigrade, centigrade

sentiment,*,tal,tally,tality,talities,talism, talist,talize,talizes,talized,talizing, talization, EMOTIONALLY SWAYED BY THE PAST

sentimeter, centimeter

sentineol, centennial

sentinse, sentence

sentipede, centipede

sentless, scent(less)

sentrul, central

sentrulize, centralize

sentry,ries, A GUARD FOR GATE/ENTRY

sents, since / sense / cent(s) / scent(s)

senttance, sentence

sentument, sentiment

sentumental, sentiment(al)

sentury, century

senu, sinew

senuee, sinew(y)

senuk, scene(nic)

senunem, synonym

senupeded, centipede

senur, sin(nner)

senurgy, synergy

senury, scene(ry)

senuster, sinister

senute, senate

senutor, senator

senutoreul, senator(ial)

senutorial, senator(ial)

senuw, sinew

senuy, sinew(y)

senyer, senior

senyority, senior(ity)

senyuee, sinew(y)

senyur, senior

seonse, se'ance

sep, seep / sip / sipe

sepage, seep(age)

sepal,*,led,lous,loid, PART OF A FLOWER

separable,bility,eness,bly, ABLE TO BE SEPARATED "prefixes: in"

separador, separator

separashen, separate(tion)

separate,*,ed,ting,tion,ely,eness,tist, tism,tistic,tive,tor, DIVIDE/BREAK APART FROM THE WHOLE "prefixes: bio"

separator,*, THAT WHICH ENCOURAGES SEPARATION

separet, separate

separite, separate

sepausatory, suppository

sepd, sip(pped) / seep(ed)

sepea, sepia

sepege, seep(age)

sepej, seep(age)

sepena, subpoena

seperabul, separable

seperader, separator

seperashen, separate(tion)

seperate, separate

seperately, separate(tly)

seperation, separate(tion)

seperatly, separate(tly)

seperator, separator

seperible, separable

seperubil, separable

sepeu, sepia

sephelis, syphilis

sephules, syphilis

sepia, A COLOR/PIGMENT, A FISH

sepige, seep(age)

sepij, seep(age)

sepil, sepal
sepirable, separable
sepirador, separator
sepirashen, separate(tion)
sepirate, separate
sepiration, separate(tion)
sepirator, separator
sepirlative, superlative
sepiruble, separable
sepkonshes, subconscious
sepkontrakt, subcontract
seplant, supplant
seple, sepal
sepli, supply
seplier, supply(lier)
sepling, sibling
sepliur, supply(lier)
seply, supply
sepol, sepal
seport, support
seportive, support(ive)
sepose, suppose
seposetory, suppository
seposubly, suppose(dly)
sepozatory, suppository
sepoze, suppose
sepozubly, suppose(dly)
seprabul, separable
seprashen, separate(tion)
seprat, separate
sepratisem, separate(tism)
seprative, separate(tive)
sepratly, separate(tly)
seprator, separator
seprechen, suppress(ion)
sepreem, supreme
sepreme, supreme
sepres, suppress
sepreshen, suppress(ion)
sepret, separate
sepretion, suppress(ion)
sepretism, separate(tism)
sepretive, separate(tive)
sepretly, separate(tly)
sepribul, separable
seprino, soprano
seprit, separate
sepritesm, separate(tism)
sepritly, separate(tly)
sepruble, separable
seprut, separate
seprutly, separate(tly)
septar, scepter
septek, septic / styptic

september, A MONTH OF THE YEAR
    (ENGLISH)
septer, scepter
septic,*,cally,city, THAT WHICH CAUSES
    PUTREFACTION OR SEPSIS, OF
    BEING ROTTEN
septik, styptic
septimber, september
septir, scepter
septisity, septic(ity)
septor, scepter
septupil, septuple
septuple,*,ed,ling, SEVEN TIMES/FOLD
septur, scepter
sepuge, seep(age)
sepuj, seep(age)
sepul, sepal
sepurabul, separable
sepurador, separator
sepurashen, separate(tion)
sepurate, separate
sepurately, separate(tly)
sepurater, separator
sepuration, separate(tion)
sepurb, superb
sepurblee, superb(ly)
sepurible, separable
sepurlative, superlative
sequel,*,litis, CONTINUATION ON THE
    STORY
sequence,*,ed,cing,cy,er,ntial,ntially,
    SERIES/PARTS ALIGNED IN ORDER/
    PATTERN
sequenshil, sequence(ntial)
sequer, secure
sequerity, secure(rity)
sequerly, secure(ly)
sequill, sequel
sequin,*,ned, SMALL REFLECTIVE
    DECORATIONS USED ON CLOTHING
sequir, secure
sequoia,*, TYPE OF TREE, A TRIBE
seqwen, sequin
ser, seer / sir / sear
seraget, surrogate
seran, saran
seranade, serenade
serandipity, serendipity
serandipudy, serendipity
serap, syrup
serape,*, OUTER GARMENT/BLANKET/
    SHAWL
serashen, serrate(tion)
serated, serrate(d)

seration, serrate(tion)
serbent, serpent
sercafigus, sarcophagus
sercamscribe, circumscribe
sercas, circus
sercemscribe, circumscribe
serch, search
sercharj, surcharge
serchuble, search(able)
sercit, circuit
sercle, circle
sercomscribe, circumscribe
sercophagus, sarcophagus
sercot, circuit
sercumfurens, circumference
sercumscribe, circumscribe
sercumsize, circumcise
sercumstans, circumstance
sercus, circus
sercut, circuit
serdafication, certificate(tion)
serdanly, certain(ly)
serdatude, certitude
serdenly, certain(ly)
serdufication, certificate(tion)
serdufy, certify
serdunly, certain(ly)
serdutude, certitude
sereal, serial / cereal / surreal
serealism, surrealism
serebral, cerebral
serebrul, cerebral
serees, series
serel, sorrel / surreal
serelism, surrealism
serenade,*,ed,ding,er, SOLITARY
    PERFORMANCE BY SOMEONE FOR
    SOMEONE IN PARTICULAR
serender, surrender
serendipity,tous, UNEXPECTED/
    ACCIDENTAL HAPPY ENDING
serene,nly,eness,nity,nities, TRANQUIL/
    PEACEFUL
sereol, serial / cereal
serep, syrup
sereul, serial / cereal
sereulizum, surrealism
sereus, serious
sereusly, serious(ly)
serf,*,fage,fdom,fhood,fish, WORKER
    WHO BELONGED WITH THE LAND
    (or see surf/serve)
serface, surface
serfdum, serf(dom)

serfee, surf(y)
serfej, serf(age)
serfes, surface
serfis, surface / service
serfuge, serf(age)
serfunt, servant
serfur, surf(er)
serfus, surface / service
sergd, surge(d)
serge, A TWILLED FABRIC (or see surge)
sergeant,*,ncy, A RANK/POSITION
    WITHIN THE U.S. MILITARY/POLICE
sergen, surgeon
sergent, sergeant / surgent
sergeon, surgeon
sergery, surgery
sergikul, surgical
sergin, surgeon
sergiry, surgery
sergon, surgeon
sergree, surgery
sergukle, surgical
serguree, surgery
serial,lly,list,lize,lization, SUCCESSIVE
    NUMBER/SERIES (or see cereal)
    "prefixes: uni"
seriasis, psoriasis
series, CORRESPONDING/SUCCESSIVE
    EVENTS/ITEMS
serim, serum
serimony, ceremony
serinade, serenade
serinder, surrender
serindipity, serendipity
serindipudy, serendipity
serious,sly,sness, EARNEST/SOLEMN/
    GRAVE
serip, syrup
seris, scirrhus / cirrus
seriulesm, surrealism
serius, serious
seriusis, psoriasis
serjakle, surgical
serjaree, surgery
serje, surge / serge
serjen, surgeon
serjent, sergeant / surgent
serjikul, surgical
serjint, sergeant / surgent
serjon, surgeon
serjree, surgery
serjukle, surgical
serkemscribe, circumscribe
serkemsize, circumcise

serkes, circus
serket, circuit
serkimscribe, circumscribe
serkimsize, circumcise
serkimstans, circumstance
serkis, circus
serkit, circuit
serkle, circle
serkofegus, sarcophagus
serkofigus, sarcophagus
serkomscribe, circumscribe
serkulate, circulate
serkuler, circular
serkumfurense, circumference
serkumsize, circumcise
serkumstans, circumstance
serkus, circus
serkut, circuit
serlee, surly
serloin, sirloin
serly, surly
serman, sermon
sermize, surmise
sermon,*,nic,nize,nizer, A RELIGIOUS
    DISCOURSE
sermun, sermon
serogate, surrogate
serondipity, serendipity
serong, sarong
serope, serape
seroredy, sorority
serority, sorority
seros, scirrhus / cirrus
seround, surround
serownd, surround
serpas, surpass
serpent,*, A SNAKE
serpentene, serpentine
serpentine, SHAPED/MOVEMENT OF A
    SNAKE
serpint, serpent
serpintene, serpentine
serplus, surplus
serprize, surprise
serrate,*,ed,ting,tion, JAGGED/
    TOOTHED OUTLINE LIKE A SAW
serrender, surrender
sersharge, surcharge
sertafy, certify
sertanle, certain(ly)
sertatude, certitude
sertefication, certificate(tion)
sertenly, certain(ly)
sertification, certificate(tion)

sertificut, certificate
sertifikashen, certificate(tion)
sertifucate, certificate
sertin, certain
sertinle, certain(ly)
sertinly, certain(ly)
sertufie, certify
sertunly, certain(ly)
seruget, surrogate
serum,*, A FLUID OF INOCULATION
serumony, ceremony
serunade, serenade
serundipety, serendipity
serundipudy, serendipity
serup, syrup
serus, cirrus / scirrhus
serva, survey
servaer, survey(or)
servailense, surveillance
servalinse, surveillance
servant,*, ONE EMPLOYED/OWNED TO
    PERFORM DOMESTIC CHORES/
    WORK
servatood, servitude
servatude, servitude
servaur, survey(or)
servayer, survey(or)
serve,*,ed,ving,er,vant,vice,vitude, ONE
    WHO PUTS A BALL INTO PLAY,
    PERFORM DUTIES FOR OTHERS
    "prefixes: sub"
serveilinse, surveillance
servent, servant
serveor, survey(or)
serves, service
serveyor, survey(or)
service,*,ed,cing,eable,eability,
    eableness,eably, PROVIDE OR
    ACCOMMODATE SOMEONE/
    SOMETHING "prefixes: dis/inter"
servife, survive
serviks, cervix
servint, servant
servisuble, service(cable)
servitude, TO BE IN THE SERVICE OF
    OTHERS
servive, survive
serviver, survive(vor)
servivul, survive(val)
servunt, servant
servusable, service(cable)
servutude, servitude
ses, see(s) / sea(s) / seize / cease
sesal, sizzle

sesame,*, AN EDIBLE SEED
sesan, season
sesdamadik, system(atic)
sesdamatic, system(atic)
sesdan, sustain
sesdum, system
sesdumadik, system(atic)
sesdumatic, system(atic)
sesede, secede
sesee, sissy
sesel, sizzle
sesen, season
seseptability, susceptible(bility)
seseptif, susceptive
seseptive, susceptive
sesers, scissor(s)
seset, secede
sesetion, secession
seshell, seashell
seshon, session
sesil, sizzle
sesime, sesame
sesin, season
sesion, session
sesirs, scissor(s)
sesle, sizzle
sesmek, seism(ic)
sesmic, seism(ic)
sesmical, seism(ical)
sesmik, seism(ic)
sesome, sesame
seson, season
sesors, scissor(s)
sespend, suspend
sespishus, suspicious
session,*,nal, A PERIOD/COURSE/
     SPECIFIC OF TIME "prefixes: inter"
sest, cyst / zest
sestain, sustain
sestane, sustain
sestanuble, sustain(able)
sester, sister
sestim, system
sestir, sister
sestum, system
sestumatic, system(atic)
sestur, sister
sesturly, sister(ly)
sesturn, cistern
sesul, sizzle
sesume, sesame
sesun, season
sesurs, scissor(s)
sesy, sissy

set,*,tting,ttee,tter,sat, COLLECTIONOF
     SIMILAR ITEMS, PUT INTO PLACE
     (or see sit/seat/said) "prefixes: in/
     over/pre/re/sub/un/under"
setal, settle
setalment, settle(ment)
setament, sediment
setamentary, sediment(ary)
setamint, sediment
setanic, satanic
setanikul, satanic(al)
setantary, sedentary
setchuashen, situate(tion)
setee, set(ttee)
setel, settle
setelment, settle(ment)
setemint, sediment
setemintary, sediment(ary)
setentary, sedentary
seter, set(tter)
seterical, satire(rical)
seth, seethe / scythe
setil, settle
setilment, settle(ment)
setintary, sedentary
setion, session
setir, set(tter)
setle, settle
setling, seedling / settle(ling)
setlment, settle(ment)
settle,*,ed,ling,ement,er, FINAL
     AGREEMENT, BECOME STATIONARY
     "prefixes: re/un"
setuashen, situate(tion)
setuation, situate(tion)
setul, settle
setulers, settle(rs)
setulment, settle(ment)
setumentary, sediment(ary)
setuntary, sedentary
setur, set(tter) / seat(er) / seed(er)
sety, city
seubil, see(able)
seuble, see(able)
seuler, cellular
seur, sear / seer
sev, sieve
sevan, seven
sevandy, seventy
sevant, savant
sevanteen, seventeen
sevanteith, seventieth
sevanth, seventh
sevanty, seventy

sevanu, savanna
sevarul, several
seven,*,nteen,nth,ntieth,nty, A
     NUMBER
sevendeith, seventieth
sevendy, seventy
seventeen, A DOUBLE DIGIT NUMBER
seventh, PLACE IN THE NUMBER
     SEQUENCE WHICH COMES AFTER
     THE 6TH
seventieth, COMES AFTER THE 69TH IN
     NUMBER SEQUENCE
seventy,ties, COMES AFTER 69 IN
     NUMBER SEQUENCE
sever,*,red,ring,rable,ralty,rance, TO
     CUT OFF/ SEPARATE FROM THE
     HOST (or see severe)
several,lly, MORE THAN TWO
severance, SEPARATION/SPLIT/
     PARTING, FROM THE WORD
     "SEVER"
severe,ely,eness,rity,rities, EXTREME/
     HARSH/PUNISHING (or see sever)
severedy, severe(rity)
severinse, severance
severly, severe(ly)
severt, sever(ed)
severul, several
severunse, severance
sevik, civic
sevil, civil
sevilean, civilian
sevin, seven
sevindeith, seventieth
sevindy, seventy
sevinteen, seventeen
sevinteith, seventieth
sevinth, seventh
sevinty, seventy
seviral, several
seviranse, severance
sevird, severe(d)
sevire, severe / sever
sevirly, severe(ly)
sevirt, sever(ed)
sevirunse, severance
sevlazation, civil(ization)
sevlization, civil(ization)
sevlozation, civil(ization)
sevluzation, civil(ization)
sevol, civil
sevolazation, civil(ization)
sevon, seven
sevondeith, seventieth

sevondy, seventy

sevont, savant

sevonteen, seventeen

sevonteith, seventieth

sevor, sever

sevr, sever

sevral, several

sevrense, severance

sevrul, several

sevrunse, severance

sevt, sift / sieve(d)

sevun, seven

sevundeith, seventieth

sevundy, seventy

sevunteen, seventeen

sevunteith, seventieth

sevunth, seventh

sevunty, seventy

sevur, sever

sevural, several

sevuranse, severance

sevurd, sever(ed)

sew,*,wed,wing,wer,wn, TO JOIN/ UNITE PIECES WITH STITCHES (or see so/sow) "prefixes: over"

sewage, WASTE MATTER

sewaro, saguaro

sewd, sue(d) / sew(ed)

sewdanim, pseudonym

sewdo, pseudo

sewdonim, pseudonym

sewer,*,wage,rage, A CHANNEL FOR WASTE/WATER, SOMEONE WHO SEWS (or see sew(er))

sewfaner, souvenir

sewfineer, souvenir

sewflay, souffle'

sewfuner, souvenir

sewkrose, sucrose

sewn, PAST TENSE FOR THE WORD "SEW" (or see son/sown)

seworo, saguaro

sewpee, soup(y)

sewperb, superb

sewpurb, superb

sewpy, soup(y)

sewt, soot / suit

sewtanim, pseudonym

sewto, pseudo

sewtonim, pseudonym

sewture, suture

sex,xes,xed,xing,xless,xy,xier,xiest,xily, xiness,xual, CONCERNING THE

REPRODUCTIVE AREAS "prefixes: de/inter/over/ under/uni"

sexest, sexist

sexis, sex(es)

sexist,*, A MAN WHO EXPLOITS/ DISCRIMINATES AGAINST WOMEN "prefixes: non"

sexshen, section

sexshin, section

sexshinul, section(al)

sexshualedy, sexual(ity)

sexshuality, sexual(ity)

sexshunol, section(al)

sexshwal, sexual

sextant,*, SIXTH PART OF A CIRCLE, AN INSTRUMENT

sexteen, sixteen

sextenth, sixteen(th)

sextet,*, SIX IN A GROUP

sexth, sixth

sextile,llion, ASTRONOMICAL/ STATISTICAL EXPRESSION, 1/6TH OF ANYTHING

sextileon, sextillion

sextilion, sextillion

sextillion,*,nth, A NUMBER FOLLOWED BY 21 OR 36 ZEROS

sextint, sextant

sextion, section

sextional, section(al)

sextuple,*,ed,ling,et, SIX FOLDS/PARTS/ TIMES

sextuplet,*, SIX EQUAL

sexual,lly,lity,lize,lizes,lized,lizing, PERTAINING TO THE FIRST SEAL/ CHAKRA, FEATURE OF REPRODUCTION "prefixes: bi/de/ inter/intra/non/uni"

sexuol, sexual

sexuoly, sexual(lly)

sexus, sex(es)

sexyewality, sexual(ity)

sexyewul, sexual

sexyuality, sexual(ity)

sexyuol, sexual

seyer, sear / seer

seyons, se'ance

seyur, sear / seer

sez, seize / cease / sea(s) / see(s)

sezal, sizzle

sezen, season

sezil, sizzle

sezin, season

sezle, sizzle

sezmek, seism(ic)

sezmic, seism(ic)

sezmical, seism(ical)

sezors, scissor(s)

sezul, sizzle

sezun, season

sezurs, scissor(s)

sfarekil, sphere(rical)

sfeer, sphere

sfencks, sphinx

sfencter, sphincter

sfenktur, sphincter

sfenx, sphinx

sfer, sphere

sferakil, sphere(rical)

sfere, sphere

sferekul, sphere(rical)

sferical, sphere(rical)

sferukle, sphere(rical)

sfincter, sphincter

sfinks, sphinx

sfinktur, sphincter

sfinx, sphinx

sgoundrel, scoundrel

sgowndrul, scoundrel

sgragliest, scraggly(liest)

sgrakleur, scraggly(lier)

shabby,bbier,bbiest,bbily,bbiness, WORN, THREADBARE

shabely, shabby(bbily)

shabiness, shabby(bbiness)

shaby, shabby

shack,*,ked,king, SHANTY, PRIMITIVE HUT, CABIN (or see shag/shake)

shackle,*,ed,ling,er, A FASTENER, CUFFS "prefixes: un"

shade,*,ed,ding,dy,eless, OVERHEAD PROTECTION FROM THE SUN

shader, shatter

shadey, shade(dy)

shadir, shatter

shado, shadow

shadow,*,wed,wing,wer,wy, AREA WHERE THE LIGHT DOESN'T PENETRATE, SCREEN/PROTECT "prefixes: over"

shadur, shatter

shaem, shame

shaemful, shame(ful)

shaenk, shank

shafd, shaft / shave(d) / chafe(d)

shafe, shave / chafe

shafed, shaft / shave(d)

shaft,*,ted,ting, NARROW COLUMN/
CYLINDER (or see chafe(d)/
shave(d))
shag,gged,gging,ggy,ggier,ggiest,
CARPET, TO RETRIEVE, LOOSE
THREADS (or see shack)
shagier, shag(ggier)
shagiest, shag(ggiest) / shake(kiest)
shagy, shag(ggy)
shaim, shame
shaimless, shame(less)
shaink, shank
shak, shack / shake
shake,*,ed,king,er,ky,kier,kiest,hook,
JUMBLE, JOSTLE, VIBRATE, MOVE
UP/DOWN, BUILDING MATERIAL (or
see shack) "prefixes: un"
shaked, shack(ed) / shake(d)
shakel, shackle
shakul, shackle
shakult, shackle(d)
shakyest, shake(kiest)
shal, shall / shale / shawl
shale,*, TYPE OF CLAY/ROCK (or see
shell)
shalet, shallot
shalit, shallot
shall, COULD, ALLOWED/ABLE TO (or
see shawl)
shallot,*, PLANT BULBS USED IN
COOKING
shallow,*,wly,wness, OF LITTLE DEPTH,
SUPERFICIAL
shalo, shallow
shaloness, shallow(ness)
shalons, chalant(nce)
shalont, chalant
shalot, shallot
shalow, shallow
shalowness, shallow(ness)
shalut, shallot
sham,mmed,mming,mmer, COVER-UP
FOR THE TRUTH (or see shame)
shaman,*,nic,nism,nist,nistic, WISE
ONE WITH SPIRITUAL POWERS
shambal, shamble
shamble,*,ed,ling, UNSTEADY,
DISORDER
shambul, shamble
shame,*,ed,ming,eful,efully,efulness,
eless, DISGRACED, DISHONORED (or
see sham)
shamed, shame(d) / sham(mmed)
shamen, shaman

shamer, sham(mmer)
shamful, shame(ful)
shamin, shaman
shaminesm, shaman(ism)
shamless, shame(less)
shamonek, shaman(ic)
shamonism, shaman(ism)
shample, shamble
shampoo,*,ooed,ooing,ooer, USE SOAP
TO CLEAN HAIR/CARPET/
UPHOLSTERY
shampoor, shampoo(er)
shampu, shampoo
shampuer, shampoo(er)
shampuir, shampoo(er)
shampul, shamble
shamrock,*, PLANT
shamrok, shamrock
shanal, channel
shanalize, channelize
shananigen, shenanigan
shananugin, shenanigan
shandalere, chandelier
shandulere, chandelier
shange, change
shanil, channel
shanilize, channelize
shank,*, PART OF THE BODY
shanty,ties, ROUGH/FRONTIER
STRUCTURE
shantys, shanty(ties)
shape,*,ed,ping,pable,eless,elessness,
elessly,eliness,ely,er, OF FORM/
FIGURE "prefixes: re/un"
shapeable, shape(pable)
shaperd, shepherd
shaplis, shape(less)
shaply, shape(ly)
shapuble, shape(pable)
shar, share / chair / char
sharade, charade
sharck, shark
shard,*, FRAGMENT
share,*,ed,ring, TO DIVIDE INTO
PORTIONS "prefixes: over"
sharee, sherry
sharef, sheriff
shari, sherry
sharif, sheriff
shark,*, MARINE FISH, LIKE A SHARK
sharp,ply,pness,pen,pens,pened,pening,
pener,per,pest,pie, DISTINCT
POINT/TIP
sharpin, sharp(en)

sharpind, sharp(ened)
sharpinur, sharp(ener)
sharpnis, sharp(ness)
sharpuner, sharp(ener)
sharpy, sharp(ie)
sharry, sherry
sharuf, sheriff
shate, shade
shater, shatter
shatir, shatter
shato, shadow
shatord, shatter(ed)
shatoy, shadow(y)
shatter,*,red,ring, REDUCE TO PIECES/
FRAGMENTS
shaturd, shatter(ed)
shauk, chalk / choke / shock / chock
shavar, shave(r)
shave,*,ed,ving,er, TO REDUCE THE
SURFACE/OUTCROP, SCRATCH/
GRAZE THE SURFACE
shavir, shave(r)
shavur, shave(r)
shawer, shower
shawir, shower
shawl,*, EXTERIOR GARMENT FOR
SHOULDERS
shawmen, shaman
shawmonism, shaman(ism)
shawur, shower
she,*, THAT FEMALE
she'd, CONTRACTION OF THE WORDS
'SHE HAD/WOULD' (or see shed)
she'll, CONTRACTION OF THE WORDS
'SHE WILL' (or see shell)
sheaf,aves, BOUND STALKS, QUIVER OF
ARROWS
shear,*,red,ring,rer,horn, CUT WITH
CLIPPERS (or see sheer)
sheath,hes,hed,hing, CLOSE FITTING
CASE/COVERING, ALSO SPELLED
'SHEATHE'
sheberd, shepherd
sheburd, shepherd
shechul, special
shed,*,dded,dding, SMALL STRUCTURE
(or see she'd/sheet)
sheef, sheaf
sheek, chic
sheeld, shield
sheen,*,ned,ning,nier,niest,ny,
RADIANT/BRIGHT/LIGHT (or see
shin)
sheengul, shingle

sheep,pish,pishly,pishness, A RUMINANT ANIMAL

sheer,*,red,ring,rer,rly,rness, NAUTICAL TERM, OF LITTLE BODY/SUBSTANCE, NEAR TRANSPARENT (or see shear)

sheet,*,ted,ting, THIN/FLAT SUBSTANCE/MATERIAL

sheeth, sheath

shef, chef / chief / sheaf

shefor, shiver

sheft, shift

shefur, shiver

sheild, shield

sheilt, shield

shel, she'll / shell / shale

shelak, shellac

sheld, shield / shell(ed)

sheldur, shelter

sheldurless, shelter(less)

shelf,lves, HORIZONTAL LEDGE TO PLACE THINGS ON (or see shelve)

shelfs, shelve(s)

shell,*,lled,lling,ller, HOUSING/ PROTECTION FOR CREATURES, LAYERS OF ATOM, HAND OVER (or see she'll) "prefixes: sub"

shellac,*,ced,cing, A CHEMICAL SOLUTION, USED IN VARNISH

shelont, chalant

shelt, shell(ed)

shelter,*,red,ring,rless, COVER/ PROTECTION/REFUGE

sheltired, shelter(ed)

sheltur, shelter

shelturd, shelter(ed)

shelturless, shelter(less)

shelve,*,ed,ving,er, PLURAL FOR SHELF, LEDGE TO PLACE ITEMS

shem, shim

shemed, shim(mmed) / shimmy(mmied)

shemee, shimmy

shemir, shimmer

shemmiry, shimmer(y)

shemonic, shaman(ic)

shemur, shimmer

shemury, shimmer(y)

shemy, shimmy

shen, sheen / shin / chin

shenanigan,*, NONSENSE TRICKERY

shengle, shingle

shengul, shingle

shep, sheep / ship / chip

shepard, shepherd

sheper, ship(pper) / chip(pper)

sheperd, shepherd

shepherd,*, THAT WHICH GUARDS/ PROTECTS

shepird, shepherd

shepish, sheep(ish)

sheprek, shipwreck

shept, ship(pped) / chip(pped)

shepur, ship(pper) / chip(pper)

shepurd, shepherd

shepwreck, shipwreck

sher, sure / share / chair / cheer

sherba, sherbet

sherbert, sherbet

sherbet,*, FRUIT FLAVORED ICE DESSERT

sherbirt, sherbet

sherburt, sherbet

sherd, shear(ed) / sheer(ed) / share(d)

shered, shear(ed) / sheer(ed) / share(d)

sheredy, surety

sheri, sherry

sheridy, surety

sherif, sheriff

sheriff,*, LAW ENFORCEMENT OFFICIAL

sherir, shear(er)

sherity, surety

sherly, sure(ly)

sheror, shear(er)

sherrif, sheriff

sherry,ries, TYPE OF WINE

shert, shear(ed) / sheer(ed) / shirt

sheruf, sheriff

sherur, shear(er)

shery, sherry

shet, shed / sheet / she'd

shethd, sheath(ed)

sheult, shield

shevir, shiver

shevt, shift

shevtur, shift(er)

shevulry, chivalry

shevur, shiver

shew, shoe / chew

shewr, sure

shews, shoe(s)

shewt, chute / shoot / chew(ed)

shi, shy / she

shid, shy(hied) / she'd

shield,*,ded,ding, USED FOR DEFENSE/ PROTECTION

shier, shy(er)

shift,*,ted,ting,tingly,tingness,ter,tless, tlessly,tlessness,ty,tily,tiness, LEAVE ONE GEAR/FOCUS/PLACE/POINT TO GO TO ANOTHER "prefixes: un/up"

shiftur, shift(er)

shifur, shiver

shil, she'll / shell

shilak, shellac

shild, shield

shilee, shy(ly)

shilons, chalant(nce)

shilont, chalant

shily, shy(ly)

shim,*,mmed,mming, A THIN STRIP OF SOME MATERIAL USED TO FILL GAPS

shimanik, shaman(ic)

shimee, shimmy

shimer, shimmer

shimery, shimmer(y)

shimes, shimmy(mmies) / shim(s)

shimmer,*,ry, LIGHT/GLEAMING

shimmy,mmies,mmied,mmying, VIBRATION/WOBBLING

shimonic, shaman(ic)

shimur, shimmer

shimury, shimmer(y)

shimy, shimmy

shimyd, shimmy(mmied)

shimys, shimmy(mmies)

shin,*,nned,nning, PART OF THE LEG, SPLINT OF WOOD (or see shine/ chin)

shinanigan, shenanigan

shinanugan, shenanigan

shind, shine(d) / shin(nned)

shine,*,ed,ning,er,ny,nier,niest,niness, RADIANT/REFLECTIVE (or see chin/ shin/shiny)

shineist, shiny(niest)

shiness, shy(ness)

shineur, shiny(nier)

shingle,*,ed,ling, ROOF COVERING, PAINFUL VIRAL INFECTION

shingul, shingle

shinguled, shingle(d)

shinie, shiny

shiny, nier,niest,niness, RADIANT/ REFLECTIVE

shinyest, shiny(niest)

shinyness, shiny(niness)

ship,*,pped,pping,pper, WATER/ NAUTICAL VESSEL, SEND ITEM BY ROAD/SEA/AIR (or see chip) "prefixes: un"

shipd, ship(pped) / chip(pped)

shiper, ship(pper) / chip(pper)
shiprek, shipwreck
shipur, ship(pper) / chip(pper)
shipwreck,*,ked, BOAT WHICH WRECKS IN THE SEA
shipwrek, shipwreck
shir, sure / shy(er) / shear
shirbert, sherbet
shirbet, sherbet
shirburt, sherbet
shiredy, surety
shirety, surety
shirly, sure(ly)
shirt,*, UPPER TORSO GARMENT "prefixes: over/under"
shister, shyster
shiur, shy(er)
shivalry, chivalry
shiver,*,red,ring, SHAKE/TREMBLE FROM COLD/FEAR
shivt, shift
shivulry, chivalry
shivur, shiver
sho, show
shoal,*, SHALLOW AREA ASSOCIATED WITH A BODY OF WATER, SCHOOL OF FISH
shoar, shore / chore
shock,*,ked,king,ker,kingly, SUDDEN/ ABRUPT/UNPREDICTABLE EVENT, JOLT OF ELECTRICITY, SUDDEN IMPACT
shod,*,ddy, TO SHOE A HORSE (or see show(ed)/shoot/shoe(d)/should) "prefixes: un"
shoddy,ddier,ddiest,ddily,ddiness, INFERIOR PRODUCT/SERVICE PRODUCED TO MOCK FINE QUALITY
shode, shoddy
shody, shoddy
shoe,*,ed,eing,er, FOOT/HOOF COVERING
shofel, shovel
shofer, chauffeur
shok, chalk / choke / shock / chock
shoked, shock(ed) / choke(d) / chock(ed)
shol, shawl / shoal
sholak, shellac
sholder, shoulder
sholdur, shoulder
shole, shoal / shawl
sholont, chalant
sholtur, shoulder

shoman, shaman
shomenism, shaman(ism)
shomin, shaman
shoo, shoe
shood, should / shoe(d)
shook, PAST TENSE FOR THE WORD "SHAKE", A SET OF PREFABRICATED PARTS (or see shuck)
shoot,*,ting,ter,hot, AIM AT SOMETHING TO DISCHARGE INTO/ PIERCE/ CAPTURE AN IMAGE (or see shut/should) "prefixes: over/ under"
shop,*,pped,pping,pper, SEEK TO PURCHASE GOODS ITEMS, PLACE TO MANUFACTURE/PERFORM RETAIL ACTIVITIES (or see chop)
shoper, shop(pper)
shopur, shop(pper)
shor, shore / chore / sure
shord, shore(d) / short
shordist, short(est)
shore,*,ed,ring, PLACE WHERE BODY OF WATER MEETS LAND (or see chore) "prefixes: in"
shork, shark
shorn, PAST TENSE FOR THE WORD "SHEAR"
shorp, sharp
shors, shore(s) / chore(s)
short,*,ted,ter,test, BRIEF/ABRUPT, SMALLER/LESS THAN NORMAL (or see shore(d)/shorts)
shortir, short(er)
shortist, short(est)
shorts,*, MEDIA LENGTH, PANTS TO THE KNEES (or see shore(d)) "prefixes: under"
shortur, short(er)
shos, shoe(s)
shot, PAST TENSE FOR THE WORD 'SHOOT', TAKE A HIT OF/FROM SOMETHING, TO FILM (or see shod)"prefixes: up"
shoty, shoddy
shoud, shout
shoul, shawl
should, PAST TENSE FOR THE WORD 'SHALL'
should've, CONTRACTION OF THE WORDS 'SHOULD HAVE'
shoulder,*,red,ring, BODY PART HOLDING THE ARM, TO USE THE SHOULDER

shouldn't, CONTRACTION OF THE WORDS 'SHOULD NOT'
shout,*,ted,ting, TO SPEAK/VOICE WORDS LOUDLY
shove,*,ed,ving, TO PUSH/RAM AGAINST
shovel,*,led,ling, AN IMPLEMENT/TOOL FOR DIGGING/MOVING/SCRAPING ORGANIC MATERIAL (or see shuffle)
show,*,wed,wing,wn,wy, TO DISPLAY FOR SOMEONE
shower,*,red,ring,ry, RAIN OR THE IMITATION OF
showfer, chauffeur
showir, shower
showl, shawl
showmin, shaman
showt, shout / show(ed)
showur, shower
shoy, show(y)
shrapnel, SHELL FRAGMENTS
shrapnul, shrapnel
shreak, shriek
shred,*,dded,dding,dder, TO TEAR/CUT INTO SLIVERS/THIN STRIPS/PIECES
shredur, shred(dder)
shreek, shriek
shreful, shrivel
shrel, shrill
shrelness, shrill(ness)
shremp, shrimp
shrempy, shrimp(y)
shrenk, shrink
shrenkable, shrink(able)
shrevle, shrivel
shrevul, shrivel
shrew,*,wish,wishly,wishness, SMALL MAMMAL, TO BE ILL TEMPERED
shrewd,dly,dness, TO BE DISCERNING/ PRACTICAL
shrewtly, shrewd(ly)
shriek,*,ked,king, A SHRILL/SHARP YELL OR SHOUT SOUNDED WHEN FRIGHTENED/ANGRY
shrifle, shrivel
shril, shrill
shrill,lly,llness, PIERCING/HIGH PITCHED SOUND
shrilness, shrill(ness)
shrimp,*,py, EDIBLE CRUSTACEANS, SMALL/TINY
shrine,*, A STRUCTURE WITH RELIGIOUS IMPLICATIONS "prefixes: en"

shrink,*,runk,king,kable, BECOME SMALLER THAN ORIGINAL SIZE, SLANG FOR MENTAL DOCTOR
shrivel,*,led,ling, TO WRINKLE/SHRINK
shrivle, shrivel
shronk, shrunk
shroo, shrew
shrood, shrewd
shroodly, shrewd(ly)
shrooish, shrew(ish)
shroot, shrewd
shroud,*,ded,ding, HIDE/COVER/ CONCEAL "prefixes: en"
shrowd, shroud
shru, shrew
shrub,*,bbery,bby, LOW GROWING TREES/BUSHES "prefixes: sub/ under"
shrubery, shrub(bbery)
shrubry, shrub(bbery)
shrud, shrewd
shrudly, shrewd(ly)
shrue, shrew
shrug,*,gged,gging, USE THE SHOULDERS FOR EMOTIONAL EXPRESSION
shrunk, PAST TENSE FOR 'SHRINK' "prefix: pre"
shrupree, shrub(bbery)
shrut, shrewd
shrutly, shrewd(ly)
shryn, shrine
shu, shoe
shuch, shush
shuck,*,ked,king,ker, REMOVE HULLS/ SHELLS/OUTER HOUSING (or see shook)
shuckir, shuck(er)
shud, should / shut
shudal, shuttle
shudder,*,red,ring,ry, PHYSICAL/ EMOTIONAL RESPONSE TO SOMETHING GROTESQUE/ REPULSIVE (or see shutter)
shudel, shuttle
shuder, shutter / shudder / shoot(er)
shuderd, shudder(ed) / shutter
shudery, shudder(y)
shudil, shuttle
shudir, shutter / shudder / shoot(er)
shudol, shuttle
shudur, shutter / shudder / shoot(er)
shuf, shove
shufal, shuffle / shovel

shuffle,*,ed,ling,ler, MOVE AROUND BY DRAGGING, AN ACT IN A CARD GAME, MOVE AS A CHESS PIECE ON GAMEBOARD (or see shovel) "prefixes: re"
shufil, shuffle / shovel
shuful, shovel / shuffle
shugar, sugar
shugur, sugar
shuk, shook / shuck
shukd, shuck(ed) / shook
shuker, sugar / shuck(er)
shukur, sugar / shuck(er)
shulak, shellac
shuld, should
shulont, chalant
shun,*,nned,nning, TO AVOID
shunanegin, shenanigan
shunanigen, shenanigan
shund, shun(nned) / shunt
shuner, shun(nner)
shunir, shun(nner)
shunt,*,ted,ter, SHIFT, RID OF, MOVE ASIDE (or see shun(nned))
shuntur, shunt(er)
shur, sure / shoe(r)
shurade, charade
shurba, sherbet
shurbert, sherbet
shurbet, sherbet
shurburt, sherbet
shuredy, surety
shurity, surety
shurly, sure(ly)
shurt, shirt
shus, shoe(s)
shush, TO ENCOURAGE TO BE QUIET
shut,*,tter,tting, TO CLOSE/STOP (or see should/shoot/chute)
shutal, shuttle
shute, chute / shoot
shuter, shutter / shudder / shoot(er)
shutir, shutter / shudder / shoot(er)
shutled, shuttle(d)
shutol, shuttle
shutter,*, A HINGED FLAP/COVER OVER AN OPENING (or see shudder)
shuttle,*,ed,ling, CARRY/TRANSPORT TO ANOTHER PLACE
shutur, shutter / shudder / shoot(er)
shuve, shove
shuvel, shovel
shuvul, shovel
shuw, shoe

shuz, shoe(s)
shy,hies,hied,ying,hier,hiest,yly,yness, yster, LESS THAN WILLING TO ACCEPT/FACE HEAD-ON/ CONFRONT
shyster,*, ONE WHO IS UNETHICAL
shystur, shyster
si, sigh / see / sea
siadeka, sciatic(a)
siadika, sciatic(a)
sianide, cyanide
sianse, science
siantifek, scientific
siantist, scientist
siants, science
siatek, sciatic
siateka, sciatic(a)
siatic, sciatic
siatika, sciatic(a)
sibkonchus, subconscious
sibkontrakt, subcontract
siblengs, sibling(s)
sibling,*, LEGAL BROTHERS/SISTERS
siborg, cyborg
siburnetiks, cybernetics
sic, WORD USED FOR REPLACEMENT IN TEXT, TO ENCOURAGE SOMETHING TO ATTACK (or see sick/psyche)
sicede, secede
sicheatric, psychiatric
sichek, psychic
sichewashen, situate(tion)
sichewation, situate(tion)
sichiatric, psychiatric
sichic, psychic
sicholegist, psychology(gist)
sichologekul, psychology(gical)
sichologest, psychology(gist)
sichology, psychology
sichopath, psychopath
sichopatholagist, psychopath(ologist)
sichosis, psychosis
sichuaded, situate(d)
sichuashen, situate(tion)
sichuate, situate
sichuation, situate(tion)
sichudelic, psychedelic
sick,kish,kishness,kly,kliness,kness, PHYSICALLY/MENTALLY ILL (or see psyche)
sickal, sickle / cycle
sickle,*,ed,ling, TOOL USED FOR CUTTING GRASS/GRAIN, CRESCENT MOON SHAPE (or see cycle)

sicks, six
sickstee, sixty
sickteith, sixtieth
sickth, sixth
siclone, cyclone
sico, psycho
sicodek, psychotic
sicological, psychology(gical)
sicology, psychology
sicreshen, secrete(tion)
sicrete, secrete
sicretion, secrete(tion)
sicuer, secure
sicuerity, secure(rity)
sicuerly, secure(ly)
sicumb, succumb
sid, sigh(ed) / side / sight / seed
sidan, sedan
sidar, sit(tter) / cider / side(r)
sidashen, sedate(tion)
sidasion, sedate(tion)
sidate, sedate
sidation, sedate(tion)
side,*,ed,ding,er, BE NEAR OR BESIDE
    BUT NOT ON, POSITION OFF FROM
    CENTER (or see site/sight) "prefixes:
    under/up/sub"
sideng, side(ding) / site(ting) / sight(ing)
sider, sit(tter) / cider / side(r)
sidewse, seduce
sidir, sit(tter) / cider / side(r)
sidokshen, seduce(ction)
sidoose, seduce
sidor, sit(tter) / cider / side(r)
sids, sit(s) / set(s) / side(s)
siducshen, seduce(ction)
sidukshen, seduce(ction)
siduktion, seduce(ction)
siduktive, seduce(ctive)
sidur, sit(tter) / cider / side(r)
siduse, seduce
siduzen, citizen
siege,*,ed,ging, TAKE/STEAL CONTROL
    OF FUNCTIONS
siegur, seize(zure)
siejur, seize(zure)
sienna, A COLOR/PIGMENT
siense, science
sienses, science(s)
sientifekly, scientific(ally)
sientific, scientific
sientifikly, scientific(ally)
sientist, scientist
sier, sigh(er)

siera, sierra
sierra, SECTION OF HILLS/RANGE, A
    FISH
siesta,*, AFTERNOON NAP
sieve,*,ed,ving, STRAINER/NET FOR
    SOLIDS/LIQUIDS
sieze, seize
sif, sieve
sifal, civil
sifalis, syphilis
sifaree, safari
sifd, sieve(d) / sift
sifen, siphon
sifenul, siphon(al)
sifinal, siphon(al)
sifise, suffice
siflazation, civil(ization)
siflus, syphilis
sifol, civil
sifolization, civil(ization)
sifon, siphon
sift,*,ted,ting,ter, SEPARATION OF
    VARIOUS GRAIN SIZES, SORT FOR A
    SPECIFIC THING (or see sieve(d))
siftur, sift(er)
sifules, syphilis
sifunil, siphon(al)
sigar, cigar
sigaret, cigarette
siger, seize(zure)
sigeret, cigarette
siggesdeve, suggest(ive)
siggestion, suggest(ion)
sigh,*,hed,hing, A DEEP/RELEASING
    BREATH
sight,*,ted,ting,table,ter,tless,tlessly,
    tlessness,tly,tliness, VISUAL, ABLE
    TO SEE (or see site) "prefixes: in/
    over/un"
sigjesdeve, suggest(ive)
sigjestion, suggest(ion)
sigjestive, suggest(ive)
sigjestshen, suggest(ion)
sigma, GREEK ALPHABET LETTER
sigmu, sigma
sign,*,ned,ning,ner, WRITTEN TEXT,
    SYMBOL WITH MEANING, A
    PLACARD/ BOARD WITH WORDS/
    SYMBOLS, A SIGNATURE (or see
    sine) "prefixes: con/-re/un/under"
signacher, signature
signafiable, signify(fiable)
signafier, signify(fier)
signafy, signify

signal,*,led,ling,ler,lly,lize,lized,lizing,
    IMAGE/GESTURE USED TO
    COMMUNICATE
signature,*,tory,tories, A PERSON'S
    NAME/MARK, TO SIGN SOMETHING
    "prefixes: bio"
signefiable, signify(fiable)
signefukent, significant
signeture, signature
signifacantly, significant(ly)
significant,tly,nce,ation,ative,atively, OF
    IMPORTANCE, OUTSTANDING
    "prefixes: in"
signify,fied,fying,fiable,fier, INDICATE,
    POINT OUT
signuchur, signature
signufy, signify
signul, signal
signushure, signature
sigur, seize(zure)
siguret, cigarette
sijur, seize(zure)
sik, sick / psyche / seek
sikadelic, psychedelic
sikal, sickle / cycle
sikamore, sycamore
sike, psyche / sick / sic
sikeatree, psychiatry
sikeatric, psychiatric
sikedelic, psychedelic
sikek, psychic
sikel, sickle / cycle
sikepath, psychopath
sikeur, secure
sikeurety, secure(rity)
sikeurly, secure(ly)
sikewr, secure
sikgest, suggest
sikgestion, suggest(ion)
sikiatree, psychiatry
sikiatrist, psychiatry(rist)
sikik, psychic
sikil, sickle / cycle
sikiotrist, psychiatry(rist)
sikiutrest, psychiatry(rist)
sikiutry, psychiatry
sikjest, suggest
sikjestion, suggest(ion)
sikjestshen, suggest(ion)
sikle, sickle
siklude, seclude
siklushen, seclusion
siklusive, seclusive
siklution, seclusion

sikma, sigma
siknacher, signature
siknafier, signify(fier)
siknashure, signature
siknature, signature
siknefakent, significant
siknefy, signify
sikneture, signature
siknifakent, significant
siknify, signify
siknishure, signature
siknol, signal
siknufy, signify
siknul, signal
siknuture, signature
siko, psycho
sikodelic, psychedelic
sikodik, psychotic
sikolegy, psychology
sikologekul, psychology(gical)
sikologest, psychology(gist)
sikology, psychology
sikopath, psychopath
sikopathic, psychopath(ic)
sikopatholagist, psychopath(ologist)
sikosis, psychosis
sikotic, psychotic
sikreshen, secrete(tion)
sikresion, secrete(tion)
sikrete, secrete
siks, six
sikstee, sixty
siksteen, sixteen
siksteenth, sixteen(th)
siksteith, sixtieth
sikstiuth, sixtieth
siksty, sixty
sikteith, sixtieth
sikth, sixth
sikudelic, psychedelic
sikul, sickle / cycle
sikulest, cyclist
sikum, succumb
sikumore, sycamore
sikure, secure
sikurity, secure(rity)
sikwenshul, sequence(ntial)
sikwential, sequence(ntial)
sikwoia, sequoia
sikwoya, sequoia
siky, psyche / sick
silabes, syllabus
silabil, syllable
silacon, silicon / silicone

silakit, silica(te)
silakon, silicon / silicone
silal, salal
silami, salami
silanoid, solenoid
silanse, silence
silant, silent
silantly, silent(ly)
silantness, silent(ness)
silareum, solarium
silawet, silhouette
sild, silt
sildashen, silt(ation)
silebus, syllabus
sileca, silica
silecate, silica(te)
silective, select(ive)
silee, silly
sileka, silica
silekshen, select(ion)
silekt, select
silektif, select(ive)
silektion, select(ion)
silektive, select(ive)
silence,*,ed,cing,er, QUIET, NO SOUND
silendur, cylinder
sileness, silly(lliness)
sileng, ceiling / seal(ing)
silenium, selenium
silenoid, solenoid
silense, silence
silensur, silence(r)
silent,tly,tness, BEING QUIET, NO
    SOUND
silerium, solarium
silesit, solicit
silesitation, solicit(ation)
silesiter, solicit(er)
silesteul, celestial
sileur, silly(llier)
silewet, silhouette
silfer, silver
silferware, silverware
silfur, silver
silfurware, silverware
silfury, silver(y)
silhouete, silhouette
silhouette,*,ed,ting, THE SHAPE/
    OUTLINE OF SOMETHING
silica,ate, A NATURAL CHEMICAL
    COMPOUND
silicon, A NATURALLY OCCURING
    ELEMENT (or see silicone)

silicone,*, A SILICON SUBSTITUTE,
    MANMADE CHEMICAL (or see
    silicon)
siliest, silly(lliest)
silinder, cylinder
siliness, silly(lliness)
siling, ceiling / seal(ing)
silinoid, solenoid
silins, silence
silinser, silence(r)
silivu, saliva
silk,*,ken,ky,kily,kiness, THREAD/
    FABRIC MADE FROM SILKWORMS
silkee, silk(y)
silkeness, silk(iness)
silkun, silk(en)
sill,*, A HORIZONTAL SHELF (or see sell)
silly,llier,lliest,llies,lliness, GOOFY/
    FUNNY, NOT SERIOUS
silo,*,oed,oing, A STRUCTURE/
    HOUSING FOR GRAIN/MISSILES/
    ROCKETS
siloet, silhouette
silomee, salami
silon, salon
siloon, saloon
siloot, salute
silow, silo
silt,tation,ty, A VERY FINE DIRT/
    SEDIMENT
siltashen, silt(ation)
silubel, syllable
silubes, syllabus
silubil, syllable
siluca, silica
silucone, silicon / silicone
siludid, salute(d)
siluet, silhouette
siluka, silica
siluket, silica(te)
silukon, silicon / silicone
silune, saloon
silunoid, solenoid
siluns, silence
silunsed, silence(d)
silunser, silence(r)
silunt, silent
siluntly, silent(ly)
siluntness, silent(ness)
silute, salute
silver,red,ry,riness, A TYPE OF SOFT
    METAL, THE COLOR OF SHINY GRAY
silverware, UTENSILS COATED IN
    SILVER

silvir, silver
silvur, silver
silvurware, silverware
silvury, silver(y)
sily, silly
sim, seem / seam
simalarly, similar(ly)
simaler, similar
simalerety, similar(ity)
simalerly, similar(ly)
simaltaneus, simultaneous
simaltaneusly, simultaneous(ly)
siman, semen
simantics, semantics
simar, simmer
simashen, sum(mmation)
simation, sum(mmation)
simatry, symmetry
simbal, symbol
simbalism, symbol(ism)
simbathetik, sympathetic
simbathy, sympathy
simbeodek, symbiotic
simbeosis, symbiosis
simbeotek, symbiotic
simbethe, sympathy
simbethetic, sympathetic
simbiosis, symbiosis
simblanse, semblance
simblants, semblance
simble, symbol
simblense, semblance
simbol, cymbal / symbol
simbolek, symbol(ic)
simbolik, symbol(ic)
simbul, symbol
simbulism, symbol(ism)
simbuthe, sympathy
simbuthetic, sympathetic
simdum, symptom
simelarity, similar(ity)
simeltaneus, simultaneous
simeltaneusly, simultaneous(ly)
simelur, similar
simelurly, similar(ly)
simen, semen
siment, cement
simer, simmer
simesder, semester
simester, semester
simetrek, symmetry(ric)
simetric, symmetry(ric)
simetry, symmetry
simewlate, simulate

simfeny, symphony
simfonic, symphony(nic)
simfune, symphony
similar,rly,rity,rities, RESEMBLES
    SOMETHING ALMOST LIKE IT, NOT
    THE SAME BUT CLOSE (also spelled
    "simular") "prefixes: dis"
similur, similar
similurly, similar(ly)
simin, semen
simmer,*,red,ring, COOK GENTLY WITH
    LOW HEAT, TO CALM DOWN
simoltaneous, simultaneous
simoltaneus, simultaneous
simoltaneusly, simultaneous(ly)
simoolader, simulate(tor)
simpal, simple
simpalest, simple(st)
simpaly, simple(ly)
simpathee, sympathy
simpathetic, sympathetic
simpathize, sympathy(hize)
simpathy, sympathy
simpdum, symptom
simpel, simple
simpelest, simple(st)
simpely, simple(ly)
simpethize, sympathy(hize)
simpethy, sympathy
simphonek, symphony(nic)
simphonic, symphony(nic)
simphuny, symphony
simpithy, sympathy
simple,er,est,leness,ly,licity,licities,lify,
    lification,lifier,lism,listic,listically,
    NOT COMPLICATED, BASIC,
    UNDERSTANDABLE "prefixes: over"
simplisity, simple(licity)
simplistec, simple(listic)
simplur, simple(r)
simposeum, symposium
simpozeum, symposium
simptom, symptom
simptum, symptom
simpul, simple
simpuler, simple(r)
simpulest, simple(st)
simpuly, simple(ly)
simputhee, sympathy
simputhetic, sympathetic
simputhize, sympathy(hize)
simtem, symptom
simtum, symptom
simualtaneus, simultaneous

simuladur, simulate(tor)
simularity, similar(ity)
simularly, similar(ly)
simulashen, simulate(tion)
simulate,*,tive,tion,tor,
    REPRODUCTION OF ORIGINAL
    "prefixes: dis"
simuler, similar
simulerity, similar(ity)
simulerly, similar(ly)
simultaneous,sly,eity, HAPPENING AT
    SAME TIME
simultaneusly, simultaneous(ly)
simur, simmer
simurd, simmer(ed)
simurt, simmer(ed)
simutary, cemetery
simutree, symmetry
sin,*,nned,nning,nner,nful,nfully,
    nfulness, KNOWINGLY COMMIT AN
    IMMORAL ACT (or see sine/sign/
    seine/seen)
sinada, sonata
sinanem, synonym
sinapse, synapse
sinapsis, synapsis
sinaptek, synaptic
sinaptic, synaptic
sinareo, scenario
sinas, sinus
sinaster, sinister
sinata, sonata
sinatorial, senator(ial)
sinatur, senator
sinc, sync / sink
since, REFERRING TO THE PAST, FROM
    THEN UP UNTIL NOW, BECAUSE OF
    (or see sense/cent(s)/sin(s)/
    scent(s))
sincere,ely,rity,eness, HONEST/
    GENUINE "prefixes: in"
sincerly, sincere(ly)
sinch, cinch
sinched, singe(d) / cinch(ed)
sinchro, synchro
sinchronus, synchrony(nous)
sincht, singe(d) / cinch(ed)
sincronize, synchrony(nize)
sincrony, synchrony
sind, send / sign(ed) / sin(nned)
sinder, cinder / send(er)
sindicate, syndicate
sindication, syndicate(tion)
sindikation, syndicate(tion)

sindiket, syndicate
sindrem, syndrome
sindrulize, centralize
sindrum, syndrome
sindukit, syndicate
sindur, send(er)
sine, MATHEMATICAL FUNCTION (or
    see sign/sin)
sined, sign(ed) / sin(nned)
sinegrade, centigrade
sinek, cynic
sinekal, cynical
sinema, cinema
sinemin, cinnamon
sineority, senior(ity)
sinepede, centipede
siner, sin(nner)
sinereo, scenario
sinergy, synergy
sinerist, scenario(ist)
sines, sign(s) / sin(s) / sinus
sinester, sinister
sinetor, senator
sinetorial, senator(ial)
sinew,wy, TENDONS, TO STRENGTHEN
sinfuly, sin(fully)
sing,*,ging,ger, CREATE MELODIC
    NOTES/SONGS WITH THE VOICE/
    THROAT(or see singe/sink)
singal, single
singar, sing(er)
singe,*,ed,ging, SCORCH/SLIGHTLY
    BURN SOMETHING (or see sing/
    cinch)
singel, single
singewlerety, singular(ity)
singil, single
singir, sing(er)
single,*,ed,ling,lism,ly, ONLY ONE, NOT
    WITH OTHERS
singul, single
singular,rly,rness,rize,rity,rities, OF
    BEING ONE/ONCE, INDIVIDUAL
    "prefixes: non"
singuler, singular
singulerety, singular(ity)
singuleridy, singular(ity)
singulerly, singular(ly)
singuly, single(ly)
singur, sing(er)
singus, singe(s) / cinch(es)
sinic, cynic
sinical, cynical
sinima, cinema

sinior, senior
sinir, sin(nner)
sinister,rous,rously,rly,rness,
    SOMETHING EVIL/FOREBODING
sinj, singe / cinch
sinjd, singe(d) / cinch(ed)
sinjt, singe(d) / cinch(ed)
sink,*,sunk,king,ker,kage,kable, TO
    DESCEND/LOWER/RECLINE/
    SUBMERGE, A BASIN (or see sync)
sinkd, sink(ed)
sinkewler, singular
sinkil, single
sinkir, sink(er) / sing(er)
sinkle, single
sinkly, single(ly)
sinkranes, synchrony(nous)
sinkrenus, synchrony(nous)
sinkro, synchro
sinkronee, synchrony
sinkronize, synchrony(nize)
sinkronus, synchrony(nous)
sinkrony, synchrony
sinkt, sink(ed)
sinkul, single
sinkularedy, singular(ity)
sinkularly, singular(ly)
sinkuler, singular
sinkur, sink(er) / sing(er)
sinles, sin(less)
sinnless, sin(less)
sinoda, sonata
sinodu, sonata
sinografee, scenography
sinography, scenography
sinome, tsunami
sinonemus, synonym(ous)
sinonim, synonym
sinonimus, synonym(ous)
sinonym, synonym
sinopsis, synopsis
sinota, sonata
sinoter, senator
sins, sign(s) / sin(s) / since / sense /
    cent(s)
sinsable, sensible
sinsaredy, sincere(rity)
sinsaridy, sincere(rity)
sinsashen, sensation
sinsation, sensation
sinsative, sensitive
sinsativity, sensitive(vity)
sinsatize, sensitize
sinse, since / sense / cent(s) / scent(s)

sinseer, sincere
sinseerly, sincere(ly)
sinsere, sincere
sinseredy, sincere(rity)
sinserity, sincere(rity)
sinserly, sincere(ly)
sinsery, sensor(y)
sinsetive, sensitive
sinseur, sincere / censor / censure /
    sensor
sinshere, century
sinshewality, sensual(ity)
sinshewus, sensuous
sinshual, sensual
sinshuality, sensual(ity)
sinshuos, sensuous
sinshure, century
sinsiry, sensor(y)
sinsless, sense(less)
sinsor, censor / censure
sinsoreal, sensor(ial)
sinsory, sensor(y)
sinst, sense(d)
sinsual, sensual
sinsuble, sensible
sinsus, census / sense
sinsutive, sensitive
sinsutivity, sensitive(vity)
sinsutize, sensitize
sint, sent / cent / scent / sin(nned) /
    sign(ed)
sintaks, syntax
sintament, sentiment
sintamental, sentiment(al)
sintax, syntax
sintchuis, sensuous
sintekit, syndicate
sintement, sentiment
sinteneul, centennial
sintense, sentence
sinter, center
sinthasis, synthesis
sinthasize, synthesize
sinthedik, synthetic
sinthesis, synthesis
sinthetek, synthetic
sinthusis, synthesis
sinthusize, synthesize
sintimental, sentiment(al)
sintineul, centennial
sintinse, sentence
sintrie, sentry / centri
sintrul, central
sintrulize, centralize

sintry, sentry / centri
sintrys, sentry(ries)
sintugrade, centigrade
sintumental, sentiment(al)
sintury, century
sinu, sinew
sinuee, sinew(y)
sinugrade, centigrade
sinumeter, centimeter
sinumon, cinnamon
sinunem, synonym
sinupede, centipede
sinur, sin(nner)
sinurgy, synergy
sinus,ses,sitis, RESPIRATORY CAVITIES/
    PASSAGES IN THE FACE, BOTANICAL
    TERM
sinuster, sinister
sinutor, senator
sinutorial, senator(ial)
sinuy, sinew(y)
sinyor, senior
sinyority, senior(ity)
sinyuee, sinew(y)
siontefikly, scientific(ally)
siontest, scientist
siontifek, scientific
siontist, scientist
sip,*,pped,pping,pper,ppingly, TO
    PURSE THE LIPS TO DRINK, SMALL
    DRINKS (or see sipe/seep)
sipasetory, suppository
sipausatory, suppository
sipe,*,ed,ping, SOAK/DRIP THROUGH
    (or see sip/seep)
sipereor, superior
sipereority, superior(ity)
sipereur, superior
siperlitef, superlative
siphelis, syphilis
siphen, siphon
siphenul, siphon(al)
siphilis, syphilis
siphon,*,ned,ning,nal,nic,nless, USE
    PRESSURE/SUCTION TO RELOCATE
    FLUIDS (also spelled syphon)
siphules, syphilis
sipkonchus, subconscious
siplant, supplant
sipli, supply
siplier, supply(lier)
sipling, sibling
sipliur, supply(lier)
siply, supply

siport, support
siportef, support(ive)
siportive, support(ive)
siposatory, suppository
sipose, suppose
siposubly, suppose(dly)
sipoze, suppose
sipozubly, suppose(dly)
sipreem, supreme
sipreno, soprano
sipres, suppress
sipreshun, suppress(ion)
siptek, styptic
siptik, styptic
sipur, sip(pper)
sipurb, superb
sipurblee, superb(ly)
sipurlitef, superlative
siquential, sequence(ntial)
siquerly, secure(ly)
siquir, secure
siquirety, secure(rity)
siquoia, sequoia
sir,*, TITLE OF A MAN (or see sire)
siraded, serrate(d)
siraget, surrogate
siragit, surrogate
siramik, ceramic
siran, saran / siren
sirape, syrup / serape
sirashen, serrate(tion)
sirated, serrate(d)
siration, serrate(tion)
sircal, circle
sircas, circus
sircemscribe, circumscribe
sircharge, surcharge
sirchuble, search(able)
sircimscribe, circumscribe
sircit, circuit
sircle, circle
sircol, circle
sircomfurinse, circumference
sircomscribe, circumscribe
sircophagus, sarcophagus
sircot, circuit
sircul, circle
sircumferenc, circumference
sircumpherence, circumference
sircumsize, circumcise
sircumstans, circumstance
sircus, circus
sircut, circuit
sirdify, certify

sire,*,ed,ring, MALE PARENT OF A
    MAMMAL (or see sir)
sireal, serial / cereal / surreal
sirealism, surrealism
sireilisum, surrealism
sirel, sorrel / surreal
sirelism, surrealism
sirem, serum
siren,*, LOUD/PIERCING SOUNDS
    FROM A DEVICE, SEA NYMPHS
sirench, syringe
sirendur, surrender
sirene, serene
sireng, syringe
sirenidy, serene(nity)
sirenity, serene(nity)
sirenj, syringe
sireol, serial / cereal
sireous, serious
sirep, syrup
sires, series / sire(s) / cirrus / scirrhus
sireul, cereal / serial
sireulizum, surrealism
sireus, serious
sireusly, serious(ly)
sirf, surf / serf / serve
sirface, surface
sirfdum, serf(dom)
sirfege, serf(age)
sirfeje, serf(age)
sirfes, surface / service
sirfibul, surf(able)
sirfis, surface
sirfunt, servant
sirfur, surf(er)
sirg, surge / serge
sirgakle, surgical
sirgekul, surgical
sirgen, surgeon
sirgent, sergeant / surgent
sirgeon, surgeon
sirgon, surgeon
sirgree, surgery
sirgukle, surgical
sirguree, surgery
siriasis, psoriasis
sirim, serum
sirin, siren
sirios, serious
siriosly, serious(ly)
siris, series
sirius, serious
sirjakle, surgical
sirje, surge / serge

sirjekul, surgical
sirjen, surgeon
sirjon, surgeon
sirjree, surgery
sirjukle, surgical
sirjuree, surgery
sirkawfigus, sarcophagus
sirkemscribe, circumscribe
sirkes, circus
sirkewler, circular
sirkis, circus
sirklar, circular
sirkofegus, sarcophagus
sirkomscribe, circumscribe
sirkulate, circulate
sirkumferinse, circumference
sirkumscribe, circumscribe
sirkumsize, circumcise
sirlee, surly
sirloin,*, A CUT OF BEEF
sirly, surly
sirman, sermon
sirmize, surmise
sirmon, sermon
sirogate, surrogate
sirom, serum
siron, siren
sirong, sarong
sirope, serape / syrup
siroredy, sorority
sirority, sorority
siros, scirrhus / cirrus
siround, surround
sirownd, surround
sirpas, surpass
sirpent, serpent
sirpentene, serpentine
sirpint, serpent
sirpintent, serpentine
sirplus, surplus
sirprize, surprise
sirrated, serrate(d)
sirrus, cirrus / scirrhus
sirtenly, certain(ly)
sirtin, certain
sirtunly, certain(ly)
sirum, serum
sirun, siren
sirup, syrup
sirus, cirrus / scirrhus
sirv, serve
sirva, survey
sirvailense, surveillance
sirvalense, surveillance

sirvatood, servitude
sirvatude, servitude
sirvaur, survey(or)
sirvayer, survey(or)
sirve, serve / survey
sirveilinse, surveillance
sirveor, survey(or)
sirves, service / survey(s) / serve(s)
sirvesable, service(cable)
sirveyor, survey(or)
sirvife, survive
sirvint, servant
sirvis, service
sirvitude, servitude
sirvive, survive
sirvivul, survive(val)
sirvont, servant
sirvunt, servant
sirvusable, service(cable)
sirvutude, servitude
sirys, series
sis, size /cease / seize
sisabul, size(zable)
sisal, sizzle
sisd, size(d) / cyst
sisdamadik, system(atic)
sisdamatic, system(atic)
sisdan, sustain
sisdem, system
sisdum, system
sisdumadik, system(atic)
sisdumatic, system(atic)
sise, size / sissy
siseble, size(zable)
sisede, secede
siseded, secede(d)
sisee, sissy
sisel, sizzle
siseptible, susceptible
siseptif, susceptive
siseptive, susceptive
siseptuble, susceptible
siseptuf, susceptive
sisers, scissor(s)
siseshen, secession
sisesion, secession
siset, secede
sisetion, secession
sisle, sizzle
sismec, seism(ic)
sismic, seism(ic)
sismical, seism(ical)
sismik, seism(ic)
sisors, scissor(s)

sispend, suspend
sissy,ssies,ssified,ssiness,yness,yish,
    BEHAVE LIKE A COWARD,
    UNMASCULINE
sist, cist / cyst
sistain, sustain
sistane, sustain
sistanuble, sustain(able)
sistem, system
sister,*,rly,hood, FEMALES WHO HAVE
    A STRONG AFFINITY/RELATIONSHIP,
    FEMALE SIBLING BY LAW/BLOOD
sistre, sister
sistum, system
sistumatic, system(atic)
sistur, sister
sisturly, sister(ly)
sisturn, cistern
sisubil, size(zable)
sisuble, size(zable)
sisul, sizzle
sisurs, scissor(s)
sisus, size(s)
sisy, sissy
sit,*,tting,tter,sat, POSITION RESTING
    ON THE BUTTOCKS, WHAT
    SOMETHING OCCUPYING SPACE/
    POSITION DOES (or see set/site/
    side)
sitanic, satanic
sitanikul, satanic(al)
sitashun, citation
sitation, citation
sitchuashen, situate(tion)
sitchuate, situate
site,*, AREA OF SIGNIFICANCE (or see
    sight/side)
siter, sit(tter)/ cider/ side(r)
siterical, satire(rical)
sitesin, citizen
sith, scythe
sitir, sit(tter) / cider / side(r)
sitor, sit(tter) / cider / side(r)
sitrek, citric
sitrik, citric
sitrus, citrus
situashen, situate(tion)
situate,*,ed,ting,tion,tional,tionally,
    LOCATION/POSITION OF OBJECTS/
    EVENTS
situatid, situate(d)
situr, sit(tter) / cider
situzin, citizen
sity, city

siunide, cyanide
siunse, science
siuntest, scientist
siuntifek, scientific
siuntifekaly, scientific(ally)
siuntist, scientist
siur, sigh(er)
siv, sieve
sival, civil
sivalization, civil(ization)
sivana, savanna
sivant, savant
sivd, sieve(d) / sift
sivear, severe
sived, sieve(d) / sift
sivere, severe
siverity, severe(rity)
siverly, severe(ly)
sivic, civic
sivil, civil
sivilean, civilian
sivlazation, civil(ization)
sivluzation, civil(ization)
sivol, civil
sivolazation, civil(ization)
sivont, savant
sivt, sift / sieve(d)
sivted, sift(ed)
sivter, sift(er)
sivul, civil
sivulization, civil(ization)
siworo, saguaro
six,xes, AN ENGLISH NUMBER AFTER
    FIVE
sixis, six(es)
sixstenth, sixteen(th)
sixtee, sixty
sixteen,nth, AN ENGLISH NUMBER
    AFTER FIFTEEN, 16 PARTS OF A
    WHOLE
sixteith, sixtieth
sixten, sixteen
sixth,*, AN ENGLISH NUMBER AFTER
    THE FIFTH, OF SIX EQUAL PARTS
sixtieth, ENGLISH NUMBER AFTER 59,
    OF 60 EQUAL PARTS
sixty,ties, AN ENGLISH NUMBER AFTER
    59
sixtyn, sixteen
sixus, six(es)
siz, size /seize / sight(s) / see(s) / sea(s)
sizabil, size(zable)
sizal, sizzle
sizars, scissor(s)

sizd, size(d) / seize(d)
size,*,ed,zing,zable,zably,zableness,
    AREA/DIMENSION OF SOMETHING
    "prefixes: over/under"
sizebul, size(zable)
sizel, sizzle
sizers, scissor(s)
sizible, size(zable)
sizis, size(s)
sizle, sizzle
sizmek, seism(ic)
sizmekul, seism(ical)
sizmik, seism(ic)
sizmikul, seism(ical)
sizold, sizzle(d)
sizors, scissor(s)
siztur, sister
sizuble, size(zable)
sizul, sizzle
sizurs, scissor(s)
sizus, size(s)
sizzle,*,ed,ling,er, A COOKING/FRYING/
    SIZZLING SOUND
skab, scab
skabard, scabbard
skabbard, scabbard
skabed, scab(bbed)
skabees, scabies
skaburd, scabbard
skaby, scab(bby)
skabys, scabies
skad, scat / skate / skat / scad
skader, skate(r) / scatter
skaffold, scaffold
skafolding, scaffold(ing)
skair, scare
skairslee, scarce(ly)
skalar, scalar
skalastic, scholastic
skalb, scalp
skalber, scalp(er)
skald, scald / scale(d)
skale, scale
skalee, scaly
skaleness, scaly(liness)
skaleon, scallion
skalep, scallop
skaleun, scallion
skaley, scaly
skalip, scallop
skaliun, scallion
skallion, scallion
skallop, scallop
skalor, scalar

skalp, scalp
skalpel, scalpel
skalper, scalp(er)
skalpul, scalpel
skalt, scald / scale(d)
skalup, scallop
skaly, scaly
skalyin, scallion
skalyun, scallion
skamatek, scheme(matic)
skan, scan
skand, scan(nned)
skandal, scandal
skandelus, scandal(ous)
skandul, scandal
skandulus, scandal(ous)
skaner, scan(nner)
skanir, scan(nner)
skant, scant / scan(nned)
skantily, scant(ily)
skantuly, scant(ily)
skanur, scan(nner)
skapal, scalpel
skapala, scapula
skapel, scalpel
skapela, scapula
skapeula, scapula
skapil, scalpel
skapila, scapula
skapul, scalpel
skapula, scapula
skar, scar / scare
skarcedy, scarce(city)
skarcity, scarce(city)
skare, scare / scare(y)
skarf, scarf
skarlut, scarlet
skarse, scarce / scare(s)
skarsedy, scarce(city)
skarsly, scarce(ly)
skarsness, scarce(ness)
skarves, scarf(rves)
skat, A CARD GAME (or see scat/skate)
skatar, skate(r) / scatter
skate,*,ed,ting,er, MOVE ABOUT WITH
    ROLLERS/BLADES ATTACHED TO
    SHOES, TO MOVE IN GLIDING
    MOTION (or see skat/scat)
skater, scatter / skate(r)
skathe, scathe
skator, skate(r) / scatter
skattur, scatter / skate(r)
skatur, skate(r) / scatter
skauler, scholar

skaulerly, scholar(ly)
skavage, scavenge
skavege, scavenge
skaveger, scavenge(r)
skavenger, scavenge(r)
skavinger, scavenge(r)
skavuge, scavenge
skavunger, scavenge(r)
skawler, scholar
skawlerly, scholar(ly)
skeam, scheme
skeat, skeet
skech, sketch
skechily, sketch(ily)
skechis, sketch(es)
skecht, sketch(ed)
skechuly, sketch(ily)
skechus, sketch(es)
skechwal, schedule
skechwul, schedule
sked, ski(ed) / scare(d) / skid
skedchule, schedule
skedule, schedule
skeed, ski(ed) / skid
skeem, scheme
skeemer, skim(mmer) / scheme(r)
skeen, skein / ski(iing)
skeet, TYPE OF TRAPSHOOTING
skef, skiff
skein, FLOCK OF WILD BIRDS, BUNDLE
    OF THREAD/YARN (or see ski(iing)/
    skin)
skeing, ski(iing)
skeir, skier
skel, skill / skull / school
skelastic, scholastic
skelaten, skeleton
skelatul, skeletal
skelatun, skeleton
skeld, skill(ed)
skeled, skill(ed)
skeletal,tally, BONES OF A BODY, BASIC
    FRAMEWORK "prefixes: exo/endo"
skeletin, skeleton
skeleton,*,tal,nize,nizer, BONES OF A
    BODY, BASIC FRAMEWORK
    "prefixes: endo/exo"
skeletun, skeleton
skelful, skill(ful)
skelit, skillet
skeliton, skeleton
skelitul, skeletal
skelitun, skeleton
skelut, skillet

skelutin, skeleton
skem, scheme / skim
skematik, scheme(matic)
skemd, skim(mmed) / scheme(d)
skeme, scheme
skemer, skim(mmer) / scheme(r)
skemur, skim(mmer) / scheme(r)
sken, skein / skin
skenee, skinny
skenir, skinner
skeniur, skinny(nier)
skeniust, skinny(niest)
skenlus, skin(less)
skenur, skinner
skeny, skinny
skeor, skier
skep, skip
skepir, skipper
skeps, skip(s)
skept, skip(pped)
skeptacism, skeptic(ism)
skeptak, skeptic
skeptic,*,cal,cally,calness,cism, ONE
    WHO CHALLENGES/DOUBTS
    DOCTRINATED BELIEFS (also spelled
    "sceptic")
skeptucism, skeptic(ism)
skeptuk, skeptic
skeptusisum, skeptic(ism)
sker, scare / skier
skerd, skirt / scare(d)
skere, scare(y)
skerfy, scurvy
skerge, scourge
skerje, scourge
skers, skier(s) / scare(s) / scarce
skersedy, scarce(city)
skersity, scarce(city)
skersly, scarce(ly)
skersness, scarce(ness)
skersudy, scarce(city)
skert, skirt / scare(d)
skervy, scurvy
skery, scurry
skeryd, scurry(ried)
skes, ski(s) / sky(kies)
skeshily, sketch(ily)
sket, skeet / skit
sketch,hes,hed,hing,her,hy,hily,hiness,
    BRIEF/ROUGH OUTLINE/DRAWING/
    IDEA
sketchewl, schedule
sketsh, sketch
skeu, skew

skeuer, skewer
skeuner, schooner
skeur, skier / skewer
skew,*,wed,wing,wness, SLANTED/
    SLOPED/DISTORTED/OBLIQUE
    POSITION
skewbu, scuba
skewdur, scoot(er)
skewer,*, THIN/LONG INSTRUMENT
    FOR HOLDING MEAT/VEGETABLES
    FOR GRILLING
skewir, skewer
skewp, scoop
skewpur, scoop(er)
skewtur, scoot(er)
skewur, skewer
skezafrinea, schizophrenia
ski,*,ied,iing,ier, LONG DEVICES
    ATTACHED TO FEET TO ACHIEVE
    SPEED/ GLIDING ON VARIOUS
    SURFACES (or see sky)
skid,*,dded,dding, FRAMEWORK TO
    HELP SOMETHING SLIDE ALONG,
    SLIDE WHEN COMING TO A STOP
    (or see ski(ed)/skit)
skidesh, skittish
skidush, skittish
skier,*, SOMEONE WHO SKIS
skif, skiff
skiff,*, SMALL BOAT
skiier, skier
skiir, skier
skiis, ski(s)
skil, skill
skilastic, scholastic
skilet, skillet
skilful, skill(ful)
skilfuly, skill(fully)
skill,*,led,lful,lfully,lfulness,less, GAIN
    APTITUDE/EXPERIENCE
    PERFORMING A CRAFT/TRADE/ACT
    "prefixes: re/semi/un"
skillet,*, LONG HANDLED FRYING PAN
skilut, skillet
skim,*,mmed,mming,mmer, BE ON/
    GLANCE OVER A SURFACE, REMOVE
    THE SURFACE (or see scheme)
skimatik, scheme(matic)
skimer, skim(mmer) / scheme(r)
skin,*,nned,nning,nner,nless, SURFACE
    ORGANISM THAT PROTECTS BODILY
    FLUIDS/CONTENTS, REMOVE
    COVER/ LAYER OF PROTECTION
    FROM SOMETHING (or see skein)

skinee, skinny
skiner, skinner
skineust, skinny(niest)
sking, ski(iing)
skinles, skin(less)
skinner,*,ry, ONE WHO REMOVES SKIN
skinny,nnier,nniest, BONEY, NOT MUCH
    MUSCLE/FAT ON THE BODY
skinur, skinner
skiny, skinny
skip,*,pped,pping, PASS OVER/MISS A
    BEAT/LEVEL
skiper, skipper
skipir, skipper
skipper,*, CAPTAIN OF A SHIP/BOAT,
    AN INSECT, ONE WHO SKIPS
skipur, skipper
skir, skier
skireed, scurry(ried)
skirfy, scurvy
skirt,*,ted,ting,ter, A GARMENT WORN
    TO COVER/PROTECT THE LOWER
    TORSO, TO EVADE/PASS AROUND
    AND ISSUE/EVENT "prefixes: under"
skirvy, scurvy
skiry, scurry
skisoed, schizoid
skisophrenea, schizophrenia
skit,*, A BRIEF/SHORT PLAY
skitesh, skittish
skitish, skittish
skitsafrenea, schizophrenia
skitsophrenia, schizophrenia
skittish,hly, EASILY FRIGHTENED
skitush, skittish
skitzafrenea, schizophrenia
skiur, skewer
skizoed, schizoid
skizofrenea, schizophrenia
skizoid, schizoid
skizophrenia, schizophrenia
skof, scoff
skolar, scholar
skolarly, scholar(ly)
skolastic, scholastic
skold, scold / scald
skoleosis, scoliosis
skoler, scholar
skolerly, scholar(ly)
skoliosis, scoliosis
skolir, scholar
skolirly, scholar(ly)
skolt, scold / scald
skolur, scholar

skolurly, scholar(ly)
skomatik, scheme(matic)
skone, scone
skons, scone(s) / sconce
skonts, sconce
skoobu, scuba
skooder, scoot(er)
skool, school
skooner, schooner
skoop, scoop
skooper, scoop(er)
skoot, scoot / scute
skooter, scoot(er)
skor, scar
skorch, scorch
skore, score
skorles, score(less)
skorn, scorn
skornfuly, scorn(fully)
skorpeon, scorpion
skorpeun, scorpion
skorsh, scorch
skorur, score(r)
skoul, scowl
skour, scour
skout, scout
skouter, scout(er)
skower, scour
skowir, scour
skowl, scowl
skowndrel, scoundrel
skowr, scour
skowt, scout
skowter, scout(er)
skowurd, scour(ed)
skquer, skewer
skquir, skewer
skrabs, scrap(s) / scrape(s)
skrach, scratch
skrag, scrag
skragliest, scraggly(liest)
skragly, scrag(ily) / scraggly
skrakleur, scraggly(lier)
skrakly, scrag(ily) / scraggly
skram, scram
skrambul, scramble
skrampul, scramble
skrap, scrap / scrape
skraper, scrape(r) / scrap(pper)
skrapuble, scrap(able)
skratch, scratch
skreach, screech
skream, scream
skrean, screen

skreblur, scribble(r)
skrebul, scribble
skrech, screech
skred, screed
skreech, screech
skreed, screed
skreem, scream
skreen, screen
skreenuble, screen(able)
skremage, scrimmage
skremije, scrimmage
skremp, scrimp
skremshaw, scrimshaw
skremuge, scrimmage
skremuje, scrimmage
skren, screen
skrenuble, screen(able)
skreped, script
skrepshur, scripture
skrept, script
skrepture, scripture
skrew, screw
skrewge, scrooge
skrewje, scrooge
skrewpal, scruple
skrewpel, scruple
skrewpewlis, scrupulous
skrewpils, scruple(s)
skrewpul, scruple
skrewpules, scrupulous
skrewpulisle, scrupulous(ly)
skrewteny, scrutiny
skrewtiney, scrutiny
skrewy, screw(y)
skribe, scribe
skrible, scribble
skribler, scribble(r)
skribul, scribble
skrimage, scrimmage
skrimije, scrimmage
skrimp, scrimp
skrimshaw, scrimshaw
skrimuge, scrimmage
skrimuje, scrimmage
skriped, script
skripshur, scripture
skript, script
skripture, scripture
skripuld, scribble(d)
skrol, scrawl / scroll
skroo, screw
skrooge, scrooge
skrooje, scrooge
skrooy, screw(y)

skroul, scrawl

skrounge, scrounge

skrowl, scrawl

skrownge, scrounge / scrounge(y)

skrowngy, scrounge(y)

skrownje, scrounge / scrounge(y)

skru, screw

skrub, scrub

skrud, screw(ed)

skrudnee, scrutiny

skruf, scruff

skrufy, scruff(y)

skruge, scrooge

skruje, scrooge

skrup, scrub

skrupel, scruple

skrupeulus, scrupulous

skrupul, scruple

skrupules, scrupulous

skrupulous, scrupulous

skruteny, scrutiny

skrutiny, scrutiny

skruwe, screw(y)

skruy, screw(y)

sku, skew

skual, squall

skuar, skewer

skuba, scuba

skuder, scoot(er)

skued, squid

skueel, squeal

skuegul, squiggle

skuel, school

skuelched, squelch(ed)

skuelsh, squelch

skuer, skewer

skuesh, squish

skueshy, squish(y)

skuf, scuff

skufel, scuffle

skuful, scuffle

skuid, squid

skuigul, squiggle

skuir, skewer

skuish, squish

skuishy, squish(y)

skul, school / skull

skulastic, scholastic

skulbd, sculpt

skulbsher, sculpt(ure)

skulbshir, sculpt(ure)

skulbt, sculpt

skull,*, BONE IN THE HEAD (or see school)

skulpsher, sculpt(ure)

skulpshur, sculpt(ure)

skulpt, sculpt

skum, scum

skumatek, scheme(matic)

skumy, scum(mmy)

skuner, schooner

skunk,*, OMNIVOROUS BLACK/WHITE MAMMAL WITH STRONG SCENT GLANDS

skupe, scoop

skuper, scoop(er)

skurage, scourge

skuraje, scourge

skured, scurry(ried) / skewer(ed)

skureed, scurry(ried)

skurfy, scurvy

skurge, scourge

skurige, scourge

skurje, scourge

skurt, skirt

skurvy, scurvy

skury, scurry

skuryd, scurry(ried)

skut, skew(ed) / scoot / scute

skuter, scoot(er)

skwabil, squabble

skwabul, squabble

skwad, squad / squat

skwader, squat(ttor)

skwadir, squat(ttor)

skwadrin, squadron

skwadron, squadron

skwadur, squat(ttor)

skwair, square

skwairly, square(ly)

skwal, squall

skwaled, squalid

skwalid, squalid

skwalor, squalor

skwander, squander

skwantur, squander

skwapel, squabble

skwapul, squabble

skward, square(d)

skware, square

skwarlee, square(ly)

skwart, square(d) / squirt

skwash, squash

skwat, squad / squat

skwater, squat(ttor)

skwatir, squat(ttor)

skwatrin, squadron

skwaudren, squadron

skwauled, squalid

skwaulid, squalid

skwaulir, squalor

skwaulur, squalor

skwaut, squad / squat

skwautrin, squadron

skwautron, squadron

skweak, squeak

skwed, squid

skweegee, squeegee

skweeje, squeegee

skweek, squeak

skweel, squeal

skweemish, squeamish

skwees, squeeze

skweesir, squeeze(r)

skweeze, squeeze

skwegal, squiggle

skwegee, squeegee

skwegul, squiggle

skwegy, squeegee

skwejee, squeegee

skwel, squeal

skwelch, squelch

skweler, squeal(er)

skwelir, squeal(er)

skwelsh, squelch

skweltch, squelch

skwelur, squeal(er)

skwemesh, squeamish

skwemish, squeamish

skwent, squint

skweral, squirrel

skwerl, squirrel

skwerly, squirrel(y)

skwerm, squirm

skwermy, squirm(y)

skwerol, squirrel

skwert, squirt

skwerul, squirrel

skwes, squeeze

skweser, squeeze(r)

skwesh, squish

skweshy, squish(y)

skwesir, squeeze(r)

skwesur, squeeze(r)

skwet, squid

skweze, squeeze

skwezur, squeeze(r)

skwiarly, square(ly)

skwid, squid

skwigal, squiggle

skwigul, squiggle

skwint, squint

skwire, squire
skwirl, squirrel
skwirm, squirm
skwirmy, squirm(y)
skwirt, squirt
skwirul, squirrel
skwish, squish
skwishy, squish(y)
skwobil, squabble
skwobul, squabble
skwod, squad / squat
skwodir, squat(ttor)
skwodrin, squadron
skwodron, squadron
skwodur, squat(ttor)
skwol, squall
skwoled, squalid
skwolid, squalid
skwolor, squalor
skwondur, squander
skwontur, squander
skwopel, squabble
skwopil, squabble
skwosh, squash
skwot, squad / squat
skwoter, squat(ttor)
skwotir, squat(ttor)
skwotrin, squadron
skwotron, squadron
skwotur, squat(ttor)
skwural, squirrel
skwurl, squirrel
skwurly, squirrel(y)
skwurm, squirm
skwurmt, squirm(ed)
skwurmy, squirm(y)
skwurt, squirt
sky,kies, FIRMAMENT/FIELD ABOVE A
PLANET (or see ski)
sla, slay / sleigh
slab,*,bbed,bbing, LARGE/FLAT/SOLID
MATERIAL (or see slap)
slabt, slept / slap(pped)
slack,*,ked,king,ker,ken, NOT TAUT/
TIGHT, PAIR OF DRESS PANTS, NOT
SHARP/ALERT (or see slag)
slade, slay(ed) / slate
slader, slaughter
slae, slay / sleigh
slafe, slave
slafree, slave(ry)
slafry, slave(ry)
slag, WASTE REMNANTS FROM METALS
(or see slack)

slag hamer, sledge hammer
slai, slay / sleigh
slain, PAST TENSE FOR THE WORD
"SLAY", KILL VIOLENTLY
slak, slack
slaker, slack(er)
slakur, slack(er)
slam,*,mmed,mming,mmer, SHUT/
CLOSE/STRIKE
slamur, slam(mmer)
slan, slain
slander,*,red,ring,rer,rous,rously,
rousness, FALSE/UNTRUE
REMARKS/WORDS
slanderus, slander(ous)
slandured, slander(ed)
slanduris, slander(ous)
slang,*,gily,giness,gy, NON-STANDARD
USAGE OF WORDS, SHORT-LIVED
WORDS
slank, slang
slant,*,ted,ting, SLOPING/OBLIQUE
STANCE, NOT LEVEL, BIASED
slantur, slander
slap,*,pped,pping,pper, TO STRIKE
WITH AN OPEN HAND, A CRISP/
SHORT BLOW
slapir, slap(pper)
slapt, slap(pped) / slept
slas, sleigh(s) / slay(s) / slaw(s)
slash,hes,hed,hing,her, TO DRIVE A
SWEEPING STROKE/BLOW, TO CUT/
OPEN WITH A BLADE
slashur, slash(er)
slat,*,ted,ting,ty, THIN STRIPS OF
WOOD/METAL (or see slate/
slay(ed))
slate,*,ed,ting,ty, CLAY/SHALE/COAL
TYPES OF ROCK, AN APPOINTMENT
(or see slat/slay(ed))
slath, sloth
slau, slaw
slaudir, slaughter
slaudur, slaughter
slaughter,*,red,ring,rer,rous,rously,
VIOLENTLY KILL/DESTROY
slauterus, slaughter(ous)
slave,*,ed,ving,ery, ONE WHO IS
FORCED TO WORK FOR SOMEONE
WITHOUT PAY,WORK HARDER
THAN REASONABLE "prefixes: en"
slaven, sloven
slavenly, sloven(ly)
slavry, slave(ry)

slaw,*, COLD CABBAGE/VEGETABLE
DISH
slawb, slob
slawderus, slaughter(ous)
slawdur, slaughter
slawter, slaughter
slawterus, slaughter(ous)
slay,*,yed,ying,yer,slew,slain, KILL
VIOLENTLY (or see sleigh)
sleak, sleek
sleaken, sleek(en)
sleaknes, sleek(ness)
sleat, sleet
sleave, sleeve
sleazy,zier,ziest,zily,ziness, OF CHEAP/
POOR CHARACTER/QUALITY
sleber, sleep(er)
slebir, sleep(er)
slebry, slip(ppery)
slebt, slept
slebur, sleep(er)
sleck, slick
slecker, slick(er)
sleckly, sleek(ly)
sled,*,dded,dding,dder, TO SLIDE/GLIDE
SMOOTHLY ALONG THE GROUND
(or see sleigh/slid)
sledge hammer, LARGE/HEAVY
HAMMER
sledir, sled(dder)
sledur, sled(dder)
sleef, sleeve
sleek,ken,kens,kened,kening,ker,kly,
kness, SHINY/SMOOTH/SOOTHING
sleeknis, sleek(ness)
sleep,*,ping,slept,per,pless,py,piness,
pily, SLOW DOWN BASIC
FUNCTIONS TO REST, BECOME
UNCONSCIOUS, PLACE TO SLEEP
"prefixes: over"
sleepee, sleep(y)
sleeseist, sleazy(ziest)
sleesy, sleazy
sleet,*,ted,ting, ICY SNOW, FROZEN
PRECIPITATION
sleeve,*,ed,ving,eless, COVER FOR
MANY THINGS
sleezee, sleazy
sleezyest, sleazy(ziest)
slefs, sleeve(s)
slefur, sliver
sleg, slick
slege hamer, sledge hammer

sleigh,*,hed,hing, A CONTRAPTION DESIGNED TO GLIDE/SLIDE ALONG THE GROUND (or see sled)

sleight,*,ted,ting, ADROIT/NIMBLE OF BODY/MIND, 'SLEIGHT OF HAND' (or see slight)

sleit, slight / sleight / slate

sleje hamer, sledge hammer

slek, slick / sleek

sleker, slick(er) / sleek(er)

slekly, sleek(ly) / slick(ly)

sleknis, slick(ness) / sleek(ness)

slekur, slick(er) / sleek(er)

slem, slim

slemd, slim(mmed) / slime(d)

slemest, slim(mmest)

slemir, slim(mmer)

slemt, slim(mmed) / slime(d)

slemur, slim(mmer)

slemust, slim(mmest)

slender,rly,rness,rize, SLIM

slendir, slender

slendirness, slender(ness)

slendur, slender

slendurness, slender(ness)

sleng, sling

slenger, sling(er)

slengur, sling(er)

slenk, sling / slink

slenky, slink(y)

slenter, slender

slentur, slender

slep, sleep / slip / slept

slepd, slept / slip(pped)

sleper, sleep(er)

slepir, sleep(er)

slepless, sleep(less)

slepry, slip(ppery)

sleps, sleep(s) / slip(s)

slept, PAST TENSE FOR THE WORD 'SLEEP', TO TAKE A DEEP REST WITH EYES CLOSED

slepur, sleep(er)

slepy, sleep(y)

sler, slur

sleried, slurry(ried)

slerp, slurp

slerpt, slurp(ed)

slert, slur(rred)

slery, slurry

sleryed, slurry(ried)

slesee, sleazy

sleseer, sleazy(zier)

sleseist, sleazy(ziest)

sleseur, sleazy(zier)

slesy, sleazy

slet, sled / slid

sleter, sled(dder)

sletir, sled(dder)

slets, sleet(s)

sletur, sled(dder)

sleuth,*, TRACK/TRAIL/DETECTIVE

sleve, sleeve

sleved, sleeve(d)

slever, sliver

slevir, sliver

slevs, sleeve(s)

slevur, sliver

slew, PAST TENSE FOR THE WORD "SLAY", LARGE AMOUNT/NUMBER OF SOMETHING, TO PIVOT, ALSO "SLUE" (or see slue/slough)

slewth, sleuth

sley, slay / sleigh

slezee, sleazy

slezeist, sleazy(ziest)

slezeur, sleazy(zier)

slezy, sleazy

sli, sly

slibree, slip(ppery)

slibry, slip(ppery)

sliburee, slip(ppery)

slice,*,ed,cing,er, TO CUT

slick,kly,kness,ker,kest, SLIPPERY/ SMOOTH

slid, PAST TENSE FOR THE WORD "SLIDE", GLIDE/MOVE ALONG SMOOTHLY WITHOUT RESISTANCE (or see sled/slide/slit/sleight/slight)

slide,*,ding,er,slid, GLIDE/MOVE ALONG SMOOTHLY WITHOUT RESISTANCE (or see slid/slit/slight/ sleight)

slided, slide(d) / slight(ed)

slidlee, slight(ly)

slifur, sliver

slig, slick

slight,*,ted,ted,test,ting,tingly,tly,tness, NEGLIGENT, PETTY, SLENDER, FRAIL, DISRESPECTFUL (or see sleight)

slightist, slight(est)

slik, slick / sleek

sliker, slick(er) / sleek(er)

slikness, slick(ness)

sliknis, slick(ness)

slikur, slick(er)

slily, sly(ly)

slim,*,mmer,mmest,mmed,mming,mly, UNDER PROPORTION, SMALL, UNSUBSTANTIAL (or see slime)

slimd, slim(mmed) / slime(d)

slime,*,ed,ming,my,mier,miest,mily, miness, VISCOUS/MUCOUS/OOZEY SECRETION (or see slim)

slimed, slim(mmed) / slime(d)

slimee, slime(y)

slimely, slim(ly)

slimeness, slime(miness)

slimeur, slime(mier)

slimiest, slime(miest)

slimiur, slime(mier)

slimt, slim(mmed) / slime(d)

slimur, slim(mmer) / slim(er)

slimy, slime(y)

slimyest, slime(miest)

slinder, slender

slindurness, slender(ness)

sliness, sly(ness)

sling,*,slung,ging,ger, DEVICE DESIGNED TO STRADLE/HOLD, TO FLING (or see slink) "prefixes: un/ under"

slingt, sling(ed) / slink(ed)

slingur, sling(er)

slink,*,ked,lunk,king,ky, MOVE/CREEP/ WALK QUIETLY/SECRETIVELY, BORN PREMATURELY

slinkd, slink(ed) / sling(ed)

slinkey, slink(y)

slinkt, slink(ed) / sling(ed)

slinter, slender

slip,*,pped,pping,ppery, SLIDE/GLIDE/ FALL AWAY, LOSS OF TRACTION/ FOOTING, AN UNDERGARMENT (or see sleep)

sliparee, slip(ppery)

slipry, slip(ppery)

slipt, slip(pped)

slipuree, slip(ppery)

slirp, slurp

sliry, slurry

slise, slice

sliser, slice(r)

slit,*,tting,tter, CUT SLOTS/OPENINGS INTO (or see slid/slide/slight/ sleight/sleet)

slited, sleight(ed)/ slight(ed)/ slide(d)

slither,*,red,ring,ry, TO SNAKE/SLIDE ALONG

slithry, slither(y)

slithur, slither

slitly, slight(ly)
sliver,*,red,ring, SMALL/THIN PIECE OF MATTER WHICH SPLINTERS/ SEPARATES FROM LARGER OBJECT
slivir, sliver
slivur, sliver
slo, slaw / slow
slob,*,bbed,bbing, SOMEONE WHO IS UNKEPT/UNCLEAN/UNHEALTHY (or see slab/slop)
slobber,*,red,ring,ry, DROOL/WET SECRETION FROM THE MOUTH
slober, slobber
slobery, slobber(y)
slobur, slobber
slobury, slobber(y)
slod, slot / slow(ed)
slodder, slaughter
slode, slot / slow(ed)
sloder, slaughter
slods, slot(s)
slodur, slaughter
slodurus, slaughter(ous)
sloe, slough / slow
sloer, slow(er)
sloest, slow(est)
slof, slough
slofenly, sloven(ly)
slofun, sloven
slofunly, sloven(ly)
slogan,*, A CATCHWORD/PHRASE/ MOTTO/BATTLE CRY
slogun, slogan
sloir, slow(er)
sloist, slow(est)
sloken, slogan
slokun, slogan
slole, slow(ly)
sloly, slow(ly)
slonis, slow(ness)
sloo, slew / slue / slough
sloose, sluice
slooth, sleuth
slop,*,pped,pping,ppy,ppier,ppiest, ppily,ppiness, CARELESS, SPILLED LIQUID, NASTY FOOD, SLUSHY/ MUDDY (or see slob/slope)
slopd, slope(d) / slop(pped)
slope,*,ed,ping,er,pingly,pingness, AN INCREASE/DECREASE IN ANGLE ALONG A HORIZONTAL/VERTICAL PLANE (or see slop) "prefixes: up"
slopee, slop(ppy)
slopeir, slop(ppier)

slopely, slop(ppily)
slopery, slobber(y)
slopeur, slop(ppier)
slopily, slop(ppily)
slopiness, slop(ppiness)
slopry, slobber(y)
slopt, slope(d) / slop(pped)
slopule, slop(ppily)
slopury, slobber(y)
slopy, slop(ppy)
slopyer, slop(ppier)
slopyest, slop(ppiest)
slopyness, slop(ppiness)
slos, sloth(es)
slosh,hes,hed,hing,hy, LIQUID SPLASHING AROUND
sloshee, slosh(y)
slot,*,tted,tting, NARROW OPENING/ CUT CREATED TO ALLOW INSERTION OF SOMETHING (or see slow(ed))
sloted, slot(tted)
sloter, slaughter
sloth,*, SLOW TREE-DWELLING MAMMAL (or see slough)
slouch,hes,hed,hing,her,hily,hiness,hier, hiest, DROOPS INTO A NON-ERECT POSITION
slough,hy,hiness, SHED/CAST OFF, MARSHY/SWAMPY AREA, CONDITION OF DEGRADATION (or see slew/slue)
slour, slow(er)
sloutsh, slouch
sloutshed, slouch(ed)
sloven,nly,liness,nlier,nliest, UNTIDY/ CARELESSLY CLAD
slovin, sloven
slovinly, sloven(ly)
slovun, sloven
slovunliness, sloven(liness)
slovunly, sloven(ly)
slow,*,wed,wing,wer,west,wly,wish, wness, PERFORM AT LESS THAN NORMAL/ AVERAGE SPEED (or see slough)
slowb, slob
slowch, slouch
slowcheur, slouch(ier)
slowchily, slouch(ily)
slowist, slow(est)
slowur, slow(er)
slu, slew / slue / slough
sluce, sluice

slud, slue(d) / slough(ed) / slew(ed) / sleuth
sludch, sludge
sludchy, sludge(gy)
sludge,*,gier,giest,gy, A THICK/VISCOUS LIQUID WITH HEAVY SEDIMENT
sludgeur, sludge(gier)
sludje, sludge
slue,*,ed,uing, TO PIVOT/SWING AROUND, HAVING TO DO WITH SLEW (or see slew/slough)
sluee, slough(y)
slueness, slough(iness)
sluf, slough
slug,*,gged,gging,ggish,ggishly, ggishness,gger, REMNANT OF BULLET THAT'S BEEN SHOT, HIT/ LUG SOMETHING, GASTROPOD THAT EATS PLANTS
slugar, slugger
sluge, sludge
sluger, slugger
slugesh, slug(ggish)
slugeshness, slug(ggishness)
slugeur, sludge(gier)
slugger,*, ONE WHO HITS HARD/HEAVY
slugir, slugger
slugish, slug(ggish)
slugishnes, slug(ggishenss)
slugt, slug(gged)
slugur, slugger
slugush, slug(ggish)
slugy, sludge(gy)
sluice,*,ed,cing, A CHANNEL/CANAL OF WATER, ITEM USED TO PAN FOR GOLD
sluje, sludge
slujeir, sludge(gier)
slujy, sludge(gy)
sluk, slug
sluker, slugger
slukesh, slug(ggish)
slukir, slugger
slukishnes, slug(ggishness)
slukur, slugger
slum,*,mmed,mming,mmer, POOR/ HIGHLY POPULATED/DIRTY AREA
slumber,*,red,ring,rer,rless,rous,ry, rously,rousness, TO SLEEP, BE QUITE INACTIVE, LIGHT SLEEP/ DOZE
slumbir, slumber
slumbrus, slumber(ous)
slumbrusly, slumber(ously)

slumbrusness, slumber(ousness)
slumbry, slumber(y)
slumbur, slumber
slumd, slum(mmed)
slump,*,ped,ping, DIP IN PRODUCTION, A SURFACE/VALUE
slumper, slumber
slumpur, slumber
slumur, slum(mmer)
slung, PAST TENSE FOR "SLING"
slunk, slung
slur,*,rred,rring, TO SMEAR/SMUDGE WORDS/SPEECH, INARTICULATE, CARELESS
slureng, slurry(ing) / slur(rring)
slurp,*,ped,ping, LOUD SIPPING SOUNDS WITH MOUTH
slurry,ried,ying, SOFT/ORGANIC MATERIAL CHOPPED UP IN LIQUID
slury, slurry
sluryed, slurry(ried)
slurz, slur(s)
slus, sluice
sluse, sluice
slush,hy,hiness, BETWEEN LIQUID AND SOLID
slushyness, slush(iness)
slutch, sludge
slutge, sludge
sluth, sleuth
slutje, sludge
sluy, slough(y)
sly,yly,yness, SMOOTH/DISCREET/QUIET
slym, slim / slime
slynis, sly(ness)
slynke, slink(y)
slyse, slice
slyt, slight / slide / slid
smack,*,ked,king,ker, TO DO WITH THE MOUTH, A SHARP BLOW, DIRECT, STRAIGHT, SAILING VESSEL
smak, smack
smaker, smack(er)
smal, small
smaler, small(er)
smalest, small(est)
smalist, small(est)
small,ller,llest,llness, NOT AS LARGE COMPARED TO NORMAL/AVERAGE
smarden, smart(en)
smardest, smart(est)
smardin, smart(en)

smart,*,ted,ten,ter,test,ting,tly,tness,ty, SHARP/QUICK/ALERT/PRACTICAL
smartie, smart(y)
smartist, smart(est)
smash,hes,hed,hing,her, BLAST/CRUSH/DEMOLISH TO PIECES, DESTROY BY VIOLENT BLOWS
smashur, smash(er)
smear,*,red,ring,ry, TO SPREAD/WIPE INTO, CAUSE TO RUN TOGETHER, SLANDER
smedin, smite(tten)
smeer, smear
smeery, smeer(y)
smel, smell
smeld, smell(ed) / smelt
smelder, smelter
smeldur, smelter
smelee, smell(y)
smell,*,led,ling,ly,lt, PERCEIVE WITH THE NOSE/OLFACTORY
smelt, FISH (or see smell(ed))
smelter,*, METAL MELTING PROCESS
smely, smell(y)
smer, smear
smerk, smirk
smerker, smirk(er)
smethureens, smithereens
smetin, smite(tten)
smiden, smite(tten)
smil, smile
smile,*,ed,ling,er,ey,lier,liest, FACIAL EXPRESSION STATING THAT ALL IS WELL, FRIENDLY EXPRESSION "prefixes: un"
smily, smile(y)
smirk,*,ked,king,ker,kingly, SMUG SMILE EXPRESSING SUPERIORITY/CONCEIT
smirkd, smirk(ed)
smit, smite
smite,*,ting,mote,tten, SERIOUSLY/DEEPLY STRUCK/AFFECTED, EXACT
smiten, smite(tten)
smithereens, BLOW/SMASH TO PIECES/BITS
smithureens, smithereens
smitin, smite(tten)
smiwree, smeer(y)
smock,*, OUTER GARMENT LOOSELY COVERING MAIN TORSO (or see smoke)

smog,ggy,ggier,ggiest,gless,gginess, HEAVY AIRBORNE POLLUTION (or see smock/smoke)
smogy, smog(ggy)
smok, smock / smog / smoke
smokd, smoke(d) / smog(gged)
smoke,*,ed,king,kier,kiest,kily,kiness,er, eless,ey, CLOUD OF GAS RESULTING FROM BURNED MATERIAL (or see smock)
smokir, smoke(r)
smokless, smoke(less)
smoklus, smoke(less)
smokt, smoke(d) / smog(ed)
smokur, smoke(r)
smoky, smoke(y) / smog(ggy)
smol, small
smold, smolt
smolder,*,red,ring, SLOWLY COOK IN SMOKE WITHOUT FLAME
smoler, small(er)
smolir, small(er)
smolt, A STAGE IN SALMON/FISH GROWTH
smolter, smolder
smoltur, smolder
smolur, small(er)
smooch,hes,hed,hing, TO HUG/KISS
smooth,hes,hed,hing,her,hest,hly,hness, hen,hie, NOT ROUGH, PLEASANT TO THE SENSES
smoothie,*, A FRUIT SLUSH/DRINK
smoothin, smooth(en)
smoothnis, smooth(ness)
smoothy, smoothie
smorgasboard,*, BUFFET WITH CONGLOMERATION/SELECTION OF FOODS
smorgusboard, smorgasboard
smort, smart
smoth, smooth
smother,*,red,ring, COVER, PUT OUT, STIFLE, SUPPRESS, SUFFOCATE (or see smooth(er))
smuch, smooch / smudge
smuched, smooch(ed) / smudge(d)
smuches, smooch(es) / smudge(s)
smudeist, smut(ttiest)
smudeness, smut(ttiness)
smudeur, smut(ttier)
smudge,*,ed,ging,er, SMEAR/STAIN, A SMOLDERING FIRE/SMOKE FOR PROTECTION
smudy, smut(tty)

smug,gly,gness, SELF-SATISFIED/ CONCEITED (or see smooch)

smugal, smuggle

smugaler, smuggle(r)

smuge, smudge

smuggle,*,ed,ling,er, TRANSPORT SOMETHING ACROSS A LAWFUL BORDER WITHOUT PERMISSION

smuglir, smuggle(r)

smugul, smuggle

smuj, smudge

smuk, smug

smukil, smuggle

smuklee, smug(ly)

smukler, smuggle(r)

smukly, smug(ly)

smuknes, smug(ness)

smukul, smuggle

smukuler, smuggle(r)

smurk, smirk

smut,tted,tting,tty,ttier,ttiest,ttily, ttiness, SOOTY/SMUDGED, INDECENT LANGUAGE, PLANT AFFECTED BY FUNGUS SPORES

smuteir, smut(ttier)

smuteist, smut(ttiest)

smuteness, smut(ttiness)

smuth, smooth

smuthen, smooth(en)

smuther, smooth(er) / smother

smuthie, smoothie

smuthir, smooth(er) / smother

smuthist, smooth(est)

smuthly, smooth(ly)

smuthness, smooth(ness)

smuthy, smoothie

smuty, smut(tty)

smabur, snap(pper)

snach, snatch

snachir, snatch(er)

snack,*,ked,king, BITS OF FOOD BETWEEN MEALS (or see snake/ snag)

snael, snail

snafoo, snafu

snafu,ued,uing, UNEXPECTED/CHAOTIC TURN OF EVENTS

snag,*,gged,gging,ggy,ggier,ggiest, BE CAUGHT UP/ENTANGLED (or see snack) "prefixes: un"

snageist, snag(ggiest)

snaggier, snag(ggier)

snail,*, GASTROPOD MOLLUSK WITH SHELL

snair, snare

snak, snack / snake / snag

snakd, snack(ed) / snake(d) / snag(gged)

snake,*,ed,king,ky,kily, REPTILE WITHOUT ARMS/LEGS (or see snack)

snakey, snake(ky)

snaks, snack(s) / snake(s) / snag(s)

snakt, snack(ed) / snake(d) / snag(gged)

snale, snail

snap,*,pped,pping,pper, A QUICK/ BITING MOTION, CRISP BREAK, BRITTLE/TENSE "prefixes: un"

snaper, snap(pper)

snapper,*, A FISH

snapur, snap(pper)

snard, snare(d)

snare,*,ed,ring,er, A TRAP/NOOSE FOR CATCHING THINGS, USED FOR INSTRUMENT "prefixes: en"

snarl,*,led,ling,ler,ly,lingly, TO ENTANGLE/COMPLICATE, A THREATENING SOUND "prefixes: en/un"

snarlee, snarl(y)

snart, snare(d)

snasee, snazzy

snaseur, snazzy(zier)

snasiest, snazzy(ziest)

snasy, snazzy

snatch,hes,hed,hing,her, SUDDEN/ SWIFT MOVE TO GRASP/SEIZE SOMETHING

snaul, snail

snawt, snout

snazeir, snazzy(zier)

snazeist, snazzy(ziest)

snazeur, snazzy(zier)

snazy, snazzy

snazzy,zzier,zziest, FANCY

sneak,*,ked,king,kingly,kily,kiness,ky, ker, ENGAGE IN ACTIVITY IN A SECRETIVE MANNER

sneaker,*, TENNIS SHOES, SOMEONE WHO SNEAKS AROUND

sneakey, sneak(y)

sneakuly, sneak(ily)

snear, sneer

sneaze, sneeze

sneazy, sneeze(zy)

snech, snitch

snechur, snitch(er)

sneek, sneak

sneeker, sneaker

sneeky, sneak(y)

sneer,*,red,ring,rer,ringly, FACIAL EXPRESSION OF CONTEMPT/SCORN

sneesy, sneeze(zy)

sneeze,*,ed,zing,zy, AN INVOLUNTARY GUST OF AIR FORCED THROUGH THE NASAL PASSAGES TO RELIEVE THEM OF AN IRRITANT

snef, sniff

snefdur, snifter

snefel, sniffle

snefer, sniff(er)

sneftur, snifter

sneful, sniffle

snefur, sniff(er)

snek, sneak

sneker, sneaker

snekily, sneak(ily)

snekir, sneaker

snekuly, sneak(ily)

snekur, sneaker / snicker

sneky, sneak(y)

snep, snip

snepee, snip(ppy)

snepit, snippet

snept, snip(pped)

sner, snare / sneer

snert, snare(d) / sneer(ed)

snesy, sneeze(zy)

snetch, snitch

sneveler, snivel(ller)

snevil, snivel

snevlur, snivel(ller)

snevul, snivel

snevult, snivel(lled)

snewdy, snooty

snewp, snoop

snews, snooze

sneze, sneeze

snezy, sneeze(zy)

snibt, snip(pped) / snipe(d)

snich, snitch

snicher, snitch(er)

snicker,*,red,ring, EMOTE A NEGATIVE SNEERING LAUGH OUT OF DISRESPECT

snide,er,est,ely, INSINUATING/ SARCASTIC

snidly, snide(ly)

snif, sniff

snifal, sniffle

snifd, sniff(ed)

snifdur, snifter

snifer, sniff(er)

sniff,*,ffed,ffing,ffer, TO SMELL FOR, USE NOSE FOR DETECTION

sniffle,*,ed,ling,er, A NASAL SOUND

snifter,*, STYLE OF GLASS DRINKING VESSEL

sniftur, snifter

sniful, sniffle

snifur, sniff(er)

sniker, snicker

snikur, snicker

snip,*,pped,pping,ppy, CUT OFF A SMALL PORTION OF SOMETHING (or see snipe)

snipe,*,ed,ping,er, TYPE OF BIRD, TO SHOOT FROM A CAMOUFLAGED POSITION (or see snip)

sniped, snip(pped) / snipe(d)

snipee, snip(ppy)

snipet, snippet

snippet,*, SMALL BITS/FRAGMENTS/ PARTS

snipur, snipe(r)

sniput, snippet

snitch,hes,hed,hing,her, FINK/RAT ON SOMEONE, BE AN INFORMANT

snite, snide

snitly, snide(ly)

snivel,*,lled,lling,ller, WHINE/CRY WHILE EXCREMENTING SNOT/ MUCOUS FROM NOSE

snivlur, snivel(ller)

snivul, snivel

sno, snow

snob,*,bby,bbery,bberies,bbish,bbishly, bbishness, SOMEONE APPEARING TO DISPLAY SUPERIORITY/ SMUGNESS/SELF-RIGHTEOUSNESS

snobeshnis, snob(bbishness)

snobish, snob(bbish)

snoby, snob(bby)

snod, snow(ed) / snot

snody, snot(tty)

snoker, snooker

snoodeist, snooty(tiest)

snoody, snooty

snooker,*, GAME OF BILLIARDS

snoop,*,ped,ping,per,pier,piest,py, SOMEONE WHO IS NOSY/PRYING/ PROWLING

snoose, snooze

snooty,tier,tiest,tily,tiness, SNOBBISH, BELIEVE THEY'RE EXCLUSIVE

snooze,*,ed,zing,er, SLEEP/NAP

snop, snob

snopee, snob(bby)

snopy, snob(bby)

snore,*,ed,ring,er, EMIT LOUD BREATHING SOUND DURING SLEEP, TO SLEEP WITH THE MOUTH OPEN

snorkel,*,led,ling, UNDERWATER BREATHING APPARATUS

snorkul, snorkel

snorl, snarl

snorlingly, snarl(lingly)

snort,*,ted,ting,ty, LOUD/QUICK BURST OF AIR FORCED FROM THE NOSE

snot,tty, MUCOUS EXCREMENTED IN THE SINUS CAVITIES, SOMEONE WHO HAS AN AIR OF SUPERIORITY/ CALLOUSNESS

snotee, snot(tty)

snoud, snout

snout,*,ted, THE NOSE/MUZZLE OF ANIMALS

snow,*,wed,wing,wy, WHITE/LIGHT PRECIPITATION FALLING FROM CLOUDS, BURY/COVER/FOOL SOMEONE LIKE SNOW AS A BLANKET

snowd, snow(ed) / snout

snowee, snow(y)

snowt, snout / snow(ed)

snub,*,bbed,bbing,bness,bby,bbiness, TURNED UP NOSE WITH ATTITUDE, REBUKE/REBUFF/NEGLECT (or see snoop)

snube, snub(bby) / snoop(y)

snubed, snoop(ed) / snub(bbed)

snubiness, snub(bbiness)

snubt, snoop(ed)

snuby, snub(bby)

snudy, snooty

snuf, snuff

snuff,*,ffer,ffy,ffier,ffiest, PAST TENSE FOR THE WORD "SNIFF", PUT OUT/ EXTINGUISH/END, POWDERED TOBACCO

snuffely, snuffle(ly)

snuffle,*,ed,ling,ly, SNIFFLE/NASAL CONGESTION

snufil, snuffle

snufir, snuff(er)

snufuly, snuffle(ly)

snufur, snuff(er)

snug,gger,ggest,gged,gging,gness,ggery, FIRMLY/COMFORTABLY IN PLACE

snugelt, snuggle(d)

snuger, snug(gger)

snuggle,*,ed,ling,ly, COZY/NESTLE UP COMFORTABLY AGAINST SOMETHING/ SOMEONE

snugle, snuggle

snugly, snuggle(ly)

snugnis, snug(ness)

snugul, snuggle

snuker, snooker

snukle, snuggle

snuklee, snuggle(ly)

snupe, snoop

snuper, snoop(er)

snupy, snoop(y)

snuse, snooze

snuteir, snooty(tier)

snuteist, snooty(tiest)

snuty, snooty

snuze, snooze

snyd, snide

so, THAT WHICH IS APPROXIMATE (or see sew/sow)

soak,*,ked,king,ker, EXPOSE TO MOISTURE UNTIL SATURATED

soap,*,ped,ping,py,piness, MANMADE COMPOUND USED FOR CLEANING (or see sop)

soar,*,red,ring,rer, RISE TO GREAT HEIGHTS EITHER LITERALLY/ FIGURATIVELY (or see sore)

soaside, suicide

sob,*,bbed,bbing, CRY WITH DEEP GASPS/EMOTION (or see sop/soap/ sub)

sobcity, subsidy

sobconshos, subconscious

sobcontract, subcontract

sobdue, subdue

sobed, sob(bbed) / soap(ed) / sop(pped)

sober,*,red,ring,ringly,rness, NOT INTOXICATED/DRUNK, INFORMATION WHICH IS SERIOUS/ GRAVE IN NATURE

soberb, suburb

sobgekt, subject

sobir, sober

sobirnes, sober(ness)

sobject, subject

sobkonshus, subconscious

sobleminal, subliminal

soblime, sublime

soblimenal, subliminal

sobmarine, submarine

sobmerge, submerge
sobmesev, submissive
sobmeshin, submission
sobmesiv, submissive
sobmet, submit
sobmirge, submerge
sobmisev, submissive
sobmishon, submission
sobmit, submit
sobmuren, submarine
sobordenate, subordinate
sobordenation, subordinate(tion)
sobort, support
sobpena, subpoena
sobpina, subpoena
sobragate, subrogate
sobregate, subrogate
sobriaty, sobriety
sobriety, BEING SOBER, FREE FROM
EXCESS/EXTRAVAGANCE, SERIOUS/
GRAVE "prefixes: in"
sobriudy, sobriety
sobrogate, subrogate
sobrugate, subrogate
sobsedy, subsidy
sobsequent, subsequent
sobsikwent, subsequent
sobstans, substance
sobstanshal, substantial
sobstins, substance
sobt, sop(pped) / sob(bbed)
sobtract, subtract
sobur, sober
soburnes, sober(ness)
sobvergin, subversion
sobvershen, subversion
sobversive, subversive
sobvert, subvert
sobvirgin, subversion
sobvirsev, subversive
sobvirshen, subversion
sobvirt, subvert
sobvurgin, subversion
sobvurshen, subversion
sobvursive, subversive
sobvurt, subvert
soccer, A TYPE OF FOOTBALL GAME
socebdubility, susceptible(bility)
socer, soccer
sochably, sociable(ly)
sochalist, social(ist)
sochaly, social(lly)
sochealugist, sociology(gist)
sochebul, sociable

sochel, social
sochelize, social(ize)
sochely, social(lly)
socheolegy, sociology
socheolugist, sociology(gist)
socher, soldier
sochibly, sociable(ly)
sochibul, sociable
sochil, social
sochilest, social(ist)
sochilize, social(ize)
sochily, social(lly)
sochioligy, sociology
sochuble, sociable
sochubly, sociable(ly)
sochul, social
sochulee, social(lly)
sochulist, social(ist)
sochulize, social(ize)
sochur, soldier
sociable,bility,eness,ly, ABILITY TO
INTERACT WITH OTHERS "prefixes:
un"
social,*,lism,list,listic,listically,lite,lity,
lize,lized,lizing,lization,lizer,lly,
INTERACTION WITH OTHERS
"prefixes: sub/un"
socialest, social(ist)
socialigest, sociology(gist)
socialise, social(ize)
socialy, social(lly)
society,ties,tal, GROUPS OF PEOPLE
WITH COMMONALITIES "prefixes:
non"
socioligest, sociology(gist)
sociology,gical,gically,gist, SCIENCE OF
STUDYING HOW SOCIAL
INTERACTION IS CONDUCTED
socir, soccer
sociubly, sociable(ly)
sock,*,ked,king, A CLOTH FOOT
COVERING, BE PUNCHED BY
SOMEONE, WINDSOCK FOR WIND
DIRECTION (or see soak)
socket,*, SOMETHING WITH THE SHAPE
OF A HOLLOWED OUT/SHORT
CYLINDER WITH A BASE
sockit, socket
sockut, socket
socom, succumb
socseshan, succession
socsesion, succession
socshen, suction
socshun, suction

socur, soccer / secure
socurity, secure(rity)
socurly, secure(ly)
sod,dded,dding,ddy, TURF, GRASS WITH
ROOTS (or see sold/saw(ed)/
sought/ sew(ed))
soda,*, CARBONATED DRINK,
COMPOUNDS OF SODIUM
sodame, sodomy
sodan, sedan
sodden,nly,nness, HEAVY WITH
MOISTURE, SOGGY
soded, sod(dded) / sold
sodeim, sodium
sodemize, sodomy(mize)
sodemy, sodomy
soden, sodden
sodeum, sodium
sodimise, sodomy(mize)
sodimy, sodomy
sodin, sodden
sodinly, sodden(ly)
sodium, METALLIC/NATURAL/ACTIVE
ELEMENT
sodn, sudden
sodomy,mize,mized,mizing, HATEFUL,
SELF-CENTERED ACT OF ANAL
PENETRATION FORCED ONTO
ANOTHER
sodu, soda
sodumee, sodomy
sodumize, sodomy(mize)
sodun, sodden
sodunly, sodden(ly)
sody, sod(ddy)
soe, soy
soeal, soil
soebean, soybean
soee, soy
soeil, soil
soeled, soil(ed)
soem, psalm
soerdo, sourdough
soeul, soil
sofaree, safari
sofaren, sovereign
sofari, safari
sofecate, suffocate
sofekate, suffocate
sofeks, suffix
sofen, soft(en)
sofenir, soft(ener)
sofer, suffer
soferin, sovereign

sofeshent, sufficient
sofet, soffit
sofex, suffix
soffit,*, NECESSARY GEOMETRIC
COMPONENT OF A STRUCTURE
soficate, suffocate
sofics, suffix
sofin, soft(en)
sofineer, souvenir
sofinur, soft(ener)
sofiren, sovereign
sofise, suffice
sofishent, sufficient
sofit, soffit
sofmore, sophomore
sofomore, sophomore
sofr, suffer
sofrech, suffrage
sofren, sovereign
sofrenity, sovereign(ity)
sofrenudy, sovereign(ity)
sofrin, sovereign
sofrinedy, sovereign(ity)
sofrun, sovereign
soft,tly,tness,ten,tener,ty, SMOOTH/
GENTLE/COMFORTABLE "prefixes:
semi"
softenur, soft(ener)
softur, soft(er)
sofun, soft(en)
sofuner, souvenir / soft(ener)
sofunir, soft(ener) / souvenir
sofuren, sovereign
sofut, soffit
sogee, soggy
sogenis, soggy(gginess)
soger, soldier
soggy,ggier,ggiest,ggily,gginess,
THOROUGHLY SOAKED
sogir, soldier
sogjesgen, suggest(ion)
sogjest, suggest
sogur, soldier
sogy, soggy
sogyness, soggy(gginess)
soht, sought/ sew(ed)
soi, soy
soibeen, soybean
soil,*,led,ling,lless,lage, DIRT, ORGANIC
DECAYED MATTER "prefixes: sub"
soing, sew(ing) / sow(ing)
soirdow, sourdough
sok, sock / soak
sokd, sock(ed) / soak(ed)

soked, sock(ed) / soak(ed)
sokee, soggy
sokenis, soggy(gginess)
soker, soccer / soak(er)
soket, socket
sokeulent, succulent
sokgeschen, suggest(ion)
sokir, soccer
sokit, socket
sokl, suckle
sokshen, suction
sokt, sock(ed) / soak(ed)
sokulent, succulent
sokur, soccer
sokut, socket
soky, soggy
sokynis, soggy(gginess)
sol, sole / soul / saw
solace,*,ed,cing, PROVIDE COMFORT,
ALLEVIATION FROM WORRY/
SORROW/GRIEF
solad, solid / salad
soladerity, solidarity
solami, salami
solanoyd, solenoid
solar,rize,rizes,rized,rizing,rization,rium,
HEAT/LIGHT PRODUCED BY SUN
"prefixes: sub"
solarium,*, ENCLOSURE WHICH
ALLOWS MAXIMUM PENETRATION
OF THE SUNS RAYS
solas, solace / soul(ess) / sole(eless)
solatare, solitaire / solitary
solatarily, solitary(rily)
solatary, solitary
solatood, solitude
solatude, solitude
solcher, soldier
solchur, soldier
sold, PAST TENSE FOR THE WORD 'SELL'
"prefixes: over/un/under"
solder,*,red,ring,rer, USE OF FLUX/
SOFT METAL TO MELD SEVERAL
PIECES OF METAL TOGETHER
soldier,*,rly,rship,ry,ries, PEOPLE
TRAINED TO PARTICIPATE IN WAR/
BATTLE
soldir, solder / soldier
soldired, solder(ed)
sole,*,ely,eness,eless, ONE AND ONLY,
THE BOTTOM OF FEET/SHOES (or
see soul) "prefixes: in"
solective, select(ive)
soled, solid

soledarity, solidarity
soledify, solid(ify)
soledness, solid(ness)
solee, sole(ly)
solelukwy, soliloquy
solem, solemn
solemly, solemn(ly)
solemn,nly,nness,nity,nities,nize,
nization, OBSERVANCE OF
CELEBRATIONS/RITES, OF A GRAVE/
SERIOUS ACTIVITY OR DISPOSITION
solen, sullen
solenium, selenium
solenoid,*,dal,dally, MAGNETICALLY
CONTROLLED
soler, solar
solereum, solarium
solerize, solar(ize)
soles, solace / soul(ess) / sole(eless)
solesit, solicit
solesitation, solicit(ation)
solesiter, solicit(er)
solesment, solace(ment)
solet, solid
soletare, solitaire / solitary
soletarily, solitary(rily)
soletary, solitary
soletness, solid(ness)
soletood, solitude
soletude, solitude
solf, solve
solfely, soul(fully)
solfint, solvent
solfite, sulfite / sulfide
solfor, sulfur
solfuly, soul(fully)
solfunt, solvent
solger, soldier
solgur, soldier
solicit,*,ted,ting,tor,tation,tous,tously,
tousness, REQUEST/SEEK/APPLY/
INFLUENCE/PETITION FOR AN
ACTION/OPPORTUNITY/FUNDING
"prefixes: un"
solid,*,dly,dify,difiable,dification,dness,
dity,dities,darity, GIVE THE
IMPRESSION OF BEING HARD/FIRM/
COMPACT/THICK "prefixes: semi"
solidarity,ties, PEOPLE WHO FORM
SOLID RELATIONSHIPS BASED ON
COMMONALITIES
solidefy, solid(ify)
soliderity, solidarity
solilaquy, soliloquy

soliloquy,uies,uist,uizer, TALK TO ONESELF, SHARE THOUGHTS OUTLOUD IN FRONT OF AN AUDIENCE

solim, solemn

solimly, solemn(ly)

solin, sullen

solinoid, solenoid

solir, solar

solirise, solar(ize)

solis, solace / soul(ess) / sole(eless)

soliset, solicit

solisetation, solicit(ation)

soliseter, solicit(er)

solisment, solace(ment)

solit, solid

solitaire,ry, CARD GAME PLAYED ALONE

solitary,ries,rily,riness, OF BEING COMPLETELY ALONE, SECLUDED

solitness, solid(ness)

solitude, ALONE/REMOTE/LONELY

solivu, saliva

soljer, soldier

soljur, soldier

solking, sulk(ing)

solm, psalm

solo,*,oed,oing,oist, TO PERFORM ALONE

solomi, salami

solon, salon

solonoid, solenoid

soloon, saloon

soloot, salute

solstes, solstice

solstice,*,itial,itially, TIME OF THE YEAR BASED UPON SUN'S POSITION

solstis, solstice

solt, sold / soil(ed) / salt

soluble,eness,ly,bility,bilities,bilize, bilizes,bilized,bilizing,bilization, ABLE TO DISSOLVE IN WATER "prefixes: dis/in/re"

solud, solid

solum, solemn

solumly, solemn(ly)

solun, sullen

solune, saloon

solunoid, solenoid

solur, solar

solurize, solar(ize)

soluse, solace / soul(ess) / sole(eless)

solutare, solitaire / solitary

solutarily, solitary(rily)

solutary, solitary

solute, salute

solution,*, A COMBINATION OF CHEMICAL FORMS, THE ANSWER TO A PROBLEM, SETTLEMENT

solutood, solitude

solutude, solitude

solvant, solvent

solvashin, salvation

solve,*,ed,ving,vable,vability,vableness, er, REMEDY/FIX/UNDERSTAND (or see salve) "prefixes: in"

solvent,ency,ently, ABLE TO BE DISSOLVED

solvuble, solve(vable)

solvunt, solvent

soly, sole(ly)

solyewble, soluble(ize)

solyubel, soluble

som, psalm / sum / some

somber,rly,rness, MELANCHOLY/ GRAVE/DEPRESSING IN MOOD/ ATTITUDE

sombir, somber

sombirly, somber(ly)

sombreo, sombrero

sombrero,*, A WIDE BRIM HAT

sombur, somber

somburly, somber(ly)

somchuos, sumptuous

some, PARTIAL, AN INDEFINITE AMOUNT/DISTANCE (or see sum)

somersault,*,ted,ting, AN ENTIRE BODY MANEUVER WITH HEELS GOING OVER HEAD

somester, semester

somet, summit

something, WANT FOR, INDETERMINABLE AMOUNT/TYPE/ OBJECT OF, OPPOSITE OF NOTHING

sometime,*, UNSPECIFIED TIME

somewar, somewhere

somewat, somewhat

somewere, somewhere

somewhat, INDETERMINATE MEASURE

somewhere, UNSPECIFIED PLACE

somewot, somewhat

somewut, somewhat

somirsalt, somersault

somirsolt, somersault

somit, summit

somon, summon

somp, sump

sompchuos, sumptuous

somper, somber

somptuous, sumptuous

sompur, somber

somtheng, something

somthing, something

somtime, sometime

somting, something

somwar, somewhere

somwat, somewhat

somwer, somewhere

somwhare, somewhere

somwhere, somewhere

somwot, somewhat

somwut, somewhat

son,*,nless,nny, PARENT'S MALE OFFSPRING (or see sun/sown/ sewn)

sona, sauna

sonar, ACRONYM FOR SOUND NAVIGATION AND RANGING (or see soon(er))

sonareo, scenario

sonata, A FORM FOR INSTRUMENTS IN MUSIC

sonda, sunday

sondree, sundry

sondrys, sundry(ries)

sonec, sonic

sonek, sonic

sonereo, scenario

sonet, sonnet

song,*,gful,gless, COLLECTION/ ARRANGEMENT OF MUSICAL NOTES AND/OR ACCOMPANYING WORDS

sonic,cally, SOUNDWAVE/FREQUENCY "prefixes: sub/super"

sonik, sonic

sonit, sonnet

sonk, song

sonkles, song(less)

sonks, song(s)

sonnet,*,teer,tize,tization, A COMPLETE IDEA WRITTEN POETICALLY IN 14 LINES

sonor, sonar

sonseer, sincere

sonter, saunter

sontir, saunter

sontre, saunter

sontree, sundry

sontres, sundry(ries)

sontur, saunter

sonu, sauna

sonuk, sonic
sonut, sonnet
sooaside, suicide
soodar, suitor
soodir, suitor
soodo, pseudo
soodor, suitor
soody, soot(y)
sooet, suet
soofaneer, souvenir
soofineer, souvenir
soofla, souffle'
sooflay, souffle'
soofuneer, souvenir
sooit, suet
sookrose, sucrose
soon,ner,nest, BEFORE IT'S TOO LATE,
    CLOSE TO NOW, READILY PREFER
    (or see sun/son)
soopereur, superior
sooperfishul, superficial
sooperioredy, superior(ity)
soopireur, superior
soopirfishul, superficial
soopurb, superb
soopurfishul, superficial
soot,ty, BLACK CARBON RESULTANT OF
    BURNED MATERIAL (or see suit)
sooter, suitor
soothe,*,ed,hing,hingly,hingness, TO
    CALM, RELIEVE AGITATION
sootir, suitor
sootor, suitor
soour, sewer
soovaneer, souvenir
soovuneer, souvenir
sop,*,pped,pping,ppy, ABSORB/
    SATURATE SOMETHING WITH
    LIQUID (or see soap/soup/sob/sap)
sopausetori, suppository
sopazeshan, supposition
sopd, sop(pped) / sob(bbed) / soap(ed)
sope, soap / sop / soap(y) / sop(ppy)
soped, sop(pped) / sob(bbed) /
    soap(ed)
sopee, soap(y)
soper, sober / sob(bber) / supper
soperioredy, superior(ity)
soperiority, superior(ity)
sophisticate,*,ed,edly,tion, IMPROVED
    QUALITY OF "prefixes: un"
sophmore, sophomore

sophomore,*,ric,rical,rically, STUDENT
    IN THE SECOND YEAR OF A FOUR-
    YEAR COURSE
soplant, supplant
soport, support
sopos, suppose
soposetori, suppository
soposishon, supposition
soprano,*, HIGHEST OCTAVE ABLE TO
    BE OBTAINED BY VOICE OR
    INSTRUMENT
soprechen, suppress(ion)
sopremosy, supremacy
sopreno, soprano
sopres, suppress
sopreshen, suppress(ion)
sopretion, suppress(ion)
soprietee, sobriety
soprim, supreme
soprino, soprano
sopscrepshon, subscription
sopsekwent, subsequent
sopsequent, subsequent
sopsid, subside
sopsikwent, subsequent
sopstans, substance
sopstanshal, substantial
sopt, sop(pped) / sob(bbed) / soap(ed)
sopy, soap(y) / sop(ppy)
soquer, secure
soquerity, secure(rity)
soquerly, secure(ly)
sor, sore / soar
soran, saran
sorape, serape
sorce, source
sorcerur, sorcery(rer)
sorcery,rer,rous, USING THE "SOURCE"/
    INVISIBLE FIELD TO CREATE
    PHYSICAL THINGS/ACTIONS
sord, soar(ed) / sword / sort
sorded, sordid / sort(ed)
sordedly, sordid(ly)
sordeen, sardine
sordene, sardine
sorder, sort(er)
sordid,dly,dness, OF BEING DIRTY/
    MEAN (or see sort(ed))
sordir, sort(er)
sordud, sordid / sort(ed)
sordudly, sordid(ly)
sordur, sort(er)

sore,*,er,est,ely,eness, PAIN,
    INFLAMMATION, PERTURBED (or
    see soar/sorry)
sored, soar(ed) / sword
soree, sorry / saury
sorel, sorrel / surreal
soren, serene
sorender, surrender
sorenidy, serene(nity)
sorenity, serene(nity)
soresury, sorcery
sorf, surf
sorfas, surface
sorfis, surface
sorgem, sorghum
sorgent, sergeant / surgent
sorghum, GRAIN USED FOR MANY
    PURPOSES
sorgint, sergeant / surgent
sorgum, sorghum
sori, sorry / saury
sorial, surreal
sorialism, surreal(ism)
soriasis, psoriasis
sorily, sorry(rily)
sorinder, surrender
soriol, surreal
soriolism, surreal(ism)
sorir, sore(r)
sorist, sore(st)
soriusis, psoriasis
sorkazem, sarcasm
sorkem, sorghum
sorkum, sorghum
sorly, sore(ly)
sorness, sore(ness)
sornis, sore(ness)
soro, sorrow
soroful, sorrow(ful)
sorority,ties, FEMALE COLLEGE
    ORGANIZATIONS
sorow, sorrow
sorowful, sorrow(ful)
sorples, surplus
sorplus, surplus
sorpris, surprise
sorrel, AN EDIBLE PLANT (or see
    surreal)
sorro, sorrow
sorrow,*,wful,wfully,wfulness, GRIEF,
    SADNESS, REGRET
sorry,rrier,rriest,rrily,rriness,
    APOLOGETIC, REGRETFUL,
    RESENTFUL (or see saury)

sors, source / sore(s) / czar(s)

sorseree, sorcery

sorserer, sorcery(rer)

sorsuree, sorcery

sorsurer, sorcery(rer)

sort,*,ted,ting,ter,table, CATEGORIZE/
    COMPARTMENTALIZE/ARRANGE BY
    ASSOCIATION (or see sword/sordid)
    "prefixes: re-"

sortar, sort(er)

sorted, sordid / sort(ed)

sortedly, sordid(ly)

sortidly, sordid(ly)

sortir, sort(er)

sortud, sordid / sort(ed)

sortudly, sordid(ly)

sortur, sort(er)

sorur, sore(r)

sorva, survey

sory, saury / sorry

sorz, source / sore(s)

sos, sauce / saw(s) / sew(s)

sosbect, suspect

sosbenchen, suspension

sosbended, suspend(ed)

sosbenders, suspender(s)

sosbens, suspense

sose, saucy

sosege, sausage

soseje, sausage

soseptef, susceptive

soseptif, susceptive

soseptubility, susceptible(bility)

soser, saucer

soseshen, secession

sosetion, secession

soseur, saucy(cier)

soshable, sociable

soshaly, social(lly)

soshealegy, sociology

soshebul, sociable

soshel, social

soshelize, social(ize)

sosheolugest, sociology(gist)

sosheolugy, sociology

soshible, sociable

soshibly, sociable(ly)

soshibul, sociable

soshil, social

soshilist, social(ist)

soshilize, social(ize)

soshily, social(lly)

soshubil, sociable

soshubly, sociable(ly)

soshul, social

soshulist, social(ist)

soshulize, social(ize)

soshuly, social(lly)

sosiatal, society(tal)

sosiaty, society

sosiedle, society(tal)

sosier, saucy(cier)

sosietal, society(tal)

sosiety, society

sosige, sausage

sosije, sausage

sosiology, sociology

sosir, saucer

sosiudil, society(tal)

sosiudy, society

sosiutul, society(tal)

sosoge, sausage

sosoje, sausage

sospact, suspect

sospect, suspect

sospenchen, suspension

sospens, suspense

sospeshen, suspicion

sospeshes, suspicious

sospinchen, suspension

sospinded, suspend(ed)

sospins, suspense

sospishon, suspicion

sospishus, suspicious

sosuge, sausage

sosuje, sausage

sosur, saucer

sosy, saucy

sot, sought / suite / soot

sota, soda

sotame, sodomy

sotanic, satanic

sotay, saute / sate

sote, saute / sate

soted, saute(d)

soteim, sodium

sotemy, sodomy

soteum, sodium

sotiably, sociable(ly)

sotiabul, sociable

sotialy, social(lly)

sotu, soda

sotume, sodomy

souerdow, sourdough

souffle',*,ed, A BAKED FLUFFY DISH

soufle', souffle'

sought, PAST TENSE FOR THE WORD
    "SEEK" "prefixes: un"

souirdow, sourdough

soul,*,lful,lfully,lfulness,lless,llessly,
    llessness, INVISIBLE FIELD/DESTINY/
    SPIRIT THOUGHT TO EXIST WITHIN
    THE BODY (or see sole/sol)
    "prefixes: en/in/over"

soulenoid, solenoid

sound,*,ded,ding,der,dest,dly,dness,
    dless,dlessly,dlessness, AUDIBLE/
    HEAR WITH EARS, RELIABLE, A
    FREQUENCY, LAND NEAR WATER
    "prefixes: un"

sounly, sound(ly)

soup,*,py,pier,piest, EDIBLE LIQUID
    BASE WITH BROTH AND/OR
    VEGETABLES/MEAT

sour,*,red,ring,rish,rly,rness, GONE
    BAD/RANCID, TYPE OF TASTE
    REGISTERED ON A CERTAIN PLACE
    ON THE TONGUE

source,*,ed,cing, POINT OF
    ORIGINATION OF SOMETHING,
    BEGINNING/PRIMARY "prefixes: in/
    out"

sourcrowt, sauerkraut

sourdough,*, TYPE OF BREAD,
    NICKNAME FOR CANADIAN/
    ALASKAN NATIVES

sourkraut, sauerkraut

sourkrowt, sauerkraut

souse,*,ed,sing, BE IMMERSED/
    DRENCHED/SATURATED IN,
    INTOXICATED

soust, souse(d)

sout, sought

souted, saute(d)

south,hern,herner,hernly,herly,herlies,
    NAVIGATIONAL DIRECTION

souvaneer, souvenir

souvenir,*, A TOKEN WHICH REMINDS/
    SHOWS WHAT YOU HAVE DONE OR
    WHERE YOU HAVE BEEN

souvuneer, souvenir

sovana, savanna

sovant, savant

sovaren, sovereign

sovereign,nly,nty,nties, SELF-
    SUFFICIENT, FREE OF OUTSIDE
    CONTROL

soverin, sovereign

soverity, severe(rity)

soviren, sovereign

sovont, savant

sovren, sovereign

sovrenedy, sovereign(ity)
sovrin, sovereign
sovrinedy, sovereign(ity)
sovrun, sovereign
sovt, soft
sovtur, soft(er)
sovurin, sovereign
sow,*,wed,wing,wer,wn, TO PLANT/
    IMPLANT/PROPOGATE, FEMALE PIG
    (or see so/sewn/son/sun/souse)
sowarkraut, sauerkraut
sowd, sew(ed) / sow(ed)
sowded, sound(ded)
sower, sour
sowerdrow, sourdough
sowerkrowt, sauerkraut
sowir, sour
sowirdo, sourdough
sowirkraut, sauerkraut
sowlitare, solitaire / solitary
sown, PAST TENSE FOR THE WORD
    "SOW" (or see sewn)
sownd, sound
sownded, sound(ded)
sowndlis, sound(less)
sowndly, sound(ly)
sownly, sound(ly)
sownt, sound
sownted, sound(ded)
sowpee, sop(ppy)
sowr, sour / sow(er)
sowree, saury / sorry
sows, sauce / sow(s) / souse / saw(s)
sowsd, souse(d) / sauce(d)
sowt, sew(ed) / sow(ed) / sought
sowth, south
sowuble, soluble(ize)
sowur, sour
sowurdo, sourdough
sowurkraut, sauerkraut
sowurkrowt, sauerkraut
soy, A SOYBEAN SAUCE/CONDIMENT
soybean,*, A PLANT/LEGUME
soybeen, soybean
soyible, soluble
soyl, soil
soyld, sold / soil(ed)
soyuble, soluble(ize)
soyul, soil
soz, sauce / saw(s)
sozy, saucy
spa,*, RETREAT/RESORT/HOT TUB/
    MINERAL SPRINGS FACILITY (or see
    spay)

space,*,ed,cing,er,eless,ey,cious, PLACE
    WHERE NO APPARENT MATTER
    EXISTS, NOT OF THIS EARTH
    "prefixes: inter/sub"
spachela, spatula
spachula, spatula
spacious,sly,sness, OPEN/VAST/BROAD
    AREA
spackel, spackle
spackle,*,ed,ling,er, PASTE FOR
    REPAIRING DAMAGE
spacy, space(y)
spad, spade / spay(ed)
spadchewla, spatula
spadchula, spatula
spade,*,ed,ding, A SHOVEL/SYMBOL/
    SHAPE
spadshewlu, spatula
spadshula, spatula
spaenk, spank
spagedi, spaghetti
spagem, sphagnum
spageti, spaghetti
spaghetti, LONG/SLENDER PASTA
    MADE OF FLOUR
spagnem, sphagnum
spagnum, sphagnum
spagum, sphagnum
spaink, spank
spaircity, sparse(sity)
spairs, sparse / spare(s)
spairsly, sparse(ly)
spakel, spackle
spakil, spackle
spakul, spackle
span,*,nned,nning,nner, TOOL,
    MATCHED PAIR, SPACE/DISTANCE
    BETWEEN
spangle,*,ed,ling, SPARKLING/GLITTERY
    ORNAMENTS ON SOMETHING
spank,*,ked,king, OPEN HANDED
    SWATS ON BUTTOCKS, SPRITELY,
    LIVELY, NEW
spar,*,rred,rring,rry, PHYSICAL DISPUTE
    WITH, CRYSTAL-LINED MINERAL (or
    see spare)
sparadik, sporadic
sparadikly, sporadic(ally)
sparcity, sparse(sity)
sparckul, sparkle
spare,*,ed,ring,eable,ely,eness,ringly,
    LEFT OVER, EXTRA, TO SAVE,
    REFRAIN FROM, BOWLING

EXPRESSION (or see spar) "prefixes:
    un"
sparengly, spare(ringly)
spark,*,ked,king,ky, RESULT BETWEEN
    TWO ELECTRICAL CHARGES
    COLLIDING, PARTICLES OF
    GLOWING MATTER
sparkal, sparkle
sparkil, sparkle
sparkle,*,ed,ling,er, GLITTERY/
    FLASHING LIGHT
sparkul, sparkle
sparo, sparrow
sparrow,*, A BIRD
sparse,er,est,ely,eness,sity, RARE, NOT
    MANY OF, MEAGER (or see
    spare(s)/spar(s))
sparsedy, sparse(sity)
sparsidy, sparse(sity)
sparsly, sparse(ly)
sparsudy, sparse(sity)
spart, spare(d) / spar(rred)
spas, spa(s) / space / spay(s)
spasam, spasm
spasdek, spastic
spasdik, spastic
spase, space
spasee, space(y)
spasefik, specific
spasefikly, specific(ally)
spasem, spasm
spaser, space(r)
spashel, spatial
spashely, spatial
spashes, spacious
spashesness, spacious(ness)
spasheus, spacious
spashewla, spatula
spashil, spatial
spashily, spatial(lly)
spashis, spacious
spashisnes, spacious(ness)
spashius, spacious
spashle, spatial
spashul, spatial
spashula, spatula
spashuly, spatial(lly)
spashus, spacious
spashusnes, spacious(ness)
spasifek, specific
spasifekly, specific(ally)
spasific, specific
spasim, spasm
spasiousness, spacious(ness)

spasir, space(r)

spasm,*,modic,modical,modically, MUSCLE CONTRACTION

spasom, spasm

spastek, spastic

spastic,cally, OCCURENCE OF MUSCLE SPASMS

spastuk, spastic

spasum, spasm

spasur, space(r)

spasy, space(y)

spat, PAST TENSE FOR THE WORD "SPIT" (or see spay(ed)/spade)

spatchela, spatula

spatchula, spatula

spate, spade / spat / spay(ed)

spatial,lly,lity, SPACE WITH NO PHYSICAL MATTER APPARENT (or see special)

spatialy, spatial(lly)

spatious, spacious

spatiuly, spatial(lly)

spatshewla, spatula

spatshula, spatula

spatula,*, FLAT/BROAD BLADE HAND IMPLEMENT/TOOL

spatulu, spatula

spause, spouse

spaut, spout

spautles, spot(less)

spaw, spa

spawn,*,ned,ning, INCUBATE, GIVE BIRTH TO, PRODUCE OFFSPRING

spaws, spouse

spawt, spout

spawtles, spot(less)

spay,*,yed,ying, NEUTER TO PREVENT FROM CREATING OFFSPRING

spazam, spasm

spazdek, spastic

spazduk, spastic

spazem, spasm

spazim, spasm

spaztek, spastic

spaztuk, spastic

spazum, spasm

speach, speech

speachless, speech(less)

spead, speed

speady, speed(y)

speak,*,poke,ker,king, COMMUNICATE WITH VERBAL SOUNDS (or see speck) "prefixes: mis/un"

speakible, speak(able)

speakuble, speak(able)

speal, spiel

spear,*,red,ring, LONG SHAFT WITH SHARP POINTED/PIERCING INSTRUMENT ON ONE END

spec, speech / speak / speck

specafy, specify

specamen, specimen

specemin, specimen

specewlate, speculate

specewlum, speculum

spech, speech

spechal, special

spechalist, special(ist)

spechalize, special(ize)

spechelty, special(ity)

speches, speech(es)

spechil, special

spechilist, special(ist)

spechilize, special(ize)

spechis, speech(es)

spechle, special

spechles, speech(less)

spechlist, special(ist)

spechlize, special(ize)

spechlus, speech(less)

spechol, special / speck(le)

specholist, special(ist)

specholize, special(ize)

specholty, special(ity)

spechulist, special(ist)

spechulize, special(ize)

spechulty, special(ity)

special,*,lly,list,lty,lties,lism,list,listic, lization,lize,lizes,lized,lizing,lity, UNLIKE OTHERS, RARE, UNUSUAL, SPECIFIC CATEGORY "prefixes: sub/ un"

species, ORGANISMS GROUPED BY ABILITY TO BREED TOGETHER "prefixes: intra/sub"

specific,*,cally,city,cation, CLEARLY AND DISTINCTLY STATE/DEFINE/ MAKE KNOWN "prefixes: con/inter/ intra/non"

specifide, specify(fied)

specify,fies,fied,fying,fier,fiable, CLEARLY AND DISTINCTLY STATE/ DEFINE/MAKE KNOWN/REVEAL "prefixes: un"

specimen,*, SAMPLE/EXAMPLE OF SOMETHING

speck,*,kle,kles,kled,kling, TINY FLECKS/ SPOTS (or see specs/speak)

specktrum, spectrum

speckulashen, speculate(tion)

speckulation, speculate(tion)

specs, SHORT FOR SPECTACLES/ GLASSES/DRAWINGS (or see speck)

spectacle,*,ed, GLASSES FOR THE EYES, FOR PUBLIC EXHIBITION/VIEW "prefixes: be"

spectacul, spectacle

spectacular,rly,rity,rization,rism,rized, MOST IMPRESSIVE EVENT/ ACTIVITY/ OCCURENCE "prefixes: un"

spectader, spectator

spectadur, spectator

spectakewler, spectacular

spectator,*,rial,rship, SOMEONE WATCHING AN EVENT WITHOUT PARTICIPATING

spectecul, spectacle

specter,*, SPIRIT, GHOST APPEARANCE, APPARITION

specticle, spectacle

specticul, spectacle

spectir, specter

spector, specter

spectral,lity,lness,lly, GIVEN TO BE LIKE A SPIRIT/GHOST

spectrim, spectrum

spectrol, spectral

spectrom, spectrum

spectrul, spectral

spectrum,*, RANGE OF SOMETHING BETWEEN TWO GIVEN POINTS

spectucle, spectacle

spectur, specter

specufy, specify

speculashen, speculate(tion)

speculate,*,ed,ting,tor,tion,tive, tiveness,tory, THEORIZE BASED UPON FACTS/KNOWINGNESS

speculim, speculum

speculum,*, MEDICAL INSTRUMENT USED TO EXAMINE MORE CLOSELY

sped, PAST TENSE FOR THE WORD "SPEED"

spede, speed(y)

spedeness, speed(iness)

speder, speed(er)

spedeur, speed(ier)

spedily, speed(ily)

spedir, speed(er)

spedul, spittle

speduly, speed(ily)

spedur, speed(er)
spedy, speed(y)
speech,hes,hless,hlessness, VOCALLY EMPHASIZE SOUNDS/WORDS
speed,*,ded,ding,dier,diest,der,dy,dily, diness, RATE/VELOCITY OF MOVEMENT, TRAVEL FASTER THAN NORMAL
speedeness, speed(iness)
speeker, speak(er)
speekt, speak
speel, spiel
speer, sphere / spear
speget, spigot
spegit, spigot
spegot, spigot
spekabul, speak(able)
spekal, speck(le)
speker, speak(er)
spekeulate, speculate
spekeulatif, speculate(tive)
spekewlashen, speculate(tion)
spekewlate, speculate
spekewlation, speculate(tion)
spekewlative, speculate(tive)
spekewlem, speculum
spekible, speak(able)
spekil, speck(le)
spekir, speak(er)
spekol, speck(le)
spekor, speak(er)
speks, specs / speak(s) / speck(s)
spekt, spoke
spektadur, spectator
spektakewler, spectacular
spektakle, spectacle
spektakul, spectacle
spektakuler, spectacular
spektar, specter
spektator, spectator
spektekul, spectacle
spekter, specter
spektikul, spectacle
spektir, specter
spektor, specter
spektrality, spectral(ity)
spektram, spectrum
spektrel, spectral
spektrem, spectrum
spektrul, spectral
spektrum, spectrum
spektukul, spectacle
spektur, specter
spekuble, speak(able)

spekul, speck(le)
spekulashen, speculate(tion)
spekulate, speculate
spekulation, speculate(tion)
spekulative, speculate(tive)
spekulem, speculum
spekulotif, speculate(tive)
spekulum, speculum
spekulutive, speculate(tive)
spekur, speak(er)
spekyewlem, speculum
spekyulate, speculate
spekyulatif, speculate(tive)
spel, spiel / spell / spill
spelar, spell(er)
speld, spill(ed) / spelt / spell(ed)
speler, spell(er)
spell,*,led,ling,ler, FORMULATE LETTERS INTO ACCEPTABLE FORMAT, BE SUBCONSCIOUSLY CONTROLLED "prefixes: mis"
spellur, spell(er)
spelor, spell(er)
spelt, PAST TENSE FOR THE WORD "SPELL", A TYPE OF WHEAT (or see spell(ed)/spill(ed)/ spiel(ed))
spelur, spell(er)
spen, spin / spend
spenatch, spinach
spend,*,nt,ding,der,dy, TRADE OUTGOING FOR INCOMING (or see spent/spin(nned)) "prefixes: mis/ over/under"
spendal, spindle
spended, spent
spendir, spend(er)
spendle, spindle
spendly, spindle(y)
spendul, spindle
spenech, spinach
spenich, spinach
spent, PAST TENSE FOR THE WORD "SPEND" (or see spend)
spentle, spindle
spentul, spindle
spenuch, spinach
spenur, spin(nner)
spenutch, spinach
speol, spiel
sper, spare / spear / spur
speradik, sporadic
spercity, sparse(sity)
sperd, spear(ed) / spur(rred)
sperds, spurt(s)

sperichual, spiritual
sperichualidy, spiritual(ity)
speringly, spare(ringly)
sperit, spirit
speritshuality, spiritual(ity)
sperm,*, A METHOD OF CARRYING MALE DNA FOR PROCREATION, SEMEN "prefixes: endo"
spero, sparrow
sperow, sparrow
spers, sparse / spare(s) / spear(s) / spur(s)
spersity, sparse(sity)
sperslee, sparse(ly)
spersly, sparse(ly)
spersudy, sparse(sity)
spert, spurt / spare(d) / spear(ed)
spesaficashen, specify(fication)
spesafide, specify(fied)
spesafikation, specify(fication)
spesafy, specify
spesamen, specimen
spesamin, specimen
spesefakation, specify(fication)
spesefide, specify(fied)
spesefukation, specify(fication)
spesefy, specify
spesemin, specimen
speshal, special
speshalist, special(ist)
speshalize, special(ize)
speshelty, special(ity)
speshez, species
speshil, special
speshilest, special(ist)
speshilty, special(ity)
speshis, species
speshle, special
speshlist, special(ist)
speshlize, special(ize)
speshol, special
spesholty, special(ity)
speshul, special
speshulist, special(ist)
speshulize, special(ize)
speshulty, special(ity)
spesial, special
spesies, species
spesifakation, specify(fication)
spesifek, specific
spesificashen, specify(fication)
spesification, specify(fication)
spesifide, specify(fied)
spesifik, specific

spesifucashen, specify(fication)
spesifukation, specify(fication)
spesify, specify
spesimen, specimen
spesofecashen, specify(fication)
spesofecation, specify(fication)
spesofide, specify(fied)
spesufication, specify(fication)
spesufide, specify(fied)
spesufy, specify
spesumen, specimen
spesumin, specimen
spet, sped
spetil, spittle
spetle, spittle
spetoon, spittoon
spetul, spittle
spetune, spittoon
spetur, spit(tter)
speu, spew
speul, spiel / spill
spew,*,wed,wing,wn, RUN/FLOW
FORTH, EJECT FROM WITHIN,
VOMIT
sphagnum,nous, VARIETY OF MOSS
spharikul, sphere(rical)
spharukil, sphere(rical)
sphenctur, sphincter
sphenktur, sphincter
spherakil, sphere(rical)
sphere,*,ed,ring,ral,rical,rics,ry,ricity,
CIRCLE/AREA EXTENDED AROUND
THE CENTER WHERE DISTANCE IS
EQUAL FROM THE CENTER
"prefixes: bio/en/non"
spherekil, sphere(rical)
spherikul, sphere(rical)
sphincter,ral,rial,rate,ric, MUSCLE
WHICH CONTRACTS THE ORIFICE
ON THE LOWER TORSO
sphinkter, sphincter
sphinx,xes,xian, A FIGURE WITH THE
HEAD OF ONE THING AND BODY OF
SOMETHING DIFFERENT
sphire, sphere
spic, speak / spike / spice
spice,*,ed,cing,ery,cy, OF OR GIVEN TO
SPICES, CULINARY PLANTS
spictacular, spectacular
spictakuler, spectacular
spid, spy(pied) / spite / speed / spit
spider,*,ry, EIGHT LEGGED ARACHNID
spidful, spite(ful)
spidul, spittle

spidur, spider
spidury, spider(y)
spiel,*, TALK/EXPLAIN AT LENGTH WITH
PERSUASION
spiget, spigot
spigot,*, DEVICE/FAUCET FOR
ALLOWING/STOPPING FLOW OF
LIQUIDS
spigut, spigot
spike,*,ed,king,ker,ky, STIFF/SHARP,
USED TO IMPALE/PIERCE, SHAPED
LIKE A NAIL
spikt, spike(d)
spiktakewler, spectacular
spiktakuler, spectacular
spiky, spike(ky)
spil, spill
spill,*,lled,lling,llage, SOMETHING
LOOSE/LIQUID TO FLOW FROM
CONTAINER/SOURCE, TO DIVULGE
(or see spiel/spell) "prefixes: over"
spin,*,pun,nning,nner, TO WEAVE/
TWIST/WRAP AROUND, TELL A
STORY, PERFORM CIRCULAR
MOTION (or see spine/spend)
"prefixes: under"
spinach, VEGETABLE/PLANT
spinal,lly, ASSOCIATED WITH THE SPINE
spinatch, spinach
spind, spend / spin(nned)
spinded, spent
spinder, spend(er)
spindil, spindle
spindle,*,ed,ling,ly, A ROD/PIN, TO
WIND/SPIN/TWIST SOMETHING
AROUND
spindly, spindle(y)
spindul, spindle
spindur, spend(er)
spine,*,eless,elessly,elessness,ny,
escent,escence, BACKBONE/
VERTEBRATE OF BODIES, A LONG
CREST/SET OF PEAKS
spinech, spinach
spinel, spinal
spiner, spin(nner)
spinlesness, spine(lessness)
spinless, spine(less)
spinol, spinal
spinor, spin(nner)
spint, spent
spinter, spend(er)
spintil, spindle
spintir, spend(er)

spintul, spindle
spintur, spend(er)
spinuch, spinach
spinul, spinal
spinur, spin(nner)
spinutch, spinach
spiny, spine(y)
spir, spur / spire / spear
spiradek, sporadic
spiradik, sporadic
spiradikly, sporadic(ally)
spiral,*,led,ling,lly, REPEATED
CIRCULAR CURVE WHOSE
EVOLUTION AROUND
CONSISTENTLY ASCENDS OR
DESCENDS, CONTINUOUS
CIRCULAR MOTION IN ONE
DIRECTION OR ANOTHER
spiraly, spiral(lly)
spird, spire(d) / spur(rred) / spurt /
spear(ed)
spire,ed,ring,ry, COMING TO A POINT,
PYRAMID SHAPE
spirechualedy, spiritual(ity)
spirechuil, spiritual
spirel, spiral
spireshuil, spiritual
spiret, spirit
spiretshualety, spiritual(ity)
spirichual, spiritual
spirichualidy, spiritual(ity)
spirichuel, spiritual
spiril, spiral
spirit,*,ted,tism,tist,tistic,tual,
CHARACTER/DISPOSITION AND
ESSENCE OF ENERGY, THAT WHICH
ANIMATES/MAKES THINGS LIFELIKE
OR ALIVE, TYPE OF ALCOHOL
"prefixes: di"
spiritchuel, spiritual
spiritual,lly,lness,lism,list,listic,lity,lities,
lize,lized,lizing, IMMATERIAL
ESSENCE/SPIRIT/LIFE, OF THE
UNKNOWN, NOT PHYSICAL
spirm, sperm
spirt, spurt / spire(d)
spirul, spiral
spiruly, spiral(lly)
spisd, spice(d)
spise, spice / spice(y) / spy(pies)
spised, spice(d)
spisury, spice(ry)
spisy, spice(y)

spit,*,tted,tting,pat,tter, PROJECT/
FORCE SALIVA FROM THE MOUTH,
ROD/PIN FOR HOLDING MEAT
WHILE COOKING, NARROW
SLENDER EXTENSION OF LAND
SURROUNDED BY WATER
spital, spittle
spite,ed,ting,eful,efully,efulness, OF
MALICIOUS INTENT/DISPOSITION
spitel, spittle
spiter, spider / spit(tter)
spitful, spite(ful)
spitle, spittle
spitoon, spittoon
spittle, SECRETION BY INSECTS
spittoon,*, VESSEL FOR SPIT
spittune, spittoon
spitul, spittle
spitune, spittoon
spitur, spider / spit(tter)
spiz, spy(pies) / spice
spize, spice / spy(pies) / spice(y)
spla, splay
splach, splotch / splash
splachy, splotch(y)
splad, splat / splay(ed)
splader, splatter
spladur, splatter
splaer, splay(er)
splash,hes,hed,hing,her,hy,hily,hiness,
PARTICLES OF LIQUID SCATTERED
INTO THE AIR
splat, BACK OF A CHAIR, A TYPE OF
SOUND
splater, splatter
splator, splatter
splatter,*,red,ring, TO SPLASH A LIQUID
splatur, splatter
splaur, splay(er)
splay,*,yed,yer, SPREAD OUT/FLARE/
FAN, CREATE CURVE
splean, spleen
spledur, split(tter)
spleen,*,nful,ny, AN ORGAN IN THE
BODY, ILL HUMOR/ IRRITABLE
splen, spleen
splendant, splendent
splendedly, splendid(ly)
splendent, BRILLIANT/RADIANT IN
APPEARANCE
splender, splendor / splinter
splendid,dly,dness, GRAND/
MAGNIFICENT
splendint, splendent

splendir, splendor / splinter
splendit, splendid
splendor,*,rous, BRILLIANCE, LUSTER
(or see splinter)
splendrus, splendor(ous)
splendunt, splendent
splendur, splendor / splinter
splene, spleen / spleen(y)
splent, splint
splented, splendid
splentor, splendor / splinter
splentrus, splendor(ous)
splentur, splendor / splinter
spleny, spleen(y)
splerge, splurge
splerje, splurge
splet, split
spletor, split(tter)
splice,*,ed,cing,er, GRAFT/PIECE
TOGETHER PERFECTLY, CUT TO JOIN
splider, split(tter)
splin, spline / spleen
splindant, splendent
splinded, splendid
splindedly, splendid(ly)
splindint, splendent
splindir, splendor / splinter
splindit, splendid
splindrus, splendor(ous)
splindud, splendid
splindunt, splendent
splindur, splendor / splinter
spline,*,ed,ning, INTERNAL PART OF A
WHEEL, A SLAT, WAY TO SECURE A
PART, MATHEMATICAL EXPRESSION
(or see spleen)
splint,*,ter, USED TO REPAIR
FRACTURES
splinted, splendid
splinter,*,red,ring,ry, A SMALL SLICE/
PIECE BROKEN/CUT OFF
LENGHTWISE, A SLIVER
splintird, splinter(ed)
splintor, splendor / splinter
splintrus, splendor(ous)
splintur, splendor / splinter
splirge, splurge
splirje, splurge
splisur, splice(r)
split,*,tting,tter, BROKEN/TORN APART/
SEPARATED
splitor, split(tter)
sploch, splotch
sploche, splotch(y)

splotch,hes,hed,hing,hy,hier,hiest, AN
IRREGULAR SPOT/SPLASH OF
LIQUID/ COLOR/STAIN
splurch, splurge
splurgd, splurge(d)
splurge,*,ed,ging, TO OVER SPEND
spo, spa
spock, spoke
spod, spot
spodable, spot(able)
spoded, spot(tted)
spodee, spot(tty)
spodible, spot(able)
spodid, spot(tted)
spodlis, spot(less)
spoduble, spot(able)
spoel, spoil
spoeld, spoil(ed) / spoilt
spoeleg, spoil(age)
spoelij, spoil(age)
spoelt, spoil(ed) / spoilt
spoeluj, spoil(age)
spogedi, spaghetti
spogeti, spaghetti
spoil,*,led,ling,lage,ler,lable,lt, TO GO
BAD, DAMAGE, RENDER UNFIT
"prefixes: un"
spoild, spoil(ed) / spoilt
spoileg, spoil(age)
spoilej, spoil(age)
spoilt, PAST TENSE FOR THE WORD
"SPOIL " (or see spoil(ed))
spoiluje, spoil(age)
spoke,*,en, PAST TENSE FOR THE
WORD "SPEAK", RODS/WIRES
RADIATING FROM THE HUB OF A
WHEEL "prefixes: mis/un"
spokun, spoke(n)
spon, spawn / spoon
sponch, sponge
sponge,*,ed,ging,gy,gier,giest,giness,er,
SEA ANIMAL, SKELETON OF SEA
ANIMALS USED TO CLEAN/ABSORB
LIQUIDS
sponser, sponsor
sponsor,*,red,ring,rial,rship, SOMEONE
WHO PAYS/SUPPORTS SOMEONE
ELSE
sponsur, sponsor
spont, spawn(ed) / spoon(ed)
spontaineus, spontaneous
spontaneity,eities,eous, ABLE TO ACT
QUICKLY ON IMPULSE WITHOUT
CONSTRAINT

spontaneous,sly,sness, ACT QUICKLY ON IMPULSE WITHOUT CONSTRAINT
spontaneus, spontaneous
spontenaity, spontaneity
spontinaedy, spontaneity
spontunaity, spontaneity
sponzur, sponsor
spoof,*, TO TEASE/DECEIVE WITH GOOD INTENT
spook,*,ked,king,ky,kish, GHOST, SPECTER, APPARITION
spool,*,led,ling,ler, ROUND/CYLINDER SHAPE HOLDING LENGTHS OF SOMETHING WOUND AROUND IT
spoon,*,ned,ning,nful, UTENSIL WITH HANDLE AT ONE END AND A BOWL SHAPE ON THE OTHER
spor, spar / spore
sporadic,cal,cally, ERRATIC/ UNPREDICTABLE OCCURENCES
sporadikly, sporadic(ally)
sporded, sport(ed)
spordee, sport(y)
spordid, sport(ed)
spordy, sport(y)
spore,*,red,ring,ral,roid,riferous,rulate, REPRODUCTIVE SEEDS OF BACTERIA AND SOME PLANTS
sporol, spore(ral)
sport,*,ted,ting,tive,tively,tiveness,ty, ATHLETIC/OUTDOOR GAMES, TO CARRY, GOOD ATTITUDE
sportee, sport(y)
sportef, sport(ive)
sportif, sport(ive)
sportud, sport(ed)
sporul, spore(ral)
spos, suppose
spot,*,tted,tting,tty,ttier,ttiest,tter, table,tless,tlessly,tlessness, FLAW/ MARK/ BLEMISH, A PARTICULAR/ SPECIFIC PLACE, TO SEE "prefixes: un"
spoted, spot(tted)
spotee, spot(tty)
spotible, spot(able)
spotid, spot(tted)
spotuble, spot(able)
spoty, spot(tty)
spouse,*,sal, ONE WHO IS ENGAGED/ VOWED/MARRIED TO ANOTHER

spout,*,ted,ting,ter, PIPE/NOZZLE PROJECTING FROM VESSEL FOR LIQUID
spown, spawn
spowse, spouse
spowsul, spouse(sal)
spowt, spout
spoyl, spoil
spoyleg, spoil(age)
spoylej, spoil(age)
spra, spray
spraer, spray(er)
spraget, sprocket
spragit, sprocket
sprain,*,ned,ning, TWIST/WRENCH/ OVER STRETCH A MUSCLE IN THE BODY
spraket, sprocket
spral, sprawl
spran, sprain
spraor, spray(er)
sprat, spray(ed)
spraukit, sprocket
spraul, sprawl
spraur, spray(er)
spraut, sprout
sprawl,*,led,ling, TO EXTEND/SPREAD OUT IN IRREGULAR POSITION/ MANNER
sprawt, sprout
spray,*,yed,ying,yer, PARTICLES OF LIQUID RELEASED/FORCED INTO THE AIR
spre, spree
spread,*,ding,der, FORCE/EXTEND INTO A THIN LAYER OVER SUBSTANTIAL DISTANCE/TIME/SPACE
spred, spread
spredur, spread(er)
spree,*, TO FROLICK, HAVE A MERRY TIME
spreg, sprig
sprein, sprain / spray(ing)
sprencol, sprinkle
spreng, spring
sprengee, spring(y)
sprengy, spring(y)
sprenk, spring
sprenkal, sprinkle
sprenkil, sprinkle
sprenkler, sprinkle(r)
sprenklor, sprinkle(r)
sprenkul, sprinkle
sprenkuler, sprinkle(r)

sprent, sprint
sprentur, sprint(er)
spret, spread
spreter, spread(er)
spretur, spread(er)
sprews, spruce
spri, spry / spree
sprig,*, SMALL BRANCH FROM PLANT
sprilee, spry(ly)
sprily, spry(ly)
sprincol, sprinkle
spring,*,ging,rang,gy,gier,giest,gily, giness, A RIVULET OF WATER, COILED DEVICE "prefixes: up"
springey, spring(y)
sprinis, spry(ness)
sprink, spring
sprinkel, sprinkle
sprinkle,*,ed,ling,er, SHOOT/RELEASE/ SPRAY HEAVY DROPS OF LIQUID
sprinklor, sprinkle(r)
sprinkul, sprinkle
sprinkuler, sprinkle(r)
sprint,*,ted,ting,ter, RACE/SPEED A SHORT DISTANCE
sprintor, sprint(er)
sprintur, sprint(er)
sprocket,*, PART OF A WHEEL/CHAIN
sprogit, sprocket
sprokut, sprocket
sprol, sprawl
sproose, spruce
sprout,*,ted,ting,ter, TO GERMINATE, GROW INTO THE DAYLIGHT, SHOW GROWTH
sprowt, sprout
spruce,*,ed,cing,ely,eness,er,est, TYPE OF TREE, GET DRESSED UP, GET FANCY
sprung, PAST TENSE FOR THE WORD SPRING "prefixes: un"
spruse, spruce
spry,yly,yness, LIVELY/NIMBLE
sprynis, spry(ness)
spuc, spook
spud,*,dded,dding, POTATOE, TOOL, TO WEED OUT
spuder, sputter
spudor, sputter
spue, spew
spufe, spoof
spugedi, spaghetti
spugeti, spaghetti
spuk, spook

spuky, spook(y)

spule, spool

spun, PAST TENSE FOR THE WORD "SPIN" (or see spoon) "prefixes: over"

spunch, sponge

spune, spoon / spun

spunful, spoon(ful)

spung, sponge / spunk

spungee, sponge(gy)

spungenis, spunk(iness)

spungy, sponge(gy)

spunj, sponge

spunjy, sponge(gy)

spunk,ky,kily,kiness,kier,kiest, SPIRITED/ COURAGEOUS, TINDER FROM FUNGUS

spunkenis, spunk(iness)

spur,*,rred,rring,rious,riously,riousness, STIMULATE/ENCOURAGE TO GO ON, DEVICE FOR BOOTS/RIDING (too many definitions, please see standard dictionary) (or see spurt)

spuradek, sporadic

spuradikly, sporadic(ally)

spurm, sperm

spurt,*,ted,ting, SUDDEN JOLT/ GROWTH/MOVEMENT, SHORT PERIOD OF TIME

spusefikly, specific(ally)

spusifikly, specific(ally)

sput, spud

sputer, sputter

sputter,*,red,ring,rer, TO RAPIDLY/ INCOHERENTLY SPEAK, ERRATIC/ HALTING MOTION/SOUND

sputur, sputter

spy,pies,pied,pying, SECRET SURVEILLANCE/MONITORING

spyd, spy(pied)

spyder, spider

spydful, spite(ful)

spydur, spider

spyeng, spy(ing)

spyke, spike

spyse, spy(pies) / spice

spytur, spider

sqeek, squeak

squabble,*,ed,ling,er, MINOR SCUFFLE/ DISPUTE

squad,*,dron, SMALL GROUP OF SPECIFIC PEOPLE (or see squat)

squadir, squat(tter)

squadron,*, SMALL MILITARY/POLICE GROUP

squadur, squat(tter)

squaemish, squeamish

squaled, squalid

squalid,dly,dness,dity, NEGLECTED/ FOUL/FILTHY

squall,*,lled,lling,llier,lliest,lly, SUDDEN/ STRONG GUSTS OF WIND/RAIN/ SLEET

squalor, NEGLECTED/FOUL/FILTHY

squander,*,red,ring, RECKLESSLY LET GO OF/USE/WASTE

square,*,ed,ring,ely,eness,rish,rishly, OF BEING FOUR EQUAL SIDES, TO BE PROPORTIONAL, SOMEONE DULL, A MATH OPERATION

squarly, square(ly)

squash,hes,hed,hing, A VEGETABLE, A GAME, TO SMASH/CRUSH SOMETHING

squat,*,tted,tting,tter, REST ON HAUNCHES, LOWER THE UPPER TORSO, TO SIT (or see squad)

squator, squat(tter)

squeak,*,ked,king,kingly,ker,ky, A SHORT/SHRILL SOUND

squeal,*,led,ling,ler, LOUD/SHRILL SOUND PRODUCED BY GLEE/ HAPPINESS, TELL A TRUTH ABOUT SOMEONE WITHOUT THEIR PERMISSION

squeamish,hly,hness, UNEASY/ UNSETTLING, DISGUSTED ABOUT SOMETHING

squed, squid

squeegee,*,eed,eeing, AN INSTRUMENT/IMPLEMENT FOR REMOVING WATER/LIQUID

squeejy, squeegee

squeek, squeak

squeel, squeal

squeelur, squeal(er)

squeemish, squeamish

squeese, squeeze

squeeze,*,ed,zing,er,zingly,zable,zably, TO FORCE BY TIGHTENING GRIP

squegy, squeegee

squejy, squeegee

squel, squeal

squelch,hed,hing,her, SILENCE/CRUSH/ SUPPRESS, A SOUND

squelur, squeal(er)

squemish, squeamish

squent, squint

squerl, squirrel

squerm, squirm

squermy, squirm(y)

squert, squirt

squesh, squish

squeshy, squish(y)

squesur, squeeze(r)

squeze, squeeze

squid,*, A CEPHALOPOD FOUND IN SALT WATER

squiggle,*,ed,ling, SQUIRM/TWIST

squigy, squeegee

squint,*,ted,ting, TO CLOSE EYES TO A NARROW OPENING FOR PROTECTION

squire,*,ed,ring, MAN OF ARISTOCRATIC BIRTH, MAN WHO ESCORTS

squirel, squirrel

squirl, squirrel

squirm,*,med,ming,mer,my,mier,miest, WRITHE/WRIGGLE LIKE A WORM

squirrel,*,lly, A RODENT, TO BEHAVE LIKE A SQUIRREL

squirt,*,ted,ting, NARROW STREAM OF LIQUID EMITTED FROM AN ORIFICE

squish,hes,hed,hing,hy,hier,hiest, SQUASH/SMASH

squrt, squirt

sqwal, squall

sqwalid, squalid

srgekul, surgical

sta, stay

stab,*,bbed,bbing,bber, TO POKE/ THRUST A BLADE WITH SHARP TIP INTO SOMETHING/SOMEONE

stabalize, stabilize

stabelity, stability

stabilise, stabilize

stability,ties,ize, OF FIRM GROUND/ FORM/FOUNDATION "prefixes: in"

stabilize,*,ed,zing,er,zation, TO PROVIDE/ENSURE FIRM GROUND/ FORM "prefixes: de"

stabiludy, stability

stable,*,ed,ling,ly,eness,bilize, OF FIRM GROUND/FORM, SHELTER FOR ANIMAL "prefixes: un"

stablize, stabilize

stabulize, stabilize

stac, stack / stake / steak / stalk / stock

stacado, staccato / stoccado

staccato,*, SHARP/BRIEF MUSICAL NOTE (or see stoccado)

stachatory, statutory

stachur, stature

stachutory, statutory

stack,*, ked,king,ker, ORGANIZE/PILE/ SET UP ITEMS ONE ON TOP OF ANOTHER (or see stake/steak/stalk)

stad, staid / stay(ed) / state

stadeim, stadium

stadek, static

stades, status

stadeum, stadium

stadiem, stadium

stadik, static

stadis, status

stadium,*, A LARGE ARENA FOR PEOPLE TO GATHER

stadus, status

staf, staff / staph / stave

stafed, staff(ed)

staff,*,ffed,ffing, GROUP OF HIRED PEOPLE, LONG POLE/STICK TO BE CARRIED/ USED BY HAND (or see staph) "prefixes: over"

staft, staff(ed) / stave(d)

stag,*,gged,gging,gger, MALE IN THE DEER FAMILY, MALE UNACCOMPANIED AT A GATHERING (or see stage/stack)

stagd, stag(gged) / stage(d)

stage,*,ed,ging,er,ey, PLATFORM DESIGNED FOR PLAYS/THEATER, TO PERFORM (or see stag) "prefixes: sub"

staged, stag(gged) / stage(d)

stagee, stodgy

stager, stagger

stagger,*,red,ring,rer,ringly, TO SWAY/ WAVER/WALK UNSTEADILY, SHOCKED, HORSE/COW HIT BY A DISEASE

stagir, stagger

stagnade, stagnate

stagnant,tly,ncy, NO MOVEMENT/ MOTION

stagnashen, stagnate(tion)

stagnate,*,ed,ting,tion, QUIT MOVING, BECOME DULL/QUIET

stagnatid, stagnate(d)

stagnit, stagnant

stagnunt, stagnant

stagnut, stagnant

stagred, stagger(ed)

stagt, stag(gged) / stage(d)

stagur, stagger

stagy, stodgy

staid,dly,dness, IN PLACE OF, FIXED/ STEADY (or see stead/stay(ed))

stain,*,ned,ning,nable,ner,nless,nlessly, UNDESIRABLE MARK, PERMANENTLY PLACE/AFFIX COLOR

stair,*, STEPS MAKING A RISE IN ELEVATION (or see stare)

stak, stack / stake / steak / stalk / stock

stakabul, stack(able)

stakado, staccato / stoccado

stakato, staccato / stoccado

stakd, stack(ed) / stake(d) / stalk(ed) / stock(ed)

stake,*,ed,king, LEVERAGE/PLEDGE/ WAGER/SUPPORT FOR SOMETHING, HAVE A VESTED INTEREST IN, BROAD POINTED POST FOR STRIKING/DRIVING INTO GROUND (or see steak/stack/stalk/stock)

staked, stack(ed) / stake(d) / stalk(ed) / stock(ed)

staker, stagger / stack(er) / stalk(er) / stock(er)

stakibel, stack(able)

stakibul, stack(able)

stakir, stagger / stack(er) / stalk(er) / stock(er)

staknade, stagnate

staknashen, stagnate(tion)

staknate, stagnate

staknation, stagnate(tion)

staknunt, stagnant

stakodo, staccato / stoccado

stakoto, staccato / stoccado

stakt, stack(ed) / stake(d) / stalk(ed) / stock(ed)

stakubil, stack(able)

stakuble, stack(able)

stakur, stagger / stack(er) / stalk(er) / stock(er)

stal, stall / stale

stale,*,ed,ling,er,est,ely,eness, LOSS OF ACTION/TASTE/FLAVOR (or see stall)

staleon, stallion

staliun, stallion

stalk,*,ked,king,ker, FOLLOW SOMEONE/SOMETHING WITH INTENT WITHOUT THEIR KNOWING, MAIN PORTION OF A POLE SHAPED PLANT

stall,*,lled,lling, A DWELLING FOR HORSES, TO HESITATE/QUIT/PAUSE (or see stale)

stallion,*, MALE HORSE CAPABLE OF BREEDING

stalwart,tly,tness, UNCOMPROMISING/ STRONG IN RESOLUTION

stalwort, stalwart

stalyun, stallion

stamen,*,nal, PLANT ORGAN

stamenu, stamina

stamer, stammer

stamin, stamen

stamina, LONGEVITY IN STRENGTH

stamir, stammer

stammer,*,red,ring,ringly, PAUSE/ HESITATE IN SPEECH

stamp,*,ped,ping,per, AFFIXED TO A POSTAL LETTER, A MARK LEFT BY PRESSING

stampede,*,ed,ding, A MAD/SUDDEN RUSH IN ONE DIRECTION BY MANY

stampet, stampede

stampir, stamp(er)

stampur, stamp(er)

stamun, stamen

stamur, stammer

stan, stain

stance, A STAND/ATTITUDE/POSITION

stanchen, stanchion

stancheon, stanchion

stanchion,*, BEAM/POST FOR SUPPORT

stand,*,ding,der,tood, PARTICULAR POSITION, BE UPRIGHT IN FOOTING "prefixes: up"

standard,*,dize,dized,dizing,dization, GENERAL CONSENSUS ON METHODOLOGY/DIMENSIONS/ DEGREE OF MEASURMENT "prefixes: non/sub"

standerd, standard

standerdazation, standard(ization)

standurd, standard

standurdize, standard(ize)

stane, stain

staneble, stain(able)

stanible, stain(able)

stank, PAST TENSE FOR THE WORD "STINK"

stans, stance / stain(s) / stand(s)

stansa, stanza

stanshen, stanchion

stanshon, stanchion

stansu, stanza

stant, stand

stanuble, stain(able)

stanza,*, FOUR OR MORE IN A VERSE/ POEM

stap, stab

stapel, staple

staph, SHORT FOR STAPHYLOCOCCUS (or see staff)

staple,*,ed,ling,er, FASTENER MADE OF METAL, BASIC REQUIREMENTS FOR SURVIVAL

stapul, staple

star,*,rred,rring,rless,rry, CELESTIAL/ SHINING BODY IN SPACE, PERSON WHO ACHIEVES THE LIMELIGHT, GEOMETRIC SHAPE (or see stare/ stair/store)

staralize, sterile(lize)

starc, stark

starch,hes,hed,hing,hiness,hy, NATURALLY OCCURING CHEMICAL USED TO MAKE THINGS STIFF

starchenes, starch(iness)

stard, start / stare(d) / star(rred)

starder, starter

stardil, startle

stardul, startle

stardur, starter

stare,*,ed,ring, AFFIX EYES ONTO A SINGLE POINT WITHOUT MOVING (or see star/stair/star(rry))

stared, stare(d) / star(rred)

stareledy, sterile(lity)

starelidy, sterile(lity)

stareo, stereo

starf, starve

staril, sterile

starilety, sterile(lity)

starilize, sterile(lize)

stark,kly,kness, GRIM/DESOLATE SCENE WITH LITTLE TO ENTERTAIN THE EYE

starling,*, A BIRD

staroed, steroid

staroid, steroid

stars, stair(s) / stare(s) / star(s)

start,*,ted,ting,ter, BEGIN, INITIAL ACTION (or see stare(d)) "prefixes: up"

starter,*, ELECTRIC MOTOR, BEGIN/ INITIATE ACTION

startil, startle

startir, starter

startle,*,ed,ling, BE ALARMED/ SURPRISED BY SUDDEN ACTION/ EVENT

startul, startle

startur, starter

starul, sterile

starulize, sterile(lize)

starvashen, starvation

starvation, SERIOUSLY LACK NOURISHMENT/BASIC ESSENTIALS

starve,*,ed,ving,vation, SERIOUSLY LACK NOURISHMENT/BASIC ESSENTIALS

stas, stay(s)

stases, stasis

stash,hes,hed,hing, TO HIDE/PUT SOMETHING AWAY

stashatory, statutory

stashen, station

stashenary, stationary / stationery

stasher, stature

stashetory, statutory

stashewesk, statue(sque)

stashewtory, statutory

stashin, station / stash(ing)

stashinary, stationary / stationery

stashir, stature

stashitory, statutory

stashonery, stationary / stationery

stashoot, statute

stashu, statue

stashuary, statuary

stashuery, statuary

stashuesk, statue(sque)

stashun, station

stashunery, stationary / stationery

stashur, stature

stashute, statute

stashutory, statutory

stasis, EQUILIBRIUM, FROZEN IN TIME/ MOVEMENT, INACTIVITY

stasus, stasis

stat,*, HOSPITAL EMERGENCY EXPRESSION, SHORT FOR STATISTICS (or see state/stay(ed))

statchuesk, statue(sque)

state,*,ed,ting,ely,elier,eliest,eliness, LAND WITH SPECIFIC/DIVISIVE BORDER, CURRENT CONDITION "prefixes: inter/intra/over/re/up"

statek, static

statement,*, SUMMARY/REVIEW OF CONDITION/STATUS

states, status / state(s)

stateur, stature

stateutory, statutory

static,*,cal,cally, NO MOVEMENT/ ACTION, AT REST

statik, static

station,*, PLACE TO MOMENTARILY REST/RECEIVE SERVICES "prefixes: inter/sub"

stationary, REST, STOP, BE STILL (or see stationery) "prefixes: non"

stationery, ENVELOPE/PAPER FOR WRITING (or see stationary)

statis, status

statistic,*,cal,cally, A MATHEMATICAL ACCOUNT OF CURRENT SITUATION/ CONDITION

statiur, stature

statment, statement

statmunt, statement

stats, state(s) / stat(s)

statshu, statue

statshuery, statuary

statuary,ries, COLLECTION OF STATUES

statue,*,esque,ette, SOLID/ STATIONARY FORM CARVED/ MOLDED TO RESEMBLE SOMETHING/SOMEONE

statuery, statuary

statuesk, statue(sque)

stature, PHYSICAL DIMENSIONS OF A LIVING THING

status, CURRENT POSITION/STANDING

statute,*,tory, A FIXED PERMANENT LAW

statutory,rily, IMPOSED BY A STATUTE

stauk, stock

staunch,hly,hness, RIGID/FIRM STRUCTURE/FORM, LIQUID RESILIENT

staut, stout

stave,*,ed,ving, FIGHT OFF AN ATTACK, A ROD/POLE/STICK

stawgines, stodgy(giness)

stawk, stock / stalk

stawked, stock(ed) / stoke(d)

stawt, stout

stay,*,yed,ying, TO REMAIN BEHIND/IN ONE PLACE, DON'T FOLLOW/MOVE "prefixes: over"

stead, TO BE IN SOMEONE'S PLACE/ POSITION WHILE THEY'RE AWAY (or see steed/staid)

steadeness, steady(diness)

steadfast,tly,tness, HOLDING FIXED/ FIRM/UNWAVERING (alternate spelling for 'stedfast')

steady,dies,died,dying,dier,diest,dily, diness, FIXED/FIRM/CONSTANT "prefixes: un"

steak,*, A CUT OF BEEF (or see stake)

steal,*,ling,tole, TAKE SOMETHING FROM SOMEONE WITHOUT THEIR PERMISSION (or see steel/stile/still)

stealth,hy,hily,hiness, SECRECY

steam,*,med,ming,mer,mily,miness,my, HOT WATER TURNED TO GASEOUS STATE

stear, steer

stebel, steeple / stipple

stebul, steeple / stipple

stebulashen, stipulate(tion)

stebulation, stipulate(tion)

stebulatory, stipulate(tory)

stec, stick

stecado, staccato / stoccado

stech, stitch

sted, SHORT FOR "INSTEAD" (or see stead/steed)

stede, steady

stedeness, steady(diness)

stedes, steady(dies)

stedfast,tly,tness, HOLDING FIXED/ FIRM/UNWAVERING (alternate spelling for 'stedfast')

stedfastnes, steadfast(ness)

stedily, steady(dily)

stediness, steady(diness)

stedness, staid(ness) / stead(ness)

steduly, steady(dily)

stedy, steady

steed,*, HORSE WITH SPIRIT, STALLION (or see stead)

steel,ly,lier,liest,liness, TYPE OF METAL (or see steal/stile/still)

steenkur, stink(er)

steenky, stink(y)

steep,*,ped,ping,ply,pness,per,pen, SHARP SLOPE, SOAK/IMMERSE (or see step/steppe)

steeple,*, TALL ROOF COMING TO A POINT AT THE TOP

steer,*,red,ring,rable,rer,rage, MANIPULATE/CONTROL INTO PARTICULAR DIRECTION, CASTRATED BOVINE "prefixes: over/ under"

steerible, steer(able)

steeruble, steer(able)

stef, stiff

stefin, stiff(en)

stefnis, stiff(ness)

stegma, stigma

stegmadik, stigma(tic)

stegmatist, stigma(tist)

stein,*, BEER MUGS (or see stain/ stay(ing))

stek, stick / steak / stake

stekado, staccato / stoccado

stekato, staccato / stoccado

stekir, stick(er)

stekler, stickler

steklur, stickler

stekmu, stigma

stekodo, staccato / stoccado

stekor, stick(er)

stekoto, staccato / stoccado

stekur, stick(er)

steky, stick(y)

stel, steel / steal / still / stile / stale

stelar, stellar

stelir, stellar

stellar, OF THE STARS "prefixes: inter/ sub"

stelnis, still(ness)

stelnus, still(ness)

stelre, stellar

stels, still(s) / steal(s)

stelt, stilt / steal(ed) / still(ed)

stelth, stealth

stelur, stellar

stem,*,mmed,mming, BRANCH OF A WOODY PLANT, SUGGESTING OF A BRANCH, THE BASE/BASIS OF SOMETHING

stemely, steam(ily)

stemer, steam(er)

stemewlasheon, stimulate(tion)

stemily, steam(ily)

stemir, steam(er)

stemulashen, stimulate(tion)

stemulate, stimulate

stemulation, stimulate(tion)

stemuly, steam(ily)

stemur, steam(er)

stenaugrafer, stenograph(er)

stench, POWERFUL STINK

stenchee, stingy

stencil,*,led,ling,ler, A FORM/OUTLINE/ TEMPLATE FOR REPRODUCING

steng, sting

stengd, sting(ed) / stink

stengee, stingy

stenger, sting(er) / stink(er)

stengles, sting(less)

stengt, sting(ed) / stink

stengur, sting(er) / stink(er)

stengyness, stingy(giness)

stenjee, stingy

stenjenes, stingy(giness)

stenk, stink

stenkee, stink(y)

stenkenes, stink(iness)

stenkur, stink(er)

steno, SHORT FOR STENOGRAPHER

stenografir, stenograph(er)

stenograph,her,hers,hy,hic,hical,hically, USE OF SHORTHAND, A TYPE OF TYPEWRITER

stensh, stench

stenshee, stingy

stensil, stencil

stensul, stencil

stent, stint

step,*,pped,pping, RISE/MOVE UP, RISER, UP IN INCREMENTS (or see steep/steppe) "prefixes: mis/over"

stepel, steeple / stipple

stepend, stipend

stepeulashen, stipulate(tion)

stepewlation, stipulate(tion)

stepil, steeple / stipple

stepind, stipend

steple, steeple / stipple

steppe,*, A PLAIN WITHOUT TREES (or see step)

stepul, steeple / stipple

stepulashen, stipulate(tion)

stepulation, stipulate(tion)

ster, stare / steer / stir

steral, sterile

steralize, sterile(lize)

sterchen, sturgeon

sterd, stare(d) / steer(ed) / stir(rred)

sterdy, sturdy

stered, stare(d) / steer(ed) / stir(rred)

stereledy, sterile(lity)

stereo,*, SOUND SYSTEM, PREFIX INDICATING "THREE DIMENSIONAL OR SOLID" MOST OFTEN MODIFIES THE WORD

stergen, sturgeon

stergon, sturgeon

sterib, stirrup

sterible, steer(able)

sterile,lity,lize,lizes,lized,lizing,lization, lizer, FREE FROM BACTERIA/ CONTAMINATION, UNPRODUCTIVE "prefixes: inter/un"
sterilety, sterile(lity)
sterip, stirrup
sterjen, sturgeon
sterjon, sturgeon
sterleng, sterling
sterling, A STANDARD/DEGREE OF SILVER
stern,ner,nest,nly,nness, HIND/BACK END, BE HARSH/RIGID
sternem, sternum
sternness, stern(ess)
sternum,*, PART OF THE SKELETON
steroed, steroid
steroet, steroid
steroid,*,dal, CHEMICAL COMPOUND
sterol, sterile
steror, stir(rrer)
steroyd, steroid
stert, steer(ed) / stir(rred)
sterty, sturdy
sterub, stirrup
steruble, steer(able)
sterul, sterile
sterulize, sterile(lize)
sterup, stirrup
stesh, stitch
stetch, stitch
stethaskope, stethoscope
stethiskopek, stethoscope(pic)
stethoscope,*,pic,pical,pically,py, INSTRUMENT A MEDICAL EXAMINER USES
stethuskope, stethoscope
stethuskopik, stethoscope(pic)
stetistiks, statistic(s)
steudeo, studio
steudint, student
steul, stool
steve, stiff
stew,*,wed,wing, A THICK SOUP
steward,*,dess,desses, ONE WHO MANAGES THE AFFAIRS OF OTHERS
stewardes, steward(ess)
stewbud, stupid
stewdeis, studious
stewdent, student
stewdeo, studio
stewdeus, studious
stewdio, studio
stewg, stooge

stewj, stooge
stewlee, stool(ie)
stewp, stoop
stewpendus, stupendous
stewper, stupor
stewpid, stupid
stewpidety, stupid(ity)
stewpir, stupor
stewpud, stupid
stewpur, stupor
stewul, stool
stewurd, steward
stey, stay
sti, sty
stibe, stipe
stible, stipple
stibul, stipple
stibulashen, stipulate(tion)
stibulation, stipulate(tion)
stibulatory, stipulate(tory)
sticado, staccato / stoccado
stich, stitch
stick,*,king,ky,ker,kier,kiest,kiness,kily, tuck, A BRANCH, SOMETHING TACKY, BE AFFIXED/ADHERED TO "prefixes: un"
stickler,*, TO BE PARTICULAR, MYSTERIOUS/PUZZLING
stif, stiff
stifal, stifle
stifel, stifle
stifen, stiff(en)
stifenur, stiff(ener)
stiff,*,ffed,ffing,ffer,ffest,ffish,ffly,ffness, ffen,ffener, RIGID/TENSE/ UNBENDING/SEVERE
stifle,*,ed,ling,er,lingly, DIFFICULT TO MOVE/BREATH, OPPRESSIVE, MAMMAL'S JOINT
stifnes, stiff(ness)
stiful, stifle
stifun, stiff(en)
stifuner, stiff(ener)
stigma,*,ata,atist,atic,atically,atism, atize,atizes,atized,atizing,atization, atizer, BLEMISH/MARK, TO BRAND
stigmadik, stigma(tic)
stigmutist, stigma(tist)
stik, stick
stikado, staccato / stoccado
stiker, stick(er)
stikir, stick(er)
stikler, stickler
stiklur, stickler

stikmu, stigma
stikodo, staccato / stoccado
stikor, stick(er)
stikoto, staccato / stoccado
stikur, stick(er)
stiky, stick(y)
stil, still / stile / style
stild, still(ed) / stilt / style(d)
stile,*, FOR ASCENDING/MOUNTING, A SHAPE (or see style/still/steal/steel)
stiled, still(ed) / steal(ed) / style(d)
stiles, stylus / style(s)
stilesh, style(lish)
stilest, style(list)
stilis, stylus
stilish, style(lish)
stilishly, style(lishly)
stilize, style(lize)
still,*,lled,lling,llness, MOTIONLESS, DEVICE FOR DISTILLATION (or see stile/style/steal/steel)
stilness, still(ness)
stilnus, still(ness)
stils, still(s) / steal(s) / style(s)
stilt,*, PAIR OF LONG MANMADE LEGS (or see still(ed)/style(d))
stilus, stylus
stilush, style(lish)
stim, stem / steam
stime, stymie
stimed, stem(mmed) / stymie(d) / steam(ed)
stimee, stymie / steam(y)
stimulashen, stimulate(tion)
stimulate,*,ed,ting,tion,ant,ants,tive, tor,lus, ENCOURAGE/MOTIVATE TO MOVE/PERFORM "prefixes: bio"
stinaugrafur, stenograph(er)
stinch, stench
stinchee, stingy
stine, stein
sting,*,tung,ging,ger,gingly,gless, PAINFUL FEELING SENSATION, A COVERT OPERATION
stingd, sting(ed) / stink
stingee, stingy
stinglus, sting(less)
stingt, sting(ed) / stink
stingur, sting(er) / stink(er)
stingy,gier,giest,gily,giness, LACK GENEROSITY, TIGHT WITH RESOURCES, UNSHARING (or see sting)
stingyness, stingy(giness)

stinjee, stingy
stinjenes, stingy(giness)
stink,*,king,ky,kiness,kingly,ker,tank, tunk, FOUL/OFFENSIVE SMELL
stinkee, stink(y)
stinkur, stink(er)
stino, steno
stinografur, stenograph(er)
stinsel, stencil
stinsul, stencil
stint,*,ted,ter,tunt, LIMITED TIME/ AMOUNT, BRIEF ACTIVITY "prefixes: un"
stintud, stint(ed)
stipe, RESEMBLES A STEM
stipend,*,diary,diaries, CONSISTENT/ STEADY PAYMENT/COMPENSATION
stipeulate, stipulate
stipeulutory, stipulate(tory)
stipewlate, stipulate
stiplur, stipple(r)
stipple,ed,ling,er, MANY DOTS TO CREATE A SCENE/PICTURE
stiptek, styptic
stiptik, styptic
stipulashen, stipulate(tion)
stipulate,*,ed,ting,tion,tive,tory, AGREEMENT WITH GUIDELINES
stir,*,rred,rring,rrer,rringly, CREATE MOTION/MOVEMENT
stirafom, styrofoam
stird, stir(rred)
stirdy, sturdy
stirefom, styrofoam
stirgen, sturgeon
stirgeon, sturgeon
stirjun, sturgeon
stirleng, sterling
stirn, stern
stirnem, sternum
stirnly, stern(ly)
stirnness, stern(ess)
stirnum, sternum
stirrup,*, PART ON A HORSE SADDLE
stirt, stir(rred)
stirty, sturdy
stirufom, styrofoam
stirup, stirrup
stish, stitch
stitch,hes,hed,hing,her, SEW TOGETHER, USE OF A NEEDLE
stiulize, style(lize)
stive, stiff
sto, stow / store

stoakul, stoic(al)
stob, stop
stobur, stop(pper)
stoc, stalk / stock / stoke
stocado, staccato / stoccado
stocato, staccato / stoccado
stoccado, TO STAB/THRUST WITH A WEAPON (or se stocatta)
stoccato, staccato / stoccado
stock,*,ked,king,ker,ky, TO COLLECT/ AMASS/ACCUMULATE SOMETHING, HOLDING INTEREST IN A COMPANY (or see stalk/stoke/stocking) "prefixes: over"
stocking,*, MATERIAL FOR COVERING LEGS/FEET
stodgeness, stodgy(giness)
stodgy,gily,giness,gier,giest, DULL/NOT INTERESTING, HEAVY/THICK (or see stogy)
stodgyest, stodgy(giest)
stoec, stoic
stoecul, stoic(al)
stoeg, stow(age)
stoej, stow(age)
stoek, stoic
stoekul, stoic(al)
stof, stove / stuff
stofs, stove(s) / stuff(s)
stoge, stogy / stodgy / stooge
stogeist, stodgy(giest)
stogenis, stodgy(giness)
stogey, stogy
stogiest, stodgy(giest)
stogines, stodgy(giness)
stogy, CIGAR, BOOT (or see stodgy)
stogyest, stodgy(giest)
stogyness, stodgy(giness)
stoic,*,cal,cally,cism, SECT WHO BELIEVES FREEDOM FROM PASSION/GRIEF/ JOY IS A VIRTUE
stoicul, stoic(al)
stoig, stow(age)
stoij, stow(age)
stoikal, stoic(al)
stok, stock / stoke / stalk / stuck
stokada, staccato / stoccado
stokato, staccato / stoccado
stokd, stock(ed) / stoke(d)
stoke,*,ed,king,er, TO STIR/FEED/POKE (or see stock(y)/stalk)

stoked, stoke(d) / stack(ed) / stake(d) / stalk(ed) / stock(ed)
stokee, stock(y) / stogy
stoker, stagger / stack(er) / stalk(er) / stock(er)
stokur, stagger / stack(er) / stalk(er) / stock(er)
stoky, stock(y) / stogy
stol, stall
stold, stall(ed)
stole,en, PAST TENSE FOR THE WORD "STEAL", FUR ACCESSORY FOR THE SHOULDERS
stolin, stole(n)
stolk, stalk / stock
stolker, stalk(er)
stolun, stole(n)
stolwart, stalwart
stolwort, stalwart
stomach,*,hic,hy, POUCH IN THE BODY WHICH HOLDS FOOD FOR DIGESTION
stomek, stomach
stomik, stomach
stomp,*,ped,ping,per, USING THE FOOT FOR FORCEFUL/HEAVY STEPS (or see stump)
stompur, stomp(er)
stomuk, stomach
ston, stun / stone
stonch, staunch
stone,*,ed,ning,er,ny,nier,niest,nily, niness, ROCK UNDER HEAVY INFLUENCE OF SOMETHING
stoney, stone(ny)
stonsh, staunch
stonshly, staunch(ly)
stooart, steward
stoobid, stupid
stood, PAST TENSE FOR THE WORD 'STAND', UPRIGHT
stooerd, steward
stooge,*, TO BE TRICKED/FOILED, A COMEDIAN
stool,*,lie, SMALL SEAT WITH NO BACK/ ARMS, FECES, AN INFORMER
stoole, stool(ie)
stoop,*,ped,ping, BEND OVER, LOWER IN STATUS, SMALL PORCH
stooped, stoop(ed) / stupid
stoopedity, stupid(ity)
stooper, stupor
stoopir, stupor
stoopud, stupid

stoopufid, stupefy(fied)
stoopur, stupor
stop,*,pped,pping,ppage,pper, PUT AN END TO, HALT PROGRESS OF, BLOCK "prefixes: non/un"
stopud, stupid
stopur, stop(pper)
stor, store / star
storach, storage
storage,*, KEEP/STOCKPILE THINGS/ INFORMATION
storck, stork
stord, store(d) / star(rred)
store,*,ed,ring,er,eable,rage, PUT AWAY FOR SAFE KEEPING, RETAIL ESTABLISHMENT (or see story) "prefixes: over/under"
storech, storage
storeg, storage
storij, storage
stork,*, A BIRD
storm,*,med,ming,my, CLASHING/ MEETING OF TWO DIFFERENT ENERGY FRONTS AND THE REPURCUSSIONS AS A RESULT
stormee, storm(y)
stort, store(d) / star(rred)
storuch, storage
storug, storage
storuj, storage
story,ries,ried, A TALE/EXPLANATION OF AN EVENT/OCCURRENCE, VARIOUS FLOOR LEVELS WITHIN A BUILDING/ HOME
storyd, story(ried)
storys, story(ries)
stot, stow(ed) / stood
stoug, stow(age)
stouj, stow(age)
stout,*, SOLID/HARDY/ROBUST/ STRONG/RESISTANT
stove,*, AN APPLIANCE/APPARATUS FOR COOKING/HEATING
stovs, stove(s) / stuff(s)
stow,*,wed,wing,wage,waway, PUT/ PLACE SOMETHING/CARGO AWAY
stoweg, stow(age)
stowej, stow(age)
stowek, stoic
stowgee, stogy
stowic, stoic
stowig, stow(age)
stowij, stow(age)
stowik, stoic

stowt, stout / stow(ed)
stra, straw / stray
stradagee, strategy
stradajist, strategy(gist)
straddle,*,ed,ling,er, SIT ATOP OF SOMETHING, BE IN BETWEEN/THE MIDDLE OF, BE ON BOTH SIDES OF SOMETHING AT THE SAME TIME
strade, stray(ed) / straight / strait
stradegist, strategy(gist)
stradejist, strategy(gist)
stradel, straddle
straden, straight(ened)
strades, stratus
stradigest, strategy(gist)
stradil, straddle
stradin, straight(ened)
stradis, stratus
stradle, straddle
strados, stratus
straduge, strategy
stradugist, strategy(gist)
stradujist, strategy(gist)
stradul, straddle
stradun, straight(ened)
stradus, stratus
strae, stray
stragel, straggle
strageler, straggle(r)
stragely, straggle(ly)
straggle,er,ly,lier,liest, WANDER OFF COURSE IN IRREGULAR PATTERN, DISORGANIZED/DISHEVELED/ UNTIDY
straght, straight / strait
stragil, straggle
stragiler, straggle(r)
stragily, straggle(ly)
stragle, straggle
straglee, straggle(ly)
stragleist, straggle(st)
straglur, straggle(r)
stragul, straggle
straguly, straggle(ly)
straight,ten,tens,tened,tening,tener, BE LINEAR/LEVEL/TRUE, WITHOUT DEVIATION BETWEEN POINT A AND B (or see strait)
strain,*,ned,ning,ner, STRETCH/PUSH/ PULL TO MAXIMUM CAPACITY, SIFT/SIEVE OUT LARGER PARTICLES, REMOVE PARTICULATE MATTER "prefixes: un"
straingly, strange(ly)

strainj, strange
strait,*,ten,tly,tness, NARROW PASSAGEWAY BETWEEN TWO BODIES OF WATER, DIFFICULT/ DESPERATE POSITION, CLOSE, STRICT, TIGHT (or see straight)
strakly, straggle(ly)
stran, strain
stranch, strange
strand,*,ded,ding, ONE ALL ALONE, BE SINGLED OUT AWAY FROM OTHERS
straner, strain(er)
strangal, strangle
strange,ely,er,est,eness, UNFAMILIAR/ ODD/WEIRD
strangel, strangle
strangeulat, strangulate(tion)
strangir, strange(r)
strangist, strange(st)
strangle,*,ed,ling,er,gulate, CHOKE/ HINDER/STOP/CLOSE OFF
strangor, strange(r)
strangul, strangle
strangulashen, strangulate(tion)
strangulate,*,ed,ting,tion, CHOKE/ HINDER/STOP/CLOSE OFF
strangur, strange(r)
stranir, strain(er)
stranj, strange
stranjer, strange(r)
stranjest, strange(st)
stranjly, strange(ly)
stranjur, strange(r)
strankel, strangle
strankler, strangle(r)
strankul, strangle
strankulate, strangulate
stranor, strain(er)
stransh, strange
strant, strand
stranur, strain(er)
strap,*,pped,pping, NARROW/THIN STRIP OF SOMETHING, TIE DOWN/ FASTEN/SECURE WITH
strapeng, strap(pping)
stras, stray(s) / stress
strat, straight / strait / stray(ed)
stratagee, strategy
stratagist, strategy(gist)
strategek, strategic
strategekly, strategic(ally)
strategic,*,cal,cally, PERFORM ALONG A GUIDELINE/METHODOLOGY, HAVE A PLAN "prefixes: un"

strategy,gies,gist, HAVE A METHOD/ PLAN TO PERFORM AN ACTION/ EVENT/ PLAY

stratejik, strategic

stratejikly, strategic(ally)

stratel, straddle

straten, straight(en)

stratend, straight(ened)

strates, stratus

stratesfere, stratosphere

stratesphere, stratosphere

stratigek, strategic

stratigekly, strategic(ally)

stratigest, strategy(gist)

stratil, straddle

stratin, straight(en)

stratis, stratus

stratle, straddle

stratnur, straight(ener)

straton, straight(en)

stratoned, straight(ened)

stratos, stratus

stratosfere, stratosphere

stratosphere,ric, LAYER SEVEN MILES ABOVE EARTH "prefixes: sub"

stratugee, strategy

stratugist, strategy(gist)

stratugy, strategy

stratul, straddle

stratum,*,ta,tal,us, LAYER, LEVEL OF A SYSTEM/ FORMATION "prefixes: sub"

stratun, straight(ened)

stratuned, straight(ened)

stratus, UNIFORM/WEAK LAYER OF CLOUDS

stratusfere, stratosphere

stratusphere, stratosphere

straw,*, STALK OF GRAIN, A TUBE TO SIP LIQUIDS

stray,*,yed,ying,yer, WANDER FROM THE GROUP/CENTER

strayd, stray(ed) / straight

streak,*,ked,king,ky,kily,kiness, SMEARED AS IF WIPED, A BLURRED IMAGE

stream,*,med,ming,mer, GENTLE/ FLOWING/CONSISTENT MOVEMENT "prefixes: un/up"

strech, stretch

strecher, stretch(er)

strechnine, strychnine

strechur, stretch(er)

streekee, streak(y)

streem, stream

streemer, stream(er)

streengy, string(y)

street,*, A ROADWAY/PATH WIDE ENOUGH FOR ALL TYPES OF TRAVEL

strek, streak

strekd, strict / streak(ed)

streke, streak(y)

strekin, stricken

strekly, strict(ly)

streknine, strychnine

strekt, strict / streak(ed)

strekun, stricken

streky, streak(y)

strem, stream

stremer, stream(er)

stremur, stream(er)

streneus, strenuous

strenewus, strenuous

streng, string

strengee, string(y)

strengensees, stringent(ncies)

strengently, stringent(ly)

strengint, stringent

strength,*,hen,hened,hening,hener, STRONG ENOUGH, ENDURANCE "prefixes: under"

strenjint, stringent

strenkth, strength

strenth, strength

strenthin, strength(en)

strenues, strenuous

strenuous,sity,sness, STRAINING POINT/ CHALLENGE

strep,ptococcal,ptococcus, SHORT FOR STREPTOCOCCAL, BACTERIA AFFECTING THE THROAT (or see strip/stripe)

strepdokokus, streptococcus

strepir, stripe(r) / strip(pper)

streptococcus,cal, BACTERIA AFFECTING THE THROAT

streptokokus, streptococcus

strepur, stripe(r) / strip(pper)

stres, stress

stresh, stretch

stress,sses,ssed,ssing,ssful,ssfully,ssless, sslessness, STRETCHED BEYOND NORMAL LIMIT OF ACCEPTANCE, CHALLENGE TO DEAL WITH "prefixes: pre/un"

stret, street

stretch,hes,hed,hing,her,hability,hable, PULL AGAINST, EXTEND OUT/ BEYOND "prefixes: over/up"

streu, strew

strew,*,wed,wing,wn, SCATTER/ SPREAD ABOUT

strewn, PAST TENSE FOR THE WORD "STREW", SCATTER/THROW

striashen, striate(tion)

striate,*,ed,ting,tion, PARALLEL STREAKS/SMEARS/FURROWS "prefixes: un"

strichnine, strychnine

stricken, PAST TENSE FOR THE WORD "STRIKE", AFFLICTED WITH/ CHALLENGED, DEALT A BLOW (or see strike)

strict,ter,test,tly,tness, EXTREMELY FIRM/GUARDED/DISCIPLINED

stride,*,ed,rode,dden,ding,er, LARGE/ LONG STEPS, A TYPE OF GAIT WHEN WALKING "prefixes: over"

strife,eless,eful, OPPOSITION/ QUARREL/CONFLICT (or see strive)

strikd, strict

strike,*,king,kingly,ruck,er, DEALT A SHARP/FORCEFUL BLOW,TERM IN SPORTS, TO IGNITE (or see stricken) "prefixes: re"

striken, stricken

strikly, strict(ly)

striknine, strychnine

strikon, stricken

strikt, strict

strikun, stricken

strinewus, strenuous

string,*,ged,ging,ger,gy, THIN ROPE, LONG/THIN/TWISTED SUBSTANCE "prefixes: un"

stringensees, stringent(ncies)

stringent,tly,ncy,ncies, TO BE NARROW/ THIN/BOUND/TIGHT/STRICT/ SEVERE

stringth, strength

strinjint, stringent

strinkth, strength

strinth, strength

strinues, strenuous

strip,*,pped,pping,pper, TO REMOVE EXCESS/EXTERNAL LAYER, REMOVE CLOTHES (or see stripe)

stripd, stripe(d) / strip(pped)

stripdokokus, streptococcus

stripe,*,ped,ping,per,py,pier,piest, THIN/NARROW/LONG UNIFORM SHAPE (or see strip)

stript, stripe(d) / strip(pped)

striptokokus, streptococcus

stripur, stripe(r) / strip(pper)

strite, stride

strive,*,ed,ving, WORK/EXERT TO ACCOMPLISH A GOAL/END RESULT (or see strife)

strivt, strive(d)

stro, straw

strobe,*, STROBOSCOPE, TYPE OF LIGHT

stroganoff, TYPE OF COOKED DISH WITH PASTA

stroginof, stroganoff

stroke,*,ed,king,er, FORCE/BLOW TO MOVE SOMETHING, SWEEPING MOVEMENT, MEDICAL TERM "prefixes: up"

strol, stroll

stroler, stroll(er)

stroll,*,lled,lling,ller, A CASUAL GAIT IN WALKING, MOVE ABOUT WITH WHEELS

strolur, stroll(er)

strong,ger,gest,gly,gish, GREAT IN STRENGTH FORCE/MASS/POSITION/ MOVEMENT

strongist, strong(est)

strongur, strong(er)

stronkist, strong(est)

stronkur, strong(er)

stroodel, strudel

stroon, strewn

strope, strobe

strow, straw

stru, strew

struck, PAST TENSE FOR THE WORD "STRIKE", A SHARP/FORCEFUL BLOW, TERM IN SPORTS, TO IGNITE

structure,*,ed,ring,reless,relessness,ral, rally, PLANNED/SPECIFIC/FORM/ SHAPE/ARRANGEMENT, A DWELLING "prefixes: sub/re/un"

strudel, TYPE OF PASTRY

strudul, strudel

struen, strewn

strugel, struggle

struggle,*,ed,ling,er, TO RESIST/FIGHT/ CONTEND WITH

strugle, struggle

strugul, struggle

struk, struck

strukcher, structure

strukel, struggle

strukle, struggle

struksher, structure

strukture, structure

strukul, struggle

strum,*,mmed,mming,mmer, USE FINGERS TO LIGHTLY TRAVEL OVER SEVERAL STRINGS OF AN INSTRUMENT

strumer, strum(mmer)

strun, strewn

strung, PAST TENSE FOR THE WORD STRING "prefixes: over/un"

strut,*,tted,tting, A DEVICE USED TO BRACE/SUPPORT, TO WALK WITH A PROUD GAIT

strutegek, strategic

strutejik, strategic

strutejikly, strategic(ally)

strutigekly, strategic(ally)

struz, strew(s)

stryate, striate

strychnine, POISON ORIGINATING FROM A PLANT

stryknine, strychnine

stu, stew

stualee, stool(ie)

stuardes, steward(ess)

stuart, steward

stuartes, steward(ess)

stub,*,bbed,bbing,bby, A KNOB/STUMP, OF A THEATER TICKET, RECEIVE A STRIKING BLOW

stubble,*,ed,ly, SHORT STALKS THAT REMAIN AFTER CUTTING OFF TIP/ TOPS

stubborn,ner,nest,nly,ness, FIRMLY UNREASONABLE

stubed, stupid / stub(bbed)

stubee, stub(bby)

stubel, stubble

stubelidy, stability

stubelity, stability

stubern, stubborn

stubid, stupid

stubil, stubble

stubiledy, stability

stubility, stability

stubirn, stubborn

stuble, stubble

stuborn, stubborn

stubud, stupid

stubul, stubble

stuburn, stubborn

stucado, staccato / stoccado

stucato, staccato / stoccado

stucco,*,oed,oing, CEMENT/PLASTER USED FOR WALL COVERING

stuch, stooge / stuck

stuck, PAST TENSE FOR THE WORD STICK "prefixes: un"

stuco, stucco

stucodo, staccato / stoccado

stucoto, staccato / stoccado

stud,*,dded,dding, STALLION, BREEDING MALE, BEAM/POST/ BOARD IN WALLS/ROOF OF A STRUCTURE (or see stew(ed)/stood)

studar, stutter

stude, study

studed, study(died) / stud(dded)

studeis, studious

studens, student(s)

student,*, PERSON WHO IS LEARNING/ FORMING KNOWLEDGE ABOUT SOMETHING

studeo, studio

studer, stutter

studes, study(dies)

studeus, studious

studid, study(died) / stud(dded)

studint, student

studio,*, SPACE/ROOM FOR CREATING ARTWORK OF ANY MEDIUM

studious,sly,sness, DEVOTED TO GAINING KNOWLEDGE ABOUT SOMETHING "prefixes: un"

studir, stutter

studunt, student

studur, stutter

study,dies,died,ying, TAKE MENTAL NOTE OF, LEARN, READ UP ON, A ROOM TO READ/WRITE "prefixes: un/under"

stue, stew

stuel, stool

stuelee, stool(ie)

stuepiduty, stupid(ity)

stuerd, steward

stuerdes, steward(ess)

stuerdis, steward(ess)

stuf, stuff

stufee, stuff(y)

stuff,*,ffed,ffing,ffy,ffier,ffiest, CRAM/ FORCE/PACK SOMETHING INTO CONTAINMENT, REFERENCE TO A

BUNCH OF THINGS, TIGHTLY CONFINED

stufy, stuff(y)

stuge, stooge

stuil, stool

stuird, steward

stuirdes, steward(ess)

stuje, stooge

stuk, stuck

stukado, staccato / stoccado

stuko, stucco

stul, stool

stulie, stool(ie)

stumach, stomach

stumb, stump

stumbel, stumble

stumble,*,ed,ling,er,lingly, FAULTER/ TRIP/BUMBLE/FALL INTO

stumbul, stumble

stumek, stomach

stump,*,ped,ping,per,py,pier,piest, END OF SOMETHING WITH MAIN PART CUT OFF/ELIMINATED/REMOVED, TO BE AT A LOSS (or see stomp)

stumpee, stump(y)

stumpul, stumble

stumuk, stomach

stun,*,nned,nning,nner,nningly, BE SURPRISED/IMMOBILIZED EITHER PHYSICALLY/MENTALLY/ PSYCHOLOGICALLY OR EMOTIONALLY

stund, stun(nned) / stunt

stunk, PAST TENSE FOR THE WORD "STINK", TO SMELL FOUL

stunt,*,ted,ting,tedness, A SHORT/ UNDEVELOPED/QUICK ACT/ MOVEMENT, A STINT (or see stun(nned))

stuol, stool

stup, stoop

stupafid, stupefy(fied)

stupafie, stupefy

stuped, stupid / stub(bbed) / stoop(ed)

stupedity, stupid(ity)

stupee, stub(bby)

stupefy,fied,fying,fiedness,fyingly, faction, SHOCK/OVERWHELM/ MAKE STUPID

stupendous,sly,sness, GREAT/GRAND/ ASTONISHING

stupendus, stupendous

stuper, stupor

stupid,der,dest,dly,dness,dity,dities, BEHAVIOR GIVEN TO BE DULL/ BORING

stupify, stupefy

stupindus, stupendous

stupir, stupor

stupor,rous, MENTAL LACK OF STABILITY/SENSIBILITY

stupt, stoop(ed) / stub(bbed)

stupufie, stupefy

stupy, stub(bby)

stur, stir

sturchan, sturgeon

sturdes, steward(ess) / steward(s)

sturdy,dier,diest,dily,diness, OF FIRM/ STABLE/STRONG STATURE/FORM

sturep, stirrup

sturgen, sturgeon

sturgeon, A FISH

sturgon, sturgeon

sturip, stirrup

sturjen, sturgeon

sturjun, sturgeon

sturling, sterling

sturn, stern

sturnem, sternum

sturnim, sternum

sturnly, stern(ly)

sturnness, stern(ess)

sturnum, sternum

sturor, stir(rrer)

sturty, sturdy

stuter, stutter

stutestiks, statistic(s)

stutir, stutter

stutistiks, statistic(s)

stutor, stutter

stutter,*,red,ring,rer,ringly, STAMMER/ REPEAT SECTIONS OF WORDS IN SPEAKING

stuwardes, steward(ess)

sty,ties, SWINE ENCLOSURE, EYE INFLAMMATION

style,*,ed,ling,er,eless,elessness,lish, lishly,lishness,list,listic,listical, listically,lize,lization,lizer, MANNER OF FORM/EXPRESSION OF THE ERA "prefixes: re"

styles, style(s) / stylus

stylest, style(list)

stylis, stylus

stylus,ses, POINTED INSTRUMENT FOR THE HAND TO USE FOR WRITING/ ENGRAVING/DRAWING (or see style(list))

stymed, stymie(d)

stymie,*,ed,mying, A DIFFICULT SITUATION/POSITION, BALL POSITION IN SPORTS

styn, stein

stype, stipe

styptic,cal,city, STOPS BLEEDING

styrafom, styrofoam

styrofoam, MANMADE SPONGEY MATERIAL WITH VARIOUS USES

styrufoam, styrofoam

su, sue / zoo

suad, suede / sway(ed) / swat

suade, suede / sway(ed)

suaf, suave

suafly, suave(ly)

suage, sewage

suaje, sewage

suar, sewer

suareje, sewer(age)

suaside, suicide

suasidul, suicide(dal)

suasite, suicide

suate, suede / sway(ed) / swat

suave,er,est,ely,eness,vity, SMOOTH, PLEASANT, SOPHISTICATED

suavidy, suave(vity)

suavly, suave(ly)

sub,*, SHORT FOR SUBSTITUTE/ SUBMARINE, TYPE OF SANDWICH, PREFIX INDICATING "BELOW/ UNDER/NEAR/IN PLACE OF SECONDARY " MOST OFTEN MODIFIES THE WORD

subcity, subsidy

subconchisly, subconscious(ly)

subconchus, subconscious

subconscious,sly,sness, NOT CONSCIOUS/FULLY AWARE OF, UNDERLYING CONSCIOUSNESS

subconshes, subconscious

subconshus, subconscious

subcontract,*,ted,ting,tor, PERFORM UNDER ANOTHER PERSON'S CONTRACT

subdavejen, subdivision

subdevide, subdivide

subdevishen, subdivision

subdew, subdue

subdivide,*,ed,ding,dable,er,ision, TO DIVIDE UP INTO PARTS UNDER A CATEGORY subdivision,*, HOUSING DEVELOPMENT

subdo, subdue

subdue,*,ed,uing,uer,ual, OVERCOME, OVERPOWER, INFLUENCE

subduvide, subdivide

subduvigun, subdivision

subduvishen, subdivision

subee, soup(y)

suber, sup(pper) / super

suberb, suburb / superb

suberbea, suburb(ia)

suberben, suburb(an)

suberentendent, superintendent

subereur, superior

suberfishul, superficial

suberintendint, superintendent

subfert, subvert

subgegate, subjugate

subgekdif, subject(ive)

subgekt, subject

subgektive, subject(ive)

subgektivedy, subject(ivity)

subgigate, subjugate

subgugate, subjugate

subir, super / supper

subirb, suburb / superb

subirbea, suburb(ia)

subirben, suburb(an)

subirentendent, superintendent

subjagashen, subjugate(tion)

subjagate, subjugate

subjagation, subjugate(tion)

subject,*,ted,ting,tion,tive,tively, tiveness,tivity,tivism,tivist,tivistic, UNDER RULE/AUTHORITY/ SCRUTINY, OPEN TO CRITERIA

subjegate, subjugate

subjekt, subject

subjektef, subject(ive)

subjektivety, subject(ivity)

subjugate,*,ed,ting,tion,tor,tive, CONQUER/DOMINATE/ENSLAVE

subjugation, subjugate(tion)

subkonshus, subconscious

subkonshusly, subconscious(ly)

subkontrakt, subcontract

sublamashen, sublime(mation)

sublamate, sublime(mate)

subleminaly, subliminal(lly)

subleminul, subliminal

sublimashen, sublime(mation)

sublime,er,est,ed,ming,ely,eness,er, mate,mation,mity,mities,minal,

LOFTY/ ELEVATED/SUPERIOR/ EXALTED/HIGHER STATE OF BEING

sublimenaly, subliminal(lly)

sublimenul, subliminal

subliminal,lly, UNDERLYING, NOT FULLY AWARE OF

sublumashen, sublime(mation)

sublyme, sublime

submareen, submarine

submaren, submarine

submarine,*, BULLET SHAPED OCEAN GOING VESSEL WHICH CAN SUBMERGE/ GO UNDER WATER

submechen, submission

submerge,*,ed,ging,gible,gence,rse, BE UNDER LIQUID

submerj, submerge

submerjebul, submerge(gable)

submerse,*,ed,sing,sible,sion, SURROUND WITH LIQUID "prefixes: semi"

submershen, submerse(sion)

submersible, submerse(sible)

submertion, submerse(sion)

submeshen, submission

submesif, submissive

submesive, submissive

submet, submit

submetid, submit(tted)

submetion, submission

submichen, submission

submirj, submerge

submirse, submerse

submirshen, submerse(sion)

submirtion, submerse(sion)

submisefly, submissive(ly)

submisevly, submissive(ly)

submishen, submission

submisive, submissive

submisivly, submissive(ly)

submission,*, RELINQUISH/AGREE TO, ABIDE BY, UNDER THE AUTHORITY OF

submissive,ely,eness,ion, CAPABLE OF/ GIVEN TO SUBMIT/COMPLY/ SURRENDER

submisuf, submissive

submit,*,tted,tting,ttal,ission,issive, TO COMPLY/SURRENDER/COMMIT/ YIELD

submitid, submit(tted)

submition, submission

submoren, submarine

submuren, submarine

submurg, submerge

submurj, submerge

submurjebul, submerge(gable)

submurs, submerse

submurshen, submerse(sion)

submurtion, submerse(sion)

subordenation, subordinate(tion)

subordenit, subordinate

subordinashen, subordinate(tion)

subordinate,*,ed,ting,ely,eness,tion, LESSER IN RANK/ORDER/ SECONDARY/ DEPENDANT, BANKING TERM "prefixes: in"

subordnet, subordinate

subpenu, subpoena

subpoena,*,aed,aing, A LAWFUL PROCESS/MANDATE TO CALL SOMEONE FORTH FOR INFORMATION

subregation, subrogate(tion)

subriedy, sobriety

subriety, sobriety

subrigate, subrogate

subrigation, subrogate(tion)

subriode, sobriety

subrogashen, subrogate(tion)

subrogate,*,ed,ting,tion, REPLACE/ SUBSTITUTE SOMEONE/ SOMETHING

subsadize, subsidy(dize)

subsaqwently, subsequent(ly)

subscrebshen, subscription

subscreption, subscription

subscribe,*,ed,bing,er,iption, COMMIT PAYMENT TO RECEIVE SOMETHING, SIGNED STATEMENT "prefixes: over/un"

subscribshen, subscription

subscription,*, AGREE TO COMMIT MONEY IN EXCHANGE FOR GOODS, SIGNATURE OF COMMITMENT

subsdanshul, substantial

subsdatushen, substitute(tion)

subsdents, substance

subsdratem, substrate(tum)

subsdutoot, substitute

subsdutushin, substitute(tion)

subsdutut, substitute

subsede, subsidy

subsedens, subsidy(dence)

subsediary, subsidiary

subsedize, subsidy(dize)

subsedy, subsidy

subsekwint, subsequent

subsekwintly, subsequent(ly)

subsequent,tly,nce, AFTER/FOLLOWING IN A CERTAIN SEQUENCE/ORDER

subseqwint, subsequent

subserveint, subservient

subserveintly, subservient(ly)

subserveints, subservient(nce)

subservient,tly,nce, FACILITATES PROMOTION OF/ACT TO CREATE, TO SERVE

subsestense, subsistence

subsestinse, subsistence

subside,*,ed,ding,ence, TO SETTLE/ SINK/FALL TO A LOWER LEVEL

subsidens, subsidy(dence)

subsidiary,ries,rily, AID/ASSIST WITH A CONTRIBUTION

subsidy,dies,dize,dizes,dized,dizing, dization,dizer, ORGANIZATION/ GOVERNMENT WHO HELPS OTHERS BY PROVIDING MONEY/SERVICES TOWARD OVERALL NEEDS OF SPECIFIC PEOPLE

subsikwent, subsequent

subsikwently, subsequent(ly)

subsirveins, subservient(nce)

subsirveint, subservient

subsistence,nt, BASIC FOUNDATION WHICH SUPPORTS LIFE

subsite, subside

subsitearee, subsidiary

subsitinse, subside(nce)

subsity, subsidy

subskrebshin, subscription

subskreption, subscription

subskrib, subscribe

subskripshen, subscription

subskription, subscription

substance,*, MATTER, FIRMNESS, REAL

substancheate, substantiate

substanchel, substantial

substanchely, substantial(lly)

substanchiative, substantiate(tive)

substanchil, substantial

substanchuly, substantial(lly)

substansheate, substantiate

substansheative, substantiate(tive)

substanshul, substantial

substantial,lly,lity,lness, OF ENOUGH, MORE THAN A LITTLE, REWARDING AMOUNT "prefixes: in/un"

substantiate,*,ed,ting,tion,tive, OF SUBSTANCE, FACTUAL/REAL "prefixes: un"

substashial, substantial

substatushen, substitute(tion)

substatute, substitute

substatution, substitute(tion)

substechuent, substituent

substense, substance

substetuent, substituent

substetute, substitute

substetution, substitute(tion)

substichuent, substituent

substinse, substance

substishuent, substituent

substitoot, substitute

substituent,*, REPLACE ONE PERSON FOR ANOTHER

substitushen, substitute(tion)

substitute,*,ed,ting,tion,table,tional, tionally,tionary,tive,tively, REPLACE ONE FOR ANOTHER

substrade, substrate

substradem, substrate(tum)

substrate,*,tum,tums, LAYER BELOW

substutushen, substitute(tion)

subsukwently, subsequent(ly)

subsuquently, subsequent(ly)

subsurveanse, subservient(nce)

subsurveint, subservient

subsurviently, subservient(ly)

subtavigen, subdivision

subtle,er,eness,ety,eties,ly, NOT OBVIOUS, SLIGHT HINT OF, SUGGESTIVE WITHOUT SPECIFICS

subtract,*,ted,ting,tion,ter,tive, TAKE AWAY FROM THE WHOLE/ ORIGINAL PART

subtrakshin, subtract(ion)

subtrakshun, subtract(ion)

subtrakt, subtract

subtraktion, subtract(ion)

subur, super / supper

suburb,*,bia,ban,banite,banize, DISTRICT OUTSIDE OF MAJOR POPULATED AREA

suburbea, suburb(ia)

suburben, suburb(an)

suburintendent, superintendent

subversef, subversive

subvershen, subversion

subversion,sary, REMOVE THE BASIS/ FOUNDATION OF ANYTHING IN ORDER TO DESTROY IT

subversive,rsively,rsiveness, REMOVE THE BASIS/FOUNDATION OF ANYTHING TO DESTROY IT

subvert,*,ted,ting,ter,rsive, REMOVE BASIS/FOUNDATION OF ANYTHING IN ORDER TO DESTROY IT

subvertion, subversion

subvirsef, subversive

subvirshen, subversion

subvirsion, subversion

subvirt, subvert

subvursef, subversive

subvurshen, subversion

subvursive, subversive

subvurt, subvert

subvurtion, subversion

subwa, subway

subway,*, UNDERGROUND ELECTRIC TRAIN, A SANDWICH

succeed,*,ded,ding, IMPROVE/GAIN/ OVERCOME

succeses, success(es)

succesful, success(ful)

succesion, succession

success,es,ssful,ssfully,ssfulness, IMPROVING/GAINING/ OVERCOMING/ ADVANCING "prefixes: un"

succession,nal,nally, SEQUENCE/SERIES/ ONE AFTER THE OTHER OF SOMETHING/SOMEONE

successive,ely,eness, FOLLOW IN ORDER WITHOUT INTERRUPTION

succinct,tly,tness, BRIEF/SHORT/ SUMMARY

succor,rer, OFFER RELIEF/SUPPORT/AID IN TIME OF NEED (or see suck(er))

succsed, succeed

succulent,*,tly,nce,ncy, JUICY/ DELICIOUS TO THE PHYSICAL SENSES

succumb,*,bed, SURRENDER/RETIRE TO, FALL FOR, YIELD/GIVE WAY TO

sucdhen, suction

sucebdubility, susceptible(bility)

sucede, secede

sucenct, succinct

suceptability, susceptible(bility)

suceptable, susceptible

sucer, succor / suck(er)

sucession, succession

such, USED TO MAKE A COMPARISON WITH SOMETHING IMPLIED BY CONTEXT

sucher, suture / suck(er)

suchur, suture / suck(er)

sucinct, succinct

sucjestion, suggest(ion)

suck,*,ked,king,ker, FORCEFULLY PULL/ DRAW SOMETHING AWAY FROM ITS SOURCE, A FISH, LOLLIPOP (or see succor)

suckle,*,ed,ling, THE ACT OF BREAST FEEDING

suckshun, suction

sucol, suckle

sucom, succumb

sucor, succor / suck(er)

sucour, succor / suck(er)

sucreshen, secrete(tion)

sucrete, secrete

sucretion, secrete(tion)

sucrose, SUGAR OBTAINED FROM PLANTS

sucsashen, succession

sucseed, succeed

sucses, success

sucsesful, success(ful)

sucseshon, succession

sucsesif, successive

sucsesiflee, successive(ly)

sucsetion, succession

sucsinkt, succinct

suction, FORCEFULLY DRAW SOMETHING FROM ITS SOURCE, CREATE A VACUUM/ADHERENCE

suculent, succulent

suculint, succulent

sucumb, succumb

sucure, secure

sucurity, secure(rity)

sucurly, secure(ly)

sud, sue(d) / suds / suit

sudan, sedan

sudanem, pseudonym

sudanim, pseudonym

sudar, suitor

sudashen, sedate(tion)

sudasion, sedate(tion)

sudate, sedate

sudation, sedate(tion)

sudden,nly,nness, IMMEDIATELY, NO TIME LAPSE

sude, sue(d) / soot(y)

suden, sudden

sudenim, pseudonym

sudenly, sudden(ly)

suder, suitor

sudews, seduce

sudin, sudden

sudinem, pseudonym

sudinly, sudden(ly)

sudir, suitor

sudn, sudden

sudo, pseudo

sudon, sudden

sudonem, pseudonym

sudonim, pseudonym

sudonly, sudden(ly)

sudoose, seduce

sudor, suitor

suds,sy, BUBBLES, FOAMY, LATHER, FROTH

suducshen, seduce(ction)

suductive, seduce(ctive)

suduktion, seduce(ction)

suduktive, seduce(ctive)

sudun, sudden

sudunly, sudden(ly)

suduse, seduce

sudy, soot(y)

sue,*,ed,uing, LEGALLY ATTEMPT TO FORCE SOMEONE TO PAY MONEY FOR A WRONGDOING

suecher, suture

suede, LEATHER (or see sway(ed))

suege, sewage

sueje, sewage

suenome, tsunami

suer, sewer

suereje, sewer(age)

sueside, suicide

suesidul, suicide(dal)

suesite, suicide

suet, PART OF ANIMALS WHICH YIELDS TALLOW (or see suit/sweet)

sufaneer, souvenir

sufaree, safari

sufary, safari

sufecashen, suffocate(tion)

sufecate, suffocate

sufecation, suffocate(tion)

sufeer, severe

sufeerly, severe(ly)

sufekashen, suffocate(tion)

sufekate, suffocate

sufeks, suffix

sufeneer, souvenir

sufer, suffer / severe

suferd, suffer(ed)

sufere, severe

suferly, severe(ly)

sufestikashen, sophisticate(tion)

sufestikated, sophisticate(d)

sufestikation, sophisticate(tion)

sufex, suffix

suffer,*,red,ring,rable,rableness,rably, rer,rance, REACTION TO PAIN/ INFLICTION "prefixes: in"

suffice,ed,cing,cient, SUFFICIENT, ADEQUATE, SATISFIED

suffichent, sufficient

sufficient,tly,ncy, ENOUGH, ADEQUATE, SATISFIED "prefixes: in"

suffishent, sufficient

suffix,xes,xed,xal,xally,xion,xation, END ATTACHED TO A WORD/ SOMETHING

suffocate,*,ed,ting,tion,tive,tingly, SMOTHER, CHOKE OFF, REMOVE OXYGEN

suffrage,ette,gist, VOTING AND RIGHTS TO VOTE

suficashen, suffocate(tion)

suficate, suffocate

sufication, suffocate(tion)

sufice, suffice

suficent, sufficient

sufichent, sufficient

suficient, sufficient

suficiently, sufficient(ly)

sufikashen, suffocate(tion)

sufikate, suffocate

sufikation, suffocate(tion)

sufiks, suffix

sufiksis, suffix(es)

sufir, suffer / severe

sufird, suffer(ed)

sufirly, severe(ly)

sufise, suffice

sufishent, sufficient

sufishintly, sufficient(ly)

sufishunt, sufficient

sufistakashen, sophisticate(tion)

sufistakation, sophisticate(tion)

sufix, suffix

sufixes, suffix(es)

sufla, souffle'

suflay, souffle'

sufocashen, suffocate(tion)

sufocate, suffocate

sufocation, suffocate(tion)

sufor, suffer

suford, suffer(ed)

suforeg, suffrage

sufr, suffer

sufrage, suffrage

sufragist, suffrage(gist)

sufraje, suffrage

sufranse, suffer(ance)
sufrech, suffrage
sufreje, suffrage
sufrige, suffrage
sufrigest, suffrage(gist)
sufrije, suffrage
sufrinse, suffer(ance)
sufrugist, suffrage(gist)
sufucashen, suffocate(tion)
sufukate, suffocate
sufukation, suffocate(tion)
sufuner, souvenir
sufur, suffer
sufurd, suffer(ed)
sugar,*,rless,red,ry,rless, SUCROSE,
    SUBSTANCE OBTAINED FROM
    PLANTS "prefixes: non"
sugchestshen, suggest(ion)
suger, sugar
sugest, suggest
suggesdiv, suggest(ive)
suggest,*,ted,ting,ter,tion,tive,tively,
    tiveness,tible, OFFER A FACT/
    THEORY TO BE CONSIDERED
suggestshen, suggest(ion)
sugjesdiv, suggest(ive)
sugjesgen, suggest(ion)
sugjest, suggest
sugjestion, suggest(ion)
sugjestive, suggest(ive)
sugnefakent, significant
sugnifukent, significant
sugwaro, suguaro
suicide,*,dal,dally, TAKE ONE'S OWN
    LIFE
suicidul, suicide(dal)
suige, sewage
suir, sewer
suireje, sewer(age)
suiside, suicide
suisidul, suicide(dal)
suisite, suicide
suit,*,ted,ting,table,tability,tableness,
    tably, PANTS/JACKET SET, IN A
    CARD GAME, PROPER/AGREEABLE/
    FITTING (or see suite/sweet)
    "prefixes: un"
suite,*, TYPE OF ROOM (too many
    definitions, please consult standard
    dictionary) (or see suit/sweet)
suitor,*, ONE WHO SUES, MAN
    COURTING A WOMAN
sujest, suggest
suk, suck

sukal, suckle
sukchen, suction
sukchest, suggest
sukchun, suction
sukel, suckle
suker, succor / suck(er)
sukeurly, secure(ly)
sukewlent, succulent
sukewlunt, succulent
sukewr, secure
sukewrity, secure(rity)
sukgeshin, suggest(ion)
sukgest, suggest
sukgestion, suggest(ion)
sukgestshen, suggest(ion)
sukiatrist, psychiatry(rist)
sukiatry, psychiatry
sukil, suckle
sukini, zuchinni
sukir, succor / suck(er)
sukiulent, succulent
sukiutrest, psychiatry(rist)
sukjesdev, suggest(ive)
sukjest, suggest
sukjestion, suggest(ion)
sukjestshen, suggest(ion)
sukle, suckle
sukluded, seclude(d)
suklusion, seclusion
suklusive, seclusive
sukol, suckle
sukor, succor / suck(er)
sukour, succor / secure / suck(er)
sukqulent, succulent
sukreshen, secrete(tion)
sukresion, secrete(tion)
sukrete, secrete
sukrose, sucrose
suksed, succeed
sukses, success
suksesful, success(ful)
sukseshen, succession
suksesif, successive
suksesiflee, successive(ly)
sukshen, suction
sukshun, suction
sukul, suckle
sukulent, succulent
sukum, succumb
sukur, suck(er) / succor / secure
sukurity, secure(rity)
sukwenshul, sequence(ntial)
sukwential, sequence(ntial)
sukwoya, sequoia

sulal, salal
sulami, salami
sulareum, solarium
suldree, sultry
sulebrity, celebrity
sulective, select(ive)
suledify, solid(ify)
suleks, select(s)
sulekshen, select(ion)
sulekt, select
sulektion, select(ion)
sulektive, select(ive)
sulektof, select(ive)
suleluquy, soliloquy
sulen, sullen
sulenity, saline(nity)
sulenium, selenium
sulerium, solarium
sulesit, solicit
sulesitation, solicit(ation)
sulesiter, solicit(er)
sulesteul, celestial
sulewshen, solution
sulewtion, solution
sulfade, sulfate
sulfate,*,ed,ting, ALSO SULPHATE, A
    SULFURIC ACID SALT "prefixes: bi"
sulfats, sulfate(s)
sulfer, sulfur
sulferik, sulfur(ic)
sulfide,*, A SULFUR CHEMICAL
    COMPOUND "prefixes: bi"
sulfir, sulfur
sulfirek, sulfur(ic)
sulfite,*,tic, A SULFUR CHEMICAL
    COMPOUND "prefixes: bi"
sulfur,ric,rize,rous,rously, ALSO
    SULPHUR, NONMETALLIC ELEMENT
    "prefixes: de"
sulfurik, sulfur(ic)
sulicit, solicit
sulicitation, solicit(ation)
suliciter, solicit(er)
sulidefy, solid(ify)
sulilakwee, soliloquy
sulin, sullen
sulinidy, saline(nity)
sulisetation, solicit(ation)
sulisit, solicit
sulisiter, solicit(er)
sulitefy, solid(ify)
sulivu, saliva
sulk,*,ked,king,ky,kier,kiest,kily,kiness,
    UPSET AT NOT GETTING ENOUGH

ATTENTION, REACTION TO BEING
OFFENDED
sulkey, sulk(y)
sullen,nly,nness, ALONE/GLOOMY/
DISMAL
sulomee, salami
sulon, salon
suloon, saloon
suloot, salute
sulowl, salal
sulphade, sulfate
sulphate, sulfate
sulpher, sulfur
sulpherik, sulfur(ic)
sulphide, sulfide
sulphir, sulfur
sulphurek, sulfur(ic)
sultan,*,nic, DOMESTICATED FOWL,
DESPOT/TYRANT
sultin, sultan
sultree, sultry
sultry,rily,riness, SWEATY/HEAVY/HOT,
OVERPOWERING COMBINATION
sultun, sultan
sulun, sullen / saloon
sulushen, solution
sulute, salute
sulution, solution
sum,*,mmed,mming,mmation,
mmational,mmary, TOTAL OF,
ALTOGETHER (or see some/zoom)
sumachin, sum(mmation)
suman, summon
sumantics, semantics
sumarely, summary(rily)
sumarize, summary(rize)
sumaruly, summary(rily)
sumary, summary / summer(y)
sumashen, sum(mmation)
sumation, sum(mmation)
sumb, sump
sumbreo, sombrero
sumbrero, sombrero
sumchewus, sumptuous
sumchuis, sumptuous
sumd, sum(mmed)
sumding, something
sumedul, summit(ttal)
sumen, summon
sumener, summon(er)
sument, cement
sumer, summer
sumerily, summary(rily)
sumerise, summary(rize)

sumersolt, somersault
sumeruly, summary(rily)
sumery, summary / summer(y)
sumesder, semester
sumester, semester
sumet, summit / submit
sumetal, summit(ttal)
sumetrek, symmetry(ric)
sumetric, symmetry(ric)
sumfing, something
sumidul, summit(ttal)
sumin, summon
sumint, cement
sumir, summer
sumiry, summary / summer(y)
sumit, summit / submit
sumitul, summit(ttal)
summary,ries,rize,rizes,rized,rizing,rizer,
rist,rily,riness, CONCISE/SIMPLIFIED
SHORT VERSION
summen, summon
summer,*,red,ring,rly,ry, SEASON
FROM JUNE THROUGH SEPTEMBER
summin, summon
summit,*, THE HIGHEST PART/PEAK/
POINT/RANK OF (or see submit)
summon,*,ned,ning,ner, TO PETITION/
CALL/SEND/ORDER FOR
ATTENDANCE
sumon, summon
sumoner, summon(er)
sump, DEPRESSION WHERE POOL OF
LIQUID CAN COLLECT
sumpchewus, sumptuous
sumpshues, sumptuous
sumptues, sumptuous
sumptuous,sly,sness, IMPRESSIVE,
LUXURIOUS, MAGNIFICENT
sumshuis, sumptuous
sumt, sum(mmed)
sumteng, something
sumthing, something
sumtime, sometime
sumting, something
sumur, summer
sumuree, summary / summer(y)
sumurees, summary(ries)
sumurize, summary(rize)
sumursolt, somersault
sumury, summary / summer(y)
sumut, summit / submit
sumware, somewhere
sumwat, somewhat
sumwer, somewhere

sumwhat, somewhat
sumwhere, somewhere
sumwot, somewhat
sumwut, somewhat
sun,*,nned,nning,nny, SOLAR PLANET
THAT ALL PLANETS IN THE SYSTEM
REVOLVE AROUND (or see son/
sunn/soon)
sunada, sonata
suname, tsunami
sunapsis, synapsis
sunaptek, synaptic
sunaptic, synaptic
sunareo, scenario
sunatu, sonata
sunc, sung / sunk
sunda, sunday
sunday,*, A DAY OF THE WEEK
(ENGLISH)
sundiket, syndicate
sundree, sundry
sundres, sundry(ries)
sundry,ries, MANY SMALL THINGS
sundukit, syndicate
sune, sun(nny) / son(y)
sunelity, senile(lity)
sunereo, scenario
sunerist, scenario(ist)
sung, PAST TENSE FOR THE WORD
'SING' "prefixes: un"
sunility, senile(lity)
sunk, PAST TENSE FOR THE WORD
'SINK'
sunn, A SHRUB (or see sun/son)
sunoda, sonata
sunografee, scenography
sunome, tsunami
sunonimus, synonym(ous)
sunopsis, synopsis
sunota, sonata
sunseer, sincere
sunseerly, sincere(ly)
suntree, sundry
suny, sun(nny) / son(y)
suoge, sewage
suor, sewer
suosidel, suicide(dal)
suove, suave
sup,*,pped,pping,pper, SHORT FOR
HAVING SUPPER/DINNER, TO SIP
(or see sub/soup)
supal, supple
suparlatif, superlative
suparstishus, superstitious

supasetory, suppository
supasition, supposition
supasitory, suppository
supausatory, suppository
supazeshen, supposition
supazishen, supposition
supcity, subsidy
supconchesly, subconscious(ly)
supconshus, subconscious
supcontrakt, subcontract
supdavide, subdivide
supdavijin, subdivision
supdevid, subdivide
supdevide, subdivide
supdew, subdue
supdo, subdue
supdu, subdue
supduvide, subdivide
supe, soup(y)
supel, supple
supenu, subpoena
super,rable,rably,rableness, GREAT/
EXCESSIVE/HIGH UP/ STRONG,
PREFIX INDICATING "OVER/ABOVE/
TO A VERY HIGH DEGREE" MOST
OFTEN MODIFIES THE WORD (or
see supper)
superb,bly,bness, GRAND/SPLENDID (or
see suburb)
superbea, suburb(ia)
superentendent, superintendent
supereoredy, superior(ity)
supereority, superior(ity)
supereur, superior
superfichul, superficial
superficial,lity,lities,lly,lness, UNREAL/
ILLUSION/FAUX/FALSE LAYER
superfishul, superficial
superflewus, superfluous
superflues, superfluous
superfluous,sly,sness, EXCESS
superintendent,*, ONE WHO
OVERSEES/MANAGES
superior,*,rity,rly, RANK/AUTHORITY
OVER ANOTHER, ELEVATED, BETTER
QUALITY/GRADE
superioridy, superior(ity)
superlatif, superlative
superlative,*,ely,eness, SURPASSES ALL
DEGREES/ RANK BY COMPARISON
superlutif, superlative
supersdishen, superstition
supersteshus, superstitious

superstition,*,ous, ALLOW SOMETHING
SEEMINGLY IRRATIONAL TO
FORETELL FUTURE EVENTS
superstitious,sly,sness, ALLOW
SOMETHING SEEMINGLY
IRRATIONAL TO FORETELL FUTURE
EVENTS
supervise,*,ed,sing,sor,sory,sion,
PROVIDE OVERSIGHT/DIRECTION
TO OTHERS
supervishen, supervise(sion)
supervizury, supervise(sory)
supesition, supposition
supgekt, subject
supgektif, subject(ive)
supil, supple
supina, subpoena
supir, sup(pper) / super
supirb, suburb / superb
supirblee, superb(ly)
supirentendent, superintendent
supireority, superior(ity)
supireur, superior
supirfichul, superficial
supirfishul, superficial
supirflewus, superfluous
supirfluis, superfluous
supirlatif, superlative
supirlative, superlative
supirlutif, superlative
supirsdishen, superstition
supirsteshus, superstitious
supirstition, superstition
supirveshin, supervise(sion)
supirvise, supervise
supirvisery, supervise(ry)
supirvishen, supervise(sion)
supirvision, supervise(sion)
supizeshen, supposition
supjekt, subject
supjektid, subject(ed)
supjektif, subject(ive)
supkonchisly, subconscious(ly)
supkonchus, subconscious
supkonshesly, subconscious(ly)
supkonshus, subconscious
supkontrakt, subcontract
suplamashen, sublime(mation)
suplament, supplement
suplamentul, supplement(al)
suplamint, supplement
suplant, supplant
suple, supple
suplement, supplement

suplementul, supplement(al)
suplemint, supplement
supleminul, subliminal
supli, supply
suplier, supply(lier)
suplime, sublime
supliment, supplement
suplimentul, supplement(al)
suplimenul, subliminal
suplument, supplement
suplumentul, supplement(al)
suply, supply
suplyer, supply(lier)
supmareen, submarine
supmaren, submarine
supmerg, submerge
supmerjebul, submerge(gable)
supmerse, submerse
supmersible, submerse(sible)
supmet, submit
supmeted, submit(tted)
supmichen, submission
supmirj, submerge
supmit, submit
supmited, submit(tted)
supmureen, submarine
supmurg, submerge
supmurjebul, submerge(gable)
supmurs, submerse
supmursabul, submerse(sible)
supmurshen, submerse(sion)
supol, supple
supor, super / supper
supordenate, subordinate
supordinet, subordinate
supordunet, subordinate
suport, support
suportef, support(ive)
suportive, support(ive)
suporvise, supervise
supose, suppose
suposetory, suppository
suposidly, suppose(dly)
suposition, supposition
supository, suppository
suposubly, suppose(dly)
supozatory, suppository
supoze, suppose
supozeshin, supposition
supozetory, suppository
supozitory, suppository
supozubly, suppose(dly)
supper, DINNER, MEAL IN EVENING (or
see super)

supplament, supplement
supplamentul, supplement(al)
supplant,*,ted,ting,tation,ter,
FORCEFUL/UNDERHANDED
REMOVAL OF SOMETHING/
SOMEONE
supple,ely,ly,eness, FLEXIBLE/
GRACEFULLY CONFORMING (or see
supply)
supplement,*,ted,ting,tal,tary,tation, IN
ADDITION TO THE BASIC
supplimentul, supplement(al)
supplument, supplement
supplumentul, supplement(al)
supply,lies,lied,lying,lier, SUPPORT/
PROVIDE GOODS/SERVICES
support,*,ted,ting,tive,tively,tiveness,
ter,table,tably, TO ENABLE/
EMPOWER/ SUSTAIN/ASSIST/
STRUCTURE SOMETHING OR
SOMEONE "prefixes: in/un"
suppose,*,ed,sing,edly,sable,sably,
PROPOSE/SUGGEST/IMPLY AS TO
THE WAY SOMETHING COULD BE
"prefixes: pre"
supposition,*,nal,nally,ous,ously,ive,
HYPOTHESIS/ASSUMPTION
suppository,ries, PREPARATION FOR
INSERTION INTO ORIFICE ON THE
LOWER HALF OF THE BODY
suppreshun, suppress(ion)
suppresion, suppress(ion)
suppress,sses,ssed,ssing,ssible,ssor,
ssion,ssive,ssant, PREVENT/
RESTRAIN
suprechen, suppress(ion)
supreem, supreme
supremacy,macist, BELIEVES THEY ARE
SUPERIOR OVER OTHERS
supremasist, supremacy(cist)
supreme,ely,eness, HIGHEST OF
QUALITY/DEGREE
supremusee, supremacy
supremusist, supremacy(cist)
supremusy, supremacy
supreno, soprano
supres, suppress
supreshen, suppress(ion)
supress, suppress
supression, suppress(ion)
supretion, suppress(ion)
suprino, soprano
suprogate, subrogate
suprveshin, supervise(sion)

suprvishen, supervise(sion)
supsakwently, subsequent(ly)
supscrepshon, subscription
supsdents, substance
supsditushen, substitute(tion)
supsedy, subsidy
supsekwent, subsequent
supsekwint, subsequent
supsekwintly, subsequent(ly)
supseqwint, subsequent
supserveint, subservient
supsestinse, subsistence
supside, subside
supsideary, subsidiary
supsidinse, subside(nce)
supsikwent, subsequent
supsikwently, subsequent(ly)
supsirveint, subservient
supsistense, subsistence
supsite, subside
supskrepshen, subscription
supskrib, subscribe
supskription, subscription
supstanchily, substantial(lly)
supstans, substance
supstansheate, substantiate
supstanshol, substantial
supstanshul, substantial
supstanshulee, substantial(lly)
supstantiate, substantiate
supstatoot, substitute
supstatushen, substitute(tion)
supstense, substance
supstetoot, substitute
supstichuent, substituent
supstinse, substance
supstishuent, substituent
supstitoot, substitute
supstitushen, substitute(tion)
supstitute, substitute
supstradem, substrate(tum)
supstrate, substrate
supstratem, substrate(tum)
supsurveint, subservient
suptract, subtract
suptrakchin, subtract(ion)
suptrakshun, subtract(ion)
suptrakt, subtract
supul, supple
supur, super / supper
supurb, suburb / superb
supurblee, superb(ly)
supurfichul, superficial
supurfishul, superficial

supurintendent, superintendent
supurlative, superlative
supurlutif, superlative
supurstishus, superstitious
supurstition, superstition
supurveshin, supervise(sion)
supurvise, supervise
supurvision, supervise(sion)
supusition, supposition
supuzishen, supposition
supvert, subvert
supvurt, subvert
supwa, subway
supy, soup(y)
suquential, sequence(ntial)
suquir, secure
suquirity, secure(ly)
suquirly, secure(ly)
suqulent, succulent
sur, PREFIX INDICATING "OVER/ABOVE/
TO A VERY HIGH DEGREE," MOST
OFTEN MODIFIES THE WORD (or
see sir/sure)
suraget, surrogate
suragit, surrogate
suramik, ceramic
suran, saran
surape, serape
suratid, serrate(d)
surbent, serpent
surcal, circle
surcas, circus
surcel, circle
surces, circus
surch, serge /surge /search
surchacol, surgical
surchan, surgeon
surcharge,*,ed,ging, AN EXCESS
CHARGE/TAX OVER AND ABOVE
THE NORM
surchari, surgery
surcharj, surcharge
surches, search(es) / surge(s)
surchon, surgeon
surchuble, search(able)
surcle, circle
surcol, circle
surcumcise, circumcise
surcumfirense, circumference
surcut, circuit
sure,er,est,ely,eness, MOST CERTAINLY,
OF COURSE, INEVITABLE,
CONFIDENTLY (or see surly)
"prefixes: en/un"

sureal, surreal
surealism, surrealism
suree, surrey
sureilisum, surrealism
surel, sorrel / surreal
surelism, surrealism
surender, surrender
surene, serene
surenge, syringe
surenidy, serene(nity)
surenity, serene(nity)
surenje, syringe
sureolesum, surrealism
surety,ties, ONE WHO IS BOUND/ LIABLE/RESPONSIBLE
sureulist, surrealism(st)
sureulizum, surrealism
surf,*,fed,fing,fable,fer,fy, WHERE OCEANS WAVES BREAK, CRUISE THE INTERNET/TV (or see serf/ serve)
surface,*,ed,cing,eless,er,ficial, TOP/ EXTERNAL/OUTSIDE PORTION OF (or see service) "prefixes: bio/re/ sub/under"
surfase, surface
surfd, surf(ed)
surfeje, serf(age)
surfent, servant
surfes, surface
surfibul, surf(able)
surfis, surface / service
surft, serve(d) / surf(ed)
surfunt, servant
surfur, surf(er)
surg, surge
surgakle, surgical
surgaree, surgery
surgarge, surcharge
surgd, surge(d)
surge,*,ed,ging, ENERGETIC SWELLING/ BURST/FLUCTUATION OF SOMETHING (or see search(ed)) "prefixes: re/up"
surgen, surgeon
surgent, UPRISING, SWELLING, STRONG FLUCTUATION (or see sergeant)
surgeon,*,ncy,ncies, DOCTOR WHO PERFORMS SURGICAL PROCEDURES
surgery,ries, PERFORM A MEDICAL OPERATION "prefixes: bio"
surgical,lly, ASSOCIATED WITH MEDICAL OPERATIONS
surgikul, surgical

surgin, surgeon
surgint, surgent / sergeant
surgis, surge(s)
surgon, surgeon
surgree, surgery
surgukle, surgical
suriasis, psoriasis
suringe, syringe
surinje, syringe
surjakle, surgical
surjaree, surgery
surje, surge
surjen, surgeon
surjent, surgent / sergeant
surjikul, surgical
surjon, surgeon
surjree, surgery
surjukle, surgical
surkawfigus, sarcophagus
surkewlate, circulate
surkofegus, sarcophagus
surkulir, circular
surkumfurens, circumference
surkumstans, circumstance
surkus, circus
surlee, surly
surloen, sirloin
surloin, sirloin
surly,lier,liest,liness, ROUGH/RUDE (or see sure(ly))
surmin, sermon
surmise,*,ed,sing, ASSUME/GUESS
surmize, surmise
surmon, sermon
surogate, surrogate
surong, sarong
surope, serape
suroredy, sorority
surority, sorority
suround, surround
surownd, surround
surpass,sses,ssed,ssing,ssable,ssingly, GO BEYOND EXPECTATIONS
surpent, serpent
surpentene, serpentine
surpint, serpent
surpintene, serpentine
surplus,ses,sage, MORE THAN NEEDED/ NECESSARY, OVERABUNDANCE
surprise,*,ed,sing,sal,ser,singly, UNEXPECTEDLY SHOWING UP/ APPEARING/ OCCURING "prefixes: un"
surprize, surprise

surrated, serrate(d)
surreal,lism,list,listic,listically,lism, NOT OF THIS PLANE/ WORLD, UNREAL, TIME PERIOD IN ART
surrealism, NOT OF THIS PLANE/ WORLD, UNREAL,TIME PERIOD IN ART
surrender,*,red,ring, GIVE UP, RELINQUISH POWER
surrey, SMALL HORSE DRAWN CARRIAGE
surrogate,*,ed,ting, TO SUBSTITUTE SOMEONE AND THEIR DUTIES
surround,*,ded,ding, ENCOMPASS/ ENCIRCLE/ENCLOSE AROUND
surry, surrey
surtatude, certitude
surten, certain
surthener, south(erner)
surtifecate, certificate
surtify, certify
surva, survey
survalinse, surveillance
survas, survey(s) / service
survatood, servitude
survatude, servitude
survaur, survey(or)
survayer, survey(or)
survd, serve(d)
surveilance, surveillance
surveillance,nt, OBSERVE/WATCH OVER SOMEONE/SOMETHING, SPYING
survent, servant
surveor, survey(or)
surves, service
survesable, service(cable)
survey,*,yed,ying,yor, TO CAPTURE FACTS/VIEW/DOCUMENT AN AREA/ SITUATION
survife, survive
surviks, cervix
survint, servant
survis, service
survisable, service(cable)
survive,*,ed,ving,val,vor, REMAIN ALIVE AFTER A TRAGIC/SOLEMN EVENT
survivul, survive(val)
survont, servant
survunt, servant
survus, service
sury, surrey
susaptible, susceptible
susbect, suspect
susbend, suspend

susbenders, suspender(s)
susbind, suspend
susbinded, suspend(ed)
susbinders, suspender(s)
susceptible,eness,ly,bility, PRONE/
    LIKELY/GIVEN TO BE AFFECTED
    "prefixes: in"
susceptive,eness,vity,ible, ABLE/LIKELY
    TO BE AFFECTED "prefixes: non/un"
suscinkt, succinct
susdan, sustain
susdanuble, sustain(able)
susdeninse, sustenance
susdinense, sustenance
susede, secede
susenked, succinct
susenktly, succinct(ly)
suseptibility, susceptible(bility)
suseptible, susceptible
suseptif, susceptive
suseptive, susceptive
suseptuble, susceptible
suseptuf, susceptive
suseshen, secession
susesion, secession
susete, secede
sush, such
susiadul, society(tal)
susiete, society
susietul, society(tal)
susiety, society
susinkt, succinct
susinktly, succinct(ly)
susiudil, society(tal)
susiuty, society
suspect,*,ted,ting, LIKELY TO BE
    INVOLVED IN AN EVENT "prefixes:
    un"
suspekt, suspect
suspenchen, suspension
suspend,*,ded,ding,der,nsion,
    TEMPORARILY BAR/RELIEVE/
    REMOVE FROM DUTY, HANG IN
    THE AIR
suspender,*, SHOULDER HOLDERS FOR
    PANTS, ONE WHO SUSPENDS
suspense,eful,sive,sively,siveness, TO
    WAIT WITH UNCERTAINTY
suspensful, suspense(ful)
suspenshen, suspension
suspension, HANGING/FLOATING IN
    LIQUID
suspent, suspend
suspention, suspension

suspeshen, suspicion
suspeshesly, suspicious(ly)
suspeshus, suspicious
suspicion,*,ous, SUSPECT TO/OF, TO
    SUPPOSE WITHOUT CLEAR
    EVIDENCE
suspicious,sly,sness, SUSPECT, TO
    SUPPOSE WITHOUT CLEAR
    EVIDENCE
suspind, suspend
suspinder, suspender
suspinse, suspense
suspinsful, suspense(ful)
suspinshen, suspension
suspintion, suspension
suspishes, suspicious
suspishesly, suspicious(ly)
suspishun, suspicion
suspitious, suspicious
sustain,*,ned,ning,nable,ner,nment,
    tenance, ENDURE/CONFIRM
sustane, sustain
sustanense, sustenance
sustanible, sustain(able)
sustanuble, sustain(able)
sustenance, BASIC PROVISIONS FOR
    SURVIVAL
susteninse, sustenance
sustunense, sustenance
sut, soot / suit / suite
sutal, subtle
sutaltee, subtle(ty)
sutanic, satanic
sutanikul, satanic(al)
sutar, suitor
sutcher, suture
sutchur, suture
sutel, subtle
suteltee, subtle(ty)
suten, sudden
sutenly, sudden(ly)
suter, suitor
suterical, satire(rical)
suth, soothe
sutherly, south(erly)
suthern, south(ern)
suthirnur, south(erner)
suthurn, south(ern)
sutil, subtle
sutiltee, subtle(ty)
sutin, sudden
sutinly, sudden(ly)
sutir, suitor
sutle, subtle

sutly, subtle(ly)
suto, pseudo
sutol, subtle
sutoltee, subtle(ty)
suton, sudden
sutonem, pseudonym
sutonim, pseudonym
sutor, suitor
suts, suds
sutultee, subtle(ty)
sutun, sudden
sutunly, sudden(ly)
suture,*,ed,ring,rally, USED TO STITCH
    A WOUND CLOSED
suty, soot(y)
suvana, savanna
suvaner, souvenir
suvant, savant
suvear, severe
suvearly, severe(ly)
suveleun, civilian
suveneer, souvenir
suvere, severe
suverity, severe(rity)
suverly, severe(ly)
suviner, souvenir
suvire, severe
suvont, savant
suvuneer, souvenir
suvunir, souvenir
suwar, sewer
suwaro, saguaro
suwer, sewer
suwerige, sewer(age)
suwero, saguaro
suwir, sewer
suworo, saguaro
suwrench, syringe
suwurege, sewer(age)
svenks, sphinx
svenkter, sphincter
svenx, sphinx
svinks, sphinx
svinktur, sphincter
svinx, sphinx
swa, sway
swab,*,bbed,bbing, ABSORBENT
    MATERIAL TO DAB/ MOP/CLEAN (or
    see swap)
swabed, swap(pped) / swab(bbed)
swabt, swap(pped) / swab(bbed)
swach, swatch
swad, suede / sway(ed)

swaddle,ed,ling, TO WRAP WITH STRIPS OF CLOTH
swade, suede / sway(ed)
swadul, swaddle
swae, sway
swaf, suave
swafly, suave(ly)
swag,*,gged,gging, HANG LOOSE (or see swage)
swage,ed,ging, BLACKSMITHS TOOL (or see swag)
swager, swagger
swagger,*,red,ring,rer,ringly, STRUT LIKE A BULLY/DRUNK
swagur, swagger
swair, swear
swak, swag
swaker, swagger
swallow,*,wed,wing, TO TAKE DOWN THE THROAT, A BIRD
swalo, swallow
swalow, swallow
swam, PAST TENSE FOR THE WORD "SWIM"
swamp,*,ped,ping,py,pier,piest,piness, per, MARSHY/WATERY LAND
swan,*, A LONG-NECKED BIRD
swang, PAST TENSE FOR THE WORD "SWING" (or see swank)
swank,ker,kily,kiness,ky, SOMEONE WHO MOVES WITH AN AIR OF DASHING SMARTNESS (or see swang)
swankee, swank(y)
swap,*,pped,pping, TRADE/BARTER (or see swab)
swaped, swap(pped) / swab(bbed)
swapt, swap(pped) / swab(bbed)
swar, swear
swarm,*,med,ming,mer, GROUP OF MANY BEES/ZOOSPHORES/PEOPLE
swarn, sworn
swasteka, swastika
swastika,*, A SYMBOLIC SHAPE
swat,*,tted,tting,tter, A STRIKING BLOW (or see sway(ed)/suede)
swatch,hes, PIECE/SAMPLE OF MATERIAL
swate, suede / sway(ed) / swat
swath,hes, TRAVEL IN LONG STRIPS GOING BACK AND FORTH IN SEQUENTIAL PARALLEL MOVEMENTS
swatul, swaddle

swave, suave
swavedy, suave(vity)
swavity, suave(vity)
swavly, suave(ly)
sway,*,yed,ying,yable,yer, SWING BACK AND FORTH, SAG
swayd, suede / sway(ed)
sweap, sweep
swear,*,ring,wore,worn,rer, TO USE PROFANITY, PLEDGE, PROMISE
sweat,*,ted,ting,ty,ter, MOISTURE COMING THROUGH PORES OF SKIN TO COOL BODY DOWN, BE ANXIOUS, HEAT TO MELTING (or see sweet)
sweater,*, A KNITTED ARTICLE OF CLOTHING
swebt, swept
swech, switch
sweder, sweater / sweet(er)
swedur, sweater / sweet(er)
swedy, sweat(y) / sweet(ie)
sweep,*,ped,ping,per,wept, REMOVE LOOSE DIRT FROM FLOOR/GROUND, A GESTURE/STROKE/MOTION "prefixes: up"
sweet,*,ter,test,tly,tness,ten,tie,tish, PALATABLE/PLEASANT TASTE, WITH SUGAR (or see sweat/suit/suite) "prefixes: semi"
sweft, swift
sweg, swig
swek, swig
swel, swell
sweld, swell(ed)
swelder, swelter
sweldur, swelter
swell,*,lled,lling,wollen, TEMPORARILY BECOME
swelt, swell(ed)
swelter,*,red,ring,ringly, AFFECTED BY OPPRESSIVE HEAT
sweltir, swelter
sweltur, swelter
swem, swim
swemur, swim(mmer)
swendul, swindle
sweng, swing
swengur, swing(er)
swep, sweep / swept
sweper, sweep(er)
swept, PAST TENSE FOR THE WORD "SWEEP"
swepur, sweep(er)

swerf, swerve
swerl, swirl
swerve,*,ed,ving, SUDDENLY SWAY/ VEER DIRECTION "prefixes: un"
swesh, swish
swet, sweet / sweat
swetch, switch
swete, sweet(ie) / sweat(y)
sweten, sweet(en)
sweter, sweater / sweet(er)
swetin, sweet(en) / sweat(ing)
swetir, sweater / sweet(er)
swetle, sweet(ly)
swetur, sweater / sweet(er)
swevel, swivel
swevul, swivel
swich, switch
swifd, swift
swifdly, swift(ly)
swifdnes, swift(ness)
swift,tly,tness, RAPID MOVEMENT
swig,*,gged,gging,gger, TAKE LARGE DRINKS OF ALCOHOLIC LIQUID
swik, swig
swill,ller, FOOD FOR SWINE, TO GUZZLE
swim,*,wam,mming,mmer, USE APPENDAGES OF BODY TO MOVE THROUGH WATER
swimd, swim(mmed)
swimt, swim(mmed)
swimur, swim(mmer)
swin, swine
swindal, swindle
swindle,*,ed,ling,er, ONE WHO CHEATS/SCHEME'S/MANIPULATES MONEY FRAUDULENTLY
swindul, swindle
swine,*,nish,nishly,nishness, DOMESTICATED PIG/BOAR
swing,*,ging,ger,wang,wung, GLIDE/ MOVE/SWAY BACK AND FORTH, TYPE OF DANCE/RELATIONSHIP "prefixes: in/up"
swip, swipe
swipe,*,ed,ping, TAKE/STRIKE/HIT, MOVE ACROSS A SCANNER
swirf, swerve
swirl,*,led,ling,lly,lier,liest, MOVE IN CIRCULAR MOTION, TWIST/CURL
swirve, swerve
swish,her,hy,hingly, A SOUND, A WISPY/ QUICK/SWEEPING MOVEMENT

switch,hes,hed,hing,her, CHANGE/FLIP/ DIVERT FROM ONE WAY/SOURCE TO ANOTHER, STICK

swivel,*,led,ling,ler, MOVEMENT CONSTRAINED TO A SINGLE PIVOT POINT

swivle, swivel

swivul, swivel

swob, swap / swab

swobed, swap(pped) / swab(bbed)

swobt, swap(pped) / swab(bbed)

swoch, swatch

swodel, swaddle

swodul, swaddle

swof, suave

swofly, suave(ly)

swolen, swollen

swollen, PAST TENSE FOR THE WORD "SWELL"

swolo, swallow

swolun, swollen

swomp, swamp

swompe, swamp(y)

swomper, swamp(er)

swompy, swamp(y)

swon, swan / swoon

swond, swoon(ed)

swoon,*,ned,ning,ner,ningly, FAINT/ DIZZY FROM LACK OF OXYGEN OR FROM FEELINGS OF ELATION

swoop,*,ped,ping, DESCEND TO CAPTURE THEN ASCEND, BIRD'S MOVEMENT

swoosh,hed,hing, FAST/RUSHING SOUND/MOVEMENT

swop, swap / swab

swopt, swap(pped) / swab(bbed)

swor, swore

sword,*, A POINTED/LONG/SHARP DOUBLE-EDGED WEAPON

swore, PAST TENSE FOR THE WORD "SWEAR"

sworm, swarm

swormer, swarm(er)

sworn, PAST TENSE FOR THE WORD "SWEAR"

swosteku, swastika

swostiku, swastika

swot, swat

swotch, swatch

swoth, swath

swov, suave

swovity, suave(vity)

swovly, suave(ly)

swoztiku, swastika

swune, swoon

swung, PAST TENSE FOR THE WORD "SWING"

swup, swoop

swurf, swerve

swurl, swirl

swurve, swerve

swush, swoosh

sy, sigh

syanide, cyanide

sybernetics, cybernetics

syborg, cyborg

sycadelic, psychedelic

sycamore,*, A TREE/FRUIT

sycek, psychic

sychadelic, psychedelic

syche, psyche / sick / sic

sychic, psychic

sycho, psycho

sychologekul, psychology(gical)

sychology, psychology

sychopath, psychopath

sychosis, psychosis

sychotic, psychotic

syclone, cyclone

sycological, psychology(gical)

syfalis, syphilis

syfen, siphon

syflus, syphilis

syfules, syphilis

syfun, siphon

sykadelic, psychedelic

sykamore, sycamore

syke, psyche / sick / sic

sykeatric, psychiatric

sykek, psychic

sykiatrist, psychiatry(rist)

sykik, psychic

sykilogekul, psychology(gical)

sykle, cycle

syklist, cyclist

syko, psycho

sykodik, psychotic

sykologee, psychology

sykologest, psychology(gist)

sykopath, psychopath

sykopathic, psychopath(ic)

sykopatholagist, psychopath(ologist)

sykosis, psychosis

sykotic, psychotic

syksteen, sixteen

syl, PREFIX INDICATING "TOGETHER/ UNITED/ALIKE" MOST OFTEN MODIFIES THE WORD

sylable, syllable

sylabus, syllabus

syllable,*,ed,ling, WORD THAT CAN BE DIVIDED INTO PARTS BASED UPON PHONETIC SOUNDS "prefixes: deca/ dis"

syllabus,ses, AN OUTLINE/SUMMARY OF LECTURES/TEACHINGS

sym, PREFIX INDICATING "TOGETHER/ UNITED/ALIKE" MOST OFTEN MODIFIES THE WORD

symatry, symmetry

symbal, symbol

symbalism, symbol(ism)

symbathe, sympathy

symbathetic, sympathetic

symbeotic, symbiotic

symbethe, sympathy

symbethetic, sympathetic

symbiosis,otic, TWO LIVE BODIES COEXISTING WITH MUTUAL BENEFITS "prefixes: endo"

symbiotic,cally, TWO LIVE BODIES COEXISTING WITH MUTUAL BENEFITS "prefixes: endo"

symbol,*,lic,lical,lically,lism,list,lize,lizes, lized,lizing,lization,lizer,logy, LETTER/ SHAPE WHICH HAS MEANING (or see cymbal)

symbolek, symbol(ic)

symbulism, symbol(ism)

symbuthe, sympathy

symbuthetic, sympathetic

symdum, symptom

symetrik, symmetry(ric)

symetry, symmetry

symfeny, symphony

symfonic, symphony(nic)

symfuny, symphony

symmetry,ries,ric,rical,rically,ricalness, rize,rization, MATHEMATICAL EXPRESSION, WHERE LINES ARE CONSISTENT WITHIN GUIDELINES "prefixes: dis"

sympathetic,cally, ABILITY TO RELATE/ REVERBERATE IN FREQUENCY/ FEELINGS

sympathy,hies,hetic,hize,hizes,hized, hizing,hizer, ABILITY TO RELATE/ REVERBERATE IN FREQUENCY/ FEELINGS

sympethy, sympathy
symphonek, symphony(nic)
symphony,nies,nic,nically,nious, HARMONIC WAVES/FREQENCY, ORCHESTRA
symphuny, symphony
sympl, simple / symbol
symposeum, symposium
symposium,*, CONFERENCE/MEETING WHERE VIEWS ARE DISCUSSED
sympozeum, symposium
symptom,*,matic,matically, REACTION TO SOME UNSEEN AFFECTATION
symptum, symptom
symputhee, sympathy
symputhize, sympathy(hize)
symtem, symptom
symtum, symptom
symutree, symmetry
syn, PREFIX INDICATING "TOGETHER/ UNITED/ALIKE" MOST OFTEN MODIFIES THE WORD
synanem, synonym
synapse,*,ed,sing,ptic, WHERE TWO NERVE ENDINGS COMMUNICATE
synapsis, MEIOSIS PHASE WITH CHROMOSOMES (or see synapse)
synapsus, synapsis
synaptek, synaptic
synaptic, MEIOSIS PHASE WITH CHROMOSOMES (or see synapse)
sync, SHORT FOR SYNCHRONIZE (or see sink)
synchro, SHORT FOR SYNCHRONIZE
synchronus, synchrony(nous)
synchrony,nal,nic,nical,nically,nism, nistic,nistically,nize,nizes,nized, nizing, nous,nously,nousness, WHEN HARMONY BETWEEN THINGS/PEOPLE/ WAVES/ FREQUENCY HAPPENS SIMULTANEOUSLY "prefixes: de/ un"
syncronize, synchrony(nize)
syncrony, synchrony
syndecate, syndicate
syndicashen, syndicate(tion)
syndicate,*,ed,tion,tor, COMPANIES/ CORPORATIONS BOUND FOR A FINANCIAL VENTURE
syndikation, syndicate(tion)
syndiket, syndicate
syndrem, syndrome

syndrome,*,mic, COMBINATION OF CIRCUMSTANCES/SYMPTOMS HAPPENING AT THE SAME TIME
syndrum, syndrome
synducate, syndicate
syndukit, syndicate
synergy,gies,getic,gism,gist,gistic, gistically, PARTS WORKING TOGETHER COOPERATIVELY
synik, cynic
synikal, cynical
synirgy, synergy
synkrenus, synchrony(nous)
synkronee, synchrony
synkronize, synchrony(nize)
synkrunus, synchrony(nous)
synonemus, synonym(ous)
synonim, synonym
synonimus, synonym(ous)
synonym,*,mic,mical,mity,mize,mized, mizing,mizer,mous,mously, ABOUT THE SAME/SIMILAR CHARACTERISTICS
synopses, synopsis
synopsis, CONCENTRATED VERSION OF SOMETHING WRITTEN, SUMMARY
syntaks, syntax
syntax,xes, A GRAMMAR RULE
syntekit, syndicate
synthasis, synthesis
synthasize, synthesize
synthedik, synthetic
synthesis,sist, HUMAN MODIFICATION/ COMBINATION OF FREQUENCY/ ELEMENTS PRODUCING SOMETHING DIFFERENT "prefixes: bio"
synthesize,*,ed,zing,zation, HUMAN MODIFICATION/ COMBINATION OF FREQUENCY/ELEMENTS PRODUCING SOMETHING DIFFERENT
synthetek, synthetic
synthetic,*,cal,cally, HUMAN MADE CHEMICAL COMPOUNDS "prefixes: retro"
synthusis, synthesis
synumen, cinnamon
synunem, synonym
syphelis, syphilis
syphen, siphon
syphilis,itic, A VENEREAL DISEASE
syphin, siphon
syphon, siphon

syphules, syphilis
syrenge, syringe
syrinch, syringe
syringe,*, TUBE WITH A PISTON FOR PULLING/EXPELLING LIQUIDS
syrinje, syringe
syrip, syrup
syrup,*,py, A VISCOUS/THICK SUGAR BASED LIQUID
sysdamadik, system(atic)
sysdamatic, system(atic)
sysdem, system
sysdum, system
sysdumadik, system(atic)
sysdumatic, system(atic)
syst, cist / cyst
system,*,mless,matic,matical,matically, maticness,matism,matist,matize, matization,matizer,mic,mically,mize, mization,mizer, OF/PERTAINING TO A PLAN/METHODOLOGY WITH PARTICULAR ORDER/ ARRANGEMENT, A CLASSIFICATION "prefixes: bio/sub"
systumatic, system(atic)
syterical, satire(rical)
syth, scythe
t, tea / tee
t-shirt,*, SHORT SLEEVE/COLLARLESS SHIRT
tab,*,bbed,bbing,bby, BILL FOR SERVICE PERFORMED, A SPACER (or see tap/ tape)
tabaco, tobacco
tabako, tobacco
tabal, table
tabby,bbies,bbied,ying, STYLE OF FUR ON A CAT
tabd, tab(bbed) / tap(pped)
tabe, tabby
tabel, table
tabernacle,*,ed,ling,cular, A NICHE/ DWELLING FOR SYMBOLIC STATUE, PART OF A BOAT
taberqulosis, tuberculosis
tabeulate, tabulate
tabew, taboo
tabewlashen, tabulate(tion)
tabewlate, tabulate
tabewlation, tabulate(tion)
tabewler, tabular
tabil, table
tabirnakle, tabernacle
tablau, tableau

table,*,ed,ling, GET RID OF, USUABLE SURFACE TO SET ITEMS, PLATFORM OF INFORMATION "prefixes: re"

tableau,*, PRESENTATION/ ARRANGEMENT WITH PICTURES

tablet,*, BOUND COMPILATION OF PAPERS, PILL SHAPE, FLAT WRITING SURFACE

tablit, tablet

tablo, tableau

tabloed, tabloid

tabloid,*, GOSSIP NEWSPAPER WITH PICTURES

tabloyd, tabloid

tablut, tablet

tabogin, toboggan

taboo,*,ooed,ooing, PROHIBITED/ BANNED/DISCRIMINATED AGAINST

tabt, tape(d) / tab(bbed) / tap(pped)

tabu, taboo

tabul, table

tabular,rly, RESEMBLING/CAN BE USED AS A TABLE

tabulashen, tabulate(tion)

tabulate,*,ed,ting,tion,tor, ENTER/LIST/ FORMULATE ONTO/INTO A TABLE

tabuld, table(d)

tabuler, tabular

tabulir, tabular

taburnakle, tabernacle

taby, tabby

tacd, tact / tack(ed)

tacdil, tactile

tacdul, tactile

tacet, MUSICAL TERM/ACTION (or see tacit)

tachometer,rically,ry, A DEVICE TO MEASURE LIQUID VELOCITY/ MOVEMENT

tachomitur, tachometer

tachy, PREFIX INDICATING "RAPID" MOST OFTEN MODIFIES THE WORD

tacit,tly,tness, IMPLIED WITHOUT SPEAKING IN WORDS (or see tacet)

tack,*,ked,king,ky,ker, ATTACH/AFFIX TO, SAILING TERM, POINTED OBJECT WITH A BROAD HEAD FOR AFFIXING THINGS (or see take/tact)

tackle,*,ed,ling,er, PURSUE/ OVERCOME/ACCOMPLISH

tacksonamy, taxonomy

tacky,kiness, STICKY, DISORDERLY/ SHABBY (or see tachy)

taco,*, SHAPED CORN TORTILLA FILLED WITH FOODS

tacs, take(s) / tax / tack(s)

tacshoal, tactual

tacshuel, tactual

tact,*,tful,tfully,tfulness,tless,tlessly, tlessness, DIPLOMATIC/ APPROPRIATE IN PRESENTATION (or see tack/take)

tactakul, tactic(al)

tactek, tactic

tactekil, tactic(al)

tactic,*,cal,cally,cian, STRATEGY/PLAN TO PERFORM A MANEUVER/ EXPERIMENT/ACTION

tactick, tactic

tactikel, tactic(al)

tactile,lity, PERTAINING TO THE SENSE OF TOUCH

taction, ACT OF TOUCHING

tactual,lly, PERTAINING/GIVEN TO SENSE OF TOUCH

tactukil, tactic(al)

tada, today

tader, tater / tatter / potato

tador, tater / tatter / potato

tadpole,*, YOUNG FROG LARVAE

tadpowl, tadpole

tadur, tater / tatter / potato

tael, tail / tale / towel

taelur, tailor

taent, taint

tafe, taffy

tafedu, taffeta

tafee, taffy

tafeta, taffeta

taffeta, TYPE OF WOVEN FABRIC

taffy, A CANDY

tafy, taffy

tag,*,gged,gging, TO LABEL/IDENTIFY SOMETHING, A GAME OF CHASE (or see tack/take)

tagethur, together

tagle, toggle

tail,*,led,ling,lless, APPENDAGE ON THE REAR OF SOMETHING, TO FOLLOW SOMEONE CLOSELY (or see tale/ tell/tall/towel)

tailor,*,red,ring, CUSTOM MAKES CLOTHING

taim, thyme / time / tame

taingo, tango

taint,*,ted,ting,tless, DISTRACTING IMPREFECTION, CORRUPT/ POLLUTED

tak, tack / take / tact

takal, tackle

takamidur, tachometer

takchen, taction

takchun, taction

takd, tact / talk(ed) / tack(ed)

takdel, tactile

take,*,took,king,en, ACQUIRE FOR ONE'S SELF, REMOVE FROM SOMETHING/ SOMEONE (too many definitions, please consult standard dictionary) (or see tack/tag) "prefixes: over/re/under/up"

taked, tact / tack(ed) / took

takee, tacky / take

takel, toggle

takela, tequila

taken, PAST TENSE FOR THE WORD "TAKE"

takil, tackle / toggle

takila, tequila

takin, taken / tack(ing)

takle, tackle / toggle

tako, taco

takol, tackle

takomeder, tachometer

takomitur, tachometer

taks, take(s) / tack(s)

taksachen, tax(ation)

taksation, tax(ation)

taksebul, tax(able)

taksed, taxi(ed)

taksedermy, taxidermy

taksee, taxi

takseng, taxi(iing) / tax(ing)

takshen, taction

takshuil, tactual

takshun, taction

taksibul, tax(able)

taksidermy, taxidermy

taksieng, taxi(iing)

taksobel, tax(able)

taksonimy, taxonomy

taksuble, tax(able)

taksudirmy, taxidermy

taksy, taxi

takt, tact / tack(ed)

taktakil, tactic(al)

taktek, tactic

taktekul, tactic(al)

taktik, tactic

taktikul, tactic(al)

taktil, tactile

taktion, taction

taktuk, tactic

taktukel, tactic(al)

taktul, tactile

takul, tackle / toggle

takun, taken / tack(ing)

taky, tacky / tachy

tal, tall / towel / tale / tail

talasman, talesman / talisman

talaspore, teliospore

talc, A CHEMICAL COMPOUND (or see talk)

tale,*, A STORY (or see tail/tall/towel)

talee, tally

talen, talon

talent,*,ted, HAVE NATURAL ABILITY FOR SOMETHING

taleology, teleology

talepathee, telepathy

taleputhee, telepathy

taler, tailor / tall(er)

talerible, tolerable

tales, tail(less)

talesman, SOMEONE PICKED FROM A COURTROOM TO SERVE ON A JURY (or see talisman)

talin, talon

talint, talent

talir, tailor / tall(er)

talirate, tolerate

talirense, tolerance

talisman, A CHARM/FIGURINE FOR GOOD LUCK (or see talesman)

talk,*,ked,king,ker,kative,kativeness,kie, ky, USE THE MOUTH/VOICE TO EXPRESS THOUGHT/FEELING "prefixes: up"

talkatif, talk(ative)

tall,ller,llest,llish,llness, MORE THAN AVERAGE HEIGHT (or see tale/tail/ towel)

tallow,wy, ANIMAL FAT

tally,llies,llied,llying, REGISTER/ RECORD/LABEL, KEEP SCORE/ COUNT

talness, tall(ness)

talo, tallow

talon,*,ned, CLAWS OF A BIRD OF PREY

talor, tailor

talosman, talesman / talisman

talow, tallow

talr, tailor

talun, talon

talunt, talent

talur, tailor / tall(er)

talurashen, tolerate(tion)

talurate, tolerate

talurense, tolerance

talurent, tolerant

talurible, tolerable

talurint, tolerant

talusman, talesman / talisman

taly, tally

tambaren, tambourine

tambourine,*, A MUSICAL INSTRUMENT

tamburen, tambourine

tame,*,ed,ming,er,est,mable,mability, mableness,ely,eness,eless, TO DOMESTICATE/CONTROL, CALM DOWN, MODIFY, ALTER

tamoro, tomorrow

tamp,*,ped,ping,per,pered,pering,perer, HAMMER/ STRIKE LIGHT BLOWS, DISRUPT/CORRUPT

tampan, tampon

tampon,*, FEMININE HYGIENE PRODUCT

tampurd, tamp(ered)

tamulchuous, tumult(uous)

tamult, tumult

tan,*,nned,nning,nnish,nner, TO CHANGE/MODIFY SKIN, PREFIX INDICATING "EXTEND/EXPAND/ SPREAD/CONTINUE/SPIN OUT/ WEAVE/PUT FORTH/SHOW/ MANIFEST" MOST OFTEN MODIFIES THE WORD

tanage, tannage

tand, tan(nned)

tandem, ONE BEFORE THE OTHER

tandim, tandem

tandrem, tantrum

tandrum, tantrum

tandum, tandem

tanej, tannage

tanel, tunnel

taner, tan(nner)

tang,ged,gy,gier,giest, A SHARP SOUND/ TASTE, CHISEL STYLE TOOL

tangabul, tangible

tangarene, tangerine

tangebul, tangible

tangee, tang(y)

tangel, tangle

tangent,*,ncy,tial,tially,tally, STRAIGHT LINE RADIATING/DIVERGING AWAY FROM A COMMON POINT "prefixes: sub"

tanger, tanker

tangerine,*, A CITRUS FRUIT

tangeur, tang(ier)

tangible,*,bility,eness,ly, ABLE TO BE FELT/ACQUIRED/ACCOMPLISHED PHYSICALLY "prefixes: in"

tangibul, tangible

tangil, tangle

tangint, tangent

tangirene, tangerine

tangle,*,ed,ling,er,ly,ement, TWISTED UP, PERPLEXING, CONFUSING "prefixes: en/un"

tanglee, tangle(ly)

tanglmint, tangle(ment)

tango,*,oed,oing, A DANCE

tangol, tangle

tangubul, tangible

tangul, tangle

tangur, tanker

tangurene, tangerine

tanige, tannage

tanil, tunnel

tanir, tan(nner)

tanjable, tangible

tanjarene, tangerine

tanjebul, tangible

tanjent, tangent

tanjerine, tangerine

tanjibul, tangible

tanjint, tangent

tanjubul, tangible

tanjurene, tangerine

tank,*,ker, CONTAINER FOR LIQUIDS, A CONTAINER

tanker, CONTAINER WHICH TRANSPORTS LIQUIDS OVER A DISTANCE

tanko, tango

tankur, tanker

tannage, ACT/RESULT OF TANNING HIDES

tanol, tunnel

tanpon, tampon

tansy,sies, A BITTER HERB

tant, taunt / taint / tan(nned)

tantalize,*,ed,zing,er,zingly, ENCOURAGE/TEASE/TORMENT WITHOUT HOPES OF RECEIVING AN END RESULT tantamount, EQUIVALENT/SIMILAR TO

tantelize, tantalize

tantem, tandem

tantilize, tantalize

tantim, tandem

tantimount, tantamount

tantra,rism,rist, RITUAL INVOLVING MOVEMENT OF FIRST LEVEL ENERGY

tantrem, tantrum

tantrest, tantra(rist)

tantrim, tantrum

tantru, tantra

tantrum,*, ANGRY/EMOTIONAL OUTBURST

tantulise, tantalize

tantum, tandem

tantumownt, tantamount

tanuj, tannage

tanul, tunnel

tanur, tan(nner)

tap,*,pped,pping,pper, LIGHT BLOWS, A FAUCET/VALVE USED TO ACCESS LIQUIDS FROM A CONTAINER (or see tape) "prefixes: un"

tapastre, tapestry

tape,*,ed,ping,er, STICKY PLASTIC USED TO SECURE/WRAP/MEND, LONG FLAT FLEXIBLE DEVICE/MATERIAL (or see tap)

tapek, topic

tapekul, topical

tapeoka, tapioca

taper,*,red,ring, DESCRIPTION FOR SOMETHING LONG THAT DECREASES IN WIDTH AS IT REACHES THE END/TIP/POINT

tapestry,ries, LARGE WOVEN FABRIC/ THREADS ILLUSTRATING A DESIGN/ PICTURE

tapik, topic

tapioca, PUDDING DERIVED FROM STARCHY PLANT

tapir, tater / tatter / potato

tapistre, tapestry

taploed, tabloid

taploid, tabloid

taployd, tabloid

taps, A MUSICAL SIGNAL USED FOR LIGHTS OUT IN MILITARY (or see tap(s)/tape(s))

tapt, tape(d) / tap(pped)

tapuk, topic

tapur, taper / tap(pper)

tapustree, tapestry

taquela, tequila

taquila, tequila

tar,*,rred,rring, A WOOD/COAL COMBINATION BY-PRODUCT (or see tare/tear)

tara, terra

tarafy, terrify

taragen, tarragon

taragon, tarragon

tarain, terrain / terrane

taranchula, tarantula

tarane, terrain / terrane

taranshula, tarantula

tarantula,*, A LARGE SPIDER

tararium, terrarium

taraso, terrazzo

tarazo, terrazzo

tard, tar(rred) / tart / tare(d) / tear(ed)

tardee, tardy

tardenes, tardy(diness)

tardur, tartar

tardy,dier,diest,dily,diness, LATE

tare,*,ed,ring, METHOD OF WEIGHING GOODS (or see tar/tear/tarry)

tarebly, terrible(ly)

tarebul, terrible

tared, tare(d) / tar(rred) / tear(ed) / tarry(ried)

taref, tariff

tarefic, terrific

tarefy, terrify

tarereim, terrarium

taresdreul, terrestrial

tarestreal, terrestrial

tarestrial, terrestrial

tareur, terrier

target,*,ted,ting, A POINT/AREA TO AIM AT/FOR

targit, target

targut, target

taribul, terrible

tarier, terrier

tarif, tariff

tarifek, terrific

tariff,*, A TAX

tarific, terrific

tarify, terrify

tarit, terret

tariur, terrier

tarlatan,*, LOOSELY WOVEN MATERIAL

tarletin, tarlatan

tarluten, tarlatan

tarmac,*, MATERIAL USED FOR ROADS/ LANDING PADS/PARKING

tarmak, tarmac

tarnesh, tarnish

tarnish,hes,hed,hing,hable, OXYDATION WHICH DISCOLORS, CAUSE TO LOOSE LUSTER/SHINE/STATE OF BEING

tarnush, tarnish

tarp,*,ped,ping, A LARGE/WOVEN MATERIAL FOR COVERING/ OVERHEAD PROTECTION

tarpalene, tarpaulin

tarpaulin,*, A WEATHERPROOF MATERIAL USED FOR A COVERING

tarpeline, tarpaulin

tarpin, tarpon

tarpon,*, LARGE OCEAN FISH

tarpulene, tarpaulin

tarpun, tarpon

tarragon, AN HERB/PLANT

tarrazzo, terrazzo

tarrestrial, terrestrial

tarrif, tariff

tarry,rries,rried,ying,rrier, LOITERING/ LINGERING, NOT MOVING ALONG, COVERED IN TAR

tars, PREFIX INDICATING "EYELID/ ANKLE/ BONES" MOST OFTEN MODIFIES THE WORD

tart,*,tish,tishly,tly,tness, SOUR TASTE, PASTRY (or see tar(rred)/tear(ed)/ tare(d)/tort/torte)

tartar, CALCIUM PHOSPHATE DEPOSIT, DEPOSIT FROM WINEMAKING, A SAUCE

tartir, tartar

tartoof, tartuffe

tartuffe,ery, COMIC DEPICTING A HYPOCRITE, ALSO SPELLED TARTUFE

tartur, tartar

taru, terra

taruf, tariff

tarufy, terrify

tarutoree, territory

tary, tarry

taryd, tarry(ried)

tasc, task

tasd, taste

tasde, taste(ty)

tasel, tassel

taset, tacet / tacit

tasil, tassel

tasit, tacet / tacit

task,*,ked,king, CHORE/WORK TO BE DONE, CHALLENGE INVOLVING HARDSHIP

tasles, taste(less)

tasol, tassel

tassel,*, HANGING THREADED ORNAMENT

taste,*,ed,ting,er,eful,efully,efulness, eless,elessly,elessness,ty,tier,tiest, tily, tiness, SENSE/FEELING WITHIN THE MOUTH "prefixes: dis"

tastee, taste(ty)

tasteir, taste(tier)

tastenes, taste(tiness)

tasteur, taste(tier)

tastful, taste(ful)

tastfule, taste(fully)

tastfuly, taste(fully)

tastur, taste(r)

tasul, tassel

tat, taught / taut

tatel, tattle

tater,*, SHORT FOR POTATOE (or see tatter)

tatewist, tattoo(ist)

tatil, tattle

tatir, tater / tatter

tatle, tattle

tatlur, tattle(r)

tatoist, tattoo(ist)

tatol, tattle

tatoo, tattoo

tator, tater / tatter

tatter,*,red,ring, WORN/SHREDDED MATERIAL (or see tater)

tattle,*,ed,ling,er, TO RAT/FINK/TELL/ EXPOSE SOMEONE'S WORDS/ BEHAVIOR/ ACT

tattoo,*,ooed,ooing,ooer,ooist, TO APPLY PERMANENT INK INTO THE SKIN WITH A NEEDLE

tatuist, tattoo(ist)

tatul, tattle

tatur, tater / tatter

taturd, tatter(ed)

tauer, tower

taught, PAST TENSE FOR THE WORD "TEACH" (or see taut/tout) "prefixes: un"

taugt, taught / taut / tout

tauko, taco

tauksik, toxic

tauksufy, toxify(fication)

taul, towel / tall

tauler, tall(er)

taulir, tall(er)

taulk, talk / talc

taulky, talk(y)

taulur, tall(er)

taulurinse, tolerance

taun, town

taunt,*,ted,ting, TEASE/PROVOKE/ MANIPULATE SOMEONE TO REACT (or see tout)

taupe, A COLOR (or see toupee)

taupikul, topical

taut,ten,tly,tness, HOLD/STRETCH TIGHT (or see taught/taunt/tout)

tavern,*,ner, PLACE WHICH SELLS SPIRITS/ALCOHOLIC BEVERAGES

tavurn, tavern

tawer, tower

tawir, tower

tawn, town

tawnt, taunt

tawp, taupe / top

tawt, taught / taut / tout

tax,xes,xed,xing,xable,xability,xation, CHARGE ADDED ONTO GOODS/ RESOURCES/SERVICE COLLECTED BY THE CITY/STATE/FEDERAL GOVERNMENTS, A CHALLENGE (or see taxi) "prefixes: over/sur"

taxadermy, taxidermy

taxashen, tax(ation)

taxe, taxi

taxed, taxi(ed) / tax(ed)

taxedirmy, taxidermy

taxi,*,ied,iing, VEHICLE HIRED FOR TRANSPORTATION, NAVIGATE A PLANE/ BOAT AT SLOW SPEED, MEDICAL TERM (or see tax)

taxidermy,mies,mist, ONE WHO EMBALMS/STUFFS ANIMALS

taxieng, taxi(iing)

taxonimy, taxonomy

taxonomy,mic,mical,mically,mist, METHOD TO CLASSIFY/CATEGORIZE ANIMALS/PLANTS

taxs, tax(es)

taxsachen, tax(ation)

taxsashen, tax(ation)

taxse, taxi

taxsedermy, taxidermy

taxsible, tax(able)

taxsuble, tax(able)

taxsudermy, taxidermy

taxudermy, taxidermy

taxus, tax(es)

tayler, tailor

taylur, tailor

taynt, taint

te, tea / tee

tea,*, DRIED PLANTS STEEPED IN WATER (or see tee)

teach,hes,taught,hing,her,hable,hability, hableness,hably, TRAIN/COACH/ INSTRUCT, INFORMATION/ KNOWLEDGE BEING PASSED ON TO OTHERS "prefixes: un"

teachs, teach(es)

teachuble, teach(able)

teachur, teach(er)

teak, A TREE

teal, A COLOR (or see teil)

team,*,med,ming, GROUP ATTEMPT TO WORK/PLAY/PERFORM TOGETHER (or see teem)

teanager, teenager

tear,*,red,ring,ry,rful,rfully,rfulness, rless, TO RIP, LIQUID COMING FROM THE EYES RELATED TO AN EMOTIONAL THOUGHT/EVENT (or see tier)

tearu, tiara

tease,*,ed,sing,er,sable,singly, TAUNT/ PROVOKE/ANNOY AS A DISTRACTION

teat,*, TIT/NIPPLE/UDDER

tebaco, tobacco

tebagen, toboggan

tebako, tobacco

tebea, tibia

tebogin, toboggan

tebse, tip(sy)

tech,*, SHORT FOR TECHNICAL (or see teach)

techable, teach(able)

techer, teach(er)

teches, teach(es)

techi,*, SHORT FOR TECHNICIAN

techible, teach(able)

techir, teach(er)

techis, teach(es)

technalogical, technology(gical)

technawlugee, technology

technecal, technical

technek, technique

techneque, technique

technical,lly,lness,lity,lities, DETAILED/ SPECIFIC, SPECIFIC TO THE

LANGUAGE/ SCHOOL/TRADE
"prefixes: bio"

technikality, technical(ity)

technilogikul, technology(gical)

technique,*, METHOD OF PERFORMING
SOMETHING FOR SPECIFIC END
RESULTS

technology,gies,gist,gic,gical,gically,
INDUSTRIAL SCIENCE/ART "prefixes:
bio"

technolugee, technology

technukality, technical(ity)

techuble, teach(able)

techur, teach(er)

techus, teach(es)

tecnec, technique

tecnic, technique

tecst, text

tectonic,*,cally, SCIENCE/ART OF
CONSTRUCTING/STUDYING FORMS/
SHAPES

teda, today

tedbet, tidbit

tedbit, tidbit

teder, teeter

tedeus, tedious

tedeusly, tedious(ly)

tedious,sly,sness, DETAILED/SLOW/
MONOTONOUS

tedir, teeter

tedius, tedious

tedur, teeter

tee,*,ed,eing, A TERM IN THE GAME OF
GOLF, TO BE IRRITATED, SHAPE/
LETTER, ALL COMES TOGETHER
SUITABLY/PERFECTLY (or see tea)

teecher, teach(er)

teechuble, teach(able)

teechur, teach(er)

teek, teak

teel, teal / teil

teem,*,med,ming, OVERFLOWING/
ABUNDANT/COMING FORTH (or
see team)

teen,*,ny,nier,niest,nager, SHORT FOR
TEENAGER, SOMETHING VERY
SMALL

teenager,*, PRE-ADULT AGE (13-19
YEARS)

teeneur, teen(ier)

teenksher, tincture

teenkur, tinker

teenyer, teen(ier)

teepee,*, A CONICAL SHAPED
DWELLING COMMON TO NATIVE
AMERICANS

teers, tear(s) / tier(s)

teery, tear(y)

tees, tease / tea(s) / tee(s)

teet, teat / tit

teeter,*,red,ring, SHIFT WEIGHT BACK
AND FORTH AS IN A ROCKING
MOTION, HORIZONTAL BALANCING
MOVEMENT/MANEUVER

teeter-totter,*, SEESAW/TOY, LONG
BOARD ON A FULCRUM WHICH
MOVES UP/DOWN WITH SHIFTING
OF WEIGHT

teeth,hing,her,tooth, MORE THAN ONE
TOOTH, ACT OF GROWING FIRST
SET OF TEETH

teetur, teeter

tef, tiff

teil, A LIME TREE (or see teal)

teir, tier / tear

teird, tier(ed) / tear(ed)

tek, teak / tech

tekal, tickle

tekdile, textile

teke, tiki

tekel, tickle

tekela, tequila

teket, ticket

teki, techi / tiki

tekil, tickle

tekit, ticket

tekle, tickle

teklech, tickle(lish)

teklish, tickle(lish)

teknakaledy, technical(ity)

teknalogical, technology(gical)

teknalugee, technology

teknek, technique

teknekality, technical(ity)

teknekul, technical

tekneque, technique

teknikul, technical

teknilogikul, technology(gical)

teknolugee, technology

teknukalety, technical(ity)

teknukil, technical

teknulogical, technology(gical)

tekol, tickle

tekot, ticket

teksd, text

teksdeur, texture

teksdile, textile

tekst, text

tekster, texture

tekstile, textile

teksture, texture

tekt, text / tick(ed)

tektonek, tectonic

tektonic, tectonic

tekul, tickle

tekut, ticket

teky, tiki

tel, PREFIX INDICATING "END/FAR"
MOST OFTEN MODIFIES THE WORD
(or see teil/teal)

telacast, telecast

telafase, telophase

telafone, telephone

telafoto, telephoto

telagraf, telegraph

telagram, telegram

telagraph, telegraph

telakanesis, telekinesis

telakast, telecast

telakinetic, telekinetic

telakunesis, telekinesis

telaphase, telophase

telaphone, telephone

telaphoto, telephoto

telapromptur, teleprompter

telar, teller

telaskope, telescope

telaskopic, telescope(pic)

telathon, telethon

telatipe, teletype

telavichen, television

telavision, television

telavize, televise

teld, tell / told / till(ed)

tele, PREFIX INDICATING "DISTANCE"
MOST OFTEN MODIFIES THE WORD

telealogy, teleology

teleaspore, teliospore

telecast,*,ted,ting,ter, BROADCAST BY
TELEVISION

telefone, telephone

telefoto, telephoto

telegraf, telegraph

telegram,*, SEND MESSAGE/MONEY BY
WIRE

telegraph,her,hist,hic,hically, MESSAGE/
TRANSMISSION SENT BY USING AN
INSTRUMENT, WIRE TRANSFER

telekinesis, OBJECTS MOVING WHICH
HAVE NO VISIBLE EXPLANATION AS
TO CAUSE

telekinetic,*, OBJECTS MOVING WHICH HAVE NO VISIBLE EXPLANATION AS TO CAUSE

telekunesis, telekinesis

telekunetic, telekinetic

teleology,gism,gist, SCIENCE WHICH STUDIES ETHICS/CAUSES/ACTS IN NATURE

telepathee, telepathy

telepathy,hic,hically,hist, COMMUNICATE BY WAVELENGTH, MIND COMMUNICATION

telephone,*,nic,nically, INSTRUMENT FOR VERBAL COMMUNICATION

telephoto,ography,ographic, TAKING PHOTOS AT LONG DISTANCE

teleprompter,*, A DEVICE WHICH ENLARGES TEXT FOR THOSE ON CAMERA TO READ FROM

teleputhee, telepathy

teler, teller

telescope,*,ed,ping,pic,pically, INSTRUMENT THAT SEEMINGLY REDUCES DISTANCE BY USE OF LENSES (or see microscope)

telethon,*, A TELEVISION BROADCAST WHICH LASTS A LONG TIME

teletipe, teletype

teletype, DEVICE USED TO TRANSMIT MESSAGES

teleupromtur, teleprompter

teleuspore, teliospore

televigen, television

televijan, television

televise,*,ed,sing,sion, USING TELEVISION TO TRANSMIT/ BROADCAST

television,*,nary, VISUAL IMAGES SENT BY WAVES THROUGH DEVICE WHICH INTERPRETS THEM

teli, telly

telialegy, teleology

teliaulugy, teleology

telicast, telecast

telifone, telephone

telifoto, telephoto

teligraf, telegraph

teligram, telegram

teligraph, telegraph

telikanesis, telekinesis

telikast, telecast

telikunesis, telekinesis

teliology, teleology

teliospore,*,ric, METHOD OF FUNGI GERMINATION

teliphone, telephone

teliphoto, telephoto

telipromtur, teleprompter

telipromtur, teleprompter

telir, teller

teliskope, telescope

teliskopic, telescope(pic)

telithon, telethon

telitipe, teletype

teliuspore, teliospore

telivishen, television

telivision, television

telivize, televise

tell,*,ling,told, TO COMMUNICATE INFORMATION ALONG (or see teal/ teil) "prefixes: re"

teller,*, ONE WHO DEALS DIRECTLY WITH CUSTOMERS AT A BANK, NARRATOR, ONE WHO FACILITATES COMMUNICATION BETWEEN OTHERS

telltale,er, TATTLER, ONE WHO PASSES ALONG GOSSIP/HERESAY, A TOOL FOR NAVIGATION

telly, SHORT FOR TELEVISION

telo, PREFIX INDICATING "END/FAR" MOST OFTEN MODIFIES THE WORD

telofase, telophase

telokanesis, telekinesis

telokunesis, telekinesis

telophase,sic, BIOLOGICAL TERM

telor, teller

teloskope, telescope

teloskopic, telescope(pic)

telothon, telethon

telovishen, television

telt, till(ed) / told / tilt

teltail, telltale

teltale, telltale

telufase, telophase

telufone, telephone

telufoto, telephoto

telugraf, telegraph

telugram, telegram

telugraph, telegraph

telukanesis, telekinesis

telukast, telecast

telukenetick, telekinetic

telukinetik, telekinetic

telukunesis, telekinesis

teluphase, telophase

teluphone, telephone

teluphoto, telephoto

telupromtur, teleprompter

telur, teller

teluskope, telescope

teluskopic, telescope(pic)

teluthon, telethon

telutipe, teletype

teluvegun, television

teluvision, television

teluvize, televise

tem, team / teem

temaro, tomorrow

tembir, timber

tembrachure, temperature

tembrament, temperament

tembramentul, temper(mental)

tembrushure, temperature

tembur, timber

temd, team(ed) / teem(ed)

temed, timid

temidly, timid(ly)

temod, timid

temoro, tomorrow

tempal, temple

temparamint, temperament

tempararely, temporary(rily)

temparary, temporary

temparize, temporize

temper,*,red,ring,rament,ramental, ramentally,rance,rate,rability,rable, rer,rature, EMOTIONS WORKED INTO AN ANGRY STATE, HEATING UP CARBON MATERIAL TO FORCE MOLECULAR REALIGNMENT

tempera, tempura

temperament,*,tal,tally, OVERALL EMOTION/PHYSICAL/MENTAL TRAITS OF A PERSON/LIVING THING "prefixes: non/un"

temperarily, temporary(rily)

temperary, temporary

temperate,ely,eness, HEATING UP CARBON MATERIAL TO FORCE MOLECULAR REALIGNMENT, STABLE "prefixes: in/sub"

temperature,*, MEASUREMENT OF HOT/COLD VARIANCES

temperize, temporize

tempermint, temper(ment)

tempeshues, tempest(uous)

tempest,tuous,tuously,tuousness, BEING STORMY/WINDY/ TURBULENT

tempil, temple

tempir, temper
tempirament, temperament
tempirashure, temperature
tempirment, temper(ment)
templat, template
template,*, SOMETHING TO SUPPORT/ ALLOW THE FORM OF SOMETHING, FOR MAKING REPLICAS
temple,*,ed, RELIGIOUS STRUCTURE FOR WORSHIP, SPOT ON THE HEAD OF THE BODY
templut, template
tempo,*, THE RHYTHM OF A WAVE, RATE/SPEED/PACE OF MOVEMENT
tempol, temple
tempor, PREFIX INDICATING "TIME/ TEMPLES" MOST OFTEN MODIFIES THE WORD
temporal,lly,lness,lity,lities, OF OR GIVEN TO THIS TIME/SPACE/ DISTANCE
temporarely, temporary(rily)
temporary,rarily,riness, SHORT DURATION IN TIME
temporely, temporal(lly)
temporize,*,ed,zing,zer,zation,zingly, GAIN/DELAY/YIELD/MANIPULATE TIME
temporment, temper(ment)
temporo, PREFIX INDICATING "TIME/ TEMPLES" MOST OFTEN MODIFIES THE WORD
temporul, temporal
tempra, tempura
temprachure, temperature
tempral, temporal
tempramentul, temper(mental)
temprary, temporary
temprashure, temperature
temprature, temperature
tempremintul, temper(mental)
tempreruly, temporary(rily)
temprery, temporary
temprment, temperament
tempru, tempura
temprumintul, temper(mental)
tempt,*,ted,ting,tingly,table,ter, tingness,tress,tation, TO ENTICE/ ALLURE/ SEDUCE/INVITE
temptashen, temptation
temptation,*, APPREHENSION IN RESPONDING TO INVITATION/ ENTICEMENT/ SEDUCTION
tempul, temple

tempur, temper
tempura, BATTER DIPPED VEGETABLES/ FISH
tempurarily, temporary(rily)
tempurary, temporary
tempurely, temporal(lly)
tempureruly, temporary(rily)
tempurery, temporary
tempurize, temporize
tempurment, temper(ment)
tempust, tempest
temt, tempt / team(ed) / teem(ed)
temtashen, temptation
temtation, temptation
temted, tempt(ed)
temtres, tempt(ress)
temulchuis, tumult(uous)
temulchuous, tumult(uous)
temult, tumult
temut, timid
ten,*,nth, ENGLISH NUMBER AFTER NINE/BEFORE ELEVEN (or see tin/ teen)
tenabel, tenable
tenable,bility,eness,ly, CAN SURVIVE ATTEMPT AT BEING TAKEN/ CARRIED AWAY "prefixes: un"
tenachus, tenacious
tenacious,sly,sness,ity, PERSISTENT/ CONSISTENT, WITHOUT FAULTER
tenacity, OF BEING TENACIOUS
tenacle, tentacle
tenager, teenager
tenakle, tentacle
tenament, tenement
tenansy, tenant(ncy)
tenant,*,tncy,tcies,try, BORROWER OF LAND/STRUCTURE/PROPERTY HELD/OWNED BY ANOTHER "prefixes: sub"
tenasedy, tenacity
tenashus, tenacious
tenasity, tenacity
tenasuty, tenacity
tenat, tenet / tenant
tenatef, tentative
tenatious, tenacious
tenative, tentative
tencity, tense(sity)
tend,*,ded,ding,der,dency, HAVE LEANING AFFINITY/TENDENCY TOWARDS, TAKE CARE OF (or see tin(nned)/tent/tint)
tendatev, tentative

tendency,cies,ntious,ntiously, ntiousness, HAVE A LEANING/ INCLINATION TOWARDS, DISPOSITION/CAPABILITY OF
tendenus, tendon(dinous)
tender,*,rly,rness,rer,rize,rizes,rized, rizing,rization,rizer, SOFTENED FIBERS, SOFT/GENTLE IN NATURE/ TEMPERAMENT, OFFER TOWARDS DEBT (or see tinder)
tenderloin,*, CUT OF BEEF
tendid, tend(ed) / tint(ed)
tendin, tendon
tendinsy, tendency
tendir, tender / tinder
tendirloin, tenderloin
tendon,*,dinous,nitis, PART OF A MUSCLE
tendorize, tender(ize)
tendril,*, CURLING OF A PLANT/HAIR
tendrul, tendril
tendun, tendon
tendunitus, tendon(itis)
tendunus, tendon(dinous)
tendur, tender / tinder
tendurize, tender(ize)
tendurloin, tenderloin
tendurly, tender(ly)
tendutif, tentative
tene, teen(y) / tin(nny)
tenekle, tentacle
tenement,*,tary, DWELLING WHERE PEOPLE LIVE AS TENANTS, PERMANENT PROPERTY
tenen, tenon
tenensy, tenant(ncy)
tener, tenor
tenet,*, DOCTRINE/BELIEF/DOGMA HELD TO BE TRUE (or see tenant)
tenetif, tentative
tenetive, tentative
teneur, tenure / teen(ier)
teneust, teen(iest)
tenewus, tenuous
tenfold, TEN TIMES OVER/GREATER
teng, ting / tinge
tenible, tenable
teniest, teen(iest)
tenikle, tentacle
teniment, tenement
tenin, tenon
tenir, tenor
tenis, tennis
tenit, tenet / tenant

tenite, tonight
tenj, tinge
tenkchur, tincture
tenker, tinker
tenkil, tinkle
tenkir, tinker
tenkol, tinkle
tenkshir, tincture
tenkture, tincture
tenkul, tinkle
tenkur, tinker
tennis, A RACQUET GAME
tenon, A CARPENTRY TOOL
tenor,*, A PITCH/LEVEL OF SOUND
tenos, tennis
tenparery, temporary
tenpermint, temperament
tenpest, tempest
tenpirery, temporary
tenpist, tempest
tenplit, template
tenpo, tempo
tenpol, temple
tenporal, temporal
tenporary, temporary
tenporat, temper(ate)
tenprachur, temperature
tenpral, temporal
tenprament, temperament
tenpret, temper(ate)
tenpriment, temperament
tenprit, temper(ate)
tenprochur, temperature
tenprot, temper(ate)
tens, ten(s) / tent(s) / tense / tint(s) / tend(s)
tense,*,ed,sing,ely,eness,sity,eless,sion, sional,sionless,sive, STRETCHED/ PUSHED/STRAINED BEYOND A COMFORTABLE POSITION, TIGHT, IN RELATION TO TIME (or see tent(s))
tensul, tinsel
tent,*,ted,ting, SHARP PEAK WITH TWO EQUAL SLOPES, TEMPORARY/ PORTABLE SHELTER, SURGICAL PROCEDURE (or see tint/tend/ tin(nned))
tentacle,*,ed,cular, LONG/FLEXIBLE APPENDAGES ON A LIVING THING
tentakle, tentacle
tentative,ely,eness, TEMPORARY PLAN/ TIME, NOT CERTAIN AS OF YET
tented, tint(ed) / tent(ed) / tend(ed)

tentekle, tentacle
tentetive, tentative
tenth,*, ONE PART OUT OF TEN
tentikle, tentacle
tentukle, tentacle
tentutive, tentative
tenuble, tenable
tenues, tenuous
tenukle, tentacle
tenument, tenement
tenunsy, tenant(ncy)
tenunt, tenant
tenuous,sly,sness, DELICATE/WEAK/ FINE/DILUTED
tenur, tenor
tenure,ed,rial,rially, HOLDING/ POSSESSING PROPERTY OR POSITION
tenus, tennis
tenutef, tentative
tenutive, tentative
teny, teen(y) / tin(nny)
tenyewr, tenure
tenyewus, tenuous
tenyir, tenure
tenyur, tenure
tenzul, tinsel
tep, tip
tepakle, typical
tepd, tip(pped)
tepe, teepee
teped, tepid
tepekul, typical
teper, tip(pper)
tepid,dity,dness,dly, LUKEWARM, WARM TO TOUCH
tepikul, typical
tepod, tepid
tepor, tip(pper)
tepse, tip(sy)
tepud, tepid
tepufy, typify
tepukle, typical
tepur, tip(pper)
tequila, A LIQUOR/ALCOHOL
ter, PREFIX INDICATING "THREE" MOST OFTEN MODIFIES THE WORD
tera, PREFIX INDICATING "ONE TRILLION/MONSTER" MOST OFTEN MODIFIES THE WORD
terable, terrible
terace, terrace
terafy, terrify
teragen, tarragon

teragin, tarragon
terain, terrain / terrane
teranchula, tarantula
terane, terrain / terrane / tyranny
teranshulu, tarantula
terantula, tarantula
terareim, terrarium
terarium, terrarium
teras, terrace
terastrial, terrestrial
terat, terret
teratoreul, territory(rial)
teratory, territory
terazo, terrazzo
terazzo, terrazzo
terben, turban / turbine
terbin, turban / turbine
terbo, turbo
terbulens, turbulent(nce)
terbulent, turbulent
terbun, turban / turbine
terd, tier(ed) / tear(ed) / tour(ed)
terdle, turtle
tere, tear(y)
tereble, terrible
terefic, terrific
terefy, terrify
terene, tyranny
terer, terror
terereim, terrarium
teres, terrace
teresdreul, terrestrial
teresm, tour(ism)
terest, tour(ist)
terestrial, terrestrial
teret, turret / terret
tereur, tarry(rier) / terrier
terf, turf
terfil, tear(ful)
terful, tear(ful)
terible, terrible
teribly, terrible(ly)
terif, tariff
terifek, terrific
terify, terrify
teriny, tyranny
terir, terror
teris, terrace
terism, tour(ism)
terist, tour(ist)
terit, turret / terret
teritoree, territory
teritoreul, territory(rial)
teriur, terrier

terkoes, turquois

terkois, turquois

term,*,med,mless, INVOLVING A SPECIFIC PERIOD OF TIME, FIXED/ SPECIFIC QUANTITY/VALUE

termarek, turmeric

termd, term(ed)

termenal, terminal

termenashen, terminate(tion)

termenate, terminate

termenation, terminate(tion)

termenator, terminate(tor)

termenolegy, terminology

termenul, terminal

termerik, turmeric

terminal,*,lly,able,ableness,ably, STATION/CONDUIT/CIRCUIT, TERMINATE, COME TO AN END "prefixes: sub"

terminashen, terminate(tion)

terminate,*,ed,ting,tive,tively,tor,tion, tional, TO END

terminology,gies,gical,gically, SPECIFIC WORDS/LANGUAGE WITHIN A SCIENCE/ART TO EXPLAIN PROCESSES

terminul, terminal

termite,*, WOOD EATING INSECT

termoel, turmoil

termonel, terminal

termunate, terminate

termunolegy, terminology

tern,*, A BIRD (or see turn)

ternament, tournament

ternd, turn(ed)

ternep, turnip

terniment, tournament

ternip, turnip

ternument, tournament

teror, terror

terpentin, turpentine

terpewlent, turbulent

terpulent, turbulent

terpuntine, turpentine

terra, PLANETS MOUNTAINOUS AREA

terrace,*,ed,cing, VARIOUS LEVEL AREAS CUT INTO A SLOPE

terrain, NATURALLY SHAPED LANDSCAPE (or see terrane)

terrane, GROUP OF NATURAL FORMATIONS PARTICULARLY ROCK (or see terrain) "prefixes: sub"

terrarium,*, CONTAINER FOR PLANTS/ ANIMALS TO LIVE/BE VIEWED

terrazzo, MOSAIC PIECES OF STONE/ TILE

terrestrial,*,lly,lness, BY/OF LAND/ EARTH "prefixes: semi/sub"

terret,*, ON A SADDLE/HARNESS (or see turret)

terreur, terrier

terrible,eness,ly, HORRIBLE/AWFUL/ UNCOMFORTABLE/STRESSFUL

terrier,*, BREED OF DOG

terrif, tariff

terrific,cally, EXCELLENT/EXCITING/ WONDERFUL

terrify,fies,fied,ying,yingly, STRICKEN WITH TERROR, HORRIFY/FRIGHTEN

terrir, terror

territory,ries,rial,rially,rialism,rialist, riality,lize,lized,lization, A SPECIFIC REGION/AREA OF TURF/LAND

terror,*,rism,rist,ristic,rless,rize,rizes, rized,rizing,rization,rizer, EXTREME FEAR/ HORROR "prefixes: bio"

terrur, terror

ters, tear(s) / tier(s)

terse,er,est,ely,eness, FREE OF FRIVOLTIES/SUPERFICIALITY

tersheary, tertiary

tershury, tertiary

tert, tier(ed) / tear(ed)

tertiary,ries, THREE/THIRD/THIRDS OF SOMETHING

tertil, turtle

tertul, turtle

teru, terra

terubil, terrible

terubly, terrible(ly)

teruf, tariff

terufy, terrify

terugen, tarragon

terugin, tarragon

terur, terror

terus, terrace

terut, turret

terutoree, territory

terutoreul, territory(rial)

terutory, territory

tery, tear(y) / tarry

terz, tear(s) / tier(s)

tes, tease / test

tesabel, tease(sable)

tesdamoneul, testimony(nial)

tesdee, testy

tesdekle, testicle

tesdi, testy

tesdukle, testicle

tesdumoneul, testimony(nial)

teseble, tease(sable)

tesh, teach

teshu, tissue

tesible, tease(sable)

test,*,ted,ting,ter,ty, TO CHALLENGE, EXPERIMENT FOR REACTION, A SHELL "prefixes: pre"

testafide, testify(fied)

testafy, testify

testament,*,tary,tal, WITNESS, CREATE A WILL "prefixes: inter"

testamint, testament

testamoneul, testimony(nial)

teste, testy

testefide, testify(fied)

testefy, testify

testekle, testicle

testemint, testament

testemony, testimony

testicle,*,cular,culate, MALE REPRODUCTIVE GLANDS

testify,fies,fied,fying,fier, TO DECLARE UNDER OATH/AS A WITNESS

testikle, testicle

testikuler, testicle(cular)

testiment, testament

testimony,nies,ial, PROVIDE WRITTEN/ VERBAL ACCOUNT AS A WITNESS

testir, test(er)

testufid, testify(fied)

testufy, testify

testukle, testicle

testument, testament

testumoneul, testimony(nial)

testumony, testimony

testur, test(er)

testy,tily,tiness, TOUCHY/IRRITABLE

tesu, tissue

tesubil, tease(sable)

tesuble, tease(sable)

tesy, tizzy

tetanus, A BACTERIA WHICH ENTERS OPEN WOUNDS

tetbit, tidbit

teter, teeter

teth, teeth

tether,*,red,ring, CORD/ROPE/ STRANDS TO SECURE SOMETHING FROM MOVING AWAY (or see teeth(er))"prefixes: un"

tethur, tether

tetir, teeter

tetnus, tetanus
tetra,*, FRESH WATER TROPICAL FISH,
    PREFIX INDICATING "FOUR" MOST
    OFTEN MODIFIES THE WORD
tetru, tetra
tetur, teeter
teuburkwulosis, tuberculosis
teul, teal / tell / teil
teurd, tier(ed) / tear(ed)
teurism, tour(ism)
teusday, tuesday
tewb, tube
tewbles, tube(less)
tewbuler, tube(bular)
tewl, tool
tewm, tomb
tewnik, tunic
tewt, toot
tewth, tooth
tewthles, tooth(less)
texder, texture
texdile, textile
texsdure, texture
text,*,ted,ting,tual,tually,tualism,tualist,
    PRINTED/WRITTEN LETTERS TO
    FORM WORDS "prefixes: inter/sub"
textile,*, ANY MATERIAL THAT CAN BE
    WOVEN
texture,*,ed,ring,ral,rally, ANY RAISED/
    VARIANT PORTION OF A FLAT/
    SMOOTH SURFACE "prefixes: inter"
tez, tease
tezzy, tizzy
tha, thaw / they
thad, they'd
thael, they'll
thair, there / their / they're
thal, they'll
thalamus,mi,mic,mically, PART OF A
    BRAIN/FLOWER
thalas, thallus
thalimus, thalamus
thallus, NEW BUD OF A PLANT
    WITHOUT LEAVES, ETC.
thalumus, thalamus
thalus, thallus
thamadik, theme(matic)
than, WORD USED TO COMPARE/
    CONTRAST
thanck, thank
thang, thong / thing
thank,*,ked,king,kful,kfully,kfulness,
    kless,klessly,klessness,
    APPRECIATION/ GRATITUDE

thanklis, thank(less)
thar, there / their / they're
tharbi, thereby
thare, there / their / they're
tharepist, therapy(pist)
tharepudik, therapy(peutic)
tharepy, therapy
tharfor, therefor / therefore
tharfour, therefor / therefore
tharipist, therapy(pist)
tharipudik, therapy(peutic)
tharipy, therapy
tharof, thereof
tharupist, therapy(pist)
tharupudik, therapy(peutic)
tharupy, therapy
thasoris, thesaurus
that,*, SOMEONE/SOMETHING NOT IN
    THE IMMEDIATE AREA/TIME
    FRAME, PREVIOUSLY MENTIONED,
    A PRONOUN (or see thought)
thatch,hes,hed,hing,her, MATTED/
    LAYERED ORGANIC MATERIAL,
    SURFACE COVERING
thau, thaw / thou
thaud, thaw(ed) / thought
thaung, thong
thausend, thousand
thaut, thaw(ed) / thought
thaw,*,wed,wing, TEMPERATURE
    WARMING AWAY FROM FREEZING,
    UNFREEZING (or see thou)
thawt, thaw(ed) / thought
thayd, they'd
thayl, they'll
the, AN IDENTIFYING/SPECIFYING
    WORD PRIOR TO A NOUN (or see
    thee)
theader, theater
theadir, theater
theadrekul, theatric(al)
theadrikal, theatric(al)
theadur, theater
thealegy, theology
theam, theme
theater,*,tre, A STRUCTURE FOR
    PERFORMING THE ARTS
theatir, theater
theatrek, theatric
theatrekul, theatric(al)
theatric,*,cal,calism,cality,calize,cally,
    THE ART OF PERFORMING,
    DRAMATIC "prefixes: non"
theatur, theater

thed, they'd
thee, REFERS TO A PERSON (or see the)
theef, thief / thieves
theem, theme
theesm, theism
thef, thief / they've
thefd, theft
theft,*, STEALING
theid, they'd
theif, thief / they've
theifs, thief(s)
theil, they'll
their,*, REFERS TO PEOPLE, POSSESSIVE
    PLURAL PRONOUN (or see there/
    they're)
theism,st,stic,stical,stically, BELIEF IN
    ONE DEITY
theive, thief / thieves
thek, thick
thekin, thick(en)
thekinur, thick(ener)
thekist, thick(est)
thekit, thicket
theknur, thick(ener)
thekun, thick(en)
thekuner, thick(ener)
thekust, thick(est)
thekut, thicket
thel, they'll
them,mselves, PRONOUN REFERRING
    TO MORE THAN ONE (or see
    theme)
themadik, theme(matic)
themble, thimble
thembul, thimble
theme,*,matic,matically, A SPECIFIC
    TOPIC/SUBJECT
themselves, PLURAL PRONOUN
    POSSESSIVE
then, SIGNIFIES TIME/PLACE (or see
    thin/than)
thener, thin(nner)
theng, thing
thenir, thin(nner)
thenk, think
thenkar, think(er)
thenkur, think(er)
thenly, thin(ly)
thenur, thin(nner)
theo, PREFIX INDICATING "GOD" MOST
    OFTEN MODIFIES THE WORD (or
    see thio)

theology,gies,gian,gic,gical,gically,gize, gizer, PHILOSOPHY CONCERNING RELIGION

theolugy, theology

theory,ries,rize,rizes,rized,rizing,rem, rematic,rematically,retic,retical, retically, PRINCIPLES/TECHNIQUES/ BELIEF IN AN ATTEMPT TO EXPLAIN/ UNDERSTAND EVENTS

ther, there / their / they're

therapudik, therapy(peutic)

therapy,pies,pist,peutic,peutics, peutically,peutist, TREATMENT TO REMEDY A MALADY "prefixes: bio/ sub"

therasik, thoracic

therbi, thereby

therd, third

therdly, third(ly)

there,*, FOLLOWS NOUN/PRONOUN TO DESCRIBE PLACE/TIME/ EMPHASIS (or see their/they're)

thereby, IN WHICH CASE/INSTANCE

therefor, FOR IT/THIS/THAT (or see therefore)

therefore, IN REFERENCE TO THE BEFORE MENTIONED (or see therefor)

thereof, BECAUSE OF THAT

therepeudik, therapy(peutic)

therfor, therefor / therefore

therfour, therefor / therefore

therm,mic,mical,mal, CALORIES, PREFIX INDICATING "HEAT" MOST OFTEN MODIFIES THE WORD "prefixes: endo/exo"

thermal,*,lly, RELATED TO HEAT

thermamedur, thermometer

thermometer,*,tric,trical,trically,try, INSTRUMENT WHICH MEASURES HOT/COLD VARIANCES

thermomuder, thermometer

thermul, thermal

thero, thorough

therof, thereof

therough, thorough

therow, thorough

thers, there(s) / their(s)

thersd, thirst

thersde, thursday / thirst(y)

thersdy, thursday / thirst(y)

therst, thirst

thersty, thursday / thirst(y)

thert, third

theru, through / threw

theruf, thereof

therupist, therapy(pist)

therupudik, therapy(peutic)

therupy, therapy

thery, theory

thes, this / these

thesal, thistle

thesares, thesaurus

thesaurus,ses, BOOK OF SYNONYMS

thesbein, thespian

these, PLURAL TENSE OF "THIS" (or see this)

thesis,ses, SET/PUT DOWN/ DOCUMENT/PROVE

thesle, thistle

thesores, thesaurus

thespein, thespian

thespian,*, ACTOR/ACTRESS

thesul, thistle

thesus, thesis

theury, theory

thev, thief / thieves

thevaree, thieves(ry)

thevury, thieves(ry)

thewre, theory

they, PLURAL OF "PERSONS IN GENERAL"

they'd, CONTRACTION OF OF THE WORDS 'THEY HAD/ WOULD"

they'll, CONTRACTION OF OF THE WORDS 'THEY SHALL/ WILL'

they're, CONTRACTION OF OF THE WORDS 'THEY ARE' (or see there/ their)

they've, CONTRACTION OF THE WORDS 'THEY HAVE'

theyl, they'll

thez, this

thi, PREFIX INDICATING "SULFUR" MOST OFTEN MODIFIES THE WORD (or see the/thigh/thy/thee)

thiadur, theater

thiamen, thiamine

thiamine, VITAMIN COMPOUND

thiazine, CHEMICAL COMPOUND

thick,ken,kens,kened,kening,kener,ker, kest,kness,kly,kish,ket, HAVING NOTICEABLE DEPTH/VISCOSITY/ DENSITY, EXCESSIVE

thicket,*,ted,ty, DENSE/THICK SHRUBS

thief,*,eves, ONE WHO STEALS

thiemin, thiamine

thieves,ed,ving,ery,eries,vish,vishly, vishness, THOSE WHO STEAL

thiezene, thiazine

thigh,*, PORTION OF LEG ABOVE THE KNEE

thik, thick

thiken, thick(en)

thiket, thicket

thikist, thick(est)

thikit, thicket

thiknur, thick(ener)

thikuner, thick(ener)

thikust, thick(est)

thikut, thicket

thim, theme / them

thimadek, theme(matic)

thimadik, theme(matic)

thimas, thymus

thimatik, theme(matic)

thimble,*, DEVICE FOR PROTECTION OF FINGERTIPS

thimbul, thimble

thimes, thymus

thimomedur, thermometer

thimple, thimble

thimpul, thimble

thimselfs, themselves

thimselvs, themselves

thimus, thymus

thin,*,nned,nning,nner,nly,nness,nnish, LESS VISCOSITY/ WEIGHT/ THICKNESS/ DEPTH THAN PREFERRED/ NORMAL (or see then/ than/thine)

thind, thin(nned)

thine,hou,hy, THIRD PERSON PRONOUN MEANING YOU/ YOURS (or see thin)

thiner, thin(nner)

thing,*, GENERIC TITLE FOR THAT WHICH IS NOT KNOWN/ UNDERSTOOD, WITHOUT A NAME (or see think)

think,*,king,ker,thought,kable,kingly, TO ENGAGE THE MIND, TO SUPPOSE/ CONTEMPLATE/ CONSIDER (or see thing) "prefixes: un"

thinkur, think(er)

thinur, thin(nner)

thio, PREFIX INDICATING "SULFUR" MOST OFTEN MODIFIES THE WORD (or see theo)

thirasik, thoracic

third,*,dly, NUMBER/ONE MORE AFTER THE SECOND, 33.3% OF THE WHOLE
thirdlee, third(ly)
thirm, therm
thirmal, thermal
thirmamedur, thermometer
thirmamiter, thermometer
thirmek, therm(ic)
thirmel, thermal
thirmometur, thermometer
thirmul, thermal
thiro, thorough
thiroed, thyroid
thirogh, thorough
thiroid, thyroid
thirow, thorough
thiroyd, thyroid
thirsd, thirst
thirsde, thursday / thirst(y)
thirst,*,ty,tier,tiest,tily,tiness, STRONG DESIRE FOR LIQUIDS, CRAVE SENSORY/MENTAL INPUT
thirsty, thursday / thirst(y)
thirt, third
thirty,ties, NUMBER AFTER 29
thiry, theory
this, PRONOUN/POSSESSIVE PRESENT TIME (or see these)
thisal, thistle
thisares, thesaurus
thises, thesis
thisle, thistle
thisoris, thesaurus
thistle,*, A PLANT
thisul, thistle
thisus, thesis
thiumen, thiamine
thiuzene, thiazine
thiwroed, thyroid
thiz, this
tho, though / thou / thaw
thogh, though
thoght, thought
thoghtles, thought(less)
thong,*, SHOES, UNDER GARMENT, LEATHER STRAP
thonk, thong
thoracic,cally, THE CHEST AREA
thoraks, thorax
thorasik, thoracic
thorax,xes, THE CHEST AREA
thorn,*,ny,nless, A SHARP/PRICKLY POINT ON A PLANT/TREE
thornee, thorn(y)

thornlis, thorn(less)
thoro, thorough
thorough,hly,hness, COMPLETE/ DETAILED/ACCURATE
thorow, thorough
thos, those / thus
those, PRONOUN FOR REMOTE
thosend, thousand
thosund, thousand
thot, thaw(ed) / thought
thotful, thought(ful)
thotles, thought(less)
thou,hy,hine, THIRD PERSON PRONOUN MEANING YOU/YOURS (or see though)
though, PLURAL ADJECTIVE MEANING THAT/BUT/HOWEVER
thought,*,tful,tfully,tfulness,tless, tlessly,tlessness, PAST TENSE FOR THE WORD "THINK/CONTEMPLATE" "prefixes: un"
thousand,*,dth, ENGLISH NUMBER AFTER 999
thousend, thousand
thousind, thousand
thousund, thousand
thow, thou / thaw / though
thowsand, thousand
thowsund, thousand
thowsunth, thousand(th)
thoz, those
thrab, throb
thrach, thrash
thral, thrall
thrall, ENSLAVED/SLAVE/BONDAGE
thrash,hes,hed,hing,her, FLAIL ABOUT VIOLENTLY, TO BEAT/KICK/TALK OVER AGAIN
thraul, thrall
thre, three
thread,*,ded,ding,der,dless,dy,diness, A THIN STRAND/FILAMENT/CORD "prefixes: un"
threat,*,ten,tens,tened,tening,teningly, CHALLENGE AGAINST SOMEONE/ SOMETHINGS IDEALS/ EXPECTATIONS
threch, thresh
threchhold, threshold
threchold, threshold
thred, thread / threat
threden, threat(en)
thredined, threat(ened)
thredun, threat(en)

thredund, threat(ened)
three,*,rice, ENGLISH NUMBER AFTER TWO
threft, thrift
threfty, thrift(y)
threl, thrill
threlur, thrill(er)
thresh,hes,hed,hing,her, BEAT GRAIN
threshhold, threshold
threshold,*, A DOOR WAY/SILL, ENTRANCE "prefixes: sub"
thret, thread / threat
thretind, threat(ened)
thretund, threat(ened)
threw, PAST TENSE FOR THE WORD "THROW" (or see thru through)
thrice, THREE TIMES
thrif, thrive
thrifd, thrift / thrive(d)
thrifde, thrift(y)
thrifs, thrive(s)
thrift,ty,tily,tiness, MINDS/WATCHES/ CONTROLS SPENDING/USE OF RESOURCES (or see thrive(d))
thril, thrill
thriler, thrill(er)
thrill,*,lled,lling,ller, EMOTION EXAGERRATED IN A POSITIVE FASHION, DELIGHT
thrilur, thrill(er)
thrise, thrice
thrive,*,ed,ving,vingly,er, TO EXIST SUCCESSFULLY
thro, throe / throw / through
throat,*,ted,ty,tily,tiness, CONICAL/ HOLLOW ENTRANCE/ PASSAGEWAY, FRONT PART OF NECK
throb,*,bbed,bbing,bber, PULSATE/ VIBRATE
throd, throat / throw(n)
throdul, throttle
throe,*, AMIDST STRONG PAIN/ AGONY/EMOTIONAL TURMOIL (or see throw)
throl, thrall
throne,*,ed,ning,eless, SOVEREIGN/ AUTHORITATIVE PLACEMENT, A CHAIR (or see thrown) "prefixes: en"
throng,*, IN A CROWD/MULTITUDE OF PEOPLE/THINGS (or see thong)
thronk, throng
throsd, thrust
throst, thrust

throt, throat / throw(n)

throtal, throttle

throtil, throttle

throttle,*,ed,ling,er, CONTROL OF FLOW THROUGH AN ORIFICE/ OPENING/ THROAT

throtul, throttle

through, TO PENETRATE/PASS/MAKE IT TO THE END (or see threw)

throughout, PENETRATES/EXISTS COMPLETELY

throw,*,wing,wn, TO TOSS/ELIMINATE/ GET RID OF (or see throe/throne) "prefixes: mis/over/up"

thrown, PAST TENSE FOR THE WORD "THROW" (or see throne)

throwt, throw(n) / throat

thru, TO PENETRATE/PASS/MAKE IT TO THE END (or see threw)

thruch, thrush

thrusd, thrust

thrush, A BIRD, A CHILDRENS DISEASE

thrust,*,ted,ting,ter, TO PLUNGE/ DRIVE/FORCE FORWARD "prefixes: under/up"

thruzd, thrust

thud,*,dded,dding, A SOLID/HEAVY/ DROPPING/FALLING SOUND

thug,*, ROBBERS/IMMORAL PEOPLE

thuk, thug

thum, thumb

thumadik, theme(matic)

thumatik, theme(matic)

thumb,*,bed,bing, OPPOSABLE DIGIT ON THE HAND, USE OF THE THUMB (or see thump)

thumbt, thumb(ed) / thump(pped)

thump,*,ped,ping, FALLING/HEAVY SOUND, SOUND OF HEARTBEAT (or see thumb)

thumpt, thumb(ed) / thump(pped)

thumselfs, themselves

thunder,*,red,ring,ringly, RUMBLING SOUND IN A RAIN STORM, SOUND MADE WHEN WEATHER FRONTS CONVERGE

thuntur, thunder

thurasik, thoracic

thurd, third

thurdly, third(ly)

thurm, therm

thurmal, thermal

thurmamiter, thermometer

thurmic, therm(ic)

thurmil, thermal

thurmometer, thermometer

thurmomuder, thermometer

thuro, thorough

thurow, thorough

thursd, thirst

thursday,*, A DAY OF THE WEEK (ENGLISH)

thursde, thursday / thirst(y)

thursdy, thursday / thirst(y)

thurst, thirst

thurste, thursday / thirst(y)

thursty, thursday / thirst(y)

thurt, third

thurtly, third(ly)

thus, IN EFFECT, THEREFORE, AS A RESULT

thusares, thesaurus

thusores, thesaurus

thwart,*,ted,tedly,ting, TO INTERVENE/ WARD OFF/DISTRACT A MISSION/ EVENT OR ACTION FROM IT'S GOAL/ACCOMPLISHMENT

thwort, thwart

thy,hine,hou, THIRD PERSON PRONOUN MEANING YOU/YOURS (or see thigh)

thymas, thymus

thyme, AN HERBAL PLANT (or see time)

thymis, thymus

thymus,ses,mi, A GLAND IN THE BODY

thyroid,*,dless, GLAND/CARTILAGE IN THE THROAT OF A BODY

thyuzene, thiazine

ti, tie / tea / tee

tiara,*, SMALL CROWN/CORONET FOR HEAD

tibaco, tobacco

tibagen, toboggan

tibako, tobacco

tibea, tibia

tiberqulosis, tuberculosis

tibia,al, SHIN BONE IN LEG

tibogin, toboggan

tibse, tip(sy)

tic, A TWITCHING IN THE BODY/FACE (or see tick)

tick,*,ked,king,ker, SMALL BLOOD SUCKING INSECT, RYTHMIC CLOCK SOUND, A MARK ETCHED INTO SOMETHING, MATTRESS/PILLOW COVERING, TELEGRAPH INSTRUMENT (or see tic)

ticket,*,ted,ting, PIECE OF PAPER ISSUED WHICH BEARS INFORMATION SOLICITING YOUR PERSONAL APPEARANCE/ VISIT

tickle,*,ed,ling,er,lish,lishness, SENSATION TO SKIN/ EMOTIONS WHICH GENERATES SMILE/ LAUGHTER/ RESPONSE

ticol, tickle

tid, tide / tied / tight

tida, today

tidal,lly, CONCERNING THE EBB AND FLOW OF THE SEA/OCEAN (or see title) "prefixes: inter/sub"

tiday, today

tidbet, tidbit

tidbit,*, A SNIPPET/SMALL PORTION OF SOMETHING GREATER/LARGER

tide,*,ed,ding,eful,eless,elessness,dings, dal, CONCERNING THE RISE/FALL OF OCEAN/SEA/ECONOMICS (or see tight/tied/tidy)

tided, tidy / tide(d) / tied

tidel, tidal / title

tiden, tight(en)

tideness, tidy(diness)

tidil, tidal / title

tidin, tight(en)

tidings, INFORMATION/KNOWLEDGE SHARING

tidle, tidal / title

tidon, tight(en)

tidond, tight(ened)

tidul, tidal / title

tidun, tight(en)

tidy,dies,died,dying,dily,diness, GET/ KEEP THINGS ORGANIZED/IN ORDER "prefixes: un"

tie,*,ed,tying,ed, TO HOLD/BUNDLE/ TIGHTEN THINGS TOGETHER USING TWINE/STRING/ROPE "prefixes: re/ un/under"

tied, PAST TENSE FOR THE WORD "TIE" (or see tight/tide)

tieng, tying

tier,*,red,ring, ELEVATE IN INCREMENTAL STEPS, RISERS, A LAYERED ARRANGEMENT OF ROWS (or see tear/tire)

tiera, tiara

tif, tiff

tifes, typhus

tiff, small argument

tifis, typhus

tifoid, typhoid
tifoon, typhoon
tifun, typhoon
tifus, typhus
tigar, tiger
tiger,*,rish, LARGE WILD FELINE
tigethur, together
tight,*,tly,tness,ten,tened,tening,
    APPLY PRESSURE/RESTRAINT/
    SUPPRESSION "prefixes: up"
tights, SNUG FITTING OUTER WEAR
tigor, tiger
tigress, FEMALE WILD FELINE
tigur, tiger
tikal, tickle
tike,*, SMALL/YOUNG CHILD (or see
    tiki)
tikel, tickle
tiker, tiger / tick(er)
tiket, ticket
tiki, A CARVED MYTHOLOGICAL FIGURE,
    OF POLYNESIAN CULTURE
tikil, tickle
tikir, tiger
tikit, ticket
tikle, tickle
tiklech, tickle(lish)
tiklush, tickle(lish)
tikol, tickle
tikor, tiger
tikot, ticket
tikres, tigress
tikt, tick(ed)
tikul, tickle
tikur, tiger
tikut, ticket
tiky, tiki
til, tile / till / teach / teal
tild, tile(d) / till(ed) / tilt
tile,*,ed,ling,er, FLAT/THIN SLAB OF
    VARIOUS MATERIAL, TO STACK (or
    see till)
tilepathee, telepathy
tileputhee, telepathy
till,*,lled,lling,ller,llage, PERFORM
    LABOR, PLACE FOR MONEY IN A
    BANK, ROTATING SOIL (too many
    definitions, please see standard
    dictionary) (or see tile/teach)
tilt,*,ted,ting,ter, TO ROTATE OFF-
    CENTER, LEAN ONE WAY/ANOTHER
    (or see till(ed)/tile(d))
tim, team / time
timado, tomato

timados, tomato(es)
timaro, tomorrow
timato, tomato
timber,*,rly, TREES VIEWED AS LUMBER
    (or see timbre)
timbrachure, temperature
timbre, A TONAL QUALITY (or see
    timber)
timbrushure, temperature
timbur, timber
timd, time(d)
time,*,ed,ming,er,ely,elier,eliest,eliness,
    eless,elessness, HUMAN
    CONSTRUCT TO DIFFERENTIATE
    BETWEEN PLACE/SPACE, TO GUAGE
    HOW MANY SECONDS/ MINUTES/
    HOURS/DAYS/MONTHS/YEARS (or
    see thyme) "prefixes: over/un/
    under"
timed, timid / time(d)
timedly, timid(ly)
timet, timid
timid,dly,dity,dness, HESITANT/
    CAUTIOUS
timly, time(ly)
timod, timid
timpal, temple
timparary, temporary
timparize, temporize
timparment, temperament
timper, temper
timperal, temporal
timperary, temporary
timperashure, temperature
timperize, temporize
timperol, temporal
timperushure, temperature
timpeshues, tempest(uous)
timpest, tempest
timpestuous, tempest(uous)
timpil, temple
timplat, template
timplut, template
timpo, tempo
timpol, temple
timporarely, temporary(rily)
timporul, temporal
timprachure, temperature
timpral, temporal
timpramentul, temper(mental)
timprary, temporary
timprashure, temperature
timprature, temperature
timprery, temporary

timpromintal, temper(mental)
timprumental, temper(mental)
timptashen, temptation
timptation, temptation
timptres, tempt(ress)
timpul, temple
timpur, temper
timpura, tempura
timpurarely, temporary(rily)
timpurary, temporary
timpurize, temporize
timpurment, temperament
timpust, tempest
timt, tempt
timtashen, temptation
timtation, temptation
timted, tempt(ed)
timtres, tempt(ress)
timud, timid
timulchuis, tumult(uous)
timulchuous, tumult(uous)
timult, tumult
timur, time(r)
timut, timid
tin,*,nned,nning,nnier,nniest,nny,nnilly,
    nniness, TYPE OF METAL, USE OF
    METAL, TINSMITH (or see tenor
    tine/tint/tiny/tend/teen)
tinable, tenable
tinachus, tenacious
tinacity, tenacity
tinakle, tentacle
tinament, tenement
tinamint, tenement
tinansy, tenant(ncy)
tinant, tenant
tinasedy, tenacity
tinashus, tenacious
tinasity, tenacity
tinatef, tentative
tinatif, tentative
tinatious, tenacious
tinative, tentative
tinchd, tinge(d)
tincity, tense(sity)
tincture,*, PLANTS SUBMERGED IN
    ALCOHOL FOR MEDICINAL USE
tind, tin(nned) / tend
tindatev, tentative
tinded, tend(ed) / tint(ed)
tinden, tendon
tindensy, tendency
tindenus, tendon(dinous)

tinder,ry, USED FOR KINDLING (or see
    tender)
tinderize, tender(ize)
tinderloin, tenderloin
tinderly, tender(ly)
tindernes, tender(ness)
tindinsy, tendency
tindirloin, tenderloin
tindon, tendon
tindor, tinder / tender
tindorize, tender(ize)
tindrel, tendril
tindrul, tendril
tindun, tendon
tindur, tender / tinder
tindurize, tender(ize)
tindurloin, tenderloin
tindurly, tender(ly)
tindutif, tentative
tine,*, A POINT ON A TOOL/
    INSTRUMENT/HORN/FORK (or see
    tin/tiny)
tinekle, tentacle
tinemint, tenement
tinen, tenon
tinensy, tenant(ncy)
tinent, tenant
tiner, tenor
tines, tennis / tine(s) / time(s)
tinet, tenet / tenant
tineur, tenure
tinewus, tenuous
tinfold, tenfold
ting, A SOUND (or see tinge)
tinge,*,ed,ging, A HINT/TRACE/SMALL
    BIT OF CHANGE IN COLOR/QUALITY
    (or see ting)
tinible, tenable
tinikle, tentacle
tinir, tenor
tinit, tenet / tenant / tonight
tinj, tinge
tink, ting
tinkal, tinkle
tinkchur, tincture
tinker,*,red,ring,rer, TOY/FONDLE/
    MEND/HANDLE SOMETHING
tinkle,*,ed,ling,ly,er, A FAINT LITTLE
    SOUND
tinkol, tinkle
tinksher, tincture
tinkture, tincture
tinkul, tinkle
tinkur, tinker

tinon, tenon
tinor, tenor
tinpal, temple
tinparery, temporary
tinpermint, temperament
tinpest, tempest
tinpirery, temporary
tinpist, tempest
tinplit, template
tinpo, tempo
tinpol, temple
tinporal, temporal
tinporary, temporary
tinporat, temper(ate)
tinprachur, temperature
tinpral, temporal
tinprament, temperament
tinpret, temper(ate)
tinpriment, temperament
tinprit, temper(ate)
tinprochur, temperature
tinprot, temper(ate)
tins, tin(s) / tent(s) / tense / tint(s) /
    tend
tinse, tense / tent(s)
tinsel,*,led,ling, SHINY/METALLIC
    STRIPS FOR DECORATION
tinsil, tinsel
tinsity, tense(sity)
tinsle, tinsel
tinsness, tense(ness)
tinsul, tinsel
tint,*,ted,ting,tless, CHANGE/APPLY
    SHADE OF COLOR (or see tent/
    tense/tin(nned)/tend) "prefixes:
    under"
tintakle, tentacle
tintative, tentative
tinted, tint(ed) / tent(ed) / tend(ed)
tintetive, tentative
tinth, tenth
tintid, tint(ed) / tent(ed) / tend(ed)
tintikle, tentacle
tintuckle, tentacle
tintud, tint(ed) / tent(ed) / tend(ed)
tintukle, tentacle
tintutive, tentative
tinuble, tenable
tinuis, tenuous
tinukle, tentacle
tinument, tenement
tinunsy, tenant(ncy)
tinunt, tenant
tinur, tenor

tinus, tennis
tinutef, tentative
tinutive, tentative
tiny,nier,niest,niness, LITTLE, VERY
    SMALL IN SCALE (or see tin(nny))
tinyewr, tenure
tinyewus, tenuous
tinyir, tenure
tinyur, tenure
tinzul, tinsel
tip,*,pped,pping,pper,ppy,ppable,pless,
    psy, TO LEAN SOMETHING OFF-
    CENTER FROM ITS POINT OF
    GRAVITY (or see type)
tipakle, typical
tipd, tip(pped) / type(d)
tipe, type / tip(ppy)
tipekul, typical
tiper, tip(pper) / type(r)
tiphoon, typhoon
tiphune, typhoon
tipi, teepee / tip(ppy)
tipikul, typical
tipist, type(pist)
tipo, typo
tipography, topography
tipogrufe, topography
tipse, tip(sy)
tipt, tip(pped) / type(d)
tipufy, typify
tipukle, typical
tipur, tip(pper) / type(r)
tiquila, tequila
tir, tire / tear
tirade,*, VERBAL/VIOLENT OUTBURST
tiranchula, tarantula
tirane, terrain / terrane / tyranny
tiranekul, tyrannical
tiranikul, tyrannical
tiranshulu, tarantula
tirant, tyrant
tirantula, tarantula
tirate, tirade
tirazo, terrazzo
tirben, turban / turbine
tirbo, turbo
tirbulens, turbulent(nce)
tirbulent, turbulent
tirbun, turban / turbine
tird, tire(d)
tirdle, turtle
tire,*,ed,ring,eless,elessly,elessness,
    edly,edness,esome,esomely,

esomeness, RUN OUT OF ENERGY, USED ON WHEELS "prefixes: un"

tirene, tyranny

tirent, tyrant

tireny, tyranny

tiresdreul, terrestrial

tirestrial, terrestrial

tirf, turf

tirit, turret

tirkoes, turquois

tirkoys, turquois

tirles, tire(less)

tirlis, tire(less)

tirm, term

tirmenashen, terminate(tion)

tirmenate, terminate

tirmenation, terminate(tion)

tirmenator, terminate(tor)

tirmenolegy, terminology

tirmenul, terminal

tirminate, terminate

tirmination, terminate(tion)

tirminator, terminate(tor)

tirminolegy, terminology

tirminul, terminal

tirmite, termite

tirmoel, turmoil

tirmonel, terminal

tirmunolegy, terminology

tirn, tern / turn

tirnament, tournament

tirnep, turnip

tirnument, tournament

tirpentine, turpentine

tirpewlent, turbulent

tirpulent, turbulent

tirpuntine, turpentine

tirrazo, terrazzo

tirse, terse

tirsheary, tertiary

tirsnes, terse(ness)

tirsum, tire(some)

tirtil, turtle

tirtul, turtle

tirunt, tyrant

tirut, turret

tise, tizzy

tishew, tissue

tissue,*, A SMALL/LIGHTWEIGHT PIECE OF PAPER

tisue, tissue

tisy, tizzy

tit,*,tty,tties, NIPPLE ON FEMALE OF SPECIES, TEAT (or see tied/tight/ tights)

tital, title / tidal

titan, tight(en)

titbet, tidbit

titbit, tidbit

tite, tidy / tight / tied

titel, title / tidal

titen, tight(en)

titend, tight(ened)

titenes, tidy(diness)

tithe,*,ed,hing,hable, A PERCENTAGE TO BE GIVEN AWAY TO SOMEONE/ SOMETHING

titil, title / tidal

titind, tight(ened)

title,*,ed,ling,list, A NAME (or see tidal/ tight(ly)) "prefixes: inter/re/sub/ sur/un"

titly, tight(ly)

titond, tight(ened)

titul, title / tidal

titun, tight(en)

titund, tight(ened)

tity, tidy

tiung, tying

tizzy, A FRENZIED STATE, A DITHER

to, PREPOSITION IN THE ENGLISH LANGUAGE TO SHOW RELATIONSHIP BETWEEN PERSON/ PLACE/THING (or see toe/too/tow)

toad,*, AN AMPHIBIAN MOSTLY FOUND IN DRY TERRAIN (or see told/toe(d)/ toady)

toady,dies,died,dying,dyish,dism,diness, TO GROVEL/FLATTER OTHERS FOR SELF-SERVING REASONS

toagrife, topography

toast,*,ted,ting,ter, TO BROWN FOOD WITH A HEAT SOURCE, HONORING SOMETHING/SOMEONE BEFORE HAVING A DRINK

tobacco, PLANT WHOSE LEAVES CONTAIN NICOTINE

tobaco, tobacco

tobagen, toboggan

tobako, tobacco

toberkulosis, tuberculosis

tobogan, toboggan

toboggan,*,ner,nist, TYPE OF SLED

tobogin, toboggan

toch, touch

tocsufy, toxify(fication)

tod, toad / toe(d) / tow(ed)

toda, today

todal, total

today, THE DAY WHICH IS PRESENT NOW

toddler,*, SMALL CHILD LEARNING TO WALK

toddy,ddies, ALCOHOLIC MIXED DRINK (or see toady)

tode, toad / toddy / toe(d) / toady

todee, toddy / toady

todel, total

todem, totem

todil, total

todim, totem

todler, toddler

todlur, toddler

todom, totem

todul, total

todum, totem

tody, toddy / toady

toe,*,ed,eless,eing, INDEX ON A FOOT (or see to/tow/toy)

toel, toil

toeld, toil(ed) / told

toelet, toilet

toeng, toe(ing) / toy(ing) / tow(ing)

tofu, A SOYBEAN BASED FOOD

toga,*, A WRAP AS WORN BY ROMANS

togal, toggle

togel, toggle

together,rness, BROUGHT/COLLECTED/ ROUNDED UP INTO ONE PLACE

toggle,*,ed,ling,er, LEVER/SWITCH FOR ALTERING ELECTRICAL CURRENT, A SYSTEM DEVISED TO FACILITATE MOVEMENT

toght, taught / taut / tout

togle, toggle

togu, toga

togul, toggle

toi, toy

toid, toy(ed)

toil,*,led,ling,ler, TO LABOR/WORK VERY HARD

toild, toil(ed)

toilet,*, A FIXTURE FOR CAPTURING URING/FECES

tok, tuck / took

toka, toga

tokel, toggle

tokela, tequila

token,*, A SMALL DISK/COIN/PAPER RESEMBLING SOMETHING OF VALUE

tokik, toxic

tokil, toggle

tokila, tequila

tokin, token

tokle, toggle

toko, taco

toksakolegy, toxicology

toksek, toxic

toksen, toxin

toksikolegy, toxicology

toksufy, toxify(fication)

toksukolegy, toxicology

toksun, toxin

toku, toga

tokul, toggle

tokun, token

tol, tall / toll

tolarense, tolerance

tolarent, tolerant

tolarible, tolerable

tolarinse, tolerance

told, PAST TENSE FOR THE WORD "TELL" (or see toll(ed)) "prefixes: re/un"

tole, toll

toler, tall(er)

tolerable,eness,bility,ly, BE PATIENT WITH DESPITE THE IRRITATION "prefixes: in"

tolerance, BE PATIENT WITH DESPITE THE IRRITATION "prefixes: in"

tolerant,ntly, BE PATIENT WITH DESPITE IRRITATION "prefixes: in"

tolerashen, tolerate(tion)

tolerate,*,ed,ting,able,ance,ant,ative, ation, BE PATIENT WITH DESPITE THE IRRITATION

tolerinse, tolerance

tolerint, tolerant

tolir, tall(er)

tolirashen, tolerate(tion)

tolirate, tolerate

tolirense, tolerance

toliruble, tolerable

tolk, talk / talc

toll,*,lled,lling, BELL RINGING, A REQUIRED FEE (or see tall)

tolness, tall(ness)

tolorinse, tolerance

tolur, tall(er)

tolurashen, tolerate(tion)

tolurate, tolerate

toluration, tolerate(tion)

tolurense, tolerance

tolurent, tolerant

tolurible, tolerable

tolurinse, tolerance

tolurint, tolerant

tomado, tomato

tomaro, tomorrow

tomato,oes, A FRUIT/VEGETABLE

tomb,*, STONE ENCLOSURE FOR A LIFELESS BODY "prefixes: en"

tomoro, tomorrow

tomorrow, THE DAY AFTER TODAY

ton,*,nnage, POUNDS (or see tone/toon)

tonaledy, tone(nality)

tone,*,ed,ning,nal,nality,nally,eless, elessly,elessness, SOUND FREQUENCY, MAKE FIRM/STRONG "prefixes: over/semi/under"

tonej, ton(nnage)

tonek, tonic

tong,*, TOOL USED FOR GRASPING/ PICKING THINGS UP (or see tongue)

tongue,*,ed,uing, MOVABLE ORGAN IN THE MOUTH, PART OF A HITCH, POINT ON LAND (or see tong)

tonic,*,cally, A MIXTURE, RELATED TO TONE "prefixes: sub"

tonight, THE NIGHT OF PRESENT TENSE

tonij, ton(nnage)

tonik, tonic

tonite, tonight

tonk, tong / tongue

tonles, tone(less)

tons, taunt(s) / ton(s) / tone(s)

tonsalodemy, tonsillotomy

tonsel, tonsil

tonselodemy, tonsillotomy

tonsil,*,llotomy, TISSUE HANGING IN THE THROAT

tonsillotomy, ACT OF REMOVING THE TONSILS

tonsilotomy, tonsillotomy

tonsul, tonsil

tonsulodemy, tonsillotomy

tont, taunt

tonul, tone(nal)

too, PREPOSITION MEANING ALSO/ MORE THAN ENOUGH (or see to/ toe/tow/ two)

toob, tube

tooba, tuba

tooch, tush

toocha, touche'

took, PAST TENSE FOR THE WORD "TAKE", TO TAKE SOMETHING "prefixes: over/re/under"

tool,*,led,ling,lless, DEVICE DESIGNED TO HELP WITH WORK "prefixes: re"

toolip, tulip

toom, tomb

toomer, tumor

toomur, tumor

toon,*, SHORT FOR CARTOON (or see tune)

toona, tuna

toonek, tunic

toonik, tunic

toonu, tuna

toopa, toupee

toopay, toupee

toosday, tuesday

toosh, tush

toot,*,ted,ting, A SOUND FROM A HORN

tooth,hless,hlessly,hy,hily,hiness,teeth, ENAMELED BONE PROJECTILES IN THE MOUTH, AN OUTCROP ON GEARS

tootoo, tutu

top,*,pped,pping,pper,pless, HEAD/TIP/ UPPERMOST PART OF SOMETHING, A SPINNING TOY (or see taupe/ toupee)

topa, toupee

topagrafik, topography(hic)

topagraphical, topography(hical)

topagraphy, topography

topal, topple

topalegy, topology

tope, toupee / taupe

topeary, topiary

topek, topic

topekul, topical

toper, top(pper)

tophu, tofu

topiary,ries, THE SCIENCE OF TRIMMING PLANTS

topic,*, SUBJECT/TITLE/THEME "prefixes: sub"

topical,lly,lity,lities, THE SURFACE, SHALLOW (or see tropical)

topiery, topiary

topigrafik, topography(hic)

topigrafikul, topography(hical)

topigraphic, topography(hic)

topigraphical, topography(hical)

topil, topple

tople, topple

toples, top(pless)

topo, PREFIX INDICATING "PLACE" MOST OFTEN MODIFIES THE WORD

topography,hies,hic,hical,hically,her, A SCIENCE WHICH IDENTIFIES ELEVATIONS/DEPRESSION ON THE EARTH

topol, topple

topolegy, topology

topology,gic,gical,gically,gist, SCIENCE THAT CAN IDENTIFY ELEVATION/ DEPRESSION ON THE EARTH

topple,*,ed,ling, OVERTHROWN, COME DOWN, FALL OVER

topugrafik, topography(hic)

topugrafikul, topography(hical)

topugraphical, topography(hical)

topuk, topic

topukil, topical

topul, topple

tor, tar / tore

torc, torque

torch,hes,hed,hing, STAFF/BRANCH WITH FIRE ON THE END

torcher, torture

torcherus, torture(rous)

torchur, torture

tord, toward / tour(ed) / tar(rred) / tore

tordis, tortoise

tordus, tortoise

tore, PAST TENSE FOR THE WORD "TEAR"

torenshul, torrent(ial)

torent, torrent

torential, torrent(ial)

tores, torus

torget, target

torgut, target

torifek, terrific

torinshul, torrent(ial)

torint, torrent

toris, torus

tork, torque

torment,*,ted,ting,ter, TO EXTEND/ APPLY CRUELTY/PAIN TO SOMETHING/ SOMEONE

tormint, torment

tornado,oes,dic, A HIGH/SWIRLING WIND WHICH BEGINS IN THE SKY THEN TOUCHES THE GROUND

tornados, tornado(es)

tornato, tornado

tornesh, tarnish

tornushd, tarnish(ed)

toros, torus

torp, tarp

torpedo,oes,oed,oing, A CONICAL/ BULLET-SHAPED MISSILE THAT PROPELS ITSELF THROUGH WATER

torpedod, torpedo(ed)

torque, AN EXERTED FORCE, AN ORNAMENT

torrent,*,tial,tially, A VIOLENT/SUDDEN GUSH/RUSH OF GREAT VOLUME

torsh, torch

torshen, torsion

torsher, torture

torshun, torsion

torshur, torture

torsion,nal,nally, TO TWIST SOMETHING OPPOSINGLY

torso,*,si, THE MAIN PORTION/TRUNK OF A BODY

tort,*, WRONG/IMPROPER (or see torte/tart)

torte,*, A HEAVILY MADE CAKE (or see tort/tart)

tortelu, tortilla

tortes, tortoise

torteu, tortilla

torteus, tortuous

tortila, tortilla

tortilla,*, CORN BASED ROUND/FLAT CAKE

tortis, tortoise

tortoise, A TURTLE LIVING ON LAND

tortuous,sly,sness, OF BEING TWISTED/ CROOKED/BENT BY NATURE

torture,*,ed,ring,rable,edly,er,esome, ringly,rous,rously, PURPOSEFUL INFLICTION OF PAIN

tortus, tortoise

torus, RING SHAPED/BULGE/RIDGE

tos, toss / toe(s) / two(s) / tow(s)

tosd, toast / toss(ed)

tosday, tuesday

tosder, toast(er)

tosdur, toast(er)

toss,sses,ssed,ssing, GENTLY THROW WITH UPWARD MOTION (or see toe(s)) "prefixes: re"

tost, toast / toss(ed)

tostur, toast(er)

tot,*,tted,tting, A SMALL AMOUNT, WORD FOR YOUNG CHILD/

TODDLER, SHORT WORD FOR 'TOTAL' (or see taught/taut/tout/ tote)

total,*,led,ling,lly,lity,lize,lizer, SUM OF ALL PARTS, COMPLETELY "prefixes: re/sub"

totalitarian,*,nism, CENTRALIZED/ DICTATORIAL GOVERNMENT

tote,*,ed,ting, TO CARRY (or see tot/ taught/taut/tout)

totel, total

totem,*,mic,mism,mist,mistic, CARVED/ SYMBOLIC REPRESENTATION

toten, taut(en)

totil, total

totile, total(lly)

totim, totem

totin, taut(en)

totler, toddler

totlur, toddler

totnes, taut(ness)

totoletarian, totalitarian

totom, totem

totule, total(lly)

totum, totem

toty, toddy / toady

touch,hes,hed,hing,hable,her,hy,hily, hiness, CONTACT/PRESSURE/ EFFECT/SENSATION AFFECTING SOME PART OF THE BODY (or see touche'/tush) "prefixes: re/un"

touche', FENCING/SPORT EXPRESSION (or see touch/tush)

tough,her,hest,hen,hener,hly,hness,hy, CHALLENGING/DIFFICULT TO PENETRATE/AFFECT/CONVINCE/ ASSUME

tought, tuft

toul, towel / tool

toun, town

toupee, FALSE HAIR PIECE (or see taupe)

tour,*,red,ring,rism,rist, PERUSE/VISIT/ TRAVEL TO SITES WITHIN A SPECIFIC TIME FRAME

tournament,*, COMPETITION IN SPORTS

tousil, tousle

tousle,*,ed,ling, RUFFLE/MESS UP

tout,*,ted,ting, TO SOLICIT FOR VOTES/ SALES/INFORMATION (or see taut/ taught)

tow,*,wed,wing,wer, TO HAUL/PULL BEHIND (or see toe/two/too/to/ toe(d)) "prefixes: under"

toward,*,dly,dliness, IN THE DIRECTION OF, EXPRESSING DIRECTION "prefixes: un"

towd, tow(ed) / toe(d) / toad

towel,*,led,ling, CLOTH/MATERIAL FOR USE IN DEALING WITH LIQUID

tower,*,red,ring, VERTICAL RISE, STRUCTURE WITH GREAT HEIGHT

towir, tower

town,*,nie, DESIGNATED AREA WHERE PEOPLE LIVE/ COHABITATE/ CONDUCT BUSINESS "prefixes: up"

towsil, tousle

towst, toast

towt, tout / taut / taught

towur, tower

tox, PREFIX INDICATING "POISON" MOST OFTEN MODIFIES THE WORD

toxakology, toxicology

toxek, toxic

toxen, toxin

toxi, PREFIX INDICATING "POISON" MOST OFTEN MODIFIES THE WORD

toxic,*,cally,cant,cation,city,cities, POISONOUS "prefixes: de/endo"

toxico, PREFIX INDICATING "POISON" MOST OFTEN MODIFIES THE WORD

toxicology,gic,gical,gically,gist,cosis, SCIENCE/STUDY OF POISONS

toxify,fies,fied,fying,fication, POISONED "prefixes: de"

toxik, toxic

toxikology, toxicology

toxin,*, POISON "prefixes: endo/exo"

toxun, toxin

toy,*,yed,ying, PLAYTHING

toyl, toil

toylet, toilet

tozdur, toast(er)

tozt, toast

tra, PREFIX INDICATING "ACROSS/ OVER/BEYOND" MOST OFTEN MODIFIES THE WORD (or see tray)

trac, track / trace

trace,*,ed,cing,er,eable,eableness,eably, eless, PATH/LINE/SCENT/CLUES LEADING TO ORIGINATION/ BEGINNING POINT (or see tray(s)/ track) "prefixes: re"

trach, trash

trachea,al,ate,eitis, TUBE PLACED IN THE THROAT FOR AIR/FOOD

trachoma,atous, EYELID INFLAMMATION/INFECTION

track,*,ked,king,ker,kable,kless, klessness, PATH/RAILS TO TRANSPORT/ NAVIGATE ALONG (or see tract)

trackshen, traction

tract,*,table,tion, A STRETCH/AREA OF SPACE/TIME/ DISTANCE (or see track(ed))

tractable,tability,tableness,tably, EASILY MANIPULATED/ FORMED (or see track(able))

tracter, tractor

traction,nal,ive, FIRM GRIP FOR MOMENTUM, METHOD TO RELIEVE STRESS ON THE BODY "prefixes: re"

tractor,*, EQUIPMENT USED FOR WORK

tractur, tractor

tracuble, trace(able)

tracur, trace(r)

trade,*,ed,ding,er,dable, EXCHANGE ONE THING FOR ANOTHER (or see trait) "prefixes: over"

traden, trod(dden) / trot(tting)

tradeshenul, tradition(al)

tradeshin, tradition

tradetion, tradition

tradin, trod(dden) / trot(tting)

tradir, trade(r) / traitor

tradishenul, tradition(al)

tradition,*,nal,nally,nalism,nalist, nalistic, PRACTICED REPEATEDLY THROUGHOUT TIME

tradur, trade(r) / traitor

trae, tray

trael, trail

traf, trough

trafek, traffic

trafel, travel

traffic,cked,cking, MANY PEOPLE USING SAME ROADWAY/PATH/AVENUE/ METHOD ROUTINELY

trafik, traffic

trafil, travel

trafler, travel(er)

trafuk, traffic

traful, travel

tragedy,dies,gic, A GREAT CATASTROPHIC/DISASTROUS EVENT

tragek, tragic

tragekle, tragic(ally)

tragekt, traject

tragektery, traject(ory)

tragety, tragedy

tragic,cally, A TRAGEDY

tragide, tragedy

tragik, tragic

tragude, tragedy

trail,*,led,ling,ler, A PATH/ROUTE "prefixes: en"

trailer,*, CONTAINER ON WHEELS WITH HITCH, MOVIE PREVIEW (or see trail(er)) "prefixes: semi"

trailor, trawl(er) / trail(er) / trailer

train,*,ned,ning,ner,nable, LOCOMOTIVE/RAILWAY CARS, DISCIPLINE TO FOLLOW DIRECTIONS AS COMMANDED/ INSTRUCTED "prefixes: de/en/re"

trainkwol, tranquil

trainqwil, tranquil

trainuble, train(able)

traipse,*,ed,sing, TO WALK AROUND WITHOUT PURPOSE

trait,*, SPECIFIC QUALITIES/FEATURES (or see trade)

traitor,*,rous,rously, ONE WHO BETRAYS ANOTHER

traject,*,ted,ting,tion,tory,tories, THE CURVE/ARC OF DIRECTION WHEN AIMING/CASTING/SHOOTING

trajectery, traject(ory)

trajek, tragic

trajekle, tragic(ally)

trajekt, traject

trajektery, traject(ory)

trajide, tragedy

trajik, tragic

trajude, tragedy

trak, track / tract

trakd, track(ed) / tract

trakea, trachea

traker, track(er)

trakia, trachea

trakible, track(able) / tract(able)

trakiu, trachea

traklis, track(less)

trakomu, trachoma

trakshen, traction

trakshun, traction

trakt, track(ed) / tract

traktor, tractor

trakuble, track(able) / tract(able)

trakur, track(er)

tral, trawl / troll / trowel

trale, trail / trolley

traler, trawl(er) / trail(er) / trailer

traley, trolley

tralur, trawl(er) / trail(er) / trailer

tram,*,mmed,mming, MECHANICALLY ADJUST, TRANSPORTER ON RAILS, WOVEN SILK TECHNIQUE

trama, trauma

tramadik, trauma(tic)

tramatis, trauma(tize)

tramb, tramp

trambalen, trampoline

trambon, trombone

trambulen, trampoline

tramel, trommel

tramendus, tremendous

tramindusle, tremendous(ly)

tramol, trommel

tramp,*, STEP HEAVILY, TRAVEL ON FOOT FROM PLACE TO PLACE FOR SUBSTINENCE WITHOUT A HOME

trampalen, trampoline

trampil, trample

trample,*,ed,ling, STEP/STOMP HEAVILY CAUSING HARM/INJURY

tramplen, trampoline

trampol, trample

trampoline,*,er,nist, MATERIAL STRETCHED ACROSS A FRAME SUPPORTED BY SPRINGS TO JUMP ON

trampul, trample

trampulen, trampoline

tramu, trauma

tramul, trommel

tramutize, trauma(tize)

tran, PREFIX INDICATING "ACROSS/ OVER/BEYOND" MOST OFTEN MODIFIES THE WORD (or see train)

trance,*,ed,cing, A SUBCONSCIOUS STATE OF MIND "prefixes: en"

trancefigurashen, transfigure(ration)

trancefushen, transfuse(sion)

trane, train

traneble, train(able)

tranes, train(s) / tran(s) / trance

trangretion, transgress(ion)

tranible, train(able)

tranir, train(er)

trankwel, tranquil

tranquil,lly,lness,lize,lizes,lized,lizer, lizing,lity, PEACEFUL/CALM/ RELAXING

tranqwul, tranquil

trans, trance / train(s) / tran(s)

transacshun, transact(ion)

transact,ted,ting,tion,tional, CARRY OUT/MAKE EXCHANGE IN BUSINESS

transaktion, transact(ion)

transatif, transit(ive)

transbertashen, transport(ation)

transbir, transpire

transbirtashen, transport(ation)

transblant, transplant

transbonder, transponder

transbort, transport

transburtachen, transport(ation)

transcend,*,ded,ding,dent,dence,dency, dently,dental,dentally,dentalism, dentalist, NOT OF THE MATERIAL/ PHYSICAL PLANE/FREQUENCY

transcrepshen, transcription

transcribe,*,ed,bing,er,iption, PHYSICALLY/LITERALLY MAKE NOTATION/COPY, AVAILABLE FOR VIEWING

transcripshen, transcription

transcription,*,tional,tive, PHYSICALLY/ LITERALLY MAKE NOTATION/COPY, AVAILABLE FOR VIEWING

transdews, transduce

transdewsur, transduce(r)

transduce,*,er,ction, CHANGE ONE TYPE OF FREQUENCY/ENERGY INTO ANOTHER

transduction,*,nal, CHANGE TYPE OF FREQUENCY/ENERGY INTO ANOTHER BIOLOGICALLY

transduse, transduce

transduxshin, transduction

transeant, transient

transechen, transit(ion)

transect,*,ted,ting,tion, DIVIDE/SEVER/ CUT ACROSS

transekt, transect

transem, transom

transend, transcend

transendense, transcend(ence)

transendent, transcend(ent)

transendentul, transcend(ental)

transendul, transcend(ental)

transent, transcend

transeshenul, transit(ional)

transestur, transistor

transet, transit

transetif, transit(ive)

transetional, transit(ional)

transetory, transit(ory)

transeunt, transient

transexshen, transect(ion)

transfeks, transfix

transfer,*,rred,rring,rrer,rral,rrals,rable, rability,ree,rence,rential, MOVE/ SHIFT FROM ONE PLACE TO ANOTHER "prefixes: re"

transfermashen, transform(ation)

transfeugin, transfuse(sion)

transfews, transfuse

transfex, transfix

transfigure,*,ed,ring,rement,ration, CHANGE APPEARANCE OF

transfirens, transfer(ence)

transfirmation, transform(ation)

transfiruble, transfer(able)

transfix,xes,xed,xing,xion, HOLD/ FROZEN IN PLACE

transfor, transfer

transform,*,med,ming,mer,mation, mational,mationally,mative,mable, CHANGE FROM ONE TO ANOTHER, AN EVOLUTION "prefixes: inter/re"

transformur, transform(er)

transfujen, transfuse(sion)

transfurd, transfer(rred)

transfurens, transfer(ence)

transfurmashen, transform(ation)

transfuruble, transfer(able)

transfuse,ed,sing,sable,sion, TRANSMISSION/MOVEMENT OF LIQUID/BLOOD

transgreshen, transgress(ion)

transgresif, transgress(ive)

transgress,sses,ssed,ssing,ssive,ssor, ssively,ssion, VIOLATING A LAW

transgretion, transgress(ion)

transichenul, transit(ional)

transient,*,tly,nce,ncy, PHYSICAL TEMPORARY/PASSING

transim, transom

transind, transcend

transindense, transcend(ence)

transindentul, transcend(ental)

transishen, transit(ion)

transistor,*,rize, ELECTRONIC DEVICE

transit,*,ted,ting,tion,tional,tionally, tive,tively,tiveness,tivity,tory,torily, toriness, PASSING OVER/THROUGH/ ACROSS

transkribe, transcribe

translachen, translate(tion)

translade, translate

transladuble, translate(table)

transladur, translate(tor)

translate,*,ed,ting,tability,table,tor,tion, tional,tive, MOVE/CONVEY INFORMATION/ITEMS/EFFECT, REPRODUCE WHILE RETAINING THE ORIGINAL

translatir, translate(tor)

translatuble, translate(table)

translewsed, translucid

translewsins, translucent(nce)

translewsint, translucent

transloused, translucid

translucent,nce,ncy,ntly,cid, LIGHT CAN PENETRATE

translucid, LIGHT CAN PENETRATE

translusent, translucent

translusinse, translucent(nce)

translusit, translucid

transmechen, transmission

transmedable, transmit(ttable)

transmedal, transmit(ttal)

transmedur, transmit(tter)

transmesable, transmissible

transmeshen, transmission

transmetuble, transmit(ttable)

transmewt, transmute

transmewtuble, transmute(table)

transmichen, transmission

transmiduble, transmit(ttable)

transmidul, transmit(ttal)

transmidur, transmit(tter)

transmisability, transmissible(bility)

transmision, transmission

transmissible,bility, PASSED ALONG, MOVEABLE, ABLE TO TRANSMIT

transmission,*, GEARS WHICH ENCOURAGE MOVEMENT, EFFECTIVE COMMUNICATION

transmisuble, transmissible

transmit,*,tted,tting,ttable,ttal,ttance, ttancy,tter,ission,issible, PASS FROM ONE TO ANOTHER

transmitable, transmit(ttable)

transmiter, transmit(tter)

transmition, transmission

transmitle, transmit(ttal)

transmituble, transmit(ttable)

transmutachen, transmute(tation)

transmute,*,ted,ting,ter,table, tableness,tability,tably,tation,tative, TRANSFORM/CHANGE FROM ONE FORM TO ANOTHER

transmutible, transmute(table)

transmutuble, transmute(table)

transom,*,med, BEAM/CROSSBOAR, VENTILATION WINDOW

transparensy, transparent(ncy)

transparent,*,tly,tness,ncy,ncies, CLEAR, ALLOWS VISUAL PENETRATION

transparint, transparent

transperinsy, transparent(ncy)

transperint, transparent

transpertashen, transport(ation)

transpire,*,ed,ring,rable,ratory, SWEAT/PERSPIRE, TO HAPPEN, COME ABOUT

transpirtachen, transport(ation)

transpirtasion, transport(ation)

transplant,*,ted,ting,table,tation,ter, MOVE/TRANSFER FROM ONE LOCATION TO ANOTHER

transplantuble, transplant(able)

transponder,*, A RADIO

transporduble, transport(able)

transport,*,ted,ting,tability,table,ter, tation,tive, CARRY/RELOCATE

transportashen, transport(ation)

transportuble, transport(able)

transpose,*,ed,sing,sable,sition,sitional, MOVE

transpoz, transpose

transpurtachen, transport(ation)

transpuzishen, transpose(sition)

transum, transom

transutif, transit(ive)

transutory, transit(ory)

transverse,*,ely,sal,sally, LYING ACROSS THE SAME LINE TWICE, CROSSING

transvurs, transverse

tranuble, train(able)

tranur, train(er)

tranzacktion, transact(ion)

tranzakt, transact

tranzatef, transit(ive)

tranzbirtashen, transport(ation)

tranzblant, transplant

tranzbonder, transponder

tranzbort, transport

tranzbortuble, transport(able)

tranzdukshen, transduction

tranzdusir, transduce(r)

tranzeant, transient

tranzechen, transit(ion)

tranzekt, transect

tranzendentul, transcend(ental)

tranzeshenul, transit(ional)

tranzeshin, transit(ion)

tranzestur, transistor

tranzet, transit

tranzetory, transit(ory)

tranzfeks, transfix

tranzfermashen, transform(ation)

tranzfeugen, transfuse(sion)

tranzfewshen, transfuse(sion)

tranzfewz, transfuse

tranzfex, transfix

tranzfikyerashen, transfigure(ration)

tranzfir, transfer

tranzfix, transfix

tranzform, transform

tranzformashen, transform(ation)

tranzformur, transform(er)

tranzfujin, transfuse(sion)

tranzfur, transfer

tranzfuruble, transfer(able)

tranzgres, transgress

tranzgreshen, transgress(ion)

tranzgresif, transgress(ive)

tranzichen, transit(ion)

tranzishenul, transit(ional)

tranzit, transit

tranzitional, transit(ional)

tranzitory, transit(ory)

tranzkribe, transcribe

tranzlachen, translate(tion)

tranzlade, translate

tranzladuble, translate(table)

tranzladur, translate(tor)

tranzlate, translate

tranzlater, translate(tor)

tranzlatible, translate(table)

tranzlation, translate(tion)

tranzlewsed, translucid

tranzlewsense, translucent(nce)

tranzlewsint, translucent

tranzlousent, translucent

tranzlousid, translucid

tranzlused, translucid

tranzlusense, translucent(nce)

tranzlusent, translucent

tranzmedable, transmit(ttable)

tranzmedur, transmit(tter)

tranzmeshin, transmission

tranzmesuble, transmissible

tranzmet, transmit

tranzmetuble, transmit(ttable)

tranzmetur, transmit(tter)

tranzmeut, transmute

tranzmewtashen, transmute(tation)

tranzmichen, transmission

tranzmidul, transmit(ttal)

tranzmidur, transmit(tter)
tranzmishen, transmission
tranzmision, transmission
tranzmisuble, transmissible
tranzmit, transmit
tranzmition, transmission
tranzmitur, transmit(tter)
tranzmutachen, transmute(tation)
tranzmutasion, transmute(tation)
tranzmute, transmute
tranzmutuble, transmute(table)
tranzpazichen, transpose(sition)
tranzperint, transparent
tranzplant, transplant
tranzplantuble, transplant(able)
tranzponder, transponder
tranzporduble, transport(able)
tranzport, transport
tranzportashen, transport(ation)
tranzpoz, transpose
tranzutif, transit(ive)
tranzvurs, transverse
trap,*,pped,pping,pper, CATCH/HOLD/
    PREVENT SOMETHING FROM ITS
    NORMAL MOVEMENT/ACTION
    MUSICAL INSTRUMENT, DEVICE
    FOR TRAPPING "prefixes: en"
trapazoed, trapezoid
trapekul, tropic(al)
traper, trap(pper)
trapes, trapeze
trapeze,zist, A TYPE OF SWING
trapezoid,dal, A GEOMETRIC SHAPE
traphek, traffic
trapickul, tropic(al)
trapik, tropic
trapikul, tropic(al)
trapir, trap(pper)
trapizoed, trapezoid
trapse, traipse
trapur, trap(pper)
trapuzoed, trapezoid
tras, tray(s) / trace
trasabul, trace(able)
trase, trace / tray(s)
trash,hes,hed,hing,hily,hiness,hy,
    GARBAGE, DISPOSABLE/DISCARDED
    ITEMS
trashd, trash(ed)
trashe, trash(y)
trasible, trace(able)
trasuble, trace(able)
trat, trade / trait
trater, trade(r) / traitor

trats, trait(s) / trade(s)
tratur, trade(r) / traitor
trau, trough / trowel
traudishen, tradition
traudition, tradition
trauf, trough
traul, trawl/ troll/ trowel
traule, trolley
trauma,*,tic,tically,tism,tize,tizes,tized,
    tizing, SUDDEN/VIOLENT SHOCK TO
    THE SYSTEM
trausers, trousers
travail,*, ENDURE A HARDSHIP
travel,*,led,ling,ler, PHYSICALLY MOVE
    ABOUT/AWAY (or see travail)
    "prefixes: un"
traverse,*,ed,sing,sable,sal,ser, TO
    CROSS/ACCOMPLISH A BARRIER/
    BOUNDARY
travesty,ties,tied,tying, RIDICULE BY
    DISTORTING/DEBASING/MOCKING
    AN ACTUAL EXPERIENCE
travil, travel
travirs, traverse
travisty, travesty
travler, travel(er)
travoste, travesty
travul, travel
travusde, travesty
trawl,*,led,ling,ler, BAITED HOOKS IN A
    LONG LINE/NET FOR CATCHING
    FISH (or see troll/trowel)
trawmu, trauma
trawpek, tropic
trawpekul, tropic(al)
trawpik, tropic
trawsers, trousers
trawt, trot / trout
tray,*, SHALLOW PAN WITH SIDES FOR
    CARRYING/HOLDING ITEMS
    "prefixes: under"
traykoma, trachoma
tre, tree / tray
treacherous,sly,sness, DANGEROUS
    FOR VARIETY OF REASONS
treachery,ries,rous, RISKY, OF
    TREASON/BETRAYAL/TRICKERY
tread,*,ded,ding,der,trod,trodden,
    HEAVY/SLOW WALK, SWIM IN
    PLACE, TIRE IMPRINT (or see
    tree(d)) "prefixes: re"
tready, treaty
treason,nable,nous,nably, BEFRIEND
    THE ENEMY

treasure,*,ed,ring,rable,er,ry,
    SOMETHING WORTHY/VALUABLE
treasury,ries, MANAGES MONEY
    "prefixes: sub"
treat,*,ted,ting,ter,table,tability,ty,
    tment, TASTY MORSEL TO EAT, PAY
    THE CHARGE/BILL FOR SOMEONE,
    TAKE FINANCIAL RESPONSIBILITY AS
    AN ACT OF KINDNESS "prefixes: en/
    in/mis/pre/re"
treaty,ties,tise, WRITTEN SETTLEMENT
    OF AGREEMENT BETWEEN TWO
    POWERS/FACTIONS
treazen, treason
trebel, treble
trebeulashen, tribulation
trebeun, tribune
trebeut, tribute
trebeutery, tributary
trebewlashen, tribulation
trebewn, tribune
trebil, treble
treble,ed,ling, TREBLE CLEF, MUSICAL
    PITCH/NOTES, OF TRIPLE/THREE,
    SYMBOL
trebul, treble
trebulashen, tribulation
trebun, tribune
trebute, tribute
trebutery, tributary
trechirus, treacherous
trechury, treachery
treck, trek
tred, tread / tree(d) / treat
trede, treaty
tredid, tread(ed) / treat(ed) / trade(d)
tredment, treat(ment)
treduble, treat(able)
tree,*,eed,eeing,eeless,eelessness,
    LARGE WOODY PLANT (or see
    tread)
treety, treaty
treezin, treason
trefea, trivia
treger, treasure / trigger
tregery, treasury
tregunometry, trigonometry
tregur, treasure / trigger
trejere, treasury
trejur, treasure
trek,*,kked,kking,kker,kkie, TO
    JOURNEY/TRAVEL/MIGRATE
    SLOWLY
trekal, trickle

treked, trek(kked) / trick(ed)
trekil, trickle
trekinoses, trichinosis
trekir, trigger
trekol, trickle
trekoma, trachoma
trekt, trek(kked) / trick(ed)
trekul, trickle
trekur, trigger
trel, trill / trail
trelege, trilogy
treleim, trillium
treleon, trillion
treles, trellis
treleum, trillium
trelion, trillion
trelis, trellis
trellis,sed, DECORATIVE LATTICE
treluge, trilogy
trelus, trellis
trelyen, trillion
trem, trim
tremadik, trauma(tic)
tremar, tremor
trematik, trauma(tic)
trembil, tremble
tremble,*,ed,ling,er,lingly, VIBRATE/
    SHAKE INVOLUNTARILY
trembul, tremble
tremd, trim(mmed)
tremendous,sly,sness, SUBSTANTIAL IN
    SIZE/AMOUNT
tremendus, tremendous
tremer, trim(mmer) / tremor
tremindus, tremendous
tremor,*,rous, INVOLUNTARY
    VIBRATION/SHAKING, RESULT OF
    EARTH CRUST MOVEMENT (or see
    trim(mmer))
trempul, tremble
tremur, trim(mmer) / tremor
trench,hes,hed,hing,her,hable,hment,
    hable,hment, DITCH/FURROW DUG
    INTO A FLAT SURFACE "prefixes: en/
    re/un"
trend,*,dy, A TEMPORARY MOVEMENT
    IN DESIGN/ CLOTHING/STYLE
    "prefixes: up"
trende, trend(y)
trenedy, trinity
trenity, trinity
trenket, trinket
trenkit, trinket
trensh, trench

trent, trend
trente, trend(y)
trenute, trinity
treo, trio
trep, trip
trepul, triple / treble
tresal, trestle
tresen, treason
treser, treasure
tresere, treasury
treshery, treachery / treasury
treshure, treachery / treasure
treshures, treacherous
tresil, trestle
tresin, treason
tresir, treasure
tresle, trestle
treson, treason
trespas, trespass
trespass,sses,ssed,ssing,sser, ENTER
    ONTO PROPERTY WITHOUT
    INVITATION/ PERMISSION
tresspas, trespass
trestle,*, SUPPORT FRAME/BEAM
tresul, trestle
tresun, treason
tresure, treasure / treasury
tret, treat
trete, treaty
tretid, tread(ed) / treat(ed) / trade(d)
tretment, treat(ment)
tretuble, treat(able)
treuth, truth
trevail, travail
trevet, trivet
treveul, trivia(l)
trevia, trivia
trevit, trivet
treviul, trivia(l)
trew, drew / true
trewant, truant
trewbador, troubadour
trewent, truant
trewezm, true(uism)
trewint, truant
trewly, true(uly)
trewp, troop / troupe
trewpur, troop(er)
trews, truce
trewth, truth
trezen, treason
trezer, treasure
trezery, treasury
trezpas, trespass

trezun, treason
trezure, treasure / treasury
tri, PREFIX INDICATING "THREE" MOST
    OFTEN MODIFIES THE WORD (or
    see try)
triad,*,dic,dically, CONSISTING OF
    THREE PARTS/ELEMENTS
trial,*, A MOMENT/PERIOD/PLACE OF
    CONSIDERATION/ REVIEW/
    JUDGEMENT "prefixes: mis/re/
    under"
triamverite, triumvirate
triangewlate, triangular(ate)
triangewlur, triangular
triangle,*, THREE SIDED GEOMETRIC
    SHAPE
triangul, triangle
triangular,rity,rly,ate,ates,ated,ating,
    ation, MAKE INTO THREE SIDES/
    PARTS/ AREAS
triankl, triangle
triankulate, triangular(ate)
triankuler, triangular
triat, triad
trib, tribe
tribe,*,bal,bally,balism,balistic, PEOPLE
    OF A SOCIETY WHO SHARE
    COMMON BELIEFS/VALUES/
    MORALS "prefixes: de/sub"
tribel, tribe(bal)
tribeun, tribune
tribeunul, tribune(nal)
tribeut, tribute
tribeutary, tributary
tribewlashen, tribulation
tribewn, tribune
tribewnul, tribune(nal)
tribewtery, tributary
tribul, tribe(bal)
tribulation, TRIAL/STRESS/TROUBLE
tribune,*,nal,eship,nate, THAT WHICH
    CHAMPIONS PEOPLES RIGHTS,
    COURT OF LAW, A PLATFORM
tribunel, tribune(nal)
tribunul, tribune(nal)
tributary,ries,rily, FLOWING/
    STREAMING OF LIQUID/ WATER/
    RESOURCES/MONEY WHICH FEEDS/
    MOVES INTO A LARGER BODY
tribute,*,ulation, TO OFFER/SUPPLY
    GRATITUDE/MONEY
triceps, ARM MUSCLES
trichanosis, trichinosis

trichinosis, DISEASE IN INTESTINES CAUSED BY WORMS

trichunosis, trichinosis

trick,*,ked,king,ker,kery,keries,ky, kiness, PRANK/HOAX (or see trek)

trickle,*,ed,ling, TINY FLOWING STREAM

trickunosis, trichinosis

tricycle,*,ed,ling, THREE WHEELED BIKE

trid, tried / trite

trident,*,tate,tal, THREE PRONGED FORK/BARB, BALLISTIC MISSILE SYSTEM

tridint, trident

tried, PAST TENSE FOR THE WORD "TRY", INSIGHTED FOR A CRIME, TESTED (or see trite) "prefixes: un"

triel, trial

triemverat, triumvirate

triemverint, triumvirate

trieng, try(ing)

trifea, trivia

trifil, trifle

trifle,*,ed,ling,er,lingly,lingness, SMALL/ MINIMAL AMOUNT, NOT TAKE SERIOUSLY, IDLE TIME

triful, trifle

trigar, trigger

trigenometry, trigonometry

trigger,*,red,ring,rless, PART OF GUN WHICH RELEASES BULLET

trigonometry, MATH WITH SYMBOLS/ DESIGNS

trigur, trigger

trihedras,al,ron, OF THREE INTERSECTING LINES

trihedril, trihedron(ral)

trihedron,*,ras,ral, THREE INTERSECTING LINES

trihedrul, trihedron(ral)

trik, trick

trikal, trickle

trikanosis, trichinosis

trikel, trickle

trikenoses, trichinosis

trikery, trick(ery)

trikul, trickle

trikure, trick(ery)

triky, trick(y)

tril, trial / trill

trilabit, trilobite

triladerul, trilateral

trilateral,lity,lly, THREE SIDED

trilaturil, trilateral

trilebit, trilobite

trilege, trilogy

trilengwul, trilingual

trileon, trillion

trileum, trillium

trilingual,lly, THREE LANGUAGES

trilingwul, trilingual

trilion, trillion

trilium, trillium

trill, TYPE OF SOUND

trillion,*,nth, ONE MILLION TIMES ONE MILLION

trillium, A LAWFULLY PROTECTED PLANT

trilobite,*,tic, EXTINCT ARTHROPOD, THREE LOBES

trilogy,gies, THREE PARTS TOGETHER IN A MUSICAL/LITERARY/FILMED/ DRAMATIC WORK

trilubit, trilobite

triluge, trilogy

trilyun, trillion

trim,*,mmed,mming,mmer, TO REMOVE EXCESS, CREATE A CLEAN/ TIDY/ FINISHED APPEARANCE

trimer, trim(mmer) / tremor

trimur, trim(mmer) / tremor

trin, trine

trinch, trench

trind, trend

trine,*,nal,nity, OF THREE PARTS

trinedy, trinity

tring, try(ing)

trinity,ties, OF THREE PARTS

trinket,*, SMALL KNICK KNACK/ ORNAMENT

trinsh, trench

trint, trend

trio,*, THREE PARTS

trip,*,pped,pping,pper,ppingly, JOURNEY AWAY FROM, STUMBLE (too many definitions, please see standard dictionary) (or see tripe)

tripal, triple

tripd, trip(pped)

tripe, COW/SHEEP STOMACH, POOR IN QUALITY

tripel, triple

tripewlashen, tribulation

triple,*,ed,ling,ly,let,licate,lication, THREE OF, THREE TIMES/FOLD

tripod,*, THREE LEGGED

tripol, triple

tripot, tripod

tripul, triple

tripulashen, tribulation

tripuld, triple(d)

trisebs, triceps

trisekel, tricycle

triseps, triceps

trisycle, tricycle

trit, tried / trite / treat

trite,ely,eness, OF LITTLE INTEREST IN (or see tried)

tritle, trite(ly)

tritly, trite(ly)

tritnes, trite(ness)

triul, trial

triumf, triumph

triumfent, triumph(ant)

triumph,*,hal,hant,hantly, A GAIN/ VICTORY/SUCCESS

triumphent, triumph(ant)

triumvaret, triumvirate

triumvirate, GROUP OF THREE

triveal, trivia(l)

trivet,*, STAND WITH THREE LEGS

triveu, trivia

triveul, trivia(l)

trivia,al,alness,ality,alities,alization,alize, ally, INSIGNIFICANT/UNIMPORTANT

trivit, trivet

troc, truck

trod,*,dden, PAST TENSE FOR THE WORD "TREAD", WALK HEAVILY/ SLOWLY WITH NO AMBITION (or see trot)

troden, trod(dden) / trot(tting)

trodeshinul, tradition(al)

trodin, trod(dden) / trot(tting)

trodition, tradition

troditional, tradition(al)

troe, troy

trof, trough / trove

trofe, trophy

trofl, truffle

trofy, trophy

trogectery, traject(ory)

troi, troy

trojektery, traject(ory)

trok, truck

trol, trawl / troll / trowel

trole, trolley / troll

troll,*,ller, TYPE OF SINGING, DRAGGING A HOOK, IMAGINARY CREATURE (or see trawl)

trolley,*, A CART/VEHICLE WITH WHEELS ON RAILS

troly, trolley
troma, trauma
tromatizd, trauma(tized)
trombone,*, A MUSICAL INSTRUMENT
tromel, trommel
trommel, ROUND SCREEN FOR SEPARATING VARIOUS SIZES OF ORGANIC MATERIAL
tromp,*,ped,ping, BIG/HEAVY FOOT STEPS, BEAT SOMEONE EXCESSIVELY (or see trump)
trompet, trumpet
tromu, trauma
tromul, trommel
tromutize, trauma(tize)
troobudor, troubadour
troop,*,ped,ping,per, AN ASSEMBLY/ GROUP/FLOCK (or see troupe)
troos, truce
tropeckul, tropic(al)
tropek, tropic
tropekul, tropic(al)
tropes, trapeze
trophe, trophy
trophy,hies,hic, MOUNTED HEAD OF ANIMAL, A COIN/ FIGURINE DESIGNED FOR AWARD/ ACHIEVEMENT
tropic,*,cal,cally, CONTINUOUS WARM WEATHER CLIMATE "prefixes: inter/ semi/sub"
tropickul, tropic(al)
tropik, tropic
tropikul, tropic(al)
trost, trust
trot,*,tted,tting,tter, STYLE OF WALKING/RUNNING (or see trout/ trod)
trotin, trod(dden) / trot(tting)
troubadour, POETS OF ANTIQUITY
trouble,*,ed,ling,esome,esomely, esomeness,lous, DIFFICULT/ CHALLENGING "prefixes: un"
trouf, trough / trove
trough,*, VESSEL FOR ANIMALS TO FEED/DRINK, RECTANGULAR/ SHALLOW CHANNEL/SHAPE
troul, trowel / troll
troupe,*,ped,ping, THEATER GROUP/ PERFORMERS (or see troop)
trousers, PANTS
trout, TYPE OF FISH
trouwl, trowel
trove,*, A FIND / DISCOVERY

trovers, traverse
trowel,*,led,ling,ler, HAND TOOL TO WORK PLASTER/MUD/MORTAR
trowsers, trousers
trowt, trout
trowzurs, trousers
troy, MEASUREMENT FOR WEIGHT OF PRECIOUS METALS
tru, true / through / thru / drew
truant,*,tly,ncy, NOT AT SCHOOL WITHOUT GOOD REASON
trubador, troubadour
trubel, trouble
trubidor, troubadour
trubudor, troubadour
trubul, trouble
truc, truck / truce
truce, COME TO AGREEMENT AFTER FIGHT/ARGUMENT (or see truss)
truch, trudge
truck,*,ked,king,ker, VEHICLE FOR HAULING/MOVING
trudeshin, tradition
trudeshinul, tradition(al)
trudge,*,ed,ging, WALK SLOWLY WITH HEAVY FEET
trudishenul, tradition(al)
trudition, tradition
truditional, tradition(al)
true,uly,uism,eness,uth, ACCURATE/ FACTUAL/REAL/STRAIGHT UP/ON THE LEVEL "prefixes: un"
truent, truant
truews, truce
truezm, true(uism)
trufal, truffle
truffle,*,ed, AN EDIBLE FUNGI, A CANDY
truful, truffle
trug, trudge
trugekt, traject
trugektery, traject(ory)
truint, truant
truizm, true(uism)
truj, trudge
trujd, trudge(d)
trujectery, traject(ory)
trujekt, traject
trujektery, traject(ory)
truk, truck
truker, truck(er)
trule, true(uly)
trumadik, trauma(tic)
trumendus, tremendous

trumindus, tremendous
trump,*,ped,ping,per,pery, OVERRANK/ SURPASS/DECEIVE (or see tromp)
trumpd, trump(ed) / tromp(ed)
trumpet,*,ter, BRASS HORNED INSTRUMENT
trumput, trumpet
trunc, trunk
truncate,*,ed,ting,tion, CUT OFF TIP/ END/PART OF, CUT SHORT
trundel, trundle
trundle,er, CIRCLE/WHEEL FOR ROTATION
trundul, trundle
trunk,*, MAIN BODY/PART FROM WHICH ALL THINGS EXTEND BEYOND, CONTAINER FOR ITEMS, ELEPHANT NOSE
trunkate, truncate
trupe, troop / troupe
trupel, trouble
truper, troop(er)
trupes, trapeze
trupir, troop(er)
trupl, trouble
trups, troop(s) / troupe(s)
trupul, trouble
trupur, troop(er)
trus, truce / truss
truse, truce / truss
truss,sses,sser, TO BOLSTER/SECURE/ SUPPORT WITH BEAMS/TIES/ROPE (or see truce)
trust,*,ted,ting,tee,tful,tfully,tfulness,ty, tiness, PLACE HOPE/ FAITH/BELIEF/ CONFIDENCE IN "prefixes: dis/en/ mis"
truste, trust(y)
truth,*,hless,hful,hfully,hfulness, ACCEPTED AS FACT/CONSTANCY/ ACTUAL "prefixes: un"
truvale, travail
truvers, traverse
truwent, truant
truz, truce / truss
try,ries,ried,ying,yingly, PUT TO THE TEST, ATTEMPT, DIFFICULT/ CHALLENGE TO ACCOMPLISH "prefixes: re"
tryd, tried / trite
trydent, trident
tryeng, try(ing)
tryn, trine
tsunami,ic, GIGANTIC TIDAL WAVE

tsunome, tsunami

tu, two / to / too

tub,*,bbable,bby,bbier,bbiest,bbiness, LARGE VESSEL/CONTAINER FOR LIQUID, ROUND LIKE A TUB (or see tube)

tuba,*, HORNED INSTRUMENT

tubaco, tobacco

tubagen, toboggan

tubako, tobacco

tube,*,ed,bing,er,eless,erous,bular, bularity,bule,bulous, CYLINDER/ ROUND SHAPE (or see tub)

tubequlosis, tuberculosis

tuberculosis,ous,ously, DISEASE OF THE LUNGS

tuberquelosis, tuberculosis

tubeulur, tube(bular)

tubir, tube(ber)

tubirquelosis, tuberculosis

tubles, tube(less)

tubogin, toboggan

tubu, tuba

tubur, tube(ber)

tuby, tub(bby)

tuc, took / tuck

tuch, touch / tush

tucha, touche'

tuche, touch(y) / touche'

tuchible, touch(able)

tuck,*,ked,king,ker,kered, TO PULL/ SECURE EDGES, PLACE AWAY SAFELY, WEARY/TIRED FROM WORKING

tuda, today

tuder, tutor

tudur, tutor

tuel, tool

tuesday,*, A DAY OF THE WEEK (ENGLISH)

tuf, tough

tufen, tough(en)

tufer, tough(er)

tufest, tough(est)

tuff, tough

tufin, tough(en)

tufir, tough(er)

tufist, tough(est)

tuft,*,ty,tier,tiest, CLUMP/CLUSTER/ BUNCH OF THREADS/ HAIR/ MATERIAL/ FUR

tufun, tough(en)

tufur, tough(er)

tug,*,gged,gging, TO PULL/DRAG/HAUL

tugethur, together

tugt, tug(gged)

tuil, tool

tuk, tuck / tug / took

tukd, tuck(ed) / tug(gged)

tuke, took

tukela, tequila

tukila, tequila

tuksedo, tuxedo

tuksido, tuxedo

tukt, tuck(ed) / tug

tukurd, tuck(ered)

tul, tool

tule, tool

tulep, tulip

tuleputhee, telepathy

tulip,*, A FLOWER

tum, tomb

tumaro, tomorrow

tumato, tomato

tumauro, tomorrow

tumbel, tumble

tumble,*,ed,ling,er, BE TOSSED ABOUT, A DRINKING VESSEL/CAM/LOCKING PART, BOLT ACTION, ACROBATICS

tumblir, tumble(r)

tumbul, tumble

tumer, tumor

tumerus, tumor(ous)

tumor,*,rous, A CLUMP/MASS OF TISSUE

tumoro, tomorrow

tumulchewus, tumult(uous)

tumulchuis, tumult(uous)

tumult,tuary,tuous,tuously,tuousness, DISTURBANCE/AGITATED/ DISORDER

tumures, tumor(ous)

tun, tune / toon / ton

tuna,*, SALT WATER FISH

tunacity, tenacity

tunaledy, tone(nality)

tunasedy, tenacity

tunasity, tenacity

tundra, ARCTIC PLAINS AROUND NORTH/SOUTH POLES

tundru, tundra

tune,*,ed,ning,er,eful,efully,efulness, eless, SET/ADJUST HARMONY/ FREQUENCY (or see toon) "prefixes: de"

tuneg, ton(nnage)

tunej, ton(nnage)

tunek, tunic

tunel, tunnel

tungsten,nic, METAL ELEMENT, TYPE OF FILAMENT IN LIGHT BULBS

tungstin, tungsten

tunic,*, LONG GARMENT, A COVERING

tunig, ton(nnage)

tunij, ton(nnage)

tunil, tunnel

tunir, tune(r)

tunite, tonight

tunl, tunnel

tunnel,*,led,ling,ler, TUBULAR SHAPED OPENING GOING INTO A SURFACE

tunor, tune(r)

tuns, tune(s) / ton(s) / toon(s)

tunsten, tungsten

tunstun, tungsten

tunt, tune(d)

tuntru, tundra

tunu, tuna

tunuk, tunic

tunul, tunnel

tunur, tune(r)

tup, tub

tupa, toupee

tupagrufe, topography

tupay, toupee

tupe, tube / tub(bby)

tupht, tuft

tupography, topography

tupogrufe, topography

tupuler, tube(bular)

tuquela, tequila

tuquila, tequila

tur, tour

turain, terrain / terrane

turanchula, tarantula

turane, terrain / terrane

turanshulu, tarantula

turantula, tarantula

turareum, terrarium

turazo, terrazzo

turban,*, LONG SCARF WRAPPED AS A HEADDRESS (or see turbine)

turben, turban / turbine

turbeulent, turbulent

turbin, turban / turbine

turbine,*, MOTOR WITH ROTORS SUPPLIED BY A CONSTANT FLOW (or see turban)

turbo,*, POWERED BY/AS IF BY A TURBINE MOTOR

turbon, turban / turbine

turbulens, turbulent(nce)

turbulent,tly,nce, ROUGH/ERRATIC/ RANDOM FLOW

turcoys, turquois

turd, tour(ed)

turdul, turtle

ture, tour

turefic, terrific

turenshul, torrent(ial)

turereum, terrarium

turesdreul, terrestrial

turestrial, terrestrial

turet, turret

turf,*,fy,fier,fiest, GRASS/ORGANIC MATERIAL FORMING A SURFACE BLANKET

turifek, terrific

turific, terrific

turist, tour(ist)

turisum, tour(ism)

turit, turret

turkes, turkey(s)

turkey,*, EDIBLE BIRD

turkie, turkey

turkois, turquois

turky, turkey

turm, term

turmaric, turmeric

turmenashen, terminate(tion)

turmenate, terminate

turmenator, terminate(tor)

turmenolegy, terminology

turmenul, terminal

turmeric, SPICE FROM A PLANT

turmeruk, turmeric

turminashen, terminate(tion)

turminate, terminate

turmination, terminate(tion)

turminator, terminate(tor)

turminolegy, terminology

turminul, terminal

turmoel, turmoil

turmoil, STATE OF STRESS/CONFUSION

turmonel, terminal

turn,*,ned,ning, CHANGE DIRECTION, ROTATE/CURVE/BEND IN COURSE "prefixes: over/up"

turnado, tornado

turnament, tournament

turnato, tornado

turnep, turnip

turniment, tournament

turnip,*, A VEGETABLE

turnument, tournament

turpentine, MINERAL SPIRIT WITH VOLATILE OIL

turpewlent, turbulent

turpulent, turbulent

turpuntine, turpentine

turquois, BLUE/GREEN GEMSTONE

turrestrial, terrestrial

turret,*, CYLINDRICAL OUTCROP AS SEEN ON CASTLES

turse, terse

tursheare, tertiary

turshury, tertiary

tursnes, terse(ness)

turtle,*, REPTILE WITH A SHELL

turut, turret

tusday, tuesday

tush,hes, REAR END, BUTTOCK (or see touch)

tusha, touche'

tusk,*,ked, LARGE EXTERIOR TOOTH

tusled, tousle(d)

tute, toot

tuter, tutor

tuth, tooth

tuthee, tooth(y)

tuthles, tooth(less)

tutir, tutor

tutolatarian, totalitarian

tutor,*,red,ring,rage,rial,elage, TO MENTOR/TEACH OR BE A GUARDIAN OF SOMEONE "prefixes: un"

tutu,*, OUTER GARMENT DANCERS WEAR

tutur, tutor

tuxedo, FORMAL ATTIRE FOR MEN

twain, RIVERBOAT TERM

twalth, twelfth

twan, twain

twang,gy, A VIBRATIONAL TONE

twank, twang

twead, tweed

tweak,*,ked,king,ker,ky, TO ADJUST

tweat, tweet

tweazer, tweezer

twed, tweed

twede, tweed(y)

tweder, tweeter

twedul, twiddle

twedur, tweeter

tweed,*,dy,dier,diest,diness, TYPE OF WOOL/WEAVE

tweek, tweak

tweenkul, twinkle

tweet,*, SOUND OF A BIRD

tweeter, TYPE OF SPEAKER FOR SOUND EQUIPMENT

tweezer,*, TOOL FOR PLUCKING/ PINCHING

tweg, twig

twek, tweak / twig

tweke, tweak(y)

twelf, twelve

twelfth,*, ONE OUT OF TWELVE

twelth, twelfth

twelve,*, ENGLISH NUMBER AFTER ELEVEN

twelvth, twelfth

twen, twin

twench, twinge

twende, twenty

twenge, twinge

twenj, twinge

twenkul, twinkle

twenteith, twentieth

twentes, twenty(ties)

twentie, twenty

twentieth, ONE PART OF TWENTY PARTS

twenty,ties,tieth, ENGLISH NUMBER AFTER NINETEEN

twentys, twenty(ties)

twerl, twirl

twerp, A DEROGATORY SLANG

tweser, tweezer

twest, twist

twesur, tweezer

twet, tweet

twetur, tweeter

twezer, tweezer

twhirl, twirl

twice, TWO TIMES

twidal, twiddle

twiddle,*,ed,ding,er, TO ROTATE ONE AROUND ANOTHER, IDLY TOY WITH SOMETHING

twidul, twiddle

twig,*,ggy, PART OF A WOODY BRANCH

twik, twig

twilid, twilight

twilight, SUNSET/SUNRISE

twilite, twilight

twin,*, TWO IDENTICAL/SIMILAR (or see twine)

twinch, twinge

twindy, twenty

twine,*,ed,ning, BRAIDED/TWISTED ROPE/THREAD (or see twin) "prefixes: en/inter"

twinge,*,ed,ging, SHARP/SUDDEN JERK RELATED TO PAINFUL SCENE/ EXPERIENCE

twinj, twinge

twinkal, twinkle

twinkle,*,ed,ling,er, SPARKLE/GLEAM OF LIGHT

twintieth, twentieth

twinty, twenty

twirl,*,led,ling,ler,ly, SPIN/WHIRL AROUND

twirp,*, DEROGATORY SLANG

twis, twice

twist,*,ted,ting,ter,ty, COILED ROTATION IN ACTION "prefixes: en/ in/inter/re"

two,*, ENGLISH NUMBER AFTER ONE (or see too/to)

twoberkeuloses, tuberculosis

twobu, tuba

twobuler, tube(bular)

twocha, touche'

twonik, tunic

twonu, tuna

twopa, toupee

tworl, twirl

twotwo, tutu

twurl, twirl

twurp, twerp / twirp

ty, tie

tydengs, tidings

tyeng, tying

tyfoed, typhoid

tyfus, typhus

tying, PRESENT PARTICIPLE FOR THE WORD 'TIE', TO FASTEN/LOOP/ ATTACH STRING/CORD, TO AFFIX "prefixes: re/un/under"

tyk, tike / tick

tynkshur, tincture

type,*,ed,ping,er,eable,eability,pist, USE OF A MACHINE TO CREATE TEXT (or see tip) "prefixes: mis/pre/ re/sub/un"

typecul, typical

typefy, typify

typhis, typhus

typhoid, DISEASE OF THE INTESTINES

typhoon,*, HURRICANE

typhus,hous, A DISEASE CAUSED BY FLEAS

typical,lly,lness,lity, PREDICTABLE/ CHARACTERISTIC

typicul, typical

typify,fies,fied,fying,fication, SYMBOLIZES

typikul, typical

typo,*, TEXT ERROR

typukle, typical

tyrane, tyranny

tyranekal, tyrannical

tyranikul, tyrannical

tyrannical,lly,lness, OF BEING CRUEL/ PREDATORY

tyranny,nnies,nnous,nnously, nnousness,nnize,nnizes,nnized, nnizing,nnizer, nnic,nnical,nnically, nnicalness,nnicide, EVENT INVOLVING CRUEL/VICIOUS PREDATOR WHO EXPLOITS VICTIMS

tyrant,*,nny, CRUEL VICIOUS PREDATOR, ONE WHO EXPLOITS VICTIMS

tyreny, tyranny

u, you / yew / ewe

ubart, apart

ubat, abate

ubatment, abate(ment)

ubedeins, obedience

ubedeint, obedient

ubeding, abet(tting)

ubedy, uppity

ubel, appeal

ubelaty, ability

ubelte, ability

ubet, abet

ubeting, abet(tting)

ubikwety, ubiquity

ubilde, ability

ubiledy, ability

ubilte, ability

ubiquity,tous,tary,tously,tousness, OMNIPRESENT, EXISTS EVERYWHERE

ubity, uppity

ubleveus, oblivious

ubli, apply

ublid, apply(lied)

ublig, oblige(d)

ublij, oblige(d)

ubliveus, oblivious

ubliz, apply(lies)

ubolesh, abolish

ubord, aboard / abort

uborded, abort(ed)

ubort, abort / aboard

ubprnetis, apprentice

ubpropreat, appropriate

ubrenis, apprentice

ubresheate, appreciate

ubreshen, oppress(ion)

ubretiate, appreciate

ubreveashen, abbreviate(tion)

ubreveat, abbreviate

ubriged, abridged

ubroch, approach

ubrod, abroad

ubroof, approve

ubropreat, appropriate

ubrosh, approach

ubruf, approve

ubruv, approve

ubsakwently, subsequent(ly)

ubserd, absurd

ubsesd, obsess(ed)

ubseshen, obsess(ion)

ubset, upset

ubsolv, absolve

ubstane, abstain

ubstrakshen, obstruct(ion) / abstract(ion)

ubstrukt, obstruct

ubtane, obtain

ubtrude, obtrude

ubtrusive, obtrusive

ubzerd, absurd

ubzerve, observe

ubzolv, absolve

ubzorb, absorb

ubzurv, observe

ucemble, assemble

ucend, ascend

ucenshen, ascension

uchamed, ashamed

ucher, assure

ucide, aside

ucimbul, assemble

ucinshen, ascension

ucompany, accompany

ucumpany, accompany

ucumulate, accumulate

udalize, utilize

udapt, adapt

udder,*, TEATS ON A MILKING ANIMALS (or see utter)

udendum, addendum

uder, odor / otter / outer / utter / udder

uderus, uterus

udeshen, edition / add(ition)
udindum, addendum
udir, odor / otter / outer / utter / udder
udirens, utter(ance)
udirus, uterus
udishen, edition / add(ition)
udopt, adopt
udor, udder / utter / adore / odor/ otter
udrausety, atrocity
udroit, adroit
udrosity, atrocity
udulize, utilize
udur, odor / otter / outer / utter / udder
ufael, avail
ufermutif, affirm(ative)
ufeshent, efficient
ufileashen, affiliate(tion)
ufileate, affiliate
ufishent, efficient
ugilede, agile(ty)
ugilety, agile(ty)
ugle, ugly
ugleist, ugly(liest)
ugleur, ugly(lier)
ugly,lies,lier,liest, UNATTRACTIVE
ugre, agree
ugresev, aggressive
ugreshen, aggression
ugresuv, aggressive
ugretion, aggression
uhbart, apart
uhbli, apply
uhblid, apply(lied)
uhbliz, apply(lies)
uhbprnetis, apprentice
uhbpropreat, appropriate
uhbrenis, apprentice
uhbresheate, appreciate
uhbreshete, appreciate
uhbretiate, appreciate
uhbroch, approach
uhbroof, approve
uhbropreat, appropriate
uhbrosh, approach
uhbruhf, approve
uhcemble, assemble
uhcend, ascend
uhcenshen, ascension
uhchamed, ashamed
uhcher, assure
uhcide, aside
uhcimbul, assemble

uhcinshen, ascension
uhdrausety, atrocity
uhdrosity, atrocity
uhod, ahold
uhold, ahold
uhpairent, apparent
uhpairul, apparel
uhpalugize, apology(gize)
uhpalugy, apology(gize)
uhparent, apparent
uhpart, apart
uhpartment, apartment
uhparul, apparel
uhpastrufe, apostrophe
uhpauluge, apology
uhpaulugize, apology(gize)
uhpaurtment, apartment
uhpaustrufe, apostrophe
uhpealing, appeal(ing)
uhpearanc, appearance
uhpearinse, appearance
uhpeel, appeal
uhpel, appeal
uhperense, appearance
uhperent, apparent
uhperinse, appearance
uhperul, apparel
uhpil, appeal
uhplaud, applaud
uhplaus, applause
uhpli, apply
uhplod, applaud
uhplos, applause
uhpoent, appoint
uhpoentment, appointment
uhpoint, appoint
uhpointment, appointment
uhpoluge, apology
uhpolugize, apology(gize)
uhport, apart
uhportment, apartment
uhpostrufe, apostrophe
uhpotment, appointment
uhpoynt, appoint
uhppearanc, appearance
uhpperinse, appearance
uhpperul, apparel
uhpplaud, applaud
uhpplause, applause
uhpplod, applaud
uhpply, apply
uhpprentis, apprentice
uhppreshiate, appreciate
uhppropriate, appropriate

uhpprove, approve
uhpproximate, approximate
uhpproximately, approximate(ly)
uhpraisul, appraisal
uhprased, appraise(d)
uhpraz, appraise
uhprazul, appraisal
uhpreceashun, appreciate(tion)
uhprecheat, appreciate
uhpreciate, appreciate
uhprenis, apprentice
uhprentis, apprentice
uhpresheate, appreciate
uhpresheation, appreciate(tion)
uhpreshete, appreciate
uhpreshetion, appreciate(tion)
uhpretiate, appreciate
uhprintes, apprentice
uhprisheate, appreciate
uhproach, approach
uhprobreat, appropriate
uhproch, approach
uhproksamit, approximate
uhproksamitly, approximate(ly)
uhproksumit, approximate
uhproksumitly, approximate(ly)
uhproof, approve
uhproovul, approve(val)
uhpropreit, appropriate
uhprosh, approach
uhproximate, approximate
uhproximatly, approximate(ly)
uhpruhf, approve
uhpruhval, approve(val)
uhrain, arraign
uhraingment, arrange(ment)
uhrainment, arraign(ment)
uhrane, arraign
uhrangment, arrange(ment)
uhranjment, arrange(ment)
uhranment, arraign(ment)
uhrear, arrear
uhreighnment, arraign(ment)
uhreinment, arraign(ment)
uhrena, arena
uhrer, arrear
uhrest, arrest
uhriful, arrival
uhrina, arena
uhrivul, arrival
uhroma, aroma
uhround, around
uhrouz, arouse
uhrownd, around

uhrows, arouse
uhrrear, arrear
uhrrest, arrest
uhrrivol, arrival
uhsacin, assassin
uhsail, assail
uhsal, assail
uhsalant, assail(ant)
uhsalt, assault
uhsasen, assassin
uhsault, assault
uhsberugus, asparagus
uhscend, ascend
uhscention, ascension
uhsdonesh, astonish
uhsdrawnumy, astronomy
uhsdronumy, astronomy
uhsemble, assemble
uhsemelate, assimilate
uhsemilate, assimilate
uhsemlate, assimilate
uhsend, ascend
uhsenshen, ascension
uhsent, assent
uhsention, ascension
uhsershen, assert(ion)
uhsert, assert
uhsertion, assert(ion)
uhses, assess / use(s)
uhsesment, assessment
uhsest, assist
uhsestens, assist(ance)
uhsestins, assist(ance)
uhseum, assume
uhsfekseate, asphyxiate
uhshamed, ashamed
uhside, aside
uhsign, assign
uhsilem, asylum
uhsimbul, assemble
uhsimelate, assimilate
uhsin, assign
uhsind, ascend
uhsinment, assignment
uhsinshen, ascension
uhsint, assent
uhsirshen, assert(ion)
uhsirt, assert
uhsirtion, assert(ion)
uhsist, assist
uhsistens, assist(ance)
uhsleep, asleep
uhslep, asleep
uhsocheat, associate

uhsocheation, associate(tion)
uhsociate, associate
uhsociation, associate(tion)
uhsolt, assault
uhsosheashun, associate(tion)
uhsosheut, associate
uhsoshiat, associate
uhsoshiation, associate(tion)
uhsparugus, asparagus
uhsperugus, asparagus
uhsphikseate, asphyxiate
uhspire, aspire
uhssal, assail
uhssasin, assassin
uhssenble, assemble
uhstonish, astonish
uhstraunume, astronomy
uhstronumy, astronomy
uhstrownumy, astronomy
uhsum, assume
uhsumpshen, assumption
uhsur, assure
uhsurt, assert
uhsylim, asylum
uhtach, attach
uhtachment, attach(ment)
uhtack, attack
uhtain, attain
uhtainable, attain(able) / obtain(able)
uhtak, attack
uhtanable, attain(able) / obtain(able)
uhtane, attain
uhtanmint, attain(ment)
uhtash, attach
uhtempt, attempt
uhtemt, attempt
uhtend, attend
uhtendens, attend(ance)
uhtending, attend(ing)
uhtenshen, attention
uhtentef, attentive
uhtentefness, attentive(ness)
uhtention, attention
uhtentive, attentive
uhtimt, attempt
uhtind, attend
uhtindens, attend(ance)
uhtinding, attend(ing)
uhtinshen, attention
uhtintef, attentive
uhtintion, attention
uhtintive, attentive
uhtintiveness, attentive(ness)
uhtire, attire

uhtrausety, atrocity
uhtrochus, atrocious
uhtroshes, atrocious
uhtrosity, atrocity
uhwrest, arrest
uhwround, around
uhwrous, arouse
ujar, ajar
ujaur, ajar
ujiledy, agile(lity)
ujilety, agile(lity)
ujor, ajar
ukalale, ukulele
ukaumplish, accomplish
ukews, accuse
ukilale, ukulele
ukle, ugly
ukomplesh, accomplish
ukomplis, accomplice
ukomplish, accomplish
ukomudate, accommodate
ukord, accord
ukordant, accord(ant)
ukount, account
ukresif, aggressive
ukulale, ukulele
ukulayle, ukulele
ukulele,*, SMALL FOUR STRING GUITAR
ukumpany, accompany
ukumplish, accomplish
ukumulate, accumulate
ukumulation, accumulate(tion)
ukustemed, accustom(ed)
ukuz, accuse
ukwire, acquire
ularm, alarm
ulcer,*,red,rate,rated,rating,ration,
    rative,rous,rousness, FESTERED
    SORES IN THE LINING OF THE
    STOMACH
ulceradid, ulcer(ated)
ulcir, ulcer
ulcirashen, ulcer(ation)
ulcur, ulcer
uldamatum, ultimatum
uldamitle, ultimate(ly)
uldimatum, ultimatum
uldimetle, ultimate(ly)
uldrusonek, ultrasonic
uldumatum, ultimatum
uldumetle, ultimate(ly)
ule, you'll / yule
ulecit, elicit / illicit
uliens, alliance

ulif, alive
ulike, alike
ulin, align
ulinment, align(ment)
ulions, alliance
uliptic, elliptic
uliset, elicit / illicit
uliv, alive
uloof, aloof
ulope, elope
ulostrious, illustrious
ulow, allow
ulowanse, allowance
ulser, ulcer
ulseradid, ulcer(ated)
ulserashen, ulcer(ation)
ulsirashen, ulcer(ation)
ulsur, ulcer
ulsurashen, ulcer(ation)
ulsurated, ulcer(ated)
ultamatem, ultimatum
ultament, ultimate
ultametle, ultimate(ly)
ultemit, ultimate
ultereur, ulterior
ulterior,rly, UNDERLYING, SECRETIVE,
    NOT UP FRONT (or see alterior)
ultimate,ely,eness, THE GREATEST OF
    ALL
ultimatum,ta, FINAL, DO THIS OR A
    PENALTY RESULTS
ultimetly, ultimate(ly)
ultireor, ulterior
ultra, THE GREATEST/MOST/BEST/
    EXTREME
ultrasonic,*, ABOVE 20,000
    VIBRATIONS PER SECOND
ultru, ultra
ultrusonek, ultrasonic
ultumetle, ultimate(ly)
ultumint, ultimate
ultumit, ultimate
uluf, aloof
ulustrious, illustrious
um, them
umaunt, amount
umbelikul, umbilical
umbilical,ate,ated,ation, RELATING TO
    THE NAVEL
umbrella,*, DOME-SHAPED COVER FOR
    PROTECTION "prefixes: sub"
umeba, amoeba
umend, amend
umindment, amend(ment)

umonea, ammonia
umount, amount
umpede, impede
un, PREFIX INDICATING THAT "NOT/
    REVERSAL" MOST OFTEN MODIFIES
    THE WORD (or see prefix in/en)
unable, NOT ABLE/CAPABLE(or see
    enable/inability)
unabridged, IN ITS FULL LENGTH
unabriged, unabridged
unacceptable, WILL NOT BE ALLOWED,
    NOT ACCEPTABLE
unacdev, enact(ive) / inactive
unacebtible, unacceptable
unacorn, unicorn
unacseptible, unacceptable
unactive, enact(ive) / inactive
unacurate, innacurate
unacycle, unicycle
unadime, anatomy
unafekachen, unification
unafi, unify
unafid, unify(fied)
unafiuble, unify(fiable)
unaform, uniform
unaformety, uniform(ity)
unaformly, uniform(ly)
unakdev, enact(ive)/ inactive
unakorn, unicorn
unakseptible, unacceptable
unaktef, inactive / enact(ive)
unaktive, enact(ive) / inactive
unakuret, inaccurate
unamoly, anomaly
unanamus, unanimous
unanimous,sly,mity, AGREED TO BY
    TWO OR MORE PEOPLE
unanomus, unanimous
unapel, unable
unapl, unable
unappreciative, inappreciative
unapresheative, inappreciative
unapropreat, inappropriate
unasen, unison
unasikle, unicycle
unasycle, unicycle
unat, innate
unate, unity
unaterein, unitary(rian)
unatery, unitary
unathekol, (un)ethic(al)
unathical, (un)ethic(al)
unatize, unite(tize)
unaty, unity

unaumily, anomaly
unavers, universe
unaversal, universal
unaversity, university
unaversule, universal(lly)
unavirs, universe
unavirsity, university
unavirsul, universal
unavurs, universe
unavursal, universal
unavursity, university
unaxseptible, unacceptable
unbanone, unbeknown
unbanonst, unbeknown(st)
unbeknown,nst, NOT KNOWN
unbenon, unbeknown
unbenonst, unbeknown(st)
unbenownst, unbeknown(st)
unbinone, unbeknown
unbinonst, unbeknown(st)
unbunownst, unbeknown(st)
uncal, uncle
uncane, uncanny
uncanily, uncanny(nnily)
uncanines, uncanny(niness)
uncanny,nnier,nniest,nily,nnniness, NOT
    FORESEEN/ORDINARY
uncanuly, uncanny(nily)
uncany, uncanny
uncase, encase
uncased, encase(d)
uncel, uncle
unchues, unction(tuous)
uncil, uncle
uncle,*, THE BROTHER OF A FATHER/
    MOTHER
uncoherent, incoherent
unconscionable,eness,ly, COMPLETELY
    UNACCEPTABLE
uncroach, encroach
uncrust, encrust
uncshen, unction
uncshuosity, unction(tuosity)
unction,*,tuous,tuosity,tuously,
    tousness, INSINCERE FLATTERY/
    CHARM, VERY SOFT/RICH, OILY/
    SOOTHING SUBSTANCE
undemic, endemic
under, PREFIX INDICATING THAT
    "BELOW/INCOMPLETE" MOST
    OFTEN MODIFIES THE WORD
undergerd, undergird
undergird,*,ded,ding,rt, SUPPORT/
    SECURE FROM BELOW

underhand,ded,dedly,dedness, DISHONEST

undermine,*,ed,ning,er, REMOVE CREDIBILITY OF SOMEONE, ETCH AWAY AT THE FOUNDATION/ BASE/ FOOTING OF SOMETHING/ SOMEONE

underneath, BELOW/UNDERSIDE/ LOWER, NOT VISIBLE

underneeth, underneath

underneth, underneath

underpass,sses, ROAD UNDER A BRIDGE

underpin,*,nned,nning,nnings, SUPPORT/FOUNDATION FOR SOMETHING

understand,*,tood,ding,dability,dable, dably,dingly, KNOW/ COMPREHEND/ PERCEIVE "prefixes: mis"

understate,*,ed,ting,ement,ements, NOT FULLY RELEASING THE FACTS/ IMPORTANCE

understood, PAST TENSE FOR THE WORD "UNDERSTAND"

underway, ACTIVELY MOVING ALONG, IN THE PROCESS TOWARDS COMPLETION

underwear, UNDER CLOTHING

undes, undies

undeulate, undulate

undewlashen, undulate(tion)

undewlate, undulate

undewlated, undulate(d)

undewly, unduly

undies, SHORT FOR UNDERWEAR

undirhand, underhand

undirhandedly, underhand(edly)

undirhandid, underhand(ed)

undirmind, undermine(d)

undirmine, undermine

undirneth, underneath

undirstand, understand

undirstood, understood

undirstude, understood

undirwa, underway

undirwar, underwear

undole, unduly

undoly, unduly

undoole, unduly

undulashen, undulate(tion)

undulate,*,ed,ting,tion,tory,ant, WAVE MOTION

unduly, BEYOND MODERATION, UNLAWFUL

undurhand, underhand

undurhandidly, underhand(edly)

undurmind, undermine(d)

undurmine, undermine

undurneth, underneath

undurstand, understand

undurstood, understood

undurstude, understood

undurwa, underway

uneak, unique

unearth,*,hed,hing,hly,hliness, REMOVE FROM THE EARTH/DIRT, SOLVE A MYSTERY, NOT OF THIS PLANE/REALITY

unebreated, inebriate(d)

unebriated, inebriate(d)

unebriged, unabridged

unecorn, unicorn

unecycle, unicycle

uneek, unique

uneekle, unique(ly)

uneeknes, unique(ness)

unefi, unify

unefid, unify(fied)

unefikashen, unification

uneform, uniform

uneformedy, uniform(ity)

uneformety, uniform(ity)

uneformly, uniform(ly)

unefy, unify

unegma, enigma / enema

unek, unique

unekle, unique(ly)

uneknes, unique(ness)

unekorn, unicorn

unekwitable, inequitable

unekwity, inequity

unekwul, inequal

uneladeral, unilateral

unelateral, unilateral

unema, enema / anemia

unemea, anemia / enema

unemek, anemic

uneonize, union(ize)

uneque, unique

unequitable, inequitable

unequity, inequity

unerth, unearth

unerthd, unearth(ed)

unesikul, unicycle

uneson, unison

unesunus, unison(ous)

unesycle, unicycle

unet, unit

unetarean, unitary(rian)

unetary, unitary

unete, unity

unethecal, (un)ethic(al)

unethical, (un)ethic(al)

unety, unity

uneversal, universal

unevursal, universal

unferl, unfurl

unflagging,gingly, TIRELESS, UNCHANGING

unflagingly, unflagging(ly)

unflapable, unflappable

unflappable,bility,ly, ABLE TO MAINTAIN CONSISTENT COMPOSURE NO MATTER WHAT

unfleched, unfledged

unfledged, INMATURE, LACKS ADULT FEATHERS

unflegd, unfledged

unflejd, unfledged

unfortunate,*,ely,eness, WILL/DID NOT TURN OUT AS PLANNED

unfurl,*,led,ling, TO UNROLL OR SPREAD OUT

ungainly,liness, AWKWARD IN MOVEMENT/APPEARANCE

unganly, ungainly

ungulate,*,ed, MAMMAL WITH HOOVES

uni, PREFIX INDICATING THAT "ONE/ SINGLE" MOST OFTEN MODIFIES THE WORD

unibreated, inebriate(d)

unicorn,*, A MYTHOLOGICAL HORSE WITH A HORN COMING FROM IT'S FOREHEAD

unicycle,*,ling, ONE-WHEELED CYCLE (or monocycle)

unifekachen, unification

unifi, unify

unification, BROUGHT TOGETHER AS ONE/UNIFIED PART

unifid, unify(fied)

unifikachen, unification

uniform,*,med,mly,mity,mness, mitarian,mitarianism, NEAR EXACT IN FORM/ SHAPE/APPEARANCE/ CHARACTER

uniformedy, uniform(ity)

uniformety, uniform(ity)

unify,fies,fied,fier,fying,fiable,fication, ABILITY TO BE BROUGHT TOGETHER AS ONE/UNIFIED PART "prefixes: non/re/un"

unifyable, unify(fiable)

unigma, enigma / enema

unikle, unique(ly)

unilateral,*,lly,lism,list, ONE UNIFIED/ LATERAL SIDE OF AN AXIS/LINEAGE/ ORGANISM/PART

unimea, anemia / enema

union,*,nism,nist,nize,nized,nizing, nization,nism, BRING/FORM TOGETHER AS ONE, ALL PARTS COMING TOGETHER WORKING AS ONE (or see onion) "prefixes: dis/ re"

unique,ely,eness, UNMATCHED, ONE OF A KIND

unirth, unearth

unirthd, unearth(ed)

unisen, unison

unisikul, unicycle

unison,nal,nous, ONE IN SOUND

unisycle, unicycle

unit,*,tage,ty, ONE PART/COMPONENT OF THE WHOLE "prefixes: sub"

unitarein, unitary(rian)

unitary,rian,rianism, CHARACTER WITHIN A UNIT, AS A UNIT

unite,*,ed,ting,table,er,edly,tive,tize, tizes,tized,tizing,tization,ty, ALL PARTS/ SECTIONS/FACTIONS COMING TOGETHER/ FUNCTIONING AS ONE/WHOLE (or see unity) "prefixes: dis/re"

uniterein, unitary(rian)

unituble, unite(table)

unity, ALL AS ONE, A JOINING (or see unite) "prefixes: dis"

universal,*,lly,lness,lism,list,lity,lities, lize,lization, APPLIES/ACCEPTED/ RELATING TO EVERYWHERE/ EVERYONE/EVERYTHING

universe,*, OF ONE, ALL TOGETHER

university,ties, A PLACE OF HIGHER EDUCATION

univurs, universe

univursal, universal

univursity, university

univursuly, universal(lly)

unjulate, ungulate

unkal, uncle

unkanely, uncanny(nily)

unkanenes, uncanny(niness)

unkany, uncanny

unkapacitated, incapacitate(d)

unkarnate, incarnate

unkase, encase

unkel, uncle

unkoherent, incoherent

unkonsheonable, unconscionable

unkroch, encroach

unkrust, encrust

unkshen, unction

unkshues, unction(tuous)

unkshuosedy, unction(tuosity)

unkshuosity, unction(tuosity)

unktion, unction

unkul, uncle

unles, unless

unless, OR, IN PLACE OF, AN EXCEPTION

unoculate, inoculate

unogeration, inaugurate(tion)

unoint, anoint

unokulate, inoculate

unomaly, anomaly

unovers, universe

unoversity, university

unowgeration, inaugurate(tion)

unoy, annoy

unroole, unruly

unruly,lier,liest,liness, NOT OBEDIENT/ CONFORMING

unsanitere, insanitary

unsbekable, unspeakable

unsboken, unspoken

unshuous, unction(tuous)

unspeakable,eness,ly,poken, NOT MAKE VERBAL SOUNDS, NOT MEANT TO BE SAID/SPOKEN

unspoken, NOT MAKE VERBAL SOUNDS, NOT TO BE SAID/SPOKEN

untel, until

until, TIME BETWEEN NOW AND THE FUTURE/NEXT TIME

unto, SAME AS THE WORD 'UNTIL', SOMETHING ACCOMPLISHED (or see onto)

untoward,*,dly,dness, NOT APPROPRIATE/PROPER, ADVERSE

untuord, untoward

untuosity, unction(tuosity)

untuword, untoward

untwo, unto / onto

untwoward, untoward

unubriged, unabridged

unucorn, unicorn

unufikachen, unification

unufikashen, unification

unuformady, uniform(ity)

unukorn, unicorn

unupropreat, inappropriate

unurth, unearth

unurthd, unearth(ed)

unusin, unison

unut, unit

unuvers, universe

unuversity, university

unuversule, universal(lly)

unuvirs, universe

unvasef, invasive

unvashen, invasion

unweting, unwitting

unwetingly, unwitting(ly)

unwitting,gly, NOT KNOWING/AWARE

unwrule, unruly

unyen, union / onion

unyon, union / onion

unyunize, union(ize)

up, DIRECTION TOWARDS THE SKY, PREFIX INDICATING THAT "MOST RECENTLY/HIGHER" MOST OFTEN MODIFIES THE WORD "prefixes: re"

upairent, apparent

upairul, apparel

upald, appall(lled)

upalugize, apology(gize)

upalugy, apology(gize)

upar, upper

uparent, apparent

upart, apart

upartment, apartment

uparul, apparel

upastrufe, apostrophe

upauld, appall(lled)

upauluge, apology

upaulugize, apology(gize)

upaurtment, apartment

upaustrufe, apostrophe

upbeat, HIGHER NOTE/FREQUENCY/ ATTITUDE

upbet, upbeat

upealing, appeal(ing)

upearanc, appearance

upearinse, appearance

upedy, uppity

upeel, appeal

upel, appeal

uper, upper

uperense, appearance

uperent, apparent
uperinse, appearance
uperul, apparel
upety, uppity
upheave,*,ed,ving,val, A LIFTING/ RISING OF
upheeve, upheave
uphev, upheave
uphevel, upheave(val)
uphevul, upheave(val)
uphold,*,held,ding, SUPPORT/ MAINTAIN
upholestury, upholstery
upholsdure, upholstery
upholster,*,red,ring,rer,ry, OF COVERING FURNITURE "prefixes: re"
upholstery,ries,rer, FABRICS FOR COVERING "prefixes: re"
upholsture, upholstery
upil, appeal
upir, upper
upity, uppity
upland, HIGHER REGION/GROUND
uplaud, applaud
uplaus, applause
uplefeus, oblivious
uplend, upland
upleveus, oblivious
upli, apply
uplifeus, oblivious
uplige, oblige(d)
upliveus, oblivious
uplod, applaud
uplos, applause
upoent, appoint
upoentment, appointment
upoint, appoint
upointment, appointment
upold, appall(lled) / uphold
upolstri, upholstery
upoluge, apology
upolugize, apology(gize)
upon, VERY CLOSE TO, UP ON
upord, aboard
uport, apart
uportment, apartment
upostrufe, apostrophe
upotment, appointment
upov, above
upoynt, appoint
uppearanc, appearance
upper, THE HIGHER LEVEL
upperinse, appearance

upperul, apparel
uppity,yness, SOMEONE BEHAVING STUCK-UP
upplaud, applaud
upplause, applause
upplod, applaud
upply, apply
upprentis, apprentice
uppreshiate, appreciate
uppropriate, appropriate
upprove, approve
upproximate, approximate
upproximately, approximate(ly)
upraisul, appraisal
uprased, appraise(d)
uprasef, abrasive
uprasul, appraisal
upraz, appraise
uprazel, appraisal
uprazif, abrasive
upreceashun, appreciate(tion)
uprecheat, appreciate
upreciate, appreciate
uprenis, apprentice
uprentis, apprentice
upresheat, appreciate
upresheate, appreciate
upresheation, appreciate(tion)
upreshen, oppress(ion)
upreshetion, appreciate(tion)
upress, oppress
upression, oppress(ion)
upretiate, appreciate
upreveate, abbreviate
upright,tly,tness, BE VERTICAL, BE IN THE RIGHT
uprintes, apprentice
uprise,*,rose,sing, STAND UP FOR/ AGAINST/WITH, RISE UP
uprisheate, appreciate
uprite, upright
uproach, approach
uproar,rious,riously,riousness, COMMOTION/DISTURBANCE, ELEVATED EMOTIONAL STATE
uprobreat, appropriate
uproch, approach
uproksamit, approximate
uproksumit, approximate
uproksumitly, approximate(ly)
uproof, approve
uproot,*,ted,ting,ter, REMOVE ROOTS FROM THE GROUND
uproovul, approve(val)

upropreit, appropriate
upror, uproar
uprose, PAST TENSE FOR THE WORD UPRISE
uprosh, approach
uproximate, approximate
uproximatly, approximate(ly)
upruf, approve
uprut, uproot
uprutid, uproot(ed)
upruv, approve
upruval, approve(val)
upserd, absurd
upsesed, obsess(ed)
upseshion, obsess(ion)
upset,*,tting, A DISTURBANCE/ IMBALANCE
upsolv, absolve
upstag, upstage
upstage,*,ed,ging, TO DISTRACT THE AUDIENCE FROM SOMEONE ELSE, BACK OF THE STAGE
upstairs, GO TO UPPER LEVEL BY MEANS OF STAIRS
upstaj, upstage
upstajd, upstage(d)
upstars, upstairs
upsters, upstairs
upsurd, absurd
uptane, obtain
uptrood, obtrude
uptroosiv, obtrusive
uptrude, obtrude
upur, upper
upward,*, MOVE UP
upwerd, upward
upwholstery, upholstery
upwird, upward
upwort, upward
upwright, upright
upwrite, upright
upwror, uproar
upwruted, uproot(ed)
upwurd, upward
upzolv, absolve
uracer, eraser
uradiate, irradiate
uradik, erotic / erratic
urain, arraign
uraingment, arrange(ment)
urainment, arraign(ment)
uralogy, urology
uran, urine / arraign
uraneum, uranium

urangment, arrange(ment)
uranium, A METAL CHEMICAL
uranjment, arrange(ment)
uranment, arraign(ment)
uranology,gies,gical, STUDY OF
    ASTRONOMY/THE HEAVENS
urase, erase
uraser, eraser
urater, ureter
urathane, urethane
uraudik, erotic
urban,nism,nist,nistic,nistically,nite,nity,
    nities,nize,nizes,nized,nizing,
    nization, LIFE ON THE OUTSKIRTS
    OF CITY "prefixes: sub"
urben, urban
urbenite, urban(ite)
urbon, urban
urbonite, urban(ite)
urchen, urchin
urchin,*, A SEA CREATURE
urea,al,eic, CHEMICAL IN URINE
urear, arrear
uregenal, origin(al)
uregenate, originate
ureighnment, arraign(ment)
ureik, urea(eic)
ureinment, arraign(ment)
urejenate, originate
urejinal, origin(al)
urek, uric
uren, urine
urena, arena
urenaded, urinate(d)
urenary, urinary
urenate, urinate
urenology, uranology
urenul, urinal
urer, arrear
urest, arrest
ureter,ral,ric, CANAL FROM KIDNEY TO
    BLADDER CONTAINED WITHIN THE
    BODY
uretha, urethra
urethane, A MANMADE CHEMICAL
urethra,*,al, TUBE IN THE BODY WHICH
    FUNNELS URINE FOR DISCHARGE
urgd, urge(d)
urge,*,ed,ging,er,gingly,ency,ent,ently,
    OVERWHELMING DESIRE TO
    ACCOMPLISH/FULFILL
urgint, urge(nt)
urgis, urge(s)
uri, awry

uria, urea
uric, OF THE URINE
urif, arrive
uriful, arrival
uriginal, origin(al)
uriginate, originate
urijenal, origin(al)
urik, uric
urin, urine
urina, arena
urinal, A DEVICE/VESSEL FOR MALE'S
    TO URINATE INTO
urinary, OF THE URINE
urinate,*,ed,ting,tion, ACT OF
    RELEASING/DISCHARGING URINE
urine, LIQUID WASTE SECRETION
urinery, urinary
urinology, uranology
urinul, urinal
uriter, ureter
urithane, urethane
urithra, urethra
uriv, arrive
urivul, arrival
urj, urge
urjd, urge(d)
urjent, urge(nt)
urjinse, urge(ncy)
urli, early
urn,*, VESSEL USED TO MAKE BUTTER,
    HOLD CONTENTS (or see earn/
    yearn/urine)
urodik, erotic
urolegy, urology
urology,gic,gical,gist, FIELD OF SCIENCE
    STUDYING THE URINARY TRACT
urolugy, urology
uroma, aroma
uron, urine
uround, around
urouz, arouse
urownd, around
urows, arouse
urrear, arrear
urrest, arrest
urrivol, arrival
urs, your(s)
urunal, urinal
urunate, urinate
urunery, urinary
urunology, uranology
us, PEOPLE INCLUDING SELF (or see
    ooze/use/yew(s))
usabil, usable

usable,*,bility,ly,eness, ABLE TO BE
    USED "prefixes: re/un"
usacin, assassin
usage,*, ABILITY TO BE USED/UTILIZED
    "prefixes: mis"
usail, assail
usal, assail
usalant, assail(ant)
usalt, assault
usary, usury
usasen, assassin
usault, assault
usberugus, asparagus
uscend, ascend
uscention, ascension
usd, use(d)
usdonesh, astonish
usdrawnumy, astronomy
usdronumy, astronomy
use,*,ed,sing,sable,sability,sage,sance,
    eful,efully,efulness,eless,elessly,
    elessness,er,sable, EMPLOY/
    EXPLOIT/UTILIZE TO ACCOMPLISH/
    ACHIEVE SUCCESS, EXPLOIT
    RESOURCES (or see yew(s))
    "prefixes: dis/mis/multi/non/over/
    re/un/under"
useage, usage
usebil, usable
useble, usable
usech, usage
usedik, acetic / acidic / ascetic
useful,lly,lness, ABLE TO BE UTILIZED
    EASILY
useg, usage
usej, usage
useless,sly,sness, NOT ABLE TO BE
    UTILIZED EASILY
uselis, useless
usemble, assemble
usemelate, assimilate
usemilate, assimilate
usemlate, assimilate
usend, ascend
usenshen, ascension
usent, assent
usention, ascension
user,*, ONE WHO EXPLOITS OTHERS/
    RESOURCES, THOSE WHO USE
    DRUGS (or see usury)
usere, usury
userp, usurp
userped, usurp(ed)
usershen, assert(ion)

usert, assert
usertev, assert(ive)
usertion, assert(ion)
usery, usury
uses, assess / use(s)
useshun, accession
usesment, assessment
usest, assist
usestens, assist(ance)
usestins, assist(ance)
useum, assume
usfekseat, asphyxiate
usfikseat, asphyxiate
usfixeat, asphyxiate
usful, useful
ushamed, ashamed
usher,*,red,ring, TENDS TO GUESTS AT
     PUBLIC GATHERING, INDUCE/
     ESCORT/ BRING ABOUT(or see
     assure)
ushir, usher / assure
ushwaly, usual(lly)
ushwule, usual(lly)
usibil, usable
usible, usable
usich, usage
uside, aside
usig, usage
usign, assign
usij, usage
usilem, asylum
usimbul, assemble
usimelate, assimilate
usin, assign
usind, ascend
usinment, assignment
usinshen, ascension
usint, assent
usir, user
usirshen, assert(ion)
usirt, assert
usirtif, assert(ive)
usirtion, assert(ion)
usiry, usury
usist, assist
usistens, assist(ance)
usitic, acetic / acidic / ascetic
usleep, asleep
uslep, asleep
uslis, useless
uslus, useless
usocheat, associate
usocheation, associate(tion)
usociate, associate

usociation, associate(tion)
usofegus, esophagus
usog, usage
usolt, assault
usordid, assorted
usortment, assortment
usosheashun, associate(tion)
usosheut, associate
usoshiat, associate
usoshiation, associate(tion)
usparugus, asparagus
usperugus, asparagus
usphikseate, asphyxiate
uspire, aspire
usry, usury
ussal, assail
ussasin, assassin
ussemble, assemble
ust, use(d)
ustonish, astonish
ustraunume, astronomy
ustronumy, astronomy
ustrownumy, astronomy
usual,lly,lness, MOST COMMON/
     PREDICTABLE "prefixes: un"
usuch, usage
usug, usage
usuj, usage
usum, assume
usumpshen, assumption
usumshen, assumption
usur, user / assure
usure, usury
usurp,*,ped,ping,pation,per, TO
     UNLAWFULLY ASSUME POSSESSION
     OF
usurt, assert
usury,ries,rer,rious,riously,riousness,
     CHARGE EXORBITANT/UNLAWFUL
     AMOUNT OF INTEREST FOR A LOAN
usylim, asylum
utachment, attach(ment)
utack, attack
utain, attain
utainable, attain(able) / obtain(able)
utak, attack
utanable, attain(able) / obtain(able)
utane, attain
utanmint, attain(ment)
utash, attach
uteludy, utility
utempt, attempt
utemt, attempt
utend, attend

utendens, attend(ance)
utending, attend(ing)
utenshen, attention
utensil,*, DEVICE/INSTRUMENT/TOOL
     FOR WORK
utensul, utensil
utentef, attentive
utentefness, attentive(ness)
utention, attention
utentive, attentive
uter, odor / otter / outer / utter / udder
uterus,ri, HOME FOR EMBRYO IN
     FEMALE MAMMALS "prefixes:
     intra"
utest, attest
uther, other
utilatarian, utilitarian
utilety, utility
utilitarian,*,nism, FOCUS ON USEFUL/
     PRACTICALITY
utility,ties,ize, A USEFUL SERVICE FOR
     THE COMMON GOOD OF THE
     PEOPLE "prefixes: dis"
utilize,*,ed,zing,zable,zation,zer, MAKE
     USE OF "prefixes: mis/re"
utilude, utility
utiluty, utility
utimt, attempt
utind, attend
utindens, attend(ance)
utinding, attend(ing)
utinsel, utensil
utinshen, attention
utinsul, utensil
utintef, attentive
utintion, attention
utintive, attentive
utintiveness, attentive(ness)
utir, odor / otter / outer / utter / udder
     / attire
utmost, BEST / HIGHEST IN ORDER OF
     IMPORTANCE
utopia,an, IDEAL SITUATION
utor, odor / otter / outer / utter / udder
utrausety, atrocity
utrochus, atrocious
utroshes, atrocious
utrosity, atrocity
utter,*,red,ring,rance,rable,rer, TO
     SPEAK (or see udder) "prefixes: un"
utur, odor / otter / outer / utter / udder
uturd, utter(ed)
uvale, avail
uvert, avert / advert / overt

uvou, avow
uvow, avow
uwa, away
uwil, awhile
uwrest, arrest
uwround, around
uwrous, arouse
uzd, use(d)
uzing, use(sing) / ooze(zing)
uzre, usury / use(r)
vacabeulery, vocabulary
vacalate, vacillate
vacancy,ncies, UNOCCUPIED DWELLING
vacant,tly,tness,ncy, DWELLING
NEEDING/WITHOUT OCCUPANCY
vacashend, vacation(ed)
vacashun, vacation
vacate,*,ed,ting, TO LEAVE
PERMANENTLY
vacation,*,ned,ning,nless,ner,nist, GO
AWAY FOR A BRIEF VISIT/
EXCURSION WITH THE INTENT OF
ENJOYMENT/RELAXATION
vaccen, vaccine
vaccenate, vaccinate
vaccilate, vacillate
vaccinate,*,ned,tion, INOCULATE WITH
A CHEMICAL/MEDICINE TO AFFECT
THE BODY
vaccine,*,nal, USED TO STIMULATE THE
BODY TO PRODUCE ANTIBODIES,
USED TO PROTECT AGAINST A
VIRUS
vacculate, vacillate
vaccum, vacuum
vacelate, vacillate
vacenity, vicinity
vacensy, vacancy
vacent, vacant
vachaina, vagina
vacilate, vacillate
vacillate,*,ed,ting,tingly,tion,tor,tory,
MOVE BACK AND FORTH, TO AND
FRO, FLUCTUATE BETWEEN TWO
POINTS
vacinate, vaccinate
vacine, vaccine
vacinity, vicinity
vacsenate, vaccinate
vacsinate, vaccinate
vacsination, vaccinate(tion)
vacum, vacuum

vacuole,*,lar,late,lates,lated,lating,
lization, LACKING SUBSTANCE/
INTELLIGENCE/AWARENESS
vacuous,sly,sness, LACKS SUBSTANCE/
INTELLIGENCE/AWARENESS
vacuum,*,med,ming, MACHINE USED
TO PULL/SUCK/PICK UP, SPACE
CREATED BY REMOVING PARTICLES
vacuus, vacuous
vad, vat
vag, vague
vagabond,*,dish,dism, ONE WHO
ROAMS WITHOUT A PERMANENT
HOME/ SUSTENANCE
vagary,ried,rious,riously, WHIMSICAL,
UNPREDICTABLE IN MOVEMENT/
BEHAVIOR
vage, vague
vagebond, vagabond
vagenul, vagina(l)
vagery, vagary
vagina,*,al,ally, TUBULAR SHAPED
CANAL FOUND IN PLANTS/FEMALE
BODIES
vaginul, vagina(l)
vagiry, vagary
vagist, vague(st)
vagle, vague(ly)
vagly, vague(ly)
vagobond, vagabond
vagrant,*,tly,ncy,ncies, HOMELESS
WHO WANDER/ROAM
vagre, vagary
vagrense, vagrant(ncy)
vagrent, vagrant
vagrunse, vagrant(ncy)
vagry, vagary
vagubond, vagabond
vague,er,est,ely,eness, HAZY, UNCLEAR
vagury, vagary
vagust, vague(st)
vahement, vehemence(nt)
vahemins, vehemence
vail,*, TO LOWER/REMOVE (or see vale/
veil/vile)
vain,nly,nness, TO ATTEMPT WITHOUT
SUCCESS, BE SELF-ABSORBED WITH
ONE'S OWN SHALLOW VALUES (or
see vane/vein)
vajenul, vagina(l)
vajina, vagina
vajinul, vagina(l)
vajunal, vagina(l)
vak, vague

vakabeulery, vocabulary
vakabulery, vocabulary
vakachend, vacation(ed)
vakachun, vacation
vakadid, vacate(d)
vakashen, vacation
vakashend, vacation(ed)
vakashun, vacation
vakat, vacate
vakatid, vacate(d)
vakchenashin, vaccinate(tion)
vakchunashen, vaccinate(tion)
vake, vague
vakense, vacant(ncy)
vakent, vacant
vakently, vacant(ly)
vakeum, vacuum
vakeuol, vacuole
vakinse, vacant(ncy)
vakint, vacant
vakium, vaccum
vakle, vague(ly)
vakly, vague(ly)
vakoum, vacuum
vakrent, vagrant
vakrint, vagrant
vakseen, vaccine
vaksen, vaccine
vaksenate, vaccinate
vakshenashin, vaccinate(tion)
vaksinate, vaccinate
vaksination, vaccinate(tion)
vaksine, vaccine
vaksunashen, vaccinate(tion)
vakual, vacuole
vakum, vacuum
vakumd, vacuum(ed)
vakunse, vacant(ncy)
vakunt, vacant
vakuol, vacuole
vakuous, vacuous
vakuus, vacuous
vakyewm, vacuum
vakyewol, vacuole
vakyual, vacuole
vakyum, vacuum
val, vail / vale / veil
vala, valet
valacity, velocity
valadectory, valedictory
valadiction, valediction
valadiktorean, valedictorian
valance,es,ed, SHORT CURTAIN (or see
valence) "prefixes: uni"

valans, valance / valence
valantine, valentine
valatil, volatile
vale, A VALLEY (or see vail/veil/valley/ valet)
valeant, valiant
valed, valid / veil(ed)
valediction, A VALEDICTORY
valedictorian, ONE WHO SPEAKS AT A SCHOOL COMMENCEMENT
valedictory,ries, SCHOOL FINAL/ FAREWELL CEREMONY
valediktorian, valedictorian
valediktory, valedictory
valedity, valid(ity)
valei, valley
valeint, valiant
valence,cy,nt, A WAY TO MEASURE THE STRENGTH OF AN ATOM (or see valance) "prefixes: bi"
valens, valance / valence
valent, valence(nt) / valiant
valentine,*, TO HONOR ONE WHOM YOU ARE ATTRACTED TO IN A ROMANTIC WAY
valer, valor
valerean, valerian
valerian, AN HERB
valerus, valor(ous)
valet, ONE WHO PARKS CARS FOR GUESTS AT AN EVENT/PUBLIC PLACE
valeubul, value(uable)
valeunt, valiant
valeuntly, valiant(ly)
valey, valley
valf, valve
valiant,tly,tness, OF COURAGE/ STRONG/BRAVE
valid,dly,dness,date,dates,dating,dation, dity,dities,dness, REAL, FACTUAL, ACTUAL, TO ACKNOWLEDGE AUTHENTICITY "prefixes: in/un"
validectory, valedictory
validete, valid(ity)
validety, valid(ity)
validiction, valediction
validictorian, valedictorian
validiktory, valedictory
valie, valley
valins, valance / valence
valint, valence(nt) / valiant
valintine, valentine
valir, valor

valirus, valor(ous)
valit, valid
valitel, volatile
valkano, volcano
valley,*, AREA BETWEEN THE MOUNTAINS AT THE LOWEST POINTS
valoor, velour / velure / valor
valor,rous,rously,rousness, QUALITY ATTRIBUTED TO MALE WHO DISPLAYS BRAVERY/FIRM RESOLVE (or see velour/velure)
valosedy, velocity
valosety, velocity
valotel, volatile
valu, value
valubel, value(uable)
valubul, value(uable)
valud, valid / value(d)
valudectory, valedictory
valudikshen, valediction
valudiktory, valedictory
value,*,ed,uing,eless,elessness,uable, uableness,uably,uate,uator,uation, uational,uationally, WHAT SOMETHING IS WORTH "prefixes: de/dis/in/un/ under"
valules, value(less)
valum, volume
valuns, valance
valuntery, voluntary
valuntine, valentine
valupshuis, voluptuous
valuptuous, voluptuous
valur, velour / velure / valor
valut, valid
valutel, volatile
valv, valve
valve,*,eless, AN APETURE/OPENING TO REGULATE FLOW OF AIR/ LIQUID/ MOLECULES "prefixes: bi/ un/uni"
valy, valley
valyant, valiant
valyently, valiant(ly)
valyew, value
valyewbul, value(uable)
valyint, valiant
valyu, value
valyubil, value(uable)
valyuble, value(uable)
valyum, volume
valyunt, valiant
valyuntle, valiant(ly)

vamb, vamp
vambir, vampire
vamp,*,ped,ping, MOVE BITS/PIECES AROUND TO CHANGE FLOW/ DIRECTION OF SOMETHING, IMPROVISE
vampire,*,ric,rism, ONE THAT DWELLS IN THE NIGHT AND USES BLOOD FOR SUSTENANCE
van,*,nned,nning, TYPE OF VEHICLE (or see vane/vain/vein/feign) "prefixes: de"
vandal,*,lic,lism,listic,lize,lizes,lized, lizing, BREAK IN AND DESTROY ANOTHERS PROPERTY
vandel, vandal
vandelism, vandal(ism)
vandelize, vandal(ize)
vandiktif, vindictive
vandil, vandal
vandilize, vandal(ize)
vandulism, vandal(ism)
vandulize, vandal(ize)
vane,*,ed,eless, DEVICE MOUNTED TO DISPLAY WIND DIRECTION, FEATHER ON AN ARROW (or see van/vain/vein/feign)
vanech, vanish
vanedy, vanity
vaneer, veneer
vanela, vanilla
vaner, veneer
vanesh, vanish
vaneshd, vanish(ed)
vanesht, vanish(ed)
vanety, vanity
vangard, vanguard
vangart, vanguard
vanguard, THE FEW WHO ARE AHEAD OF THE GROUP
vanich, vanish
vanide, vanity
vanila, vanilla
vanilla, TYPE OF FRUIT/BEAN
vanish,hes,hed,hing, TO DISAPPEAR
vanishd, vanish(ed)
vanity,ties, OF BEING VAIN, SELF- ABSORBED WITH SHALLOW VALUES
vankuesh, vanquish
vankwesh, vanquish
vankwish, vanquish
vankwishd, vanquish(ed)
vanquesh, vanquish
vanqueshd, vanquish(ed)

vanquish,hes,hed,hing,hable, OVERCOME/SUBDUE/DEFEAT

vanqwesh, vanquish

vanqweshd, vanquish(ed)

vanqwish, vanquish

vantage,*, A SUPERIOR POSITION/ LOCATION

vantech, vantage

vantej, vantage

vantich, vantage

vantig, vantage

vantuj, vantage

vanude, vanity

vanush, vanish

vanushd, vanish(ed)

vanute, vanity

vaper, vapor

vaperize, vapor(ize)

vapir, vapor

vapirize, vapor(ize)

vapor,*,rer,rish,rishness,rific,ring,rize, rizes,rized,rizing,rizable,rization, rizer, rous,rously,rousness,rosity,ry, FUMES/CLOUD EMITTED/GIVEN OFF BY SOMETHING WHEN EXPOSED TO THE AIR

vapur, vapor

vapurize, vapor(ize)

vaqium, vacuum

vaqum, vacuum

varashis, veracious / voracious

varcity, varsity

vare, vary / very

vareagashen, variegate(tion)

vareashen, variate(tion)

vareation, variate(tion)

vared, vary(ried)

varefication, verify(fication)

varefy, verify

vareins, variant(nce)

vareint, variant

vares, vary(ries)

vareuble, variable

vareuns, variant(nce)

vareunt, variant

vareus, vary(rious)

vari, vary / very

variable,*,bility,eness,ly, CHANGE IN VALUE OF SOMETHING, THE GIVENS IN AN EQUATION, RATE OF SPEED/FLOW/FREQUENCY "prefixes: in"

variant,*,nce, RANGE OF SPEED/FLOW/ FREQUENCY

variate,tion,tional,tionally,tive,tively, RATE OF CHANGE/ FLOW/SPEED/ DIRECTION/FREQUENCY "prefixes: bi"

variedy, variety

variegate,*,ed,ting,tion, OF A VARIETY

variety,ties,tal,tally, A RANGE OF CHOICES

varificashen, verify(fication)

varify, verify

varis, vary(ries)

variuble, variable

variugashen, variegate(tion)

variuns, variant(nce)

varius, vary(rious)

variuty, variety

varment, A TROUBLESOME ANIMAL

varmint, varment

varmun, varment

varnesh, varnish

varneshd, varnish(ed)

varnish,hes,hed,hing,her,hy, TRANSPARENT CHEMICAL COATING FOR PROTECTION "prefixes: un"

varnush, varnish

varsedy, varsity

varsety, varsity

varsity,ties, TYPE OF SCHOOL SPORTS TEAM

varsudes, varsity(ties)

varsuty, varsity

varufi, verify

vary,ries,ried,ying,yingly,rious,riously, riousness, MOVEABLE RANGE/RATE OF CHANGE/SELECTION (or see very)

varyd, vary(ried)

varys, vary(ries)

vas, vase

vasalashen, vacillate(tion)

vasalate, vacillate

vasalation, vacillate(tion)

vascular,rity,rly, FLOW WITHIN A SYSTEM "prefixes: intra/non"

vasd, vast

vase,*, A CONTAINER

vasectomy,mies, SURGICAL PROCEDURE FOR MALES

vasektumy, vasectomy

vaselashen, vacillate(tion)

vaselate, vacillate

vaselation, vacillate(tion)

vasenedy, vicinity

vasenety, vicinity

vasilashen, vacillate(tion)

vasilate, vacillate

vasilation, vacillate(tion)

vasinedy, vicinity

vasinety, vicinity

vaskeuler, vascular

vaskewler, vascular

vaskiular, vascular

vaskuler, vascular

vasnes, vast(ness)

vasqueler, vascular

vasquler, vascular

vast,tly,tness,ty,tier,tiest,titude,tity, GREAT AMOUNT IN RANGE/ DEGREES/ FREQUENCY/AREA

vasul, vessel

vasulashen, vacillate(tion)

vasulate, vacillate

vasulation, vacillate(tion)

vat,*,tted,tting, A VESSEL FOR LIQUIDS

vau, vow

vauch, vouch

vaucher, vouch(er)

vaud, vow(ed)

vaudku, vodka

vaul, vowel

vaulatil, volatile

vaulcano, volcano

vaule, volley

vaulenteer, volunteer

vauli, volley

vaulinter, volunteer

vaulkano, volcano

vault,*,ted,ting,ter, HOLDING/ CONTAINER TO PROTECT VALUABLES, ARCHED HEIGHT WITHIN A DWELLING/SPACE/ CONTAINER, LEAP HIGH (or see volt)

vaulum, volume

vauluntery, voluntary

vaulutil, volatile

vauly, volley

vaumet, vomit

vaumit, vomit

vaush, vouch

vausher, vouch(er)

vautku, vodka

vauz, vase

vaw, vow

vawch, vouch

vawcher, vouch(er)

vawd, vow(ed)

vawl, vowel

vawle, volley
vaygari, vagary
vea, via
veakul, vehicle
veal, MEAT FROM THE CALF OF A
 BOVINE
vecenity, vicinity
vechen, vision
vechenary, vision(ary)
veches, vicious
vechetal, vegetal
vechetarian, vegetarian
vechetate, vegetate
vechitarian, vegetarian
vechtable, vegetable
vechualize, visual(ize)
vechulante, vigil(ante)
vechun, vision
vechunary, vision(ary)
vechus, vicious
vechutarian, vegetarian
vecinity, vicinity
vecks, vex
vectomize, victim(ize)
vectumizashen, victim(ization)
vectumize, victim(ize)
vedeo, video
vederan, veteran
vedio, video
vedo, veto
vedod, veto(ed)
vedran, veteran
vedrify, vitrify
vedurin, veteran
veer,*,red,ring,ringly, SWERVE IN
 MOVEMENT, MOVE TOWARDS
 PARTICULAR DIRECTION
vegatashen, vegetate(tion)
vegatate, vegetate
vegatuble, vegetable
vegduble, vegetable
vegel, vigil
vegelante, vigil(ante)
veger, vigor
vegerus, vigor(ous)
vegetable,*, CATEGORY OF EDIBLE
 PLANTS
vegetal, OF BEING A VEGETABLE
vegetarian,*,nism, EATS PRIMARILY
 VEGETABLES "prefixes: non"
vegetate,*,ed,ting,tion,tional,tionless,
 tive,tively,tivness, SIT/AGE/RIPEN
 AS A VEGETABLE WITHOUT
 MOVEMENT "prefixes: re"

vegetuble, vegetable
vegetul, vegetal
vegil, vigil
vegilante, vigil(ante)
vegilent, vigil(ant)
veginu, vagina
vegir, vigor
vegirus, vigor(ous)
vegitashen, vegetate(tion)
vegitate, vegetate
vegiterean, vegetarian
vegituble, vegetable
vegitul, vegetal
vegolante, vigil(ante)
vegorus, vigor(ous)
vegtable, vegetable
vegtuble, vegetable
vegual, visual
vegulante, vigil(ante)
veguol, visual
veguolize, visual(ize)
vegur, vigor
vegurus, vigor(ous)
vegutarean, vegetarian
vegutashen, vegetate(tion)
vegutate, vegetate
vehecle, vehicle
vehekul, vehicle
vehemence,cy,nt,ntly, STRONG/
 FORCEFUL FEELINGS BROUGHT ON
 BY AN EMOTIONAL STATE/PASSION,
 STRONG/FORCEFUL EVENT
vehemint, vehemence(nt)
vehicle,*,cular, MOVING/POWERED
 VESSELS
vehicul, vehicle
vehikul, vehicle
veic, vague
veig, vague
veigary, vagary
veikle, vehicle
veil,*,led,ling, THIN/TRANSPARENT/
 REMOVABLE COVER (or see vail/
 vale) "prefixes: un"
vein,*,ned,ning,nal,ny,nlet, TUBE/
 CHANNEL THAT ALLOWS FLOW OF
 LIQUID (or see vane/vain) "prefixes:
 de"
veis, vase
veiwed, view(ed)
vejalante, vigil(ante)
vejalent, vigil(ant)
vejatashen, vegetate(tion)
vejatate, vegetate

vejaterean, vegetarian
vejdible, vegetable
vejduble, vegetable
vejetarean, vegetarian
vejetashen, vegetate(tion)
vejetul, vegetal
vejewelize, visual(ize)
vejinu, vagina
vejitarean, vegetarian
vejitashen, vegetate(tion)
vejitate, vegetate
vejitul, vegetal
vejolent, vigil(ant)
vejtuble, vegetable
vejual, visual
vejulante, vigil(ante)
vejulent, vigil(ant)
vejuolize, visual(ize)
vejutarean, vegetarian
vejutashen, vegetate(tion)
vejutate, vegetate
vekabeulery, vocabulary
vekabulery, vocabulary
veker, vigor
vekir, vigor
vekor, vigor
veks, vex
veksashen, vex(ation)
veksation, vex(ation)
vektem, victim
vektemize, victim(ize)
vektumize, victim(ize)
vekur, vigor
vel, vale / vail / veil
vela, villa
velafy, vilify
velage, villa(ge)
velanus, villain(ous)
velarean, valerian
velcom, welcome
veledictore, valedictory
veledictorean, valedictorian
veledictori, valedictory
velefy, vilify
velege, villa(ge)
velej, villa(ge)
velen, villain
velenus, villain(ous)
velidety, valid(ity)
velin, villain
velocity,ties,tize,tizes,tized,tizing,
 tization, RATE/AMOUNT OF
 MOVEMENT/ SPEED
velon, villain

velour,*,red,ring, TYPE OF FABRIC/ VELVET (or see velure)
velu, villa
veluch, villa(ge)
velufy, vilify
velug, villa(ge)
veluj, villa(ge)
velun, villain
velunus, villain(ous)
velure,*,ed,ring, TYPE OF FABRIC (or see velour)
velutch, villa(ge)
velvet,*,ted,ting,teen,ty, THICK/SILKY/ SOFT FABRIC
velvity, velvet(y)
velvude, velvet(y)
velvut, velvet
vem, vim
vemens, vehemence
venager, vinegar
venagrey, vinaigrette
venaker, vinegar
venam, venom
venamus, venom(ous)
venasin, venison
vench, venge
vencher, venture
venchful, venge(ful)
venchurd, venture(d)
vend,*,ded,ding,der,dition, TO SELL (or see vent)
vendacation, vindicate(tion)
vendalashen, ventilate(tion)
vendalate, ventilate
vendalation, ventilate(tion)
vendecate, vindicate
vendecation, vindicate(tion)
vendeda, vendetta
vendekduf, vindictive
vendektif, vindictive
vendetta,*, HAS A STRONG/DEEP GRUDGE/DISPUTE/DISAGREEMENT WITH
vendicashen, vindicate(tion)
vendicate, vindicate
vendiktif, vindictive
venducation, vindicate(tion)
vendulashen, ventilate(tion)
veneer,*,red,ring,rer,rable,rability, rableness, THIN OVERLAYMENT USED FOR SURFACING
venegrey, vinaigrette
venela, vanilla
venem, venom

venemus, venom(ous)
venerate,*,ed,ting,tor,tion,able,ability, ableness,ably, CANONIZE/ WORSHIP/ PUT IN HIGH ESTEEM OVER ONESELF
venew, venue
venge,*,ed,ging,eance,eful,efully, efulness, SEEK AVENGE FOR A WRONG, BE VINDICTIVE/ RELENTLESS IN PURSUIT OF SATISFACTION
vengens, venge(ance)
vengful, venge(ful)
venguns, venge(ance)
veniger, vinegar
venigra, vinaigrette
venila, vanilla
venim, venom
venimus, venom(ous)
venir, veneer
venirate, venerate
venison, TERM FOR THE MEAT OF THE DEER FAMILY
venj, venge
venjens, venge(ance)
venjful, venge(ful)
venjuns, venge(ance)
veno, vino
venom,*,mous,mously,mousness, POISON
venomus, venom(ous)
venorate, venerate
venosen, venison
vensable, vincible
vensher, venture
vensubul, vincible
vent,*,ted,ting, ALLOWS THE RELEASE OF AIR/STEAM/HEAT/EMOTIONS (or see vend) "prefixes: bio"
ventag, vintage
ventalashen, ventilate(tion)
ventalate, ventilate
ventalation, ventilate(tion)
venteg, vintage
ventej, vintage
ventilashen, ventilate(tion)
ventilate,*,ed,ting,tion,tive,tor,tory, ENCOURAGE THE FLOW OF AIR
ventricle,*,cular,culus,culi, TUBES/ ARTERIES "prefixes: inter/intra"
ventrikul, ventricle
ventriloquist,tic,sm,uy,ial,ially,ize, TO THROW/PROJECT THE VOICE WITHOUT MOVING THE LIPS

ventrilukwist, ventriloquist
ventrukle, ventricle
ventuge, vintage
ventuj, vintage
venture,*,ed,ring, GO ON BRAVE/ DARING ADVENTURE, MOVE TOWARDS UNKNOWN TERRITORY
venu, venue
venue,*, WAYS/PATHS, A LEGAL TERM
venuger, vinegar
venugray, vinaigrette
venuker, vinegar
venumus, venom(ous)
venurate, venerate
venusin, venison
venyou, venue
veol, vail / vale / veil / veal
ver, veer
veracious,sly,sness, TRUTHFUL/ UNERRING (or see voracious)
veracity,ties, EAGERNESS/SUPPORT FOR THE TRUTH
verafecation, verify(fication)
verafikashen, verify(fication)
verafy, verify
verasedy, veracity / voracity
verashes, voracious / veracious
verasious, voracious / veracious
verasity, veracity / voracity
verb,*,bal, WORD WHICH DENOTES ACTION
verbadum, verbatim
verbal,lly,lism,list,listic,lize,lizes,lized, lizing,lization,lizer, VOICE/SPEAK FROM THE MOUTH, MAKE THOUGHTS HEARD "prefixes: non"
verbatim, EXACT WORDS
verbatum, verbatim
verble, verbal / verbal(lly)
verblize, verbal(ize)
verboly, verbal(lly)
verbose,ely,eness,sity, TOO WORDY, USES TOO MANY WORDS TO DESCRIBE/COMMUNICATE
verbosity, verbose(sity)
verbosudy, verbose(sity)
verbule, verbal / verbal(lly)
verbulize, verbal(ize)
verch, verge
verchen, version / virgin
verchew, virtue
verchewul, virtual
verchoo, virtue
verchualedy, virtual(ity)

verchuality, virtual(ity)
verchuol, virtual
verd, veer(ed)
verdabra, vertebra
verdacal, vertical
verdago, vertigo
verdekly, vertical(lly)
verdekt, verdict
verdekul, vertical
verdibra, vertebra
verdical, vertical
verdict,*, FINAL DECISION/JUDGEMENT
verdigo, vertigo
verdikly, vertical(lly)
verdikul, vertical
verdubra, vertebra
verdukol, vertical
vere, vary / very
vereability, variable(lity)
vereabl, variable
vereant, variant
vereas, vary(rious)
vereashen, variate(tion)
vereate, variate
vereation, variate(tion)
vered, vary(ried)
verefikashen, verify(fication)
verefukashen, verify(fication)
verefy, verify
veregate, variegate
veres, vary(ries)
vereuble, variable
vereugate, variegate
vereuns, variant(nce)
vereunt, variant
vereus, vary(rious)
verge,*,ed,ging, EDGE/RIM/PIVOT/
    PEAK PRIOR TO
vergen, version / virgin
vergun, version / virgin
veri, vary / very
veriabol, variable
veriagashen, variegate(tion)
veriagate, variegate
veriant, variant
veriants, variant(nce)
veriate, variate
verient, variant
verietal, variety(tal)
veriety, variety
verifikashen, verify(fication)
verifucation, verify(fication)
verify,fies,fied,fying,fication,ficative,
    ficatory,fiability,fiable,fiableness,

fier, AUTHENTICATE/
    ACKNOWLEDGE/RECOGNIZE FOR
    TRUTH
verigate, variegate
veriubility, variable(lity)
veriuble, variable
veriugate, variegate
veriuns, variant(nce)
verius, vary(rious)
verj, verge
verjen, version / virgin
vermakulite, vermiculite
vermekulite, vermiculite
vermen, vermin
vermiculite, TYPE OF ROCK
vermikewlite, vermiculite
vermin,nous,nously, ANNOYING/PESTY
    LIVING THING IN GREAT
    QUANTITIES
vermiqulite, vermiculite
vermooth, vermouth
vermouth, ALCOHOLIC APERITIF
vermuth, vermouth
vernacular,rly,rism, WORD USED AS IT
    ORIGINATED, NATIVE USE OF
    WORD
vernakular, vernacular
verp, verb
verply, verbal(lly)
verpul, verbal
vers, verse / veer(s)
versatile,ely,eness,lity, ABLE TO
    CONFORM TO MANY GIVEN
    SITUATIONS
versatilety, versatile(lity)
verse,*,ed,sing,sify,sifies,sified,sifying,
    sifier,sification, ONE PART/STANZA
    OF A GREATER PIECE/STORY, TO
    MAKE VERSE (or see versus)
versetul, versatile
vershin, version
vershu, virtue
vershuality, virtual(ity)
vershun, version
version,*, ONE PART/VIEW/
    PERSPECTIVE OF A STORY/EVENT
versis, verse(s) / versus
versital, versatile
versitilety, versatile(lity)
versus, AGAINST, TWO PERSPECTIVES
    IN OPPOSITION (or see verse(s))
versutil, versatile
versutilety, versatile(lity)
vert, veer(ed)

vertabra, vertebra
vertebra,*,al,ally,ate,ation, A BONE IN
    THE SPINE "prefixes: inter"
vertego, vertigo
vertekul, vertical
vertibra, vertebra
vertical,lity,lness,lly, OPPOSED TO THE
    HORIZONTAL, AN UPRIGHT
    POSITION
verticly, vertical(lly)
vertigo,oes, DIZZY
vertikul, vertical
vertucly, vertical(lly)
vertue, virtue
vertugo, vertigo
verufecation, verify(fication)
verufikashen, verify(fication)
verufy, verify
verul, virile
very, MUCH/LOTS, GREAT AMOUNT (or
    see vary)
veryus, vary(rious)
vesa, visa
vesabul, visible
vesatashen, visit(ation)
vesater, visit(or)
vesatir, visit(or)
vesatude, vicissitude
vescosedy, viscous(ity)
vescosity, viscous(ity)
vescosudy, viscous(ity)
vesdabule, vestibule
vesdubule, vestibule
vesectomy, vasectomy
vesel, vessel
vesenedy, vicinity
vesenety, vicinity
vesetashen, visit(ation)
veseter, visit(or)
veshen, vision
veshenary, vision(ary)
veshes, vicious
veshuel, visual
veshun, vision
veshunary, vision(ary)
veshus, vicious
vesil, vessel
vesinedy, vicinity
vesinety, vicinity
vesit, visit
vesitashen, visit(ation)
vesiter, visit(or)
vesitude, vicissitude
veskes, viscous

veskosedy, viscous(ity)
veskosity, viscous(ity)
veskus, viscous
vesle, vessel
vessel,*, A CONTAINER
vest,*,ted,ting, SLEEVELESS OUTER
GARMENT, POSSESS POWER/
POSITION
vestabule, vestibule
vestibule,*,ed,ling,lar,late, A CHAMBER/
CAVITY
vestubule, vestibule
vesu, visa
vesubel, visible
vesubiledy, visibility
vesuble, visible / visible(ly)
vesul, vessel
vesut, visit
vesutashen, visit(ation)
vesuter, visit(or)
vesutude, vicissitude
vet,*, SHORT FOR VETERINARIAN AND
VETERAN
vetaren, veteran
veteran,*, ONES WHO SURVIVED A
WAR/BATTLE OR GAINED WISDOM
THOROUGH STUDY/ SERVICE
vetiren, veteran
veto,oes,oed,oing,oer, TO REJECT/
FORBID
vetod, veto(ed)
vetos, veto(es)
vetran, veteran
vetrefy, vitrify
vetrify, vitrify
veturen, veteran
veu, via / view
veud, view(ed)
veukle, vehicle
veva, viva
veved, vivid
vevidly, vivid(ly)
vevu, viva
vew, view
vex,xes,xed,xing,xingly,xation,xatious,
xatiously,xatiousness,xedly,xedness,
TO PLAGUE/IRRITATE/CAUSE
COMMOTION
vexashen, vex(ation)
veygari, vagary
veyude, view(ed)
vezabel, visible
vezabelity, visibility
vezabiledy, visibility

vezatashen, visit(ation)
vezibiledy, visibility
vezit, visit
vezitashen, visit(ation)
vezubelity, visibility
vezubiledy, visibility
vezutashen, visit(ation)
via, BY WAY/MEANS OF
viable,bility,ly, POSSIBLE/CAPABLE
"prefixes: non"
viabul, viable
viaduct,*, CHANNELS WHICH ALLOW
FLOW/TRANSPORT
viaduk, viaduct
vial,*,led,ling, SMALL BOTTLE (or see
vile)
vialashen, violate(tion)
vialate, violate
vialation, violate(tion)
vialen, violin
vialens, violent(nce)
vialet, violet
vialin, violin
vialint, violent
vialunt, violent
vibd, vibe(d)
vibe,*,bing, SHORT FOR VIBRATION, A
RYTHMIC SYNCHRONICITY,
RESOUNDS WELL TOGETHER
vibrachun, vibrate(tion)
vibraded, vibrate(d)
vibrant,ncy,tly, PULSING WITH ENERGY/
LIFE
vibrashen, vibrate(tion)
vibrate,*,ed,ting,tion,tor,ant,
PULSATING RYTHM/WAVES
vibratid, vibrate(d)
vibrator,*,ry, MACHINE PRODUCING
PULSES OF WAVES/FREQUENCY
vibrensy, vibrant(ncy)
vibrent, vibrant
vibrently, vibrant(ly)
vibrinsy, vibrant(ncy)
vibrutory, vibrator(y)
vicabulary, vocabulary
vice,*, REPLACING ONE INFERIOR WITH
ANOTHER, INSTEAD OF (or see vise)
vicenity, vicinity
vichen, vision
vichenary, vision(ary)
viches, vicious
vichol, vigil
vichos, vicious
vichualize, visual(ize)

vichulante, vigil(ante)
vichun, vision
vichunary, vision(ary)
vichus, vicious
vichwal, visual
vichwulize, visual(ize)
vicinity,ties, WITHIN THE AREA
vicious,sly,sness, HATEFUL DISPOSITION,
LASHING OUT WITH DARK/
NEGATIVE EMOTION
vicisitude, vicissitude
vicissitude,dinary,dinous, TO MOVE
FROM ONE FREQUENCY TO
ANOTHER, A MUTATION
victamize, victim(ize)
victem, victim
victim,*,mize,mizes,mized,mizing,
mization,mizer, RECEIVER OF ILL
WILL, HELPLESS, INABILITY TO GAIN
POWER IN A SITUATION
victomizashen, victim(ization)
victomize, victim(ize)
victum, victim
victumizashen, victim(ization)
victumize, victim(ize)
vidal, vital
vidamen, vitamin
videl, vital
videmen, vitamin
video,*,oed,oing, MOVING/VISUAL
FILM WITH MANY FRAMES/
PICTURES
vidio, video
vidl, vital
vidrefy, vitrify
vidul, vital
vidumen, vitamin
vidumin, vitamin
vieble, viable
viebul, viable
viecol, vehicle
vieduk, viaduct
vielashen, violate(tion)
vielate, violate
view,*,wed,wing,wer, TO SEE WITH THE
EYES "prefixes: over/pre"
vigalanty, vigil(ante)
vigalent, vigil(ant)
vigel, vigil
vigelent, vigil(ant)
vigeng, viking
viger, vigor
vigerus, vigor(ous)

vigil,la,lance,lant,lantly,lante,lantism, TO WATCH OVER, PAY CAREFUL ATTENTION TO "prefixes: in"

viging, viking
viginu, vagina
vigir, vigor
vigirus, vigor(ous)
vigolante, vigil(ante)
vigor,*,rous,roso,rously,rousness, OF VITALITY/STRENGTH "prefixes: in"
vigorus, vigor(ous)
vigual, visual
vigulante, vigil(ante)
vigulent, vigil(ant)
viguol, visual
vigur, vigor
vigurus, vigor(ous)
vijalante, vigil(ante)
vijalent, vigil(ant)
vijewelize, visual(ize)
vijinu, vagina
vijolent, vigil(ant)
vijual, visual
vijulante, vigil(ante)
vijulent, vigil(ant)
vijwel, visual
vijwul, visual
vijwulize, visual(ize)
vikabeulery, vocabulary
vikabulery, vocabulary
vikeng, viking
viker, vigor
viking,*, SCANDINAVIAN WARRIOR
vikir, vigor
vikor, vigor
viktem, victim
viktemizashen, victim(ization)
viktemize, victim(ize)
viktim, victim
viktumizashen, victim(ization)
viktumize, victim(ize)
vikur, vigor
vila, valet / villa
vilafy, vilify
vilage, villa(ge)
vilan, villain
vilanus, villain(ous)
vilarean, valerian
vile,*,ely,eness, DISGUSTING (or see vial/villa/valet)
vilefy, vilify
vilege, villa(ge)
vilej, villa(ge)
vilen, villain / violin

vilenus, villain(ous)
vilerean, valerian
vilet, valet
vilify,fies,fied,fier,vying,fication, TO DEFACE/SLANDER/DEGRADE
vilij, villa(ge)
vilin, villain / violin
vilinus, villain(ous)
villa,*,age,ager,agery, A RURAL/ COUNTRY TOWN (or see valet)
villain,*,nous,nously,nousness,ny,nies, THE BAD GUY/ANTAGONIST, OF EVIL CHARACTER
villian, villain
vilofi, vilify
vilon, villain
vilosedy, velocity
vilosety, velocity
vilu, villa
viluch, villa(ge)
vilufy, vilify
vilug, villa(ge)
viluj, villa(ge)
vilun, villain
vilunus, villain(ous)
vilur, velure / velour
vilutch, villa(ge)
vim, OF STRENGTH/ENTHUSIASM
vin, vine
vinager, vinegar
vinagra, vinaigrette
vinagrette, vinaigrette
vinaigrette, SALAD DRESSING WITH MOSTLY VINEGAR
vinaker, vinegar
vinal, vinyl
vinamus, venom(ous)
vinasin, venison
vinch, venge
vincher, venture
vinchful, venge(ful)
vinchurd, venture(d)
vincible,lity,eness, CAN BE OVERCOME/ CONQUERED
vind, vend / vent
vindalashen, ventilate(tion)
vindalate, ventilate
vindecate, vindicate
vindedu, vendetta
vindekdef, vindictive
vindektif, vindictive
vindeta, vendetta
vindetta, vendetta
vindicashen, vindicate(tion)

vindicate,*,ed,ting,able,ation,ative,ator, atory,ctive, TO BE LIBERATED BY AVENGING
vindictef, vindictive
vindictive,ely,eness, HAS A REVENGE
vindikduv, vindictive
vindiktif, vindictive
vinducation, vindicate(tion)
vindulashen, ventilate(tion)
vindulate, ventilate
vine,*,ey, A TRAILING PLANT SUCH AS IVY/GRAPE
vineer, veneer
vinegar,*,ry,rish, RESULT OF FERMENTATION
vinegre, vinaigrette
vinegrette, vinaigrette
vinel, vinyl
vinemus, venom(ous)
viner, veneer
vinerate, venerate
vinew, venue
ving, venge
vingents, venge(ance)
vingful, venge(ful)
viniger, vinegar
vinigre, vinaigrette
vinigrette, vinaigrette
vinil, vinyl
vinila, vanilla
vinj, venge
vinjents, venge(ance)
vinjful, venge(ful)
vino, WINE
vinol, vinyl
vinosen, venison
vinsable, vincible
vinsher, venture
vinsuble, vincible
vint, vint / vend
vintage, RESULT OF A SUPERIOR CROP SEASON
vintalashen, ventilate(tion)
vintalate, ventilate
vintalation, ventilate(tion)
vinteg, vintage
vintelate, ventilate
vintilate, ventilate
vintrecal, ventricle
vintrecular, ventricle(cular)
vintrelukwist, ventriloquist
vintrical, ventricle
vintrikul, ventricle
vintrikuler, ventricle(cular)

vintrilukwist, ventriloquist
vintrukle, ventricle
vintuge, vintage
vintuj, vintage
vintulate, ventilate
vintur, venture
vintured, venture(d)
vinu, venue
vinuger, vinegar
vinugrey, vinaigrette
vinuker, vinegar
vinul, vinyl
vinumus, venom(ous)
vinurate, venerate
vinusen, venison
viny, vine(y)
vinyl, TYPE OF PLASTIC
vinyou, venue
viola, STRINGED INSTRUMENT
violadid, violate(d)
violashen, violate(tion)
violate,*,ed,ting,tive,tor,tion, TO BASH
    BOUNDARIES/LAWS SET FORTH BY
    PEOPLE/NATURE "prefixes: in"
violen, violin
violens, violent(nce)
violent,tly,nce, USE OF AGGRESSIVE
    FORCE "prefixes: non"
violet, DARK COLOR OF RED/BLUE
violin,*, STRINGED INSTRUMENT
violint, violent
violunt, violent
vipe, vibe
viper,*,rish,rous,rously, POISONOUS
    SNAKE
vipir, viper
viporus, viper(ous)
viprus, viper(ous)
vipur, viper
vir, veer
viracedy, veracity / voracity
viracious, voracious / veracious
viracity, veracity / voracity
viral,lly, OF A VIRUS (or see virile)
    "prefixes: non/retro"
viralent, virulent
viralint, virulent
virasedy, veracity / voracity
virashes, voracious / veracious
virasious, voracious / veracious
virasity, veracity
virb, verb
virbadum, verbatim
virbatum, verbatim

virble, verbal
virblize, verbal(ize)
virbly, verbal(lly)
virboly, verbal(lly)
virbos, verbose
virbosity, verbose(sity)
virbosudy, verbose(sity)
virbul, verbal
virbule, verbal(lly)
virbulize, verbal(ize)
virch, verge
virchen, version
virchew, virtue
virchewul, virtual
virchoo, virtue
virchual, virtual
virchualedy, virtual(ity)
virchuality, virtual(ity)
virchuil, virtual
virchuol, virtual
virdabra, vertebra
virdago, vertigo
virdego, vertigo
virdek, verdict
virdekly, vertical(lly)
virdekul, vertical
virdibra, vertebra
virdict, verdict
virdigo, vertigo
virdikly, vertical(lly)
virdikt, verdict
virdikul, vertical
virdubra, vertebra
virdugo, vertigo
virdukil, vertical
virdukly, vertical(lly)
virel, viral / virile
vires, virus
virge, verge
virgen, version / virgin
virgin,*,nal, PRISTINE/NATURAL,
    HASN'T BEEN EXPLOITED/ ALTERED
    (or see version)
virgun, version / virgin
virile,lity,lism, HEALTHY MASCULINE
    QUALITIES (or see viral)
viris, virus
viriudy, variety
viriuty, variety
virje, verge
virjen, virgin
virjin, version / virgin
virmeculite, vermiculite
virmen, vermin

virmikewlite, vermiculite
virmikulite, vermiculite
virmin, vermin
virmiqulite, vermiculite
virmooth, vermouth
virmuth, vermouth
virnakuler, vernacular
virol, viral / virile
virolent, virulent
viros, virus
virp, verb
virply, verbal(lly)
virpul, verbal
virs, verse
virsatil, versatile
virsatilety, versatile(lity)
virsetal, versatile
virshen, version
virshuality, virtual(ity)
virsutil, versatile
virsutilety, versatile(lity)
virtebra, vertebra
virtego, vertigo
virtekul, vertical
virtibra, vertebra
virtigo, vertigo
virtikul, vertical
virtual,lity,lly, NOT PHYSICAL TO THE
    TOUCH
virtue,uosity,uosities,uoso,uous,uously,
    uousness, KNOWS OF EXCELLENCE,
    ONE WITH SUPRA KNOWLEDGE
virtugo, vertigo
virtukle, vertical(lly)
virul, viral / virile
virulent, VERY BITTER/POISONOUS/
    DANGEROUS
virulint, virulent
virus,ses, LIVING ORGANISM "prefixes:
    pro/retro/sub"
visa,aed,aing, A PASS/PASSPORT
visabelity, visibility
visabil, visible
visabiledy, visibility
visabilety, visibility
visably, visible(ly)
visatashen, visit(ation)
visater, visit(or)
visatude, vicissitude
viscos, viscous
viscosedy, viscous(ity)
viscosity, viscous(ity)

viscous,sly,sness,osity, TEXTURE/ CONSISTENCY OF SYRUP "prefixes: non"
viscus, viscous
vise,*,ed,sing, A TOOL/PRESS FOR GRIPING/HOLDING ITEMS IN PLACE (or see vice)
visectomy, vasectomy
visekteme, vasectomy
visenedy, vicinity
visenety, vicinity
viser, visor
viset, visit
visetashen, visit(ation)
visetation, visit(ation)
viseter, visit(or)
visetude, vicissitude
vishen, vision
vishenary, vision(ary)
vishes, vicious
vishon, vision
vishos, vicious
vishuel, visual
vishun, vision
vishunary, vision(ary)
vishus, vicious
visibility,ties, THE DEGREE OF ABILITY TO SEE WITH THE NAKED EYE
visible,eness,ly, ABLE TO BE SEEN WITH THE EYE
visinedy, vicinity
visinety, vicinity
vision,*,nal,nally,nary,naries,nariness, nless, TO CONCEIVE/VIEW THAT BEYOND OUR EYE'S ABILITY, ABILITY TO SEE "prefixes: en/pre"
visir, visor
visit,*,ted,ting,table,tant,tation,tational, tatorial,tor, GO SEE SOMEONE/ SOMETHING BRIEFLY, RECEIVE GUESTS, BE A GUEST
visitashen, visit(ation)
visiter, visit(or)
visitude, vicissitude
viskes, viscous
viskosedy, viscous(ity)
viskosity, viscous(ity)
viskus, viscous
visor,*, GUARD/SHIELD TO PROTECT SUN'S GLARES
vista,*, A LONG/STRETCHING VIEW
visu, visa

visual,*,lly,lize,lization,lizer, USE OF EYES TO SEE, TO SEE AS IF WITH THE EYES "prefixes: non"
visubel, visible
visubelity, visibility
visubiledy, visibility
visuble, visible / visible(ly)
visur, visor
visut, visit
visutashen, visit(ation)
visutation, visit(ation)
visuter, visit(or)
visutude, vicissitude
vital,*,lly,lness,lism,listic,lity,lities,lize, lizes,lized,lizing,lization, LIFE ENERGY/ PROPERTIES, ESSENTIAL PROCESSES FOR CONTINUATION OF LIFE "prefixes: de/intra"
vitaledy, vital(ity)
vitalidy, vital(ity)
vitamen, vitamin
vitamin,*, ORGANIC NUTRIENTS/ MINERALS
vitel, vital
vitemen, vitamin
vitl, vital
vito, veto
vitrify,fies,fied,fying,fiability,fiable, BECOME/CHANGE INTO GLASS "prefixes: de"
vitul, vital
vitumen, vitamin
vitumin, vitamin
viu, view
viubil, viable
viuble, viable
viud, view(ed)
viuduk, viaduct
viuladid, violate(d)
viulashen, violate(tion)
viulation, violate(tion)
viulens, violent(nce)
viulet, violet
viva,acity,acities, LIFE
vivaches, vivacious
vivachusnes, vivacious(ness)
vivacious,sly,sness,ity,ities, BOUNDING WITH LIFE/ENERGY/ SPIRIT
vivashes, vivacious
vivashous, vivacious
vivashusnes, vivacious(ness)
vived, vivid
vivedly, vivid(ly)

vivid,dly,dness, BRIGHT/DRAMATIC/ CLEAR
vivu, viva
viyudukt, viaduct
vizabelity, visibility
vizabil, visible
vizabiledy, visibility
vizably, visible(ly)
vizatashen, visit(ation)
vizater, visit(or)
vizer, visor
vizet, visit
vizetashen, visit(ation)
vizetur, visit(or)
vizibelity, visibility
vizibiledy, visibility
vizibul, visible
vizir, visor
vizit, visit
vizitashen, visit(ation)
viziter, visit(or)
vizivelity, visibility
vizor, visor
vizubel, visible
vizubelity, visibility
vizubiledy, visibility
vizuble, visible
vizubly, visible(ly)
vizur, visor
vizutashen, visit(ation)
vizuter, visit(or)
vocabeulery, vocabulary
vocabulary,ries, WORDS IN A PARTICULAR LANGUAGE USED FOR COMMUNICATION
vocal,*,lly,lness,lize,lizes,lized,lizing, lization,list,lism,lizer, USING THE VOICE "prefixes: de/inter/sub/uni"
vocalise, vocal(ize)
vocashen, vocation
vocashenul, vocation(al)
vocation,*,nal,nally, AN ACQUIRED/ NATURAL SKILL/ PROFESSION USED TO EARN MONEY "prefixes: in"
vocel, vocal
vocul, vocal
voculize, vocal(ize)
voded, vote(d)
vodef, votive
voder, vote(r)
vodev, votive
vodid, vote(d)
vodif, votive
vodir, vote(r)

vodiv, votive

vodka, ALCOHOLIC SPIRITS

vodur, vote(r)

voed, void

voeg, voyage

voej, voyage

voes, voice

voezd, voice(d)

vog, vogue

vogue, IN FASHION

voice,*,ed,cing,eful,efulness,eless, elessly,elessness, SOUND COMING FROM THE MOUTH "prefixes: de/ un"

void,*,ded,ding,dable,dableness,der, dness,dance, ONE VAST NOTHING MATERIALLY ALL THINGS POTENTIALLY, RETURN TO NOTHING

voig, voyage

voij, voyage

vois, voice

voist, voice(d)

vok, vogue

vokabeulery, vocabulary

vokabulery, vocabulary

vokalize, vocal(ize)

vokashen, vocation

vokashenul, vocation(al)

vokation, vocation

vokationul, vocation(al)

vokeishon, vocation

vokel, vocal

vokelize, vocal(ize)

vokil, vocal

vokilize, vocal(ize)

vokul, vocal

vokulize, vocal(ize)

volanteer, volunteer

volanterd, volunteer(ed)

volatel, volatile

volatile,eness,lity,lize,lization, ABLE TO CHANGE SUDDENLY IN COMPOSITION, EXPLOSIVE "prefixes: de"

volcano,oes,nic,nically,nism,nicity,nist, nize,nizes,nized,nizing,nization, MOUNTAIN ERUPTION FROM ITS CORE

volcher, vulture

vold, vault / volt

vole, volley

volee, volley

volenter, volunteer

volenterd, volunteer(ed)

volentery, voluntary

voleum, volume

volgar, vulgar

voli, volley

volinter, volunteer

volisity, velocity

volitel, volatile

volkano, volcano

volley,*,yed,ying,yer, TO GO BACK AND FORTH, DISCHARGE OF MANY THINGS AT ONCE

volly, volley

volnerable, vulnerable

volnirable, vulnerable

volnrable, vulnerable

volopchuis, voluptuous

volosedy, velocity

volshur, vulture

volt,*,tage,taic, ELECTRICAL MEASUREMENT OF POWER (or see vault)

voltaec, voltaic

voltage,*, TYPE OF ELECTRICAL ACTION "prefixes: over"

voltaic,*, TYPE OF ELECTRICAL ACTION

voltauk, voltaic

voltshur, vulture

volume,*,ed,ming,minous,minously, minosity, LEVEL OF SOUND/ FREQUENCY, MANY THINGS BROUGHT TOGETHER, FORM OF MEASUREMENT

voluntary,rism,rist,ristic,ries,rily,riness, teer, FREELY OFFER SERVICE WITHOUT EXPECTING PAY/MONEY/ EXCHANGE "prefixes: in"

volunteer,*,red,ring, FREELY OFFER SERVICE WITHOUT EXPECTING PAY/ MONEY/EXCHANGE

volunter, volunteer

volunterd, volunteer(ed)

voluntery, voluntary

voluptuous,sly,sness, OF SENSUALITY

volutel, volatile

volutil, volatile

volva,ate, FUNGI MEMBRANE (or see vulva)

voly, volley

volyewm, volume

vomet, vomit

vomit,*,ted,ting,tous,tory,tories, turition,tus, THE ENERGETIC DISCHARGE OF CONTENTS OF THE STOMACH THROUGH THE MOUTH

vomut, vomit

voner, veneer

voodoo, FICTITIOUS PRACTICE OF SORCERY

voracious,sly,sness, DEVOUR WITH EXTREME GREED/ENTHUSIASM (or see veracious)

voracity,ious, VORACIOUS/EAGER/ RAVENOUS CONSUMPTION, GREAT APPETITE FOR (or see veracity)

vorashus, voracious / veracious

vorasity, veracity

vordes, vortice

vordex, vortex

vorteks, vortex

vortes, vortice

vortesis, vortex(es) / vortice(s)

vortex,xes,tices,tical,tically,ticose, A SWIRLING/SPIRAL MOVEMENT

vortice,*,cal,cally,cose, SWIRLING/ SPIRAL MOVEMENT AS IN A VORTEX

vortisus, vortex(es)

vos, vase

vosektumy, vasectomy

vot, vote

vote,*,ed,ting,er,eless, TO MAKE A CHOICE/DECISION BETWEEN TWO OR MORE THINGS

votef, votive

voteve, votive

votid, vote(d)

votif, votive

votive, DEDICATED WITH A VOW

votka, vodka

votku, vodka

votuve, votive

vouch,hes,hed,hing,her,hee, CONFIRM/ ATTEST/UPHOLD THE LEGITIMACY/ VALIDITY OF SOMEONE/ SOMETHING

vouchd, vouch(ed)

voug, voyage

vouj, voyage

voul, vowel

vow,*,wed,wing, TAKE AN OATH, SWEAR TO UPHOLD

vowch, vouch

vowchur, vouch(er)

vowel,*, ONE OF SIX LETTERS OF THE ENGLISH ALPHABET WITH CERTAIN CHARACTERISTICS "prefixes: semi"

vowl, vowel
voyage,*,ed,ging,er, A JOURNEY/TRIP
    BY SEA
voyd, void
voyg, voyage
voyj, voyage
voys, voice
voyst, voice(d)
voz, vase
vucabeulery, vocabulary
vucinity, vicinity
vud, view(ed)
vudu, voodoo
vue, view
vugina, vagina
vuhemint, vehemence(nt)
vujina, vagina
vukabulery, vocabulary
vula, valet
vularean, valerian
vulchur, vulture
vuledity, valid(ity)
vulerean, valerian
vulerian, valerian
vulet, valet
vulfa, vulva / volva
vulgar,rly,rness,rian,rism,rity,rities,rize,
    rization,rizer, OFF COLOR IN
    BEHAVIOR/LANGUAGE/
    MANNERISM
vulgaredy, vulgar(ity)
vulger, vulgar
vulgeredy, vulgar(ity)
vulgurly, vulgar(ly)
vulidete, valid(ity)
vulnerable,bility,eness,bly, NOT WELL
    PROTECTED "prefixes: in"
vulnuruble, vulnerable
vulopchues, voluptuous
vulosedy, velocity
vulosety, velocity
vulsher, vulture
vulture,*, A LARGE SCAVENGER BIRD
vulupchuis, voluptuous
vuluptuis, voluptuous
vuluptuous, voluptuous
vulur, velour / velure
vulva, EXTERNAL FEMALE GENITALIA
    (or see volva)
vuneer, veneer
vunela, vanilla
vuner, veneer
vunila, vanilla
vuracious, voracious / veracious

vurashes, voracious / veracious
vurasity, veracity
vurb, verb
vurbadum, verbatim
vurbatum, verbatim
vurbelize, verbal(ize)
vurblize, verbal(ize)
vurbose, verbose
vurbuliz, verbal(ize)
vurchen, version / virgin
vurchew, virtue
vurchewul, virtual
vurchoo, virtue
vurchual, virtual
vurchuol, virtual
vurdabra, vertebra
vurdago, vertigo
vurdekly, vertical(lly)
vurdekt, verdict
vurdekul, vertical
vurdibra, vertebra
vurdigo, vertigo
vurdikly, vertical(lly)
vurdikt, verdict
vurdikul, vertical
vurdubra, vertebra
vurdukil, vertical
vurge, verge
vurgen, version / virgin
vurgun, version / virgin
vuriedy, variety
vurietal, variety(tal)
vuriety, variety
vurje, verge
vurjen, version / virgin
vurjun, version / virgin
vurmeculite, vermiculite
vurmikulite, vermiculite
vurmouth, vermouth
vurmuth, vermouth
vurnaculer, vernacular
vurnakuler, vernacular
vurp, verb
vurple, verbal / verbal(lly)
vurs, verse
vursatilety, versatile(lity)
vursitelity, versatile(lity)
vurtabra, vertebra
vurtego, vertigo
vurtekul, vertical
vurtibra, vertebra
vurtigo, vertigo
vurtikul, vertical
vurtue, virtue

vurtugo, vertigo
vusectemy, vasectomy
vusekteme, vasectomy
vusenedy, vicinity
vusinity, vicinity
vyle, vial / vile
wa, way / weigh / whey
wabel, wobble
wabul, wobble
wac, wake / walk / wok / whack
wach, wage / wash / watch / wake /
    wok / walk
wacher, washer / wage(r)
waches, wage(s) / watch(es)
wachir, washer / wage(r)
wachis, wage(s) / watch(es)
wachul, waggle
wachus, wage(s) / wash(es)
wack, wake / walk / wok / whack
wacks, wax / whack(s) / walk(s)
wacky,kily,kiness, SILLY, ERRATIC,
    CRAZY
wackyness, wacky(kiness)
wacs, wax / whack(s) / walk(s) / wake(s)
    / wok(s)
wad,*,dded,dding, CRUMPLE/CRINKLE/
    ROLL SOMETHING UP INTO A BALL
    SHAPE (or see wade/what/watt/
    wait/weight)
waddle,*,ed,ling,er,ly, MOVE BACK AND
    FORTH IN MOVEMENT SUCH AS A
    PENGUIN WALKING
wade,*,ed,ding,er,ers, WALK/
    NAVIGATE THROUGH SHALLOW
    WATER/ LIQUID/RESISTANT
    MATERIAL (or see wait/wad/
    weight)
wadel, waddle / what'll
wader, wader / water / waiter
wadercres, watercress
waderfol, waterfall
waderproof, waterproof
waderpruf, waterproof
waders, LONG RUBBER BOOTS FOR
    FEET TO PROTECT AGAINST DEEP
    WATER (or see waiter(s))
wadertite, watertight
wadevr, whatever
wadid, wad(dded) / wait(ed) / wed(ed)
wadil, waddle / what'll
wadir, wader / water / waiter
wadirproof, waterproof
wadirpruf, waterproof
wadirs, waders / waiter(s) / water(s)

wadirtite, watertight

wadle, waddle / what'll

wadol, waddle / what'll

wador, wader / water / waiter

wadres, waitress

wadrus, waitress

wadud, wad(dded) / wait(ed) / wade(d)

wadul, waddle / what'll

wadur, wader / water / waiter

wadurd, water(ed)

wadurfol, waterfall

wadurproof, waterproof

wadurpruf, waterproof

wadurs, waders / waiter(s) / water(s)

wae, way / weigh / whey

wael, whale / wail / wale

waen, wain / wane

waest, waist / waste

waet, wait / weight

waf, wave

wafd, waft / raft / wave(d) / waive(d)

wafe, wave / wave(vy)

wafel, waffle

wafer,*, THIN SLICE OF SOMETHING (or see waiver)

waffle,*,ed,ling, BATTER COOKED IN A WAFFLE MAKER

wafil, waffle

wafir, wafer / waiver

wafle, waffle

waflis, wave(less)

wafor, wafer / waiver

waft,*,ted,ting,ty,tage, SMALL PENNANT SHAPED FLAG, BE CARRIED ALONG ,FLOAT (or see raft/wave(d)/waive(d))

waful, waffle

wafur, wafer / waiver

wag,*,gged,gging,gger,ggle,ggles,ggled, ggling, QUICKLY MOVE BACK AND FORTH SUCH AS A DOGS TAIL (or see wage)

wagd, wag(gged) / wage(d)

wage,*,ed,ging,eless,er,erer, MONEY EARNED BY WORKING,MAKE A BET, CREATE CONFLICT/WAR (or see wag) "prefixes: un"

wagel, waggle

wagen, wagon

waggle,*,ed,ling,ly,ggingly, QUICKLY MOVE BACK AND FORTH SUCH AS A DOGS TAIL

wagil, waggle

wagin, wagon

wagir, wage(r)

wagle, waggle / waggle(ly)

wagly, waggle(ly)

wagon,*,ner, VESSEL WITH BOX SHAPED BASE AND FOUR WHEELS FOR CARRYING THINGS

wagul, waggle

wagun, wake(n) / wagon

wagur, wage(r)

wail,*,led,ling,ler,lingly,lful,lfully, VERY HEAVY/LOUD/ PAINFUL CRY (or see wale/whale)

wain, TYPE OF WAGON (or see wane)

wainscot,ted,ting, WOOD/SUBSTANCE ONLY COVERING LOWER HALF OF A WALL

wainskot, wainscot

waist, MIDDLE SECTION/MIDRIFF OF A BODY BETWEEN RIBCAGE AND HIPS (or see waste)

wait,*,ted,ting,ter, TEMPORARILY PAUSE/STOP MOMENTUM TO SERVICE ANOTHER'S NEEDS (or see wade/weight)

waiter,*, ONE WHO SERVES PATRONS FOOD AT A RESTAURANT/CAFE/ DINER (or see waders)

waitress,ses, FEMALES WHO SERVE PATRONS FOOD AT A RESTAURANT/ CAFE/ DINER

waive,*,ed,ving,er, RELINQUISH/LET GO OF YOUR RIGHTS TO SOMETHING (or see wave)

waiver,*, A TEMPORARY PASS, TO GIVE UP RIGHTS

wajd, wage(d)

wajer, wage(r)

wajur, wage(r)

wak, walk / whack / wake / wok

wake,*,en,woke,eful,efully,efulness, eless,king, BE AWARE OF PHYSICAL REALITY AFTER BEING ASLEEP, WAVE CAUSED BY MOVEMENT, RITUAL PERFORMED FOR DECEASED (or see whack/wok/ wacky)

waken, wake(n) / wagon

wakenes, wacky(kiness)

waker, walker / wake(n) / whack(er)

wakin, wake(n) / wagon

wakle, waggle

wakon, wake(n) / wagon

waks, wax / whack(s) / walk(s) / wake(s) / wok(s)

wakse, wax(y)

wakser, wax(er)

waksy, wax(y)

wakul, waggle

wakun, wake(n) / wagon

waky, wacky

wakynes, wacky(kiness)

wal, wall / wail / whale

wald, wail(ed) / wale(d) / wall(ed)

wale,*,ed,ling, A WELT CAUSED BY A WHIPPING, SUPPORT FOR OUTSIDE PLANKING OF A BOAT (or see wail/ whale/wall)

walep, wallop

walet, wallet

walip, wallop

walit, wallet

walk,*,ked,king,ker, MOVING/ TRAVELING ON FOOT

walker,*, A DEVICE TO HELP PEOPLE WALK (or see walk(er))

walkor, walk(er) / walker

wall,*,lled,lling, VERTICAL SECTION OF A DWELLING/STRUCTURE (or see wail/wale)

wallet,*, HOLDER FOR MONEY AND I.D.

wallit, wallet

wallop,*,ped,ping, THRASH/STRIKE A BLOW TO

wallow,*,wed,wing,wer, LIKE A PIG SQUIRMING IN THE MUD, TO LIE/BE DEEP INTO SOMETHING

wallut, wallet

walnut,*, A NUT

walo, wallow

walod, wallow(ed)

walop, wallop

waloped, wallop(ed)

walow, wallow

walowed, wallow(ed)

walres, walrus

walrus,ses, A CARNIVOROUS/MARINE MAMMAL

wals, waltz / wall(s) / wale(s) / wail(s)

walts, waltz

waltsd, waltz(ed)

waltz,zes,zed,zing,zer, DANCE TO 3/4 TIME MUSIC

walup, wallop

waluped, wallop(ed)

walupt, wallop(ed)

walut, wallet

walz, waltz

walzed, waltz(ed)

wamp, whomp

wan,*, WASHED OUT/WEAK IN COLOR/ ENERGY/MOTION (or see wain/ wane/ won/one)

wand,*, SLENDER STICK USED FOR MANY PURPOSES (or see want/ won't)

wander,*,red,ring,ringly,rer, TO MOVE/ TRAVEL AIMLESSLY ABOUT (or see wonder)

wanderful, wonderful

wandurer, wander(er)

wane,*,ed,ning,ey,nier,niest, ON THE DOWNSIDE OF A PEAK/WAVE, TO DIMINISH (or see wan/wain)

wans, once

wanscoat, wainscot

wanskot, wainscot

want,*,ted,ting, DESIRE SOMETHING (or see won't/wand)

wanten, wanton

wanton,nly,nness, WANT FOR NOTHING, FREE/UNBOUND/ UNRESTRAINED

wantun, wanton

wantunes, wanton(nness)

wantunle, wanton(ly)

wapen, weapon

wapun, weapon

war,*,rred,rring,rless, DISPLAY OF HOSTILITY/OPPOSITION BETWEEN FORCES (or see wore/wear/where/ ware/we're/weir) "prefixes: pre"

warale, weary(rily)

warant, warrant

warante, warrant(y)

waras, whereas

warbil, warble

warble,*,ed,ling,er, TYPE OF VIBRATION/SOUND, A TUMOR/ SWELLING

warbler,*, A BIRD

warbul, warble

ward,*,ded,ding,den, TERRITORY/AREA, FEND OFF, DEFEND AGAINST (or see word/wart/war(rred)/where'd)

warden,*, A PAID OVERSEER IN A PRISON SYSTEM

wardon, warden

wardrobe,*, COLLECTION OF CLOTHING, PLACE WHERE CLOTHING IS KEPT

wardun, warden

ware,*, BE WATCHFUL OF, SPECIAL ITEMS OF USE/VALUE (or see war/ wear/ where/weary)

warefur, wherever

wareir, warrior

warele, weary(rily)

waren, warren

warent, warrant

warente, warrant(y)

warenty, warrant(y)

wareur, warrior

warevur, wherever

warf, wharf

warier, warrior

warily, weary(rily)

warin, warren

warint, warrant

warinte, warrant(y)

warinted, warrant(ed)

warinty, warrant(y)

warl, where'll

warm,*,med,ming,mer,mest,mth,mly, mish,mness, TEMPERATURE BETWEEN HOT/COLD, BECOME COMFORTABLE WITH (or see worm)

warmist, warm(est)

warn,*,ned,ning,ningly, TO CAUTION SOMEONE AGAINST HARM/ PUNISHMENT (or see worn/warren)

warp,*,ped,ping, BECOME TWISTED/ BENT/BOWED IN SHAPE

warrant,*,ted,ting,ty,ties,ter, GUARANTEE/CONTRACT/ AUTHORIZATION "prefixes: un"

warren,*, ENCLOSURE FOR BREEDING GAME

warrior,*, BRAVE FIGHTER IN WARFARE

warrun, warren

wars, war(s) / where(s) / wear(s) / was / worse / worst

warsh, wash

warshd, wash(ed)

wart,*,ted,ty, A BUMPY SKIN GROWTH FROM A VIRUS

wartrobe, wardrobe

warule, weary(rily)

warun, warren

warunt, warrant

warunte, warrant(y)

warunted, warrant(ed)

warunty, warrant(y)

warwithal, wherewithal

wary,rier,riest,rily,riness, BE CAUTIOUS/ CAREFUL OF (or see weary) "prefixes: un"

was, PAST TENSE FOR THE WORD "IS" (or see weigh(s)/way(s))

wasd, waist / waste

wash,hes,hed,hing,her,hable,hy, TO CLEANSE WITH WATER/LIQUID "prefixes: pre/un"

washe, wash(y)

washeble, wash(able)

washepl, wash(able)

washer,*, APPLIANCE TO WASH CLOTHES/PARTS, SOMEONE WHO WASHES

washible, wash(able)

washipl, wash(able)

washir, washer

washt, wash(ed)

washuble, wash(able)

washur, washer

wasn't, CONTRACTION OF THE WORDS "WAS NOT", PAST TENSE FOR THE WORD "IS NOT"

wasp,*, A STINGING/FLYING INSECT

wast, waist / waste

waste,*,ed,ting,er,tage,eness,tingly, MORE THAN NECESSARY, LEFTOVERS, REMAINS OF SOMETHING (or see waist)

wastid, waste(d)

wat, wait / weight / what / watt / wade / wad

watal, waddle / what'll

watch,hes,hed,hing,hful,hfully,hfulness, MONITOR/LOOK AFTER, A DEVICE WORN ON THE WRIST "prefixes: un"

wated, wade(d) / wait(ed) / wad(dded)

watel, waddle / what'll

water,*,red,ring,ry,rless, CLEAR/ NATURAL SOLUTION THAT CONFORMS TO ICE/LIQUID/GAS "prefixes: un/under"

watercress, AN EDIBLE PLANT

waterd, water(ed)

waterfall, A DOWNFLOWING OF WATER

waterfaul, waterfall

waterfol, waterfall

waterkres, watercress

waterproof,*,fed,fing,fer, WATER CANNOT PENETRATE

waterpruf, waterproof

waters, waders / waiter(s) / water(s)
watertight,tness, SEALS AGAINST WATER ENTERING
watertite, watertight
watever, whatever
watevur, whatever
watid, wade(d) / wait(ed) / wad(dded)
watil, waddle / what'll
watir, wader / water / waiter
watird, water(ed)
watirfal, waterfall
watirfol, waterfall
watirkres, watercress
watirproof, waterproof
watirpruf, waterproof
watirs, waders / waiter(s) / water(s)
watl, waddle / what'll
watle, waddle / what'll
wator, wader / water / waiter
watres, waitress
watrus, waitress
watt,*,ttage, MEASURE OF ELECTRICITY (or see what/wad)
watud, wade(d) / wait(ed) / wad(dded)
watul, waddle / what'll
watur, wader / water / waiter
waturcres, watercress
waturfal, waterfall
waturfol, waterfall
waturproof, waterproof
waturpruf, waterproof
waturs, waders / waiter(s) / water(s)
waubel, wobble
waubil, wobble
wauch, watch
wauchful, watch(ful)
wauded, wade(d) / wait(ed) / wad(dded)
waudel, waddle / what'll
wauder, water
waudertight, watertight
waudid, wade(d) / wait(ed) / wad(dded)
waudil, waddle / what'll
waudul, waddle / what'll
waufel, waffle
wauful, waffle
wauk, wok / walk
waul, whale / wail / wale / wall
waulep, wallop
waulet, wallet
waulk, walk
waulker, walk(er) / walker
waulkur, walk(er) / walker

waulnut, walnut
waulo, wallow
waulop, wallop
waulow, wallow
waults, waltz
waulup, wallop
waulut, wallet
waun, won / one
waund, wound
waunder, wander / wonder
waunt, want
wauper, whopper
waupur, whopper
waur, war(s) / where(s) / wear(s) / was / worse / worst
waurl, where'll
waurp, warp
waurs, war(s) / where(s) / wear(s) / was / worse / worst
waut, watt / what / wad
wautercres, watercress
wautertite, watertight
wavd, wave(d) / waive(d)
wave,*,ed,ving,eless,vy,vily,viness,er, SERPENTINE ACTION DISPLAYING UP/DOWN/BACK/FORTH MOVEMENTS
wavenes, wave(viness)
waver,*, FLUCTUATE UP/DOWN/BACK/ FORTH (or see waiver/wafer) "prefixes: un"
wavir, waiver / wafer
wavles, wave(less)
wavur, waiver / wafer
wavynes, wave(viness)
wax,xes,xed,xing,xer,xen,xy,xier,xiest, xiness, INCREASE IN INTENSITY/ SIZE/ STRENGTH, MATTER PRODUCED BY BEE/PETROLEUM (or see whack(s)/ wake(s))
waxin, wax(en)
waxse, wax(y)
way,*,yless, METHOD, FASHION, STYLE, DIRECTION (or see weigh/whey)
wayv, wave
waz, way(s) / weigh(s) / was
wazp, wasp
we, MORE THAN ONE WITH SELF INCLUDED (or see wee/whee/ whey)
we'd, CONTRACTION OF THE WORDS "WE WOULD/HAD" (or see wed/ weed/ wheat/whet)

we'll, CONTRACTION OF THE WORDS "WE WILL" (or see well/wheel)
we're, CONTRACTION OF THE WORDS "WE ARE" (or see were/where/ weir/ whirr)
we've, CONTRACTION OF THE WORDS "WE HAVE" (or see weave)
weak,ker,kest,ken,kened,kening,kish, kishly,kishness,kener,kling,kly, kliness, kness, LACKING IN SKILL/ STRENGTH/KNOWLEDGE (or see week)
weald,*, PRISTINE/UNCULTIVATED FIELD AMIDST A FOREST (or see wield/ wheel(ed))
wealth,hy,hier,hiest,hily,hiness, AN OVER ABUNDANCE, MORE THAN ONE NEEDS
wean,*,ned,ning,ner,nling, SLOWLY REDUCE NEED FOR NOURISHMENT FROM THE MOTHER/PRIMARY FOOD SOURCE (or see ween)
weane, weeny
weapan, weapon
weape, weep(y)
weaped, weep(ed) / wept / reap(ed)
weapen, weapon
weapon,*,nry,nless, TOOL/ INSTRUMENT FOR PROTECTION OR TO HURT/KILL "prefixes: bio"
weapun, weapon
weapy, weep(y)
wear,*,ring,wore,worn,rable, USE SOMETHING UNTIL NO LONGER NEW, COVERING, CLOTHING (or see ware/where/we're/weir)
weard, weird
weary,rier,riest,ried,rying,rily,riness, riful,rifully,rifulness,riless,risome, risomely,risomeness, TIRED/ EXHAUSTED/FATIGUED (or see wary) "prefixes: un"
weasel,*,led,ling, CARNIVOROUS/ SLINKY/RODENT/MAMMAL
weather,*,red,ring,rability,rly,rliness, ELEMENTS/ATMOSPHERE AROUND THE EARTH (or see whether/ wether/wither)
weathur, weather / wether / wither / whether
weave,*,woven,ving,er, CRISS-CROSS PERPENDICULAR FIBERS ONE INTO/ THROUGH/ACROSS THE OTHER (or see we've) "prefixes: in/inter"

web,*,bbed,bbing,bby, INTERCONNECTING STRANDS CRISSCROSSING ONE ANOTHER, A NET, STRETCHED SKIN ON DUCK FEET (or see wept)

webd, web(bbed) / wept / weep(ed)

webt, web(bbed) / wept / weep(ed)

wech, which / witch / wedge

wechd, wedge(d)

wecht, wedge(d)

wed,*,dded,dding, GET MARRIED (or see wet/we'd/weed/whet/wheat)

weded, wed(dded) / weed(ed) / wet(tted)

wedeir, weed(er) / wet(tter)

wedel, whittle

weder, weed(er) / wet(tter) / weather

wedge,*,ed,ging,gie,gier,giest, A TRIANGULAR SHAPE, METHOD FOR RAISING/LEVELING

wedible, wet(able)

wedid, wed(dded) / weed(ed) / wet(tted)

wediest, weed(iest)

wedil, wheedle / whittle

wedir, weed(er) / wet(tter) / weather

wedle, wheedle / whittle

wedlock, MARRIAGE

wedlok, wedlock

wednesday,*, A DAY OF THE WEEK (ENGLISH)

wedo, widow

wedol, wheedle / whittle

wedr, weed(er) / wet(tter) / weather

wedth, width

wedud, wed(dded) / weed(ed) / wet(tted)

wedul, wheedle / whittle

wedur, weed(er) / wet(tter) / weather

wee, TINY/SMALL (or see we/whee)

weed,*,ded,ding,dy,dier,diest,dless,der, dily,diness, PLANTS MISUNDERSTOOD/ UNDERAPPRECIATED FOR THEIR MEDICINAL QUALITIES (or see we'd)

week,*,kly, SEVEN DAYS IN A ROW (or see weak) "prefixes: bi/semi"

weekle, week(ly)

weels, wheel(s) / wield(s)

ween,*,ned,ning, DESIRE/EXPECT SOMETHING (or see wean)

weeny,nies,nier,niest,nsy, TINY/SMALL, A TYPE OF HOTDOG/WEINER

---

weep,*,ped,ping,py,pier,piest, PASSIONATE/SAD/INTENSE CRYING, AN OOZING/LEAKING/DRIPPING OF FLUIDS (or see wept/reap)

weery, weary

weevil,*,led,ly, AN INSECT/BEETLE WHICH BORES INTO PLANTS

wef, weave / we've

weful, weevil

weg, wedge / wig

wegal, wiggle

wegd, wedge(d)

wege, wedge / wedge(gy)

weged, wedge(d) / wig(gged)

wegis, wedge(s)

wegle, wiggle

wegul, wiggle

wegus, wedge(s)

weigh,*,hed,hing,hable,her,ht, THE ACT OF MEASURING THE WEIGHT OF SOMETHING, TO FEEL WEIGHT (or see way/whey)

weight,*,ted,ting,ty,tier,tiest,tless, tlessly,tlessness,ty,tier,tiest,tily, tiness, MEASUREMENT OF VOLUME/DENSITY/MASS (or see wait/whet) "prefixes: over/under"

weild, wield / weald / weld

weiner,*, A HOTDOG/SMOKED SAUSAGE, ALSO SPELLED 'WIENER', SHORT FOR WIENER WURST VIENNESE SAUSAGE (or see wean(er))

weir,*, WALL/DAM BUILT TO SLOW DOWN THE FLOW OF WATER (or see were/ we're/wear/where)

weird,der,dest,dly,dness, STRANGE/ UNCOMMON/UNKNOWN/ UNLIKELY

wej, wedge

wejt, wedge(d)

wek, weak / week / wick

weked, wicked / wick(ed)

weker, wicker

wekle, week(ly)

wekur, wicker / weak(er)

wel, well / we'll / wheel

welcome,*,ed,ming,ely,eness,er, INVITE/HONOR/ENCOURAGE/ ACKNOWLEDGE THE ARRIVAL OF SOMETHING/SOMEONE

welcomnes, welcome(ness)

welcum, welcome

---

weld,*,ded,ding,der,dability,dable, dment, FUSE TWO PIECES OF SUBSTANCE TOGETHER USING A FILLER, HERB (or see wheel(ed)/ wield/weald)

weldid, weld(ed) / wield(ed)

weldir, weld(er) / wield(er)

weldmint, weld(ment)

welduble, weld(able) / wield(able)

weldur, weld(er) / wield(er)

weldurnes, wilderness

weler, wheel(er)

welfare,rism, ABLE TO FARE WELL AND FUNCTION NORMALLY/PROPERLY

welfer, welfare

welkem, welcome

welkumd, welcome(d)

welkumt, welcome(d)

well,*,lled,lling, FIT, HEALTHY, STRUCTURE THAT HOLDS WATER SEEPING UP FROM A SPRING, WORD POSED AS A QUESTION, ALSO, IN ADDITION TO (or see will/ we'll/ wheel) "prefixes: un/up"

wellth, wealth

welo, willow

wels, wheel(s) / wield(s)

welt,*, DISCOLORED/RAISED AREA ON THE SKIN WHERE DAMAGE OCCURED (or see weld/weild/ wheel(ed)/weald/wilt)

welter, weld(er) / wield(er)

welth, wealth

welthe, wealth(y)

weltheist, wealth(iest)

welthenes, wealth(iness)

weltheur, wealth(ier)

welur, wheel(er)

wem, whim

weman, women

wemin, women

wempe, wimp(y)

wemped, wimp(ed)

wemper, whimper

wempur, whimper

wemsekul, whimsical

wemsukil, whimsical

wen, wean / ween / win / when

wenar, win(nner) / whine(r) / weiner

wence, wince

wench,hes,hing, DEROGATORY WORD FOR A WOMAN WHO IS FROM THE COUNTRY/PROMISCUOUS (or see winch/wrench) wenchis, wench(es) / winch(es) / wrench(es)

wencht, wench(ed) / winch(ed) / wrench(ed)

wend,*,ded,ding, TRAVELING ALONG A PATH/ROUTE (or see wean(ed)/ ween(ed)/wind)

wende, wind(y)

wendeur, wind(ier)

wendy, wind(y)

wene, weeny / whinny / weiner

wenefer, whenever

wenefur, whenever

wener, win(nner) / whine(r) / weiner / wean(er)

weng, wing / wink

wenging, wing(ing)

wenie, weeny / weiner / whinny

wenir, win(nner) / weiner

wenk, wing / wink

wenking, wing(ing)

wenor, win(nner) / whine(r) / weiner

wens, whence / win(s) / wince

wensda, wednesday

wensh, wench / winch / wrench

wenshd, wench(ed) / winch(ed) / wrench(ed)

went, PAST TENSE FOR THE WORD "GO" (or see wind) "prefixes: under"

wenter, winter

wentre, wintery

wentur, winter

wenur, win(nner) / whine(r) / weiner

weny, weeny / whinny / weiner

wenzda, wednesday

wep, web / weep / whip

wepd, web(bbed) / wept / weep(ed)

wepe, weep(y)

weped, weep(ed) / wept / reap(ed)

wepen, whip(pping) / weapon

wepenre, weapon(ry)

weperwil, whippoorwill

wepeur, weep(ier)

wepin, whip(pping) / weapon

wepinre, weapon(ry)

wept, PAST TENSE FOR THE WORD 'WEEP', CRY (or see web(bbed)) "prefixes: un"

wepun, whip(pping) / weapon

wepunre, weapon(ry)

wepurwil, whippoorwill

wepy, weep(y)

wepyer, weep(ier)

wer, wear/ ware / where / we're / were / weir

werable, wear(able)

werafir, wherever

weras, whereas

werd, word / weird / where'd

werder, weird(er)

werdest, weird(est)

werdist, weird(est)

werdly, weird(ly)

werdnes, weird(ness)

were, PAST TENSE FOR THE WORD "WAS/IS" (or see where/we're/ whirr/weary/wire/weir/ worry)

wereble, wear(able)

werefur, wherever

weren't, CONTRACTION OF THE WORDS "WERE NOT"

werever, wherever

weri, wary / weary / worry

werible, wear(able)

werkd, work(ed)

werkt, work(ed)

werkuble, work(able)

werl, whirl / whorl / where'll

werld, whirl(ed) / world / whorl(ed)

werlpool, whirlpool

werlpul, whirlpool

werlwend, whirlwind

werlwind, whirlwind

werm, worm

wernd, weren't / warn(ed)

wernt, weren't

wers, where's / wear(s) / ware(s) / worse / worst

wershep, worship

wership, worship

wert, weird / word / where'd

werth, worth

werubel, wear(able)

weruble, wear(able)

werwithal, wherewithal

wery, weary / wary / worry

wes, wheeze

wesal, weasel

wesd, whiz(zzed)

wesdim, wisdom

wesdum, wisdom

wesdwurd, west(ward)

wesel, whistle

weseld, weasel(ed)

wesenes, wheeze(ziness)

weserd, wizard

weses, whiz(zzes)

wesh, wish

weshd, wish(ed)

wesil, weasel

wesk, whisk

weskd, whisk(ed)

weske, whiskey

wesker, whisker

weskur, whisker

wesky, whiskey

wesol, weasel / whistle

wesp, wisp

wespe, wisp(y)

wesper, whisper

wesperd, whisper(ed)

wespur, whisper

wespurd, whisper(ed)

wespy, wisp(y)

west,terly,tern,ternize,ternized,ting, tward, ONE OF THE FOUR DIRECTIONS ON THE EARTH

westirea, wisteria

westirly, west(erly)

westirn, west(ern)

westirnise, west(ernize)

westle, whistle

westorn, west(ern)

westornize, west(ernize)

westurle, west(erly)

westurly, west(erly)

westurn, west(ern)

westurnise, west(ernize)

westwerd, west(ward)

westwurd, west(ward)

wesul, weasel / whistle

wesuld, weasel(ed) / whistle(d)

wesuls, weasel(s) / whistle(s)

wesurd, wizard

wesus, whiz(zzes)

wet,*,tted,tting,tter,ttest,tly,tness, ttable,ttish, BATHED/COATED/ AFFECTED BY A LIQUID (or see wheat/wed/whet/we'd/weed/wit)

wetch, which / witch

wetel, whittle

weter, wet(tter) / whet(tter)

wetesh, wet(ish)

weth, with

wethar, weather / wether / wither / whether

wethaut, without

wethdrau, withdraw

wethdro, withdraw

wethdron, withdraw(n)

wethdroul, withdraw(al)

wetheld, withheld
wethen, within
wether, A RAM/BUCK THAT HAS BEEN CASTRATED (or see weather/wither/whether)
wethhold, withhold
wethin, within
wethir, weather / wether / wither / whether
wethold, withhold
wethout, without
wethrdraul, withdraw(al)
wethstand, withstand
wethstood, withstood
wethstud, withstood
wethur, weather / wether / wither / whether
wethurle, weather(ly)
wetir, wet(tter) / whet(tter)
wetl, whittle
wetlok, wedlock
wetnes, witness / wet(ness)
wetnus, witness / wet(ness)
wetnusd, witness(ed)
weto, widow
wetuble, wet(able)
wetul, whittle
wetur, wet(tter) / whet(tter)
wety, wit(tty)
weuld, wield / weald / weld
weurd, weird
weurdest, weird(est)
weurl, where'll / whirl
wev, weave / we've
wevd, weave(d)
wevel, weevil
wevor, weave(r)
wevul, weevil
wevur, weave(r)
wewre, weary
wey, way / weigh / whey
wez, wheeze / whiz
wezard, wizard
wezd, whiz(zzed)
weze, wheeze(zy)
wezel, weasel
wezeld, weasel(ed)
wezil, weasel
wezines, wheeze(ziness)
wezt, west
wezul, weasel
wezuld, weasel(ed)
wezurd, wizard

whack,*,ked,king,ky, A SOUND, A SLAPPING ACTION
whad, wad / what / wade / wait
whaddle, waddle / what'll
whadul, waddle / what'll
whake, wacky / wake
whakiness, wacky(kiness)
whaky, wacky
whale,*,ed,ling,er, LARGE AQUATIC MAMMAL, CETACEAN, TO BEAT/THRASH/WHIP (or see wale/wail)
whalep, wallop
whalup, wallop
whar, wear / ware / where / we're
wharas, whereas
whard, where'd
whare, where / ware / wear / were
wharevur, wherever
wharf,es, PLACE FOR BOATS TO DOCK AND UNLOAD/LOAD ALONG A BODY OF WATER
whars, where's / ware(s) / wear(s)
wharwithal, wherewithal
what,*, A GENERAL WORD USED TO ASK A QUESTION OR LEARN MORE ABOUT SOMETHING (or see watt)
what'll, CONTRACTION OF THE WORDS "WHAT WILL/ SHALL" (or see waddle)
whatel, what'll / waddle
whatever, EITHER WAY, NOT THAT IMPORTANT
whatul, what'll / waddle
wheat,*, A GRAIN (or see weight/weed/we'd)
wheb, web
whech, which / witch
whed, wed / we'd / weed / wheat
whedil, wheedle / whittle
whedlok, wedlock
whedul, wheedle / whittle
whee, EXPRESSION OF JOY, SUDDEN EXCITEMENT (or see we/wee)
wheedle,*,ed,ling,er,lingly, USE WORDS TO COAX/ENTICE SOMEONE TO GIVE YOU SOMETHING (or see whittle)
wheel,*,led,ling,ler, ROUND SHAPED DEVICE USED TO ROLL/TRANSPORT (or see we'll/well/weld/weald)
wheeze,*,ed,zing,zily,ziness,zy,ziness, RASPY BREATHING SOUND DUE TO LUNG IRRITATION
wheld, wheel(ed) / weld / wield / weald

whelm,*,med,ming, OVERTAKE, OVERPOWER, SUBMERGE "prefixes: over/under"
whem, whim
when, REFERENCE TO TIME (or see win/wean/ween)
whence, REFERS TO "FROM/ORIGIN/WHEN" (or see wince)
whenever, NO SPECIFIC TIME
whenevur, whenever
whens, whence / wean(s) / wince
whent, went
whep, whip
whepurwil, whippoorwill
wher, where / were / we're / ware / weir
wheras, whereas
wherd, where'd / weird
where,*, IN REFERENCE TO PLACE (or see ware/were/we're/whirr)
where'd, CONTRACTION OF THE WORDS "WHERE DID" (or see weird)
where'll, CONTRACTION OF THE WORDS "WHERE WILL", SLANG WORD (or see whirl)
where's, CONTRACTION OF THE WORDS "WHERE IS" (or see ware(s)/wear(s))
whereas, ALTHOUGH, EXCEPT THAT, OTHER THAN
wherever, NO SPECIFIC PLACE
wherewithal, TO HAVE THE RESOURCES/TIME
wherl, whirl / whorl / where'll
wherlpool, whirlpool
wherlwind, whirlwind
whers, where's / wear(s) / ware(s)
whert, where'd / weird
wherwithal, wherewithal
whesk, whisk
whesky, whiskey
whet,*,tted,tting, SMALL AMOUNT REMOVED/ADDED/CARVED OUT (or see wet/wheat/wit/wed)
whether, WHEN ONE OF SEVERAL CHOICES HASN'T BEEN DECIDED, REFERRING TO CHOICE (or see weather/wether/wither)
whetle, whittle
whetlok, wedlock
whetul, whittle

whew, DEEP SIGH OF RELIEF AFTER A STRESSFUL MOMENT (or see woo/ hue/ who)

whey, INGREDIENT IN SOME ANIMALS MILK (or see way/weigh)

whez, whiz / wheeze

wheze, wheeze(zy)

whezines, wheeze(ziness)

which, CHOICE BETWEEN, CHOOSE ONE (or see witch)

whid, wide / white

while, REFERENCE TO TIME,IN THE MEANTIME, DURING THE SAME TIME (or see will/wile)

whim,msy,msies,msical, SPONTANEOUS, WITHOUT MUCH FORETHOUGHT

whimper,*,red,ring,rer, SOFT CRYING/ WHINING SOUND

whimsical,lly,lity,lness, WITH A FRIVOLOUS NATURE, ADVENTUROUS/FANTASY

whine,*,ed,ning,ey,er, A NASAL/NEEDY/ PLEADING/WANTING SOUND (or see wine/whinny)

whinefur, whenever

whinevur, whenever

whinny,nnies,nnied,nnying, SOUND A HORSE MAKES (or see whine(y))

whint, went

whiny, whine(y) / whinny

whip,*,pped,pping,pper, BEAT/WORK INTO A LATHER, LONG DEVICE MADE OF WOVEN LEATHER STRIPS (or see wipe)

whiperwil, whippoorwill

whippoorwill, A BIRD

whipurwil, whippoorwill

whirl,*,led,ling,ler,ly, SPIN AROUND (or see whorl)

whirlpool,*, A CIRCULAR/SPIRAL MOTION IN THE WATER

whirlwind,*, CIRCULAR/SPIRAL MOTION IN THE WIND

whirr,*,rred,rring, TYPE OF SOUND LIKE A MOTOR/SPIRAL (or see were/ we're/ where/whirl)

whisel, whistle

whisk,*,ked,king, BRUSH AWAY AS IF BY THE WIND

whisker,*,red,ry, LONG SENSITIVE/ SENSORY HAIRS AROUND ANIMALS NOSE/ SNOUT, FACIAL HAIR

whiskey, ALCOHOL FERMENTATION

whisky, whiskey

whisol, whistle

whisper,*,red,ring,rer,ry, SPEAK QUIETLY/FAINTLY

whistle,*,ed,ling,er, FORCED AIR FROM BETWEEN PURSED LIPS PRODUCING SOUND

whisul, whistle

whit, white / wit / wide

white,*,ed,ting,er,est,en,ener,eness, ening, COLOR PRODUCED BY ALL COLORS OF THE LIGHT SPECTRUM, CALCIUM CARBONATE

whitle, whittle

whittle,*,ed,ling,er, SHAVE OFF SMALL PORTIONS/SLIVERS OF WOOD

whitul, whittle

whity, wit(tty)

whiz,zzes,zzed,zzing, TO STREAK BY QUICKLY AS IF BLOWN BY A STRONG WIND

who,*, TO REFER TO "IN GENERAL" WITHOUT USING A NAME/TITLE/ DESCRIPTION OF (or see whoa/hue/ whew/woo)

who'd, CONTRACTION OF THE WORDS "WHO HAD/ WOULD/COULD"

who'll, CONTRACTION OF THE WORDS "WHO WILL/SHALL"

who's, CONTRACTION OF THE WORDS "WHO IS/HAS" (or see whose/hose)

whoa, WORD TO GET A HORSE TO STOP (or see woo/whew/woe)

whodel, waddle / what'll

whodul, waddle / what'll

whoever, IN REFERENCE TO ANYBODY, SOMEONE WHOSE NAME/TITLE IS NOT KNOWN AT THE TIME

whole,eness,esome,lly, ENTIRE THING, ALL OF IT, WELL-ROUNDED, COMPLETE (or see hole/holy/ wholly)

wholesale,ling,er, SELL WITHOUT PRICE MARK-UP

wholesome,ely,eness, COMPLETE, WELL-ROUNDED "prefixes: un"

wholly, COMPLETE IN ITS ENTIRETY (or see holy/hole/whole(y))

wholsail, wholesale

wholsel, wholesale

wholsem, wholesome

wholsum, wholesome

wholupt, wallop(ed)

wholy, wholly / whole(y)

whom, OBJECTIVE PRONOUN OF "WHO"

whomever, OBJECTIVE CASE OF "WHOEVER"

whomp,*,ped,ping, A SOUND, COMPLETE VICTORY

whoop,*,ped,ping, A TYPE OF SOUND USED IN WAR CRIES, GET A SPANKING/BEATING

whoosh,hes,hed,hing, ACTION/SOUND AS IF SWEPT UP BY THE WIND

whoper, whopper

whopper,*, GREAT/GIANT/HUGE

whore,*,ed,ring, DEROGATORY TERM FOR A PROMISCUOUS FEMALE

whorf, wharf

whorl,*,led,ling, LIKE A WHIRL/SWIRL AS IF TURNED ABOUT BY THE WIND, SPIRAL (or see whirl)

whose, BELONGS TO SOMEONE/ SOMETHING IN PARTICULAR (or see who's)

whot, what / watt

whud, what / would

whudel, what'll / waddle

whudevur, whatever

whudul, what'll / waddle

whuever, whoever

whup, whoop

whurlwind, whirlwind

whut, what / would

whutel, what'll / waddle

whutever, whatever

whutul, what'll / waddle

why, A GENERAL QUESTION DESIRING AN ANSWER

wi, we / whee / why / wee

wic, witch / which / week / wick

wich, which / witch

wick,*,ked,king,ker, SLOWLY SOAK UP LIQUID, A WOVEN COTTON FOR LAMP OIL (or see wig)

wicked,dly,dness, EVIL/MALICIOUSNESS INTENT (or see wick(ed))

wicker, FURNITURE BUILT OF WOODY/ WOVEN MATERIAL

wid, wide / ride / white / with / wit / weed / we'd

wide,er,est,en,eness,ener,dth, DIMENSION OF GIRTH/ BREADTH, EXTENT/SPREAD OF (or see white/ width)

widel, whittle

wider, wither / wide(r) / white(r) / ride(r)

widin, within / wide(n)

widl, whittle

wido, widow

widow,*,wer, SPOUSE WHO LOST MATE TO DEATH

widt, width / with / wit

width,*, MEASUREMENT/DISTANCE OF ONE SIDE OF SOMETHING

widul, whittle

wiel, while / will / well / wile

wield,*,ded,ding,dable,der,dy, USE/ GIVEN TO POWER/COMMAND (or see weld/wheel(ed)/wealed/wild) "prefixes: un"

wiener, weiner / wean(er)

wif, wife / weave / we've / with

wife,ely,ives, FEMALE LEGALLY BONDED IN MARRIAGE

wifes, wives

wifs, wives

wig,*,gged,gging, FALSE HAIR FOR THE HEAD, TO FREAK OUT/ACT NUTS, BE UNCHARACTERISTICALLY UNPREDICTABLE (or see wick)

wiged, wig(gged)

wiggle,*,ed,ling, MOVE QUICKLY FROM SIDE TO SIDE (or see wriggle)

wigul, wiggle

wik, wick / weak / week

wiked, wicked

wiker, wicker

wikur, wicker

wil, while / will / well / wile

wild,der,dest,dly, UNCONTROLLABLE, NO RESTRAINT IN ACTIONS (or see wile(d)/will(ed))

wilderness, UNTAMED/NATURAL FOREST

wildist, wild(est)

wildurnes, wilderness

wile,ed, LURE/ENTICE AWAY FROM (or see while/will)

will,*,lled,lling,llful,llfully,llfulness,llingly, llingness, DESIRE/INCLINATION TO MAKE HAPPEN, LEGAL DOCUMENT OUTLINING DIVISION OF PROPERTY AFTER DEATH (or see well/wile/ while) "prefixes: un"

willdernes, wilderness

willow,*,wy, A TREE, LIKE THE TREE

wilo, willow

wilow, willow

wilt,*,ted,ting, DROOP FROM LACK OF NOURISHMENT AS A PLANT DOES (or see welt)

wim, whim

wiman, women

wimon, women

wimp,*,ped,ping,py, LACK OF COURAGE/STRENGTH

wimpur, whimper

wimsecal, whimsical

wimsikul, whimsical

win,*,nning,nner,won,nnable, ADVANTAGE IN COMPETITION (or see when/whine/wine)

wince,*,ed,cing, TO FLINCH (or see whence)

winch,hes,hed,hing, PULL/HOIST SOMETHING BY MEANS OF A DEVICE (or see wench/wrench)

winchd, wench(ed) / winch(ed) / wrench(ed)

winchis, wench(es) / winch(es) / wrench(es)

wind,*,ded,ding,dy,dier,diest,wound, dless, AIR MOVING FASTER THAN A BREEZE,TURN SOMETHING UNTIL TIGHT/TAUT (or see went) "prefixes: en/in/re/un/up"

wine,*,ning, FRUIT/FLOWERS THAT HAVE BEEN CAREFULLY AGED/ FERMENTED (or see whine/whinny)

wined, wine(d) / whine(d) / wind

winefer, whenever

winefur, whenever

winer, win(nner) / whine(r) / weiner

winey, whine(y) / weeny

wing,*,ged,ging,gless, BIRD/INSECT/ PLANE ARMS, TO AD LIB "prefixes: under"

wini, weeny / whine(y)

wink,*,ked,king, QUICK BLINK OF ONE EYE "prefixes: un"

winor, win(nner) / whine(r) / weiner / wean(er)

winsday, wednesday

winsh, wench / winch / wrench

winshd, wench(ed) / winch(ed) / wrench(ed)

wint, went / wend / whine(d) / wind

winter,*,red,ring,ry, SEASON BETWEEN FALL/AUTUMN/ SPRING "prefixes: over"

wintre, winter / wintry

wintry,rier,riest, LIKE WINTER

wintur, winter

winur, win(nner) / whine(r) / weiner / wean(er)

winy, whine(y) / whinny

wip, whip / wipe

wipd, whip(pped) / wipe(d)

wipe,*,ed,ping,er, REMOVE CONTAMINANT/SURFACE DEBRIS/ MATERIAL TO CREATE SMOOTH PLANE/SURFACE (or see whip)

wipen, whip(pping) / wipe(ping)

wiperwil, whippoorwill

wipon, whip(pping) / wipe(ping)

wipt, whip(pped) / wipe(d)

wipun, whip(pping) / wipe(ping)

wipurwil, whippoorwill

wir, wire / were / wear / ware / where / we're / whirr / weir

wird, word / wire(d)

wire,*,ed,ring,eless,ry, METAL STRAND (or see were/whirr/weir) "prefixes: pre/re/un/under"

wiri, worry / weary

wirk, work

wirkeble, work(able)

wirkt, work(ed)

wirkuble, work(able)

wirkur, work(er)

wirl, whirl / whorl

wirld, whirl(ed) / world / whorl(ed)

wirleng, whirl(ing)

wirles, wire(less)

wirlpul, whirlpool

wirlwind, whirlwind

wirm, worm

wirnt, weren't

wirpool, whirlpool

wirs, worse / worst

wirshep, worship

wirshup, worship

wirth, worth

wirthe, worth(y)

wirthy, worth(y)

wis, wise / whiz

wisd, whiz(zzed)

wisdem, wisdom

wisdom, KNOWLEDGE GAINED BY EXPERIENCE "prefixes: un"

wisdum, wisdom

wise,er,est,ely,eness,sdom, KNOWLEDGE GAINED BY EXPERIENCE "prefixes: un"

wisel, whistle

wiserd, wizard

wises, whiz(zzes) / wise(s)

wish,hes,hed,hing,hful,hfully,hfulness, HOPE/IMAGINE FOR THE FUTURE "prefixes: un"

wishus, wish(es)

wisk, whisk

wiskd, whisk(ed)

wiske, whiskey

wisker, whisker

wiskur, whisker

wisky, whiskey

wisol, whistle / weasel

wisp,*,py, LIGHT, AIRY, OF LITTLE WEIGHT

wispe, wisp(y)

wisper, whisper

wisperd, whisper(ed)

wispur, whisper

wispurer, whisper(er)

wisteria, A FLOWERING BUSH

wistle, whistle

wisul, whistle

wisurd, wizard

wisus, whiz(zzes)

wit,*,tted,tting,tty,ttier,ttiest, QUICK IN MIND/RESPONSE (or see with/wet/ white/write/wheat) "prefixes: un"

witch,hes,hing,hy,hery, TERM FOR A FEMALE WHO GIVES IMPRESSION THEY HAVE SUPER POWER (or see which)

wite, wit(tty) / white

witel, whittle

with, PREFIX INDICATING 'BACK/AWAY/ AGAINST' MOST OFTEN MODIFIES THE WORD (or see width)

withaut, without

withdrau, withdraw

withdraw,*,wing,wal,wn,hdrew, PULL/ MOVE BACK, RETREAT

withdro, withdraw

withdron, withdraw(n)

witheld, withheld

withen, within

wither,*,red,ring, SHRIVEL/SHRINK FROM LACK OF NOURISHMENT/ MOISTURE, MEASUREMENT OF SOME QUADRUPED ANIMALS AT THE SHOULDER (or see weather/ wether/whether)

withheld, PAST TENSE FOR THE WORD 'WITHHOLD', TO HOLD BACK

withhold,*,ding,held, THE ACT OF HOLDING BACK, REFRAIN FROM MAKING VISIBLE/APPARENT

within, CONTAINED, NOT VISIBLE/ APPARENT

withold, withhold

withor, wither

without, LACKING, NOT HAVING

withstand,*,ding,tood, TO STAND AGAINST, TOLERATE

withstood, PAST TENSE FOR THE WORD 'WITHSTAND'

withstud, withstood

withur, wither

witle, whittle

witness,sses,ssed,ssing, HAVE KNOWINGNESS OF, HAVING SEEN

witnus, witness

witol, whittle

witul, whittle

wity, wit(tty)

wives, PLURAL WORD FOR 'WIFE', MORE THAN ONE WIFE

wiz, wise / whiz

wizard,*,dry, A PERSON WHO PARTAKES IN ACTIONS INVOLVING MYSTICAL POWER

wizd, whiz(zzed)

wizer, wise(r)

wizerd, wizard

wizest, wise(st)

wizur, wise(r)

wizurd, wizard

wo, whoa / woo / woe / whew

wobble,*,ed,ling,ly, LACKS STABILITY IN POSITION, NOT STEADY

wobul, wobble

woc, walk / woke / wok

woch, wash / watch

wochd, watch(ed)

woches, watch(es)

wochful, watch(ful)

wocht, watch(ed)

wochus, watch(es)

wod, wad / wood / would / what / wait

wodent, wouldn't

woder, water

wodercres, watercress

wodere, water(y)

woderfol, waterfall

woderkres, watercress

wodertite, watertight

wodery, water(y)

wodid, wad(dded) / wait(ed) / wade(d)

wodil, waddle / what'll

wodint, wouldn't

wodir, water

wodirfal, waterfall

wodirkres, watercress

wodirtite, watertight

wodul, waddle / what'll

wodur, water

wodurkres, watercress

wodurtite, watertight

woe,*,eful,efully,efulness, SORROW/ LAMENT (or see woo/whoa)

wofel, waffle

woful, waffle

wok,*, VESSEL FOR COOKING (or see woke/walk)

woke, PAST TENSE FOR 'WAKE' (or see wok/walk)

woken, PAST TENSE FOR 'WAKE', BRING TO CONSCIOUSNESS FROM A DEEP SLEEP

wokin, woken

wokun, woken

wol, wall / wool

wold, wall(ed)/ wail(ed) / would

wolen, wool(en)

wolep, wallop

wolet, wallet

wolf,lves,fing, OF THE WILD CANINE/ CANID FAMILY

wolin, wool(en)

wolip, wallop

wolipd, wallop(ed)

woliped, wallop(ed)

wolit, wallet

wolk, walk / woke

wolken, walk(ing)

wolker, walk(er) / walker

wolkur, walk(er) / walker

wolnut, walnut

wolo, wallow

wolod, wallow(ed)

wolopd, wallop(ed)

wolopt, wallop(ed)

wolres, walrus

wolrus, walrus

wolsem, wholesome

wolst, waltz(ed)

wolts, waltz

woltsd, waltz(ed)

woltz, waltz

wolup, wallop

wolupt, wallop(ed)

wolut, wallet

wolveren, wolverine

wolverine,*, ANIMAL IN THE WEASEL FAMILY NOT RELATED TO WOLVES

wolves, PLURAL FOR 'WOLF', IN THE CANID FAMILY

wolwrus, walrus

wolz, waltz

wom, womb

woman,men,nism,nless,nly,nliness, AN ADULT FEMALE

womanhood, GROWING INTO ADULT FEMALE HUMAN

womanize,*,ed,zing,er, MEN WHO DENIGRATE WOMEN

womb,*, FEMALE ORGAN THAT CREATES LIFE "prefixes: en"

women, PLURAL FOR "WOMAN"

womin, woman / women

womp, whomp

won, PAST TENSE WORD FOR 'WIN' (or see one/wan)

won't, CONTRACTION OF THE WORDS 'WILL NOT' (or see want)

wond, wand / won / wane(d) / wan(ed)

wonder,*,red,ring,rful, QUESTION, PONDER, MARVEL (or see wander)

wonderd, wander(ed) / wonder(ed)

wonderful,lly,lness, FULL OF AWE, IMPRESSED

wondurd, wander(ed) / wonder(ed)

wondurer, wander(er)

wons, once / want(s) / win(s)

wonten, wanton

wontenes, wanton(nness)

wonter, wander / wonder

wonton, wanton

wontunes, wanton(nness)

wontunle, wanton(ly)

woo,*,oed,oing,oingly,oer, PERFORM ACTS TO GAIN ATTENTION/ AFFECTION/APPROVAL FROM SOMEONE (or see whew/woe/ whoa)

wood,*,ded,den,dy,dsy,dless, FIBROUS/ NATURAL MATERIAL, STEM/BASE OF A TREE/BUSH, HEAVILY TREED/ BUSHY AREA (or see would) "prefixes: under"

woofer,*, LOUDSPEAKER IN SOUND SYSTEM

woofur, woofer

wool,*,len,ly, HAIR FROM THE FLEECE OF ANIMALS

woolvs, wolves

woom, womb

woop, whoop

woose, woozy

woosh, whoosh

woosy, woozy

woozy,zily,ziness,zier,zies, FEELING OUT OF SORTS/UNSTABLE/SLIGHTLY DRUNK

woper, whopper

wopur, whopper

wor, war / wore

worant, warrant

worbeld, warble(d)

worbild, warble(d)

worbler, warbler

worblur, warbler

worbuld, warble(d)

word,*,ded,ding,dy,dily,diness,dless, dlessly,dlessness, LETTERS ARRANGED TOGETHER TO CREATE MEANING, USING TOO MANY WORDS TO DESCRIBE (or see war(rred)/ward/where'd/wart) "prefixes: re"

worden, warden

wordon, warden

wordrob, wardrobe

wordun, warden

wore, PAST TENSE FOR THE WORD 'WEAR' (or see war)

woreir, warrior

woren, warren

worent, warrant

worented, warrant(ed)

worentes, warrant(ies)

worenty, warrant(y)

woreur, warrior

worf, wharf

worier, warrior

worin, warren

worint, warrant

worinte, warrant(y)

worinted, warrant(ed)

worinty, warrant(y)

work,*,ked,king,ker,kable,kability, kableness, PERFORM ACTIONS/ TASKS TO ACCOMPLISH A DESIRED RESULT "prefixes: over/re/un"

workuble, work(able)

worl, whirl / whorl

world,*,dly,liness, OF/BELONGS TO THIS PLANET "prefixes: un/under"

worm,*,med,ming,mer,my, AN INVERTEBRATE WHICH LIVES MOSTLY CONCEALED FROM VIEW (or see warm)

wormd, warm(ed) / worm(ed)

wormer, warm(er) / worm(er)

wormest, warm(est)

wormle, warm(ly)

wormth, warm(th)

wormur, warm(er)

wormust, warm(est)

worn, PAST TENSE FOR THE WORD 'WEAR', USED MANY TIMES (or see warn) "prefixes: un"

wornd, warn(ed)

wornt, warn(ed) / weren't

worp, warp

worpd, warp(ed)

worry,rries,rried,rying,rrisome,yingly, rrier, BE CONCERNED/ FEARFUL ABOUT SOMETHING WHICH MAY/ MAY NOT HAPPEN

worse,st,en, MORE THAN BAD, MORE TROUBLE THAN EXPECTED/ ANTICIPATED (or see worst)

worsen,*,ned,ning,st, CONTINUES TO GET WORST/ DETERIORATE

worsh, wash

worshep, worship

worship,*,pped,pping,pper, ONE WHO IDOLIZES/ADORES SOMEONE/ SOMETHING

worst, MORE EXTREME THAN WORSE, MORE TROUBLE THAN EXPECTED/ ANTICIPATED (or see worse)

wort, wart / word / ward

worth,hier,hiest,hiness,hless,hlessly,hy, hily, VALUE/QUALITY OF SOMETHING/ SOMEONE "prefixes: un"

worun, warren

worunt, warrant

worunty, warrant(y)

wory, worry

wos, was / woe(s)

wosh, wash

woshd, wash(ed)

woshepl, wash(able)

wosher, washer

woshir, washer

wosht, wash(ed)

woshuble, wash(able)

woshur, washer

wosnt, wasn't

wosp, wasp

wosy, woozy

wot, watt / what / wad

wotch, watch

wotertite, watertight

woturd, water(ed)

would, PERHAPS WILL BE DONE/ ACCOMPLISHED, POSSIBLE (or see wood)

would've, CONTRACTION OF THE WORDS 'WOULD HAVE'

wouldn't, CONTRACTION OF THE WORDS 'WOULD NOT', WILL NOT BE DONE/ ACCOMPLISHED

wound,*,ded,ding,dless, PHYSICALLY HARMED/INJURED, PAST TENSE FOR THE WORD 'WIND' "prefixes: en/un"

wount, won't

wove,en, PAST TENSE FOR THE WORD 'WEAVE' "prefixes: inter"

wownt, won't

woz, was

wozp, wasp

wozy, woozy

wra, ray / raw

wrack,*,ked,king,kful, WRECKED/ RUINED, PERTAINING TO CLOUDS (or see rack)

wrak, rack / rake / wrack / rag

wrangle,*,ed,ling,er, BE CONFRONTATIONAL/ ARGUMENTATIVE, TO ROUND UP CATTLE

wrangul, wrangle

wrap,*,pped,pping,pper, COVER/ SURROUND SOMETHING, TO PACKAGE UP (or see rap) "prefixes: en/un"

wrased, raise(d) / race(d) / erase(d)

wrath,hful,hfully, EXTREMELY ANGRY/ PUNISHING/REVENGEFUL

wreak,*,ked,king, CAUSE CONFUSION/ DAMAGE AS IF BY MEANS OF RAGE/ VENGEANCE (or see reek/wreck)

wreath,*,hless, CIRCULAR GARLAND OF VARIOUS PLANT/ORGANIC MATERIAL, CIRCULAR SHAPE, NOUN (or see wreathe)

wreathe,*,hed,hing, THE ACTION OF CIRCLING/ENCIRCLING, VERB (or see wreath) "prefixes: en"

wrech, wretch / reach

wreck,*,ked,king,ker, CRASH/ALTER/ DESTROY (or see wreak)

wrecker,*, A TRUCK THAT TOWS VEHICLES

wreek, wreak / reak

wreeth, wreath / wreathe

wregul, wriggle

wreker, wrecker

wrekur, wrecker

wren,*, A SMALL BIRD

wrench,hes,hed,hing, A HAND TOOL USED FOR TURNING/TWISTING, TWIST SOMETHING AROUND (or see winch/wench)

wrer, rear / rare / wear

wresil, wrestle

wrest,*,ted,ting, TO FORCIBLY TWIST/ WRING/REMOVE FROM GRASP/ POWER (or see wrist)

wrestle,*,ed,ling,er, FORCIBLY ATTEMPT TO MANEUVER/ MANIPULATE

wresul, wrestle

wretch,hed,hedly,hedness, POOR/ MISERABLE/UNHAPPY PERSON

wreth, wreath / wreathe

wriggle,*,ed,ling,ly, TO SQUIRM/ WRITHE/MOVE IN TWISTING/ TURNING MOTIONS (or see wiggle)

wright, PROFESSIONAL INVOLVED IN ART/HAND WORK, AN ARTISAN (or see right/rite/writ)

wrigle, wriggle

wrigul, wriggle

wrin, wren

wrinch, wrench

wring,*,ging,rung, TWIST SOMETHING AROUND TIGHTLY CREATING COMPRESSION (or see ring)

wrinkle,*,ed,ling,ly, LINES, CREASES

wrist, A JOINT THE ARM (or see wrest)

writ, WRITTEN COURT ORDER (or see write/right/rite)

write,*,tten,ting,rote,table,tability, PUT WORDS/MUSIC INTO PHYSICAL/ VISIBLE FORM (or see writ/right/ rite/wright) "prefixes: over/pre/re/ under"

writer,*, SOMEONE WHO WRITES (or see writ/right/rite/wright) "prefixes: under"

writhe,*,ed,hing, TWIST/SQUIRM EMOTIONALLY AND/OR PHYSICALLY

written, PAST TENSE FOR THE WORD WRITE "prefixes: un"

wrk, work

wrm, worm/ warm

wrom, worm / warm

wron, worn / warn

wrong,*,ged,ging,gly,gness, NOT SUITABLE/CORRECT/PROPER/ NORMAL

wrot, wrought / wrote / rote

wrote, PAST TENSE FOR THE WORD "WRITE" (or see rote/wrought/rot) "prefixes: under"

wrought, DECORATIVE METALWORK, PAST TENSE FOR THE WORD "WREAK", TWISTED WITH WORRY/ PAIN "prefixes: over"

wrout, wrought

wrudikulus, ridiculous

wrudiquelus, ridiculous

wrung, PAST TENSE FOR THE WORD "WRING" (or see rung)

wry,rier,riest,yly,yness, TWISTEDLY IRONIC, OUT OF SHAPE (or see rye)

wryth, writhe

wu, whew / woo / what

wud, would / wood / what

wudal, what'll / waddle

wudent, wouldn't

wudever, whatever

wudil, what'll / waddle

wudint, wouldn't

wudul, what'll / waddle

wue, whew / woo

wufer, woofer

wufir, woofer

wufs, wolves

wul, wool

wulen, wool(en)

wulf, wolf

wulferene, wolverine

wulin, wool(en)

wulveren, wolverine

wulviren, wolverine

wulvs, wolves

wum, womb

wumen, woman / women

wumin, woman / women

wuminhud, womanhood

wuminizer, womanize(r)

wund, wound

wunderful, wonderful

wunefur, whenever

wunevur, whenever

wup, whoop

wur, were / whirr

wurd, word / where'd

wure, worry
wuri, worry
wurk, work
wurkd, work(ed)
wurkebul, work(able)
wurker, work(er)
wurkt, work(ed)
wurl, whirl / whorl
wurld, whirl(ed) / world / whorl(ed)
wurlpool, whirlpool
wurlpul, whirlpool
wurls, whirl(s) / whorl(s)
wurlt, whirl(ed) / world / whorl(ed)
wurlwend, whirlwind
wurlwind, whirlwind
wurm, worm
wurnt, weren't
wurs, worse / worst
wursen, worsen
wurshep, worship
wurshup, worship
wurst, worst
wurth, worth
wurthe, worth(y)
wurthy, worth(y)
wury, worry
wus, was / woo(s)
wuse, woozy
wush, whoosh
wusi, woozy
wusnt, wasn't
wut, what / would / wood
wutefer, whatever
wutel, what'll / waddle
wutever, whatever
wutil, what'll / waddle
wutul, what'll / waddle
wuz, was
wuznt, wasn't
wuzy, woozy
wy, why
x, ex
x-ray,*,yed,ying, RADIATION WHICH
    PENETRATES PHYSICAL MASS
xagurate, exaggerate
xajurate, exaggerate
xakut, execute
xam, exam
xamen, examine
xamin, examine
xampel, example
xampul, example
xamun, examine

xanth, PREFIX INDICATING "YELLOW"
    MOST OFTEN MODIFIES THE WORD
xaspurate, exasperate
xaust, exhaust
xchang, exchange
xdra, extra
xdru, extra
xekute, execute
xemplify, exemplify
xempt, exempt
xen, PREFIX INDICATING "STRANGE"
    MOST OFTEN MODIFIES THE WORD
xeno, PREFIX INDICATING "STRANGE"
    MOST OFTEN MODIFIES THE WORD
xenon, A GAS
xenophobe,bia,bic, IRRATIONAL/
    EXTREME HATRED/CONTEMPT FOR
    FOREIGN PEOPLE
xer, PREFIX INDICATING "DRY" MOST
    OFTEN MODIFIES THE WORD
xerafit, xerophyte
xeraphyte, xerophyte
xero, PREFIX INDICATING "DRY" MOST
    OFTEN MODIFIES THE WORD
xerophily,lous, SURVIVES IN DRY/HOT
    REGIONS
xerophyte,*,tic,tically,tism, DROUGHT/
    HEAT RESISTANT PLANT
xet, exit
xhale, exhale
xibit, exhibit
xil, exile
xilene, xylene
ximplify, exemplify
xiraphyte, xerophyte
xist, exist
xit, exit
xklud, exclude
xklumashen, exclamation
xkurshen, excursion
xkuse, excuse
xkuvate, excavate
xodik, exotic
xpand, expand
xpans, expanse / expense / expand(s)
xpekt, expect
xpel, expel
xpens, expense
xpereins, experience
xperumint, experiment
xpir, expire
xplan, explain
xplod, explode
xplor, explore

xployt, exploit
xport, export
xpoz, expose
xpres, express
xpudeshin, expedition
xpurt, expert
xsalint, excellent
xsed, exceed
xsel, excel / accel / axle
xsept, except
xses, excess
xsit, excite / exit
xsploshen, explosion
xsplosive, explosive
xsulent, excellent
xsurpt, excerpt
xsursiz, exercise / exorcise
xtend, extend
xtenshen, extension
xtenuate, extenuate
xtereur, exterior
xtinkt, extinct
xtra, extra
xtradite, extradite
xtrakt, extract
xtrem, extreme
xtrordenair, extraordinaire
xtrordinery, extraordinary
xtru, extra
xturnol, external
xukute, execute
xurt, exert
xyl, PREFIX INDICATING "WOOD" MOST
    OFTEN MODIFIES THE WORD
xylafon, xylophone
xylagraf, xylograph
xylaphone, xylophone
xylatomy, xylotomy
xylaudomy, xylotomy
xylem, THAT WHICH FORMS WOODY
    FIBER/TISSUE/STEM IN PLANTS
xylene,*,lol, A CHEMICAL
xylo, PREFIX INDICATING "WOOD"
    MOST OFTEN MODIFIES THE WORD
xylofon, xylophone
xylograph,*,her,hy,hic,hical,hically,
    WOOD CARVINGS USED TO
    EMBOSS SOMETHING ELSE
xylophone,*,nist, MUSICAL
    INSTRUMENT
xylose, A CHEMICAL
xylotomy,mic,mical,mous,mist, THE
    ART OF CUTTING WOOD
xylum, xylem

y, why
y'all, CONTRACTION FOR THE WORDS "YOU ALL" (or see yell)
ya, yaw / ye / yea / yeah
yacht,*,ting, PLEASURE SHIP
yahoo,*, EXPRESSION OF JOY, ROWDY PEOPLE
yal, yawl / y'all / yowl / you'll
yam,*, TYPE OF POTATO
yank,*,ked,king, TO SWIFTLY JERK/PULL
yard,*,dage, ENGLISH MEASUREMENT OF DISTANCE/LENGTH, THREE FEET, AREA FOR SPECIAL USE
yareu, urea
yareul, urea(l)
yarn,*, SPUN THREADS
yarrow, A WILD HERB
yart, yard
yat, yacht
yau, yaw / ye / yea / yeah
yaul, yawl / y'all / yowl / you'll
yaupon, SHRUB HOLLY
yaurd, yard
yaw,*,wed,wing, VERTICAL ROLL/TILT ON A SHIP/VESSEL/CRAFT
yawl,*, TYPE OF BOAT (or see y'all/ yowl)
yawn,*,ned,ning, EXAGERRATED STRETCHING OF JAW WHILE DEEPLY INHALING
ye, ANOTHER EXPRESSION OF "YOU"
yea,*, VERBAL VOTE OF "YES" (or see yeah)
yeah, SAME MEANING AS "YES" (or see yea)
year,*,rly, DAYS "prefixes: bi/semi"
yearling,*, AN ANIMAL IN ITS SECOND YEAR OF LIFE
yearn,*,ned,ning, LONG FOR/WANT SOMETHING
yeast,*,ted,ting,ty, A FUNGUS THAT ACTIVATES FOOD TOWARD FERMENTATION
yeild, yield
yel, yell
yeld, yell(ed) / yield
yell,*,lled,lling, TO VOICE/VOCALIZE LOUDLY (or see yield)
yellow,*,wed,wing,wer,west, A COLOR "prefixes: non"
yelp,*,ped,ping, HIGH-PITCHED SOUND DOG MAKES ASSOCIATED WITH PAIN
yelt, yell(ed) / yield

yeoman,*,men,menly, A NAVAL TERM/ POSITION, ATTENDANT TO NOBILITY
yep, yip / yes
yepe, yippee
yer, your / you're
yeraneum, uranium
yerater, ureter
yerathan, urethane
yereik, urea(eic)
yerek, uric
yerethu, urethra
yerin, urine
yerinary, urinary
yerinate, urinate
yerolegy, urology
yerolugy, urology
yers, your(s)
yerun, urine
yerunal, urinal
yerunology, uranology
yes,ses, AFFIRMATIVE/CONFIRM/ APPROVE
yeseg, usage
yest, yeast
yesterday, THE DAY BEFORE TODAY
yet, EXCEPT/BUT, IN REFERENCE TO TIME
yeu, ewe / you / yew
yeuld, yield / yell(ed)
yew,*, A TREE (or see you/ewe)
yewbikwite, ubiquity
yewcaliptus, eucalyptus
yewderis, uterus
yewdirus, uterus
yewdulize, utilize
yewjuale, usual(lly)
yewkalale, ukulele
yewkulale, ukulele
yewl, yule / you'll
yewnafid, unify(fied)
yewnaform, uniform
yewnaformedy, uniform(ity)
yewnasen, unison
yewnasikul, unicycle
yewnatery, unitary
yewnaversul, universal
yewnek, unique
yewnekorn, unicorn
yewneladeral, unilateral
yewnelateral, unilateral
yewnesikul, unicycle
yewnet, unit
yewnety, unity

yewnevers, universe
yewnikorn, unicorn
yewniladeral, unilateral
yewnilateral, unilateral
yewnit, unit
yewnitary, unitary
yewnite, unite
yewnufikashen, unification
yewnusen, unison
yewnusikul, unicycle
yewnutarean, unitary(rian)
yewnuversul, universal
yewnyun, union
yewsd, use(d)
yewshwul, usual
yewtensul, utensil
yewtilutarean, utilitarian
yewtilute, utility
yewtinsul, utensil
yewtopea, utopia
yewtulize, utilize
yewturis, uterus
yield,*,ded,ding, GIVE WAY TO, GAIN/ PRODUCE "prefixes: un"
yip,*,pped,pping,pper,ppee, SOUND/ BARK FROM A DOG (or see yep)
yipe, yippee
yippee, JUBILANT SOUND OF JOY
yipy, yippee
yir, your / you're / year
yiraneum, uranium
yirathan, urethane
yirek, uric
yiren, urine
yirenary, urinary
yirenate, urinate
yirenul, urinal
yirethu, urethra
yiruter, ureter
yo, yaw / ye / yea / yeah
yoc, yoke / yolk
yocert, yogurt
yocurt, yogurt
yodel,*,led,ling,ler, FALSETTO SOUND COMING FROM THE THROAT
yoeman, yeoman
yoga, FORM OF MEDITATIVE EXERCISE
yoge, yogi
yogi,ic, TEACHES/PRACTICES THE ART OF YOGA
yogurt, FOOD WITH PUDDING TEXTURE/CONSISTENCE(CY)
yok, yoke / yolk

yoke,*,ed,king, HARNESS (or see yolk)
    "prefixes: un"
yokel,*, A LOCAL/COUNTRY TYPE
    PERSON
yokert, yogurt
yokirt, yogurt
yokurt, yogurt
yol, yawl / y'all / yowl / you'll
yolk,*, YELLOW PART OF EGG, EMBRYO
    (or see yoke)
yoman, yeoman
yonder, WAY OVER THERE
yoni, FEMALE GENITALIA
yor, your / you're
yord, yard
yorn, yarn
yot, yacht
you, REFERRING TO A PERSON OTHER
    THAN SELF (or see yew/ewe)
you'll, CONTRACTION FOR THE WORDS
    'YOU WILL'
you're, CONTRACTION FOR THE
    WORDS 'YOU ARE' (or see your)
youbikwite, ubiquity
youdulize, utilize
youduris, uterus
youl, yule / you'll
younanemus, unanimous
younaversul, universal
younavirsity, university
youneladeral, unilateral
younelateral, unilateral
younevirsul, universal
younevursity, university
young,ger,gest,gish,gster, YOUTHFUL,
    EARLIER YEARS
youngster,*, YOUNG PEOPLE/CHILDREN
youniversity, university
youniversul, universal
younivurs, universe
younuvers, universe
your,*, IN REFERENCE TO SOMEONE
    ELSE'S POSSESSION (or see you're)
yourself,lves, MAKING REFERENCE TO
    SOMEONE ELSE
yous, use
yousd, use(d)
youseg, usage
youser, user
youserp, usurp
yousery, usury
yousful, useful
youshwule, usual(lly)
yousles, useless

youslus, useless
youtensul, utensil
youth,hful, YOUNG
youthful,lly,lness, OF BEING YOUNG
youtilady, utility
youtilutarean, utilitarian
youtilute, utility
youtopea, utopia
youtulize, utilize
youturis, uterus
youz, use
yowl,*,led,ling,ler, MOURNFUL CRY OF
    ANIMAL/PERSON (or see jowl)
yu, you/ yew/ ewe
yubikwite, ubiquity
yuderus, uterus
yuduris, uterus
yue, ewe / you / yew
yukaliptus, eucalyptus
yukulale, ukulele
yul, yule / you'll
yule, PAGAN FESTIVAL AROUND
    CHRISTMAS (or see you'll)
yunanemus, unanimous
yuneform, uniform
yuneladeral, unilateral
yunelateral, unilateral
yup, yip / yes
yuraneum, uranium
yuranium, uranium
yurathen, urethane
yureik, urea(eic)
yurek, uric
yuren, urine
yurenal, urinal
yurenary, urinary
yurenat, urinate
yurethu, urethra
yureu, urea
yureul, urea(l)
yurin, urine
yuritur, ureter
yurolegy, urology
yurolugy, urology
yuron, urine
yurs, your(s)
yurt,*, TENT/DOME STRUCTURE/
    DWELLING
yusd, use(d)
yuseg, usage
yuser, user
yuserp, usurp
yusful, useful
yushuel, usual

yushwul, usual
yusig, usage
yusir, user
yusirp, usurp
yusiry, usury
yuslus, useless
yust, use(d)
yutopea, utopia
yutulize, utilize
yuturis, uterus
yuwl, yawl / y'all / yowl / you'll
yuze, use
yuzer, user
yuzir, user
yuzur, use
zar, czar
zderty, sturdy
zdirdy, sturdy
zdurdee, sturdy
zdurty, sturdy
zeal,lous,lously,lousness, PASSIONATE/
    EXUBERANT/EAGER EMOTIONS
zealot,*, ONE WHO IS FANATICAL/GETS
    CARRIED AWAY BY EMOTIONS
zebra,*, AFRICAN STRIPED HORSE
zebru, zebra
zefir, zephyr
zegzag, zig-zag
zel, zeal
zeleon, zillion
zeles, zeal(ous)
zelet, zealot
zelis, zeal(ous)
zelit, zealot
zelus, zeal(ous)
zelut, zealot
zenafobia, xenophobe(bia)
zeneth, zenith
zeng, zing
zenge, zing(y)
zenith,hal, HIGHEST/FARTHEST PEAK/
    POINT
zenk, zinc
zenofob, xenophobe
zenofobic, xenophobe(bic)
zenon, xenon
zenuth, zenith
zenya, zinnia
zep, zip
zephir, zephyr
zephyr, FRAGILE/GENTLE WIND/FABRIC
zepur, zipper
zerafit, xerophyte
zeraufilus, xerophily(lous)

zerconium, zirconium
zero,oes,oed,oing, NUMBER INDICATING NIL/NOTHING, TARGET IN ON
zerofele, xerophily
zerofelus, xerophily(lous)
zerofit, xerophyte
zerofule, xerophily
zerofulus, xerophily(lous)
zest,ty,tful,tfrully,tfulness, WITH ENERGY/SPICE/GUSTO
zethur, zither
zigzag,*, GO BACK AND FORTH WHILE MOVING IN SPECIFIC DIRECTION
zilafon, xylophone
zilagraf, xylograph
zilaudime, xylotomy
zilaugrafur, xylograph(er)
zilauteme, xylotomy
zilefon, xylophone
zilegraf, xylograph
zilem, xylem
zilen, xylene
zileon, zillion
zilion, zillion
ziliphone, xylophone
zillion,*, EXTREMELY HIGH NUMBER
zilodeme, xylotomy
zilograf, xylograph
zilom, xylem
zilos, xylose
ziloteme, xylotomy
zilufon, xylophone
zilugraf, xylograph
zilum, xylem
ziluphone, xylophone
zimerge, zymurgy
zimolege, zymology
zimurge, zymurgy
zinafobia, xenophobe(bia)
zinafobic, xenophobe(bic)
zinc,ced,cing,cic,coid,cous,cky,cy,cite, A METAL
zing,*,ged,ging,gy, A SPEEDY/SHRILL SOUND/ACTION WHICH HAPPENS VERY QUICKLY, FAST, SPEEDY
zinia, zinnia
zink, zinc
zinnia,*, A FLOWER
zinya, zinnia
zip,*,pped,pping,ppy,pper, FAST/SWIFT "prefixes: un"
zipd, zip(pped)
zipe, zip(ppy)

ziped, zip(pped)
ziper, zipper
zipper,*,red,ring, A CLOSING DEVICE
zipur, zipper
zirafule, xerophily
zirconium, ON THE PERIODIC TABLE OF ELEMENTS
zirkoneum, zirconium
zirofit, xerophyte
ziruphyte, xerophyte
zither,*, AN INSTRUMENT
zithur, zither
zoademy, zootomy
zoagrafe, zoography
zodeak, zodiac
zodiac,*,cal, DEPICTION OF CONSTELLATIONS AND HOW THEY RELATE TO HUMANS
zoezu, zoysia
zoisa, zoysia
zombe, zombie
zombie,*, SOMEONE WHO IS ROBOTIC/ CONTROLLED BY A NON-HUMAN FORCE
zone,*,ed,ning,nal,nate,nated,nation, A SPECIFIC AREA DESIGNATED FOR SPECIFIC PURPOSES "prefixes: bi/ inter/intra"
zoo,*,oography,oology,oometry, oomorphic,oophyte,ootomy, PLACE WHERE ANIMALS ARE AVAILABLE FOR VIEWING PUBLIC, PREFIX INDICATING 'ANIMAL' MOST OFTEN MODIFIES THE WORD
zoodeme, zootomy
zoofit, zoophyte
zoography,her,hic,hical,hically, RELATED TO THE STUDY OF ANIMALS AND THEIR BEHAVIOR
zoogrufe, zoography
zoology,gical,gically,gist, SCIENCE OF STUDYING ANIMALS AND THEIR BEHAVIOR
zoom,*,med,ming, TO DECREASE DISTANCE BETWEEN OBSERVER AND THE OBSERVED
zoometry,ric,rical,rist, SCIENCE WHICH STUDIES ANIMALS AND THEIR SIZES/ PROPORTIONS
zoomorfik, zoomorphic
zoomorphic,ism, PORTRAY/ASCRIBE ANIMALS AS IF HAVING HUMAN FEELINGS/ BEHAVIORS/ CHARACTERISTICS

zoophyte,*,tic,tical, ANIMALS THAT RESEMBLE PLANTS
zootomy,mic,mical,mist, STUDY/ DISSECTION OF THE ANATOMY OF ANIMALS
zorgem, sorghum
zorgum, sorghum
zorkum, sorghum
zoysa, zoysia
zoysia, A GRASS
zu, zoo
zuamorfik, zoomorphic
zuchene, zuchinni
zuchinni,*, A VEGETABLE
zufit, zoophyte
zukene, zuchinni
zukine, zuchinni
zum, zoom
zumd, zoom(ed)
zuografe, zoography
zuolege, zoology
zuometre, zoometry
zurconium, zirconium
zurkoneum, zirconium
zyg, PREFIX INDICATING 'UNION/PAIR' MOST OFTEN MODIFIES THE WORD
zygo, PREFIX INDICATING 'UNION/PAIR' MOST OFTEN MODIFIES THE WORD
zym, PREFIX INDICATING 'UNION/PAIR' MOST OFTEN MODIFIES THE WORD
zymerge, zymurgy
zymirgy, zymurgy
zymo, PREFIX INDICATING 'UNION/ PAIR' MOST OFTEN MODIFIES THE WORD
zymolege, zymology
zymology,gic, SCIENCE DEALING WITH FERMENTATION
zymurgy, STUDY OF THE PRINCIPLES OF FERMENTATION

Printed in Great Britain
by Amazon

25301986R10256